About the Authors

Jim Kurose

Jim Kurose is a Distinguished University Professor of Computer Science at the University of Massachusetts, Amherst.

Dr. Kurose has received a number of recognitions for his educational activities including Outstanding Teacher Awards from the National Technological University (eight times), the University of Massachusetts, and the Northeast Association of Graduate Schools. He received the IEEE Taylor Booth Education Medal and was recognized for his leadership of Massachusetts' Commonwealth Information Technology Initiative. He has been the recipient of a GE Fellowship, an IBM Faculty Development Award, and a Lilly Teaching Fellowship.

Dr. Kurose is a former Editor-in-Chief of *IEEE Transactions on Communications* and of *IEEE/ACM Transactions on Networking*. He has been active in the program committees for *IEEE Infocom, ACM SIGCOMM, ACM Internet Measurement Conference*, and *ACM SIGMETRICS* for a number of years and has served as Technical Program Co-Chair for those conferences. He is a Fellow of the IEEE and the ACM. His research interests include network protocols and architecture, network measurement, sensor networks, multimedia communication, and modeling and performance evaluation. He holds a PhD in Computer Science from Columbia University.

Keith Ross

Keith Ross is the Leonard J. Shustek Chair Professor and Head of the Computer Science Department at Polytechnic Institute of NYU. Before joining NYU-Poly in 2003, he was a professor at the University of Pennsylvania (13 years) and a professor at Eurecom Institute (5 years). He received a B.S.E.E from Tufts University, a M.S.E.E. from Columbia University, and a Ph.D. in Computer and Control Engineering from The University of Michigan. Keith Ross is also the founder and original CEO of Wimba, which develops online multimedia applications for e-learning and was acquired by Blackboard in 2010.

Professor Ross's research interests are in security and privacy, social networks, peer-to-peer networking, Internet measurement, video streaming, content distribution networks, and stochastic modeling. He is an IEEE Fellow, recipient of the Infocom 2009 Best Paper Award, and recipient of 2011 and 2008 Best Paper Awards for Multimedia Communications (awarded by IEEE Communications Society). He has served on numerous journal editorial boards and conference program committees, including *IEEE/ACM Transactions on Networking, ACM SIGCOMM, ACM CoNext, and ACM Internet Measurement Conference*. He also has served as an advisor to the Federal Trade Commission on P2P file sharing.

To Julie and our three precious
ones—Chris, Charlie, and Nina
JFK

A big THANKS to my professors, colleagues,
and students all over the world.
KWR

Preface

Welcome to the sixth edition of *Computer Networking: A Top-Down Approach*. Since the publication of the first edition 12 years ago, our book has been adopted for use at many hundreds of colleges and universities, translated into 14 languages, and used by over one hundred thousand students and practitioners worldwide. We've heard from many of these readers and have been overwhelmed by the positive response.

What's New in the Sixth Edition?

We think one important reason for this success has been that our book continues to offer a fresh and timely approach to computer networking instruction. We've made changes in this sixth edition, but we've also kept unchanged what we believe (and the instructors and students who have used our book have confirmed) to be the most important aspects of this book: its top-down approach, its focus on the Internet and a modern treatment of computer networking, its attention to both principles and practice, and its accessible style and approach toward learning about computer networking. Nevertheless, the sixth edition has been revised and updated substantially:

- The Companion Web site has been significantly expanded and enriched to include VideoNotes and interactive exercises, as discussed later in this Preface.

- In Chapter 1, the treatment of access networks has been modernized, and the description of the Internet ISP ecosystem has been substantially revised, accounting for the recent emergence of content provider networks, such as Google's. The presentation of packet switching and circuit switching has also been reorganized, providing a more topical rather than historical orientation.

- In Chapter 2, Python has replaced Java for the presentation of socket programming. While still explicitly exposing the key ideas behind the socket API, Python code is easier to understand for the novice programmer. Moreover, unlike Java, Python provides access to raw sockets, enabling students to build a larger variety of network applications. Java-based socket programming labs have been replaced with corresponding Python labs, and a new Python-based ICMP Ping lab has been added. As always, when material is retired from the book, such as Java-based socket programming material, it remains available on the book's Companion Web site (see following text).

- In Chapter 3, the presentation of one of the reliable data transfer protocols has been simplified and a new sidebar on TCP splitting, commonly used to optimize the performance of cloud services, has been added.

- In Chapter 4, the section on router architectures has been significantly updated, reflecting recent developments and practices in the field. Several new integrative sidebars involving DNS, BGP, and OSPF are included.

- Chapter 5 has been reorganized and streamlined, accounting for the ubiquity of switched Ethernet in local area networks and the consequent increased use of Ethernet in point-to-point scenarios. Also, a new section on data center networking has been added.

- Chapter 6 has been updated to reflect recent advances in wireless networks, particularly cellular data networks and 4G services and architecture.

- Chapter 7, which focuses on multimedia networking, has gone through a major revision. The chapter now includes an in-depth discussion of streaming video, including adaptive streaming, and an entirely new and modernized discussion of CDNs. A newly added section describes the Netflix, YouTube, and Kankan video streaming systems. The material that has been removed to make way for these new topics is still available on the Companion Web site.

- Chapter 8 now contains an expanded discussion on endpoint authentication.

- Significant new material involving end-of-chapter problems has been added. As with all previous editions, homework problems have been revised, added, and removed.

Audience

This textbook is for a first course on computer networking. It can be used in both computer science and electrical engineering departments. In terms of programming languages, the book assumes only that the student has experience with C, C++, Java, or Python (and even then only in a few places). Although this book is more precise and analytical than many other introductory computer networking texts, it rarely uses any mathematical concepts that are not taught in high school. We have made a deliberate effort to avoid using any advanced calculus, probability, or stochastic process concepts (although we've included some homework problems for students with this advanced background). The book is therefore appropriate for undergraduate courses and for first-year graduate courses. It should also be useful to practitioners in the telecommunications industry.

What Is Unique about This Textbook?

The subject of computer networking is enormously complex, involving many concepts, protocols, and technologies that are woven together in an intricate manner. To cope with this scope and complexity, many computer networking texts are often organized around the "layers" of a network architecture. With a layered organization, students can see through the complexity of computer networking— they learn about the distinct concepts and protocols in one part of the architecture while seeing the big picture of how all parts fit together. From a pedagogical perspective, our personal experience has been that such a layered approach indeed works well. Nevertheless, we have found that the traditional approach of teaching—bottom up; that is, from the physical layer towards the application layer—is not the best approach for a modern course on computer networking.

A Top-Down Approach

Our book broke new ground 12 years ago by treating networking in a top-down manner—that is, by beginning at the application layer and working its way down toward the physical layer. The feedback we received from teachers and students alike have confirmed that this top-down approach has many advantages and does indeed work well pedagogically. First, it places emphasis on the application layer (a "high growth area" in networking). Indeed, many of the recent revolutions in computer networking—including the Web, peer-to-peer file sharing, and media streaming—have taken place at the application layer. An early emphasis on application-layer issues differs from the approaches taken in most other texts, which have only a small amount of material on network applications, their requirements, application-layer paradigms (e.g., client-server and peer-to-peer), and application programming inter-faces. Second, our experience as instructors (and that of many instructors who have used this text) has been that teaching networking applications near the beginning of the course is a powerful motivational tool. Students are thrilled to learn about how networking applications work—applications such as e-mail and the Web, which most students use on a daily basis. Once a student understands the applications, the student can then understand the network services needed to support these applications. The student can then, in turn, examine the various ways in which such services might be provided and implemented in the lower layers. Covering applications early thus provides motivation for the remainder of the text.

Third, a top-down approach enables instructors to introduce network application development at an early stage. Students not only see how popular applications and protocols work, but also learn how easy it is to create their own network applications and application-level protocols. With the top-down approach, students get early exposure to the notions of socket programming, service models, and protocols—important concepts that resurface in all subsequent layers. By providing socket programming examples in Python, we highlight the central ideas without confusing students with complex code. Undergraduates in electrical engineering and computer science should not have difficulty following the Python code.

An Internet Focus

Although we dropped the phrase "Featuring the Internet" from the title of this book with the fourth edition, this doesn't mean that we dropped our focus on the Internet! Indeed, nothing could be further from the case! Instead, since the Internet has become so pervasive, we felt that any networking textbook must have a significant focus on the Internet, and thus this phrase was somewhat unnecessary. We continue to use the Internet's architecture and protocols as primary vehicles for studying fundamental computer networking concepts. Of course, we also include concepts and protocols from other network architectures. But the spotlight is clearly on the Internet, a fact reflected in our organizing the book around the Internet's five-layer architecture: the application, transport, network, link, and physical layers.

Another benefit of spotlighting the Internet is that most computer science and electrical engineering students are eager to learn about the Internet and its protocols. They know that the Internet has been a revolutionary and disruptive technology and can see that it is profoundly changing our world. Given the enormous relevance of the Internet, students are naturally curious about what is "under the hood." Thus, it is easy for an instructor to get students excited about basic principles when using the Internet as the guiding focus.

Teaching Networking Principles

Two of the unique features of the book—its top-down approach and its focus on the Internet—have appeared in the titles of our book. If we could have squeezed a *third* phrase into the subtitle, it would have contained the word *principles*. The field of networking is now mature enough that a number of fundamentally important issues can be identified. For example, in the transport layer, the fundamental issues include reliable communication over an unreliable network layer, connection establishment/teardown and handshaking, congestion and flow control, and multiplexing. Two fundamentally important network-layer issues are determining "good" paths between two routers and interconnecting a large number of heterogeneous networks. In the link layer, a fundamental problem is sharing a multiple access channel. In network security, techniques for providing confidentiality, authentication, and message integrity are all based on cryptographic fundamentals. This text identifies fundamental networking issues and studies approaches towards addressing these issues. The student learning these principles will gain knowledge with a long "shelf life"—long after today's network standards and protocols have become obsolete, the principles they embody will remain important and relevant. We believe that the combination of using the Internet to get the student's foot in the door and then emphasizing fundamental issues and solution approaches will allow the student to quickly understand just about any networking technology.

The Web Site

Each new copy of this textbook includes six months of access to a Companion Web site for all book readers at http://www.pearsoninternationaleditions.com/kurose-ross, which includes:

* *Interactive learning material.* An important new component of the sixth edition is the significantly expanded online and interactive learning material. The book's Companion Web site now contains VideoNotes—video presentations of

important topics thoughout the book done by the authors, as well as walk-throughs of solutions to problems similar to those at the end of the chapter. We've also added Interactive Exercises that can create (and present solutions for) problems similar to selected end-of-chapter problems. Since students can generate (and view solutions for) an unlimited number of similar problem instances, they can work until the material is truly mastered. We've seeded the Web site with VideoNotes and online problems for chapters 1 through 5 and will continue to actively add and update this material over time. As in earlier editions, the Web site contains the interactive Java applets that animate many key networking concepts. The site also has interactive quizzes that permit students to check their basic understanding of the subject matter. Professors can integrate these interactive features into their lectures or use them as mini labs.

- *Additional technical material.* As we have added new material in each edition of our book, we've had to remove coverage of some existing topics to keep the book at manageable length. For example, to make room for the new material in this edition, we've removed material on ATM networks and the RTSP protocol for multimedia. Material that appeared in earlier editions of the text is still of interest, and can be found on the book's Web site.

- *Programming assignments.* The Web site also provides a number of detailed programming assignments, which include building a multithreaded Web server, building an e-mail client with a GUI interface, programming the sender and receiver sides of a reliable data transport protocol, programming a distributed routing algorithm, and more.

- *Wireshark labs.* One's understanding of network protocols can be greatly deepened by seeing them in action. The Web site provides numerous Wireshark assignments that enable students to actually observe the sequence of messages exchanged between two protocol entities. The Web site includes separate Wireshark labs on HTTP, DNS, TCP, UDP, IP, ICMP, Ethernet, ARP, WiFi, SSL, and on tracing all protocols involved in satisfying a request to fetch a web page. We'll continue to add new labs over time.

Pedagogical Features

We have each been teaching computer networking for more than 20 years. Together, we bring more than 50 years of teaching experience to this text, during which time we have taught many thousands of students. We have also been active researchers in computer networking during this time. (In fact, Jim and Keith first met each other as master's students in a computer networking course taught by Mischa Schwartz in 1979 at Columbia University.) We think all this gives us a good perspective on where networking has been and where it is likely to go in the future. Nevertheless, we have resisted temptations to bias the material in this book towards our own pet research projects. We figure you can visit our personal Web sites if you are interested in our research. Thus, this book is about modern computer networking—it is about contemporary protocols and technologies as well as the underlying principles behind these protocols and technologies. We also believe that learning (and teaching!) about networking can be fun. A sense of humor, use of analogies, and real-world examples in this book will hopefully make this material more fun.

Supplements for Instructors

We provide a complete supplements package to aid instructors in teaching this course. This material can be accessed from Pearson's Instructor Resource Center (http://www.pearsoninternationaleditions.com/kurose-ross). Visit the Instructor Resource Center to learn about accessing these instructor's supplements.

- *PowerPoint® slides.* We provide PowerPoint slides for all nine chapters. The slides have been completely updated with this sixth edition. The slides cover each chapter in detail. They use graphics and animations (rather than relying only on monotonous text bullets) to make the slides interesting and visually appealing. We provide the original PowerPoint slides so you can customize them to best suit your own teaching needs. Some of these slides have been contributed by other instructors who have taught from our book.
- *Homework solutions.* We provide a solutions manual for the homework problems in the text, programming assignments, and Wireshark labs. As noted earlier, we've introduced many new homework problems in the first five chapters of the book.

Chapter Dependencies

The first chapter of this text presents a self-contained overview of computer networking. Introducing many key concepts and terminology, this chapter sets the stage for the rest of the book. All of the other chapters directly depend on this first chapter. After completing Chapter 1, we recommend instructors cover Chapters 2 through 5 in sequence, following our top-down philosophy. Each of these five chapters leverages material from the preceding chapters. After completing the first five chapters, the instructor has quite a bit of flexibility. There are no interdependencies among the last four chapters, so they can be taught in any order. However, each of the last four chapters depends on the material in the first five chapters. Many instructors first teach the first five chapters and then teach one of the last four chapters for "dessert."

One Final Note: We'd Love to Hear from You

We encourage students and instructors to e-mail us with any comments they might have about our book. It's been wonderful for us to hear from so many instructors and students from around the world about our first four editions. We've incorporated many of these suggestions into later editions of the book. We also encourage instructors to send us new homework problems (and solutions) that would complement the current homework problems. We'll post these on the instructor-only portion of the Web site. We also encourage instructors and students to create new Java applets that illustrate the concepts and protocols in this book. If you have an applet that you think would be appropriate for this text, please submit it to us. If the applet (including notation and terminology) is appropriate, we'll be happy to include it on the text's Web site, with an appropriate reference to the applet's authors.

So, as the saying goes, "Keep those cards and letters coming!" Seriously, please *do* continue to send us interesting URLs, point out typos, disagree with any of our claims, and tell us what works and what doesn't work. Tell us what you think should or shouldn't be included in the next edition. Send your e-mail to kurose@cs.umass.edu and ross@poly.edu.

Acknowledgments

Since we began writing this book in 1996, many people have given us invaluable help and have been influential in shaping our thoughts on how to best organize and teach a networking course. We want to say A BIG THANKS to everyone who has helped us from the earliest first drafts of this book, up to this fifth edition. We are also *very* thankful to the many hundreds of readers from around the world—students, faculty, practitioners—who have sent us thoughts and comments on earlier editions of the book and suggestions for future editions of the book. Special thanks go out to:

Al Aho (Columbia University)
Hisham Al-Mubaid (University of Houston-Clear Lake)
Pratima Akkunoor (Arizona State University)
Paul Amer (University of Delaware)
Shamiul Azom (Arizona State University)
Lichun Bao (University of California at Irvine)
Paul Barford (University of Wisconsin)
Bobby Bhattacharjee (University of Maryland)
Steven Bellovin (Columbia University)
Pravin Bhagwat (Wibhu)
Supratik Bhattacharyya (previously at Sprint)
Ernst Biersack (Eurécom Institute)

Shahid Bokhari (University of Engineering & Technology, Lahore)
Jean Bolot (Technicolor Research)
Daniel Brushteyn (former University of Pennsylvania student)
Ken Calvert (University of Kentucky)
Evandro Cantu (Federal University of Santa Catarina)
Jeff Case (SNMP Research International)
Jeff Chaltas (Sprint)
Vinton Cerf (Google)
Byung Kyu Choi (Michigan Technological University)
Bram Cohen (BitTorrent, Inc.)
Constantine Coutras (Pace University)
John Daigle (University of Mississippi)
Edmundo A. de Souza e Silva (Federal University of Rio de Janeiro)
Philippe Decuetos (Eurécom Institute)
Christophe Diot (Technicolor Research)
Prithula Dhunghel (Akamai)
Deborah Estrin (University of California, Los Angeles)
Michalis Faloutsos (University of California at Riverside)
Wu-chi Feng (Oregon Graduate Institute)
Sally Floyd (ICIR, University of California at Berkeley)
Paul Francis (Max Planck Institute)
Lixin Gao (University of Massachusetts)
JJ Garcia-Luna-Aceves (University of California at Santa Cruz)
Mario Gerla (University of California at Los Angeles)
David Goodman (NYU-Poly)
Yang Guo (Alcatel/Lucent Bell Labs)
Tim Griffin (Cambridge University)
Max Hailperin (Gustavus Adolphus College)
Bruce Harvey (Florida A&M University, Florida State University)
Carl Hauser (Washington State University)
Rachelle Heller (George Washington University)
Phillipp Hoschka (INRIA/W3C)
Wen Hsin (Park University)
Albert Huang (former University of Pennsylvania student)
Cheng Huang (Microsoft Research)
Esther A. Hughes (Virginia Commonwealth University)
Van Jacobson (Xerox PARC)
Pinak Jain (former NYU-Poly student)
Jobin James (University of California at Riverside)
Sugih Jamin (University of Michigan)
Shivkumar Kalyanaraman (IBM Research, India)
Jussi Kangasharju (University of Helsinki)
Sneha Kasera (University of Utah)
Parviz Kermani (formerly of IBM Research)
Hyojin Kim (former University of Pennsylvania student)

Leonard Kleinrock (University of California at Los Angeles)
David Kotz (Dartmouth College)
Beshan Kulapala (Arizona State University)
Rakesh Kumar (Bloomberg)
Miguel A. Labrador (University of South Florida)
Simon Lam (University of Texas)
Steve Lai (Ohio State University)
Tom LaPorta (Penn State University)
Tim-Berners Lee (World Wide Web Consortium)
Arnaud Legout (INRIA)
Lee Leitner (Drexel University)
Brian Levine (University of Massachusetts)
Chunchun Li (former NYU-Poly student)
Yong Liu (NYU-Poly)
William Liang (former University of Pennsylvania student)
Willis Marti (Texas A&M University)
Nick McKeown (Stanford University)
Josh McKinzie (Park University)
Deep Medhi (University of Missouri, Kansas City)
Bob Metcalfe (International Data Group)
Sue Moon (KAIST)
Jenni Moyer (Comcast)
Erich Nahum (IBM Research)
Christos Papadopoulos (Colorado Sate University)
Craig Partridge (BBN Technologies)
Radia Perlman (Intel)
Jitendra Padhye (Microsoft Research)
Vern Paxson (University of California at Berkeley)
Kevin Phillips (Sprint)
George Polyzos (Athens University of Economics and Business)
Sriram Rajagopalan (Arizona State University)
Ramachandran Ramjee (Microsoft Research)
Ken Reek (Rochester Institute of Technology)
Martin Reisslein (Arizona State University)
Jennifer Rexford (Princeton University)
Leon Reznik (Rochester Institute of Technology)
Pablo Rodrigez (Telefonica)
Sumit Roy (University of Washington)
Avi Rubin (Johns Hopkins University)
Dan Rubenstein (Columbia University)
Douglas Salane (John Jay College)
Despina Saparilla (Cisco Systems)
John Schanz (Comcast)
Henning Schulzrinne (Columbia University)
Mischa Schwartz (Columbia University)

Ardash Sethi (University of Delaware)
Harish Sethu (Drexel University)
K. Sam Shanmugan (University of Kansas)
Prashant Shenoy (University of Massachusetts)
Clay Shields (Georgetown University)
Subin Shrestra (University of Pennsylvania)
Bojie Shu (former NYU-Poly student)
Mihail L. Sichitiu (NC State University)
Peter Steenkiste (Carnegie Mellon University)
Tatsuya Suda (University of California at Irvine)
Kin Sun Tam (State University of New York at Albany)
Don Towsley (University of Massachusetts)
David Turner (California State University, San Bernardino)
Nitin Vaidya (University of Illinois)
Michele Weigle (Clemson University)
David Wetherall (University of Washington)
Ira Winston (University of Pennsylvania)
Di Wu (Sun Yat-sen University)
Shirley Wynn (NYU-Poly)
Raj Yavatkar (Intel)
Yechiam Yemini (Columbia University)
Ming Yu (State University of New York at Binghamton)
Ellen Zegura (Georgia Institute of Technology)
Honggang Zhang (Suffolk University)
Hui Zhang (Carnegie Mellon University)
Lixia Zhang (University of California at Los Angeles)
Meng Zhang (former NYU-Poly student)
Shuchun Zhang (former University of Pennsylvania student)
Xiaodong Zhang (Ohio State University)
ZhiLi Zhang (University of Minnesota)
Phil Zimmermann (independent consultant)
Cliff C. Zou (University of Central Florida)

We also want to thank the entire Addison-Wesley team—in particular, Michael Hirsch, Marilyn Lloyd, and Emma Snider—who have done an absolutely outstanding job on this sixth edition (and who have put up with two very finicky authors who seem congenitally unable to meet deadlines!). Thanks also to our artists, Janet Theurer and Patrice Rossi Calkin, for their work on the beautiful figures in this book, and to Andrea Stefanowicz and her team at PreMediaGlobal for their wonderful production work on this edition. Finally, a most special thanks go to Michael Hirsch, our editor at Addison-Wesley, and Susan Hartman, our former editor at Addison-Wesley. This book would not be what it is (and may well not have been at all) without their graceful management, constant encouragement, nearly infinite patience, good humor, and perseverance.

The publishers would like to thank B. R. Chandavarkar of the National Institute of Technology Karnataka, Surathkal, for reviewing the content of the International Edition.

Table of Contents

Chapter 6 Wireless and Mobile Networks 539

COMPUTER

SIXTH EDITION

NETWORKING

A Top-Down Approach

Computer Networks and the Internet

Today's Internet is arguably the largest engineered system ever created by mankind, with hundreds of millions of connected computers, communication links, and switches; with billions of users who connect via laptops, tablets, and smartphones; and with an array of new Internet-connected devices such as sensors, Web cams, game consoles, picture frames, and even washing machines. Given that the Internet is so large and has so many diverse components and uses, is there any hope of understanding how it works? Are there guiding principles and structure that can provide a foundation for understanding such an amazingly large and complex system? And if so, is it possible that it actually could be both interesting *and* fun to learn about computer networks? Fortunately, the answers to all of these questions is a resounding YES! Indeed, it's our aim in this book to provide you with a modern introduction to the dynamic field of computer networking, giving you the principles and practical insights you'll need to understand not only today's networks, but tomorrow's as well.

This first chapter presents a broad overview of computer networking and the Internet. Our goal here is to paint a broad picture and set the context for the rest of this book, to see the forest through the trees. We'll cover a lot of ground in this introductory chapter and discuss a lot of the pieces of a computer network, without losing sight of the big picture.

We'll structure our overview of computer networks in this chapter as follows. After introducing some basic terminology and concepts, we'll first examine the basic hardware and software components that make up a network. We'll begin at the network's edge and look at the end systems and network applications running in the network. We'll then explore the core of a computer network, examining the links and the switches that transport data, as well as the access networks and physical media that connect end systems to the network core. We'll learn that the Internet is a network of networks, and we'll learn how these networks connect with each other.

After having completed this overview of the edge and core of a computer network, we'll take the broader and more abstract view in the second half of this chapter. We'll examine delay, loss, and throughput of data in a computer network and provide simple quantitative models for end-to-end throughput and delay: models that take into account transmission, propagation, and queuing delays. We'll then introduce some of the key architectural principles in computer networking, namely, protocol layering and service models. We'll also learn that computer networks are vulnerable to many different types of attacks; we'll survey some of these attacks and consider how computer networks can be made more secure. Finally, we'll close this chapter with a brief history of computer networking.

1.1 What Is the Internet?

In this book, we'll use the public Internet, a specific computer network, as our principal vehicle for discussing computer networks and their protocols. But what *is* the Internet? There are a couple of ways to answer this question. First, we can describe the nuts and bolts of the Internet, that is, the basic hardware and software components that make up the Internet. Second, we can describe the Internet in terms of a networking infrastructure that provides services to distributed applications. Let's begin with the nuts-and-bolts description, using Figure 1.1 to illustrate our discussion.

1.1.1 A Nuts-and-Bolts Description

The Internet is a computer network that interconnects hundreds of millions of computing devices throughout the world. Not too long ago, these computing devices were primarily traditional desktop PCs, Linux workstations, and so-called servers that store and transmit information such as Web pages and e-mail messages. Increasingly, however, nontraditional Internet end systems such as laptops, smartphones, tablets, TVs, gaming consoles, Web cams, automobiles, environmental sensing devices, picture frames, and home electrical and security systems are being connected to the Internet. Indeed, the term *computer network* is beginning to sound a bit dated, given the many nontraditional devices that are being hooked up to the Internet. In Internet jargon, all of these devices are called **hosts** or **end systems**. As of July 2011, there were

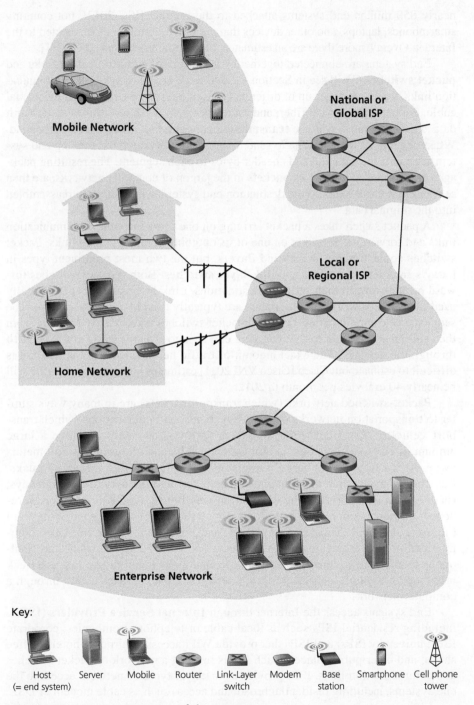

Key:

Host
(= end system)   Server   Mobile   Router   Link-Layer   Modem   Base   Smartphone   Cell phone
                                             switch   station   tower

Figure 1.1 ♦ Some pieces of the Internet

nearly 850 million end systems attached to the Internet [ISC 2012], not counting smartphones, laptops, and other devices that are only intermittently connected to the Internet. Overall, more there are an estimated 2 billion Internet users [ITU 2011].

End systems are connected together by a network of **communication links** and **packet switches**. We'll see in Section 1.2 that there are many types of communication links, which are made up of different types of physical media, including coaxial cable, copper wire, optical fiber, and radio spectrum. Different links can transmit data at different rates, with the **transmission rate** of a link measured in bits/second. When one end system has data to send to another end system, the sending end system segments the data and adds header bytes to each segment. The resulting packages of information, known as **packets** in the jargon of computer networks, are then sent through the network to the destination end system, where they are reassembled into the original data.

A packet switch takes a packet arriving on one of its incoming communication links and forwards that packet on one of its outgoing communication links. Packet switches come in many shapes and flavors, but the two most prominent types in today's Internet are **routers** and **link-layer switches**. Both types of switches forward packets toward their ultimate destinations. Link-layer switches are typically used in access networks, while routers are typically used in the network core. The sequence of communication links and packet switches traversed by a packet from the sending end system to the receiving end system is known as a **route** or **path** through the network. The exact amount of traffic being carried in the Internet is difficult to estimate but Cisco [Cisco VNI 2011] estimates global Internet traffic will be nearly 40 exabytes per month in 2012.

Packet-switched networks (which transport packets) are in many ways similar to transportation networks of highways, roads, and intersections (which transport vehicles). Consider, for example, a factory that needs to move a large amount of cargo to some destination warehouse located thousands of kilometers away. At the factory, the cargo is segmented and loaded into a fleet of trucks. Each of the trucks then independently travels through the network of highways, roads, and intersections to the destination warehouse. At the destination warehouse, the cargo is unloaded and grouped with the rest of the cargo arriving from the same shipment. Thus, in many ways, packets are analogous to trucks, communication links are analogous to highways and roads, packet switches are analogous to intersections, and end systems are analogous to buildings. Just as a truck takes a path through the transportation network, a packet takes a path through a computer network.

End systems access the Internet through **Internet Service Providers (ISPs)**, including residential ISPs such as local cable or telephone companies; corporate ISPs; university ISPs; and ISPs that provide WiFi access in airports, hotels, coffee shops, and other public places. Each ISP is in itself a network of packet switches and communication links. ISPs provide a variety of types of network access to the end systems, including residential broadband access such as cable modem or DSL, high-speed local area network access, wireless access, and 56 kbps dial-up modem access. ISPs also provide Internet access to content providers, connecting Web sites directly to the Internet. The Internet is all about connecting end systems to each other, so the ISPs that provide access to end systems must also be interconnected. These lower-tier ISPs are interconnected through national and international upper-tier ISPs such as Level 3 Communications, AT&T, Sprint, and NTT. An upper-tier ISP consists of high-speed routers interconnected with high-speed fiber-optic links. Each ISP network, whether upper-tier or lower-tier, is managed independently, runs the IP protocol (see below), and conforms to certain naming and address conventions. We'll examine ISPs and their interconnection more closely in Section 1.3.

End systems, packet switches, and other pieces of the Internet run **protocols** that control the sending and receiving of information within the Internet. The **Transmission Control Protocol (TCP)** and the **Internet Protocol (IP)** are two of the most important protocols in the Internet. The IP protocol specifies the format of the packets that are sent and received among routers and end systems. The Internet's principal protocols are collectively known as **TCP/IP**. We'll begin looking into protocols in this introductory chapter. But that's just a start—much of this book is concerned with computer network protocols!

Given the importance of protocols to the Internet, it's important that everyone agree on what each and every protocol does, so that people can create systems and products that interoperate. This is where standards come into play. **Internet standards** are developed by the Internet Engineering Task Force (IETF)[IETF 2012]. The IETF standards documents are called **requests for comments (RFCs)**. RFCs started out as general requests for comments (hence the name) to resolve network and protocol design problems that faced the precursor to the Internet [Allman 2011]. RFCs tend to be quite technical and detailed. They define protocols such as TCP, IP, HTTP (for the Web), and SMTP (for e-mail). There are currently more than 6,000 RFCs. Other bodies also specify standards for network components, most notably for network links. The IEEE 802 LAN/MAN Standards Committee [IEEE 802 2012], for example, specifies the Ethernet and wireless WiFi standards.

1.1.2 A Services Description

Our discussion above has identified many of the pieces that make up the Internet. But we can also describe the Internet from an entirely different angle—namely, as *an infrastructure that provides services to applications*. These applications include electronic mail, Web surfing, social networks, instant messaging, Voice-over-IP (VoIP), video streaming, distributed games, peer-to-peer (P2P) file sharing, television over the Internet, remote login, and much, much more. The applications are said to be **distributed applications**, since they involve multiple end systems that exchange data with each other. Importantly, Internet applications run on end systems—they do not run in the packet switches in the network core. Although packet switches facilitate the exchange of data among end systems, they are not concerned with the application that is the source or sink of data.

Let's explore a little more what we mean by an infrastructure that provides services to applications. To this end, suppose you have an exciting new idea for a distributed Internet application, one that may greatly benefit humanity or one that may simply make you rich and famous. How might you go about transforming this idea into an actual Internet application? Because applications run on end systems, you are going to need to write programs that run on the end systems. You might, for example, write your programs in Java, C, or Python. Now, because you are developing a distributed Internet application, the programs running on the different end systems will need to send data to each other. And here we get to a central issue—one that leads to the alternative way of describing the Internet as a platform for applications. How does one program running on one end system instruct the Internet to deliver data to another program running on another end system?

End systems attached to the Internet provide an **Application Programming Interface (API)** that specifies how a program running on one end system asks the Internet infrastructure to deliver data to a specific destination program running on another end system. This Internet API is a set of rules that the sending program must follow so that the Internet can deliver the data to the destination program. We'll discuss the Internet API in detail in Chapter 2. For now, let's draw upon a simple analogy, one that we will frequently use in this book. Suppose Alice wants to send a letter to Bob using the postal service. Alice, of course, can't just write the letter (the data) and drop the letter out her window. Instead, the postal service requires that Alice put the letter in an envelope; write Bob's full name, address, and zip code in the center of the envelope; seal the envelope; put a stamp in the upper-right-hand corner of the envelope; and finally, drop the envelope into an official postal service mailbox. Thus, the postal service has its own "postal service API," or set of rules, that Alice must follow to have the postal service deliver her letter to Bob. In a similar manner, the Internet has an API that the program sending data must follow to have the Internet deliver the data to the program that will receive the data.

The postal service, of course, provides more than one service to its customers. It provides express delivery, reception confirmation, ordinary use, and many more services. In a similar manner, the Internet provides multiple services to its applications. When you develop an Internet application, you too must choose one of the Internet's services for your application. We'll describe the Internet's services in Chapter 2.

We have just given two descriptions of the Internet; one in terms of its hardware and software components, the other in terms of an infrastructure for providing services to distributed applications. But perhaps you are still confused as to what the

Internet is. What are packet switching and TCP/IP? What are routers? What kinds of communication links are present in the Internet? What is a distributed application? How can a toaster or a weather sensor be attached to the Internet? If you feel a bit overwhelmed by all of this now, don't worry—the purpose of this book is to introduce you to both the nuts and bolts of the Internet and the principles that govern how and why it works. We'll explain these important terms and questions in the following sections and chapters.

1.1.3 What Is a Protocol?

Now that we've got a bit of a feel for what the Internet is, let's consider another important buzzword in computer networking: *protocol*. What is a protocol? What does a protocol do*?*

A Human Analogy

It is probably easiest to understand the notion of a computer network protocol by first considering some human analogies, since we humans execute protocols all of the time. Consider what you do when you want to ask someone for the time of day. A typical exchange is shown in Figure 1.2. Human protocol (or good manners, at least) dictates that one first offer a greeting (the first "Hi" in Figure 1.2) to initiate communication with someone else. The typical response to a "Hi" is a returned "Hi" message. Implicitly, one then takes a cordial "Hi" response as an indication that one can proceed and ask for the time of day. A different response to the initial "Hi" (such as "Don't bother me!" or "I don't speak English," or some unprintable reply) might indicate an unwillingness or inability to communicate. In this case, the human protocol would be not to ask for the time of day. Sometimes one gets no response at all to a question, in which case one typically gives up asking that person for the time. Note that in our human protocol, *there are specific messages we send, and specific actions we take in response to the received reply messages or other events* (such as no reply within some given amount of time). Clearly, transmitted and received messages, and actions taken when these messages are sent or received or other events occur, play a central role in a human protocol. If people run different protocols (for example, if one person has manners but the other does not, or if one understands the concept of time and the other does not) the protocols do not interoperate and no useful work can be accomplished. The same is true in networking—it takes two (or more) communicating entities running the same protocol in order to accomplish a task.

   Let's consider a second human analogy. Suppose you're in a college class (a computer networking class, for example!). The teacher is droning on about protocols and you're confused. The teacher stops to ask, "Are there any questions?" (a

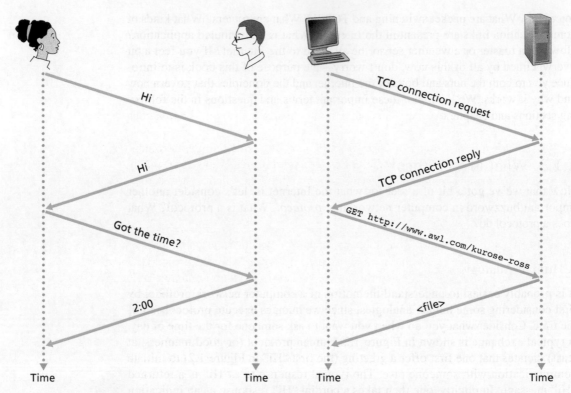

Figure 1.2 ♦ A human protocol and a computer network protocol

message that is transmitted to, and received by, all students who are not sleeping). You raise your hand (transmitting an implicit message to the teacher). Your teacher acknowledges you with a smile, saying "Yes . . ." (a transmitted message encouraging you to ask your question—teachers *love* to be asked questions), and you then ask your question (that is, transmit your message to your teacher). Your teacher hears your question (receives your question message) and answers (transmits a reply to you). Once again, we see that the transmission and receipt of messages, and a set of conventional actions taken when these messages are sent and received, are at the heart of this question-and-answer protocol.

Network Protocols

A network protocol is similar to a human protocol, except that the entities exchanging messages and taking actions are hardware or software components of some device (for example, computer, smartphone, tablet, router, or other network-capable device). All activity in the Internet that involves two or more communicating remote entities is governed by a protocol. For example, hardware-implemented protocols in two physically connected computers control the flow of bits on the "wire" between the two network interface cards; congestion-control protocols in end systems control the rate at which packets are transmitted between sender and receiver; protocols in routers determine a packet's path from source to destination. Protocols are running everywhere in the Internet, and consequently much of this book is about computer network protocols.

As an example of a computer network protocol with which you are probably familiar, consider what happens when you make a request to a Web server, that is, when you type the URL of a Web page into your Web browser. The scenario is illustrated in the right half of Figure 1.2. First, your computer will send a connection request message to the Web server and wait for a reply. The Web server will eventually receive your connection request message and return a connection reply message. Knowing that it is now OK to request the Web document, your computer then sends the name of the Web page it wants to fetch from that Web server in a GET message. Finally, the Web server returns the Web page (file) to your computer.

Given the human and networking examples above, the exchange of messages and the actions taken when these messages are sent and received are the key defining elements of a protocol:

> A **protocol** defines the format and the order of messages exchanged between two or more communicating entities, as well as the actions taken on the transmission and/or receipt of a message or other event.

The Internet, and computer networks in general, make extensive use of protocols. Different protocols are used to accomplish different communication tasks. As you read through this book, you will learn that some protocols are simple and straightforward, while others are complex and intellectually deep. Mastering the field of computer networking is equivalent to understanding the what, why, and how of networking protocols.

1.2 The Network Edge

In the previous section we presented a high-level overview of the Internet and networking protocols. We are now going to delve a bit more deeply into the components of a computer network (and the Internet, in particular). We begin in this section at the edge of a network and look at the components with which we are most familiar—namely, the computers, smartphones and other devices that we use on a daily basis. In the next section we'll move from the network edge to the network core and examine switching and routing in computer networks.

CASE HISTORY

A DIZZYING ARRAY OF INTERNET END SYSTEMS

Not too long ago, the end-system devices connected to the Internet were primarily traditional computers such as desktop machines and powerful servers. Beginning in the late 1990s and continuing today, a wide range of interesting devices are being connected to the Internet, leveraging their ability to send and receive digital data. Given the Internet's ubiquity, its well-defined (standardized) protocols, and the availability of Internet-ready commodity hardware, it's natural to use Internet technology to network these devices together and to Internet-connected servers.

Many of these devices are based in the home—video game consoles (e.g., Microsoft's Xbox), Internet-ready televisions, digital picture frames that download and display digital pictures, washing machines, refrigerators, and even a toaster that downloads meteorological information and burns an image of the day's forecast (e.g., mixed clouds and sun) on your morning toast [BBC 2001]. IP-enabled phones with GPS capabilities put location-dependent services (maps, information about nearby services or people) at your fingertips. Networked sensors embedded into the physical environment allow monitoring of buildings, bridges, seismic activity, wildlife habitats, river estuaries, and the weather. Biomedical devices can be embedded and networked in a body-area network. With so many diverse devices being networked together, the Internet is indeed becoming an "Internet of things" [ITU 2005b].

Recall from the previous section that in computer networking jargon, the computers and other devices connected to the Internet are often referred to as end systems. They are referred to as end systems because they sit at the edge of the Internet, as shown in Figure 1.3. The Internet's end systems include desktop computers (e.g., desktop PCs, Macs, and Linux boxes), servers (e.g., Web and e-mail servers), and mobile computers (e.g., laptops, smartphones, and tablets). Furthermore, an increasing number of non-traditional devices are being attached to the Internet as end systems (see sidebar).

End systems are also referred to as *hosts* because they host (that is, run) application programs such as a Web browser program, a Web server program, an e-mail client program, or an e-mail server program. Throughout this book we will use the terms hosts and end systems interchangeably; that is, *host = end system*. Hosts are sometimes further divided into two categories: **clients** and **servers**. Informally, clients tend to be desktop and mobile PCs, smartphones, and so on, whereas servers tend to be more powerful machines that store and distribute Web pages, stream video, relay e-mail, and so on. Today, most of the servers from which we receive

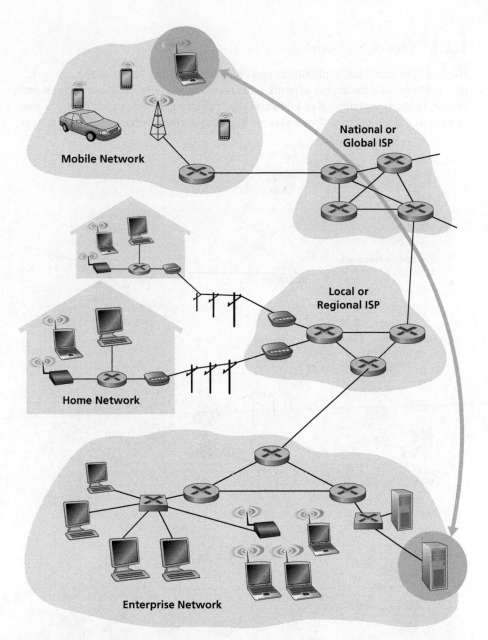

Figure 1.3 ♦ End-system interaction

search results, e-mail, Web pages, and videos reside in large **data centers**. For example, Google has 30–50 data centers, with many having more than one hundred thousand servers.

1.2.1 Access Networks

Having considered the applications and end systems at the "edge of the network," let's next consider the access network—the network that physically connects an end system to the first router (also known as the "edge router") on a path from the end system to any other distant end system. Figure 1.4 shows several types of access

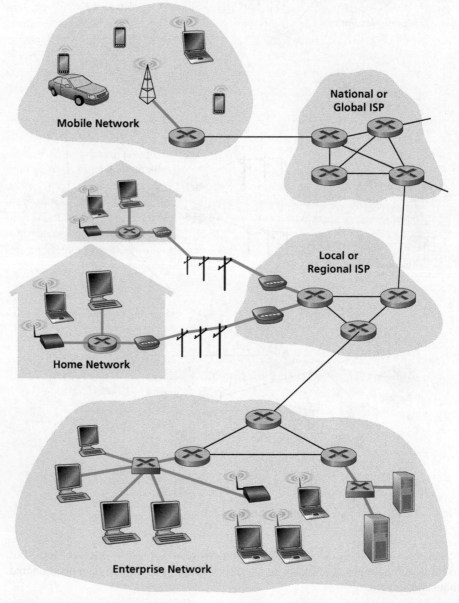

Figure 1.4 ♦ Access networks

networks with thick, shaded lines, and the settings (home, enterprise, and wide-area mobile wireless) in which they are used.

Home Access: DSL, Cable, FTTH, Dial-Up, and Satellite

In developed countries today, more than 65 percent of the households have Internet access, with Korea, Netherlands, Finland, and Sweden leading the way with more than 80 percent of households having Internet access, almost all via a high-speed broadband connection [ITU 2011]. Finland and Spain have recently declared high-speed Internet access to be a "legal right." Given this intense interest in home access, let's begin our overview of access networks by considering how homes connect to the Internet.

Today, the two most prevalent types of broadband residential access are **digital subscriber line (DSL)** and cable. A residence typically obtains DSL Internet access from the same local telephone company (telco) that provides its wired local phone access. Thus, when DSL is used, a customer's telco is also its ISP. As shown in Figure 1.5, each customer's DSL modem uses the existing telephone line (twisted-pair copper wire, which we'll discuss in Section 1.2.2) to exchange data with a digital subscriber line access multiplexer (DSLAM) located in the telco's local central office (CO). The home's DSL modem takes digital data and translates it to high-frequency tones for transmission over telephone wires to the CO; the analog signals from many such houses are translated back into digital format at the DSLAM.

The residential telephone line carries both data and traditional telephone signals simultaneously, which are encoded at different frequencies:

- A high-speed downstream channel, in the 50 kHz to 1 MHz band
- A medium-speed upstream channel, in the 4 kHz to 50 kHz band
- An ordinary two-way telephone channel, in the 0 to 4 kHz band

This approach makes the single DSL link appear as if there were three separate links, so that a telephone call and an Internet connection can share the DSL link at the same time. (We'll describe this technique of frequency-division multiplexing in

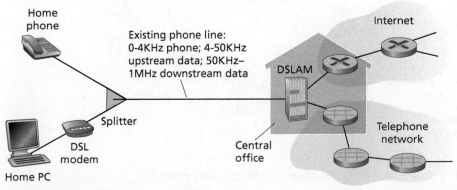

Figure 1.5 ♦ DSL Internet access

Section 1.3.1). On the customer side, a splitter separates the data and telephone signals arriving to the home and forwards the data signal to the DSL modem. On the telco side, in the CO, the DSLAM separates the data and phone signals and sends the data into the Internet. Hundreds or even thousands of households connect to a single DSLAM [Dischinger 2007].

The DSL standards define transmission rates of 12 Mbps downstream and 1.8 Mbps upstream [ITU 1999], and 24 Mbps downstream and 2.5 Mbps upstream [ITU 2003]. Because the downstream and upstream rates are different, the access is said to be asymmetric. The actual downstream and upstream transmission rates achieved may be less than the rates noted above, as the DSL provider may purposefully limit a residential rate when tiered service (different rates, available at different prices) are offered, or because the maximum rate can be limited by the distance between the home and the CO, the gauge of the twisted-pair line and the degree of electrical interference. Engineers have expressly designed DSL for short distances between the home and the CO; generally, if the residence is not located within 5 to 10 miles of the CO, the residence must resort to an alternative form of Internet access.

While DSL makes use of the telco's existing local telephone infrastructure, **cable Internet access** makes use of the cable television company's existing cable television infrastructure. A residence obtains cable Internet access from the same company that provides its cable television. As illustrated in Figure 1.6, fiber optics connect the cable head end to neighborhood-level junctions, from which traditional coaxial cable is then used to reach individual houses and apartments. Each neighborhood junction typically supports 500 to 5,000 homes. Because both fiber and coaxial cable are employed in this system, it is often referred to as hybrid fiber coax (HFC).

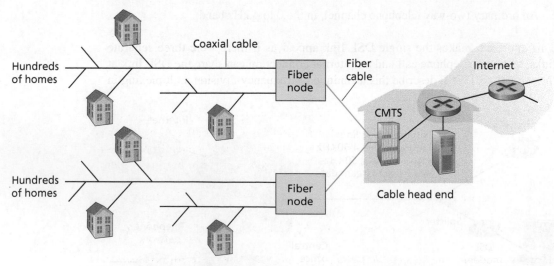

Figure 1.6 ♦ A hybrid fiber-coaxial access network

Cable internet access requires special modems, called cable modems. As with a DSL modem, the cable modem is typically an external device and connects to the home PC through an Ethernet port. (We will discuss Ethernet in great detail in Chapter 5.) At the cable head end, the cable modem termination system (CMTS) serves a similar function as the DSL network's DSLAM—turning the analog signal sent from the cable modems in many downstream homes back into digital format. Cable modems divide the HFC network into two channels, a downstream and an upstream channel. As with DSL, access is typically asymmetric, with the downstream channel typically allocated a higher transmission rate than the upstream channel. The DOCSIS 2.0 standard defines downstream rates up to 42.8 Mbps and upstream rates of up to 30.7 Mbps. As in the case of DSL networks, the maximum achievable rate may not be realized due to lower contracted data rates or media impairments.

One important characteristic of cable Internet access is that it is a shared broadcast medium. In particular, every packet sent by the head end travels downstream on every link to every home and every packet sent by a home travels on the upstream channel to the head end. For this reason, if several users are simultaneously downloading a video file on the downstream channel, the actual rate at which each user receives its video file will be significantly lower than the aggregate cable downstream rate. On the other hand, if there are only a few active users and they are all Web surfing, then each of the users may actually receive Web pages at the full cable downstream rate, because the users will rarely request a Web page at exactly the same time. Because the upstream channel is also shared, a distributed multiple access protocol is needed to coordinate transmissions and avoid collisions. (We'll discuss this collision issue in some detail in Chapter 5.)

Although DSL and cable networks currently represent more than 90 percent of residential broadband access in the United States, an up-and-coming technology that promises even higher speeds is the deployment of **fiber to the home (FTTH)** [FTTH Council 2011a]. As the name suggests, the FTTH concept is simple—provide an optical fiber path from the CO directly to the home. In the United States, Verizon has been particularly aggressive with FTTH with its FIOS service [Verizon FIOS 2012].

There are several competing technologies for optical distribution from the CO to the homes. The simplest optical distribution network is called direct fiber, with one fiber leaving the CO for each home. More commonly, each fiber leaving the central office is actually shared by many homes; it is not until the fiber gets relatively close to the homes that it is split into individual customer-specific fibers. There are two competing optical-distribution network architectures that perform this splitting: active optical networks (AONs) and passive optical networks (PONs). AON is essentially switched Ethernet, which is discussed in Chapter 5.

Here, we briefly discuss PON, which is used in Verizon's FIOS service. Figure 1.7 shows FTTH using the PON distribution architecture. Each home has

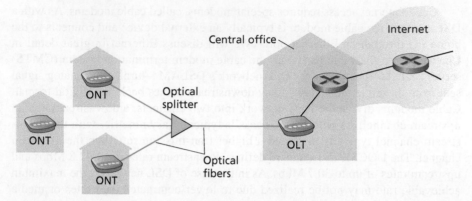

Figure 1.7 ◆ FTTH Internet access

an optical network terminator (ONT), which is connected by dedicated optical
fiber to a neighborhood splitter. The splitter combines a number of homes (typically
less than 100) onto a single, shared optical fiber, which connects to an optical line
terminator (OLT) in the telco's CO. The OLT, providing conversion between optical
and electrical signals, connects to the Internet via a telco router. In the home, users
connect a home router (typically a wireless router) to the ONT and access the Internet via this home router. In the PON architecture, all packets sent from OLT to the
splitter are replicated at the splitter (similar to a cable head end).

FTTH can potentially provide Internet access rates in the gigabits per second
range. However, most FTTH ISPs provide different rate offerings, with the higher
rates naturally costing more money. The average downstream speed of US FTTH
customers was approximately 20 Mbps in 2011 (compared with 13 Mbps for cable
access networks and less than 5 Mbps for DSL) [FTTH Council 2011b].

Two other access network technologies are also used to provide Internet access
to the home. In locations where DSL, cable, and FTTH are not available (e.g., in
some rural settings), a satellite link can be used to connect a residence to the Internet at speeds of more than 1 Mbps; StarBand and HughesNet are two such satellite
access providers. Dial-up access over traditional phone lines is based on the same
model as DSL—a home modem connects over a phone line to a modem in the ISP.
Compared with DSL and other broadband access networks, dial-up access is excru-
ciatingly slow at 56 kbps.

Access in the Enterprise (and the Home): Ethernet and WiFi

On corporate and university campuses, and increasingly in home settings, a local area
network (LAN) is used to connect an end system to the edge router. Although there
are many types of LAN technologies, Ethernet is by far the most prevalent access
technology in corporate, university, and home networks. As shown in Figure 1.8,
Ethernet users use twisted-pair copper wire to connect to an Ethernet switch, a

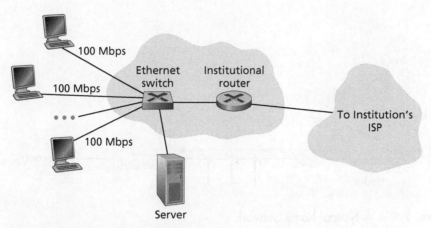

Figure 1.8 ♦ Ethernet Internet access

technology discussed in detail in Chapter 5. The Ethernet switch, or a network of such interconnected switches, is then in turn connected into the larger Internet. With Ethernet access, users typically have 100 Mbps access to the Ethernet switch, whereas servers may have 1 Gbps or even 10 Gbps access.

Increasingly, however, people are accessing the Internet wirelessly from laptops, smartphones, tablets, and other devices (see earlier sidebar on "A Dizzying Array of Devices"). In a wireless LAN setting, wireless users transmit/receive packets to/from an access point that is connected into the enterprise's network (most likely including wired Ethernet), which in turn is connected to the wired Internet. A wireless LAN user must typically be within a few tens of meters of the access point. Wireless LAN access based on IEEE 802.11 technology, more colloquially known as WiFi, is now just about everywhere—universities, business offices, cafes, airports, homes, and even in airplanes. In many cities, one can stand on a street corner and be within range of ten or twenty base stations (for a browseable global map of 802.11 base stations that have been discovered and logged on a Web site by people who take great enjoyment in doing such things, see [wigle.net 2012]). As discussed in detail in Chapter 6, 802.11 today provides a shared transmission rate of up to 54 Mbps.

Even though Ethernet and WiFi access networks were initially deployed in enterprise (corporate, university) settings, they have recently become relatively common components of home networks. Many homes combine broadband residential access (that is, cable modems or DSL) with these inexpensive wireless LAN technologies to create powerful home networks [Edwards 2011]. Figure 1.9 shows a typical home network. This home network consists of a roaming laptop as well as a wired PC; a base station (the wireless access point), which communicates with the wireless PC; a cable modem, providing broadband access to the Internet; and a router, which interconnects the base station and the stationary PC with the cable modem. This network allows household members to have broadband access to the Internet with one member roaming from the kitchen to the backyard to the bedrooms.

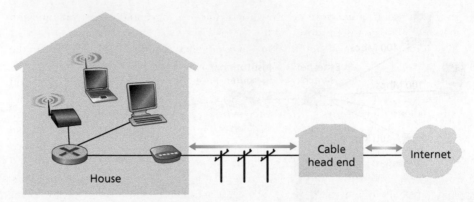

Figure 1.9 ♦ A typical home network

Wide-Area Wireless Access: 3G and LTE

Increasingly, devices such as iPhones, BlackBerrys, and Android devices are being used to send email, surf the Web, Tweet, and download music while on the run. These devices employ the same wireless infrastructure used for cellular telephony to send/receive packets through a base station that is operated by the cellular network provider. Unlike WiFi, a user need only be within a few tens of kilometers (as opposed to a few tens of meters) of the base station.

Telecommunications companies have made enormous investments in so-called third-generation (3G) wireless, which provides packet-switched wide-area wireless Internet access at speeds in excess of 1 Mbps. But even higher-speed wide-area access technologies—a fourth-generation (4G) of wide-area wireless networks—are already being deployed. LTE (for "Long-Term Evolution"—a candidate for Bad Acronym of the Year Award) has its roots in 3G technology, and can potentially achieve rates in excess of 10 Mbps. LTE downstream rates of many tens of Mbps have been reported in commercial deployments. We'll cover the basic principles of wireless networks and mobility, as well as WiFi, 3G, and LTE technologies (and more!) in Chapter 6.

1.2.2 Physical Media

In the previous subsection, we gave an overview of some of the most important network access technologies in the Internet. As we described these technologies, we also indicated the physical media used. For example, we said that HFC uses a combination of fiber cable and coaxial cable. We said that DSL and Ethernet use copper wire. And we said that mobile access networks use the radio spectrum.

In this subsection we provide a brief overview of these and other transmission media that are commonly used in the Internet.

In order to define what is meant by a physical medium, let us reflect on the brief life of a bit. Consider a bit traveling from one end system, through a series of links and routers, to another end system. This poor bit gets kicked around and transmitted many, many times! The source end system first transmits the bit, and shortly thereafter the first router in the series receives the bit; the first router then transmits the bit, and shortly thereafter the second router receives the bit; and so on. Thus our bit, when traveling from source to destination, passes through a series of transmitter-receiver pairs. For each transmitter-receiver pair, the bit is sent by propagating electromagnetic waves or optical pulses across a **physical medium**. The physical medium can take many shapes and forms and does not have to be of the same type for each transmitter-receiver pair along the path. Examples of physical media include twisted-pair copper wire, coaxial cable, multimode fiber-optic cable, terrestrial radio spectrum, and satellite radio spectrum. Physical media fall into two categories: **guided media** and **unguided media**. With guided media, the waves are guided along a solid medium, such as a fiber-optic cable, a twisted-pair copper wire, or a coaxial cable. With unguided media, the waves propagate in the atmosphere and in outer space, such as in a wireless LAN or a digital satellite channel.

But before we get into the characteristics of the various media types, let us say a few words about their costs. The actual cost of the physical link (copper wire, fiber-optic cable, and so on) is often relatively minor compared with other networking costs. In particular, the labor cost associated with the installation of the physical link can be orders of magnitude higher than the cost of the material. For this reason, many builders install twisted pair, optical fiber, and coaxial cable in every room in a building. Even if only one medium is initially used, there is a good chance that another medium could be used in the near future, and so money is saved by not having to lay additional wires in the future.

Twisted-Pair Copper Wire

The least expensive and most commonly used guided transmission medium is twisted-pair copper wire. For over a hundred years it has been used by telephone networks. In fact, more than 99 percent of the wired connections from the telephone handset to the local telephone switch use twisted-pair copper wire. Most of us have seen twisted pair in our homes and work environments. Twisted pair consists of two insulated copper wires, each about 1 mm thick, arranged in a regular spiral pattern. The wires are twisted together to reduce the electrical interference from similar pairs close by. Typically, a number of pairs are bundled together in a cable by wrapping the pairs in a protective shield. A wire pair constitutes a single communication link. **Unshielded twisted pair (UTP)** is commonly used for computer networks within a building, that is, for LANs. Data rates for LANs using twisted pair today range from 10 Mbps to 10 Gbps. The data rates that can be achieved depend on the thickness of the wire and the distance between transmitter and receiver.

When fiber-optic technology emerged in the 1980s, many people disparaged twisted pair because of its relatively low bit rates. Some people even felt that fiber-optic technology would completely replace twisted pair. But twisted pair did not give up so easily. Modern twisted-pair technology, such as category 6a cable, can achieve data rates of 10 Gbps for distances up to a hundred meters. In the end, twisted pair has emerged as the dominant solution for high-speed LAN networking.

As discussed earlier, twisted pair is also commonly used for residential Internet access. We saw that dial-up modem technology enables access at rates of up to 56 kbps over twisted pair. We also saw that DSL (digital subscriber line) technology has enabled residential users to access the Internet at tens of Mbps over twisted pair (when users live close to the ISP's modem).

Coaxial Cable

Like twisted pair, coaxial cable consists of two copper conductors, but the two conductors are concentric rather than parallel. With this construction and special insulation and shielding, coaxial cable can achieve high data transmission rates. Coaxial cable is quite common in cable television systems. As we saw earlier, cable television systems have recently been coupled with cable modems to provide residential users with Internet access at rates of tens of Mbps. In cable television and cable Internet access, the transmitter shifts the digital signal to a specific frequency band, and the resulting analog signal is sent from the transmitter to one or more receivers. Coaxial cable can be used as a guided **shared medium**. Specifically, a number of end systems can be connected directly to the cable, with each of the end systems receiving whatever is sent by the other end systems.

Fiber Optics

An optical fiber is a thin, flexible medium that conducts pulses of light, with each pulse representing a bit. A single optical fiber can support tremendous bit rates, up to tens or even hundreds of gigabits per second. They are immune to electromagnetic interference, have very low signal attenuation up to 100 kilometers, and are very hard to tap. These characteristics have made fiber optics the preferred long-haul guided transmission media, particularly for overseas links. Many of the long-distance telephone networks in the United States and elsewhere now use fiber optics exclusively. Fiber optics is also prevalent in the backbone of the Internet. However, the high cost of optical devices—such as transmitters, receivers, and switches—has hindered their deployment for short-haul transport, such as in a LAN or into the home in a residential access network. The Optical Carrier (OC) standard link speeds range from 51.8 Mbps to 39.8 Gbps; these specifications are often referred to as OC-n, where the link speed equals $n \times 51.8$ Mbps. Standards in use today include OC-1, OC-3, OC-12, OC-24, OC-48, OC-96, OC-192, OC-768. [Mukherjee 2006, Ramaswamy 2010] provide coverage of various aspects of optical networking.

Terrestrial Radio Channels

Radio channels carry signals in the electromagnetic spectrum. They are an attractive medium because they require no physical wire to be installed, can penetrate walls, provide connectivity to a mobile user, and can potentially carry a signal for long distances. The characteristics of a radio channel depend significantly on the propagation environment and the distance over which a signal is to be carried. Environmental considerations determine path loss and shadow fading (which decrease the signal strength as the signal travels over a distance and around/through obstructing objects), multipath fading (due to signal reflection off of interfering objects), and interference (due to other transmissions and electromagnetic signals).

Terrestrial radio channels can be broadly classified into three groups: those that operate over very short distance (e.g., with one or two meters); those that operate in local areas, typically spanning from ten to a few hundred meters; and those that operate in the wide area, spanning tens of kilometers. Personal devices such as wireless headsets, keyboards, and medical devices operate over short distances; the wireless LAN technologies described in Section 1.2.1 use local-area radio channels; the cellular access technologies use wide-area radio channels. We'll discuss radio channels in detail in Chapter 6.

Satellite Radio Channels

A communication satellite links two or more Earth-based microwave transmitter/ receivers, known as ground stations. The satellite receives transmissions on one frequency band, regenerates the signal using a repeater (discussed below), and transmits the signal on another frequency. Two types of satellites are used in communications: **geostationary satellites** and **low-earth orbiting (LEO) satellites**.

Geostationary satellites permanently remain above the same spot on Earth. This stationary presence is achieved by placing the satellite in orbit at 36,000 kilometers above Earth's surface. This huge distance from ground station through satellite back to ground station introduces a substantial signal propagation delay of 280 milliseconds. Nevertheless, satellite links, which can operate at speeds of hundreds of Mbps, are often used in areas without access to DSL or cable-based Internet access.

LEO satellites are placed much closer to Earth and do not remain permanently above one spot on Earth. They rotate around Earth (just as the Moon does) and may communicate with each other, as well as with ground stations. To provide continuous coverage to an area, many satellites need to be placed in orbit. There are currently many low-altitude communication systems in development. Lloyd's satellite constellations Web page [Wood 2012] provides and collects information on satellite constellation systems for communications. LEO satellite technology may be used for Internet access sometime in the future.

1.3 The Network Core

Having examined the Internet's edge, let us now delve more deeply inside the network core—the mesh of packet switches and links that interconnects the Internet's end systems. Figure 1.10 highlights the network core with thick, shaded lines.

1.3.1 Packet Switching

In a network application, end systems exchange **messages** with each other. Messages can contain anything the application designer wants. Messages may perform a control function (for example, the "Hi" messages in our handshaking example in Figure 1.2) or can contain data, such as an email message, a JPEG image, or an MP3 audio file. To send a message from a source end system to a destination end system, the source breaks long messages into smaller chunks of data known as **packets**. Between source and destination, each packet travels through communication links and **packet switches** (for which there are two predominant types, **routers** and **link-layer switches**). Packets are transmitted over each communication link at a rate equal to the *full* transmission rate of the link. So, if a source end system or a packet switch is sending a packet of L bits over a link with transmission rate R bits/sec, then the time to transmit the packet is L/R seconds.

Store-and-Forward Transmission

Most packet switches use **store-and-forward transmission** at the inputs to the links. Store-and-forward transmission means that the packet switch must receive the entire packet before it can begin to transmit the first bit of the packet onto the outbound link. To explore store-and-forward transmission in more detail, consider a simple network consisting of two end systems connected by a single router, as shown in Figure 1.11. A router will typically have many incident links, since its job is to switch an incoming packet onto an outgoing link; in this simple example, the router has the rather simple task of transferring a packet from one (input) link to the only other attached link. In this example, the source has three packets, each consisting of L bits, to send to the destination. At the snapshot of time shown in Figure 1.11, the source has transmitted some of packet 1, and the front of packet 1 has already arrived at the router. Because the router employs store-and-forwarding, at this instant of time, the router cannot transmit the bits it has received; instead it

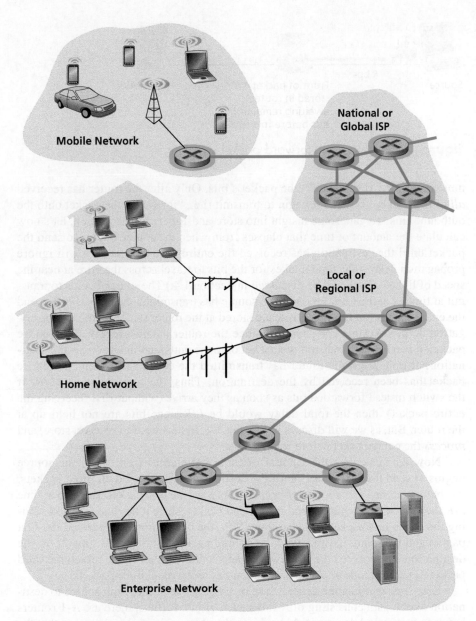

National or
Global ISP

Mobile Network

Local or
Regional ISP

Home Network

Enterprise Network

Figure 1.10 ♦ The network core

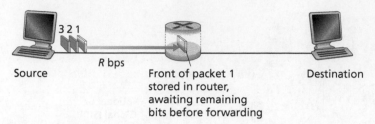

Figure 1.11 ♦ Store-and-forward packet switching

must first buffer (i.e., "store") the packet's bits. Only after the router has received *all* of the packet's bits can it begin to transmit (i.e., "forward") the packet onto the outbound link. To gain some insight into store-and-forward transmission, let's now calculate the amount of time that elapses from when the source begins to send the packet until the destination has received the entire packet. (Here we will ignore propagation delay—the time it takes for the bits to travel across the wire at near the speed of light—which will be discussed in Section 1.4.) The source begins to transmit at time 0; at time L/R seconds, the source has transmitted the entire packet, and the entire packet has been received and stored at the router (since there is no propagation delay). At time L/R seconds, since the router has just received the entire packet, it can begin to transmit the packet onto the outbound link towards the destination; at time $2L/R$, the router has transmitted the entire packet, and the entire packet has been received by the destination. Thus, the total delay is $2L/R$. If the switch instead forwarded bits as soon as they arrive (without first receiving the entire packet), then the total delay would be L/R since bits are not held up at the router. But, as we will discuss in Section 1.4, routers need to receive, store, and *process* the entire packet before forwarding.

Now let's calculate the amount of time that elapses from when the source begins to send the first packet until the destination has received all three packets. As before, at time L/R, the router begins to forward the first packet. But also at time L/R the source will begin to send the second packet, since it has just finished sending the entire first packet. Thus, at time $2L/R$, the destination has received the first packet and the router has received the second packet. Similarly, at time $3L/R$, the destination has received the first two packets and the router has received the third packet. Finally, at time $4L/R$ the destination has received all three packets!

Let's now consider the general case of sending one packet from source to destination over a path consisting of N links each of rate R (thus, there are N-1 routers between source and destination). Applying the same logic as above, we see that the end-to-end delay is:

$$d_{\text{end-to-end}} = N\frac{L}{R} \qquad (1.1)$$

You may now want to try to determine what the delay would be for P packets sent over a series of N links.

Queuing Delays and Packet Loss

Each packet switch has multiple links attached to it. For each attached link, the packet switch has an **output buffer** (also called an **output queue**), which stores packets that the router is about to send into that link. The output buffers play a key role in packet switching. If an arriving packet needs to be transmitted onto a link but finds the link busy with the transmission of another packet, the arriving packet must wait in the output buffer. Thus, in addition to the store-and-forward delays, packets suffer output buffer **queuing delays**. These delays are variable and depend on the level of congestion in the network. Since the amount of buffer space is finite, an arriving packet may find that the buffer is completely full with other packets waiting for transmission. In this case, **packet loss** will occur—either the arriving packet or one of the already-queued packets will be dropped.

Figure 1.12 illustrates a simple packet-switched network. As in Figure 1.11, packets are represented by three-dimensional slabs. The width of a slab represents the number of bits in the packet. In this figure, all packets have the same width and hence the same length. Suppose Hosts A and B are sending packets to Host E. Hosts A and B first send their packets along 10 Mbps Ethernet links to the first router. The router then directs these packets to the 1.5 Mbps link. If, during a short interval of time, the arrival rate of packets to the router (when converted to bits per second) exceeds 1.5 Mbps, congestion will occur at the router as packets queue in the link's output buffer before being transmitted onto the link. For example, if Host A and B each send a burst of five packets back-to-back at the same time, then most of these packets will spend some time waiting in the queue. The situation is, in fact, entirely analogous to many common-day situations—for example, when we wait in line for a bank teller or wait in front of a tollbooth. We'll examine this queuing delay in more detail in Section 1.4.

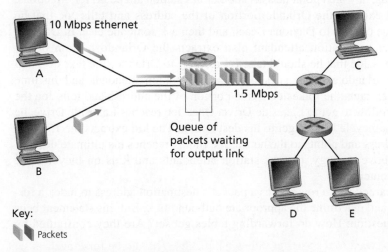

10 Mbps Ethernet

A

B

1.5 Mbps

Queue of
packets waiting
for output link

C

D E

Key:

Packets

Figure 1.12 ◆ Packet switching

Forwarding Tables and Routing Protocols

Earlier, we said that a router takes a packet arriving on one of its attached communication links and forwards that packet onto another one of its attached communication links. But how does the router determine which link it should forward the packet onto? Packet forwarding is actually done in different ways in different types of computer networks. Here, we briefly describe how it is done in the Internet.

In the Internet, every end system has an address called an IP address. When a source end system wants to send a packet to a destination end system, the source includes the destination's IP address in the packet's header. As with postal addresses, this address has a hierarchical structure. When a packet arrives at a router in the network, the router examines a portion of the packet's destination address and forwards the packet to an adjacent router. More specifically, each router has a **forwarding table** that maps destination addresses (or portions of the destination addresses) to that router's outbound links. When a packet arrives at a router, the router examines the address and searches its forwarding table, using this destination address, to find the appropriate outbound link. The router then directs the packet to this outbound link.

The end-to-end routing process is analogous to a car driver who does not use maps but instead prefers to ask for directions. For example, suppose Joe is driving from Philadelphia to 156 Lakeside Drive in Orlando, Florida. Joe first drives to his neighborhood gas station and asks how to get to 156 Lakeside Drive in Orlando, Florida. The gas station attendant extracts the Florida portion of the address and tells Joe that he needs to get onto the interstate highway I-95 South, which has an entrance just next to the gas station. He also tells Joe that once he enters Florida, he should ask someone else there. Joe then takes I-95 South until he gets to Jacksonville, Florida, at which point he asks another gas station attendant for directions. The attendant extracts the Orlando portion of the address and tells Joe that he should continue on I-95 to Daytona Beach and then ask someone else. In Daytona Beach, another gas station attendant also extracts the Orlando portion of the address and tells Joe that he should take I-4 directly to Orlando. Joe takes I-4 and gets off at the Orlando exit. Joe goes to another gas station attendant, and this time the attendant extracts the Lakeside Drive portion of the address and tells Joe the road he must follow to get to Lakeside Drive. Once Joe reaches Lakeside Drive, he asks a kid on a bicycle how to get to his destination. The kid extracts the 156 portion of the address and points to the house. Joe finally reaches his ultimate destination. In the above analogy, the gas station attendants and kids on bicycles are analogous to routers.

We just learned that a router uses a packet's destination address to index a forwarding table and determine the appropriate outbound link. But this statement begs yet another question: How do forwarding tables get set? Are they configured by hand in each and every router, or does the Internet use a more automated procedure? This issue will be studied in depth in Chapter 4. But to whet your appetite here, we'll note now that the Internet has a number of special **routing protocols** that are used to automatically set the forwarding tables. A routing protocol may, for example, determine the shortest path from each router to each destination and use the shortest path results to configure the forwarding tables in the routers.

How would you actually like to see the end-to-end route that packets take in the Internet? We now invite you to get your hands dirty by interacting with the Traceroute program. Simply visit the site www.traceroute.org, choose a source in a particular country, and trace the route from that source to your computer. (For a discussion of Traceroute, see Section 1.4.)

1.3.2 Circuit Switching

There are two fundamental approaches to moving data through a network of links and switches: **circuit switching** and **packet switching**. Having covered packet-switched networks in the previous subsection, we now turn our attention to circuit-switched networks.

In circuit-switched networks, the resources needed along a path (buffers, link transmission rate) to provide for communication between the end systems are *reserved* for the duration of the communication session between the end systems. In packet-switched networks, these resources are *not* reserved; a session's messages use the resources on demand, and as a consequence, may have to wait (that is, queue) for access to a communication link. As a simple analogy, consider two restaurants, one that requires reservations and another that neither requires reservations nor accepts them. For the restaurant that requires reservations, we have to go through the hassle of calling before we leave home. But when we arrive at the restaurant we can, in principle, immediately be seated and order our meal. For the restaurant that does not require reservations, we don't need to bother to reserve a table. But when we arrive at the restaurant, we may have to wait for a table before we can be seated.

Traditional telephone networks are examples of circuit-switched networks. Consider what happens when one person wants to send information (voice or facsimile) to another over a telephone network. Before the sender can send the information, the network must establish a connection between the sender and the receiver. This is a *bona fide* connection for which the switches on the path between the sender and receiver maintain connection state for that connection. In the jargon of telephony, this connection is called a **circuit**. When the network establishes the circuit, it also reserves a constant transmission rate in the network's links (representing a fraction of each link's transmission capacity) for the duration of the connection. Since a given transmission rate has been reserved for this sender-to-receiver connection, the sender can transfer the data to the receiver at the *guaranteed* constant rate.

Figure 1.13 illustrates a circuit-switched network. In this network, the four circuit switches are interconnected by four links. Each of these links has four circuits, so that each link can support four simultaneous connections. The hosts (for example, PCs and workstations) are each directly connected to one of the switches. When two hosts want to communicate, the network establishes a dedicated **end-to-end connection** between the two hosts. Thus, in order for Host A to communicate with Host B, the network must first reserve one circuit on each of two links. In this example, the dedicated end-to-end connection uses the second circuit in the first link and the fourth circuit in the second link. Because each link has four circuits, for each link used by the end-to-end connection, the connection gets one fourth of the link's total transmission capacity for the duration of the connection. Thus, for example, if each link between adjacent switches has a transmission rate of 1 Mbps, then each end-to-end circuit-switch connection gets 250 kbps of dedicated transmission rate.

In contrast, consider what happens when one host wants to send a packet to another host over a packet-switched network, such as the Internet. As with circuit switching, the packet is transmitted over a series of communication links. But different from circuit switching, the packet is sent into the network without reserving any link resources whatsoever. If one of the links is congested because other packets need to be transmitted over the link at the same time, then the packet will have to wait in a buffer at the sending side of the transmission link and suffer a delay. The Internet makes its best effort to deliver packets in a timely manner, but it does not make any guarantees.

Multiplexing in Circuit-Switched Networks

A circuit in a link is implemented with either **frequency-division multiplexing (FDM)** or **time-division multiplexing (TDM)**. With FDM, the frequency spectrum of a link is divided up among the connections established across the link.

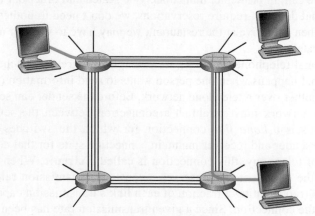

Figure 1.13 ♦ A simple circuit-switched network consisting of four switches and four links

Specifically, the link dedicates a frequency band to each connection for the duration of the connection. In telephone networks, this frequency band typically has a width of 4 kHz (that is, 4,000 hertz or 4,000 cycles per second). The width of the band is called, not surprisingly, the **bandwidth**. FM radio stations also use FDM to share the frequency spectrum between 88 MHz and 108 MHz, with each station being allocated a specific frequency band.

For a TDM link, time is divided into frames of fixed duration, and each frame is divided into a fixed number of time slots. When the network establishes a connection across a link, the network dedicates one time slot in every frame to this connection. These slots are dedicated for the sole use of that connection, with one time slot available for use (in every frame) to transmit the connection's data.

Figure 1.14 illustrates FDM and TDM for a specific network link supporting up to four circuits. For FDM, the frequency domain is segmented into four bands, each of bandwidth 4 kHz. For TDM, the time domain is segmented into frames, with four time slots in each frame; each circuit is assigned the same dedicated slot in the revolving TDM frames. For TDM, the transmission rate of a circuit is equal to the frame rate multiplied by the number of bits in a slot. For example, if the link transmits 8,000 frames per second and each slot consists of 8 bits, then the transmission rate of each circuit is 64 kbps.

Proponents of packet switching have always argued that circuit switching is wasteful because the dedicated circuits are idle during **silent periods**. For example,

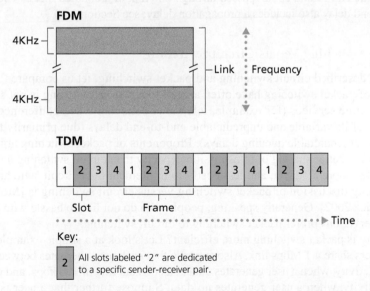

Figure 1.14 ◆ With FDM, each circuit continuously gets a fraction of the bandwidth. With TDM, each circuit gets all of the bandwidth periodically during brief intervals of time (that is, during slots)

when one person in a telephone call stops talking, the idle network resources (frequency bands or time slots in the links along the connection's route) cannot be used by other ongoing connections. As another example of how these resources can be underutilized, consider a radiologist who uses a circuit-switched network to remotely access a series of x-rays. The radiologist sets up a connection, requests an image, contemplates the image, and then requests a new image. Network resources are allocated to the connection but are not used (i.e., are wasted) during the radiologist's contemplation periods. Proponents of packet switching also enjoy pointing out that establishing end-to-end circuits and reserving end-to-end transmission capacity is complicated and requires complex signaling software to coordinate the operation of the switches along the end-to-end path.

Before we finish our discussion of circuit switching, let's work through a numerical example that should shed further insight on the topic. Let us consider how long it takes to send a file of 640,000 bits from Host A to Host B over a circuit-switched network. Suppose that all links in the network use TDM with 24 slots and have a bit rate of 1.536 Mbps. Also suppose that it takes 500 msec to establish an end-to-end circuit before Host A can begin to transmit the file. How long does it take to send the file? Each circuit has a transmission rate of (1.536 Mbps)/24 = 64 kbps, so it takes (640,000 bits)/(64 kbps) = 10 seconds to transmit the file. To this 10 seconds we add the circuit establishment time, giving 10.5 seconds to send the file. Note that the transmission time is independent of the number of links: The transmission time would be 10 seconds if the end-to-end circuit passed through one link or a hundred links. (The actual end-to-end delay also includes a propagation delay; see Section 1.4.)

Packet Switching Versus Circuit Switching

Having described circuit switching and packet switching, let us compare the two. Critics of packet switching have often argued that packet switching is not suitable for real-time services (for example, telephone calls and video conference calls) because of its variable and unpredictable end-to-end delays (due primarily to variable and unpredictable queuing delays). Proponents of packet switching argue that (1) it offers better sharing of transmission capacity than circuit switching and (2) it is simpler, more efficient, and less costly to implement than circuit switching. An interesting discussion of packet switching versus circuit switching is [Molinero-Fernandez 2002]. Generally speaking, people who do not like to hassle with restaurant reservations prefer packet switching to circuit switching.

Why is packet switching more efficient? Let's look at a simple example. Suppose users share a 1 Mbps link. Also suppose that each user alternates between periods of activity, when a user generates data at a constant rate of 100 kbps, and periods of inactivity, when a user generates no data. Suppose further that a user is active only 10 percent of the time (and is idly drinking coffee during the remaining 90 percent of the time). With circuit switching, 100 kbps must be *reserved* for *each* user at all times. For example, with circuit-switched TDM, if a one-second frame is divided into 10 time slots of 100 ms each, then each user would be allocated one time slot per frame.

Thus, the circuit-switched link can support only 10 (= 1 Mbps/100 kbps) simultaneous users. With packet switching, the probability that a specific user is active is 0.1 (that is, 10 percent). If there are 35 users, the probability that there are 11 or more simultaneously active users is approximately 0.0004. (Homework Problem P8 outlines how this probability is obtained.) When there are 10 or fewer simultaneously active users (which happens with probability 0.9996), the aggregate arrival rate of data is less than or equal to 1 Mbps, the output rate of the link. Thus, when there are 10 or fewer active users, users' packets flow through the link essentially without delay, as is the case with circuit switching. When there are more than 10 simultaneously active users, then the aggregate arrival rate of packets exceeds the output capacity of the link, and the output queue will begin to grow. (It continues to grow until the aggregate input rate falls back below 1 Mbps, at which point the queue will begin to diminish in length.) Because the probability of having more than 10 simultaneously active users is minuscule in this example, packet switching provides essentially the same performance as circuit switching, *but does so while allowing for more than three times the number of users.*

Let's now consider a second simple example. Suppose there are 10 users and that one user suddenly generates one thousand 1,000-bit packets, while other users remain quiescent and do not generate packets. Under TDM circuit switching with 10 slots per frame and each slot consisting of 1,000 bits, the active user can only use its one time slot per frame to transmit data, while the remaining nine time slots in each frame remain idle. It will be 10 seconds before all of the active user's one million bits of data has been transmitted. In the case of packet switching, the active user can continuously send its packets at the full link rate of 1 Mbps, since there are no other users generating packets that need to be multiplexed with the active user's packets. In this case, all of the active user's data will be transmitted within 1 second.

The above examples illustrate two ways in which the performance of packet switching can be superior to that of circuit switching. They also highlight the crucial difference between the two forms of sharing a link's transmission rate among multiple data streams. Circuit switching pre-allocates use of the transmission link regardless of demand, with allocated but unneeded link time going unused. Packet switching on the other hand allocates link use *on demand.* Link transmission capacity will be shared on a packet-by-packet basis only among those users who have packets that need to be transmitted over the link.

Although packet switching and circuit switching are both prevalent in today's telecommunication networks, the trend has certainly been in the direction of packet switching. Even many of today's circuit-switched telephone networks are slowly migrating toward packet switching. In particular, telephone networks often use packet switching for the expensive overseas portion of a telephone call.

1.3.3 A Network of Networks

We saw earlier that end systems (PCs, smartphones, Web servers, mail servers, and so on) connect into the Internet via an access ISP. The access ISP can provide either wired or wireless connectivity, using an array of access technologies including DSL, cable, FTTH, Wi-Fi, and cellular. Note that the access ISP does not have to be a telco or a cable company; instead it can be, for example, a university (providing Internet access to students, staff, and faculty), or a company (providing access for its employees). But connecting end users and content providers into an access ISP is only a small piece of solving the puzzle of connecting the billions of end systems that make up the Internet. To complete this puzzle, the access ISPs themselves must be interconnected. This is done by creating a *network of networks*—understanding this phrase is the key to understanding the Internet.

Over the years, the network of networks that forms the Internet has evolved into a very complex structure. Much of this evolution is driven by economics and national policy, rather than by performance considerations. In order to understand today's Internet network structure, let's incrementally build a series of network structures, with each new structure being a better approximation of the complex Internet that we have today. Recall that the overarching goal is to interconnect the access ISPs so that all end systems can send packets to each other. One naive approach would be to have each access ISP *directly* connect with every other access ISP. Such a mesh design is, of course, much too costly for the access ISPs, as it would require each access ISP to have a separate communication link to each of the hundreds of thousands of other access ISPs all over the world.

Our first network structure, *Network Structure 1*, interconnects all of the access ISPs with a *single global transit ISP*. Our (imaginary) global transit ISP is a network of routers and communication links that not only spans the globe, but also has at least one router near each of the hundreds of thousands of access ISPs. Of course, it would be very costly for the global ISP to build such an extensive network. To be profitable, it would naturally charge each of the access ISPs for connectivity, with the pricing reflecting (but not necessarily directly proportional to) the amount of traffic an access ISP exchanges with the global ISP. Since the access ISP pays the global transit ISP, the access ISP is said to be a **customer** and the global transit ISP is said to be a **provider**.

Now if some company builds and operates a global transit ISP that is profitable, then it is natural for other companies to build their own global transit ISPs and compete with the original global transit ISP. This leads to *Network Structure 2*, which consists of the hundreds of thousands of access ISPs and *multiple* global transit ISPs. The access ISPs certainly prefer Network Structure 2 over Network Structure 1 since they can now choose among the competing global transit providers as a function of their pricing and services. Note, however, that the global transit ISPs themselves must interconnect: Otherwise access ISPs connected to one of the global transit providers would not be able to communicate with access ISPs connected to the other global transit providers.

Network Structure 2, just described, is a two-tier hierarchy with global transit providers residing at the top tier and access ISPs at the bottom tier. This assumes that global transit ISPs are not only capable of getting close to each and every access ISP, but also find it economically desirable to do so. In reality, although some ISPs do have impressive global coverage and do directly connect with many access ISPs, no ISP has presence in each and every city in the world. Instead, in any given region, there may be a **regional ISP** to which the access ISPs in the region connect. Each regional ISP then connects to **tier-1 ISPs**. Tier-1 ISPs are similar to our (imaginary) global transit ISP; but tier-1 ISPs, which actually do exist, do not have a presence in every city in the world. There are approximately a dozen tier-1 ISPs, including Level 3 Communications, AT&T, Sprint, and NTT. Interestingly, no group officially sanctions tier-1 status; as the saying goes—if you have to ask if you're a member of a group, you're probably not.

Returning to this network of networks, not only are there multiple competing tier-1 ISPs, there may be multiple competing regional ISPs in a region. In such a hierarchy, each access ISP pays the regional ISP to which it connects, and each regional ISP pays the tier-1 ISP to which it connects. (An access ISP can also connect directly to a tier-1 ISP, in which case it pays the tier-1 ISP). Thus, there is customer-provider relationship at each level of the hierarchy. Note that the tier-1 ISPs do not pay anyone as they are at the top of the hierarchy. To further complicate matters, in some regions, there may be a larger regional ISP (possibly spanning an entire country) to which the smaller regional ISPs in that region connect; the larger regional ISP then connects to a tier-1 ISP. For example, in China, there are access ISPs in each city, which connect to provincial ISPs, which in turn connect to national ISPs, which finally connect to tier-1 ISPs [Tian 2012]. We refer to this multi-tier hierarchy, which is still only a crude approximation of today's Internet, as *Network Structure 3*.

To build a network that more closely resembles today's Internet, we must add points of presence (PoPs), multi-homing, peering, and Internet exchange points (IXPs) to the hierarchical Network Structure 3. PoPs exist in all levels of the hierarchy, except for the bottom (access ISP) level. A **PoP** is simply a group of one or more routers (at the same location) in the provider's network where customer ISPs can connect into the provider ISP. For a customer network to connect to a provider's PoP, it can lease a high-speed link from a third-party telecommunications provider to directly connect one of its routers to a router at the PoP. Any ISP (except for tier-1 ISPs) may choose to **multi-home**, that is, to connect to two or more provider ISPs. So, for example, an access ISP may multi-home with two regional ISPs, or it may multi-home with two regional ISPs and also with a tier-1 ISP. Similarly, a regional ISP may multi-home with multiple tier-1 ISPs. When an

ISP multi-homes, it can continue to send and receive packets into the Internet even if one of its providers has a failure.

As we just learned, customer ISPs pay their provider ISPs to obtain global Internet interconnectivity. The amount that a customer ISP pays a provider ISP reflects the amount of traffic it exchanges with the provider. To reduce these costs, a pair of nearby ISPs at the same level of the hierarchy can **peer**, that is, they can directly connect their networks together so that all the traffic between them passes over the direct connection rather than through upstream intermediaries. When two ISPs peer, it is typically settlement-free, that is, neither ISP pays the other. As noted earlier, tier-1 ISPs also peer with one another, settlement-free. For a readable discussion of peering and customer-provider relationships, see [Van der Berg 2008]. Along these same lines, a third-party company can create an **Internet Exchange Point (IXP)** (typically in a stand-alone building with its own switches), which is a meeting point where multiple ISPs can peer together. There are roughly 300 IXPs in the Internet today [Augustin 2009]. We refer to this ecosystem—consisting of access ISPs, regional ISPs, tier-1 ISPs, PoPs, multi-homing, peering, and IXPs—as *Network Structure 4*.

We now finally arrive at *Network Structure 5,* which describes the Internet of 2012. Network Structure 5, illustrated in Figure 1.15, builds on top of Network Structure 4 by adding **content provider networks**. Google is currently one of the leading examples of such a content provider network. As of this writing, it is estimated that Google has 30 to 50 data centers distributed across North America, Europe, Asia, South America, and Australia. Some of these data centers house over one hundred thousand servers, while other data centers are smaller, housing only hundreds of servers. The Google data centers are all interconnected via Google's private TCP/IP network, which spans the entire globe but is nevertheless separate from the public Internet. Importantly, the Google private network only

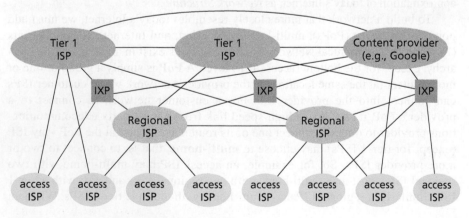

Figure 1.15 ♦ Interconnection of ISPs

carries traffic to/from Google servers. As shown in Figure 1.15, the Google private network attempts to "bypass" the upper tiers of the Internet by peering (settlement free) with lower-tier ISPs, either by directly connecting with them or by connecting with them at IXPs [Labovitz 2010]. However, because many access ISPs can still only be reached by transiting through tier-1 networks, the Google network also connects to tier-1 ISPs, and pays those ISPs for the traffic it exchanges with them. By creating its own network, a content provider not only reduces its payments to upper-tier ISPs, but also has greater control of how its services are ultimately delivered to end users. Google's network infrastructure is described in greater detail in Section 7.2.4.

In summary, today's Internet—a network of networks—is complex, consisting of a dozen or so tier-1 ISPs and hundreds of thousands of lower-tier ISPs. The ISPs are diverse in their coverage, with some spanning multiple continents and oceans, and others limited to narrow geographic regions. The lower-tier ISPs connect to the higher-tier ISPs, and the higher-tier ISPs interconnect with one another. Users and content providers are customers of lower-tier ISPs, and lower-tier ISPs are customers of higher-tier ISPs. In recent years, major content providers have also created their own networks and connect directly into lower-tier ISPs where possible.

1.4 Delay, Loss, and Throughput in Packet-Switched Networks

Back in Section 1.1 we said that the Internet can be viewed as an infrastructure that provides services to distributed applications running on end systems. Ideally, we would like Internet services to be able to move as much data as we want between any two end systems, instantaneously, without any loss of data. Alas, this is a lofty goal, one that is unachievable in reality. Instead, computer networks necessarily constrain throughput (the amount of data per second that can be transferred) between end systems, introduce delays between end systems, and can actually lose packets. On one hand, it is unfortunate that the physical laws of reality introduce delay and loss as well as constrain throughput. On the other hand, because computer networks have these problems, there are many fascinating issues surrounding how to deal with the problems—more than enough issues to fill a course on computer networking and to motivate thousands of PhD theses! In this section, we'll begin to examine and quantify delay, loss, and throughput in computer networks.

1.4.1 Overview of Delay in Packet-Switched Networks

Recall that a packet starts in a host (the source), passes through a series of routers, and ends its journey in another host (the destination). As a packet travels from one node (host or router) to the subsequent node (host or router) along this path, the

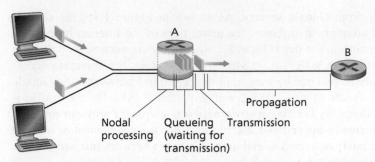

Figure 1.16 ♦ The nodal delay at router A

packet suffers from several types of delays at *each* node along the path. The most important of these delays are the **nodal processing delay, queuing delay, transmission delay,** and **propagation delay**; together, these delays accumulate to give a **total nodal delay**. The performance of many Internet applications—such as search, Web browsing, email, maps, instant messaging, and voice-over-IP—are greatly affected by network delays. In order to acquire a deep understanding of packet switching and computer networks, we must understand the nature and importance of these delays.

Types of Delay

Let's explore these delays in the context of Figure 1.16. As part of its end-to-end route between source and destination, a packet is sent from the upstream node through router A to router B. Our goal is to characterize the nodal delay at router A. Note that router A has an outbound link leading to router B. This link is preceded by a queue (also known as a buffer). When the packet arrives at router A from the upstream node, router A examines the packet's header to determine the appropriate outbound link for the packet and then directs the packet to this link. In this example, the outbound link for the packet is the one that leads to router B. A packet can be transmitted on a link only if there is no other packet currently being transmitted on the link and if there are no other packets preceding it in the queue; if the link is currently busy or if there are other packets already queued for the link, the newly arriving packet will then join the queue.

Processing Delay

The time required to examine the packet's header and determine where to direct the packet is part of the **processing delay**. The processing delay can also include other factors, such as the time needed to check for bit-level errors in the packet that occurred in transmitting the packet's bits from the upstream node to router A. Processing delays in high-speed routers are typically on the order of microseconds or less. After this nodal processing, the router directs the packet to the queue that precedes the link to router B. (In Chapter 4 we'll study the details of how a router operates.)

Queuing Delay

At the queue, the packet experiences a **queuing delay** as it waits to be transmitted onto the link. The length of the queuing delay of a specific packet will depend on the number of earlier-arriving packets that are queued and waiting for transmission onto the link. If the queue is empty and no other packet is currently being transmitted, then our packet's queuing delay will be zero. On the other hand, if the traffic is heavy and many other packets are also waiting to be transmitted, the queuing delay will be long. We will see shortly that the number of packets that an arriving packet might expect to find is a function of the intensity and nature of the traffic arriving at the queue. Queuing delays can be on the order of microseconds to milliseconds in practice.

Transmission Delay

Assuming that packets are transmitted in a first-come-first-served manner, as is common in packet-switched networks, our packet can be transmitted only after all the packets that have arrived before it have been transmitted. Denote the length of the packet by L bits, and denote the transmission rate of the link from router A to router B by R bits/sec. For example, for a 10 Mbps Ethernet link, the rate is $R = 10$ Mbps; for a 100 Mbps Ethernet link, the rate is $R = 100$ Mbps. The **transmission delay** is L/R. This is the amount of time required to push (that is, transmit) all of the packet's bits into the link. Transmission delays are typically on the order of microseconds to milliseconds in practice.

Propagation Delay

Once a bit is pushed into the link, it needs to propagate to router B. The time required to propagate from the beginning of the link to router B is the **propagation delay**. The bit propagates at the propagation speed of the link. The propagation speed depends on the physical medium of the link (that is, fiber optics, twisted-pair copper wire, and so on) and is in the range of

$$2 \cdot 10^8 \text{ meters/sec to } 3 \cdot 10^8 \text{ meters/sec}$$

which is equal to, or a little less than, the speed of light. The propagation delay is the distance between two routers divided by the propagation speed. That is, the propagation delay is d/s, where d is the distance between router A and router B and s is the propagation speed of the link. Once the last bit of the packet propagates to node B, it and all the preceding bits of the packet are stored in router B. The whole process then continues with router B now performing the forwarding. In wide-area networks, propagation delays are on the order of milliseconds.

Comparing Transmission and Propagation Delay

Newcomers to the field of computer networking sometimes have difficulty understanding the difference between transmission delay and propagation delay. The difference is subtle but important. The transmission delay is the amount of time required for the router to push out the packet; it is a function of the packet's length and the transmission rate of the link, but has nothing to do with the distance between the two routers. The propagation delay, on the other hand, is the time it takes a bit to propagate from one router to the next; it is a function of the distance between the two routers, but has nothing to do with the packet's length or the transmission rate of the link.

An analogy might clarify the notions of transmission and propagation delay. Consider a highway that has a tollbooth every 100 kilometers, as shown in Figure 1.17. You can think of the highway segments between tollbooths as links and the tollbooths as routers. Suppose that cars travel (that is, propagate) on the highway at a rate of 100 km/hour (that is, when a car leaves a tollbooth, it instantaneously accelerates to 100 km/hour and maintains that speed between tollbooths). Suppose next that 10 cars, traveling together as a caravan, follow each other in a fixed order. You can think of each car as a bit and the caravan as a packet. Also suppose that each tollbooth services (that is, transmits) a car at a rate of one car per 12 seconds, and that it is late at night so that the caravan's cars are the only cars on the highway. Finally, suppose that whenever the first car of the caravan arrives at a tollbooth, it waits at the entrance until the other nine cars have arrived and lined up behind it. (Thus the entire caravan must be stored at the tollbooth before it can begin to be forwarded.) The time required for the tollbooth to push the entire caravan onto the highway is (10 cars)/(5 cars/minute) = 2 minutes. This time is analogous to the transmission delay in a router. The time required for a car to travel from the exit of one tollbooth to the next tollbooth is 100 km/(100 km/hour) = 1 hour. This time is analogous to propagation delay. Therefore, the time from when the caravan is stored in front of a tollbooth until the caravan is stored in front of the next tollbooth is the sum of transmission delay and propagation delay—in this example, 62 minutes.

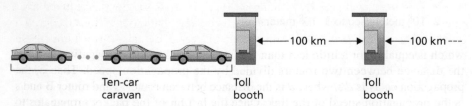

Figure 1.17 ♦ Caravan analogy

Let's explore this analogy a bit more. What would happen if the tollbooth service time for a caravan were greater than the time for a car to travel between tollbooths? For example, suppose now that the cars travel at the rate of 1,000 km/hour and the tollbooth services cars at the rate of one car per minute. Then the traveling delay between two tollbooths is 6 minutes and the time to serve a caravan is 10 minutes. In this case, the first few cars in the caravan will arrive at the second tollbooth before the last cars in the caravan leave the first tollbooth. This situation also arises in packet-switched networks—the first bits in a packet can arrive at a router while many of the remaining bits in the packet are still waiting to be transmitted by the preceding router.

If a picture speaks a thousand words, then an animation must speak a million words. The companion Web site for this textbook provides an interactive Java applet that nicely illustrates and contrasts transmission delay and propagation delay. The reader is highly encouraged to visit that applet. [Smith 2009] also provides a very readable discussion of propagation, queueing, and transmission delays.

If we let d_{proc}, d_{queue}, d_{trans}, and d_{prop} denote the processing, queuing, transmission, and propagation delays, then the total nodal delay is given by

$$d_{nodal} = d_{proc} + d_{queue} + d_{trans} + d_{prop}$$

The contribution of these delay components can vary significantly. For example, d_{prop} can be negligible (for example, a couple of microseconds) for a link connecting two routers on the same university campus; however, d_{prop} is hundreds of milliseconds for two routers interconnected by a geostationary satellite link, and can be the dominant term in d_{nodal}. Similarly, d_{trans} can range from negligible to significant. Its contribution is typically negligible for transmission rates of 10 Mbps and higher (for example, for LANs); however, it can be hundreds of milliseconds for large Internet packets sent over low-speed dial-up modem links. The processing delay, d_{proc}, is often negligible; however, it strongly influences a router's maximum throughput, which is the maximum rate at which a router can forward packets.

1.4.2 Queuing Delay and Packet Loss

The most complicated and interesting component of nodal delay is the queuing delay, d_{queue}. In fact, queuing delay is so important and interesting in computer networking that thousands of papers and numerous books have been written about it [Bertsekas 1991; Daigle 1991; Kleinrock 1975, 1976; Ross 1995]. We give only a high-level, intuitive discussion of queuing delay here; the more curious reader may want to browse through some of the books (or even eventually write a PhD thesis on the subject!). Unlike the other three delays (namely, d_{proc}, d_{trans}, and d_{prop}), the queuing delay can vary from packet to packet. For example, if 10 packets arrive at an empty queue at the same time, the first packet transmitted will suffer no queuing delay, while the last packet transmitted will suffer a relatively large queuing delay (while it waits for the other nine packets to be transmitted). Therefore, when characterizing queuing delay, one typically uses statistical measures, such as average queuing delay, variance of queuing delay, and the probability that the queuing delay exceeds some specified value.

When is the queuing delay large and when is it insignificant? The answer to this question depends on the rate at which traffic arrives at the queue, the transmission rate of the link, and the nature of the arriving traffic, that is, whether the traffic arrives periodically or arrives in bursts. To gain some insight here, let a denote the average rate at which packets arrive at the queue (a is in units of packets/sec). Recall that R is the transmission rate; that is, it is the rate (in bits/sec) at which bits are pushed out of the queue. Also suppose, for simplicity, that all packets consist of L bits. Then the average rate at which bits arrive at the queue is La bits/sec. Finally, assume that the queue is very big, so that it can hold essentially an infinite number of bits. The ratio La/R, called the **traffic intensity**, often plays an important role in estimating the extent of the queuing delay. If $La/R > 1$, then the average rate at which bits arrive at the queue exceeds the rate at which the bits can be transmitted from the queue. In this unfortunate situation, the queue will tend to increase without bound and the queuing delay will approach infinity! Therefore, one of the golden rules in traffic engineering is: *Design your system so that the traffic intensity is no greater than 1*.

Now consider the case $La/R \leq 1$. Here, the nature of the arriving traffic impacts the queuing delay. For example, if packets arrive periodically—that is, one packet arrives every L/R seconds—then every packet will arrive at an empty queue and there will be no queuing delay. On the other hand, if packets arrive in bursts but periodically, there can be a significant average queuing delay. For example, suppose N packets arrive simultaneously every $(L/R)N$ seconds. Then the first packet transmitted has no queuing delay; the second packet transmitted has a queuing delay of L/R seconds; and more generally, the nth packet transmitted has a queuing delay of $(n - 1)L/R$ seconds. We leave it as an exercise for you to calculate the average queuing delay in this example.

The two examples of periodic arrivals described above are a bit academic. Typically, the arrival process to a queue is *random;* that is, the arrivals do not follow any pattern and the packets are spaced apart by random amounts of time. In this more realistic case, the quantity La/R is not usually sufficient to fully characterize the queueing delay statistics. Nonetheless, it is useful in gaining an intuitive understanding of the extent of the queuing delay. In particular, if the traffic intensity is close to zero, then packet arrivals are few and far between and it is unlikely that an arriving packet will find another packet in the queue. Hence, the average queuing delay will be close to zero. On the other hand, when the traffic intensity is close to 1, there will be intervals of time when the arrival rate exceeds the transmission capacity (due to variations in packet arrival rate), and a queue will form during these periods of time; when the arrival rate is less than the transmission capacity, the length of the queue will shrink. Nonetheless, as the traffic intensity approaches 1, the average queue length gets larger and larger. The qualitative dependence of average queuing delay on the traffic intensity is shown in Figure 1.18.

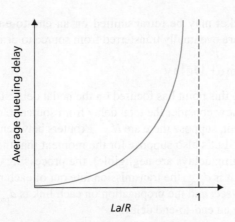

Figure 1.18 ♦ Dependence of average queuing delay on traffic intensity

One important aspect of Figure 1.18 is the fact that as the traffic intensity approaches 1, the average queuing delay increases rapidly. A small percentage increase in the intensity will result in a much larger percentage-wise increase in delay. Perhaps you have experienced this phenomenon on the highway. If you regularly drive on a road that is typically congested, the fact that the road is typically congested means that its traffic intensity is close to 1. If some event causes an even slightly larger-than-usual amount of traffic, the delays you experience can be huge.

To really get a good feel for what queuing delays are about, you are encouraged once again to visit the companion Web site, which provides an interactive Java applet for a queue. If you set the packet arrival rate high enough so that the traffic intensity exceeds 1, you will see the queue slowly build up over time.

Packet Loss

In our discussions above, we have assumed that the queue is capable of holding an infinite number of packets. In reality a queue preceding a link has finite capacity, although the queuing capacity greatly depends on the router design and cost. Because the queue capacity is finite, packet delays do not really approach infinity as the traffic intensity approaches 1. Instead, a packet can arrive to find a full queue. With no place to store such a packet, a router will **drop** that packet; that is, the packet will be **lost**. This overflow at a queue can again be seen in the Java applet for a queue when the traffic intensity is greater than 1.

From an end-system viewpoint, a packet loss will look like a packet having been transmitted into the network core but never emerging from the network at the destination. The fraction of lost packets increases as the traffic intensity increases. Therefore, performance at a node is often measured not only in terms of delay, but also in terms of the probability of packet loss. As we'll discuss in the subsequent chapters, a lost packet may be retransmitted on an end-to-end basis in order to ensure that all data are eventually transferred from source to destination

1.4.3 End-to-End Delay

Our discussion up to this point has focused on the nodal delay, that is, the delay at a single router. Let's now consider the total delay from source to destination. To get a handle on this concept, suppose there are $N - 1$ routers between the source host and the destination host. Let's also suppose for the moment that the network is uncongested (so that queuing delays are negligible), the processing delay at each router and at the source host is d_{proc}, the transmission rate out of each router and out of the source host is R bits/sec, and the propagation on each link is d_{prop}. The nodal delays accumulate and give an end-to-end delay,

$$d_{end\text{-}end} = N\,(d_{proc} + d_{trans} + d_{prop}) \tag{1.2}$$

where, once again, $d_{trans} = L/R,$ where L is the packet size. Note that Equation 1.2 is a generalization of Equation 1.1, which did not take into account processing and propagation delays. We leave it to you to generalize Equation 1.2 to the case of heterogeneous delays at the nodes and to the presence of an average queuing delay at each node.

Traceroute

VideoNote
Using Traceroute to discover network paths and measure network delay

To get a hands-on feel for end-to-end delay in a computer network, we can make use of the Traceroute program. Traceroute is a simple program that can run in any Internet host. When the user specifies a destination hostname, the program in the source host sends multiple, special packets toward that destination. As these packets work their way toward the destination, they pass through a series of routers. When a router receives one of these special packets, it sends back to the source a short message that contains the name and address of the router.

More specifically, suppose there are $N - 1$ routers between the source and the destination. Then the source will send N special packets into the network, with each packet addressed to the ultimate destination. These N special packets are marked 1 through N, with the first packet marked 1 and the last packet marked N. When the nth router receives the nth packet marked n, the router does not forward the packet toward its destination, but instead sends a message back to the source. When the destination host receives the Nth packet, it too returns a message back to the source. The source records the time that elapses between when it sends a packet and when it receives the corresponding return message; it also records the name and address of the router (or the destination host) that returns the message. In this manner, the source can reconstruct the route taken by packets flowing from source to destination, and the source can determine the round-trip delays to all the intervening routers. Traceroute actually repeats the experiment just described three times, so the source actually sends $3 \cdot N$ packets to the destination. RFC 1393 describes Traceroute in detail.

Here is an example of the output of the Traceroute program, where the route was being traced from the source host gaia.cs.umass.edu (at the University of Massachusetts) to the host cis.poly.edu (at Polytechnic University in Brooklyn). The output has six columns: the first column is the n value described above, that is, the number of the router along the route; the second column is the name of the router; the third column is the address of the router (of the form xxx.xxx.xxx.xxx); the last three columns are the round-trip delays for three experiments. If the source receives fewer than three messages from any given router (due to packet loss in the network), Traceroute places an asterisk just after the router number and reports fewer than three round-trip times for that router.

```
1 cs-gw (128.119.240.254) 1.009 ms 0.899 ms 0.993 ms
2 128.119.3.154 (128.119.3.154) 0.931 ms 0.441 ms 0.651 ms
3 border4-rt-gi-1-3.gw.umass.edu (128.119.2.194) 1.032 ms 0.484 ms 0.451 ms
4 acr1-ge-2-1-0.Boston.cw.net (208.172.51.129) 10.006 ms 8.150 ms 8.460 ms
5 agr4-loopback.NewYork.cw.net (206.24.194.104) 12.272 ms 14.344 ms 13.267 ms
6 acr2-loopback.NewYork.cw.net (206.24.194.62) 13.225 ms 12.292 ms 12.148 ms
7 pos10-2.core2.NewYork1.Level3.net (209.244.160.133) 12.218 ms 11.823 ms 11.793 ms
8 gige9-1-52.hsipaccess1.NewYork1.Level3.net (64.159.17.39) 13.081 ms 11.556 ms 13.297 ms
9 p0-0.polyu.bbnplanet.net (4.25.109.122) 12.716 ms 13.052 ms 12.786 ms
10 cis.poly.edu (128.238.32.126) 14.080 ms 13.035 ms 12.802 ms
```

In the trace above there are nine routers between the source and the destination. Most of these routers have a name, and all of them have addresses. For example, the name of Router 3 is `border4-rt-gi-1-3.gw.umass.edu` and its address is `128.119.2.194`. Looking at the data provided for this same router, we see that in the first of the three trials the round-trip delay between the source and the router was 1.03 msec. The round-trip delays for the subsequent two trials were 0.48 and 0.45 msec. These round-trip delays include all of the delays just discussed, including transmission delays, propagation delays, router processing delays, and queuing delays. Because the queuing delay is varying with time, the round-trip delay of packet n sent to a router n can sometimes be longer than the round-trip delay of packet $n+1$ sent to router $n+1$. Indeed, we observe this phenomenon in the above example: the delays to Router 6 are larger than the delays to Router 7!

Want to try out Traceroute for yourself? We *highly* recommended that you visit http://www.traceroute.org, which provides a Web interface to an extensive list of sources for route tracing. You choose a source and supply the hostname for any destination. The Traceroute program then does all the work. There are a number of free software programs that provide a graphical interface to Traceroute; one of our favorites is PingPlotter [PingPlotter 2012].

End System, Application, and Other Delays

In addition to processing, transmission, and propagation delays, there can be additional significant delays in the end systems. For example, an end system wanting to transmit a packet into a shared medium (e.g., as in a WiFi or cable modem scenario) may *purposefully* delay its transmission as part of its protocol for sharing the medium with other end systems; we'll consider such protocols in detail in Chapter 5. Another important delay is media packetization delay, which is present in Voice-over-IP (VoIP) applications. In VoIP, the sending side must first fill a packet with encoded digitized speech before passing the packet to the Internet. This time to fill a packet—called the packetization delay—can be significant and can impact the user-perceived quality of a VoIP call. This issue will be further explored in a homework problem at the end of this chapter.

1.4.4 Throughput in Computer Networks

In addition to delay and packet loss, another critical performance measure in computer networks is end-to-end throughput. To define throughput, consider transferring a large file from Host A to Host B across a computer network. This transfer might be, for example, a large video clip from one peer to another in a P2P file sharing system. The **instantaneous throughput** at any instant of time is the rate (in bits/sec) at which Host B is receiving the file. (Many applications, including many P2P file sharing systems, display the instantaneous throughput during downloads in the user interface—perhaps you have observed this before!) If the file consists of F bits and the transfer takes T seconds for Host B to receive all F bits, then the **average throughput** of the file transfer is F/T bits/sec. For some applications, such as Internet telephony, it is desirable to have a low delay and an instantaneous throughput consistently above some threshold (for example, over 24 kbps for some Internet telephony applications and over 256 kbps for some real-time video applications). For other applications, including those involving file transfers, delay is not critical, but it is desirable to have the highest possible throughput.

To gain further insight into the important concept of throughput, let's consider a few examples. Figure 1.19(a) shows two end systems, a server and a client, connected by two communication links and a router. Consider the throughput for a file transfer from the server to the client. Let R_s denote the rate of the link between the server and the router; and R_c denote the rate of the link between the router and the client. Suppose that the only bits being sent in the entire network are those from the server to the client. We now ask, in this ideal scenario, what is the server-to-client throughput? To answer this question, we may think of bits as *fluid* and communication links as *pipes*. Clearly, the server cannot pump bits through its link at a rate faster than R_s bps; and the router cannot forward bits at a rate faster than R_c bps. If $R_s < R_c$, then the bits pumped by the server will "flow" right through the router and arrive at the client at a rate of R_s bps, giving a throughput of R_s bps. If, on the other hand, $R_c < R_s$, then the router will not be able to forward bits as quickly as it receives them. In this case, bits will only leave the router at rate R_c, giving an

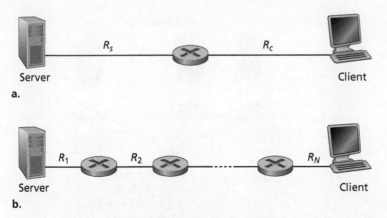

Figure 1.19 ♦ Throughput for a file transfer from server to client

end-to-end throughput of R_c. (Note also that if bits continue to arrive at the router at rate R_s, and continue to leave the router at R_c, the backlog of bits at the router waiting for transmission to the client will grow and grow—a most undesirable situation!) Thus, for this simple two-link network, the throughput is $\min\{R_c, R_s\}$, that is, it is the transmission rate of the **bottleneck link**. Having determined the throughput, we can now approximate the time it takes to transfer a large file of F bits from server to client as $F/\min\{R_s, R_c\}$. For a specific example, suppose you are downloading an MP3 file of $F = 32$ million bits, the server has a transmission rate of $R_s = 2$ Mbps, and you have an access link of $R_c = 1$ Mbps. The time needed to transfer the file is then 32 seconds. Of course, these expressions for throughput and transfer time are only approximations, as they do not account for store-and-forward and processing delays as well as protocol issues.

Figure 1.19(b) now shows a network with N links between the server and the client, with the transmission rates of the N links being $R_1, R_2,..., R_N$. Applying the same analysis as for the two-link network, we find that the throughput for a file transfer from server to client is $\min\{R_1, R_2,..., R_N\}$, which is once again the transmission rate of the bottleneck link along the path between server and client.

Now consider another example motivated by today's Internet. Figure 1.20(a) shows two end systems, a server and a client, connected to a computer network. Consider the throughput for a file transfer from the server to the client. The server is connected to the network with an access link of rate R_s and the client is connected to the network with an access link of rate R_c. Now suppose that all the links in the core of the communication network have very high transmission rates, much higher than R_s and R_c. Indeed, today, the core of the Internet is over-provisioned with high speed links that experience little congestion. Also suppose that the only bits being sent in the entire network are those from the server to the client. Because the core of the computer network is like a wide pipe in this example, the rate at which bits can flow

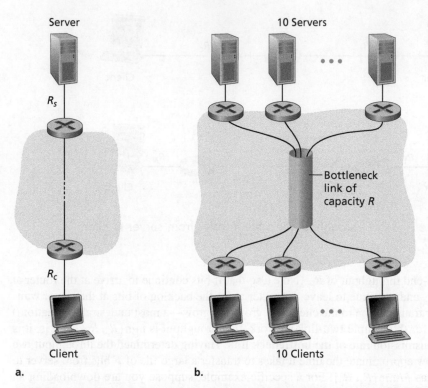

Figure 1.20 ♦ End-to-end throughput: (a) Client downloads a file from server; (b) 10 clients downloading with 10 servers

from source to destination is again the minimum of R_s and R_c, that is, throughput = $\min\{R_s, R_c\}$. Therefore, the constraining factor for throughput in today's Internet is typically the access network.

For a final example, consider Figure 1.20(b) in which there are 10 servers and 10 clients connected to the core of the computer network. In this example, there are 10 simultaneous downloads taking place, involving 10 client-server pairs. Suppose that these 10 downloads are the only traffic in the network at the current time. As shown in the figure, there is a link in the core that is traversed by all 10 downloads. Denote R for the transmission rate of this link R. Let's suppose that all server access links have the same rate R_s, all client access links have the same rate R_c, and the transmission rates of all the links in the core—except the one common link of rate R—are much larger than R_s, R_c, and R. Now we ask, what are the throughputs of the downloads? Clearly, if the rate of the common link, R, is large—say a hundred times larger than both R_s and R_c—then the throughput for each download will once again be $\min\{R_s, R_c\}$. But what if the rate of the common link is of the same order as R_s and R_c? What will the throughput be in this case? Let's take a look at a specific example. Suppose R_s = 2 Mbps, R_c = 1 Mbps, R = 5 Mbps, and the common link divides its transmission rate equally among the 10 downloads. Then the bottleneck for each download is no longer in the access network, but is now instead the shared link in the core, which only provides each download with 500 kbps of throughput. Thus the end-to-end throughput for each download is now reduced to 500 kbps.

The examples in Figure 1.19 and Figure 1.20(a) show that throughput depends on the transmission rates of the links over which the data flows. We saw that when there is no other intervening traffic, the throughput can simply be approximated as the minimum transmission rate along the path between source and destination. The example in Figure 1.20(b) shows that more generally the throughput depends not only on the transmission rates of the links along the path, but also on the intervening traffic. In particular, a link with a high transmission rate may nonetheless be the bottleneck link for a file transfer if many other data flows are also passing through that link. We will examine throughput in computer networks more closely in the homework problems and in the subsequent chapters.

1.5 Protocol Layers and Their Service Models

From our discussion thus far, it is apparent that the Internet is an *extremely* complicated system. We have seen that there are many pieces to the Internet: numerous applications and protocols, various types of end systems, packet switches, and various types of link-level media. Given this enormous complexity, is there any hope of organizing a network architecture, or at least our discussion of network architecture? Fortunately, the answer to both questions is yes.

1.5.1 Layered Architecture

Before attempting to organize our thoughts on Internet architecture, let's look for a human analogy. Actually, we deal with complex systems all the time in our everyday life. Imagine if someone asked you to describe, for example, the airline system. How would you find the structure to describe this complex system that has ticketing agents, baggage checkers, gate personnel, pilots, airplanes, air traffic control, and a worldwide system for routing airplanes? One way to describe this system might be to describe the series of actions you take (or others take for you) when you fly on an airline. You purchase your ticket, check your bags, go to the gate, and eventually get loaded onto the plane. The plane takes off and is routed to its destination. After your plane lands, you deplane at the gate and claim your bags. If the trip was bad, you complain about the flight to the ticket agent (getting nothing for your effort). This scenario is shown in Figure 1.21.

Already, we can see some analogies here with computer networking: You are being shipped from source to destination by the airline; a packet is shipped from

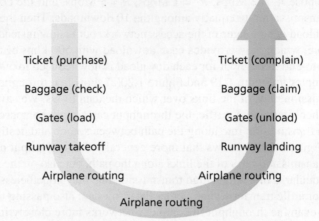

Ticket (purchase)   Ticket (complain)

Baggage (check)   Baggage (claim)

Gates (load)   Gates (unload)

Runway takeoff   Runway landing

Airplane routing   Airplane routing

Airplane routing

Figure 1.21 ♦ Taking an airplane trip: actions

source host to destination host in the Internet. But this is not quite the analogy we are after. We are looking for some *structure* in Figure 1.21. Looking at Figure 1.21, we note that there is a ticketing function at each end; there is also a baggage function for already-ticketed passengers, and a gate function for already-ticketed and already-baggage-checked passengers. For passengers who have made it through the gate (that is, passengers who are already ticketed, baggage-checked, and through the gate), there is a takeoff and landing function, and while in flight, there is an airplane-routing function. This suggests that we can look at the functionality in Figure 1.21 in a *horizontal* manner, as shown in Figure 1.22.

Figure 1.22 has divided the airline functionality into layers, providing a framework in which we can discuss airline travel. Note that each layer, combined with the

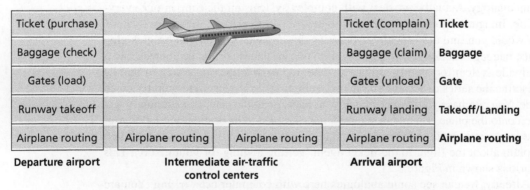

Ticket (purchase)			Ticket (complain)	**Ticket**
Baggage (check)			Baggage (claim)	**Baggage**
Gates (load)			Gates (unload)	**Gate**
Runway takeoff			Runway landing	**Takeoff/Landing**
Airplane routing	Airplane routing	Airplane routing	Airplane routing	**Airplane routing**
Departure airport	**Intermediate air-traffic control centers**		**Arrival airport**	

Figure 1.22 ♦ Horizontal layering of airline functionality

layers below it, implements some functionality, some *service*. At the ticketing layer and below, airline-counter-to-airline-counter transfer of a person is accomplished. At the baggage layer and below, baggage-check-to-baggage-claim transfer of a person and bags is accomplished. Note that the baggage layer provides this service only to an already-ticketed person. At the gate layer, departure-gate-to-arrival-gate transfer of a person and bags is accomplished. At the takeoff/landing layer, runway-to-runway transfer of people and their bags is accomplished. Each layer provides its service by (1) performing certain actions within that layer (for example, at the gate layer, loading and unloading people from an airplane) and by (2) using the services of the layer directly below it (for example, in the gate layer, using the runway-to-runway passenger transfer service of the takeoff/landing layer).

A layered architecture allows us to discuss a well-defined, specific part of a large and complex system. This simplification itself is of considerable value by providing modularity, making it much easier to change the implementation of the service provided by the layer. As long as the layer provides the same service to the layer above it, and uses the same services from the layer below it, the remainder of the system remains unchanged when a layer's implementation is changed. (Note that changing the implementation of a service is very different from changing the service itself!) For example, if the gate functions were changed (for instance, to have people board and disembark by height), the remainder of the airline system would remain unchanged since the gate layer still provides the same function (loading and unloading people); it simply implements that function in a different manner after the change. For large and complex systems that are constantly being updated, the ability to change the implementation of a service without affecting other components of the system is another important advantage of layering.

Protocol Layering

But enough about airlines. Let's now turn our attention to network protocols. To provide structure to the design of network protocols, network designers organize protocols—and the network hardware and software that implement the protocols—in **layers**. Each protocol belongs to one of the layers, just as each function in the airline architecture in Figure 1.22 belonged to a layer. We are again interested in the **services** that a layer offers to the layer above—the so-called **service model** of a layer. Just as in the case of our airline example, each layer provides its service by (1) performing certain actions within that layer and by (2) using the services of the layer directly below it. For example, the services provided by layer n may include reliable delivery of messages from one edge of the network to the other. This might be implemented by using an unreliable edge-to-edge message delivery service of layer $n - 1$, and adding layer n functionality to detect and retransmit lost messages.

A protocol layer can be implemented in software, in hardware, or in a combination of the two. Application-layer protocols—such as HTTP and SMTP—are almost

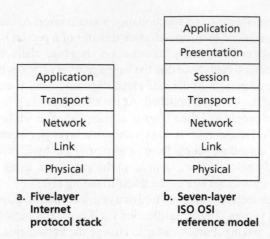

Figure 1.23 ♦ The Internet protocol stack (a) and OSI reference model (b)

always implemented in software in the end systems; so are transport-layer protocols. Because the physical layer and data link layers are responsible for handling communication over a specific link, they are typically implemented in a network interface card (for example, Ethernet or WiFi interface cards) associated with a given link. The network layer is often a mixed implementation of hardware and software. Also note that just as the functions in the layered airline architecture were distributed among the various airports and flight control centers that make up the system, so too is a layer *n* protocol *distributed* among the end systems, packet switches, and other components that make up the network. That is, there's often a piece of a layer *n* protocol in each of these network components.

Protocol layering has conceptual and structural advantages [RFC 3439]. As we have seen, layering provides a structured way to discuss system components. Modularity makes it easier to update system components. We mention, however, that some researchers and networking engineers are vehemently opposed to layering [Wakeman 1992]. One potential drawback of layering is that one layer may duplicate lower-layer functionality. For example, many protocol stacks provide error recovery on both a per-link basis and an end-to-end basis. A second potential drawback is that functionality at one layer may need information (for example, a timestamp value) that is present only in another layer; this violates the goal of separation of layers.

When taken together, the protocols of the various layers are called the **protocol stack**. The Internet protocol stack consists of five layers: the physical, link, network, transport, and application layers, as shown in Figure 1.23(a). If you examine the Table of Contents, you will see that we have roughly organized this book using the layers of the Internet protocol stack. We take a **top-down approach**, first covering the application layer and then proceeding downward.

Application Layer

The application layer is where network applications and their application-layer protocols reside. The Internet's application layer includes many protocols, such as the HTTP protocol (which provides for Web document request and transfer), SMTP (which provides for the transfer of e-mail messages), and FTP (which provides for the transfer of files between two end systems). We'll see that certain network functions, such as the translation of human-friendly names for Internet end systems like www.ietf.org to a 32-bit network address, are also done with the help of a specific application-layer protocol, namely, the domain name system (DNS). We'll see in Chapter 2 that it is very easy to create and deploy our own new application-layer protocols.

An application-layer protocol is distributed over multiple end systems, with the application in one end system using the protocol to exchange packets of information with the application in another end system. We'll refer to this packet of information at the application layer as a **message**.

Transport Layer

The Internet's transport layer transports application-layer messages between application endpoints. In the Internet there are two transport protocols, TCP and UDP, either of which can transport application-layer messages. TCP provides a connection-oriented service to its applications. This service includes guaranteed delivery of application-layer messages to the destination and flow control (that is, sender/receiver speed matching). TCP also breaks long messages into shorter segments and provides a congestion-control mechanism, so that a source throttles its transmission rate when the network is congested. The UDP protocol provides a connectionless service to its applications. This is a no-frills service that provides no reliability, no flow control, and no congestion control. In this book, we'll refer to a transport-layer packet as a **segment**.

Network Layer

The Internet's network layer is responsible for moving network-layer packets known as **datagrams** from one host to another. The Internet transport-layer protocol (TCP or UDP) in a source host passes a transport-layer segment and a destination address to the network layer, just as you would give the postal service a letter with a destination address. The network layer then provides the service of delivering the segment to the transport layer in the destination host.

The Internet's network layer includes the celebrated IP Protocol, which defines the fields in the datagram as well as how the end systems and routers act on these fields. There is only one IP protocol, and all Internet components that have a network layer must run the IP protocol. The Internet's network layer also contains routing protocols that determine the routes that datagrams take between sources and destinations. The Internet has many routing protocols. As we saw in Section 1.3, the Internet is a network of networks, and within a network, the network administrator can run any routing protocol desired. Although the network layer contains both the IP protocol and numerous routing protocols, it is often simply referred to as the IP layer, reflecting the fact that IP is the glue that binds the Internet together.

Link Layer

The Internet's network layer routes a datagram through a series of routers between the source and destination. To move a packet from one node (host or router) to the next node in the route, the network layer relies on the services of the link layer. In particular, at each node, the network layer passes the datagram down to the link layer, which delivers the datagram to the next node along the route. At this next node, the link layer passes the datagram up to the network layer.

The services provided by the link layer depend on the specific link-layer protocol that is employed over the link. For example, some link-layer protocols provide reliable delivery, from transmitting node, over one link, to receiving node. Note that this reliable delivery service is different from the reliable delivery service of TCP, which provides reliable delivery from one end system to another. Examples of link-layer protocols include Ethernet, WiFi, and the cable access network's DOCSIS protocol. As datagrams typically need to traverse several links to travel from source to destination, a datagram may be handled by different link-layer protocols at different links along its route. For example, a datagram may be handled by Ethernet on one link and by PPP on the next link. The network layer will receive a different service from each of the different link-layer protocols. In this book, we'll refer to the link-layer packets as **frames**.

Physical Layer

While the job of the link layer is to move entire frames from one network element to an adjacent network element, the job of the physical layer is to move the *individual bits* within the frame from one node to the next. The protocols in this layer are again link dependent and further depend on the actual transmission medium of the link (for example, twisted-pair copper wire, single-mode fiber optics). For example, Ethernet has many physical-layer protocols: one for twisted-pair copper wire, another for coaxial cable, another for fiber, and so on. In each case, a bit is moved across the link in a different way.

The OSI Model

Having discussed the Internet protocol stack in detail, we should mention that it is not the only protocol stack around. In particular, back in the late 1970s, the International Organization for Standardization (ISO) proposed that computer networks be organized around seven layers, called the Open Systems Interconnection (OSI) model [ISO 2012]. The OSI model took shape when the protocols that were to become the Internet protocols were in their infancy, and were but one of many different protocol suites under development; in fact, the inventors of the original OSI model probably did not have the Internet in mind when creating it. Nevertheless, beginning in the late 1970s, many training and university courses picked up on the ISO mandate and organized courses around the seven-layer model. Because of its early impact on networking education, the seven-layer model continues to linger on in some networking textbooks and training courses.

The seven layers of the OSI reference model, shown in Figure 1.23(b), are: application layer, presentation layer, session layer, transport layer, network layer, data link layer, and physical layer. The functionality of five of these layers is roughly the same as their similarly named Internet counterparts. Thus, let's consider the two additional layers present in the OSI reference model—the presentation layer and the session layer. The role of the presentation layer is to provide services that allow communicating applications to interpret the meaning of data exchanged. These services include data compression and data encryption (which are self-explanatory) as well as data description (which, as we will see in Chapter 9, frees the applications from having to worry about the internal format in which data are represented/stored—formats that may differ from one computer to another). The session layer provides for delimiting and synchronization of data exchange, including the means to build a checkpointing and recovery scheme.

The fact that the Internet lacks two layers found in the OSI reference model poses a couple of interesting questions: Are the services provided by these layers unimportant? What if an application *needs* one of these services? The Internet's answer to both of these questions is the same—it's up to the application developer. It's up to the application developer to decide if a service is important, and if the service *is* important, it's up to the application developer to build that functionality into the application.

1.5.2 Encapsulation

Figure 1.24 shows the physical path that data takes down a sending end system's protocol stack, up and down the protocol stacks of an intervening link-layer switch and router, and then up the protocol stack at the receiving end system. As we discuss later in this book, routers and link-layer switches are both packet switches. Similar to end systems, routers and link-layer switches organize their networking hardware and software into layers. But routers and link-layer switches do not implement *all* of the layers in the protocol stack; they typically implement only the bottom layers. As shown in Figure 1.24, link-layer switches implement layers 1 and 2; routers implement layers 1 through 3. This means, for example, that Internet routers are capable of implementing the IP protocol (a layer 3 protocol), while link-layer switches are not. We'll see later that while link-layer switches do not recognize IP addresses, they

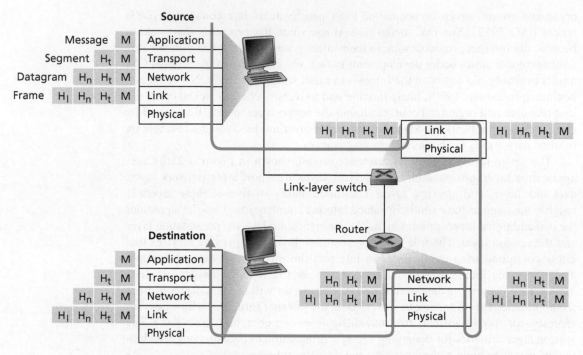

Figure 1.24 ♦ Hosts, routers, and link-layer switches; each contains a different set of layers, reflecting their differences in functionality

are capable of recognizing layer 2 addresses, such as Ethernet addresses. Note that hosts implement all five layers; this is consistent with the view that the Internet architecture puts much of its complexity at the edges of the network.

Figure 1.24 also illustrates the important concept of **encapsulation**. At the sending host, an **application-layer message** (M in Figure 1.24) is passed to the transport layer. In the simplest case, the transport layer takes the message and appends additional information (so-called transport-layer header information, H_t in Figure 1.24) that will be used by the receiver-side transport layer. The application-layer message and the transport-layer header information together constitute the **transport-layer segment**. The transport-layer segment thus encapsulates the application-layer message. The added information might include information allowing the receiver-side transport layer to deliver the message up to the appropriate application, and error-detection bits that allow the receiver to determine whether bits in the message have been changed in route. The transport layer then passes the segment to the network layer, which adds network-layer header information (H_n in Figure 1.24) such as source and destination end system addresses, creating a **network-layer datagram**. The datagram is then passed to the link layer, which (of course!) will add its own link-layer header information and create a **link-layer frame**. Thus, we see that at each layer, a packet has two types of fields: header fields and a **payload field**. The payload is typically a packet from the layer above.

A useful analogy here is the sending of an interoffice memo from one corporate branch office to another via the public postal service. Suppose Alice, who is in one branch office, wants to send a memo to Bob, who is in another branch office. The *memo* is analogous to the *application-layer message*. Alice puts the memo in an interoffice envelope with Bob's name and department written on the front of the envelope. The *interoffice envelope* is analogous to a *transport-layer segment*—it contains header information (Bob's name and department number) and it encapsulates the application-layer message (the memo). When the sending branch-office mailroom receives the interoffice envelope, it puts the interoffice envelope inside yet another envelope, which is suitable for sending through the public postal service. The sending mailroom also writes the postal address of the sending and receiving branch offices on the postal envelope. Here, the *postal envelope* is analogous to the *datagram*—it encapsulates the transport-layer segment (the interoffice envelope), which encapsulates the original message (the memo). The postal service delivers the postal envelope to the receiving branch-office mailroom. There, the process of de-encapsulation is begun. The mailroom extracts the interoffice memo and forwards it to Bob. Finally, Bob opens the envelope and removes the memo.

The process of encapsulation can be more complex than that described above. For example, a large message may be divided into multiple transport-layer segments (which might themselves each be divided into multiple network-layer datagrams). At the receiving end, such a segment must then be reconstructed from its constituent datagrams.

1.6 Networks Under Attack

The Internet has become mission critical for many institutions today, including large and small companies, universities, and government agencies. Many individuals also rely on the Internet for many of their professional, social, and personal activities. But behind all this utility and excitement, there is a dark side, a side where "bad guys" attempt to wreak havoc in our daily lives by damaging our Internet-connected computers, violating our privacy, and rendering inoperable the Internet services on which we depend.

The field of network security is about how the bad guys can attack computer networks and about how we, soon-to-be experts in computer networking, can defend networks against those attacks, or better yet, design new architectures that are immune to such attacks in the first place. Given the frequency and variety of existing attacks as well as the threat of new and more destructive future attacks, network security has become a central topic in the field of computer networking. One of the features of this textbook is that it brings network security issues to the forefront.

Since we don't yet have expertise in computer networking and Internet protocols, we'll begin here by surveying some of today's more prevalent security-related problems. This will whet our appetite for more substantial discussions in the upcoming chapters. So we begin here by simply asking, what can go wrong? How are computer networks vulnerable? What are some of the more prevalent types of attacks today?

The bad guys can put malware into your host via the Internet

We attach devices to the Internet because we want to receive/send data from/to the Internet. This includes all kinds of good stuff, including Web pages, e-mail messages, MP3s, telephone calls, live video, search engine results, and so on. But, unfortunately, along with all that good stuff comes malicious stuff—collectively known as **malware**—that can also enter and infect our devices. Once malware infects our device it can do all kinds of devious things, including deleting our files; installing spyware that collects our private information, such as social security numbers, passwords, and keystrokes, and then sends this (over the Internet, of course!) back to the bad guys. Our compromised host may also be enrolled in a network of thousands of similarly compromised devices, collectively known as a **botnet**, which the bad guys control and leverage for spam e-mail distribution or distributed denial-of-service attacks (soon to be discussed) against targeted hosts.

Much of the malware out there today is **self-replicating**: once it infects one host, from that host it seeks entry into other hosts over the Internet, and from the newly infected hosts, it seeks entry into yet more hosts. In this manner, self-replicating malware can spread exponentially fast. Malware can spread in the form of a virus or a worm. **Viruses** are malware that require some form of user interaction to infect the user's device. The classic example is an e-mail attachment containing malicious executable code. If a user receives and opens such an attachment, the user inadvertently runs the malware on the device. Typically, such e-mail viruses are self-replicating: once executed, the virus may send an identical message with an identical malicious attachment to, for example, every recipient in the user's address book. **Worms** are malware that can enter a device without any explicit user interaction. For example, a user may be running a vulnerable network application to which an attacker can send malware. In some cases, without any user intervention, the application may accept the malware from the Internet and

1.6 • NETWORKS UNDER ATTACK   **83**

run it, creating a worm. The worm in the newly infected device then scans the Internet, searching for other hosts running the same vulnerable network application. When it finds other vulnerable hosts, it sends a copy of itself to those hosts. Today, malware, is pervasive and costly to defend against. As you work through this textbook, we encourage you to think about the following question: What can computer network designers do to defend Internet-attached devices from malware attacks?

The bad guys can attack servers and network infrastructure

Another broad class of security threats are known as **denial-of-service (DoS) attacks**. As the name suggests, a DoS attack renders a network, host, or other piece of infrastructure unusable by legitimate users. Web servers, e-mail servers, DNS servers (discussed in Chapter 2), and institutional networks can all be subject to DoS attacks. Internet DoS attacks are extremely common, with thousands of DoS attacks occurring every year [Moore 2001; Mirkovic 2005]. Most Internet DoS attacks fall into one of three categories:

- *Vulnerability attack.* This involves sending a few well-crafted messages to a vulnerable application or operating system running on a targeted host. If the right sequence of packets is sent to a vulnerable application or operating system, the service can stop or, worse, the host can crash.
- *Bandwidth flooding.* The attacker sends a deluge of packets to the targeted host—so many packets that the target's access link becomes clogged, preventing legitimate packets from reaching the server.
- *Connection flooding.* The attacker establishes a large number of half-open or fully open TCP connections (TCP connections are discussed in Chapter 3) at the target host. The host can become so bogged down with these bogus connections that it stops accepting legitimate connections.

Let's now explore the bandwidth-flooding attack in more detail. Recalling our delay and loss analysis discussion in Section 1.4.2, it's evident that if the server has an access rate of R bps, then the attacker will need to send traffic at a rate of approximately R bps to cause damage. If R is very large, a single attack source may not be able to generate enough traffic to harm the server. Furthermore, if all the traffic emanates from a single source, an upstream router may be able to detect the attack and block all traffic from that source before the traffic gets near the server. In a **distributed DoS (DDoS)** attack, illustrated in Figure 1.25, the attacker controls multiple sources and has each source blast traffic at the target. With this approach, the aggregate traffic rate across all the controlled sources needs to be approximately R to cripple the

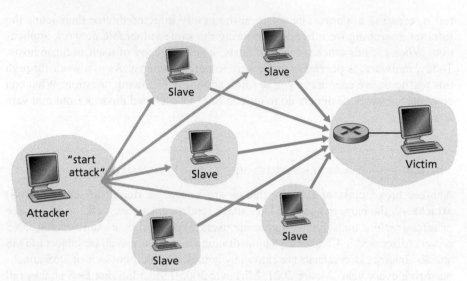

Figure 1.25 ♦ A distributed denial-of-service attack

service. DDoS attacks leveraging botnets with thousands of comprised hosts are a common occurrence today [Mirkovic 2005]. DDos attacks are much harder to detect and defend against than a DoS attack from a single host.

We encourage you to consider the following question as you work your way through this book: What can computer network designers do to defend against DoS attacks? We will see that different defenses are needed for the three types of DoS attacks.

The bad guys can sniff packets

Many users today access the Internet via wireless devices, such as WiFi-connected laptops or handheld devices with cellular Internet connections (covered in Chapter 6). While ubiquitous Internet access is extremely convenient and enables marvelous new applications for mobile users, it also creates a major security vulnerability—by placing a passive receiver in the vicinity of the wireless transmitter, that receiver can obtain a copy of every packet that is transmitted! These packets can contain all kinds of sensitive information, including passwords, social security numbers, trade secrets, and private personal messages. A passive receiver that records a copy of every packet that flies by is called a **packet sniffer**.

Sniffers can be deployed in wired environments as well. In wired broadcast environments, as in many Ethernet LANs, a packet sniffer can obtain copies of broadcast packets sent over the LAN. As described in Section 1.2, cable access technologies also broadcast packets and are thus vulnerable to sniffing. Furthermore, a bad guy who gains access to an institution's access router or access link to the Internet may be able to plant a sniffer that makes a copy of every packet going to/from the organization. Sniffed packets can then be analyzed offline for sensitive information.

Packet-sniffing software is freely available at various Web sites and as commercial products. Professors teaching a networking course have been known to assign lab exercises that involve writing a packet-sniffing and application-layer data reconstruction program. Indeed, the Wireshark [Wireshark 2012] labs associated with this text (see the introductory Wireshark lab at the end of this chapter) use exactly such a packet sniffer!

Because packet sniffers are passive—that is, they do not inject packets into the channel—they are difficult to detect. So, when we send packets into a wireless channel, we must accept the possibility that some bad guy may be recording copies of our packets. As you may have guessed, some of the best defenses against packet sniffing involve cryptography. We will examine cryptography as it applies to network security in Chapter 8.

The bad guys can masquerade as someone you trust

It is surprisingly easy (*you* will have the knowledge to do so shortly as you proceed through this text!) to create a packet with an arbitrary source address, packet content, and destination address and then transmit this hand-crafted packet into the Internet, which will dutifully forward the packet to its destination. Imagine the unsuspecting receiver (say an Internet router) who receives such a packet, takes the (false) source address as being truthful, and then performs some command embedded in the packet's contents (say modifies its forwarding table). The ability to inject packets into the Internet with a false source address is known as **IP spoofing**, and is but one of many ways in which one user can masquerade as another user.

To solve this problem, we will need *end-point authentication,* that is, a mechanism that will allow us to determine with certainty if a message originates from where we think it does. Once again, we encourage you to think about how this can be done for network applications and protocols as you progress through the chapters of this book. We will explore mechanisms for end-point authentication in Chapter 8.

In closing this section, it's worth considering how the Internet got to be such an insecure place in the first place. The answer, in essence, is that the Internet was originally designed to be that way, based on the model of "a group of mutually trusting users attached to a transparent network" [Blumenthal 2001]—a model in which (by definition) there is no need for security. Many aspects of the original Internet architecture deeply reflect this notion of mutual trust. For example, the ability for one user to send a packet to any other user is the default rather than a requested/granted capability, and user identity is taken at declared face value, rather than being authenticated by default.

But today's Internet certainly does not involve "mutually trusting users." Nonetheless, today's users still need to communicate when they don't necessarily trust each other, may wish to communicate anonymously, may communicate indirectly through third parties (e.g., Web caches, which we'll study in Chapter 2, or mobility-assisting agents, which we'll study in Chapter 6), and may distrust the hardware, software, and even the air through which they communicate. We now have many security-related challenges before us as we progress through this book: We should seek defenses against sniffing, end-point masquerading, man-in-the-middle attacks, DDoS attacks, malware, and more. We should keep in mind that communication among mutually trusted users is the exception rather than the rule. Welcome to the world of modern computer networking!

1.7 History of Computer Networking and the Internet

Sections 1.1 through 1.6 presented an overview of the technology of computer networking and the Internet. You should know enough now to impress your family and friends! However, if you really want to be a big hit at the next cocktail party, you should sprinkle your discourse with tidbits about the fascinating history of the Internet [Segaller 1998].

1.7.1 The Development of Packet Switching: 1961–1972

The field of computer networking and today's Internet trace their beginnings back to the early 1960s, when the telephone network was the world's dominant communication network. Recall from Section 1.3 that the telephone network uses circuit switching to transmit information from a sender to a receiver—an appropriate choice given that voice is transmitted at a constant rate between sender and receiver. Given the increasing importance of computers in the early 1960s and the advent of timeshared computers, it was perhaps natural to consider how to hook computers together so that they could be shared among geographically distributed users. The traffic generated by such users was likely to be *bursty*— intervals of activity, such as the sending of a command to a remote computer, followed by periods of inactivity while waiting for a reply or while contemplating the received response.

Three research groups around the world, each unaware of the others' work [Leiner 1998], began inventing packet switching as an efficient and robust alternative to circuit switching. The first published work on packet-switching techniques was that of Leonard Kleinrock [Kleinrock 1961; Kleinrock 1964], then a graduate student at MIT. Using queuing theory, Kleinrock's work elegantly demonstrated the effectiveness of the packet-switching approach for bursty traffic sources. In 1964, Paul Baran [Baran 1964] at the Rand Institute had begun investigating the use of packet switching for secure voice over military networks, and at the National Physical Laboratory in England, Donald Davies and Roger Scantlebury were also developing their ideas on packet switching.

The work at MIT, Rand, and the NPL laid the foundations for today's Internet. But the Internet also has a long history of a let's-build-it-and-demonstrate-it attitude that also dates back to the 1960s. J. C. R. Licklider [DEC 1990] and Lawrence Roberts, both colleagues of Kleinrock's at MIT, went on to lead the computer science program at the Advanced Research Projects Agency (ARPA) in the United States. Roberts published an overall plan for the ARPAnet [Roberts 1967], the first packet-switched computer network and a direct ancestor of today's public Internet. On Labor Day in 1969, the first packet switch was installed at UCLA under Kleinrock's supervision, and three additional packet switches were installed shortly thereafter at the Stanford Research Institute (SRI), UC Santa Barbara, and the University of Utah (Figure 1.26). The fledgling precursor to the

Figure 1.26 ◆ An early packet switch

Internet was four nodes large by the end of 1969. Kleinrock recalls the very first use of the network to perform a remote login from UCLA to SRI, crashing the system [Kleinrock 2004].

By 1972, ARPAnet had grown to approximately 15 nodes and was given its first public demonstration by Robert Kahn. The first host-to-host protocol between ARPAnet end systems, known as the network-control protocol (NCP), was completed [RFC 001]. With an end-to-end protocol available, applications could now be written. Ray Tomlinson wrote the first e-mail program in 1972.

1.7.2 Proprietary Networks and Internetworking: 1972–1980

The initial ARPAnet was a single, closed network. In order to communicate with an ARPAnet host, one had to be actually attached to another ARPAnet IMP. In the early to mid-1970s, additional stand-alone packet-switching networks besides ARPAnet came into being: ALOHANet, a microwave network linking universities on the Hawaiian islands [Abramson 1970], as well as DARPA's packet-satellite [RFC 829] and packet-radio networks [Kahn 1978]; Telenet, a BBN commercial packet-switching network based on ARPAnet technology; Cyclades, a French packet-switching network pioneered by Louis Pouzin [Think 2012]; Time-sharing networks such as Tymnet and the GE Information Services network, among others, in the late 1960s and early 1970s [Schwartz 1977]; IBM's SNA (1969–1974), which paralleled the ARPAnet work [Schwartz 1977].

The number of networks was growing. With perfect hindsight we can see that the time was ripe for developing an encompassing architecture for connecting networks together. Pioneering work on interconnecting networks (under the sponsorship of the Defense Advanced Research Projects Agency (DARPA)), in essence creating a *network of networks,* was done by Vinton Cerf and Robert Kahn [Cerf 1974]; the term *internetting* was coined to describe this work.

These architectural principles were embodied in TCP. The early versions of TCP, however, were quite different from today's TCP. The early versions of TCP combined a reliable in-sequence delivery of data via end-system retransmission (still part of today's TCP) with forwarding functions (which today are performed by IP). Early experimentation with TCP, combined with the recognition of the importance of an unreliable, non-flow-controlled, end-to-end transport service for applications such as packetized voice, led to the separation of IP out of TCP and the development of the UDP protocol. The three key Internet protocols that we see today—TCP, UDP, and IP—were conceptually in place by the end of the 1970s.

In addition to the DARPA Internet-related research, many other important networking activities were underway. In Hawaii, Norman Abramson was developing ALOHAnet, a packet-based radio network that allowed multiple remote sites on the Hawaiian Islands to communicate with each other. The ALOHA protocol

[Abramson 1970] was the first multiple-access protocol, allowing geographically distributed users to share a single broadcast communication medium (a radio frequency). Metcalfe and Boggs built on Abramson's multiple-access protocol work when they developed the Ethernet protocol [Metcalfe 1976] for wire-based shared broadcast networks. Interestingly, Metcalfe and Boggs' Ethernet protocol was motivated by the need to connect multiple PCs, printers, and shared disks [Perkins 1994]. Twenty-five years ago, well before the PC revolution and the explosion of networks, Metcalfe and Boggs were laying the foundation for today's PC LANs.

1.7.3 A Proliferation of Networks: 1980–1990

By the end of the 1970s, approximately two hundred hosts were connected to the ARPAnet. By the end of the 1980s the number of hosts connected to the public Internet, a confederation of networks looking much like today's Internet, would reach a hundred thousand. The 1980s would be a time of tremendous growth.

Much of that growth resulted from several distinct efforts to create computer networks linking universities together. BITNET provided e-mail and file transfers among several universities in the Northeast. CSNET (computer science network) was formed to link university researchers who did not have access to ARPAnet. In 1986, NSFNET was created to provide access to NSF-sponsored supercomputing centers. Starting with an initial backbone speed of 56 kbps, NSFNET's backbone would be running at 1.5 Mbps by the end of the decade and would serve as a primary backbone linking regional networks.

In the ARPAnet community, many of the final pieces of today's Internet architecture were falling into place. January 1, 1983 saw the official deployment of TCP/IP as the new standard host protocol for ARPAnet (replacing the NCP protocol). The transition [RFC 801] from NCP to TCP/IP was a flag day event—all hosts were required to transfer over to TCP/IP as of that day. In the late 1980s, important extensions were made to TCP to implement host-based congestion control [Jacobson 1988]. The DNS, used to map between a human-readable Internet name (for example, gaia.cs.umass.edu) and its 32-bit IP address, was also developed [RFC 1034].

Paralleling this development of the ARPAnet (which was for the most part a US effort), in the early 1980s the French launched the Minitel project, an ambitious plan to bring data networking into everyone's home. Sponsored by the French government, the Minitel system consisted of a public packet-switched network (based on the X.25 protocol suite), Minitel servers, and inexpensive terminals with built-in low-speed modems. The Minitel became a huge success in 1984 when the French government gave away a free Minitel terminal to each French household that wanted one. Minitel sites included free sites—such as a telephone directory site—as well as private sites, which collected a usage-based fee from each user. At its peak in the mid 1990s, it offered more than 20,000 services, ranging from home banking to specialized research databases. The Minitel was in a large proportion of French homes 10 years before most Americans had ever heard of the Internet.

1.7.4 The Internet Explosion: The 1990s

The 1990s were ushered in with a number of events that symbolized the continued evolution and the soon-to-arrive commercialization of the Internet. ARPAnet, the progenitor of the Internet, ceased to exist. In 1991, NSFNET lifted its restrictions on the use of NSFNET for commercial purposes. NSFNET itself would be decommissioned in 1995, with Internet backbone traffic being carried by commercial Internet Service Providers.

The main event of the 1990s was to be the emergence of the World Wide Web application, which brought the Internet into the homes and businesses of millions of people worldwide. The Web served as a platform for enabling and deploying hundreds of new applications that we take for granted today, including search (e.g., Google and Bing) Internet commerce (e.g., Amazon and eBay) and social networks (e.g., Facebook).

The Web was invented at CERN by Tim Berners-Lee between 1989 and 1991 [Berners-Lee 1989], based on ideas originating in earlier work on hypertext from the 1940s by Vannevar Bush [Bush 1945] and since the 1960s by Ted Nelson [Xanadu 2012]. Berners-Lee and his associates developed initial versions of HTML, HTTP, a Web server, and a browser—the four key components of the Web. Around the end of 1993 there were about two hundred Web servers in operation, this collection of servers being just a harbinger of what was about to come. At about this time several researchers were developing Web browsers with GUI interfaces, including Marc Andreessen, who along with Jim Clark, formed Mosaic Communications, which later became Netscape Communications Corporation [Cusumano 1998; Quittner 1998]. By 1995, university students were using Netscape browsers to surf the Web on a daily basis. At about this time companies—big and small—began to operate Web servers and transact commerce over the Web. In 1996, Microsoft started to make browsers, which started the browser war between Netscape and Microsoft, which Microsoft won a few years later [Cusumano 1998].

The second half of the 1990s was a period of tremendous growth and innovation for the Internet, with major corporations and thousands of startups creating Internet products and services. By the end of the millennium the Internet was supporting hundreds of popular applications, including four killer applications:

• E-mail, including attachments and Web-accessible e-mail

• The Web, including Web browsing and Internet commerce

- Instant messaging, with contact lists
- Peer-to-peer file sharing of MP3s, pioneered by Napster

Interestingly, the first two killer applications came from the research community, whereas the last two were created by a few young entrepreneurs.

The period from 1995 to 2001 was a roller-coaster ride for the Internet in the financial markets. Before they were even profitable, hundreds of Internet startups made initial public offerings and started to be traded in a stock market. Many companies were valued in the billions of dollars without having any significant revenue streams. The Internet stocks collapsed in 2000–2001, and many startups shut down. Nevertheless, a number of companies emerged as big winners in the Internet space, including Microsoft, Cisco, Yahoo, e-Bay, Google, and Amazon.

1.7.5 The New Millennium

Innovation in computer networking continues at a rapid pace. Advances are being made on all fronts, including deployments of faster routers and higher transmission speeds in both access networks and in network backbones. But the following developments merit special attention:

- Since the beginning of the millennium, we have been seeing aggressive deployment of broadband Internet access to homes—not only cable modems and DSL but also fiber to the home, as discussed in Section 1.2. This high-speed Internet access has set the stage for a wealth of video applications, including the distribution of user-generated video (for example, YouTube), on-demand streaming of movies and television shows (e.g., Netflix) , and multi-person video conference (e.g., Skype).

- The increasing ubiquity of high-speed (54 Mbps and higher) public WiFi networks and medium-speed (up to a few Mbps) Internet access via 3G and 4G cellular telephony networks is not only making it possible to remain constantly connected while on the move, but also enabling new location-specific applications. The number of wireless devices connecting to the Internet surpassed the number of wired devices in 2011. This high-speed wireless access has set the stage for the rapid emergence of hand-held computers (iPhones, Androids, iPads, and so on), which enjoy constant and untethered access to the Internet.

- Online social networks, such as Facebook and Twitter, have created massive people networks on top of the Internet. Many Internet users today "live" primarily within Facebook. Through their APIs, the online social networks create platforms for new networked applications and distributed games.

- As discussed in Section 1.3.3, online service providers, such as Google and Microsoft, have deployed their own extensive private networks, which not only connect together their globally distributed data centers, but are used to bypass the Internet as much as possible by peering directly with lower-tier ISPs. As a result, Google provides search results and email access almost instantaneously, as if their data centers were running within one's own computer.

- Many Internet commerce companies are now running their applications in the "cloud"—such as in Amazon's EC2, in Google's Application Engine, or in Microsoft's Azure. Many companies and universities have also migrated their Internet applications (e.g., email and Web hosting) to the cloud. Cloud companies not only provide applications scalable computing and storage environments, but also provide the applications implicit access to their high-performance private networks.

1.8 Summary

In this chapter we've covered a tremendous amount of material! We've looked at the various pieces of hardware and software that make up the Internet in particular and computer networks in general. We started at the edge of the network, looking at end systems and applications, and at the transport service provided to the applications running on the end systems. We also looked at the link-layer technologies and physical media typically found in the access network. We then dove deeper inside the network, into the network core, identifying packet switching and circuit switching as the two basic approaches for transporting data through a telecommunication network, and we examined the strengths and weaknesses of each approach. We also examined the structure of the global Internet, learning that the Internet is a network of networks. We saw that the Internet's hierarchical structure, consisting of higher- and lower-tier ISPs, has allowed it to scale to include thousands of networks.

In the second part of this introductory chapter, we examined several topics central to the field of computer networking. We first examined the causes of delay, throughput and packet loss in a packet-switched network. We developed simple quantitative models for transmission, propagation, and queuing delays as well as for throughput; we'll make extensive use of these delay models in the homework problems throughout this book. Next we examined protocol layering and service models, key architectural principles in networking that we will also refer back to throughout this book. We also surveyed some of the more prevalent security attacks in the Internet day. We finished our introduction to networking with a brief history of computer networking. The first chapter in itself constitutes a mini-course in computer networking.

So, we have indeed covered a tremendous amount of ground in this first chapter! If you're a bit overwhelmed, don't worry. In the following chapters we'll revisit all of these ideas, covering them in much more detail (that's a promise, not a threat!). At this point, we hope you leave this chapter with a still-developing intuition for the pieces that make up a network, a still-developing command of the vocabulary of networking (don't be shy about referring back to this chapter), and an ever-growing desire to learn more about networking. That's the task ahead of us for the rest of this book.

Road-Mapping This Book

Before starting any trip, you should always glance at a road map in order to become familiar with the major roads and junctures that lie ahead. For the trip we are about to embark on, the ultimate destination is a deep understanding of the how, what, and why of computer networks. Our road map is the sequence of chapters of this book:

1. Computer Networks and the Internet
2. Application Layer
3. Transport Layer
4. Network Layer
5. Link Layer and Local Area Networks
6. Wireless and Mobile Networks
7. Multimedia Networking
8. Security in Computer Networks
9. Network Management

Chapters 2 through 5 are the four core chapters of this book. You should notice that these chapters are organized around the top four layers of the five-layer Internet protocol stack, one chapter for each layer. Further note that our journey will begin at the top of the Internet protocol stack, namely, the application layer, and will work its way downward. The rationale behind this top-down journey is that once we understand the applications, we can understand the network services needed to support these applications. We can then, in turn, examine the various ways in which such services might be implemented by a network architecture. Covering applications early thus provides motivation for the remainder of the text.

The second half of the book—Chapters 6 through 9—zooms in on four enormously important (and somewhat independent) topics in modern computer networking. In Chapter 6, we examine wireless and mobile networks, including wireless LANs (including WiFi and Bluetooth), Cellular telephony networks (including GSM, 3G, and 4G), and mobility (in both IP and GSM networks). In Chapter 7 (Multimedia Networking) we examine audio and video applications such as Internet phone, video conferencing, and streaming of stored media. We also look at how a packet-switched network can be designed to provide consistent quality of service to audio and video applications. In Chapter 8 (Security in Computer Networks), we first look at the underpinnings of encryption and network security, and then we examine how the basic theory is being applied in a broad range of Internet contexts. The last chapter (Network Management) examines the key issues in network management as well as the primary Internet protocols used for network management.

Homework Problems and Questions

Chapter 1 Review Questions

SECTION 1.1

R1. In a computer network, how are end systems or hosts connected to each other? What are the different types of physical media for communication?

R2. The word *protocol* is often used to describe diplomatic relations. How does Wikipedia describe diplomatic protocol?

R3. Why are standards important for protocols?

SECTION 1.2

R4. List six access technologies. Classify each one as home access, enterprise access, or wide-area wireless access.

R5. What is DSL? Is it mainly for commercial or for domestic use? Mention how subscription to DSL is done.

R6. List the available residential access technologies in your city. For each type of access, provide the advertised downstream rate, upstream rate, and monthly price.

R7. What is the transmission rate of Ethernet LANs?

R8. The mobile standards 1G, 2G, 3G, etc. differ in their transmission rates. What are the typical transmission rates of 3G and 4G?

R9. With guided media, the waves are guided along a solid medium. With unguided media, the waves propagate in the atmosphere and in outer space. Give examples of guided and unguided media.

R10. Describe the two types of satellites used in communications.

SECTION 1.3

R11. Suppose there is exactly one packet switch between a sending host and a receiving host. The transmission rates between the sending host and the switch and between the switch and the receiving host are R_1 and R_2, respectively. Assuming that the switch uses store-and-forward packet switching, what is the total end-to-end delay to send a packet of length L? (Ignore queuing, propagation delay, and processing delay.)

R12. What is the role of output queue in packet switching?

R13. Suppose users share a 2 Mbps link. Also suppose each user transmits continuously at 1 Mbps when transmitting, but each user transmits only 20 percent of the time. (See the discussion of statistical multiplexing in Section 1.3.)

a. When circuit switching is used, how many users can be supported?

b. For the remainder of this problem, suppose packet switching is used. Why will there be essentially no queuing delay before the link if two or fewer users transmit at the same time? Why will there be a queuing delay if three users transmit at the same time?

c. Find the probability that a given user is transmitting.

d. Suppose now there are three users. Find the probability that at any given time, all three users are transmitting simultaneously. Find the fraction of time during which the queue grows.

R14. A circuit in a link is implemented with either frequency-division multiplexing (FDM) or time-division multiplexing (TDM). What is the difference between FDM and TDM links?

R15. Some content providers have created their own networks. Describe Google's network. What motivates content providers to create these networks?

SECTION 1.4

R16. Consider sending a packet from a source host to a destination host over a fixed route. List the delay components in the end-to-end delay. Which of these delays are constant and which are variable?

R17. Visit the Transmission Versus Propagation Delay applet at the companion Web site. Among the rates, propagation delay, and packet sizes available, find a combination for which the sender finishes transmitting before the first bit of the packet reaches the receiver. Find another combination for which the first bit of the packet reaches the receiver before the sender finishes transmitting.

R18. How long does it take a packet of length 1,000 bytes to propagate over a link of distance 2,500 km, propagation speed $2.5 \cdot 10^8$ m/s, and transmission rate 2 Mbps? More generally, how long does it take a packet of length L to propagate over a link of distance d, propagation speed s, and transmission rate R bps? Does this delay depend on packet length? Does this delay depend on transmission rate?

R19. Suppose Host A wants to send a large file to Host B. The path from Host A to Host B has three links, of rates $R_1 = 500$ kbps, $R_2 = 2$ Mbps, and $R_3 = 1$ Mbps.

a. Assuming no other traffic in the network, what is the throughput for the file transfer?

b. Suppose the file is 4 million bytes. Dividing the file size by the throughput, roughly how long will it take to transfer the file to Host B?

c. Repeat (a) and (b), but now with R_2 reduced to 100 kbps.

R20. Suppose end system A wants to send a large file to end system B. At a very high level, describe how end system A creates packets from the file. When one of these packets arrives to a packet switch, what information in the packet does the switch use to determine the link onto which the packet is forwarded? Why is packet switching in the Internet analogous to driving from one city to another and asking directions along the way?

R21. Visit the Queuing and Loss applet at the companion Web site. What is the maximum emission rate and the minimum transmission rate? With those rates, what is the traffic intensity? Run the applet with these rates and determine how long it takes for packet loss to occur. Then repeat the experiment a second time and determine again how long it takes for packet loss to occur. Are the values different? Why or why not?

SECTION 1.5

R22. Network protocol stack is designed in layers, and communication between two hosts happens in peer-to-peer fashion. What is the motivation behind protocol layering?

R23. Does layering have any disadvantages?

R24. What is an application-layer message? A transport-layer segment? A network-layer datagram? A link-layer frame?

R25. Which layers in the Internet protocol stack does a router process? Which layers does a link-layer switch process? Which layers does a host process?

SECTION 1.6

R26. How does a self-replicating malware spread itself?

R27. Describe how a botnet can be created, and how it can be used for a DDoS attack.

R28. Suppose Alice and Bob are sending packets to each other over a computer network. Suppose Trudy positions herself in the network so that she can capture all the packets sent by Alice and send whatever she wants to Bob; she can also capture all the packets sent by Bob and send whatever she wants to Alice. List some of the malicious things Trudy can do from this position.

 Problems

P1. Design and describe an application-level protocol to be used between an automatic teller machine and a bank's centralized computer. Your protocol should allow a user's card and password to be verified, the account balance (which is maintained at the centralized computer) to be queried, and an account withdrawal to be made (that is, money disbursed to the user). Your protocol entities should be able to handle the all-too-common case in which there is not enough money in the account to cover the withdrawal. Specify your protocol by listing the messages exchanged and the action taken by the automatic teller machine or the bank's centralized computer on transmission and receipt of messages. Sketch the operation of your protocol for the case of a simple withdrawal with no errors, using a diagram similar to that in Figure 1.2. Explicitly state the assumptions made by your protocol about the underlying end-to-end transport service.

P2. According to Equation 1.1, the propagation delay for sending one packet across N links is NL/R, where L is the packet length and R is the transmission rate. Assuming the transmission rate to be constant at R, what will be the propagation delay for sending P packets each of length L across:

a. 1 link?

b. 2 links?

c. N links?

P3. The entire treatise on propagation delay in Section 1.3.1 assumes that all packets are of the same length L. Let us now relax this constraint and allow for variable length packets. Suppose P packets of lengths $L_1, L_2, ..., L_P$ are to be sent back to back across a network. What will be the net propagation delay across:

a. 1 link?

b. 2 links?

c. N links?

P4. Consider the circuit-switched network in Figure 1.13. Recall that there are 4 circuits on each link. Label the four switches A, B, C and D, going in the clockwise direction.

a. What is the maximum number of simultaneous connections that can be in progress at any one time in this network?

b. Suppose that all connections are between switches A and C. What is the maximum number of simultaneous connections that can be in progress?

c. Suppose we want to make four connections between switches A and C, and another four connections between switches B and D. Can we route these calls through the four links to accommodate all eight connections?

P5. Suppose we want to send a file of 160,000 bits from Host A to Host B over a circuit-switched network. Suppose that all links in the network use TDM with 12 slots and have a bit rate of 1.536 Mbps. Also suppose that it takes 600 msec to establish an end-to-end circuit before Host A can begin to transmit the file. How long does it take to send the file?

VideoNote
**Exploring propagation
delay and transmission
delay**

P6. This elementary problem begins to explore propagation delay and transmission delay, two central concepts in data networking. Consider two hosts, A and B, connected by a single link of rate R bps. Suppose that the two hosts are separated by m meters, and suppose the propagation speed along the link is s meters/sec. Host A is to send a packet of size L bits to Host B.

a. Express the propagation delay, d_{prop}, in terms of m and s.

b. Determine the transmission time of the packet, d_{trans}, in terms of L and R.

c. Ignoring processing and queuing delays, obtain an expression for the end-to-end delay.

d. Suppose Host A begins to transmit the packet at time $t = 0$. At time $t = d_{trans}$, where is the last bit of the packet?

e. Suppose d_{prop} is greater than d_{trans}. At time $t = d_{trans}$, where is the first bit of the packet?

f. Suppose d_{prop} is less than d_{trans}. At time $t = d_{trans}$, where is the first bit of the packet?

g. Suppose $s = 2.5 \cdot 10^8$, $L = 120$ bits, and $R = 56$ kbps. Find the distance m so that d_{prop} equals d_{trans}.

P7. In this problem, we consider sending real-time voice from Host A to Host B over a packet-switched network (VoIP). Host A converts analog voice to a digital 128 kbps bit stream on the fly. Host A then groups the bits into 64-byte packets. There is one link between Host A and B; its transmission rate is 4 Mbps and its propagation delay is 8 msec. As soon as Host A gathers a packet, it sends it to Host B. As soon as Host B receives an entire packet, it converts the packet's bits to an analog signal. How much time elapses from the time a bit is created (from the original analog signal at Host A) until the bit is decoded (as part of the analog signal at Host B)? What about the second bit? What about the other bits?

P8. Suppose users share a 3 Mbps link. Also suppose each user requires 150 kbps when transmitting, but each user transmits only 10 percent of the time. (See the discussion of packet switching versus circuit switching in Section 1.3.)

a. When circuit switching is used, how many users can be supported?

b. For the remainder of this problem, suppose packet switching is used. Find the probability that a given user is transmitting.

c. Suppose there are 120 users. Find the probability that at any given time, exactly n users are transmitting simultaneously. (*Hint*: Use the binomial distribution.)

d. Find the probability that there are 21 or more users transmitting simultaneously.

P9. A 2 Gbps link supports a maximum of 5,000 users under circuit switching.

    a. At what rate are the users generating data?

    b. Now consider packet switching and a user population of N users. If the probability that a specific user is active is p, what is the probability that exactly half of the users are sending data?

P10. Consider a packet of length L which begins at end system A and travels over three links to a destination end system. These three links are connected by two packet switches. Let d_i, s_i, and R_i denote the length, propagation speed, and the transmission rate of link i, for $i = 1, 2, 3$. The packet switch delays each packet by d_{proc}. Assuming no queuing delays, in terms of d_i, s_i, R_i, ($i = 1,2,3$), and L, what is the total end-to-end delay for the packet? Suppose now the packet is 1,500 bytes, the propagation speed on all three links is $2.5 \cdot 10^8$ m/s, the transmission rates of all three links are 2 Mbps, the packet switch processing delay is 3 msec, the length of the first link is 5,000 km, the length of the second link is 4,000 km, and the length of the last link is 1,000 km. For these values, what is the end-to-end delay?

P11. In the above problem, suppose $R_1 = R_2 = R_3 = R$ and $d_{proc} = 0$. Further suppose the packet switch does not store-and-forward packets but instead immediately transmits each bit it receives before waiting for the entire packet to arrive. What is the end-to-end delay?

P12. A packet switch receives a packet and determines the outbound link to which the packet should be forwarded. When the packet arrives, one other packet is halfway done being transmitted on this outbound link and four other packets are waiting to be transmitted. Packets are transmitted in order of arrival. Suppose all packets are 1,500 bytes and the link rate is 2 Mbps. What is the queuing delay for the packet? More generally, what is the queuing delay when all packets have length L, the transmission rate is R, x bits of the currently-being-transmitted packet have been transmitted, and n packets are already in the queue?

P13. (a) Suppose N packets arrive simultaneously to a link at which no packets are currently being transmitted or queued. Each packet is of length L and the link has transmission rate R. What is the average queuing delay for the N packets?

    (b) Now suppose that N such packets arrive to the link every LN/R seconds. What is the average queuing delay of a packet?

P14. Consider the queuing delay in a router buffer. Let I denote traffic intensity; that is, $I = La/R$. Suppose that the queuing delay takes the form $IL/R (1 - I)$ for $I < 1$.

   a. Provide a formula for the total delay, that is, the queuing delay plus the transmission delay.

   b. Plot the total delay as a function of L/R.

P15. Let a denote the rate of packets arriving at a link in packets/sec, and let μ denote the link's transmission rate in packets/sec. Based on the formula for the total delay (i.e., the queuing delay plus the transmission delay) derived in the previous problem, derive a formula for the total delay in terms of a and μ.

P16. Consider a router buffer preceding an outbound link. In this problem, you will use Little's formula, a famous formula from queuing theory. Let N denote the average number of packets in the buffer plus the packet being transmitted. Let a denote the rate of packets arriving at the link. Let d denote the average total delay (i.e., the queuing delay plus the transmission delay) experienced by a packet. Little's formula is $N = a \cdot d$. Suppose that the average packet arrival rate average is 750 packets/sec, assuming there is no packet loss. If the average packet queuing delay is 10 msec and the link's transmission rate is 100 packets/sec, what is the average number of packets in the buffer?

P17. a. Generalize Equation 1.2 in Section 1.4.3 for heterogeneous processing rates, transmission rates, and propagation delays.

   b. Repeat (a), but now also suppose that there is an average queuing delay of d_{queue} at each node.

P18. Perform a Traceroute between source and destination on the same continent at three different hours of the day.

   a. Find the average and standard deviation of the round-trip delays at each of the three hours.

   b. Find the number of routers in the path at each of the three hours. Did the paths change during any of the hours?

   c. Try to identify the number of ISP networks that the Traceroute packets pass through from source to destination. Routers with similar names and/or similar IP addresses should be considered as part of the same ISP. In your experiments, do the largest delays occur at the peering interfaces between adjacent ISPs?

   d. Repeat the above for a source and destination on different continents. Compare the intra-continent and inter-continent results.

P19. (a) Visit the site www.traceroute.org and perform traceroutes from two different cities in France to the same destination host in the United States. How many links are the same in the two traceroutes? Is the transatlantic link the same?

(b) Repeat (a) but this time choose one city in France and another city in Germany.

(c) Pick a city in the United States, and perform traceroutes to two hosts, each in a different city in China. How many links are common in the two traceroutes? Do the two traceroutes diverge before reaching China?

P20. Consider the throughput example corresponding to Figure 1.20(b). Now suppose that there are M client-server pairs rather than 10. Denote R_s, R_c, and R for the rates of the server links, client links, and network link. Assume all other links have abundant capacity and that there is no other traffic in the network besides the traffic generated by the M client-server pairs. Derive a general expression for throughput in terms of R_s, R_c, R, and M.

P21. Consider Figure 1.19(b). Now suppose that there are M paths between the server and the client. No two paths share any link. Path k ($k = 1, \ldots, M$) consists of N links with transmission rates $R_1^k, R_2^k, \ldots, R_N^k$. If the server can only use one path to send data to the client, what is the maximum throughput that the server can achieve? If the server can use all M paths to send data, what is the maximum throughput that the server can achieve?

P22. Consider Figure 1.19(b). Suppose that each link between the server and the client has a packet loss probability p, and the packet loss probabilities for these links are independent. What is the probability that a packet (sent by the server) is successfully received by the receiver? If a packet is lost in the path from the server to the client, then the server will re-transmit the packet. On average, how many times will the server re-transmit the packet in order for the client to successfully receive the packet?

P23. Consider Figure 1.19(a). Assume that we know the bottleneck link along the path from the server to the client is the first link with rate R_s bits/sec. Suppose we send a pair of packets back to back from the server to the client, and there is no other traffic on this path. Assume each packet of size L bits, and both links have the same propagation delay d_{prop}.

a. What is the packet inter-arrival time at the destination? That is, how much time elapses from when the last bit of the first packet arrives until the last bit of the second packet arrives?

b. Now assume that the second link is the bottleneck link (i.e., $R_c < R_s$). Is it possible that the second packet queues at the input queue of the second link? Explain. Now suppose that the server sends the second packet T seconds after sending the first packet. How large must T be to ensure no queuing before the second link? Explain.

P24. Suppose you would like to urgently deliver 300 terabytes data from Boston to Los Angeles. You have available a 1 Gbps dedicated link for data transfer. Would you prefer to transmit the data via this link or instead use FedEx overnight delivery? Explain.

P25. Suppose two hosts, A and B, are separated by 20,000 kilometers and are connected by a direct link of $R = 2$ Mbps. Suppose the propagation speed over the link is $2.5 \cdot 10^8$ meters/sec.

    a. Calculate the bandwidth-delay product, $R \cdot d_{prop}$.

    b. Consider sending a file of 800,000 bits from Host A to Host B. Suppose the file is sent continuously as one large message. What is the maximum number of bits that will be in the link at any given time?

    c. Provide an interpretation of the bandwidth-delay product.

    d. What is the width (in meters) of a bit in the link? Is it longer than a football field?

    e. Derive a general expression for the width of a bit in terms of the propagation speed s, the transmission rate R, and the length of the link m.

P26. Referring to problem P25, suppose we can modify R. For what value of R is the width of a bit as long as the length of the link?

P27. Consider problem P25 but now with a link of $R = 1$ Gbps.

    a. Calculate the bandwidth-delay product, $R \cdot d_{prop}$.

    b. Consider sending a file of 800,000 bits from Host A to Host B. Suppose the file is sent continuously as one big message. What is the maximum number of bits that will be in the link at any given time?

    c. What is the width (in meters) of a bit in the link?

P28. Refer again to problem P25.

    a. How long does it take to send the file, assuming it is sent continuously?

    b. Suppose now the file is broken up into 20 packets with each packet containing 40,000 bits. Suppose that each packet is acknowledged by the receiver and the transmission time of an acknowledgment packet is negligible. Finally, assume that the sender cannot send a packet until the preceding one is acknowledged. How long does it take to send the file?

    c. Compare the results from (a) and (b).

P29. Suppose there is a 10 Mbps microwave link between a geostationary satellite and its base station on Earth. Every minute the satellite takes a digital photo and sends it to the base station. Assume a propagation speed of $2.4 \cdot 10^8$ meters/sec.

    a. What is the propagation delay of the link?

    b. What is the bandwidth-delay product, $R \cdot d_{prop}$?

    c. Let x denote the size of the photo. What is the minimum value of x for the microwave link to be continuously transmitting?

P30. Consider the airline travel analogy in our discussion of layering in Section 1.5, and the addition of headers to protocol data units as they flow down the protocol stack. Is there an equivalent notion of header information that is added to passengers and baggage as they move down the airline protocol stack?

P31. In modern packet-switched networks, including the Internet, the source host segments long, application-layer messages (for example, an image or a music file) into smaller packets and sends the packets into the network. The receiver then reassembles the packets back into the original message. We refer to this process as *message segmentation*. Figure 1.27 illustrates the end-to-end transport of a message with and without message segmentation. Consider a message that is $8 \cdot 10^6$ bits long that is to be sent from source to destination in Figure 1.27. Suppose each link in the figure is 2 Mbps. Ignore propagation, queuing, and processing delays.

a. Consider sending the message from source to destination *without* message segmentation. How long does it take to move the message from the source host to the first packet switch? Keeping in mind that each switch uses store-and-forward packet switching, what is the total time to move the message from source host to destination host?

b. Now suppose that the message is segmented into 800 packets, with each packet being 10,000 bits long. How long does it take to move the first packet from source host to the first switch? When the first packet is being sent from the first switch to the second switch, the second packet is being sent from the source host to the first switch. At what time will the second packet be fully received at the first switch?

c. How long does it take to move the file from source host to destination host when message segmentation is used? Compare this result with your answer in part (a) and comment.

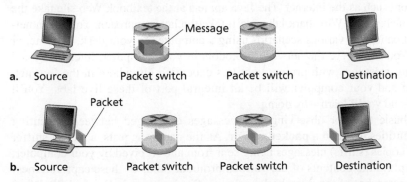

Figure 1.27 ♦ End-to-end message transport: (a) without message segmentation; (b) with message segmentation

d. In addition to reducing delay, what are reasons to use message segmentation?

e. Discuss the drawbacks of message segmentation.

P32. Experiment with the Message Segmentation applet at the book's Web site. Do the delays in the applet correspond to the delays in the previous problem? How do link propagation delays affect the overall end-to-end delay for packet switching (with message segmentation) and for message switching?

P33. Consider sending a large file of F bits from Host A to Host B. There are three links (and two switches) between A and B, and the links are uncongested (that is, no queuing delays). Host A segments the file into segments of S bits each and adds 80 bits of header to each segment, forming packets of $L = 80 + S$ bits. Each link has a transmission rate of R bps. Find the value of S that minimizes the delay of moving the file from Host A to Host B. Disregard propagation delay.

P34. Skype offers a service that allows you to make a phone call from a PC to an ordinary phone. This means that the voice call must pass through both the Internet and through a telephone network. Discuss how this might be done.

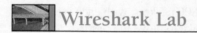 Wireshark Lab

"Tell me and I forget. Show me and I remember. Involve me and I understand."

Chinese proverb

One's understanding of network protocols can often be greatly deepened by seeing them in action and by playing around with them—observing the sequence of messages exchanged between two protocol entities, delving into the details of protocol operation, causing protocols to perform certain actions, and observing these actions and their consequences. This can be done in simulated scenarios or in a real network environment such as the Internet. The Java applets at the textbook Web site take the first approach. In the Wireshark labs, we'll take the latter approach. You'll run network applications in various scenarios using a computer on your desk, at home, or in a lab. You'll observe the network protocols in your computer, interacting and exchanging messages with protocol entities executing elsewhere in the Internet. Thus, you and your computer will be an integral part of these live labs. You'll observe—and you'll learn—by doing.

The basic tool for observing the messages exchanged between executing protocol entities is called a **packet sniffer**. As the name suggests, a packet sniffer passively copies (sniffs) messages being sent from and received by your computer; it also displays the contents of the various protocol fields of these captured messages. A screenshot of the Wireshark packet sniffer is shown in Figure 1.28. Wireshark is a free packet sniffer that runs on Windows, Linux/Unix, and Mac

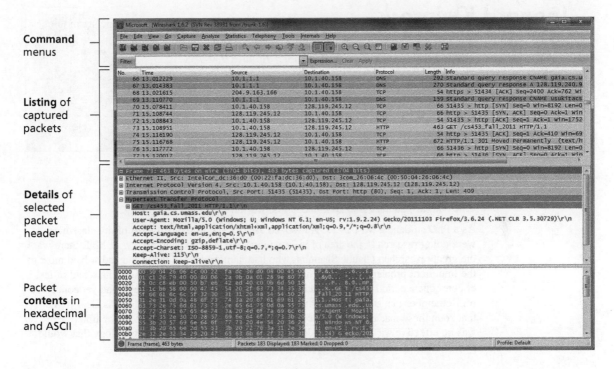

Command menus

Listing of captured packets

Details of selected packet header

Packet **contents** in hexadecimal and ASCII

Figure 1.28 ♦ A Wireshark screen shot (Wireshark screenshot reprinted by permission of the Wireshark Foundation.)

computers. Throughout the textbook, you will find Wireshark labs that allow you to explore a number of the protocols studied in the chapter. In this first Wireshark lab, you'll obtain and install a copy of Wireshark, access a Web site, and capture and examine the protocol messages being exchanged between your Web browser and the Web server.

You can find full details about this first Wireshark lab (including instructions about how to obtain and install Wireshark) at the Web site http://www.awl.com/kurose-ross.

Leonard Kleinrock

Leonard Kleinrock is a professor of computer science at the University of California, Los Angeles. In 1969, his computer at UCLA became the first node of the Internet. His creation of packet-switching principles in 1961 became the technology behind the Internet. He received his B.E.E. from the City College of New York (CCNY) and his masters and PhD in electrical engineering from MIT.

What made you decide to specialize in networking/Internet technology?

As a PhD student at MIT in 1959, I looked around and found that most of my classmates were doing research in the area of information theory and coding theory. At MIT, there was the great researcher, Claude Shannon, who had launched these fields and had solved most of the important problems already. The research problems that were left were hard and of lesser consequence. So I decided to launch out in a new area that no one else had yet conceived of. Remember that at MIT I was surrounded by lots of computers, and it was clear to me that soon these machines would need to communicate with each other. At the time, there was no effective way for them to do so, so I decided to develop the technology that would permit efficient and reliable data networks to be created.

What was your first job in the computer industry? What did it entail?

I went to the evening session at CCNY from 1951 to 1957 for my bachelor's degree in electrical engineering. During the day, I worked first as a technician and then as an engineer at a small, industrial electronics firm called Photobell. While there, I introduced digital technology to their product line. Essentially, we were using photoelectric devices to detect the presence of certain items (boxes, people, etc.) and the use of a circuit known then as a *bistable multivibrator* was just the kind of technology we needed to bring digital processing into this field of detection. These circuits happen to be the building blocks for computers, and have come to be known as *flip-flops* or *switches* in today's vernacular.

What was going through your mind when you sent the first host-to-host message (from UCLA to the Stanford Research Institute)?

Frankly, we had no idea of the importance of that event. We had not prepared a special message of historic significance, as did so many inventors of the past (Samuel Morse with "What hath God wrought." or Alexander Graham Bell with "Watson, come here! I want you." or Neal Amstrong with "That's one small step for a man, one giant leap for mankind.") Those guys were *smart*! They understood media and public relations. All we wanted to do was to login to the SRI computer. So we typed the "L", which was correctly received, we typed the "o" which was received, and then we typed the "g" which caused the SRI host computer to crash! So, it turned out that our message was the shortest and perhaps the most prophetic message ever, namely "Lo!" as in "Lo and behold!"

Earlier that year, I was quoted in a UCLA press release saying that once the network was up and running, it would be possible to gain access to computer utilities from our homes and offices as easily as we gain access to electricity and telephone connectivity. So my vision at that time was that the Internet would be ubiquitous, always on, always available, anyone with any device could connect from any location, and it would be invisible. However, I never anticipated that my 99-year-old mother would use the Internet—and indeed she did!

What is your vision for the future of networking?

The easy part of the vision is to predict the infrastructure itself. I anticipate that we see considerable deployment of nomadic computing, mobile devices, and smart spaces. Indeed, the availability of lightweight, inexpensive, high-performance, portable computing, and communication devices (plus the ubiquity of the Internet) has enabled us to become nomads. Nomadic computing refers to the technology that enables end users who travel from place to place to gain access to Internet services in a transparent fashion, no matter where they travel and no matter what device they carry or gain access to. The harder part of the vision is to predict the applications and services, which have consistently surprised us in dramatic ways (email, search technologies, the world-wide-web, blogs, social networks, user generation, and sharing of music, photos, and videos, etc.). We are on the verge of a new class of surprising and innovative mobile applications delivered to our hand-held devices.

The next step will enable us to move out from the netherworld of cyberspace to the physical world of smart spaces. Our environments (desks, walls, vehicles, watches, belts, and so on) will come alive with technology, through actuators, sensors, logic, processing, storage, cameras, microphones, speakers, displays, and communication. This embedded technology will allow our environment to provide the IP services we want. When I walk into a room, the room will know I entered. I will be able to communicate with my environment naturally, as in spoken English; my requests will generate replies that present Web pages to me from wall displays, through my eyeglasses, as speech, holograms, and so forth.

Looking a bit further out, I see a networking future that includes the following additional key components. I see intelligent software agents deployed across the network whose function it is to mine data, act on that data, observe trends, and carry out tasks dynamically and adaptively. I see considerably more network traffic generated not so much by humans, but by these embedded devices and these intelligent software agents. I see large collections of self-organizing systems controlling this vast, fast network. I see huge amounts of information flashing across this network instantaneously with this information undergoing enormous processing and filtering. The Internet will essentially be a pervasive global nervous system. I see all these things and more as we move headlong through the twenty-first century.

What people have inspired you professionally?

By far, it was Claude Shannon from MIT, a brilliant researcher who had the ability to relate his mathematical ideas to the physical world in highly intuitive ways. He was on my PhD thesis committee.

Do you have any advice for students entering the networking/Internet field?

The Internet and all that it enables is a vast new frontier, full of amazing challenges. There is room for great innovation. Don't be constrained by today's technology. Reach out and imagine what could be and then make it happen.

CHAPTER | 2

Application Layer

Network applications are the *raisons d'être* of a computer network—if we couldn't conceive of any useful applications, there wouldn't be any need for networking protocols that support these applications. Since the Internet's inception, numerous useful and entertaining applications have indeed been created. These applications have been the driving force behind the Internet's success, motivating people in homes, schools, governments, and businesses to make the Internet an integral part of their daily activities.

Internet applications include the classic text-based applications that became popular in the 1970s and 1980s: text email, remote access to computers, file transfers, and newsgroups. They include *the* killer application of the mid-1990s, the World Wide Web, encompassing Web surfing, search, and electronic commerce. They include instant messaging and P2P file sharing, the two killer applications introduced at the end of the millennium. Since 2000, we have seen an explosion of popular voice and video applications, including: voice-over-IP (VoIP) and video conferencing over IP such as Skype; user-generated video distribution such as YouTube; and movies on demand such as Netflix. During this same period we have also seen the immergence of highly engaging multi-player online games, including Second Life and World of Warcraft. And most recently, we have seen the emergence of a new generation of social networking applications, such as Facebook and Twitter, which have created engaging human networks on top of the Internet's network of routers and communication links. Clearly, there has been no slowing down of new and exciting Internet applications. Perhaps some of the readers of this text will create the next generation of killer Internet applications!

In this chapter we study the conceptual and implementation aspects of network applications. We begin by defining key application-layer concepts, including network services required by applications, clients and servers, processes, and transport-layer interfaces. We examine several network applications in detail, including the Web, e-mail, DNS, and peer-to-peer (P2P) file distribution (Chapter 8 focuses on multimedia applications, including streaming video and VoIP). We then cover network application development, over both TCP and UDP. In particular, we study the socket API and walk through some simple client-server applications in Python. We also provide several fun and interesting socket programming assignments at the end of the chapter.

The application layer is a particularly good place to start our study of protocols. It's familiar ground. We're acquainted with many of the applications that rely on the protocols we'll study. It will give us a good feel for what protocols are all about and will introduce us to many of the same issues that we'll see again when we study transport, network, and link layer protocols.

2.1 Principles of Network Applications

Suppose you have an idea for a new network application. Perhaps this application will be a great service to humanity, or will please your professor, or will bring you great wealth, or will simply be fun to develop. Whatever the motivation may be, let's now examine how you transform the idea into a real-world network application.

At the core of network application development is writing programs that run on different end systems and communicate with each other over the network. For example, in the Web application there are two distinct programs that communicate with each other: the browser program running in the user's host (desktop, laptop, tablet, smartphone, and so on); and the Web server program running in the Web server host. As another example, in a P2P file-sharing system there is a program in each host that participates in the file-sharing community. In this case, the programs in the various hosts may be similar or identical.

Thus, when developing your new application, you need to write software that will run on multiple end systems. This software could be written, for example, in C, Java, or Python. Importantly, you do not need to write software that runs on network-core devices, such as routers or link-layer switches. Even if you wanted to write application software for these network-core devices, you wouldn't be able to do so. As we learned in Chapter 1, and as shown earlier in Figure 1.24, network-core devices do not function at the application layer but instead function at lower layers—specifically at the network layer and below. This basic design—namely, confining application software to the end systems—as shown in Figure 2.1, has facilitated the rapid development and deployment of a vast array of network applications.

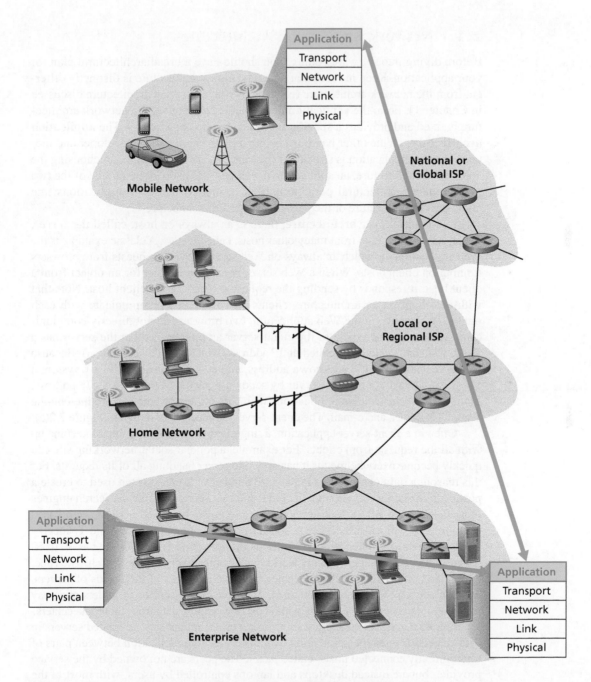

Figure 2.1 ♦ Communication for a network application takes place between end systems at the application layer

2.1.1 Network Application Architectures

Before diving into software coding, you should have a broad architectural plan for your application. Keep in mind that an application's architecture is distinctly different from the network architecture (e.g., the five-layer Internet architecture discussed in Chapter 1). From the application developer's perspective, the network architecture is fixed and provides a specific set of services to applications. The **application architecture**, on the other hand, is designed by the application developer and dictates how the application is structured over the various end systems. In choosing the application architecture, an application developer will likely draw on one of the two predominant architectural paradigms used in modern network applications: the client-server architecture or the peer-to-peer (P2P) architecture

In a **client-server architecture**, there is an always-on host, called the *server*, which services requests from many other hosts, called *clients*. A classic example is the Web application for which an always-on Web server services requests from browsers running on client hosts. When a Web server receives a request for an object from a client host, it responds by sending the requested object to the client host. Note that with the client-server architecture, clients do not directly communicate with each other; for example, in the Web application, two browsers do not directly communicate. Another characteristic of the client-server architecture is that the server has a fixed, well-known address, called an IP address (which we'll discuss soon). Because the server has a fixed, well-known address, and because the server is always on, a client can always contact the server by sending a packet to the server's IP address. Some of the better-known applications with a client-server architecture include the Web, FTP, Telnet, and e-mail. The client-server architecture is shown in Figure 2.2(a).

Often in a client-server application, a single-server host is incapable of keeping up with all the requests from clients. For example, a popular social-networking site can quickly become overwhelmed if it has only one server handling all of its requests. For this reason, a **data center**, housing a large number of hosts, is often used to create a powerful virtual server. The most popular Internet services—such as search engines (e.g., Google and Bing), Internet commerce (e.g., Amazon and e-Bay), Web-based email (e.g., Gmail and Yahoo Mail), social networking (e.g., Facebook and Twitter)—employ one or more data centers. As discussed in Section 1.3.3, Google has 30 to 50 data centers distributed around the world, which collectively handle search, YouTube, Gmail, and other services. A data center can have hundreds of thousands of servers, which must be powered and maintained. Additionally, the service providers must pay recurring interconnection and bandwidth costs for sending data from their data centers.

In a **P2P architecture**, there is minimal (or no) reliance on dedicated servers in data centers. Instead the application exploits direct communication between pairs of intermittently connected hosts, called *peers*. The peers are not owned by the service provider, but are instead desktops and laptops controlled by users, with most of the peers residing in homes, universities, and offices. Because the peers communicate without passing through a dedicated server, the architecture is called peer-to-peer. Many of today's most popular and traffic-intensive applications are based on P2P architectures. These applications include file sharing (e.g., BitTorrent), peer-assisted

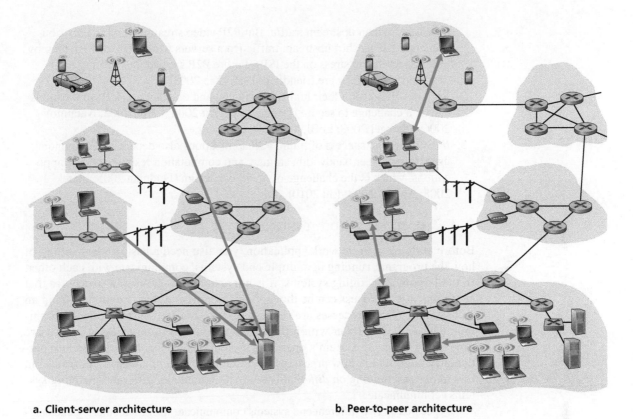

a. Client-server architecture   b. Peer-to-peer architecture

Figure 2.2 ♦ (a) Client-server architecture; (b) P2P architecture

download acceleration (e.g., Xunlei), Internet Telephony (e.g., Skype), and IPTV (e.g., Kankan and PPstream). The P2P architecture is illustrated in Figure 2.2(b). We mention that some applications have hybrid architectures, combining both client-server and P2P elements. For example, for many instant messaging applications, servers are used to track the IP addresses of users, but user-to-user messages are sent directly between user hosts (without passing through intermediate servers).

One of the most compelling features of P2P architectures is their **self-scalability**. For example, in a P2P file-sharing application, although each peer generates workload by requesting files, each peer also adds service capacity to the system by distributing files to other peers. P2P architectures are also cost effective, since they normally don't require significant server infrastructure and server bandwidth (in contrast with clients-server designs with datacenters). However, future P2P applications face three major challenges:

1. *ISP Friendly.* Most residential ISPs (including DSL and cable ISPs) have been dimensioned for "asymmetrical" bandwidth usage, that is, for much more

downstream than upstream traffic. But P2P video streaming and file distribution applications shift upstream traffic from servers to residential ISPs, thereby putting significant stress on the ISPs. Future P2P applications need to be designed so that they are friendly to ISPs [Xie 2008].

2. *Security.* Because of their highly distributed and open nature, P2P applications can be a challenge to secure [Doucer 2002; Yu 2006; Liang 2006; Naoumov 2006; Dhungel 2008; LeBlond 2011].

3. *Incentives.* The success of future P2P applications also depends on convincing users to volunteer bandwidth, storage, and computation resources to the applications, which is the challenge of incentive design [Feldman 2005; Piatek 2008; Aperjis 2008; Liu 2010].

2.1.2 Processes Communicating

Before building your network application, you also need a basic understanding of how the programs, running in multiple end systems, communicate with each other. In the jargon of operating systems, it is not actually programs but **processes** that communicate. A process can be thought of as a program that is running within an end system. When processes are running on the same end system, they can communicate with each other with interprocess communication, using rules that are governed by the end system's operating system. But in this book we are not particularly interested in how processes in the same host communicate, but instead in how processes running on *different* hosts (with potentially different operating systems) communicate.

Processes on two different end systems communicate with each other by exchanging **messages** across the computer network. A sending process creates and sends messages into the network; a receiving process receives these messages and possibly responds by sending messages back. Figure 2.1 illustrates that processes communicating with each other reside in the application layer of the five-layer protocol stack.

Client and Server Processes

A network application consists of pairs of processes that send messages to each other over a network. For example, in the Web application a client browser process exchanges messages with a Web server process. In a P2P file-sharing system, a file is transferred from a process in one peer to a process in another peer. For each pair of communicating processes, we typically label one of the two processes as the **client** and the other process as the **server**. With the Web, a browser is a client process and a Web server is a server process. With P2P file sharing, the peer that is downloading the file is labeled as the client, and the peer that is uploading the file is labeled as the server.

You may have observed that in some applications, such as in P2P file sharing, a process can be both a client and a server. Indeed, a process in a P2P file-sharing system can both upload and download files. Nevertheless, in the context of any given communication session between a pair of processes, we can still label one process as the client and the other process as the server. We define the client and server processes as follows:

> *In the context of a communication session between a pair of processes, the process that initiates the communication (that is, initially contacts the other process at the beginning of the session) is labeled as the **client**. The process that waits to be contacted to begin the session is the **server**.*

In the Web, a browser process initializes contact with a Web server process; hence the browser process is the client and the Web server process is the server. In P2P file sharing, when Peer A asks Peer B to send a specific file, Peer A is the client and Peer B is the server in the context of this specific communication session. When there's no confusion, we'll sometimes also use the terminology "client side and server side of an application." At the end of this chapter, we'll step through simple code for both the client and server sides of network applications.

The Interface Between the Process and the Computer Network

As noted above, most applications consist of pairs of communicating processes, with the two processes in each pair sending messages to each other. Any message sent from one process to another must go through the underlying network. A process sends messages into, and receives messages from, the network through a software interface called a **socket**. Let's consider an analogy to help us understand processes and sockets. A process is analogous to a house and its socket is analogous to its door. When a process wants to send a message to another process on another host, it shoves the message out its door (socket). This sending process assumes that there is a transportation infrastructure on the other side of its door that will transport the message to the door of the destination process. Once the message arrives at the destination host, the message passes through the receiving process's door (socket), and the receiving process then acts on the message

Figure 2.3 illustrates socket communication between two processes that communicate over the Internet. (Figure 2.3 assumes that the underlying transport protocol used by the processes is the Internet's TCP protocol.) As shown in this figure, a socket is the interface between the application layer and the transport layer within a host. It is also referred to as the **Application Programming Interface (API)** between the application and the network, since the socket is the programming interface with which network applications are built. The application developer has control of everything on the application-layer side of the socket but has little control of the transport-layer side of the socket. The only control that the application developer has on the transport-layer side is (1) the choice of transport protocol and (2) perhaps the ability to fix a few transport-layer parameters such as maximum buffer and maximum segment sizes (to be covered in Chapter 3). Once the application developer chooses a transport protocol (if a choice is available),

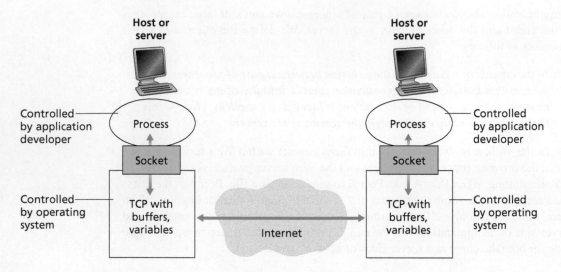

Figure 2.3 ♦ Application processes, sockets, and underlying transport protocol

the application is built using the transport-layer services provided by that protocol. We'll explore sockets in some detail in Section 2.7.

Addressing Processes

In order to send postal mail to a particular destination, the destination needs to have an address. Similarly, in order for a process running on one host to send packets to a process running on another host, the receiving process needs to have an address. To identify the receiving process, two pieces of information need to be specified: (1) the address of the host and (2) an identifier that specifies the receiving process in the destination host.

In the Internet, the host is identified by its **IP address**. We'll discuss IP addresses in great detail in Chapter 4. For now, all we need to know is that an IP address is a 32-bit quantity that we can think of as uniquely identifying the host. In addition to knowing the address of the host to which a message is destined, the sending process must also identify the receiving process (more specifically, the receiving socket) running in the host. This information is needed because in general a host could be running many network applications. A destination **port number** serves this purpose. Popular applications have been assigned specific port numbers. For example, a Web server is identified by port number 80. A mail server process (using the SMTP protocol) is identified by port number 25. A list of well-known port numbers for all Internet standard protocols can be found at http://www.iana.org. We'll examine port numbers in detail in Chapter 3.

2.1.3 Transport Services Available to Applications

Recall that a socket is the interface between the application process and the transport-layer protocol. The application at the sending side pushes messages through the socket. At the other side of the socket, the transport-layer protocol has the responsibility of getting the messages to the socket of the receiving process.

Many networks, including the Internet, provide more than one transport-layer protocol. When you develop an application, you must choose one of the available transport-layer protocols. How do you make this choice? Most likely, you would study the services provided by the available transport-layer protocols, and then pick the protocol with the services that best match your application's needs. The situation is similar to choosing either train or airplane transport for travel between two cities. You have to choose one or the other, and each transportation mode offers different services. (For example, the train offers downtown pickup and drop-off, whereas the plane offers shorter travel time.)

What are the services that a transport-layer protocol can offer to applications invoking it? We can broadly classify the possible services along four dimensions: reliable data transfer, throughput, timing, and security.

Reliable Data Transfer

As discussed in Chapter 1, packets can get lost within a computer network. For example, a packet can overflow a buffer in a router, or can be discarded by a host or router after having some of its bits corrupted. For many applications—such as electronic mail, file transfer, remote host access, Web document transfers, and financial applications—data loss can have devastating consequences (in the latter case, for either the bank or the customer!). Thus, to support these applications, something has to be done to guarantee that the data sent by one end of the application is delivered correctly and completely to the other end of the application. If a protocol provides such a guaranteed data delivery service, it is said to provide **reliable data transfer**. One important service that a transport-layer protocol can potentially provide to an application is process-to-process reliable data transfer. When a transport protocol provides this service, the sending process can just pass its data into the socket and know with complete confidence that the data will arrive without errors at the receiving process.

When a transport-layer protocol doesn't provide reliable data transfer, some of the data sent by the sending process may never arrive at the receiving process. This may be acceptable for **loss-tolerant applications**, most notably multimedia applications such as conversational audio/video that can tolerate some amount of data loss. In these multimedia applications, lost data might result in a small glitch in the audio/video—not a crucial impairment.

Throughput

In Chapter 1 we introduced the concept of available throughput, which, in the context of a communication session between two processes along a network path, is the rate at which the sending process can deliver bits to the receiving process. Because other sessions will be sharing the bandwidth along the network path, and because these other sessions will be coming and going, the available throughput can fluctuate with time. These observations lead to another natural service that a transport-layer protocol could provide, namely, guaranteed available throughput at some specified rate. With such a service, the application could request a guaranteed throughput of r bits/sec, and the transport protocol would then ensure that the available throughput is always at least r bits/sec. Such a guaranteed throughput service would appeal to many applications. For example, if an Internet telephony application encodes voice at 32 kbps, it needs to send data into the network and have data delivered to the receiving application at this rate. If the transport protocol cannot provide this throughput, the application would need to encode at a lower rate (and receive enough throughput to sustain this lower coding rate) or may have to give up, since receiving, say, half of the needed throughput is of little or no use to this Internet telephony application. Applications that have throughput requirements are said to be **bandwidth-sensitive applications**. Many current multimedia applications are bandwidth sensitive, although some multimedia applications may use adaptive coding techniques to encode digitized voice or video at a rate that matches the currently available throughput.

While bandwidth-sensitive applications have specific throughput requirements, **elastic applications** can make use of as much, or as little, throughput as happens to be available. Electronic mail, file transfer, and Web transfers are all elastic applications. Of course, the more throughput, the better. There's an adage that says that one cannot be too rich, too thin, or have too much throughput!

Timing

A transport-layer protocol can also provide timing guarantees. As with throughput guarantees, timing guarantees can come in many shapes and forms. An example guarantee might be that every bit that the sender pumps into the socket arrives at the receiver's socket no more than 100 msec later. Such a service would be appealing to interactive real-time applications, such as Internet telephony, virtual environments, teleconferencing, and multiplayer games, all of which require tight timing constraints on data delivery in order to be effective. (See Chapter 7, [Gauthier 1999; Ramjee 1994].) Long delays in Internet telephony, for example, tend to result in unnatural pauses in the conversation; in a multiplayer game or virtual interactive environment, a long delay between taking an action and seeing the response from the environment (for example, from another player at the end of an end-to-end connection) makes the application feel less realistic. For non-real-time applications, lower delay is always preferable to higher delay, but no tight constraint is placed on the end-to-end delays.

Security

Finally, a transport protocol can provide an application with one or more security services. For example, in the sending host, a transport protocol can encrypt all data transmitted by the sending process, and in the receiving host, the transport-layer protocol can decrypt the data before delivering the data to the receiving process. Such a service would provide confidentiality between the two processes, even if the data is somehow observed between sending and receiving processes. A transport protocol can also provide other security services in addition to confidentiality, including data integrity and end-point authentication, topics that we'll cover in detail in Chapter 8.

2.1.4 Transport Services Provided by the Internet

Up until this point, we have been considering transport services that a computer network *could* provide in general. Let's now get more specific and examine the type of transport services provided by the Internet. The Internet (and, more generally, TCP/IP networks) makes two transport protocols available to applications, UDP and TCP. When you (as an application developer) create a new network application for the Internet, one of the first decisions you have to make is whether to use UDP or TCP. Each of these protocols offers a different set of services to the invoking applications. Figure 2.4 shows the service requirements for some selected applications.

Application	Data Loss	Throughput	Time-Sensitive
File transfer/download	No loss	Elastic	No
E-mail	No loss	Elastic	No
Web documents	No loss	Elastic (few kbps)	No
Internet telephony/ Video conferencing	Loss-tolerant	Audio: few kbps–1Mbps Video: 10 kbps–5 Mbps	Yes: 100s of msec
Streaming stored audio/video	Loss-tolerant	Same as above	Yes: few seconds
Interactive games	Loss-tolerant	Few kbps–10 kbps	Yes: 100s of msec
Instant messaging	No loss	Elastic	Yes and no

Figure 2.4 ◆ Requirements of selected network applications

TCP Services

The TCP service model includes a connection-oriented service and a reliable data transfer service. When an application invokes TCP as its transport protocol, the application receives both of these services from TCP.

*   *Connection-oriented service.* TCP has the client and server exchange transport-layer control information with each other *before* the application-level messages begin to flow. This so-called handshaking procedure alerts the client and server, allowing them to prepare for an onslaught of packets. After the handshaking phase, a **TCP connection** is said to exist between the sockets of the two processes. The connection is a full-duplex connection in that the two processes can send messages to each other over the connection at the same time. When the application finishes sending messages, it must tear down the connection. In Chapter 3 we'll discuss connection-oriented service in detail and examine how it is implemented.

FOCUS ON SECURITY

SECURING TCP

Neither TCP nor UDP provide any encryption—the data that the sending process passes into its socket is the same data that travels over the network to the destination process. So, for example, if the sending process sends a password in cleartext (i.e., unencrypted) into its socket, the cleartext password will travel over all the links between sender and receiver, potentially getting sniffed and discovered at any of the intervening links. Because privacy and other security issues have become critical for many applications, the Internet community has developed an enhancement for TCP, called **Secure Sockets Layer (SSL)**. TCP-enhanced-with-SSL not only does everything that traditional TCP does but also provides critical process-to-process security services, including encryption, data integrity, and end-point authentication. We emphasize that SSL is not a third Internet transport protocol, on the same level as TCP and UDP, but instead is an enhancement of TCP, with the enhancements being implemented in the application layer. In particular, if an application wants to use the services of SSL, it needs to include SSL code (existing, highly optimized libraries and classes) in both the client and server sides of the application. SSL has its own socket API that is similar to the traditional TCP socket API. When an application uses SSL, the sending process passes cleartext data to the SSL socket; SSL in the sending host then encrypts the data and passes the encrypted data to the TCP socket. The encrypted data travels over the Internet to the TCP socket in the receiving process. The receiving socket passes the encrypted data to SSL, which decrypts the data. Finally, SSL passes the cleartext data through its SSL socket to the receiving process. We'll cover SSL in some detail in Chapter 8.

- *Reliable data transfer service.* The communicating processes can rely on TCP to deliver all data sent without error and in the proper order. When one side of the application passes a stream of bytes into a socket, it can count on TCP to deliver the same stream of bytes to the receiving socket, with no missing or duplicate bytes.

TCP also includes a congestion-control mechanism, a service for the general welfare of the Internet rather than for the direct benefit of the communicating processes. The TCP congestion-control mechanism throttles a sending process (client or server) when the network is congested between sender and receiver. As we will see in Chapter 3, TCP congestion control also attempts to limit each TCP connection to its fair share of network bandwidth.

UDP Services

UDP is a no-frills, lightweight transport protocol, providing minimal services. UDP is connectionless, so there is no handshaking before the two processes start to communicate. UDP provides an unreliable data transfer service—that is, when a process sends a message into a UDP socket, UDP provides *no* guarantee that the message will ever reach the receiving process. Furthermore, messages that do arrive at the receiving process may arrive out of order.

UDP does not include a congestion-control mechanism, so the sending side of UDP can pump data into the layer below (the network layer) at any rate it pleases. (Note, however, that the actual end-to-end throughput may be less than this rate due to the limited transmission capacity of intervening links or due to congestion).

Services Not Provided by Internet Transport Protocols

We have organized transport protocol services along four dimensions: reliable data transfer, throughput, timing, and security. Which of these services are provided by TCP and UDP? We have already noted that TCP provides reliable end-to-end data transfer. And we also know that TCP can be easily enhanced at the application layer with SSL to provide security services. But in our brief description of TCP and UDP, conspicuously missing was any mention of throughput or timing guarantees—services *not* provided by today's Internet transport protocols. Does this mean that time-sensitive applications such as Internet telephony cannot run in today's Internet? The answer is clearly no—the Internet has been hosting time-sensitive applications for many years. These applications often work fairly well because they have been designed to cope, to the greatest extent possible, with this lack of guarantee. We'll investigate several of these design tricks in Chapter 7. Nevertheless, clever design has its limitations when delay is excessive, or the end-to-end throughput is limited. In summary, today's Internet can often provide satisfactory service to time-sensitive applications, but it cannot provide any timing or throughput guarantees.

Application	Application-Layer Protocol	Underlying Transport Protocol
Electronic mail	SMTP [RFC 5321]	TCP
Remote terminal access	Telnet [RFC 854]	TCP
Web	HTTP [RFC 2616]	TCP
File transfer	FTP [RFC 959]	TCP
Streaming multimedia	HTTP (e.g., YouTube)	TCP
Internet telephony	SIP [RFC 3261], RTP [RFC 3550], or proprietary (e.g., Skype)	UDP or TCP

Figure 2.5 ♦ Popular Internet applications, their application-layer protocols, and their underlying transport protocols

Figure 2.5 indicates the transport protocols used by some popular Internet applications. We see that e-mail, remote terminal access, the Web, and file transfer all use TCP. These applications have chosen TCP primarily because TCP provides reliable data transfer, guaranteeing that all data will eventually get to its destination. Because Internet telephony applications (such as Skype) can often tolerate some loss but require a minimal rate to be effective, developers of Internet telephony applications usually prefer to run their applications over UDP, thereby circumventing TCP's congestion control mechanism and packet overheads. But because many firewalls are configured to block (most types of) UDP traffic, Internet telephony applications often are designed to use TCP as a backup if UDP communication fails.

2.1.5 Application-Layer Protocols

We have just learned that network processes communicate with each other by sending messages into sockets. But how are these messages structured? What are the meanings of the various fields in the messages? When do the processes send the messages? These questions bring us into the realm of application-layer protocols. An **application-layer protocol** defines how an application's processes, running on different end systems, pass messages to each other. In particular, an application-layer protocol defines:

* The types of messages exchanged, for example, request messages and response messages

* The syntax of the various message types, such as the fields in the message and how the fields are delineated

- The semantics of the fields, that is, the meaning of the information in the fields
- Rules for determining when and how a process sends messages and responds to messages

Some application-layer protocols are specified in RFCs and are therefore in the public domain. For example, the Web's application-layer protocol, HTTP (the HyperText Transfer Protocol [RFC 2616]), is available as an RFC. If a browser developer follows the rules of the HTTP RFC, the browser will be able to retrieve Web pages from any Web server that has also followed the rules of the HTTP RFC. Many other application-layer protocols are proprietary and intentionally not available in the public domain. For example, Skype uses proprietary application-layer protocols.

It is important to distinguish between network applications and application-layer protocols. An application-layer protocol is only one piece of a network application (albeit, a very important piece of the application from our point of view!). Let's look at a couple of examples. The Web is a client-server application that allows users to obtain documents from Web servers on demand. The Web application consists of many components, including a standard for document formats (that is, HTML), Web browsers (for example, Firefox and Microsoft Internet Explorer), Web servers (for example, Apache and Microsoft servers), and an application-layer protocol. The Web's application-layer protocol, HTTP, defines the format and sequence of messages exchanged between browser and Web server. Thus, HTTP is only one piece (albeit, an important piece) of the Web application. As another example, an Internet e-mail application also has many components, including mail servers that house user mailboxes; mail clients (such as Microsoft Outlook) that allow users to read and create messages; a standard for defining the structure of an e-mail message; and application-layer protocols that define how messages are passed between servers, how messages are passed between servers and mail clients, and how the contents of message headers are to be interpreted. The principal application-layer protocol for electronic mail is SMTP (Simple Mail Transfer Protocol) [RFC 5321]. Thus, e-mail's principal application-layer protocol, SMTP, is only one piece (albeit, an important piece) of the e-mail application.

2.1.6 Network Applications Covered in This Book

New public domain and proprietary Internet applications are being developed every day. Rather than covering a large number of Internet applications in an encyclopedic manner, we have chosen to focus on a small number of applications that are both pervasive and important. In this chapter we discuss five important applications: the Web, file transfer, electronic mail, directory service, and P2P applications. We first discuss the Web, not only because it is an enormously popular application, but also because its application-layer protocol, HTTP, is straightforward and easy to understand. After covering the Web, we briefly examine FTP, because it provides a nice contrast to HTTP. We then discuss electronic mail, the Internet's first killer application. E-mail is more complex than the Web in the sense that it makes use of not one but several application-layer protocols. After e-mail, we cover DNS, which provides a directory service for the Internet. Most users do not interact with DNS directly; instead, users invoke DNS indirectly through other applications (including the Web, file transfer, and electronic mail). DNS illustrates nicely how a piece of core network functionality (network-name to network-address translation) can be implemented at the application layer in the Internet. Finally, we discuss in this chapter several P2P applications, focusing on file sharing applications, and distributed lookup services. In Chapter 7, we'll cover multimedia applications, including streaming video and voice-over-IP.

2.2 The Web and HTTP

Until the early 1990s the Internet was used primarily by researchers, academics, and university students to log in to remote hosts, to transfer files from local hosts to remote hosts and vice versa, to receive and send news, and to receive and send electronic mail. Although these applications were (and continue to be) extremely useful, the Internet was essentially unknown outside of the academic and research communities. Then, in the early 1990s, a major new application arrived on the scene—the World Wide Web [Berners-Lee 1994]. The Web was the first Internet application that caught the general public's eye. It dramatically changed, and continues to change, how people interact inside and outside their work environments. It elevated the Internet from just one of many data networks to essentially the one and only data network.

Perhaps what appeals the most to users is that the Web operates *on demand*. Users receive what they want, when they want it. This is unlike traditional broadcast radio and television, which force users to tune in when the content provider makes the content available. In addition to being available on demand, the Web has many other wonderful features that people love and cherish. It is enormously easy for any individual to make information available over the Web—everyone can become a publisher at extremely low cost. Hyperlinks and search engines help us navigate through an ocean of Web sites. Graphics stimulate our senses. Forms, JavaScript, Java applets, and many other devices enable us to interact with pages and sites. And the Web serves as a platform for many killer applications emerging after 2003, including YouTube, Gmail, and Facebook.

2.2.1 Overview of HTTP

The **HyperText Transfer Protocol (HTTP)**, the Web's application-layer protocol, is at the heart of the Web. It is defined in [RFC 1945] and [RFC 2616]. HTTP is implemented in two programs: a client program and a server program. The client program and server program, executing on different end systems, talk to each other by exchanging HTTP messages. HTTP defines the structure of these messages and how the client and server exchange the messages. Before explaining HTTP in detail, we should review some Web terminology.

A **Web page** (also called a document) consists of objects. An **object** is simply a file—such as an HTML file, a JPEG image, a Java applet, or a video clip—that is addressable by a single URL. Most Web pages consist of a **base HTML file** and several referenced objects. For example, if a Web page contains HTML text and five JPEG images, then the Web page has six objects: the base HTML file plus the five images. The base HTML file references the other objects in the page with the objects' URLs. Each URL has two components: the hostname of the server that houses the object and the object's path name. For example, the URL

`http://www.someSchool.edu/someDepartment/picture.gif`

has `www.someSchool.edu` for a hostname and `/someDepartment/picture.gif` for a path name. Because **Web browsers** (such as Internet Explorer and Firefox) implement the client side of HTTP, in the context of the Web, we will use the words *browser* and *client* interchangeably. **Web servers**, which implement the server side of HTTP, house Web objects, each addressable by a URL. Popular Web servers include Apache and Microsoft Internet Information Server.

HTTP defines how Web clients request Web pages from Web servers and how servers transfer Web pages to clients. We discuss the interaction between client and server in detail later, but the general idea is illustrated in Figure 2.6. When a user requests a Web page (for example, clicks on a hyperlink), the browser sends HTTP request messages for the objects in the page to the server. The server receives the requests and responds with HTTP response messages that contain the objects.

HTTP uses TCP as its underlying transport protocol (rather than running on top of UDP). The HTTP client first initiates a TCP connection with the server. Once the connection is established, the browser and the server processes access TCP through their socket interfaces. As described in Section 2.1, on the client side the socket interface is the door between the client process and the TCP connection; on the server side it is the

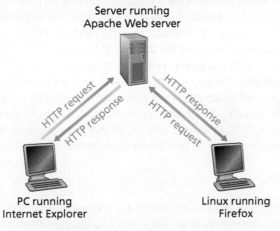

Server running
Apache Web server

PC running
Internet Explorer

Linux running
Firefox

Figure 2.6 ♦ HTTP request-response behavior

door between the server process and the TCP connection. The client sends HTTP request messages into its socket interface and receives HTTP response messages from its socket interface. Similarly, the HTTP server receives request messages from its socket interface and sends response messages into its socket interface. Once the client sends a message into its socket interface, the message is out of the client's hands and is "in the hands" of TCP. Recall from Section 2.1 that TCP provides a reliable data transfer service to HTTP. This implies that each HTTP request message sent by a client process eventually arrives intact at the server; similarly, each HTTP response message sent by the server process eventually arrives intact at the client. Here we see one of the great advantages of a layered architecture—HTTP need not worry about lost data or the details of how TCP recovers from loss or reordering of data within the network. That is the job of TCP and the protocols in the lower layers of the protocol stack.

It is important to note that the server sends requested files to clients without storing any state information about the client. If a particular client asks for the same object twice in a period of a few seconds, the server does not respond by saying that it just served the object to the client; instead, the server resends the object, as it has completely forgotten what it did earlier. Because an HTTP server maintains no information about the clients, HTTP is said to be a **stateless protocol**. We also remark that the Web uses the client-server application architecture, as described in Section 2.1. A Web server is always on, with a fixed IP address, and it services requests from potentially millions of different browsers.

2.2.2 Non-Persistent and Persistent Connections

In many Internet applications, the client and server communicate for an extended period of time, with the client making a series of requests and the server responding to each of the requests. Depending on the application and on how the application is being used, the series of requests may be made back-to-back, periodically at regular intervals, or intermittently. When this client-server interaction is taking place over TCP, the application developer needs to make an important decision—should each request/response pair be sent over a *separate* TCP connection, or should all of the requests and their corresponding responses be sent over the *same* TCP connection? In the former approach, the application is said to use **non-persistent connections**; and in the latter approach, **persistent connections**. To gain a deep understanding of this design issue, let's examine the advantages and disadvantages of persistent connections in the context of a specific application, namely, HTTP, which can use both non-persistent connections and persistent connections. Although HTTP uses persistent connections in its default mode, HTTP clients and servers can be configured to use non-persistent connections instead.

HTTP with Non-Persistent Connections

Let's walk through the steps of transferring a Web page from server to client for the case of non-persistent connections. Let's suppose the page consists of a base HTML file and 10 JPEG images, and that all 11 of these objects reside on the same server. Further suppose the URL for the base HTML file is

```
http://www.someSchool.edu/someDepartment/home.index
```

Here is what happens:

1. The HTTP client process initiates a TCP connection to the server `www.someSchool.edu` on port number 80, which is the default port number for HTTP. Associated with the TCP connection, there will be a socket at the client and a socket at the server.
2. The HTTP client sends an HTTP request message to the server via its socket. The request message includes the path name `/someDepartment/home.index`. (We will discuss HTTP messages in some detail below.)
3. The HTTP server process receives the request message via its socket, retrieves the object `/someDepartment/home.index` from its storage (RAM or disk), encapsulates the object in an HTTP response message, and sends the response message to the client via its socket.
4. The HTTP server process tells TCP to close the TCP connection. (But TCP doesn't actually terminate the connection until it knows for sure that the client has received the response message intact.)
5. The HTTP client receives the response message. The TCP connection terminates. The message indicates that the encapsulated object is an HTML file. The client extracts the file from the response message, examines the HTML file, and finds references to the 10 JPEG objects.
6. The first four steps are then repeated for each of the referenced JPEG objects.

As the browser receives the Web page, it displays the page to the user. Two different browsers may interpret (that is, display to the user) a Web page in somewhat different ways. HTTP has nothing to do with how a Web page is interpreted by a client. The HTTP specifications ([RFC 1945] and [RFC 2616]) define only the communication protocol between the client HTTP program and the server HTTP program.

The steps above illustrate the use of non-persistent connections, where each TCP connection is closed after the server sends the object—the connection does not persist for other objects. Note that each TCP connection transports exactly one request message and one response message. Thus, in this example, when a user requests the Web page, 11 TCP connections are generated.

In the steps described above, we were intentionally vague about whether the client obtains the 10 JPEGs over 10 serial TCP connections, or whether some of the JPEGs are obtained over parallel TCP connections. Indeed, users can configure modern browsers to control the degree of parallelism. In their default modes, most browsers open 5 to 10 parallel TCP connections, and each of these connections handles one request-response transaction. If the user prefers, the maximum number of parallel connections can be set to one, in which case the 10 connections are established serially. As we'll see in the next chapter, the use of parallel connections shortens the response time.

Before continuing, let's do a back-of-the-envelope calculation to estimate the amount of time that elapses from when a client requests the base HTML file until the entire file is received by the client. To this end, we define the **round-trip time (RTT)**, which is the time it takes for a small packet to travel from client to server and then back to the client. The RTT includes packet-propagation delays, packet-queuing delays in intermediate routers and switches, and packet-processing delays. (These delays were discussed in Section 1.4.) Now consider what happens when a user clicks on a hyperlink. As shown in Figure 2.7, this causes the browser to initiate a TCP connection between the browser and the Web server; this involves a "three-way handshake"—the client sends a small TCP segment to the server, the server acknowledges and responds with a small TCP segment, and, finally, the client acknowledges back to the server. The first two parts of the three-way handshake take one RTT. After completing the first two parts of the handshake, the client sends the HTTP request message combined with the third part of

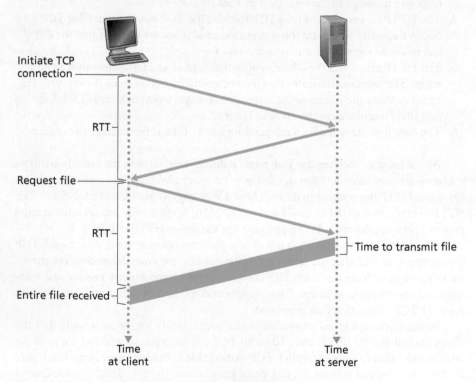

Figure 2.7 ♦ Back-of-the-envelope calculation for the time needed to request and receive an HTML file

the three-way handshake (the acknowledgment) into the TCP connection. Once the request message arrives at the server, the server sends the HTML file into the TCP connection. This HTTP request/response eats up another RTT. Thus, roughly, the total response time is two RTTs plus the transmission time at the server of the HTML file.

HTTP with Persistent Connections

Non-persistent connections have some shortcomings. First, a brand-new connection must be established and maintained for *each requested object*. For each of these connections, TCP buffers must be allocated and TCP variables must be kept in both the client and server. This can place a significant burden on the Web server, which may be serving requests from hundreds of different clients simultaneously. Second, as we just described, each object suffers a delivery delay of two RTTs— one RTT to establish the TCP connection and one RTT to request and receive an object.

With persistent connections, the server leaves the TCP connection open after sending a response. Subsequent requests and responses between the same client and server can be sent over the same connection. In particular, an entire Web page (in the example above, the base HTML file and the 10 images) can be sent over a single persistent TCP connection. Moreover, multiple Web pages residing on the same server can be sent from the server to the same client over a single persistent TCP connection. These requests for objects can be made back-to-back, without waiting for replies to pending requests (pipelining). Typically, the HTTP server closes a connection when it isn't used for a certain time (a configurable timeout interval). When the server receives the back-to-back requests, it sends the objects back-to-back. The default mode of HTTP uses persistent connections with pipelining. We'll quantitatively compare the performance of non-persistent and persistent connections in the homework problems of Chapters 2 and 3. You are also encouraged to see [Heidemann 1997; Nielsen 1997].

2.2.3 HTTP Message Format

The HTTP specifications [RFC 1945; RFC 2616] include the definitions of the HTTP message formats. There are two types of HTTP messages, request messages and response messages, both of which are discussed below.

HTTP Request Message

Below we provide a typical HTTP request message:

```
GET /somedir/page.html HTTP/1.1
Host: www.someschool.edu
```

```
Connection: close
User-agent: Mozilla/5.0
Accept-language: fr
```

We can learn a lot by taking a close look at this simple request message. First of all, we see that the message is written in ordinary ASCII text, so that your ordinary computer-literate human being can read it. Second, we see that the message consists of five lines, each followed by a carriage return and a line feed. The last line is followed by an additional carriage return and line feed. Although this particular request message has five lines, a request message can have many more lines or as few as one line. The first line of an HTTP request message is called the **request line**; the subsequent lines are called the **header lines**. The request line has three fields: the method field, the URL field, and the HTTP version field. The method field can take on several different values, including GET, POST, HEAD, PUT, and DELETE. The great majority of HTTP request messages use the GET method. The GET method is used when the browser requests an object, with the requested object identified in the URL field. In this example, the browser is requesting the object /somedir/page.html. The version is self-explanatory; in this example, the browser implements version HTTP/1.1.

Now let's look at the header lines in the example. The header line Host: www.someschool.edu specifies the host on which the object resides. You might think that this header line is unnecessary, as there is already a TCP connection in place to the host. But, as we'll see in Section 2.2.5, the information provided by the host header line is required by Web proxy caches. By including the Connection: close header line, the browser is telling the server that it doesn't want to bother with persistent connections; it wants the server to close the connection after sending the requested object. The User-agent: header line specifies the user agent, that is, the browser type that is making the request to the server. Here the user agent is Mozilla/5.0, a Firefox browser. This header line is useful because the server can actually send different versions of the same object to different types of user agents. (Each of the versions is addressed by the same URL.) Finally, the Accept-language: header indicates that the user prefers to receive a French version of the object, if such an object exists on the server; otherwise, the server should send its default version. The Accept-language: header is just one of many content negotiation headers available in HTTP.

Having looked at an example, let's now look at the general format of a request message, as shown in Figure 2.8. We see that the general format closely follows our earlier example. You may have noticed, however, that after the header lines (and the additional carriage return and line feed) there is an "entity body." The entity body is empty with the GET method, but is used with the POST method. An HTTP client often uses the POST method when the user fills out a form—for example, when a user provides search words to a search engine. With a POST message, the user is still requesting a Web page from the server, but the specific contents of the Web page

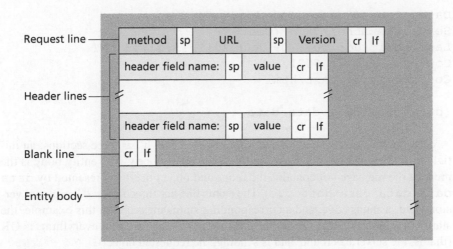

Figure 2.8 ♦ General format of an HTTP request message

depend on what the user entered into the form fields. If the value of the method field is POST, then the entity body contains what the user entered into the form fields.

We would be remiss if we didn't mention that a request generated with a form does not necessarily use the POST method. Instead, HTML forms often use the GET method and include the inputted data (in the form fields) in the requested URL. For example, if a form uses the GET method, has two fields, and the inputs to the two fields are monkeys and bananas, then the URL will have the structure www.somesite.com/animalsearch?monkeys&bananas. In your day-to-day Web surfing, you have probably noticed extended URLs of this sort.

The HEAD method is similar to the GET method. When a server receives a request with the HEAD method, it responds with an HTTP message but it leaves out the requested object. Application developers often use the HEAD method for debugging. The PUT method is often used in conjunction with Web publishing tools. It allows a user to upload an object to a specific path (directory) on a specific Web server. The PUT method is also used by applications that need to upload objects to Web servers. The DELETE method allows a user, or an application, to delete an object on a Web server.

HTTP Response Message

Below we provide a typical HTTP response message. This response message could be the response to the example request message just discussed.

```
HTTP/1.1 200 OK
Connection: close
```

```
Date: Tue, 09 Aug 2011 15:44:04 GMT
Server: Apache/2.2.3 (CentOS)
Last-Modified: Tue, 09 Aug 2011 15:11:03 GMT
Content-Length: 6821
Content-Type: text/html

(data data data data data ...)
```

Let's take a careful look at this response message. It has three sections: an initial **status line**, six **header lines**, and then the **entity body**. The entity body is the meat of the message—it contains the requested object itself (represented by data data data data data ...). The status line has three fields: the protocol version field, a status code, and a corresponding status message. In this example, the status line indicates that the server is using HTTP/1.1 and that everything is OK (that is, the server has found, and is sending, the requested object).

Now let's look at the header lines. The server uses the Connection: close header line to tell the client that it is going to close the TCP connection after sending the message. The Date: header line indicates the time and date when the HTTP response was created and sent by the server. Note that this is not the time when the object was created or last modified; it is the time when the server retrieves the object from its file system, inserts the object into the response message, and sends the response message. The Server: header line indicates that the message was generated by an Apache Web server; it is analogous to the User-agent: header line in the HTTP request message. The Last-Modified: header line indicates the time and date when the object was created or last modified. The Last-Modified: header, which we will soon cover in more detail, is critical for object caching, both in the local client and in network cache servers (also known as proxy servers). The Content-Length: header line indicates the number of bytes in the object being sent. The Content-Type: header line indicates that the object in the entity body is HTML text. (The object type is officially indicated by the Content-Type: header and not by the file extension.)

Having looked at an example, let's now examine the general format of a response message, which is shown in Figure 2.9. This general format of the response message matches the previous example of a response message. Let's say a few additional words about status codes and their phrases. The status code and associated phrase indicate the result of the request. Some common status codes and associated phrases include:

- 200 OK: Request succeeded and the information is returned in the response.
- 301 Moved Permanently: Requested object has been permanently moved; the new URL is specified in Location: header of the response message. The client software will automatically retrieve the new URL.

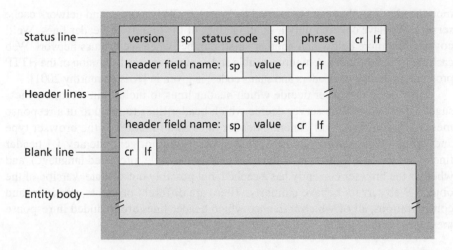

Figure 2.9 ♦ General format of an HTTP response message

- **400 Bad Request:** This is a generic error code indicating that the request could not be understood by the server.
- **404 Not Found:** The requested document does not exist on this server.
- **505 HTTP Version Not Supported:** The requested HTTP protocol version is not supported by the server.

How would you like to see a real HTTP response message? This is highly recommended and very easy to do! First Telnet into your favorite Web server. Then type in a one-line request message for some object that is housed on the server. For example, if you have access to a command prompt, type:

```
telnet cis.poly.edu 80
```

```
GET /~ross/ HTTP/1.1
Host: cis.poly.edu
```

(Press the carriage return twice after typing the last line.) This opens a TCP connection to port 80 of the host `cis.poly.edu` and then sends the HTTP request message. You should see a response message that includes the base HTML file of Professor Ross's homepage. If you'd rather just see the HTTP message lines and not receive the object itself, replace GET with HEAD. Finally, replace /~ross/ with /~banana/ and see what kind of response message you get.

In this section we discussed a number of header lines that can be used within HTTP request and response messages. The HTTP specification defines many, many

VideoNote
Using Wireshark to investigate the HTTP protocol

more header lines that can be inserted by browsers, Web servers, and network cache servers. We have covered only a small number of the totality of header lines. We'll cover a few more below and another small number when we discuss network Web caching in Section 2.2.5. A highly readable and comprehensive discussion of the HTTP protocol, including its headers and status codes, is given in [Krishnamurthy 2001].

How does a browser decide which header lines to include in a request message? How does a Web server decide which header lines to include in a response message? A browser will generate header lines as a function of the browser type and version (for example, an HTTP/1.0 browser will not generate any 1.1 header lines), the user configuration of the browser (for example, preferred language), and whether the browser currently has a cached, but possibly out-of-date, version of the object. Web servers behave similarly: There are different products, versions, and configurations, all of which influence which header lines are included in response messages.

2.2.4 User-Server Interaction: Cookies

We mentioned above that an HTTP server is stateless. This simplifies server design and has permitted engineers to develop high-performance Web servers that can handle thousands of simultaneous TCP connections. However, it is often desirable for a Web site to identify users, either because the server wishes to restrict user access or because it wants to serve content as a function of the user identity. For these purposes, HTTP uses cookies. Cookies, defined in [RFC 6265], allow sites to keep track of users. Most major commercial Web sites use cookies today.

As shown in Figure 2.10, cookie technology has four components: (1) a cookie header line in the HTTP response message; (2) a cookie header line in the HTTP request message; (3) a cookie file kept on the user's end system and managed by the user's browser; and (4) a back-end database at the Web site. Using Figure 2.10, let's walk through an example of how cookies work. Suppose Susan, who always accesses the Web using Internet Explorer from her home PC, contacts Amazon.com for the first time. Let us suppose that in the past she has already visited the eBay site. When the request comes into the Amazon Web server, the server creates a unique identification number and creates an entry in its back-end database that is indexed by the identification number. The Amazon Web server then responds to Susan's browser, including in the HTTP response a `Set-cookie:` header, which contains the identification number. For example, the header line might be:

```
Set-cookie: 1678
```

When Susan's browser receives the HTTP response message, it sees the `Set-cookie:` header. The browser then appends a line to the special cookie file that it manages. This line includes the hostname of the server and the identification number in the `Set-cookie:` header. Note that the cookie file already has an entry for

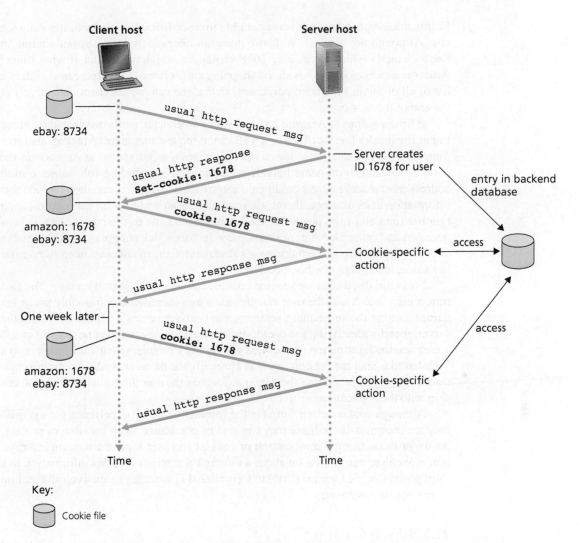

Key:

🗄️ Cookie file

Figure 2.10 ♦ Keeping user state with cookies

eBay, since Susan has visited that site in the past. As Susan continues to browse the Amazon site, each time she requests a Web page, her browser consults her cookie file, extracts her identification number for this site, and puts a cookie header line that includes the identification number in the HTTP request. Specifically, each of her HTTP requests to the Amazon server includes the header line:

```
Cookie: 1678
```

In this manner, the Amazon server is able to track Susan's activity at the Amazon site. Although the Amazon Web site does not necessarily know Susan's name, it knows exactly which pages user 1678 visited, in which order, and at what times! Amazon uses cookies to provide its shopping cart service—Amazon can maintain a list of all of Susan's intended purchases, so that she can pay for them collectively at the end of the session.

If Susan returns to Amazon's site, say, one week later, her browser will continue to put the header line `Cookie: 1678` in the request messages. Amazon also recommends products to Susan based on Web pages she has visited at Amazon in the past. If Susan also registers herself with Amazon—providing full name, e-mail address, postal address, and credit card information—Amazon can then include this information in its database, thereby associating Susan's name with her identification number (and all of the pages she has visited at the site in the past!). This is how Amazon and other e-commerce sites provide "one-click shopping"—when Susan chooses to purchase an item during a subsequent visit, she doesn't need to re-enter her name, credit card number, or address.

From this discussion we see that cookies can be used to identify a user. The first time a user visits a site, the user can provide a user identification (possibly his or her name). During the subsequent sessions, the browser passes a cookie header to the server, thereby identifying the user to the server. Cookies can thus be used to create a user session layer on top of stateless HTTP. For example, when a user logs in to a Web-based e-mail application (such as Hotmail), the browser sends cookie information to the server, permitting the server to identify the user throughout the user's session with the application.

Although cookies often simplify the Internet shopping experience for the user, they are controversial because they can also be considered as an invasion of privacy. As we just saw, using a combination of cookies and user-supplied account information, a Web site can learn a lot about a user and potentially sell this information to a third party. Cookie Central [Cookie Central 2012] includes extensive information on the cookie controversy.

2.2.5 Web Caching

A **Web cache**—also called a **proxy server**—is a network entity that satisfies HTTP requests on the behalf of an origin Web server. The Web cache has its own disk storage and keeps copies of recently requested objects in this storage. As shown in Figure 2.11, a user's browser can be configured so that all of the user's HTTP requests are first directed to the Web cache. Once a browser is configured, each browser request for an object is first directed to the Web cache. As an example, suppose a browser is requesting the object `http://www.someschool.edu/campus.gif`. Here is what happens:

1. The browser establishes a TCP connection to the Web cache and sends an HTTP request for the object to the Web cache.

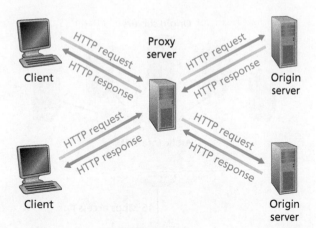

Figure 2.11 ♦ Clients requesting objects through a Web cache

2. The Web cache checks to see if it has a copy of the object stored locally. If it does, the Web cache returns the object within an HTTP response message to the client browser.
3. If the Web cache does not have the object, the Web cache opens a TCP connection to the origin server, that is, to `www.someschool.edu`. The Web cache then sends an HTTP request for the object into the cache-to-server TCP connection. After receiving this request, the origin server sends the object within an HTTP response to the Web cache.
4. When the Web cache receives the object, it stores a copy in its local storage and sends a copy, within an HTTP response message, to the client browser (over the existing TCP connection between the client browser and the Web cache).

Note that a cache is both a server and a client at the same time. When it receives requests from and sends responses to a browser, it is a server. When it sends requests to and receives responses from an origin server, it is a client.

Typically a Web cache is purchased and installed by an ISP. For example, a university might install a cache on its campus network and configure all of the campus browsers to point to the cache. Or a major residential ISP (such as AOL) might install one or more caches in its network and preconfigure its shipped browsers to point to the installed caches.

Web caching has seen deployment in the Internet for two reasons. First, a Web cache can substantially reduce the response time for a client request, particularly if the bottleneck bandwidth between the client and the origin server is much less than the bottleneck bandwidth between the client and the cache. If there is a high-speed connection between the client and the cache, as there often is, and if the cache has the requested object, then the cache will be able to deliver the object rapidly to the client. Second, as we will soon illustrate with an example, Web caches can substantially reduce traffic on

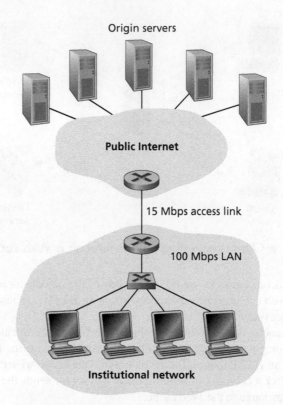

Figure 2.12 ♦ Bottleneck between an institutional network and the Internet

an institution's access link to the Internet. By reducing traffic, the institution (for example, a company or a university) does not have to upgrade bandwidth as quickly, thereby reducing costs. Furthermore, Web caches can substantially reduce Web traffic in the Internet as a whole, thereby improving performance for all applications.

To gain a deeper understanding of the benefits of caches, let's consider an example in the context of Figure 2.12. This figure shows two networks—the institutional network and the rest of the public Internet. The institutional network is a high-speed LAN. A router in the institutional network and a router in the Internet are connected by a 15 Mbps link. The origin servers are attached to the Internet but are located all over the globe. Suppose that the average object size is 1 Mbits and that the average request rate from the institution's browsers to the origin servers is 15 requests per second. Suppose that the HTTP request messages are negligibly small and thus create no traffic in the networks or in the access link (from institutional router to Internet router). Also suppose that the amount of time it takes from when the router on the Internet side of the access link in Figure 2.12 forwards an HTTP request (within an IP datagram) until it receives the response (typically within many IP datagrams) is two seconds on average. Informally, we refer to this last delay as the "Internet delay."

The total response time—that is, the time from the browser's request of an object until its receipt of the object—is the sum of the LAN delay, the access delay (that is, the delay between the two routers), and the Internet delay. Let's now do a very crude calculation to estimate this delay. The traffic intensity on the LAN (see Section 1.4.2) is

$$(15 \text{ requests/sec}) \cdot (1 \text{ Mbits/request})/(100 \text{ Mbps}) = 0.15$$

whereas the traffic intensity on the access link (from the Internet router to institution router) is

$$(15 \text{ requests/sec}) \cdot (1 \text{ Mbits/request})/(15 \text{ Mbps}) = 1$$

A traffic intensity of 0.15 on a LAN typically results in, at most, tens of milliseconds of delay; hence, we can neglect the LAN delay. However, as discussed in Section 1.4.2, as the traffic intensity approaches 1 (as is the case of the access link in Figure 2.12), the delay on a link becomes very large and grows without bound. Thus, the average response time to satisfy requests is going to be on the order of minutes, if not more, which is unacceptable for the institution's users. Clearly something must be done.

One possible solution is to increase the access rate from 15 Mbps to, say, 100 Mbps. This will lower the traffic intensity on the access link to 0.15, which translates to negligible delays between the two routers. In this case, the total response time will roughly be two seconds, that is, the Internet delay. But this solution also means that the institution must upgrade its access link from 15 Mbps to 100 Mbps, a costly proposition.

Now consider the alternative solution of not upgrading the access link but instead installing a Web cache in the institutional network. This solution is illustrated in Figure 2.13. Hit rates—the fraction of requests that are satisfied by a cache—typically range from 0.2 to 0.7 in practice. For illustrative purposes, let's suppose that the cache provides a hit rate of 0.4 for this institution. Because the clients and the cache are connected to the same high-speed LAN, 40 percent of the requests will be satisfied almost immediately, say, within 10 milliseconds, by the cache. Nevertheless, the remaining 60 percent of the requests still need to be satisfied by the origin servers. But with only 60 percent of the requested objects passing through the access link, the traffic intensity on the access link is reduced from 1.0 to 0.6. Typically, a traffic intensity less than 0.8 corresponds to a small delay, say, tens of milliseconds, on a 15 Mbps link. This delay is negligible compared with the two-second Internet delay. Given these considerations, average delay therefore is

$$0.4 \cdot (0.01 \text{ seconds}) + 0.6 \cdot (2.01 \text{ seconds})$$

which is just slightly greater than 1.2 seconds. Thus, this second solution provides an even lower response time than the first solution, and it doesn't require the institution to upgrade its link to the Internet. The institution does, of course, have to purchase

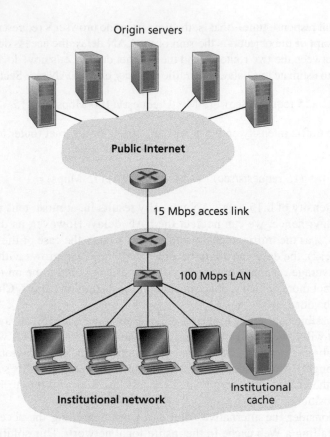

Origin servers

Public Internet

15 Mbps access link

100 Mbps LAN

Institutional network

Institutional cache

Figure 2.13 ♦ Adding a cache to the institutional network

and install a Web cache. But this cost is low—many caches use public-domain software that runs on inexpensive PCs.

Through the use of **Content Distribution Networks (CDNs)**, Web caches are increasingly playing an important role in the Internet. A CDN company installs many geographically distributed caches throughout the Internet, thereby localizing much of the traffic. There are shared CDNs (such as Akamai and Limelight) and dedicated CDNs (such as Google and Microsoft). We will discuss CDNs in more detail in Chapter 7.

2.2.6 The Conditional GET

Although caching can reduce user-perceived response times, it introduces a new problem—the copy of an object residing in the cache may be stale. In other words, the object housed in the Web server may have been modified since the copy was cached at the client. Fortunately, HTTP has a mechanism that allows a cache to verify that its objects are up to date. This mechanism is called the **conditional GET**. An HTTP request message is a so-called conditional GET message if (1) the request message uses the GET method and (2) the request message includes an If-Modified-Since: header line.

To illustrate how the conditional GET operates, let's walk through an example. First, on the behalf of a requesting browser, a proxy cache sends a request message to a Web server:

```
GET /fruit/kiwi.gif HTTP/1.1
Host: www.exotiquecuisine.com
```

Second, the Web server sends a response message with the requested object to the cache:

```
HTTP/1.1 200 OK
Date: Sat, 8 Oct 2011 15:39:29
Server: Apache/1.3.0 (Unix)
Last-Modified: Wed, 7 Sep 2011 09:23:24
Content-Type: image/gif

(data data data data data ...)
```

The cache forwards the object to the requesting browser but also caches the object locally. Importantly, the cache also stores the last-modified date along with the object. Third, one week later, another browser requests the same object via the cache, and the object is still in the cache. Since this object may have been modified at the Web server in the past week, the cache performs an up-to-date check by issuing a conditional GET. Specifically, the cache sends:

```
GET /fruit/kiwi.gif HTTP/1.1
Host: www.exotiquecuisine.com
If-modified-since: Wed, 7 Sep 2011 09:23:24
```

Note that the value of the If-modified-since: header line is exactly equal to the value of the Last-Modified: header line that was sent by the server one week ago. This conditional GET is telling the server to send the object only if the object has been modified since the specified date. Suppose the object has not been modified since 7 Sep 2011 09:23:24. Then, fourth, the Web server sends a response message to the cache:

```
HTTP/1.1 304 Not Modified
Date: Sat, 15 Oct 2011 15:39:29
Server: Apache/1.3.0 (Unix)

(empty entity body)
```

We see that in response to the conditional GET, the Web server still sends a response message but does not include the requested object in the response message. Including the requested object would only waste bandwidth and increase user-perceived response time, particularly if the object is large. Note that this last response message has 304 Not Modified in the status line, which tells the cache that it can go ahead and forward its (the proxy cache's) cached copy of the object to the requesting browser.

This ends our discussion of HTTP, the first Internet protocol (an application-layer protocol) that we've studied in detail. We've seen the format of HTTP messages and the actions taken by the Web client and server as these messages are sent and received. We've also studied a bit of the Web's application infrastructure, including caches, cookies, and back-end databases, all of which are tied in some way to the HTTP protocol.

2.3 File Transfer: FTP

In a typical FTP session, the user is sitting in front of one host (the local host) and wants to transfer files to or from a remote host. In order for the user to access the remote account, the user must provide a user identification and a password. After providing this authorization information, the user can transfer files from the local file system to the remote file system and vice versa. As shown in Figure 2.14, the user interacts with FTP through an FTP user agent. The user first provides the hostname of the remote host, causing the FTP client process in the local host to establish a TCP connection with the FTP server process in the remote host. The user then provides the user identification and password, which are sent over the TCP connection as part of FTP commands. Once the server has authorized the user, the user copies one or more files stored in the local file system into the remote file system (or vice versa).

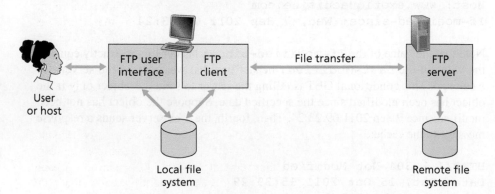

Figure 2.14 ◆ FTP moves files between local and remote file systems

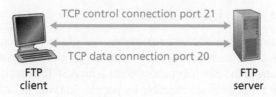

TCP control connection port 21

TCP data connection port 20

FTP
client

FTP
server

Figure 2.15 ♦ Control and data connections

HTTP and FTP are both file transfer protocols and have many common characteristics; for example, they both run on top of TCP. However, the two application-layer protocols have some important differences. The most striking difference is that FTP uses two parallel TCP connections to transfer a file, a **control connection** and a **data connection**. The control connection is used for sending control information between the two hosts—information such as user identification, password, commands to change remote directory, and commands to "put" and "get" files. The data connection is used to actually send a file. Because FTP uses a separate control connection, FTP is said to send its control information **out-of-band**. HTTP, as you recall, sends request and response header lines into the same TCP connection that carries the transferred file itself. For this reason, HTTP is said to send its control information **in-band**. In the next section, we'll see that SMTP, the main protocol for electronic mail, also sends control information in-band. The FTP control and data connections are illustrated in Figure 2.15.

When a user starts an FTP session with a remote host, the client side of FTP (user) first initiates a control TCP connection with the server side (remote host) on server port number 21. The client side of FTP sends the user identification and password over this control connection. The client side of FTP also sends, over the control connection, commands to change the remote directory. When the server side receives a command for a file transfer over the control connection (either to, or from, the remote host), the server side initiates a TCP data connection to the client side. FTP sends exactly one file over the data connection and then closes the data connection. If, during the same session, the user wants to transfer another file, FTP opens another data connection. Thus, with FTP, the control connection remains open throughout the duration of the user session, but a new data connection is created for each file transferred within a session (that is, the data connections are non-persistent).

Throughout a session, the FTP server must maintain **state** about the user. In particular, the server must associate the control connection with a specific user account, and the server must keep track of the user's current directory as the user wanders about the remote directory tree. Keeping track of this state information for each ongoing user session significantly constrains the total number of sessions that FTP can maintain simultaneously. Recall that HTTP, on the other hand, is stateless—it does not have to keep track of any user state.

2.3.1 FTP Commands and Replies

We end this section with a brief discussion of some of the more common FTP commands and replies. The commands, from client to server, and replies, from server to client, are sent across the control connection in 7-bit ASCII format. Thus, like HTTP commands, FTP commands are readable by people. In order to delineate successive commands, a carriage return and line feed end each command. Each command consists of four uppercase ASCII characters, some with optional arguments. Some of the more common commands are given below:

- `USER username:` Used to send the user identification to the server.
- `PASS password:` Used to send the user password to the server.
- `LIST:` Used to ask the server to send back a list of all the files in the current remote directory. The list of files is sent over a (new and non-persistent) data connection rather than the control TCP connection.
- `RETR filename:` Used to retrieve (that is, get) a file from the current directory of the remote host. This command causes the remote host to initiate a data connection and to send the requested file over the data connection.
- `STOR filename:` Used to store (that is, put) a file into the current directory of the remote host.

There is typically a one-to-one correspondence between the command that the user issues and the FTP command sent across the control connection. Each command is followed by a reply, sent from server to client. The replies are three-digit numbers, with an optional message following the number. This is similar in structure to the status code and phrase in the status line of the HTTP response message. Some typical replies, along with their possible messages, are as follows:

- `331 Username OK, password required`
- `125 Data connection already open; transfer starting`
- `425 Can't open data connection`
- `452 Error writing file`

Readers who are interested in learning about the other FTP commands and replies are encouraged to read RFC 959.

2.4 Electronic Mail in the Internet

Electronic mail has been around since the beginning of the Internet. It was the most popular application when the Internet was in its infancy [Segaller 1998], and has become more and more elaborate and powerful over the years. It remains one of the Internet's most important and utilized applications.

As with ordinary postal mail, e-mail is an asynchronous communication medium—people send and read messages when it is convenient for them, without having to coordinate with other people's schedules. In contrast with postal mail, electronic mail is fast, easy to distribute, and inexpensive. Modern e-mail has many powerful features, including messages with attachments, hyperlinks, HTML-formatted text, and embedded photos.

In this section, we examine the application-layer protocols that are at the heart of Internet e-mail. But before we jump into an in-depth discussion of these protocols, let's take a high-level view of the Internet mail system and its key components.

Figure 2.16 presents a high-level view of the Internet mail system. We see from this diagram that it has three major components: **user agents**, **mail servers**, and the

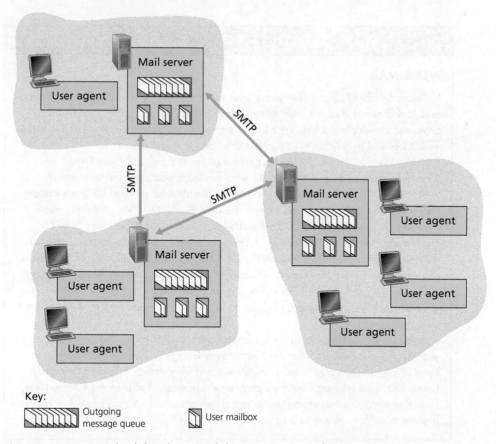

Figure 2.16 ♦ A high-level view of the Internet e-mail system

Simple Mail Transfer Protocol (SMTP). We now describe each of these components in the context of a sender, Alice, sending an e-mail message to a recipient, Bob. User agents allow users to read, reply to, forward, save, and compose messages. Microsoft Outlook and Apple Mail are examples of user agents for e-mail. When Alice is finished composing her message, her user agent sends the message to her mail server, where the message is placed in the mail server's outgoing message queue. When Bob wants to read a message, his user agent retrieves the message from his mailbox in his mail server.

Mail servers form the core of the e-mail infrastructure. Each recipient, such as Bob, has a **mailbox** located in one of the mail servers. Bob's mailbox manages and maintains the messages that have been sent to him. A typical message starts its journey in the sender's user agent, travels to the sender's mail server, and travels to the recipient's mail server, where it is deposited in the recipient's mailbox.

CASE HISTORY

WEB E-MAIL

In December 1995, just a few years after the Web was "invented," Sabeer Bhatia and Jack Smith visited the Internet venture capitalist Draper Fisher Jurvetson and proposed developing a free Web-based e-mail system. The idea was to give a free e-mail account to anyone who wanted one, and to make the accounts accessible from the Web. In exchange for 15 percent of the company, Draper Fisher Jurvetson financed Bhatia and Smith, who formed a company called Hotmail. With three full-time people and 14 part-time people who worked for stock options, they were able to develop and launch the service in July 1996. Within a month after launch, they had 100,000 subscribers. In December 1997, less than 18 months after launching the service, Hotmail had over 12 million subscribers and was acquired by Microsoft, reportedly for $400 million. The success of Hotmail is often attributed to its "first-mover advantage" and to the intrinsic "viral marketing" of e-mail. (Perhaps some of the students reading this book will be among the new entrepreneurs who conceive and develop first-mover Internet services with inherent viral marketing.)

Web e-mail continues to thrive, becoming more sophisticated and powerful every year. One of the most popular services today is Google's gmail, which offers gigabytes of free storage, advanced spam filtering and virus detection, e-mail encryption (using SSL), mail fetching from third-party e-mail services, and a search-oriented interface. Asynchronous messaging within social networks, such as Facebook, has also become popular in recent years.

2.4 • ELECTRONIC MAIL IN THE INTERNET

When Bob wants to access the messages in his mailbox, the mail server containing his mailbox authenticates Bob (with usernames and passwords). Alice's mail server must also deal with failures in Bob's mail server. If Alice's server cannot deliver mail to Bob's server, Alice's server holds the message in a **message queue** and attempts to transfer the message later. Reattempts are often done every 30 minutes or so; if there is no success after several days, the server removes the message and notifies the sender (Alice) with an e-mail message.

SMTP is the principal application-layer protocol for Internet electronic mail. It uses the reliable data transfer service of TCP to transfer mail from the sender's mail server to the recipient's mail server. As with most application-layer protocols, SMTP has two sides: a client side, which executes on the sender's mail server, and a server side, which executes on the recipient's mail server. Both the client and server sides of SMTP run on every mail server. When a mail server sends mail to other mail servers, it acts as an SMTP client. When a mail server receives mail from other mail servers, it acts as an SMTP server.

2.4.1 SMTP

SMTP, defined in RFC 5321, is at the heart of Internet electronic mail. As mentioned above, SMTP transfers messages from senders' mail servers to the recipients' mail servers. SMTP is much older than HTTP. (The original SMTP RFC dates back to 1982, and SMTP was around long before that.) Although SMTP has numerous wonderful qualities, as evidenced by its ubiquity in the Internet, it is nevertheless a legacy technology that possesses certain archaic characteristics. For example, it restricts the body (not just the headers) of all mail messages to simple 7-bit ASCII. This restriction made sense in the early 1980s when transmission capacity was scarce and no one was e-mailing large attachments or large image, audio, or video files. But today, in the multimedia era, the 7-bit ASCII restriction is a bit of a pain—it requires binary multimedia data to be encoded to ASCII before being sent over SMTP; and it requires the corresponding ASCII message to be decoded back to binary after SMTP transport. Recall from Section 2.2 that HTTP does not require multimedia data to be ASCII encoded before transfer.

To illustrate the basic operation of SMTP, let's walk through a common scenario. Suppose Alice wants to send Bob a simple ASCII message.

1. Alice invokes her user agent for e-mail, provides Bob's e-mail address (for example, bob@someschool.edu), composes a message, and instructs the user agent to send the message.
2. Alice's user agent sends the message to her mail server, where it is placed in a message queue.

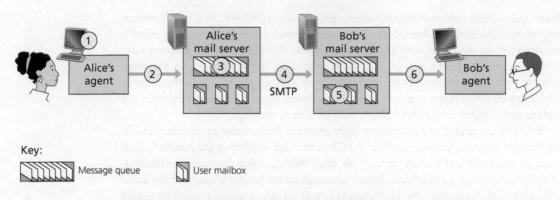

Key:

▨ Message queue   ▧ User mailbox

Figure 2.17 ♦ Alice sends a message to Bob

3. The client side of SMTP, running on Alice's mail server, sees the message in the message queue. It opens a TCP connection to an SMTP server, running on Bob's mail server.
4. After some initial SMTP handshaking, the SMTP client sends Alice's message into the TCP connection.
5. At Bob's mail server, the server side of SMTP receives the message. Bob's mail server then places the message in Bob's mailbox.
6. Bob invokes his user agent to read the message at his convenience.

The scenario is summarized in Figure 2.17.

It is important to observe that SMTP does not normally use intermediate mail servers for sending mail, even when the two mail servers are located at opposite ends of the world. If Alice's server is in Hong Kong and Bob's server is in St. Louis, the TCP connection is a direct connection between the Hong Kong and St. Louis servers. In particular, if Bob's mail server is down, the message remains in Alice's mail server and waits for a new attempt—the message does not get placed in some intermediate mail server.

Let's now take a closer look at how SMTP transfers a message from a sending mail server to a receiving mail server. We will see that the SMTP protocol has many similarities with protocols that are used for face-to-face human interaction. First, the client SMTP (running on the sending mail server host) has TCP establish a connection to port 25 at the server SMTP (running on the receiving mail server host). If the server is down, the client tries again later. Once this connection is established, the server and client perform some application-layer handshaking—just as humans often introduce themselves before transferring information from one to another, SMTP clients and servers introduce themselves before transferring information. During this SMTP handshaking phase, the

SMTP client indicates the e-mail address of the sender (the person who generated the message) and the e-mail address of the recipient. Once the SMTP client and server have introduced themselves to each other, the client sends the message. SMTP can count on the reliable data transfer service of TCP to get the message to the server without errors. The client then repeats this process over the same TCP connection if it has other messages to send to the server; otherwise, it instructs TCP to close the connection.

Let's next take a look at an example transcript of messages exchanged between an SMTP client (C) and an SMTP server (S). The hostname of the client is `crepes.fr` and the hostname of the server is `hamburger.edu`. The ASCII text lines prefaced with `C:` are exactly the lines the client sends into its TCP socket, and the ASCII text lines prefaced with `S:` are exactly the lines the server sends into its TCP socket. The following transcript begins as soon as the TCP connection is established.

```
S: 220 hamburger.edu
C: HELO crepes.fr
S: 250 Hello crepes.fr, pleased to meet you
C: MAIL FROM: <alice@crepes.fr>
S: 250 alice@crepes.fr ... Sender ok
C: RCPT TO: <bob@hamburger.edu>
S: 250 bob@hamburger.edu ... Recipient ok
C: DATA
S: 354 Enter mail, end with "." on a line by itself
C: Do you like ketchup?
C: How about pickles?
C: .
S: 250 Message accepted for delivery
C: QUIT
S: 221 hamburger.edu closing connection
```

In the example above, the client sends a message ("Do you like ketchup? How about pickles?") from mail server `crepes.fr` to mail server `hamburger.edu`. As part of the dialogue, the client issued five commands: `HELO` (an abbreviation for HELLO), `MAIL FROM`, `RCPT TO`, `DATA`, and `QUIT`. These commands are self-explanatory. The client also sends a line consisting of a single period, which indicates the end of the message to the server. (In ASCII jargon, each message ends with `CRLF.CRLF`, where `CR` and `LF` stand for carriage return and line feed, respectively.) The server issues replies to each command, with each reply having a reply code and some (optional) English-language explanation. We mention here that SMTP uses persistent connections: If the sending mail server has several messages to send to the same receiving mail server, it can send all of the messages over the same TCP connection. For each message, the client begins the process with a new `MAIL FROM: crepes.fr`, designates the end of message with an isolated period, and issues `QUIT` only after all messages have been sent.

It is highly recommended that you use Telnet to carry out a direct dialogue with an SMTP server. To do this, issue

```
telnet serverName 25
```

where `serverName` is the name of a local mail server. When you do this, you are simply establishing a TCP connection between your local host and the mail server. After typing this line, you should immediately receive the `220` reply from the server. Then issue the SMTP commands `HELO`, `MAIL FROM`, `RCPT TO`, `DATA`, `CRLF.CRLF`, and `QUIT` at the appropriate times. It is also highly recommended that you do Programming Assignment 3 at the end of this chapter. In that assignment, you'll build a simple user agent that implements the client side of SMTP. It will allow you to send an e-mail message to an arbitrary recipient via a local mail server.

2.4.2 Comparison with HTTP

Let's now briefly compare SMTP with HTTP. Both protocols are used to transfer files from one host to another: HTTP transfers files (also called objects) from a Web server to a Web client (typically a browser); SMTP transfers files (that is, e-mail messages) from one mail server to another mail server. When transferring the files, both persistent HTTP and SMTP use persistent connections. Thus, the two protocols have common characteristics. However, there are important differences. First, HTTP is mainly a **pull protocol**—someone loads information on a Web server and users use HTTP to pull the information from the server at their convenience. In particular, the TCP connection is initiated by the machine that wants to receive the file. On the other hand, SMTP is primarily a **push protocol**—the sending mail server pushes the file to the receiving mail server. In particular, the TCP connection is initiated by the machine that wants to send the file.

A second difference, which we alluded to earlier, is that SMTP requires each message, including the body of each message, to be in 7-bit ASCII format. If the message contains characters that are not 7-bit ASCII (for example, French characters with accents) or contains binary data (such as an image file), then the message has to be encoded into 7-bit ASCII. HTTP data does not impose this restriction.

A third important difference concerns how a document consisting of text and images (along with possibly other media types) is handled. As we learned in Section 2.2, HTTP encapsulates each object in its own HTTP response message. Internet mail places all of the message's objects into one message.

2.4.3 Mail Message Formats

When Alice writes an ordinary snail-mail letter to Bob, she may include all kinds of peripheral header information at the top of the letter, such as Bob's address, her own return address, and the date. Similarly, when an e-mail message is sent from one person to another, a header containing peripheral information precedes the body of the message itself. This peripheral information is contained in a series of header lines, which are defined in RFC 5322. The header lines and the body of the message are separated by a blank line (that is, by `CRLF`). RFC 5322 specifies the exact format for mail header lines as well as their semantic interpretations. As with HTTP, each header line contains readable text, consisting of a keyword followed by a colon followed by a value. Some of the keywords are required and others are optional. Every header must have a `From:` header line and a `To:` header line; a header may include a `Subject:` header line as well as other optional header lines. It is important to note that these header lines are *different* from the SMTP commands we studied in Section 2.4.1 (even though they contain some common words such as "*from*" and "*to*"). The commands in that section were part of the SMTP handshaking protocol; the header lines examined in this section are part of the mail message itself.

A typical message header looks like this:

```
From: alice@crepes.fr
To: bob@hamburger.edu
Subject: Searching for the meaning of life.
```

After the message header, a blank line follows; then the message body (in ASCII) follows. You should use Telnet to send a message to a mail server that contains some header lines, including the `Subject:` header line. To do this, issue `telnet serverName 25,` as discussed in Section 2.4.1.

2.4.4 Mail Access Protocols

Once SMTP delivers the message from Alice's mail server to Bob's mail server, the message is placed in Bob's mailbox. Throughout this discussion we have tacitly assumed that Bob reads his mail by logging onto the server host and then executing a mail reader that runs on that host. Up until the early 1990s this was the standard way of doing things. But today, mail access uses a client-server architecture—the typical user reads e-mail with a client that executes on the user's end system, for example, on an office PC, a laptop, or a smartphone. By executing a mail client on a local PC, users enjoy a rich set of features, including the ability to view multimedia messages and attachments.

Given that Bob (the recipient) executes his user agent on his local PC, it is natural to consider placing a mail server on his local PC as well. With this approach,

Alice's mail server would dialogue directly with Bob's PC. There is a problem with this approach, however. Recall that a mail server manages mailboxes and runs the client and server sides of SMTP. If Bob's mail server were to reside on his local PC, then Bob's PC would have to remain always on, and connected to the Internet, in order to receive new mail, which can arrive at any time. This is impractical for many Internet users. Instead, a typical user runs a user agent on the local PC but accesses its mailbox stored on an always-on shared mail server. This mail server is shared with other users and is typically maintained by the user's ISP (for example, university or company).

Now let's consider the path an e-mail message takes when it is sent from Alice to Bob. We just learned that at some point along the path the e-mail message needs to be deposited in Bob's mail server. This could be done simply by having Alice's user agent send the message directly to Bob's mail server. And this could be done with SMTP—indeed, SMTP has been designed for pushing e-mail from one host to another. However, typically the sender's user agent does not dialogue directly with the recipient's mail server. Instead, as shown in Figure 2.18, Alice's user agent uses SMTP to push the e-mail message into her mail server, then Alice's mail server uses SMTP (as an SMTP client) to relay the e-mail message to Bob's mail server. Why the two-step procedure? Primarily because without relaying through Alice's mail server, Alice's user agent doesn't have any recourse to an unreachable destination mail server. By having Alice first deposit the e-mail in her own mail server, Alice's mail server can repeatedly try to send the message to Bob's mail server, say every 30 minutes, until Bob's mail server becomes operational. (And if Alice's mail server is down, then she has the recourse of complaining to her system administrator!) The SMTP RFC defines how the SMTP commands can be used to relay a message across multiple SMTP servers.

But there is still one missing piece to the puzzle! How does a recipient like Bob, running a user agent on his local PC, obtain his messages, which are sitting in a mail server within Bob's ISP? Note that Bob's user agent can't use SMTP to obtain the messages because obtaining the messages is a pull operation, whereas SMTP is a

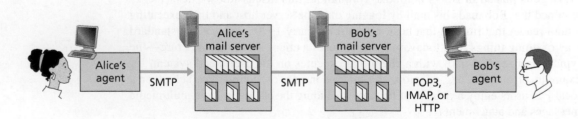

Figure 2.18 ◆ E-mail protocols and their communicating entities

push protocol. The puzzle is completed by introducing a special mail access protocol that transfers messages from Bob's mail server to his local PC. There are currently a number of popular mail access protocols, including **Post Office Protocol—Version 3 (POP3)**, **Internet Mail Access Protocol (IMAP)**, and HTTP.

Figure 2.18 provides a summary of the protocols that are used for Internet mail: SMTP is used to transfer mail from the sender's mail server to the recipient's mail server; SMTP is also used to transfer mail from the sender's user agent to the sender's mail server. A mail access protocol, such as POP3, is used to transfer mail from the recipient's mail server to the recipient's user agent.

POP3

POP3 is an extremely simple mail access protocol. It is defined in [RFC 1939], which is short and quite readable. Because the protocol is so simple, its functionality is rather limited. POP3 begins when the user agent (the client) opens a TCP connection to the mail server (the server) on port 110. With the TCP connection established, POP3 progresses through three phases: authorization, transaction, and update. During the first phase, authorization, the user agent sends a username and a password (in the clear) to authenticate the user. During the second phase, transaction, the user agent retrieves messages; also during this phase, the user agent can mark messages for deletion, remove deletion marks, and obtain mail statistics. The third phase, update, occurs after the client has issued the `quit` command, ending the POP3 session; at this time, the mail server deletes the messages that were marked for deletion.

In a POP3 transaction, the user agent issues commands, and the server responds to each command with a reply. There are two possible responses: `+OK` (sometimes followed by server-to-client data), used by the server to indicate that the previous command was fine; and `-ERR`, used by the server to indicate that something was wrong with the previous command.

The authorization phase has two principal commands: `user <username>` and `pass <password>`. To illustrate these two commands, we suggest that you Telnet directly into a POP3 server, using port 110, and issue these commands. Suppose that `mailServer` is the name of your mail server. You will see something like:

```
telnet mailServer 110
+OK POP3 server ready
user bob
+OK
pass hungry
+OK user successfully logged on
```

If you misspell a command, the POP3 server will reply with an `-ERR` message.

Now let's take a look at the transaction phase. A user agent using POP3 can often be configured (by the user) to "download and delete" or to "download and keep." The sequence of commands issued by a POP3 user agent depends on which of these two modes the user agent is operating in. In the download-and-delete mode, the user agent will issue the list, retr, and dele commands. As an example, suppose the user has two messages in his or her mailbox. In the dialogue below, C: (standing for client) is the user agent and S: (standing for server) is the mail server. The transaction will look something like:

```
C: list
S: 1 498
S: 2 912
S: .
C: retr 1
S: (blah blah ...
S: ................
S: .........blah)
S: .
C: dele 1
C: retr 2
S: (blah blah ...
S: ................
S: .........blah)
S: .
C: dele 2
C: quit
S: +OK POP3 server signing off
```

The user agent first asks the mail server to list the size of each of the stored messages. The user agent then retrieves and deletes each message from the server. Note that after the authorization phase, the user agent employed only four commands: list, retr, dele, and quit. The syntax for these commands is defined in RFC 1939. After processing the quit command, the POP3 server enters the update phase and removes messages 1 and 2 from the mailbox.

A problem with this download-and-delete mode is that the recipient, Bob, may be nomadic and may want to access his mail messages from multiple machines, for example, his office PC, his home PC, and his portable computer. The download-and-delete mode partitions Bob's mail messages over these three machines; in particular, if Bob first reads a message on his office PC, he will not be able to reread the message from his portable at home later in the evening. In the download-and-keep mode, the user agent leaves the messages on the mail server after downloading them. In this case, Bob can reread messages from different machines; he can access a message from work and access it again later in the week from home.

During a POP3 session between a user agent and the mail server, the POP3 server maintains some state information; in particular, it keeps track of which user messages have been marked deleted. However, the POP3 server does not carry state information across POP3 sessions. This lack of state information across sessions greatly simplifies the implementation of a POP3 server.

IMAP

With POP3 access, once Bob has downloaded his messages to the local machine, he can create mail folders and move the downloaded messages into the folders. Bob can then delete messages, move messages across folders, and search for messages (by sender name or subject). But this paradigm—namely, folders and messages in the local machine—poses a problem for the nomadic user, who would prefer to maintain a folder hierarchy on a remote server that can be accessed from any computer. This is not possible with POP3—the POP3 protocol does not provide any means for a user to create remote folders and assign messages to folders.

To solve this and other problems, the IMAP protocol, defined in [RFC 3501], was invented. Like POP3, IMAP is a mail access protocol. It has many more features than POP3, but it is also significantly more complex. (And thus the client and server side implementations are significantly more complex.)

An IMAP server will associate each message with a folder; when a message first arrives at the server, it is associated with the recipient's INBOX folder. The recipient can then move the message into a new, user-created folder, read the message, delete the message, and so on. The IMAP protocol provides commands to allow users to create folders and move messages from one folder to another. IMAP also provides commands that allow users to search remote folders for messages matching specific criteria. Note that, unlike POP3, an IMAP server maintains user state information across IMAP sessions—for example, the names of the folders and which messages are associated with which folders.

Another important feature of IMAP is that it has commands that permit a user agent to obtain components of messages. For example, a user agent can obtain just the message header of a message or just one part of a multipart MIME message. This feature is useful when there is a low-bandwidth connection (for example, a slow-speed modem link) between the user agent and its mail server. With a low-bandwidth connection, the user may not want to download all of the messages in its mailbox, particularly avoiding long messages that might contain, for example, an audio or video clip.

Web-Based E-Mail

More and more users today are sending and accessing their e-mail through their Web browsers. Hotmail introduced Web-based access in the mid 1990s. Now Web-based e-mail is also provided by Google, Yahoo!, as well as just about every major university and corporation. With this service, the user agent is an ordinary Web browser, and the user communicates with its remote mailbox via HTTP. When a recipient, such as Bob, wants to access a message in his mailbox, the e-mail message is sent from Bob's mail server to Bob's browser using the HTTP protocol rather than the POP3 or IMAP protocol. When a sender, such as Alice, wants to send an e-mail message, the e-mail message is sent from her browser to her mail server over HTTP rather than over SMTP. Alice's mail server, however, still sends messages to, and receives messages from, other mail servers using SMTP.

2.5 DNS—The Internet's Directory Service

We human beings can be identified in many ways. For example, we can be identified by the names that appear on our birth certificates. We can be identified by our social security numbers. We can be identified by our driver's license numbers. Although each of these identifiers can be used to identify people, within a given context one identifier may be more appropriate than another. For example, the computers at the IRS (the infamous tax-collecting agency in the United States) prefer to use fixed-length social security numbers rather than birth certificate names. On the other hand, ordinary people prefer the more mnemonic birth certificate names rather than social security numbers. (Indeed, can you imagine saying, "Hi. My name is 132-67-9875. Please meet my husband, 178-87-1146.")

Just as humans can be identified in many ways, so too can Internet hosts. One identifier for a host is its **hostname**. Hostnames—such as `cnn.com`, `www.yahoo.com`, `gaia.cs.umass.edu`, and `cis.poly.edu`—are mnemonic and are therefore appreciated by humans. However, hostnames provide little, if any, information about the location within the Internet of the host. (A hostname such as `www.eurecom.fr`, which ends with the country code `.fr`, tells us that the host is probably in France, but doesn't say much more.) Furthermore, because hostnames can consist of variable-length alphanumeric characters, they would be difficult to process by routers. For these reasons, hosts are also identified by so-called **IP addresses**.

We discuss IP addresses in some detail in Chapter 4, but it is useful to say a few brief words about them now. An IP address consists of four bytes and has a rigid hierarchical structure. An IP address looks like `121.7.106.83`, where each period separates one of the bytes expressed in decimal notation from 0 to 255. An IP address is hierarchical because as we scan the address from left to right, we obtain more and more specific information about where the host is located in the Internet (that is, within which network, in the network of networks). Similarly, when we scan a postal address from bottom to top, we obtain more and more specific information about where the addressee is located.

2.5.1 Services Provided by DNS

We have just seen that there are two ways to identify a host—by a hostname and by an IP address. People prefer the more mnemonic hostname identifier, while routers prefer fixed-length, hierarchically structured IP addresses. In order to reconcile these preferences, we need a directory service that translates hostnames to IP addresses. This is the main task of the Internet's **domain name system (DNS)**. The DNS is (1) a distributed database implemented in a hierarchy of **DNS servers**, and (2) an application-layer protocol that allows hosts to query the distributed database. The DNS servers are often UNIX machines running the Berkeley Internet Name Domain (BIND) software [BIND 2012]. The DNS protocol runs over UDP and uses port 53.

DNS is commonly employed by other application-layer protocols—including HTTP, SMTP, and FTP—to translate user-supplied hostnames to IP addresses. As an example, consider what happens when a browser (that is, an HTTP client), running on some user's host, requests the URL `www.someschool.edu/index.html`. In order for the user's host to be able to send an HTTP request message to the Web server `www.someschool.edu`, the user's host must first obtain the IP address of `www.someschool.edu`. This is done as follows.

1. The same user machine runs the client side of the DNS application.
2. The browser extracts the hostname, `www.someschool.edu`, from the URL and passes the hostname to the client side of the DNS application.
3. The DNS client sends a query containing the hostname to a DNS server.
4. The DNS client eventually receives a reply, which includes the IP address for the hostname.
5. Once the browser receives the IP address from DNS, it can initiate a TCP connection to the HTTP server process located at port 80 at that IP address.

We see from this example that DNS adds an additional delay—sometimes substantial—to the Internet applications that use it. Fortunately, as we discuss below, the desired IP address is often cached in a "nearby" DNS server, which helps to reduce DNS network traffic as well as the average DNS delay.

DNS provides a few other important services in addition to translating hostnames to IP addresses:

- **Host aliasing.** A host with a complicated hostname can have one or more alias names. For example, a hostname such as `relay1.west-coast.enterprise.com` could have, say, two aliases such as `enterprise.com` and `www.enterprise.com`. In this case, the hostname `relay1.west-coast.enterprise.com` is said to be a **canonical hostname**. Alias hostnames, when present, are typically more mnemonic than canonical hostnames.

PRINCIPLES IN PRACTICE

DNS: CRITICAL NETWORK FUNCTIONS VIA THE CLIENT-SERVER PARADIGM

Like HTTP, FTP, and SMTP, the DNS protocol is an application-layer protocol since it (1) runs between communicating end systems using the client-server paradigm and (2) relies on an underlying end-to-end transport protocol to transfer DNS messages between communicating end systems. In another sense, however, the role of the DNS is quite different from Web, file transfer, and e-mail applications. Unlike these applications, the DNS is not an application with which a user directly interacts. Instead, the DNS provides a core Internet function—namely, translating hostnames to their underlying IP addresses, for user applications and other software in the Internet. We noted in Section 1.2 that much of the complexity in the Internet architecture is located at the "edges" of the network. The DNS, which implements the critical name-to-address translation process using clients and servers located at the edge of the network, is yet another example of that design philosophy.

DNS can be invoked by an application to obtain the canonical hostname for a supplied alias hostname as well as the IP address of the host.

• **Mail server aliasing.** For obvious reasons, it is highly desirable that e-mail addresses be mnemonic. For example, if Bob has an account with Hotmail, Bob's e-mail address might be as simple as bob@hotmail.com. However, the hostname of the Hotmail mail server is more complicated and much less mnemonic than simply hotmail.com (for example, the canonical hostname might be something like relay1.west-coast.hotmail.com). DNS can be invoked by a mail application to obtain the canonical hostname for a supplied alias hostname as well as the IP address of the host. In fact, the MX record (see below) permits a company's mail server and Web server to have identical (aliased) hostnames; for example, a company's Web server and mail server can both be called enterprise.com.

• **Load distribution.** DNS is also used to perform load distribution among replicated servers, such as replicated Web servers. Busy sites, such as cnn.com, are replicated over multiple servers, with each server running on a different end system and each having a different IP address. For replicated Web servers, a *set* of IP addresses is thus associated with one canonical hostname. The DNS database contains this set of IP addresses. When clients make a DNS query for a name mapped to a set of addresses, the server responds with the entire set of IP addresses, but rotates the ordering of the addresses within each reply. Because a client typically sends its HTTP request message to the IP address that is listed first in the set, DNS rotation distributes the traffic among the replicated servers.

DNS rotation is also used for e-mail so that multiple mail servers can have the same alias name. Also, content distribution companies such as Akamai have used DNS in more sophisticated ways [Dilley 2002] to provide Web content distribution (see Chapter 7).

The DNS is specified in RFC 1034 and RFC 1035, and updated in several additional RFCs. It is a complex system, and we only touch upon key aspects of its operation here. The interested reader is referred to these RFCs and the book by Albitz and Liu [Albitz 1993]; see also the retrospective paper [Mockapetris 1988], which provides a nice description of the what and why of DNS, and [Mockapetris 2005].

2.5.2 Overview of How DNS Works

We now present a high-level overview of how DNS works. Our discussion will focus on the hostname-to-IP-address translation service.

Suppose that some application (such as a Web browser or a mail reader) running in a user's host needs to translate a hostname to an IP address. The application will invoke the client side of DNS, specifying the hostname that needs to be translated. (On many UNIX-based machines, `gethostbyname()` is the function call that an application calls in order to perform the translation.) DNS in the user's host then takes over, sending a query message into the network. All DNS query and reply messages are sent within UDP datagrams to port 53. After a delay, ranging from milliseconds to seconds, DNS in the user's host receives a DNS reply message that provides the desired mapping. This mapping is then passed to the invoking application. Thus, from the perspective of the invoking application in the user's host, DNS is a black box providing a simple, straightforward translation service. But in fact, the black box that implements the service is complex, consisting of a large number of DNS servers distributed around the globe, as well as an application-layer protocol that specifies how the DNS servers and querying hosts communicate.

A simple design for DNS would have one DNS server that contains all the mappings. In this centralized design, clients simply direct all queries to the single DNS server, and the DNS server responds directly to the querying clients. Although the simplicity of this design is attractive, it is inappropriate for today's Internet, with its vast (and growing) number of hosts. The problems with a centralized design include:

* **A single point of failure.** If the DNS server crashes, so does the entire Internet!
* **Traffic volume.** A single DNS server would have to handle all DNS queries (for all the HTTP requests and e-mail messages generated from hundreds of millions of hosts).

- **Distant centralized database.** A single DNS server cannot be "close to" all the querying clients. If we put the single DNS server in New York City, then all queries from Australia must travel to the other side of the globe, perhaps over slow and congested links. This can lead to significant delays.
- **Maintenance.** The single DNS server would have to keep records for all Internet hosts. Not only would this centralized database be huge, but it would have to be updated frequently to account for every new host.

In summary, a centralized database in a single DNS server simply *doesn't scale.* Consequently, the DNS is distributed by design. In fact, the DNS is a wonderful example of how a distributed database can be implemented in the Internet.

A Distributed, Hierarchical Database

In order to deal with the issue of scale, the DNS uses a large number of servers, organized in a hierarchical fashion and distributed around the world. No single DNS server has all of the mappings for all of the hosts in the Internet. Instead, the mappings are distributed across the DNS servers. To a first approximation, there are three classes of DNS servers—root DNS servers, top-level domain (TLD) DNS servers, and authoritative DNS servers—organized in a hierarchy as shown in Figure 2.19. To understand how these three classes of servers interact, suppose a DNS client wants to determine the IP address for the hostname `www.amazon.com`. To a first approximation, the following events will take place. The client first contacts one of the root servers, which returns IP addresses for TLD servers for the top-level domain `com`. The client then contacts one of these TLD servers, which returns the IP address of an authoritative server for `amazon.com`. Finally, the client contacts one of the authoritative servers for `amazon.com`, which returns the IP address

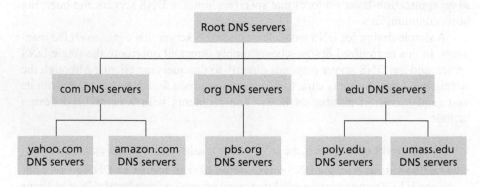

Figure 2.19 ✦ Portion of the hierarchy of DNS servers

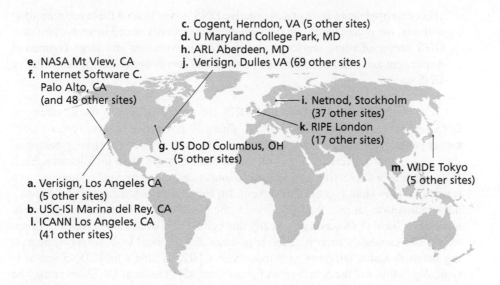

e. NASA Mt View, CA
f. Internet Software C.
Palo Alto, CA
(and 48 other sites)

c. Cogent, Herndon, VA (5 other sites)
d. U Maryland College Park, MD
h. ARL Aberdeen, MD
j. Verisign, Dulles VA (69 other sites)

i. Netnod, Stockholm
(37 other sites)
k. RIPE London
(17 other sites)

g. US DoD Columbus, OH
(5 other sites)

m. WIDE Tokyo
(5 other sites)

a. Verisign, Los Angeles CA
(5 other sites)
b. USC-ISI Marina del Rey, CA
l. ICANN Los Angeles, CA
(41 other sites)

Figure 2.20 ♦ DNS root servers in 2012 (name, organization, location)

for the hostname www.amazon.com. We'll soon examine this DNS lookup process in more detail. But let's first take a closer look at these three classes of DNS servers:

- **Root DNS servers.** In the Internet there are 13 root DNS servers (labeled A through M), most of which are located in North America. An October 2006 map of the root DNS servers is shown in Figure 2.20; a list of the current root DNS servers is available via [Root-servers 2012]. Although we have referred to each of the 13 root DNS servers as if it were a single server, each "server" is actually a network of replicated servers, for both security and reliability purposes. All together, there are 247 root servers as of fall 2011.

- **Top-level domain (TLD) servers.** These servers are responsible for top-level domains such as com, org, net, edu, and gov, and all of the country top-level domains such as uk, fr, ca, and jp. The company Verisign Global Registry Services maintains the TLD servers for the com top-level domain, and the company Educause maintains the TLD servers for the edu top-level domain. See [IANA TLD 2012] for a list of all top-level domains.

- **Authoritative DNS servers.** Every organization with publicly accessible hosts (such as Web servers and mail servers) on the Internet must provide publicly accessible DNS records that map the names of those hosts to IP addresses. An organization's authoritative DNS server houses these DNS records. An organization can choose to implement its own authoritative DNS server to hold these records; alternatively, the organization can pay to have these records stored in an authoritative DNS server of some service provider. Most universities and large companies implement and maintain their own primary and secondary (backup) authoritative DNS server.

The root, TLD, and authoritative DNS servers all belong to the hierarchy of DNS servers, as shown in Figure 2.19. There is another important type of DNS server called the **local DNS server**. A local DNS server does not strictly belong to the hierarchy of servers but is nevertheless central to the DNS architecture. Each ISP—such as a university, an academic department, an employee's company, or a residential ISP—has a local DNS server (also called a default name server). When a host connects to an ISP, the ISP provides the host with the IP addresses of one or more of its local DNS servers (typically through DHCP, which is discussed in Chapter 4). You can easily determine the IP address of your local DNS server by accessing network status windows in Windows or UNIX. A host's local DNS server is typically "close to" the host. For an institutional ISP, the local DNS server may be on the same LAN as the host; for a residential ISP, it is typically separated from the host by no more than a few routers. When a host makes a DNS query, the query is sent to the local DNS server, which acts a proxy, forwarding the query into the DNS server hierarchy, as we'll discuss in more detail below.

Let's take a look at a simple example. Suppose the host `cis.poly.edu` desires the IP address of `gaia.cs.umass.edu`. Also suppose that Polytechnic's local DNS server is called `dns.poly.edu` and that an authoritative DNS server for `gaia.cs.umass.edu` is called `dns.umass.edu`. As shown in Figure 2.21, the host `cis.poly.edu` first sends a DNS query message to its local DNS server, `dns.poly.edu`. The query message contains the hostname to be translated, namely, `gaia.cs.umass.edu`. The local DNS server forwards the query message to a root DNS server. The root DNS server takes note of the edu suffix and returns to the local DNS server a list of IP addresses for TLD servers responsible for edu. The local DNS server then resends the query message to one of these TLD servers. The TLD server takes note of the `umass.edu` suffix and responds with the IP address of the authoritative DNS server for the University of Massachusetts, namely, `dns.umass.edu`. Finally, the local DNS server resends the query message directly to `dns.umass.edu`, which responds with the IP address of `gaia.cs.umass.edu`. Note that in this example, in order to obtain the mapping for one hostname, eight DNS messages were sent: four query messages and four reply messages! We'll soon see how DNS caching reduces this query traffic.

Our previous example assumed that the TLD server knows the authoritative DNS server for the hostname. In general this not always true. Instead, the TLD server may know only of an intermediate DNS server, which in turn knows the authoritative DNS server for the hostname. For example, suppose again that the University of

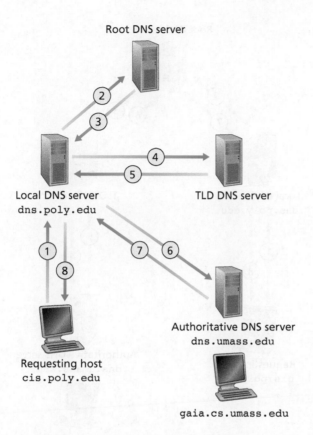

Figure 2.21 ♦ Interaction of the various DNS servers

Massachusetts has a DNS server for the university, called `dns.umass.edu`. Also suppose that each of the departments at the University of Massachusetts has its own DNS server, and that each departmental DNS server is authoritative for all hosts in the department. In this case, when the intermediate DNS server, `dns.umass.edu`, receives a query for a host with a hostname ending with `cs.umass.edu`, it returns to `dns.poly.edu` the IP address of `dns.cs.umass.edu`, which is authoritative for all hostnames ending with `cs.umass.edu`. The local DNS server `dns.poly.edu` then sends the query to the authoritative DNS server, which returns the desired mapping to the local DNS server, which in turn returns the mapping to the requesting host. In this case, a total of 10 DNS messages are sent!

The example shown in Figure 2.21 makes use of both **recursive queries** and **iterative queries**. The query sent from `cis.poly.edu` to `dns.poly.edu` is a recursive query, since the query asks `dns.poly.edu` to obtain the mapping on its

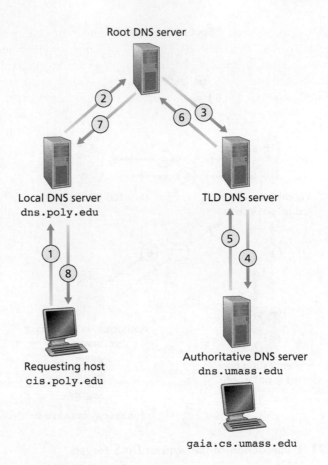

Root DNS server

Local DNS server
`dns.poly.edu`

TLD DNS server

Requesting host
`cis.poly.edu`

Authoritative DNS server
`dns.umass.edu`

`gaia.cs.umass.edu`

Figure 2.22 ♦ Recursive queries in DNS

behalf. But the subsequent three queries are iterative since all of the replies are directly returned to `dns.poly.edu`. In theory, any DNS query can be iterative or recursive. For example, Figure 2.22 shows a DNS query chain for which all of the queries are recursive. In practice, the queries typically follow the pattern in Figure 2.21: The query from the requesting host to the local DNS server is recursive, and the remaining queries are iterative.

DNS Caching

Our discussion thus far has ignored **DNS caching**, a critically important feature of the DNS system. In truth, DNS extensively exploits DNS caching in order to improve the delay performance and to reduce the number of DNS messages ricocheting around the Internet. The idea behind DNS caching is very simple. In a query chain, when a DNS server receives a DNS reply (containing, for example, a mapping from a hostname to an IP address), it can cache the mapping in its local memory. For example, in Figure 2.21, each time the local DNS server `dns.poly.edu` receives a reply from some DNS server, it can cache any of the information contained in the reply. If a hostname/IP address pair is cached in a DNS server and another query arrives to the DNS server for the same hostname, the DNS server can provide the desired IP address, even if it is not authoritative for the hostname. Because hosts and mappings between hostnames and IP addresses are by no means permanent, DNS servers discard cached information after a period of time (often set to two days).

As an example, suppose that a host `apricot.poly.edu` queries `dns.poly.edu` for the IP address for the hostname `cnn.com`. Furthermore, suppose that a few hours later, another Polytechnic University host, say, `kiwi.poly.edu`, also queries `dns.poly.edu` with the same hostname. Because of caching, the local DNS server will be able to immediately return the IP address of `cnn.com` to this second requesting host without having to query any other DNS servers. A local DNS server can also cache the IP addresses of TLD servers, thereby allowing the local DNS server to bypass the root DNS servers in a query chain (this often happens).

2.5.3 DNS Records and Messages

The DNS servers that together implement the DNS distributed database store **resource records (RRs)**, including RRs that provide hostname-to-IP address mappings. Each DNS reply message carries one or more resource records. In this and the following subsection, we provide a brief overview of DNS resource records and messages; more details can be found in [Abitz 1993] or in the DNS RFCs [RFC 1034; RFC 1035].

A resource record is a four-tuple that contains the following fields:

```
(Name, Value, Type, TTL)
```

TTL is the time to live of the resource record; it determines when a resource should be removed from a cache. In the example records given below, we ignore the TTL field. The meaning of Name and Value depend on Type:

* If Type=A, then Name is a hostname and Value is the IP address for the hostname. Thus, a Type A record provides the standard hostname-to-IP address mapping. As an example, (relay1.bar.foo.com, 145.37.93.126, A) is a Type A record.
* If Type=NS, then Name is a domain (such as foo.com) and Value is the hostname of an authoritative DNS server that knows how to obtain the IP addresses for hosts in the domain. This record is used to route DNS queries further along in

the query chain. As an example, (`foo.com, dns.foo.com, NS`) is a Type NS record.

- If `Type=CNAME`, then `Value` is a canonical hostname for the alias hostname `Name`. This record can provide querying hosts the canonical name for a hostname. As an example, (`foo.com, relay1.bar.foo.com, CNAME`) is a CNAME record.

- If `Type=MX`, then `Value` is the canonical name of a mail server that has an alias hostname `Name`. As an example, (`foo.com, mail.bar.foo.com, MX`) is an MX record. MX records allow the hostnames of mail servers to have simple aliases. Note that by using the MX record, a company can have the same aliased name for its mail server and for one of its other servers (such as its Web server). To obtain the canonical name for the mail server, a DNS client would query for an MX record; to obtain the canonical name for the other server, the DNS client would query for the CNAME record.

If a DNS server is authoritative for a particular hostname, then the DNS server will contain a Type A record for the hostname. (Even if the DNS server is not authoritative, it may contain a Type A record in its cache.) If a server is not authoritative for a hostname, then the server will contain a Type NS record for the domain that includes the hostname; it will also contain a Type A record that provides the IP address of the DNS server in the `Value` field of the NS record. As an example, suppose an edu TLD server is not authoritative for the host `gaia.cs.umass.edu`. Then this server will contain a record for a domain that includes the host `gaia.cs.umass.edu`, for example, (`umass.edu, dns.umass.edu, NS`). The edu TLD server would also contain a Type A record, which maps the DNS server `dns.umass.edu` to an IP address, for example, (`dns.umass.edu, 128.119.40.111, A`).

DNS Messages

Earlier in this section, we referred to DNS query and reply messages. These are the only two kinds of DNS messages. Furthermore, both query and reply messages have the same format, as shown in Figure 2.23. The semantics of the various fields in a DNS message are as follows:

- The first 12 bytes is the *header section,* which has a number of fields. The first field is a 16-bit number that identifies the query. This identifier is copied into the reply message to a query, allowing the client to match received replies with sent queries. There are a number of flags in the flag field. A 1-bit query/reply flag indicates whether the message is a query (0) or a reply (1). A 1-bit authoritative flag is set in a reply message when a DNS server is an authoritative server for a queried name. A 1-bit recursion-desired flag is set when a client (host or DNS server) desires that the DNS server perform recursion when it doesn't have the record. A 1-bit recursion-available field is set in a reply if the DNS server supports recursion. In the header,

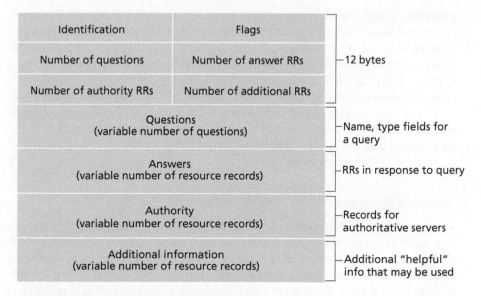

Figure 2.23 ♦ DNS message format

there are also four number-of fields. These fields indicate the number of occurrences of the four types of data sections that follow the header.

*   The *question section* contains information about the query that is being made. This section includes (1) a name field that contains the name that is being queried, and (2) a type field that indicates the type of question being asked about the name—for example, a host address associated with a name (Type A) or the mail server for a name (Type MX).

*   In a reply from a DNS server, the *answer section* contains the resource records for the name that was originally queried. Recall that in each resource record there is the `Type` (for example, A, NS, CNAME, and MX), the `Value`, and the `TTL`. A reply can return multiple RRs in the answer, since a hostname can have multiple IP addresses (for example, for replicated Web servers, as discussed earlier in this section).

*   The *authority section* contains records of other authoritative servers.

*   The *additional section* contains other helpful records. For example, the answer field in a reply to an MX query contains a resource record providing the canonical hostname of a mail server. The additional section contains a Type A record providing the IP address for the canonical hostname of the mail server.

How would you like to send a DNS query message directly from the host you're working on to some DNS server? This can easily be done with the **nslookup**

program, which is available from most Windows and UNIX platforms. For example, from a Windows host, open the Command Prompt and invoke the nslookup program by simply typing "nslookup." After invoking nslookup, you can send a DNS query to any DNS server (root, TLD, or authoritative). After receiving the reply message from the DNS server, nslookup will display the records included in the reply (in a human-readable format). As an alternative to running nslookup from your own host, you can visit one of many Web sites that allow you to remotely employ nslookup. (Just type "nslookup" into a search engine and you'll be brought to one of these sites.) The DNS Wireshark lab at the end of this chapter will allow you to explore the DNS in much more detail.

Inserting Records into the DNS Database

The discussion above focused on how records are retrieved from the DNS database. You might be wondering how records get into the database in the first place. Let's look at how this is done in the context of a specific example. Suppose you have just created an exciting new startup company called Network Utopia. The first thing you'll surely want to do is register the domain name `networkutopia.com` at a registrar. A **registrar** is a commercial entity that verifies the uniqueness of the domain name, enters the domain name into the DNS database (as discussed below), and collects a small fee from you for its services. Prior to 1999, a single registrar, Network Solutions, had a monopoly on domain name registration for `com`, `net`, and `org` domains. But now there are many registrars competing for customers, and the Internet Corporation for Assigned Names and Numbers (ICANN) accredits the various registrars. A complete list of accredited registrars is available at `http://www.internic.net`.

When you register the domain name `networkutopia.com` with some registrar, you also need to provide the registrar with the names and IP addresses of your primary and secondary authoritative DNS servers. Suppose the names and IP addresses are `dns1.networkutopia.com`, `dns2.networkutopia.com`, `212.212.212.1`, and `212.212.212.2`. For each of these two authoritative DNS servers, the registrar would then make sure that a Type NS and a Type A record are entered into the TLD com servers. Specifically, for the primary authoritative server for `networkutopia.com`, the registrar would insert the following two resource records into the DNS system:

```
(networkutopia.com, dns1.networkutopia.com, NS)

(dns1.networkutopia.com, 212.212.212.1, A)
```

You'll also have to make sure that the Type A resource record for your Web server `www.networkutopia.com` and the Type MX resource record for your mail server `mail.networkutopia.com` are entered into your authoritative DNS servers. (Until recently, the contents of each DNS server were configured statically,

FOCUS ON SECURITY

DNS VULNERABILITIES

We have seen that DNS is a critical component of the Internet infrastructure, with many important services - including the Web and e-mail - simply incapable of functioning without it. We therefore naturally ask, how can DNS be attacked? Is DNS a sitting duck, waiting to be knocked out of service, while taking most Internet applications down with it?

The first type of attack that comes to mind is a DDoS bandwidth-flooding attack (see Section 1.6) against DNS servers. For example, an attacker could attempt to send to each DNS root server a deluge of packets, so many that the majority of legitimate DNS queries never get answered. Such a large-scale DDoS attack against DNS root servers actually took place on October 21, 2002. In this attack, the attackers leveraged a botnet to send truck loads of ICMP ping messages to each of the 13 DNS root servers. (ICMP messages are discussed in Chapter 4. For now, it suffices to know that ICMP packets are special types of IP datagrams.) Fortunately, this large-scale attack caused minimal damage, having little or no impact on users' Internet experience. The attackers did succeed at directing a deluge of packets at the root servers. But many of the DNS root servers were protected by packet filters, configured to always block all ICMP ping messages directed at the root servers. These protected servers were thus spared and functioned as normal. Furthermore, most local DNS servers cache the IP addresses of top-level-domain servers, allowing the query process to often bypass the DNS root servers.

A potentially more effective DDoS attack against DNS would be send a deluge of DNS queries to top-level-domain servers, for example, to all the top-level-domain servers that handle the .com domain. It would be harder to filter DNS queries directed to DNS servers; and top-level-domain servers are not as easily bypassed as are root servers. But the severity of such an attack would be partially mitigated by caching in local DNS servers.

DNS could potentially be attacked in other ways. In a man-in-the-middle attack, the attacker intercepts queries from hosts and returns bogus replies. In the DNS poisoning attack, the attacker sends bogus replies to a DNS server, tricking the server into accepting bogus records into its cache. Either of these attacks could be used, for example, to redirect an unsuspecting Web user to the attacker's Web site. These attacks, however, are difficult to implement, as they require intercepting packets or throttling servers [Skoudis 2006].

Another important DNS attack is not an attack on the DNS service per se, but instead exploits the DNS infrastructure to launch a DDoS attack against a targeted host (for example, your university's mail server). In this attack, the attacker sends DNS queries to many authoritative DNS servers, with each query having the spoofed source address of the targeted host. The DNS servers then send their replies directly to the targeted host. If the queries can be crafted in such a way that a response is much larger

for example, from a configuration file created by a system manager. More recently, an UPDATE option has been added to the DNS protocol to allow data to be dynamically added or deleted from the database via DNS messages. [RFC 2136] and [RFC 3007] specify DNS dynamic updates.)

Once all of these steps are completed, people will be able to visit your Web site and send e-mail to the employees at your company. Let's conclude our discussion of DNS by verifying that this statement is true. This verification also helps to solidify what we have learned about DNS. Suppose Alice in Australia wants to view the Web page www.networkutopia.com. As discussed earlier, her host will first send a DNS query to her local DNS server. The local DNS server will then contact a TLD com server. (The local DNS server will also have to contact a root DNS server if the address of a TLD com server is not cached.) This TLD server contains the Type NS and Type A resource records listed above, because the registrar had these resource records inserted into all of the TLD com servers. The TLD com server sends a reply to Alice's local DNS server, with the reply containing the two resource records. The local DNS server then sends a DNS query to 212.212.212.1, asking for the Type A record corresponding to www.networkutopia.com. This record provides the IP address of the desired Web server, say, 212.212.71.4, which the local DNS server passes back to Alice's host. Alice's browser can now initiate a TCP connection to the host 212.212.71.4 and send an HTTP request over the connection. Whew! There's a lot more going on than what meets the eye when one surfs the Web!

2.6 Peer-to-Peer Applications

The applications described in this chapter thus far—including the Web, e-mail, and DNS—all employ client-server architectures with significant reliance on always-on infrastructure servers. Recall from Section 2.1.1 that with a P2P architecture, there is minimal (or no) reliance on always-on infrastructure servers. Instead, pairs of intermittently connected hosts, called peers, communicate directly with each other.

The peers are not owned by a service provider, but are instead desktops and laptops controlled by users.

In this section we'll examine two different applications that are particularly well-suited for P2P designs. The first is file distribution, where the application distributes a file from a single source to a large number of peers. File distribution is a nice place to start our investigation of P2P, as it clearly exposes the self-scalability of P2P architectures. As a specific example for file distribution, we'll describe the popular BitTorrent system. The second P2P application we'll examine is a database distributed over a large community of peers. For this application, we'll explore the concept of a Distributed Hash Table (DHT).

2.6.1 P2P File Distribution

We begin our foray into P2P by considering a very natural application, namely, distributing a large file from a single server to a large number of hosts (called peers). The file might be a new version of the Linux operating system, a software patch for an existing operating system or application, an MP3 music file, or an MPEG video file. In client-server file distribution, the server must send a copy of the file to each of the peers—placing an enormous burden on the server and consuming a large amount of server bandwidth. In P2P file distribution, each peer can redistribute any portion of the file it has received to any other peers, thereby assisting the server in the distribution process. As of 2012, the most popular P2P file distribution protocol is BitTorrent. Originally developed by Bram Cohen, there are now many different independent BitTorrent clients conforming to the BitTorrent protocol, just as there are a number of Web browser clients that conform to the HTTP protocol. In this subsection, we first examine the self-scalability of P2P architectures in the context of file distribution. We then describe BitTorrent in some detail, highlighting its most important characteristics and features.

Scalability of P2P Architectures

To compare client-server architectures with peer-to-peer architectures, and illustrate the inherent self-scalability of P2P, we now consider a simple quantitative model for distributing a file to a fixed set of peers for both architecture types. As shown in Figure 2.24, the server and the peers are connected to the Internet with access links. Denote the upload rate of the server's access link by u_s, the upload rate of the ith peer's access link by u_i, and the download rate of the ith peer's access link by d_i. Also denote the size of the file to be distributed (in bits) by F and the number of peers that want to obtain a copy of the file by N. The **distribution time** is the time it takes to get a copy of the file to all N peers. In our analysis of the distribution time below, for both client-server and P2P architectures, we make the simplifying (and generally accurate [Akella 2003]) assumption that the Internet core has abundant

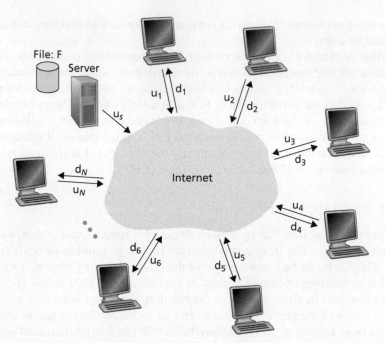

Figure 2.24 ♦ An illustrative file distribution problem

bandwidth, implying that all of the bottlenecks are in access networks. We also suppose that the server and clients are not participating in any other network applications, so that all of their upload and download access bandwidth can be fully devoted to distributing this file.

Let's first determine the distribution time for the client-server architecture, which we denote by D_{cs}. In the client-server architecture, none of the peers aids in distributing the file. We make the following observations:

• The server must transmit one copy of the file to each of the N peers. Thus the server must transmit NF bits. Since the server's upload rate is u_s, the time to distribute the file must be at least NF/u_s.

• Let d_{min} denote the download rate of the peer with the lowest download rate, that is, $d_{min} = min\{d_1, d_p, ..., d_N\}$. The peer with the lowest download rate cannot obtain all F bits of the file in less than F/d_{min} seconds. Thus the minimum distribution time is at least F/d_{min}.

Putting these two observations together, we obtain

$$D_{cs} \geq max\left\{\frac{NF}{u_s}, \frac{F}{d_{min}}\right\}.$$

This provides a lower bound on the minimum distribution time for the client-server architecture. In the homework problems you will be asked to show that the server can schedule its transmissions so that the lower bound is actually achieved. So let's take this lower bound provided above as the actual distribution time, that is,

$$D_{cs} = \max\left\{\frac{NF}{u_s}, \frac{F}{d_{min}}\right\} \tag{2.1}$$

We see from Equation 2.1 that for N large enough, the client-server distribution time is given by NF/u_s. Thus, the distribution time increases linearly with the number of peers N. So, for example, if the number of peers from one week to the next increases a thousand-fold from a thousand to a million, the time required to distribute the file to all peers increases by 1,000.

Let's now go through a similar analysis for the P2P architecture, where each peer can assist the server in distributing the file. In particular, when a peer receives some file data, it can use its own upload capacity to redistribute the data to other peers. Calculating the distribution time for the P2P architecture is somewhat more complicated than for the client-server architecture, since the distribution time depends on how each peer distributes portions of the file to the other peers. Nevertheless, a simple expression for the minimal distribution time can be obtained [Kumar 2006]. To this end, we first make the following observations:

- At the beginning of the distribution, only the server has the file. To get this file into the community of peers, the server must send each bit of the file at least once into its access link. Thus, the minimum distribution time is at least F/u_s. (Unlike the client-server scheme, a bit sent once by the server may not have to be sent by the server again, as the peers may redistribute the bit among themselves.)

- As with the client-server architecture, the peer with the lowest download rate cannot obtain all F bits of the file in less than F/d_{min} seconds. Thus the minimum distribution time is at least F/d_{min}.

- Finally, observe that the total upload capacity of the system as a whole is equal to the upload rate of the server plus the upload rates of each of the individual peers, that is, $u_{total} = u_s + u_1 + \dots + u_N$. The system must deliver (upload) F bits to each of the N peers, thus delivering a total of NF bits. This cannot be done at a rate faster than u_{total}. Thus, the minimum distribution time is also at least $NF/(u_s + u_1 + \dots + u_N)$.

Putting these three observations together, we obtain the minimum distribution time for P2P, denoted by D_{P2P}.

$$D_{P2P} \geq \max\left\{\frac{F}{u_s}, \frac{F}{d_{min}}, \frac{NF}{u_s + \sum_{i=1}^{N} u_i}\right\} \tag{2.2}$$

Equation 2.2 provides a lower bound for the minimum distribution time for the P2P architecture. It turns out that if we imagine that each peer can redistribute a bit as soon as it receives the bit, then there is a redistribution scheme that actually achieves this lower bound [Kumar 2006]. (We will prove a special case of this result in the homework.) In reality, where chunks of the file are redistributed rather than individual bits, Equation 2.2 serves as a good approximation of the actual minimum distribution time. Thus, let's take the lower bound provided by Equation 2.2 as the actual minimum distribution time, that is,

$$D_{P2P} = \max \left\{ \frac{F}{u_s}, \frac{F}{d_{min}}, \frac{NF}{u_s + \sum_{i=1}^{N} u_i} \right\} \qquad (2.3)$$

Figure 2.25 compares the minimum distribution time for the client-server and P2P architectures assuming that all peers have the same upload rate u. In Figure 2.25, we have set $F/u = 1$ hour, $u_s = 10u$, and $d_{min} \geq u_s$. Thus, a peer can transmit the entire file in one hour, the server transmission rate is 10 times the peer upload rate, and (for simplicity) the peer download rates are set large enough so as not to have an effect. We see from Figure 2.25 that for the client-server architecture, the distribution time increases linearly and without bound as the number of peers increases. However, for the P2P architecture, the minimal distribution time is not only always less than the distribution time of the client-server architecture; it is also less than one hour for *any* number of peers N. Thus, applications with the P2P architecture can be self-scaling. This scalability is a direct consequence of peers being redistributors as well as consumers of bits.

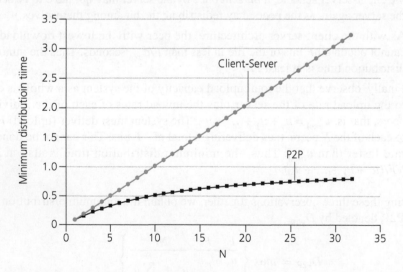

Figure 2.25 ♦ Distribution time for P2P and client-server architectures

BitTorrent

BitTorrent is a popular P2P protocol for file distribution [Chao 2011]. In BitTorrent lingo, the collection of all peers participating in the distribution of a particular file is called a *torrent*. Peers in a torrent download equal-size *chunks* of the file from one another, with a typical chunk size of 256 KBytes. When a peer first joins a torrent, it has no chunks. Over time it accumulates more and more chunks. While it downloads chunks it also uploads chunks to other peers. Once a peer has acquired the entire file, it may (selfishly) leave the torrent, or (altruistically) remain in the torrent and continue to upload chunks to other peers. Also, any peer may leave the torrent at any time with only a subset of chunks, and later rejoin the torrent.

Let's now take a closer look at how BitTorrent operates. Since BitTorrent is a rather complicated protocol and system, we'll only describe its most important mechanisms, sweeping some of the details under the rug; this will allow us to see the forest through the trees. Each torrent has an infrastructure node called a *tracker*. When a peer joins a torrent, it registers itself with the tracker and periodically informs the tracker that it is still in the torrent. In this manner, the tracker keeps track of the peers that are participating in the torrent. A given torrent may have fewer than ten or more than a thousand peers participating at any instant of time.

As shown in Figure 2.26, when a new peer, Alice, joins the torrent, the tracker randomly selects a subset of peers (for concreteness, say 50) from the set of participating peers, and sends the IP addresses of these 50 peers to Alice. Possessing this list of peers, Alice attempts to establish concurrent TCP connections with all the peers on this list. Let's call all the peers with which Alice succeeds in establishing a TCP connection "neighboring peers." (In Figure 2.26, Alice is shown to have only three neighboring peers. Normally, she would have many more.) As time evolves, some of these peers may leave and other peers (outside the initial 50) may attempt to establish TCP connections with Alice. So a peer's neighboring peers will fluctuate over time.

At any given time, each peer will have a subset of chunks from the file, with different peers having different subsets. Periodically, Alice will ask each of her neighboring peers (over the TCP connections) for the list of the chunks they have. If Alice has L different neighbors, she will obtain L lists of chunks. With this knowledge, Alice will issue requests (again over the TCP connections) for chunks she currently does not have.

So at any given instant of time, Alice will have a subset of chunks and will know which chunks her neighbors have. With this information, Alice will have two important decisions to make. First, which chunks should she request first from her neighbors? And second, to which of her neighbors should she send requested chunks? In deciding which chunks to request, Alice uses a technique called **rarest first**. The idea is to determine, from among the chunks she does not have, the chunks that are the rarest among her neighbors (that is, the chunks that have the fewest repeated copies among her neighbors) and then request those rarest chunks first. In this manner, the rarest chunks get more quickly redistributed, aiming to (roughly) equalize the numbers of copies of each chunk in the torrent.

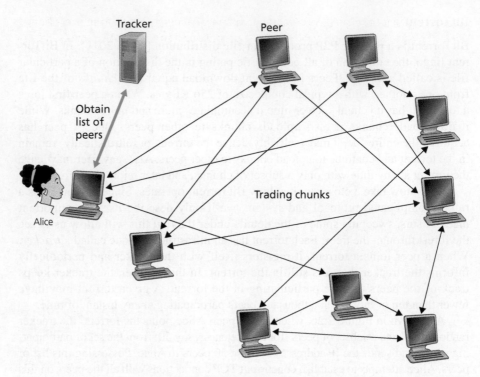

Figure 2.26 ♦ File distribution with BitTorrent

To determine which requests she responds to, BitTorrent uses a clever trading algorithm. The basic idea is that Alice gives priority to the neighbors that are currently supplying her data *at the highest rate*. Specifically, for each of her neighbors, Alice continually measures the rate at which she receives bits and determines the four peers that are feeding her bits at the highest rate. She then reciprocates by sending chunks to these same four peers. Every 10 seconds, she recalculates the rates and possibly modifies the set of four peers. In BitTorrent lingo, these four peers are said to be **unchoked**. Importantly, every 30 seconds, she also picks one additional neighbor at random and sends it chunks. Let's call the randomly chosen peer Bob. In BitTorrent lingo, Bob is said to be **optimistically unchoked**. Because Alice is sending data to Bob, she may become one of Bob's top four uploaders, in which case Bob would start to send data to Alice. If the rate at which Bob sends data to Alice is high enough, Bob could then, in turn, become one of Alice's top four uploaders. In other words, every 30 seconds, Alice will randomly choose a new trading partner and initiate trading with that partner. If the two peers are satisfied with the trading, they will put each other in their top four lists and continue trading with each other until one of the peers finds a better partner. The effect is that peers capable of uploading at compatible rates tend to find each other. The random neighbor selection also allows new peers to get chunks, so that they can have something to trade. All other neighboring peers besides these five peers (four "top" peers and one probing peer) are "choked," that is, they do not receive any chunks from Alice. BitTorrent has a number of interesting mechanisms that are not discussed here, including pieces (mini-chunks), pipelining, random first selection, endgame mode, and anti-snubbing [Cohen 2003].

The incentive mechanism for trading just described is often referred to as tit-for-tat [Cohen 2003]. It has been shown that this incentive scheme can be circumvented [Liogkas 2006; Locher 2006; Piatek 2007]. Nevertheless, the BitTorrent ecosystem is wildly successful, with millions of simultaneous peers actively sharing files in hundreds of thousands of torrents. If BitTorrent had been designed without tit-for-tat (or a variant), but otherwise exactly the same, BitTorrent would likely not even exist now, as the majority of the users would have been freeriders [Saroiu 2002].

Interesting variants of the BitTorrent protocol are proposed [Guo 2005; Piatek 2007]. Also, many of the P2P live streaming applications, such as PPLive and ppstream, have been inspired by BitTorrent [Hei 2007].

2.6.2 Distributed Hash Tables (DHTs)

In this section, we will consider how to implement a simple database in a P2P network. Let's begin by describing a centralized version of this simple database, which will simply contain (key, value) pairs. For example, the keys could be social security numbers and the values could be the corresponding human names; in this case, an example key-value pair is (156-45-7081, Johnny Wu). Or the keys could be content names (e.g., names of movies, albums, and software), and the value could be the IP address at which the content is stored; in this case, an example key-value pair is (Led Zeppelin IV, 128.17.123.38). We query the database with a key. If there are one or more key-value pairs in the database that match the query key, the database returns the corresponding values. So, for example, if the database stores social security numbers and their corresponding human names, we can query with a specific social security number, and the database returns the name of the human who has that social security number. Or, if the database stores content names and their corresponding IP addresses, we can query with a specific content name, and the database returns the IP addresses that store the specific content.

Building such a database is straightforward with a client-server architecture that stores all the (key, value) pairs in one central server. So in this section, we'll instead consider how to build a distributed, P2P version of this database that will store the (key, value) pairs over millions of peers. In the P2P system, each peer will only hold a small subset of the totality of the (key, value) pairs. We'll allow any peer to query the distributed database with a particular key. The distributed database will then locate the peers that have the corresponding (key, value) pairs and return the key-value pairs to the querying peer. Any peer will also be allowed to insert new key-value pairs into the database. Such a distributed database is referred to as a **distributed hash table (DHT)**.

Before describing how we can create a DHT, let's first describe a specific example DHT service in the context of P2P file sharing. In this case, a key is the content name and the value is the IP address of a peer that has a copy of the content. So, if Bob and Charlie each have a copy of the latest Linux distribution, then the DHT database will include the following two key-value pairs: (Linux, IP_{Bob}) and (Linux, $IP_{Charlie}$). More specifically, since the DHT database is distributed over the peers, some peer, say Dave, will be responsible for the key "Linux" and will have the corresponding key-value pairs. Now suppose Alice wants to obtain a copy of Linux. Clearly, she first needs to know which peers have a copy of Linux before she can begin to download it. To this end, she queries the DHT with "Linux" as the key. The DHT then determines that the peer Dave is responsible for the key "Linux." The DHT then contacts peer Dave, obtains from Dave the key-value pairs (Linux, IP_{Bob}) and (Linux, $IP_{Charlie}$), and passes them on to Alice. Alice can then download the latest Linux distribution from either IP_{Bob} or $IP_{Charlie}$.

Now let's return to the general problem of designing a DHT for general key-value pairs. One naïve approach to building a DHT is to randomly scatter the (key, value) pairs across all the peers and have each peer maintain a list of the IP addresses of all participating peers. In this design, the querying peer sends its query to all other peers, and the peers containing the (key, value) pairs that match the key can respond with their matching pairs. Such an approach is completely unscalable, of course, as it would require each peer to not only know about all other peers (possibly millions of such peers!) but even worse, have each query sent to *all* peers.

We now describe an elegant approach to designing a DHT. To this end, let's first assign an identifier to each peer, where each identifier is an integer in the range $[0, 2^n - 1]$ for some fixed n. Note that each such identifier can be expressed by an n-bit representation. Let's also require each key to be an integer in the same range. The astute reader may have observed that the example keys described a little earlier (social security numbers and content names) are not integers. To create integers out of such keys, we will use a hash function that maps each key (e.g., social security number) to an integer in the range $[0, 2^n - 1]$. A hash function is a many-to-one function for which two different inputs can have the same output (same integer), but the likelihood of the having the same output is extremely small. (Readers who are unfamiliar with hash functions may want to visit Chapter 7, in which hash functions are discussed in some detail.) The hash function is assumed to be available to all peers in the system. Henceforth, when we refer to the "key," we are referring to the hash of the original key. So, for example, if the original key is "Led Zeppelin IV," the key used in the DHT will be the integer that equals the hash of "Led Zeppelin IV." As you may have guessed, this is why "Hash" is used in the term "Distributed Hash Function."

Let's now consider the problem of storing the (key, value) pairs in the DHT. The central issue here is defining a rule for assigning keys to peers. Given that each peer has an integer identifier and that each key is also an integer in the same range, a natural approach is to assign each (key, value) pair to the peer whose identifier is the *closest* to the key. To implement such a scheme, we'll need to define what is meant by "closest," for which many conventions are possible. For convenience, let's define the closest peer as the *closest successor of the key*. To gain some insight here, let's take a look at a specific example. Suppose $n = 4$ so that all the peer and key identifiers are in the range [0, 15]. Further suppose that there are eight peers in the system with identifiers 1, 3, 4, 5, 8, 10, 12, and 15. Finally, suppose we want to store the (key, value) pair (11, Johnny Wu) in one of the eight peers. But in which peer? Using our closest convention, since peer 12 is the closest successor for key 11, we therefore store the pair (11, Johnny Wu) in the peer 12. [To complete our definition of closest, if the key is exactly equal to one of the peer identifiers, we store the (key, value) pair in that matching peer; and if the key is larger than all the peer identifiers, we use a modulo-2^n convention, storing the (key, value) pair in the peer with the smallest identifier.]

Now suppose a peer, Alice, wants to insert a (key, value) pair into the DHT. Conceptually, this is straightforward: She first determines the peer whose identifier is closest to the key; she then sends a message to that peer, instructing it to store the (key, value) pair. But how does Alice determine the peer that is closest to the key? If Alice were to keep track of all the peers in the system (peer IDs and corresponding IP addresses), she could locally determine the closest peer. But such an approach requires e*ach* peer to keep track of *all* other peers in the DHT—which is completely impractical for a large-scale system with millions of peers.

Circular DHT

To address this problem of scale, let's now consider organizing the peers into a circle. In this circular arrangement, each peer only keeps track of its immediate successor and immediate predecessor (modulo 2^n). An example of such a circle is shown in Figure 2.27(a). In this example, n is again 4 and there are the same eight

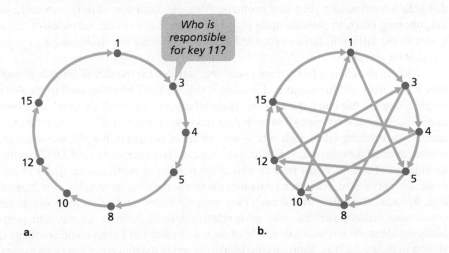

Figure 2.27 ◆ (a) A circular DHT. Peer 3 wants to determine who is responsible for key 11. (b) A circular DHT with shortcuts

peers from the previous example. Each peer is only aware of its immediate successor and predecessor; for example, peer 5 knows the IP address and identifier for peers 8 and 4 but does not necessarily know anything about any other peers that may be in the DHT. This circular arrangement of the peers is a special case of an **overlay network**. In an overlay network, the peers form an abstract logical network which resides above the "underlay" computer network consisting of physical links, routers, and hosts. The links in an overlay network are not physical links, but are simply virtual liaisons between pairs of peers. In the overlay in Figure 2.27(a), there are eight peers and eight overlay links; in the overlay in Figure 2.27(b) there are eight peers and 16 overlay links. A single overlay link typically uses many physical links and physical routers in the underlay network.

Using the circular overlay in Figure 2.27(a), now suppose that peer 3 wants to determine which peer in the DHT is responsible for key 11. Using the circular overlay, the origin peer (peer 3) creates a message saying "Who is responsible for key 11?" and sends this message clockwise around the circle. Whenever a peer receives such a message, because it knows the identifier of its successor and predecessor, it can determine whether it is responsible for (that is, closest to) the key in question. If a peer is not responsible for the key, it simply sends the message to its successor. So, for example, when peer 4 receives the message asking about key 11, it determines that it is not responsible for the key (because its successor is closer to the key), so it just passes the message along to peer 5. This process continues until the message arrives at peer 12, who determines that it is the closest peer to key 11. At this point, peer 12 can send a message back to the querying peer, peer 3, indicating that it is responsible for key 11.

The circular DHT provides a very elegant solution for reducing the amount of overlay information each peer must manage. In particular, each peer needs only to be aware of two peers, its immediate successor and its immediate predecessor. But this solution introduces yet a new problem. Although each peer is only aware of two neighboring peers, to find the node responsible for a key (in the worst case), all N nodes in the DHT will have to forward a message around the circle; $N/2$ messages are sent on average.

Thus, in designing a DHT, there is tradeoff between the number of neighbors each peer has to track and the number of messages that the DHT needs to send to resolve a single query. On one hand, if each peer tracks all other peers (mesh overlay), then only one message is sent per query, but each peer has to keep track of N peers. On the other hand, with a circular DHT, each peer is only aware of two peers, but $N/2$ messages are sent on average for each query. Fortunately, we can refine our designs of DHTs so that the number of neighbors per peer as well as the number of messages per query is kept to an acceptable size. One such refinement is to use the circular overlay as a foundation, but add "shortcuts" so that each peer not only keeps track of its immediate successor and predecessor, but also of a relatively small number of shortcut peers scattered about the circle. An example of such a circular DHT with some shortcuts is shown in Figure 2.27(b). Shortcuts are used to expedite the routing of query messages. Specifically, when a peer receives a message that is querying for a key, it forwards the message to the neighbor (successor neighbor or one of the shortcut neighbors) which is the closet to the key. Thus, in Figure 2.27(b), when peer 4 receives the message asking about key 11, it determines that the closet peer to the key (among its neighbors) is its shortcut neighbor 10 and then forwards the message directly to peer 10. Clearly, shortcuts can significantly reduce the number of messages used to process a query.

The next natural question is "How many shortcut neighbors should a peer have, and which peers should be these shortcut neighbors? This question has received significant attention in the research community [Balakrishnan 2003; Androutsellis-Theotokis 2004]. Importantly, it has been shown that the DHT can be designed so that both the number of neighbors per peer as well as the number of messages per query is $O(\log N)$, where N is the number of peers. Such designs strike a satisfactory compromise between the extreme solutions of using mesh and circular overlay topologies.

Peer Churn

In P2P systems, a peer can come or go without warning. Thus, when designing a DHT, we also must be concerned about maintaining the DHT overlay in the presence of such peer churn. To get a big-picture understanding of how this could be accomplished, let's once again consider the circular DHT in Figure 2.27(a). To handle peer churn, we will now require each peer to track (that is, know the IP address of) its first and second successors; for example, peer 4 now tracks both peer 5 and peer 8. We also require each peer to periodically verify that its two successors are alive (for example, by periodically sending ping messages to them and asking for responses). Let's now consider how the DHT is maintained when a peer abruptly leaves. For example, suppose peer 5 in Figure 2.27(a) abruptly leaves. In this case, the two peers preceding the departed peer (4 and 3) learn that 5 has departed, since it no longer responds to ping messages. Peers 4 and 3 thus need to update their successor state information. Let's consider how peer 4 updates its state:

1. Peer 4 replaces its first successor (peer 5) with its second successor (peer 8).
2. Peer 4 then asks its new first successor (peer 8) for the identifier and IP address of its immediate successor (peer 10). Peer 4 then makes peer 10 its second successor.

In the homework problems, you will be asked to determine how peer 3 updates its overlay routing information.

Having briefly addressed what has to be done when a peer leaves, let's now consider what happens when a peer wants to join the DHT. Let's say a peer with identifier 13 wants to join the DHT, and at the time of joining, it only knows about peer 1's existence in the DHT. Peer 13 would first send peer 1 a message, saying "what will be 13's predecessor and successor?" This message gets forwarded through the DHT until it reaches peer 12, who realizes that it will be 13's predecessor and that its current successor, peer 15, will become 13's successor. Next, peer 12 sends this predecessor and successor information to peer 13. Peer 13 can now join the DHT by making peer 15 its successor and by notifying peer 12 that it should change its immediate successor to 13.

DHTs have been finding widespread use in practice. For example, BitTorrent uses the Kademlia DHT to create a distributed tracker. In the BitTorrent, the key is the torrent identifier and the value is the IP addresses of all the peers currently participating in the torrent [Falkner 2007, Neglia 2007]. In this manner, by querying the DHT with a torrent identifier, a newly arriving BitTorrent peer can determine the peer that is responsible for the identifier (that is, for tracking the peers in the torrent). After having found that peer, the arriving peer can query it for a list of other peers in the torrent.

2.7 Socket Programming: Creating Network Applications

Now that we've looked at a number of important network applications, let's explore how network application programs are actually created. Recall from Section 2.1 that a typical network application consists of a pair of programs—a client program and a server program—residing in two different end systems. When these two programs are executed, a client process and a server process are created, and these processes communicate with each other by reading from, and writing to, sockets. When creating a network application, the developer's main task is therefore to write the code for both the client and server programs.

There are two types of network applications. One type is an implementation whose operation is specified in a protocol standard, such as an RFC or some other standards document; such an application is sometimes referred to as "open," since the rules specifying its operation are known to all. For such an implementation, the client and server programs must conform to the rules dictated by the RFC. For example, the client program could be an implementation of the client side of the FTP protocol, described in Section 2.3 and explicitly defined in RFC 959; similarly, the server program could be an implementation of the FTP server protocol, also explicitly defined in RFC 959. If one developer writes code for the client program and another developer writes code for the server program, and both developers carefully follow the rules of the RFC, then the two programs will be able to interoperate. Indeed, many of today's network applications involve communication between client and server programs that have been created by independent developers—for example, a Firefox browser communicating with an Apache Web server, or a BitTorrent client communicating with BitTorrent tracker.

The other type of network application is a proprietary network application. In this case the client and server programs employ an application-layer protocol that has *not* been openly published in an RFC or elsewhere. A single developer (or development team) creates both the client and server programs, and the developer has complete control over what goes in the code. But because the code does not implement an open protocol, other independent developers will not be able to develop code that interoperates with the application.

In this section, we'll examine the key issues in developing a client-server application, and we'll "get our hands dirty" by looking at code that implements a very simple client-server application. During the development phase, one of the first decisions the developer must make is whether the application is to run over TCP or over UDP. Recall that TCP is connection oriented and provides a reliable byte-stream channel through which data flows between two end systems. UDP is connectionless and sends independent packets of data from one end system to the other, without any guarantees about delivery. Recall also that when a client or server program implements a protocol defined by an RFC, it should use the well-known port number associated with the protocol; conversely, when developing a proprietary application, the developer must be careful to avoid using such well-known port numbers. (Port numbers were briefly discussed in Section 2.1. They are covered in more detail in Chapter 3.)

We introduce UDP and TCP socket programming by way of a simple UDP application and a simple TCP application. We present the simple UDP and TCP applications in Python. We could have written the code in Java, C, or C++, but we chose Python mostly because Python clearly exposes the key socket concepts. With Python there are fewer lines of code, and each line can be explained to the novice programmer without difficulty. But there's no need to be frightened if you are not familiar with Python. You should be able to easily follow the code if you have experience programming in Java, C, or C++.

If you are interested in client-server programming with Java, you are encouraged to see the companion Web site for this textbook; in fact, you can find there all the examples in this section (and associated labs) in Java. For readers who are interested in client-server programming in C, there are several good references available [Donahoo 2001; Stevens 1997; Frost 1994; Kurose 1996]; our Python examples below have a similar look and feel to C.

2.7.1 Socket Programming with UDP

In this subsection, we'll write simple client-server programs that use UDP; in the following section, we'll write similar programs that use TCP.

Recall from Section 2.1 that processes running on different machines communicate with each other by sending messages into sockets. We said that each process is analogous to a house and the process's socket is analogous to a door. The application resides on one side of the door in the house; the transport-layer protocol resides on the other side of the door in the outside world. The application developer has control of everything on the application-layer side of the socket; however, it has little control of the transport-layer side.

Now let's take a closer look at the interaction between two communicating processes that use UDP sockets. Before the sending process can push a packet of data out the socket door, when using UDP, it must first attach a destination address to the packet. After the packet passes through the sender's socket, the Internet will use this destination address to route the packet through the Internet to the socket in the receiving process. When the packet arrives at the receiving socket, the receiving process will retrieve the packet through the socket, and then inspect the packet's contents and take appropriate action.

So you may be now wondering, what goes into the destination address that is attached to the packet? As you might expect, the destination host's IP address is part of the destination address. By including the destination IP address in the packet, the routers in the Internet will be able to route the packet through the Internet to the destination host. But because a host may be running many network application processes, each with one or more sockets, it is also necessary to identify the particular socket in the destination host. When a socket is created, an identifier, called a **port number**, is assigned to it. So, as you might expect, the packet's destination address also includes the socket's port number. In summary, the sending process attaches to the packet a destination address which consists of the destination host's IP address and the destination socket's port number. Moreover, as we shall soon see, the sender's source address—consisting of the IP address of the source host and the port number of the source socket—are also attached to the packet. However, attaching the source address to the packet is typically *not* done by the UDP application code; instead it is automatically done by the underlying operating system.

We'll use the following simple client-server application to demonstrate socket programming for both UDP and TCP:

1. The client reads a line of characters (data) from its keyboard and sends the data to the server.
2. The server receives the data and converts the characters to uppercase.
3. The server sends the modified data to the client.
4. The client receives the modified data and displays the line on its screen.

Figure 2.28 highlights the main socket-related activity of the client and server that communicate over the UDP transport service.

Now let's get our hands dirty and take a look at the client-server program pair for a UDP implementation of this simple application. We also provide a detailed, line-by-line analysis after each program. We'll begin with the UDP client, which will send a simple application-level message to the server. In order for the server to be able to receive and reply to the client's message, it must be ready and running—that is, it must be running as a process before the client sends its message.

The client program is called UDPClient.py, and the server program is called UDPServer.py. In order to emphasize the key issues, we intentionally provide code that is minimal. "Good code" would certainly have a few more auxiliary lines, in

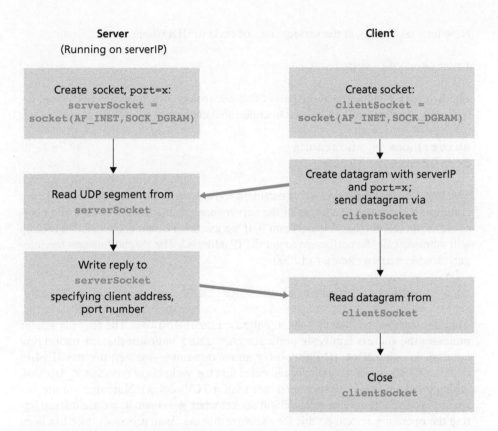

Figure 2.28 ♦ The client-server application using UDP

particular for handling error cases. For this application, we have arbitrarily chosen 12000 for the server port number.

UDPClient.py

Here is the code for the client side of the application:

```
from socket import *
serverName = 'hostname'
serverPort = 12000
clientSocket = socket(socket.AF_INET, socket.SOCK_DGRAM)
message = raw_input('Input lowercase sentence:')
clientSocket.sendto(message,(serverName, serverPort))
modifiedMessage, serverAddress = clientSocket.recvfrom(2048)
print modifiedMessage
clientSocket.close()
```

Now let's take a look at the various lines of code in UDPClient.py.

```
from socket import *
```

The `socket` module forms the basis of all network communications in Python. By including this line, we will be able to create sockets within our program.

```
serverName = 'hostname'
serverPort = 12000
```

The first line sets the string `serverName` to hostname. Here, we provide a string containing either the IP address of the server (e.g., "128.138.32.126") or the hostname of the server (e.g., "cis.poly.edu"). If we use the hostname, then a DNS lookup will automatically be performed to get the IP address.) The second line sets the integer variable `serverPort` to 12000.

```
clientSocket = socket(socket.AF_INET, socket.SOCK_DGRAM)
```

This line creates the client's socket, called `clientSocket`. The first parameter indicates the address family; in particular, `AF_INET` indicates that the underlying network is using IPv4. (Do not worry about this now—we will discuss IPv4 in Chapter 4.) The second parameter indicates that the socket is of type `SOCK_DGRAM`, which means it is a UDP socket (rather than a TCP socket). Note that we are not specifying the port number of the client socket when we create it; we are instead letting the operating system do this for us. Now that the client process's door has been created, we will want to create a message to send through the door.

```
message = raw_input('Input lowercase sentence:')
```

`raw_input()` is a built-in function in Python. When this command is executed, the user at the client is prompted with the words "Input lowercase sentence:" The user then uses her keyboard to input a line, which is put into the variable `message`. Now that we have a socket and a message, we will want to send the message through the socket to the destination host.

```
clientSocket.sendto(message,(serverName, serverPort))
```

In the above line, the method `sendto()` attaches the destination address (`serverName, serverPort`) to the message and sends the resulting packet into the process's socket, `clientSocket`. (As mentioned earlier, the source address is also attached to the packet, although this is done automatically rather than explicitly by the code.) Sending a client-to-server message via a UDP socket is that simple! After sending the packet, the client waits to receive data from the server.

```
modifiedMessage, serverAddress = clientSocket.recvfrom(2048)
```

With the above line, when a packet arrives from the Internet at the client's socket, the packet's data is put into the variable `modifiedMessage` and the packet's source address is put into the variable `serverAddress`. The variable `serverAddress` contains both the server's IP address and the server's port number. The program UDPClient doesn't actually need this server address information, since it already knows the server address from the outset; but this line of Python provides the server address nevertheless. The method `recvfrom` also takes the buffer size 2048 as input. (This buffer size works for most purposes.)

```
print modifiedMessage
```

This line prints out modifiedMessage on the user's display. It should be the original line that the user typed, but now capitalized.

```
clientSocket.close()
```

This line closes the socket. The process then terminates.

UDPServer.py

Let's now take a look at the server side of the application:

```
from socket import *
serverPort = 12000
serverSocket = socket(AF_INET, SOCK_DGRAM)
serverSocket.bind(('', serverPort))
print "The server is ready to receive"
while 1:
        message, clientAddress = serverSocket.recvfrom(2048)
        modifiedMessage = message.upper()
        serverSocket.sendto(modifiedMessage, clientAddress)
```

Note that the beginning of UDPServer is similar to UDPClient. It also imports the socket module, also sets the integer variable `serverPort` to 12000, and also creates a socket of type `SOCK_DGRAM` (a UDP socket). The first line of code that is significantly different from UDPClient is:

```
serverSocket.bind(('', serverPort))
```

The above line binds (that is, assigns) the port number 12000 to the server's socket. Thus in UDPServer, the code (written by the application developer) is explicitly assigning a port number to the socket. In this manner, when anyone sends a packet to port 12000 at the IP address of the server, that packet will be directed to this socket. UDPServer then enters a while loop; the while loop will allow UDPServer to receive and process packets from clients indefinitely. In the while loop, UDPServer waits for a packet to arrive.

```
message, clientAddress = serverSocket.recvfrom(2048)
```

This line of code is similar to what we saw in UDPClient. When a packet arrives at the server's socket, the packet's data is put into the variable `message` and the packet's source address is put into the variable `clientAddress`. The variable clientAddress contains both the client's IP address and the client's port number. Here, UDPServer *will* make use of this address information, as it provides a return address, similar to the return address with ordinary postal mail. With this source address information, the server now knows to where it should direct its reply.

```
modifiedMessage = message.upper()
```

This line is the heart of our simple application. It takes the line sent by the client and uses the method `upper()` to capitalize it.

```
serverSocket.sendto(modifiedMessage, clientAddress)
```

This last line attaches the client's address (IP address and port number) to the capitalized message, and sends the resulting packet into the server's socket. (As mentioned earlier, the server address is also attached to the packet, although this is done automatically rather than explicitly by the code.) The Internet will then deliver the packet to this client address. After the server sends the packet, it remains in the while loop, waiting for another UDP packet to arrive (from any client running on any host).

To test the pair of programs, you install and compile UDPClient.py in one host and UDPServer.py in another host. Be sure to include the proper hostname or IP address of the server in UDPClient.py. Next, you execute UDPServer.py, the compiled server program, in the server host. This creates a process in the server that idles until it is contacted by some client. Then you execute UDPClient.py, the compiled client program, in the client. This creates a process in the client. Finally, to use the application at the client, you type a sentence followed by a carriage return.

To develop your own UDP client-server application, you can begin by slightly modifying the client or server programs. For example, instead of converting all the letters to uppercase, the server could count the number of times the letter *s* appears and return this number. Or you can modify the client so that after receiving a capitalized sentence, the user can continue to send more sentences to the server.

2.7.2 Socket Programming with TCP

Unlike UDP, TCP is a connection-oriented protocol. This means that before the client and server can start to send data to each other, they first need to handshake and establish a TCP connection. One end of the TCP connection is attached to the client socket and the other end is attached to a server socket. When creating the TCP connection, we associate with it the client socket address (IP address and port number) and the server socket address (IP address and port number). With the TCP connection established, when one side wants to send data to the other side, it just drops the data into the TCP connection via its socket. This is different from UDP, for which the server must attach a destination address to the packet before dropping it into the socket.

Now let's take a closer look at the interaction of client and server programs in TCP. The client has the job of initiating contact with the server. In order for the server to be able to react to the client's initial contact, the server has to be ready. This implies two things. First, as in the case of UDP, the TCP server must be running as a process before the client attempts to initiate contact. Second, the server program must have a special door—more precisely, a special socket—that welcomes some initial contact from a client process running on an arbitrary host. Using our house/door analogy for a process/socket, we will sometimes refer to the client's initial contact as "knocking on the welcoming door."

With the server process running, the client process can initiate a TCP connection to the server. This is done in the client program by creating a TCP socket. When the client creates its TCP socket, it specifies the address of the welcoming socket in the server, namely, the IP address of the server host and the port number of the socket. After creating its socket, the client initiates a three-way handshake and establishes a TCP connection with the server. The three-way handshake, which takes place within the transport layer, is completely invisible to the client and server programs.

During the three-way handshake, the client process knocks on the welcoming door of the server process. When the server "hears" the knocking, it creates a new door—more precisely, a *new* socket that is dedicated to that particular client. In our example below, the welcoming door is a TCP socket object that we call `serverSocket`; the newly created socket dedicated to the client making the connection is called `connectionSocket`. Students who are encountering TCP sockets for the first time sometimes confuse the welcoming socket (which is the initial point of contact for all clients wanting to communicate with the server), and each newly created server-side connection socket that is subsequently created for communicating with each client.

From the application's perspective, the client's socket and the server's connection socket are directly connected by a pipe. As shown in Figure 2.29, the client process can send arbitrary bytes into its socket, and TCP guarantees that the server process will receive (through the connection socket) each byte in the order sent. TCP thus provides a reliable service between the client and server processes. Furthermore, just as people can go in and out the same door, the client process not only sends bytes

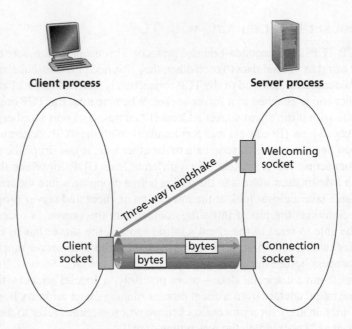

Client process

Server process

Welcoming socket

Three-way handshake

Client socket

bytes

bytes

Connection socket

Figure 2.29 ♦ The `TCPServer` process has two sockets

into but also receives bytes from its socket; similarly, the server process not only receives bytes from but also sends bytes into its connection socket.

We use the same simple client-server application to demonstrate socket programming with TCP: The client sends one line of data to the server, the server capitalizes the line and sends it back to the client. Figure 2.30 highlights the main socket-related activity of the client and server that communicate over the TCP transport service.

TCPClient.py

Here is the code for the client side of the application:

```
from socket import *
serverName = 'servername'
serverPort = 12000
clientSocket = socket(AF_INET, SOCK_STREAM)
clientSocket.connect((serverName,serverPort))
sentence = raw_input('Input lowercase sentence:')
clientSocket.send(sentence)
modifiedSentence = clientSocket.recv(1024)
print 'From Server:', modifiedSentence
clientSocket.close()
```

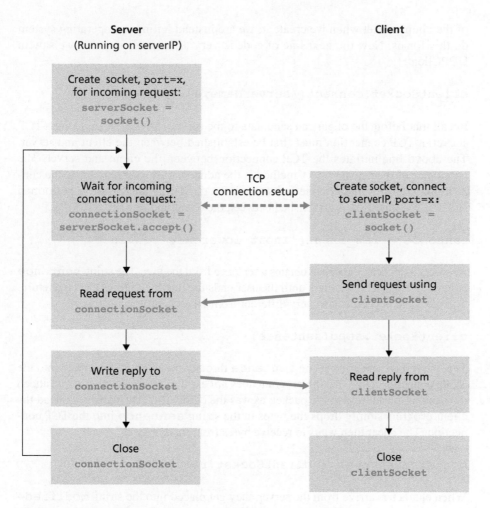

Figure 2.30 ♦ The client-server application using TCP

Let's now take a look at the various lines in the code that differ significantly from the UDP implementation. The first such line is the creation of the client socket.

```
clientSocket = socket(AF_INET, SOCK_STREAM)
```

This line creates the client's socket, called `clientSocket`. The first parameter again indicates that the underlying network is using IPv4. The second parameter indicates that the socket is of type `SOCK_STREAM`, which means it is a TCP socket (rather than a UDP socket). Note that we are again not specifying the port number of the client socket when we create it; we are instead letting the operating system do this for us. Now the next line of code is very different from what we saw in UDPClient:

```
clientSocket.connect((serverName,serverPort))
```

Recall that before the client can send data to the server (or vice versa) using a TCP socket, a TCP connection must first be established between the client and server. The above line initiates the TCP connection between the client and server. The parameter of the `connect()` method is the address of the server side of the connection. After this line of code is executed, the three-way handshake is performed and a TCP connection is established between the client and server.

```
sentence = raw_input('Input lowercase sentence:')
```

As with UDPClient, the above obtains a sentence from the user. The string `sentence` continues to gather characters until the user ends the line by typing a carriage return. The next line of code is also very different from UDPClient:

```
clientSocket.send(sentence)
```

The above line sends the string `sentence` through the client's socket and into the TCP connection. Note that the program does *not* explicitly create a packet and attach the destination address to the packet, as was the case with UDP sockets. Instead the client program simply drops the bytes in the string `sentence` into the TCP connection. The client then waits to receive bytes from the server.

```
modifiedSentence = clientSocket.recv(2048)
```

When characters arrive from the server, they get placed into the string `modified-Sentence`. Characters continue to accumulate in `modifiedSentence` until the line ends with a carriage return character. After printing the capitalized sentence, we close the client's socket:

```
clientSocket.close()
```

This last line closes the socket and, hence, closes the TCP connection between the client and the server. It causes TCP in the client to send a TCP message to TCP in the server (see Section 3.5).

TCPServer.py

Now let's take a look at the server program.

```
from socket import *
serverPort = 12000
serverSocket = socket(AF_INET,SOCK_STREAM)
serverSocket.bind(('',serverPort))
serverSocket.listen(1)
print 'The server is ready to receive'
while 1:
    connectionSocket, addr = serverSocket.accept()
    sentence = connectionSocket.recv(1024)
    capitalizedSentence = sentence.upper()
    connectionSocket.send(capitalizedSentence)
    connectionSocket.close()
```

Let's now take a look at the lines that differ significantly from UDPServer and TCP-Client. As with TCPClient, the server creates a TCP socket with:

```
serverSocket=socket(AF_INET,SOCK_STREAM)
```

Similar to UDPServer, we associate the server port number, `serverPort`, with this socket:

```
serverSocket.bind(('',serverPort))
```

But with TCP, `serverSocket` will be our welcoming socket. After establishing this welcoming door, we will wait and listen for some client to knock on the door:

```
serverSocket.listen(1)
```

This line has the server listen for TCP connection requests from the client. The parameter specifies the maximum number of queued connections (at least 1).

```
connectionSocket, addr = serverSocket.accept()
```

When a client knocks on this door, the program invokes the `accept()` method for serverSocket, which creates a new socket in the server, called `connectionSocket`, dedicated to this particular client. The client and server then complete the handshaking, creating a TCP connection between the client's `clientSocket` and the server's `connectionSocket`. With the TCP connection established, the client and server can now send bytes to each other over the connection. With TCP, all bytes sent from one side not are not only guaranteed to arrive at the other side but also guaranteed arrive in order.

```
connectionSocket.close()
```

In this program, after sending the modified sentence to the client, we close the connection socket. But since `serverSocket` remains open, another client can now knock on the door and send the server a sentence to modify.

This completes our discussion of socket programming in TCP. You are encouraged to run the two programs in two separate hosts, and also to modify them to achieve slightly different goals. You should compare the UDP program pair with the TCP program pair and see how they differ. You should also do many of the socket programming assignments described at the ends of Chapters 2, 4, and 7. Finally, we hope someday, after mastering these and more advanced socket programs, you will write your own popular network application, become very rich and famous, and remember the authors of this textbook!

2.8 Summary

In this chapter, we've studied the conceptual and the implementation aspects of network applications. We've learned about the ubiquitous client-server architecture adopted by many Internet applications and seen its use in the HTTP, FTP, SMTP, POP3, and DNS protocols. We've studied these important application-level protocols, and their corresponding associated applications (the Web, file transfer, e-mail, and DNS) in some detail. We've also learned about the increasingly prevalent P2P architecture and how it is used in many applications. We've examined how the socket API can be used to build network applications. We've walked through the use of sockets for connection-oriented (TCP) and connectionless (UDP) end-to-end transport services. The first step in our journey down the layered network architecture is now complete!

At the very beginning of this book, in Section 1.1, we gave a rather vague, barebones definition of a protocol: "the format and the order of messages exchanged between two or more communicating entities, as well as the actions taken on the transmission and/or receipt of a message or other event." The material in this chapter, and in particular our detailed study of the HTTP, FTP, SMTP, POP3, and DNS protocols, has now added considerable substance to this definition. Protocols are a key concept in networking; our study of application protocols has now given us the opportunity to develop a more intuitive feel for what protocols are all about.

In Section 2.1, we described the service models that TCP and UDP offer to applications that invoke them. We took an even closer look at these service models when we developed simple applications that run over TCP and UDP in Section 2.7. However, we have said little about how TCP and UDP provide these service models. For example, we know that TCP provides a reliable data service, but we haven't said yet how it does so. In the next chapter we'll take a careful look at not only the *what,* but also the *how* and *why* of transport protocols.

Equipped with knowledge about Internet application structure and application-level protocols, we're now ready to head further down the protocol stack and examine the transport layer in Chapter 3.

 # Homework Problems and Questions

Chapter 2 Review Questions

SECTION 2.1

R1. What are the two distinct programs that communicate with each other in case of a Web application?

R2. What is the difference between network architecture and application architecture?

R3. Give examples of applications with a client-server architecture.

R4. A popular social networking site can quickly become overwhelmed if it has only one server handling all of its requests. How is this tackled in practice?

R5. Some applications have hybrid architectures, combining both client-server and P2P elements. Give an example of such an application.

R6. Suppose you wanted to do a transaction from a remote client to a server as fast as possible. Would you use UDP or TCP? Why?

R7. Many networks, including the Internet, provide more than one transport-layer protocol. When you develop an application, you must choose one of the available transport-layer protocols. How do you make this choice?

R8. List the four broad classes of services that a transport protocol can provide. For each of the service classes, indicate if either UDP or TCP (or both) provides such a service.

R9. Recall that TCP can be enhanced with SSL to provide process-to-process security services, including encryption. Does SSL operate at the transport layer or the application layer? If the application developer wants TCP to be enhanced with SSL, what does the developer have to do?

SECTIONS 2.2–2.5

R10. What is the role of HTTP? Why is it called a stateless protocol?

R11. Why do HTTP, FTP, SMTP, and POP3 run on top of TCP rather than on UDP?

R12. Consider an e-commerce site that wants to keep a purchase record for each of its customers. Describe how this can be done with cookies.

R13. Although caching can reduce user-perceived response times, it introduces a new problem—the copy of an object residing in the cache may be stale. In other words, the object housed in the Web server may have been modified since the copy was cached at the client. How is this handled by HTTP?

R14. Telnet into a Web server and send a multiline request message. Include in the request message the `If-modified-since:` header line to force a response message with the `304 Not Modified` status code.

R15. What kind of state information is maintained by an FTP server?

R16. Suppose Alice, with a Web-based e-mail account (such as Hotmail or gmail), sends a message to Bob, who accesses his mail from his mail server using POP3. Discuss how the message gets from Alice's host to Bob's host. Be sure to list the series of application-layer protocols that are used to move the message between the two hosts.

R17. Print out the header of an e-mail message you have recently received. How many `Received:` header lines are there? Analyze each of the header lines in the message.

R18. With the TCP connection established, POP3 progresses through three phases. List them.

R19. Is it possible for an organization's Web server and mail server to have exactly the same alias for a hostname (for example, `foo.com`)? What would be the type for the RR that contains the hostname of the mail server?

R20. Look over your received emails, and examine the header of a message sent from a user with an .edu email address. Is it possible to determine from the header the IP address of the host from which the message was sent? Do the same for a message sent from a gmail account.

SECTION 2.6

R21. In BitTorrent, suppose Alice provides chunks to Bob throughout a 30-second interval. Will Bob necessarily return the favor and provide chunks to Alice in this same interval? Why or why not?

R22. Consider a new peer Alice that joins BitTorrent without possessing any chunks. Without any chunks, she cannot become a top-four uploader for any of the other peers, since she has nothing to upload. How then will Alice get her first chunk?

R23. In designing a DHT, there is trade-off between the number of neighbors each peer has to track and the number of messages that the DHT needs to send to resolve single query. Why?

R24. Consider a DHT with a mesh overlay topology (that is, every peer tracks all peers in the system). What are the advantages and disadvantages of such a design? What are the advantages and disadvantages of a circular DHT (with no shortcuts)?

R25. What is peer churn?

SECTION 2.7

R26. In Section 2.7, the UDP server described needed only one socket, whereas the TCP server needed two sockets. Why? If the TCP server were to support *n* simultaneous connections, each from a different client host, how many sockets would the TCP server need?

R27. For the client-server application over TCP described in Section 2.7, why must the server program be executed before the client program? For the client-server application over UDP, why may the client program be executed before the server program?

 Problems

P1. True or false?

a. Processes on two different end systems communicate with each other by exchanging messages across the computer network.

b. A client server architecture achieves perfect security.

c. Socket is a hardware interface through which a process sends messages into, and receives messages from the network.

d. No data loss is tolerated in multimedia applications such as conversational audio/video.

e. Developing a new network application for the Internet often requires one to decide whether to choose UDP or TCP.

P2. Read RFC 959 for FTP. List all of the client commands that are supported by the RFC.

P3. An application layer protocol defines four items. What are those?

P4. Consider the following string of ASCII characters that were captured by Wireshark when the browser sent an HTTP GET message (i.e., this is the actual content of an HTTP GET message). The characters *<cr><lf>* are carriage return and line-feed characters (that is, the italized character string *<cr>* in the text below represents the single carriage-return character that was contained at that point in the HTTP header). Answer the following questions, indicating where in the HTTP GET message below you find the answer.

```
GET /cs453/index.html HTTP/1.1<cr><lf>Host: gai
a.cs.umass.edu<cr><lf>User-Agent: Mozilla/5.0 (
Windows;U; Windows NT 5.1; en-US; rv:1.7.2) Gec
ko/20040804 Netscape/7.2 (ax) <cr><lf>Accept:ex
t/xml, application/xml, application/xhtml+xml, text
/html;q=0.9, text/plain;q=0.8,image/png,*/*;q=0.5
<cr><lf>Accept-Language: en-us,en;q=0.5<cr><lf>Accept-
Encoding: zip,deflate<cr><lf>Accept-Charset: ISO
-8859-1,utf-8;q=0.7,*;q=0.7<cr><lf>Keep-Alive: 300<cr>
<lf>Connection:keep-alive<cr><lf><cr><lf>
```

    a. What is the URL of the document requested by the browser?

    b. What version of HTTP is the browser running?

    c. Does the browser request a non-persistent or a persistent connection?

    d. What is the IP address of the host on which the browser is running?

    e. What type of browser initiates this message? Why is the browser type needed in an HTTP request message?

P5. The text below shows the reply sent from the server in response to the HTTP GET message in the question above. Answer the following questions, indicating where in the message below you find the answer.

```
HTTP/1.1 200 OK<cr><lf>Date: Tue, 07 Mar 2008
12:39:45GMT<cr><lf>Server: Apache/2.0.52 (Fedora)
<cr><lf>Last-Modified: Sat, 10 Dec2005 18:27:46
GMT<cr><lf>ETag: "526c3-f22-a88a4c80"<cr><lf>Accept-
Ranges: bytes<cr><lf>Content-Length: 3874<cr><lf>
Keep-Alive: timeout=max=100<cr><lf>Connection:
Keep-Alive<cr><lf>Content-Type: text/html; charset=
ISO-8859-1<cr><lf><cr><lf><!doctype html public "-
//w3c//dtd html 4.0 transitional//en"><lf><html><lf>
<head><lf> <meta http-equiv="Content-Type"
content="text/html; charset=iso-8859-1"><lf> <meta
name="GENERATOR" content="Mozilla/4.79 [en] (Windows NT
5.0; U) Netscape]"><lf> <title>CMPSCI 453 / 591 /
NTU-ST550A Spring 2005 homepage</title><lf></head><lf>
<much more document text following here (not shown)>
```

    a. Was the server able to successfully find the document or not? What time was the document reply provided?

    b. When was the document last modified?

    c. How many bytes are there in the document being returned?

    d. What are the first 5 bytes of the document being returned? Did the server agree to a persistent connection?

P6. Obtain the HTTP/1.1 specification (RFC 2616). Answer the following questions:

    a. Explain the mechanism used for signaling between the client and server to indicate that a persistent connection is being closed. Can the client, the server, or both signal the close of a connection?

    b. What encryption services are provided by HTTP?

    c. Can a client open three or more simultaneous connections with a given server?

    d. Either a server or a client may close a transport connection between them if either one detects the connection has been idle for some time. Is it possible that one side starts closing a connection while the other side is transmitting data via this connection? Explain.

P7. Suppose within your Web browser you click on a link to obtain a Web page. The IP address for the associated URL is not cached in your local host, so a DNS lookup is necessary to obtain the IP address. Suppose that n DNS servers are visited before your host receives the IP address from DNS; visiting k of them incurs an RTT of D_1 per DNS and visiting each of the remaining incurs an RTT of D_2. Further suppose that the Web page associated with the link contains m very small objects. Suppose the HTTP running is non-persistent and let RTT_0 denote the RTT between the local host and the server for each object. Assuming zero transmission time of each object, how much time elapses from when the client clicks on the link until the client receives all the objects?

P8. Referring to Problem P7, suppose 3 DNS servers are visited and the value of k is 2. Further, the HTML file references 5 very small objects on the same server. Neglecting transmission times, how much time elapses with

    a. Non-persistent HTTP with no parallel TCP connections?

    b. Non-persistent HTTP with the browser configured for 5 parallel connections?

    c. Persistent HTTP?

P9. Consider Figure 2.12, for which there is an institutional network connected to the Internet and assume that the access link is of 16 Mbps. Suppose that the average object size is 960,000 bits and that the average request rate from the institution's browsers to the origin servers is 15 requests per second. Also suppose that the amount of time it takes from when the router on the Internet side of the access link forwards an HTTP request until it receives the response is 2 seconds on average. Model the total average response time as the sum of the average access delay (that is, the delay from Internet router to institution router) and the average Internet delay. For the average access delay, use $\Delta(1 - \Delta\beta)$, where Δ is the average time required to send an object over the access link and β is the arrival rate of objects to the access link.

    a. Find the total average response time.

    b. Now suppose a cache is installed in the institutional LAN. Suppose the miss rate is 0.4. Find the total response time.

P10. Consider a short, 15-meter link, over which a sender can transmit at a rate of 160 bits/sec in both directions. Suppose that packets containing data are 200,000 bits long, and packets containing only control (e.g., ACK or handshaking) are 100 bits long. Assume that N parallel connections each get $1/N$ of the link bandwidth. Now consider the HTTP protocol, and suppose that each downloaded object is 200 Kbits long, and that the initial downloaded object contains 10 referenced objects from the same sender. Would parallel downloads via parallel instances of non-persistent HTTP make sense in this case? Now consider persistent HTTP. Do you expect significant gains over the non-persistent case? Justify and explain your answer.

P11. Consider the scenario introduced in the previous problem. Now suppose that the link is shared by Bob with four other users. Bob uses parallel instances of non-persistent HTTP, and the other four users use non-persistent HTTP without parallel downloads.

  a. Do Bob's parallel connections help him get Web pages more quickly? Why or why not?

  b. If all five users open five parallel instances of non-persistent HTTP, then would Bob's parallel connections still be beneficial? Why or why not?

P12. Write a simple TCP program for a server that accepts lines of input from a client and prints the lines onto the server's standard output. (You can do this by modifying the TCPServer.py program in the text.) Compile and execute your program. On any other machine that contains a Web browser, set the proxy server in the browser to the host that is running your server program; also configure the port number appropriately. Your browser should now send its GET request messages to your server, and your server should display the messages on its standard output. Use this platform to determine whether your browser generates conditional GET messages for objects that are locally cached.

P13. Explain the difference between control and data connection in FTP.

P14. How does SMTP differ from HTTP in terms of data format?

P15. Read RFC 5321 for SMTP. What does MTA stand for? Consider the following received spam email (modified from a real spam email). Assuming only the originator of this spam email is malacious and all other hosts are honest, identify the malacious host that has generated this spam email.

```
From - Fri Nov 07 13:41:30 2008
Return-Path: <tennis5@pp33head.com>
Received: from barmail.cs.umass.edu
(barmail.cs.umass.edu [128.119.240.3]) by cs.umass.edu
(8.13.1/8.12.6) for <hg@cs.umass.edu>; Fri, 7 Nov 2008
13:27:10 -0500
```

```
Received: from asusus-4b96 (localhost [127.0.0.1]) by
barmail.cs.umass.edu (Spam Firewall) for
<hg@cs.umass.edu>; Fri,  7 Nov 2008 13:27:07 -0500
(EST)
Received: from asusus-4b96 ([58.88.21.177]) by
barmail.cs.umass.edu for <hg@cs.umass.edu>; Fri,
07 Nov 2008 13:27:07 -0500 (EST)
Received: from [58.88.21.177] by
inbnd55.exchangeddd.com; Sat, 8 Nov 2008 01:27:07 +0700
From: "Jonny" <tennis5@pp33head.com>
To: <hg@cs.umass.edu>
Subject: How to secure your savings
```

P16. What is the primary advantage of IMAP over POP3?

P17. Consider accessing your e-mail with POP3.

   a. Suppose you have configured your POP mail client to operate in the
      download-and-delete mode. Complete the following transaction:

```
C: list
S: 1 498
S: 2 912
S: .
C: retr 1
S: blah blah ...
S: .........blah
S: .
?
?
```

   b. Suppose you have configured your POP mail client to operate in the
      download-and-keep mode. Complete the following transaction:

```
C: list
S: 1 498
S: 2 912
S: .
C: retr 1
S: blah blah ...
S: .........blah
S: .
?
?
```

    c. Suppose you have configured your POP mail client to operate in the download-and-keep mode. Using your transcript in part (b), suppose you retrieve messages 1 and 2, exit POP, and then five minutes later you again access POP to retrieve new e-mail. Suppose that in the five-minute interval no new messages have been sent to you. Provide a transcript of this second POP session.

P18. a. What is a *whois* database?

    b. Use various whois databases on the Internet to obtain the names of two DNS servers. Indicate which whois databases you used.

    c. Use nslookup on your local host to send DNS queries to three DNS servers: your local DNS server and the two DNS servers you found in part (b). Try querying for Type A, NS, and MX reports. Summarize your findings.

    d. Use nslookup to find a Web server that has multiple IP addresses. Does the Web server of your institution (school or company) have multiple IP addresses?

    e. Use the ARIN whois database to determine the IP address range used by your university.

    f. Describe how an attacker can use whois databases and the nslookup tool to perform reconnaissance on an institution before launching an attack.

    g. Discuss why whois databases should be publicly available.

P19. In this problem, we use the useful *dig* tool available on Unix and Linux hosts to explore the hierarchy of DNS servers. Recall that in Figure 2.21, a DNS server higher in the DNS hierarchy delegates a DNS query to a DNS server lower in the hierarchy, by sending back to the DNS client the name of that lower-level DNS server. First read the man page for *dig*, and then answer the following questions.

    a. Starting with a root DNS server (from one of the root servers [a-m].root-servers.net), initiate a sequence of queries for the IP address for your department's Web server by using *dig*. Show the list of the names of DNS servers in the delegation chain in answering your query.

    b. Repeat part a) for several popular Web sites, such as google.com, yahoo.com, or amazon.com.

P20. Consider what happens when a browser (that is, an HTTP client), running on some user's host, requests the URL www.somesite.com/index.html. In order for the user's host to be able to send an HTTP request message to the Web server www.somesite.com, the user's host must first obtain the IP address of www.somesite.com. Explain the steps through which the IP address for such a hostname is obtained by the client.

P21. Suppose that your department has a local DNS server for all computers in the department. You are an ordinary user (i.e., not a network/system administrator). Can you determine if an external Web site was likely accessed from a computer in your department a couple of seconds ago? Explain.

P22. Consider distributing a file of $F = 15$ Gbits to N peers. The server has an upload rate of $u_s = 30$ Mbps, and each peer has a download rate of $d_i = 2$ Mbps and an upload rate of u. For $N = 10$, 100, and 1,000 and $u = 300$ Kbps, 700 Kbps, and 2 Mbps, prepare a chart giving the minimum distribution time for each of the combinations of N and u for both client-server distribution and P2P distribution.

P23. Consider distributing a file of F bits to N peers using a client-server architecture. Assume a fluid model where the server can simultaneously transmit to multiple peers, transmitting to each peer at different rates, as long as the combined rate does not exceed u_s.

a. Suppose that $u_s/N \le d_{min}$. Specify a distribution scheme that has a distribution time of NF/u_s.

b. Suppose that $u_s/N \ge d_{min}$. Specify a distribution scheme that has a distribution time of F/d_{min}.

c. Conclude that the minimum distribution time is in general given by $\max\{NF/u_s, F/d_{min}\}$.

P24. Consider distributing a file of F bits to N peers using a P2P architecture. Assume a fluid model. For simplicity assume that d_{min} is very large, so that peer download bandwidth is never a bottleneck.

a. Suppose that $u_s \le (u_s + u_1 + \ldots + u_N)/N$. Specify a distribution scheme that has a distribution time of F/u_s.

b. Suppose that $u_s \ge (u_s + u_1 + \ldots + u_N)/N$. Specify a distribution scheme that has a distribution time of $NF/(u_s + u_1 + \ldots + u_N)$.

c. Conclude that the minimum distribution time is in general given by $\max\{F/u_s, NF/(u_s + u_1 + \ldots + u_N)\}$.

P25. Consider a network with N hosts. Each host is connected to certain number of other hosts. This number is called the degree of a host. Is there any upper-bound for the degree?

P26. Suppose Bob joins a BitTorrent torrent, but he does not want to upload any data to any other peers (so called free-riding).

a. Bob claims that he can receive a complete copy of the file that is shared by the swarm. Is Bob's claim possible? Why or why not?

b. Bob further claims that he can further make his "free-riding" more efficient by using a collection of multiple computers (with distinct IP addresses) in the computer lab in his department. How can he do that?

P27. In the circular DHT example in Section 2.6.2, suppose that peer 3 learns that peer 5 has left. How does peer 3 update its successor state information? Which peer is now its first successor? Its second successor?

VideoNote
**Walking through
distributed hash tables**

P28. In the circular DHT example in Section 2.6.2, suppose that a new peer 6 wants to join the DHT and peer 6 initially only knows peer 15's IP address. What steps are taken?

P29. Because an integer in $[0, 2^n - 1]$ can be expressed as an n-bit binary number in a DHT, each key can be expressed as $k = (k_0, k_1, \ldots, k_{n-1})$, and each peer identifier can be expressed $p = (p_0, p_1, \ldots, p_{n-1})$. Let's now define the XOR distance between a key k and peer p as

$$d(k, p) = \sum_{j=0}^{n-1} |k_j - p_j| 2^j$$

Describe how this metric can be used to assign (key, value) pairs to peers. (To learn about how to build an efficient DHT using this natural metric, see [Maymounkov 2002] in which the Kademlia DHT is described.)

P30. As DHTs are overlay networks, they may not necessarily match the underlay physical network well in the sense that two neighboring peers might be physically very far away; for example, one peer could be in Asia and its neighbor could be in North America. If we randomly and uniformly assign identifiers to newly joined peers, would this assignment scheme cause such a mismatch? Explain. And how would such a mismatch affect the DHT's performance?

P31. Install and compile the Python programs TCPClient and UDPClient on one host and TCPServer and UDPServer on another host.

a. Suppose you run TCPClient before you run TCPServer. What happens? Why?

b. Suppose you run UDPClient before you run UDPServer. What happens? Why?

c. What happens if you use different port numbers for the client and server sides?

P32. Suppose that in UDPClient.py, after we create the socket, we add the line:

```
clientSocket.bind(('', 5432))
```

Will it become necessary to change UDPServer.py? What are the port numbers for the sockets in UDPClient and UDPServer? What were they before making this change?

P33. At any given instant of time, a peer in a torrent has a subset of chunks and will know which chunks its neighbors have. With this information, how does it decide which chunks should it request first from its neighbors? To which of its neighbors should it send requested chunks?

P34. One naïve approach to building a DHT is to randomly scatter the (key, value) pairs across all the peers and have each peer maintain a list of the IP addresses of all participating peers. In this design, the querying peer sends its query to all other peers, and the peers containing the (key, value) pairs that match the key can respond with their matching pairs. Explain why such an approach is completely unscalable.

P35. What is the trade-off in designing a DHT with respect to the number of neighbors?

P36. Justify the advantages of Python over C/C++ for writing Socket programs.

 Socket Programming Assignments

The companion Web site includes six socket programming assignments. The first four assignments are summarized below. The fifth assignment makes use of the ICMP protocol and is summarized at the end of Chapter 4. The sixth assignment employs multimedia protocols and is summarized at the end of Chapter 7. It is highly recommended that students complete several, if not all, of these assignments. Students can find full details of these assignments, as well as important snippets of the Python code, at the Web site http://www.awl.com/kurose-ross.

Assignment 1: Web Server

In this assignment, you will develop a simple Web server in Python that is capable of processing only one request. Specifically, your Web server will (i) create a connection socket when contacted by a client (browser); (ii) receive the HTTP request from this connection; (iii) parse the request to determine the specific file being requested; (iv) get the requested file from the server's file system; (v) create an HTTP response message consisting of the requested file preceded by header lines; and (vi) send the response over the TCP connection to the requesting browser. If a browser requests a file that is not present in your server, your server should return a "404 Not Found" error message.

In the companion Web site, we provide the skeleton code for your server. Your job is to complete the code, run your server, and then test your server by sending requests from browsers running on different hosts. If you run your server on a host that already has a Web server running on it, then you should use a different port than port 80 for your Web server.

Assignment 2: UDP Pinger

In this programming assignment, you will write a client ping program in Python. Your client will send a simple ping message to a server, receive a corresponding pong message back from the server, and determine the delay between when the client sent the ping message and received the pong message. This delay is called the Round Trip Time (RTT). The functionality provided by the client and server is similar to the functionality provided by standard ping program available in modern operating systems. However, standard ping programs use the Internet Control Message Protocol (ICMP) (which we will study in Chapter 4). Here we will create a nonstandard (but simple!) UDP-based ping program.

Your ping program is to send 10 ping messages to the target server over UDP. For each message, your client is to determine and print the RTT when the corresponding pong message is returned. Because UDP is an unreliable protocol, a packet sent by the client or server may be lost. For this reason, the client cannot wait indefinitely for a reply to a ping message. You should have the client wait up to one second for a reply from the server; if no reply is received, the client should assume that the packet was lost and print a message accordingly.

In this assignment, you will be given the complete code for the server (available in the companion Web site). Your job is to write the client code, which will be very similar to the server code. It is recommended that you first study carefully the server code. You can then write your client code, liberally cutting and pasting lines from the server code.

Assignment 3: Mail Client

The goal of this programming assignment is to create a simple mail client that sends email to any recipient. Your client will need to establish a TCP connection with a mail server (e.g., a Google mail server), dialogue with the mail server using the SMTP protocol, send an email message to a recipient (e.g., your friend) via the mail server, and finally close the TCP connection with the mail server.

For this assignment, the companion Web site provides the skeleton code for your client. Your job is to complete the code and test your client by sending email to different user accounts. You may also try sending through different servers (for example, through a Google mail server and through your university mail server).

Assignment 4: Multi-Threaded Web Proxy

In this assignment, you will develop a Web proxy. When your proxy receives an HTTP request for an object from a browser, it generates a new HTTP request for the same object and sends it to the origin server. When the proxy receives the corresponding HTTP response with the object from the origin server, it creates a new HTTP response, including the object, and sends it to the client. This proxy will be multi-threaded, so that it will be able to handle multiple requests at the same time.

For this assignment, the companion Web site provides the skeleton code for the proxy server. Your job is to complete the code, and then test it by having different browsers request Web objects via your proxy.

Wireshark Lab: HTTP

Having gotten our feet wet with the Wireshark packet sniffer in Lab 1, we're now ready to use Wireshark to investigate protocols in operation. In this lab, we'll explore several aspects of the HTTP protocol: the basic GET/reply interaction, HTTP message formats, retrieving large HTML files, retrieving HTML files with embedded URLs, persistent and non-persistent connections, and HTTP authentication and security.

VideoNote
Using Wireshark to investigate the HTTP protocol

As is the case with all Wireshark labs, the full description of this lab is available at this book's Web site, http://www.awl.com/kurose-ross.

Wireshark Lab: DNS

In this lab, we take a closer look at the client side of the DNS, the protocol that translates Internet hostnames to IP addresses. Recall from Section 2.5 that the client's role in the DNS is relatively simple—a client sends a query to its local DNS server and receives a response back. Much can go on under the covers, invisible to the DNS clients, as the hierarchical DNS servers communicate with each other to either recursively or iteratively resolve the client's DNS query. From the DNS client's standpoint, however, the protocol is quite simple—a query is formulated to the local DNS server and a response is received from that server. We observe DNS in action in this lab.

As is the case with all Wireshark labs, the full description of this lab is available at this book's Web site, http://www.awl.com/kurose-ross.

Marc Andreessen

Marc Andreessen is the co-creator of Mosaic, the Web browser that popularized the World Wide Web in 1993. Mosaic had a clean, easily understood interface and was the first browser to display images in-line with text. In 1994, Marc Andreessen and Jim Clark founded Netscape, whose browser was by far the most popular browser through the mid-1990s. Netscape also developed the Secure Sockets Layer (SSL) protocol and many Internet server products, including mail servers and SSL-based Web servers. He is now a co-founder and general partner of venture capital firm Andreessen Horowitz, overseeing portfolio development with holdings that include Facebook, Foursquare, Groupon, Jawbone, Twitter, and Zynga. He serves on numerous boards, including Bump, eBay, Glam Media, Facebook, and Hewlett-Packard. He holds a BS in Computer Science from the University of Illinois at Urbana-Champaign.

How did you become interested in computing? Did you always know that you wanted to work in information technology?

The video game and personal computing revolutions hit right when I was growing up— personal computing was the new technology frontier in the late 70's and early 80's. And it wasn't just Apple and the IBM PC, but hundreds of new companies like Commodore and Atari as well. I taught myself to program out of a book called "Instant Freeze-Dried BASIC" at age 10, and got my first computer (a TRS-80 Color Computer—look it up!) at age 12.

Please describe one or two of the most exciting projects you have worked on during your career. What were the biggest challenges?

Undoubtedly the most exciting project was the original Mosaic web browser in '92–'93— and the biggest challenge was getting anyone to take it seriously back then. At the time, everyone thought the interactive future would be delivered as "interactive television" by huge companies, not as the Internet by startups.

What excites you about the future of networking and the Internet? What are your biggest concerns?

The most exciting thing is the huge unexplored frontier of applications and services that programmers and entrepreneurs are able to explore—the Internet has unleashed creativity at a level that I don't think we've ever seen before. My biggest concern is the principle of unintended consequences—we don't always know the implications of what we do, such as the Internet being used by governments to run a new level of surveillance on citizens.

Is there anything in particular students should be aware of as Web technology advances?

The rate of change—the most important thing to learn is how to learn—how to flexibly adapt to changes in the specific technologies, and how to keep an open mind on the new opportunities and possibilities as you move through your career.

What people inspired you professionally?

Vannevar Bush, Ted Nelson, Doug Engelbart, Nolan Bushnell, Bill Hewlett and Dave Packard, Ken Olsen, Steve Jobs, Steve Wozniak, Andy Grove, Grace Hopper, Hedy Lamarr, Alan Turing, Richard Stallman.

What are your recommendations for students who want to pursue careers in computing and information technology?

Go as deep as you possibly can on understanding how technology is created, and then complement with learning how business works.

Can technology solve the world's problems?

No, but we advance the standard of living of people through economic growth, and most economic growth throughout history has come from technology—so that's as good as it gets.

3

Transport Layer

Residing between the application and network layers, the transport layer is a central piece of the layered network architecture. It has the critical role of providing communication services directly to the application processes running on different hosts. The pedagogic approach we take in this chapter is to alternate between discussions of transport-layer principles and discussions of how these principles are implemented in existing protocols; as usual, particular emphasis will be given to Internet protocols, in particular the TCP and UDP transport-layer protocols.

We'll begin by discussing the relationship between the transport and network layers. This sets the stage for examining the first critical function of the transport layer—extending the network layer's delivery service between two end systems to a delivery service between two application-layer processes running on the end systems. We'll illustrate this function in our coverage of the Internet's connectionless transport protocol, UDP.

We'll then return to principles and confront one of the most fundamental problems in computer networking—how two entities can communicate reliably over a medium that may lose and corrupt data. Through a series of increasingly complicated (and realistic!) scenarios, we'll build up an array of techniques that transport protocols use to solve this problem. We'll then show how these principles are embodied in TCP, the Internet's connection-oriented transport protocol.

We'll next move on to a second fundamentally important problem in networking—controlling the transmission rate of transport-layer entities in order to avoid, or

recover from, congestion within the network. We'll consider the causes and consequences of congestion, as well as commonly used congestion-control techniques.
After obtaining a solid understanding of the issues behind congestion control, we'll
study TCP's approach to congestion control.

3.1 Introduction and Transport-Layer Services

In the previous two chapters we touched on the role of the transport layer and the
services that it provides. Let's quickly review what we have already learned about
the transport layer.

A transport-layer protocol provides for **logical communication** between application processes running on different hosts. By *logical communication*, we mean
that from an application's perspective, it is as if the hosts running the processes were
directly connected; in reality, the hosts may be on opposite sides of the planet, connected via numerous routers and a wide range of link types. Application processes
use the logical communication provided by the transport layer to send messages to
each other, free from the worry of the details of the physical infrastructure used to
carry these messages. Figure 3.1 illustrates the notion of logical communication.

As shown in Figure 3.1, transport-layer protocols are implemented in the end
systems but not in network routers. On the sending side, the transport layer converts
the application-layer messages it receives from a sending application process into
transport-layer packets, known as transport-layer **segments** in Internet terminology.
This is done by (possibly) breaking the application messages into smaller chunks and
adding a transport-layer header to each chunk to create the transport-layer segment.
The transport layer then passes the segment to the network layer at the sending end
system, where the segment is encapsulated within a network-layer packet (a datagram) and sent to the destination. It's important to note that network routers act only
on the network-layer fields of the datagram; that is, they do not examine the fields of
the transport-layer segment encapsulated with the datagram. On the receiving side,
the network layer extracts the transport-layer segment from the datagram and passes
the segment up to the transport layer. The transport layer then processes the received
segment, making the data in the segment available to the receiving application.

More than one transport-layer protocol may be available to network applications.
For example, the Internet has two protocols—TCP and UDP. Each of these protocols
provides a different set of transport-layer services to the invoking application.

3.1.1 Relationship Between Transport and Network Layers

Recall that the transport layer lies just above the network layer in the protocol stack.
Whereas a transport-layer protocol provides logical communication between
processes running on different hosts, a network-layer protocol provides logical

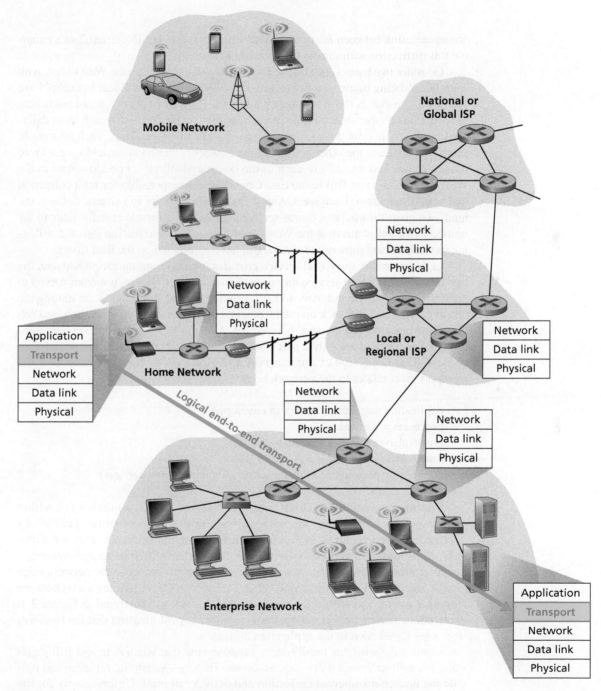

Figure 3.1 ♦ The transport layer provides logical rather than physical communication between application processes

communication between *hosts*. This distinction is subtle but important. Let's examine this distinction with the aid of a household analogy.

Consider two houses, one on the East Coast and the other on the West Coast, with each house being home to a dozen kids. The kids in the East Coast household are cousins of the kids in the West Coast household. The kids in the two households love to write to each other—each kid writes each cousin every week, with each letter delivered by the traditional postal service in a separate envelope. Thus, each household sends 144 letters to the other household every week. (These kids would save a lot of money if they had e-mail!) In each of the households there is one kid—Ann in the West Coast house and Bill in the East Coast house—responsible for mail collection and mail distribution. Each week Ann visits all her brothers and sisters, collects the mail, and gives the mail to a postal-service mail carrier, who makes daily visits to the house. When letters arrive at the West Coast house, Ann also has the job of distributing the mail to her brothers and sisters. Bill has a similar job on the East Coast.

In this example, the postal service provides logical communication between the two houses—the postal service moves mail from house to house, not from person to person. On the other hand, Ann and Bill provide logical communication among the cousins—Ann and Bill pick up mail from, and deliver mail to, their brothers and sisters. Note that from the cousins' perspective, Ann and Bill *are* the mail service, even though Ann and Bill are only a part (the end-system part) of the end-to-end delivery process. This household example serves as a nice analogy for explaining how the transport layer relates to the network layer:

> application messages = letters in envelopes
> processes = cousins
> hosts (also called end systems) = houses
> transport-layer protocol = Ann and Bill
> network-layer protocol = postal service (including mail carriers)

Continuing with this analogy, note that Ann and Bill do all their work within their respective homes; they are not involved, for example, in sorting mail in any intermediate mail center or in moving mail from one mail center to another. Similarly, transport-layer protocols live in the end systems. Within an end system, a transport protocol moves messages from application processes to the network edge (that is, the network layer) and vice versa, but it doesn't have any say about how the messages are moved within the network core. In fact, as illustrated in Figure 3.1, intermediate routers neither act on, nor recognize, any information that the transport layer may have added to the application messages.

Continuing with our family saga, suppose now that when Ann and Bill go on vacation, another cousin pair—say, Susan and Harvey—substitute for them and provide the household-internal collection and delivery of mail. Unfortunately for the two families, Susan and Harvey do not do the collection and delivery in exactly the same way as Ann and Bill. Being younger kids, Susan and Harvey pick up and drop off the mail less frequently and occasionally lose letters (which are sometimes chewed up by the family dog). Thus, the cousin-pair Susan and Harvey do not provide the same set of services (that is, the same service model) as Ann and Bill. In an analogous manner, a computer network may make available multiple transport protocols, with each protocol offering a different service model to applications.

The possible services that Ann and Bill can provide are clearly constrained by the possible services that the postal service provides. For example, if the postal service doesn't provide a maximum bound on how long it can take to deliver mail between the two houses (for example, three days), then there is no way that Ann and Bill can guarantee a maximum delay for mail delivery between any of the cousin pairs. In a similar manner, the services that a transport protocol can provide are often constrained by the service model of the underlying network-layer protocol. If the network-layer protocol cannot provide delay or bandwidth guarantees for transport-layer segments sent between hosts, then the transport-layer protocol cannot provide delay or bandwidth guarantees for application messages sent between processes.

Nevertheless, certain services *can* be offered by a transport protocol even when the underlying network protocol doesn't offer the corresponding service at the network layer. For example, as we'll see in this chapter, a transport protocol can offer reliable data transfer service to an application even when the underlying network protocol is unreliable, that is, even when the network protocol loses, garbles, or duplicates packets. As another example (which we'll explore in Chapter 8 when we discuss network security), a transport protocol can use encryption to guarantee that application messages are not read by intruders, even when the network layer cannot guarantee the confidentiality of transport-layer segments.

3.1.2 Overview of the Transport Layer in the Internet

Recall that the Internet, and more generally a TCP/IP network, makes two distinct transport-layer protocols available to the application layer. One of these protocols is **UDP** (User Datagram Protocol), which provides an unreliable, connectionless service to the invoking application. The second of these protocols is **TCP** (Transmission Control Protocol), which provides a reliable, connection-oriented service to the invoking application. When designing a network application, the application developer must specify one of these two transport protocols. As we saw in Section 2.7, the application developer selects between UDP and TCP when creating sockets.

To simplify terminology, when in an Internet context, we refer to the transport-layer packet as a *segment*. We mention, however, that the Internet literature (for example, the RFCs) also refers to the transport-layer packet for TCP as a segment but often refers to the packet for UDP as a datagram. But this same Internet literature also uses the term *datagram* for the network-layer packet! For an introductory book on computer networking such as this, we believe that it is less confusing to refer to both TCP and UDP packets as segments, and reserve the term *datagram* for the network-layer packet.

Before proceeding with our brief introduction of UDP and TCP, it will be useful to say a few words about the Internet's network layer. (We'll learn about the network layer in detail in Chapter 4.) The Internet's network-layer protocol has a name—IP, for Internet Protocol. IP provides logical communication between hosts. The IP service model is a **best-effort delivery service**. This means that IP makes its "best effort" to deliver segments between communicating hosts, *but it makes no guarantees*. In particular, it does not guarantee segment delivery, it does not guarantee orderly delivery of segments, and it does not guarantee the integrity of the data in the segments. For these reasons, IP is said to be an **unreliable service**. We also mention here that every host has at least one network-layer address, a so-called IP address. We'll examine IP addressing in detail in Chapter 4; for this chapter we need only keep in mind that *each host has an IP address*.

Having taken a glimpse at the IP service model, let's now summarize the service models provided by UDP and TCP. The most fundamental responsibility of UDP and TCP is to extend IP's delivery service between two end systems to a delivery service between two processes running on the end systems. Extending host-to-host delivery to process-to-process delivery is called **transport-layer multiplexing** and **demultiplexing**. We'll discuss transport-layer multiplexing and demultiplexing in the next section. UDP and TCP also provide integrity checking by including error-detection fields in their segments' headers. These two minimal transport-layer services—process-to-process data delivery and error checking—are the only two services that UDP provides! In particular, like IP, UDP is an unreliable service—it does not guarantee that data sent by one process will arrive intact (or at all!) to the destination process. UDP is discussed in detail in Section 3.3.

TCP, on the other hand, offers several additional services to applications. First and foremost, it provides **reliable data transfer**. Using flow control, sequence numbers, acknowledgments, and timers (techniques we'll explore in detail in this chapter), TCP ensures that data is delivered from sending process to receiving process, correctly and in order. TCP thus converts IP's unreliable service between end systems into a reliable data transport service between processes. TCP also provides **congestion control**. Congestion control is not so much a service provided to the invoking application as it is a service for the Internet as a whole, a service for the general good. Loosely speaking, TCP congestion control prevents any one TCP connection from swamping the links and routers between communicating hosts with an excessive amount of traffic. TCP strives to give each connection traversing a congested link an equal share of the link bandwidth. This is done by regulating the rate at which the sending sides of TCP connections can send traffic into the network. UDP traffic, on the other hand, is unregulated. An application using UDP transport can send at any rate it pleases, for as long as it pleases.

A protocol that provides reliable data transfer and congestion control is necessarily complex. We'll need several sections to cover the principles of reliable data transfer and congestion control, and additional sections to cover the TCP protocol itself. These topics are investigated in Sections 3.4 through 3.8. The approach taken in this chapter is to alternate between basic principles and the TCP protocol. For example, we'll first discuss reliable data transfer in a general setting and then discuss how TCP specifically provides reliable data transfer. Similarly, we'll first discuss congestion control in a general setting and then discuss how TCP performs congestion control. But before getting into all this good stuff, let's first look at transport-layer multiplexing and demultiplexing.

3.2 Multiplexing and Demultiplexing

In this section, we discuss transport-layer multiplexing and demultiplexing, that is, extending the host-to-host delivery service provided by the network layer to a process-to-process delivery service for applications running on the hosts. In order to keep the discussion concrete, we'll discuss this basic transport-layer service in the context of the Internet. We emphasize, however, that a multiplexing/demultiplexing service is needed for all computer networks.

At the destination host, the transport layer receives segments from the network layer just below. The transport layer has the responsibility of delivering the data in these segments to the appropriate application process running in the host. Let's take a look at an example. Suppose you are sitting in front of your computer, and you are downloading Web pages while running one FTP session and two Telnet sessions. You therefore have four network application processes running—two Telnet processes, one FTP process, and one HTTP process. When the transport layer in your computer receives data from the network layer below, it needs to direct the received data to one of these four processes. Let's now examine how this is done.

First recall from Section 2.7 that a process (as part of a network application) can have one or more **sockets**, doors through which data passes from the network to the process and through which data passes from the process to the network. Thus, as shown in Figure 3.2, the transport layer in the receiving host does not actually deliver data directly to a process, but instead to an intermediary socket. Because at any given time there can be more than one socket in the receiving host, each socket has a unique identifier. The format of the identifier depends on whether the socket is a UDP or a TCP socket, as we'll discuss shortly.

Now let's consider how a receiving host directs an incoming transport-layer segment to the appropriate socket. Each transport-layer segment has a set of fields in the segment for this purpose. At the receiving end, the transport layer examines these fields to identify the receiving socket and then directs the segment to that socket. This job of delivering the data in a transport-layer segment to the correct socket is called **demultiplexing**. The job of gathering data chunks at the source host from different sockets, encapsulating each data chunk with header information (that will later be used in demultiplexing) to create segments, and passing the segments to the network layer is called **multiplexing**. Note that the transport layer in the middle host in Figure 3.2 must demultiplex segments arriving from the network layer below to either process P_1 or P_2 above; this is done by directing the arriving segment's data to the corresponding process's socket. The transport layer in the middle host must also

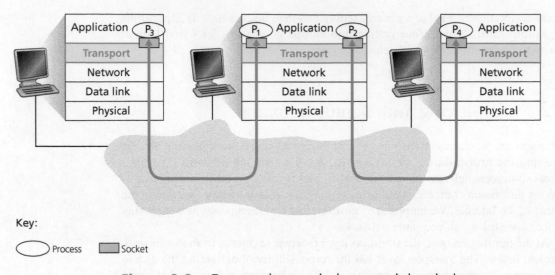

Key:

⬭ Process   ▢ Socket

Figure 3.2 ♦ Transport-layer multiplexing and demultiplexing

gather outgoing data from these sockets, form transport-layer segments, and pass these segments down to the network layer. Although we have introduced multiplexing and demultiplexing in the context of the Internet transport protocols, it's important to realize that they are concerns whenever a single protocol at one layer (at the transport layer or elsewhere) is used by multiple protocols at the next higher layer.

To illustrate the demultiplexing job, recall the household analogy in the previous section. Each of the kids is identified by his or her name. When Bill receives a batch of mail from the mail carrier, he performs a demultiplexing operation by observing to whom the letters are addressed and then hand delivering the mail to his brothers and sisters. Ann performs a multiplexing operation when she collects letters from her brothers and sisters and gives the collected mail to the mail person.

Now that we understand the roles of transport-layer multiplexing and demultiplexing, let us examine how it is actually done in a host. From the discussion above, we know that transport-layer multiplexing requires (1) that sockets have unique identifiers, and (2) that each segment have special fields that indicate the socket to which the segment is to be delivered. These special fields, illustrated in Figure 3.3, are the **source port number field** and the **destination port number field**. (The UDP and TCP segments have other fields as well, as discussed in the subsequent sections of this chapter.) Each port number is a 16-bit number, ranging from 0 to 65535. The port numbers ranging from 0 to 1023 are called **well-known port numbers** and are restricted, which means that they are reserved for use by well-known application protocols such as HTTP (which uses port number 80) and FTP (which uses port number 21). The list of well-known port numbers is given in RFC 1700 and is updated at http://www.iana.org [RFC 3232]. When we develop a new

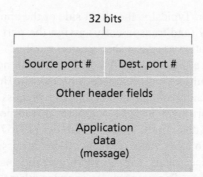

32 bits

Source port # | Dest. port #

Other header fields

Application
data
(message)

Figure 3.3 ♦ Source and destination port-number fields in a transport-layer
segment

application (such as the simple application developed in Section 2.7), we must
assign the application a port number.

It should now be clear how the transport layer *could* implement the demultiplexing service: Each socket in the host could be assigned a port number, and when a segment arrives at the host, the transport layer examines the destination port number in
the segment and directs the segment to the corresponding socket. The segment's data
then passes through the socket into the attached process. As we'll see, this is basically how UDP does it. However, we'll also see that multiplexing/demultiplexing in
TCP is yet more subtle.

Connectionless Multiplexing and Demultiplexing

Recall from Section 2.7.1 that the Python program running in a host can create a
UDP socket with the line

```
clientSocket = socket(socket.AF_INET, socket.SOCK_DGRAM)
```

When a UDP socket is created in this manner, the transport layer automatically
assigns a port number to the socket. In particular, the transport layer assigns a port
number in the range 1024 to 65535 that is currently not being used by any other UDP
port in the host. Alternatively, we can add a line into our Python program after we
create the socket to associate a specific port number (say, 19157) to this UDP socket
via the socket bind() method:

```
clientSocket.bind(('', 19157))
```

If the application developer writing the code were implementing the server side of a
"well-known protocol," then the developer would have to assign the corresponding

well-known port number. Typically, the client side of the application lets the transport layer automatically (and transparently) assign the port number, whereas the server side of the application assigns a specific port number.

With port numbers assigned to UDP sockets, we can now precisely describe UDP multiplexing/demultiplexing. Suppose a process in Host A, with UDP port 19157, wants to send a chunk of application data to a process with UDP port 46428 in Host B. The transport layer in Host A creates a transport-layer segment that includes the application data, the source port number (19157), the destination port number (46428), and two other values (which will be discussed later, but are unimportant for the current discussion). The transport layer then passes the resulting segment to the network layer. The network layer encapsulates the segment in an IP datagram and makes a best-effort attempt to deliver the segment to the receiving host. If the segment arrives at the receiving Host B, the transport layer at the receiving host examines the destination port number in the segment (46428) and delivers the segment to its socket identified by port 46428. Note that Host B could be running multiple processes, each with its own UDP socket and associated port number. As UDP segments arrive from the network, Host B directs (demultiplexes) each segment to the appropriate socket by examining the segment's destination port number.

It is important to note that a UDP socket is fully identified by a two-tuple consisting of a destination IP address and a destination port number. As a consequence, if two UDP segments have different source IP addresses and/or source port numbers, but have the same *destination* IP address and *destination* port number, then the two segments will be directed to the same destination process via the same destination socket.

You may be wondering now, what is the purpose of the source port number? As shown in Figure 3.4, in the A-to-B segment the source port number serves as part of a "return address"—when B wants to send a segment back to A, the destination port in the B-to-A segment will take its value from the source port value of the A-to-B segment. (The complete return address is A's IP address and the source port number.) As an example, recall the UDP server program studied in Section 2.7. In `UDPServer.py`, the server uses the `recvfrom()` method to extract the client-side (source) port number from the segment it receives from the client; it then sends a new segment to the client, with the extracted source port number serving as the destination port number in this new segment.

Connection-Oriented Multiplexing and Demultiplexing

In order to understand TCP demultiplexing, we have to take a close look at TCP sockets and TCP connection establishment. One subtle difference between a TCP socket and a UDP socket is that a TCP socket is identified by a four-tuple: (source IP address, source port number, destination IP address, destination port number). Thus, when a TCP segment arrives from the network to a host, the host uses all four values to direct (demultiplex) the segment to the appropriate socket. In particular, and in contrast with UDP, two arriving TCP segments with different source IP

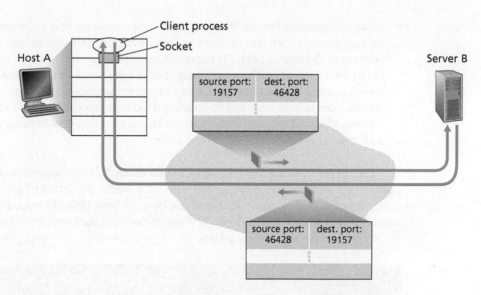

Host A

Client process
Socket

| source port: 19157 | dest. port: 46428 |

Server B

| source port: 46428 | dest. port: 19157 |

Figure 3.4 ♦ The inversion of source and destination port numbers

addresses or source port numbers will (with the exception of a TCP segment carrying the original connection-establishment request) be directed to two different sockets. To gain further insight, let's reconsider the TCP client-server programming example in Section 2.7.2:

- The TCP server application has a "welcoming socket," that waits for connection-establishment requests from TCP clients (see Figure 2.29) on port number 12000.
- The TCP client creates a socket and sends a connection establishment request segment with the lines:

```
clientSocket = socket(AF_INET, SOCK_STREAM)
clientSocket.connect((serverName,12000))
```

- A connection-establishment request is nothing more than a TCP segment with destination port number 12000 and a special connection-establishment bit set in the TCP header (discussed in Section 3.5). The segment also includes a source port number that was chosen by the client.
- When the host operating system of the computer running the server process receives the incoming connection-request segment with destination port 12000, it locates the server process that is waiting to accept a connection on port number 12000. The server process then creates a new socket:

```
connectionSocket, addr = serverSocket.accept()
```

- Also, the transport layer at the server notes the following four values in the connection-request segment: (1) the source port number in the segment, (2) the IP address of the source host, (3) the destination port number in the segment, and (4) its own IP address. The newly created connection socket is identified by these four values; all subsequently arriving segments whose source port, source IP address, destination port, and destination IP address match these four values will be demultiplexed to this socket. With the TCP connection now in place, the client and server can now send data to each other.

The server host may support many simultaneous TCP connection sockets, with each socket attached to a process, and with each socket identified by its own four-tuple. When a TCP segment arrives at the host, all four fields (source IP address, source port, destination IP address, destination port) are used to direct (demultiplex) the segment to the appropriate socket.

FOCUS ON SECURITY

PORT SCANNING

We've seen that a server process waits patiently on an open port for contact by a remote client. Some ports are reserved for well-known applications (e.g., Web, FTP, DNS, and SMTP servers); other ports are used by convention by popular applications (e.g., the Microsoft 2000 SQL server listens for requests on UDP port 1434). Thus, if we determine that a port is open on a host, we may be able to map that port to a specific application running on the host. This is very useful for system administrators, who are often interested in knowing which network applications are running on the hosts in their networks. But attackers, in order to "case the joint," also want to know which ports are open on target hosts. If a host is found to be running an application with a known security flaw (e.g., a SQL server listening on port 1434 was subject to a buffer overflow, allowing a remote user to execute arbitrary code on the vulnerable host, a flaw exploited by the Slammer worm [CERT 2003–04]), then that host is ripe for attack.

Determining which applications are listening on which ports is a relatively easy task. Indeed there are a number of public domain programs, called port scanners, that do just that. Perhaps the most widely used of these is nmap, freely available at http://nmap.org and included in most Linux distributions. For TCP, nmap sequentially scans ports, looking for ports that are accepting TCP connections. For UDP, nmap again sequentially scans ports, looking for UDP ports that respond to transmitted UDP segments. In both cases, nmap returns a list of open, closed, or unreachable ports. A host running nmap can attempt to scan any target host *anywhere* in the Internet. We'll revisit nmap in Section 3.5.6, when we discuss TCP connection management.

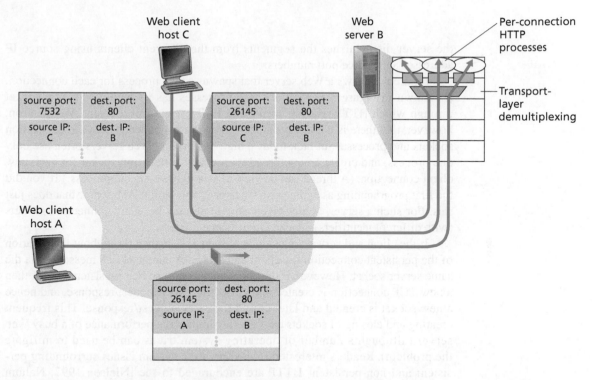

Figure 3.5 ♦ Two clients, using the same destination port number (80) to communicate with the same Web server application

The situation is illustrated in Figure 3.5, in which Host C initiates two HTTP sessions to server B, and Host A initiates one HTTP session to B. Hosts A and C and server B each have their own unique IP address—A, C, and B, respectively. Host C assigns two different source port numbers (26145 and 7532) to its two HTTP connections. Because Host A is choosing source port numbers independently of C, it might also assign a source port of 26145 to its HTTP connection. But this is not a problem—server B will still be able to correctly demultiplex the two connections having the same source port number, since the two connections have different source IP addresses.

Web Servers and TCP

Before closing this discussion, it's instructive to say a few additional words about Web servers and how they use port numbers. Consider a host running a Web server, such as an Apache Web server, on port 80. When clients (for example, browsers) send segments to the server, *all* segments will have destination port 80. In particular, both the initial connection-establishment segments and the segments carrying HTTP request messages will have destination port 80. As we have just described, the server distinguishes the segments from the different clients using source IP addresses and source port numbers.

Figure 3.5 shows a Web server that spawns a new process for each connection. As shown in Figure 3.5, each of these processes has its own connection socket through which HTTP requests arrive and HTTP responses are sent. We mention, however, that there is not always a one-to-one correspondence between connection sockets and processes. In fact, today's high-performing Web servers often use only one process, and create a new thread with a new connection socket for each new client connection. (A thread can be viewed as a lightweight subprocess.) If you did the first programming assignment in Chapter 2, you built a Web server that does just this. For such a server, at any given time there may be many connection sockets (with different identifiers) attached to the same process.

If the client and server are using persistent HTTP, then throughout the duration of the persistent connection the client and server exchange HTTP messages via the same server socket. However, if the client and server use non-persistent HTTP, then a new TCP connection is created and closed for every request/response, and hence a new socket is created and later closed for every request/response. This frequent creating and closing of sockets can severely impact the performance of a busy Web server (although a number of operating system tricks can be used to mitigate the problem). Readers interested in the operating system issues surrounding persistent and non-persistent HTTP are encouraged to see [Nielsen 1997; Nahum 2002].

Now that we've discussed transport-layer multiplexing and demultiplexing, let's move on and discuss one of the Internet's transport protocols, UDP. In the next section we'll see that UDP adds little more to the network-layer protocol than a multiplexing/demultiplexing service.

3.3 Connectionless Transport: UDP

In this section, we'll take a close look at UDP, how it works, and what it does. We encourage you to refer back to Section 2.1, which includes an overview of the UDP service model, and to Section 2.7.1, which discusses socket programming using UDP.

To motivate our discussion about UDP, suppose you were interested in designing a no-frills, bare-bones transport protocol. How might you go about doing this? You might first consider using a vacuous transport protocol. In particular, on the sending side, you might consider taking the messages from the application process and passing them directly to the network layer; and on the receiving side, you might consider taking the messages arriving from the network layer and passing them directly to the application process. But as we learned in the previous section, we have to do a little more than nothing! At the very least, the transport layer has to provide a multiplexing/demultiplexing service in order to pass data between the network layer and the correct application-level process.

UDP, defined in [RFC 768], does just about as little as a transport protocol can do. Aside from the multiplexing/demultiplexing function and some light error checking, it adds nothing to IP. In fact, if the application developer chooses UDP instead of TCP, then the application is almost directly talking with IP. UDP takes messages from the application process, attaches source and destination port number fields for the multiplexing/demultiplexing service, adds two other small fields, and passes the resulting segment to the network layer. The network layer encapsulates the transport-layer segment into an IP datagram and then makes a best-effort attempt to deliver the segment to the receiving host. If the segment arrives at the receiving host, UDP uses the destination port number to deliver the segment's data to the correct application process. Note that with UDP there is no handshaking between sending and receiving transport-layer entities before sending a segment. For this reason, UDP is said to be *connectionless*.

DNS is an example of an application-layer protocol that typically uses UDP. When the DNS application in a host wants to make a query, it constructs a DNS query message and passes the message to UDP. Without performing any handshaking with the UDP entity running on the destination end system, the host-side UDP adds header fields to the message and passes the resulting segment to the network layer. The network layer encapsulates the UDP segment into a datagram and sends the datagram to a name server. The DNS application at the querying host then waits for a reply to its query. If it doesn't receive a reply (possibly because the underlying network lost the query or the reply), either it tries sending the query to another name server, or it informs the invoking application that it can't get a reply.

Now you might be wondering why an application developer would ever choose to build an application over UDP rather than over TCP. Isn't TCP always preferable, since TCP provides a reliable data transfer service, while UDP does not? The answer is no, as many applications are better suited for UDP for the following reasons:

• *Finer application-level control over what data is sent, and when.* Under UDP, as soon as an application process passes data to UDP, UDP will package the data inside a UDP segment and immediately pass the segment to the network layer. TCP, on the other hand, has a congestion-control mechanism that throttles the transport-layer TCP sender when one or more links between the source and destination hosts become excessively congested. TCP will also continue to resend a segment until the receipt of the segment has been acknowledged by the destination, regardless of how long reliable delivery takes. Since real-time applications often require a minimum sending rate, do not want to overly delay segment transmission, and can tolerate some data loss, TCP's service model is not particularly well matched to these applications' needs. As discussed below, these applications can use UDP and implement, as part of the application, any additional functionality that is needed beyond UDP's no-frills segment-delivery service.

- *No connection establishment.* As we'll discuss later, TCP uses a three-way hand-shake before it starts to transfer data. UDP just blasts away without any formal pre-liminaries. Thus UDP does not introduce any delay to establish a connection. This is probably the principal reason why DNS runs over UDP rather than TCP—DNS would be much slower if it ran over TCP. HTTP uses TCP rather than UDP, since reliability is critical for Web pages with text. But, as we briefly discussed in Section 2.2, the TCP connection-establishment delay in HTTP is an important contributor to the delays associated with downloading Web documents.

- *No connection state.* TCP maintains connection state in the end systems. This connection state includes receive and send buffers, congestion-control parameters, and sequence and acknowledgment number parameters. We will see in Section 3.5 that this state information is needed to implement TCP's reliable data transfer service and to provide congestion control. UDP, on the other hand, does not maintain connection state and does not track any of these parameters. For this reason, a server devoted to a particular application can typically support many more active clients when the application runs over UDP rather than TCP.

- *Small packet header overhead.* The TCP segment has 20 bytes of header overhead in every segment, whereas UDP has only 8 bytes of overhead.

Figure 3.6 lists popular Internet applications and the transport protocols that they use. As we expect, e-mail, remote terminal access, the Web, and file transfer run over TCP—all these applications need the reliable data transfer service of TCP. Nevertheless, many important applications run over UDP rather than TCP. UDP is used for RIP routing table updates (see Section 4.6.1). Since RIP updates are sent periodically (typically every five minutes), lost updates will be replaced by more recent updates, thus making the lost, out-of-date update useless. UDP is also used to carry network management (SNMP; see Chapter 9) data. UDP is preferred to TCP in this case, since network management applications must often run when the network is in a stressed state—precisely when reliable, congestion-controlled data transfer is difficult to achieve. Also, as we mentioned earlier, DNS runs over UDP, thereby avoiding TCP's connection-establishment delays.

As shown in Figure 3.6, both UDP and TCP are used today with multimedia applications, such as Internet phone, real-time video conferencing, and streaming of stored audio and video. We'll take a close look at these applications in Chapter 7. We just mention now that all of these applications can tolerate a small amount of packet loss, so that reliable data transfer is not absolutely critical for the application's success. Furthermore, real-time applications, like Internet phone and video conferencing, react very poorly to TCP's congestion control. For these reasons, developers of multimedia applications may choose to run their applications over UDP instead of TCP. However, TCP is increasingly being used for streaming media transport. For example, [Sripanidkulchai 2004] found that nearly 75% of on-demand and live streaming used TCP. When packet loss rates are low, and with some organizations

Application	Application-Layer Protocol	Underlying Transport Protocol
Electronic mail	SMTP	TCP
Remote terminal access	Telnet	TCP
Web	HTTP	TCP
File transfer	FTP	TCP
Remote file server	NFS	Typically UDP
Streaming multimedia	typically proprietary	UDP or TCP
Internet telephony	typically proprietary	UDP or TCP
Network management	SNMP	Typically UDP
Routing protocol	RIP	Typically UDP
Name translation	DNS	Typically UDP

Figure 3.6 ♦ Popular Internet applications and their underlying transport protocols

blocking UDP traffic for security reasons (see Chapter 8), TCP becomes an increasingly attractive protocol for streaming media transport.

Although commonly done today, running multimedia applications over UDP is controversial. As we mentioned above, UDP has no congestion control. But congestion control is needed to prevent the network from entering a congested state in which very little useful work is done. If everyone were to start streaming high-bit-rate video without using any congestion control, there would be so much packet overflow at routers that very few UDP packets would successfully traverse the source-to-destination path. Moreover, the high loss rates induced by the uncontrolled UDP senders would cause the TCP senders (which, as we'll see, *do* decrease their sending rates in the face of congestion) to dramatically decrease their rates. Thus, the lack of congestion control in UDP can result in high loss rates between a UDP sender and receiver, and the crowding out of TCP sessions—a potentially serious problem [Floyd 1999]. Many researchers have proposed new mechanisms to force all sources, including UDP sources, to perform adaptive congestion control [Mahdavi 1997; Floyd 2000; Kohler 2006: RFC 4340].

Before discussing the UDP segment structure, we mention that it *is* possible for an application to have reliable data transfer when using UDP. This can be done if reliability is built into the application itself (for example, by adding acknowledgment and retransmission mechanisms, such as those we'll study in the next section). But this is a nontrivial task that would keep an application developer busy debugging for a long time. Nevertheless, building reliability directly into the application allows the application to "have its cake and eat it too." That is, application processes can communicate reliably without being subjected to the transmission-rate constraints imposed by TCP's congestion-control mechanism.

3.3.1 UDP Segment Structure

The UDP segment structure, shown in Figure 3.7, is defined in RFC 768. The application data occupies the data field of the UDP segment. For example, for DNS, the data field contains either a query message or a response message. For a streaming audio application, audio samples fill the data field. The UDP header has only four fields, each consisting of two bytes. As discussed in the previous section, the port numbers allow the destination host to pass the application data to the correct process running on the destination end system (that is, to perform the demultiplexing function). The length field specifies the number of bytes in the UDP segment (header plus data). An explicit length value is needed since the size of the data field may differ from one UDP segment to the next. The checksum is used by the receiving host to check whether errors have been introduced into the segment. In truth, the checksum is also calculated over a few of the fields in the IP header in addition to the UDP segment. But we ignore this detail in order to see the forest through the trees. We'll discuss the checksum calculation below. Basic principles of error detection are described in Section 5.2. The length field specifies the length of the UDP segment, including the header, in bytes.

3.3.2 UDP Checksum

The UDP checksum provides for error detection. That is, the checksum is used to determine whether bits within the UDP segment have been altered (for example, by noise in the links or while stored in a router) as it moved from source to destination. UDP at the sender side performs the 1s complement of the sum of all the 16-bit words in the segment, with any overflow encountered during the sum being

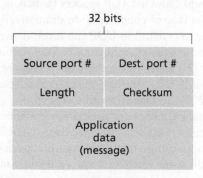

Figure 3.7 ◆ UDP segment structure

wrapped around. This result is put in the checksum field of the UDP segment. Here we give a simple example of the checksum calculation. You can find details about efficient implementation of the calculation in RFC 1071 and performance over real data in [Stone 1998; Stone 2000]. As an example, suppose that we have the following three 16-bit words:

0110011001100000
0101010101010101
1000111100001100

The sum of first two of these 16-bit words is

0110011001100000
<u>0101010101010101</u>
1011101110110101

Adding the third word to the above sum gives

1011101110110101
<u>1000111100001100</u>
0100101011000010

Note that this last addition had overflow, which was wrapped around. The 1s complement is obtained by converting all the 0s to 1s and converting all the 1s to 0s. Thus the 1s complement of the sum 0100101011000010 is 1011010100111101, which becomes the checksum. At the receiver, all four 16-bit words are added, including the checksum. If no errors are introduced into the packet, then clearly the sum at the receiver will be 1111111111111111. If one of the bits is a 0, then we know that errors have been introduced into the packet.

You may wonder why UDP provides a checksum in the first place, as many link-layer protocols (including the popular Ethernet protocol) also provide error checking. The reason is that there is no guarantee that all the links between source and destination provide error checking; that is, one of the links may use a link-layer protocol that does not provide error checking. Furthermore, even if segments are correctly transferred across a link, it's possible that bit errors could be introduced when a segment is stored in a router's memory. Given that neither link-by-link reliability nor in-memory error detection is guaranteed, UDP must provide error detection at the transport layer, *on an end-end basis*, if the end-end data transfer service is to provide error detection. This is an example of the celebrated **end-end principle** in system design [Saltzer 1984], which states that since certain functionality (error detection, in this case) must be implemented on an end-end basis: "functions placed at the lower levels may be redundant or of little value when compared to the cost of providing them at the higher level."

Because IP is supposed to run over just about any layer-2 protocol, it is useful for the transport layer to provide error checking as a safety measure. Although UDP provides error checking, it does not do anything to recover from an error. Some implementations of UDP simply discard the damaged segment; others pass the damaged segment to the application with a warning.

That wraps up our discussion of UDP. We will soon see that TCP offers reliable data transfer to its applications as well as other services that UDP doesn't offer. Naturally, TCP is also more complex than UDP. Before discussing TCP, however, it will be useful to step back and first discuss the underlying principles of reliable data transfer.

3.4 Principles of Reliable Data Transfer

In this section, we consider the problem of reliable data transfer in a general context. This is appropriate since the problem of implementing reliable data transfer occurs not only at the transport layer, but also at the link layer and the application layer as well. The general problem is thus of central importance to networking. Indeed, if one had to identify a "top-ten" list of fundamentally important problems in all of networking, this would be a candidate to lead the list. In the next section we'll examine TCP and show, in particular, that TCP exploits many of the principles that we are about to describe.

Figure 3.8 illustrates the framework for our study of reliable data transfer. The service abstraction provided to the upper-layer entities is that of a reliable channel through which data can be transferred. With a reliable channel, no transferred data bits are corrupted (flipped from 0 to 1, or vice versa) or lost, and all are delivered in the order in which they were sent. This is precisely the service model offered by TCP to the Internet applications that invoke it.

It is the responsibility of a **reliable data transfer protocol** to implement this service abstraction. This task is made difficult by the fact that the layer *below* the reliable data transfer protocol may be unreliable. For example, TCP is a reliable data transfer protocol that is implemented on top of an unreliable (IP) end-to-end network layer. More generally, the layer beneath the two reliably communicating end points might consist of a single physical link (as in the case of a link-level data transfer protocol) or a global internetwork (as in the case of a transport-level protocol). For our purposes, however, we can view this lower layer simply as an unreliable point-to-point channel.

In this section, we will incrementally develop the sender and receiver sides of a reliable data transfer protocol, considering increasingly complex models of the underlying channel. For example, we'll consider what protocol mechanisms are needed when the underlying channel can corrupt bits or lose entire packets. One assumption we'll adopt throughout our discussion here is that packets will be delivered in the order in which they were sent, with some packets possibly being lost; that is, the underlying channel will not reorder packets. Figure 3.8(b) illustrates the interfaces for our data transfer protocol. The sending side of the data transfer protocol will be invoked from above by a call to `rdt_send()`. It will pass the data to be delivered to the upper layer at the receiving side. (Here `rdt` stands for *reliable data transfer* protocol and `_send`

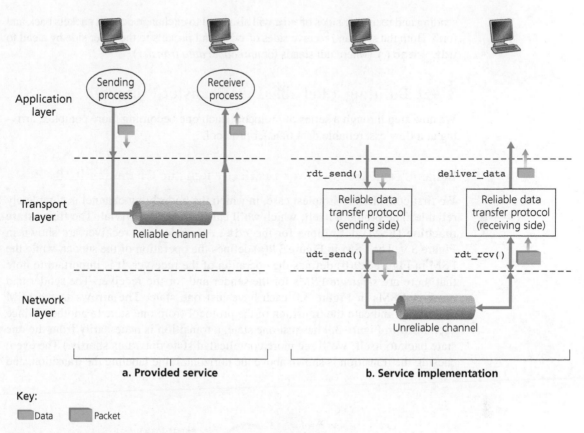

Figure 3.8 ♦ Reliable data transfer: Service model and service implementation

indicates that the sending side of `rdt` is being called. The first step in developing any protocol is to choose a good name!) On the receiving side, `rdt_rcv()` will be called when a packet arrives from the receiving side of the channel. When the `rdt` protocol wants to deliver data to the upper layer, it will do so by calling `deliver_data()`. In the following we use the terminology "packet" rather than transport-layer "segment." Because the theory developed in this section applies to computer networks in general and not just to the Internet transport layer, the generic term "packet" is perhaps more appropriate here.

In this section we consider only the case of **unidirectional data transfer**, that is, data transfer from the sending to the receiving side. The case of reliable **bidirectional** (that is, full-duplex) **data transfer** is conceptually no more difficult but considerably more tedious to explain. Although we consider only unidirectional data transfer, it is important to note that the sending and receiving sides of our protocol will nonetheless need to transmit packets in *both* directions, as indicated in Figure 3.8. We will see shortly that, in addition to exchanging packets containing the data to be transferred, the sending and receiving sides of `rdt` will also need to exchange control packets back and forth. Both the send and receive sides of `rdt` send packets to the other side by a call to `udt_send()` (where udt stands for *unreliable data transfer*).

3.4.1 Building a Reliable Data Transfer Protocol

We now step through a series of protocols, each one becoming more complex, arriving at a flawless, reliable data transfer protocol.

Reliable Data Transfer over a Perfectly Reliable Channel: rdt1.0

We first consider the simplest case, in which the underlying channel is completely reliable. The protocol itself, which we'll call `rdt1.0`, is trivial. The **finite-state machine (FSM)** definitions for the `rdt1.0` sender and receiver are shown in Figure 3.9. The FSM in Figure 3.9(a) defines the operation of the sender, while the FSM in Figure 3.9(b) defines the operation of the receiver. It is important to note that there are *separate* FSMs for the sender and for the receiver. The sender and receiver FSMs in Figure 3.9 each have just one state. The arrows in the FSM description indicate the transition of the protocol from one state to another. (Since each FSM in Figure 3.9 has just one state, a transition is necessarily from the one state back to itself; we'll see more complicated state diagrams shortly.) The event causing the transition is shown above the horizontal line labeling the transition, and

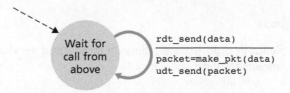

```
                            rdt_send(data)
 Wait for                   ─────────────────────
 call from                  packet=make_pkt(data)
 above                      udt_send(packet)
```

a. rdt1.0: sending side

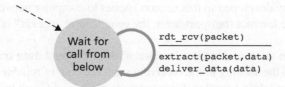

```
                            rdt_rcv(packet)
 Wait for                   ─────────────────────
 call from                  extract(packet,data)
 below                      deliver_data(data)
```

b. rdt1.0: receiving side

Figure 3.9 ♦ `rdt1.0` – A protocol for a completely reliable channel

the actions taken when the event occurs are shown below the horizontal line. When no action is taken on an event, or no event occurs and an action is taken, we'll use the symbol Λ below or above the horizontal, respectively, to explicitly denote the lack of an action or event. The initial state of the FSM is indicated by the dashed arrow. Although the FSMs in Figure 3.9 have but one state, the FSMs we will see shortly have multiple states, so it will be important to identify the initial state of each FSM.

The sending side of `rdt` simply accepts data from the upper layer via the `rdt_send(data)` event, creates a packet containing the data (via the action `make_pkt(data)`) and sends the packet into the channel. In practice, the `rdt_send(data)` event would result from a procedure call (for example, to `rdt_send()`) by the upper-layer application.

On the receiving side, rdt receives a packet from the underlying channel via the `rdt_rcv(packet)` event, removes the data from the packet (via the action `extract (packet, data)`) and passes the data up to the upper layer (via the action `deliver_data(data)`). In practice, the `rdt_rcv(packet)` event would result from a procedure call (for example, to `rdt_rcv()`) from the lower-layer protocol.

In this simple protocol, there is no difference between a unit of data and a packet. Also, all packet flow is from the sender to receiver; with a perfectly reliable channel there is no need for the receiver side to provide any feedback to the sender since nothing can go wrong! Note that we have also assumed that the receiver is able to receive data as fast as the sender happens to send data. Thus, there is no need for the receiver to ask the sender to slow down!

Reliable Data Transfer over a Channel with Bit Errors: `rdt2.0`

A more realistic model of the underlying channel is one in which bits in a packet may be corrupted. Such bit errors typically occur in the physical components of a network as a packet is transmitted, propagates, or is buffered. We'll continue to assume for the moment that all transmitted packets are received (although their bits may be corrupted) in the order in which they were sent.

Before developing a protocol for reliably communicating over such a channel, first consider how people might deal with such a situation. Consider how you yourself might dictate a long message over the phone. In a typical scenario, the message taker might say "OK" after each sentence has been heard, understood, and recorded. If the message taker hears a garbled sentence, you're asked to repeat the garbled sentence. This message-dictation protocol uses both **positive acknowledgments** ("OK") and **negative acknowledgments** ("Please repeat that."). These control messages allow the receiver to let the sender know what has been received correctly, and what has been received in error and thus requires repeating. In a computer network setting, reliable data transfer protocols based on such retransmission are known as **ARQ (Automatic Repeat reQuest) protocols**.

Fundamentally, three additional protocol capabilities are required in ARQ protocols to handle the presence of bit errors:

- *Error detection.* First, a mechanism is needed to allow the receiver to detect when bit errors have occurred. Recall from the previous section that UDP uses the Internet checksum field for exactly this purpose. In Chapter 5 we'll examine error-detection and -correction techniques in greater detail; these techniques allow the receiver to detect and possibly correct packet bit errors. For now, we need only know that these techniques require that extra bits (beyond the bits of original data to be transferred) be sent from the sender to the receiver; these bits will be gathered into the packet checksum field of the `rdt2.0` data packet.

- *Receiver feedback.* Since the sender and receiver are typically executing on different end systems, possibly separated by thousands of miles, the only way for the sender to learn of the receiver's view of the world (in this case, whether or not a packet was received correctly) is for the receiver to provide explicit feedback to the sender. The positive (ACK) and negative (NAK) acknowledgment replies in the message-dictation scenario are examples of such feedback. Our `rdt2.0` protocol will similarly send ACK and NAK packets back from the receiver to the sender. In principle, these packets need only be one bit long; for example, a 0 value could indicate a NAK and a value of 1 could indicate an ACK.

- *Retransmission.* A packet that is received in error at the receiver will be retransmitted by the sender.

Figure 3.10 shows the FSM representation of `rdt2.0`, a data transfer protocol employing error detection, positive acknowledgments, and negative acknowledgments.

The send side of `rdt2.0` has two states. In the leftmost state, the send-side protocol is waiting for data to be passed down from the upper layer. When the `rdt_send(data)` event occurs, the sender will create a packet (`sndpkt`) containing the data to be sent, along with a packet checksum (for example, as discussed in Section 3.3.2 for the case of a UDP segment), and then send the packet via the `udt_send(sndpkt)` operation. In the rightmost state, the sender protocol is waiting for an ACK or a NAK packet from the receiver. If an ACK packet is received (the notation `rdt_rcv(rcvpkt) && isACK (rcvpkt)` in Figure 3.10 corresponds to this event), the sender knows that the most recently transmitted packet has been received correctly and thus the protocol returns to the state of waiting for data from the upper layer. If a NAK is received, the protocol retransmits the last packet and waits for an ACK or NAK to be returned by the receiver in response to the retransmitted data packet. It is important to note that when the sender is in the wait-for-ACK-or-NAK state, it *cannot* get more data from the upper layer; that is, the `rdt_send()` event can not occur; that will happen only after the sender receives an ACK and leaves this state. Thus, the sender will not send a new piece of data until it is sure that the receiver has

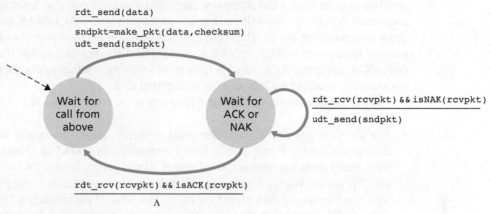

a. **rdt2.0: sending side**

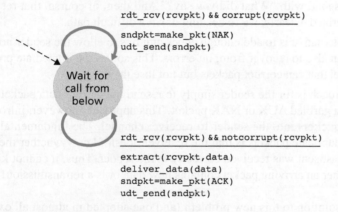

b. **rdt2.0: receiving side**

Figure 3.10 ♦ rdt2.0–A protocol for a channel with bit errors

correctly received the current packet. Because of this behavior, protocols such as rdt2.0 are known as **stop-and-wait** protocols.

The receiver-side FSM for rdt2.0 still has a single state. On packet arrival, the receiver replies with either an ACK or a NAK, depending on whether or not the received packet is corrupted. In Figure 3.10, the notation rdt_rcv(rcvpkt) && corrupt(rcvpkt) corresponds to the event in which a packet is received and is found to be in error.

Protocol rdt2.0 may look as if it works but, unfortunately, it has a fatal flaw. In particular, we haven't accounted for the possibility that the ACK or NAK packet could be corrupted! (Before proceeding on, you should think about how this problem may be fixed.) Unfortunately, our slight oversight is not as innocuous as it may seem. Minimally, we will need to add checksum bits to ACK/NAK packets in order to detect such errors. The more difficult question is how the protocol should recover from errors in ACK or NAK packets. The difficulty here is that if an ACK or NAK is corrupted, the sender has no way of knowing whether or not the receiver has correctly received the last piece of transmitted data.

Consider three possibilities for handling corrupted ACKs or NAKs:

- For the first possibility, consider what a human might do in the message-dictation scenario. If the speaker didn't understand the "OK" or "Please repeat that" reply from the receiver, the speaker would probably ask, "What did you say?" (thus introducing a new type of sender-to-receiver packet to our protocol). The receiver would then repeat the reply. But what if the speaker's "What did you say?" is corrupted? The receiver, having no idea whether the garbled sentence was part of the dictation or a request to repeat the last reply, would probably then respond with "What did *you* say?" And then, of course, that response might be garbled. Clearly, we're heading down a difficult path.

- A second alternative is to add enough checksum bits to allow the sender not only to detect, but also to recover from, bit errors. This solves the immediate problem for a channel that can corrupt packets but not lose them.

- A third approach is for the sender simply to resend the current data packet when it receives a garbled ACK or NAK packet. This approach, however, introduces **duplicate packets** into the sender-to-receiver channel. The fundamental difficulty with duplicate packets is that the receiver doesn't know whether the ACK or NAK it last sent was received correctly at the sender. Thus, it cannot know *a priori* whether an arriving packet contains new data or is a retransmission!

A simple solution to this new problem (and one adopted in almost all existing data transfer protocols, including TCP) is to add a new field to the data packet and have the sender number its data packets by putting a **sequence number** into this field. The receiver then need only check this sequence number to determine whether or not the received packet is a retransmission. For this simple case of a stop-and-wait protocol, a 1-bit sequence number will suffice, since it will allow the receiver to know whether the sender is resending the previously transmitted packet (the sequence number of the received packet has the same sequence number as the most recently received packet) or a new packet (the sequence number changes, moving "forward" in modulo-2 arithmetic). Since we are currently assuming a channel that does not lose packets, ACK and NAK packets do not themselves need to indicate the sequence number of the packet they are acknowledging. The sender knows that a received ACK or NAK packet (whether garbled or not) was generated in response to its most recently transmitted data packet.

Figures 3.11 and 3.12 show the FSM description for `rdt2.1`, our fixed version of `rdt2.0`. The `rdt2.1` sender and receiver FSMs each now have twice as many states as before. This is because the protocol state must now reflect whether the packet currently being sent (by the sender) or expected (at the receiver) should have a sequence number of 0 or 1. Note that the actions in those states where a 0-numbered packet is being sent or expected are mirror images of those where a 1-numbered packet is being sent or expected; the only differences have to do with the handling of the sequence number.

Protocol `rdt2.1` uses both positive and negative acknowledgments from the receiver to the sender. When an out-of-order packet is received, the receiver sends a positive acknowledgment for the packet it has received. When a corrupted packet is received, the receiver sends a negative acknowledgment. We can accomplish the same effect as a NAK if, instead of sending a NAK, we send an ACK for the last correctly received packet. A sender that receives two ACKs for the same packet (that is, receives **duplicate ACKs**) knows that the receiver did not correctly receive the packet following the packet that is being ACKed twice. Our NAK-free reliable data

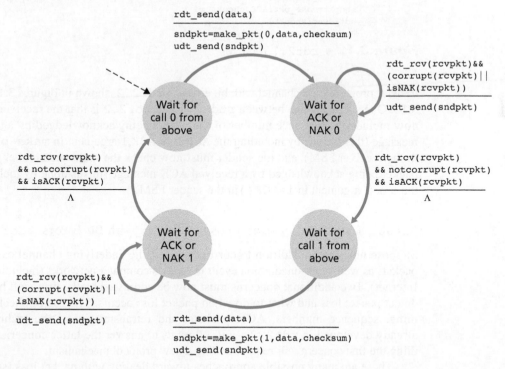

Figure 3.11 ♦ rdt2.1 sender

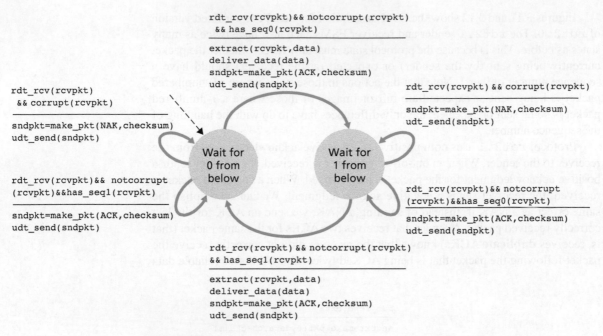

```
rdt_rcv(rcvpkt)&& notcorrupt(rcvpkt)
 && has_seq0(rcvpkt)
_____
extract(rcvpkt,data)
deliver_data(data)
sndpkt=make_pkt(ACK,checksum)
udt_send(sndpkt)
```

```
rdt_rcv(rcvpkt)
 && corrupt(rcvpkt)
_____
sndpkt=make_pkt(NAK,checksum)
udt_send(sndpkt)
```

```
rdt_rcv(rcvpkt)&& notcorrupt
(rcvpkt)&&has_seq1(rcvpkt)
_____
sndpkt=make_pkt(ACK,checksum)
udt_send(sndpkt)
```

Wait for 0 from below   Wait for 1 from below

```
rdt_rcv(rcvpkt) && corrupt(rcvpkt)
_____
sndpkt=make_pkt(NAK,checksum)
udt_send(sndpkt)
```

```
rdt_rcv(rcvpkt)&& notcorrupt
(rcvpkt)&&has_seq0(rcvpkt)
_____
sndpkt=make_pkt(ACK,checksum)
udt_send(sndpkt)
```

```
rdt_rcv(rcvpkt) && notcorrupt(rcvpkt)
 && has_seq1(rcvpkt)
_____
extract(rcvpkt,data)
deliver_data(data)
sndpkt=make_pkt(ACK,checksum)
udt_send(sndpkt)
```

Figure 3.12 ♦ rdt2.1 receiver

transfer protocol for a channel with bit errors is `rdt2.2`, shown in Figures 3.13 and 3.14. One subtle change between `rtdt2.1` and `rdt2.2` is that the receiver must now include the sequence number of the packet being acknowledged by an ACK message (this is done by including the ACK,0 or ACK,1 argument in `make_pkt()` in the receiver FSM), and the sender must now check the sequence number of the packet being acknowledged by a received ACK message (this is done by including the 0 or 1 argument in `isACK()` in the sender FSM).

Reliable Data Transfer over a Lossy Channel with Bit Errors: `rdt3.0`

Suppose now that in addition to corrupting bits, the underlying channel can *lose* packets as well, a not-uncommon event in today's computer networks (including the Internet). Two additional concerns must now be addressed by the protocol: how to detect packet loss and what to do when packet loss occurs. The use of checksumming, sequence numbers, ACK packets, and retransmissions—the techniques already developed in `rdt2.2`—will allow us to answer the latter concern. Handling the first concern will require adding a new protocol mechanism.

There are many possible approaches toward dealing with packet loss (several more of which are explored in the exercises at the end of the chapter). Here, we'll put the burden of detecting and recovering from lost packets on the sender. Suppose

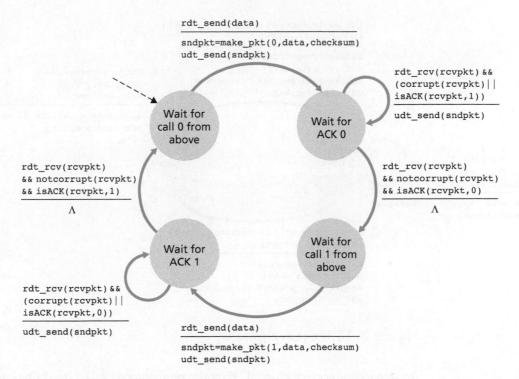

Figure 3.13 ♦ rdt2.2 sender

that the sender transmits a data packet and either that packet, or the receiver's ACK of that packet, gets lost. In either case, no reply is forthcoming at the sender from the receiver. If the sender is willing to wait long enough so that it is *certain* that a packet has been lost, it can simply retransmit the data packet. You should convince yourself that this protocol does indeed work.

But how long must the sender wait to be certain that something has been lost? The sender must clearly wait at least as long as a round-trip delay between the sender and receiver (which may include buffering at intermediate routers) plus whatever amount of time is needed to process a packet at the receiver. In many networks, this worst-case maximum delay is very difficult even to estimate, much less know with certainty. Moreover, the protocol should ideally recover from packet loss as soon as possible; waiting for a worst-case delay could mean a long wait until error recovery is initiated. The approach thus adopted in practice is for the sender to judiciously choose a time value such that packet loss is likely, although not guaranteed, to have happened. If an ACK is not received within this time, the packet is retransmitted. Note that if a packet experiences a particularly large delay, the sender may retransmit the packet even though neither the data packet nor its ACK have been lost. This introduces the possibility of **duplicate data packets** in

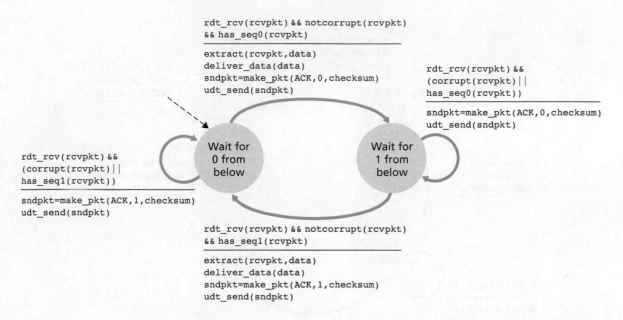

rdt_rcv(rcvpkt) && notcorrupt(rcvpkt)
&& has_seq0(rcvpkt)
_____

extract(rcvpkt,data)
deliver_data(data)
sndpkt=make_pkt(ACK,0,checksum)
udt_send(sndpkt)

rdt_rcv(rcvpkt) &&
(corrupt(rcvpkt)||
has_seq0(rcvpkt))
_____

sndpkt=make_pkt(ACK,0,checksum)
udt_send(sndpkt)

Wait for
0 from
below

Wait for
1 from
below

rdt_rcv(rcvpkt) &&
(corrupt(rcvpkt)||
has_seq1(rcvpkt))
_____

sndpkt=make_pkt(ACK,1,checksum)
udt_send(sndpkt)

rdt_rcv(rcvpkt) && notcorrupt(rcvpkt)
&& has_seq1(rcvpkt)
_____

extract(rcvpkt,data)
deliver_data(data)
sndpkt=make_pkt(ACK,1,checksum)
udt_send(sndpkt)

Figure 3.14 ♦ rdt2.2 receiver

the sender-to-receiver channel. Happily, protocol rdt2.2 already has enough functionality (that is, sequence numbers) to handle the case of duplicate packets.

From the sender's viewpoint, retransmission is a panacea. The sender does not know whether a data packet was lost, an ACK was lost, or if the packet or ACK was simply overly delayed. In all cases, the action is the same: retransmit. Implementing a time-based retransmission mechanism requires a **countdown timer** that can interrupt the sender after a given amount of time has expired. The sender will thus need to be able to (1) start the timer each time a packet (either a first-time packet or a retransmission) is sent, (2) respond to a timer interrupt (taking appropriate actions), and (3) stop the timer.

Figure 3.15 shows the sender FSM for rdt3.0, a protocol that reliably transfers data over a channel that can corrupt or lose packets; in the homework problems, you'll be asked to provide the receiver FSM for rdt3.0. Figure 3.16 shows how the protocol operates with no lost or delayed packets and how it handles lost data packets. In Figure 3.16, time moves forward from the top of the diagram toward the bottom of the diagram; note that a receive time for a packet is necessarily later than the send time for a packet as a result of transmission and propagation delays. In Figures 3.16(b)–(d), the send-side brackets indicate the times at which a timer is set and later times out. Several of the more subtle aspects of this protocol are explored in the exercises at the end of this chapter. Because packet sequence numbers alternate between 0 and 1, protocol rdt3.0 is sometimes known as the **alternating-bit protocol**.

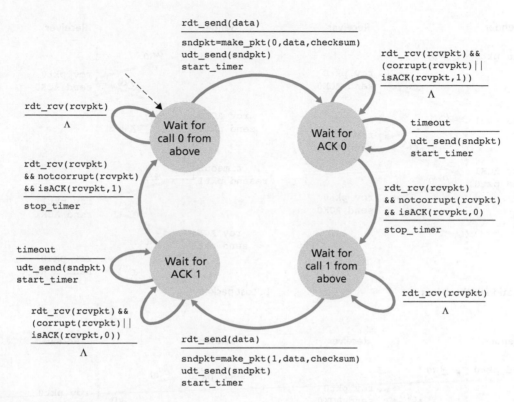

Figure 3.15 ♦ rdt3.0 sender

We have now assembled the key elements of a data transfer protocol. Checksums, sequence numbers, timers, and positive and negative acknowledgment packets each play a crucial and necessary role in the operation of the protocol. We now have a working reliable data transfer protocol!

VideoNote
Developing a protocol
and FSM representation
for a simple application-
layer protocol

3.4.2 Pipelined Reliable Data Transfer Protocols

Protocol rdt3.0 is a functionally correct protocol, but it is unlikely that anyone would be happy with its performance, particularly in today's high-speed networks. At the heart of rdt3.0's performance problem is the fact that it is a stop-and-wait protocol.

To appreciate the performance impact of this stop-and-wait behavior, consider an idealized case of two hosts, one located on the West Coast of the United States and the other located on the East Coast, as shown in Figure 3.17. The speed-of-light round-trip propagation delay between these two end systems, RTT, is approximately 30 milliseconds. Suppose that they are connected by a channel with a transmission rate, R, of 1 Gbps (10^9 bits per second). With a packet size, L, of 1,000 bytes

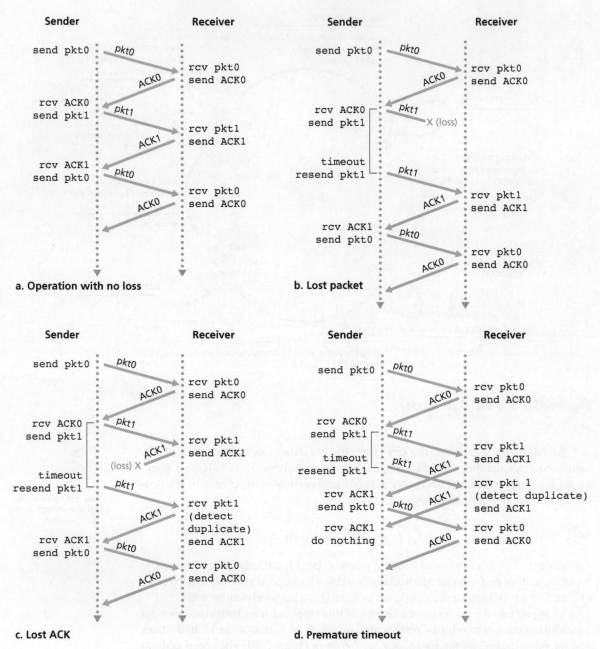

Figure 3.16 ♦ Operation of `rdt3.0`, the alternating-bit protocol

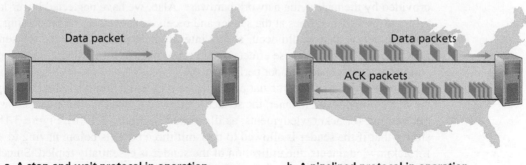

a. A stop-and-wait protocol in operation   b. A pipelined protocol in operation

Figure 3.17 ♦ Stop-and-wait versus pipelined protocol

(8,000 bits) per packet, including both header fields and data, the time needed to actually transmit the packet into the 1 Gbps link is

$$d_{trans} = \frac{L}{R} = \frac{8000 \text{ bits/packet}}{10^9 \text{ bits/sec}} = 8 \text{ microseconds}$$

Figure 3.18(a) shows that with our stop-and-wait protocol, if the sender begins sending the packet at $t = 0$, then at $t = L/R = 8$ microseconds, the last bit enters the channel at the sender side. The packet then makes its 15-msec cross-country journey, with the last bit of the packet emerging at the receiver at $t = RTT/2 + L/R = 15.008$ msec. Assuming for simplicity that ACK packets are extremely small (so that we can ignore their transmission time) and that the receiver can send an ACK as soon as the last bit of a data packet is received, the ACK emerges back at the sender at $t = RTT + L/R = 30.008$ msec. At this point, the sender can now transmit the next message. Thus, in 30.008 msec, the sender was sending for only 0.008 msec. If we define the **utilization** of the sender (or the channel) as the fraction of time the sender is actually busy sending bits into the channel, the analysis in Figure 3.18(a) shows that the stop-and-wait protocol has a rather dismal sender utilization, U_{sender}, of

$$U_{sender} = \frac{L/R}{RTT + L/R} = \frac{.008}{30.008} = 0.00027$$

That is, the sender was busy only 2.7 hundredths of one percent of the time! Viewed another way, the sender was able to send only 1,000 bytes in 30.008 milliseconds, an effective throughput of only 267 kbps—even though a 1 Gbps link was available! Imagine the unhappy network manager who just paid a fortune for a gigabit capacity link but manages to get a throughput of only 267 kilobits per second! This is a graphic example of how network protocols can limit the capabilities provided by the underlying network hardware. Also, we have neglected lower-layer protocol-processing times at the sender and receiver, as well as the processing and queuing delays that would occur at any intermediate routers between the sender and receiver. Including these effects would serve only to further increase the delay and further accentuate the poor performance.

The solution to this particular performance problem is simple: Rather than operate in a stop-and-wait manner, the sender is allowed to send multiple packets without waiting for acknowledgments, as illustrated in Figure 3.17(b). Figure 3.18(b) shows that if the sender is allowed to transmit three packets before having to wait for acknowledgments, the utilization of the sender is essentially tripled. Since the many in-transit sender-to-receiver packets can be visualized as filling a pipeline, this technique is known as **pipelining**. Pipelining has the following consequences for reliable data transfer protocols:

- The range of sequence numbers must be increased, since each in-transit packet (not counting retransmissions) must have a unique sequence number and there may be multiple, in-transit, unacknowledged packets.

- The sender and receiver sides of the protocols may have to buffer more than one packet. Minimally, the sender will have to buffer packets that have been transmitted but not yet acknowledged. Buffering of correctly received packets may also be needed at the receiver, as discussed below.

- The range of sequence numbers needed and the buffering requirements will depend on the manner in which a data transfer protocol responds to lost, corrupted, and overly delayed packets. Two basic approaches toward pipelined error recovery can be identified: **Go-Back-N** and **selective repeat**.

3.4.3 Go-Back-N (GBN)

In a **Go-Back-N (GBN) protocol**, the sender is allowed to transmit multiple packets (when available) without waiting for an acknowledgment, but is constrained to have no more than some maximum allowable number, N, of unacknowledged packets in the pipeline. We describe the GBN protocol in some detail in this section. But before reading on, you are encouraged to play with the GBN applet (an awesome applet!) at the companion Web site.

Figure 3.19 shows the sender's view of the range of sequence numbers in a GBN protocol. If we define `base` to be the sequence number of the oldest unacknowledged packet and `nextseqnum` to be the smallest unused sequence number (that is, the sequence number of the next packet to be sent), then four intervals in the range of sequence numbers can be identified. Sequence numbers in the interval [0,base-1] correspond to packets that have already been transmitted and acknowledged. The interval [base,nextseqnum-1] corresponds to packets that have been sent but not yet acknowledged. Sequence numbers in the interval [nextseqnum,base+N-1] can

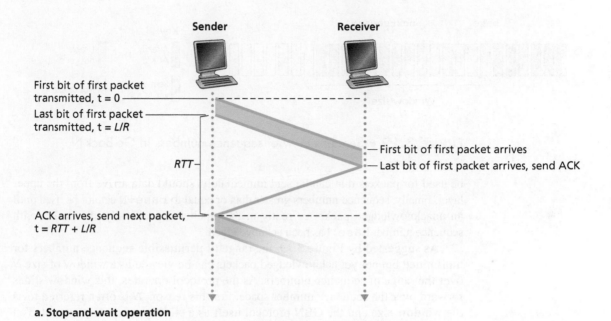

a. Stop-and-wait operation

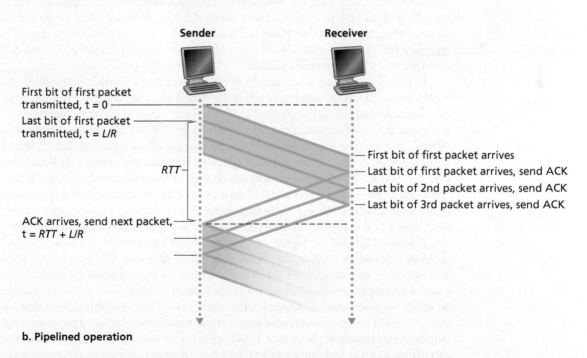

b. Pipelined operation

Figure 3.18 ♦ Stop-and-wait and pipelined sending

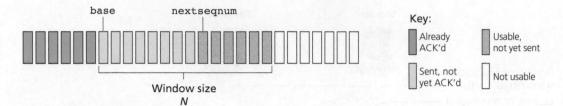

Figure 3.19 ♦ Sender's view of sequence numbers in Go-Back-N

be used for packets that can be sent immediately, should data arrive from the upper layer. Finally, sequence numbers greater than or equal to `base+N` cannot be used until an unacknowledged packet currently in the pipeline (specifically, the packet with sequence number `base`) has been acknowledged.

As suggested by Figure 3.19, the range of permissible sequence numbers for transmitted but not yet acknowledged packets can be viewed as a window of size N over the range of sequence numbers. As the protocol operates, this window slides forward over the sequence number space. For this reason, N is often referred to as the **window size** and the GBN protocol itself as a **sliding-window protocol**. You might be wondering why we would even limit the number of outstanding, unacknowledged packets to a value of N in the first place. Why not allow an unlimited number of such packets? We'll see in Section 3.5 that flow control is one reason to impose a limit on the sender. We'll examine another reason to do so in Section 3.7, when we study TCP congestion control.

In practice, a packet's sequence number is carried in a fixed-length field in the packet header. If k is the number of bits in the packet sequence number field, the range of sequence numbers is thus $[0, 2^k - 1]$. With a finite range of sequence numbers, all arithmetic involving sequence numbers must then be done using modulo 2^k arithmetic. (That is, the sequence number space can be thought of as a ring of size 2^k, where sequence number $2^k - 1$ is immediately followed by sequence number 0.) Recall that `rdt3.0` had a 1-bit sequence number and a range of sequence numbers of $[0,1]$. Several of the problems at the end of this chapter explore the consequences of a finite range of sequence numbers. We will see in Section 3.5 that TCP has a 32-bit sequence number field, where TCP sequence numbers count bytes in the byte stream rather than packets.

Figures 3.20 and 3.21 give an extended FSM description of the sender and receiver sides of an ACK-based, NAK-free, GBN protocol. We refer to this FSM description as an *extended FSM* because we have added variables (similar to programming-language variables) for `base` and `nextseqnum`, and added operations on these variables and conditional actions involving these variables. Note that the extended FSM specification is now beginning to look somewhat like a programming-language specification. [Bochman 1984] provides an excellent survey of additional extensions to FSM techniques as well as other programming-language-based techniques for specifying protocols.

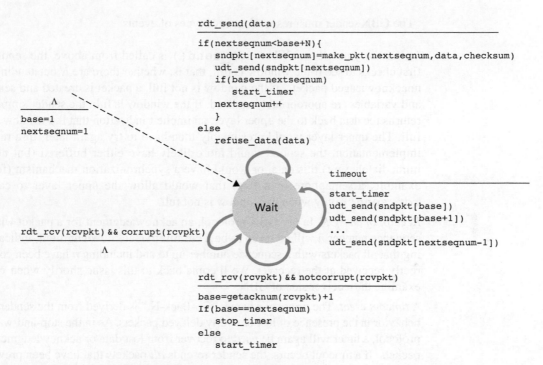

```
                              rdt_send(data)

                              if(nextseqnum<base+N){
                                  sndpkt[nextseqnum]=make_pkt(nextseqnum,data,checksum)
                                  udt_send(sndpkt[nextseqnum])
                                  if(base==nextseqnum)
                                      start_timer
                                  nextseqnum++
                                  }
                              else
                                  refuse_data(data)

        Λ
        base=1                                        timeout
        nextseqnum=1
                                                      start_timer
                                                      udt_send(sndpkt[base])
                                     Wait             udt_send(sndpkt[base+1])
                                                      ...
                                                      udt_send(sndpkt[nextseqnum-1])
 rdt_rcv(rcvpkt) && corrupt(rcvpkt)
        Λ

                              rdt_rcv(rcvpkt) && notcorrupt(rcvpkt)

                              base=getacknum(rcvpkt)+1
                              If(base==nextseqnum)
                                  stop_timer
                              else
                                  start_timer
```

Figure 3.20 ♦ Extended FSM description of GBN sender

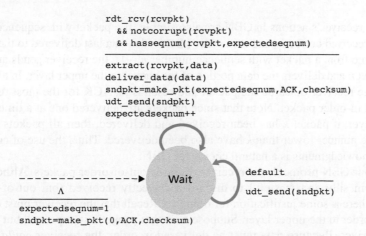

```
                              rdt_rcv(rcvpkt)
                                  && notcorrupt(rcvpkt)
                                  && hasseqnum(rcvpkt,expectedseqnum)

                              extract(rcvpkt,data)
                              deliver_data(data)
                              sndpkt=make_pkt(expectedseqnum,ACK,checksum)
                              udt_send(sndpkt)
                              expectedseqnum++

                                                      default

                                     Wait             udt_send(sndpkt)
        Λ
        expectedseqnum=1
        sndpkt=make_pkt(0,ACK,checksum)
```

Figure 3.21 ♦ Extended FSM description of GBN receiver

The GBN sender must respond to three types of events:

- *Invocation from above.* When `rdt_send()` is called from above, the sender first checks to see if the window is full, that is, whether there are N outstanding, unacknowledged packets. If the window is not full, a packet is created and sent, and variables are appropriately updated. If the window is full, the sender simply returns the data back to the upper layer, an implicit indication that the window is full. The upper layer would presumably then have to try again later. In a real implementation, the sender would more likely have either buffered (but not immediately sent) this data, or would have a synchronization mechanism (for example, a semaphore or a flag) that would allow the upper layer to call `rdt_send()` only when the window is not full.

- *Receipt of an ACK.* In our GBN protocol, an acknowledgment for a packet with sequence number n will be taken to be a **cumulative acknowledgment**, indicating that all packets with a sequence number up to and including n have been correctly received at the receiver. We'll come back to this issue shortly when we examine the receiver side of GBN.

- *A timeout event.* The protocol's name, "Go-Back-N," is derived from the sender's behavior in the presence of lost or overly delayed packets. As in the stop-and-wait protocol, a timer will again be used to recover from lost data or acknowledgment packets. If a timeout occurs, the sender resends *all* packets that have been previously sent but that have not yet been acknowledged. Our sender in Figure 3.20 uses only a single timer, which can be thought of as a timer for the oldest transmitted but not yet acknowledged packet. If an ACK is received but there are still additional transmitted but not yet acknowledged packets, the timer is restarted. If there are no outstanding, unacknowledged packets, the timer is stopped.

The receiver's actions in GBN are also simple. If a packet with sequence number n is received correctly and is in order (that is, the data last delivered to the upper layer came from a packet with sequence number $n - 1$), the receiver sends an ACK for packet n and delivers the data portion of the packet to the upper layer. In all other cases, the receiver discards the packet and resends an ACK for the most recently received in-order packet. Note that since packets are delivered one at a time to the upper layer, if packet k has been received and delivered, then all packets with a sequence number lower than k have also been delivered. Thus, the use of cumulative acknowledgments is a natural choice for GBN.

In our GBN protocol, the receiver discards out-of-order packets. Although it may seem silly and wasteful to discard a correctly received (but out-of-order) packet, there is some justification for doing so. Recall that the receiver must deliver data in order to the upper layer. Suppose now that packet n is expected, but packet $n + 1$ arrives. Because data must be delivered in order, the receiver *could* buffer (save) packet $n + 1$ and then deliver this packet to the upper layer after it had later received and delivered packet *n*. However, if packet *n* is lost, both it and packet *n* + 1 will eventually be retransmitted as a result of the GBN retransmission rule at the sender. Thus, the receiver can simply discard packet *n* + 1. The advantage of this approach is the simplicity of receiver buffering—the receiver need not buffer *any* out-of-order packets. Thus, while the sender must maintain the upper and lower bounds of its window and the position of `nextseqnum` within this window, the only piece of information the receiver need maintain is the sequence number of the next in-order packet. This value is held in the variable `expectedseqnum`, shown in the receiver FSM in Figure 3.21. Of course, the disadvantage of throwing away a correctly received packet is that the subsequent retransmission of that packet might be lost or garbled and thus even more retransmissions would be required.

Figure 3.22 shows the operation of the GBN protocol for the case of a window size of four packets. Because of this window size limitation, the sender sends packets 0 through 3 but then must wait for one or more of these packets to be acknowledged before proceeding. As each successive ACK (for example, `ACK0` and `ACK1`) is received, the window slides forward and the sender can transmit one new packet (pkt4 and pkt5, respectively). On the receiver side, packet 2 is lost and thus packets 3, 4, and 5 are found to be out of order and are discarded.

Before closing our discussion of GBN, it is worth noting that an implementation of this protocol in a protocol stack would likely have a structure similar to that of the extended FSM in Figure 3.20. The implementation would also likely be in the form of various procedures that implement the actions to be taken in response to the various events that can occur. In such **event-based programming**, the various procedures are called (invoked) either by other procedures in the protocol stack, or as the result of an interrupt. In the sender, these events would be (1) a call from the upper-layer entity to invoke `rdt_send()`, (2) a timer interrupt, and (3) a call from the lower layer to invoke `rdt_rcv()` when a packet arrives. The programming exercises at the end of this chapter will give you a chance to actually implement these routines in a simulated, but realistic, network setting.

We note here that the GBN protocol incorporates almost all of the techniques that we will encounter when we study the reliable data transfer components of TCP in Section 3.5. These techniques include the use of sequence numbers, cumulative acknowledgments, checksums, and a timeout/retransmit operation.

3.4.4 Selective Repeat (SR)

The GBN protocol allows the sender to potentially "fill the pipeline" in Figure 3.17 with packets, thus avoiding the channel utilization problems we noted with stop-and-wait protocols. There are, however, scenarios in which GBN itself suffers from performance problems. In particular, when the window size and bandwidth-delay product are both large, many packets can be in the pipeline. A single packet error can thus cause GBN to retransmit a large number of packets, many unnecessarily. As the probability of channel errors increases, the pipeline can become filled with

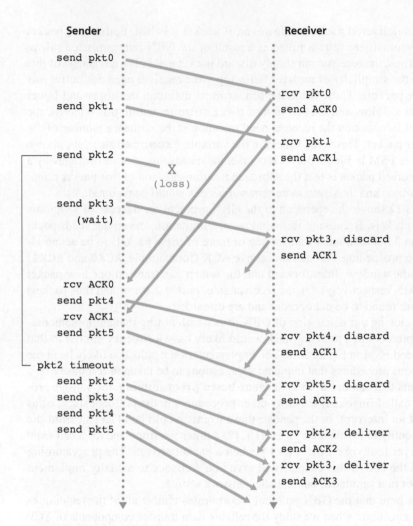

Figure 3.22 ♦ Go-Back-N in operation

these unnecessary retransmissions. Imagine, in our message-dictation scenario, that if every time a word was garbled, the surrounding 1,000 words (for example, a window size of 1,000 words) had to be repeated. The dictation would be slowed by all of the reiterated words.

As the name suggests, selective-repeat protocols avoid unnecessary retransmissions by having the sender retransmit only those packets that it suspects were received in error (that is, were lost or corrupted) at the receiver. This individual, as-needed, retransmission will require that the receiver *individually* acknowledge correctly received packets. A window size of *N* will again be used to limit the number

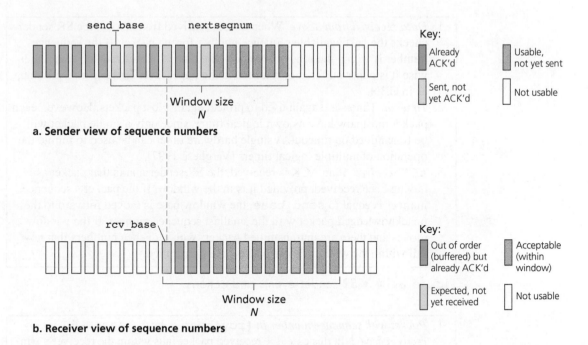

Figure 3.23 ♦ Selective-repeat (SR) sender and receiver views of sequence-number space

of outstanding, unacknowledged packets in the pipeline. However, unlike GBN, the sender will have already received ACKs for some of the packets in the window. Figure 3.23 shows the SR sender's view of the sequence number space. Figure 3.24 details the various actions taken by the SR sender.

The SR receiver will acknowledge a correctly received packet whether or not it is in order. Out-of-order packets are buffered until any missing packets (that is, packets with lower sequence numbers) are received, at which point a batch of packets can be delivered in order to the upper layer. Figure 3.25 itemizes the various actions taken by the SR receiver. Figure 3.26 shows an example of SR operation in the presence of lost packets. Note that in Figure 3.26, the receiver initially buffers packets 3, 4, and 5, and delivers them together with packet 2 to the upper layer when packet 2 is finally received.

It is important to note that in Step 2 in Figure 3.25, the receiver reacknowledges (rather than ignores) already received packets with certain sequence numbers *below* the current window base. You should convince yourself that this reacknowledgment is indeed needed. Given the sender and receiver sequence number spaces in Figure 3.23, for example, if there is no ACK for packet `send_base` propagating from the receiver to the sender, the sender will eventually retransmit packet `send_base`, even though it is clear (to us, not the sender!) that the receiver has already received

---

1. *Data received from above.* When data is received from above, the SR sender checks the next available sequence number for the packet. If the sequence number is within the sender's window, the data is packetized and sent; otherwise it is either buffered or returned to the upper layer for later transmission, as in GBN.
2. *Timeout.* Timers are again used to protect against lost packets. However, each packet must now have its own logical timer, since only a single packet will be transmitted on timeout. A single hardware timer can be used to mimic the operation of multiple logical timers [Varghese 1997].
3. *ACK received.* If an ACK is received, the SR sender marks that packet as having been received, provided it is in the window. If the packet's sequence number is equal to `send_base`, the window base is moved forward to the unacknowledged packet with the smallest sequence number. If the window moves and there are untransmitted packets with sequence numbers that now fall within the window, these packets are transmitted.

Figure 3.24 ♦ SR sender events and actions

---

1. *Packet with sequence number in* [`rcv_base, rcv_base+N-1`] *is correctly received.* In this case, the received packet falls within the receiver's window and a selective ACK packet is returned to the sender. If the packet was not previously received, it is buffered. If this packet has a sequence number equal to the base of the receive window (`rcv_base` in Figure 3.22), then this packet, and any previously buffered and consecutively numbered (beginning with `rcv_base`) packets are delivered to the upper layer. The receive window is then moved forward by the number of packets delivered to the upper layer. As an example, consider Figure 3.26. When a packet with a sequence number of `rcv_base=2` is received, it and packets 3, 4, and 5 can be delivered to the upper layer.
2. *Packet with sequence number in* [`rcv_base-N, rcv_base-1`] *is correctly received.* In this case, an ACK must be generated, even though this is a packet that the receiver has previously acknowledged.
3. *Otherwise.* Ignore the packet.

Figure 3.25 ♦ SR receiver events and actions

that packet. If the receiver were not to acknowledge this packet, the sender's window would never move forward! This example illustrates an important aspect of SR protocols (and many other protocols as well). The sender and receiver will not always have an identical view of what has been received correctly and what has not. For SR protocols, this means that the sender and receiver windows will not always coincide.

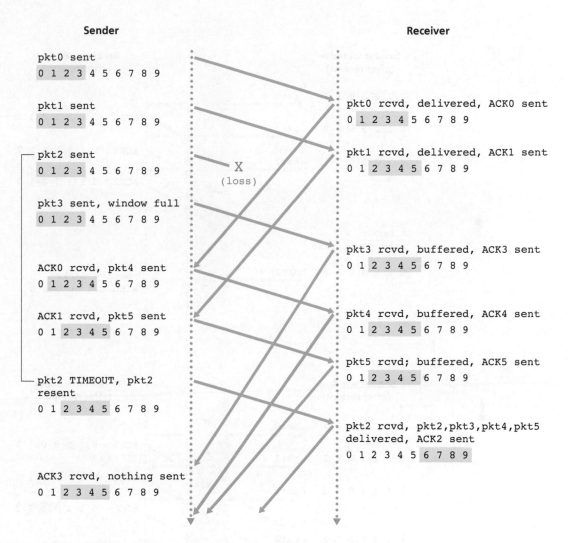

Figure 3.26 ♦ SR operation

The lack of synchronization between sender and receiver windows has important consequences when we are faced with the reality of a finite range of sequence numbers. Consider what could happen, for example, with a finite range of four packet sequence numbers, 0, 1, 2, 3, and a window size of three. Suppose packets 0 through 2 are transmitted and correctly received and acknowledged at the receiver. At this point, the receiver's window is over the fourth, fifth, and sixth packets, which have sequence numbers 3, 0, and 1, respectively. Now consider two scenarios. In the first scenario, shown in Figure 3.27(a), the ACKs for the first three packets are lost and

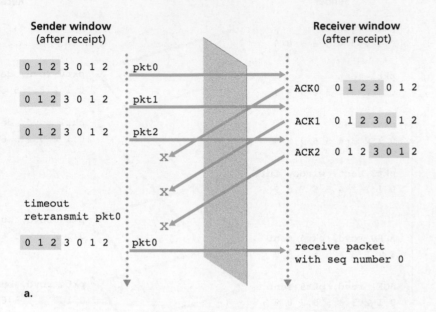

a.

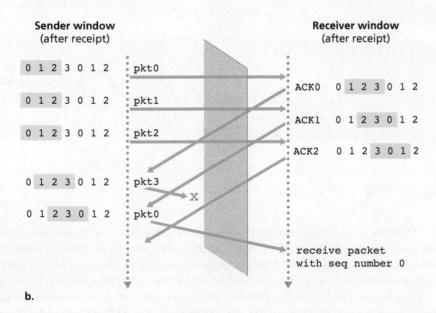

b.

Figure 3.27 ♦ SR receiver dilemma with too-large windows: A new packet or a retransmission?

the sender retransmits these packets. The receiver thus next receives a packet with sequence number 0—a copy of the first packet sent.

In the second scenario, shown in Figure 3.27(b), the ACKs for the first three packets are all delivered correctly. The sender thus moves its window forward and sends the fourth, fifth, and sixth packets, with sequence numbers 3, 0, and 1, respectively. The packet with sequence number 3 is lost, but the packet with sequence number 0 arrives—a packet containing *new* data.

Now consider the receiver's viewpoint in Figure 3.27, which has a figurative curtain between the sender and the receiver, since the receiver cannot "see" the actions taken by the sender. All the receiver observes is the sequence of messages it receives from the channel and sends into the channel. As far as it is concerned, the two scenarios in Figure 3.27 are *identical*. There is no way of distinguishing the retransmission of the first packet from an original transmission of the fifth packet. Clearly, a window size that is 1 less than the size of the sequence number space won't work. But how small must the window size be? A problem at the end of the chapter asks you to show that the window size must be less than or equal to half the size of the sequence number space for SR protocols.

At the companion Web site, you will find an applet that animates the operation of the SR protocol. Try performing the same experiments that you did with the GBN applet. Do the results agree with what you expect?

This completes our discussion of reliable data transfer protocols. We've covered a *lot* of ground and introduced numerous mechanisms that together provide for reliable data transfer. Table 3.1 summarizes these mechanisms. Now that we have seen all of these mechanisms in operation and can see the "big picture," we encourage you to review this section again to see how these mechanisms were incrementally added to cover increasingly complex (and realistic) models of the channel connecting the sender and receiver, or to improve the performance of the protocols.

Let's conclude our discussion of reliable data transfer protocols by considering one remaining assumption in our underlying channel model. Recall that we have assumed that packets cannot be reordered within the channel between the sender and receiver. This is generally a reasonable assumption when the sender and receiver are connected by a single physical wire. However, when the "channel" connecting the two is a network, packet reordering can occur. One manifestation of packet reordering is that old copies of a packet with a sequence or acknowledgment number of x can appear, even though neither the sender's nor the receiver's window contains x. With packet reordering, the channel can be thought of as essentially buffering packets and spontaneously emitting these packets at *any* point in the future. Because sequence numbers may be reused, some care must be taken to guard against such duplicate packets. The approach taken in practice is to ensure that a sequence number is not reused until the sender is "sure" that any previously sent packets with sequence number x are no longer in the network. This is done by assuming that a packet cannot "live" in the network for longer than some fixed maximum amount of time. A maximum packet lifetime of approximately three minutes is assumed in the TCP extensions

Mechanism	Use, Comments
Checksum	Used to detect bit errors in a transmitted packet.
Timer	Used to timeout/retransmit a packet, possibly because the packet (or its ACK) was lost within the channel. Because timeouts can occur when a packet is delayed but not lost (premature timeout), or when a packet has been received by the receiver but the receiver-to-sender ACK has been lost, duplicate copies of a packet may be received by a receiver.
Sequence number	Used for sequential numbering of packets of data flowing from sender to receiver. Gaps in the sequence numbers of received packets allow the receiver to detect a lost packet. Packets with duplicate sequence numbers allow the receiver to detect duplicate copies of a packet.
Acknowledgment	Used by the receiver to tell the sender that a packet or set of packets has been received correctly. Acknowledgments will typically carry the sequence number of the packet or packets being acknowledged. Acknowledgments may be individual or cumulative, depending on the protocol.
Negative acknowledgment	Used by the receiver to tell the sender that a packet has not been received correctly. Negative acknowledgments will typically carry the sequence number of the packet that was not received correctly.
Window, pipelining	The sender may be restricted to sending only packets with sequence numbers that fall within a given range. By allowing multiple packets to be transmitted but not yet acknowledged, sender utilization can be increased over a stop-and-wait mode of operation. We'll see shortly that the window size may be set on the basis of the receiver's ability to receive and buffer messages, or the level of congestion in the network, or both.

Table 3.1 ♦ Summary of reliable data transfer mechanisms and their use

for high-speed networks [RFC 1323]. [Sunshine 1978] describes a method for using sequence numbers such that reordering problems can be completely avoided.

3.5 Connection-Oriented Transport: TCP

Now that we have covered the underlying principles of reliable data transfer, let's turn to TCP—the Internet's transport-layer, connection-oriented, reliable transport protocol. In this section, we'll see that in order to provide reliable data transfer, TCP relies on many of the underlying principles discussed in the previous section, including error detection, retransmissions, cumulative acknowledgments, timers, and header fields for sequence and acknowledgment numbers. TCP is defined in RFC 793, RFC 1122, RFC 1323, RFC 2018, and RFC 2581.

3.5.1 The TCP Connection

TCP is said to be **connection-oriented** because before one application process can begin to send data to another, the two processes must first "handshake" with each other—that is, they must send some preliminary segments to each other to establish the parameters of the ensuing data transfer. As part of TCP connection establishment, both sides of the connection will initialize many TCP state variables (many of which will be discussed in this section and in Section 3.7) associated with the TCP connection.

The TCP "connection" is not an end-to-end TDM or FDM circuit as in a circuit-switched network. Nor is it a virtual circuit (see Chapter 1), as the connection state resides entirely in the two end systems. Because the TCP protocol runs only in the end systems and not in the intermediate network elements (routers and link-layer switches), the intermediate network elements do not maintain TCP connection state.

CASE HISTORY

VINTON CERF, ROBERT KAHN, AND TCP/IP

In the early 1970s, packet-switched networks began to proliferate, with the ARPAnet—the precursor of the Internet—being just one of many networks. Each of these networks had its own protocol. Two researchers, Vinton Cerf and Robert Kahn, recognized the importance of interconnecting these networks and invented a cross-network protocol called TCP/IP, which stands for Transmission Control Protocol/Internet Protocol. Although Cerf and Kahn began by seeing the protocol as a single entity, it was later split into its two parts, TCP and IP, which operated separately. Cerf and Kahn published a paper on TCP/IP in May 1974 in *IEEE Transactions on Communications Technology* [Cerf 1974].

The TCP/IP protocol, which is the bread and butter of today's Internet, was devised before PCs, workstations, smartphones, and tablets, before the proliferation of Ethernet, cable, and DSL, WiFi, and other access network technologies, and before the Web, social media, and streaming video. Cerf and Kahn saw the need for a networking protocol that, on the one hand, provides broad support for yet-to-be-defined applications and, on the other hand, allows arbitrary hosts and link-layer protocols to interoperate.

In 2004, Cerf and Kahn received the ACM's Turing Award, considered the "Nobel Prize of Computing" for "pioneering work on internetworking, including the design and implementation of the Internet's basic communications protocols, TCP/IP, and for inspired leadership in networking."

In fact, the intermediate routers are completely oblivious to TCP connections; they see datagrams, not connections.

A TCP connection provides a **full-duplex service**: If there is a TCP connection between Process A on one host and Process B on another host, then application-layer data can flow from Process A to Process B at the same time as application-layer data flows from Process B to Process A. A TCP connection is also always **point-to-point**, that is, between a single sender and a single receiver. So-called "multicasting" (see Section 4.7)—the transfer of data from one sender to many receivers in a single send operation—is not possible with TCP. With TCP, two hosts are company and three are a crowd!

Let's now take a look at how a TCP connection is established. Suppose a process running in one host wants to initiate a connection with another process in another host. Recall that the process that is initiating the connection is called the *client process*, while the other process is called the *server process*. The client application process first informs the client transport layer that it wants to establish a connection to a process in the server. Recall from Section 2.7.2, a Python client program does this by issuing the command

```
clientSocket.connect((serverName,serverPort))
```

where `serverName` is the name of the server and `serverPort` identifies the process on the server. TCP in the client then proceeds to establish a TCP connection with TCP in the server. At the end of this section we discuss in some detail the connection-establishment procedure. For now it suffices to know that the client first sends a special TCP segment; the server responds with a second special TCP segment; and finally the client responds again with a third special segment. The first two segments carry no payload, that is, no application-layer data; the third of these segments may carry a payload. Because three segments are sent between the two hosts, this connection-establishment procedure is often referred to as a **three-way handshake**.

Once a TCP connection is established, the two application processes can send data to each other. Let's consider the sending of data from the client process to the server process. The client process passes a stream of data through the socket (the door of the process), as described in Section 2.7. Once the data passes through the door, the data is in the hands of TCP running in the client. As shown in Figure 3.28, TCP directs this data to the connection's **send buffer**, which is one of the buffers that is set aside during the initial three-way handshake. From time to time, TCP will grab chunks of data from the send buffer and pass the data to the network layer. Interestingly, the TCP specification [RFC 793] is very laid back about specifying when TCP should actually send buffered data, stating that TCP should "send that data in segments at its own convenience." The maximum amount of data that can be grabbed and placed in a segment is limited by the **maximum segment size (MSS)**. The MSS is typically set by first determining the length of the largest link-layer frame that can be sent by the local sending host (the so-called **maximum**

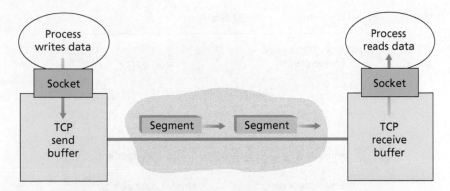

Figure 3.28 ♦ TCP send and receive buffers

transmission unit, **MTU**), and then setting the MSS to ensure that a TCP segment (when encapsulated in an IP datagram) plus the TCP/IP header length (typically 40 bytes) will fit into a single link-layer frame. Both Ethernet and PPP link-layer protocols have an MTU of 1,500 bytes. Thus a typical value of MSS is 1460 bytes. Approaches have also been proposed for discovering the path MTU—the largest link-layer frame that can be sent on all links from source to destination [RFC 1191]—and setting the MSS based on the path MTU value. Note that the MSS is the maximum amount of application-layer data in the segment, not the maximum size of the TCP segment including headers. (This terminology is confusing, but we have to live with it, as it is well entrenched.)

TCP pairs each chunk of client data with a TCP header, thereby forming **TCP segments**. The segments are passed down to the network layer, where they are separately encapsulated within network-layer IP datagrams. The IP datagrams are then sent into the network. When TCP receives a segment at the other end, the segment's data is placed in the TCP connection's receive buffer, as shown in Figure 3.28. The application reads the stream of data from this buffer. Each side of the connection has its own send buffer and its own receive buffer. (You can see the online flow-control applet at http://www.awl.com/kurose-ross, which provides an animation of the send and receive buffers.)

We see from this discussion that a TCP connection consists of buffers, variables, and a socket connection to a process in one host, and another set of buffers, variables, and a socket connection to a process in another host. As mentioned earlier, no buffers or variables are allocated to the connection in the network elements (routers, switches, and repeaters) between the hosts.

3.5.2 TCP Segment Structure

Having taken a brief look at the TCP connection, let's examine the TCP segment structure. The TCP segment consists of header fields and a data field. The data field contains a chunk of application data. As mentioned above, the MSS limits the

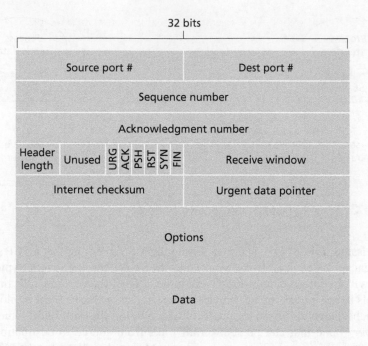

Figure 3.29 ◆ TCP segment structure

maximum size of a segment's data field. When TCP sends a large file, such as an image as part of a Web page, it typically breaks the file into chunks of size MSS (except for the last chunk, which will often be less than the MSS). Interactive applications, however, often transmit data chunks that are smaller than the MSS; for example, with remote login applications like Telnet, the data field in the TCP segment is often only one byte. Because the TCP header is typically 20 bytes (12 bytes more than the UDP header), segments sent by Telnet may be only 21 bytes in length.

Figure 3.29 shows the structure of the TCP segment. As with UDP, the header includes **source and destination port numbers**, which are used for multiplexing/demultiplexing data from/to upper-layer applications. Also, as with UDP, the header includes a **checksum field**. A TCP segment header also contains the following fields:

- The 32-bit **sequence number field** and the 32-bit **acknowledgment number field** are used by the TCP sender and receiver in implementing a reliable data transfer service, as discussed below.

- The 16-bit **receive window** field is used for flow control. We will see shortly that it is used to indicate the number of bytes that a receiver is willing to accept.

- The 4-bit **header length field** specifies the length of the TCP header in 32-bit words. The TCP header can be of variable length due to the TCP options field.

(Typically, the options field is empty, so that the length of the typical TCP header is 20 bytes.)

- The optional and variable-length **options field** is used when a sender and receiver negotiate the maximum segment size (MSS) or as a window scaling factor for use in high-speed networks. A time-stamping option is also defined. See RFC 854 and RFC 1323 for additional details.

- The **flag field** contains 6 bits. The **ACK bit** is used to indicate that the value carried in the acknowledgment field is valid; that is, the segment contains an acknowledgment for a segment that has been successfully received. The **RST**, **SYN**, and **FIN** bits are used for connection setup and teardown, as we will discuss at the end of this section. Setting the **PSH** bit indicates that the receiver should pass the data to the upper layer immediately. Finally, the **URG** bit is used to indicate that there is data in this segment that the sending-side upper-layer entity has marked as "urgent." The location of the last byte of this urgent data is indicated by the 16-bit **urgent data pointer field**. TCP must inform the receiving-side upper-layer entity when urgent data exists and pass it a pointer to the end of the urgent data. (In practice, the PSH, URG, and the urgent data pointer are not used. However, we mention these fields for completeness.)

Sequence Numbers and Acknowledgment Numbers

Two of the most important fields in the TCP segment header are the sequence number field and the acknowledgment number field. These fields are a critical part of TCP's reliable data transfer service. But before discussing how these fields are used to provide reliable data transfer, let us first explain what exactly TCP puts in these fields.

TCP views data as an unstructured, but ordered, stream of bytes. TCP's use of sequence numbers reflects this view in that sequence numbers are over the stream of transmitted bytes and *not* over the series of transmitted segments. The **sequence number for a segment** is therefore the byte-stream number of the first byte in the segment. Let's look at an example. Suppose that a process in Host A wants to send a stream of data to a process in Host B over a TCP connection. The TCP in Host A will implicitly number each byte in the data stream. Suppose that the data stream consists of a file consisting of 500,000 bytes, that the MSS is 1,000 bytes, and that the first byte of the data stream is numbered 0. As shown in Figure 3.30, TCP constructs 500 segments out of the data stream. The first segment gets assigned sequence number 0, the second segment gets assigned sequence number 1,000, the third segment gets assigned sequence number 2,000, and so on. Each sequence number is inserted in the sequence number field in the header of the appropriate TCP segment.

Now let's consider acknowledgment numbers. These are a little trickier than sequence numbers. Recall that TCP is full-duplex, so that Host A may be receiving data from Host B while it sends data to Host B (as part of the same TCP connection). Each of the segments that arrive from Host B has a sequence number for the data

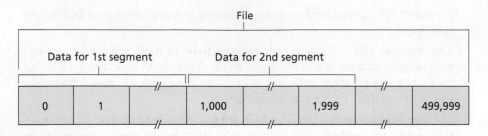

Figure 3.30 ♦ Dividing file data into TCP segments

flowing from B to A. *The acknowledgment number that Host A puts in its segment is the sequence number of the next byte Host A is expecting from Host B.* It is good to look at a few examples to understand what is going on here. Suppose that Host A has received all bytes numbered 0 through 535 from B and suppose that it is about to send a segment to Host B. Host A is waiting for byte 536 and all the subsequent bytes in Host B's data stream. So Host A puts 536 in the acknowledgment number field of the segment it sends to B.

As another example, suppose that Host A has received one segment from Host B containing bytes 0 through 535 and another segment containing bytes 900 through 1,000. For some reason Host A has not yet received bytes 536 through 899. In this example, Host A is still waiting for byte 536 (and beyond) in order to re-create B's data stream. Thus, A's next segment to B will contain 536 in the acknowledgment number field. Because TCP only acknowledges bytes up to the first missing byte in the stream, TCP is said to provide **cumulative acknowledgments**.

This last example also brings up an important but subtle issue. Host A received the third segment (bytes 900 through 1,000) before receiving the second segment (bytes 536 through 899). Thus, the third segment arrived out of order. The subtle issue is: What does a host do when it receives out-of-order segments in a TCP connection? Interestingly, the TCP RFCs do not impose any rules here and leave the decision up to the people programming a TCP implementation. There are basically two choices: either (1) the receiver immediately discards out-of-order segments (which, as we discussed earlier, can simplify receiver design), or (2) the receiver keeps the out-of-order bytes and waits for the missing bytes to fill in the gaps. Clearly, the latter choice is more efficient in terms of network bandwidth, and is the approach taken in practice.

In Figure 3.30, we assumed that the initial sequence number was zero. In truth, both sides of a TCP connection randomly choose an initial sequence number. This is done to minimize the possibility that a segment that is still present in the network from an earlier, already-terminated connection between two hosts is mistaken for a valid segment in a later connection between these same two hosts (which also happen to be using the same port numbers as the old connection) [Sunshine 1978].

Telnet: A Case Study for Sequence and Acknowledgment Numbers

Telnet, defined in RFC 854, is a popular application-layer protocol used for remote login. It runs over TCP and is designed to work between any pair of hosts. Unlike the bulk data transfer applications discussed in Chapter 2, Telnet is an interactive application. We discuss a Telnet example here, as it nicely illustrates TCP sequence and acknowledgment numbers. We note that many users now prefer to use the SSH protocol rather than Telnet, since data sent in a Telnet connection (including passwords!) is not encrypted, making Telnet vulnerable to eavesdropping attacks (as discussed in Section 8.7).

Suppose Host A initiates a Telnet session with Host B. Because Host A initiates the session, it is labeled the client, and Host B is labeled the server. Each character typed by the user (at the client) will be sent to the remote host; the remote host will send back a copy of each character, which will be displayed on the Telnet user's screen. This "echo back" is used to ensure that characters seen by the Telnet user have already been received and processed at the remote site. Each character thus traverses the network twice between the time the user hits the key and the time the character is displayed on the user's monitor.

Now suppose the user types a single letter, 'C,' and then grabs a coffee. Let's examine the TCP segments that are sent between the client and server. As shown in Figure 3.31, we suppose the starting sequence numbers are 42 and 79 for the client and server, respectively. Recall that the sequence number of a segment is the sequence number of the first byte in the data field. Thus, the first segment sent from the client will have sequence number 42; the first segment sent from the server will have sequence number 79. Recall that the acknowledgment number is the sequence number of the next byte of data that the host is waiting for. After the TCP connection is established but before any data is sent, the client is waiting for byte 79 and the server is waiting for byte 42.

As shown in Figure 3.31, three segments are sent. The first segment is sent from the client to the server, containing the 1-byte ASCII representation of the letter 'C' in its data field. This first segment also has 42 in its sequence number field, as we just described. Also, because the client has not yet received any data from the server, this first segment will have 79 in its acknowledgment number field.

The second segment is sent from the server to the client. It serves a dual purpose. First it provides an acknowledgment of the data the server has received. By putting 43 in the acknowledgment field, the server is telling the client that it has successfully received everything up through byte 42 and is now waiting for bytes 43 onward. The second purpose of this segment is to echo back the letter 'C.' Thus, the second segment has the ASCII representation of 'C' in its data field. This second segment has the sequence number 79, the initial sequence number of the server-to-client data flow of this TCP connection, as this is the very first byte of data that the server is sending. Note that the acknowledgment for client-to-server data is carried in a segment carrying server-to-client data; this acknowledgment is said to be **piggybacked** on the server-to-client data segment.

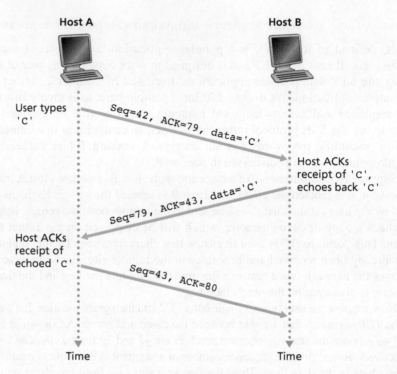

Figure 3.31 ♦ Sequence and acknowledgment numbers for a simple
Telnet application over TCP

The third segment is sent from the client to the server. Its sole purpose is to acknowledge the data it has received from the server. (Recall that the second segment contained data—the letter 'C'—from the server to the client.) This segment has an empty data field (that is, the acknowledgment is not being piggybacked with any client-to-server data). The segment has 80 in the acknowledgment number field because the client has received the stream of bytes up through byte sequence number 79 and it is now waiting for bytes 80 onward. You might think it odd that this segment also has a sequence number since the segment contains no data. But because TCP has a sequence number field, the segment needs to have some sequence number.

3.5.3 Round-Trip Time Estimation and Timeout

TCP, like our `rdt` protocol in Section 3.4, uses a timeout/retransmit mechanism to recover from lost segments. Although this is conceptually simple, many subtle issues arise when we implement a timeout/retransmit mechanism in an actual protocol such as TCP. Perhaps the most obvious question is the length of the timeout intervals. Clearly, the timeout should be larger than the connection's round-trip time (RTT), that is, the time from when a segment is sent until it is acknowledged. Otherwise, unnecessary retransmissions would be sent. But how much larger? How should the RTT be estimated in the first place? Should a timer be associated with each and every unacknowledged segment? So many questions! Our discussion in this section is based on the TCP work in [Jacobson 1988] and the current IETF recommendations for managing TCP timers [RFC 6298].

Estimating the Round-Trip Time

Let's begin our study of TCP timer management by considering how TCP estimates the round-trip time between sender and receiver. This is accomplished as follows. The sample RTT, denoted `SampleRTT`, for a segment is the amount of time between when the segment is sent (that is, passed to IP) and when an acknowledgment for the segment is received. Instead of measuring a `SampleRTT` for every transmitted segment, most TCP implementations take only one `SampleRTT` measurement at a time. That is, at any point in time, the `SampleRTT` is being estimated for only one of the transmitted but currently unacknowledged segments, leading to a new value of `SampleRTT` approximately once every RTT. Also, TCP never computes a `SampleRTT` for a segment that has been retransmitted; it only measures `SampleRTT` for segments that have been transmitted once [Karn 1987]. (A problem at the end of the chapter asks you to consider why.)

Obviously, the `SampleRTT` values will fluctuate from segment to segment due to congestion in the routers and to the varying load on the end systems. Because of this fluctuation, any given `SampleRTT` value may be atypical. In order to estimate a typical RTT, it is therefore natural to take some sort of average of the `SampleRTT` values. TCP maintains an average, called `EstimatedRTT`, of the `SampleRTT` values. Upon obtaining a new `SampleRTT`, TCP updates `EstimatedRTT` according to the following formula:

$$\texttt{EstimatedRTT} = (1 - \alpha) \cdot \texttt{EstimatedRTT} + \alpha \cdot \texttt{SampleRTT}$$

The formula above is written in the form of a programming-language statement—the new value of `EstimatedRTT` is a weighted combination of the previous value of `EstimatedRTT` and the new value for `SampleRTT`. The recommended value of α is $\alpha = 0.125$ (that is, 1/8) [RFC 6298], in which case the formula above becomes:

$$\texttt{EstimatedRTT} = 0.875 \cdot \texttt{EstimatedRTT} + 0.125 \cdot \texttt{SampleRTT}$$

Note that `EstimatedRTT` is a weighted average of the `SampleRTT` values. As discussed in a homework problem at the end of this chapter, this weighted average puts more weight on recent samples than on old samples. This is natural, as the

PRINCIPLES IN PRACTICE

TCP provides reliable data transfer by using positive acknowledgments and timers in much the same way that we studied in Section 3.4. TCP acknowledges data that has been received correctly, and it then retransmits segments when segments or their corresponding acknowledgments are thought to be lost or corrupted. Certain versions of TCP also have an implicit NAK mechanism—with TCP's fast retransmit mechanism, the receipt of three duplicate ACKs for a given segment serves as an implicit NAK for the following segment, triggering retransmission of that segment before timeout. TCP uses sequences of numbers to allow the receiver to identify lost or duplicate segments. Just as in the case of our reliable data transfer protocol, `rdt3.0`, TCP cannot itself tell for certain if a segment, or its ACK, is lost, corrupted, or overly delayed. At the sender, TCP's response will be the same: retransmit the segment in question.

TCP also uses pipelining, allowing the sender to have multiple transmitted but yet-to-be-acknowledged segments outstanding at any given time. We saw earlier that pipelining can greatly improve a session's throughput when the ratio of the segment size to round-trip delay is small. The specific number of outstanding, unacknowledged segments that a sender can have is determined by TCP's flow-control and congestion-control mechanisms. TCP flow control is discussed at the end of this section; TCP congestion control is discussed in Section 3.7. For the time being, we must simply be aware that the TCP sender uses pipelining.

more recent samples better reflect the current congestion in the network. In statistics, such an average is called an **exponential weighted moving average (EWMA)**. The word "exponential" appears in EWMA because the weight of a given `SampleRTT` decays exponentially fast as the updates proceed. In the homework problems you will be asked to derive the exponential term in `EstimatedRTT`.

Figure 3.32 shows the `SampleRTT` values and `EstimatedRTT` for a value of α = 1/8 for a TCP connection between `gaia.cs.umass.edu` (in Amherst, Massachusetts) to `fantasia.eurecom.fr` (in the south of France). Clearly, the variations in the `SampleRTT` are smoothed out in the computation of the `EstimatedRTT`.

In addition to having an estimate of the RTT, it is also valuable to have a measure of the variability of the RTT. [RFC 6298] defines the RTT variation, `DevRTT`, as an estimate of how much `SampleRTT` typically deviates from `EstimatedRTT`:

$$\text{DevRTT} = (1 - \beta) \cdot \text{DevRTT} + \beta \cdot | \text{SampleRTT} - \text{EstimatedRTT} |$$

Note that `DevRTT` is an EWMA of the difference between `SampleRTT` and `EstimatedRTT`. If the `SampleRTT` values have little fluctuation, then `DevRTT` will be small; on the other hand, if there is a lot of fluctuation, `DevRTT` will be large. The recommended value of β is 0.25.

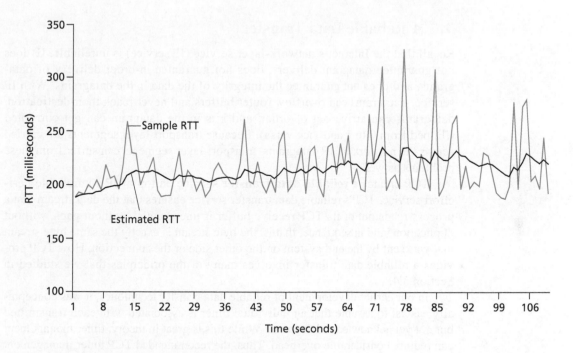

Figure 3.32 ♦ RTT samples and RTT estimates

Setting and Managing the Retransmission Timeout Interval

Given values of `EstimatedRTT` and `DevRTT`, what value should be used for TCP's timeout interval? Clearly, the interval should be greater than or equal to `EstimatedRTT`, or unnecessary retransmissions would be sent. But the timeout interval should not be too much larger than `EstimatedRTT`; otherwise, when a segment is lost, TCP would not quickly retransmit the segment, leading to large data transfer delays. It is therefore desirable to set the timeout equal to the `EstimatedRTT` plus some margin. The margin should be large when there is a lot of fluctuation in the `SampleRTT` values; it should be small when there is little fluctuation. The value of `DevRTT` should thus come into play here. All of these considerations are taken into account in TCP's method for determining the retransmission timeout interval:

```
TimeoutInterval = EstimatedRTT + 4 · DevRTT
```

An initial `TimeoutInterval` value of 1 second is recommended [RFC 6298]. Also, when a timeout occurs, the value of `TimeoutInterval` is doubled to avoid a premature timeout occurring for a subsequent segment that will soon be acknowledged. However, as soon as a segment is received and `EstimatedRTT` is updated, the `TimeoutInterval` is again computed using the formula above.

3.5.4 Reliable Data Transfer

Recall that the Internet's network-layer service (IP service) is unreliable. IP does not guarantee datagram delivery, does not guarantee in-order delivery of datagrams, and does not guarantee the integrity of the data in the datagrams. With IP service, datagrams can overflow router buffers and never reach their destination, datagrams can arrive out of order, and bits in the datagram can get corrupted (flipped from 0 to 1 and vice versa). Because transport-layer segments are carried across the network by IP datagrams, transport-layer segments can suffer from these problems as well.

TCP creates a **reliable data transfer service** on top of IP's unreliable best-effort service. TCP's reliable data transfer service ensures that the data stream that a process reads out of its TCP receive buffer is uncorrupted, without gaps, without duplication, and in sequence; that is, the byte stream is exactly the same byte stream that was sent by the end system on the other side of the connection. How TCP provides a reliable data transfer involves many of the principles that we studied in Section 3.4.

In our earlier development of reliable data transfer techniques, it was conceptually easiest to assume that an individual timer is associated with each transmitted but not yet acknowledged segment. While this is great in theory, timer management can require considerable overhead. Thus, the recommended TCP timer management procedures [RFC 6298] use only a *single* retransmission timer, even if there are multiple transmitted but not yet acknowledged segments. The TCP protocol described in this section follows this single-timer recommendation.

We will discuss how TCP provides reliable data transfer in two incremental steps. We first present a highly simplified description of a TCP sender that uses only timeouts to recover from lost segments; we then present a more complete description that uses duplicate acknowledgments in addition to timeouts. In the ensuing discussion, we suppose that data is being sent in only one direction, from Host A to Host B, and that Host A is sending a large file.

Figure 3.33 presents a highly simplified description of a TCP sender. We see that there are three major events related to data transmission and retransmission in the TCP sender: data received from application above; timer timeout; and ACK receipt. Upon the occurrence of the first major event, TCP receives data from the application, encapsulates the data in a segment, and passes the segment to IP. Note that each segment includes a sequence number that is the byte-stream number of the first data byte in the segment, as described in Section 3.5.2. Also note that if the timer is already not running for some other segment, TCP starts the timer when the segment is passed to IP. (It is helpful to think of the timer as being associated with the oldest unacknowledged segment.) The expiration interval for this timer is the `TimeoutInterval`, which is calculated from `EstimatedRTT` and `DevRTT`, as described in Section 3.5.3.

```
/* Assume sender is not constrained by TCP flow or congestion control, that data from above is less
than MSS in size, and that data transfer is in one direction only. */

NextSeqNum=InitialSeqNumber
SendBase=InitialSeqNumber

loop (forever) {
    switch(event)

        event: data received from application above
            create TCP segment with sequence number NextSeqNum
            if (timer currently not running)
                start timer
            pass segment to IP
            NextSeqNum=NextSeqNum+length(data)
            break;

        event: timer timeout
            retransmit not-yet-acknowledged segment with
                smallest sequence number
            start timer
            break;

        event: ACK received, with ACK field value of y
            if (y > SendBase) {
                SendBase=y
                if (there are currently any not-yet-acknowledged segments)
                    start timer
            }
            break;

    } /* end of loop forever */
```

Figure 3.33 ♦ Simplified TCP sender

The second major event is the timeout. TCP responds to the timeout event by retransmitting the segment that caused the timeout. TCP then restarts the timer.

The third major event that must be handled by the TCP sender is the arrival of an acknowledgment segment (ACK) from the receiver (more specifically, a segment containing a valid ACK field value). On the occurrence of this event, TCP compares the ACK value y with its variable SendBase. The TCP state variable SendBase is the sequence number of the oldest unacknowledged byte. (Thus SendBase−1 is the sequence number of the last byte that is known to have been received correctly and in order at the receiver.) As indicated earlier, TCP uses cumulative acknowledgments, so that y acknowledges the receipt of all bytes before byte number y. If y > SendBase, then the ACK is acknowledging one or more previously unacknowledged segments. Thus the sender updates its `SendBase` variable; it also restarts the timer if there currently are any not-yet-acknowledged segments.

A Few Interesting Scenarios

We have just described a highly simplified version of how TCP provides reliable data transfer. But even this highly simplified version has many subtleties. To get a good feeling for how this protocol works, let's now walk through a few simple scenarios. Figure 3.34 depicts the first scenario, in which Host A sends one segment to Host B. Suppose that this segment has sequence number 92 and contains 8 bytes of data. After sending this segment, Host A waits for a segment from B with acknowledgment number 100. Although the segment from A is received at B, the acknowledgment from B to A gets lost. In this case, the timeout event occurs, and Host A retransmits the same segment. Of course, when Host B receives the retransmission, it observes from the sequence number that the segment contains data that has already been received. Thus, TCP in Host B will discard the bytes in the retransmitted segment.

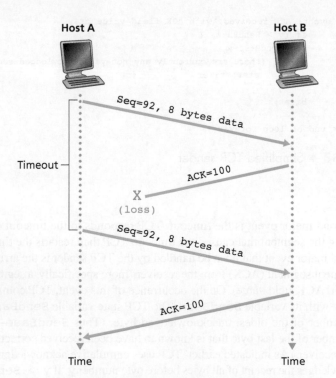

Figure 3.34 ♦ Retransmission due to a lost acknowledgment

In a second scenario, shown in Figure 3.35, Host A sends two segments back to back. The first segment has sequence number 92 and 8 bytes of data, and the second segment has sequence number 100 and 20 bytes of data. Suppose that both segments arrive intact at B, and B sends two separate acknowledgments for each of these segments. The first of these acknowledgments has acknowledgment number 100; the second has acknowledgment number 120. Suppose now that neither of the acknowledgments arrives at Host A before the timeout. When the timeout event occurs, Host A resends the first segment with sequence number 92 and restarts the timer. As long as the ACK for the second segment arrives before the new timeout, the second segment will not be retransmitted.

In a third and final scenario, suppose Host A sends the two segments, exactly as in the second example. The acknowledgment of the first segment is lost in the network, but just before the timeout event, Host A receives an acknowledgment with acknowledgment number 120. Host A therefore knows that Host B has received *everything* up through byte 119; so Host A does not resend either of the two segments. This scenario is illustrated in Figure 3.36.

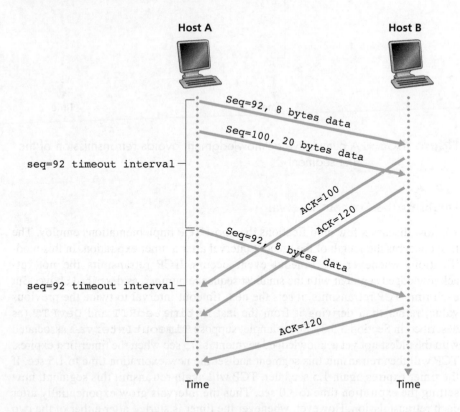

Figure 3.35 ♦ Segment 100 not retransmitted

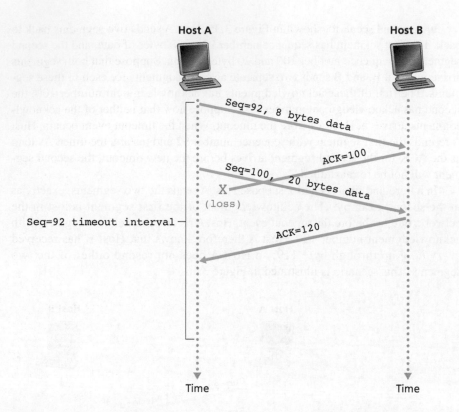

Host A   Host B

Seq=92, 8 bytes data

ACK=100

Seq=100, 20 bytes data

X
(loss)

Seq=92 timeout interval

ACK=120

Time   Time

Figure 3.36 ♦ A cumulative acknowledgment avoids retransmission of the first segment

Doubling the Timeout Interval

We now discuss a few modifications that most TCP implementations employ. The first concerns the length of the timeout interval after a timer expiration. In this modification, whenever the timeout event occurs, TCP retransmits the not-yet-acknowledged segment with the smallest sequence number, as described above. But each time TCP retransmits, it sets the next timeout interval to twice the previous value, rather than deriving it from the last `EstimatedRTT` and `DevRTT` (as described in Section 3.5.3). For example, suppose `TimeoutInterval` associated with the oldest not yet acknowledged segment is .75 sec when the timer first expires. TCP will then retransmit this segment and set the new expiration time to 1.5 sec. If the timer expires again 1.5 sec later, TCP will again retransmit this segment, now setting the expiration time to 3.0 sec. Thus the intervals grow exponentially after each retransmission. However, whenever the timer is started after either of the two other events (that is, data received from application above, and ACK received), the

`TimeoutInterval` is derived from the most recent values of `EstimatedRTT` and `DevRTT`.

This modification provides a limited form of congestion control. (More comprehensive forms of TCP congestion control will be studied in Section 3.7.) The timer expiration is most likely caused by congestion in the network, that is, too many packets arriving at one (or more) router queues in the path between the source and destination, causing packets to be dropped and/or long queuing delays. In times of congestion, if the sources continue to retransmit packets persistently, the congestion may get worse. Instead, TCP acts more politely, with each sender retransmitting after longer and longer intervals. We will see that a similar idea is used by Ethernet when we study CSMA/CD in Chapter 5.

Fast Retransmit

One of the problems with timeout-triggered retransmissions is that the timeout period can be relatively long. When a segment is lost, this long timeout period forces the sender to delay resending the lost packet, thereby increasing the end-to-end delay. Fortunately, the sender can often detect packet loss well before the timeout event occurs by noting so-called duplicate ACKs. A **duplicate ACK** is an ACK that reacknowledges a segment for which the sender has already received an earlier acknowledgment. To understand the sender's response to a duplicate ACK, we must look at why the receiver sends a duplicate ACK in the first place. Table 3.2 summarizes the TCP receiver's ACK generation policy [RFC 5681]. When a TCP receiver receives a segment with a sequence number that is larger than the next, expected, in-order sequence number, it detects a gap in the data stream—that is, a missing segment. This gap could be the result of lost or reordered segments within the network.

Event	TCP Receiver Action
Arrival of in-order segment with expected sequence number. All data up to expected sequence number already acknowledged.	Delayed ACK. Wait up to 500 msec for arrival of another in-order segment. If next in-order segment does not arrive in this interval, send an ACK.
Arrival of in-order segment with expected sequence number. One other in-order segment waiting for ACK transmission.	Immediately send single cumulative ACK, ACKing both in-order segments.
Arrival of out-of-order segment with higher-than-expected sequence number. Gap detected.	Immediately send duplicate ACK, indicating sequence number of next expected byte (which is the lower end of the gap).
Arrival of segment that partially or completely fills in gap in received data.	Immediately send ACK, provided that segment starts at the lower end of gap.

Table 3.2 ♦ TCP ACK Generation Recommendation [RFC 5681]

Since TCP does not use negative acknowledgments, the receiver cannot send an explicit negative acknowledgment back to the sender. Instead, it simply reacknowledges (that is, generates a duplicate ACK for) the last in-order byte of data it has received. (Note that Table 3.2 allows for the case that the receiver does not discard out-of-order segments.)

Because a sender often sends a large number of segments back to back, if one segment is lost, there will likely be many back-to-back duplicate ACKs. If the TCP sender receives three duplicate ACKs for the same data, it takes this as an indication that the segment following the segment that has been ACKed three times has been lost. (In the homework problems, we consider the question of why the sender waits for three duplicate ACKs, rather than just a single duplicate ACK.) In the case that three duplicate ACKs are received, the TCP sender performs a **fast retransmit** [RFC 5681], retransmitting the missing segment *before* that segment's timer expires. This is shown in Figure 3.37, where the second segment is lost, then retransmitted before its timer expires. For TCP with fast retransmit, the following code snippet replaces the ACK received event in Figure 3.33:

```
event: ACK received, with ACK field value of y
        if (y > SendBase) {
                SendBase=y
                if (there are currently any not yet
                              acknowledged segments)
                     start timer
                }
        else { /* a duplicate ACK for already ACKed
                segment */
            increment number of duplicate ACKs
                received for y
            if (number of duplicate ACKS received
                for y==3)
                /* TCP fast retransmit */
                resend segment with sequence number y
        }
        break;
```

We noted earlier that many subtle issues arise when a timeout/retransmit mechanism is implemented in an actual protocol such as TCP. The procedures above, which have evolved as a result of more than 20 years of experience with TCP timers, should convince you that this is indeed the case!

Go-Back-N or Selective Repeat?

Let us close our study of TCP's error-recovery mechanism by considering the following question: Is TCP a GBN or an SR protocol? Recall that TCP acknowledgments are cumulative and correctly received but out-of-order segments are not individually

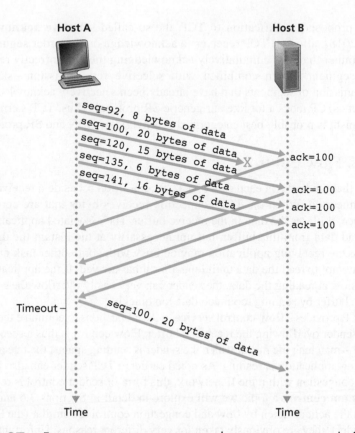

Figure 3.37 ♦ Fast retransmit: retransmitting the missing segment before the segment's timer expires

ACKed by the receiver. Consequently, as shown in Figure 3.33 (see also Figure 3.19), the TCP sender need only maintain the smallest sequence number of a transmitted but unacknowledged byte (`SendBase`) and the sequence number of the next byte to be sent (`NextSeqNum`). In this sense, TCP looks a lot like a GBN-style protocol. But there are some striking differences between TCP and Go-Back-N. Many TCP implementations will buffer correctly received but out-of-order segments [Stevens 1994]. Consider also what happens when the sender sends a sequence of segments 1, 2, . . . , N, and all of the segments arrive in order without error at the receiver. Further suppose that the acknowledgment for packet n < N gets lost, but the remaining N − 1 acknowledgments arrive at the sender before their respective timeouts. In this example, GBN would retransmit not only packet n, but also all of the subsequent packets n + 1, n + 2, . . . , N. TCP, on the other hand, would retransmit at most one segment, namely, segment n. Moreover, TCP would not even retransmit segment n if the acknowledgment for segment n + 1 arrived before the timeout for segment n.

A proposed modification to TCP, the so-called **selective acknowledgment** [RFC 2018], allows a TCP receiver to acknowledge out-of-order segments selectively rather than just cumulatively acknowledging the last correctly received, in-order segment. When combined with selective retransmission—skipping the retransmission of segments that have already been selectively acknowledged by the receiver—TCP looks a lot like our generic SR protocol. Thus, TCP's error-recovery mechanism is probably best categorized as a hybrid of GBN and SR protocols.

3.5.5 Flow Control

Recall that the hosts on each side of a TCP connection set aside a receive buffer for the connection. When the TCP connection receives bytes that are correct and in sequence, it places the data in the receive buffer. The associated application process will read data from this buffer, but not necessarily at the instant the data arrives. Indeed, the receiving application may be busy with some other task and may not even attempt to read the data until long after it has arrived. If the application is relatively slow at reading the data, the sender can very easily overflow the connection's receive buffer by sending too much data too quickly.

TCP provides a **flow-control service** to its applications to eliminate the possibility of the sender overflowing the receiver's buffer. Flow control is thus a speed-matching service—matching the rate at which the sender is sending against the rate at which the receiving application is reading. As noted earlier, a TCP sender can also be throttled due to congestion within the IP network; this form of sender control is referred to as **congestion control**, a topic we will explore in detail in Sections 3.6 and 3.7. Even though the actions taken by flow and congestion control are similar (the throttling of the sender), they are obviously taken for very different reasons. Unfortunately, many authors use the terms interchangeably, and the savvy reader would be wise to distinguish between them. Let's now discuss how TCP provides its flow-control service. In order to see the forest for the trees, we suppose throughout this section that the TCP implementation is such that the TCP receiver discards out-of-order segments.

TCP provides flow control by having the *sender* maintain a variable called the **receive window**. Informally, the receive window is used to give the sender an idea of how much free buffer space is available at the receiver. Because TCP is full-duplex, the sender at each side of the connection maintains a distinct receive window. Let's investigate the receive window in the context of a file transfer. Suppose that Host A is sending a large file to Host B over a TCP connection. Host B allocates a receive buffer to this connection; denote its size by `RcvBuffer`. From time to time, the application process in Host B reads from the buffer. Define the following variables:

- `LastByteRead`: the number of the last byte in the data stream read from the buffer by the application process in B
- `LastByteRcvd`: the number of the last byte in the data stream that has arrived from the network and has been placed in the receive buffer at B

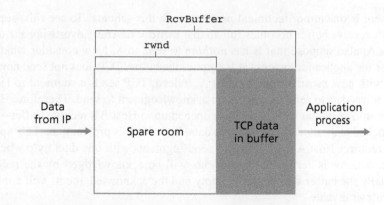

Figure 3.38 ♦ The receive window (`rwnd`) and the receive buffer (`RcvBuffer`)

Because TCP is not permitted to overflow the allocated buffer, we must have

LastByteRcvd − LastByteRead ≤ RcvBuffer

The receive window, denoted `rwnd` is set to the amount of spare room in the buffer:

rwnd = RcvBuffer − [LastByteRcvd − LastByteRead]

Because the spare room changes with time, `rwnd` is dynamic. The variable `rwnd` is illustrated in Figure 3.38.

How does the connection use the variable `rwnd` to provide the flow-control service? Host B tells Host A how much spare room it has in the connection buffer by placing its current value of `rwnd` in the receive window field of every segment it sends to A. Initially, Host B sets `rwnd` = `RcvBuffer`. Note that to pull this off, Host B must keep track of several connection-specific variables.

Host A in turn keeps track of two variables, `LastByteSent` and `Last-ByteAcked`, which have obvious meanings. Note that the difference between these two variables, `LastByteSent − LastByteAcked`, is the amount of unacknowledged data that A has sent into the connection. By keeping the amount of unacknowledged data less than the value of `rwnd`, Host A is assured that it is not overflowing the receive buffer at Host B. Thus, Host A makes sure throughout the connection's life that

LastByteSent − LastByteAcked ≤ rwnd

There is one minor technical problem with this scheme. To see this, suppose Host B's receive buffer becomes full so that `rwnd = 0`. After advertising `rwnd = 0` to Host A, also suppose that B has *nothing* to send to A. Now consider what happens. As the application process at B empties the buffer, TCP does not send new segments with new `rwnd` values to Host A; indeed, TCP sends a segment to Host A only if it has data to send or if it has an acknowledgment to send. Therefore, Host A is never informed that some space has opened up in Host B's receive buffer—Host A is blocked and can transmit no more data! To solve this problem, the TCP specification requires Host A to continue to send segments with one data byte when B's receive window is zero. These segments will be acknowledged by the receiver. Eventually the buffer will begin to empty and the acknowledgments will contain a nonzero `rwnd` value.

The online site at http://www.awl.com/kurose-ross for this book provides an interactive Java applet that illustrates the operation of the TCP receive window.

Having described TCP's flow-control service, we briefly mention here that UDP does not provide flow control. To understand the issue, consider sending a series of UDP segments from a process on Host A to a process on Host B. For a typical UDP implementation, UDP will append the segments in a finite-sized buffer that "precedes" the corresponding socket (that is, the door to the process). The process reads one entire segment at a time from the buffer. If the process does not read the segments fast enough from the buffer, the buffer will overflow and segments will get dropped.

3.5.6 TCP Connection Management

In this subsection we take a closer look at how a TCP connection is established and torn down. Although this topic may not seem particularly thrilling, it is important because TCP connection establishment can significantly add to perceived delays (for example, when surfing the Web). Furthermore, many of the most common network attacks—including the incredibly popular SYN flood attack—exploit vulnerabilities in TCP connection management. Let's first take a look at how a TCP connection is established. Suppose a process running in one host (client) wants to initiate a connection with another process in another host (server). The client application process first informs the client TCP that it wants to establish a connection to a process in the server. The TCP in the client then proceeds to establish a TCP connection with the TCP in the server in the following manner:

• *Step 1.* The client-side TCP first sends a special TCP segment to the server-side TCP. This special segment contains no application-layer data. But one of the flag bits in the segment's header (see Figure 3.29), the SYN bit, is set to 1. For this reason, this special segment is referred to as a SYN segment. In addition, the client randomly chooses an initial sequence number (`client_isn`) and puts this number in the sequence number field of the initial TCP SYN segment. This segment is encapsulated within an IP datagram and sent to the server. There has been considerable interest in properly randomizing the choice of the `client_isn` in order to avoid certain security attacks [CERT 2001–09].

- *Step 2.* Once the IP datagram containing the TCP SYN segment arrives at the server host (assuming it does arrive!), the server extracts the TCP SYN segment from the datagram, allocates the TCP buffers and variables to the connection, and sends a connection-granted segment to the client TCP. (We'll see in Chapter 8 that the allocation of these buffers and variables before completing the third step of the three-way handshake makes TCP vulnerable to a denial-of-service attack known as SYN flooding.) This connection-granted segment also contains no application-layer data. However, it does contain three important pieces of information in the segment header. First, the SYN bit is set to 1. Second, the acknowledgment field of the TCP segment header is set to `client_isn+1`. Finally, the server chooses its own initial sequence number (`server_isn`) and puts this value in the sequence number field of the TCP segment header. This connection-granted segment is saying, in effect, "I received your SYN packet to start a connection with your initial sequence number, `client_isn`. I agree to establish this connection. My own initial sequence number is `server_isn`." The connection-granted segment is referred to as a **SYNACK segment**.

- *Step 3.* Upon receiving the SYNACK segment, the client also allocates buffers and variables to the connection. The client host then sends the server yet another segment; this last segment acknowledges the server's connection-granted segment (the client does so by putting the value `server_isn+1` in the acknowledgment field of the TCP segment header). The SYN bit is set to zero, since the connection is established. This third stage of the three-way handshake may carry client-to-server data in the segment payload.

Once these three steps have been completed, the client and server hosts can send segments containing data to each other. In each of these future segments, the SYN bit will be set to zero. Note that in order to establish the connection, three packets are sent between the two hosts, as illustrated in Figure 3.39. For this reason, this connection-establishment procedure is often referred to as a **three-way handshake**. Several aspects of the TCP three-way handshake are explored in the homework problems (Why are initial sequence numbers needed? Why is a three-way handshake, as opposed to a two-way handshake, needed?). It's interesting to note that a rock climber and a belayer (who is stationed below the rock climber and whose job it is to handle the climber's safety rope) use a three-way-handshake communication protocol that is identical to TCP's to ensure that both sides are ready before the climber begins ascent.

All good things must come to an end, and the same is true with a TCP connection. Either of the two processes participating in a TCP connection can end the connection. When a connection ends, the "resources" (that is, the buffers and variables) in the hosts are deallocated. As an example, suppose the client decides to close the connection, as shown in Figure 3.40. The client application process issues a close

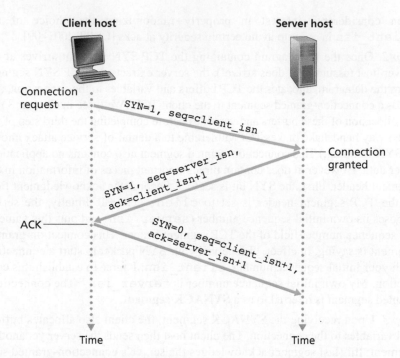

Figure 3.39 ♦ TCP three-way handshake: segment exchange

command. This causes the client TCP to send a special TCP segment to the server process. This special segment has a flag bit in the segment's header, the FIN bit (see Figure 3.29), set to 1. When the server receives this segment, it sends the client an acknowledgment segment in return. The server then sends its own shutdown segment, which has the FIN bit set to 1. Finally, the client acknowledges the server's shutdown segment. At this point, all the resources in the two hosts are now deallocated.

During the life of a TCP connection, the TCP protocol running in each host makes transitions through various **TCP states**. Figure 3.41 illustrates a typical sequence of TCP states that are visited by the *client* TCP. The client TCP begins in the CLOSED state. The application on the client side initiates a new TCP connection (by creating a Socket object in our Java examples as in the Python examples from Chapter 2). This causes TCP in the client to send a SYN segment to TCP in the server. After having sent the SYN segment, the client TCP enters the SYN_SENT state. While in the SYN_SENT state, the client TCP waits for a segment from the server TCP that includes an acknowledgment for the client's previous segment and has the SYN bit set to 1. Having received such a segment, the client TCP enters the ESTABLISHED state. While in the ESTABLISHED state, the TCP client can send and receive TCP segments containing payload (that is, application-generated) data.

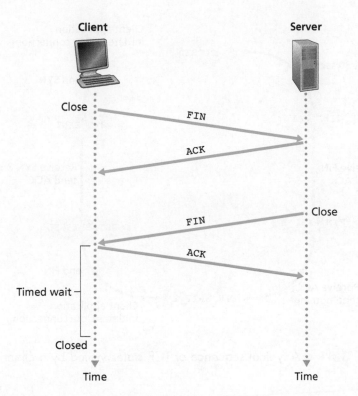

Figure 3.40 ♦ Closing a TCP connection

Suppose that the client application decides it wants to close the connection. (Note that the server could also choose to close the connection.) This causes the client TCP to send a TCP segment with the FIN bit set to 1 and to enter the FIN_WAIT_1 state. While in the FIN_WAIT_1 state, the client TCP waits for a TCP segment from the server with an acknowledgment. When it receives this segment, the client TCP enters the FIN_WAIT_2 state. While in the FIN_WAIT_2 state, the client waits for another segment from the server with the FIN bit set to 1; after receiving this segment, the client TCP acknowledges the server's segment and enters the TIME_WAIT state. The TIME_WAIT state lets the TCP client resend the final acknowledgment in case the ACK is lost. The time spent in the TIME_WAIT state is implementation-dependent, but typical values are 30 seconds, 1 minute, and 2 minutes. After the wait, the connection formally closes and all resources on the client side (including port numbers) are released.

Figure 3.42 illustrates the series of states typically visited by the server-side TCP, assuming the client begins connection teardown. The transitions are self-explanatory. In these two state-transition diagrams, we have only shown how a TCP connection is normally established and shut down. We have not described what

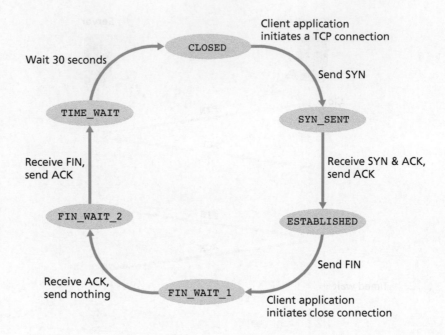

Figure 3.41 ♦ A typical sequence of TCP states visited by a client TCP

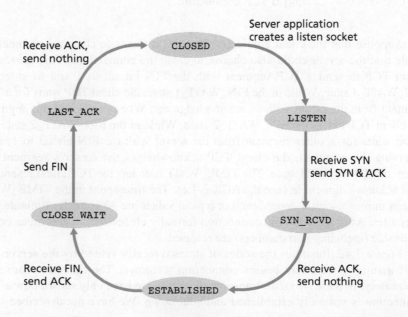

Figure 3.42 ♦ A typical sequence of TCP states visited by a server-side TCP

FOCUS ON SECURITY

THE SYN FLOOD ATTACK

We've seen in our discussion of TCP's three-way handshake that a server allocates and initializes connection variables and buffers in response to a received SYN. The server then sends a SYNACK in response, and awaits an ACK segment from the client. If the client does not send an ACK to complete the third step of this 3-way handshake, eventually (often after a minute or more) the server will terminate the half-open connection and reclaim the allocated resources.

This TCP connection management protocol sets the stage for a classic Denial of Service (DoS) attack known as the **SYN flood attack**. In this attack, the attacker(s) send a large number of TCP SYN segments, without completing the third handshake step. With this deluge of SYN segments, the server's connection resources become exhausted as they are allocated (but never used!) for half-open connections; legitimate clients are then denied service. Such SYN flooding attacks were among the first documented DoS attacks [CERT SYN 1996]. Fortunately, an effective defense known as **SYN cookies** [RFC 4987] are now deployed in most major operating systems. SYN cookies work as follows:

o When the server receives a SYN segment, it does not know if the segment is coming from a legitimate user or is part of a SYN flood attack. So, instead of creating a half-open TCP connection for this SYN, the server creates an initial TCP sequence number that is a complicated function (hash function) of source and destination IP addresses and port numbers of the SYN segment, as well as a secret number only known to the server. This carefully crafted initial sequence number is the so-called "cookie." The server then sends the client a SYNACK packet with this special initial sequence number. *Importantly, the server does not remember the cookie or any other state information corresponding to the SYN.*

o A legitimate client will return an ACK segment. When the server receives this ACK, it must verify that the ACK corresponds to some SYN sent earlier. But how is this done if the server maintains no memory about SYN segments? As you may have guessed, it is done with the cookie. Recall that for a legitimate ACK, the value in the acknowledgment field is equal to the initial sequence number in the SYNACK (the cookie value in this case) plus one (see Figure 3.39). The server can then run the same hash function using the source and destination IP address and port numbers in the SYNACK (which are the same as in the original SYN) and the secret number. If the result of the function plus one is the same as the acknowledgment (cookie) value in the client's SYNACK, the server concludes that the ACK corresponds to an earlier SYN segment and is hence valid. The server then creates a fully open connection along with a socket.

o On the other hand, if the client does not return an ACK segment, then the original SYN has done no harm at the server, since the server hasn't yet allocated any resources in response to the original bogus SYN.

happens in certain pathological scenarios, for example, when both sides of a connection want to initiate or shut down at the same time. If you are interested in learning about this and other advanced issues concerning TCP, you are encouraged to see Stevens' comprehensive book [Stevens 1994].

Our discussion above has assumed that both the client and server are prepared to communicate, i.e., that the server is listening on the port to which the client sends its SYN segment. Let's consider what happens when a host receives a TCP segment whose port numbers or source IP address do not match with any of the ongoing sockets in the host. For example, suppose a host receives a TCP SYN packet with destination port 80, but the host is not accepting connections on port 80 (that is, it is not running a Web server on port 80). Then the host will send a special reset segment to the source. This TCP segment has the RST flag bit (see Section 3.5.2) set to 1. Thus, when a host sends a reset segment, it is telling the source "I don't have a socket for that segment. Please do not resend the segment." When a host receives a UDP packet whose destination port number doesn't match with an ongoing UDP socket, the host sends a special ICMP datagram, as discussed in Chapter 4.

Now that we have a good understanding of TCP connection management, let's revisit the nmap port-scanning tool and examine more closely how it works. To explore a specific TCP port, say port 6789, on a target host, nmap will send a TCP SYN segment with destination port 6789 to that host. There are three possible outcomes:

• *The source host receives a TCP SYNACK segment from the target host*. Since this means that an application is running with TCP port 6789 on the target post, nmap returns "open."
• *The source host receives a TCP RST segment from the target host*. This means that the SYN segment reached the target host, but the target host is not running an application with TCP port 6789. But the attacker at least knows that the segments destined to the host at port 6789 are not blocked by any firewall on the path between source and target hosts. (Firewalls are discussed in Chapter 8.)
• *The source receives nothing*. This likely means that the SYN segment was blocked by an intervening firewall and never reached the target host.

Nmap is a powerful tool, which can "case the joint" not only for open TCP ports, but also for open UDP ports, for firewalls and their configurations, and even for the versions of applications and operating systems. Most of this is done by manipulating TCP connection-management segments [Skoudis 2006]. You can download nmap from www.nmap.org.

This completes our introduction to error control and flow control in TCP. In Section 3.7 we'll return to TCP and look at TCP congestion control in some depth. Before doing so, however, we first step back and examine congestion-control issues in a broader context.

3.6 Principles of Congestion Control

In the previous sections, we examined both the general principles and specific TCP mechanisms used to provide for a reliable data transfer service in the face of packet loss. We mentioned earlier that, in practice, such loss typically results from the overflowing of router buffers as the network becomes congested. Packet retransmission thus treats a symptom of network congestion (the loss of a specific transport-layer segment) but does not treat the cause of network congestion—too many sources attempting to send data at too high a rate. To treat the cause of network congestion, mechanisms are needed to throttle senders in the face of network congestion.

In this section, we consider the problem of congestion control in a general context, seeking to understand why congestion is a bad thing, how network congestion is manifested in the performance received by upper-layer applications, and various approaches that can be taken to avoid, or react to, network congestion. This more general study of congestion control is appropriate since, as with reliable data transfer, it is high on our "top-ten" list of fundamentally important problems in networking. We conclude this section with a discussion of congestion control in the **available bit-rate (ABR)** service in **asynchronous transfer mode (ATM)** networks. The following section contains a detailed study of TCP's congestion-control algorithm.

3.6.1 The Causes and the Costs of Congestion

Let's begin our general study of congestion control by examining three increasingly complex scenarios in which congestion occurs. In each case, we'll look at why congestion occurs in the first place and at the cost of congestion (in terms of resources not fully utilized and poor performance received by the end systems). We'll not (yet) focus on how to react to, or avoid, congestion but rather focus on the simpler issue of understanding what happens as hosts increase their transmission rate and the network becomes congested.

Scenario 1: Two Senders, a Router with Infinite Buffers

We begin by considering perhaps the simplest congestion scenario possible: Two hosts (A and B) each have a connection that shares a single hop between source and destination, as shown in Figure 3.43.

Let's assume that the application in Host A is sending data into the connection (for example, passing data to the transport-level protocol via a socket) at an average rate of λ_{in} bytes/sec. These data are original in the sense that each unit of data is sent into the socket only once. The underlying transport-level protocol is a

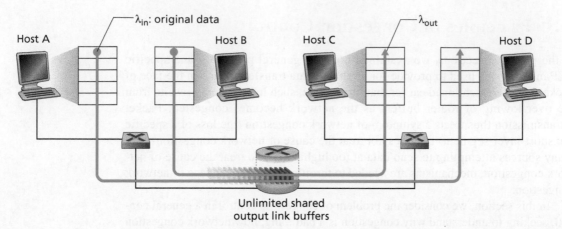

Figure 3.43 ♦ Congestion scenario 1: Two connections sharing a single hop with infinite buffers

simple one. Data is encapsulated and sent; no error recovery (for example, retransmission), flow control, or congestion control is performed. Ignoring the additional overhead due to adding transport- and lower-layer header information, the rate at which Host A offers traffic to the router in this first scenario is thus λ_{in} bytes/sec. Host B operates in a similar manner, and we assume for simplicity that it too is sending at a rate of λ_{in} bytes/sec. Packets from Hosts A and B pass through a router and over a shared outgoing link of capacity R. The router has buffers that allow it to store incoming packets when the packet-arrival rate exceeds the outgoing link's capacity. In this first scenario, we assume that the router has an infinite amount of buffer space.

Figure 3.44 plots the performance of Host A's connection under this first scenario. The left graph plots the **per-connection throughput** (number of bytes per second at the receiver) as a function of the connection-sending rate. For a sending rate between 0 and $R/2$, the throughput at the receiver equals the sender's sending rate—everything sent by the sender is received at the receiver with a finite delay. When the sending rate is above $R/2$, however, the throughput is only $R/2$. This upper limit on throughput is a consequence of the sharing of link capacity between two connections. The link simply cannot deliver packets to a receiver at a steady-state rate that exceeds $R/2$. No matter how high Hosts A and B set their sending rates, they will each never see a throughput higher than $R/2$.

Achieving a per-connection throughput of $R/2$ might actually appear to be a good thing, because the link is fully utilized in delivering packets to their destinations. The right-hand graph in Figure 3.44, however, shows the consequence of operating near link capacity. As the sending rate approaches $R/2$ (from the left), the average delay becomes larger and larger. When the sending rate exceeds $R/2$, the

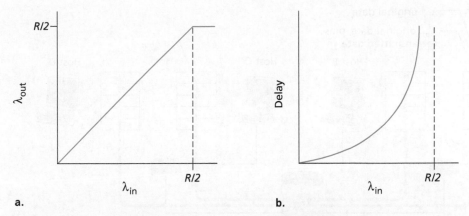

Figure 3.44 ♦ Congestion scenario 1: Throughput and delay as a function of host sending rate

average number of queued packets in the router is unbounded, and the average delay between source and destination becomes infinite (assuming that the connections operate at these sending rates for an infinite period of time and there is an infinite amount of buffering available). Thus, while operating at an aggregate throughput of near R may be ideal from a throughput standpoint, it is far from ideal from a delay standpoint. *Even in this (extremely) idealized scenario, we've already found one cost of a congested network—large queuing delays are experienced as the packet-arrival rate nears the link capacity.*

Scenario 2: Two Senders and a Router with Finite Buffers

Let us now slightly modify scenario 1 in the following two ways (see Figure 3.45). First, the amount of router buffering is assumed to be finite. A consequence of this real-world assumption is that packets will be dropped when arriving to an already-full buffer. Second, we assume that each connection is reliable. If a packet containing a transport-level segment is dropped at the router, the sender will eventually retransmit it. Because packets can be retransmitted, we must now be more careful with our use of the term *sending rate*. Specifically, let us again denote the rate at which the application sends original data into the socket by λ_{in} bytes/sec. The rate at which the transport layer sends segments (containing original data *and* retransmitted data) into the network will be denoted λ'_{in} bytes/sec. λ'_{in} is sometimes referred to as the **offered load** to the network.

The performance realized under scenario 2 will now depend strongly on how retransmission is performed. First, consider the unrealistic case that Host A is able to somehow (magically!) determine whether or not a buffer is free in the router and thus sends a packet only when a buffer is free. In this case, no loss would occur,

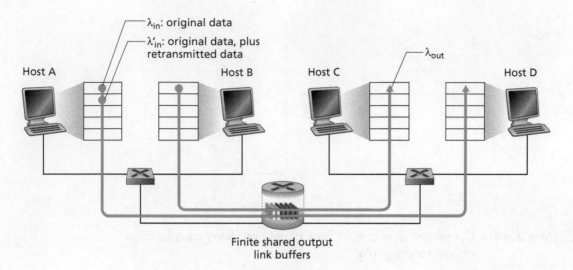

Figure 3.45 ♦ Scenario 2: Two hosts (with retransmissions) and a router with finite buffers

λ_{in} would be equal to λ'_{in}, and the throughput of the connection would be equal to λ_{in}. This case is shown in Figure 3.46(a). From a throughput standpoint, performance is ideal—everything that is sent is received. Note that the average host sending rate cannot exceed $R/2$ under this scenario, since packet loss is assumed never to occur.

Consider next the slightly more realistic case that the sender retransmits only when a packet is known for certain to be lost. (Again, this assumption is a bit of a stretch. However, it is possible that the sending host might set its timeout large enough to be virtually assured that a packet that has not been acknowledged has been lost.) In this case, the performance might look something like that shown in Figure 3.46(b). To appreciate what is happening here, consider the case that the offered load, λ'_{in} (the rate of original data transmission plus retransmissions), equals $R/2$. According to Figure 3.46(b), at this value of the offered load, the rate at which data are delivered to the receiver application is $R/3$. Thus, out of the $0.5R$ units of data transmitted, $0.333R$ bytes/sec (on average) are original data and $0.166R$ bytes/sec (on average) are retransmitted data. *We see here another cost of a congested network—the sender must perform retransmissions in order to compensate for dropped (lost) packets due to buffer overflow.*

Finally, let us consider the case that the sender may time out prematurely and retransmit a packet that has been delayed in the queue but not yet lost. In this case, both the original data packet and the retransmission may reach the receiver. Of

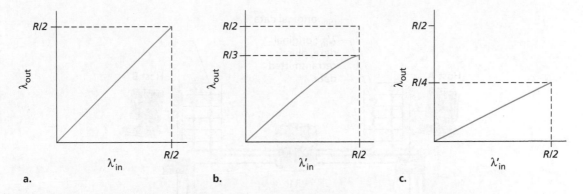

Figure 3.46 ◆ Scenario 2 performance with finite buffers

course, the receiver needs but one copy of this packet and will discard the retransmission. In this case, the work done by the router in forwarding the retransmitted copy of the original packet was wasted, as the receiver will have already received the original copy of this packet. The router would have better used the link transmission capacity to send a different packet instead. *Here then is yet another cost of a congested network—unneeded retransmissions by the sender in the face of large delays may cause a router to use its link bandwidth to forward unneeded copies of a packet.* Figure 3.46 (c) shows the throughput versus offered load when each packet is assumed to be forwarded (on average) twice by the router. Since each packet is forwarded twice, the throughput will have an asymptotic value of $R/4$ as the offered load approaches $R/2$.

Scenario 3: Four Senders, Routers with Finite Buffers, and Multihop Paths

In our final congestion scenario, four hosts transmit packets, each over overlapping two-hop paths, as shown in Figure 3.47. We again assume that each host uses a timeout/retransmission mechanism to implement a reliable data transfer service, that all hosts have the same value of λ_{in}, and that all router links have capacity R bytes/sec.

Let's consider the connection from Host A to Host C, passing through routers R1 and R2. The A–C connection shares router R1 with the D–B connection and shares router R2 with the B–D connection. For extremely small values of λ_{in}, buffer overflows are rare (as in congestion scenarios 1 and 2), and the throughput approximately equals the offered load. For slightly larger values of λ_{in}, the corresponding throughput is also larger, since more original data is being transmitted into the

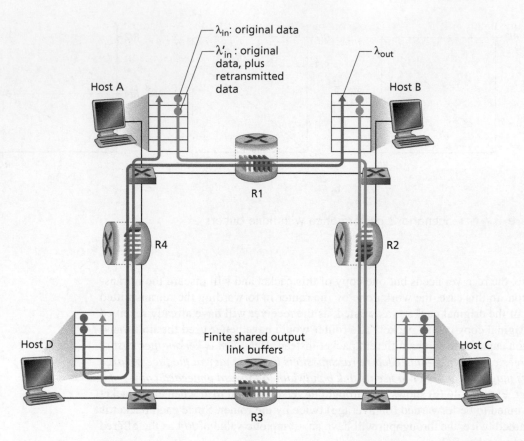

Figure 3.47 ♦ Four senders, routers with finite buffers, and multihop paths

network and delivered to the destination, and overflows are still rare. Thus, for small values of λ_{in}, an increase in λ_{in} results in an increase in λ_{out}.

Having considered the case of extremely low traffic, let's next examine the case that λ_{in} (and hence λ'_{in}) is extremely large. Consider router R2. The A–C traffic arriving to router R2 (which arrives at R2 after being forwarded from R1) can have an arrival rate at R2 that is at most R, the capacity of the link from R1 to R2, regardless of the value of λ_{in}. If λ'_{in} is extremely large for all connections (including the B–D connection), then the arrival rate of B–D traffic at R2 can be much larger than that of the A–C traffic. Because the A–C and B–D traffic must compete at router R2 for the limited amount of buffer space, the amount of A–C traffic that successfully gets through R2 (that is, is not lost due to buffer overflow) becomes smaller and smaller as the offered load from B–D gets larger and larger. In the limit, as the offered load approaches infinity, an empty buffer at R2 is immediately filled by a B–D packet, and the throughput of the A–C connection at R2 goes to zero. This, in turn, *implies that the A–C end-to-end throughput goes to zero* in the limit of heavy traffic. These considerations give rise to the offered load versus throughput tradeoff shown in Figure 3.48.

The reason for the eventual decrease in throughput with increasing offered load is evident when one considers the amount of wasted work done by the network. In the high-traffic scenario outlined above, whenever a packet is dropped at a second-hop router, the work done by the first-hop router in forwarding a packet to the second-hop router ends up being "wasted." The network would have been equally well off (more accurately, equally bad off) if the first router had simply discarded that packet and remained idle. More to the point, the transmission capacity used at the first router to forward the packet to the second router could have been much more profitably used to transmit a different packet. (For example, when selecting a packet for transmission, it might be better for a router to give priority to packets that have already traversed some number of upstream routers.) *So here we see yet another cost of dropping a packet due to congestion—when a packet is dropped along a path, the transmission capacity that was used at each of the upstream links to forward that packet to the point at which it is dropped ends up having been wasted.*

3.6.2 Approaches to Congestion Control

In Section 3.7, we'll examine TCP's specific approach to congestion control in great detail. Here, we identify the two broad approaches to congestion control that are taken in practice and discuss specific network architectures and congestion-control protocols embodying these approaches.

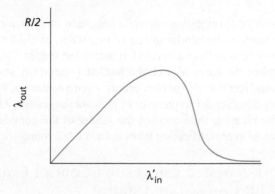

Figure 3.48 ♦ Scenario 3 performance with finite buffers and multihop paths

At the broadest level, we can distinguish among congestion-control approaches by whether the network layer provides any explicit assistance to the transport layer for congestion-control purposes:

• *End-to-end congestion control.* In an end-to-end approach to congestion control, the network layer provides *no explicit support* to the transport layer for congestion-control purposes. Even the presence of congestion in the network must be inferred by the end systems based only on observed network behavior (for example, packet loss and delay). We will see in Section 3.7 that TCP must necessarily take this end-to-end approach toward congestion control, since the IP layer provides no feedback to the end systems regarding network congestion. TCP segment loss (as indicated by a timeout or a triple duplicate acknowledgment) is taken as an indication of network congestion and TCP decreases its window size accordingly. We will also see a more recent proposal for TCP congestion control that uses increasing round-trip delay values as indicators of increased network congestion.

• *Network-assisted congestion control.* With network-assisted congestion control, network-layer components (that is, routers) provide explicit feedback to the sender regarding the congestion state in the network. This feedback may be as simple as a single bit indicating congestion at a link. This approach was taken in the early IBM SNA [Schwartz 1982] and DEC DECnet [Jain 1989; Ramakrishnan 1990] architectures, was recently proposed for TCP/IP networks [Floyd TCP 1994; RFC 3168], and is used in ATM available bit-rate (ABR) congestion control as well, as discussed below. More sophisticated network feedback is also possible. For example, one form of ATM ABR congestion control that we will study shortly allows a router to inform the sender explicitly of the transmission rate it (the router) can support on an outgoing link. The XCP protocol [Katabi 2002] provides router-computed feedback to each source, carried in the packet header, regarding how that source should increase or decrease its transmission rate.

For network-assisted congestion control, congestion information is typically fed back from the network to the sender in one of two ways, as shown in Figure 3.49. Direct feedback may be sent from a network router to the sender. This form of notification typically takes the form of a **choke packet** (essentially saying, "I'm congested!"). The second form of notification occurs when a router marks/updates a field in a packet flowing from sender to receiver to indicate congestion. Upon receipt of a marked packet, the receiver then notifies the sender of the congestion indication. Note that this latter form of notification takes at least a full round-trip time.

3.6.3 Network-Assisted Congestion-Control Example: ATM ABR Congestion Control

We conclude this section with a brief case study of the congestion-control algorithm in ATM ABR—a protocol that takes a network-assisted approach toward congestion control. We stress that our goal here is not to describe aspects of the ATM architecture

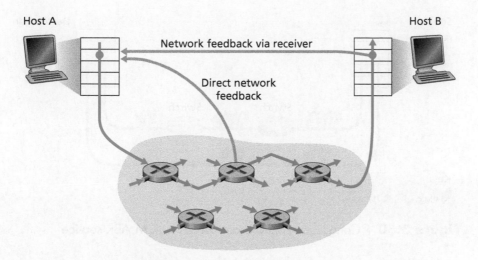

Host A   Host B

Network feedback via receiver

Direct network
feedback

Figure 3.49 ♦ Two feedback pathways for network-indicated congestion
information

in great detail, but rather to illustrate a protocol that takes a markedly different
approach toward congestion control from that of the Internet's TCP protocol. Indeed,
we only present below those few aspects of the ATM architecture that are needed to
understand ABR congestion control.

Fundamentally ATM takes a virtual-circuit (VC) oriented approach toward
packet switching. Recall from our discussion in Chapter 1, this means that each
switch on the source-to-destination path will maintain state about the source-to-
destination VC. This per-VC state allows a switch to track the behavior of individual senders (e.g., tracking their average transmission rate) and to take
source-specific congestion-control actions (such as explicitly signaling to the
sender to reduce its rate when the switch becomes congested). This per-VC state
at network switches makes ATM ideally suited to perform network-assisted congestion control.

ABR has been designed as an elastic data transfer service in a manner reminis-
cent of TCP. When the network is underloaded, ABR service should be able to take
advantage of the spare available bandwidth; when the network is congested, ABR
service should throttle its transmission rate to some predetermined minimum transmission rate. A detailed tutorial on ATM ABR congestion control and traffic management is provided in [Jain 1996].

Figure 3.50 shows the framework for ATM ABR congestion control. In our
discussion we adopt ATM terminology (for example, using the term *switch* rather
than *router*, and the term *cell* rather than *packet*). With ATM ABR service, data
cells are transmitted from a source to a destination through a series of intermediate switches. Interspersed with the data cells are **resource-management cells**

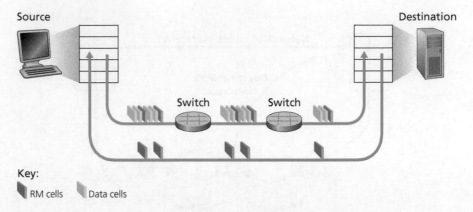

Figure 3.50 ♦ Congestion-control framework for ATM ABR service

(RM cells); these RM cells can be used to convey congestion-related information among the hosts and switches. When an RM cell arrives at a destination, it will be turned around and sent back to the sender (possibly after the destination has modified the contents of the RM cell). It is also possible for a switch to generate an RM cell itself and send this RM cell directly to a source. RM cells can thus be used to provide both direct network feedback and network feedback via the receiver, as shown in Figure 3.50.

ATM ABR congestion control is a rate-based approach. That is, the sender explicitly computes a maximum rate at which it can send and regulates itself accordingly. ABR provides three mechanisms for signaling congestion-related information from the switches to the receiver:

- *EFCI bit.* Each *data cell* contains an **explicit forward congestion indication (EFCI) bit**. A congested network switch can set the EFCI bit in a data cell to 1 to signal congestion to the destination host. The destination must check the EFCI bit in all received data cells. When an RM cell arrives at the destination, if the most recently received data cell had the EFCI bit set to 1, then the destination sets the congestion indication bit (the CI bit) of the RM cell to 1 and sends the RM cell back to the sender. Using the EFCI in data cells and the CI bit in RM cells, a sender can thus be notified about congestion at a network switch.

- *CI and NI bits.* As noted above, sender-to-receiver RM cells are interspersed with data cells. The rate of RM cell interspersion is a tunable parameter, with the default value being one RM cell every 32 data cells. These RM cells have a **congestion indication (CI) bit** and a **no increase (NI) bit** that can be set by a congested network switch. Specifically, a switch can set the NI bit in a passing RM cell to 1 under mild congestion and can set the CI bit to 1 under severe congestion conditions. When a destination host receives an RM cell, it will send the RM cell back to the sender with its CI and NI bits intact (except that CI may be set to 1 by the destination as a result of the EFCI mechanism described above).

- *ER setting.* Each RM cell also contains a 2-byte **explicit rate (ER) field**. A congested switch may lower the value contained in the ER field in a passing RM cell. In this manner, the ER field will be set to the minimum supportable rate of all switches on the source-to-destination path.

An ATM ABR source adjusts the rate at which it can send cells as a function of the CI, NI, and ER values in a returned RM cell. The rules for making this rate adjustment are rather complicated and a bit tedious. The interested reader is referred to [Jain 1996] for details.

3.7 TCP Congestion Control

In this section we return to our study of TCP. As we learned in Section 3.5, TCP provides a reliable transport service between two processes running on different hosts. Another key component of TCP is its congestion-control mechanism. As indicated in the previous section, TCP must use end-to-end congestion control rather than network-assisted congestion control, since the IP layer provides no explicit feedback to the end systems regarding network congestion.

The approach taken by TCP is to have each sender limit the rate at which it sends traffic into its connection as a function of perceived network congestion. If a TCP sender perceives that there is little congestion on the path between itself and the destination, then the TCP sender increases its send rate; if the sender perceives that there is congestion along the path, then the sender reduces its send rate. But this approach raises three questions. First, how does a TCP sender limit the rate at which it sends traffic into its connection? Second, how does a TCP sender perceive that there is congestion on the path between itself and the destination? And third, what algorithm should the sender use to change its send rate as a function of perceived end-to-end congestion?

Let's first examine how a TCP sender limits the rate at which it sends traffic into its connection. In Section 3.5 we saw that each side of a TCP connection consists of a receive buffer, a send buffer, and several variables (`LastByteRead`, `rwnd`, and so on). The TCP congestion-control mechanism operating at the sender keeps track of an additional variable, the **congestion window**. The congestion window, denoted `cwnd`, imposes a constraint on the rate at which a TCP sender can send traffic into the network. Specifically, the amount of unacknowledged data at a sender may not exceed the minimum of cwnd and rwnd, that is:

$$\texttt{LastByteSent} - \texttt{LastByteAcked} \leq \min\{\texttt{cwnd, rwnd}\}$$

In order to focus on congestion control (as opposed to flow control), let us henceforth assume that the TCP receive buffer is so large that the receive-window constraint can be ignored; thus, the amount of unacknowledged data at the sender is solely limited by cwnd. We will also assume that the sender always has data to send, i.e., that all segments in the congestion window are sent.

The constraint above limits the amount of unacknowledged data at the sender and therefore indirectly limits the sender's send rate. To see this, consider a connection for which loss and packet transmission delays are negligible. Then, roughly, at the beginning of every RTT, the constraint permits the sender to send cwnd bytes of data into the connection; at the end of the RTT the sender receives acknowledgments for the data. *Thus the sender's send rate is roughly cwnd/RTT bytes/sec. By adjusting the value of cwnd, the sender can therefore adjust the rate at which it sends data into its connection.*

Let's next consider how a TCP sender perceives that there is congestion on the path between itself and the destination. Let us define a "loss event" at a TCP sender as the occurrence of either a timeout or the receipt of three duplicate ACKs from the receiver. (Recall our discussion in Section 3.5.4 of the timeout event in Figure 3.33 and the subsequent modification to include fast retransmit on receipt of three duplicate ACKs.) When there is excessive congestion, then one (or more) router buffers along the path overflows, causing a datagram (containing a TCP segment) to be dropped. The dropped datagram, in turn, results in a loss event at the sender—either a timeout or the receipt of three duplicate ACKs—which is taken by the sender to be an indication of congestion on the sender-to-receiver path.

Having considered how congestion is detected, let's next consider the more optimistic case when the network is congestion-free, that is, when a loss event doesn't occur. In this case, acknowledgments for previously unacknowledged segments will be received at the TCP sender. As we'll see, TCP will take the arrival of these acknowledgments as an indication that all is well—that segments being transmitted into the network are being successfully delivered to the destination—and will use acknowledgments to increase its congestion window size (and hence its transmission rate). Note that if acknowledgments arrive at a relatively slow rate (e.g., if the end-end path has high delay or contains a low-bandwidth link), then the congestion window will be increased at a relatively slow rate. On the other hand, if acknowledgments arrive at a high rate, then the congestion window will be increased more quickly. Because TCP uses acknowledgments to trigger (or clock) its increase in congestion window size, TCP is said to be **self-clocking**.

Given the *mechanism* of adjusting the value of cwnd to control the sending rate, the critical question remains: *How* should a TCP sender determine the rate at which it should send? If TCP senders collectively send too fast, they can congest the network, leading to the type of congestion collapse that we saw in Figure 3.48. Indeed, the version of TCP that we'll study shortly was developed in response to observed Internet congestion collapse [Jacobson 1988] under earlier versions of TCP. However, if TCP senders are too cautious and send too slowly, they could under utilize the bandwidth in the network; that is, the TCP senders could send at a higher rate without congesting the network. How then do the TCP senders determine their sending rates such that they don't congest the network but at the same time make use of all the available bandwidth? Are TCP senders explicitly coordinated, or is there a distributed approach in which the TCP senders can set their sending rates based only on local information? TCP answers these questions using the following guiding principles:

* *A lost segment implies congestion, and hence, the TCP sender's rate should be decreased when a segment is lost.* Recall from our discussion in Section 3.5.4, that a timeout event or the receipt of four acknowledgments for a given segment (one original ACK and then three duplicate ACKs) is interpreted as an implicit "loss event" indication of the segment following the quadruply ACKed segment, triggering a retransmission of the lost segment. From a congestion-control standpoint, the question is how the TCP sender should decrease its congestion window size, and hence its sending rate, in response to this inferred loss event.

* *An acknowledged segment indicates that the network is delivering the sender's segments to the receiver, and hence, the sender's rate can be increased when an ACK arrives for a previously unacknowledged segment.* The arrival of acknowledgments is taken as an implicit indication that all is well—segments are being successfully delivered from sender to receiver, and the network is thus not congested. The congestion window size can thus be increased.

* *Bandwidth probing.* Given ACKs indicating a congestion-free source-to-destination path and loss events indicating a congested path, TCP's strategy for adjusting its transmission rate is to increase its rate in response to arriving ACKs until a loss event occurs, at which point, the transmission rate is decreased. The TCP sender thus increases its transmission rate to probe for the rate that at which congestion onset begins, backs off from that rate, and then to begins probing again to see if the congestion onset rate has changed. The TCP sender's behavior is perhaps analogous to the child who requests (and gets) more and more goodies until finally he/she is finally told "No!", backs off a bit, but then begins making requests

again shortly afterwards. Note that there is no explicit signaling of congestion state by the network—ACKs and loss events serve as implicit signals—and that each TCP sender acts on local information asynchronously from other TCP senders.

Given this overview of TCP congestion control, we're now in a position to consider the details of the celebrated **TCP congestion-control algorithm**, which was first described in [Jacobson 1988] and is standardized in [RFC 5681]. The algorithm has three major components: (1) slow start, (2) congestion avoidance, and (3) fast recovery. Slow start and congestion avoidance are mandatory components of TCP, differing in how they increase the size of cwnd in response to received ACKs. We'll see shortly that slow start increases the size of cwnd more rapidly (despite its name!) than congestion avoidance. Fast recovery is recommended, but not required, for TCP senders.

Slow Start

When a TCP connection begins, the value of cwnd is typically initialized to a small value of 1 MSS [RFC 3390], resulting in an initial sending rate of roughly MSS/RTT. For example, if MSS = 500 bytes and RTT = 200 msec, the resulting initial sending rate is only about 20 kbps. Since the available bandwidth to the TCP sender may be much larger than MSS/RTT, the TCP sender would like to find the amount of available bandwidth quickly. Thus, in the **slow-start** state, the value of cwnd begins at 1 MSS and increases by 1 MSS every time a transmitted segment is first acknowledged. In the example of Figure 3.51, TCP sends the first segment into the network and waits for an acknowledgment. When this acknowledgment arrives, the TCP sender increases the congestion window by one MSS and sends out two maximum-sized segments. These segments are then acknowledged, with the sender increasing the congestion window by 1 MSS for each of the acknowledged segments, giving a congestion window of 4 MSS, and so on. This process results in a doubling of the sending rate every RTT. Thus, the TCP send rate starts slow but grows exponentially during the slow start phase.

But when should this exponential growth end? Slow start provides several answers to this question. First, if there is a loss event (i.e., congestion) indicated by a timeout, the TCP sender sets the value of cwnd to 1 and begins the slow start process anew. It also sets the value of a second state variable, ssthresh (shorthand for "slow start threshold") to cwnd/2—half of the value of the congestion window value when congestion was detected. The second way in which slow start may end is directly tied to the value of ssthresh. Since ssthresh is half the value of cwnd when congestion was last detected, it might be a bit reckless to keep doubling cwnd when it reaches or surpasses the value of ssthresh. Thus, when the value of cwnd equals ssthresh, slow start ends and TCP transitions into congestion avoidance mode. As we'll see, TCP increases

PRINCIPLES IN PRACTICE

TCP SPLITTING: OPTIMIZING THE PERFORMANCE OF CLOUD SERVICES

For cloud services such as search, e-mail, and social networks, it is desirable to provide a high-level of responsiveness, ideally giving users the illusion that the services are running within their own end systems (including their smartphones). This can be a major challenge, as users are often located far away from the data centers that are responsible for serving the dynamic content associated with the cloud services. Indeed, if the end system is far from a data center, then the RTT will be large, potentially leading to poor response time performance due to TCP slow start.

As a case study, consider the delay in receiving a response for a search query. Typically, the server requires three TCP windows during slow start to deliver the response [Pathak 2010]. Thus the time from when an end system initiates a TCP connection until the time when it receives the last packet of the response is roughly $4 \cdot \text{RTT}$ (one RTT to set up the TCP connection plus three RTTs for the three windows of data) plus the processing time in the data center. These RTT delays can lead to a noticeable delay in returning search results for a significant fraction of queries. Moreover, there can be significant packet loss in access networks, leading to TCP retransmissions and even larger delays.

One way to mitigate this problem and improve user-perceived performance is to (1) deploy front-end servers closer to the users, and (2) utilize **TCP splitting** by breaking the TCP connection at the front-end server. With TCP splitting, the client establishes a TCP connection to the nearby front-end, and the front-end maintains a persistent TCP connection to the data center with a very large TCP congestion window [Tariq 2008, Pathak 2010, Chen 2011]. With this approach, the response time roughly becomes $4 \cdot \text{RTT}_{FE} + \text{RTT}_{BE} +$ processing time, where RTT_{FE} is the round-trip time between client and front-end server, and RTT_{BE} is the round-trip time between the front-end server and the data center (back-end server). If the front-end server is close to client, then this response time approximately becomes RTT plus processing time, since RTT_{FE} is negligibly small and RTT_{BE} is approximately RTT. In summary, TCP splitting can reduce the networking delay roughly from $4 \cdot \text{RTT}$ to RTT, significantly improving user-perceived performance, particularly for users who are far from the nearest data center. TCP splitting also helps reduce TCP retransmission delays caused by losses in access networks. Today, Google and Akamai make extensive use of their CDN servers in access networks (see Section 3.7) to perform TCP splitting for the cloud services they support [Chen 2011].

`cwnd` more cautiously when in congestion-avoidance mode. The final way in which slow start can end is if three duplicate ACKs are detected, in which case TCP performs a fast retransmit (see Section 3.5.4) and enters the fast recovery state, as discussed below. TCP's behavior in slow start is summarized in the FSM

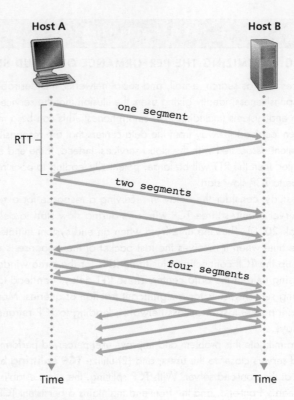

Figure 3.51 ♦ TCP slow start

description of TCP congestion control in Figure 3.52. The slow-start algorithm traces it roots to [Jacobson 1988]; an approach similar to slow start was also proposed independently in [Jain 1986].

Congestion Avoidance

On entry to the congestion-avoidance state, the value of cwnd is approximately half its value when congestion was last encountered—congestion could be just around the corner! Thus, rather than doubling the value of cwnd every RTT, TCP adopts a more conservative approach and increases the value of cwnd by just a single MSS every RTT [RFC 5681]. This can be accomplished in several ways. A common approach is for the TCP sender to increase cwnd by MSS bytes (MSS/cwnd) whenever a new acknowledgment arrives. For example, if MSS is 1,460 bytes and cwnd is 14,600 bytes, then 10 segments are being sent within an RTT. Each arriving ACK (assuming one ACK per segment) increases the congestion window size by 1/10

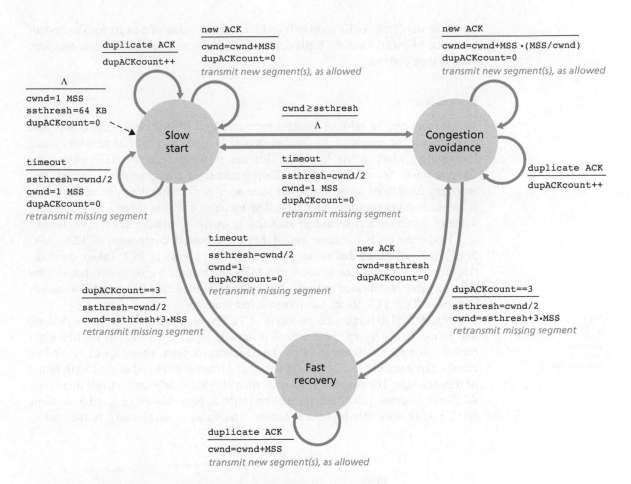

Figure 3.52 ♦ FSM description of TCP congestion control

MSS, and thus, the value of the congestion window will have increased by one MSS after ACKs when all 10 segments have been received.

But when should congestion avoidance's linear increase (of 1 MSS per RTT) end? TCP's congestion-avoidance algorithm behaves the same when a timeout occurs. As in the case of slow start: The value of `cwnd` is set to 1 MSS, and the value of `ssthresh` is updated to half the value of `cwnd` when the loss event occurred. Recall, however, that a loss event also can be triggered by a triple duplicate ACK event. In this case, the network is continuing to deliver segments from sender to receiver (as indicated by the receipt of duplicate ACKs). So TCP's behavior to this type of loss event should be less drastic than with a timeout-indicated loss: TCP halves the value of `cwnd` (adding in 3 MSS for good measure to account for the triple duplicate ACKs received) and records the value of `ssthresh` to be half the value of `cwnd` when the triple duplicate ACKs were received. The fast-recovery state is then entered.

Fast Recovery

In fast recovery, the value of `cwnd` is increased by 1 MSS for every duplicate ACK received for the missing segment that caused TCP to enter the fast-recovery state. Eventually, when an ACK arrives for the missing segment, TCP enters the congestion-avoidance state after deflating `cwnd`. If a timeout event occurs, fast recovery transitions to the slow-start state after performing the same actions as in slow start and congestion avoidance: The value of `cwnd` is set to 1 MSS, and the value of `ssthresh` is set to half the value of `cwnd` when the loss event occurred.

Fast recovery is a recommended, but not required, component of TCP [RFC 5681]. It is interesting that an early version of TCP, known as **TCP Tahoe**, unconditionally cut its congestion window to 1 MSS and entered the slow-start phase after either a timeout-indicated or triple-duplicate-ACK-indicated loss event. The newer version of TCP, **TCP Reno**, incorporated fast recovery.

Figure 3.53 illustrates the evolution of TCP's congestion window for both Reno and Tahoe. In this figure, the threshold is initially equal to 8 MSS. For the first eight transmission rounds, Tahoe and Reno take identical actions. The congestion window climbs exponentially fast during slow start and hits the threshold at the fourth round of transmission. The congestion window then climbs linearly until a triple duplicate-ACK event occurs, just after transmission round 8. Note that the congestion window is 12 • *MSS* when this loss event occurs. The value of `ssthresh` is then set to

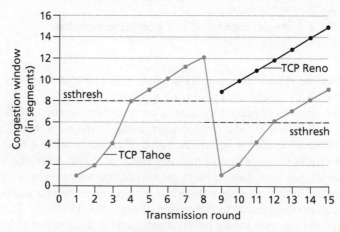

Figure 3.53 ♦ Evolution of TCP's congestion window (Tahoe and Reno)

$0.5 \cdot$ cwnd $= 6 \cdot$ MSS. Under TCP Reno, the congestion window is set to cwnd $= 6 \cdot$ MSS and then grows linearly. Under TCP Tahoe, the congestion window is set to 1 MSS and grows exponentially until it reaches the value of ssthresh, at which point it grows linearly.

Figure 3.52 presents the complete FSM description of TCP's congestion-control algorithms—slow start, congestion avoidance, and fast recovery. The figure also indicates where transmission of new segments or retransmitted segments can occur. Although it is important to distinguish between TCP error control/retransmission and TCP congestion control, it's also important to appreciate how these two aspects of TCP are inextricably linked.

TCP Congestion Control: Retrospective

Having delved into the details of slow start, congestion avoidance, and fast recovery, it's worthwhile to now step back and view the forest from the trees. Ignoring the initial slow-start period when a connection begins and assuming that losses are indicated by triple duplicate ACKs rather than timeouts, TCP's congestion control consists of linear (additive) increase in cwnd of 1 MSS per RTT and then a halving (multiplicative decrease) of cwnd on a triple duplicate-ACK event. For this reason, TCP congestion control is often referred to as an **additive-increase, multiplicative-decrease (AIMD)** form of congestion control. AIMD congestion control gives rise to the "saw tooth" behavior shown in Figure 3.54, which also nicely illustrates our earlier intuition of TCP "probing" for bandwidth—TCP linearly increases its congestion window size (and hence its transmission rate) until a triple duplicate-ACK event occurs. It then decreases its congestion window size by a factor of two but then again begins increasing it linearly, probing to see if there is additional available bandwidth.

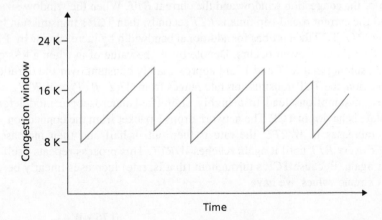

Time

Figure 3.54 ◆ Additive-increase, multiplicative-decrease congestion control

As noted previously, many TCP implementations use the Reno algorithm [Padhye 2001]. Many variations of the Reno algorithm have been proposed [RFC 3782; RFC 2018]. The TCP Vegas algorithm [Brakmo 1995; Ahn 1995] attempts to avoid congestion while maintaining good throughput. The basic idea of Vegas is to (1) detect congestion in the routers between source and destination *before* packet loss occurs, and (2) lower the rate linearly when this imminent packet loss is detected. Imminent packet loss is predicted by observing the RTT. The longer the RTT of the packets, the greater the congestion in the routers. Linux supports a number of congestion-control algorithms (including TCP Reno and TCP Vegas) and allows a system administrator to configure which version of TCP will be used. The default version of TCP in Linux version 2.6.18 was set to CUBIC [Ha 2008], a version of TCP developed for high-bandwidth applications. For a recent survey of the many flavors of TCP, see [Afanasyev 2010].

TCP's AIMD algorithm was developed based on a tremendous amount of engineering insight and experimentation with congestion control in operational networks. Ten years after TCP's development, theoretical analyses showed that TCP's congestion-control algorithm serves as a distributed asynchronous-optimization algorithm that results in several important aspects of user and network performance being simultaneously optimized [Kelly 1998]. A rich theory of congestion control has since been developed [Srikant 2004].

Macroscopic Description of TCP Throughput

Given the saw-toothed behavior of TCP, it's natural to consider what the average throughput (that is, the average rate) of a long-lived TCP connection might be. In this analysis we'll ignore the slow-start phases that occur after timeout events. (These phases are typically very short, since the sender grows out of the phase exponentially fast.) During a particular round-trip interval, the rate at which TCP sends data is a function of the congestion window and the current *RTT*. When the window size is *w* bytes and the current round-trip time is *RTT* second*s*, then TCP's transmission rate is roughly *w/RTT*. TCP then probes for additional bandwidth by increasing *w* by 1 MSS each *RTT* until a loss event occurs. Denote by *W* the value of *w* when a loss event occurs. Assuming that *RTT* and *W* are approximately constant over the duration of the connection, the TCP transmission rate ranges from $W/(2 \cdot RTT)$ to *W/RTT*.

These assumptions lead to a highly simplified macroscopic model for the steady-state behavior of TCP. The network drops a packet from the connection when the rate increases to *W/RTT;* the rate is then cut in half and then increases by MSS/*RTT* every *RTT* until it again reaches *W/RTT*. This process repeats itself over and over again. Because TCP's throughput (that is, rate) increases linearly between the two extreme values, we have

$$\text{average throughput of a connection} = \frac{0.75 \cdot W}{RTT}$$

Using this highly idealized model for the steady-state dynamics of TCP, we can also derive an interesting expression that relates a connection's loss rate to its available bandwidth [Mahdavi 1997]. This derivation is outlined in the homework problems. A more sophisticated model that has been found empirically to agree with measured data is [Padhye 2000].

TCP Over High-Bandwidth Paths

It is important to realize that TCP congestion control has evolved over the years and indeed continues to evolve. For a summary of current TCP variants and discussion of TCP evolution, see [Floyd 2001, RFC 5681, Afanasyev 2010]. What was good for the Internet when the bulk of the TCP connections carried SMTP, FTP, and Telnet traffic is not necessarily good for today's HTTP-dominated Internet or for a future Internet with services that are still undreamed of.

The need for continued evolution of TCP can be illustrated by considering the high-speed TCP connections that are needed for grid- and cloud-computing applications. For example, consider a TCP connection with 1,500-byte segments and a 100 ms *RTT*, and suppose we want to send data through this connection at 10 Gbps. Following [RFC 3649], we note that using the TCP throughput formula above, in order to achieve a 10 Gbps throughput, the average congestion window size would need to be 83,333 segments. That's a *lot* of segments, leading us to be rather concerned that one of these 83,333 in-flight segments might be lost. What would happen in the case of a loss? Or, put another way, what fraction of the transmitted segments could be lost that would allow the TCP congestion-control algorithm specified in Figure 3.52 still to achieve the desired 10 Gbps rate? In the homework questions for this chapter, you are led through the derivation of a formula relating the throughput of a TCP connection as a function of the loss rate (L), the round-trip time (RTT), and the maximum segment size (MSS):

$$\text{average throughput of a connection} = \frac{1.22 \cdot MSS}{RTT \sqrt{L}}$$

Using this formula, we can see that in order to achieve a throughput of 10 Gbps, today's TCP congestion-control algorithm can only tolerate a segment loss probability of $2 \cdot 10^{-10}$ (or equivalently, one loss event for every 5,000,000,000 segments)—a very low rate. This observation has led a number of researchers to investigate new versions of TCP that are specifically designed for such high-speed environments; see [Jin 2004; RFC 3649; Kelly 2003; Ha 2008] for discussions of these efforts.

3.7.1 Fairness

Consider K TCP connections, each with a different end-to-end path, but all passing through a bottleneck link with transmission rate R bps. (By *bottleneck link*, we mean that for each connection, all the other links along the connection's path are not congested and have abundant transmission capacity as compared with the transmission capacity of the bottleneck link.) Suppose each connection is transferring a large file and there is no UDP traffic passing through the bottleneck link. A congestion-control mechanism is said to be *fair* if the average transmission rate of each connection is approximately R/K; that is, each connection gets an equal share of the link bandwidth.

Is TCP's AIMD algorithm fair, particularly given that different TCP connections may start at different times and thus may have different window sizes at a given point in time? [Chiu 1989] provides an elegant and intuitive explanation of why TCP congestion control converges to provide an equal share of a bottleneck link's bandwidth among competing TCP connections.

Let's consider the simple case of two TCP connections sharing a single link with transmission rate R, as shown in Figure 3.55. Assume that the two connections have the same MSS and RTT (so that if they have the same congestion window size, then they have the same throughput), that they have a large amount of data to send, and that no other TCP connections or UDP datagrams traverse this shared link. Also, ignore the slow-start phase of TCP and assume the TCP connections are operating in CA mode (AIMD) at all times.

Figure 3.56 plots the throughput realized by the two TCP connections. If TCP is to share the link bandwidth equally between the two connections, then the realized throughput should fall along the 45-degree arrow (equal bandwidth share) emanating from the origin. Ideally, the sum of the two throughputs should equal R. (Certainly, each connection receiving an equal, but zero, share of the link capacity is not a desirable situation!) So the goal should be to have the achieved throughputs fall somewhere near the intersection of the equal bandwidth share line and the full bandwidth utilization line in Figure 3.56.

Suppose that the TCP window sizes are such that at a given point in time, connections 1 and 2 realize throughputs indicated by point A in Figure 3.56. Because the amount of link bandwidth jointly consumed by the two connections is less than

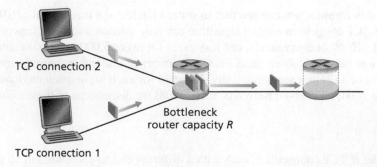

TCP connection 2

TCP connection 1

Bottleneck router capacity R

Figure 3.55 ♦ Two TCP connections sharing a single bottleneck link

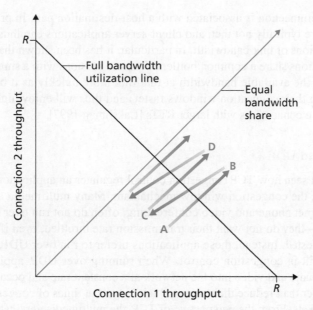

Figure 3.56 ♦ Throughput realized by TCP connections 1 and 2

R, no loss will occur, and both connections will increase their window by 1 MSS per RTT as a result of TCP's congestion-avoidance algorithm. Thus, the joint throughput of the two connections proceeds along a 45-degree line (equal increase for both connections) starting from point *A*. Eventually, the link bandwidth jointly consumed by the two connections will be greater than *R,* and eventually packet loss will occur. Suppose that connections 1 and 2 experience packet loss when they realize throughputs indicated by point *B*. Connections 1 and 2 then decrease their windows by a factor of two. The resulting throughputs realized are thus at point *C,* halfway along a vector starting at *B* and ending at the origin. Because the joint bandwidth use is less than *R* at point *C,* the two connections again increase their throughputs along a 45-degree line starting from *C*. Eventually, loss will again occur, for example, at point *D,* and the two connections again decrease their window sizes by a factor of two, and so on. You should convince yourself that the bandwidth realized by the two connections eventually fluctuates along the equal bandwidth share line. You should also convince yourself that the two connections will converge to this behavior regardless of where they are in the two-dimensional space! Although a number of idealized assumptions lie behind this scenario, it still provides an intuitive feel for why TCP results in an equal sharing of bandwidth among connections.

In our idealized scenario, we assumed that only TCP connections traverse the bottleneck link, that the connections have the same RTT value, and that only a single TCP connection is associated with a host-destination pair. In practice, these conditions are typically not met, and client-server applications can thus obtain very unequal portions of link bandwidth. In particular, it has been shown that when multiple connections share a common bottleneck, those sessions with a smaller RTT are able to grab the available bandwidth at that link more quickly as it becomes free (that is, open their congestion windows faster) and thus will enjoy higher throughput than those connections with larger RTTs [Lakshman 1997].

Fairness and UDP

We have just seen how TCP congestion control regulates an application's transmission rate via the congestion window mechanism. Many multimedia applications, such as Internet phone and video conferencing, often do not run over TCP for this very reason—they do not want their transmission rate throttled, even if the network is very congested. Instead, these applications prefer to run over UDP, which does not have built-in congestion control. When running over UDP, applications can pump their audio and video into the network at a constant rate and occasionally lose packets, rather than reduce their rates to "fair" levels at times of congestion and not lose any packets. From the perspective of TCP, the multimedia applications running over UDP are not being fair—they do not cooperate with the other connections nor adjust their transmission rates appropriately. Because TCP congestion control will decrease its transmission rate in the face of increasing congestion (loss), while UDP sources need not, it is possible for UDP sources to crowd out TCP traffic. An area of research today is thus the development of congestion-control mechanisms for the Internet that prevent UDP traffic from bringing the Internet's throughput to a grinding halt [Floyd 1999; Floyd 2000; Kohler 2006].

Fairness and Parallel TCP Connections

But even if we could force UDP traffic to behave fairly, the fairness problem would still not be completely solved. This is because there is nothing to stop a TCP-based application from using multiple parallel connections. For example, Web browsers often use multiple parallel TCP connections to transfer the multiple objects within a Web page. (The exact number of multiple connections is configurable in most browsers.) When an application uses multiple parallel connections, it gets a larger fraction of the bandwidth in a congested link. As an example, consider a link of rate R supporting nine ongoing client-server applications, with each of the applications using one TCP connection. If a new application comes along and also uses one TCP connection, then each application gets approximately the same transmission rate of $R/10$. But if this new application instead uses 11 parallel TCP connections, then the new application gets an unfair allocation of more than $R/2$. Because Web traffic is so pervasive in the Internet, multiple parallel connections are not uncommon.

3.8 Summary

We began this chapter by studying the services that a transport-layer protocol can provide to network applications. At one extreme, the transport-layer protocol can be very simple and offer a no-frills service to applications, providing only a multiplexing/demultiplexing function for communicating processes. The Internet's UDP protocol is an example of such a no-frills transport-layer protocol. At the other extreme, a transport-layer protocol can provide a variety of guarantees to applications, such as reliable delivery of data, delay guarantees, and bandwidth guarantees. Nevertheless, the services that a transport protocol can provide are often constrained by the service model of the underlying network-layer protocol. If the network-layer protocol cannot provide delay or bandwidth guarantees to transport-layer segments, then the transport-layer protocol cannot provide delay or bandwidth guarantees for the messages sent between processes.

We learned in Section 3.4 that a transport-layer protocol can provide reliable data transfer even if the underlying network layer is unreliable. We saw that providing reliable data transfer has many subtle points, but that the task can be accomplished by carefully combining acknowledgments, timers, retransmissions, and sequence numbers.

Although we covered reliable data transfer in this chapter, we should keep in mind that reliable data transfer can be provided by link-, network-, transport-, or application-layer protocols. Any of the upper four layers of the protocol stack can implement acknowledgments, timers, retransmissions, and sequence numbers and provide reliable data transfer to the layer above. In fact, over the years, engineers and computer scientists have independently designed and implemented link-, network-, transport-, and application-layer protocols that provide reliable data transfer (although many of these protocols have quietly disappeared).

In Section 3.5, we took a close look at TCP, the Internet's connection-oriented and reliable transport-layer protocol. We learned that TCP is complex, involving connection management, flow control, and round-trip time estimation, as well as reliable data transfer. In fact, TCP is actually more complex than our description—we intentionally did not discuss a variety of TCP patches, fixes, and improvements that are widely implemented in various versions of TCP. All of this complexity, however, is hidden from the network application. If a client on one host wants to send data reliably to a server on another host, it simply opens a TCP socket to the server and pumps data into that socket. The client-server application is blissfully unaware of TCP's complexity.

In Section 3.6, we examined congestion control from a broad perspective, and in Section 3.7, we showed how TCP implements congestion control. We learned that congestion control is imperative for the well-being of the network. Without congestion control, a network can easily become gridlocked, with little or no data being transported end-to-end. In Section 3.7 we learned that TCP implements an end-to-end congestion-control mechanism that additively increases its transmission rate when the TCP connection's path is judged to be congestion-free, and multiplicatively decreases its transmission rate when loss occurs. This mechanism also strives to give each TCP connection passing through a congested link an equal share of the link bandwidth. We also examined in some depth the impact of TCP connection establishment and slow start on latency. We observed that in many important scenarios, connection establishment and slow start significantly contribute to end-to-end delay. We emphasize once more that while TCP congestion control has evolved over the years, it remains an area of intensive research and will likely continue to evolve in the upcoming years.

Our discussion of specific Internet transport protocols in this chapter has focused on UDP and TCP—the two "work horses" of the Internet transport layer. However, two decades of experience with these two protocols has identified circumstances in which neither is ideally suited. Researchers have thus been busy developing additional transport-layer protocols, several of which are now IETF proposed standards.

The Datagram Congestion Control Protocol (DCCP) [RFC 4340] provides a low-overhead, message-oriented, UDP-like unreliable service, but with an application-selected form of congestion control that is compatible with TCP. If reliable or semi-reliable data transfer is needed by an application, then this would be performed within the application itself, perhaps using the mechanisms we have studied in Section 3.4. DCCP is envisioned for use in applications such as streaming media (see Chapter 7) that can exploit the tradeoff between timeliness and reliability of data delivery, but that want to be responsive to network congestion.

The Stream Control Transmission Protocol (SCTP) [RFC 4960, RFC 3286] is a reliable, message-oriented protocol that allows several different application-level "streams" to be multiplexed through a single SCTP connection (an approach known as "multi-streaming"). From a reliability standpoint, the different streams within the connection are handled separately, so that packet loss in one stream does not affect the delivery of data in other streams. SCTP also allows data to be transferred over two outgoing paths when a host is connected to two or more networks, optional delivery of out-of-order data, and a number of other features. SCTP's flow- and congestion-control algorithms are essentially the same as in TCP.

The TCP-Friendly Rate Control (TFRC) protocol [RFC 5348] is a congestion-control protocol rather than a full-fledged transport-layer protocol. It specifies a congestion-control mechanism that could be used in anther transport protocol such as DCCP (indeed one of the two application-selectable protocols available in DCCP is TFRC). The goal of TFRC is to smooth out the "saw tooth" behavior (see Figure 3.54) in TCP congestion control, while maintaining a long-term sending rate that is "reasonably" close to that of TCP. With a smoother sending rate than TCP, TFRC is well-suited for multimedia applications such as IP telephony or streaming media where such a smooth rate is important. TFRC is an "equation-based" protocol that uses the measured packet loss rate as input to an equation [Padhye 2000] that estimates what TCP's throughput would be if a TCP session experiences that loss rate. This rate is then taken as TFRC's target sending rate.

Only the future will tell whether DCCP, SCTP, or TFRC will see widespread deployment. While these protocols clearly provide enhanced capabilities over TCP and UDP, TCP and UDP have proven themselves "good enough" over the years. Whether "better" wins out over "good enough" will depend on a complex mix of technical, social, and business considerations.

In Chapter 1, we said that a computer network can be partitioned into the "network edge" and the "network core." The network edge covers everything that happens in the end systems. Having now covered the application layer and the transport layer, our discussion of the network edge is complete. It is time to explore the network core! This journey begins in the next chapter, where we'll study the network layer, and continues into Chapter 5, where we'll study the link layer.

 # Homework Problems and Questions

Chapter 3 Review Questions

SECTIONS 3.1–3.3

R1. Suppose the network layer provides the following service. The network layer in the source host accepts a segment of maximum size 1,200 bytes and a destination host address from the transport layer. The network layer then guarantees to deliver the segment to the transport layer at the destination host. Suppose many network application processes can be running at the destination host.

   a. Design the simplest possible transport-layer protocol that will get application data to the desired process at the destination host. Assume the operating system in the destination host has assigned a 4-byte port number to each running application process.

   b. Modify this protocol so that it provides a "return address" to the destination process.

   c. In your protocols, does the transport layer "have to do anything" in the core of the computer network?

R2. Consider a planet where everyone belongs to a family of six, every family lives in its own house, each house has a unique address, and each person in a given house has a unique name. Suppose this planet has a mail service that delivers letters from source house to destination house. The mail service requires that (1) the letter be in an envelope, and that (2) the address of the destination house (and nothing more) be clearly written on the envelope. Suppose each family has a delegate family member who collects and distributes letters for the other family members. The letters do not necessarily provide any indication of the recipients of the letters.

    a. Using the solution to Problem R1 above as inspiration, describe a protocol that the delegates can use to deliver letters from a sending family member to a receiving family member.

    b. In your protocol, does the mail service ever have to open the envelope and examine the letter in order to provide its service?

R3. Consider a TCP connection between Host A and Host B. Suppose that the TCP segments traveling from Host A to Host B have source port number 37 and destination port number 61. What are the source and destination port numbers for the segments traveling from Host B to Host A?

R4. For IP Telephony and IP Videoconferencing, which one of TCP and UDP would be preferable? Justify your answer.

R5. Compare the size of overheads between TCP and UDP.

R6. When an application runs over UDP, which layer takes the extra overhead to ensure reliability of the data?

R7. Suppose a process in Host C has a UDP socket with port number 6789. Suppose both Host A and Host B each send a UDP segment to Host C with destination port number 6789. Will both of these segments be directed to the same socket at Host C? If so, how will the process at Host C know that these two segments originated from two different hosts?

R8. Suppose that a Web server runs in Host C on port 80. Suppose this Web server uses persistent connections, and is currently receiving requests from two different Hosts, A and B. Are all of the requests being sent through the same socket at Host C? If they are being passed through different sockets, do both of the sockets have port 80? Discuss and explain.

SECTION 3.4

R9. What is the meaning of positive and negative acknowledgements?

R10. List the three possibilities for handling corrupted ACKs or NAKs, in `rdt` protocol.

R11. With the help of FSM, describe the two states of the sender side and one state of the receiver side of `rdt 2.0`.

R12. Visit the Go-Back-N Java applet at the companion Web site.

    a. Have the source send five packets, and then pause the animation before any of the five packets reach the destination. Then kill the first packet and resume the animation. Describe what happens.

    b. Repeat the experiment, but now let the first packet reach the destination and kill the first acknowledgment. Describe again what happens.

    c. Finally, try sending six packets. What happens?

R13. Repeat R12, but now with the Selective Repeat Java applet. How are Selective Repeat and Go-Back-N different?

SECTION 3.5

R14. True or false?

a. Host A is sending Host B a large file over a TCP connection. Assume Host B has no data to send Host A. Host B will not send acknowledgments to Host A because Host B cannot piggyback the acknowledgments on data.

b. The size of the TCP `rwnd` never changes throughout the duration of the connection.

c. Suppose Host A is sending Host B a large file over a TCP connection. The number of unacknowledged bytes that A sends cannot exceed the size of the receive buffer.

d. Suppose Host A is sending a large file to Host B over a TCP connection. If the sequence number for a segment of this connection is m, then the sequence number for the subsequent segment will necessarily be $m + 1$.

e. The TCP segment has a field in its header for `rwnd`.

f. Suppose that the last `SampleRTT` in a TCP connection is equal to 1 sec. The current value of `TimeoutInterval` for the connection will necessarily be ≥ 1 sec.

g. Suppose Host A sends one segment with sequence number 38 and 4 bytes of data over a TCP connection to Host B. In this same segment the acknowledgment number is necessarily 42.

R15. Suppose Host A sends two TCP segments back to back to Host B over a TCP connection. The first segment has sequence number 65; the second has sequence number 92.

a. How much data is in the first segment?

b. Suppose that the first segment is lost but the second segment arrives at B. In the acknowledgment that Host B sends to Host A, what will be the acknowledgment number?

R16. Why does TCP protocol run only in the end systems and not in the intermediate network elements, routers and link layer switches?

SECTION 3.7

R17. Suppose two TCP connections are present over some bottleneck link of rate R bps. Both connections have a huge file to send (in the same direction over the bottleneck link). The transmissions of the files start at the same time. What transmission rate would TCP like to give to each of the connections?

R18. Why is TCP congestion control often referred to as an additive-increase, multiplicative decrease (AIMD) form of congestion control?

R19. TCP congestion control decreases its transmission rate in the face of increasing congestion (loss), while UDP sources need not, and it is possible for UDP sources to crowd out TCP traffic. Does it mean that TCP is fairer than UDP?

 Problems

P1. Suppose Client A initiates a Telnet session with Server S. At about the same time, Client B also initiates a Telnet session with Server S. Provide possible source and destination port numbers for

a. The segments sent from A to S.

b. The segments sent from B to S.

c. The segments sent from S to A.

d. The segments sent from S to B.

e. If A and B are different hosts, is it possible that the source port number in the segments from A to S is the same as that from B to S?

f. How about if they are the same host?

P2. Consider Figure 3.5. What are the source and destination port values in the segments flowing from the server back to the clients' processes? What are the IP addresses in the network-layer datagrams carrying the transport-layer segments?

P3. UDP and TCP use 1s complement for their checksums. Suppose you have the following three 8-bit bytes: 00100011, 01001110, 01010100. What is the 1s complement of the sum of these 8-bit bytes? (Note that although UDP and TCP use 16-bit words in computing the checksum, for this problem you are being asked to consider 8-bit sums.) Show all work. With the 1s complement scheme, how does the receiver detect errors? Is it possible that a 1-bit error will go undetected? How about a 2-bit error?

P4. a. Suppose you have the following 2 bytes: 11000100 and 00100100. What is the 1s complement of the sum of these 2 bytes?

b. Suppose you have the following 2 bytes: 01001010 and 10100101. What is the 1s complement of the sum of these 2 bytes?

c. If 1s complement of the two bytes in (a) are added, what will be the 1s complement of the sum?

P5. Suppose that the UDP receiver computes the Internet checksum for the received UDP segment and finds that it matches the value carried in the checksum field. Describe a scenario in which bit errors occur, but the receiver cannot detect that error has occurred.

P6. The receive window, denoted by variable `rwnd`, as shown in Fig. 3.38, is set to the amount of spare room in the buffer, i.e. `rwnd` = `RcvBuffer` − [`LastByteRcvd` − `LastByteRead`]. How does the connection use the variable `rwnd` to provide the flow-control service?

P7. Refer to Problem P6. Suppose that Host B's receive buffer becomes full so that `rwnd` = 0. Assume that after advertising `rwnd` = 0 to Host A, B has nothing to send to A. Since TCP sends a segment to Host A only if it has data to send or if it has an acknowledgment to send, Host A is never informed that some space has opened up in Host B's receive buffer. Hence, Host A is blocked and can transmit no more data! How can this problem be solved?

P8. Draw the FSM for the receiver side of protocol `rdt3.0`.

P9. Give a trace of the operation of protocol `rdt3.0` when data packets and acknowledgment packets are garbled. Your trace should be similar to that used in Figure 3.16.

P10. Consider a channel that can lose packets but has a maximum delay that is known. Modify protocol `rdt2.1` to include sender timeout and retransmit. Informally argue why your protocol can communicate correctly over this channel.

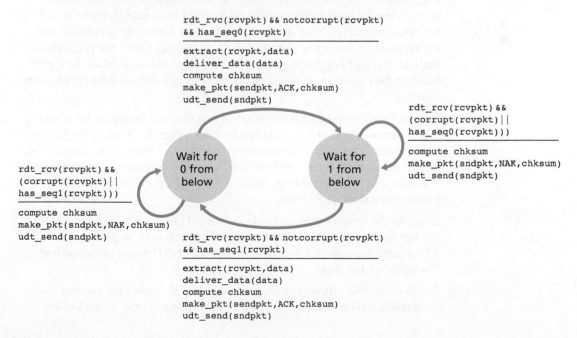

Figure 3.57 ♦ An incorrect receiver for protocol `rdt 2.1`

P11. Consider the `rdt2.2` receiver in Figure 3.14, and the creation of a new packet in the self-transition (i.e., the transition from the state back to itself) in the Wait-for-0-from-below and the Wait-for-1-from-below states: `sndpkt=make_pkt(ACK,1,checksum)` and `sndpkt=make_pkt(ACK,0,checksum)`. Would the protocol work correctly if this action were removed from the self-transition in the Wait-for-1-from-below state? Justify your answer. What if this event were removed from the self-transition in the Wait-for-0-from-below state? [*Hint*: In this latter case, consider what would happen if the first sender-to-receiver packet were corrupted.]

P12. The sender side of `rdt3.0` simply ignores (that is, takes no action on) all received packets that are either in error or have the wrong value in the `acknum` field of an acknowledgment packet. Suppose that in such circumstances, `rdt3.0` were simply to retransmit the current data packet. Would the protocol still work? (*Hint*: Consider what would happen if there were only bit errors; there are no packet losses but premature timeouts can occur. Consider how many times the *n*th packet is sent, in the limit as *n* approaches infinity.)

P13. Consider the `rdt 3.0` protocol. Draw a diagram showing that if the network connection between the sender and receiver can reorder messages (that is, that two messages propagating in the medium between the sender and receiver can be reordered), then the alternating-bit protocol will not work correctly (make sure you clearly identify the sense in which it will not work correctly). Your diagram should have the sender on the left and the receiver on the right, with the time axis running down the page, showing data (D) and acknowledgment (A) message exchange. Make sure you indicate the sequence number associated with any data or acknowledgment segment.

P14. Consider a reliable data transfer protocol that uses only negative acknowledgments. Suppose the sender sends data only infrequently. Would a NAK-only protocol be preferable to a protocol that uses ACKs? Why? Now suppose the sender has a lot of data to send and the end-to-end connection experiences few losses. In this second case, would a NAK-only protocol be preferable to a protocol that uses ACKs? Why?

P15. Consider the cross-country example shown in Figure 3.17. How big would the window size have to be for the channel utilization to be greater than 97 percent? Suppose that the size of a packet is 1,200 bytes, including both header fields and data.

P16. Either of the two processes participating in a TCP connection can end the connection. When a connection ends, the "resources" (that is, the buffers and variables) in the hosts are deallocated. Suppose the client decides to close the connection. Describe the sequence of steps that follow to end this connection.

P17. Consider two network entities, A and B, which are connected by a perfect bi-directional channel (i.e., any message sent will be received correctly; the channel will not corrupt, lose, or re-order packets). A and B are to deliver data messages to each other in an alternating manner: First, A must deliver a message to B, then B must deliver a message to A, then A must deliver a message to B and so on. If an entity is in a state where it should not attempt to deliver a message to the other side, and there is an event like `rdt_send(data)` call from above that attempts to pass data down for transmission to the other side, this call from above can simply be ignored with a call to `rdt_unable_to_send(data)`, which informs the higher layer that it is currently not able to send data. [Note: This simplifying assumption is made so you don't have to worry about buffering data.]

Draw a FSM specification for this protocol (one FSM for A, and one FSM for B!). Note that you do not have to worry about a reliability mechanism here; the main point of this question is to create a FSM specification that reflects the synchronized behavior of the two entities. You should use the following events and actions that have the same meaning as protocol rdt1.0 in Figure 3.9: `rdt_send(data)`, `packet = make_pkt(data)`, `udt_send(packet)`, `rdt_rcv(packet)`, `extract(packet,data)`, `deliver_data(data)`. Make sure your protocol reflects the strict alternation of sending between A and B. Also, make sure to indicate the initial states for A and B in your FSM descriptions.

P18. In the generic SR protocol that we studied in Section 3.4.4, the sender transmits a message as soon as it is available (if it is in the window) without waiting for an acknowledgment. Suppose now that we want an SR protocol that sends messages two at a time. That is, the sender will send a pair of messages and will send the next pair of messages only when it knows that both messages in the first pair have been received correctly.

Suppose that the channel may lose messages but will not corrupt or reorder messages. Design an error-control protocol for the unidirectional reliable transfer of messages. Give an FSM description of the sender and receiver. Describe the format of the packets sent between sender and receiver, and vice versa. If you use any procedure calls other than those in Section 3.4 (for example, `udt_send()`, `start_timer()`, `rdt_rcv()`, and so on), clearly state their actions. Give an example (a timeline trace of sender and receiver) showing how your protocol recovers from a lost packet.

P19. Consider a scenario in which Host A wants to simultaneously send packets to Hosts B and C. A is connected to B and C via a broadcast channel—a packet sent by A is carried by the channel to both B and C. Suppose that the broad-cast channel connecting A, B, and C can independently lose and corrupt packets (and so, for example, a packet sent from A might be correctly received by B, but not by C). Design a stop-and-wait-like error-control proto-col for reliably transferring packets from A to B and C, such that A will not get new data from the upper layer until it knows that both B and C have cor-rectly received the current packet. Give FSM descriptions of A and C. (*Hint:* The FSM for B should be essentially the same as for C.) Also, give a descrip-tion of the packet format(s) used.

P20. Consider a scenario in which Host A and Host B want to send messages to Host C. Hosts A and C are connected by a channel that can lose and corrupt (but not reorder) messages. Hosts B and C are connected by another chan-nel (independent of the channel connecting A and C) with the same proper-ties. The transport layer at Host C should alternate in delivering messages from A and B to the layer above (that is, it should first deliver the data from a packet from A, then the data from a packet from B, and so on). Design a stop-and-wait-like error-control protocol for reliably transferring packets from A and B to C, with alternating delivery at C as described above. Give FSM descriptions of A and C. (*Hint:* The FSM for B should be essentially the same as for A.) Also, give a description of the packet format(s) used.

P21. Suppose we have two network entities, A and B. B has a supply of data mes-sages that will be sent to A according to the following conventions. When A gets a request from the layer above to get the next data (D) message from B, A must send a request (R) message to B on the A-to-B channel. Only when B receives an R message can it send a data (D) message back to A on the B-to-A channel. A should deliver exactly one copy of each D message to the layer above. R messages can be lost (but not corrupted) in the A-to-B channel; D messages, once sent, are always delivered correctly. The delay along both channels is unknown and variable.

Design (give an FSM description of) a protocol that incorporates the appro-priate mechanisms to compensate for the loss-prone A-to-B channel and implements message passing to the layer above at entity A, as discussed above. Use only those mechanisms that are absolutely necessary.

P22. Consider the GBN protocol with a sender window size of 4 and a sequence number range of 1,024. Suppose that at time t, the next in-order packet that the receiver is expecting has a sequence number of k. Assume that the medium does not reorder messages. Answer the following questions:

a. What are the possible sets of sequence numbers inside the sender's win-dow at time t? Justify your answer.

b. What are all possible values of the ACK field in all possible messages cur-rently propagating back to the sender at time t? Justify your answer.

P23. Consider the GBN and SR protocols. Suppose the sequence number space is of size k. What is the largest allowable sender window that will avoid the occurrence of problems such as that in Figure 3.27 for each of these protocols?

P24. When both the client and server are prepared to communicate, i.e., that the server is listening on the port to which the client sends its SYN segment, TCP connection can be easily established. Now, consider what happens when a host receives a TCP segment whose port numbers or source IP address do not match with any of the ongoing sockets in the host. For example, suppose a host receives a TCP SYN packet with destination port 80, but the host is not accepting connections on port 80 (that is, it is not running a Web server on port 80). What will happen in this case?

P25. Consider the same situation as described in Problem P24. However, the protocol is UDP, instead of TCP. Describe what will happen.

P26. Consider transferring an enormous file of L bytes from Host A to Host B. Assume an MSS of 512 bytes.

    a. What is the maximum value of L such that TCP sequence numbers are not exhausted? Recall that the TCP sequence number field has 4 bytes.

    b. For the L you obtain in (a), find how long it takes to transmit the file. Assume that a total of 64 bytes of transport, network, and data-link header are added to each segment before the resulting packet is sent out over a 156 Mbps link. Ignore flow control and congestion control so A can pump out the segments back to back and continuously.

P27. Host A and B are communicating over a TCP connection, and Host B has already received from A all bytes up through byte 126. Suppose Host A then sends two segments to Host B back-to-back. The first and second segments contain 80 and 40 bytes of data, respectively. In the first segment, the sequence number is 127, the source port number is 302, and the destination port number is 80. Host B sends an acknowledgment whenever it receives a segment from Host A.

    a. In the second segment sent from Host A to B, what are the sequence number, source port number, and destination port number?

    b. If the first segment arrives before the second segment, in the acknowledgment of the first arriving segment, what is the acknowledgment number, the source port number, and the destination port number?

c. If the second segment arrives before the first segment, in the acknowledgment of the first arriving segment, what is the acknowledgment number?

d. Suppose the two segments sent by A arrive in order at B. The first acknowledgment is lost and the second acknowledgment arrives after the first timeout interval. Draw a timing diagram, showing these segments and all other segments and acknowledgments sent. (Assume there is no additional packet loss.) For each segment in your figure, provide the sequence number and the number of bytes of data; for each acknowledgment that you add, provide the acknowledgment number.

P28. Host A and B are directly connected with a 80 Mbps link. There is one TCP connection between the two hosts, and Host A is sending to Host B an enormous file over this connection. Host A can send its application data into its TCP socket at a rate as high as 100 Mbps but Host B can read out of its TCP receive buffer at a maximum rate of 40 Mbps. Describe the effect of TCP flow control.

P29. That packets cannot be reordered within the channel between the sender and receiver is generally a reasonable assumption when the sender and receiver are connected by a single physical wire. However, when the "channel" connecting the two is a network, packet reordering can occur. One manifestation of packet reordering is that old copies of a packet with a sequence or acknowledgment number of x can appear, even though neither the sender's nor the receiver's window contains x. With packet reordering, the channel can be thought of as essentially buffering packets and spontaneously emitting these packets at any point in the future. What care must be taken to guard against such duplicate packets?

P30. Suppose that Host A has received one segment from Host B containing bytes 0 through 465 and another segment containing bytes 800 through 900. For some reason Host A has not yet received bytes 466 through 799. Thus, the third segment arrived out of order. What does a host do when it receives out-of-order segments in a TCP connection?

P31. Suppose that the five measured `SampleRTT` values (see Section 3.5.3) are 106 ms, 120 ms, 140 ms, 90 ms, and 115 ms. Compute the `EstimatedRTT` after each of these SampleRTT values is obtained, using a value of $\alpha = 0.125$ and assuming that the value of `EstimatedRTT` was 100 ms just before the first of these five samples were obtained. Compute also the `DevRTT` after each sample is obtained, assuming a value of $\beta = 0.25$ and assuming the value of `DevRTT` was 5 ms just before the first of these five samples was obtained. Last, compute the TCP `TimeoutInterval` after each of these samples is obtained.

P32. Consider the TCP procedure for estimating RTT. Suppose that $\alpha = 0.1$. Let $\texttt{SampleRTT}_1$ be the most recent sample RTT, let $\texttt{SampleRTT}_2$ be the next most recent sample RTT, and so on.

   a. For a given TCP connection, suppose four acknowledgments have been returned with corresponding sample RTTs: $\texttt{SampleRTT}_4$, $\texttt{SampleRTT}_3$, $\texttt{SampleRTT}_2$, and $\texttt{SampleRTT}_1$. Express $\texttt{EstimatedRTT}$ in terms of the four sample RTTs.

   b. Generalize your formula for n sample RTTs.

   c. For the formula in part (b) let n approach infinity. Comment on why this averaging procedure is called an exponential moving average.

P33. Given values of $\texttt{EstimatedRTT}$ and $\texttt{DevRTT}$, what value should be used for TCP's timeout interval?

P34. What is the utility of the TCP state variable $\texttt{SendBase}$?

P35. Each time TCP retransmits, it sets the next timeout interval to twice the previous value, rather than deriving it from the last $\texttt{EstimatedRTT}$ and $\texttt{DevRTT}$. Why?

P36. One of the problems with timeout-triggered retransmissions is that the timeout period can be relatively long. When a segment is lost, this long timeout period forces the sender to delay resending the lost packet, thereby increasing the end-to-end delay. Is there any remedy for this?

P37. Compare GBN, SR, and TCP (no delayed ACK). Assume that the timeout values for all three protocols are sufficiently long such that 5 consecutive data segments and their corresponding ACKs can be received (if not lost in the channel) by the receiving host (Host B) and the sending host (Host A) respectively. Suppose Host A sends 5 data segments to Host B, and the 2nd segment (sent from A) is lost. In the end, all 5 data segments have been correctly received by Host B.

   a. How many segments has Host A sent in total and how many ACKs has Host B sent in total? What are their sequence numbers? Answer this question for all three protocols.

   b. If the timeout values for all three protocol are much longer than 5 RTT, then which protocol successfully delivers all five data segments in shortest time interval?

P38. In our description of TCP in Figure 3.53, the value of the threshold, $\texttt{ssthresh}$, is set as $\texttt{ssthresh=cwnd/2}$ in several places and $\texttt{ssthresh}$ value is referred to as being set to half the window size when a loss event occurred. Must the rate at which the sender is sending when the loss event occurred be approximately equal to $\texttt{cwnd}$ segments per RTT? Explain your answer. If your answer is no, can you suggest a different manner in which $\texttt{ssthresh}$ should be set?

VideoNote
**Examining the
behavior of TCP**

P39. What is selective acknowledgement and selective retransmission? What does TCP look like when they are combined?

P40. Consider Figure 3.58. Assuming TCP Reno is the protocol experiencing the behavior shown above, answer the following questions. In all cases, you should provide a short discussion justifying your answer.

a. Identify the intervals of time when TCP slow start is operating.

b. Identify the intervals of time when TCP congestion avoidance is operating.

c. After the 16th transmission round, is segment loss detected by a triple duplicate ACK or by a timeout?

d. After the 22nd transmission round, is segment loss detected by a triple duplicate ACK or by a timeout?

e. What is the initial value of `ssthresh` at the first transmission round?

f. What is the value of `ssthresh` at the 18th transmission round?

g. What is the value of `ssthresh` at the 24th transmission round?

h. During what transmission round is the 70th segment sent?

i. Assuming a packet loss is detected after the 26th round by the receipt of a triple duplicate ACK, what will be the values of the congestion window size and of `ssthresh`?

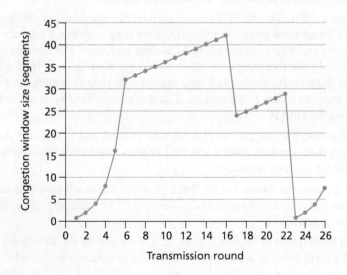

Figure 3.58 ♦ TCP window size as a function of time

j. Suppose TCP Tahoe is used (instead of TCP Reno), and assume that triple duplicate ACKs are received at the 16th round. What are the `ssthresh` and the congestion window size at the 19th round?

k. Again suppose TCP Tahoe is used, and there is a timeout event at 22nd round. How many packets have been sent out from 17th round till 22nd round, inclusive?

P41. Both congestion control and flow control throttle the sender. Then how are they different? Through which variable at the sender side does TCP provide flow control?

P42. "When a packet is dropped along a path, the transmission capacity that was used at each of the upstream links to forward that packet to the point at which it is dropped ends up having been wasted." Justify this statement.

P43. Host A is sending an enormous file to Host B over a TCP connection. Over this connection there is never any packet loss and the timers never expire. Denote the transmission rate of the link connecting Host A to the Internet by R bps. Suppose that the process in Host A is capable of sending data into its TCP socket at a rate S bps, where $S = 10 \cdot R$. Further suppose that the TCP receive buffer is large enough to hold the entire file, and the send buffer can hold only one percent of the file. What would prevent the process in Host A from continuously passing data to its TCP socket at rate S bps? TCP flow control? TCP congestion control? Or something else? Elaborate.

P44. Consider sending a large file from a host to another over a TCP connection that has no loss.

a. Suppose TCP uses AIMD for its congestion control without slow start. Assuming `cwnd` increases by 1 MSS every time a batch of ACKs is received and assuming approximately constant round-trip times, how long does it take for `cwnd` increase from 6 MSS to 12 MSS (assuming no loss events)?

b. What is the average throughout (in terms of MSS and RTT) for this connection up through time = 6 RTT?

P45. Recall the macroscopic description of TCP throughput. In the period of time from when the connection's rate varies from $W/(2 \cdot RTT)$ to W/RTT, only one packet is lost (at the very end of the period).

a. Show that the loss rate (fraction of packets lost) is equal to

$$L = \text{loss rate} = \frac{1}{\frac{3}{8}W^2 + \frac{3}{4}W}$$

b. Use the result above to show that if a connection has loss rate L, then its average rate is approximately given by

$$\approx \frac{1.22 \cdot MSS}{RTT \sqrt{L}}$$

P46. Consider that only a single TCP (Reno) connection uses one 15Mbps link which does not buffer any data. Suppose that this link is the only congested link between the sending and receiving hosts. Assume that the TCP sender has a huge file to send to the receiver, and the receiver's receive buffer is much larger than the congestion window. We also make the following assumptions: each TCP segment size is 1,200 bytes; the two-way propagation delay of this connection is 160 msec; and this TCP connection is always in congestion avoidance phase, that is, ignore slow start.

a. What is the maximum window size (in segments) that this TCP connection can achieve?

b. What is the average window size (in segments) and average throughput (in bps) of this TCP connection?

c. How long would it take for this TCP connection to reach its maximum window again after recovering from a packet loss?

P47. Consider the scenario described in the previous problem. Suppose that the 15Mbps link can buffer a finite number of segments. Argue that in order for the link to always be busy sending data, we would like to choose a buffer size that is at least the product of the link speed C and the two-way propagation delay between the sender and the receiver.

P48. Repeat Problem 46, but replacing the 10 Mbps link with a 10 Gbps link. Note that in your answer to part c, you will realize that it takes a very long time for the congestion window size to reach its maximum window size after recovering from a packet loss. Sketch a solution to solve this problem.

P49. Let T (measured by RTT) denote the time interval that a TCP connection takes to increase its congestion window size from $W/2$ to W, where W is the maximum congestion window size. Argue that T is a function of TCP's average throughput.

P50. Consider a simplified TCP's AIMD algorithm where the congestion window size is measured in number of segments, not in bytes. In additive increase, the congestion window size increases by one segment in each RTT. In multiplicative decrease, the congestion window size decreases by half (if the result is not an integer, round down to the nearest integer). Suppose that two TCP connections, C_1 and C_2, share a single congested link of speed 30 segments per second. Assume that both C_1 and C_2 are in the congestion avoidance phase. Connection C_1's RTT is 50 msec and connection C_2's RTT is 100 msec. Assume that when the data rate in the link exceeds the link's speed, all TCP connections experience data segment loss.

a. If both C_1 and C_2 at time t_0 have a congestion window of 10 segments, what are their congestion window sizes after 1000 msec?

b. In the long run, will these two connections get the same share of the bandwidth of the congested link? Explain.

P51. Consider the network described in the previous problem. Now suppose that the two TCP connections, C1 and C2, have the same RTT of 100 msec. Suppose that at time t_0, C1's congestion window size is 15 segments but C2's congestion window size is 10 segments.

a. What are their congestion window sizes after 2200msec?

b. In the long run, will these two connections get about the same share of the bandwidth of the congested link?

c. We say that two connections are synchronized, if both connections reach their maximum window sizes at the same time and reach their minimum window sizes at the same time. In the long run, will these two connections get synchronized eventually? If so, what are their maximum window sizes?

d. Will this synchronization help to improve the utilization of the shared link? Why? Sketch some idea to break this synchronization.

P52. Consider a modification to TCP's congestion control algorithm. Instead of additive increase, we can use multiplicative increase. A TCP sender increases its window size by a small positive constant a $(0 < a < 1)$ whenever it receives a valid ACK. Find the functional relationship between loss rate L and maximum congestion window W. Argue that for this modified TCP, regardless of TCP's average throughput, a TCP connection always spends the same amount of time to increase its congestion window size from $W/2$ to W.

P53. In our discussion of TCP futures in Section 3.7, we noted that to achieve a throughput of 10 Gbps, TCP could only tolerate a segment loss probability of $2 \cdot 10^{-10}$ (or equivalently, one loss event for every 5,000,000,000 segments). Show the derivation for the values of $2 \cdot 10^{-10}$ (1 out of 5,000,000) for the RTT and MSS values given in Section 3.7. If TCP needed to support a 100 Gbps connection, what would the tolerable loss be?

P54. In our discussion of TCP congestion control in Section 3.7, we implicitly assumed that the TCP sender always had data to send. Consider now the case that the TCP sender sends a large amount of data and then goes idle (since it has no more data to send) at t_1. TCP remains idle for a relatively long period of time and then wants to send more data at t_2. What are the advantages and disadvantages of having TCP use the cwnd and ssthresh values from t_1 when starting to send data at t_2? What alternative would you recommend? Why?

P55. In this problem we investigate whether either UDP or TCP provides a degree of end-point authentication.

a. Consider a server that receives a request within a UDP packet and responds to that request within a UDP packet (for example, as done by a DNS server). If a client with IP address X spoofs its address with address Y, where will the server send its response?

b. Suppose a server receives a SYN with IP source address Y, and after responding with a SYNACK, receives an ACK with IP source address Y with the correct acknowledgment number. Assuming the server chooses a random initial sequence number and there is no "man-in-the-middle," can the server be certain that the client is indeed at Y (and not at some other address X that is spoofing Y)?

P56. In this problem, we consider the delay introduced by the TCP slow-start phase. Consider a client and a Web server directly connected by one link of rate R. Suppose the client wants to retrieve an object whose size is exactly equal to 15 S, where S is the maximum segment size (MSS). Denote the round-trip time between client and server as RTT (assumed to be constant). Ignoring protocol headers, determine the time to retrieve the object (including TCP connection establishment) when

a. $4 S/R > S/R + RTT > 2S/R$

b. $S/R + RTT > 4 S/R$

c. $S/R > RTT$.

 Programming Assignments

Implementing a Reliable Transport Protocol

In this laboratory programming assignment, you will be writing the sending and receiving transport-level code for implementing a simple reliable data transfer protocol. There are two versions of this lab, the alternating-bit-protocol version and the GBN version. This lab should be fun—your implementation will differ very little from what would be required in a real-world situation.

Since you probably don't have standalone machines (with an OS that you can modify), your code will have to execute in a simulated hardware/software environment. However, the programming interface provided to your routines—the code that would call your entities from above and from below—is very close to what is done in an actual UNIX environment. (Indeed, the software interfaces described in this programming assignment are much more realistic than the infinite loop senders and receivers that many texts describe.) Stopping and starting timers are also simulated, and timer interrupts will cause your timer handling routine to be activated.

The full lab assignment, as well as code you will need to compile with your own code, are available at this book's Web site: http://www.awl.com/kurose-ross.

Wireshark Lab: Exploring TCP

In this lab, you'll use your Web browser to access a file from a Web server. As in earlier Wireshark labs, you'll use Wireshark to capture the packets arriving at your computer. Unlike earlier labs, you'll *also* be able to download a Wireshark-readable packet trace from the Web server from which you downloaded the file. In this server trace, you'll find the packets that were generated by your own access of the Web server. You'll analyze the client- and server-side traces to explore aspects of TCP. In particular, you'll evaluate the performance of the TCP connection between your computer and the Web server. You'll trace TCP's window behavior, and infer packet loss, retransmission, flow control and congestion control behavior, and estimated roundtrip time.

As is the case with all Wireshark labs, the full description of this lab is available at this book's Web site, http://www.awl.com/kurose-ross.

Wireshark Lab: Exploring UDP

In this short lab, you'll do a packet capture and analysis of your favorite application that uses UDP (for example, DNS or a multimedia application such as Skype). As we learned in Section 3.3, UDP is a simple, no-frills transport protocol. In this lab, you'll investigate the header fields in the UDP segment as well as the checksum calculation.

As is the case with all Wireshark labs, the full description of this lab is available at this book's Web site, http://www.awl.com/kurose-ross.

Van Jacobson

Van Jacobson is a Research Fellow at PARC. Prior to that, he was co-founder and Chief Scientist of Packet Design. Before that, he was Chief Scientist at Cisco. Before joining Cisco, he was head of the Network Research Group at Lawrence Berkeley National Laboratory and taught at UC Berkeley and Stanford. Van received the ACM SIGCOMM Award in 2001 for outstanding lifetime contribution to the field of communication networks and the IEEE Kobayashi Award in 2002 for "contributing to the understanding of network congestion and developing congestion control mechanisms that enabled the successful scaling of the Internet". He was elected to the U.S. National Academy of Engineering in 2004.

Please describe one or two of the most exciting projects you have worked on during your career. What were the biggest challenges?

School teaches us lots of ways to find answers. In every interesting problem I've worked on, the challenge has been finding the right question. When Mike Karels and I started looking at TCP congestion, we spent months staring at protocol and packet traces asking "Why is it failing?". One day in Mike's office, one of us said "The reason I can't figure out why it fails is because I don't understand how it ever worked to begin with." That turned out to be the right question and it forced us to figure out the "ack clocking" that makes TCP work. After that, the rest was easy.

More generally, where do you see the future of networking and the Internet?

For most people, the Web is the Internet. Networking geeks smile politely since we know the Web is an application running over the Internet but what if they're right? The Internet is about enabling conversations between pairs of hosts. The Web is about distributed information production and consumption. "Information propagation" is a very general view of communication of which "pairwise conversation" is a tiny subset. We need to move into the larger tent. Networking today deals with broadcast media (radios, PONs, etc.) by pretending it's a point-to-point wire. That's massively inefficient. Terabits-per-second of data are being exchanged all over the World via thumb drives or smart phones but we don't know how to treat that as "networking". ISPs are busily setting up caches and CDNs to scalably distribute video and audio. Caching is a necessary part of the solution but there's no part of today's networking—from Information, Queuing or Traffic Theory down to the Internet protocol specs—that tells us how to engineer and deploy it. I think and hope that over the next few years, networking will evolve to embrace the much larger vision of communication that underlies the Web.

What people inspired you professionally?

When I was in grad school, Richard Feynman visited and gave a colloquium. He talked about a piece of Quantum theory that I'd been struggling with all semester and his explanation was so simple and lucid that what had been incomprehensible gibberish to me became obvious and inevitable. That ability to see and convey the simplicity that underlies our complex world seems to me a rare and wonderful gift.

What are your recommendations for students who want careers in computer science and networking?

It's a wonderful field—computers and networking have probably had more impact on society than any invention since the book. Networking is fundamentally about connecting stuff, and studying it helps you make intellectual connections: Ant foraging & Bee dances demonstrate protocol design better than RFCs, traffic jams or people leaving a packed stadium are the essence of congestion, and students finding flights back to school in a post-Thanksgiving blizzard are the core of dynamic routing. If you're interested in lots of stuff and want to have an impact, it's hard to imagine a better field.

4

The Network Layer

We learned in the previous chapter that the transport layer provides various forms of process-to-process communication by relying on the network layer's host-to-host communication service. We also learned that the transport layer does so without any knowledge about how the network layer actually implements this service. So perhaps you're now wondering, what's under the hood of the host-to-host communication service, what makes it tick?

In this chapter, we'll learn exactly how the network layer implements the host-to-host communication service. We'll see that unlike the transport and application layers, there is a piece of the network layer in each and every host and router in the network. Because of this, network-layer protocols are among the most challenging (and therefore among the most interesting!) in the protocol stack.

The network layer is also one of the most complex layers in the protocol stack, and so we'll have a lot of ground to cover here. We'll begin our study with an overview of the network layer and the services it can provide. We'll then examine two broad approaches towards structuring network-layer packet delivery—the datagram and the virtual-circuit model—and see the fundamental role that addressing plays in delivering a packet to its destination host.

In this chapter, we'll make an important distinction between the **forwarding** and **routing** functions of the network layer. Forwarding involves the transfer of a packet from an incoming link to an outgoing link within a *single* router. Routing involves *all* of a network's routers, whose collective interactions via routing protocols determine the paths that packets take on their trips from source to destination node. This will be an important distinction to keep in mind as you progress through this chapter.

In order to deepen our understanding of packet forwarding, we'll look "inside" a router—at its hardware architecture and organization. We'll then look at packet forwarding in the Internet, along with the celebrated Internet Protocol (IP). We'll investigate network-layer addressing and the IPv4 datagram format. We'll then explore network address translation (NAT), datagram fragmentation, the Internet Control Message Protocol (ICMP), and IPv6.

We'll then turn our attention to the network layer's routing function. We'll see that the job of a routing algorithm is to determine good paths (equivalently, routes) from senders to receivers. We'll first study the theory of routing algorithms, concentrating on the two most prevalent classes of algorithms: link-state and distance-vector algorithms. Since the complexity of routing algorithms grows considerably as the number of network routers increases, hierarchical routing approaches will also be of interest. We'll then see how theory is put into practice when we cover the Internet's intra-autonomous system routing protocols (RIP, OSPF, and IS-IS) and its inter-autonomous system routing protocol, BGP. We'll close this chapter with a discussion of broadcast and multicast routing.

In summary, this chapter has three major parts. The first part, Sections 4.1 and 4.2, covers network-layer functions and services. The second part, Sections 4.3 and 4.4, covers forwarding. Finally, the third part, Sections 4.5 through 4.7, covers routing.

4.1 Introduction

Figure 4.1 shows a simple network with two hosts, H1 and H2, and several routers on the path between H1 and H2. Suppose that H1 is sending information to H2, and consider the role of the network layer in these hosts and in the intervening routers. The network layer in H1 takes segments from the transport layer in H1, encapsulates each segment into a datagram (that is, a network-layer packet), and then sends the datagrams to its nearby router, R1. At the receiving host, H2, the network layer receives the datagrams from its nearby router R2, extracts the transport-layer segments, and delivers the segments up to the transport layer at H2. The primary role of the routers is to forward datagrams from input links to output links. Note that the routers in Figure 4.1 are shown with a truncated protocol stack, that is, with no upper layers above the network layer, because (except for control purposes) routers do not run application- and transport-layer protocols such as those we examined in Chapters 2 and 3.

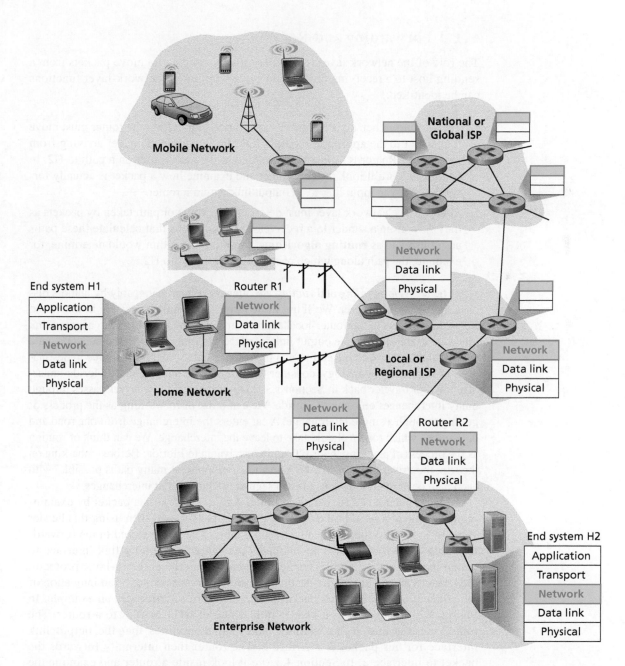

Figure 4.1 ♦ The network layer

4.1.1 Forwarding and Routing

The role of the network layer is thus deceptively simple—to move packets from a sending host to a receiving host. To do so, two important network-layer functions can be identified:

- *Forwarding.* When a packet arrives at a router's input link, the router must move the packet to the appropriate output link. For example, a packet arriving from Host H1 to Router R1 must be forwarded to the next router on a path to H2. In Section 4.3, we'll look inside a router and examine how a packet is actually forwarded from an input link to an output link within a router.

- *Routing.* The network layer must determine the route or path taken by packets as they flow from a sender to a receiver. The algorithms that calculate these paths are referred to as **routing algorithms**. A routing algorithm would determine, for example, the path along which packets flow from H1 to H2.

The terms *forwarding* and *routing* are often used interchangeably by authors discussing the network layer. We'll use these terms much more precisely in this book. *Forwarding* refers to the router-local action of transferring a packet from an input link interface to the appropriate output link interface. *Routing* refers to the network-wide process that determines the end-to-end paths that packets take from source to destination. Using a driving analogy, consider the trip from Pennsylvania to Florida undertaken by our traveler back in Section 1.3.1. During this trip, our driver passes through many interchanges en route to Florida. We can think of forwarding as the process of getting through a single interchange: A car enters the interchange from one road and determines which road it should take to leave the interchange. We can think of routing as the process of planning the trip from Pennsylvania to Florida: Before embarking on the trip, the driver has consulted a map and chosen one of many paths possible, with each path consisting of a series of road segments connected at interchanges.

Every router has a **forwarding table**. A router forwards a packet by examining the value of a field in the arriving packet's header, and then using this header value to index into the router's forwarding table. The value stored in the forwarding table entry for that header indicates the router's outgoing link interface to which that packet is to be forwarded. Depending on the network-layer protocol, the header value could be the destination address of the packet or an indication of the connection to which the packet belongs. Figure 4.2 provides an example. In Figure 4.2, a packet with a header field value of 0111 arrives to a router. The router indexes into its forwarding table and determines that the output link interface for this packet is interface 2. The router then internally forwards the packet to interface 2. In Section 4.3, we'll look inside a router and examine the forwarding function in much greater detail.

You might now be wondering how the forwarding tables in the routers are configured. This is a crucial issue, one that exposes the important interplay between

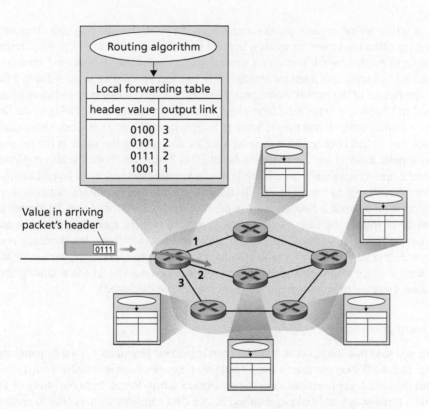

Figure 4.2 ◆ Routing algorithms determine values in forwarding tables

routing and forwarding. As shown in Figure 4.2, the routing algorithm determines the values that are inserted into the routers' forwarding tables. The routing algorithm may be centralized (e.g., with an algorithm executing on a central site and downloading routing information to each of the routers) or decentralized (i.e., with a piece of the distributed routing algorithm running in each router). In either case, a router receives routing protocol messages, which are used to configure its forwarding table. The distinct and different purposes of the forwarding and routing functions can be further illustrated by considering the hypothetical (and unrealistic, but technically feasible) case of a network in which all forwarding tables are configured directly by human network operators physically present at the routers. In this case, *no* routing protocols would be required! Of course, the human operators would need to interact with each other to ensure that the forwarding tables were configured in such a way that packets reached their intended destinations. It's also likely that human configuration would be more error-prone and much slower to respond to changes in the network topology than a routing protocol. We're thus fortunate that all networks have both a forwarding *and* a routing function!

While we're on the topic of terminology, it's worth mentioning two other terms that are often used interchangeably, but that we will use more carefully. We'll reserve the term *packet switch* to mean a general packet-switching device that transfers a packet from input link interface to output link interface, according to the value in a field in the header of the packet. Some packet switches, called **link-layer switches** (examined in Chapter 5), base their forwarding decision on values in the fields of the link-layer frame; switches are thus referred to as link-layer (layer 2) devices. Other packet switches, called **routers**, base their forwarding decision on the value in the network-layer field. Routers are thus network-layer (layer 3) devices, but must also implement layer 2 protocols as well, since layer 3 devices require the services of layer 2 to implement their (layer 3) functionality. (To fully appreciate this important distinction, you might want to review Section 1.5.2, where we discuss network-layer datagrams and link-layer frames and their relationship.) To confuse matters, marketing literature often refers to "layer 3 switches" for routers with Ethernet interfaces, but these are really layer 3 devices. Since our focus in this chapter is on the network layer, we use the term *router* in place of *packet switch*. We'll even use the term *router* when talking about packet switches in virtual-circuit networks (soon to be discussed).

Connection Setup

We just said that the network layer has two important functions, forwarding and routing. But we'll soon see that in some computer networks there is actually a third important network-layer function, namely, **connection setup**. Recall from our study of TCP that a three-way handshake is required before data can flow from sender to receiver. This allows the sender and receiver to set up the needed state information (for example, sequence number and initial flow-control window size). In an analogous manner, some network-layer architectures—for example, ATM, frame relay, and MPLS (which we will study in Section 5.8)—require the routers along the chosen path from source to destination to handshake with each other in order to set up state before network-layer data packets within a given source-to-destination connection can begin to flow. In the network layer, this process is referred to as *connection setup*. We'll examine connection setup in Section 4.2.

4.1.2 Network Service Models

Before delving into the network layer, let's take the broader view and consider the different types of service that might be offered by the network layer. When the transport layer at a sending host transmits a packet into the network (that is, passes it down to the network layer at the sending host), can the transport layer rely on the network layer to deliver the packet to the destination? When multiple packets are sent, will they be delivered to the transport layer in the receiving host in the order in which they were sent? Will the amount of time between the sending of two sequential packet transmissions be the same as the amount of time between their reception? Will the network provide any feedback about congestion in the network? What is the abstract view (properties) of the channel connecting the transport layer in the sending and receiving hosts? The answers to these questions and others are determined by the service model provided by the network layer. The **network service model** defines the characteristics of end-to-end transport of packets between sending and receiving end systems.

Let's now consider some possible services that the network layer could provide. In the sending host, when the transport layer passes a packet to the network layer, specific services that could be provided by the network layer include:

- *Guaranteed delivery*. This service guarantees that the packet will eventually arrive at its destination.
- *Guaranteed delivery with bounded delay*. This service not only guarantees delivery of the packet, but delivery within a specified host-to-host delay bound (for example, within 100 msec).

Furthermore, the following services could be provided to a *flow of packets* between a given source and destination:

- *In-order packet delivery*. This service guarantees that packets arrive at the destination in the order that they were sent.
- *Guaranteed minimal bandwidth*. This network-layer service emulates the behavior of a transmission link of a specified bit rate (for example, 1 Mbps) between sending and receiving hosts. As long as the sending host transmits bits (as part of packets) at a rate below the specified bit rate, then no packet is lost and each packet arrives within a prespecified host-to-host delay (for example, within 40 msec).
- *Guaranteed maximum jitter*. This service guarantees that the amount of time between the transmission of two successive packets at the sender is equal to the amount of time between their receipt at the destination (or that this spacing changes by no more than some specified value).
- *Security services*. Using a secret session key known only by a source and destination host, the network layer in the source host could encrypt the payloads of all datagrams being sent to the destination host. The network layer in the destination host would then be responsible for decrypting the payloads. With such a service, confidentiality would be provided to all transport-layer segments (TCP and UDP) between the source and destination hosts. In addition to confidentiality, the network layer could provide data integrity and source authentication services.

This is only a partial list of services that a network layer could provide—there are countless variations possible.

The Internet's network layer provides a single service, known as **best-effort service**. From Table 4.1, it might appear that *best-effort service* is a euphemism for

Network Architecture	Service Model	Bandwidth Guarantee	No-Loss Guarantee	Ordering	Timing	Congestion Indication
Internet	Best Effort	None	None	Any order possible	Not maintained	None
ATM	CBR	Guaranteed constant rate	Yes	In order	Maintained	Congestion will not occur
ATM	ABR	Guaranteed minimum	None	In order	Not maintained	Congestion indication provided

Table 4.1 ♦ Internet, ATM CBR, and ATM ABR service models

no service at all. With best-effort service, timing between packets is not guaranteed to be preserved, packets are not guaranteed to be received in the order in which they were sent, nor is the eventual delivery of transmitted packets guaranteed. Given this definition, a network that delivered *no* packets to the destination would satisfy the definition of best-effort delivery service. As we'll discuss shortly, however, there are sound reasons for such a minimalist network-layer service model.

Other network architectures have defined and implemented service models that go beyond the Internet's best-effort service. For example, the ATM network architecture [MFA Forum 2012, Black 1995] provides for multiple service models, meaning that different connections can be provided with different classes of service within the same network. A discussion of how an ATM network provides such services is well beyond the scope of this book; our aim here is only to note that alternatives do exist to the Internet's best-effort model. Two of the more important ATM service models are constant bit rate and available bit rate service:

- *Constant bit rate (CBR) ATM network service.* This was the first ATM service model to be standardized, reflecting early interest by the telephone companies in ATM and the suitability of CBR service for carrying real-time, constant bit rate audio and video traffic. The goal of CBR service is conceptually simple—to provide a flow of packets (known as cells in ATM terminology) with a virtual pipe whose properties are the same as if a dedicated fixed-bandwidth transmission link existed between sending and receiving hosts. With CBR service, a flow of ATM cells is carried across the network in such a way that a cell's end-to-end delay, the variability in a cell's end-to-end delay (that is, the jitter), and the fraction of cells that are lost or delivered late are all guaranteed to be less than specified values. These values are agreed upon by the sending host and the ATM network when the CBR connection is first established.

- *Available bit rate (ABR) ATM network service.* With the Internet offering so-called best-effort service, ATM's ABR might best be characterized as being a slightly-better-than-best-effort service. As with the Internet service model, cells may be lost under ABR service. Unlike in the Internet, however, cells cannot be reordered (although they may be lost), and a minimum cell transmission rate (MCR) is guaranteed to a connection using ABR service. If the network has enough free resources at a given time, a sender may also be able to send cells successfully at a higher rate than the MCR. Additionally, as we saw in Section 3.6, ATM ABR service can provide feedback to the sender (in terms of a congestion notification bit, or an explicit rate at which to send) that controls how the sender adjusts its rate between the MCR and an allowable peak cell rate.

4.2 Virtual Circuit and Datagram Networks

Recall from Chapter 3 that a transport layer can offer applications connectionless service or connection-oriented service between two processes. For example, the Internet's transport layer provides each application a choice between two services: UDP, a connectionless service; or TCP, a connection-oriented service. In a similar manner, a network layer can provide connectionless service or connection service between two hosts. Network-layer connection and connectionless services in many ways parallel transport-layer connection-oriented and connectionless services. For example, a network-layer connection service begins with handshaking between the source and destination hosts; and a network-layer connectionless service does not have any handshaking preliminaries.

Although the network-layer connection and connectionless services have some parallels with transport-layer connection-oriented and connectionless services, there are crucial differences:

- In the network layer, these services are host-to-host services provided by the network layer for the transport layer. In the transport layer these services are process-to-process services provided by the transport layer for the application layer.

- In all major computer network architectures to date (Internet, ATM, frame relay, and so on), the network layer provides either a host-to-host connectionless service or a host-to-host connection service, but not both. Computer networks that provide only a connection service at the network layer are called **virtual-circuit (VC) networks**; computer networks that provide only a connectionless service at the network layer are called **datagram networks**.

- The implementations of connection-oriented service in the transport layer and the connection service in the network layer are fundamentally different. We saw in the previous chapter that the transport-layer connection-oriented service is implemented at the edge of the network in the end systems; we'll see shortly that the network-layer connection service is implemented in the routers in the network core as well as in the end systems.

Virtual-circuit and datagram networks are two fundamental classes of computer networks. They use very different information in making their forwarding decisions. Let's now take a closer look at their implementations.

4.2.1 Virtual-Circuit Networks

While the Internet is a datagram network, many alternative network architectures—including those of ATM and frame relay—are virtual-circuit networks and, therefore, use connections at the network layer. These network-layer connections are called **virtual circuits (VCs)**. Let's now consider how a VC service can be implemented in a computer network.

A VC consists of (1) a path (that is, a series of links and routers) between the source and destination hosts, (2) VC numbers, one number for each link along the path, and (3) entries in the forwarding table in each router along the path. A packet belonging to a virtual circuit will carry a VC number in its header. Because a virtual circuit may have a different VC number on each link, each intervening router must replace the VC number of each traversing packet with a new VC number. The new VC number is obtained from the forwarding table.

To illustrate the concept, consider the network shown in Figure 4.3. The numbers next to the links of R1 in Figure 4.3 are the link interface numbers. Suppose now that Host A requests that the network establish a VC between itself and Host B. Suppose also that the network chooses the path A-R1-R2-B and assigns VC numbers 12, 22, and 32 to the three links in this path for this virtual circuit. In this case, when a packet in this VC leaves Host A, the value in the VC number field in the packet header is 12; when it leaves R1, the value is 22; and when it leaves R2, the value is 32.

How does the router determine the replacement VC number for a packet traversing the router? For a VC network, each router's forwarding table includes VC

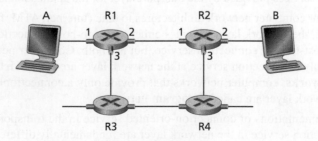

Figure 4.3 ♦ A simple virtual circuit network

number translation; for example, the forwarding table in R1 might look something like this:

Incoming Interface	Incoming VC #	Outgoing Interface	Outgoing VC #
1	12	2	22
2	63	1	18
3	7	2	17
1	97	3	87
...	...	...	...

Whenever a new VC is established across a router, an entry is added to the forwarding table. Similarly, whenever a VC terminates, the appropriate entries in each table along its path are removed.

You might be wondering why a packet doesn't just keep the same VC number on each of the links along its route. The answer is twofold. First, replacing the number from link to link reduces the length of the VC field in the packet header. Second, and more importantly, VC setup is considerably simplified by permitting a different VC number at each link along the path of the VC. Specifically, with multiple VC numbers, each link in the path can choose a VC number independently of the VC numbers chosen at other links along the path. If a common VC number were required for all links along the path, the routers would have to exchange and process a substantial number of messages to agree on a common VC number (e.g., one that is not being used by any other existing VC at these routers) to be used for a connection.

In a VC network, the network's routers must maintain **connection state information** for the ongoing connections. Specifically, each time a new connection is established across a router, a new connection entry must be added to the router's forwarding table; and each time a connection is released, an entry must be removed from the table. Note that even if there is no VC-number translation, it is still necessary to maintain connection state information that associates VC numbers with output interface numbers. The issue of whether or not a router maintains connection state information for each ongoing connection is a crucial one—one that we'll return to repeatedly in this book.

There are three identifiable phases in a virtual circuit:

- *VC setup.* During the setup phase, the sending transport layer contacts the network layer, specifies the receiver's address, and waits for the network to set up the VC. The network layer determines the path between sender and receiver, that is, the series of links and routers through which all packets of the VC will travel. The network layer also determines the VC number for each link along the path. Finally, the network layer adds an entry in the forwarding table in each router along the path. During VC setup, the network layer may also reserve resources (for example, bandwidth) along the path of the VC.

• *Data transfer.* As shown in Figure 4.4, once the VC has been established, packets can begin to flow along the VC.

• *VC teardown.* This is initiated when the sender (or receiver) informs the network layer of its desire to terminate the VC. The network layer will then typically inform the end system on the other side of the network of the call termination and update the forwarding tables in each of the packet routers on the path to indicate that the VC no longer exists.

There is a subtle but important distinction between VC setup at the network layer and connection setup at the transport layer (for example, the TCP three-way handshake we studied in Chapter 3). Connection setup at the transport layer involves only the two end systems. During transport-layer connection setup, the two end systems alone determine the parameters (for example, initial sequence number and flow-control window size) of their transport-layer connection. Although the two end systems are aware of the transport-layer connection, the routers within the network are completely oblivious to it. On the other hand, with a VC network layer, *routers along the path between the two end systems are involved in VC setup, and each router is fully aware of all the VCs passing through it.*

The messages that the end systems send into the network to initiate or terminate a VC, and the messages passed between the routers to set up the VC (that is, to modify connection state in router tables) are known as **signaling messages**, and the protocols

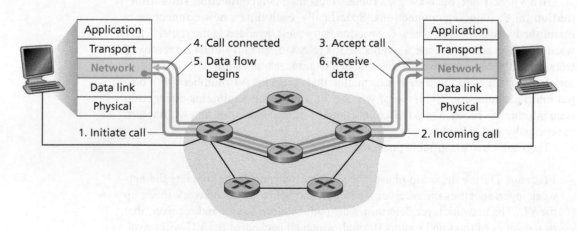

Figure 4.4 ♦ Virtual-circuit setup

used to exchange these messages are often referred to as **signaling protocols**. VC setup is shown pictorially in Figure 4.4. We'll not cover VC signaling protocols in this book; see [Black 1997] for a general discussion of signaling in connection-oriented networks and [ITU-T Q.2931 1995] for the specification of ATM's Q.2931 signaling protocol.

4.2.2 Datagram Networks

In a **datagram network**, each time an end system wants to send a packet, it stamps the packet with the address of the destination end system and then pops the packet into the network. As shown in Figure 4.5, there is no VC setup and routers do not maintain any VC state information (because there are no VCs!).

As a packet is transmitted from source to destination, it passes through a series of routers. Each of these routers uses the packet's destination address to forward the packet. Specifically, each router has a forwarding table that maps destination addresses to link interfaces; when a packet arrives at the router, the router uses the packet's destination address to look up the appropriate output link interface in the forwarding table. The router then intentionally forwards the packet to that output link interface.

To get some further insight into the lookup operation, let's look at a specific example. Suppose that all destination addresses are 32 bits (which just happens to be the length of the destination address in an IP datagram). A brute-force implementation of the forwarding table would have one entry for every possible destination address. Since there are more than 4 billion possible addresses, this option is totally out of the question.

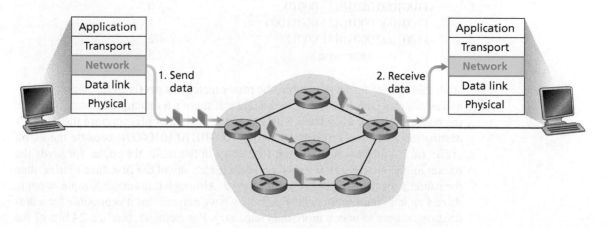

Figure 4.5 ♦ Datagram network

Now let's further suppose that our router has four links, numbered 0 through 3, and that packets are to be forwarded to the link interfaces as follows:

Destination Address Range	Link Interface
11001000 00010111 00010000 00000000 through 11001000 00010111 00010111 11111111	0
11001000 00010111 00011000 00000000 through 11001000 00010111 00011000 11111111	1
11001000 00010111 00011001 00000000 through 11001000 00010111 00011111 11111111	2
otherwise	3

Clearly, for this example, it is not necessary to have 4 billion entries in the router's forwarding table. We could, for example, have the following forwarding table with just four entries:

Prefix Match	Link Interface
11001000 00010111 00010	0
11001000 00010111 00011000	1
11001000 00010111 00011	2
otherwise	3

With this style of forwarding table, the router matches a **prefix** of the packet's destination address with the entries in the table; if there's a match, the router forwards the packet to a link associated with the match. For example, suppose the packet's destination address is 11001000 00010111 00010110 10100001; because the 21-bit prefix of this address matches the first entry in the table, the router forwards the packet to link interface 0. If a prefix doesn't match any of the first three entries, then the router forwards the packet to interface 3. Although this sounds simple enough, there's an important subtlety here. You may have noticed that it is possible for a destination address to match more than one entry. For example, the first 24 bits of the address 11001000 00010111 00011000 10101010 match the second entry in the table, and the first 21 bits of the address match the third entry in the table. When there are multiple matches, the router uses the **longest prefix matching rule**; that is, it finds the longest matching entry in the table and forwards the packet to the link interface associated with the longest prefix match. We'll see exactly why this longest prefix-matching rule is used when we study Internet addressing in more detail in Section 4.4.

Although routers in datagram networks maintain no connection state information, they nevertheless maintain forwarding state information in their forwarding tables. However, the time scale at which this forwarding state information changes is relatively slow. Indeed, in a datagram network the forwarding tables are modified by the routing algorithms, which typically update a forwarding table every one-to-five minutes or so. In a VC network, a forwarding table in a router is modified whenever a new connection is set up through the router or whenever an existing connection through the router is torn down. This could easily happen at a microsecond timescale in a backbone, tier-1 router.

Because forwarding tables in datagram networks can be modified at any time, a series of packets sent from one end system to another may follow different paths through the network and may arrive out of order. [Paxson 1997] and [Jaiswal 2003] present interesting measurement studies of packet reordering and other phenomena in the public Internet.

4.2.3 Origins of VC and Datagram Networks

The evolution of datagram and VC networks reflects their origins. The notion of a virtual circuit as a central organizing principle has its roots in the telephony world, which uses real circuits. With call setup and per-call state being maintained at the routers within the network, a VC network is arguably more complex than a datagram network (although see [Molinero-Fernandez 2002] for an interesting comparison of the complexity of circuit- versus packet-switched networks). This, too, is in keeping with its telephony heritage. Telephone networks, by necessity, had their complexity within the network, since they were connecting dumb end-system devices such as rotary telephones. (For those too young to know, a rotary phone is an analog telephone with no buttons—only a dial.)

The Internet as a datagram network, on the other hand, grew out of the need to connect computers together. Given more sophisticated end-system devices, the Internet architects chose to make the network-layer service model as simple as possible. As we have already seen in Chapters 2 and 3, additional functionality (for example, in-order delivery, reliable data transfer, congestion control, and DNS name resolution) is then implemented at a higher layer, in the end systems. This inverts the model of the telephone network, with some interesting consequences:

• Since the resulting Internet network-layer service model makes minimal (no!) service guarantees, it imposes minimal requirements on the network layer. This makes it easier to interconnect networks that use very different link-layer technologies (for example, satellite, Ethernet, fiber, or radio) that have very different transmission rates and loss characteristics. We will address the interconnection of IP networks in detail in Section 4.4.

• As we saw in Chapter 2, applications such as e-mail, the Web, and even some network infrastructure services such as the DNS are implemented in hosts (servers) at the network edge. The ability to add a new service simply by attaching a host to the network and defining a new application-layer protocol (such as HTTP) has allowed new Internet applications such as the Web to be deployed in a remarkably short period of time.

4.3 What's Inside a Router?

Now that we've overviewed the network layer's services and functions, let's turn our attention to its **forwarding function**—the actual transfer of packets from a router's incoming links to the appropriate outgoing links at that router. We already took a brief look at a few aspects of forwarding in Section 4.2, namely, addressing and longest prefix matching. We mention here in passing that the terms *forwarding* and *switching* are often used interchangeably by computer-networking researchers and practitioners; we'll use both terms interchangeably in this textbook as well.

A high-level view of a generic router architecture is shown in Figure 4.6. Four router components can be identified:

• *Input ports.* An input port performs several key functions. It performs the physical layer function of terminating an incoming physical link at a router; this is shown in the leftmost box of the input port and the rightmost box of the output port in Figure 4.6. An input port also performs link-layer functions needed to interoperate with the link layer at the other side of the incoming link; this is represented by the middle boxes in the input and output ports. Perhaps most crucially, the lookup function is also performed at the input port; this will occur in the rightmost box of the input port. It is here that the forwarding table is consulted to determine the router output port to which an arriving packet will be forwarded via the switching fabric. Control packets (for example, packets carrying routing protocol information) are forwarded from an input port to the routing processor. Note that the term *port* here— referring to the physical input and output router interfaces—is distinctly different from the software ports associated with network applications and sockets discussed in Chapters 2 and 3.

• *Switching fabric.* The switching fabric connects the router's input ports to its output ports. This switching fabric is completely contained within the router— a network inside of a network router!

• *Output ports.* An output port stores packets received from the switching fabric and transmits these packets on the outgoing link by performing the necessary link-layer and physical-layer functions. When a link is bidirectional (that is,

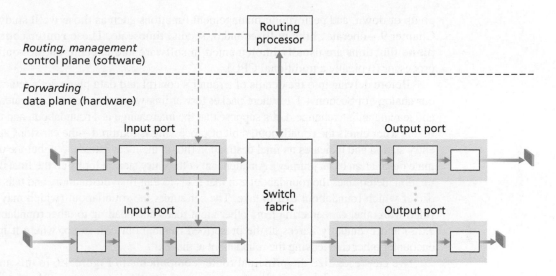

Figure 4.6 ♦ Router architecture

carries traffic in both directions), an output port will typically be paired with the input port for that link on the same line card (a printed circuit board containing one or more input ports, which is connected to the switching fabric).

• *Routing processor.* The routing processor executes the routing protocols (which we'll study in Section 4.6), maintains routing tables and attached link state information, and computes the forwarding table for the router. It also performs the network management functions that we'll study in Chapter 9.

Recall that in Section 4.1.1 we distinguished between a router's forwarding and routing functions. A router's input ports, output ports, and switching fabric together implement the forwarding function and are almost always implemented in hardware, as shown in Figure 4.6. These forwarding functions are sometimes collectively referred to as the **router forwarding plane**. To appreciate why a hardware implementation is needed, consider that with a 10 Gbps input link and a 64-byte IP datagram, the input port has only 51.2 ns to process the datagram before another datagram may arrive. If N ports are combined on a line card (as is often done in practice), the datagram-processing pipeline must operate N times faster—far too fast for software implementation. Forwarding plane hardware can be implemented either using a router vendor's own hardware designs, or constructed using purchased merchant-silicon chips (e.g., as sold by companies such as Intel and Broadcom).

While the forwarding plane operates at the nanosecond time scale, a router's control functions—executing the routing protocols, responding to attached links that go up or down, and performing management functions such as those we'll study in Chapter 9—operate at the millisecond or second timescale. These **router control plane** functions are usually implemented in software and execute on the routing processor (typically a traditional CPU).

Before delving into the details of a router's control and data plane, let's return to our analogy of Section 4.1.1, where packet forwarding was compared to cars entering and leaving an interchange. Let's suppose that the interchange is a roundabout, and that before a car enters the roundabout, a bit of processing is required—the car stops at an entry station and indicates its final destination (not at the local roundabout, but the ultimate destination of its journey). An attendant at the entry station looks up the final destination, determines the roundabout exit that leads to that final destination, and tells the driver which roundabout exit to take. The car enters the roundabout (which may be filled with other cars entering from other input roads and heading to other roundabout exits) and eventually leaves at the prescribed roundabout exit ramp, where it may encounter other cars leaving the roundabout at that exit.

We can recognize the principal router components in Figure 4.6 in this analogy—the entry road and entry station correspond to the input port (with a lookup function to determine to local outgoing port); the roundabout corresponds to the switch fabric; and the roundabout exit road corresponds to the output port. With this analogy, it's instructive to consider where bottlenecks might occur. What happens if cars arrive blazingly fast (for example, the roundabout is in Germany or Italy!) but the station attendant is slow? How fast must the attendant work to ensure there's no backup on an entry road? Even with a blazingly fast attendant, what happens if cars traverse the roundabout slowly—can backups still occur? And what happens if most of the entering cars all want to leave the roundabout at the same exit ramp—can backups occur at the exit ramp or elsewhere? How should the roundabout operate if we want to assign priorities to different cars, or block certain cars from entering the roundabout in the first place? These are all analogous to critical questions faced by router and switch designers.

In the following subsections, we'll look at router functions in more detail. [Iyer 2008, Chao 2001; Chuang 2005; Turner 1988; McKeown 1997a; Partridge 1998] provide a discussion of specific router architectures. For concreteness, the ensuing discussion assumes a datagram network in which forwarding decisions are based on the packet's destination address (rather than a VC number in a virtual-circuit network). However, the concepts and techniques are quite similar for a virtual-circuit network.

4.3.1 Input Processing

A more detailed view of input processing is given in Figure 4.7. As discussed above, the input port's line termination function and link-layer processing implement the physical and link layers for that individual input link. The lookup performed in the input port is central to the router's operation—it is here that the router uses the forwarding table to look up the output port to which an arriving packet will be

CASE HISTORY

CISCO SYSTEMS: DOMINATING THE NETWORK CORE

As of this writing 2012, Cisco employs more than 65,000 people. How did this gorilla of a networking company come to be? It all started in 1984 in the living room of a Silicon Valley apartment.

Len Bosak and his wife Sandy Lerner were working at Stanford University when they had the idea to build and sell Internet routers to research and academic institutions, the primary adopters of the Internet at that time. Sandy Lerner came up with the name Cisco (an abbreviation for San Francisco), and she also designed the company's bridge logo. Corporate headquarters was their living room, and they financed the project with credit cards and moonlighting consulting jobs. At the end of 1986, Cisco's revenues reached $250,000 a month. At the end of 1987, Cisco succeeded in attracting venture capital— $2 million from Sequoia Capital in exchange for one-third of the company. Over the next few years, Cisco continued to grow and grab more and more market share. At the same time, relations between Bosak/Lerner and Cisco management became strained. Cisco went public in 1990; in the same year Lerner and Bosak left the company.

Over the years, Cisco has expanded well beyond the router market, selling security, wireless caching, Ethernet switch, datacenter infrastructure, video conferencing, and voice-over IP products and services. However, Cisco is facing increased international competition, including from Huawei, a rapidly growing Chinese network-gear company. Other sources of competition for Cisco in the router and switched Ethernet space include Alcatel-Lucent and Juniper.

forwarded via the switching fabric. The forwarding table is computed and updated by the routing processor, with a shadow copy typically stored at each input port. The forwarding table is copied from the routing processor to the line cards over a separate bus (e.g., a PCI bus) indicated by the dashed line from the routing processor to the input line cards in Figure 4.6. With a shadow copy, forwarding decisions can be made locally, at each input port, without invoking the centralized routing processor on a per-packet basis and thus avoiding a centralized processing bottleneck.

Given the existence of a forwarding table, lookup is conceptually simple—we just search through the forwarding table looking for the longest prefix match, as described

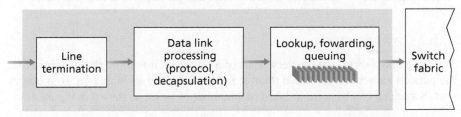

Figure 4.7 ♦ Input port processing

in Section 4.2.2. But at Gigabit transmission rates, this lookup must be performed in nanoseconds (recall our earlier example of a 10 Gbps link and a 64-byte IP datagram). Thus, not only must lookup be performed in hardware, but techniques beyond a simple linear search through a large table are needed; surveys of fast lookup algorithms can be found in [Gupta 2001, Ruiz-Sanchez 2001]. Special attention must also be paid to memory access times, resulting in designs with embedded on-chip DRAM and faster SRAM (used as a DRAM cache) memories. Ternary Content Address Memories (TCAMs) are also often used for lookup. With a TCAM, a 32-bit IP address is presented to the memory, which returns the content of the forwarding table entry for that address in essentially constant time. The Cisco 8500 has a 64K CAM for each input port.

Once a packet's output port has been determined via the lookup, the packet can be sent into the switching fabric. In some designs, a packet may be temporarily blocked from entering the switching fabric if packets from other input ports are currently using the fabric. A blocked packet will be queued at the input port and then scheduled to cross the fabric at a later point in time. We'll take a closer look at the blocking, queuing, and scheduling of packets (at both input ports and output ports) in Section 4.3.4. Although "lookup" is arguably the most important action in input port processing, many other actions must be taken: (1) physical- and link-layer processing must occur, as discussed above; (2) the packet's version number, checksum and time-to-live field—all of which we'll study in Section 4.4.1—must be checked and the latter two fields rewritten; and (3) counters used for network management (such as the number of IP datagrams received) must be updated.

Let's close our discussion of input port processing by noting that the input port steps of looking up an IP address ("match") then sending the packet into the switching fabric ("action") is a specific case of a more general "match plus action" abstraction that is performed in many networked devices, not just routers. In link-layer switches (covered in Chapter 5), link-layer destination addresses are looked up and several actions may be taken in addition to sending the frame into the switching fabric towards the output port. In firewalls (covered in Chapter 8)—devices that filter out selected incoming packets—an incoming packet whose header matches a given criteria (e.g., a combination of source/destination IP addresses and transport-layer port numbers) may be prevented from being forwarded (action). In a network address translator (NAT, covered in Section 4.4), an incoming packet whose transport-layer port number matches a given value will have its port number rewritten before forwarding (action). Thus, the "match plus action" abstraction is both powerful and prevalent in network devices.

4.3.2 Switching

The switching fabric is at the very heart of a router, as it is through this fabric that the packets are actually switched (that is, forwarded) from an input port to an output port. Switching can be accomplished in a number of ways, as shown in Figure 4.8:

• *Switching via memory.* The simplest, earliest routers were traditional computers, with switching between input and output ports being done under direct control of

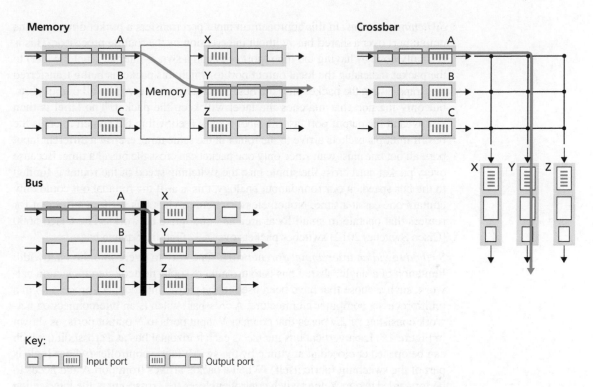

Figure 4.8 ♦ Three switching techniques

the CPU (routing processor). Input and output ports functioned as traditional I/O devices in a traditional operating system. An input port with an arriving packet first signaled the routing processor via an interrupt. The packet was then copied from the input port into processor memory. The routing processor then extracted the destination address from the header, looked up the appropriate output port in the forwarding table, and copied the packet to the output port's buffers. In this scenario, if the memory bandwidth is such that B packets per second can be written into, or read from, memory, then the overall forwarding throughput (the total rate at which packets are transferred from input ports to output ports) must be less than $B/2$. Note also that two packets cannot be forwarded at the same time, even if they have different destination ports, since only one memory read/write over the shared system bus can be done at a time.

Many modern routers switch via memory. A major difference from early routers, however, is that the lookup of the destination address and the storing of the packet into the appropriate memory location are performed by processing on the input line cards. In some ways, routers that switch via memory look very much like shared-memory multiprocessors, with the processing on a line card switching (writing) packets into the memory of the appropriate output port. Cisco's Catalyst 8500 series switches [Cisco 8500 2012] forward packets via a shared memory.

- *Switching via a bus.* In this approach, an input port transfers a packet directly to the output port over a shared bus, without intervention by the routing processor. This is typically done by having the input port pre-pend a switch-internal label (header) to the packet indicating the local output port to which this packet is being transferred and transmitting the packet onto the bus. The packet is received by all output ports, but only the port that matches the label will keep the packet. The label is then removed at the output port, as this label is only used within the switch to cross the bus. If multiple packets arrive to the router at the same time, each at a different input port, all but one must wait since only one packet can cross the bus at a time. Because every packet must cross the single bus, the switching speed of the router is limited to the bus speed; in our roundabout analogy, this is as if the roundabout could only contain one car at a time. Nonetheless, switching via a bus is often sufficient for routers that operate in small local area and enterprise networks. The Cisco 5600 [Cisco Switches 2012] switches packets over a 32 Gbps backplane bus.

- *Switching via an interconnection network.* One way to overcome the bandwidth limitation of a single, shared bus is to use a more sophisticated interconnection network, such as those that have been used in the past to interconnect processors in a multiprocessor computer architecture. A crossbar switch is an interconnection network consisting of $2N$ buses that connect N input ports to N output ports, as shown in Figure 4.8. Each vertical bus intersects each horizontal bus at a crosspoint, which can be opened or closed at any time by the switch fabric controller (whose logic is part of the switching fabric itself). When a packet arrives from port A and needs to be forwarded to port Y, the switch controller closes the crosspoint at the intersection of busses A and Y, and port A then sends the packet onto its bus, which is picked up (only) by bus Y. Note that a packet from port B can be forwarded to port X at the same time, since the A-to-Y and B-to-X packets use different input and output busses. Thus, unlike the previous two switching approaches, crossbar networks are capable of forwarding multiple packets in parallel. However, if two packets from two different input ports are destined to the same output port, then one will have to wait at the input, since only one packet can be sent over any given bus at a time.

More sophisticated interconnection networks use multiple stages of switching elements to allow packets from different input ports to proceed towards the same output port at the same time through the switching fabric. See [Tobagi 1990] for a survey of switch architectures. Cisco 12000 family switches [Cisco 12000 2012] use an interconnection network.

4.3.3 Output Processing

Output port processing, shown in Figure 4.9, takes packets that have been stored in the output port's memory and transmits them over the output link. This includes selecting and de-queueing packets for transmission, and performing the needed link-layer and physical-layer transmission functions.

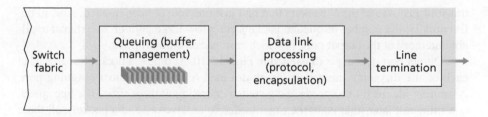

Figure 4.9 ♦ Output port processing

4.3.4 Where Does Queueing Occur?

If we consider input and output port functionality and the configurations shown in Figure 4.8, it's clear that packet queues may form at both the input ports *and* the output ports, just as we identified cases where cars may wait at the inputs and outputs of the traffic intersection in our roundabout analogy. The location and extent of queueing (either at the input port queues or the output port queues) will depend on the traffic load, the relative speed of the switching fabric, and the line speed. Let's now consider these queues in a bit more detail, since as these queues grow large, the router's memory can eventually be exhausted and **packet loss** will occur when no memory is available to store arriving packets. Recall that in our earlier discussions, we said that packets were "lost within the network" or "dropped at a router." It is here, at these queues within a router, where such packets are actually dropped and lost.

Suppose that the input and output line speeds (transmission rates) all have an identical transmission rate of R_{line} packets per second, and that there are N input ports and N output ports. To further simplify the discussion, let's assume that all packets have the same fixed length, and the packets arrive to input ports in a synchronous manner. That is, the time to send a packet on any link is equal to the time to receive a packet on any link, and during such an interval of time, either zero or one packet can arrive on an input link. Define the switching fabric transfer rate R_{switch} as the rate at which packets can be moved from input port to output port. If R_{switch} is N times faster than R_{line}, then only negligible queuing will occur at the input ports. This is because even in the worst case, where all N input lines are receiving packets, and all packets are to be forwarded to the same output port, each batch of N packets (one packet per input port) can be cleared through the switch fabric before the next batch arrives.

But what can happen at the output ports? Let's suppose that R_{switch} is still N times faster than R_{line}. Once again, packets arriving at each of the N input ports are destined to the same output port. In this case, in the time it takes to send a single packet onto the outgoing link, N new packets will arrive at this output port. Since the output port can transmit only a single packet in a unit of time (the packet transmission time), the N arriving packets will have to queue (wait) for transmission over the outgoing link. Then N more packets can possibly arrive in the time it takes to transmit just one of the N packets that had just previously been queued. And so on. Eventually, the number of queued packets can grow large enough to exhaust available memory at the output port, in which case packets are dropped.

Output port queuing is illustrated in Figure 4.10. At time t, a packet has arrived at each of the incoming input ports, each destined for the uppermost outgoing port. Assuming identical line speeds and a switch operating at three times the line speed, one time unit later (that is, in the time needed to receive or send a packet), all three original packets have been transferred to the outgoing port and are queued awaiting transmission. In the next time unit, one of these three packets will have been transmitted over the outgoing link. In our example, two *new* packets have arrived at the incoming side of the switch; one of these packets is destined for this uppermost output port.

Given that router buffers are needed to absorb the fluctuations in traffic load, the natural question to ask is how *much* buffering is required. For many years, the rule of thumb [RFC 3439] for buffer sizing was that the amount of buffering (B) should be equal to an average round-trip time $(RTT,$ say 250 msec) times the link capacity (C). This result is based on an analysis of the queueing dynamics of a relatively small number of TCP flows [Villamizar 1994]. Thus, a 10 Gbps link with an RTT of 250 msec would need an amount of buffering equal to $B = RTT \cdot C = 2.5$ Gbits of buffers. Recent

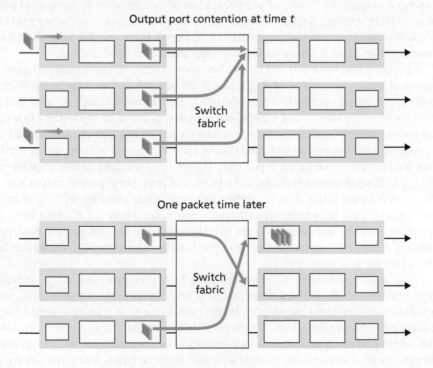

Figure 4.10 ♦ Output port queuing

theoretical and experimental efforts [Appenzeller 2004], however, suggest that when there are a large number of TCP flows (N) passing through a link, the amount of buffering needed is $B = RTT \cdot C/\sqrt{N}$. With a large number of flows typically passing through large backbone router links (see, e.g., [Fraleigh 2003]), the value of N can be large, with the decrease in needed buffer size becoming quite significant. [Appenzellar 2004; Wischik 2005; Beheshti 2008] provide very readable discussions of the buffer sizing problem from a theoretical, implementation, and operational standpoint.

A consequence of output port queuing is that a **packet scheduler** at the output port must choose one packet among those queued for transmission. This selection might be done on a simple basis, such as first-come-first-served (FCFS) scheduling, or a more sophisticated scheduling discipline such as weighted fair queuing (WFQ), which shares the outgoing link fairly among the different end-to-end connections that have packets queued for transmission. Packet scheduling plays a crucial role in providing **quality-of-service guarantees**. We'll thus cover packet scheduling extensively in Chapter 7. A discussion of output port packet scheduling disciplines is [Cisco Queue 2012].

Similarly, if there is not enough memory to buffer an incoming packet, a decision must be made to either drop the arriving packet (a policy known as **drop-tail**) or remove one or more already-queued packets to make room for the newly arrived packet. In some cases, it may be advantageous to drop (or mark the header of) a packet *before* the buffer is full in order to provide a congestion signal to the sender. A number of packet-dropping and -marking policies (which collectively have become known as **active queue management** (**AQM**) algorithms) have been proposed and analyzed [Labrador 1999, Hollot 2002]. One of the most widely studied and implemented AQM algorithms is the **Random Early Detection** (**RED**) algorithm. Under RED, a weighted average is maintained for the length of the output queue. If the average queue length is less than a minimum threshold, min_{th}, when a packet arrives, the packet is admitted to the queue. Conversely, if the queue is full or the average queue length is greater than a maximum threshold, max_{th}, when a packet arrives, the packet is marked or dropped. Finally, if the packet arrives to find an average queue length in the interval $[min_{th}, max_{th}]$, the packet is marked or dropped with a probability that is typically some function of the average queue length, min_{th}, and max_{th}. A number of probabilistic marking/dropping functions have been proposed, and various versions of RED have been analytically modeled, simulated, and/or implemented. [Christiansen 2001] and [Floyd 2012] provide overviews and pointers to additional reading.

If the switch fabric is not fast enough (relative to the input line speeds) to transfer *all* arriving packets through the fabric without delay, then packet queuing can also occur at the input ports, as packets must join input port queues to wait their turn to be transferred through the switching fabric to the output port. To illustrate an important consequence of this queuing, consider a crossbar switching fabric and suppose that (1) all link speeds are identical, (2) that one packet can be transferred from any one input port to a given output port in the same amount of time it takes for a packet to be received on an input link, and (3) packets are moved from a given input queue to their desired output queue in an FCFS manner. Multiple packets can be transferred in parallel, as long as their output ports are different. However, if two packets at the front of two input queues are destined for the same output queue, then one of the packets will be blocked and must wait at the input queue—the switching fabric can transfer only one packet to a given output port at a time.

Figure 4.11 shows an example in which two packets (darkly shaded) at the front of their input queues are destined for the same upper-right output port. Suppose that the switch fabric chooses to transfer the packet from the front of the upper-left queue. In this case, the darkly shaded packet in the lower-left queue must wait. But not only must this darkly shaded packet wait, so too must the lightly shaded packet that is queued behind that packet in the lower-left queue, even though there is *no* contention for the middle-right output port (the destination for the lightly shaded packet). This phenomenon is known as **head-of-the-line** (**HOL**) **blocking** in an

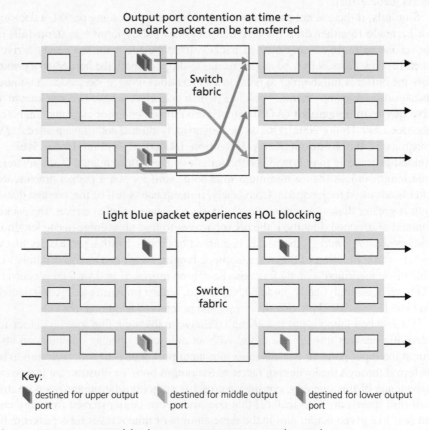

Figure 4.11 ♦ HOL blocking at an input queued switch

input-queued switch—a queued packet in an input queue must wait for transfer through the fabric (even though its output port is free) because it is blocked by another packet at the head of the line. [Karol 1987] shows that due to HOL blocking, the input queue will grow to unbounded length (informally, this is equivalent to saying that significant packet loss will occur) under certain assumptions as soon as the packet arrival rate on the input links reaches only 58 percent of their capacity. A number of solutions to HOL blocking are discussed in [McKeown 1997b].

4.3.5 The Routing Control Plane

In our discussion thus far and in Figure 4.6, we've implicitly assumed that the routing control plane fully resides and executes in a routing processor within the router. The network-wide routing control plane is thus decentralized—with different pieces (e.g., of a routing algorithm) executing at different routers and interacting by sending control messages to each other. Indeed, today's Internet routers and the routing algorithms we'll study in Section 4.6 operate in exactly this manner. Additionally, router and switch vendors bundle their hardware data plane and software control plane together into closed (but inter-operable) platforms in a vertically integrated product.

Recently, a number of researchers [Caesar 2005a, Casado 2009, McKeown 2008] have begun exploring new router control plane architectures in which part of the control plane is implemented in the routers (e.g., local measurement/reporting of link state, forwarding table installation and maintenance) along with the data plane, and part of the control plane can be implemented externally to the router (e.g., in a centralized server, which could perform route calculation). A well-defined API dictates how these two parts interact and communicate with each other. These researchers argue that separating the software control plane from the hardware data plane (with a minimal router-resident control plane) can simplify routing by replacing distributed routing calculation with centralized routing calculation, and enable network innovation by allowing different customized control planes to operate over fast hardware data planes.

4.4 The Internet Protocol (IP): Forwarding and Addressing in the Internet

Our discussion of network-layer addressing and forwarding thus far has been without reference to any specific computer network. In this section, we'll turn our attention to how addressing and forwarding are done in the Internet. We'll see that Internet addressing and forwarding are important components of the Internet Protocol (IP). There are two versions of IP in use today. We'll first examine the widely deployed IP protocol version 4, which is usually referred to simply as IPv4

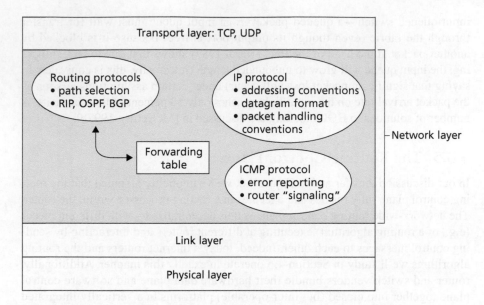

Figure 4.12 ♦ A look inside the Internet's network layer

[RFC 791]. We'll examine IP version 6 [RFC 2460; RFC 4291], which has been proposed to replace IPv4, at the end of this section.

But before beginning our foray into IP, let's take a step back and consider the components that make up the Internet's network layer. As shown in Figure 4.12, the Internet's network layer has three major components. The first component is the IP protocol, the topic of this section. The second major component is the routing component, which determines the path a datagram follows from source to destination. We mentioned earlier that routing protocols compute the forwarding tables that are used to forward packets through the network. We'll study the Internet's routing protocols in Section 4.6. The final component of the network layer is a facility to report errors in datagrams and respond to requests for certain network-layer information. We'll cover the Internet's network-layer error- and information-reporting protocol, the Internet Control Message Protocol (ICMP), in Section 4.4.3.

4.4.1 Datagram Format

Recall that a network-layer packet is referred to as a *datagram*. We begin our study of IP with an overview of the syntax and semantics of the IPv4 datagram. You might be thinking that nothing could be drier than the syntax and semantics of a packet's bits. Nevertheless, the datagram plays a central role in the Internet—every networking student and professional needs to see it, absorb it, and master it. The

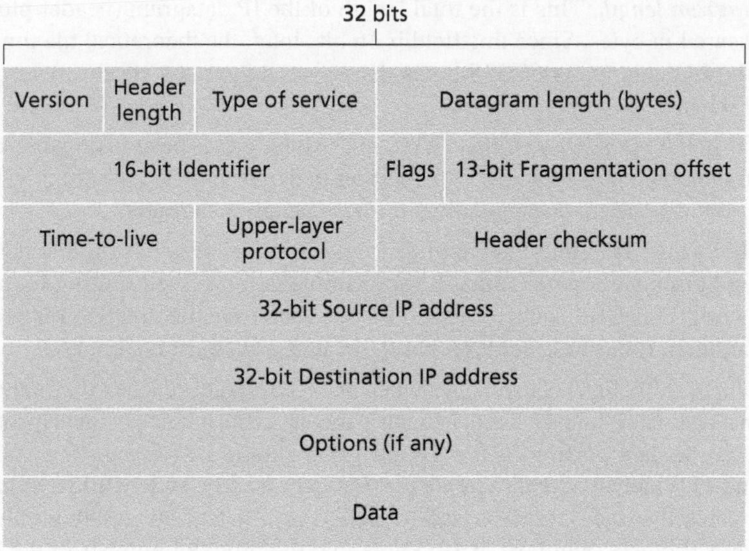

32 bits

Version	Header length	Type of service	Datagram length (bytes)	
16-bit Identifier			Flags	13-bit Fragmentation offset
Time-to-live		Upper-layer protocol	Header checksum	
32-bit Source IP address				
32-bit Destination IP address				
Options (if any)				
Data				

Figure 4.13 ♦ IPv4 datagram format

IPv4 datagram format is shown in Figure 4.13. The key fields in the IPv4 datagram are the following:

- *Version number.* These 4 bits specify the IP protocol version of the datagram. By looking at the version number, the router can determine how to interpret the remainder of the IP datagram. Different versions of IP use different datagram formats. The datagram format for the current version of IP, IPv4, is shown in Figure 4.13. The datagram format for the new version of IP (IPv6) is discussed at the end of this section.

- *Header length.* Because an IPv4 datagram can contain a variable number of options (which are included in the IPv4 datagram header), these 4 bits are needed to determine where in the IP datagram the data actually begins. Most IP datagrams do not contain options, so the typical IP datagram has a 20-byte header.

- *Type of service.* The type of service (TOS) bits were included in the IPv4 header to allow different types of IP datagrams (for example, datagrams particularly requiring low delay, high throughput, or reliability) to be distinguished from each other. For example, it might be useful to distinguish real-time datagrams (such as those used by an IP telephony application) from non-real-time traffic (for example, FTP). The specific level of service to be provided is a policy issue determined by the router's administrator. We'll explore the topic of differentiated service in Chapter 7.

- *Datagram length.* This is the total length of the IP datagram (header plus data), measured in bytes. Since this field is 16 bits long, the theoretical maximum size of the IP datagram is 65,535 bytes. However, datagrams are rarely larger than 1,500 bytes.

- *Identifier, flags, fragmentation offset.* These three fields have to do with so-called IP fragmentation, a topic we will consider in depth shortly. Interestingly, the new version of IP, IPv6, does not allow for fragmentation at routers.

- *Time-to-live.* The time-to-live (TTL) field is included to ensure that datagrams do not circulate forever (due to, for example, a long-lived routing loop) in the network. This field is decremented by one each time the datagram is processed by a router. If the TTL field reaches 0, the datagram must be dropped.

- *Protocol.* This field is used only when an IP datagram reaches its final destination. The value of this field indicates the specific transport-layer protocol to which the data portion of this IP datagram should be passed. For example, a value of 6 indicates that the data portion is passed to TCP, while a value of 17 indicates that the data is passed to UDP. For a list of all possible values, see [IANA Protocol Numbers 2012]. Note that the protocol number in the IP datagram has a role that is analogous to the role of the port number field in the transport-layer segment. The protocol number is the glue that binds the network and transport layers together, whereas the port number is the glue that binds the transport and application layers together. We'll see in Chapter 5 that the link-layer frame also has a special field that binds the link layer to the network layer.

- *Header checksum.* The header checksum aids a router in detecting bit errors in a received IP datagram. The header checksum is computed by treating each 2 bytes in the header as a number and summing these numbers using 1s complement arithmetic. As discussed in Section 3.3, the 1s complement of this sum, known as the Internet checksum, is stored in the checksum field. A router computes the header checksum for each received IP datagram and detects an error condition if the checksum carried in the datagram header does not equal the computed checksum. Routers typically discard datagrams for which an error has been detected. Note that the checksum must be recomputed and stored again at each router, as the TTL field, and possibly the options field as well, may change. An interesting discussion of fast algorithms for computing the Internet checksum is [RFC 1071]. A question often asked at this point is, why does TCP/IP perform error checking at both the transport and network layers? There are several reasons for this repetition. First, note that only the IP header is checksummed at the IP layer, while the TCP/UDP checksum is computed over the entire TCP/UDP segment. Second, TCP/UDP and IP do not necessarily both have to belong to the same protocol stack. TCP can, in principle, run over a different protocol (for example, ATM) and IP can carry data that will not be passed to TCP/UDP.

- *Source and destination IP addresses.* When a source creates a datagram, it inserts its IP address into the source IP address field and inserts the address of the ultimate destination into the destination IP address field. Often the source host determines the destination address via a DNS lookup, as discussed in Chapter 2. We'll discuss IP addressing in detail in Section 4.4.2.

* *Options.* The options fields allow an IP header to be extended. Header options were meant to be used rarely—hence the decision to save overhead by not including the information in options fields in every datagram header. However, the mere existence of options does complicate matters—since datagram headers can be of variable length, one cannot determine a priori where the data field will start. Also, since some datagrams may require options processing and others may not, the amount of time needed to process an IP datagram at a router can vary greatly. These considerations become particularly important for IP processing in high-performance routers and hosts. For these reasons and others, IP options were dropped in the IPv6 header, as discussed in Section 4.4.4.

* *Data (payload).* Finally, we come to the last and most important field—the *raison d'être* for the datagram in the first place! In most circumstances, the data field of the IP datagram contains the transport-layer segment (TCP or UDP) to be delivered to the destination. However, the data field can carry other types of data, such as ICMP messages (discussed in Section 4.4.3).

Note that an IP datagram has a total of 20 bytes of header (assuming no options). If the datagram carries a TCP segment, then each (nonfragmented) datagram carries a total of 40 bytes of header (20 bytes of IP header plus 20 bytes of TCP header) along with the application-layer message.

IP Datagram Fragmentation

We'll see in Chapter 5 that not all link-layer protocols can carry network-layer packets of the same size. Some protocols can carry big datagrams, whereas other protocols can carry only little packets. For example, Ethernet frames can carry up to 1,500 bytes of data, whereas frames for some wide-area links can carry no more than 576 bytes. The maximum amount of data that a link-layer frame can carry is called the maximum transmission unit (MTU). Because each IP datagram is encapsulated within the link-layer frame for transport from one router to the next router, the MTU of the link-layer protocol places a hard limit on the length of an IP datagram. Having a hard limit on the size of an IP datagram is not much of a problem. What is a problem is that each of the links along the route between sender and destination can use different link-layer protocols, and each of these protocols can have different MTUs.

To understand the forwarding issue better, imagine that *you* are a router that interconnects several links, each running different link-layer protocols with different MTUs. Suppose you receive an IP datagram from one link. You check your forwarding table to determine the outgoing link, and this outgoing link has an MTU that is smaller than the length of the IP datagram. Time to panic—how are you going to squeeze this oversized IP datagram into the payload field of the link-layer frame?

The solution is to fragment the data in the IP datagram into two or more smaller IP datagrams, encapsulate each of these smaller IP datagrams in a separate link-layer frame; and send these frames over the outgoing link. Each of these smaller datagrams is referred to as a **fragment**.

Fragments need to be reassembled before they reach the transport layer at the destination. Indeed, both TCP and UDP are expecting to receive complete, unfragmented segments from the network layer. The designers of IPv4 felt that reassembling datagrams in the routers would introduce significant complication into the protocol and put a damper on router performance. (If you were a router, would you want to be reassembling fragments on top of everything else you had to do?) Sticking to the principle of keeping the network core simple, the designers of IPv4 decided to put the job of datagram reassembly in the end systems rather than in network routers.

When a destination host receives a series of datagrams from the same source, it needs to determine whether any of these datagrams are fragments of some original, larger datagram. If some datagrams are fragments, it must further determine when it has received the last fragment and how the fragments it has received should be pieced back together to form the original datagram. To allow the destination host to perform these reassembly tasks, the designers of IP (version 4) put *identification, flag,* and *fragmentation offset* fields in the IP datagram header. When a datagram is created, the sending host stamps the datagram with an identification number as well as source and destination addresses. Typically, the sending host increments the identification number for each datagram it sends. When a router needs to fragment a datagram, each resulting datagram (that is, fragment) is stamped with the source address, destination address, and identification number of the original datagram. When the destination receives a series of datagrams from the same sending host, it can examine the identification numbers of the datagrams to determine which of the datagrams are actually fragments of the same larger datagram. Because IP is an unreliable service, one or more of the fragments may never arrive at the destination. For this reason, in order for the destination host to be absolutely sure it has received the last fragment of the original datagram, the last fragment has a flag bit set to 0, whereas all the other fragments have this flag bit set to 1. Also, in order for the destination host to determine whether a fragment is missing (and also to be able to reassemble the fragments in their proper order), the offset field is used to specify where the fragment fits within the original IP datagram.

Figure 4.14 illustrates an example. A datagram of 4,000 bytes (20 bytes of IP header plus 3,980 bytes of IP payload) arrives at a router and must be forwarded to a link with an MTU of 1,500 bytes. This implies that the 3,980 data bytes in the original datagram must be allocated to three separate fragments (each of which is also an IP datagram). Suppose that the original datagram is stamped with an identification number of 777. The characteristics of the three fragments are shown in Table 4.2. The values in Table 4.2 reflect the requirement that the amount of original payload data in all but the last fragment be a multiple of 8 bytes, and that the offset value be specified in units of 8-byte chunks.

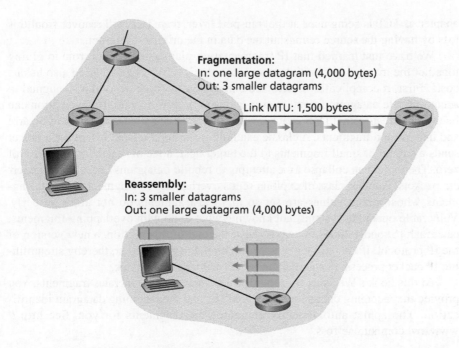

Fragmentation:
In: one large datagram (4,000 bytes)
Out: 3 smaller datagrams

Link MTU: 1,500 bytes

Reassembly:
In: 3 smaller datagrams
Out: one large datagram (4,000 bytes)

Figure 4.14 ♦ IP fragmentation and reassembly

At the destination, the payload of the datagram is passed to the transport layer only after the IP layer has fully reconstructed the original IP datagram. If one or more of the fragments does not arrive at the destination, the incomplete datagram is discarded and not passed to the transport layer. But, as we learned in the previous

Fragment	Bytes	ID	Offset	Flag
1st fragment	1,480 bytes in the data field of the IP datagram	identification = 777	offset = 0 (meaning the data should be inserted beginning at byte 0)	flag = 1 (meaning there is more)
2nd fragment	1,480 bytes of data	identification = 777	offset = 185 (meaning the data should be inserted beginning at byte 1,480. Note that $185 \cdot 8 = 1,480$)	flag = 1 (meaning there is more)
3rd fragment	1,020 bytes (= 3,980–1,480–1,480) of data	identification = 777	offset = 370 (meaning the data should be inserted beginning at byte 2,960. Note that $370 \cdot 8 = 2,960$)	flag = 0 (meaning this is the last fragment)

Table 4.2 ♦ IP fragments

chapter, if TCP is being used at the transport layer, then TCP will recover from this loss by having the source retransmit the data in the original datagram.

We have just learned that IP fragmentation plays an important role in gluing together the many disparate link-layer technologies. But fragmentation also has its costs. First, it complicates routers and end systems, which need to be designed to accommodate datagram fragmentation and reassembly. Second, fragmentation can be used to create lethal DoS attacks, whereby the attacker sends a series of bizarre and unexpected fragments. A classic example is the Jolt2 attack, where the attacker sends a stream of small fragments to the target host, none of which has an offset of zero. The target can collapse as it attempts to rebuild datagrams out of the degenerate packets. Another class of exploits sends overlapping IP fragments, that is, fragments whose offset values are set so that the fragments do not align properly. Vulnerable operating systems, not knowing what to do with overlapping fragments, can crash [Skoudis 2006]. As we'll see at the end of this section, a new version of the IP protocol, IPv6, does away with fragmentation altogether, thereby streamlining IP packet processing and making IP less vulnerable to attack.

At this book's Web site, we provide a Java applet that generates fragments. You provide the incoming datagram size, the MTU, and the incoming datagram identification. The applet automatically generates the fragments for you. See http://www.awl.com/kurose-ross.

4.4.2 IPv4 Addressing

We now turn our attention to IPv4 addressing. Although you may be thinking that addressing must be a straightforward topic, hopefully by the end of this chapter you'll be convinced that Internet addressing is not only a juicy, subtle, and interesting topic but also one that is of central importance to the Internet. Excellent treatments of IPv4 addressing are [3Com Addressing 2012] and the first chapter in [Stewart 1999].

Before discussing IP addressing, however, we'll need to say a few words about how hosts and routers are connected into the network. A host typically has only a single link into the network; when IP in the host wants to send a datagram, it does so over this link. The boundary between the host and the physical link is called an **interface**. Now consider a router and its interfaces. Because a router's job is to receive a datagram on one link and forward the datagram on some other link, a router necessarily has two or more links to which it is connected. The boundary between the router and any one of its links is also called an interface. A router thus has multiple interfaces, one for each of its links. Because every host and router is capable of sending and receiving IP datagrams, IP requires each host and router interface to have its own IP address. Thus, an IP address is technically associated with an interface, rather than with the host or router containing that interface.

Each IP address is 32 bits long (equivalently, 4 bytes), and there are thus a total of 2^{32} possible IP addresses. By approximating 2^{10} by 10^3, it is easy to see that there are about 4 billion possible IP addresses. These addresses are typically written in so-called **dotted-decimal notation**, in which each byte of the address is written in its decimal form and is separated by a period (dot) from other bytes in the address. For example, consider the IP address 193.32.216.9. The 193 is the decimal equivalent of the first 8 bits of the address; the 32 is the decimal equivalent of the second 8 bits of the address, and so on. Thus, the address 193.32.216.9 in binary notation is

$$11000001 \ 00100000 \ 11011000 \ 00001001$$

Each interface on every host and router in the global Internet must have an IP address that is globally unique (except for interfaces behind NATs, as discussed at the end of this section). These addresses cannot be chosen in a willy-nilly manner, however. A portion of an interface's IP address will be determined by the subnet to which it is connected.

Figure 4.15 provides an example of IP addressing and interfaces. In this figure, one router (with three interfaces) is used to interconnect seven hosts. Take a close look at the IP addresses assigned to the host and router interfaces, as there are several things to notice. The three hosts in the upper-left portion of Figure 4.15, and the router interface to which they are connected, all have an IP address of the form 223.1.1.xxx. That is, they all have the same leftmost 24 bits in their IP address. The four interfaces are also interconnected to each other by a network *that contains no routers*. This network

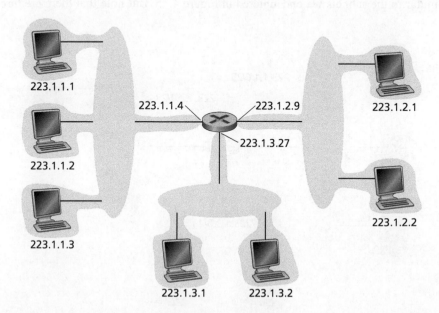

223.1.1.1

223.1.1.4   223.1.2.9   223.1.2.1

223.1.3.27

223.1.1.2

223.1.2.2

223.1.1.3

223.1.3.1   223.1.3.2

Figure 4.15 ♦ Interface addresses and subnets

could be interconnected by an Ethernet LAN, in which case the interfaces would be interconnected by an Ethernet switch (as we'll discuss in Chapter 5), or by a wireless access point (as we'll discuss in Chapter 6). We'll represent this routerless network connecting these hosts as a cloud for now, and dive into the internals of such networks in Chapters 5 and 6.

In IP terms, this network interconnecting three host interfaces and one router interface forms a **subnet** [RFC 950]. (A subnet is also called an *IP network* or simply a *network* in the Internet literature.) IP addressing assigns an address to this subnet: 223.1.1.0/24, where the /24 notation, sometimes known as a **subnet mask**, indicates that the leftmost 24 bits of the 32-bit quantity define the subnet address. The subnet 223.1.1.0/24 thus consists of the three host interfaces (223.1.1.1, 223.1.1.2, and 223.1.1.3) and one router interface (223.1.1.4). Any additional hosts attached to the 223.1.1.0/24 subnet would be *required* to have an address of the form 223.1.1.xxx. There are two additional subnets shown in Figure 4.15: the 223.1.2.0/24 network and the 223.1.3.0/24 subnet. Figure 4.16 illustrates the three IP subnets present in Figure 4.15.

The IP definition of a subnet is not restricted to Ethernet segments that connect multiple hosts to a router interface. To get some insight here, consider Figure 4.17, which shows three routers that are interconnected with each other by point-to-point links. Each router has three interfaces, one for each point-to-point link and one for the broadcast link that directly connects the router to a pair of hosts. What subnets are present here? Three subnets, 223.1.1.0/24, 223.1.2.0/24, and 223.1.3.0/24, are similar to the subnets we encountered in Figure 4.15. But note that there are three

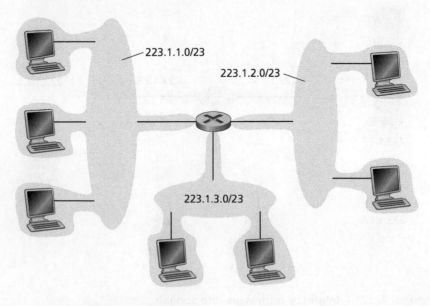

Figure 4.16 ♦ Subnet addresses

additional subnets in this example as well: one subnet, 223.1.9.0/24, for the interfaces that connect routers R1 and R2; another subnet, 223.1.8.0/24, for the interfaces that connect routers R2 and R3; and a third subnet, 223.1.7.0/24, for the interfaces that connect routers R3 and R1. For a general interconnected system of routers and hosts, we can use the following recipe to define the subnets in the system:

> *To determine the subnets, detach each interface from its host or router, creating islands of isolated networks, with interfaces terminating the end points of the isolated networks. Each of these isolated networks is called a **subnet**.*

If we apply this procedure to the interconnected system in Figure 4.17, we get six islands or subnets.

From the discussion above, it's clear that an organization (such as a company or academic institution) with multiple Ethernet segments and point-to-point links will have multiple subnets, with all of the devices on a given subnet having the same subnet address. In principle, the different subnets could have quite different subnet addresses. In practice, however, their subnet addresses often have much in common. To understand why, let's next turn our attention to how addressing is handled in the global Internet.

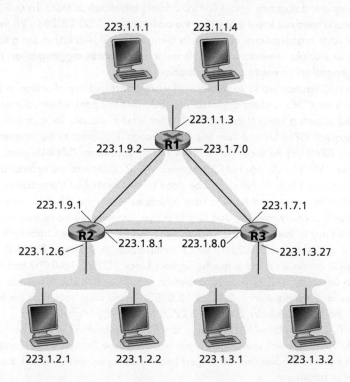

Figure 4.17 ♦ Three routers interconnecting six subnets

The Internet's address assignment strategy is known as **Classless Interdomain Routing** (**CIDR**—pronounced *cider*) [RFC 4632]. CIDR generalizes the notion of subnet addressing. As with subnet addressing, the 32-bit IP address is divided into two parts and again has the dotted-decimal form *a.b.c.d/x*, where *x* indicates the number of bits in the first part of the address.

The *x* most significant bits of an address of the form *a.b.c.d/x* constitute the network portion of the IP address, and are often referred to as the **prefix** (or *network prefix*) of the address. An organization is typically assigned a block of contiguous addresses, that is, a range of addresses with a common prefix (see the Principles in Practice sidebar). In this case, the IP addresses of devices within the organization will share the common prefix. When we cover the Internet's BGP

PRINCIPLES IN PRACTICE

This example of an ISP that connects eight organizations to the Internet nicely illustrates how carefully allocated CIDRized addresses facilitate routing. Suppose, as shown in Figure 4.18, that the ISP (which we'll call Fly-By-Night-ISP) advertises to the outside world that it should be sent any datagrams whose first 20 address bits match 200.23.16.0/20. The rest of the world need not know that within the address block 200.23.16.0/20 there are in fact eight other organizations, each with its own subnets. This ability to use a single prefix to advertise multiple networks is often referred to as **address aggregation** (also **route aggregation** or **route summarization**).

Address aggregation works extremely well when addresses are allocated in blocks to ISPs and then from ISPs to client organizations. But what happens when addresses are not allocated in such a hierarchical manner? What would happen, for example, if Fly-By-Night-ISP acquires ISPs-R-Us and then has Organization 1 connect to the Internet through its subsidiary ISPs-R-Us? As shown in Figure 4.18, the subsidiary ISPs-R-Us owns the address block 199.31.0.0/16, but Organization 1's IP addresses are unfortunately outside of this address block. What should be done here? Certainly, Organization 1 could renumber all of its routers and hosts to have addresses within the ISPs-R-Us address block. But this is a costly solution, and Organization 1 might well be reassigned to another subsidiary in the future. The solution typically adopted is for Organization 1 to keep its IP addresses in 200.23.18.0/23. In this case, as shown in Figure 4.19, Fly-By-Night-ISP continues to advertise the address block 200.23.16.0/20 and ISPs-R-Us continues to advertise 199.31.0.0/16. However, ISPs-R-Us now *also* advertises the block of addresses for Organization 1, 200.23.18.0/23. When other routers in the larger Internet see the address blocks 200.23.16.0/20 (from Fly-By-Night-ISP) and 200.23.18.0/23 (from ISPs-R-Us) and want to route to an address in the block 200.23.18.0/23, they will use longest prefix matching (see Section 4.2.2), and route toward ISPs-R-Us, as it advertises the longest (most specific) address prefix that matches the destination address.

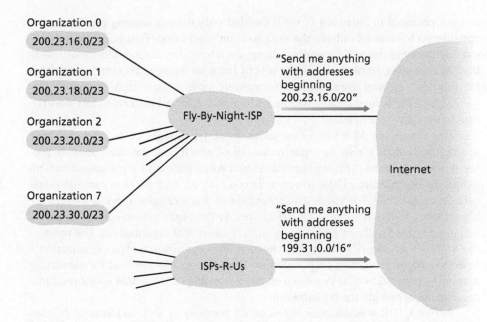

Figure 4.18 ♦ Hierarchical addressing and route aggregation

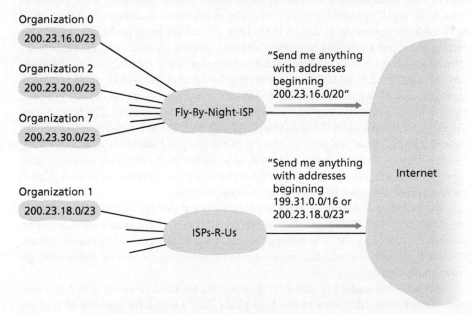

Figure 4.19 ♦ ISPs-R-Us has a more specific route to Organization 1

routing protocol in Section 4.6, we'll see that only these x leading prefix bits are considered by routers outside the organization's network. That is, when a router outside the organization forwards a datagram whose destination address is inside the organization, only the leading x bits of the address need be considered. This considerably reduces the size of the forwarding table in these routers, since a *single* entry of the form *a.b.c.d/x* will be sufficient to forward packets to *any* destination within the organization.

The remaining $32-x$ bits of an address can be thought of as distinguishing among the devices *within* the organization, all of which have the same network prefix. These are the bits that will be considered when forwarding packets at routers *within* the organization. These lower-order bits may (or may not) have an additional subnetting structure, such as that discussed above. For example, suppose the first 21 bits of the CIDRized address a.b.c.d/21 specify the organization's network prefix and are common to the IP addresses of all devices in that organization. The remaining 11 bits then identify the specific hosts in the organization. The organization's internal structure might be such that these 11 rightmost bits are used for subnetting within the organization, as discussed above. For example, a.b.c.d/24 might refer to a specific subnet within the organization.

Before CIDR was adopted, the network portions of an IP address were constrained to be 8, 16, or 24 bits in length, an addressing scheme known as **classful addressing**, since subnets with 8-, 16-, and 24-bit subnet addresses were known as class A, B, and C networks, respectively. The requirement that the subnet portion of an IP address be exactly 1, 2, or 3 bytes long turned out to be problematic for supporting the rapidly growing number of organizations with small and medium-sized subnets. A class C (/24) subnet could accommodate only up to $2^8 - 2 = 254$ hosts (two of the $2^8 = 256$ addresses are reserved for special use)—too small for many organizations. However, a class B (/16) subnet, which supports up to 65,634 hosts, was too large. Under classful addressing, an organization with, say, 2,000 hosts was typically allocated a class B (/16) subnet address. This led to a rapid depletion of the class B address space and poor utilization of the assigned address space. For example, the organization that used a class B address for its 2,000 hosts was allocated enough of the address space for up to 65,534 interfaces—leaving more than 63,000 addresses that could not be used by other organizations.

We would be remiss if we did not mention yet another type of IP address, the IP broadcast address 255.255.255.255. When a host sends a datagram with destination address 255.255.255.255, the message is delivered to all hosts on the same subnet. Routers optionally forward the message into neighboring subnets as well (although they usually don't).

Having now studied IP addressing in detail, we need to know how hosts and subnets get their addresses in the first place. Let's begin by looking at how an organization gets a block of addresses for its devices, and then look at how a device (such as a host) is assigned an address from within the organization's block of addresses.

Obtaining a Block of Addresses

In order to obtain a block of IP addresses for use within an organization's subnet, a network administrator might first contact its ISP, which would provide addresses from a larger block of addresses that had already been allocated to the ISP. For example, the ISP may itself have been allocated the address block 200.23.16.0/20. The ISP, in turn, could divide its address block into eight equal-sized contiguous address blocks and give one of these address blocks out to each of up to eight organizations that are supported by this ISP, as shown below. (We have underlined the subnet part of these addresses for your convenience.)

ISP's block	200.23.16.0/20	<u>11001000 00010111 0001</u>0000 00000000
Organization 0	200.23.16.0/23	<u>11001000 00010111 0001000</u>0 00000000
Organization 1	200.23.18.0/23	<u>11001000 00010111 0001001</u>0 00000000
Organization 2	200.23.20.0/23	<u>11001000 00010111 0001010</u>0 00000000
. . .	. . .	. . .
Organization 7	200.23.30.0/23	<u>11001000 00010111 0001111</u>0 00000000

While obtaining a set of addresses from an ISP is one way to get a block of addresses, it is not the only way. Clearly, there must also be a way for the ISP itself to get a block of addresses. Is there a global authority that has ultimate responsibility for managing the IP address space and allocating address blocks to ISPs and other organizations? Indeed there is! IP addresses are managed under the authority of the Internet Corporation for Assigned Names and Numbers (ICANN) [ICANN 2012], based on guidelines set forth in [RFC 2050]. The role of the nonprofit ICANN organization [NTIA 1998] is not only to allocate IP addresses, but also to manage the DNS root servers. It also has the very contentious job of assigning domain names and resolving domain name disputes. The ICANN allocates addresses to regional Internet registries (for example, ARIN, RIPE, APNIC, and LACNIC, which together form the Address Supporting Organization of ICANN [ASO-ICANN 2012]), and handle the allocation/management of addresses within their regions.

Obtaining a Host Address: the Dynamic Host Configuration Protocol

Once an organization has obtained a block of addresses, it can assign individual IP addresses to the host and router interfaces in its organization. A system administrator will typically manually configure the IP addresses into the router (often remotely, with a network management tool). Host addresses can also be configured manually, but more often this task is now done using the **Dynamic Host Configuration Protocol (DHCP)** [RFC 2131]. DHCP allows a host to obtain (be allocated) an IP address automatically. A network administrator can configure DHCP so that a given host receives the same IP address each time it connects to the network, or a host may be assigned a **temporary IP address** that will be different each time the host connects to the network. In addition to host IP address assignment, DHCP also allows a host to learn additional information, such as its subnet mask, the address of its first-hop router (often called the default gateway), and the address of its local DNS server.

Because of DHCP's ability to automate the network-related aspects of connecting a host into a network, it is often referred to as a **plug-and-play protocol**. This capability makes it *very* attractive to the network administrator who would otherwise have to perform these tasks manually! DHCP is also enjoying widespread use in residential Internet access networks and in wireless LANs, where hosts join and leave the network frequently. Consider, for example, the student who carries a laptop from a dormitory room to a library to a classroom. It is likely that in each location, the student will be connecting into a new subnet and hence will need a new IP address at each location. DHCP is ideally suited to this situation, as there are many users coming and going, and addresses are needed for only a limited amount of time. DHCP is similarly useful in residential ISP access networks. Consider, for example, a residential ISP that has 2,000 customers, but no more than 400 customers are ever online at the same time. In this case, rather than needing a block of 2,048 addresses, a DHCP server that assigns addresses dynamically needs only a block of 512 addresses (for example, a block of the form a.b.c.d/23). As the hosts join and leave, the DHCP server needs to update its list of available IP addresses. Each time a host joins, the DHCP server allocates an arbitrary address from its current pool of available addresses; each time a host leaves, its address is returned to the pool.

DHCP is a client-server protocol. A client is typically a newly arriving host wanting to obtain network configuration information, including an IP address for itself. In the simplest case, each subnet (in the addressing sense of Figure 4.17) will have a DHCP server. If no server is present on the subnet, a DHCP relay agent (typically a router) that knows the address of a DHCP server for that network is needed. Figure 4.20 shows a DHCP server attached to subnet 223.1.2/24, with the router serving as the relay agent for arriving clients attached to subnets 223.1.1/24 and 223.1.3/24. In our discussion below, we'll assume that a DHCP server is available on the subnet.

For a newly arriving host, the DHCP protocol is a four-step process, as shown in Figure 4.21 for the network setting shown in Figure 4.20. In this figure, `yiaddr` (as in "your Internet address") indicates the address being allocated to the newly arriving client. The four steps are:

• *DHCP server discovery.* The first task of a newly arriving host is to find a DHCP server with which to interact. This is done using a **DHCP discover message**, which a client sends within a UDP packet to port 67. The UDP packet is encapsulated in an IP datagram. But to whom should this datagram be sent? The host doesn't even know the IP address of the network to which it is attaching, much

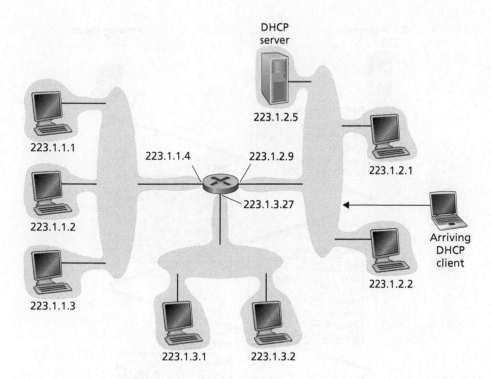

223.1.1.1

223.1.1.4   223.1.2.9

DHCP
server

223.1.2.5

223.1.2.1

223.1.3.27

Arriving
DHCP
client

223.1.1.2

223.1.1.3

223.1.2.2

223.1.3.1   223.1.3.2

Figure 4.20 ♦ DHCP client-server scenario

less the address of a DHCP server for this network. Given this, the DHCP client creates an IP datagram containing its DHCP discover message along with the broadcast destination IP address of 255.255.255.255 and a "this host" source IP address of 0.0.0.0. The DHCP client passes the IP datagram to the link layer, which then broadcasts this frame to all nodes attached to the subnet (we will cover the details of link-layer broadcasting in Section 5.4).

• *DHCP server offer(s).* A DHCP server receiving a DHCP discover message responds to the client with a **DHCP offer message** that is broadcast to all nodes on the subnet, again using the IP broadcast address of 255.255.255.255. (You might want to think about why this server reply must also be broadcast). Since several DHCP servers can be present on the subnet, the client may find itself in the enviable position of being able to choose from among several offers. Each server offer message contains the transaction ID of the received discover message, the proposed IP address for the client, the network mask, and an IP **address lease time**—the amount of time for which the IP address will be valid. It is common for the server to set the lease time to several hours or days [Droms 2002].

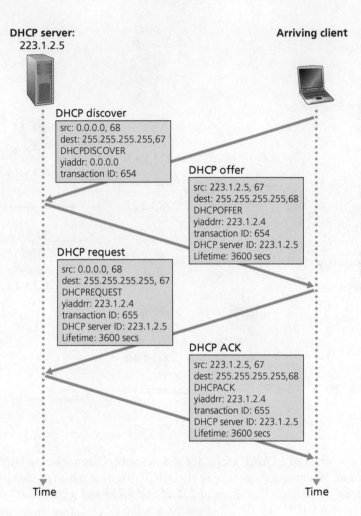

Figure 4.21 ◆ DHCP client-server interaction

- *DHCP request.* The newly arriving client will choose from among one or more server offers and respond to its selected offer with a **DHCP request message**, echoing back the configuration parameters.

- *DHCP ACK.* The server responds to the DHCP request message with a **DHCP ACK message**, confirming the requested parameters.

Once the client receives the DHCP ACK, the interaction is complete and the client can use the DHCP-allocated IP address for the lease duration. Since a client may want to use its address beyond the lease's expiration, DHCP also provides a mechanism that allows a client to renew its lease on an IP address.

The value of DHCP's plug-and-play capability is clear, considering the fact that the alternative is to manually configure a host's IP address. Consider the student who moves from classroom to library to dorm room with a laptop, joins a new subnet, and thus obtains a new IP address at each location. It is unimaginable that a system administrator would have to reconfigure laptops at each location, and few students (except those taking a computer networking class!) would have the expertise to configure their laptops manually. From a mobility aspect, however, DHCP does have shortcomings. Since a new IP address is obtained from DHCP each time a node connects to a new subnet, a TCP connection to a remote application cannot be maintained as a mobile node moves between subnets. In Chapter 6, we will examine mobile IP—a recent extension to the IP infrastructure that allows a mobile node to use a single permanent address as it moves between subnets. Additional details about DHCP can be found in [Droms 2002] and [dhc 2012]. An open source reference implementation of DHCP is available from the Internet Systems Consortium [ISC 2012].

Network Address Translation (NAT)

Given our discussion about Internet addresses and the IPv4 datagram format, we're now well aware that every IP-capable device needs an IP address. With the proliferation of small office, home office (SOHO) subnets, this would seem to imply that whenever a SOHO wants to install a LAN to connect multiple machines, a range of addresses would need to be allocated by the ISP to cover all of the SOHO's machines. If the subnet grew bigger (for example, the kids at home have not only their own computers, but have smartphones and networked Game Boys as well), a larger block of addresses would have to be allocated. But what if the ISP had already allocated the contiguous portions of the SOHO network's current address range? And what typical homeowner wants (or should need) to know how to manage IP addresses in the first place? Fortunately, there is a simpler approach to address allocation that has found increasingly widespread use in such scenarios: **network address translation** (**NAT**) [RFC 2663; RFC 3022; Zhang 2007].

Figure 4.22 shows the operation of a NAT-enabled router. The NAT-enabled router, residing in the home, has an interface that is part of the home network on the right of Figure 4.22. Addressing within the home network is exactly as we have seen above—all four interfaces in the home network have the same subnet address of 10.0.0/24. The address space 10.0.0.0/8 is one of three portions of the IP address space that is reserved in [RFC 1918] for a private network or a **realm** with private addresses, such as the home network in Figure 4.22. A *realm with private addresses* refers to a network whose addresses only have meaning to devices within that network. To see why this is important, consider the fact that there are hundreds of

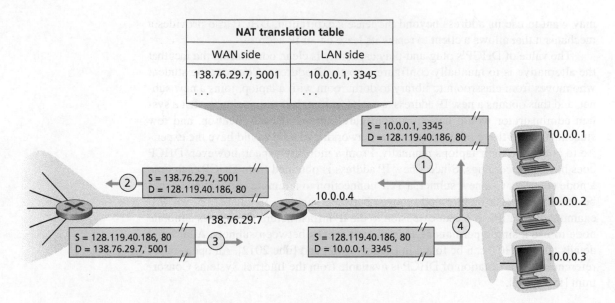

Figure 4.22 ♦ Network address translation

thousands of home networks, many using the same address space, 10.0.0.0/24. Devices within a given home network can send packets to each other using 10.0.0.0/24 addressing. However, packets forwarded *beyond* the home network into the larger global Internet clearly cannot use these addresses (as either a source or a destination address) because there are hundreds of thousands of networks using this block of addresses. That is, the 10.0.0.0/24 addresses can only have meaning within the given home network. But if private addresses only have meaning within a given network, how is addressing handled when packets are sent to or received from the global Internet, where addresses are necessarily unique? The answer lies in understanding NAT.

The NAT-enabled router does not *look* like a router to the outside world. Instead the NAT router behaves to the outside world as a *single* device with a *single* IP address. In Figure 4.22, all traffic leaving the home router for the larger Internet has a source IP address of 138.76.29.7, and all traffic entering the home router must have a destination address of 138.76.29.7. In essence, the NAT-enabled router is hiding the details of the home network from the outside world. (As an aside, you might wonder where the home network computers get their addresses and where the router gets its single IP address. Often, the answer is the same—DHCP! The router gets its address from the ISP's DHCP server, and the router runs a DHCP server to provide addresses to computers within the NAT-DHCP-router-controlled home network's address space.)

If all datagrams arriving at the NAT router from the WAN have the same destination IP address (specifically, that of the WAN-side interface of the NAT router), then how does the router know the internal host to which it should forward a given datagram? The trick is to use a **NAT translation table** at the NAT router, and to include port numbers as well as IP addresses in the table entries.

Consider the example in Figure 4.22. Suppose a user sitting in a home network behind host 10.0.0.1 requests a Web page on some Web server (port 80) with IP address 128.119.40.186. The host 10.0.0.1 assigns the (arbitrary) source port number 3345 and sends the datagram into the LAN. The NAT router receives the datagram, generates a new source port number 5001 for the datagram, replaces the source IP address with its WAN-side IP address 138.76.29.7, and replaces the original source port number 3345 with the new source port number 5001. When generating a new source port number, the NAT router can select any source port number that is not currently in the NAT translation table. (Note that because a port number field is 16 bits long, the NAT protocol can support over 60,000 simultaneous connections with a single WAN-side IP address for the router!) NAT in the router also adds an entry to its NAT translation table. The Web server, blissfully unaware that the arriving datagram containing the HTTP request has been manipulated by the NAT router, responds with a datagram whose destination address is the IP address of the NAT router, and whose destination port number is 5001. When this datagram arrives at the NAT router, the router indexes the NAT translation table using the destination IP address and destination port number to obtain the appropriate IP address (10.0.0.1) and destination port number (3345) for the browser in the home network. The router then rewrites the datagram's destination address and destination port number, and forwards the datagram into the home network.

NAT has enjoyed widespread deployment in recent years. But we should mention that many purists in the IETF community loudly object to NAT. First, they argue, port numbers are meant to be used for addressing processes, not for addressing hosts. (This violation can indeed cause problems for servers running on the home network, since, as we have seen in Chapter 2, server processes wait for incoming requests at well-known port numbers.) Second, they argue, routers are supposed to process packets only up to layer 3. Third, they argue, the NAT protocol violates the so-called end-to-end argument; that is, hosts should be talking directly with each other, without interfering nodes modifying IP addresses and port numbers. And fourth, they argue, we should use IPv6 (see Section 4.4.4) to solve the shortage of IP addresses, rather than recklessly patching up the problem with a stopgap solution like NAT. But like it or not, NAT has become an important component of the Internet.

Yet another major problem with NAT is that it interferes with P2P applications, including P2P file-sharing applications and P2P Voice-over-IP applications. Recall from Chapter 2 that in a P2P application, any participating Peer A should be able to initiate a TCP connection to any other participating Peer B. The essence of the problem is that if Peer B is behind a NAT, it cannot act as a server and accept TCP connections. As we'll see in the homework problems, this NAT problem can be circumvented if Peer A is not behind a NAT. In this case, Peer A can first contact Peer B through an intermediate Peer C, which is not behind a NAT and to which B has established an ongoing TCP connection. Peer A can then ask Peer B, via Peer C, to initiate a TCP connection directly back to Peer A. Once the direct P2P TCP connection is established between Peers A and B, the two peers can exchange messages or files. This hack, called **connection reversal**, is actually used by many P2P applications for **NAT traversal**. If both Peer A and Peer B are behind their own NATs, the situation is a bit trickier but can be handled using application relays, as we saw with Skype relays in Chapter 2.

UPnP

NAT traversal is increasingly provided by Universal Plug and Play (UPnP), which is a protocol that allows a host to discover and configure a nearby NAT [UPnP Forum 2012]. UPnP requires that both the host and the NAT be UPnP compatible. With UPnP, an application running in a host can request a NAT mapping between its (*private IP address, private port number*) and the (*public IP address, public port number*) for some requested public port number. If the NAT accepts the request and creates the mapping, then nodes from the outside can initiate TCP connections to (*public IP address, public port number*). Furthermore, UPnP lets the application know the value of (*public IP address, public port number*), so that the application can advertise it to the outside world.

As an example, suppose your host, behind a UPnP-enabled NAT, has private address 10.0.0.1 and is running BitTorrent on port 3345. Also suppose that the public IP address of the NAT is 138.76.29.7. Your BitTorrent application naturally wants to be able to accept connections from other hosts, so that it can trade chunks with them. To this end, the BitTorrent application in your host asks the NAT to create a "hole" that maps (10.0.0.1, 3345) to (138.76.29.7, 5001). (The public port number 5001 is chosen by the application.) The BitTorrent application in your host could also advertise to its tracker that it is available at (138.76.29.7, 5001). In this manner, an external host running BitTorrent can contact the tracker and learn that your BitTorrent application is running at (138.76.29.7, 5001). The external host can send a TCP SYN packet to (138.76.29.7, 5001). When the NAT receives the SYN packet, it will change the destination IP address and port number in the packet to (10.0.0.1, 3345) and forward the packet through the NAT.

In summary, UPnP allows external hosts to initiate communication sessions to NATed hosts, using either TCP or UDP. NATs have long been a nemesis for P2P applications; UPnP, providing an effective and robust NAT traversal solution, may be their savior. Our discussion of NAT and UPnP here has been necessarily brief. For more detailed discussions of NAT see [Huston 2004, Cisco NAT 2012].

4.4.3 Internet Control Message Protocol (ICMP)

Recall that the network layer of the Internet has three main components: the IP protocol, discussed in the previous section; the Internet routing protocols (including RIP, OSPF, and BGP), which are covered in Section 4.6; and ICMP, which is the subject of this section.

ICMP, specified in [RFC 792], is used by hosts and routers to communicate network-layer information to each other. The most typical use of ICMP is for error reporting. For example, when running a Telnet, FTP, or HTTP session, you may have encountered an error message such as "Destination network unreachable." This message had its origins in ICMP. At some point, an IP router was unable to find a path to the host specified in your Telnet, FTP, or HTTP application. That router created and sent a type-3 ICMP message to your host indicating the error.

ICMP is often considered part of IP but architecturally it lies just above IP, as ICMP messages are carried inside IP datagrams. That is, ICMP messages are carried as IP payload, just as TCP or UDP segments are carried as IP payload. Similarly, when a host receives an IP datagram with ICMP specified as the upper-layer protocol, it demultiplexes the datagram's contents to ICMP, just as it would demultiplex a datagram's content to TCP or UDP.

ICMP messages have a type and a code field, and contain the header and the first 8 bytes of the IP datagram that caused the ICMP message to be generated in the first place (so that the sender can determine the datagram that caused the error). Selected ICMP message types are shown in Figure 4.23. Note that ICMP messages are used not only for signaling error conditions.

The well-known ping program sends an ICMP type 8 code 0 message to the specified host. The destination host, seeing the echo request, sends back a type 0 code 0 ICMP echo reply. Most TCP/IP implementations support the `ping` server directly in the operating system; that is, the server is not a process. Chapter 11 of [Stevens 1990] provides the source code for the ping client program. Note that the client program needs to be able to instruct the operating system to generate an ICMP message of type 8 code 0.

Another interesting ICMP message is the source quench message. This message is seldom used in practice. Its original purpose was to perform congestion control—to allow a congested router to send an ICMP source quench message to a host to force that host to reduce its transmission rate. We have seen in Chapter 3 that TCP has its own congestion-control mechanism that operates at the transport layer, without the use of network-layer feedback such as the ICMP source quench message.

In Chapter 1 we introduced the Traceroute program, which allows us to trace a route from a host to any other host in the world. Interestingly, Traceroute is implemented with ICMP messages. To determine the names and addresses of the routers between source and destination, Traceroute in the source sends a series of ordinary IP datagrams to the destination. Each of these datagrams carries a UDP segment with an unlikely UDP port number. The first of these datagrams has a TTL of 1, the

ICMP Type	Code	Description
0	0	echo reply (to ping)
3	0	destination network unreachable
3	1	destination host unreachable
3	2	destination protocol unreachable
3	3	destination port unreachable
3	6	destination network unknown
3	7	destination host unknown
4	0	source quench (congestion control)
8	0	echo request
9	0	router advertisement
10	0	router discovery
11	0	TTL expired
12	0	IP header bad

Figure 4.23 ♦ ICMP message types

second of 2, the third of 3, and so on. The source also starts timers for each of the datagrams. When the nth datagram arrives at the nth router, the nth router observes that the TTL of the datagram has just expired. According to the rules of the IP protocol, the router discards the datagram and sends an ICMP warning message to the source (type 11 code 0). This warning message includes the name of the router and its IP address. When this ICMP message arrives back at the source, the source obtains the round-trip time from the timer and the name and IP address of the nth router from the ICMP message.

How does a Traceroute source know when to stop sending UDP segments? Recall that the source increments the TTL field for each datagram it sends. Thus, one of the datagrams will eventually make it all the way to the destination host. Because this datagram contains a UDP segment with an unlikely port number, the destination host sends a port unreachable ICMP message (type 3 code 3) back to the source. When the source host receives this particular ICMP message, it knows it does not need to send additional probe packets. (The standard Traceroute program actually sends sets of three packets with the same TTL; thus the Traceroute output provides three results for each TTL.)

FOCUS ON SECURITY

INSPECTING DATAGRAMS: FIREWALLS AND INTRUSION DETECTION SYSTEMS

Suppose you are assigned the task of administering a home, departmental, university, or corporate network. Attackers, knowing the IP address range of your network, can easily send IP datagrams to addresses in your range. These datagrams can do all kinds of devious things, including mapping your network with ping sweeps and port scans, crashing vulnerable hosts with malformed packets, flooding servers with a deluge of ICMP packets, and infecting hosts by including malware in the packets. As the network administrator, what are you going to do about all those bad guys out there, each capable of sending malicious packets into your network? Two popular defense mechanisms to malicious packet attacks are firewalls and intrusion detection systems (IDSs).

As a network administrator, you may first try installing a firewall between your network and the Internet. (Most access routers today have firewall capability.) Firewalls inspect the datagram and segment header fields, denying suspicious datagrams entry into the internal network. For example, a firewall may be configured to block all ICMP echo request packets, thereby preventing an attacker from doing a traditional ping sweep across your IP address range. Firewalls can also block packets based on source and destination IP addresses and port numbers. Additionally, firewalls can be configured to track TCP connections, granting entry only to datagrams that belong to approved connections.

Additional protection can be provided with an IDS. An IDS, typically situated at the network boundary, performs "deep packet inspection," examining not only header fields but also the payloads in the datagram (including application-layer data). An IDS has a database of packet signatures that are known to be part of attacks. This database is automatically updated as new attacks are discovered. As packets pass through the IDS, the IDS attempts to match header fields and payloads to the signatures in its signature database. If such a match is found, an alert is created. An intrusion prevention system (IPS) is similar to an IDS, except that it actually blocks packets in addition to creating alerts. In Chapter 8, we'll explore firewalls and IDSs in more detail.

Can firewalls and IDSs fully shield your network from all attacks? The answer is clearly no, as attackers continually find new attacks for which signatures are not yet available. But firewalls and traditional signature-based IDSs are useful in protecting your network from known attacks.

In this manner, the source host learns the number and the identities of routers that lie between it and the destination host and the round-trip time between the two hosts. Note that the Traceroute client program must be able to instruct the operating system to generate UDP datagrams with specific TTL values and must also be able to be notified by its operating system when ICMP messages arrive. Now that you understand how Traceroute works, you may want to go back and play with it some more.

4.4.4 IPv6

In the early 1990s, the Internet Engineering Task Force began an effort to develop a successor to the IPv4 protocol. A prime motivation for this effort was the realization that the 32-bit IP address space was beginning to be used up, with new subnets and IP nodes being attached to the Internet (and being allocated unique IP addresses) at a breathtaking rate. To respond to this need for a large IP address space, a new IP protocol, IPv6, was developed. The designers of IPv6 also took this opportunity to tweak and augment other aspects of IPv4, based on the accumulated operational experience with IPv4.

The point in time when IPv4 addresses would be completely allocated (and hence no new networks could attach to the Internet) was the subject of considerable debate. The estimates of the two leaders of the IETF's Address Lifetime Expectations working group were that addresses would become exhausted in 2008 and 2018, respectively [Solensky 1996]. In February 2011, IANA allocated out the last remaining pool of unassigned IPv4 addresses to a regional registry. While these registries still have available IPv4 addresses within their pool, once these addresses are exhausted, there are no more available address blocks that can be allocated from a central pool [Huston 2011a]. Although the mid-1990s estimates of IPv4 address depletion suggested that a considerable amount of time might be left until the IPv4 address space was exhausted, it was realized that considerable time would be needed to deploy a new technology on such an extensive scale, and so the Next Generation IP (IPng) effort [Bradner 1996; RFC 1752] was begun. The result of this effort was the specification of IP version 6 (IPv6) [RFC 2460] which we'll discuss below. (An often-asked question is what happened to IPv5? It was initially envisioned that the ST-2 protocol would become IPv5, but ST-2 was later dropped.) Excellent sources of information about IPv6 are [Huitema 1998, IPv6 2012].

IPv6 Datagram Format

The format of the IPv6 datagram is shown in Figure 4.24. The most important changes introduced in IPv6 are evident in the datagram format:

• *Expanded addressing capabilities.* IPv6 increases the size of the IP address from 32 to 128 bits. This ensures that the world won't run out of IP addresses. Now, every grain of sand on the planet can be IP-addressable. In addition to unicast and multicast addresses, IPv6 has introduced a new type of address, called an **anycast address**, which allows a datagram to be delivered to any one of a group of hosts. (This feature could be used, for example, to send an HTTP GET to the nearest of a number of mirror sites that contain a given document.)

• *A streamlined 40-byte header.* As discussed below, a number of IPv4 fields have been dropped or made optional. The resulting 40-byte fixed-length header allows

32 bits

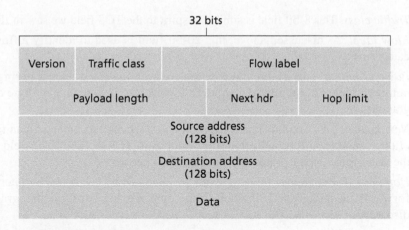

Version	Traffic class	Flow label	
Payload length		Next hdr	Hop limit
Source address (128 bits)			
Destination address (128 bits)			
Data			

Figure 4.24 ◆ IPv6 datagram format

for faster processing of the IP datagram. A new encoding of options allows for more flexible options processing.

- *Flow labeling and priority.* IPv6 has an elusive definition of a **flow**. RFC 1752 and RFC 2460 state that this allows "labeling of packets belonging to particular flows for which the sender requests special handling, such as a nondefault quality of service or real-time service." For example, audio and video transmission might likely be treated as a flow. On the other hand, the more traditional applications, such as file transfer and e-mail, might not be treated as flows. It is possible that the traffic carried by a high-priority user (for example, someone paying for better service for their traffic) might also be treated as a flow. What is clear, however, is that the designers of IPv6 foresee the eventual need to be able to differentiate among the flows, even if the exact meaning of a flow has not yet been determined. The IPv6 header also has an 8-bit traffic class field. This field, like the TOS field in IPv4, can be used to give priority to certain datagrams within a flow, or it can be used to give priority to datagrams from certain applications (for example, ICMP) over datagrams from other applications (for example, network news).

As noted above, a comparison of Figure 4.24 with Figure 4.13 reveals the simpler, more streamlined structure of the IPv6 datagram. The following fields are defined in IPv6:

- *Version.* This 4-bit field identifies the IP version number. Not surprisingly, IPv6 carries a value of 6 in this field. Note that putting a 4 in this field does not create a valid IPv4 datagram. (If it did, life would be a lot simpler—see the discussion below regarding the transition from IPv4 to IPv6.)

- *Traffic class.* This 8-bit field is similar in spirit to the TOS field we saw in IPv4.
- *Flow label.* As discussed above, this 20-bit field is used to identify a flow of datagrams.
- *Payload length.* This 16-bit value is treated as an unsigned integer giving the number of bytes in the IPv6 datagram following the fixed-length, 40-byte datagram header.
- *Next header.* This field identifies the protocol to which the contents (data field) of this datagram will be delivered (for example, to TCP or UDP). The field uses the same values as the protocol field in the IPv4 header.
- *Hop limit.* The contents of this field are decremented by one by each router that forwards the datagram. If the hop limit count reaches zero, the datagram is discarded.
- *Source and destination addresses.* The various formats of the IPv6 128-bit address are described in RFC 4291.
- *Data.* This is the payload portion of the IPv6 datagram. When the datagram reaches its destination, the payload will be removed from the IP datagram and passed on to the protocol specified in the next header field.

The discussion above identified the purpose of the fields that are included in the IPv6 datagram. Comparing the IPv6 datagram format in Figure 4.24 with the IPv4 datagram format that we saw in Figure 4.13, we notice that several fields appearing in the IPv4 datagram are no longer present in the IPv6 datagram:

- *Fragmentation/Reassembly.* IPv6 does not allow for fragmentation and reassembly at intermediate routers; these operations can be performed only by the source and destination. If an IPv6 datagram received by a router is too large to be forwarded over the outgoing link, the router simply drops the datagram and sends a "Packet Too Big" ICMP error message (see below) back to the sender. The sender can then resend the data, using a smaller IP datagram size. Fragmentation and reassembly is a time-consuming operation; removing this functionality from the routers and placing it squarely in the end systems considerably speeds up IP forwarding within the network.
- *Header checksum.* Because the transport-layer (for example, TCP and UDP) and link-layer (for example, Ethernet) protocols in the Internet layers perform checksumming, the designers of IP probably felt that this functionality was sufficiently redundant in the network layer that it could be removed. Once again, fast processing of IP packets was a central concern. Recall from our discussion of IPv4 in Section 4.4.1 that since the IPv4 header contains a TTL field (similar to the hop limit field in IPv6), the IPv4 header checksum needed to be recomputed at every router. As with fragmentation and reassembly, this too was a costly operation in IPv4.

- *Options.* An options field is no longer a part of the standard IP header. However, it has not gone away. Instead, the options field is one of the possible next headers pointed to from within the IPv6 header. That is, just as TCP or UDP protocol headers can be the next header within an IP packet, so too can an options field. The removal of the options field results in a fixed-length, 40-byte IP header.

Recall from our discussion in Section 4.4.3 that the ICMP protocol is used by IP nodes to report error conditions and provide limited information (for example, the echo reply to a ping message) to an end system. A new version of ICMP has been defined for IPv6 in RFC 4443. In addition to reorganizing the existing ICMP type and code definitions, ICMPv6 also added new types and codes required by the new IPv6 functionality. These include the "Packet Too Big" type, and an "unrecognized IPv6 options" error code. In addition, ICMPv6 subsumes the functionality of the Internet Group Management Protocol (IGMP) that we'll study in Section 4.7. IGMP, which is used to manage a host's joining and leaving of multicast groups, was previously a separate protocol from ICMP in IPv4.

Transitioning from IPv4 to IPv6

Now that we have seen the technical details of IPv6, let us consider a very practical matter: How will the public Internet, which is based on IPv4, be transitioned to IPv6? The problem is that while new IPv6-capable systems can be made backward-compatible, that is, can send, route, and receive IPv4 datagrams, already deployed IPv4-capable systems are not capable of handling IPv6 datagrams. Several options are possible [Huston 2011b].

One option would be to declare a flag day—a given time and date when all Internet machines would be turned off and upgraded from IPv4 to IPv6. The last major technology transition (from using NCP to using TCP for reliable transport service) occurred almost 25 years ago. Even back then [RFC 801], when the Internet was tiny and still being administered by a small number of "wizards," it was realized that such a flag day was not possible. A flag day involving hundreds of millions of machines and millions of network administrators and users is even more unthinkable today. RFC 4213 describes two approaches (which can be used either alone or together) for gradually integrating IPv6 hosts and routers into an IPv4 world (with the long-term goal, of course, of having all IPv4 nodes eventually transition to IPv6).

Probably the most straightforward way to introduce IPv6-capable nodes is a **dual-stack** approach, where IPv6 nodes also have a complete IPv4 implementation. Such a node, referred to as an IPv6/IPv4 node in RFC 4213, has the ability to send and receive both IPv4 and IPv6 datagrams. When interoperating with an IPv4 node, an IPv6/IPv4 node can use IPv4 datagrams; when interoperating with an IPv6 node, it can speak IPv6. IPv6/IPv4 nodes must have both IPv6 and IPv4 addresses. They must furthermore be able to determine whether another node is IPv6-capable or IPv4-only. This problem can be solved using the DNS (see Chapter 2), which can return an IPv6 address if the node name being resolved is IPv6-capable, or otherwise return an IPv4 address. Of course, if the node issuing the DNS request is only IPv4-capable, the DNS returns only an IPv4 address.

In the dual-stack approach, if either the sender or the receiver is only IPv4-capable, an IPv4 datagram must be used. As a result, it is possible that two IPv6-capable nodes can end up, in essence, sending IPv4 datagrams to each other. This is illustrated in Figure 4.25. Suppose Node A is IPv6-capable and wants to send an IP datagram to Node F, which is also IPv6-capable. Nodes A and B can exchange an IPv6 datagram. However, Node B must create an IPv4 datagram to send to C. Certainly, the data field of the IPv6 datagram can be copied into the data field of the IPv4 datagram and appropriate address mapping can be done. However, in performing the conversion from IPv6 to IPv4, there will be IPv6-specific fields in the IPv6 datagram (for example, the flow identifier field) that have no counterpart in IPv4. The information in these fields will be lost. Thus, even though E and F can exchange IPv6 datagrams, the arriving IPv4 datagrams at E from D do not contain all of the fields that were in the original IPv6 datagram sent from A.

An alternative to the dual-stack approach, also discussed in RFC 4213, is known as **tunneling**. Tunneling can solve the problem noted above, allowing, for example, E to receive the IPv6 datagram originated by A. The basic idea behind tunneling is the following. Suppose two IPv6 nodes (for example, B and E in Figure 4.25) want to interoperate using IPv6 datagrams but are connected to each other by intervening IPv4 routers. We refer to the intervening set of IPv4 routers between two IPv6 routers as a **tunnel**, as illustrated in Figure 4.26. With tunneling, the IPv6 node on the sending side of the tunnel (for example, B) takes the *entire* IPv6 datagram and puts it in the data (payload) field of an IPv4 datagram.

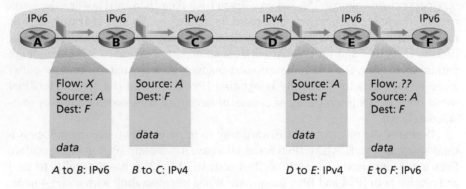

Figure 4.25 ♦ A dual-stack approach

Logical view

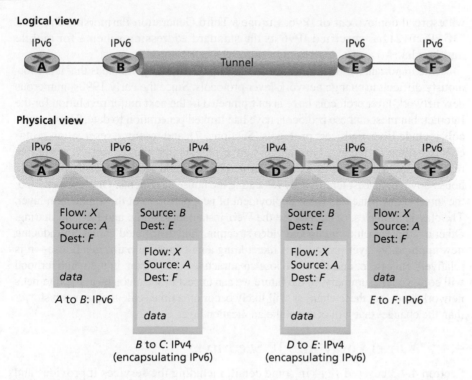

Figure 4.26 ♦ Tunneling

This IPv4 datagram is then addressed to the IPv6 node on the receiving side of the tunnel (for example, E) and sent to the first node in the tunnel (for example, C). The intervening IPv4 routers in the tunnel route this IPv4 datagram among themselves, just as they would any other datagram, blissfully unaware that the IPv4 datagram itself contains a complete IPv6 datagram. The IPv6 node on the receiving side of the tunnel eventually receives the IPv4 datagram (it is the destination of the IPv4 datagram!), determines that the IPv4 datagram contains an IPv6 datagram, extracts the IPv6 datagram, and then routes the IPv6 datagram exactly as it would if it had received the IPv6 datagram from a directly connected IPv6 neighbor.

We end this section by noting that while the adoption of IPv6 was initially slow to take off [Lawton 2001], momentum has been building recently. See [Huston 2008b] for discussion of IPv6 deployment as of 2008; see [NIST IPv6 2012] for a snapshot of US IPv6 deployment. The proliferation of devices such as IP-enabled phones and other portable devices provides an additional push for more widespread deployment of IPv6. Europe's Third Generation Partnership Program [3GPP 2012] has specified IPv6 as the standard addressing scheme for mobile multimedia.

One important lesson that we can learn from the IPv6 experience is that it is enormously difficult to change network-layer protocols. Since the early 1990s, numerous new network-layer protocols have been trumpeted as the next major revolution for the Internet, but most of these protocols have had limited penetration to date. These protocols include IPv6, multicast protocols (Section 4.7), and resource reservation protocols (Chapter 7). Indeed, introducing new protocols into the network layer is like replacing the foundation of a house—it is difficult to do without tearing the whole house down or at least temporarily relocating the house's residents. On the other hand, the Internet has witnessed rapid deployment of new protocols at the application layer. The classic examples, of course, are the Web, instant messaging, and P2P file sharing. Other examples include audio and video streaming and distributed games. Introducing new application-layer protocols is like adding a new layer of paint to a house—it is relatively easy to do, and if you choose an attractive color, others in the neighborhood will copy you. In summary, in the future we can expect to see changes in the Internet's network layer, but these changes will likely occur on a time scale that is much slower than the changes that will occur at the application layer.

4.4.5 A Brief Foray into IP Security

Section 4.4.3 covered IPv4 in some detail, including the services it provides and how those services are implemented. While reading through that section, you may have noticed that there was no mention of any security services. Indeed, IPv4 was designed in an era (the 1970s) when the Internet was primarily used among mutually-trusted networking researchers. Creating a computer network that integrated a multitude of link-layer technologies was already challenging enough, without having to worry about security.

But with security being a major concern today, Internet researchers have moved on to design new network-layer protocols that provide a variety of security services. One of these protocols is IPsec, one of the more popular secure network-layer protocols and also widely deployed in Virtual Private Networks (VPNs). Although IPsec and its cryptographic underpinnings are covered in some detail in Chapter 8, we provide a brief, high-level introduction into IPsec services in this section.

IPsec has been designed to be backward compatible with IPv4 and IPv6. In particular, in order to reap the benefits of IPsec, we don't need to replace the protocol stacks in *all* the routers and hosts in the Internet. For example, using the transport mode (one of two IPsec "modes"), if two hosts want to securely communicate, IPsec needs to be available only in those two hosts. All other routers and hosts can continue to run vanilla IPv4.

For concreteness, we'll focus on IPsec's transport mode here. In this mode, two hosts first establish an IPsec session between themselves. (Thus IPsec is connection-oriented!) With the session in place, all TCP and UDP segments sent between the two hosts enjoy the security services provided by IPsec. On the sending side, the transport layer passes a segment to IPsec. IPsec then encrypts the segment, appends additional security fields to the segment, and encapsulates the resulting payload in an ordinary IP datagram. (It's actually a little more complicated than this, as we'll see in Chapter 8.) The sending host then sends the datagram into the Internet, which transports it to the destination host. There, IPsec decrypts the segment and passes the unencrypted segment to the transport layer.

The services provided by an IPsec session include:

- *Cryptographic agreement.* Mechanisms that allow the two communicating hosts to agree on cryptographic algorithms and keys.
- *Encryption of IP datagram payloads.* When the sending host receives a segment from the transport layer, IPsec encrypts the payload. The payload can only be decrypted by IPsec in the receiving host.
- *Data integrity.* IPsec allows the receiving host to verify that the datagram's header fields and encrypted payload were not modified while the datagram was en route from source to destination.
- *Origin authentication.* When a host receives an IPsec datagram from a trusted source (with a trusted key—see Chapter 8), the host is assured that the source IP address in the datagram is the actual source of the datagram.

When two hosts have an IPsec session established between them, all TCP and UDP segments sent between them will be encrypted and authenticated. IPsec therefore provides blanket coverage, securing all communication between the two hosts for all network applications.

A company can use IPsec to communicate securely in the nonsecure public Internet. For illustrative purposes, we'll just look at a simple example here. Consider a company that has a large number of traveling salespeople, each possessing a company laptop computer. Suppose the salespeople need to frequently consult sensitive company information (for example, pricing and product information) that is stored on a server in the company's headquarters. Further suppose that the salespeople also need to send sensitive documents to each other. How can this be done with IPsec? As you might guess, we install IPsec in the server and in all of the salespeople's laptops. With IPsec installed in these hosts, whenever a salesperson needs to communicate with the server or with another salesperson, the communication session will be secure.

4.5 Routing Algorithms

So far in this chapter, we've mostly explored the network layer's forwarding function. We learned that when a packet arrives to a router, the router indexes a forwarding table and determines the link interface to which the packet is to be directed. We also learned that routing algorithms, operating in network routers, exchange and compute the information that is used to configure these forwarding tables. The interplay between routing algorithms and forwarding tables was shown in Figure 4.2. Having explored forwarding in some depth we now turn our attention to the other major topic of this chapter, namely, the network layer's critical routing function. Whether the network layer provides a datagram service (in which case different packets between a given source-destination pair may take different routes) or a VC service (in which case all packets between a given source and destination will take the same path), the network layer must nonetheless determine the path that packets take from senders to receivers. We'll see that the job of routing is to determine good paths (equivalently, routes), from senders to receivers, through the network of routers.

Typically a host is attached directly to one router, the **default router** for the host (also called the **first-hop router** for the host). Whenever a host sends a packet, the packet is transferred to its default router. We refer to the default router of the source host as the **source router** and the default router of the destination host as the **destination router**. The problem of routing a packet from source host to destination host clearly boils down to the problem of routing the packet from source router to destination router, which is the focus of this section.

The purpose of a routing algorithm is then simple: given a set of routers, with links connecting the routers, a routing algorithm finds a "good" path from source router to destination router. Typically, a good path is one that has the least cost. We'll see, however, that in practice, real-world concerns such as policy issues (for example, a rule such as "router x, belonging to organization Y, should not forward any packets originating from the network owned by organization Z") also come into play to complicate the conceptually simple and elegant algorithms whose theory underlies the practice of routing in today's networks.

A graph is used to formulate routing problems. Recall that a **graph** $G = (N,E)$ is a set N of nodes and a collection E of edges, where each edge is a pair of nodes from N. In the context of network-layer routing, the nodes in the graph represent routers—the points at which packet-forwarding decisions are made—and the edges connecting these nodes represent the physical links between these routers. Such a graph abstraction of a computer network is shown in Figure 4.27. To view some graphs representing real network maps, see [Dodge 2012, Cheswick 2000]; for a discussion of how well different graph-based models model the Internet, see [Zegura 1997, Faloutsos 1999, Li 2004].

As shown in Figure 4.27, an edge also has a value representing its cost. Typically, an edge's cost may reflect the physical length of the corresponding link (for example, a transoceanic link might have a higher cost than a short-haul terrestrial link), the link speed, or the monetary cost associated with a link. For our purposes, we'll simply take the edge costs as a given and won't worry about how they are determined. For any edge (x,y) in E, we denote $c(x,y)$ as the cost of the edge between nodes x and y. If the pair (x,y) does not belong to E, we set $c(x,y) = \infty$. Also, throughout we consider only undirected graphs (i.e., graphs whose edges do not have a direction), so that edge (x,y) is the same as edge (y,x) and that $c(x,y) = c(y,x)$. Also, a node y is said to be a **neighbor** of node x if (x,y) belongs to E.

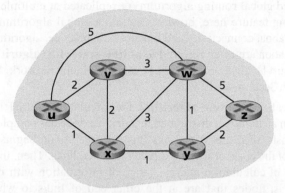

Figure 4.27 ♦ Abstract graph model of a computer network

Given that costs are assigned to the various edges in the graph abstraction, a natural goal of a routing algorithm is to identify the least costly paths between sources and destinations. To make this problem more precise, recall that a **path** in a graph $G = (N,E)$ is a sequence of nodes $(x_1, x_2,..., x_p)$ such that each of the pairs (x_1,x_2), $(x_2,x_3),...,(x_{p-1},x_p)$ are edges in E. The cost of a path $(x_1,x_2,..., x_p)$ is simply the sum of all the edge costs along the path, that is, $c(x_1,x_2) + c(x_2,x_3) + ...+ c(x_{p-1},x_p)$. Given any two nodes x and y, there are typically many paths between the two nodes, with each path having a cost. One or more of these paths is a **least-cost path**. The least-cost problem is therefore clear: Find a path between the source and destination that has least cost. In Figure 4.27, for example, the least-cost path between source node u and destination node w is (u, x, y, w) with a path cost of 3. Note that if all edges in the graph have the same cost, the least-cost path is also the **shortest path** (that is, the path with the smallest number of links between the source and the destination).

As a simple exercise, try finding the least-cost path from node u to z in Figure 4.27 and reflect for a moment on how you calculated that path. If you are like most people, you found the path from u to z by examining Figure 4.27, tracing a few routes from u to z, and somehow convincing yourself that the path you had chosen had the least cost among all possible paths. (Did you check all of the 17 possible paths between u and z? Probably not!) Such a calculation is an example of a centralized routing algorithm—the routing algorithm was run in one location, your brain, with complete information about the network. Broadly, one way in which we can classify routing algorithms is according to whether they are global or decentralized.

• A **global routing algorithm** computes the least-cost path between a source and destination using complete, global knowledge about the network. That is, the algorithm takes the connectivity between all nodes and all link costs as inputs. This then requires that the algorithm somehow obtain this information before actually performing the calculation. The calculation itself can be run at one site (a centralized global routing algorithm) or replicated at multiple sites. The key distinguishing feature here, however, is that a global algorithm has complete information about connectivity and link costs. In practice, algorithms with global state information are often referred to as **link-state (LS) algorithms**, since the algorithm must be aware of the cost of each link in the network. We'll study LS algorithms in Section 4.5.1.

* In a **decentralized routing algorithm**, the calculation of the least-cost path is carried out in an iterative, distributed manner. No node has complete information about the costs of all network links. Instead, each node begins with only the knowledge of the costs of its own directly attached links. Then, through an iterative process of calculation and exchange of information with its neighboring nodes (that is, nodes that are at the other end of links to which it itself is attached), a node gradually calculates the least-cost path to a destination or set of destinations. The decentralized routing algorithm we'll study below in Section 4.5.2 is called a distance-vector (DV) algorithm, because each node maintains a vector of estimates of the costs (distances) to all other nodes in the network.

A second broad way to classify routing algorithms is according to whether they are static or dynamic. In **static routing algorithms**, routes change very slowly over time, often as a result of human intervention (for example, a human manually editing a router's forwarding table). **Dynamic routing algorithms** change the routing paths as the network traffic loads or topology change. A dynamic algorithm can be run either periodically or in direct response to topology or link cost changes. While dynamic algorithms are more responsive to network changes, they are also more susceptible to problems such as routing loops and oscillation in routes.

A third way to classify routing algorithms is according to whether they are load-sensitive or load-insensitive. In a **load-sensitive algorithm**, link costs vary dynamically to reflect the current level of congestion in the underlying link. If a high cost is associated with a link that is currently congested, a routing algorithm will tend to choose routes around such a congested link. While early ARPAnet routing algorithms were load-sensitive [McQuillan 1980], a number of difficulties were encountered [Huitema 1998]. Today's Internet routing algorithms (such as RIP, OSPF, and BGP) are **load-insensitive**, as a link's cost does not explicitly reflect its current (or recent past) level of congestion.

4.5.1 The Link-State (LS) Routing Algorithm

Recall that in a link-state algorithm, the network topology and all link costs are known, that is, available as input to the LS algorithm. In practice this is accomplished by having each node broadcast link-state packets to *all* other nodes in the network, with each link-state packet containing the identities and costs of its attached links. In practice (for example, with the Internet's OSPF routing protocol, discussed in Section 4.6.1) this is often accomplished by a **link-state broadcast** algorithm [Perlman 1999]. We'll cover broadcast algorithms in Section 4.7. The result of the nodes' broadcast is that all nodes have an identical and complete view of the network. Each node can then run the LS algorithm and compute the same set of least-cost paths as every other node.

The link-state routing algorithm we present below is known as *Dijkstra's algorithm*, named after its inventor. A closely related algorithm is Prim's algorithm; see [Cormen 2001] for a general discussion of graph algorithms. Dijkstra's algorithm computes the least-cost path from one node (the source, which we will refer to as u) to all other nodes in the network. Dijkstra's algorithm is iterative and has the property that after the kth iteration of the algorithm, the least-cost paths are known to k destination nodes, and among the least-cost paths to all destination nodes, these k paths will have the k smallest costs. Let us define the following notation:

- $D(v)$: cost of the least-cost path from the source node to destination v as of this iteration of the algorithm.
- $p(v)$: previous node (neighbor of v) along the current least-cost path from the source to v.
- N' : subset of nodes; v is in N' if the least-cost path from the source to v is definitively known.

The global routing algorithm consists of an initialization step followed by a loop. The number of times the loop is executed is equal to the number of nodes in the network. Upon termination, the algorithm will have calculated the shortest paths from the source node u to every other node in the network.

Link-State (LS) Algorithm for Source Node u

```
1   Initialization:
2      N' = {u}
3      for all nodes v
4        if v is a neighbor of u
5           then D(v) = c(u,v)
6        else D(v) = ∞
7
8   Loop
9      find w not in N' such that D(w) is a minimum
10     add w to N'
11     update D(v) for each neighbor v of w and not in N':
12           D(v) = min( D(v), D(w) + c(w,v) )
13     /* new cost to v is either old cost to v or known
14       least path cost to w plus cost from w to v */
15  until N'= N
```

As an example, let's consider the network in Figure 4.27 and compute the least-cost paths from u to all possible destinations. A tabular summary of the algorithm's computation is shown in Table 4.3, where each line in the table gives the values of the algorithm's variables at the end of the iteration. Let's consider the few first steps in detail.

- In the initialization step, the currently known least-cost paths from u to its directly attached neighbors, v, x, and w, are initialized to 2, 1, and 5, respectively. Note in particular that the cost to w is set to 5 (even though we will soon see that a lesser-cost path does indeed exist) since this is the cost of the direct (one hop) link from u to w. The costs to y and z are set to infinity because they are not directly connected to u.

- In the first iteration, we look among those nodes not yet added to the set N' and find that node with the least cost as of the end of the previous iteration. That node is x, with a cost of 1, and thus x is added to the set N'. Line 12 of the LS algorithm is then performed to update $D(v)$ for all nodes v, yielding the results shown in the second line (Step 1) in Table 4.3. The cost of the path to v is unchanged. The cost of the path to w (which was 5 at the end of the initialization) through node x is found to have a cost of 4. Hence this lower-cost path is selected and w's predecessor along the shortest path from u is set to x. Similarly, the cost to y (through x) is computed to be 2, and the table is updated accordingly.

- In the second iteration, nodes v and y are found to have the least-cost paths (2), and we break the tie arbitrarily and add y to the set N' so that N' now contains u, x, and y. The cost to the remaining nodes not yet in N', that is, nodes v, w, and z, are updated via line 12 of the LS algorithm, yielding the results shown in the third row in the Table 4.3.

- And so on. . . .

When the LS algorithm terminates, we have, for each node, its predecessor along the least-cost path from the source node. For each predecessor, we also

step	N'	D(v),p(v)	D(w),p(w)	D(x),p(x)	D(y),p(y)	D(z),p(z)
0	u	2,u	5,u	1,u	∞	∞
1	ux	2,u	4,x		2,x	∞
2	uxy	2,u	3,y			4,y
3	uxyv		3,y			4,y
4	uxyvw					4,y
5	uxyvwz					

Table 4.3 ♦ Running the link-state algorithm on the network in Figure 4.27

have *its* predecessor, and so in this manner we can construct the entire path from the source to all destinations. The forwarding table in a node, say node u, can then be constructed from this information by storing, for each destination, the next-hop node on the least-cost path from u to the destination. Figure 4.28 shows the resulting least-cost paths and forwarding table in u for the network in Figure 4.27.

What is the computational complexity of this algorithm? That is, given n nodes (not counting the source), how much computation must be done in the worst case to find the least-cost paths from the source to all destinations? In the first iteration, we need to search through all n nodes to determine the node, w, not in N' that has the minimum cost. In the second iteration, we need to check $n - 1$ nodes to determine the minimum cost; in the third iteration $n - 2$ nodes, and so on. Overall, the total number of nodes we need to search through over all the iterations is $n(n + 1)/2$, and thus we say that the preceding implementation of the LS algorithm has worst-case complexity of order n squared: $O(n^2)$. (A more sophisticated implementation of this algorithm, using a data structure known as a heap, can find the minimum in line 9 in logarithmic rather than linear time, thus reducing the complexity.)

Before completing our discussion of the LS algorithm, let us consider a pathology that can arise. Figure 4.29 shows a simple network topology where link costs are equal to the load carried on the link, for example, reflecting the delay that would be experienced. In this example, link costs are not symmetric; that is, $c(u,v)$ equals $c(v,u)$ only if the load carried on both directions on the link (u,v) is the same. In this example, node z originates a unit of traffic destined for w, node x also originates a unit of traffic destined for w, and node y injects an amount of traffic equal to e, also destined for w. The initial routing is shown in Figure 4.29(a) with the link costs corresponding to the amount of traffic carried.

When the LS algorithm is next run, node y determines (based on the link costs shown in Figure 4.29(a)) that the clockwise path to w has a cost of 1, while the counterclockwise path to w (which it had been using) has a cost of $1 + e$. Hence y's

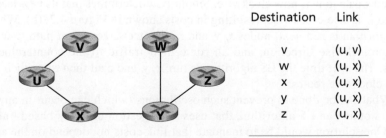

Figure 4.28 ♦ Least cost path and forwarding table for node

Destination	Link
v	(u, v)
w	(u, x)
x	(u, x)
y	(u, x)
z	(u, x)

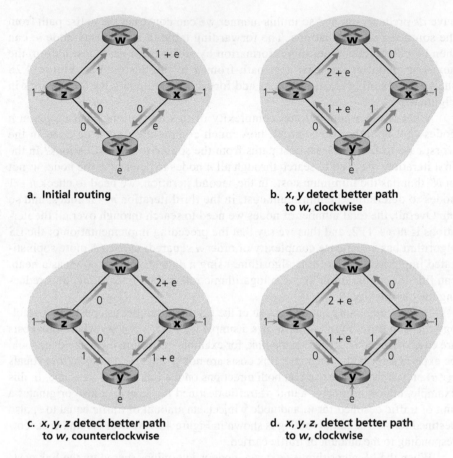

a. Initial routing

b. x, y detect better path to w, clockwise

c. x, y, z detect better path to w, counterclockwise

d. x, y, z, detect better path to w, clockwise

Figure 4.29 ♦ Oscillations with congestion-sensitive routing

least-cost path to w is now clockwise. Similarly, x determines that its new least-cost path to w is also clockwise, resulting in costs shown in Figure 4.29(b). When the LS algorithm is run next, nodes x, y, and z all detect a zero-cost path to w in the counterclockwise direction, and all route their traffic to the counterclockwise routes. The next time the LS algorithm is run, x, y, and z all then route their traffic to the clockwise routes.

What can be done to prevent such oscillations (which can occur in any algorithm, not just an LS algorithm, that uses a congestion or delay-based link metric)? One solution would be to mandate that link costs not depend on the amount of traffic carried—an unacceptable solution since one goal of routing is to avoid highly congested (for example, high-delay) links. Another solution is to ensure that not all routers run the LS algorithm at the same time. This seems a more reasonable solution, since we would hope that even if routers ran the LS algorithm with the same periodicity, the execution instance of the algorithm would not be the same at each node. Interestingly, researchers have found that routers in the Internet can self-synchronize among themselves [Floyd Synchronization 1994]. That is, even though they initially execute the algorithm with the same period but at different instants of time, the algorithm execution instance can eventually become, and remain, synchronized at the routers. One way to avoid such self-synchronization is for each router to randomize the time it sends out a link advertisement.

Having studied the LS algorithm, let's consider the other major routing algorithm that is used in practice today—the distance-vector routing algorithm.

4.5.2 The Distance-Vector (DV) Routing Algorithm

Whereas the LS algorithm is an algorithm using global information, the **distance-vector (DV)** algorithm is iterative, asynchronous, and distributed. It is *distributed* in that each node receives some information from one or more of its *directly attached* neighbors, performs a calculation, and then distributes the results of its calculation back to its neighbors. It is *iterative* in that this process continues on until no more information is exchanged between neighbors. (Interestingly, the algorithm is also self-terminating—there is no signal that the computation should stop; it just stops.) The algorithm is *asynchronous* in that it does not require all of the nodes to operate in lockstep with each other. We'll see that an asynchronous, iterative, self-terminating, distributed algorithm is much more interesting and fun than a centralized algorithm!

Before we present the DV algorithm, it will prove beneficial to discuss an important relationship that exists among the costs of the least-cost paths. Let $d_x(y)$ be the cost of the least-cost path from node x to node y. Then the least costs are related by the celebrated Bellman-Ford equation, namely,

$$d_x(y) = \min_v \{c(x,v) + d_v(y)\}, \tag{4.1}$$

where the min_v in the equation is taken over all of x's neighbors. The Bellman-Ford equation is rather intuitive. Indeed, after traveling from x to v, if we then take the least-cost path from v to y, the path cost will be $c(x,v) + d_v(y)$. Since we must begin by traveling to some neighbor v, the least cost from x to y is the minimum of $c(x,v) + d_v(y)$ taken over all neighbors v.

But for those who might be skeptical about the validity of the equation, let's check it for source node u and destination node z in Figure 4.27. The source node u

has three neighbors: nodes v, x, and w. By walking along various paths in the graph, it is easy to see that $d_v(z) = 5$, $d_x(z) = 3$, and $d_w(z) = 3$. Plugging these values into Equation 4.1, along with the costs $c(u,v) = 2$, $c(u,x) = 1$, and $c(u,w) = 5$, gives $d_u(z) = \min\{2 + 5, 5 + 3, 1 + 3\} = 4$, which is obviously true and which is exactly what the Dijskstra algorithm gave us for the same network. This quick verification should help relieve any skepticism you may have.

The Bellman-Ford equation is not just an intellectual curiosity. It actually has significant practical importance. In particular, the solution to the Bellman-Ford equation provides the entries in node x's forwarding table. To see this, let v^* be any neighboring node that achieves the minimum in Equation 4.1. Then, if node x wants to send a packet to node y along a least-cost path, it should first forward the packet to node v^*. Thus, node x's forwarding table would specify node v^* as the next-hop router for the ultimate destination y. Another important practical contribution of the Bellman-Ford equation is that it suggests the form of the neighbor-to-neighbor communication that will take place in the DV algorithm.

The basic idea is as follows. Each node x begins with $D_x(y)$, an estimate of the cost of the least-cost path from itself to node y, for all nodes in N. Let $\boldsymbol{D}_x = [D_x(y): y$ in $N]$ be node x's distance vector, which is the vector of cost estimates from x to all other nodes, y, in N. With the DV algorithm, each node x maintains the following routing information:

- For each neighbor v, the cost $c(x,v)$ from x to directly attached neighbor, v
- Node x's distance vector, that is, $\boldsymbol{D}_x = [D_x(y): y$ in $N]$, containing x's estimate of its cost to all destinations, y, in N
- The distance vectors of each of its neighbors, that is, $\boldsymbol{D}_v = [D_v(y): y$ in $N]$ for each neighbor v of x

In the distributed, asynchronous algorithm, from time to time, each node sends a copy of its distance vector to each of its neighbors. When a node x receives a new distance vector from any of its neighbors v, it saves v's distance vector, and then uses the Bellman-Ford equation to update its own distance vector as follows:

$$D_x(y) = \min_v\{c(x,v) + D_v(y)\} \quad \text{for each node } y \text{ in } N$$

If node x's distance vector has changed as a result of this update step, node x will then send its updated distance vector to each of its neighbors, which can in turn update their own distance vectors. Miraculously enough, as long as all the nodes continue to exchange their distance vectors in an asynchronous fashion, each cost estimate $D_x(y)$ converges to $d_x(y)$, the actual cost of the least-cost path from node x to node y [Bertsekas 1991]!

Distance-Vector (DV) Algorithm

At each node, x:

```
1   Initialization:
2       for all destinations y in N:
3           D_x(y) = c(x,y)    /* if y is not a neighbor then c(x,y) = ∞ */
4       for each neighbor w
5           D_w(y) = ? for all destinations y in N
6       for each neighbor w
7           send distance vector D_x = [D_x(y): y in N] to w
8
9   loop
10      wait (until I see a link cost change to some neighbor w or
11             until I receive a distance vector from some neighbor w)
12
13      for each y in N:
14          D_x(y) = min_v{c(x,v) + D_v(y)}
15
16      if D_x(y) changed for any destination y
17          send distance vector D_x = [D_x(y): y in N] to all neighbors
18
19  forever
```

In the DV algorithm, a node x updates its distance-vector estimate when it either sees a cost change in one of its directly attached links or receives a distance-vector update from some neighbor. But to update its own forwarding table for a given destination y, what node x really needs to know is not the shortest-path distance to y but instead the neighboring node $v^*(y)$ that is the next-hop router along the shortest path to y. As you might expect, the next-hop router $v^*(y)$ is the neighbor v that achieves the minimum in Line 14 of the DV algorithm. (If there are multiple neighbors v that achieve the minimum, then $v^*(y)$ can be any of the minimizing neighbors.) Thus, in Lines 13–14, for each destination y, node x also determines $v^*(y)$ and updates its forwarding table for destination y.

Recall that the LS algorithm is a global algorithm in the sense that it requires each node to first obtain a complete map of the network before running the Dijkstra algorithm. The DV algorithm is *decentralized* and does not use such global information. Indeed, the only information a node will have is the costs of the links to its directly attached neighbors and information it receives from these neighbors. Each node waits for an update from any neighbor (Lines 10–11), calculates its new distance vector when receiving an update (Line 14), and distributes its new distance vector to its neighbors (Lines 16–17). DV-like algorithms are used in many routing protocols in practice, including the Internet's RIP and BGP, ISO IDRP, Novell IPX, and the original ARPAnet.

Figure 4.30 illustrates the operation of the DV algorithm for the simple three-node network shown at the top of the figure. The operation of the algorithm is illustrated in a synchronous manner, where all nodes simultaneously receive distance vectors from their neighbors, compute their new distance vectors, and inform their neighbors if their distance vectors have changed. After studying this example, you

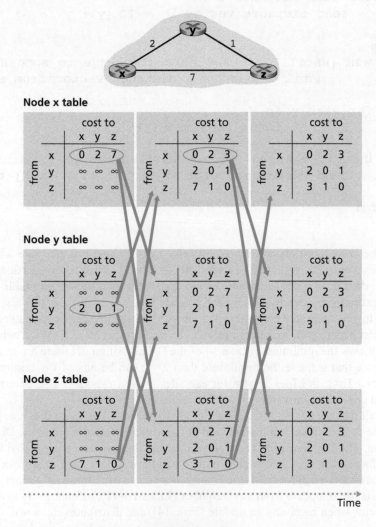

Figure 4.30 ♦ Distance-vector (DV) algorithm

should convince yourself that the algorithm operates correctly in an asynchronous manner as well, with node computations and update generation/reception occurring at any time.

The leftmost column of the figure displays three initial **routing tables** for each of the three nodes. For example, the table in the upper-left corner is node x's initial routing table. Within a specific routing table, each row is a distance vector—specifically, each node's routing table includes its own distance vector and that of each of its neighbors. Thus, the first row in node x's initial routing table is $D_x = [D_x(x), D_x(y), D_x(z)] = [0, 2, 7]$. The second and third rows in this table are the most recently received distance vectors from nodes y and z, respectively. Because at initialization node x has not received anything from node y or z, the entries in the second and third rows are initialized to infinity.

After initialization, each node sends its distance vector to each of its two neighbors. This is illustrated in Figure 4.30 by the arrows from the first column of tables to the second column of tables. For example, node x sends its distance vector $D_x = [0, 2, 7]$ to both nodes y and z. After receiving the updates, each node recomputes its own distance vector. For example, node x computes

$$D_x(x) = 0$$
$$D_x(y) = \min\{c(x,y) + D_y(y), c(x,z) + D_z(y)\} = \min\{2 + 0, 7 + 1\} = 2$$
$$D_x(z) = \min\{c(x,y) + D_y(z), c(x,z) + D_z(z)\} = \min\{2 + 1, 7 + 0\} = 3$$

The second column therefore displays, for each node, the node's new distance vector along with distance vectors just received from its neighbors. Note, for example, that node x's estimate for the least cost to node z, $D_x(z)$, has changed from 7 to 3. Also note that for node x, neighboring node y achieves the minimum in line 14 of the DV algorithm; thus at this stage of the algorithm, we have at node x that $v^*(y) = y$ and $v^*(z) = y$.

After the nodes recompute their distance vectors, they again send their updated distance vectors to their neighbors (if there has been a change). This is illustrated in Figure 4.30 by the arrows from the second column of tables to the third column of tables. Note that only nodes x and z send updates: node y's distance vector didn't change so node y doesn't send an update. After receiving the updates, the nodes then recompute their distance vectors and update their routing tables, which are shown in the third column.

The process of receiving updated distance vectors from neighbors, recomputing routing table entries, and informing neighbors of changed costs of the least-cost path to a destination continues until no update messages are sent. At this point, since no update messages are sent, no further routing table calculations will occur and the algorithm will enter a quiescent state; that is, all nodes will be performing the wait in Lines 10–11 of the DV algorithm. The algorithm remains in the quiescent state until a link cost changes, as discussed next.

Distance-Vector Algorithm: Link-Cost Changes and Link Failure

When a node running the DV algorithm detects a change in the link cost from itself to a neighbor (Lines 10–11), it updates its distance vector (Lines 13–14) and, if there's a change in the cost of the least-cost path, informs its neighbors (Lines 16–17) of its new distance vector. Figure 4.31(a) illustrates a scenario where the link cost from y to x changes from 4 to 1. We focus here only on y' and z's distance table entries to destination x. The DV algorithm causes the following sequence of events to occur:

- At time t_0, y detects the link-cost change (the cost has changed from 4 to 1), updates its distance vector, and informs its neighbors of this change since its distance vector has changed.

- At time t_1, z receives the update from y and updates its table. It computes a new least cost to x (it has decreased from a cost of 5 to a cost of 2) and sends its new distance vector to its neighbors.

- At time t_2, y receives z's update and updates its distance table. y's least costs do not change and hence y does not send any message to z. The algorithm comes to a quiescent state.

Thus, only two iterations are required for the DV algorithm to reach a quiescent state. The good news about the decreased cost between x and y has propagated quickly through the network.

Let's now consider what can happen when a link cost *increases*. Suppose that the link cost between x and y increases from 4 to 60, as shown in Figure 4.31(b).

1. Before the link cost changes, $D_y(x) = 4$, $D_y(z) = 1$, $D_z(y) = 1$, and $D_z(x) = 5$. At time t_0, y detects the link-cost change (the cost has changed from 4 to 60). y computes its new minimum-cost path to x to have a cost of

$$D_y(x) = \min\{c(y,x) + D_x(x),\ c(y,z) + D_z(x)\} = \min\{60 + 0,\ 1 + 5\} = 6$$

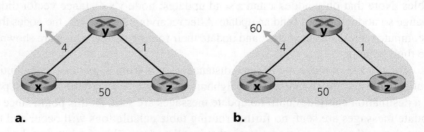

a.   b.

Figure 4.31 ◆ Changes in link cost

Of course, with our global view of the network, we can see that this new cost via z is *wrong*. But the only information node y has is that its direct cost to x is 60 and that z has last told y that z could get to x with a cost of 5. So in order to get to x, y would now route through z, fully expecting that z will be able to get to x with a cost of 5. As of t_1 we have a **routing loop**—in order to get to x, y routes through z, and z routes through y. A routing loop is like a black hole—a packet destined for x arriving at y or z as of t_1 will bounce back and forth between these two nodes forever (or until the forwarding tables are changed).

2. Since node y has computed a new minimum cost to x, it informs z of its new distance vector at time t_1.

3. Sometime after t_1, z receives y's new distance vector, which indicates that y's minimum cost to x is 6. z knows it can get to y with a cost of 1 and hence computes a new least cost to x of $D_z(x) = \min\{50 + 0, 1 + 6\} = 7$. Since z's least cost to x has increased, it then informs y of its new distance vector at t_2.

4. In a similar manner, after receiving z's new distance vector, y determines $D_y(x) = 8$ and sends z its distance vector. z then determines $D_z(x) = 9$ and sends y its distance vector, and so on.

How long will the process continue? You should convince yourself that the loop will persist for 44 iterations (message exchanges between y and z)—until z eventually computes the cost of its path via y to be greater than 50. At this point, z will (finally!) determine that its least-cost path to x is via its direct connection to x. y will then route to x via z. The result of the bad news about the increase in link cost has indeed traveled slowly! What would have happened if the link cost $c(y, x)$ had changed from 4 to 10,000 and the cost $c(z, x)$ had been 9,999? Because of such scenarios, the problem we have seen is sometimes referred to as the count-to-infinity problem.

Distance-Vector Algorithm: Adding Poisoned Reverse

The specific looping scenario just described can be avoided using a technique known as *poisoned reverse*. The idea is simple—if z routes through y to get to destination x, then z will advertise to y that its distance to x is infinity, that is, z will advertise to y that $D_z(x) = \infty$ (even though z knows $D_z(x) = 5$ in truth). z will continue telling this little white lie to y as long as it routes to x via y. Since y believes that z has no path to x, y will never attempt to route to x via z, as long as z continues to route to x via y (and lies about doing so).

Let's now see how poisoned reverse solves the particular looping problem we encountered before in Figure 4.31(b). As a result of the poisoned reverse, y's distance table indicates $D_z(x) = \infty$. When the cost of the (x, y) link changes from 4 to 60 at time t_0, y updates its table and continues to route directly to x, albeit at a higher cost of 60, and informs z of its new cost to x, that is, $D_y(x) = 60$. After receiving the update at t_1, z immediately shifts its route to x to be via the direct (z, x) link at a cost of 50. Since this is a new least-cost path to x, and since the path no longer passes through y, z now informs y that $D_z(x) = 50$ at t_2. After receiving the update from z, y updates its distance table with $D_y(x) = 51$. Also, since z is now on y's least-cost path to x, y poisons the reverse path from z to x by informing z at time t_3 that $D_y(x) = \infty$ (even though y knows that $D_y(x) = 51$ in truth).

Does poisoned reverse solve the general count-to-infinity problem? It does not. You should convince yourself that loops involving three or more nodes (rather than simply two immediately neighboring nodes) will not be detected by the poisoned reverse technique.

A Comparison of LS and DV Routing Algorithms

The DV and LS algorithms take complementary approaches towards computing routing. In the DV algorithm, each node talks to *only* its directly connected neighbors, but it provides its neighbors with least-cost estimates from itself to *all* the nodes (that it knows about) in the network. In the LS algorithm, each node talks with *all* other nodes (via broadcast), but it tells them *only* the costs of its directly connected links. Let's conclude our study of LS and DV algorithms with a quick comparison of some of their attributes. Recall that N is the set of nodes (routers) and E is the set of edges (links).

- *Message complexity.* We have seen that LS requires each node to know the cost of each link in the network. This requires $O(|N| \, |E|)$ messages to be sent. Also, whenever a link cost changes, the new link cost must be sent to all nodes. The DV algorithm requires message exchanges between directly connected neighbors at each iteration. We have seen that the time needed for the algorithm to converge can depend on many factors. When link costs change, the DV algorithm will propagate the results of the changed link cost only if the new link cost results in a changed least-cost path for one of the nodes attached to that link.

- *Speed of convergence.* We have seen that our implementation of LS is an $O(|N|^2)$ algorithm requiring $O(|N| \, |E|)$) messages. The DV algorithm can converge slowly and can have routing loops while the algorithm is converging. DV also suffers from the count-to-infinity problem.

- *Robustness.* What can happen if a router fails, misbehaves, or is sabotaged? Under LS, a router could broadcast an incorrect cost for one of its attached links (but no others). A node could also corrupt or drop any packets it received as part of an LS broadcast. But an LS node is computing only its own forwarding tables; other nodes are performing similar calculations for themselves. This means route calculations are somewhat separated under LS, providing a degree of robustness. Under DV, a node can advertise incorrect least-cost paths to any or all destinations. (Indeed, in 1997, a malfunctioning router in a small ISP provided national backbone routers with erroneous routing information. This caused other routers to flood the malfunctioning router with traffic and caused large portions of the Internet to become disconnected for up to several hours [Neumann 1997].) More generally, we note that, at each iteration, a node's calculation in DV is passed on to its neighbor and then indirectly to its neighbor's neighbor on the next iteration. In this sense, an incorrect node calculation can be diffused through the entire network under DV.

In the end, neither algorithm is an obvious winner over the other; indeed, both algorithms are used in the Internet.

Other Routing Algorithms

The LS and DV algorithms we have studied are not only widely used in practice, they are essentially the *only* routing algorithms used in practice today in the Internet. Nonetheless, many routing algorithms have been proposed by researchers over the past 30 years, ranging from the extremely simple to the very sophisticated and complex. A broad class of routing algorithms is based on viewing packet traffic as flows between sources and destinations in a network. In this approach, the routing problem can be formulated mathematically as a constrained optimization problem known as a network flow problem [Bertsekas 1991]. Yet another set of routing algorithms we mention here are those derived from the telephony world. These **circuit-switched routing algorithms** are of interest to packet-switched data networking in cases where per-link resources (for example, buffers, or a fraction of the link bandwidth) are to be reserved for each connection that is routed over the link. While the formulation of the routing problem might appear quite different from the least-cost routing formulation we have seen in this chapter, there are a number of similarities, at least as far as the path-finding algorithm (routing algorithm) is concerned. See [Ash 1998; Ross 1995; Girard 1990] for a detailed discussion of this research area.

4.5.3 Hierarchical Routing

In our study of LS and DV algorithms, we've viewed the network simply as a collection of interconnected routers. One router was indistinguishable from another in the sense that all routers executed the same routing algorithm to compute routing paths through the entire network. In practice, this model and its view of a homogenous set of routers all executing the same routing algorithm is a bit simplistic for at least two important reasons:

*   *Scale.* As the number of routers becomes large, the overhead involved in computing, storing, and communicating routing information (for example,

LS updates or least-cost path changes) becomes prohibitive. Today's public Internet consists of hundreds of millions of hosts. Storing routing information at each of these hosts would clearly require enormous amounts of memory. The overhead required to broadcast LS updates among all of the routers in the public Internet would leave no bandwidth left for sending data packets! A distance-vector algorithm that iterated among such a large number of routers would surely never converge. Clearly, something must be done to reduce the complexity of route computation in networks as large as the public Internet.

- *Administrative autonomy.* Although researchers tend to ignore issues such as a company's desire to run its routers as it pleases (for example, to run whatever routing algorithm it chooses) or to hide aspects of its network's internal organization from the outside, these are important considerations. Ideally, an organization should be able to run and administer its network as it wishes, while still being able to connect its network to other outside networks.

Both of these problems can be solved by organizing routers into **autonomous systems (ASs)**, with each AS consisting of a group of routers that are typically under the same administrative control (e.g., operated by the same ISP or belonging to the same company network). Routers within the same AS all run the same routing algorithm (for example, an LS or DV algorithm) and have information about each other—exactly as was the case in our idealized model in the preceding section. The routing algorithm running within an autonomous system is called an **intra-autonomous system routing protocol**. It will be necessary, of course, to connect ASs to each other, and thus one or more of the routers in an AS will have the added task of being responsible for forwarding packets to destinations outside the AS; these routers are called **gateway routers**.

Figure 4.32 provides a simple example with three ASs: AS1, AS2, and AS3. In this figure, the heavy lines represent direct link connections between pairs of routers. The thinner lines hanging from the routers represent subnets that are directly connected to the routers. AS1 has four routers—1a, 1b, 1c, and 1d—which run the intra-AS routing protocol used within AS1. Thus, each of these four routers knows how to forward packets along the optimal path to any destination within AS1. Similarly, autonomous systems AS2 and AS3 each have three routers. Note that the intra-AS routing protocols running in AS1, AS2, and AS3 need not be the same. Also note that the routers 1b, 1c, 2a, and 3a are all gateway routers.

It should now be clear how the routers in an AS determine routing paths for source-destination pairs that are internal to the AS. But there is still a big missing piece to the end-to-end routing puzzle. How does a router, within some AS, know how to route a packet to a destination that is outside the AS? It's easy to answer this question if the AS has only one gateway router that connects to only one other AS. In this case, because the AS's intra-AS routing algorithm has determined the least-cost path from each internal router to the gateway router, each

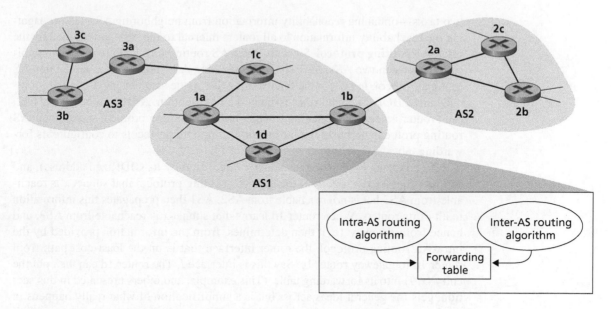

Figure 4.32 ♦ An example of interconnected autonomous systems

internal router knows how it should forward the packet. The gateway router, upon receiving the packet, forwards the packet on the one link that leads outside the AS. The AS on the other side of the link then takes over the responsibility of routing the packet to its ultimate destination. As an example, suppose router 2b in Figure 4.32 receives a packet whose destination is outside of AS2. Router 2b will then forward the packet to either router 2a or 2c, as specified by router 2b's forwarding table, which was configured by AS2's intra-AS routing protocol. The packet will eventually arrive to the gateway router 2a, which will forward the packet to 1b. Once the packet has left 2a, AS2's job is done with this one packet.

So the problem is easy when the source AS has only one link that leads outside the AS. But what if the source AS has two or more links (through two or more gateway routers) that lead outside the AS? Then the problem of knowing where to forward the packet becomes significantly more challenging. For example, consider a router in AS1 and suppose it receives a packet whose destination is outside the AS. The router should clearly forward the packet to one of its two gateway routers, 1b or 1c, but which one? To solve this problem, AS1 needs (1) to learn which destinations are reachable via AS2 and which destinations are reachable via AS3, and (2) to propagate this reachability information to all the routers within AS1, so that each router can configure its forwarding table to handle external-AS destinations. These two tasks—obtaining reachability information from neighboring ASs and propagating the reachability information to all routers internal to the AS—are handled by the **inter-AS routing protocol**. Since the inter-AS routing protocol involves communication between two ASs, the two communicating ASs must run the same inter-AS routing protocol. In fact, in the Internet all ASs run the same inter-AS routing protocol, called BGP4, which is discussed in the next section. As shown in Figure 4.32, each router receives information from an intra-AS routing protocol and an inter-AS routing protocol, and uses the information from both protocols to configure its forwarding table.

As an example, consider a subnet x (identified by its CIDRized address), and suppose that AS1 learns from the inter-AS routing protocol that subnet x is reachable from AS3 but is *not* reachable from AS2. AS1 then propagates this information to all of its routers. When router 1d learns that subnet x is reachable from AS3, and hence from gateway 1c, it then determines, from the information provided by the intra-AS routing protocol, the router interface that is on the least-cost path from router 1d to gateway router 1c. Say this is interface I. The router 1d can then put the entry (x, I) into its forwarding table. (This example, and others presented in this section, gets the general ideas across but is a simplification of what really happens in the Internet. In the next section we'll provide a more detailed description, albeit more complicated, when we discuss BGP.)

Following up on the previous example, now suppose that AS2 and AS3 connect to other ASs, which are not shown in the diagram. Also suppose that AS1 learns from the inter-AS routing protocol that subnet x is reachable both from AS2, via gateway 1b, and from AS3, via gateway 1c. AS1 would then propagate this information to all its routers, including router 1d. In order to configure its forwarding table, router 1d would have to determine to which gateway router, 1b or 1c, it should direct packets that are destined for subnet x. One approach, which is often employed in practice, is to use **hot-potato routing**. In hot-potato routing, the AS gets rid of the packet (the hot potato) as quickly as possible (more precisely, as inexpensively as possible). This is done by having a router send the packet to the gateway router that has the smallest router-to-gateway cost among all gateways with a path to the destination. In the context of the current example, hot-potato routing, running in 1d, would use information from the intra-AS routing protocol to determine the path costs to 1b and 1c, and then choose the path with the least cost. Once this path is chosen, router 1d adds an entry for subnet x in its forwarding table. Figure 4.33 summarizes the actions taken at router 1d for adding the new entry for x to the forwarding table.

When an AS learns about a destination from a neighboring AS, the AS can advertise this routing information to some of its other neighboring ASs. For example, suppose AS1 learns from AS2 that subnet x is reachable via AS2. AS1 could then tell AS3 that x is reachable via AS1. In this manner, if AS3 needs to route a packet destined to x, AS3 would forward the packet to AS1, which would in turn forward the packet to AS2. As we'll see in our discussion of BGP, an AS has quite a bit of

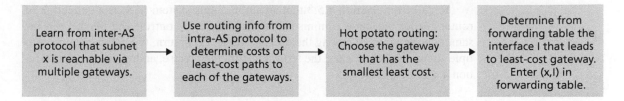

| Learn from inter-AS protocol that subnet x is reachable via multiple gateways. | → | Use routing info from intra-AS protocol to determine costs of least-cost paths to each of the gateways. | → | Hot potato routing: Choose the gateway that has the smallest least cost. | → | Determine from forwarding table the interface I that leads to least-cost gateway. Enter (x,I) in forwarding table. |

Figure 4.33 ♦ Steps in adding an outside-AS destination in a router's forwarding table

flexibility in deciding which destinations it advertises to its neighboring ASs. This is a *policy* decision, typically depending more on economic issues than on technical issues.

Recall from Section 1.5 that the Internet consists of a hierarchy of interconnected ISPs. So what is the relationship between ISPs and ASs? You might think that the routers in an ISP, and the links that interconnect them, constitute a single AS. Although this is often the case, many ISPs partition their network into multiple ASs. For example, some tier-1 ISPs use one AS for their entire network; others break up their ISP into tens of interconnected ASs.

In summary, the problems of scale and administrative authority are solved by defining autonomous systems. Within an AS, all routers run the same intra-AS routing protocol. Among themselves, the ASs run the same inter-AS routing protocol. The problem of scale is solved because an intra-AS router need only know about routers within its AS. The problem of administrative authority is solved since an organization can run whatever intra-AS routing protocol it chooses; however, each pair of connected ASs needs to run the same inter-AS routing protocol to exchange reachability information.

In the following section, we'll examine two intra-AS routing protocols (RIP and OSPF) and the inter-AS routing protocol (BGP) that are used in today's Internet. These case studies will nicely round out our study of hierarchical routing.

4.6 Routing in the Internet

Having studied Internet addressing and the IP protocol, we now turn our attention to the Internet's routing protocols; their job is to determine the path taken by a datagram between source and destination. We'll see that the Internet's routing protocols embody many of the principles we learned earlier in this chapter. The link-state and distance-vector approaches studied in Sections 4.5.1 and 4.5.2 and the notion of an autonomous system considered in Section 4.5.3 are all central to how routing is done in today's Internet.

Recall from Section 4.5.3 that an autonomous system (AS) is a collection of routers under the same administrative and technical control, and that all run the same routing protocol among themselves. Each AS, in turn, typically contains multiple subnets (where we use the term subnet in the precise, addressing sense in Section 4.4.2).

4.6.1 Intra-AS Routing in the Internet: RIP

An intra-AS routing protocol is used to determine how routing is performed within an autonomous system (AS). Intra-AS routing protocols are also known as **interior gateway protocols**. Historically, two routing protocols have been used extensively for routing within an autonomous system in the Internet: the **Routing Information Protocol (RIP)** and **Open Shortest Path First (OSPF)**. A routing protocol closely related to OSPF is the **IS-IS** protocol [RFC 1142, Perlman 1999]. We first discuss RIP and then consider OSPF.

RIP was one of the earliest intra-AS Internet routing protocols and is still in widespread use today. It traces its origins and its name to the Xerox Network Systems (XNS) architecture. The widespread deployment of RIP was due in great part to its inclusion in 1982 in the Berkeley Software Distribution (BSD) version of UNIX supporting TCP/IP. RIP version 1 is defined in [RFC 1058], with a backward-compatible version 2 defined in [RFC 2453].

RIP is a distance-vector protocol that operates in a manner very close to the idealized DV protocol we examined in Section 4.5.2. The version of RIP specified in RFC 1058 uses hop count as a cost metric; that is, each link has a cost of 1. In the DV algorithm in Section 4.5.2, for simplicity, costs were defined between pairs of routers. In RIP (and also in OSPF), costs are actually from source router to a destination subnet. RIP uses the term *hop*, which is the number of subnets traversed along the shortest path from source router to destination subnet, including the destination subnet. Figure 4.34 illustrates an AS with six leaf subnets. The table in the figure indicates the number of hops from the source A to each of the leaf subnets.

The maximum cost of a path is limited to 15, thus limiting the use of RIP to autonomous systems that are fewer than 15 hops in diameter. Recall that in DV protocols, neighboring routers exchange distance vectors with each other. The distance vector for any one router is the current estimate of the shortest path distances from that router to the subnets in the AS. In RIP, routing updates are exchanged between neighbors approximately every 30 seconds using a **RIP response message**. The response message sent by a router or host contains a list of up to 25 destination subnets within the AS, as well as the sender's distance to each of those subnets. Response messages are also known as **RIP advertisements**.

Let's take a look at a simple example of how RIP advertisements work. Consider the portion of an AS shown in Figure 4.35. In this figure, lines connecting the routers denote subnets. Only selected routers (*A, B, C,* and *D*) and subnets (*w, x, y,*

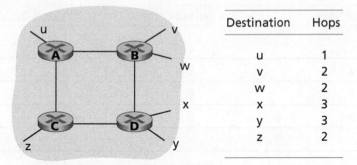

Destination	Hops
u	1
v	2
w	2
x	3
y	3
z	2

Figure 4.34 ♦ Number of hops from source router A to various subnets

and z) are labeled. Dotted lines indicate that the AS continues on; thus this autonomous system has many more routers and links than are shown.

Each router maintains a RIP table known as a **routing table**. A router's routing table includes both the router's distance vector and the router's forwarding table. Figure 4.36 shows the routing table for router D. Note that the routing table has three columns. The first column is for the destination subnet, the second column indicates the identity of the next router along the shortest path to the destination subnet, and the third column indicates the number of hops (that is, the number of subnets that have to be traversed, including the destination subnet) to get to the destination subnet along the shortest path. For this example, the table indicates that to send a datagram from router D to destination subnet w, the datagram should first be forwarded to neighboring router A; the table also indicates that destination subnet w is two hops away along the shortest path. Similarly, the table indicates that subnet z is seven hops away via router B. In principle, a routing table will have one row for each subnet in the AS, although RIP version 2 allows subnet entries to be aggregated using route aggregation techniques similar to those we examined in

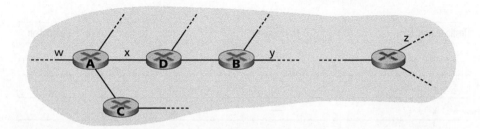

Figure 4.35 ♦ A portion of an autonomous system

Destination Subnet	Next Router	Number of Hops to Destination
w	A	2
y	B	2
z	B	7
x	—	1
. . . .	. . . .	. . . .

Figure 4.36 ♦ Routing table in router *D* before receiving advertisement from router *A*

Section 4.4. The table in Figure 4.36, and the subsequent tables to come, are only partially complete.

Now suppose that 30 seconds later, router *D* receives from router *A* the advertisement shown in Figure 4.37. Note that this advertisement is nothing other than the routing table information from router *A*! This information indicates, in particular, that subnet *z* is only four hops away from router *A*. Router *D*, upon receiving this advertisement, merges the advertisement (Figure 4.37) with the old routing table (Figure 4.36). In particular, router *D* learns that there is now a path through router *A* to subnet *z* that is shorter than the path through router *B*. Thus, router *D* updates its routing table to account for the shorter shortest path, as shown in Figure 4.38. How is it, you might ask, that the shortest path to subnet *z* has become shorter? Possibly, the decentralized distance-vector algorithm is still in the process of converging (see Section 4.5.2), or perhaps new links and/or routers were added to the AS, thus changing the shortest paths in the AS.

Let's next consider a few of the implementation aspects of RIP. Recall that RIP routers exchange advertisements approximately every 30 seconds. If a router does not hear from its neighbor at least once every 180 seconds, that neighbor is considered to be no longer reachable; that is, either the neighbor has died or the

Destination Subnet	Next Router	Number of Hops to Destination
z	C	4
w	—	1
x	—	1
. . . .	. . . .	. . . .

Figure 4.37 ♦ Advertisement from router A

Destination Subnet	Next Router	Number of Hops to Destination
w	A	2
y	B	2
z	A	5
....	....	....

Figure 4.38 ♦ Routing table in router *D* after receiving advertisement from router *A*

connecting link has gone down. When this happens, RIP modifies the local routing table and then propagates this information by sending advertisements to its neighboring routers (the ones that are still reachable). A router can also request information about its neighbor's cost to a given destination using RIP's request message. Routers send RIP request and response messages to each other over UDP using port number 520. The UDP segment is carried between routers in a standard IP datagram. The fact that RIP uses a transport-layer protocol (UDP) on top of a network-layer protocol (IP) to implement network-layer functionality (a routing algorithm) may seem rather convoluted (it is!). Looking a little deeper at how RIP is implemented will clear this up.

Figure 4.39 sketches how RIP is typically implemented in a UNIX system, for example, a UNIX workstation serving as a router. A process called *routed* (pronounced "route dee") executes RIP, that is, maintains routing information and exchanges messages with *routed* processes running in neighboring routers. Because RIP is implemented as an application-layer process (albeit a very special one that is able to

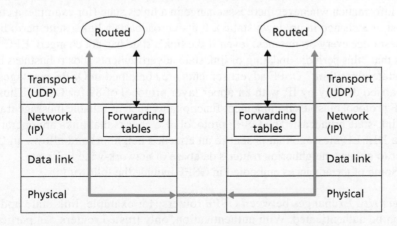

Figure 4.39 ♦ Implementation of RIP as the *routed* daemon

manipulate the routing tables within the UNIX kernel), it can send and receive messages over a standard socket and use a standard transport protocol. As shown, RIP is implemented as an application-layer protocol (see Chapter 2) running over UDP. If you're interested in looking at an implementation of RIP (or the OSPF and BGP protocols that we will study shortly), see [Quagga 2012].

4.6.2 Intra-AS Routing in the Internet: OSPF

Like RIP, OSPF routing is widely used for intra-AS routing in the Internet. OSPF and its closely related cousin, IS-IS, are typically deployed in upper-tier ISPs whereas RIP is deployed in lower-tier ISPs and enterprise networks. The Open in OSPF indicates that the routing protocol specification is publicly available (for example, as opposed to Cisco's EIGRP protocol). The most recent version of OSPF, version 2, is defined in RFC 2328, a public document.

OSPF was conceived as the successor to RIP and as such has a number of advanced features. At its heart, however, OSPF is a link-state protocol that uses flooding of link-state information and a Dijkstra's least-cost path algorithm. With OSPF, a router constructs a complete topological map (that is, a graph) of the entire autonomous system. The router then locally runs Dijkstra's shortest-path algorithm to determine a shortest-path tree to all *subnets*, with itself as the root node. Individual link costs are configured by the network administrator (see Principles and Practice: Setting OSPF Weights). The administrator might choose to set all link costs to 1, thus achieving minimum-hop routing, or might choose to set the link weights to be inversely proportional to link capacity in order to discourage traffic from using low-bandwidth links. OSPF does not mandate a policy for how link weights are set (that is the job of the network administrator), but instead provides the mechanisms (protocol) for determining least-cost path routing for the given set of link weights.

With OSPF, a router broadcasts routing information to *all* other routers in the autonomous system, not just to its neighboring routers. A router broadcasts link-state information whenever there is a change in a link's state (for example, a change in cost or a change in up/down status). It also broadcasts a link's state periodically (at least once every 30 minutes), even if the link's state has not changed. RFC 2328 notes that "this periodic updating of link state advertisements adds robustness to the link state algorithm." OSPF advertisements are contained in OSPF messages that are carried directly by IP, with an upper-layer protocol of 89 for OSPF. Thus, the OSPF protocol must itself implement functionality such as reliable message transfer and link-state broadcast. The OSPF protocol also checks that links are operational (via a HELLO message that is sent to an attached neighbor) and allows an OSPF router to obtain a neighboring router's database of network-wide link state.

Some of the advances embodied in OSPF include the following:

• *Security.* Exchanges between OSPF routers (for example, link-state updates) can be authenticated. With authentication, only trusted routers can participate in the OSPF protocol within an AS, thus preventing malicious intruders (or networking students taking their newfound knowledge out for a joyride) from injecting incorrect information into router tables. By default, OSPF packets between routers are not authenticated and could be forged. Two types of authentication can be configured—simple and MD5 (see Chapter 8 for a discussion on MD5 and authentication in general). With simple authentication, the same password is configured on each router. When a router sends an OSPF packet, it includes the password in plaintext. Clearly, simple authentication is not very secure. MD5 authentication is based on shared secret keys that are configured in all the routers. For each OSPF packet that it sends, the router computes the MD5 hash of the content of the OSPF packet appended with the secret key. (See the discussion of message authentication codes in Chapter 7.) Then the router includes the resulting hash value in the OSPF packet. The receiving router, using the preconfigured secret key, will compute an MD5 hash of the packet and compare it with the hash value that the packet carries, thus verifying the packet's authenticity. Sequence numbers are also used with MD5 authentication to protect against replay attacks.

* *Multiple same-cost paths.* When multiple paths to a destination have the same cost, OSPF allows multiple paths to be used (that is, a single path need not be chosen for carrying all traffic when multiple equal-cost paths exist).

* *Integrated support for unicast and multicast routing.* Multicast OSPF (MOSPF) [RFC 1584] provides simple extensions to OSPF to provide for multicast routing (a topic we cover in more depth in Section 4.7.2). MOSPF uses the existing OSPF link database and adds a new type of link-state advertisement to the existing OSPF link-state broadcast mechanism.

* *Support for hierarchy within a single routing domain.* Perhaps the most significant advance in OSPF is the ability to structure an autonomous system hierarchically. Section 4.5.3 has already looked at the many advantages of hierarchical routing structures. We cover the implementation of OSPF hierarchical routing in the remainder of this section.

An OSPF autonomous system can be configured hierarchically into areas. Each area runs its own OSPF link-state routing algorithm, with each router in an area broadcasting its link state to all other routers in that area. Within each area, one or more **area border routers** are responsible for routing packets outside the area. Lastly, exactly one OSPF area in the AS is configured to be the **backbone** area. The primary role of the backbone area is to route traffic between the other areas in the AS. The backbone always contains all area border routers in the AS and may contain nonborder routers as well. Inter-area routing within the AS requires that the packet be first routed to an area border router (intra-area routing), then routed through the backbone to the area border router that is in the destination area, and then routed to the final destination.

SETTING OSPF LINK WEIGHTS

Our discussion of link-state routing has implicitly assumed that link weights are set, a routing algorithm such as OSPF is run, and traffic flows according to the routing tables computed by the LS algorithm. In terms of cause and effect, the link weights are given (i.e., they come first) and result (via Dijkstra's algorithm) in routing paths that minimize overall cost. In this viewpoint, link weights reflect the cost of using a link (e.g., if link weights are inversely proportional to capacity, then the use of high-capacity links would have smaller weights and thus be more attractive from a routing standpoint) and Disjkstra's algorithm serves to minimize overall cost.

In practice, the cause and effect relationship between link weights and routing paths may be reversed, with network operators configuring link weights in order to obtain routing paths that achieve certain traffic engineering goals [Fortz 2000, Fortz 2002]. For example, suppose a network operator has an estimate of traffic flow entering the network at each ingress point and destined for each egress point. The operator may then want to put in place a specific routing of ingress-to-egress flows that minimizes the maximum utilization over all of the network's links. But with a routing algorithm such as OSPF, the operator's main "knobs" for tuning the routing of flows through the network are the link weights. Thus, in order to achieve the goal of minimizing the maximum link utilization, the operator must find the set of link weights that achieves this goal. This is a reversal of the cause and effect relationship—the desired routing of flows is known, and the OSPF link weights must be found such that the OSPF routing algorithm results in this desired routing of flows.

OSPF is a relatively complex protocol, and our coverage here has been necessarily brief; [Huitema 1998; Moy 1998; RFC 2328] provide additional details.

4.6.3 Inter-AS Routing: BGP

We just learned how ISPs use RIP and OSPF to determine optimal paths for source-destination pairs that are internal to the same AS. Let's now examine how paths are determined for source-destination pairs that span multiple ASs. The **Border Gateway Protocol** version 4, specified in RFC 4271 (see also [RFC 4274), is the *de facto* standard inter-AS routing protocol in today's Internet. It is commonly referred to as BGP4 or simply as **BGP**. As an inter-AS routing protocol (see Section 4.5.3), BGP provides each AS a means to

1. Obtain subnet reachability information from neighboring ASs.
2. Propagate the reachability information to all routers internal to the AS.
3. Determine "good" routes to subnets based on the reachability information and on AS policy.

Most importantly, BGP allows each subnet to advertise its existence to the rest of the Internet. A subnet screams "I exist and I am here," and BGP makes sure that all the ASs in the Internet know about the subnet and how to get there. If it weren't for BGP, each subnet would be isolated—alone and unknown by the rest of the Internet.

BGP Basics

BGP is extremely complex; entire books have been devoted to the subject and many issues are still not well understood [Yannuzzi 2005]. Furthermore, even after having read the books and RFCs, you may find it difficult to fully master BGP without having practiced BGP for many months (if not years) as a designer or administrator of an upper-tier ISP. Nevertheless, because BGP is an absolutely critical protocol for the Internet—in essence, it is the protocol that glues the whole thing together—we need to acquire at least a rudimentary understanding of how it works. We begin by describing how BGP might work in the context of the simple example network we studied earlier in Figure 4.32. In this description, we build on our discussion of hierarchical routing in Section 4.5.3; we encourage you to review that material.

In BGP, pairs of routers exchange routing information over semipermanent TCP connections using port 179. The semi-permanent TCP connections for the network in Figure 4.32 are shown in Figure 4.40. There is typically one such BGP TCP connection for each link that directly connects two routers in two different ASs; thus, in Figure 4.40, there is a TCP connection between gateway routers 3a and 1c and another TCP connection between gateway routers 1b and 2a. There are also semipermanent BGP TCP connections between routers within an AS. In particular, Figure 4.40 displays a common configuration of one TCP connection for each pair of routers internal to an AS, creating a mesh of TCP connections within each AS. For each TCP connection, the two routers at the end of the connection are called **BGP peers**, and the TCP connection along with all the BGP messages sent over the

VideoNote
Gluing the Internet together

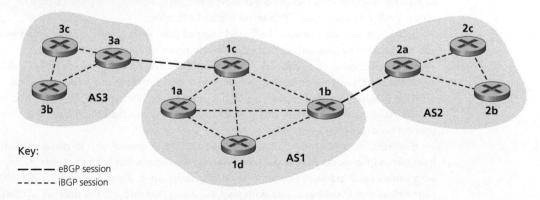

Key:

— — — eBGP session

------ iBGP session

Figure 4.40 ♦ eBGP and iBGP sessions

PRINCIPLES IN PRACTICE

OBTAINING INTERNET PRESENCE: PUTTING THE PUZZLE TOGETHER

Suppose you have just created a small that has a number of servers, including a public Web server that describes your company's products and services, a mail server from which your employees obtain their email messages, and a DNS server. Naturally, you would like the entire world to be able to surf your Web site in order to learn about your exciting products and services. Moreover, you would like your employees to be able to send and receive email to potential customers throughout the world.

To meet these goals, you first need to obtain Internet connectivity, which is done by contracting with, and connecting to, a local ISP. Your company will have a gateway router, which will be connected to a router in your local ISP. This connection might be a DSL connection through the existing telephone infrastructure, a leased line to the ISP's router, or one of the many other access solutions described in Chapter 1. Your local ISP will also provide you with an IP address range, e.g., a /24 address range consisting of 256 addresses. Once you have your physical connectivity and your IP address range, you will assign one of the IP addresses (in your address range) to your Web server, one to your mail server, one to your DNS server, one to your gateway router, and other IP addresses to other servers and networking devices in your company's network.

In addition to contracting with an ISP, you will also need to contract with an Internet registrar to obtain a domain name for your company, as described in Chapter 2. For example, if your company's name is, say, Xanadu Inc., you will naturally try to obtain the domain name xanadu.com. Your company must also obtain presence in the DNS system. Specifically, because outsiders will want to contact your DNS server to obtain the IP addresses of your servers, you will also need to provide your registrar with the IP address of your DNS server. Your registrar will then put an entry for your DNS server (domain name and corresponding IP address) in the .com top-level-domain servers, as described in Chapter 2. After this step is completed, any user who knows your domain name (e.g., xanadu.com) will be able to obtain the IP address of your DNS server via the DNS system.

So that people can discover the IP addresses of your Web server, in your DNS server you will need to include entries that map the host name of your Web server (e.g., www.xanadu.com) to its IP address. You will want to have similar entries for other publicly available servers in your company, including your mail server. In this manner, if Alice wants to browse your Web server, the DNS system will contact your DNS server, find the IP address of your Web server, and give it to Alice. Alice can then establish a TCP connection directly with your Web server.

However, there still remains one other necessary and crucial step to allow outsiders from around the world access your Web server. Consider what happens when Alice, who knows the IP address of your Web server, sends an IP datagram (e.g., a TCP SYN segment) to that IP address. This datagram will be routed through the Internet, visiting a series of routers in many different ASes, and eventually reach your Web server. When any one of the routers receives the datagram, it is going to look for an entry in its forwarding table to determine on which outgoing port it should forward the datagram. Therefore, each of the routers needs to know about the existence of your company's /24 prefix (or some aggregate entry). How does a router become aware of your company's prefix? As we have just seen, it becomes aware of it from BGP! Specifically, when your company contracts with a local ISP and gets assigned a prefix (i.e., an address range), your local ISP will use BGP to advertise this prefix to the ISPs to which it connects. Those ISPs will then, in turn, use BGP to propagate the advertisement. Eventually, all Internet routers will know about your prefix (or about some aggregate that includes your prefix) and thus be able to appropriately forward datagrams destined to your Web and mail servers.

---

connection is called a **BGP session**. Furthermore, a BGP session that spans two ASs is called an **external BGP (eBGP) session**, and a BGP session between routers in the same AS is called an **internal BGP (iBGP) session**. In Figure 4.40, the eBGP sessions are shown with the long dashes; the iBGP sessions are shown with the short dashes. Note that BGP session lines in Figure 4.40 do not always correspond to the physical links in Figure 4.32.

BGP allows each AS to learn which destinations are reachable via its neighboring ASs. In BGP, destinations are not hosts but instead are CIDRized **prefixes**, with each prefix representing a subnet or a collection of subnets. Thus, for example, suppose there are four subnets attached to AS2: 138.16.64/24, 138.16.65/24, 138.16.66/24, and 138.16.67/24. Then AS2 could aggregate the prefixes for these four subnets and use BGP to advertise the single prefix to 138.16.64/22 to AS1. As another example, suppose that only the first three of those four subnets are in AS2 and the fourth subnet, 138.16.67/24, is in AS3. Then, as described in the Principles and Practice in Section 4.4.2, because routers use longest-prefix matching for forwarding datagrams, AS3 could advertise to AS1 the more specific prefix 138.16.67/24 and AS2 could *still* advertise to AS1 the aggregated prefix 138.16.64/22.

Let's now examine how BGP would distribute prefix reachability information over the BGP sessions shown in Figure 4.40. As you might expect, using the eBGP session between the gateway routers 3a and 1c, AS3 sends AS1 the list of prefixes that are reachable from AS3; and AS1 sends AS3 the list of prefixes that are reachable from AS1. Similarly, AS1 and AS2 exchange prefix reachability information through their gateway routers 1b and 2a. Also as you may expect, when a gateway router (in any AS) receives eBGP-learned prefixes, the gateway router uses its iBGP sessions to distribute the prefixes to the other routers in the AS. Thus, all the routers in AS1 learn about AS3 prefixes, including the gateway router 1b. The gateway router 1b (in AS1) can therefore re-advertise AS3's prefixes to AS2. When a router (gateway or not) learns about a new prefix, it creates an entry for the prefix in its forwarding table, as described in Section 4.5.3.

Path Attributes and BGP Routes

Having now a preliminary understanding of BGP, let's get a little deeper into it (while still brushing some of the less important details under the rug!). In BGP, an autonomous system is identified by its globally unique **autonomous system number (ASN)** [RFC 1930]. (Technically, not every AS has an ASN. In particular, a so-called stub AS that carries only traffic for which it is a source or destination will not typically have an ASN; we ignore this technicality in our discussion in order to better see the forest for the trees.) AS numbers, like IP addresses, are assigned by ICANN regional registries [ICANN 2012].

When a router advertises a prefix across a BGP session, it includes with the prefix a number of **BGP attributes**. In BGP jargon, a prefix along with its attributes is called a **route**. Thus, BGP peers advertise routes to each other. Two of the more important attributes are AS-PATH and NEXT-HOP:

- *AS-PATH*. This attribute contains the ASs through which the advertisement for the prefix has passed. When a prefix is passed into an AS, the AS adds its ASN to the AS-PATH attribute. For example, consider Figure 4.40 and suppose that prefix 138.16.64/24 is first advertised from AS2 to AS1; if AS1 then advertises the prefix to AS3, AS-PATH would be AS2 AS1. Routers use the AS-PATH attribute to detect and prevent looping advertisements; specifically, if a router sees that its AS is contained in the path list, it will reject the advertisement. As we'll soon discuss, routers also use the AS-PATH attribute in choosing among multiple paths to the same prefix.

- Providing the critical link between the inter-AS and intra-AS routing protocols, the NEXT-HOP attribute has a subtle but important use. *The NEXT-HOP is the router interface that begins the AS-PATH*. To gain insight into this attribute, let's again refer to Figure 4.40. Consider what happens when the gateway router 3a in AS3 advertises a route to gateway router 1c in AS1 using eBGP. The route includes the advertised prefix, which we'll call x, and an AS-PATH to the prefix. This advertisement also includes the NEXT-HOP, which is the IP address of the router 3a interface that leads to 1c. (Recall that a router has multiple IP addresses, one for each of its interfaces.) Now consider what happens when router 1d learns about this route from iBGP. After learning about this route to x, router 1d may want to forward packets to x along the route, that is, router 1d may want to include the entry (x, l) in its forwarding table, where l is its interface that begins the least-cost path from 1d towards the gateway router 1c. To determine l, 1d provides the IP address in the NEXT-HOP attribute to its intra-AS routing module. Note that the intra-AS routing algorithm has determined the least-cost path to all subnets attached to the routers in AS1, including to the subnet for the link between 1c and 3a. From this least-cost path from 1d to the 1c-3a subnet, 1d determines its router interface l that begins this path and then adds the entry (x, l) to its forwarding table. Whew! In summary, the NEXT-HOP attribute is used by routers to properly configure their forwarding tables.

- Figure 4.41 illustrates another situation where the NEXT-HOP is needed. In this figure, AS1 and AS2 are connected by two peering links. A router in AS1 could learn

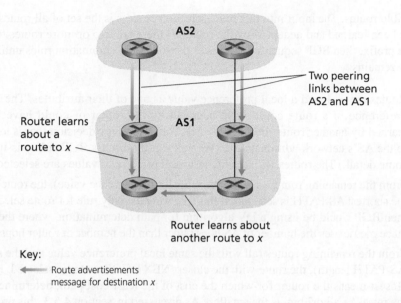

Key:

◀———— Route advertisements
message for destination x

Figure 4.41 ♦ NEXT-HOP attributes in advertisements are used to determine which peering link to use

about two different routes to the same prefix x. These two routes could have the same AS-PATH to x, but could have different NEXT-HOP values corresponding to the different peering links. Using the NEXT-HOP values and the intra-AS routing algorithm, the router can determine the cost of the path to each peering link, and then apply hot-potato routing (see Section 4.5.3) to determine the appropriate interface.

BGP also includes attributes that allow routers to assign preference metrics to the routes, and an attribute that indicates how the prefix was inserted into BGP at the origin AS. For a full discussion of route attributes, see [Griffin 2012; Stewart 1999; Halabi 2000; Feamster 2004; RFC 4271].

When a gateway router receives a route advertisement, it uses its **import policy** to decide whether to accept or filter the route and whether to set certain attributes such as the router preference metrics. The import policy may filter a route because the AS may not want to send traffic over one of the ASs in the route's AS-PATH. The gateway router may also filter a route because it already knows of a preferable route to the same prefix.

BGP Route Selection

As described earlier in this section, BGP uses eBGP and iBGP to distribute routes to all the routers within ASs. From this distribution, a router may learn about more than one route to any one prefix, in which case the router must select one of the possible routes. The input into this route selection process is the set of all routes that have been learned and accepted by the router. If there are two or more routes to the same prefix, then BGP sequentially invokes the following elimination rules until one route remains:

- Routes are assigned a local preference value as one of their attributes. The local preference of a route could have been set by the router or could have been learned by another router in the same AS. This is a policy decision that is left up to the AS's network administrator. (We will shortly discuss BGP policy issues in some detail.) The routes with the highest local preference values are selected.

- From the remaining routes (all with the same local preference value), the route with the shortest AS-PATH is selected. If this rule were the only rule for route selection, then BGP would be using a DV algorithm for path determination, where the distance metric uses the number of AS hops rather than the number of router hops.

- From the remaining routes (all with the same local preference value and the same AS-PATH length), the route with the closest NEXT-HOP router is selected. Here, closest means the router for which the cost of the least-cost path, determined by the intra-AS algorithm, is the smallest. As discussed in Section 4.5.3, this process is called hot-potato routing.

- If more than one route still remains, the router uses BGP identifiers to select the route; see [Stewart 1999].

The elimination rules are even more complicated than described above. To avoid nightmares about BGP, it's best to learn about BGP selection rules in small doses!

PRINCIPLES IN PRACTICE

PUTTING IT ALL TOGETHER: HOW DOES AN ENTRY GET INTO A ROUTER'S FORWARDING TABLE?

Recall that an entry in a router's forwarding table consists of a prefix (e.g., 138.16.64/22) and a corresponding router output port (e.g., port 7). When a packet arrives to the router, the packet's destination IP address is compared with the prefixes in the forwarding table to find the one with the longest prefix match. The packet is then forwarded (within the router) to the router port associated with that prefix. Let's now summarize how a routing entry (prefix and associated port) gets entered into a forwarding table. This simple exercise will tie together a lot of what we just learned about routing and forwarding. To make things interesting, let's assume that the prefix is a "foreign prefix," that is, it does not belong to the router's AS but to some other AS.

In order for a prefix to get entered into the router's forwarding table, the router has to *first become aware* of the prefix (corresponding to a subnet or an aggregation of subnets). As we have just learned, the router becomes aware of the prefix via a BGP route advertisement. Such an advertisement may be sent to it over an eBGP session (from a router in another AS) or over an iBGP session (from a router in the same AS).

After the router becomes aware of the prefix, it needs to determine the appropriate output port to which datagrams destined to that prefix will be forwarded, before it can enter that prefix in its forwarding table. If the router receives more than one route advertisement for this prefix, the router uses the BGP route selection process, as described earlier in this subsection, to find the "best" route for the prefix. Suppose such a best route has been selected. As described earlier, the selected route includes a NEXT-HOP attribute, which is the IP address of the first router outside the router's AS along this best route. As described above, the router then uses its intra-AS routing protocol (typically OSPF) to determine the shortest path to the NEXT-HOP router. The router finally determines the port number to associate with the prefix by identifying the first link along that shortest path. The router can then (finally!) enter the prefix-port pair into its forwarding table! The forwarding table computed by the routing processor (see Figure 4.6) is then pushed to the router's input port line cards.

Routing Policy

Let's illustrate some of the basic concepts of BGP routing policy with a simple example. Figure 4.42 shows six interconnected autonomous systems: A, B, C, W, X, and Y. It is important to note that A, B, C, W, X, and Y are ASs, not routers. Let's assume that autonomous systems W, X, and Y are stub networks and that A, B, and C are backbone provider networks. We'll also assume that A, B, and C, all peer with each other, and provide full BGP information to their customer networks. All traffic entering a **stub network** must be destined for that network, and all traffic leaving a stub network must have originated in that network. W and Y are clearly stub networks. X is a **multi-homed stub network,** since it is connected to the rest of the network via two different providers (a scenario that is becoming increasingly common in practice). However, like W and Y, X itself must be the source/destination of all traffic leaving/entering X. But how will this stub network behavior be implemented and enforced? How will X be prevented from forwarding traffic between B and C? This can easily be

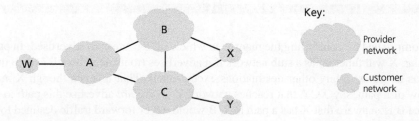

Key:

Provider network

Customer network

Figure 4.42 ♦ A simple BGP scenario

WHY ARE THERE DIFFERENT INTER-AS AND INTRA-AS ROUTING PROTOCOLS?

Having now studied the details of specific inter-AS and intra-AS routing protocols deployed in today's Internet, let's conclude by considering perhaps the most fundamental question we could ask about these protocols in the first place (hopefully, you have been wondering this all along, and have not lost the forest for the trees!): Why are different inter-AS and intra-AS routing protocols used?

The answer to this question gets at the heart of the differences between the goals of routing within an AS and among ASs:

• *Policy.* Among ASs, policy issues dominate. It may well be important that traffic originating in a given AS not be able to pass through another specific AS. Similarly, a given AS may well want to control what transit traffic it carries between other ASs. We have seen that BGP carries path attributes and provides for controlled distribution of routing information so that such policy-based routing decisions can be made. Within an AS, everything is nominally under the same administrative control, and thus policy issues play a much less important role in choosing routes within the AS.

• *Scale.* The ability of a routing algorithm and its data structures to scale to handle routing to/among large numbers of networks is a critical issue in inter-AS routing. Within an AS, scalability is less of a concern. For one thing, if a single administrative domain becomes too large, it is always possible to divide it into two ASs and perform inter-AS routing between the two new ASs. (Recall that OSPF allows such a hierarchy to be built by splitting an AS into areas.)

• *Performance.* Because inter-AS routing is so policy oriented, the quality (for example, performance) of the routes used is often of secondary concern (that is, a longer or more costly route that satisfies certain policy criteria may well be taken over a route that is shorter but does not meet that criteria). Indeed, we saw that among ASs, there is not even the notion of cost (other than AS hop count) associated with routes. Within a single AS, however, such policy concerns are of less importance, allowing routing to focus more on the level of performance realized on a route.

accomplished by controlling the manner in which BGP routes are advertised. In particular, X will function as a stub network if it advertises (to its neighbors B and C) that it has no paths to any other destinations except itself. That is, even though X may know of a path, say XCY, that reaches network Y, it will *not* advertise this path to B. Since B is unaware that X has a path to Y, B would never forward traffic destined to Y (or C) via X. This simple example illustrates how a selective route advertisement policy can be used to implement customer/provider routing relationships.

Let's next focus on a provider network, say AS B. Suppose that B has learned (from A) that A has a path AW to W. B can thus install the route BAW into its routing information base. Clearly, B also wants to advertise the path BAW to its customer, X, so that X knows that it can route to W via B. But should B advertise the path BAW to C? If it does so, then C could route traffic to W via CBAW. If A, B, and C are all backbone providers, than B might rightly feel that it should not have to shoulder the burden (and cost!) of carrying transit traffic between A and C. B might rightly feel that it is A's and C's job (and cost!) to make sure that C can route to/from A's customers via a direct connection between A and C. There are currently no official standards that govern how backbone ISPs route among themselves. However, a rule of thumb followed by commercial ISPs is that any traffic flowing across an ISP's backbone network must have either a source or a destination (or both) in a network that is a customer of that ISP; otherwise the traffic would be getting a free ride on the ISP's network. Individual peering agreements (that would govern questions such as those raised above) are typically negotiated between pairs of ISPs and are often confidential; [Huston 1999a] provides an interesting discussion of peering agreements. For a detailed description of how routing policy reflects commercial relationships among ISPs, see [Gao 2001; Dmitiropoulos 2007]. For a discussion of BGP routing polices from an ISP standpoint, see [Caesar 2005b].

As noted above, BGP is the *de facto* standard for inter-AS routing for the public Internet. To see the contents of various BGP routing tables (large!) extracted from routers in tier-1 ISPs, see http://www.routeviews.org. BGP routing tables often contain tens of thousands of prefixes and corresponding attributes. Statistics about the size and characteristics of BGP routing tables are presented in [Potaroo 2012].

This completes our brief introduction to BGP. Understanding BGP is important because it plays a central role in the Internet. We encourage you to see the references [Griffin 2012; Stewart 1999; Labovitz 1997; Halabi 2000; Huitema 1998; Gao 2001; Feamster 2004; Caesar 2005b; Li 2007] to learn more about BGP.

4.7 Broadcast and Multicast Routing

Thus far in this chapter, our focus has been on routing protocols that support unicast (i.e., point-to-point) communication, in which a single source node sends a packet to a single destination node. In this section, we turn our attention to broadcast and multicast routing protocols. In **broadcast routing**, the network layer provides a service of delivering a packet sent from a source node to all other nodes in the network; **multicast routing** enables a single source node to send a copy of a packet to a subset of the other network nodes. In Section 4.7.1 we'll consider broadcast routing algorithms and their embodiment in routing protocols. We'll examine multicast routing in Section 4.7.2.

4.7.1 Broadcast Routing Algorithms

Perhaps the most straightforward way to accomplish broadcast communication is for the sending node to send a separate copy of the packet to each destination, as shown in Figure 4.43(a). Given *N* destination nodes, the source node simply makes *N* copies of the packet, addresses each copy to a different destination, and then transmits the *N* copies to the *N* destinations using unicast routing. This **N-way-unicast** approach to broadcasting is simple—no new network-layer routing protocol, packet-duplication, or forwarding functionality is needed. There are, however, several drawbacks to this approach. The first drawback is its inefficiency. If the source node is connected to the rest of the network via a single link, then *N* separate copies of the (same) packet will traverse this single link. It would clearly be more efficient to send only a single copy of a packet over this first hop and then have the node at the other end of the first hop make and forward any additional needed copies. That is, it would be more efficient for the network nodes themselves (rather than just the source node) to create duplicate copies of a packet. For example, in Figure 4.43(b), only a single copy of a packet traverses the R1-R2 link. That packet is then duplicated at R2, with a single copy being sent over links R2-R3 and R2-R4.

The additional drawbacks of *N*-way-unicast are perhaps more subtle, but no less important. An implicit assumption of *N*-way-unicast is that broadcast recipients, and their addresses, are known to the sender. But how is this information obtained? Most likely, additional protocol mechanisms (such as a broadcast membership or destination-registration protocol) would be required. This would add more overhead and, importantly, additional complexity to a protocol that had initially seemed quite simple. A final drawback of *N*-way-unicast relates to the purposes for which broadcast is to be used. In Section 4.5, we learned that link-state routing protocols use broadcast to disseminate the link-state information that is used to compute unicast routes. Clearly, in situations where broadcast is used to create and update unicast routes, it would be unwise (at best!) to rely on the unicast routing infrastructure to achieve broadcast.

Duplicate creation/transmission

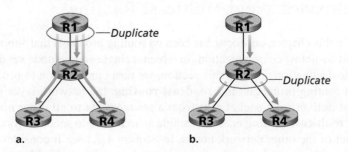

Figure 4.43 ◆ Source-duplication versus in-network duplication

Given the several drawbacks of N-way-unicast broadcast, approaches in which the network nodes themselves play an active role in packet duplication, packet forwarding, and computation of the broadcast routes are clearly of interest. We'll examine several such approaches below and again adopt the graph notation introduced in Section 4.5. We again model the network as a graph, $G = (N,E)$, where N is a set of nodes and a collection E of edges, where each edge is a pair of nodes from N. We'll be a bit sloppy with our notation and use N to refer to both the set of nodes, as well as the cardinality ($|N|$) or size of that set when there is no confusion.

Uncontrolled Flooding

The most obvious technique for achieving broadcast is a **flooding** approach in which the source node sends a copy of the packet to all of its neighbors. When a node receives a broadcast packet, it duplicates the packet and forwards it to all of its neighbors (except the neighbor from which it received the packet). Clearly, if the graph is connected, this scheme will eventually deliver a copy of the broadcast packet to all nodes in the graph. Although this scheme is simple and elegant, it has a fatal flaw (before you read on, see if you can figure out this fatal flaw): If the graph has cycles, then one or more copies of each broadcast packet will cycle indefinitely. For example, in Figure 4.43, R2 will flood to R3, R3 will flood to R4, R4 will flood to R2, and R2 will flood (again!) to R3, and so on. This simple scenario results in the endless cycling of two broadcast packets, one clockwise, and one counterclockwise. But there can be an even more calamitous fatal flaw: When a node is connected to more than two other nodes, it will create and forward multiple copies of the broadcast packet, each of which will create multiple copies of itself (at other nodes with more than two neighbors), and so on. This **broadcast storm**, resulting from the endless multiplication of broadcast packets, would eventually result in so many broadcast packets being created that the network would be rendered useless. (See the homework questions at the end of the chapter for a problem analyzing the rate at which such a broadcast storm grows.)

Controlled Flooding

The key to avoiding a broadcast storm is for a node to judiciously choose when to flood a packet and (e.g., if it has already received and flooded an earlier copy of a packet) when not to flood a packet. In practice, this can be done in one of several ways.

In **sequence-number-controlled flooding**, a source node puts its address (or other unique identifier) as well as a **broadcast sequence number** into a broadcast packet, then sends the packet to all of its neighbors. Each node maintains a list of the source address and sequence number of each broadcast packet it has already received, duplicated, and forwarded. When a node receives a broadcast packet, it first checks whether the packet is in this list. If so, the packet is dropped; if not, the packet is duplicated and forwarded to all the node's neighbors (except the node from which the packet has just been received). The Gnutella protocol, discussed in Chapter 2, uses sequence-number-controlled flooding to broadcast queries in its overlay network. (In Gnutella, message duplication and forwarding is performed at the application layer rather than at the network layer.)

A second approach to controlled flooding is known as **reverse path forwarding (RPF)** [Dalal 1978], also sometimes referred to as reverse path broadcast (RPB). The idea behind RPF is simple, yet elegant. When a router receives a broadcast packet with a given source address, it transmits the packet on all of its outgoing links (except the one on which it was received) only if the packet arrived on the link that is on its own shortest unicast path back to the source. Otherwise, the router simply discards the incoming packet without forwarding it on any of its outgoing links. Such a packet can be dropped because the router knows it either will receive or has already received a copy of this packet on the link that is on its own shortest path back to the sender. (You might want to convince yourself that this will, in fact, happen and that looping and broadcast storms will not occur.) Note that RPF does not use unicast routing to actually deliver a packet to a destination, nor does it require that a router know the complete shortest path from itself to the source. RPF need only know the next neighbor on its unicast shortest path to the sender; it uses this neighbor's identity only to determine whether or not to flood a received broadcast packet.

Figure 4.44 illustrates RPF. Suppose that the links drawn with thick lines represent the least-cost paths from the receivers to the source (A). Node A initially broadcasts a source-A packet to nodes C and B. Node B will forward the source-A packet it has received from A (since A is on its least-cost path to A) to both C and D. B will ignore (drop, without forwarding) any source-A packets it receives from any other

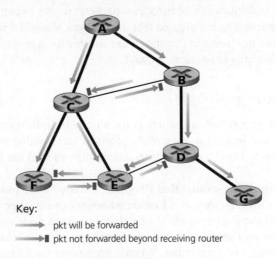

Key:

→ pkt will be forwarded

→▮ pkt not forwarded beyond receiving router

Figure 4.44 ♦ Reverse path forwarding

nodes (for example, from routers *C* or *D*). Let us now consider node *C*, which will receive a source-*A* packet directly from *A* as well as from *B*. Since *B* is not on *C*'s own shortest path back to *A*, *C* will ignore any source-*A* packets it receives from *B*. On the other hand, when *C* receives a source-*A* packet directly from *A*, it will forward the packet to nodes *B*, *E*, and *F*.

Spanning-Tree Broadcast

While sequence-number-controlled flooding and RPF avoid broadcast storms, they do not completely avoid the transmission of redundant broadcast packets. For example, in Figure 4.44, nodes *B*, *C*, *D*, *E*, and *F* receive either one or two redundant packets. Ideally, every node should receive only one copy of the broadcast packet. Examining the tree consisting of the nodes connected by thick lines in Figure 4.45(a), you can see that if broadcast packets were forwarded only along links within this tree, each and every network node would receive exactly one copy of the broadcast packet—exactly the solution we were looking for! This tree is an example of a **spanning tree**—a tree that contains each and every node in a graph. More formally, a spanning tree of a graph *G* = (*N*,*E*) is a graph *G'* = (*N*,*E'*) such that *E'* is a subset of *E*, *G'* is connected, *G'* contains no cycles, and *G'* contains all the original nodes in *G*. If each link has an associated cost and the cost of a tree is the sum of the link costs, then a spanning tree whose cost is the minimum of all of the graph's spanning trees is called (not surprisingly) a **minimum spanning tree**.

Thus, another approach to providing broadcast is for the network nodes to first construct a spanning tree. When a source node wants to send a broadcast packet, it sends the packet out on all of the incident links that belong to the spanning tree. A node receiving a broadcast packet then forwards the packet to all its neighbors in the

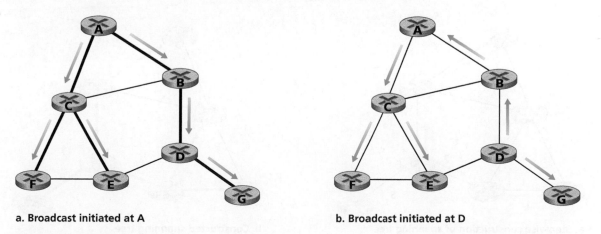

a. Broadcast initiated at A   b. Broadcast initiated at D

Figure 4.45 ♦ Broadcast along a spanning tree

spanning tree (except the neighbor from which it received the packet). Not only does spanning tree eliminate redundant broadcast packets, but once in place, the spanning tree can be used by any node to begin a broadcast, as shown in Figures 4.45(a) and 4.45(b). Note that a node need not be aware of the entire tree; it simply needs to know which of its neighbors in *G* are spanning-tree neighbors.

The main complexity associated with the spanning-tree approach is the creation and maintenance of the spanning tree. Numerous distributed spanning-tree algorithms have been developed [Gallager 1983, Gartner 2003]. We consider only one simple algorithm here. In the **center-based approach** to building a spanning tree, a center node (also known as a **rendezvous point** or a **core**) is defined. Nodes then unicast tree-join messages addressed to the center node. A tree-join message is forwarded using unicast routing toward the center until it either arrives at a node that already belongs to the spanning tree or arrives at the center. In either case, the path that the tree-join message has followed defines the branch of the spanning tree between the edge node that initiated the tree-join message and the center. One can think of this new path as being grafted onto the existing spanning tree.

Figure 4.46 illustrates the construction of a center-based spanning tree. Suppose that node *E* is selected as the center of the tree. Suppose that node *F* first joins the tree and forwards a tree-join message to *E*. The single link *EF* becomes the initial spanning tree. Node *B* then joins the spanning tree by sending its tree-join message to *E*. Suppose that the unicast path route to *E* from *B* is via *D*. In this case, the tree-join message results in the path *BDE* being grafted onto the spanning tree. Node *A* next joins the spanning group by forwarding its tree-join message towards *E*. If *A*'s unicast path to *E* is through *B*, then since *B* has already joined the spanning tree, the arrival of *A*'s tree-join message at *B* will result in the *AB* link being immediately grafted onto the spanning tree. Node *C* joins the spanning tree next by forwarding its tree-join message directly to *E*. Finally, because the unicast routing from *G* to *E*

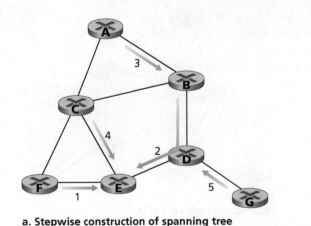

a. Stepwise construction of spanning tree

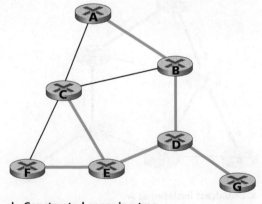

b. Constructed spanning tree

Figure 4.46 ♦ Center-based construction of a spanning tree

must be via node *D*, when *G* sends its tree-join message to *E*, the *GD* link is grafted onto the spanning tree at node *D*.

Broadcast Algorithms in Practice

Broadcast protocols are used in practice at both the application and network layers. Gnutella [Gnutella 2009] uses application-level broadcast in order to broadcast queries for content among Gnutella peers. Here, a link between two distributed application-level peer processes in the Gnutella network is actually a TCP connection. Gnutella uses a form of sequence-number-controlled flooding in which a 16-bit identifier and a 16-bit payload descriptor (which identifies the Gnutella message type) are used to detect whether a received broadcast query has been previously received, duplicated, and forwarded. Gnutella also uses a time-to-live (TTL) field to limit the number of hops over which a flooded query will be forwarded. When a Gnutella process receives and duplicates a query, it decrements the TTL field before forwarding the query. Thus, a flooded Gnutella query will only reach peers that are within a given number (the initial value of TTL) of application-level hops from the query initiator. Gnutella's flooding mechanism is thus sometimes referred to as *limited-scope flooding*.

A form of sequence-number-controlled flooding is also used to broadcast link-state advertisements (LSAs) in the OSPF [RFC 2328, Perlman 1999] routing algorithm, and in the Intermediate-System-to-Intermediate-System (IS-IS) routing algorithm [RFC 1142, Perlman 1999]. OSPF uses a 32-bit sequence number, as well as a 16-bit age field to identify LSAs. Recall that an OSPF node broadcasts LSAs for its attached links periodically, when a link cost to a neighbor changes, or when a link goes up/down. LSA sequence numbers are used to detect duplicate LSAs, but also serve a second important function in OSPF. With flooding, it is possible for an LSA generated by the source at time *t* to arrive *after* a newer LSA that was generated by the same source at time $t + \delta$. The sequence numbers used by the source node allow an older LSA to be distinguished from a newer LSA. The age field serves a purpose similar to that of a TTL value. The initial age field value is set to zero and is incremented at each hop as it is flooded, and is also incremented as it sits in a router's memory waiting to be flooded. Although we have only briefly described the LSA flooding algorithm here, we note that designing LSA broadcast protocols can be very tricky business indeed. [RFC 789; Perlman 1999] describe an incident in which incorrectly transmitted LSAs by two malfunctioning routers caused an early version of an LSA flooding algorithm to take down the entire ARPAnet!

4.7.2 Multicast

We've seen in the previous section that with broadcast service, packets are delivered to each and every node in the network. In this section we turn our attention to **multicast** service, in which a multicast packet is delivered to only a *subset* of network nodes. A number of emerging network applications require the delivery of packets from one or more senders to a group of receivers. These applications include bulk data transfer (for example, the transfer of a software upgrade from the software developer to users needing the upgrade), streaming continuous media (for example, the transfer of the audio, video, and text of a live lecture to a set of distributed lecture participants), shared data applications (for example, a whiteboard or teleconferencing application that is shared among many distributed participants), data feeds (for example, stock quotes), Web cache updating, and interactive gaming (for example, distributed interactive virtual environments or multiplayer games).

In multicast communication, we are immediately faced with two problems—how to identify the receivers of a multicast packet and how to address a packet sent to these receivers. In the case of unicast communication, the IP address of the receiver (destination) is carried in each IP unicast datagram and identifies the single recipient; in the case of broadcast, *all* nodes need to receive the broadcast packet, so no destination addresses are needed. But in the case of multicast, we now have multiple receivers. Does it make sense for each multicast packet to carry the IP addresses of all of the multiple recipients? While this approach might be workable with a small number of recipients, it would not scale well to the case of hundreds or thousands of receivers; the amount of addressing information in the datagram would swamp the amount of data actually carried in the packet's payload field. Explicit identification of the receivers by the sender also requires that the sender know the identities and addresses of all of the receivers. We will see shortly that there are cases where this requirement might be undesirable.

For these reasons, in the Internet architecture (and other network architectures such as ATM [Black 1995]), a multicast packet is addressed using **address indirection**. That is, a single identifier is used for the group of receivers, and a copy of the packet that is addressed to the group using this single identifier is delivered to all of the multicast receivers associated with that group. In the Internet, the single identifier that represents a group of receivers is a class D multicast IP address. The group of receivers associated with a class D address is referred to as a **multicast group**. The multicast group abstraction is illustrated in Figure 4.47. Here, four hosts (shown in shaded color) are associated with the multicast group address of 226.17.30.197 and will receive all datagrams addressed to that multicast address. The difficulty that we must still address is the fact that each host has a unique IP unicast address that is completely independent of the address of the multicast group in which it is participating.

While the multicast group abstraction is simple, it raises a host (pun intended) of questions. How does a group get started and how does it terminate? How is the group address chosen? How are new hosts added to the group (either as senders or receivers)? Can anyone join a group (and send to, or receive from, that group) or is group membership restricted and, if so, by whom? Do group members know the identities of the other group members as part of the network-layer protocol? How do the network nodes interoperate with each other to deliver a multicast datagram to all group members? For the Internet, the answers to all of these questions involve the Internet Group Management Protocol [RFC 3376]. So, let us next briefly consider IGMP and then return to these broader questions.

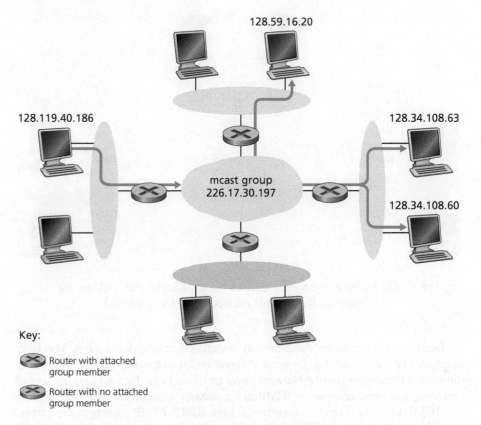

Figure 4.47 ♦ The multicast group: A datagram addressed to the group is delivered to all members of the multicast group

Internet Group Management Protocol

The IGMP protocol version 3 [RFC 3376] operates between a host and its directly attached router (informally, we can think of the directly attached router as the first-hop router that a host would see on a path to any other host outside its own local network, or the last-hop router on any path to that host), as shown in Figure 4.48. Figure 4.48 shows three first-hop multicast routers, each connected to its attached hosts via one outgoing local interface. This local interface is attached to a LAN in this example, and while each LAN has multiple attached hosts, at most a few of these hosts will typically belong to a given multicast group at any given time.

IGMP provides the means for a host to inform its attached router that an application running on the host wants to join a specific multicast group. Given that the scope of IGMP interaction is limited to a host and its attached router, another protocol is clearly required to coordinate the multicast routers (including the attached routers) throughout

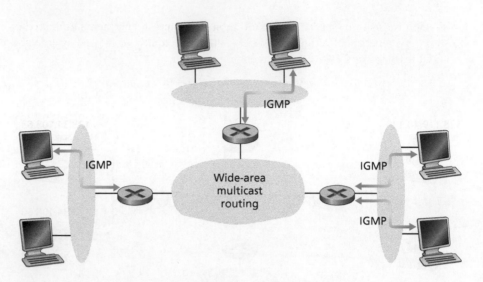

Figure 4.48 ♦ The two components of network-layer multicast in the Internet: IGMP and multicast routing protocols

the Internet, so that multicast datagrams are routed to their final destinations. This latter functionality is accomplished by network-layer multicast routing algorithms, such as those we will consider shortly. Network-layer multicast in the Internet thus consists of two complementary components: IGMP and multicast routing protocols.

IGMP has only three message types. Like ICMP, IGMP messages are carried (encapsulated) within an IP datagram, with an IP protocol number of 2. The `membership_query` message is sent by a router to all hosts on an attached interface (for example, to all hosts on a local area network) to determine the set of all multicast groups that have been joined by the hosts on that interface. Hosts respond to a `membership_query` message with an IGMP `membership_report` message. `membership_report` messages can also be generated by a host when an application first joins a multicast group without waiting for a `membership_query` message from the router. The final type of IGMP message is the `leave_group` message. Interestingly, this message is optional. But if it is optional, how does a router detect when a host leaves the multicast group? The answer to this question is that the router *infers* that a host is no longer in the multicast group if it no longer responds to a `membership_query` message with the given group address. This is an example of what is sometimes called **soft state** in an Internet protocol. In a soft-state protocol, the state (in this case of IGMP, the fact that there are hosts joined to a given multicast group) is removed via a timeout event (in this case, via a periodic `membership_query` message from the router) if it is not explicitly refreshed (in this case, by a `membership_report` message from an attached host).

The term soft state was coined by Clark [Clark 1988], who described the notion of periodic state refresh messages being sent by an end system, and suggested that with such refresh messages, state could be lost in a crash and then automatically restored by subsequent refresh messages—all transparently to the end system and without invoking any explicit crash-recovery procedures:

> *". . . the state information would not be critical in maintaining the desired type of service associated with the flow. Instead, that type of service would be enforced by the end points, which would periodically send messages to ensure that the proper type of service was being associated with the flow. In this way, the state information associated with the flow could be lost in a crash without permanent disruption of the service features being used. I call this concept "soft state," and it may very well permit us to achieve our primary goals of survivability and flexibility. . ."*

It has been argued that soft-state protocols result in simpler control than hard-state protocols, which not only require state to be explicitly added and removed, but also require mechanisms to recover from the situation where the entity responsible for removing state has terminated prematurely or failed. Interesting discussions of soft state can be found in [Raman 1999; Ji 2003; Lui 2004].

Multicast Routing Algorithms

The **multicast routing problem** is illustrated in Figure 4.49. Hosts joined to the multicast group are shaded in color; their immediately attached router is also shaded in color. As shown in Figure 4.49, only a subset of routers (those with attached hosts that are joined to the multicast group) actually needs to receive the multicast traffic. In Figure 4.49, only routers A, B, E, and F need to receive the multicast traffic. Since none of the hosts attached to router D are joined to the multicast group and since router C has no attached hosts, neither C nor D needs to receive the multicast group traffic. The goal of multicast routing, then, is to find a tree of links that connects all of the routers that have attached hosts belonging to the multicast group. Multicast packets will then be routed along this tree from the sender to all of the hosts belonging to the multicast tree. Of course, the tree may contain routers that do not have attached hosts belonging to the multicast group (for example, in Figure 4.49, it is impossible to connect routers A, B, E, and F in a tree without involving either router C or D).

In practice, two approaches have been adopted for determining the multicast routing tree, both of which we have already studied in the context of broadcast routing, and so we will only mention them in passing here. The two approaches differ according to whether a single group-shared tree is used to distribute the traffic for *all* senders in the group, or whether a source-specific routing tree is constructed for each individual sender.

• *Multicast routing using a group-shared tree.* As in the case of spanning-tree broadcast, multicast routing over a group-shared tree is based on building a tree that includes all edge routers with attached hosts belonging to the multicast group. In practice, a center-based approach is used to construct the multicast routing tree, with edge routers with attached hosts belonging to the multicast group sending

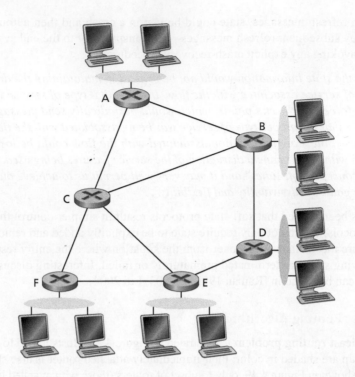

Figure 4.49 ♦ Multicast hosts, their attached routers, and other routers

(via unicast) join messages addressed to the center node. As in the broadcast case, a join message is forwarded using unicast routing toward the center until it either arrives at a router that already belongs to the multicast tree or arrives at the center. All routers along the path that the join message follows will then forward received multicast packets to the edge router that initiated the multicast join. A critical question for center-based tree multicast routing is the process used to select the center. Center-selection algorithms are discussed in [Wall 1980; Thaler 1997; Estrin 1997].

• *Multicast routing using a source-based tree*. While group-shared tree multicast routing constructs a single, shared routing tree to route packets from *all* senders, the second approach constructs a multicast routing tree for *each* source in the multicast group. In practice, an RPF algorithm (with source node x) is used to construct a multicast forwarding tree for multicast datagrams originating at source x. The RPF broadcast algorithm we studied earlier requires a bit of tweaking for use in multicast. To see why, consider router D in Figure 4.50. Under broadcast RPF, it would forward packets to router G, even though router G has no attached hosts that are joined to the multicast group. While this is not so bad for this case where D has only a single downstream router, G, imagine what would happen if there were thousands of routers downstream from D! Each of these thousands of routers would receive unwanted multicast packets.

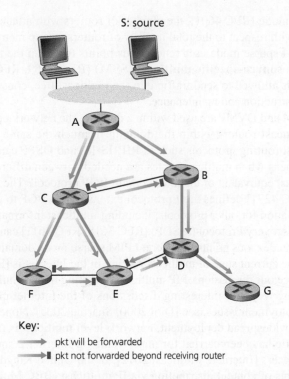

Figure 4.50 ♦ Reverse path forwarding, the multicast case

(This scenario is not as far-fetched as it might seem. The initial MBone [Casner 1992; Macedonia 1994], the first global multicast network, suffered from precisely this problem at first.). The solution to the problem of receiving unwanted multicast packets under RPF is known as **pruning**. A multicast router that receives multicast packets and has no attached hosts joined to that group will send a prune message to its upstream router. If a router receives prune messages from each of its downstream routers, then it can forward a prune message upstream.

Multicast Routing in the Internet

The first multicast routing protocol used in the Internet was the **Distance-Vector Multicast Routing Protocol (DVMRP)** [RFC 1075]. DVMRP implements source-based trees with reverse path forwarding and pruning. DVMRP uses an RPF algorithm with pruning, as discussed above. Perhaps the most widely used Internet multicast routing protocol is the **Protocol-Independent Multicast (PIM) routing protocol**, which explicitly recognizes two multicast distribution scenarios. In dense mode [RFC 3973], multicast group members are densely located; that is, many or most of the routers in the area need to be involved in routing multicast datagrams. PIM dense mode is a flood-and-prune reverse path forwarding technique similar in spirit to DVMRP.

In sparse mode [RFC 4601], the number of routers with attached group members is small with respect to the total number of routers; group members are widely dispersed. PIM sparse mode uses rendezvous points to set up the multicast distribution tree. In **source-specific multicast (SSM)** [RFC 3569, RFC 4607], only a single sender is allowed to send traffic into the multicast tree, considerably simplifying tree construction and maintenance.

When PIM and DVMP are used within a domain, the network operator can configure IP multicast routers within the domain, in much the same way that intradomain unicast routing protocols such as RIP, IS-IS, and OSPF can be configured. But what happens when multicast routes are needed between different domains? Is there a multicast equivalent of the inter-domain BGP protocol? The answer is (literally) yes. [RFC 4271] defines multiprotocol extensions to BGP to allow it to carry routing information for other protocols, including multicast information. The Multicast Source Discovery Protocol (MSDP) [RFC 3618, RFC 4611] can be used to connect together rendezvous points in different PIM sparse mode domains. An excellent overview of the current state of multicast routing in the Internet is [RFC 5110].

Let us close our discussion of IP multicast by noting that IP multicast has yet to take off in a big way. For interesting discussions of the Internet multicast service model and deployment issues, see [Diot 2000, Sharma 2003]. Nonetheless, in spite of the lack of widespread deployment, network-level multicast is far from "dead." Multicast traffic has been carried for many years on Internet 2, and the networks with which it peers [Internet2 Multicast 2012]. In the United Kingdom, the BBC is engaged in trials of content distribution via IP multicast [BBC Multicast 2012]. At the same time, application-level multicast, as we saw with PPLive in Chapter 2 and in other peer-to-peer systems such as End System Multicast [Chu 2002], provides multicast distribution of content among peers using application-layer (rather than network-layer) multicast protocols. Will future multicast services be primarily implemented in the network layer (in the network core) or in the application layer (at the network's edge)? While the current craze for content distribution via peer-to-peer approaches tips the balance in favor of application-layer multicast at least in the near-term future, progress continues to be made in IP multicast, and sometimes the race ultimately goes to the slow and steady.

4.8 Summary

In this chapter, we began our journey into the network core. We learned that the network layer involves each and every host and router in the network. Because of this, network-layer protocols are among the most challenging in the protocol stack.

We learned that a router may need to process millions of flows of packets between different source-destination pairs at the same time. To permit a router to process such a large number of flows, network designers have learned over the years that the router's tasks should be as simple as possible. Many measures can be taken to make the router's job easier, including using a datagram network layer rather than a virtual-circuit network layer, using a streamlined and fixed-sized header (as in IPv6), eliminating fragmentation (also done in IPv6), and providing the one and only best-effort service. Perhaps the most important trick here is *not* to keep track of individual flows, but instead base routing decisions solely on hierarchically structured destination addresses in the datagrams. It is interesting to note that the postal service has been using this approach for many years.

In this chapter, we also looked at the underlying principles of routing algorithms. We learned how routing algorithms abstract the computer network to a graph with nodes and links. With this abstraction, we can exploit the rich theory of shortest-path routing in graphs, which has been developed over the past 40 years in the operations research and algorithms communities. We saw that there are two broad approaches: a centralized (global) approach, in which each node obtains a complete map of the network and independently applies a shortest-path routing algorithm; and a decentralized approach, in which individual nodes have only a partial picture of the entire network, yet the nodes work together to deliver packets along the shortest routes. We also studied how hierarchy is used to deal with the problem of scale by partitioning large networks into independent administrative domains called autonomous systems (ASs). Each AS independently routes its datagrams through the AS, just as each country independently routes its postal mail through the country. We learned how centralized, decentralized, and hierarchical approaches are embodied in the principal routing protocols in the Internet: RIP, OSPF, and BGP. We concluded our study of routing algorithms by considering broadcast and multicast routing.

Having completed our study of the network layer, our journey now takes us one step further down the protocol stack, namely, to the link layer. Like the network layer, the link layer is also part of the network core. But we will see in the next chapter that the link layer has the much more localized task of moving packets between nodes on the same link or LAN. Although this task may appear on the surface to be trivial compared with that of the network layer's tasks, we will see that the link layer involves a number of important and fascinating issues that can keep us busy for a long time.

 Homework Problems and Questions

Chapter 4 Review Questions

SECTIONS 4.1–4.2

R1. Let's review some of the terminology used in this textbook. What is the difference between a *segment*, *datagram* and *frame*? Recall that both routers and link-layer switches are called *packet switches*. Which one of them forwards a packet based on the packet's IP address and which one forwards a packet based on the packet's MAC address?

R2. What is the network service model?

R3. List the different services provided to a flow of packets between a given source and destination by the network layer.

R4. Explain the implementation of virtual-circuit (VC) services in a computer network.

R5. A packet belonging to a virtual circuit will carry a VC number in its header. Because a virtual circuit may have a different VC number on each link, each intervening router must replace the VC number of each traversing packet with a new VC number. Why doesn't a packet just keep the same VC number on each of the links along its route?

R6. In a datagram network, how a packet is transmitted from source to destination?

SECTION 4.3

R7. What does each input port of a high speed router store to facilitate fast forwarding decisions?

R8. Switching in a router forwards data from an input port to an output port. What is the advantage of switching via an interconnection network over switching via memory and switching via bus?

R9. What is the role of a *packet scheduler* at the output port of a router?

R10. What is a drop-tail policy? What are AQM algorithms? Which is the most widely studied and implemented AQM algorithm? How does it work?

R11. What is HOL blocking? Does it occur in input ports or output ports?

SECTION 4.4

R12. A router has eight interfaces. How many IP addresses will it have?

R13. What is the 32-bit binary equivalent of the IP address 202.3.14.25?

R14. Visit a host that uses DHCP to obtain its IP address, network mask, default router, and IP address of its local DNS server. List these values.

R15. Suppose there are four routers between a source host and a destination host. Ignoring fragmentation, an IP datagram sent from the source host to the destination host will travel over how many interfaces? How many forwarding tables will be indexed to move the datagram from the source to the destination?

R16. Suppose an application generates chunks of 40 bytes of data every 20 msec, and each chunk gets encapsulated in a TCP segment and then an IP datagram. What percentage of each datagram will be overhead, and what percentage will be application data?

R17. Suppose Host A sends Host B a TCP segment encapsulated in an IP datagram. When Host B receives the datagram, how does the network layer in Host B know it should pass the segment (that is, the payload of the datagram) to TCP rather than to UDP or to something else?

R18. Suppose you purchase a wireless router and connect it to your cable modem. Also suppose that your ISP dynamically assigns your connected device (that is, your wireless router) one IP address. Also suppose that you have five PCs at home that use 802.11 to wirelessly connect to your wireless router. How are IP addresses assigned to the five PCs? Does the wireless router use NAT? Why or why not?

R19. Compare and contrast the IPv4 and the IPv6 header fields. Do they have any fields in common?

R20. It has been said that when IPv6 tunnels through IPv4 routers, IPv6 treats the IPv4 tunnels as link-layer protocols. Do you agree with this statement? Why or why not?

SECTION 4.5

R21. Compare and contrast static and dynamic routing algorithms.

R22. In the graph used to formulate the routing problem, what does an edge cost represent?

R23. How is a least cost path calculated in a decentralized routing algorithm?

SECTION 4.6

R24. Consider Figure 4.37. Starting with the original table in *D,* suppose that *D* receives from *A* the following advertisement:

Destination Subnet	Next Router	Number of Hops to Destination
z	C	10
w	—	1
x	—	1
....	....	....

Will the table in *D* change? If so how?

R25. What is an import policy for the gateway router?

R26. Fill in the blank: RIP advertisements typically announce the number of hops to various destinations. BGP updates, on the other hand, announce the _____ to the various destinations.

R27. Why are different inter-AS and intra-AS protocols used in the Internet?

R28. Why are policy considerations as important for intra-AS protocols, such as OSPF and RIP, as they are for an inter-AS routing protocol like BGP?

R29. Define and contrast the following terms: *subnet*, *prefix*, and *BGP route*.

R30. How does BGP use the NEXT-HOP attribute? How does it use the AS-PATH attribute?

R31. Describe how a network administrator of an upper-tier ISP can implement policy when configuring BGP.

SECTION 4.7

R32. What is an important difference between implementing the broadcast abstraction via multiple unicasts, and a single network- (router-) supported broadcast?

R33. For each of the three general approaches we studied for broadcast communication (uncontrolled flooding, controlled flooding, and spanning-tree broadcast), are the following statements true or false? You may assume that no packets are lost due to buffer overflow and all packets are delivered on a link in the order in which they were sent.

   a. A node may receive multiple copies of the same packet.

   b. A node may forward multiple copies of a packet over the same outgoing link.

R34. When a host joins a multicast group, must it change its IP address to that of the multicast group it is joining?

R35. What are the roles played by the IGMP protocol and a wide-area multicast routing protocol?

R36. What is the difference between a group-shared tree and a source-based tree in the context of multicast routing?

 Problems

P1. In this question, we consider some of the pros and cons of virtual-circuit and datagram networks.

   a. Suppose that routers were subjected to conditions that might cause them to fail fairly often. Would this argue in favor of a VC or datagram architecture? Why?

   b. Suppose that a source node and a destination require that a fixed amount of capacity always be available at all routers on the path between the source and destination node, for the exclusive use of traffic flowing between this source and destination node. Would this argue in favor of a VC or datagram architecture? Why?

   c. Suppose that the links and routers in the network never fail and that routing paths used between all source/destination pairs remains constant. In this scenario, does a VC or datagram architecture have more control traffic overhead? Why?

P2. Consider a virtual-circuit network. Suppose the VC number is a 4-bit field.

    a. What is the maximum number of virtual circuits that can be carried over a link?

    b. Suppose a central node determines paths and VC numbers at connection setup. Suppose the same VC number is used on each link along the VC's path. Describe how the central node might determine the VC number at connection setup. Is it possible that there are fewer VCs in progress than the maximum as determined in part (a) yet there is no common free VC number?

    c. Suppose that different VC numbers are permitted in each link along a VC's path. During connection setup, after an end-to-end path is determined, describe how the links can choose their VC numbers and configure their forwarding tables in a decentralized manner, without reliance on a central node.

P3. A bare-bones forwarding table in a VC network has four columns. What is the meaning of the values in each of these columns? A bare-bones forwarding table in a datagram network has two columns. What is the meaning of the values in each of these columns?

P4. Consider the network below.

    a. Suppose that this network is a datagram network. Show the forwarding table in router A, such that all traffic destined to host H3 is forwarded through interface 3.

    b. Suppose that this network is a datagram network. Can you write down a forwarding table in router A, such that all traffic from H1 destined to host H3 is forwarded through interface 3, while all traffic from H2 destined to host H3 is forwarded through interface 4? (Hint: this is a trick question.)

    c. Now suppose that this network is a virtual circuit network and that there is one ongoing call between H1 and H3, and another ongoing call between H2 and H3. Write down a forwarding table in router A, such that all traffic from H1 destined to host H3 is forwarded through interface 3, while all traffic from H2 destined to host H3 is forwarded through interface 4.

    d. Assuming the same scenario as (c), write down the forwarding tables in nodes B, C, and D.

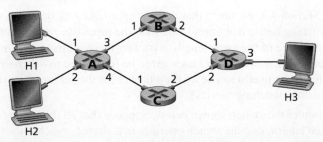

P5. Consider a VC network with a 2-bit field for the VC number. Suppose that the network wants to set up a virtual circuit over four links: link A, link B, link C, and link D. Suppose that each of these links is currently carrying two other virtual circuits, and the VC numbers of these other VCs are as follows:

Link A	Link B	Link C	Link D
00	01	10	11
01	10	11	00

In answering the following questions, keep in mind that each of the existing VCs may only be traversing one of the four links.

a. If each VC is required to use the same VC number on all links along its path, what VC number could be assigned to the new VC?

b. If each VC is permitted to have different VC numbers in the different links along its path (so that forwarding tables must perform VC number translation), how many different combinations of four VC numbers (one for each of the four links) could be used?

P6. The value of DHCP's plug-and-play capability is clear, considering the fact that the alternative is to manually configure a host's IP address. Does it have any shortcomings?

P7. Suppose two packets arrive to two different input ports of a router at exactly the same time. Also suppose there are no other packets anywhere in the router.

a. Suppose the two packets are to be forwarded to two *different* output ports. Is it possible to forward the two packets through the switch fabric at the same time when the fabric uses a *shared bus*?

b. Suppose the two packets are to be forwarded to two *different* output ports. Is it possible to forward the two packets through the switch fabric at the same time when the fabric uses a *crossbar*?

c. Suppose the two packets are to be forwarded to the *same* output port. Is it possible to forward the two packets through the switch fabric at the same time when the fabric uses a *crossbar*?

P8. In Section 4.3, we noted that the maximum queuing delay is $(n-1)D$ if the switching fabric is n times faster than the input line rates. Suppose that all packets are of the same length, n packets arrive at the same time to the n input ports, and all n packets want to be forwarded to *different* output ports. What is the maximum delay for a packet for the (a) memory, (b) bus, and (c) crossbar switching fabrics?

P9. Consider the switch shown below. Suppose that all datagrams have the same fixed length, that the switch operates in a slotted, synchronous manner, and that in one time slot a datagram can be transferred from an input port to an output port. The switch fabric is a crossbar so that at most one datagram can be transferred to a given output port in a time slot, but different output ports can receive datagrams from different input ports in a single time slot. What is the minimal number of time slots needed to transfer the packets shown from input ports to their output ports, assuming any input queue scheduling order you want (i.e., it need not have HOL blocking)? What is the largest number of slots needed, assuming the worst-case scheduling order you can devise, assuming that a non-empty input queue is never idle?

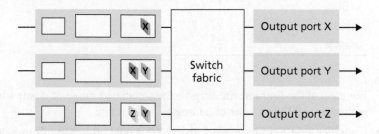

P10. Consider a datagram network using 32-bit host addresses. Suppose a router has four links, numbered 0 through 3, and packets are to be forwarded to the link interfaces as follows:

Destination Address Range	Link Interface
11100000 00000000 00000000 00000000 through 11100000 00000000 11111111 11111111	0
11100000 00000001 00000000 00000000 through 11100000 00000001 11111111 11111111	1
11100000 00000010 00000000 00000000 through 11100001 11111111 11111111 11111111	2
otherwise	3

a. Provide a forwarding table that has five entries, uses longest prefix matching, and forwards packets to the correct link interfaces.

b. Describe how your forwarding table determines the appropriate link interface for datagrams with destination addresses:

> 11111000 10010001 01010001 01010101
> 11100000 00000000 11000011 00111100
> 11100001 10000000 00010001 01110111

P11. Consider a datagram network using 8-bit host addresses. Suppose a router uses longest prefix matching and has the following forwarding table:

Prefix Match	Interface
00	0
01	1
100	2
otherwise	3

For each of the four interfaces, give the associated range of destination host addresses and the number of addresses in the range.

P12. Consider a datagram network using 8-bit host addresses. Suppose a router uses longest prefix matching and has the following forwarding table:

Prefix Match	Interface
11	0
101	1
100	2
otherwise	3

For each of the four interfaces, give the associated range of destination host addresses and the number of addresses in the range.

P13. Consider a router that interconnects three subnets: Subnet 1, Subnet 2, and Subnet 3. Suppose all of the interfaces in each of these three subnets are required to have the prefix 223.1.17/24. Also suppose that Subnet 1 is required to support up to 62 interfaces, Subnet 2 is to support up to 106 interfaces, and Subnet 3 is to support up to 15 interfaces. Provide three network addresses (of the form a.b.c.d/x) that satisfy these constraints.

P14. Suppose there are 35 hosts in a subnet. What should the IP address structure look like?

P15. What is the problem of NAT in P2P applications? How can it be avoided? Is there a special name for this solution?

P16. Consider a subnet with prefix 192.168.56.128/26. Give an example of one IP address (of form xxx.xxx.xxx.xxx) that can be assigned to this network. Suppose an ISP owns the block of addresses of the form 192.168.56.32/26. Suppose it wants to create four subnets from this block, with each block having the same number of IP addresses. What are the prefixes (of form a.b.c.d/x) for the four subnets?

P17. Consider the topology shown in Figure 4.17. Denote the three subnets with hosts (starting clockwise at 12:00) as Networks A, B, and C. Denote the subnets without hosts as Networks D, E, and F.

a. Assign network addresses to each of these six subnets, with the following constraints: All addresses must be allocated from 214.97.254/23; Subnet A should have enough addresses to support 250 interfaces; Subnet B should have enough addresses to support 120 interfaces; and Subnet C should have enough addresses to support 120 interfaces. Of course, subnets D, E and F should each be able to support two interfaces. For each subnet, the assignment should take the form a.b.c.d/x or a.b.c.d/x − e.f.g.h/y.

b. Using your answer to part (a), provide the forwarding tables (using longest prefix matching) for each of the three routers.

P18. IPsec has been designed to be backward compatible with IPv4 and IPv6. In particular, in order to reap the benefits of IPsec, we don't need to replace the protocol stacks in all the routers and hosts in the Internet. For example, using the transport mode (one of two IPsec "modes"), if two hosts want to securely communicate, IPsec needs to be available only in those two hosts. Discuss the services provided by an IPsec session.

P19. Consider sending a 1600-byte datagram into a link that has an MTU of 500 bytes. Suppose the original datagram is stamped with the identification number 291. How many fragments are generated? What are the values in the various fields in the IP datagram(s) generated related to fragmentation?

P20. Suppose datagrams are limited to 1,200 bytes (including header) between source Host A and destination Host B. Assuming a 20-byte IP header, how many datagrams would be required to send an MP3 consisting of 4 million bytes? Explain how you computed your answer.

P21. Consider the network setup in Figure 4.22. Suppose that the ISP instead assigns the router the address 24.34.112.235 and that the network address of the home network is 192.168.1/24.

a. Assign addresses to all interfaces in the home network.

b. Suppose each host has two ongoing TCP connections, all to port 80 at host 128.119.40.86. Provide the six corresponding entries in the NAT translation table.

P22. Suppose you are interested in detecting the number of hosts behind a NAT. You observe that the IP layer stamps an identification number sequentially on each IP packet. The identification number of the first IP packet generated by a host is a random number, and the identification numbers of the subsequent IP packets are sequentially assigned. Assume all IP packets generated by hosts behind the NAT are sent to the outside world.

   a. Based on this observation, and assuming you can sniff all packets sent by the NAT to the outside, can you outline a simple technique that detects the number of unique hosts behind a NAT? Justify your answer.

   b. If the identification numbers are not sequentially assigned but randomly assigned, would your technique work? Justify your answer.

P23. In this problem we'll explore the impact of NATs on P2P applications. Suppose a peer with username Arnold discovers through querying that a peer with username Bernard has a file it wants to download. Also suppose that Bernard and Arnold are both behind a NAT. Try to devise a technique that will allow Arnold to establish a TCP connection with Bernard without application-specific NAT configuration. If you have difficulty devising such a technique, discuss why.

P24. Looking at Figure 4.27, enumerate the paths from y to u through w that do not contain any loops.

P25. Repeat Problem P24 for paths from x to z through w, z to u through w, and z to w through u.

P26. Consider the following network. With the indicated link costs, use Dijkstra's shortest-path algorithm to compute the shortest path from x to all network nodes. Show how the algorithm works by computing a table similar to Table 4.3.

VideoNote
Dijkstra's algorithm:
discussion and example

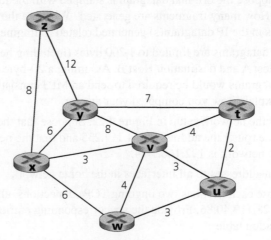

P27. Consider the network shown in Problem P26. Using Dijkstra's algorithm, and showing your work using a table similar to Table 4.3, do the following:

  a. Compute the shortest path from t to all network nodes.

  b. Compute the shortest path from u to all network nodes.

  c. Compute the shortest path from v to all network nodes.

  d. Compute the shortest path from w to all network nodes.

  e. Compute the shortest path from y to all network nodes.

  f. Compute the shortest path from z to all network nodes.

P28. Consider the network shown below, and assume that each node initially knows the costs to each of its neighbors. Consider the distance-vector algorithm and show the distance table entries at node z.

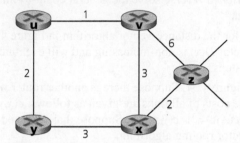

P29. Consider a general topology (that is, not the specific network shown above) and a synchronous version of the distance-vector algorithm. Suppose that at each iteration, a node exchanges its distance vectors with its neighbors and receives their distance vectors. Assuming that the algorithm begins with each node knowing only the costs to its immediate neighbors, what is the maximum number of iterations required before the distributed algorithm converges? Justify your answer.

P30. Consider the network fragment shown below. x has only two attached neighbors, w and y. w has a minimum-cost path to destination u (not shown) of 5, and y has a minimum-cost path to u of 6. The complete paths from w and y to u (and between w and y) are not shown. All link costs in the network have strictly positive integer values.

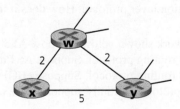

    a. Give x's distance vector for destinations w, y, and u.

    b. Give a link-cost change for either $c(x,w)$ or $c(x,y)$ such that x will inform its neighbors of a new minimum-cost path to u as a result of executing the distance-vector algorithm.

    c. Give a link-cost change for either $c(x,w)$ or $c(x,y)$ such that x will *not* inform its neighbors of a new minimum-cost path to u as a result of executing the distance-vector algorithm.

P31. Consider the three-node topology shown in Figure 4.30. Rather than having the link costs shown in Figure 4.30, the link costs are $c(x,y) = 3$, $c(y,z) = 6$, $c(z,x) = 4$. Compute the distance tables after the initialization step and after each iteration of a synchronous version of the distance-vector algorithm (as we did in our earlier discussion of Figure 4.30).

P32. Can the *poisoned reverse* solve the general count-to-infinity problem? Justify your answer.

P33. Argue that for the distance-vector algorithm in Figure 4.30, each value in the distance vector $D(x)$ is non-increasing and will eventually stabilize in a finite number of steps.

P34. Consider Figure 4.31. Suppose there is another router w, connected to router y and z. The costs of all links are given as follows: $c(x,y) = 4$, $c(x,z) = 50$, $c(y,w) = 1$, $c(z,w) = 1$, $c(y,z) = 3$. Suppose that poisoned reverse is used in the distance-vector routing algorithm.

    a. When the distance vector routing is stabilized, router w, y, and z inform their distances to x to each other. What distance values do they tell each other?

    b. Now suppose that the link cost between x and y increases to 60. Will there be a count-to-infinity problem even if poisoned reverse is used? Why or why not? If there is a count-to-infinity problem, then how many iterations are needed for the distance-vector routing to reach a stable state again? Justify your answer.

    c. How do you modify $c(y,z)$ such that there is no count-to-infinity problem at all if $c(y,x)$ changes from 4 to 60?

P35. What is the message complexity of LS routing algorithm?

P36. RIP is an application layer protocol. How does it implement network-layer functionality?

P37. Consider the network shown below. Suppose AS3 and AS2 are running OSPF for their intra-AS routing protocol. Suppose AS1 and AS4 are running RIP for their intra-AS routing protocol. Suppose eBGP and iBGP are used for the inter-AS routing protocol. Initially suppose there is *no* physical link between AS2 and AS4.

a. Router 3c learns about prefix *x* from which routing protocol: OSPF, RIP, eBGP, or iBGP?

b. Router 3a learns about *x* from which routing protocol?

c. Router 1c learns about *x* from which routing protocol?

d. Router 1d learns about *x* from which routing protocol?

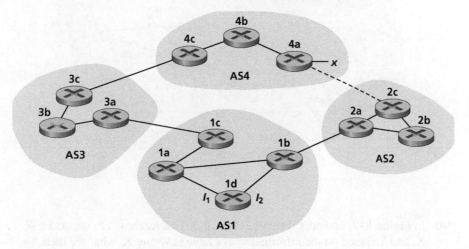

P38. Referring to the previous problem, once router 1d learns about *x* it will put an entry (x, I) in its forwarding table.

a. Will I be equal to I_1 or I_2 for this entry? Explain why in one sentence.

b. Now suppose that there is a physical link between AS2 and AS4, shown by the dotted line. Suppose router 1d learns that *x* is accessible via AS2 as well as via AS3. Will I be set to I_1 or I_2? Explain why in one sentence.

c. Now suppose there is another AS, called AS5, which lies on the path between AS2 and AS4 (not shown in diagram). Suppose router 1d learns that *x* is accessible via AS2 AS5 AS4 as well as via AS3 AS4. Will I be set to I_1 or I_2? Explain why in one sentence.

P39. Consider the following network. ISP B provides national backbone service to regional ISP A. ISP C provides national backbone service to regional ISP D. Each ISP consists of one AS. B and C peer with each other in two places using BGP. Consider traffic going from A to D. B would prefer to hand that traffic over to C on the West Coast (so that C would have to absorb the cost of carrying the traffic cross-country), while C would prefer to get the traffic via its East Coast peering point with B (so that B would have carried the traffic across the country). What BGP mechanism might C use, so that B would hand over A-to-D traffic at its East Coast peering point? To answer this question, you will need to dig into the BGP specification.

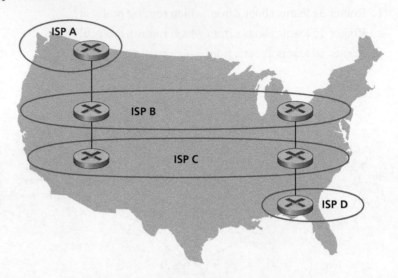

P40. In Figure 4.42, consider the path information that reaches stub networks W, X, and Y. Based on the information available at W and X, what are their respective views of the network topology? Justify your answer. The topology view at Y is shown below.

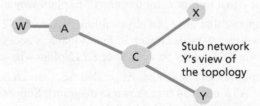

P41. Consider Figure 4.42. B would never forward traffic destined to Y via X based on BGP routing. But there are some very popular applications for which data packets go to X first and then flow to Y. Identify one such application, and describe how data packets follow a path not given by BGP routing.

P42. In Figure 4.42, suppose that there is another stub network V that is a customer of ISP A. Suppose that B and C have a peering relationship, and A is a customer of both B and C. Suppose that A would like to have the traffic destined to W to come from B only, and the traffic destined to V from either B or C. How should A advertise its routes to B and C? What AS routes does C receive?

P43. Suppose ASs X and Z are not directly connected but instead are connected by AS Y. Further suppose that X has a peering agreement with Y, and that Y has a peering agreement with Z. Finally, suppose that Z wants to transit all of Y's traffic but does not want to transit X's traffic. Does BGP allow Z to implement this policy?

P44. Consider the seven-node network (with nodes labeled *t* to *z*) in Problem P26. Show the minimal-cost tree rooted at *z* that includes (as end hosts) nodes *u*, *v*, *w*, and *y*. Informally argue why your tree is a minimal-cost tree.

P45. Consider the two basic approaches identified for achieving broadcast, unicast emulation and network-layer (i.e., router-assisted) broadcast, and suppose spanning-tree broadcast is used to achive network-layer broadcast. Consider a single sender and 32 receivers. Suppose the sender is connected to the receivers by a binary tree of routers. What is the cost of sending a broadcast packet, in the cases of unicast emulation and network-layer broadcast, for this topology? Here, each time a packet (or copy of a packet) is sent over a single link, it incurs a unit of cost. What topology for interconnecting the sender, receivers, and routers will bring the cost of unicast emulation and true network-layer broadcast as far apart as possible? You can choose as many routers as you'd like.

P46. Consider the operation of the reverse path forwarding (RPF) algorithm in Figure 4.44. Using the same topology, find a set of paths from all nodes to the source node *A* (and indicate these paths in a graph using thicker-shaded lines as in Figure 4.44) such that if these paths were the least-cost paths, then node *B* would receive a copy of *A*'s broadcast message from nodes *A*, *C*, and *D* under RPF.

P47. Consider the topology shown in Figure 4.44. Suppose that all links have unit cost and that node *E* is the broadcast source. Using arrows like those shown in Figure 4.44 indicate links over which packets will be forwarded using RPF, and links over which packets will not be forwarded, given that node *E* is the source.

P48. What are two most important BGP attributes?

P49. Consider the topology shown in Figure 4.46, and suppose that each link has unit cost. Suppose node *C* is chosen as the center in a center-based multicast routing algorithm. Assuming that each attached router uses its least-cost path to node *C* to send join messages to *C*, draw the resulting center-based routing tree. Is the resulting tree a minimum-cost tree? Justify your answer.

P50. How does flooding lead to a broadcast storm?

P51. In Section 4.5.1, we studied Dijkstra's link-state routing algorithm for computing the unicast paths that are individually the least-cost paths from the source to all destinations. The union of these paths might be thought of as forming a **least-unicast-cost path tree** (or a shortest unicast path tree, if all link costs are identical). By constructing a counterexample, show that the least-cost path tree is *not* always the same as a minimum spanning tree.

P52. Consider a network in which all nodes are connected to three other nodes. In a single time step, a node can receive all transmitted broadcast packets from its neighbors, duplicate the packets, and send them to all of its neighbors (except to the node that sent a given packet). At the next time step, neighboring nodes can receive, duplicate, and forward these packets, and so on. Suppose that uncontrolled flooding is used to provide broadcast in such a network. At time step t, how many copies of the broadcast packet will be transmitted, assuming that during time step 1, a single broadcast packet is transmitted by the source node to its three neighbors.

P53. We saw in Section 4.7 that there is no network-layer protocol that can be used to identify the hosts participating in a multicast group. Given this, how can multicast applications learn the identities of the hosts that are participating in a multicast group?

P54. Design (give a pseudocode description of) an application-level protocol that maintains the host addresses of all hosts participating in a multicast group. Specifically identify the network service (unicast or multicast) that is used by your protocol, and indicate whether your protocol is sending messages in-band or out-of-band (with respect to the application data flow among the multicast group participants) and why.

P55. What is the size of the multicast address space? Suppose now that two multicast groups randomly choose a multicast address. What is the probability that they choose the same address? Suppose now that 1,000 multicast groups are ongoing at the same time and choose their multicast group addresses at random. What is the probability that they interfere with each other?

 # Socket Programming Assignment

At the end of Chapter 2, there are four socket programming assignments. Below, you will find a fifth assignment which employs ICMP, a protocol discussed in this chapter.

Assignment 5: ICMP Ping

Ping is a popular networking application used to test from a remote location whether a particular host is up and reachable. It is also often used to measure latency between the client host and the target host. It works by sending ICMP "echo request" packets (i.e., ping packets) to the target host and listening for ICMP "echo response" replies (i.e., pong packets). Ping measures the RRT, records packet loss, and calculates a statistical summary of multiple ping-pong exchanges (the minimum, mean, max, and standard deviation of the round-trip times).

In this lab, you will write your own Ping application in Python. Your application will use ICMP. But in order to keep your program simple, you will not exactly follow the official specification in RFC 1739. Note that you will only need to write the client side of the program, as the functionality needed on the server side is built into almost all operating systems. You can find full details of this assignment, as well as important snippets of the Python code, at the Web site http://www.awl.com/kurose-ross.

Programming Assignment

In this programming assignment, you will be writing a "distributed" set of procedures that implements a distributed asynchronous distance-vector routing for the network shown below.

You are to write the following routines that will "execute" asynchronously within the emulated environment provided for this assignment. For node 0, you will write the routines:

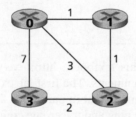

- *rtinit0()*. This routine will be called once at the beginning of the emulation. *rtinit0()* has no arguments. It should initialize your distance table in node 0 to reflect the direct costs of 1, 3, and 7 to nodes 1, 2, and 3, respectively. In the figure above, all links are bidirectional and the costs in both directions are identical. After initializing the distance table and any other data structures needed by your node 0 routines, it should then send its directly connected neighbors (in this case, 1, 2, and 3) the cost of its minimum-cost paths to all other network nodes. This minimum-cost information is sent to neighboring nodes in a routing update packet by calling the routine *tolayer2()*, as described in the full assignment. The format of the routing update packet is also described in the full assignment.
- *rtupdate0(struct rtpkt *rcvdpkt)*. This routine will be called when node 0 receives a routing packet that was sent to it by one of its directly connected neighbors. The parameter **rcvdpkt* is a pointer to the packet that was received. *rtupdate0()* is the "heart" of the distance-vector algorithm. The values it receives in a routing update packet from some other node *i* contain *i*'s current shortest-path costs to all other network nodes. *rtupdate0()* uses these received

values to update its own distance table (as specified by the distance-vector algorithm). If its own minimum cost to another node changes as a result of the
update, node 0 informs its directly connected neighbors of this change in minimum cost by sending them a routing packet. Recall that in the distance-vector
algorithm, only directly connected nodes will exchange routing packets. Thus,
nodes 1 and 2 will communicate with each other, but nodes 1 and 3 will not
communicate with each other.

Similar routines are defined for nodes 1, 2, and 3. Thus, you will write eight procedures in all: *rtinit0(), rtinit1(), rtinit2(), rtinit3(), rtupdate0(), rtupdate1(), rtup-
date2(),* and *rtupdate3().* These routines will together implement a distributed,
asynchronous computation of the distance tables for the topology and costs shown
in the figure on the preceding page.

You can find the full details of the programming assignment, as well as C code
that you will need to create the simulated hardware/software environment, at
http://www.awl.com/kurose-ross. A Java version of the assignment is also available.

 ## Wireshark Labs

In the companion Web site for this textbook, http://www.awl.com/kurose-ross,
you'll find two Wireshark lab assignments. The first lab examines the operation of
the IP protocol, and the IP datagram format in particular. The second lab explores
the use of the ICMP protocol in the ping and traceroute commands.

Vinton G. Cerf

Vinton G. Cerf is Vice President and Chief Internet Evangelist for Google. He served for over 16 years at MCI in various positions, ending up his tenure there as Senior Vice President for Technology Strategy. He is widely known as the co-designer of the TCP/IP protocols and the architecture of the Internet. During his time from 1976 to 1982 at the US Department of Defense Advanced Research Projects Agency (DARPA), he played a key role leading the development of Internet and Internet-related data packet and security techniques. He received the US Presidential Medal of Freedom in 2005 and the US National Medal of Technology in 1997. He holds a BS in Mathematics from Stanford University and an MS and PhD in computer science from UCLA.

What brought you to specialize in networking?

I was working as a programmer at UCLA in the late 1960s. My job was supported by the US Defense Advanced Research Projects Agency (called ARPA then, called DARPA now). I was working in the laboratory of Professor Leonard Kleinrock on the Network Measurement Center of the newly created ARPAnet. The first node of the ARPAnet was installed at UCLA on September 1, 1969. I was responsible for programming a computer that was used to capture performance information about the ARPAnet and to report this information back for comparison with mathematical models and predictions of the performance of the network.

Several of the other graduate students and I were made responsible for working on the so-called host-level protocols of the ARPAnet—the procedures and formats that would allow many different kinds of computers on the network to interact with each other. It was a fascinating exploration into a new world (for me) of distributed computing and communication.

Did you imagine that IP would become as pervasive as it is today when you first designed the protocol?

When Bob Kahn and I first worked on this in 1973, I think we were mostly very focused on the central question: How can we make heterogeneous packet networks interoperate with one another, assuming we cannot actually change the networks themselves? We hoped that we could find a way to permit an arbitrary collection of packet-switched networks to be interconnected in a transparent fashion, so that host computers could communicate end-to-end without having to do any translations in between. I think we knew that we were dealing with powerful and expandable technology but I doubt we had a clear image of what the world would be like with hundreds of millions of computers all interlinked on the Internet.

What do you now envision for the future of networking and the Internet? What major challenges/obstacles do you think lie ahead in their development?

I believe the Internet itself and networks in general will continue to proliferate. Already there is convincing evidence that there will be billions of Internet-enabled devices on the Internet, including appliances like cell phones, refrigerators, personal digital assistants, home servers, televisions, as well as the usual array of laptops, servers, and so on. Big challenges include support for mobility, battery life, capacity of the access links to the network, and ability to scale the optical core of the network up in an unlimited fashion. Designing an interplanetary extension of the Internet is a project in which I am deeply engaged at the Jet Propulsion Laboratory. We will need to cut over from IPv4 [32-bit addresses] to IPv6 [128 bits]. The list is long!

Who has inspired you professionally?

My colleague Bob Kahn; my thesis advisor, Gerald Estrin; my best friend, Steve Crocker (we met in high school and he introduced me to computers in 1960!); and the thousands of engineers who continue to evolve the Internet today.

Do you have any advice for students entering the networking/Internet field?

Think outside the limitations of existing systems—imagine what might be possible; but then do the hard work of figuring out how to get there from the current state of affairs. Dare to dream: A half dozen colleagues and I at the Jet Propulsion Laboratory have been working on the design of an interplanetary extension of the terrestrial Internet. It may take decades to implement this, mission by mission, but to paraphrase: "A man's reach should exceed his grasp, or what are the heavens for?"

The Link Layer: Links, Access Networks, and LANs

In the previous chapter, we learned that the network layer provides a communication service between *any* two network hosts. Between the two hosts, datagrams travel over a series of communication links, some wired and some wireless, starting at the source host, passing through a series of packet switches (switches and routers) and ending at the destination host. As we continue down the protocol stack, from the network layer to the link layer, we naturally wonder how packets are sent across the *individual links* that make up the end-to-end communication path. How are the network-layer datagrams encapsulated in the link-layer frames for transmission over a single link? Are different link-layer protocols used in the different links along the communication path? How are transmission conflicts in broadcast links resolved? Is there addressing at the link layer and, if so, how does the link-layer addressing operate with the network-layer addressing we learned about in Chapter 4? And what exactly is the difference between a switch and a router? We'll answer these and other important questions in this chapter.

In discussing the link layer, we'll see that there are two fundamentally different types of link-layer channels. The first type are broadcast channels, which connect multiple hosts in wireless LANs, satellite networks, and hybrid fiber-coaxial cable (HFC)

459

access networks. Since many hosts are connected to the same broadcast communication channel, a so-called medium access protocol is needed to coordinate frame transmission. In some cases, a central controller may be used to coordinate transmissions; in other cases, the hosts themselves coordinate transmissions. The second type of link-layer channel is the point-to-point communication link, such as that often found between two routers connected by a long-distance link, or between a user's office computer and the nearby Ethernet switch to which it is connected. Coordinating access to a point-to-point link is simpler; the reference material on this book's web site has a detailed discussion of the Point-to-Point Protocol (PPP), which is used in settings ranging from dial-up service over a telephone line to high-speed point-to-point frame transport over fiber-optic links.

We'll explore several important link-layer concepts and technologies in this chapter. We'll dive deeper into error detection and correction, a topic we touched on briefly in Chapter 3. We'll consider multiple access networks and switched LANs, including Ethernet—by far the most prevalent wired LAN technology. We'll also look at virtual LANs, and data center networks. Although WiFi, and more generally wireless LANs, are link-layer topics, we'll postpone our study of these important topics until Chapter 6.

5.1 Introduction to the Link Layer

Let's begin with some important terminology. We'll find it convenient in this chapter to refer to any device that runs a link-layer (i.e., layer 2) protocol as a **node**. Nodes include hosts, routers, switches, and WiFi access points (discussed in Chapter 6). We will also refer to the communication channels that connect adjacent nodes along the communication path as **links**. In order for a datagram to be transferred from source host to destination host, it must be moved over each of the *individual links* in the end-to-end path. As an example, in the company network shown at the bottom of Figure 5.1, consider sending a datagram from one of the wireless hosts to one of the servers. This datagram will actually pass through six links: a WiFi link between sending host and WiFi access point, an Ethernet link between the access point and a link-layer switch; a link between the link-layer switch and the router, a link between the two routers; an Ethernet link between the router and a link-layer switch; and finally an Ethernet link between the switch and the server. Over a given link, a transmitting node encapsulates the datagram in a **link-layer frame** and transmits the frame into the link.

In order to gain further insight into the link layer and how it relates to the network layer, let's consider a transportation analogy. Consider a travel agent who is planning a trip for a tourist traveling from Princeton, New Jersey, to Lausanne, Switzerland. The travel agent decides that it is most convenient for the tourist to take a limousine from Princeton to JFK airport, then a plane from JFK airport to Geneva's airport, and finally a train from Geneva's airport to Lausanne's train station. Once the travel agent makes the three reservations, it is the responsibility of the Princeton limousine company to get the tourist from Princeton to JFK; it is the responsibility of the airline company to

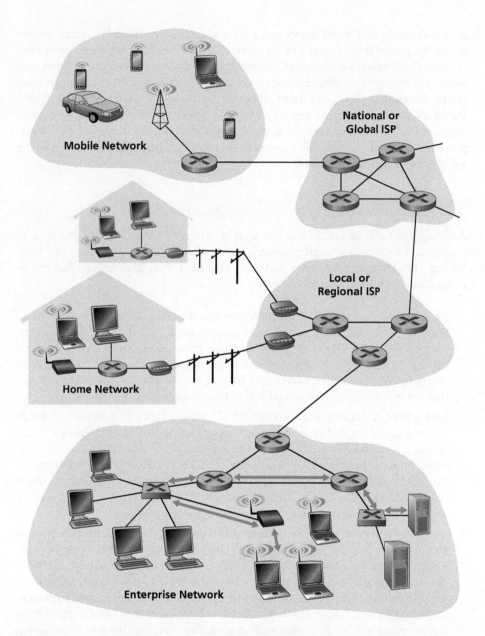

Figure 5.1 ♦ Six link-layer hops between wireless host and server

get the tourist from JFK to Geneva; and it is the responsibility of the Swiss train service to get the tourist from Geneva to Lausanne. Each of the three segments of the trip is "direct" between two "adjacent" locations. Note that the three transportation segments are managed by different companies and use entirely different transportation modes (limousine, plane, and train). Although the transportation modes are different, they each provide the basic service of moving passengers from one location to an adjacent location. In this transportation analogy, the tourist is a datagram, each transportation segment is a link, the transportation mode is a link-layer protocol, and the travel agent is a routing protocol.

5.1.1 The Services Provided by the Link Layer

Although the basic service of any link layer is to move a datagram from one node to an adjacent node over a single communication link, the details of the provided service can vary from one link-layer protocol to the next. Possible services that can be offered by a link-layer protocol include:

- *Framing.* Almost all link-layer protocols encapsulate each network-layer datagram within a link-layer frame before transmission over the link. A frame consists of a data field, in which the network-layer datagram is inserted, and a number of header fields. The structure of the frame is specified by the link-layer protocol. We'll see several different frame formats when we examine specific link-layer protocols in the second half of this chapter.

- *Link access.* A medium access control (MAC) protocol specifies the rules by which a frame is transmitted onto the link. For point-to-point links that have a single sender at one end of the link and a single receiver at the other end of the link, the MAC protocol is simple (or nonexistent)—the sender can send a frame whenever the link is idle. The more interesting case is when multiple nodes share a single broadcast link—the so-called multiple access problem. Here, the MAC protocol serves to coordinate the frame transmissions of the many nodes.

- *Reliable delivery.* When a link-layer protocol provides reliable delivery service, it guarantees to move each network-layer datagram across the link without error. Recall that certain transport-layer protocols (such as TCP) also provide a reliable delivery service. Similar to a transport-layer reliable delivery service, a link-layer reliable delivery service can be achieved with acknowledgments and retransmissions (see Section 3.4). A link-layer reliable delivery service is often used for links that are prone to high error rates, such as a wireless link, with the goal of correcting an error locally—on the link where the error occurs—rather than forcing an end-to-end retransmission of the data by a transport- or application-layer protocol. However, link-layer reliable delivery can be considered an unnecessary overhead for low bit-error links, including fiber, coax, and many twisted-pair copper links. For this reason, many wired link-layer protocols do not provide a reliable delivery service.

- *Error detection and correction.* The link-layer hardware in a receiving node can incorrectly decide that a bit in a frame is zero when it was transmitted as a one, and vice versa. Such bit errors are introduced by signal attenuation and electromagnetic noise. Because there is no need to forward a datagram that has an error, many link-layer protocols provide a mechanism to detect such bit errors. This is done by having the transmitting node include error-detection bits in the frame, and having the receiving node perform an error check. Recall from Chapters 3 and 4 that the Internet's transport layer and network layer also provide a limited form of error detection—the Internet checksum. Error detection in the link layer is usually more sophisticated and is implemented in hardware. Error correction is similar to error detection, except that a receiver not only detects when bit errors have occurred in the frame but also determines exactly where in the frame the errors have occurred (and then corrects these errors).

5.1.2 Where Is the Link Layer Implemented?

Before diving into our detailed study of the link layer, let's conclude this introduction by considering the question of where the link layer is implemented. We'll focus here on an end system, since we learned in Chapter 4 that the link layer is implemented in a router's line card. Is a host's link layer implemented in hardware or software? Is it implemented on a separate card or chip, and how does it interface with the rest of a host's hardware and operating system components?

Figure 5.2 shows a typical host architecture. For the most part, the link layer is implemented in a **network adapter**, also sometimes known as a **network interface card (NIC)**. At the heart of the network adapter is the link-layer controller, usually a single, special-purpose chip that implements many of the link-layer services (framing, link access, error detection, and so on). Thus, much of a link-layer controller's functionality is implemented in hardware. For example, Intel's 8254x controller [Intel 2012] implements the Ethernet protocols we'll study in Section 5.5; the Atheros AR5006 [Atheros 2012] controller implements the 802.11 WiFi protocols we'll study in Chapter 6. Until the late 1990s, most network adapters were physically separate cards (such as a PCMCIA card or a plug-in card fitting into a PC's PCI card slot) but increasingly, network adapters are being integrated onto the host's motherboard—a so-called LAN-on-motherboard configuration.

On the sending side, the controller takes a datagram that has been created and stored in host memory by the higher layers of the protocol stack, encapsulates the datagram in a link-layer frame (filling in the frame's various fields), and then transmits the frame into the communication link, following the link-access protocol. On the receiving side, a controller receives the entire frame, and extracts the network-layer datagram. If the link layer performs error detection, then it is the sending controller that sets the error-detection bits in the frame header and it is the receiving controller that performs error detection.

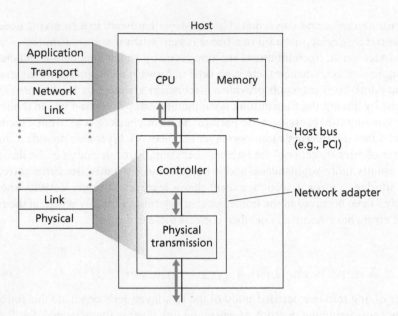

Figure 5.2 ♦ Network adapter: its relationship to other host components and to protocol stack functionality

Figure 5.2 shows a network adapter attaching to a host's bus (e.g., a PCI or PCI-X bus), where it looks much like any other I/O device to the other host components. Figure 5.2 also shows that while most of the link layer is implemented in hardware, part of the link layer is implemented in software that runs on the host's CPU. The software components of the link layer implement higher-level link-layer functionality such as assembling link-layer addressing information and activating the controller hardware. On the receiving side, link-layer software responds to controller interrupts (e.g., due to the receipt of one or more frames), handling error conditions and passing a datagram up to the network layer. Thus, the link layer is a combination of hardware and software—the place in the protocol stack where software meets hardware. Intel [2012] provides a readable overview (as well as a detailed description) of the 8254x controller from a software-programming point of view.

5.2 Error-Detection and -Correction Techniques

In the previous section, we noted that **bit-level error detection and correction**—detecting and correcting the corruption of bits in a link-layer frame sent from one node to another physically connected neighboring node—are two services often provided by the link layer. We saw in Chapter 3 that error-detection and -correction services are also often offered at the transport layer as well. In this section, we'll examine a few of the simplest techniques that can be used to detect and, in some cases, correct such bit errors. A full treatment of the theory and implementation of this topic is itself the topic of many textbooks (for example, [Schwartz 1980] or [Bertsekas 1991]), and our treatment here is necessarily brief. Our goal here is to develop an intuitive feel for the capabilities that error-detection and -correction techniques provide, and to see how a few simple techniques work and are used in practice in the link layer.

Figure 5.3 illustrates the setting for our study. At the sending node, data, *D,* to be protected against bit errors is augmented with error-detection and -correction bits (*EDC*). Typically, the data to be protected includes not only the datagram passed down from the network layer for transmission across the link, but also link-level addressing information, sequence numbers, and other fields in the link frame header. Both *D* and *EDC* are sent to the receiving node in a link-level frame. At the receiving node, a sequence of bits, *D′* and *EDC′* is received. Note that *D′* and *EDC′* may differ from the original *D* and *EDC* as a result of in-transit bit flips.

The receiver's challenge is to determine whether or not *D′* is the same as the original *D*, given that it has only received *D′* and *EDC′*. The exact wording of the receiver's decision in Figure 5.3 (we ask whether an error is detected, not whether an error has occurred!) is important. Error-detection and -correction techniques

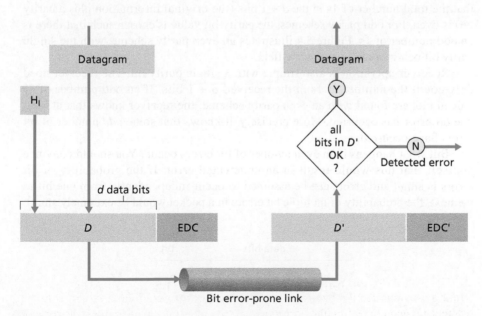

Figure 5.3 ♦ Error-detection and -correction scenario

allow the receiver to sometimes, *but not always,* detect that bit errors have occurred. Even with the use of error-detection bits there still may be **undetected bit errors**; that is, the receiver may be unaware that the received information contains bit errors. As a consequence, the receiver might deliver a corrupted datagram to the network layer, or be unaware that the contents of a field in the frame's header has been corrupted. We thus want to choose an error-detection scheme that keeps the probability of such occurrences small. Generally, more sophisticated error-detection and-correction techniques (that is, those that have a smaller probability of allowing undetected bit errors) incur a larger overhead—more computation is needed to compute and transmit a larger number of error-detection and -correction bits.

Let's now examine three techniques for detecting errors in the transmitted data—parity checks (to illustrate the basic ideas behind error detection and correction), checksumming methods (which are more typically used in the transport layer), and cyclic redundancy checks (which are more typically used in the link layer in an adapter).

5.2.1 Parity Checks

Perhaps the simplest form of error detection is the use of a single **parity bit**. Suppose that the information to be sent, D in Figure 5.4, has d bits. In an even parity scheme, the sender simply includes one additional bit and chooses its value such that the total number of 1s in the $d + 1$ bits (the original information plus a parity bit) is even. For odd parity schemes, the parity bit value is chosen such that there is an odd number of 1s. Figure 5.4 illustrates an even parity scheme, with the single parity bit being stored in a separate field.

Receiver operation is also simple with a single parity bit. The receiver need only count the number of 1s in the received $d + 1$ bits. If an odd number of 1-valued bits are found with an even parity scheme, the receiver knows that at least one bit error has occurred. More precisely, it knows that some *odd* number of bit errors have occurred.

But what happens if an even number of bit errors occur? You should convince yourself that this would result in an undetected error. If the probability of bit errors is small and errors can be assumed to occur independently from one bit to the next, the probability of multiple bit errors in a packet would be extremely small.

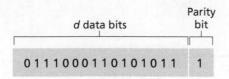

Figure 5.4 ◆ One-bit even parity

In this case, a single parity bit might suffice. However, measurements have shown that, rather than occurring independently, errors are often clustered together in "bursts." Under burst error conditions, the probability of undetected errors in a frame protected by single-bit parity can approach 50 percent [Spragins 1991]. Clearly, a more robust error-detection scheme is needed (and, fortunately, is used in practice!). But before examining error-detection schemes that are used in practice, let's consider a simple generalization of one-bit parity that will provide us with insight into error-correction techniques.

Figure 5.5 shows a two-dimensional generalization of the single-bit parity scheme. Here, the d bits in D are divided into i rows and j columns. A parity value is computed for each row and for each column. The resulting $i + j + 1$ parity bits comprise the link-layer frame's error-detection bits.

Suppose now that a single bit error occurs in the original d bits of information. With this **two-dimensional parity** scheme, the parity of both the column and the row containing the flipped bit will be in error. The receiver can thus not only *detect* the fact that a single bit error has occurred, but can use the column and row indices of the column and row with parity errors to actually identify the bit that was corrupted and *correct* that error! Figure 5.5 shows an example in

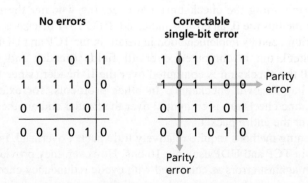

Figure 5.5 ♦ Two-dimensional even parity

which the 1-valued bit in position (2,2) is corrupted and switched to a 0—an error that is both detectable and correctable at the receiver. Although our discussion has focused on the original d bits of information, a single error in the parity bits themselves is also detectable and correctable. Two-dimensional parity can also detect (but not correct!) any combination of two errors in a packet. Other properties of the two-dimensional parity scheme are explored in the problems at the end of the chapter.

The ability of the receiver to both detect and correct errors is known as **forward error correction (FEC)**. These techniques are commonly used in audio storage and playback devices such as audio CDs. In a network setting, FEC techniques can be used by themselves, or in conjunction with link-layer ARQ techniques similar to those we examined in Chapter 3. FEC techniques are valuable because they can decrease the number of sender retransmissions required. Perhaps more important, they allow for immediate correction of errors at the receiver. This avoids having to wait for the round-trip propagation delay needed for the sender to receive a NAK packet and for the retransmitted packet to propagate back to the receiver—a potentially important advantage for real-time network applications [Rubenstein 1998] or links (such as deep-space links) with long propagation delays. Research examining the use of FEC in error-control protocols includes [Biersack 1992; Nonnenmacher 1998; Byers 1998; Shacham 1990].

5.2.2 Checksumming Methods

In checksumming techniques, the d bits of data in Figure 5.4 are treated as a sequence of k-bit integers. One simple checksumming method is to simply sum these k-bit integers and use the resulting sum as the error-detection bits. The **Internet checksum** is based on this approach—bytes of data are treated as 16-bit integers and summed. The 1s complement of this sum then forms the Internet checksum that is carried in the segment header. As discussed in Section 3.3, the receiver checks the checksum by taking the 1s complement of the sum of the received data (including the checksum) and checking whether the result is all 1 bits. If any of the bits are 0, an error is indicated. RFC 1071 discusses the Internet checksum algorithm and its implementation in detail. In the TCP and UDP protocols, the Internet checksum is computed over all fields (header and data fields included). In IP the checksum is computed over the IP header (since the UDP or TCP segment has its own checksum). In other protocols, for example, XTP [Strayer 1992], one checksum is computed over the header and another checksum is computed over the entire packet.

Checksumming methods require relatively little packet overhead. For example, the checksums in TCP and UDP use only 16 bits. However, they provide relatively weak protection against errors as compared with cyclic redundancy check, which is discussed below and which is often used in the link layer. A natural question at this point is, Why is checksumming used at the transport layer and cyclic redundancy check used at the link layer? Recall that the transport layer is typically implemented in software in a host as part of the host's operating system. Because transport-layer error detection is implemented in software, it is important to have a simple and fast error-detection scheme such as checksumming. On the other hand, error detection at the link layer is implemented in dedicated hardware in adapters, which can rapidly perform the more complex CRC operations. Feldmeier [Feldmeier 1995] presents fast software implementation techniques for not only weighted checksum codes, but CRC (see below) and other codes as well.

5.2.3 Cyclic Redundancy Check (CRC)

An error-detection technique used widely in today's computer networks is based on **cyclic redundancy check (CRC) codes**. CRC codes are also known as **polynomial codes**, since it is possible to view the bit string to be sent as a polynomial whose coefficients are the 0 and 1 values in the bit string, with operations on the bit string interpreted as polynomial arithmetic.

CRC codes operate as follows. Consider the d-bit piece of data, D, that the sending node wants to send to the receiving node. The sender and receiver must first agree on an $r + 1$ bit pattern, known as a **generator**, which we will denote as G. We will require that the most significant (leftmost) bit of G be a 1. The key idea behind CRC codes is shown in Figure 5.6. For a given piece of data, D, the sender will choose r additional bits, R, and append them to D such that the resulting $d + r$ bit pattern (interpreted as a binary number) is exactly divisible by G (i.e., has no remainder) using modulo-2 arithmetic. The process of error checking with CRCs is thus simple: The receiver divides the $d + r$ received bits by G. If the remainder is nonzero, the receiver knows that an error has occurred; otherwise the data is accepted as being correct.

All CRC calculations are done in modulo-2 arithmetic without carries in addition or borrows in subtraction. This means that addition and subtraction are identical, and both are equivalent to the bitwise exclusive-or (XOR) of the operands. Thus, for example,

```
1011 XOR 0101 = 1110
1001 XOR 1101 = 0100
```

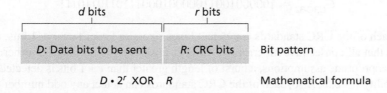

Figure 5.6 ♦ CRC

Also, we similarly have

```
1011 - 0101 = 1110
1001 - 1101 = 0100
```

Multiplication and division are the same as in base-2 arithmetic, except that any required addition or subtraction is done without carries or borrows. As in regular binary arithmetic, multiplication by 2^k left shifts a bit pattern by k places. Thus, given D and R, the quantity $D \cdot 2^r$ XOR R yields the $d + r$ bit pattern shown in Figure 5.6. We'll use this algebraic characterization of the $d + r$ bit pattern from Figure 5.6 in our discussion below.

Let us now turn to the crucial question of how the sender computes R. Recall that we want to find R such that there is an n such that

$$D \cdot 2^r \text{ XOR } R = nG$$

That is, we want to choose R such that G divides into $D \cdot 2^r$ XOR R without remainder. If we XOR (that is, add modulo-2, without carry) R to both sides of the above equation, we get

$$D \cdot 2^r = nG \text{ XOR } R$$

This equation tells us that if we divide $D \cdot 2^r$ by G, the value of the remainder is precisely R. In other words, we can calculate R as

$$R = \text{remainder} \frac{D \cdot 2^r}{G}$$

Figure 5.7 illustrates this calculation for the case of $D = 101110$, $d = 6$, $G = 1001$, and $r = 3$. The 9 bits transmitted in this case are 101110 011. You should check these calculations for yourself and also check that indeed $D \cdot 2^r = 101011 \cdot G$ XOR R.

International standards have been defined for 8-, 12-, 16-, and 32-bit generators, G. The CRC-32 32-bit standard, which has been adopted in a number of link-level IEEE protocols, uses a generator of

$$G_{\text{CRC-32}} = 100000100110000010001110110110111$$

Each of the CRC standards can detect burst errors of fewer than $r + 1$ bits. (This means that all consecutive bit errors of r bits or fewer will be detected.) Furthermore, under appropriate assumptions, a burst of length greater than $r + 1$ bits is detected with probability $1 - 0.5^r$. Also, each of the CRC standards can detect any odd number of bit errors. See [Williams 1993] for a discussion of implementing CRC checks. The theory

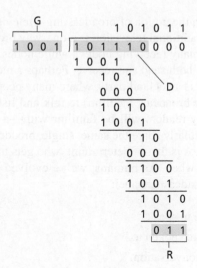

Figure 5.7 ♦ A sample CRC calculation

behind CRC codes and even more powerful codes is beyond the scope of this text. The text [Schwartz 1980] provides an excellent introduction to this topic.

5.3 Multiple Access Links and Protocols

In the introduction to this chapter, we noted that there are two types of network links: point-to-point links and broadcast links. A **point-to-point link** consists of a single sender at one end of the link and a single receiver at the other end of the link. Many link-layer protocols have been designed for point-to-point links; the point-to-point protocol (PPP) and high-level data link control (HDLC) are two such protocols that we'll cover later in this chapter. The second type of link, a **broadcast link**, can have multiple sending and receiving nodes all connected to the same, single, shared broadcast channel. The term *broadcast* is used here because when any one node transmits a frame, the channel broadcasts the frame and each of the other nodes receives a copy. Ethernet and wireless LANs are examples of broadcast link-layer technologies. In this section we'll take a step back from specific link-layer protocols and first examine a problem of central importance to the link layer: how to coordinate the access of multiple sending and receiving nodes to a shared broadcast channel—the **multiple access problem**. Broadcast channels are often used in LANs, networks that are geographically concentrated in a single building (or on a corporate or university campus). Thus, we'll also look at how multiple access channels are used in LANs at the end of this section.

We are all familiar with the notion of broadcasting—television has been using it since its invention. But traditional television is a one-way broadcast (that is, one fixed node transmitting to many receiving nodes), while nodes on a computer network broadcast channel can both send and receive. Perhaps a more apt human analogy for a broadcast channel is a cocktail party, where many people gather in a large room (the air providing the broadcast medium) to talk and listen. A second good analogy is something many readers will be familiar with—a classroom—where teacher(s) and student(s) similarly share the same, single, broadcast medium. A central problem in both scenarios is that of determining who gets to talk (that is, transmit into the channel), and when. As humans, we've evolved an elaborate set of protocols for sharing the broadcast channel:

"Give everyone a chance to speak."

"Don't speak until you are spoken to."

"Don't monopolize the conversation."

"Raise your hand if you have a question."

"Don't interrupt when someone is speaking."

"Don't fall asleep when someone is talking."

Computer networks similarly have protocols—so-called **multiple access protocols**—by which nodes regulate their transmission into the shared broadcast channel. As shown in Figure 5.8, multiple access protocols are needed in a wide variety of network settings, including both wired and wireless access networks, and satellite networks. Although technically each node accesses the broadcast channel through its adapter, in this section we will refer to the *node* as the sending and receiving device. In practice, hundreds or even thousands of nodes can directly communicate over a broadcast channel.

Because all nodes are capable of transmitting frames, more than two nodes can transmit frames at the same time. When this happens, all of the nodes receive multiple frames at the same time; that is, the transmitted frames **collide** at all of the receivers. Typically, when there is a collision, none of the receiving nodes can make any sense of any of the frames that were transmitted; in a sense, the signals of the colliding frames become inextricably tangled together. Thus, all the frames involved in the collision are lost, and the broadcast channel is wasted during the collision interval. Clearly, if many nodes want to transmit frames frequently, many transmissions will result in collisions, and much of the bandwidth of the broadcast channel will be wasted.

In order to ensure that the broadcast channel performs useful work when multiple nodes are active, it is necessary to somehow coordinate the transmissions of the active nodes. This coordination job is the responsibility of the multiple access protocol. Over the past 40 years, thousands of papers and hundreds of PhD dissertations have been written on multiple access protocols; a comprehensive survey of the first 20 years of

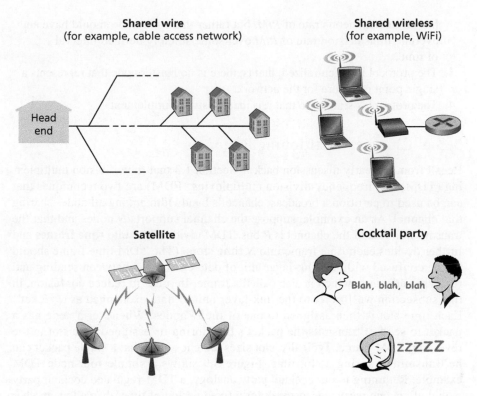

Figure 5.8 ♦ Various multiple access channels

this body of work is [Rom 1990]. Furthermore, active research in multiple access protocols continues due to the continued emergence of new types of links, particularly new wireless links.

Over the years, dozens of multiple access protocols have been implemented in a variety of link-layer technologies. Nevertheless, we can classify just about any multiple access protocol as belonging to one of three categories: **channel partitioning protocols**, **random access protocols**, and **taking-turns protocols**. We'll cover these categories of multiple access protocols in the following three subsections.

Let's conclude this overview by noting that, ideally, a multiple access protocol for a broadcast channel of rate R bits per second should have the following desirable characteristics:

1. When only one node has data to send, that node has a throughput of R bps.
2. When M nodes have data to send, each of these nodes has a throughput of R/M bps. This need not necessarily imply that each of the M nodes always

has an instantaneous rate of R/M, but rather that each node should have an average transmission rate of R/M over some suitably defined interval of time.

3. The protocol is decentralized; that is, there is no master node that represents a single point of failure for the network.

4. The protocol is simple, so that it is inexpensive to implement.

5.3.1 Channel Partitioning Protocols

Recall from our early discussion back in Section 1.3 that time-division multiplexing (TDM) and frequency-division multiplexing (FDM) are two techniques that can be used to partition a broadcast channel's bandwidth among all nodes sharing that channel. As an example, suppose the channel supports N nodes and that the transmission rate of the channel is R bps. TDM divides time into **time frames** and further divides each time frame into N **time slots**. (The TDM time frame should not be confused with the link-layer unit of data exchanged between sending and receiving adapters, which is also called a frame. In order to reduce confusion, in this subsection we'll refer to the link-layer unit of data exchanged as a packet.) Each time slot is then assigned to one of the N nodes. Whenever a node has a packet to send, it transmits the packet's bits during its assigned time slot in the revolving TDM frame. Typically, slot sizes are chosen so that a single packet can be transmitted during a slot time. Figure 5.9 shows a simple four-node TDM example. Returning to our cocktail party analogy, a TDM-regulated cocktail party would allow one partygoer to speak for a fixed period of time, then allow another partygoer to speak for the same amount of time, and so on. Once everyone had had a chance to talk, the pattern would repeat.

TDM is appealing because it eliminates collisions and is perfectly fair: Each node gets a dedicated transmission rate of R/N bps during each frame time. However, it has two major drawbacks. First, a node is limited to an average rate of R/N bps even when it is the only node with packets to send. A second drawback is that a node must always wait for its turn in the transmission sequence—again, even when it is the only node with a frame to send. Imagine the partygoer who is the only one with anything to say (and imagine that this is the even rarer circumstance where everyone wants to hear what that one person has to say). Clearly, TDM would be a poor choice for a multiple access protocol for this particular party.

While TDM shares the broadcast channel in time, FDM divides the R bps channel into different frequencies (each with a bandwidth of R/N) and assigns each frequency to one of the N nodes. FDM thus creates N smaller channels of R/N bps out of the single, larger R bps channel. FDM shares both the advantages and drawbacks of TDM. It avoids collisions and divides the bandwidth fairly among the N nodes. However, FDM also shares a principal disadvantage with TDM—a node is limited to a bandwidth of R/N, even when it is the only node with packets to send.

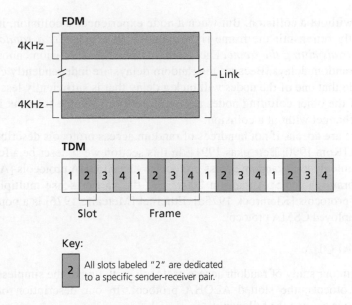

Figure 5.9 ◆ A four-node TDM and FDM example

A third channel partitioning protocol is **code division multiple access (CDMA)**. While TDM and FDM assign time slots and frequencies, respectively, to the nodes, CDMA assigns a different *code* to each node. Each node then uses its unique code to encode the data bits it sends. If the codes are chosen carefully, CDMA networks have the wonderful property that different nodes can transmit *simultaneously* and yet have their respective receivers correctly receive a sender's encoded data bits (assuming the receiver knows the sender's code) in spite of interfering transmissions by other nodes. CDMA has been used in military systems for some time (due to its anti-jamming properties) and now has widespread civilian use, particularly in cellular telephony. Because CDMA's use is so tightly tied to wireless channels, we'll save our discussion of the technical details of CDMA until Chapter 6. For now, it will suffice to know that CDMA codes, like time slots in TDM and frequencies in FDM, can be allocated to the multiple access channel users.

5.3.2 Random Access Protocols

The second broad class of multiple access protocols are random access protocols. In a random access protocol, a transmitting node always transmits at the full rate of the channel, namely, *R* bps. When there is a collision, each node involved in the collision repeatedly retransmits its frame (that is, packet) until its frame gets through without a collision. But when a node experiences a collision, it doesn't necessarily retransmit the frame right away. *Instead it waits a random delay before retransmitting the frame.* Each node involved in a collision chooses independent random delays. Because the random delays are independently chosen, it is possible that one of the nodes will pick a delay that is sufficiently less than the delays of the other colliding nodes and will therefore be able to sneak its frame into the channel without a collision.

There are dozens if not hundreds of random access protocols described in the literature [Rom 1990; Bertsekas 1991]. In this section we'll describe a few of the most commonly used random access protocols—the ALOHA protocols [Abramson 1970; Abramson 1985; Abramson 2009] and the carrier sense multiple access (CSMA) protocols [Kleinrock 1975b]. Ethernet [Metcalfe 1976] is a popular and widely deployed CSMA protocol.

Slotted ALOHA

Let's begin our study of random access protocols with one of the simplest random access protocols, the slotted ALOHA protocol. In our description of slotted ALOHA, we assume the following:

- All frames consist of exactly L bits.
- Time is divided into slots of size L/R seconds (that is, a slot equals the time to transmit one frame).
- Nodes start to transmit frames only at the beginnings of slots.
- The nodes are synchronized so that each node knows when the slots begin.
- If two or more frames collide in a slot, then all the nodes detect the collision event before the slot ends.

Let p be a probability, that is, a number between 0 and 1. The operation of slotted ALOHA in each node is simple:

- When the node has a fresh frame to send, it waits until the beginning of the next slot and transmits the entire frame in the slot.
- If there isn't a collision, the node has successfully transmitted its frame and thus need not consider retransmitting the frame. (The node can prepare a new frame for transmission, if it has one.)
- If there is a collision, the node detects the collision before the end of the slot. The node retransmits its frame in each subsequent slot with probability p until the frame is transmitted without a collision.

By retransmitting with probability p, we mean that the node effectively tosses a biased coin; the event heads corresponds to "retransmit," which occurs with probability p. The event tails corresponds to "skip the slot and toss the coin again in the next slot"; this occurs with probability $(1 - p)$. All nodes involved in the collision toss their coins independently.

Slotted ALOHA would appear to have many advantages. Unlike channel partitioning, slotted ALOHA allows a node to transmit continuously at the full rate, R, when that node is the only active node. (A node is said to be active if it has frames to send.) Slotted ALOHA is also highly decentralized, because each node detects collisions and independently decides when to retransmit. (Slotted ALOHA does, however, require the slots to be synchronized in the nodes; shortly we'll discuss an unslotted version of the ALOHA protocol, as well as CSMA protocols, none of which require such synchronization.) Slotted ALOHA is also an extremely simple protocol.

Slotted ALOHA works well when there is only one active node, but how efficient is it when there are multiple active nodes? There are two possible efficiency concerns here. First, as shown in Figure 5.10, when there are multiple active nodes, a certain fraction of the slots will have collisions and will therefore be "wasted." The second concern is that another fraction of the slots will be *empty* because all active nodes refrain from transmitting as a result of the probabilistic transmission policy. The only "unwasted" slots will be those in which exactly one node transmits. A slot in which exactly one node transmits is said to be a **successful slot**. The **efficiency** of a slotted multiple access protocol is defined to be the long-run fraction of successful slots in the case when there are a large number of active nodes, each always having a large number of frames to send.

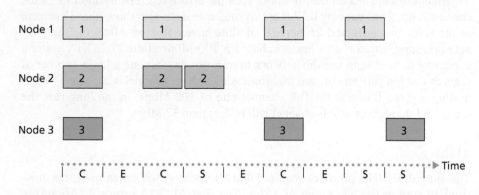

Key:

C = Collision slot
E = Empty slot
S = Successful slot

Figure 5.10 ♦ Nodes 1, 2, and 3 collide in the first slot. Node 2 finally succeeds in the fourth slot, node 1 in the eighth slot, and node 3 in the ninth slot

Note that if no form of access control were used, and each node were to immediately retransmit after each collision, the efficiency would be zero. Slotted ALOHA clearly increases the efficiency beyond zero, but by how much?

We now proceed to outline the derivation of the maximum efficiency of slotted ALOHA. To keep this derivation simple, let's modify the protocol a little and assume that each node attempts to transmit a frame in each slot with probability p. (That is, we assume that each node always has a frame to send and that the node transmits with probability p for a fresh frame as well as for a frame that has already suffered a collision.) Suppose there are N nodes. Then the probability that a given slot is a successful slot is the probability that one of the nodes transmits and that the remaining $N - 1$ nodes do not transmit. The probability that a given node transmits is p; the probability that the remaining nodes do not transmit is $(1 - p)^{N-1}$. Therefore the probability a given node has a success is $p(1 - p)^{N-1}$. Because there are N nodes, the probability that any one of the N nodes has a success is $Np(1 - p)^{N-1}$.

Thus, when there are N active nodes, the efficiency of slotted ALOHA is $Np(1 - p)^{N-1}$. To obtain the *maximum* efficiency for N active nodes, we have to find the p^* that maximizes this expression. (See the homework problems for a general outline of this derivation.) And to obtain the maximum efficiency for a large number of active nodes, we take the limit of $Np^*(1 - p^*)^{N-1}$ as N approaches infinity. (Again, see the homework problems.) After performing these calculations, we'll find that the maximum efficiency of the protocol is given by $1/e = 0.37$. That is, when a large number of nodes have many frames to transmit, then (at best) only 37 percent of the slots do useful work. Thus the effective transmission rate of the channel is not R bps but only $0.37 R$ bps! A similar analysis also shows that 37 percent of the slots go empty and 26 percent of slots have collisions. Imagine the poor network administrator who has purchased a 100-Mbps slotted ALOHA system, expecting to be able to use the network to transmit data among a large number of users at an aggregate rate of, say, 80 Mbps! Although the channel is capable of transmitting a given frame at the full channel rate of 100 Mbps, in the long run, the successful throughput of this channel will be less than 37 Mbps.

Aloha

The slotted ALOHA protocol required that all nodes synchronize their transmissions to start at the beginning of a slot. The first ALOHA protocol [Abramson 1970] was actually an unslotted, fully decentralized protocol. In pure ALOHA, when a frame first arrives (that is, a network-layer datagram is passed down from the network layer at the sending node), the node immediately transmits the frame in its entirety into the broadcast channel. If a transmitted frame experiences a collision with one or more other transmissions, the node will then immediately (after completely transmitting its collided frame) retransmit the frame with probability p. Otherwise, the node waits for a frame transmission time. After this wait, it then transmits the frame with probability p, or waits (remaining idle) for another frame time with probability $1 - p$.

To determine the maximum efficiency of pure ALOHA, we focus on an individual node. We'll make the same assumptions as in our slotted ALOHA analysis and take the frame transmission time to be the unit of time. At any given time, the probability that a node is transmitting a frame is p. Suppose this frame begins transmission at time t_0. As shown in Figure 5.11, in order for this frame to be successfully transmitted, no other nodes can begin their transmission in the interval of time $[t_0 - 1, t_0]$. Such a transmission would overlap with the beginning of the transmission of node i's frame. The probability that all other nodes do not begin a transmission in this interval is $(1 - p)^{N-1}$. Similarly, no other node can begin a transmission while node i is transmitting, as such a transmission would overlap with the latter part of node i's transmission. The probability that all other nodes do not begin a transmission in this interval is also $(1 - p)^{N-1}$. Thus, the probability that a given node has a successful transmission is $p(1 - p)^{2(N-1)}$. By taking limits as in the slotted ALOHA case, we find that the maximum efficiency of the pure ALOHA protocol is only $1/(2e)$—exactly half that of slotted ALOHA. This then is the price to be paid for a fully decentralized ALOHA protocol.

Carrier Sense Multiple Access (CSMA)

In both slotted and pure ALOHA, a node's decision to transmit is made independently of the activity of the other nodes attached to the broadcast channel. In particular, a node neither pays attention to whether another node happens to be transmitting when it begins to transmit, nor stops transmitting if another node begins to interfere with its transmission. In our cocktail party analogy, ALOHA protocols are quite like

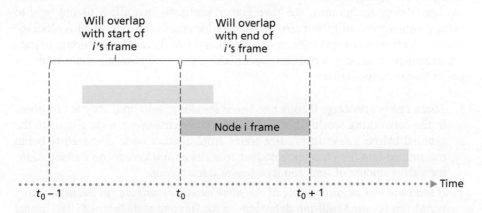

Figure 5.11 ♦ Interfering transmissions in pure ALOHA

CASE HISTORY

NORM ABRAMSON AND ALOHANET

Norm Abramson, a PhD engineer, had a passion for surfing and an interest in packet switching. This combination of interests brought him to the University of Hawaii in 1969. Hawaii consists of many mountainous islands, making it difficult to install and operate land-based networks. When not surfing, Abramson thought about how to design a network that does packet switching over radio. The network he designed had one central host and several secondary nodes scattered over the Hawaiian Islands. The network had two channels, each using a different frequency band. The downlink channel broadcasted packets from the central host to the secondary hosts; and the upstream channel sent packets from the secondary hosts to the central host. In addition to sending informational packets, the central host also sent on the downstream channel an acknowledgment for each packet successfully received from the secondary hosts.

Because the secondary hosts transmitted packets in a decentralized fashion, collisions on the upstream channel inevitably occurred. This observation led Abramson to devise the pure ALOHA protocol, as described in this chapter. In 1970, with continued funding from ARPA, Abramson connected his ALOHAnet to the ARPAnet. Abramson's work is important not only because it was the first example of a radio packet network, but also because it inspired Bob Metcalfe. A few years later, Metcalfe modified the ALOHA protocol to create the CSMA/CD protocol and the Ethernet LAN.

a boorish partygoer who continues to chatter away regardless of whether other people are talking. As humans, we have human protocols that allow us not only to behave with more civility, but also to decrease the amount of time spent "colliding" with each other in conversation and, consequently, to increase the amount of data we exchange in our conversations. Specifically, there are two important rules for polite human conversation:

• *Listen before speaking.* If someone else is speaking, wait until they are finished. In the networking world, this is called **carrier sensing**—a node listens to the channel before transmitting. If a frame from another node is currently being transmitted into the channel, a node then waits until it detects no transmissions for a short amount of time and then begins transmission.

• *If someone else begins talking at the same time, stop talking.* In the networking world, this is called **collision detection**—a transmitting node listens to the channel while it is transmitting. If it detects that another node is transmitting an interfering frame, it stops transmitting and waits a random amount of time before repeating the sense-and-transmit-when-idle cycle.

These two rules are embodied in the family of **carrier sense multiple access (CSMA)** and **CSMA with collision detection (CSMA/CD)** protocols [Kleinrock 1975b; Metcalfe 1976; Lam 1980; Rom 1990]. Many variations on CSMA and CSMA/CD have been proposed. Here, we'll consider a few of the most important, and fundamental, characteristics of CSMA and CSMA/CD.

The first question that you might ask about CSMA is why, if all nodes perform carrier sensing, do collisions occur in the first place? After all, a node will refrain from transmitting whenever it senses that another node is transmitting. The answer to the question can best be illustrated using space-time diagrams [Molle 1987]. Figure 5.12 shows a space-time diagram of four nodes (A, B, C, D) attached to a linear broadcast bus. The horizontal axis shows the position of each node in space; the vertical axis represents time.

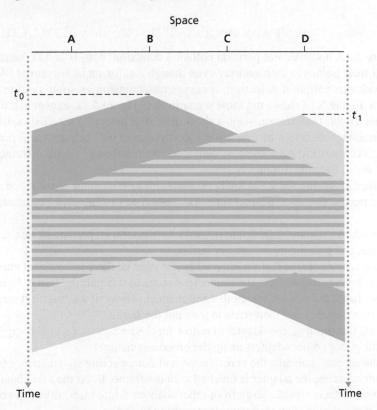

Figure 5.12 ♦ Space-time diagram of two CSMA nodes with colliding transmissions

At time t_0, node B senses the channel is idle, as no other nodes are currently transmitting. Node B thus begins transmitting, with its bits propagating in both directions along the broadcast medium. The downward propagation of B's bits in Figure 5.12 with increasing time indicates that a nonzero amount of time is needed for B's bits actually to propagate (albeit at near the speed of light) along the broadcast medium. At time t_1 $(t_1 > t_0)$, node D has a frame to send. Although node B is currently transmitting at time t_1, the bits being transmitted by B have yet to reach D, and thus D senses the channel idle at t_1. In accordance with the CSMA protocol, D thus begins transmitting its frame. A short time later, B's transmission begins to interfere with D's transmission at D. From Figure 5.12, it is evident that the end-to-end **channel propagation delay** of a broadcast channel—the time it takes for a signal to propagate from one of the nodes to another—will play a crucial role in determining its performance. The longer this propagation delay, the larger the chance that a carrier-sensing node is not yet able to sense a transmission that has already begun at another node in the network.

Carrier Sense Multiple Access with Collision Dection (CSMA/CD)

In Figure 5.12, nodes do not perform collision detection; both B and D continue to transmit their frames in their entirety even though a collision has occurred. When a node performs collision detection, it ceases transmission as soon as it detects a collision. Figure 5.13 shows the same scenario as in Figure 5.12, except that the two nodes each abort their transmission a short time after detecting a collision. Clearly, adding collision detection to a multiple access protocol will help protocol performance by not transmitting a useless, damaged (by interference with a frame from another node) frame in its entirety.

Before analyzing the CSMA/CD protocol, let us now summarize its operation from the perspective of an adapter (in a node) attached to a broadcast channel:

1. The adapter obtains a datagram from the network layer, prepares a link-layer frame, and puts the frame adapter buffer.
2. If the adapter senses that the channel is idle (that is, there is no signal energy entering the adapter from the channel), it starts to transmit the frame. If, on the other hand, the adapter senses that the channel is busy, it waits until it senses no signal energy and then starts to transmit the frame.
3. While transmitting, the adapter monitors for the presence of signal energy coming from other adapters using the broadcast channel.
4. If the adapter transmits the entire frame without detecting signal energy from other adapters, the adapter is finished with the frame. If, on the other hand, the adapter detects signal energy from other adapters while transmitting, it aborts the transmission (that is, it stops transmitting its frame).
5. After aborting, the adapter waits a random amount of time and then returns to step 2.

Space

A   B   C   D

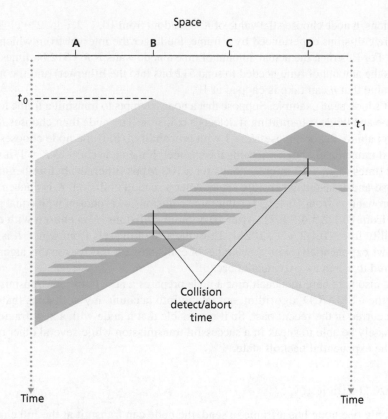

t_0

t_1

Collision
detect/abort
time

Time   Time

Figure 5.13 ♦ CSMA with collision detection

The need to wait a random (rather than fixed) amount of time is hopefully clear—if
two nodes transmitted frames at the same time and then both waited the same fixed
amount of time, they'd continue colliding forever. But what is a good interval
of time from which to choose the random backoff time? If the interval is large and
the number of colliding nodes is small, nodes are likely to wait a large amount
of time (with the channel remaining idle) before repeating the sense-and-transmit-
when-idle step. On the other hand, if the interval is small and the number of colliding nodes is large, it's likely that the chosen random values will be nearly the same,
and transmitting nodes will again collide. What we'd like is an interval that is short
when the number of colliding nodes is small, and long when the number of colliding nodes is large.

The **binary exponential backoff** algorithm, used in Ethernet as well as in
DOCSIS cable network multiple access protocols [DOCSIS 2011], elegantly solves
this problem. Specifically, when transmitting a frame that has already experienced

n collisions, a node chooses the value of K at random from $\{0, 1, 2, \ldots 2^n-1\}$. Thus, the more collisions experienced by a frame, the larger the interval from which K is chosen. For Ethernet, the actual amount of time a node waits is $K \cdot 512$ bit times (i.e., K times the amount of time needed to send 512 bits into the Ethernet) and the maximum value that n can take is capped at 10.

Let's look at an example. Suppose that a node attempts to transmit a frame for the first time and while transmitting it detects a collision. The node then chooses $K = 0$ with probability 0.5 or chooses $K = 1$ with probability 0.5. If the node chooses $K = 0$, then it immediately begins sensing the channel. If the node chooses $K = 1$, it waits 512 bit times (e.g., 5.12 microseconds for a 100 Mbps Ethernet) before beginning the sense-and-transmit-when-idle cycle. After a second collision, K is chosen with equal probability from $\{0,1,2,3\}$. After three collisions, K is chosen with equal probability from $\{0,1,2,3,4,5,6,7\}$. After 10 or more collisions, K is chosen with equal probability from $\{0,1,2, \ldots, 1023\}$. Thus, the size of the sets from which K is chosen grows exponentially with the number of collisions; for this reason this algorithm is referred to as binary exponential backoff.

We also note here that each time a node prepares a new frame for transmission, it runs the CSMA/CD algorithm, not taking into account any collisions that may have occurred in the recent past. So it is possible that a node with a new frame will immediately be able to sneak in a successful transmission while several other nodes are in the exponential backoff state.

CSMA/CD Efficiency

When only one node has a frame to send, the node can transmit at the full channel rate (e.g., for Ethernet typical rates are 10 Mbps, 100 Mbps, or 1 Gbps). However, if many nodes have frames to transmit, the effective transmission rate of the channel can be much less. We define the **efficiency of CSMA/CD** to be the long-run fraction of time during which frames are being transmitted on the channel without collisions when there is a large number of active nodes, with each node having a large number of frames to send. In order to present a closed-form approximation of the efficiency of Ethernet, let d_{prop} denote the maximum time it takes signal energy to propagate between any two adapters. Let d_{trans} be the time to transmit a maximum-size frame (approximately 1.2 msecs for a 10 Mbps Ethernet). A derivation of the efficiency of CSMA/CD is beyond the scope of this book (see [Lam 1980] and [Bertsekas 1991]). Here we simply state the following approximation:

$$\text{Efficiency} = \frac{1}{1 + 5d_{prop}/d_{trans}}$$

We see from this formula that as d_{prop} approaches 0, the efficiency approaches 1. This matches our intuition that if the propagation delay is zero, colliding nodes will abort immediately without wasting the channel. Also, as d_{trans} becomes very large, efficiency approaches 1. This is also intuitive because when a frame grabs the channel, it will hold on to the channel for a very long time; thus, the channel will be doing productive work most of the time.

5.3.3 Taking-Turns Protocols

Recall that two desirable properties of a multiple access protocol are (1) when only one node is active, the active node has a throughput of R bps, and (2) when M nodes are active, then each active node has a throughput of nearly R/M bps. The ALOHA and CSMA protocols have this first property but not the second. This has motivated researchers to create another class of protocols—the **taking-turns protocols**. As with random access protocols, there are dozens of taking-turns protocols, and each one of these protocols has many variations. We'll discuss two of the more important protocols here. The first one is the **polling protocol**. The polling protocol requires one of the nodes to be designated as a master node. The master node **polls** each of the nodes in a round-robin fashion. In particular, the master node first sends a message to node 1, saying that it (node 1) can transmit up to some maximum number of frames. After node 1 transmits some frames, the master node tells node 2 it (node 2) can transmit up to the maximum number of frames. (The master node can determine when a node has finished sending its frames by observing the lack of a signal on the channel.) The procedure continues in this manner, with the master node polling each of the nodes in a cyclic manner.

The polling protocol eliminates the collisions and empty slots that plague random access protocols. This allows polling to achieve a much higher efficiency. But it also has a few drawbacks. The first drawback is that the protocol introduces a polling delay—the amount of time required to notify a node that it can transmit. If, for example, only one node is active, then the node will transmit at a rate less than R bps, as the master node must poll each of the inactive nodes in turn each time the active node has sent its maximum number of frames. The second drawback, which is potentially more serious, is that if the master node fails, the entire channel becomes inoperative. The 802.15 protocol and the Bluetooth protocol we will study in Section 6.3 are examples of polling protocols.

The second taking-turns protocol is the **token-passing protocol**. In this protocol there is no master node. A small, special-purpose frame known as a **token** is exchanged among the nodes in some fixed order. For example, node 1 might always send the token to node 2, node 2 might always send the token to node 3, and node N might always send the token to node 1. When a node receives a token, it holds onto the token only if it has some frames to transmit; otherwise, it immediately forwards the token to the next node. If a node does have frames to transmit when it receives the token, it sends up to a maximum number of frames and then forwards the token to the next node. Token passing is decentralized and highly efficient. But it has its problems as well. For example, the failure of one node can crash the entire channel. Or if a node accidentally neglects to release the token, then some recovery procedure must be invoked to get the token back in circulation. Over the years many token-passing protocols have been developed, including the fiber distributed data interface (FDDI) protocol [Jain 1994] and the IEEE 802.5 token ring protocol [IEEE 802.5 2012], and each one had to address these as well as other sticky issues.

5.3.4 DOCSIS: The Link-Layer Protocol for Cable Internet Access

In the previous three subsections, we've learned about three broad classes of multiple access protocols: channel partitioning protocols, random access protocols, and taking turns protocols. A cable access network will make for an excellent case study here, as we'll find aspects of *each* of these three classes of multiple access protocols with the cable access network!

Recall from Section 1.2.1, that a cable access network typically connects several thousand residential cable modems to a cable modem termination system (CMTS) at the cable network headend. The Data-Over-Cable Service Interface Specifications (DOCSIS) [DOCSIS 2011] specifies the cable data network architecture and its protocols. DOCSIS uses FDM to divide the downstream (CMTS to modem) and upstream (modem to CMTS) network segments into multiple frequency channels. Each downstream channel is 6 MHz wide, with a maximum throughput of approximately 40 Mbps per channel (although this data rate is seldom seen at a cable modem in practice); each upstream channel has a maximum channel width of 6.4 MHz, and a maximum upstream throughput of approximately 30 Mbps. Each upstream and downstream channel is a broadcast channel. Frames transmitted on the downstream channel by the CMTS are received by all cable modems receiving that channel; since there is just a single CMTS transmitting into the downstream channel, however, there is no multiple access problem. The upstream direction, however, is more interesting and technically challenging, since multiple cable modems share the same upstream channel (frequency) to the CMTS, and thus collisions can potentially occur.

As illustrated in Figure 5.14, each upstream channel is divided into intervals of time (TDM-like), each containing a sequence of mini-slots during which cable modems can transmit to the CMTS. The CMTS explicitly grants permission to individual cable modems to transmit during specific mini-slots. The CMTS accomplishes this by sending a control message known as a MAP message on a downstream channel to specify which cable modem (with data to send) can transmit during which mini-slot for the interval of time specified in the control message. Since mini-slots are explicitly allocated to cable modems, the CMTS can ensure there are no colliding transmissions during a mini-slot.

But how does the CMTS know which cable modems have data to send in the first place? This is accomplished by having cable modems send mini-slot-request frames to the CMTS during a special set of interval mini-slots that are dedicated

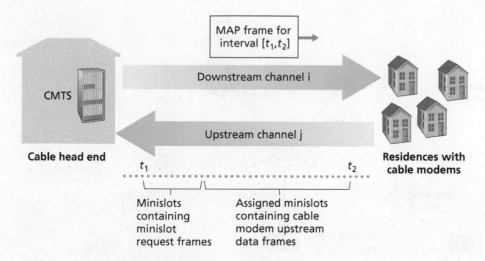

MAP frame for interval [t_1, t_2]

Downstream channel i

CMTS

Upstream channel j

Cable head end

Residences with cable modems

t_1 t_2

Minislots containing minislot request frames

Assigned minislots containing cable modem upstream data frames

Figure 5.14 ♦ Upstream and downstream channels between CMTS and cable modems

for this purpose, as shown in Figure 5.14. These mini-slot-request frames are transmitted in a random access manner and so may collide with each other. A cable modem can neither sense whether the upstream channel is busy nor detect collisions. Instead, the cable modem infers that its mini-slot-request frame experienced a collision if it does not receive a response to the requested allocation in the next downstream control message. When a collision is inferred, a cable modem uses binary exponential backoff to defer the retransmission of its mini-slot -request frame to a future time slot. When there is little traffic on the upstream channel, a cable modem may actually transmit data frames during slots nominally assigned for mini-slot-request frames (and thus avoid having to wait for a mini-slot assignment).

A cable access network thus serves as a terrific example of multiple access protocols in action—FDM, TDM, random access, and centrally allocated time slots all within one network!

5.4 Switched Local Area Networks

Having covered broadcast networks and multiple access protocols in the previous section, let's turn our attention next to switched local networks. Figure 5.15 shows a switched local network connecting three departments, two servers and a router with four switches. Because these switches operate at the link layer, they switch link-layer frames (rather than network-layer datagrams), don't recognize

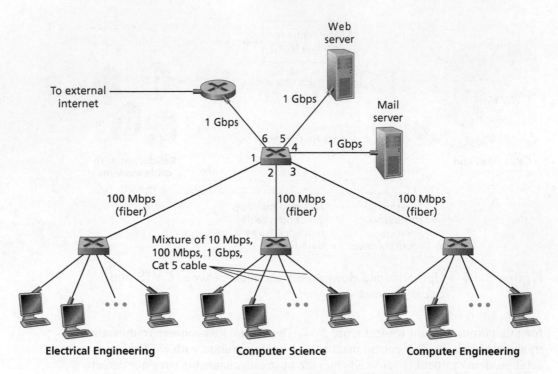

To external internet

Web server

Mail server

1 Gbps

1 Gbps

1 Gbps

1 Gbps

6 5
1   4
2   3

100 Mbps (fiber)

100 Mbps (fiber)

100 Mbps (fiber)

Mixture of 10 Mbps, 100 Mbps, 1 Gbps, Cat 5 cable

Electrical Engineering   **Computer Science**   **Computer Engineering**

Figure 5.15 ♦ An institutional network connected together by four switches

network-layer addresses, and don't use routing algorithms like RIP or OSPF to determine paths through the network of layer-2 switches. Instead of using IP addresses, we will soon see that they use link-layer addresses to forward link-layer frames through the network of switches. We'll begin our study of switched LANs by first covering link-layer addressing (Section 5.4.1). We then examine the celebrated Ethernet protocol (Section 5.5.2). After examining link-layer addressing and Ethernet, we'll look at how link-layer switches operate (Section 5.4.3), and then see (Section 5.4.4) how these switches are often used to build large-scale LANs.

5.4.1 Link-Layer Addressing and ARP

Hosts and routers have link-layer addresses. Now you might find this surprising, recalling from Chapter 4 that hosts and routers have network-layer addresses as well. You might be asking, why in the world do we need to have addresses at both the network and link layers? In addition to describing the syntax and function of the link-layer addresses, in this section we hope to shed some light on why the two layers of addresses are useful and, in fact, indispensable. We'll also cover the Address Resolution Protocol (ARP), which provides a mechanism to translate IP addresses to link-layer addresses.

MAC Addresses

In truth, it is not hosts and routers that have link-layer addresses but rather their adapters (that is, network interfaces) that have link-layer addresses. A host or router with multiple network interfaces will thus have multiple link-layer addresses associated with it, just as it would also have multiple IP addresses associated with it. It's important to note, however, that link-layer switches do not have link-layer addresses associated with their interfaces that connect to hosts and routers. This is because the job of the link-layer switch is to carry datagrams between hosts and routers; a switch does this job transparently, that is, without the host or router having to explicitly address the frame to the intervening switch. This is illustrated in Figure 5.16. A link-layer address is variously called a **LAN address**, a **physical address,** or a **MAC address**. Because MAC address seems to be the most popular term, we'll henceforth refer to link-layer addresses as MAC addresses. For most LANs (including Ethernet and 802.11 wireless LANs), the MAC address is 6 bytes long, giving 2^{48} possible MAC addresses. As shown in Figure 5.16, these 6-byte addresses are typically expressed in hexadecimal notation, with each byte of the address expressed as a pair of hexadecimal numbers. Although MAC addresses were designed to be permanent, it is now possible to

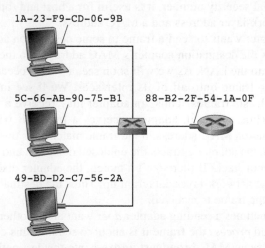

Figure 5.16 ♦ Each interface connected to a LAN has a unique MAC address

change an adapter's MAC address via software. For the rest of this section, however, we'll assume that an adapter's MAC address is fixed.

One interesting property of MAC addresses is that no two adapters have the same address. This might seem surprising given that adapters are manufactured in many countries by many companies. How does a company manufacturing adapters in Taiwan make sure that it is using different addresses from a company manufacturing adapters in Belgium? The answer is that the IEEE manages the MAC address space. In particular, when a company wants to manufacture adapters, it purchases a chunk of the address space consisting of 2^{24} addresses for a nominal fee. IEEE allocates the chunk of 2^{24} addresses by fixing the first 24 bits of a MAC address and letting the company create unique combinations of the last 24 bits for each adapter.

An adapter's MAC address has a flat structure (as opposed to a hierarchical structure) and doesn't change no matter where the adapter goes. A laptop with an Ethernet interface always has the same MAC address, no matter where the computer goes. A smartphone with an 802.11 interface always has the same MAC address, no matter where the smartphone goes. Recall that, in contrast, IP addresses have a hierarchical structure (that is, a network part and a host part), and a host's IP addresses needs to be changed when the host moves, i.e, changes the network to which it is attached. An adapter's MAC address is analogous to a person's social security number, which also has a flat addressing structure and which doesn't change no matter where the person goes. An IP address is analogous to a person's postal address, which is hierarchical and which must be changed whenever a person moves. Just as a person may find it useful to have both a postal address and a social security number, it is useful for a host and router interfaces to have both a network-layer address and a MAC address.

When an adapter wants to send a frame to some destination adapter, the sending adapter inserts the destination adapter's MAC address into the frame and then sends the frame into the LAN. As we will soon see, a switch occassionally broadcasts an incoming frame onto all of its interfaces. We'll see in Chapter 6 that 802.11 also broadcasts frames. Thus, an adapter may receive a frame that isn't addressed to it. Thus, when an adapter receives a frame, it will check to see whether the destination MAC address in the frame matches its own MAC address. If there is a match, the adapter extracts the enclosed datagram and passes the datagram up the protocol stack. If there isn't a match, the adapter discards the frame, without passing the network-layer datagram up. Thus, the destination only will be interrupted when the frame is received.

However, sometimes a sending adapter *does* want all the other adapters on the LAN to receive and *process* the frame it is about to send. In this case, the sending adapter inserts a special MAC **broadcast address** into the destination address field of the frame. For LANs that use 6-byte addresses (such as Ethernet and 802.11), the broadcast address is a string of 48 consecutive 1s (that is, FF-FF-FF-FF-FF-FF in hexadecimal notation).

PRINCIPLES IN PRACTICE

KEEPING THE LAYERS INDEPENDENT

There are several reasons why hosts and router interfaces have MAC addresses in addition to network-layer addresses. First, LANs are designed for arbitrary network-layer protocols, not just for IP and the Internet. If adapters were assigned IP addresses rather than "neutral" MAC addresses, then adapters would not easily be able to support other network-layer protocols (for example, IPX or DECnet). Second, if adapters were to use network-layer addresses instead of MAC addresses, the network-layer address would have to be stored in the adapter RAM and reconfigured every time the adapter was moved (or powered up). Another option is to not use any addresses in the adapters and have each adapter pass the data (typically, an IP datagram) of each frame it receives up the protocol stack. The network layer could then check for a matching network-layer address. One problem with this option is that the host would be interrupted by every frame sent on the LAN, including by frames that were destined for other hosts on the same broadcast LAN. In summary, in order for the layers to be largely independent building blocks in a network architecture, different layers need to have their own addressing scheme. We have now seen three types of addresses: host names for the application layer, IP addresses for the network layer, and MAC addresses for the link layer.

Address Resolution Protocol (ARP)

Because there are both network-layer addresses (for example, Internet IP addresses) and link-layer addresses (that is, MAC addresses), there is a need to translate between them. For the Internet, this is the job of the **Address Resolution Protocol (ARP)** [RFC 826].

To understand the need for a protocol such as ARP, consider the network shown in Figure 5.17. In this simple example, each host and router has a single IP address and single MAC address. As usual, IP addresses are shown in dotted-decimal notation and MAC addresses are shown in hexadecimal notation. For the purposes of this discussion, we will assume in this section that the switch broadcasts all frames; that is, whenever a switch receives a frame on one interface, it forwards the frame on all of its other interfaces. In the next section, we will provide a more accurate explanation of how switches operate.

Now suppose that the host with IP address 222.222.222.220 wants to send an IP datagram to host 222.222.222.222. In this example, both the source and destination are in the same subnet, in the addressing sense of Section 4.4.2. To send a datagram, the source must give its adapter not only the IP datagram but also the MAC address for destination 222.222.222.222. The sending adapter will then construct a link-layer frame containing the destination's MAC address and send the frame into the LAN.

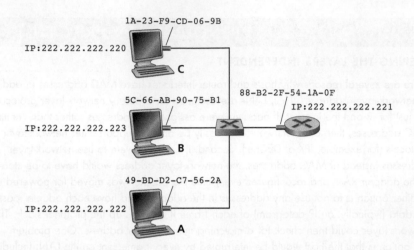

Figure 5.17 ♦ Each interface on a LAN has an IP address and a MAC address

The important question addressed in this section is, How does the sending host determine the MAC address for the destination host with IP address 222.222.222.222? As you might have guessed, it uses ARP. An ARP module in the sending host takes any IP address on the same LAN as input, and returns the corresponding MAC address. In the example at hand, sending host 222.222.222.220 provides its ARP module the IP address 222.222.222.222, and the ARP module returns the corresponding MAC address 49-BD-D2-C7-56-2A.

So we see that ARP resolves an IP address to a MAC address. In many ways it is analogous to DNS (studied in Section 2.5), which resolves host names to IP addresses. However, one important difference between the two resolvers is that DNS resolves host names for hosts anywhere in the Internet, whereas ARP resolves IP addresses only for hosts and router interfaces on the same subnet. If a node in California were to try to use ARP to resolve the IP address for a node in Mississippi, ARP would return with an error.

Now that we have explained what ARP does, let's look at how it works. Each host and router has an **ARP table** in its memory, which contains mappings of IP addresses to MAC addresses. Figure 5.18 shows what an ARP table in host 222.222.222.220 might look like. The ARP table also contains a time-to-live (TTL) value, which indicates when each mapping will be deleted from the table. Note that a table does not necessarily contain an entry for every host and router on the subnet; some may have never been entered into the table, and others may have expired. A typical expiration time for an entry is 20 minutes from when an entry is placed in an ARP table.

IP Address	MAC Address	TTL
222.222.222.221	88-B2-2F-54-1A-0F	13:45:00
222.222.222.223	5C-66-AB-90-75-B1	13:52:00

Figure 5.18 ♦ A possible ARP table in 222.222.222.220

Now suppose that host 222.222.222.220 wants to send a datagram that is IP-addressed to another host or router on that subnet. The sending host needs to obtain the MAC address of the destination given the IP address. This task is easy if the sender's ARP table has an entry for the destination node. But what if the ARP table doesn't currently have an entry for the destination? In particular, suppose 222.222.222.220 wants to send a datagram to 222.222.222.222. In this case, the sender uses the ARP protocol to resolve the address. First, the sender constructs a special packet called an **ARP packet**. An ARP packet has several fields, including the sending and receiving IP and MAC addresses. Both ARP query and response packets have the same format. The purpose of the ARP query packet is to query all the other hosts and routers on the subnet to determine the MAC address corresponding to the IP address that is being resolved.

Returning to our example, 222.222.222.220 passes an ARP query packet to the adapter along with an indication that the adapter should send the packet to the MAC broadcast address, namely, FF-FF-FF-FF-FF-FF. The adapter encapsulates the ARP packet in a link-layer frame, uses the broadcast address for the frame's destination address, and transmits the frame into the subnet. Recalling our social security number/postal address analogy, an ARP query is equivalent to a person shouting out in a crowded room of cubicles in some company (say, AnyCorp): "What is the social security number of the person whose postal address is Cubicle 13, Room 112, AnyCorp, Palo Alto, California?" The frame containing the ARP query is received by all the other adapters on the subnet, and (because of the broadcast address) each adapter passes the ARP packet within the frame up to its ARP module. Each of these ARP modules checks to see if its IP address matches the destination IP address in the ARP packet. The one with a match sends back to the querying host a response ARP packet with the desired mapping. The querying host 222.222.222.220 can then update its ARP table and send its IP datagram, encapsulated in a link-layer frame whose destination MAC is that of the host or router responding to the earlier ARP query.

There are a couple of interesting things to note about the ARP protocol. First, the query ARP message is sent within a broadcast frame, whereas the response ARP message is sent within a standard frame. Before reading on you should think about why this is so. Second, ARP is plug-and-play; that is, an ARP table gets built automatically—it doesn't have to be configured by a system administrator. And if a host becomes disconnected from the subnet, its entry is eventually deleted from the other ARP tables in the subnet.

Students often wonder if ARP is a link-layer protocol or a network-layer protocol. As we've seen, an ARP packet is encapsulated within a link-layer frame and thus lies architecturally above the link layer. However, an ARP packet has fields containing link-layer addresses and thus is arguably a link-layer protocol, but it also contains network-layer addresses and thus is also arguably a network-layer protocol. In the end, ARP is probably best considered a protocol that straddles the boundary between the link and network layers—not fitting neatly into the simple layered protocol stack we studied in Chapter 1. Such are the complexities of real-world protocols!

Sending a Datagram off the Subnet

It should now be clear how ARP operates when a host wants to send a datagram to another host *on the same subnet.* But now let's look at the more complicated situation when a host on a subnet wants to send a network-layer datagram to a host *off the subnet* (that is, across a router onto another subnet). Let's discuss this issue in the context of Figure 5.19, which shows a simple network consisting of two subnets interconnected by a router.

There are several interesting things to note about Figure 5.19. Each host has exactly one IP address and one adapter. But, as discussed in Chapter 4, a router has an IP address for *each* of its interfaces. For each router interface there is also an ARP module (in the router) and an adapter. Because the router in Figure 5.19 has two interfaces, it has two IP addresses, two ARP modules, and two adapters. Of course, each adapter in the network has its own MAC address.

Also note that Subnet 1 has the network address 111.111.111/24 and that Subnet 2 has the network address 222.222.222/24. Thus all of the interfaces connected to Subnet 1 have addresses of the form 111.111.111.xxx and all of the interfaces connected to Subnet 2 have addresses of the form 222.222.222.xxx.

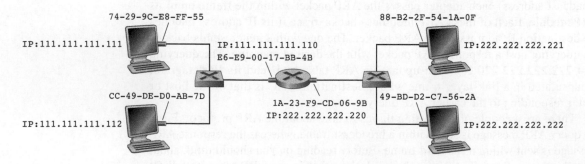

Figure 5.19 ♦ Two subnets interconnected by a router

Now let's examine how a host on Subnet 1 would send a datagram to a host on Subnet 2. Specifically, suppose that host 111.111.111.111 wants to send an IP datagram to a host 222.222.222.222. The sending host passes the datagram to its adapter, as usual. But the sending host must also indicate to its adapter an appropriate destination MAC address. What MAC address should the adapter use? One might be tempted to guess that the appropriate MAC address is that of the adapter for host 222.222.222.222, namely, 49-BD-D2-C7-56-2A. This guess, however, would be wrong! If the sending adapter were to use that MAC address, then none of the adapters on Subnet 1 would bother to pass the IP datagram up to its network layer, since the frame's destination address would not match the MAC address of any adapter on Subnet 1. The datagram would just die and go to datagram heaven.

If we look carefully at Figure 5.19, we see that in order for a datagram to go from 111.111.111.111 to a host on Subnet 2, the datagram must first be sent to the router interface 111.111.111.110, which is the IP address of the first-hop router on the path to the final destination. Thus, the appropriate MAC address for the frame is the address of the adapter for router interface 111.111.111.110, namely, E6-E9-00-17-BB-4B. How does the sending host acquire the MAC address for 111.111.111.110? By using ARP, of course! Once the sending adapter has this MAC address, it creates a frame (containing the datagram addressed to 222.222.222.222) and sends the frame into Subnet 1. The router adapter on Subnet 1 sees that the link-layer frame is addressed to it, and therefore passes the frame to the network layer of the router. Hooray—the IP datagram has successfully been moved from source host to the router! But we are not finished. We still have to move the datagram from the router to the destination. The router now has to determine the correct interface on which the datagram is to be forwarded. As discussed in Chapter 4, this is done by consulting a forwarding table in the router. The forwarding table tells the router that the datagram is to be forwarded via router interface 222.222.222.220. This interface then passes the datagram to its adapter, which encapsulates the datagram in a new frame and sends the frame into Subnet 2. This time, the destination MAC address of the frame is indeed the MAC address of the ultimate destination. And how does the router obtain this destination MAC address? From ARP, of course!

ARP for Ethernet is defined in RFC 826. A nice introduction to ARP is given in the TCP/IP tutorial, RFC 1180. We'll explore ARP in more detail in the homework problems.

VideoNote
Sending a datagram between subnets: link-layer and network-layer addressing

5.4.2 Ethernet

Ethernet has pretty much taken over the wired LAN market. In the 1980s and the early 1990s, Ethernet faced many challenges from other LAN technologies, including token ring, FDDI, and ATM. Some of these other technologies succeeded in capturing a part of the LAN market for a few years. But since its invention in the mid-1970s, Ethernet has continued to evolve and grow and has held on to its dominant position. Today, Ethernet is by far the most prevalent wired LAN technology, and it is likely to remain so for the foreseeable future. One might say that Ethernet has been to local area networking what the Internet has been to global networking.

There are many reasons for Ethernet's success. First, Ethernet was the first widely deployed high-speed LAN. Because it was deployed early, network administrators became intimately familiar with Ethernet—its wonders and its quirks—and were reluctant to switch over to other LAN technologies when they came on the scene. Second, token ring, FDDI, and ATM were more complex and expensive than Ethernet, which further discouraged network administrators from switching over. Third, the most compelling reason to switch to another LAN technology (such as FDDI or ATM) was usually the higher data rate of the new technology; however, Ethernet always fought back, producing versions that operated at equal data rates or higher. Switched Ethernet was also introduced in the early 1990s, which further increased its effective data rates. Finally, because Ethernet has been so popular, Ethernet hardware (in particular, adapters and switches) has become a commodity and is remarkably cheap.

The original Ethernet LAN was invented in the mid-1970s by Bob Metcalfe and David Boggs. The original Ethernet LAN used a coaxial bus to interconnect the nodes. Bus topologies for Ethernet actually persisted throughout the 1980s and into the mid-1990s. Ethernet with a bus topology is a broadcast LAN—all transmitted frames travel to and are processed by *all* adapters connected to the bus. Recall that we covered Ethernet's CSMA/CD multiple access protocol with binary exponential backoff in Section 5.3.2.

By the late 1990s, most companies and universities had replaced their LANs with Ethernet installations using a hub-based star topology. In such an installation the hosts (and routers) are directly connected to a hub with twisted-pair copper wire. A **hub** is a physical-layer device that acts on individual bits rather than frames. When a bit, representing a zero or a one, arrives from one interface, the hub simply re-creates the bit, boosts its energy strength, and transmits the bit onto all the other interfaces. Thus, Ethernet with a hub-based star topology is also a broadcast LAN—whenever a hub receives a bit from one of its interfaces, it sends a copy out on all of its other interfaces. In particular, if a hub receives frames from two different interfaces at the same time, a collision occurs and the nodes that created the frames must retransmit.

In the early 2000s Ethernet experienced yet another major evolutionary change. Ethernet installations continued to use a star topology, but the hub at the center was replaced with a **switch**. We'll be examining switched Ethernet in depth later in this chapter. For now, we only mention that a switch is not only "collision-less" but is also a bona-fide store-and-forward packet switch; but unlike routers, which operate up through layer 3, a switch operates only up through layer 2.

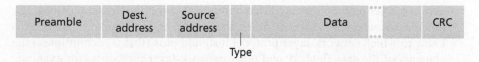

Figure 5.20 ♦ Ethernet frame structure

Ethernet Frame Structure

We can learn a lot about Ethernet by examining the Ethernet frame, which is shown in Figure 5.20. To give this discussion about Ethernet frames a tangible context, let's consider sending an IP datagram from one host to another host, with both hosts on the same Ethernet LAN (for example, the Ethernet LAN in Figure 5.17.) (Although the payload of our Ethernet frame is an IP datagram, we note that an Ethernet frame can carry other network-layer packets as well.) Let the sending adapter, adapter A, have the MAC address AA-AA-AA-AA-AA-AA and the receiving adapter, adapter B, have the MAC address BB-BB-BB-BB-BB-BB. The sending adapter encapsulates the IP datagram within an Ethernet frame and passes the frame to the physical layer. The receiving adapter receives the frame from the physical layer, extracts the IP datagram, and passes the IP datagram to the network layer. In this context, let's now examine the six fields of the Ethernet frame, as shown in Figure 5.20.

* *Data field (46 to 1,500 bytes)*. This field carries the IP datagram. The maximum transmission unit (MTU) of Ethernet is 1,500 bytes. This means that if the IP datagram exceeds 1,500 bytes, then the host has to fragment the datagram, as discussed in Section 4.4.1. The minimum size of the data field is 46 bytes. This means that if the IP datagram is less than 46 bytes, the data field has to be "stuffed" to fill it out to 46 bytes. When stuffing is used, the data passed to the network layer contains the stuffing as well as an IP datagram. The network layer uses the length field in the IP datagram header to remove the stuffing.

* *Destination address (6 bytes)*. This field contains the MAC address of the destination adapter, BB-BB-BB-BB-BB-BB. When adapter B receives an Ethernet frame whose destination address is either BB-BB-BB-BB-BB-BB or the MAC broadcast address, it passes the contents of the frame's data field to the network layer; if it receives a frame with any other MAC address, it discards the frame.

* *Source address (6 bytes)*. This field contains the MAC address of the adapter that transmits the frame onto the LAN, in this example, AA-AA-AA-AA-AA-AA.

* *Type field (2 bytes)*. The type field permits Ethernet to multiplex network-layer protocols. To understand this, we need to keep in mind that hosts can use other network-layer protocols besides IP. In fact, a given host may support multiple

network-layer protocols using different protocols for different applications. For this reason, when the Ethernet frame arrives at adapter B, adapter B needs to know to which network-layer protocol it should pass (that is, demultiplex) the contents of the data field. IP and other network-layer protocols (for example, Novell IPX or AppleTalk) each have their own, standardized type number. Furthermore, the ARP protocol (discussed in the previous section) has its own type number, and if the arriving frame contains an ARP packet (i.e., has a type field of 0806 hexadecimal), the ARP packet will be demultiplexed up to the ARP protocol. Note that the type field is analogous to the protocol field in the network-layer datagram and the port-number fields in the transport-layer segment; all of these fields serve to glue a protocol at one layer to a protocol at the layer above.

• *Cyclic redundancy check (CRC) (4 bytes).* As discussed in Section 5.2.3, the purpose of the CRC field is to allow the receiving adapter, adapter B, to detect bit errors in the frame.

• *Preamble (8 bytes).* The Ethernet frame begins with an 8-byte preamble field. Each of the first 7 bytes of the preamble has a value of 10101010; the last byte is 10101011. The first 7 bytes of the preamble serve to "wake up" the receiving adapters and to synchronize their clocks to that of the sender's clock. Why should the clocks be out of synchronization? Keep in mind that adapter A aims to transmit the frame at 10 Mbps, 100 Mbps, or 1 Gbps, depending on the type of Ethernet LAN. However, because nothing is absolutely perfect, adapter A will not transmit the frame at exactly the target rate; there will always be some *drift* from the target rate, a drift which is not known *a priori* by the other adapters on the LAN. A receiving adapter can lock onto adapter A's clock simply by locking onto the bits in the first 7 bytes of the preamble. The last 2 bits of the eighth byte of the preamble (the first two consecutive 1s) alert adapter B that the "important stuff" is about to come.

All of the Ethernet technologies provide connectionless service to the network layer. That is, when adapter A wants to send a datagram to adapter B, adapter A encapsulates the datagram in an Ethernet frame and sends the frame into the LAN, without first handshaking with adapter B. This layer-2 connectionless service is analogous to IP's layer-3 datagram service and UDP's layer-4 connectionless service.

Ethernet technologies provide an unreliable service to the network layer. Specifically, when adapter B receives a frame from adapter A, it runs the frame through a CRC check, but neither sends an acknowledgment when a frame passes the CRC check nor sends a negative acknowledgment when a frame fails the CRC check. When a frame fails the CRC check, adapter B simply discards the frame. Thus, adapter A has no idea whether its transmitted frame reached adapter B and passed the CRC check. This lack of reliable transport (at the link layer) helps to make Ethernet simple and cheap. But it also means that the stream of datagrams passed to the network layer can have gaps.

CASE HISTORY

BOB METCALFE AND ETHERNET

As a PhD student at Harvard University in the early 1970s, Bob Metcalfe worked on the ARPAnet at MIT. During his studies, he also became exposed to Abramson's work on ALOHA and random access protocols. After completing his PhD and just before beginning a job at Xerox Palo Alto Research Center (Xerox PARC), he visited Abramson and his University of Hawaii colleagues for three months, getting a first-hand look at ALOHAnet. At Xerox PARC, Metcalfe became exposed to Alto computers, which in many ways were the forerunners of the personal computers of the 1980s. Metcalfe saw the need to network these computers in an inexpensive manner. So armed with his knowledge about ARPAnet, ALOHAnet, and random access protocols, Metcalfe—along with colleague David Boggs—invented Ethernet.

Metcalfe and Boggs's original Ethernet ran at 2.94 Mbps and linked up to 256 hosts separated by up to one mile. Metcalfe and Boggs succeeded at getting most of the researchers at Xerox PARC to communicate through their Alto computers. Metcalfe then forged an alliance between Xerox, Digital, and Intel to establish Ethernet as a 10 Mbps Ethernet standard, ratified by the IEEE. Xerox did not show much interest in commercializing Ethernet. In 1979, Metcalfe formed his own company, 3Com, which developed and commercialized networking technology, including Ethernet technology. In particular, 3Com developed and marketed Ethernet cards in the early 1980s for the immensely popular IBM PCs. Metcalfe left 3Com in 1990, when it had 2,000 employees and $400 million in revenue.

If there are gaps due to discarded Ethernet frames, does the application at Host B see gaps as well? As we learned in Chapter 3, this depends on whether the application is using UDP or TCP. If the application is using UDP, then the application in Host B will indeed see gaps in the data. On the other hand, if the application is using TCP, then TCP in Host B will not acknowledge the data contained in discarded frames, causing TCP in Host A to retransmit. Note that when TCP retransmits data, the data will eventually return to the Ethernet adapter at which it was discarded. Thus, in this sense, Ethernet does retransmit data, although Ethernet is unaware of whether it is transmitting a brand-new datagram with brand-new data, or a datagram that contains data that has already been transmitted at least once.

Ethernet Technologies

In our discussion above, we've referred to Ethernet as if it were a single protocol standard. But in fact, Ethernet comes in *many* different flavors, with somewhat bewildering acronyms such as 10BASE-T, 10BASE-2, 100BASE-T, 1000BASE-LX, and

10GBASE-T. These and many other Ethernet technologies have been standardized over the years by the IEEE 802.3 CSMA/CD (Ethernet) working group [IEEE 802.3 2012]. While these acronyms may appear bewildering, there is actually considerable order here. The first part of the acronym refers to the speed of the standard: 10, 100, 1000, or 10G, for 10 Megabit (per second), 100 Megabit, Gigabit, and 10 Gigabit Ethernet, respectively. "BASE" refers to baseband Ethernet, meaning that the physical media only carries Ethernet traffic; almost all of the 802.3 standards are for baseband Ethernet. The final part of the acronym refers to the physical media itself; Ethernet is both a link-layer *and* a physical-layer specification and is carried over a variety of physical media including coaxial cable, copper wire, and fiber. Generally, a "T" refers to twisted-pair copper wires.

Historically, an Ethernet was initially conceived of as a segment of coaxial cable. The early 10BASE-2 and 10BASE-5 standards specify 10 Mbps Ethernet over two types of coaxial cable, each limited in length to 500 meters. Longer runs could be obtained by using a **repeater**—a physical-layer device that receives a signal on the input side, and regenerates the signal on the output side. A coaxial cable, as in Figure 5.20, corresponds nicely to our view of Ethernet as a broadcast medium—all frames transmitted by one interface are received at other interfaces, and Ethernet's CDMA/CD protocol nicely solves the multiple access problem. Nodes simply attach to the cable, and *voila*, we have a local area network!

Ethernet has passed through a series of evolutionary steps over the years, and today's Ethernet is very different from the original bus-topology designs using coaxial cable. In most installations today, nodes are connected to a switch via point-to-point segments made of twisted-pair copper wires or fiber-optic cables, as shown in Figures 5.15–5.17.

In the mid-1990s, Ethernet was standardized at 100 Mbps, 10 times faster than 10 Mbps Ethernet. The original Ethernet MAC protocol and frame format were preserved, but higher-speed physical layers were defined for copper wire (100BASE-T) and fiber (100BASE-FX, 100BASE-SX, 100BASE-BX). Figure 5.21 shows these different standards and the common Ethernet MAC protocol and frame format.

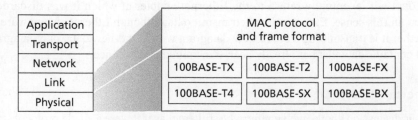

Figure 5.21 ♦ 100 Mbps Ethernet standards: a common link layer, different physical layers

100 Mbps Ethernet is limited to a 100 meter distance over twisted pair, and to several kilometers over fiber, allowing Ethernet switches in different buildings to be connected.

Gigabit Ethernet is an extension to the highly successful 10 Mbps and 100 Mbps Ethernet standards. Offering a raw data rate of 1,000 Mbps, Gigabit Ethernet maintains full compatibility with the huge installed base of Ethernet equipment. The standard for Gigabit Ethernet, referred to as IEEE 802.3z, does the following:

- Uses the standard Ethernet frame format (Figure 5.20) and is backward compatible with 10BASE-T and 100BASE-T technologies. This allows for easy integration of Gigabit Ethernet with the existing installed base of Ethernet equipment.

- Allows for point-to-point links as well as shared broadcast channels. Point-to-point links use switches while broadcast channels use hubs, as described earlier. In Gigabit Ethernet jargon, hubs are called *buffered distributors*.

- Uses CSMA/CD for shared broadcast channels. In order to have acceptable efficiency, the maximum distance between nodes must be severely restricted.

- Allows for full-duplex operation at 1,000 Mbps in both directions for point-to-point channels.

Initially operating over optical fiber, Gigabit Ethernet is now able to run over category 5 UTP cabling. 10 Gbps Ethernet (10GBASE-T) was standardized in 2007, providing yet higher Ethernet LAN capacities.

Let's conclude our discussion of Ethernet technology by posing a question that may have begun troubling you. In the days of bus topologies and hub-based star topologies, Ethernet was clearly a broadcast link (as defined in Section 5.3) in which frame collisions occurred when nodes transmitted at the same time. To deal with these collisions, the Ethernet standard included the CSMA/CD protocol, which is particularly effective for a wired broadcast LAN spanning a small geographical region. But if the prevalent use of Ethernet today is a switch-based star topology, using store-and-forward packet switching, is there really a need anymore for an Ethernet MAC protocol? As we'll see shortly, a switch coordinates its transmissions and never forwards more than one frame onto the same interface at any time. Furthermore, modern switches are full-duplex, so that a switch and a node can each send frames to each other at the same time without interference. In other words, in a switch-based Ethernet LAN there are no collisions and, therefore, there is no need for a MAC protocol!

As we've seen, today's Ethernets are *very* different from the original Ethernet conceived by Metcalfe and Boggs more than 30 years ago—speeds have increased by three orders of magnitude, Ethernet frames are carried over a variety of media, switched-Ethernets have become dominant, and now even the MAC protocol is often unnecessary! Is all of this *really* still Ethernet? The answer, of course, is "yes, by definition." It is interesting to note, however, that through all of these changes, there has indeed been one enduring constant that has remained unchanged over 30 years—Ethernet's frame format. Perhaps this then is the one true and timeless centerpiece of the Ethernet standard.

5.4.3 Link-Layer Switches

Up until this point, we have been purposefully vague about what a switch actually does and how it works. The role of the switch is to receive incoming link-layer frames and forward them onto outgoing links; we'll study this forwarding function in detail in this subsection. We'll see that the switch itself is **transparent** to the hosts and routers in the subnet; that is, a host/router addresses a frame to another host/router (rather than addressing the frame to the switch) and happily sends the frame into the LAN, unaware that a switch will be receiving the frame and forwarding it. The rate at which frames arrive to any one of the switch's output interfaces may temporarily exceed the link capacity of that interface. To accommodate this problem, switch output interfaces have buffers, in much the same way that router output interfaces have buffers for datagrams. Let's now take a closer look at how switches operate.

Forwarding and Filtering

Filtering is the switch function that determines whether a frame should be forwarded to some interface or should just be dropped. **Forwarding** is the switch function that determines the interfaces to which a frame should be directed, and then moves the frame to those interfaces. Switch filtering and forwarding are done with a **switch table**. The switch table contains entries for some, but not necessarily all, of the hosts and routers on a LAN. An entry in the switch table contains (1) a MAC address, (2) the switch interface that leads toward that MAC address, and (3) the time at which the entry was placed in the table. An example switch table for the uppermost switch in Figure 5.15 is shown in Figure 5.22.

Address	Interface	Time
62-FE-F7-11-89-A3	1	9:32
7C-BA-B2-B4-91-10	3	9:36
....	....	....

Figure 5.22 ♦ Portion of a switch table for the uppermost switch in Figure 5.15

Although this description of frame forwarding may sound similar to our discussion of datagram forwarding in Chapter 4, we'll see shortly that there are important differences. One important difference is that switches forward packets based on MAC addresses rather than on IP addresses. We will also see that a switch table is constructed in a very different manner from a router's forwarding table.

To understand how switch filtering and forwarding work, suppose a frame with destination address DD-DD-DD-DD-DD-DD arrives at the switch on interface x. The switch indexes its table with the MAC address DD-DD-DD-DD-DD-DD. There are three possible cases:

- There is no entry in the table for DD-DD-DD-DD-DD-DD. In this case, the switch forwards copies of the frame to the output buffers preceding *all* interfaces except for interface x. In other words, if there is no entry for the destination address, the switch broadcasts the frame.

- There is an entry in the table, associating DD-DD-DD-DD-DD-DD with interface x. In this case, the frame is coming from a LAN segment that contains adapter DD-DD-DD-DD-DD-DD. There being no need to forward the frame to any of the other interfaces, the switch performs the filtering function by discarding the frame.

- There is an entry in the table, associating DD-DD-DD-DD-DD-DD with interface $y \neq x$. In this case, the frame needs to be forwarded to the LAN segment attached to interface y. The switch performs its forwarding function by putting the frame in an output buffer that precedes interface y.

Let's walk through these rules for the uppermost switch in Figure 5.15 and its switch table in Figure 5.22. Suppose that a frame with destination address 62-FE-F7-11-89-A3 arrives at the switch from interface 1. The switch examines its table and sees that the destination is on the LAN segment connected to interface 1 (that is, Electrical Engineering). This means that the frame has already been broadcast on the LAN segment that contains the destination. The switch therefore filters (that is, discards) the frame. Now suppose a frame with the same destination address arrives from interface 2. The switch again examines its table and sees that the destination is in the direction of interface 1; it therefore forwards the frame to the output buffer preceding interface 1. It should be clear from this example that as long as the switch table is complete and accurate, the switch forwards frames towards destinations without any broadcasting.

In this sense, a switch is "smarter" than a hub. But how does this switch table get configured in the first place? Are there link-layer equivalents to network-layer routing protocols? Or must an overworked manager manually configure the switch table?

Self-Learning

A switch has the wonderful property (particularly for the already-overworked network administrator) that its table is built automatically, dynamically, and autonomously—without any intervention from a network administrator or from a configuration protocol. In other words, switches are **self-learning**. This capability is accomplished as follows:

1. The switch table is initially empty.
2. For each incoming frame received on an interface, the switch stores in its table (1) the MAC address in the frame's *source address field*, (2) the interface from which the frame arrived, and (3) the current time. In this manner the switch records in its table the LAN segment on which the sender resides. If every host in the LAN eventually sends a frame, then every host will eventually get recorded in the table.
3. The switch deletes an address in the table if no frames are received with that address as the source address after some period of time (the **aging time**). In this manner, if a PC is replaced by another PC (with a different adapter), the MAC address of the original PC will eventually be purged from the switch table.

Let's walk through the self-learning property for the uppermost switch in Figure 5.15 and its corresponding switch table in Figure 5.22. Suppose at time 9:39 a frame with source address 01-12-23-34-45-56 arrives from interface 2. Suppose that this address is not in the switch table. Then the switch adds a new entry to the table, as shown in Figure 5.23.

Continuing with this same example, suppose that the aging time for this switch is 60 minutes, and no frames with source address 62-FE-F7-11-89-A3 arrive to the switch between 9:32 and 10:32. Then at time 10:32, the switch removes this address from its table.

Address	Interface	Time
01-12-23-34-45-56	2	9:39
62-FE-F7-11-89-A3	1	9:32
7C-BA-B2-B4-91-10	3	9:36
....	....	....

Figure 5.23 ◆ Switch learns about the location of an adapter with address 01-12-23-34-45-56

Switches are **plug-and-play devices** because they require no intervention from a network administrator or user. A network administrator wanting to install a switch need do nothing more than connect the LAN segments to the switch interfaces. The administrator need not configure the switch tables at the time of installation or when a host is removed from one of the LAN segments. Switches are also full-duplex, meaning any switch interface can send and receive at the same time.

Properties of Link-Layer Switching

Having described the basic operation of a link-layer switch, let's now consider their features and properties. We can identify several advantages of using switches, rather than broadcast links such as buses or hub-based star topologies:

- *Elimination of collisions.* In a LAN built from switches (and without hubs), there is no wasted bandwidth due to collisions! The switches buffer frames and never transmit more than one frame on a segment at any one time. As with a router, the maximum aggregate throughput of a switch is the sum of all the switch interface rates. Thus, switches provide a significant performance improvement over LANs with broadcast links.

- *Heterogeneous links.* Because a switch isolates one link from another, the different links in the LAN can operate at different speeds and can run over different media. For example, the uppermost switch in Figure 5.22 might have three 1 Gbps 1000BASE-T copper links, two 100 Mbps 100BASE-FX fiber links, and one 100BASE-T copper link. Thus, a switch is ideal for mixing legacy equipment with new equipment.

- *Management.* In addition to providing enhanced security (see sidebar on Focus on Security), a switch also eases network management. For example, if an adapter malfunctions and continually sends Ethernet frames (called a jabbering adapter), a switch can detect the problem and internally disconnect the malfunctioning adapter. With this feature, the network administrator need not get out of bed and drive back to work in order to correct the problem. Similarly, a cable cut disconnects only that host that was using the cut cable to connect to the switch. In the days of coaxial cable, many a network manager spent hours "walking the line" (or more accurately, "crawling the floor") to find the cable break that brought down the entire network. As discussed in Chapter 9 (Network Management), switches also gather statistics on bandwidth usage, collision rates, and traffic types, and make this information available to the network manager. This information can be used to debug and correct problems, and to plan how the LAN should evolve in the future. Researchers are exploring adding yet more management functionality into Ethernet LANs in prototype deployments [Casado 2007; Koponen 2011].

FOCUS ON SECURITY

SNIFFING A SWITCHED LAN: SWITCH POISONING

When a host is connected to a switch, it typically only receives frames that are being explicity sent to it. For example, consider a switched LAN in Figure 5.17. When host A sends a frame to host B, and there is an entry for host B in the switch table, then the switch will forward the frame *only* to host B. If host C happens to be running a sniffer, host C will not be able to sniff this A-to-B frame. Thus, in a switched-LAN environment (in contrast to a broadcast link environment such as 802.11 LANs or hub–based Ethernet LANs), it is more difficult for an attacker to sniff frames. *However*, because the switch broadcasts frames that have destination addresses that are not in the switch table, the sniffer at C can still sniff some frames that are not explicitly addressed to C. Furthermore, a sniffer will be able sniff all Ethernet broadcast frames with broadcast destination address FF–FF–FF–FF–FF–FF. A well-known attack against a switch, called **switch poisoning**, is to send tons of packets to the switch with many different bogus source MAC addresses, thereby filling the switch table with bogus entries and leaving no room for the MAC addresses of the legitimate hosts. This causes the switch to broadcast most frames, which can then be picked up by the sniffer [Skoudis 2006]. As this attack is rather involved even for a sophisticated attacker, switches are significantly less vulnerable to sniffing than are hubs and wireless LANs.

Switches Versus Routers

As we learned in Chapter 4, routers are store-and-forward packet switches that forward packets using network-layer addresses. Although a switch is also a store-and-forward packet switch, it is fundamentally different from a router in that it forwards packets using MAC addresses. Whereas a router is a layer-3 packet switch, a switch is a layer-2 packet switch.

Even though switches and routers are fundamentally different, network administrators must often choose between them when installing an interconnection device. For example, for the network in Figure 5.15, the network administrator could just as easily have used a router instead of a switch to connect the department LANs, servers, and internet gateway router. Indeed, a router would permit interdepartmental communication without creating collisions. Given that both switches and routers are candidates for interconnection devices, what are the pros and cons of the two approaches?

First consider the pros and cons of switches. As mentioned above, switches are plug-and-play, a property that is cherished by all the overworked network administrators of the world. Switches can also have relatively high filtering and forwarding rates—as shown in Figure 5.24, switches have to process frames only up through layer 2, whereas routers have to process datagrams up through layer 3. On the other

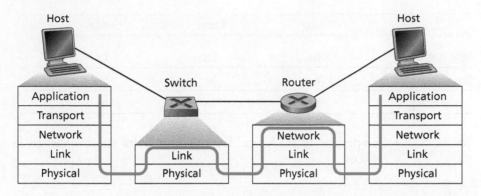

Figure 5.24 ♦ Packet processing in switches, routers, and hosts

hand, to prevent the cycling of broadcast frames, the active topology of a switched network is restricted to a spanning tree. Also, a large switched network would require large ARP tables in the hosts and routers and would generate substantial ARP traffic and processing. Furthermore, switches are susceptible to broadcast storms—if one host goes haywire and transmits an endless stream of Ethernet broadcast frames, the switches will forward all of these frames, causing the entire network to collapse.

Now consider the pros and cons of routers. Because network addressing is often hierarchical (and not flat, as is MAC addressing), packets do not normally cycle through routers even when the network has redundant paths. (However, packets can cycle when router tables are misconfigured; but as we learned in Chapter 4, IP uses a special datagram header field to limit the cycling.) Thus, packets are not restricted to a spanning tree and can use the best path between source and destination. Because routers do not have the spanning tree restriction, they have allowed the Internet to be built with a rich topology that includes, for example, multiple active links between Europe and North America. Another feature of routers is that they provide firewall protection against layer-2 broadcast storms. Perhaps the most significant drawback of routers, though, is that they are not plug-and-play—they and the hosts that connect to them need their IP addresses to be configured. Also, routers often have a larger per-packet processing time than switches, because they have to process up through the layer-3 fields. Finally, there are two different ways to pronounce the word *router*, either as "rootor" or as "rowter," and people waste a lot of time arguing over the proper pronunciation [Perlman 1999].

Given that both switches and routers have their pros and cons (as summarized in Table 5.1), when should an institutional network (for example, a university campus network or a corporate campus network) use switches, and when should it use

	Hubs	Routers	Switches
Traffic isolation	No	Yes	Yes
Plug and play	Yes	No	Yes
Optimal routing	No	Yes	No

Table 5.1 ♦ Comparison of the typical features of popular interconnection devices

routers? Typically, small networks consisting of a few hundred hosts have a few LAN segments. Switches suffice for these small networks, as they localize traffic and increase aggregate throughput without requiring any configuration of IP addresses. But larger networks consisting of thousands of hosts typically include routers within the network (in addition to switches). The routers provide a more robust isolation of traffic, control broadcast storms, and use more "intelligent" routes among the hosts in the network.

For more discussion of the pros and cons of switched versus routed networks, as well as a discussion of how switched LAN technology can be extended to accommodate two orders of magnitude more hosts than today's Ethernets, see [Meyers 2004; Kim 2008].

5.4.4 Virtual Local Area Networks (VLANs)

In our earlier discussion of Figure 5.15, we noted that modern institutional LANs are often configured hierarchically, with each workgroup (department) having its own switched LAN connected to the switched LANs of other groups via a switch hierarchy. While such a configuration works well in an ideal world, the real world is often far from ideal. Three drawbacks can be identified in the configuration in Figure 5.15:

• *Lack of traffic isolation.* Although the hierarchy localizes group traffic to within a single switch, broadcast traffic (e.g., frames carrying ARP and DHCP messages or frames whose destination has not yet been learned by a self-learning switch) must still traverse the entire institutional network. Limiting the scope of such broadcast traffic would improve LAN performance. Perhaps more importantly, it also may be desirable to limit LAN broadcast traffic for security/privacy reasons. For example, if one group contains the company's executive management team and another group contains disgruntled employees running Wireshark packet sniffers, the network manager may well prefer that the executives' traffic never even reaches employee hosts. This type of isolation could be provided by replacing the center switch in Figure 5.15 with a router. We'll see shortly that this isolation also can be achieved via a switched (layer 2) solution

- *Inefficient use of switches.* If instead of three groups, the institution had 10 groups, then 10 first-level switches would be required. If each group were small, say less than 10 people, then a single 96-port switch would likely be large enough to accommodate everyone, but this single switch would not provide traffic isolation.

- *Managing users.* If an employee moves between groups, the physical cabling must be changed to connect the employee to a different switch in Figure 5.15. Employees belonging to two groups make the problem even harder.

Fortunately, each of these difficulties can be handled by a switch that supports **virtual local area networks** (**VLANs**). As the name suggests, a switch that supports VLANs allows multiple *virtual* local area networks to be defined over a single *physical* local area network infrastructure. Hosts within a VLAN communicate with each other as if they (and no other hosts) were connected to the switch. In a port-based VLAN, the switch's ports (interfaces) are divided into groups by the network manager. Each group constitutes a VLAN, with the ports in each VLAN forming a broadcast domain (i.e., broadcast traffic from one port can only reach other ports in the group). Figure 5.25 shows a single switch with 16 ports. Ports 2 to 8 belong to the EE VLAN, while ports 9 to 15 belong to the CS VLAN (ports 1 and 16 are unassigned). This VLAN solves all of the difficulties noted above—EE and CS VLAN frames are isolated from each other, the two switches in Figure 5.15 have been replaced by a single switch, and if the user at switch port 8 joins the CS Department, the network operator simply reconfigures the VLAN software so that port 8 is now associated with the CS VLAN. One can easily

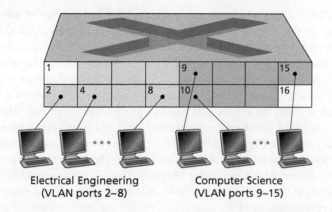

Electrical Engineering
(VLAN ports 2–8)

Computer Science
(VLAN ports 9–15)

Figure 5.25 ♦ A single switch with two configured VLANs

imagine how the VLAN switch is configured and operates—the network manager declares a port to belong to a given VLAN (with undeclared ports belonging to a default VLAN) using switch management software, a table of port-to-VLAN mappings is maintained within the switch; and switch hardware only delivers frames between ports belonging to the same VLAN.

But by completely isolating the two VLANs, we have introduced a new difficulty! How can traffic from the EE Department be sent to the CS Department? One way to handle this would be to connect a VLAN switch port (e.g., port 1 in Figure 5.25) to an external router and configure that port to belong both the EE and CS VLANs. In this case, even though the EE and CS departments share the same physical switch, the logical configuration would look as if the EE and CS departments had separate switches connected via a router. An IP datagram going from the EE to the CS department would first cross the EE VLAN to reach the router and then be forwarded by the router back over the CS VLAN to the CS host. Fortunately, switch vendors make such configurations easy for the network manager by building a single device that contains both a VLAN switch *and* a router, so a separate external router is not needed. A homework problem at the end of the chapter explores this scenario in more detail.

Returning again to Figure 5.15, let's now suppose that rather than having a separate Computer Engineering department, some EE and CS faculty are housed in a separate building, where (of course!) they need network access, and (of course!) they'd like to be part of their department's VLAN. Figure 5.26 shows a second 8-port switch, where the switch ports have been defined as belonging to the EE or the CS VLAN, as needed. But how should these two switches be interconnected? One easy solution would be to define a port belonging to the CS VLAN on each switch (similarly for the EE VLAN) and to connect these ports to each other, as shown in Figure 5.26(a). This solution doesn't scale, however, since *N* VLANS would require *N* ports on each switch simply to interconnect the two switches.

A more scalable approach to interconnecting VLAN switches is known as **VLAN trunking**. In the VLAN trunking approach shown in Figure 5.26(b), a special port on each switch (port 16 on the left switch and port 1 on the right switch) is configured as a trunk port to interconnect the two VLAN switches. The trunk port belongs to all VLANs, and frames sent to any VLAN are forwarded over the trunk link to the other switch. But this raises yet another question: How does a switch know that a frame arriving on a trunk port belongs to a particular VLAN? The IEEE has defined an extended Ethernet frame format, 802.1Q, for frames crossing a VLAN trunk. As shown in Figure 5.27, the 802.1Q frame consists of the standard Ethernet frame with a four-byte **VLAN tag** added into the header that carries the identity of the VLAN to which the frame belongs. The VLAN tag is added into a frame by the switch at the sending side of a VLAN trunk, parsed, and removed by the switch at the receiving side of the trunk. The VLAN tag itself consists of a 2-byte

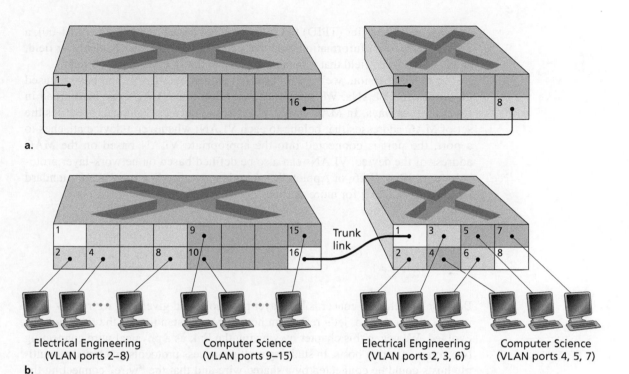

a.

b.

Electrical Engineering
(VLAN ports 2–8)

Computer Science
(VLAN ports 9–15)

Electrical Engineering
(VLAN ports 2, 3, 6)

Computer Science
(VLAN ports 4, 5, 7)

Trunk link

Figure 5.26 ♦ Connecting two VLAN switches with two VLANs: (a) two cables (b) trunked

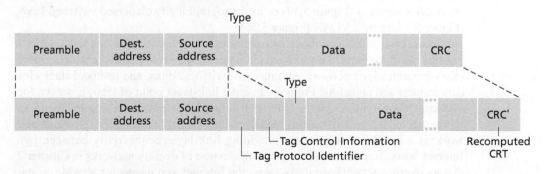

Figure 5.27 ♦ Original Ethernet frame (top), 802.1Q-tagged Ethernet VLAN frame (below)

Tag Protocol Identifier (TPID) field (with a fixed hexadecimal value of 81-00), a 2-byte Tag Control Information field that contains a 12-bit VLAN identifier field, and a 3-bit priority field that is similar in intent to the IP datagram TOS field.

In this discussion, we've only briefly touched on VLANs and have focused on port-based VLANs. We should also mention that VLANs can be defined in several other ways. In MAC-based VLANs, the network manager specifies the set of MAC addresses that belong to each VLAN; whenever a device attaches to a port, the port is connected into the appropriate VLAN based on the MAC address of the device. VLANs can also be defined based on network-layer protocols (e.g., IPv4, IPv6, or Appletalk) and other criteria. See the 802.1Q standard [IEEE 802.1q 2005] for more details.

5.5 Link Virtualization: A Network as a Link Layer

Because this chapter concerns link-layer protocols, and given that we're now nearing the chapter's end, let's reflect on how our understanding of the term *link* has evolved. We began this chapter by viewing the link as a physical wire connecting two communicating hosts. In studying multiple access protocols, we saw that multiple hosts could be connected by a shared wire and that the "wire" connecting the hosts could be radio spectra or other media. This led us to consider the link a bit more abstractly as a channel, rather than as a wire. In our study of Ethernet LANs (Figure 5.15) we saw that the interconnecting media could actually be a rather complex switched infrastructure. Throughout this evolution, however, the hosts themselves maintained the view that the interconnecting medium was simply a link-layer channel connecting two or more hosts. We saw, for example, that an Ethernet host can be blissfully unaware of whether it is connected to other LAN hosts by a single short LAN segment (Figure 5.17) or by a geographically dispersed switched LAN (Figure 5.15) or by a VLAN (Figure 5.26).

In the case of a dialup modem connection between two hosts, the link connecting the two hosts is actually the telephone network—a logically separate, global telecommunications network with its own switches, links, and protocol stacks for data transfer and signaling. From the Internet link-layer point of view, however, the dial-up connection through the telephone network is viewed as a simple "wire." In this sense, the Internet virtualizes the telephone network, viewing the telephone network as a link-layer technology providing link-layer connectivity between two Internet hosts. You may recall from our discussion of overlay networks in Chapter 2 that an overlay network similarly views the Internet as a means for providing connectivity between overlay nodes, seeking to overlay the Internet in the same way that the Internet overlays the telephone network.

In this section, we'll consider Multiprotocol Label Switching (MPLS) networks. Unlike the circuit-switched telephone network, MPLS is a packet-switched, virtual-circuit network in its own right. It has its own packet formats and forwarding behaviors. Thus, from a pedagogical viewpoint, a discussion of MPLS fits well into a study of either the network layer or the link layer. From an Internet viewpoint, however, we can consider MPLS, like the telephone network and switched-Ethernets, as a link-layer technology that serves to interconnect IP devices. Thus, we'll consider MPLS in our discussion of the link layer. Frame-relay and ATM networks can also be used to interconnect IP devices, though they represent a slightly older (but still deployed) technology and will not be covered here; see the very readable book [Goralski 1999] for details. Our treatment of MPLS will be necessarily brief, as entire books could be (and have been) written on these networks. We recommend [Davie 2000] for details on MPLS. We'll focus here primarily on how MPLS servers interconnect to IP devices, although we'll dive a bit deeper into the underlying technologies as well.

5.5.1 Multiprotocol Label Switching (MPLS)

Multiprotocol Label Switching (MPLS) evolved from a number of industry efforts in the mid-to-late 1990s to improve the forwarding speed of IP routers by adopting a key concept from the world of virtual-circuit networks: a fixed-length label. The goal was not to abandon the destination-based IP datagram-forwarding infrastructure for one based on fixed-length labels and virtual circuits, but to augment it by selectively labeling datagrams and allowing routers to forward datagrams based on fixed-length labels (rather than destination IP addresses) when possible. Importantly, these techniques work hand-in-hand with IP, using IP addressing and routing. The IETF unified these efforts in the MPLS protocol [RFC 3031, RFC 3032], effectively blending VC techniques into a routed datagram network.

Let's begin our study of MPLS by considering the format of a link-layer frame that is handled by an MPLS-capable router. Figure 5.28 shows that a link-layer frame transmitted between MPLS-capable devices has a small MPLS header added between the layer-2 (e.g., Ethernet) header and layer-3 (i.e., IP) header. RFC 3032

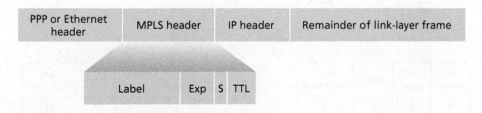

Figure 5.28 ♦ MPLS header: Located between link- and network-layer headers

defines the format of the MPLS header for such links; headers are defined for ATM and frame-relayed networks as well in other RFCs. Among the fields in the MPLS header are the label (which serves the role of the virtual-circuit identifier that we encountered back in Section 4.2.1), 3 bits reserved for experimental use, a single S bit, which is used to indicate the end of a series of "stacked" MPLS headers (an advanced topic that we'll not cover here), and a time-to-live field.

It's immediately evident from Figure 5.28 that an MPLS-enhanced frame can only be sent between routers that are both MPLS capable (since a non-MPLS-capable router would be quite confused when it found an MPLS header where it had expected to find the IP header!). An MPLS-capable router is often referred to as a **label-switched router**, since it forwards an MPLS frame by looking up the MPLS label in its forwarding table and then immediately passing the datagram to the appropriate output interface. Thus, the MPLS-capable router need *not* extract the destination IP address and perform a lookup of the longest prefix match in the forwarding table. But how does a router know if its neighbor is indeed MPLS capable, and how does a router know what label to associate with the given IP destination? To answer these questions, we'll need to take a look at the interaction among a group of MPLS-capable routers.

In the example in Figure 5.29, routers R1 through R4 are MPLS capable. R5 and R6 are standard IP routers. R1 has advertised to R2 and R3 that it (R1) can route to destination A, and that a received frame with MPLS label 6 will be forwarded to destination A. Router R3 has advertised to router R4 that it can route to destinations

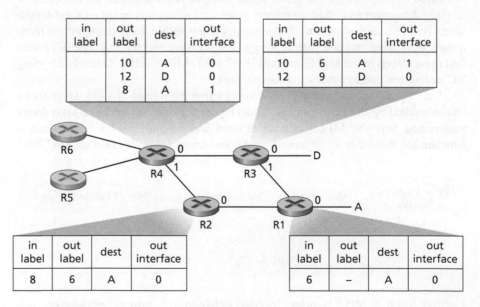

Figure 5.29 ♦ MPLS-enhanced forwarding

in label	out label	dest	out interface
10		A	0
12		D	0
8		A	1

in label	out label	dest	out interface
10	6	A	1
12	9	D	0

in label	out label	dest	out interface
8	6	A	0

in label	out label	dest	out interface
6	–	A	0

A and D, and that incoming frames with MPLS labels 10 and 12, respectively, will be switched toward those destinations. Router R2 has also advertised to router R4 that it (R2) can reach destination A, and that a received frame with MPLS label 8 will be switched toward A. Note that router R4 is now in the interesting position of having two MPLS paths to reach A: via interface 0 with outbound MPLS label 10, and via interface 1 with an MPLS label of 8. The broad picture painted in Figure 5.29 is that IP devices R5, R6, A, and D are connected together via an MPLS infrastructure (MPLS-capable routers R1, R2, R3, and R4) in much the same way that a switched LAN or an ATM network can connect together IP devices. And like a switched LAN or ATM network, the MPLS-capable routers R1 through R4 do so *without ever touching the IP header of a packet*.

In our discussion above, we've not specified the specific protocol used to distribute labels among the MPLS-capable routers, as the details of this signaling are well beyond the scope of this book. We note, however, that the IETF working group on MPLS has specified in [RFC 3468] that an extension of the RSVP protocol, known as RSVP-TE [RFC 3209], will be the focus of its efforts for MPLS signaling. We've also not discussed how MPLS actually computes the paths for packets among MPLS capable routers, nor how it gathers link-state information (e.g., amount of link bandwidth unreserved by MPLS) to use in these path computations. Existing link-state routing algorithms (e.g., OSPF) have been extended to flood this information to MPLS-capable routers. Interestingly, the actual path computation algorithms are not standardized, and are currently vendor-specific.

Thus far, the emphasis of our discussion of MPLS has been on the fact that MPLS performs switching based on labels, without needing to consider the IP address of a packet. The true advantages of MPLS and the reason for current interest in MPLS, however, lie not in the potential increases in switching speeds, but rather in the new traffic management capabilities that MPLS enables. As noted above, R4 has *two* MPLS paths to A. If forwarding were performed up at the IP layer on the basis of IP address, the IP routing protocols we studied in Chapter 4 would specify only a single, least-cost path to A. Thus, MPLS provides the ability to forward packets along routes that would not be possible using standard IP routing protocols. This is one simple form of **traffic engineering** using MPLS [RFC 3346; RFC 3272; RFC 2702; Xiao 2000], in which a network operator can override normal IP routing and force some of the traffic headed toward a given destination along one path, and other traffic destined toward the same destination along another path (whether for policy, performance, or some other reason).

It is also possible to use MPLS for many other purposes as well. It can be used to perform fast restoration of MPLS forwarding paths, e.g., to reroute traffic over a precomputed failover path in response to link failure [Kar 2000; Huang 2002; RFC 3469]. Finally, we note that MPLS can, and has, been used to implement so-called **virtual private networks** (VPNs). In implementing a VPN for a customer, an ISP uses its MPLS-enabled network to connect together the customer's various networks. MPLS can be used to isolate both the resources and addressing used by the customer's VPN from that of other users crossing the ISP's network; see [DeClercq 2002] for details.

Our discussion of MPLS has been brief, and we encourage you to consult the references we've mentioned. We note that with so many possible uses for MPLS, it appears that it is rapidly becoming the Swiss Army knife of Internet traffic engineering!

5.6 Data Center Networking

In recent years, Internet companies such as Google, Microsoft, Facebook, and Amazon (as well as their counterparts in Asia and Europe) have built massive data centers, each housing tens to hundreds of thousands of hosts, and concurrently supporting many distinct cloud applications (e.g., search, email, social networking, and e-commerce). Each data center has its own **data center network** that interconnects its hosts with each other and interconnects the data center with the Internet. In this section, we provide a brief introduction to data center networking for cloud applications.

The cost of a large data center is huge, exceeding $12 million per month for a 100,000 host data center [Greenberg 2009a]. Of these costs, about 45 percent can be attributed to the hosts themselves (which need to be replaced every 3–4 years); 25 percent to infrastructure, including transformers, uninterruptable power supplies (UPS) systems, generators for long-term outages, and cooling systems; 15 percent for electric utility costs for the power draw; and 15 percent for networking, including network gear (switches, routers and load balancers), external links, and transit traffic costs. (In these percentages, costs for equipment are amortized so that a common cost metric is applied for one-time purchases and ongoing expenses such as power.) While networking is not the largest cost, networking innovation is the key to reducing overall cost and maximizing performance [Greenberg 2009a].

The worker bees in a data center are the hosts: They serve content (e.g., Web pages and videos), store emails and documents, and collectively perform massively distributed computations (e.g., distributed index computations for search engines). The hosts in data centers, called **blades** and resembling pizza boxes, are generally commodity hosts that include CPU, memory, and disk storage. The hosts are stacked in racks, with each rack typically having 20 to 40 blades. At the top of each rack there is a switch, aptly named the **Top of Rack (TOR) switch**, that interconnects the hosts in the rack with each other and with other switches in the data center. Specifically, each host in the rack has a network interface card that connects to its TOR switch, and each TOR switch has additional ports that can be connected to other switches. Although today hosts typically have 1 Gbps Ethernet connections to their TOR switches, 10 Gbps connections may become the norm. Each host is also assigned its own data-center-internal IP address.

The data center network supports two types of traffic: traffic flowing between external clients and internal hosts and traffic flowing between internal hosts. To handle flows between external clients and internal hosts, the data center network includes one or more **border routers**, connecting the data center network to the public Internet. The data center network therefore interconnects the racks with each other and connects the racks to the border routers. Figure 5.30 shows an example of a data center network. **Data center network design**, the art of designing the interconnection network and protocols that connect the racks with each other and with the border routers, has become an important branch of computer networking research in recent years [Al-Fares 2008; Greenberg 2009a; Greenberg 2009b; Mydotr 2009; Guo 2009; Chen 2010; Abu-Libdeh 2010; Alizadeh 2010; Wang 2010; Farrington 2010; Halperin 2011; Wilson 2011; Mudigonda 2011; Ballani 2011; Curtis 2011; Raiciu 2011].

Load Balancing

A cloud data center, such as a Google or Microsoft data center, provides many applications concurrently, such as search, email, and video applications. To support requests from external clients, each application is associated with a publicly visible IP address to which clients send their requests and from which they receive responses. Inside the data center, the external requests are first directed to a **load balancer** whose job it is to distribute requests to the hosts, balancing the load across the hosts as a function of their current load. A large data center will often have several

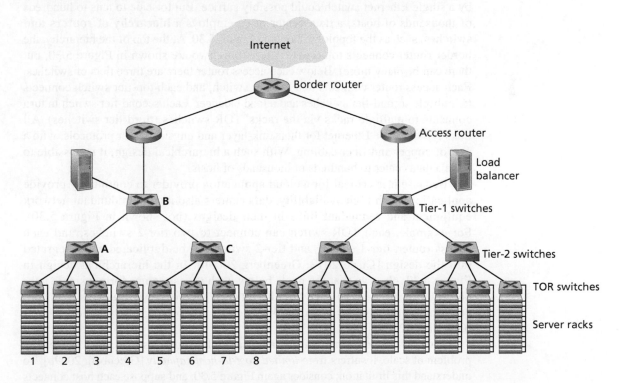

Figure 5.30 ♦ A data center network with a hierarchical topology

load balancers, each one devoted to a set of specific cloud applications. Such a load balancer is sometimes referred to as a "layer-4 switch" since it makes decisions based on the destination port number (layer 4) as well as destination IP address in the packet. Upon receiving a request for a particular application, the load balancer forwards it to one of the hosts that handles the application. (A host may then invoke the services of other hosts to help process the request.) When the host finishes processing the request, it sends its response back to the load balancer, which in turn relays the response back to the external client. The load balancer not only balances the work load across hosts, but also provides a NAT-like function, translating the public external IP address to the internal IP address of the appropriate host, and then translating back for packets traveling in the reverse direction back to the clients. This prevents clients from contacting hosts directly, which has the security benefit of hiding the internal network structure and preventing clients from directly interacting with the hosts.

Hierarchical Architecture

For a small data center housing only a few thousand hosts, a simple network consisting of a border router, a load balancer, and a few tens of racks all interconnected by a single Ethernet switch could possibly suffice. But to scale to tens to hundreds of thousands of hosts, a data center often employs a **hierarchy of routers and switches**, such as the topology shown in Figure 5.30. At the top of the hierarchy, the border router connects to access routers (only two are shown in Figure 5.30, but there can be many more). Below each access router there are three tiers of switches. Each access router connects to a top-tier switch, and each top-tier switch connects to multiple second-tier switches and a load balancer. Each second-tier switch in turn connects to multiple racks via the racks' TOR switches (third-tier switches). All links typically use Ethernet for their link-layer and physical-layer protocols, with a mix of copper and fiber cabling. With such a hierarchical design, it is possible to scale a data center to hundreds of thousands of hosts.

Because it is critical for a cloud application provider to continually provide applications with high availability, data centers also include redundant network equipment and redundant links in their designs (not shown in Figure 5.30). For example, each TOR switch can connect to two tier-2 switches, and each access router, tier-1 switch, and tier-2 switch can be duplicated and integrated into the design [Cisco 2012; Greenberg 2009b]. In the hierarchical design in Figure 5.30, observe that the hosts below each access router form a single subnet. In order to localize ARP broadcast traffic, each of these subnets is further partitioned into smaller VLAN subnets, each comprising a few hundred hosts [Greenberg 2009a].

Although the conventional hierarchical architecture just described solves the problem of scale, it suffers from *limited host-to-host capacity* [Greenberg 2009b]. To understand this limitation, consider again Figure 5.30, and suppose each host connects to its TOR switch with a 1 Gbps link, whereas the links between switches are 10 Gbps Ethernet links. Two hosts in the same rack can always communicate at a full 1 Gbps, limited only by the rate of the hosts' network interface cards. However, if there are many simultaneous flows in the data center network, the maximum rate between two hosts in *different* racks can be much less. To gain insight into this issue, consider a traffic pattern consisting of 40 simultaneous flows between 40 pairs of hosts in different racks. Specifically, suppose each of 10 hosts in rack 1 in Figure 5.30 sends a flow to a corresponding host in rack 5. Similarly, there are ten simultaneous flows between pairs of hosts in racks 2 and 6, ten simultaneous flows between racks 3 and 7, and ten simultaneous flows between racks 4 and 8. If each flow evenly shares a link's capacity with other flows traversing that link, then the 40 flows crossing the 10 Gbps A-to-B link (as well as the 10 Gbps B-to-C link) will each only receive 10 Gbps / 40 = 250 Mbps, which is significantly less than the 1 Gbps network interface card rate. The problem becomes even more acute for flows between hosts that need to travel higher up the hierarchy. One possible solution to this limitation is to deploy higher-rate switches and routers. But this would significantly increase the cost of the data center, because switches and routers with high port speeds are very expensive.

Supporting high-bandwidth host-to-host communication is important because a key requirement in data centers is flexibility in placement of computation and services [Greenberg 2009b; Farrington 2010]. For example, a large-scale Internet search engine may run on thousands of hosts spread across multiple racks with significant bandwidth requirements between all pairs of hosts. Similarly, a cloud computing service such as EC2 may wish to place the multiple virtual machines comprising a customer's service on the physical hosts with the most capacity irrespective of their location in the data center. If these physical hosts are spread across multiple racks, network bottlenecks as described above may result in poor performance.

Trends in Data Center Networking

In order to reduce the cost of data centers, and at the same time improve their delay and throughput performance, Internet cloud giants such as Google, Facebook, Amazon, and Microsoft are continually deploying new data center network designs. Although these designs are proprietary, many important trends can nevertheless be identified.

One such trend is to deploy new interconnection architectures and network protocols that overcome the drawbacks of the traditional hierarchical designs. One such approach is to replace the hierarchy of switches and routers with a **fully connected topology** [Al-Fares 2008; Greenberg 2009b; Guo 2009], such as the topology shown in Figure 5.31. In this design, each tier-1 switch connects to all of the tier-2 switches so that (1) host-to-host traffic never has to rise above the switch tiers, and (2) with n tier-1 switches, between any two tier-2 switches there are n disjoint paths. Such a design can significantly improve the host-to-host capacity. To see this, consider again our example of 40 flows. The topology in Figure 5.31 can handle such a flow pattern since there are four distinct paths between the first tier-2 switch and the second tier-2 switch, together

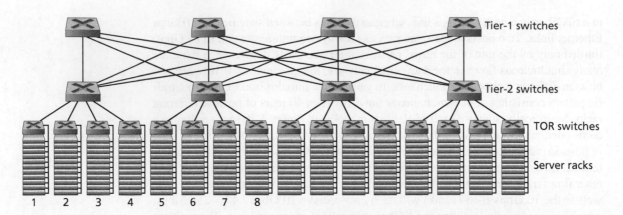

Figure 5.31 ◆ Highly-interconnected data network topology

providing an aggregate capacity of 40 Gbps between the first two tier-2 switches. Such a design not only alleviates the host-to-host capacity limitation, but also creates a more flexible computation and service environment in which communication between any two racks not connected to the same switch is logically equivalent, irrespective of their locations in the data center.

Another major trend is to employ shipping container–based modular data centers (MDCs) [YouTube 2009; Waldrop 2007]. In an MDC, a factory builds, within a standard 12-meter shipping container, a "mini data center" and ships the container to the data center location. Each container has up to a few thousand hosts, stacked in tens of racks, which are packed closely together. At the data center location, multiple containers are interconnected with each other and also with the Internet. Once a prefabricated container is deployed at a data center, it is often difficult to service. Thus, each container is designed for graceful performance degradation: as components (servers and switches) fail over time, the container continues to operate but with degraded performance. When many components have failed and performance has dropped below a threshold, the entire container is removed and replaced with a fresh one.

Building a data center out of containers creates new networking challenges. With an MDC, there are two types of networks: the container-internal networks within each of the containers and the core network connecting each container [Guo 2009; Farrington 2010]. Within each container, at the scale of up to a few thousand hosts, it is possible to build a fully connected network (as described above) using inexpensive commodity Gigabit Ethernet switches. However, the design of the core network, interconnecting hundreds to thousands of containers while providing high host-to-host bandwidth across containers for typical workloads, remains a challenging problem. A hybrid electrical/optical switch architecture for interconnecting the containers is proposed in [Farrington 2010].

When using highly interconnected topologies, one of the major issues is designing routing algorithms among the switches. One possibility [Greenberg 2009b] is to use a form of random routing. Another possibility [Guo 2009] is to deploy multiple network interface cards in each host, connect each host to multiple low-cost commodity switches, and allow the hosts themselves to intelligently route traffic among the switches. Variations and extensions of these approaches are currently being deployed in contemporary data centers. Many more innovations in data center design are likely to come; interested readers are encouraged to read the many recent papers on data center network design.

5.7 Retrospective: A Day in the Life of a Web Page Request

Now that we've covered the link layer in this chapter, and the network, transport and application layers in earlier chapters, our journey down the protocol stack is complete! In the very beginning of this book (Section 1.1), we wrote "much of this book is concerned with computer network protocols," and in the first five chapters, we've certainly seen that this is indeed the case! Before heading into the topical chapters in second part of this book, we'd like to wrap up our journey down the protocol stack by taking an integrated, holistic view of the protocols we've learned about so far. One way then to take this "big picture" view is to identify the many (many!) protocols that are involved in satisfying even the simplest request: downloading a web page. Figure 5.32 illustrates our setting: a student, Bob, connects a laptop to his school's Ethernet switch and downloads a web page (say the home page of www.google.com). As we now know, there's a *lot* going on "under the hood" to satisfy this seemingly simple request. A Wireshark lab at the end of this chapter examines trace files containing a number of the packets involved in similar scenarios in more detail.

5.7.1 Getting Started: DHCP, UDP, IP, and Ethernet

Let's suppose that Bob boots up his laptop and then connects it to an Ethernet cable connected to the school's Ethernet switch, which in turn is connected to the school's router, as shown in Figure 5.32. The school's router is connected to an ISP, in this example, comcast.net. In this example, comcast.net is providing the DNS service for the school; thus, the DNS server resides in the Comcast network rather than the school network. We'll assume that the DHCP server is running within the router, as is often the case.

When Bob first connects his laptop to the network, he can't do anything (e.g., download a Web page) without an IP address. Thus, the first network-related action taken by Bob's laptop is to run the DHCP protocol to obtain an IP address, as well as other information, from the local DHCP server:

1. The operating system on Bob's laptop creates a **DHCP request message** (Section 4.4.2) and puts this message within a **UDP segment** (Section 3.3) with destination port 67 (DHCP server) and source port 68 (DHCP client). The UDP segment is then placed within an **IP datagram** (Section 4.4.1) with a broadcast

VideoNote
A day in the life of a Web page request

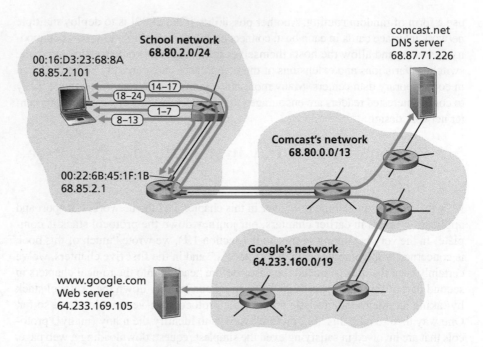

Figure 5.32 ♦ A day in the life of a Web page request: network setting and actions

IP destination address (255.255.255.255) and a source IP address of 0.0.0.0, since Bob's laptop doesn't yet have an IP address.

2. The IP datagram containing the DHCP request message is then placed within an **Ethernet frame** (Section 5.4.2). The Ethernet frame has a destination MAC addresses of FF:FF:FF:FF:FF:FF so that the frame will be broadcast to all devices connected to the switch (hopefully including a DHCP server); the frame's source MAC address is that of Bob's laptop, 00:16:D3:23:68:8A.

3. The broadcast Ethernet frame containing the DHCP request is the first frame sent by Bob's laptop to the Ethernet switch. The switch broadcasts the incoming frame on all outgoing ports, including the port connected to the router.

4. The router receives the broadcast Ethernet frame containing the DHCP request on its interface with MAC address 00:22:6B:45:1F:1B and the IP datagram is extracted from the Ethernet frame. The datagram's broadcast IP destination address indicates that this IP datagram should be processed by upper layer protocols at this node, so the datagram's payload (a UDP segment) is thus **demultiplexed** (Section 3.2) up to UDP, and the DHCP request message is extracted from the UDP segment. The DHCP server now has the DHCP request message.

5. Let's suppose that the DHCP server running within the router can allocate IP addresses in the **CIDR** (Section 4.4.2) block 68.85.2.0/24. In this example, all IP addresses used within the school are thus within Comcast's address block.

Let's suppose the DHCP server allocates address 68.85.2.101 to Bob's laptop. The DHCP server creates a **DHCP ACK message** (Section 4.4.2) containing this IP address, as well as the IP address of the DNS server (68.87.71.226), the IP address for the default gateway router (68.85.2.1), and the subnet block (68.85.2.0/24) (equivalently, the "network mask"). The DHCP message is put inside a UDP segment, which is put inside an IP datagram, which is put inside an Ethernet frame. The Ethernet frame has a source MAC address of the router's interface to the home network (00:22:6B:45:1F:1B) and a destination MAC address of Bob's laptop (00:16:D3:23:68:8A).

6. The Ethernet frame containing the DHCP ACK is sent (unicast) by the router to the switch. Because the switch is **self-learning** (Section 5.4.3) and previously received an Ethernet frame (containing the DHCP request) from Bob's laptop, the switch knows to forward a frame addressed to 00:16:D3:23:68:8A only to the output port leading to Bob's laptop.

7. Bob's laptop receives the Ethernet frame containing the DHCP ACK, extracts the IP datagram from the Ethernet frame, extracts the UDP segment from the IP datagram, and extracts the DHCP ACK message from the UDP segment. Bob's DHCP client then records its IP address and the IP address of its DNS server. It also installs the address of the default gateway into its **IP forwarding table** (Section 4.1). Bob's laptop will send all datagrams with destination address outside of its subnet 68.85.2.0/24 to the default gateway. At this point, Bob's laptop has initialized its networking components and is ready to begin processing the Web page fetch. (Note that only the last two DHCP steps of the four presented in Chapter 4 are actually necessary.)

5.7.2 Still Getting Started: DNS and ARP

When Bob types the URL for www.google.com into his Web browser, he begins the long chain of events that will eventually result in Google's home page being displayed by his Web browser. Bob's Web browser begins the process by creating a **TCP socket** (Section 2.7) that will be used to send the **HTTP request** (Section 2.2) to www.google.com. In order to create the socket, Bob's laptop will need to know the IP address of www.google.com. We learned in Section 2.5, that the **DNS protocol** is used to provide this name-to-IP-address translation service.

8. The operating system on Bob's laptop thus creates a **DNS query message** (Section 2.5.3), putting the string "www.google.com" in the question section of the DNS message. This DNS message is then placed within a UDP segment with a destination port of 53 (DNS server). The UDP segment is then placed within an IP datagram with an IP destination address of 68.87.71.226 (the address of the DNS server returned in the DHCP ACK in step 5) and a source IP address of 68.85.2.101.

9. Bob's laptop then places the datagram containing the DNS query message in an Ethernet frame. This frame will be sent (addressed, at the link layer) to the gateway router in Bob's school's network. However, even though Bob's laptop

knows the IP address of the school's gateway router (68.85.2.1) via the DHCP ACK message in step 5 above, it doesn't know the gateway router's MAC address. In order to obtain the MAC address of the gateway router, Bob's laptop will need to use the **ARP protocol** (Section 5.4.1).

10. Bob's laptop creates an **ARP query** message with a target IP address of 68.85.2.1 (the default gateway), places the ARP message within an Ethernet frame with a broadcast destination address (FF:FF:FF:FF:FF:FF) and sends the Ethernet frame to the switch, which delivers the frame to all connected devices, including the gateway router.

11. The gateway router receives the frame containing the ARP query message on the interface to the school network, and finds that the target IP address of 68.85.2.1 in the ARP message matches the IP address of its interface. The gateway router thus prepares an **ARP reply**, indicating that its MAC address of 00:22:6B:45:1F:1B corresponds to IP address 68.85.2.1. It places the ARP reply message in an Ethernet frame, with a destination address of 00:16:D3:23:68:8A (Bob's laptop) and sends the frame to the switch, which delivers the frame to Bob's laptop.

12. Bob's laptop receives the frame containing the ARP reply message and extracts the MAC address of the gateway router (00:22:6B:45:1F:1B) from the ARP reply message.

13. Bob's laptop can now (*finally!*) address the Ethernet frame containing the DNS query to the gateway router's MAC address. Note that the IP datagram in this frame has an IP destination address of 68.87.71.226 (the DNS server), while the frame has a destination address of 00:22:6B:45:1F:1B (the gateway router). Bob's laptop sends this frame to the switch, which delivers the frame to the gateway router.

5.7.3 Still Getting Started: Intra-Domain Routing to the DNS Server

14. The gateway router receives the frame and extracts the IP datagram containing the DNS query. The router looks up the destination address of this datagram (68.87.71.226) and determines from its forwarding table that the datagram should be sent to the leftmost router in the Comcast network in Figure 5.32. The IP datagram is placed inside a link-layer frame appropriate for the link connecting the school's router to the leftmost Comcast router and the frame is sent over this link.

15. The leftmost router in the Comcast network receives the frame, extracts the IP datagram, examines the datagram's destination address (68.87.71.226) and determines the outgoing interface on which to forward the datagram towards the DNS server from its forwarding table, which has been filled in by Comcast's intra-domain protocol (such as **RIP**, **OSPF** or **IS-IS**, Section 4.6) as well as the **Internet's inter-domain protocol**, **BGP**.

16. Eventually the IP datagram containing the DNS query arrives at the DNS server. The DNS server extracts the DNS query message, looks up the name www.google.com in its DNS database (Section 2.5), and finds the **DNS resource**

record that contains the IP address (64.233.169.105) for www.google.com. (assuming that it is currently cached in the DNS server). Recall that this cached data originated in the **authoritative DNS server** (Section 2.5.2) for googlecom. The DNS server forms a **DNS reply message** containing this hostname-to-IP-address mapping, and places the DNS reply message in a UDP segment, and the segment within an IP datagram addressed to Bob's laptop (68.85.2.101). This datagram will be forwarded back through the Comcast network to the school's router and from there, via the Ethernet switch to Bob's laptop.

17. Bob's laptop extracts the IP address of the server www.google.com from the DNS message. *Finally,* after a *lot* of work, Bob's laptop is now ready to contact the www.google.com server!

5.7.4 Web Client-Server Interaction: TCP and HTTP

18. Now that Bob's laptop has the IP address of www.google.com, it can create the **TCP socket** (Section 2.7) that will be used to send the **HTTP GET** message (Section 2.2.3) to www.google.com. When Bob creates the TCP socket, the TCP in Bob's laptop must first perform a **three-way handshake** (Section 3.5.6) with the TCP in www.google.com. Bob's laptop thus first creates a **TCP SYN** segment with destination port 80 (for HTTP), places the TCP segment inside an IP datagram with a destination IP address of 64.233.169.105 (www.google.com), places the datagram inside a frame with a destination MAC address of 00:22:6B:45:1F:1B (the gateway router) and sends the frame to the switch.

19. The routers in the school network, Comcast's network, and Google's network forward the datagram containing the TCP SYN towards www.google.com, using the forwarding table in each router, as in steps 14–16 above. Recall that the router forwarding table entries governing forwarding of packets over the intcr-domain link between the Comcast and Google networks are determined by the **BGP** protocol (Section 4.6.3).

20. Eventually, the datagram containing the TCP SYN arrives at www.google.com. The TCP SYN message is extracted from the datagram and demultiplexed to the welcome socket associated with port 80. A connection socket (Section 2.7) is created for the TCP connection between the Google HTTP server and Bob's laptop. A TCP SYNACK (Section 3.5.6) segment is generated, placed inside a datagram addressed to Bob's laptop, and finally placed inside a link-layer frame appropriate for the link connecting www.google.com to its first-hop router.

21. The datagram containing the TCP SYNACK segment is forwarded through the Google, Comcast, and school networks, eventually arriving at the Ethernet card in Bob's laptop. The datagram is demultiplexed within the operating system to the TCP socket created in step 18, which enters the connected state.

22. With the socket on Bob's laptop now (*finally!*) ready to send bytes to www.google .com, Bob's browser creates the HTTP GET message (Section 2.2.3) containing the URL to be fetched. The HTTP GET message is then written into the socket, with the

GET message becoming the payload of a TCP segment. The TCP segment is placed in a datagram and sent and delivered to www.google.com as in steps 18–20 above.

23. The HTTP server at www.google.com reads the HTTP GET message from the TCP socket, creates an **HTTP response** message (Section 2.2), places the requested Web page content in the body of the HTTP response message, and sends the message into the TCP socket.

24. The datagram containing the HTTP reply message is forwarded through the Google, Comcast, and school networks, and arrives at Bob's laptop. Bob's Web browser program reads the HTTP response from the socket, extracts the html for the Web page from the body of the HTTP response, and finally (*finally!*) displays the Web page!

Our scenario above has covered a lot of networking ground! If you've understood most or all of the above example, then you've also covered a lot of ground since you first read Section 1.1, where we wrote "much of this book is concerned with computer network protocols" and you may have wondered what a protocol actually was! As detailed as the above example might seem, we've omitted a number of possible additional protocols (e.g., NAT running in the school's gateway router, wireless access to the school's network, security protocols for accessing the school network or encrypting segments or datagrams, network management protocols), and considerations (Web caching, the DNS hierarchy) that one would encounter in the public Internet. We'll cover a number of these topics and more in the second part of this book.

Lastly, we note that our example above was an integrated and holistic, but also very "nuts and bolts," view of many of the protocols that we've studied in the first part of this book. The example focused more on the "how" than the "why." For a broader, more reflective view on the design of network protocols in general, see [Clark 1988, RFC 5218].

5.8 Summary

In this chapter, we've examined the link layer—its services, the principles underlying its operation, and a number of important specific protocols that use these principles in implementing link-layer services.

We saw that the basic service of the link layer is to move a network-layer datagram from one node (host, switch, router, WiFi access point) to an adjacent node. We saw that all link-layer protocols operate by encapsulating a network-layer datagram within a link-layer frame before transmitting the frame over the link to the adjacent node. Beyond this common framing function, however, we learned that different link-layer protocols provide very different link access, delivery, and transmission services. These differences are due in part to the wide variety of link types over which link-layer protocols must operate. A simple point-to-point link has a single sender and receiver communicating over a single "wire." A multiple access link is shared among many senders and receivers; consequently, the link-layer protocol for a multiple access channel has a protocol (its multiple access protocol) for coordinating link access. In the case of MPLS, the "link" connecting two adjacent nodes (for example, two IP routers that are adjacent in an IP sense—that they are next-hop IP routers toward some destination) may actually be a *network* in and of itself. In one sense, the idea of a network being considered as a link should not seem odd. A telephone link connecting a home modem/computer to a remote modem/router, for example, is actually a path through a sophisticated and complex telephone *network*.

Among the principles underlying link-layer communication, we examined error-detection and -correction techniques, multiple access protocols, link-layer addressing, virtualization (VLANs), and the construction of extended switched LANs and data center networks. Much of the focus today at the link layer is on these switched networks. In the case of error detection/correction, we examined how it is possible to add additional bits to a frame's header in order to detect, and in some cases correct, bit-flip errors that might occur when the frame is transmitted over the link. We covered simple parity and checksumming schemes, as well as the more robust cyclic redundancy check. We then moved on to the topic of multiple access protocols. We identified and studied three broad approaches for coordinating access to a broadcast channel: channel partitioning approaches (TDM, FDM), random access approaches (the ALOHA protocols and CSMA protocols), and taking-turns approaches (polling and token passing). We studied the cable access network and found that it uses many of these multiple access methods. We saw that a consequence of having multiple nodes share a single broadcast channel was the need to provide node addresses at the link layer. We learned that link-layer addresses were quite different from network-layer addresses and that, in the case of the Internet, a special protocol (ARP—the Address Resolution Protocol) is used to translate between these two forms of addressing and studied the hugely successful Ethernet protocol in detail. We then examined how nodes sharing a broadcast channel form a LAN and how multiple LANs can be connected together to form larger LANs—all *without* the intervention of network-layer routing to interconnect these local nodes. We also learned how multiple virtual LANs can be created on a single physical LAN infrastructure.

We ended our study of the link layer by focusing on how MPLS networks provide link-layer services when they interconnect IP routers and an overview of the network designs for today's massive data centers.We wrapped up this chapter (and indeed the first five chapters) by identifying the many protocols that are needed to fetch a simple Web page. Having covered the link layer, *our journey down the protocol stack is now ove*r! Certainly, the physical layer lies below the link layer, but the details of the physical layer are probably best left for another course (for example, in communication theory, rather than computer networking). We have, however, touched upon several aspects of the physical layer in this chapter and in Chapter 1 (our discussion of physical media in Section 1.2). We'll consider the physical layer again when we study wireless link characteristics in the next chapter.

Although our journey down the protocol stack is over, our study of computer networking is not yet at an end. In the following four chapters we cover wireless networking, multimedia networking, network security, and network management. These four topics do not fit conveniently into any one layer; indeed, each topic crosscuts many layers. Understanding these topics (billed as advanced topics in some networking texts) thus requires a firm foundation in all layers of the protocol stack—a foundation that our study of the link layer has now completed!

 Homework Problems and Questions

Chapter 5 Review Questions

SECTIONS 5.1–5.2

R1. What is framing in link layer?

R2. If all the links in the Internet were to provide reliable delivery service, would the TCP reliable delivery service be redundant? Why or why not?

R3. Name three error-detection strategies employed by link layer.

SECTION 5.3

R4. Suppose two nodes start to transmit at the same time a packet of length L over a broadcast channel of rate R. Denote the propagation delay between the two nodes as d_{prop}. Will there be a collision if $d_{prop} < L/R$? Why or why not?

R5. In Section 5.3, we listed four desirable characteristics of a broadcast channel. Which of these characteristics does slotted ALOHA have? Which of these characteristics does token passing have?

R6. In CSMA/CD, after the fifth collision, what is the probability that a node chooses $K = 4$? The result $K = 4$ corresponds to a delay of how many seconds on a 10 Mbps Ethernet?

R7. While TDM and FDM assign time slots and frequencies, CDMA assigns a different code to each node. Explain the basic principle in which CDMA works.

R8. Why does collision occur in CSMA, if all nodes perform carrier sensing before transmission?

SECTION 5.4

R9. How big is the MAC address space? The IPv4 address space? The IPv6 address space?

R10. Suppose nodes A, B, and C each attach to the same broadcast LAN (through their adapters). If A sends thousands of IP datagrams to B with each encapsulating frame addressed to the MAC address of B, will C's adapter process these frames? If so, will C's adapter pass the IP datagrams in these frames to the network layer C? How would your answers change if A sends frames with the MAC broadcast address?

R11. When a company wants to manufacture adapters, it purchases a chunk of the address space consisting of 2^{24} addresses for a nominal fee. IEEE allocates the chunk of 2^{24} addresses by fixing the first 24 bits of a MAC address. How many adapters can such a company manufacture?

R12. For the network in Figure 5.19, the router has two ARP modules, each with its own ARP table. Is it possible that the same MAC address appears in both tables?

R13. What is a hub used for?

R14. Consider Figure 5.15. How many subnetworks are there, in the addressing sense of Section 4.4?

R15. Each host and router has an ARP table in its memory. What are the contents of this table?

R16. The Ethernet frame begins with an 8-byte preamble field. The purpose of the first 7 bytes is to "wake up" the receiving adapters and to synchronize their clocks to that of the sender's clock. What are the contents of the 8 bytes? What is the purpose of the last byte?

 Problems

P1. Suppose the information content of a packet is the bit pattern 1010 0111 0101 1001 and an even parity scheme is being used. What would the value of the field containing the parity bits be for the case of a two-dimensional parity scheme? Your answer should be such that a minimum-length checksum field is used.

P2. Consider the following two-dimensional parity matrix.

0 1 0 1
1 0 1 0
0 1 0 1
1 0 1 0

Give an example of a double bit error that can be detected but cannot be corrected.

P3. Suppose the information portion of a packet contains six bytes consisting of the 8-bit unsigned binary ASCII representation of string "CHKSUM"; compute the Internet checksum for this data.

P4. Compute the Internet checksum for each of the following:

a. the binary representation of the numbers 1 through 6.

b. the ASCII representation of the letters C through H (uppercase).

c. the ASCII representation of the letters c through h (lowercase).

P5. Consider the generator, G = 1001, and suppose that D has the value 11000111010. What is the value of R?

P6. Rework the previous problem, but suppose that D has the value

a. 01101010101.

b. 11111010101.

c. 10001100001.

P7. In this problem, we explore some of the properties of the CRC. For the generator G (=1001) given in Section 5.2.3, answer the following questions.

   a. Why can it detect any single bit error in data D?

   b. Can the above G detect any odd number of bit errors? Why?

P8. In Section 5.3, we provided an outline of the derivation of the efficiency of slotted ALOHA. In this problem we'll complete the derivation.

   a. Recall that when there are N active nodes, the efficiency of slotted ALOHA is $Np(1-p)^{N-1}$. Find the value of p that maximizes this expression.

   b. Using the value of p found in (a), find the efficiency of slotted ALOHA by letting N approach infinity. *Hint*: $(1-1/N)^N$ approaches $1/e$ as N approaches infinity.

P9. Show that the maximum efficiency of pure ALOHA is $1/(2e)$. *Note*: This problem is easy if you have completed the problem above!

P10. Consider two nodes, A and B, that use the slotted ALOHA protocol to contend for a channel. Suppose node A has more data to transmit than node B, and node A's retransmission probability p_A is greater than node B's retransmission probability, p_B.

   a. Provide a formula for node A's average throughput. What is the total efficiency of the protocol with these two nodes?

   b. If $p_A = 2p_B$, is node A's average throughput twice as large as that of node B? Why or why not? If not, how can you choose p_A and p_B to make that happen?

   c. In general, suppose there are N nodes, among which node A has retransmission probability $2p$ and all other nodes have retransmission probability p. Provide expressions to compute the average throughputs of node A and of any other node.

P11. Suppose four active nodes—nodes A, B, C and D—are competing for access to a channel using slotted ALOHA. Assume each node has an infinite number of packets to send. Each node attempts to transmit in each slot with probability p. The first slot is numbered slot 1, the second slot is numbered slot 2, and so on.

   a. What is the probability that node A succeeds for the first time in slot 5?

   b. What is the probability that some node (either A, B, C or D) succeeds in slot 4?

   c. What is the probability that the first success occurs in slot 3?

   d. What is the efficiency of this four-node system?

P12. Graph the efficiency of slotted ALOHA and pure ALOHA as a function of p for the following values of N:

   a. $N=15$.

   b. $N=25$.

   c. $N=35$.

P13. Consider a broadcast channel with N nodes and a transmission rate of R bps. Suppose the broadcast channel uses polling (with an additional polling node) for multiple access. Suppose the amount of time from when a node completes transmission until the subsequent node is permitted to transmit (that is, the polling delay) is d_{poll}. Suppose that within a polling round, a given node is allowed to transmit at most Q bits. What is the maximum throughput of the broadcast channel?

P14. Consider three LANs interconnected by two routers, as shown in Figure 5.33.

   a. Assign IP addresses to all of the interfaces. For Subnet 1 use addresses of the form 192.168.1.xxx; for Subnet 2 uses addresses of the form 192.168.2.xxx; and for Subnet 3 use addresses of the form 192.168.3.xxx.

   b. Assign MAC addresses to all of the adapters.

   c. Consider sending an IP datagram from Host E to Host B. Suppose all of the ARP tables are up to date. Enumerate all the steps, as done for the single-router example in Section 5.4.1.

   d. Repeat (c), now assuming that the ARP table in the sending host is empty (and the other tables are up to date).

P15. Consider Figure 5.33. Now we replace the router between subnets 1 and 2 with a switch S1, and label the router between subnets 2 and 3 as R1.

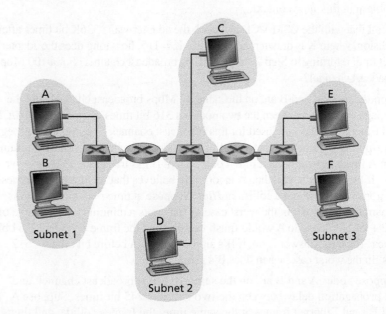

Figure 5.33 ♦ Three subnets, interconnected by routers

VideoNote
Sending a datagram
between subnets: link-
layer and network-layer
addressing

a. Consider sending an IP datagram from Host E to Host F. Will Host E ask router R1 to help forward the datagram? Why? In the Ethernet frame containing the IP datagram, what are the source and destination IP and MAC addresses?

b. Suppose E would like to send an IP datagram to B, and assume that E's ARP cache does not contain B's MAC address. Will E perform an ARP query to find B's MAC address? Why? In the Ethernet frame (containing the IP datagram destined to B) that is delivered to router R1, what are the source and destination IP and MAC addresses?

c. Suppose Host A would like to send an IP datagram to Host B, and neither A's ARP cache contains B's MAC address nor does B's ARP cache contain A's MAC address. Further suppose that the switch S1's forwarding table contains entries for Host B and router R1 only. Thus, A will broadcast an ARP request message. What actions will switch S1 perform once it receives the ARP request message? Will router R1 also receive this ARP request message? If so, will R1 forward the message to Subnet 3? Once Host B receives this ARP request message, it will send back to Host A an ARP response message. But will it send an ARP query message to ask for A's MAC address? Why? What will switch S1 do once it receives an ARP response message from Host B?

P16. Consider the previous problem, but suppose now that the router between subnets 2 and 3 is replaced by a switch. Answer questions (a)–(c) in the previous problem in this new context.

P17. Recall that with the CSMA/CD protocol, the adapter waits 536K bit times after a collision, where K is drawn randomly. For K = 115, how long does the adapter wait until returning to Step 2 for a 10 Mbps broadcast channel? For a 100 Mbps broadcast channel?

P18. Suppose nodes A and B are on the same 12 Mbps broadcast channel, and the propagation delay between the two nodes is 316 bit times. Suppose CSMA/CD and Ethernet packets are used for this broadcast channel. Suppose node A begins transmitting a frame and, before it finishes, node B begins transmitting a frame. Can A finish transmitting before it detects that B has transmitted? Why or why not? If the answer is yes, then A incorrectly believes that its frame was successful transmitted without a collision. *Hint:* Suppose at time $t = 0$ bits, A begins transmitting a frame. In the worst case, A transmits a minimum-sized frame of $512 + 64$ bit times. So A would finish transmitting the frame at $t = 512 + 64$ bit times. Thus, the answer is no, if B's signal reaches A before bit time $t = 512 + 64$ bits. In the worst case, when does B's signal reach A?

P19. Suppose nodes A and B are on the same 10 Mbps broadcast channel, and the propagation delay between the two nodes is 245 bit times. Suppose A and B send Ethernet frames at the same time, the frames collide, and then A and B choose different values of K in the CSMA/CD algorithm. Assuming no other nodes are active, can the retransmissions from A and B collide? For our purposes, it suffices to work out the following example. Suppose A and B begin transmission at $t = 0$ bit times. They both detect collisions at $t = 245$ bit times. Suppose $K_A = 0$ and $K_B = 1$. At what time does B schedule its retransmission? At what time does A begin transmission? (*Note*: The nodes must wait for an idle channel after returning to Step 2—see protocol.) At what time does A's signal reach B? Does B refrain from transmitting at its scheduled time?

P20. In this problem, you will derive the efficiency of a CSMA/CD-like multiple access protocol. In this protocol, time is slotted and all adapters are synchronized to the slots. Unlike slotted ALOHA, however, the length of a slot (in seconds) is much less than a frame time (the time to transmit a frame). Let S be the length of a slot. Suppose all frames are of constant length $L = kRS$, where R is the transmission rate of the channel and k is a large integer. Suppose there are N nodes, each with an infinite number of frames to send. We also assume that $d_{prop} < S$, so that all nodes can detect a collision before the end of a slot time. The protocol is as follows:

- If, for a given slot, no node has possession of the channel, all nodes contend for the channel; in particular, each node transmits in the slot with probability p. If exactly one node transmits in the slot, that node takes possession of the channel for the subsequent $k - 1$ slots and transmits its entire frame.

- If some node has possession of the channel, all other nodes refrain from transmitting until the node that possesses the channel has finished transmitting its frame. Once this node has transmitted its frame, all nodes contend for the channel.

Note that the channel alternates between two states: the productive state, which lasts exactly k slots, and the nonproductive state, which lasts for a random number of slots. Clearly, the channel efficiency is the ratio of $k/(k + x)$, where x is the expected number of consecutive unproductive slots.

a. For fixed N and p, determine the efficiency of this protocol.

b. For fixed N, determine the p that maximizes the efficiency.

c. Using the p (which is a function of N) found in (b), determine the efficiency as N approaches infinity.

d. Show that this efficiency approaches 1 as the frame length becomes large.

P21. Consider Figure 5.33 in Problem P14. Provide MAC addresses and IP addresses for the interfaces at Host A, both routers, and Host F. Suppose Host A sends a datagram to Host F. Give the source and destination MAC addresses in the frame encapsulating this IP datagram as the frame is transmitted (*i*) from A to the left router, (*ii*) from the left router to the right router, (*iii*) from the right router to F. Also give the source and destination IP addresses in the IP datagram encapsulated within the frame at each of these points in time.

P22. Suppose now that the leftmost router in Figure 5.33 is replaced by a switch. Hosts A, B, C, and D and the right router are all star-connected into this switch. Give the source and destination MAC addresses in the frame encapsulating this IP datagram as the frame is transmitted *(i)* from A to the switch, *(ii)* from the switch to the right router, *(iii)* from the right router to F. Also give the source and destination IP addresses in the IP datagram encapsulated within the frame at each of these points in time.

P23. Consider Figure 5.15. Suppose that all links are 120 Mbps. What is the maximum total aggregate throughput that can be achieved among 12 hosts (4 in each department) and 2 servers in this network? You can assume that any host or server can send to any other host or server. Why?

P24. Suppose the three departmental switches in Figure 5.15 are replaced by hubs. All links are 120 Mbps. Now answer the questions posed in Problem P23.

P25. Suppose that *all* the switches in Figure 5.15 are replaced by hubs. All links are 120 Mbps. Now answer the questions posed in Problem P23

P26. Let's consider the operation of a learning switch in the context of a network in which 6 nodes labeled A through F are star connected into an Ethernet switch. Suppose that *(i)* B sends a frame to E, *(ii)* E replies with a frame to B, *(iii)* A sends a frame to B, *(iv)* B replies with a frame to A. The switch table is initially empty. Show the state of the switch table before and after each of these events. For each of these events, identify the link(s) on which the transmitted frame will be forwarded, and briefly justify your answers.

P27. In this problem, we explore the use of small packets for Voice-over-IP applications. One of the drawbacks of a small packet size is that a large fraction of link bandwidth is consumed by overhead bytes. To this end, suppose that the packet consists of P bytes and 5 bytes of header.

  a. Consider sending a digitally encoded voice source directly. Suppose the source is encoded at a constant rate of 128 kbps. Assume each packet is entirely filled before the source sends the packet into the network. The time required to fill a packet is the **packetization delay**. In terms of L, determine the packetization delay in milliseconds.

  b. Packetization delays greater than 20 msec can cause a noticeable and unpleasant echo. Determine the packetization delay for $L = 1,500$ bytes (roughly corresponding to a maximum-sized Ethernet packet) and for $L = 50$ (corresponding to an ATM packet).

  c. Calculate the store-and-forward delay at a single switch for a link rate of $R = 622$ Mbps for $L = 1,500$ bytes, and for $L = 50$ bytes.

  d. Comment on the advantages of using a small packet size.

P28. Consider the single switch VLAN in Figure 5.25, and assume an external router is connected to switch port 1. Assign IP addresses to the EE and CS hosts and router interface. Trace the steps taken at both the network layer and the link layer to transfer an IP datagram from an EE host to a CS host (*Hint:* reread the discussion of Figure 5.19 in the text).

P29. Consider the MPLS network shown in Figure 5.29, and suppose that routers R5 and R6 are now MPLS enabled. Suppose that we want to perform traffic engineering so that packets from R6 destined for A are switched to A via R6-R4-R3-R1, and packets from R5 destined for A are switched via R5-R4-R2-R1. Show the MPLS tables in R5 and R6, as well as the modified table in R4, that would make this possible.

P30. Consider again the same scenario as in the previous problem, but suppose that packets from R6 destined for D are switched via R6-R4-R3, while packets from R5 destined to D are switched via R4-R2-R1-R3. Show the MPLS tables in all routers that would make this possible.

P31. In this problem, you will put together much of what you have learned about Internet protocols. Suppose you walk into a room, connect to Ethernet, and want to download a Web page. What are all the protocol steps that take place, starting from powering on your PC to getting the Web page? Assume there is nothing in our DNS or browser caches when you power on your PC. (*Hint:* the steps include the use of Ethernet, DHCP, ARP, DNS, TCP, and HTTP protocols.) Explicitly indicate in your steps how you obtain the IP and MAC addresses of a gateway router.

P32. Consider the data center network with hierarchical topology in Figure 5.30. Suppose now there are 80 pairs of flows, with ten flows between the first and ninth rack, ten flows between the second and tenth rack, and so on. Further suppose that all links in the network are 10 Gbps, except for the links between hosts and TOR switches, which are 1 Gbps.

a. Each flow has the same data rate; determine the maximum rate of a flow.

b. For the same traffic pattern, determine the maximum rate of a flow for the highly interconnected topology in Figure 5.31.

c. Now suppose there is a similar traffic pattern, but involving 20 hosts on each rack and 160 pairs of flows. Determine the maximum flow rates for the two topologies.

P33. Consider the hierarchical network in Figure 5.30 and suppose that the data center needs to support email and video distribution among other applications. Suppose four racks of servers are reserved for email and four racks are reserved for video. For each of the applications, all four racks must lie below a single tier-2 switch since the tier-2 to tier-1 links do not have sufficient bandwidth to support the intra-application traffic. For the email application, suppose that for 99.9 percent of the time only three racks are used, and that the video application has identical usage patterns.

a. For what fraction of time does the email application need to use a fourth rack? How about for the video application?

b. Assuming email usage and video usage are independent, for what fraction of time do (equivalently, what is the probability that) both applications need their fourth rack?

c. Suppose that it is acceptable for an application to have a shortage of servers for 0.001 percent of time or less (causing rare periods of performance degradation for users). Discuss how the topology in Figure 5.31 can be used so that only seven racks are collectively assigned to the two applications (assuming that the topology can support all the traffic).

 ## Wireshark Labs

At the companion Web site for this textbook, http://www.awl.com/kurose-ross, you'll find a Wireshark lab that examines the operation of the IEEE 802.3 protocol and the Wireshark frame format. A second Wireshark lab examines packet traces taken in a home network scenario.

AN INTERVIEW WITH...

Simon S. Lam

Simon S. Lam is Professor and Regents Chair in Computer Sciences at the University of Texas at Austin. From 1971 to 1974, he was with the ARPA Network Measurement Center at UCLA, where he worked on satellite and radio packet switching. He led a research group that invented secure sockets and prototyped, in 1993, the first secure sockets layer named Secure Network Programming, which won the 2004 ACM Software System Award. His research interests are in design and analysis of network protocols and security services. He received his BSEE from Washington State University and his MS and PhD from UCLA. He was elected to the National Academy of Engineering in 2007.

Why did you decide to specialize in networking?

When I arrived at UCLA as a new graduate student in Fall 1969, my intention was to study control theory. Then I took the queuing theory classes of Leonard Kleinrock and was very impressed by him. For a while, I was working on adaptive control of queuing systems as a possible thesis topic. In early 1972, Larry Roberts initiated the ARPAnet Satellite System project (later called Packet Satellite). Professor Kleinrock asked me to join the project. The first thing we did was to introduce a simple, yet realistic, backoff algorithm to the slotted ALOHA protocol. Shortly thereafter, I found many interesting research problems, such as ALOHA's instability problem and need for adaptive backoff, which would form the core of my thesis.

You were active in the early days of the Internet in the 1970s, beginning with your student days at UCLA. What was it like then? Did people have any inkling of what the Internet would become?

The atmosphere was really no different from other system-building projects I have seen in industry and academia. The initially stated goal of the ARPAnet was fairly modest, that is, to provide access to expensive computers from remote locations so that many more scientists could use them. However, with the startup of the Packet Satellite project in 1972 and the Packet Radio project in 1973, ARPA's goal had expanded substantially. By 1973, ARPA was building three different packet networks at the same time, and it became necessary for Vint Cerf and Bob Kahn to develop an interconnection strategy.

Back then, all of these progressive developments in networking were viewed (I believe) as logical rather than magical. No one could have envisioned the scale of the Internet and power of personal computers today. It was a decade before appearance of the first PCs. To put things in perspective, most students submitted their computer programs as decks of punched cards for batch processing. Only some students had direct access to computers, which were typically housed in a restricted area. Modems were slow and still a rarity. As a graduate student, I had only a phone on my desk, and I used pencil and paper to do most of my work.

537

Where do you see the field of networking and the Internet heading in the future?

In the past, the simplicity of the Internet's IP protocol was its greatest strength in vanquishing competition and becoming the *de facto* standard for internetworking. Unlike competitors, such as X.25 in the 1980s and ATM in the 1990s, IP can run on top of any link-layer networking technology, because it offers only a best-effort datagram service. Thus, any packet network can connect to the Internet.

Today, IP's greatest strength is actually a shortcoming. IP is like a straitjacket that confines the Internet's development to specific directions. In recent years, many researchers have redirected their efforts to the application layer only. There is also a great deal of research on wireless ad hoc networks, sensor networks, and satellite networks. These networks can be viewed either as stand-alone systems or link-layer systems, which can flourish because they are outside of the IP straitjacket.

Many people are excited about the possibility of P2P systems as a platform for novel Internet applications. However, P2P systems are highly inefficient in their use of Internet resources. A concern of mine is whether the transmission and switching capacity of the Internet core will continue to increase faster than the traffic demand on the Internet as it grows to interconnect all kinds of devices and support future P2P-enabled applications. Without substantial overprovisioning of capacity, ensuring network stability in the presence of malicious attacks and congestion will continue to be a significant challenge.

The Internet's phenomenal growth also requires the allocation of new IP addresses at a rapid rate to network operators and enterprises worldwide. At the current rate, the pool of unallocated IPv4 addresses would be depleted in a few years. When that happens, large contiguous blocks of address space can only be allocated from the IPv6 address space. Since adoption of IPv6 is off to a slow start, due to lack of incentives for early adopters, IPv4 and IPv6 will most likely co-exist on the Internet for many years to come. Successful migration from an IPv4-dominant Internet to an IPv6-dominant Internet will require a substantial global effort.

What is the most challenging part of your job?

The most challenging part of my job as a professor is teaching and motivating *every* student in my class, and *every* doctoral student under my supervision, rather than just the high achievers. The very bright and motivated may require a little guidance but not much else. I often learn more from these students than they learn from me. Educating and motivating the underachievers present a major challenge.

What impacts do you foresee technology having on learning in the future?

Eventually, almost all human knowledge will be accessible through the Internet, which will be the most powerful tool for learning. This vast knowledge base will have the potential of leveling the playing field for students all over the world. For example, motivated students in any country will be able to access the best-class Web sites, multimedia lectures, and teaching materials. Already, it was said that the IEEE and ACM digital libraries have accelerated the development of computer science researchers in China. In time, the Internet will transcend all geographic barriers to learning.

CHAPTER 6

Wireless and Mobile Networks

In the telephony world, the past 15 years have arguably been the golden years of cellular telephony. The number of worldwide mobile cellular subscribers increased from 34 million in 1993 to nearly 5.5 billion subscribers by 2011, with the number of cellular subscribers now surpassing the number of wired telephone lines. The many advantages of cell phones are evident to all—anywhere, anytime, untethered access to the global telephone network via a highly portable lightweight device. With the advent of laptops, palmtops, smartphones, and their promise of anywhere, anytime, untethered access to the global Internet, is a similar explosion in the use of wireless Internet devices just around the corner?

Regardless of the future growth of wireless Internet devices, it's already clear that wireless networks and the mobility-related services they enable are here to stay. From a networking standpoint, the challenges posed by these networks, particularly at the link layer and the network layer, are so different from traditional wired computer networks that an individual chapter devoted to the study of wireless and mobile networks (i.e., *this* chapter) is appropriate.

We'll begin this chapter with a discussion of mobile users, wireless links, and networks, and their relationship to the larger (typically wired) networks to which they connect. We'll draw a distinction between the challenges posed by the *wireless* nature of the communication links in such networks, and by the *mobility* that these wireless links enable. Making this important distinction—between wireless and

539

mobility—will allow us to better isolate, identify, and master the key concepts in each area. Note that there are indeed many networked environments in which the network nodes are wireless but not mobile (e.g., wireless home or office networks with stationary workstations and large displays), and that there are limited forms of mobility that do not require wireless links (e.g., a worker who uses a wired laptop at home, shuts down the laptop, drives to work, and attaches the laptop to the company's wired network). Of course, many of the most exciting networked environments are those in which users are both wireless *and* mobile—for example, a scenario in which a mobile user (say in the back seat of car) maintains a Voice-over-IP call and multiple ongoing TCP connections while racing down the autobahn at 160 kilometers per hour. It is here, at the intersection of wireless and mobility, that we'll find the most interesting technical challenges!

We'll begin by illustrating the setting in which we'll consider wireless communication and mobility—a network in which wireless (and possibly mobile) users are connected into the larger network infrastructure by a wireless link at the network's edge. We'll then consider the characteristics of this wireless link in Section 6.2. We include a brief introduction to code division multiple access (CDMA), a shared-medium access protocol that is often used in wireless networks, in Section 6.2. In Section 6.3, we'll examine the link-level aspects of the IEEE 802.11 (WiFi) wireless LAN standard in some depth; we'll also say a few words about Bluetooth and other wireless personal area networks. In Section 6.4, we'll provide an overview of cellular Internet access, including 3G and emerging 4G cellular technologies that provide both voice and high-speed Internet access. In Section 6.5, we'll turn our attention to mobility, focusing on the problems of locating a mobile user, routing to the mobile user, and "handing off" the mobile user who dynamically moves from one point of attachment to the network to another. We'll examine how these mobility services are implemented in the mobile IP standard and in GSM, in Sections 6.6 and 6.7, respectively. Finally, we'll consider the impact of wireless links and mobility on transport-layer protocols and networked applications in Section 6.8.

6.1 Introduction

Figure 6.1 shows the setting in which we'll consider the topics of wireless data communication and mobility. We'll begin by keeping our discussion general enough to cover a wide range of networks, including both wireless LANs such as IEEE 802.11 and cellular networks such as a 3G network; we'll drill down into a more detailed discussion of specific wireless architectures in later sections. We can identify the following elements in a wireless network:

• *Wireless hosts.* As in the case of wired networks, hosts are the end-system devices that run applications. A **wireless host** might be a laptop, palmtop, smartphone, or desktop computer. The hosts themselves may or may not be mobile.

CASE HISTORY

PUBLIC WIFI ACCESS: COMING SOON TO A LAMP POST NEAR YOU?

WiFi hotspots—public locations where users can find 802.11 wireless access—are becoming increasingly common in hotels, airports, and cafés around the world. Most college campuses offer ubiquitous wireless access, and it's hard to find a hotel that doesn't offer wireless Internet access.

Over the past decade a number of cities have designed, deployed, and operated municipal WiFi networks. The vision of providing ubiquitous WiFi access to the community as a public service (much like streetlights)—helping to bridge the digital divide by providing Internet access to all citizens and to promote economic development—is compelling. Many cities around the world, including Philadelphia, Toronto, Hong Kong, Minneapolis, London, and Auckland, have plans to provide ubiquitous wireless within the city, or have already done so to varying degrees. The goal in Philadelphia was to "turn Philadelphia into the nation's largest WiFi hotspot and help to improve education, bridge the digital divide, enhance neighborhood development, and reduce the costs of government." The ambitious program—an agreement between the city, Wireless Philadelphia (a nonprofit entity), and the Internet Service Provider Earthlink—built an operational network of 802.11b hotspots on streetlamp pole arms and traffic control devices that covered 80 percent of the city. But financial and operational concerns caused the network to be sold to a group of private investors in 2008, who later sold the network back to the city in 2010. Other cities, such as Minneapolis, Toronto, Hong Kong, and Auckland, have had success with smaller-scale efforts.

The fact that 802.11 networks operate in the unlicensed spectrum (and hence can be deployed without purchasing expensive spectrum use rights) would seem to make them financially attractive. However, 802.11 access points (see Section 6.3) have much shorter ranges than 3G cellular base stations (see Section 6.4), requiring a larger number of deployed endpoints to cover the same geographic region. Cellular data networks providing Internet access, on the other hand, operate in the licensed spectrum. Cellular providers pay billions of dollars for spectrum access rights for their networks, making cellular data networks a business rather than municipal undertaking.

• *Wireless links.* A host connects to a base station (defined below) or to another wireless host through a **wireless communication link**. Different wireless link technologies have different transmission rates and can transmit over different distances. Figure 6.2 shows two key characteristics (coverage area and link rate) of the more popular wireless network standards. (The figure is only meant to provide a rough idea of these characteristics. For example, some of these types of networks are only now being deployed, and some link rates can increase or decrease beyond the values shown depending on distance, channel conditions, and the number of users in the wireless network.) We'll cover these standards

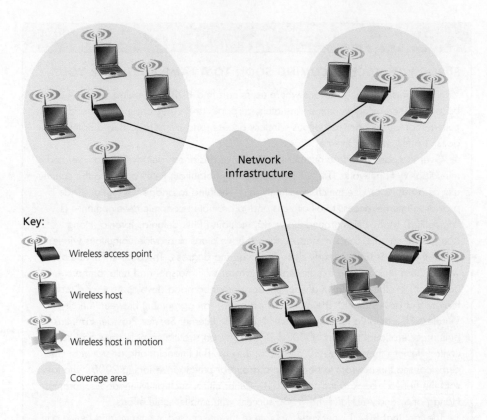

Key:

Wireless access point

Wireless host

Wireless host in motion

Coverage area

Figure 6.1 ♦ Elements of a wireless network

later in the first half of this chapter; we'll also consider other wireless link characteristics (such as their bit error rates and the causes of bit errors) in Section 6.2.

In Figure 6.1, wireless links connect wireless hosts located at the edge of the network into the larger network infrastructure. We hasten to add that wireless links are also sometimes used *within* a network to connect routers, switches, and other network equipment. However, our focus in this chapter will be on the use of wireless communication at the network edge, as it is here that many of the most exciting technical challenges, and most of the growth, are occurring.

• *Base station*. The **base station** is a key part of the wireless network infrastructure. Unlike the wireless host and wireless link, a base station has no obvious counterpart in a wired network. A base station is responsible for sending and receiving data (e.g., packets) to and from a wireless host that is associated with that base station. A base station will often be responsible for coordinating the transmission of multiple wireless hosts with which it is associated. When we say a wireless host is "associated" with a base station, we mean that (1) the host is within the wireless communication

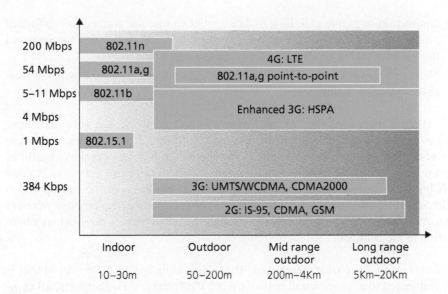

Figure 6.2 ◆ Link characteristics of selected wireless network standards

distance of the base station, and (2) the host uses that base station to relay data between it (the host) and the larger network. **Cell towers** in cellular networks and **access points** in 802.11 wireless LANs are examples of base stations.

In Figure 6.1, the base station is connected to the larger network (e.g., the Internet, corporate or home network, or telephone network), thus functioning as a link-layer relay between the wireless host and the rest of the world with which the host communicates.

Hosts associated with a base station are often referred to as operating in **infrastructure mode**, since all traditional network services (e.g., address assignment and routing) are provided by the network to which a host is connected via the base station. In **ad hoc networks**, wireless hosts have no such infrastructure with which to connect. In the absence of such infrastructure, the hosts themselves must provide for services such as routing, address assignment, DNS-like name translation, and more.

When a mobile host moves beyond the range of one base station and into the range of another, it will change its point of attachment into the larger network (i.e., change the base station with which it is associated)—a process referred to as **handoff**. Such mobility raises many challenging questions. If a host can move, how does one find the mobile host's current location in the network so that data can be forwarded to that mobile host? How is addressing performed, given that a host can be in one of many possible locations? If the host moves *during* a TCP connection or phone call, how is data routed so that the connection continues uninterrupted? These and many (many!) other questions make wireless and mobile networking an area of exciting networking research.

• *Network infrastructure.* This is the larger network with which a wireless host may wish to communicate.

Having discussed the "pieces" of a wireless network, we note that these pieces can be combined in many different ways to form different types of wireless networks. You may find a taxonomy of these types of wireless networks useful as you read on in this chapter, or read/learn more about wireless networks beyond this book. At the highest level we can classify wireless networks according to two criteria: *(i)* whether a packet in the wireless network crosses exactly *one wireless hop or multiple wireless hops*, and *(ii)* whether there is *infrastructure* such as a base station in the network:

• *Single-hop, infrastructure-based.* These networks have a base station that is connected to a larger wired network (e.g., the Internet). Furthermore, all communication is between this base station and a wireless host over a single wireless hop. The 802.11 networks you use in the classroom, café, or library; and the 3G cellular data networks that we will learn about shortly all fall in this category.

• *Single-hop, infrastructure-less.* In these networks, there is no base station that is connected to a wireless network. However, as we will see, one of the nodes in this single-hop network may coordinate the transmissions of the other nodes. Bluetooth networks (which we will study in Section 6.3.6) and 802.11 networks in ad hoc mode are single-hop, infrastructure-less networks.

• *Multi-hop, infrastructure-based.* In these networks, a base station is present that is wired to the larger network. However, some wireless nodes may have to relay their communication through other wireless nodes in order to communicate via the base station. Some wireless sensor networks and so-called **wireless mesh networks** fall in this category.

• *Multi-hop, infrastructure-less.* There is no base station in these networks, and nodes may have to relay messages among several other nodes in order to reach a destination. Nodes may also be mobile, with connectivity changing among nodes—a class of networks known as **mobile ad hoc networks (MANETs)**. If the mobile nodes are vehicles, the network is a **vehicular ad hoc network (VANET)**. As you might imagine, the development of protocols for such networks is challenging and is the subject of much ongoing research.

In this chapter, we'll mostly confine ourselves to single-hop networks, and then mostly to infrastructure-based networks.

Let's now dig deeper into the technical challenges that arise in wireless and mobile networks. We'll begin by first considering the individual wireless link, deferring our discussion of mobility until later in this chapter.

6.2 Wireless Links and Network Characteristics

Let's begin by considering a simple wired network, say a home network, with a wired Ethernet switch (see Section 5.4) interconnecting the hosts. If we replace the wired Ethernet with a wireless 802.11 network, a wireless network interface would replace the host's wired Ethernet interface, and an access point would replace the Ethernet switch, but virtually no changes would be needed at the network layer or above. This suggests that we focus our attention on the link layer when looking for important differences between wired and wireless networks. Indeed, we can find a number of important differences between a wired link and a wireless link:

- *Decreasing signal strength*. Electromagnetic radiation attenuates as it passes through matter (e.g., a radio signal passing through a wall). Even in free space, the signal will disperse, resulting in decreased signal strength (sometimes referred to as **path loss**) as the distance between sender and receiver increases.

- *Interference from other sources*. Radio sources transmitting in the same frequency band will interfere with each other. For example, 2.4 GHz wireless phones and 802.11b wireless LANs transmit in the same frequency band. Thus, the 802.11b wireless LAN user talking on a 2.4 GHz wireless phone can expect that neither the network nor the phone will perform particularly well. In addition to interference from transmitting sources, electromagnetic noise within the environment (e.g., a nearby motor, a microwave) can result in interference.

- *Multipath propagation*. **Multipath propagation** occurs when portions of the electromagnetic wave reflect off objects and the ground, taking paths of different lengths between a sender and receiver. This results in the blurring of the received signal at the receiver. Moving objects between the sender and receiver can cause multipath propagation to change over time.

For a detailed discussion of wireless channel characteristics, models, and measurements, see [Anderson 1995].

The discussion above suggests that bit errors will be more common in wireless links than in wired links. For this reason, it is perhaps not surprising that wireless link protocols (such as the 802.11 protocol we'll examine in the following section) employ not only powerful CRC error detection codes, but also link-level reliable-data-transfer protocols that retransmit corrupted frames.

Having considered the impairments that can occur on a wireless channel, let's next turn our attention to the host receiving the wireless signal. This host receives an electromagnetic signal that is a combination of a degraded form of the original signal transmitted by the sender (degraded due to the attenuation and multipath propagation effects that we discussed above, among others) and background noise in the environment. The **signal-to-noise ratio (SNR)** is a relative measure of the strength of the received signal (i.e., the information being transmitted) and this noise. The SNR is typically measured in units of decibels (dB), a unit of measure that some think is used by electrical engineers primarily to confuse computer scientists. The SNR, measured in dB, is twenty times the ratio of the base-10 logarithm of the amplitude of the received signal to the amplitude of the noise. For our purposes here, we need only know that a larger SNR makes it easier for the receiver to extract the transmitted signal from the background noise.

Figure 6.3 (adapted from [Holland 2001]) shows the bit error rate (BER)—roughly speaking, the probability that a transmitted bit is received in error at the receiver—versus the SNR for three different modulation techniques for encoding information for transmission on an idealized wireless channel. The theory of modulation and coding, as well as signal extraction and BER, is well beyond the scope of this text (see [Schwartz 1980] for a discussion of these topics). Nonetheless, Figure 6.3 illustrates several physical-layer characteristics that are important in understanding higher-layer wireless communication protocols:

- *For a given modulation scheme, the higher the SNR, the lower the BER.* Since a sender can increase the SNR by increasing its transmission power, a sender

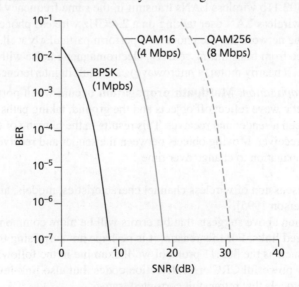

Figure 6.3 ♦ Bit error rate, transmission rate, and SNR

can decrease the probability that a frame is received in error by increasing its transmission power. Note, however, that there is arguably little practical gain in increasing the power beyond a certain threshold, say to decrease the BER from 10^{-12} to 10^{-13}. There are also *disadvantages* associated with increasing the transmission power: More energy must be expended by the sender (an important concern for battery-powered mobile users), and the sender's transmissions are more likely to interfere with the transmissions of another sender (see Figure 6.4(b)).

• *For a given SNR, a modulation technique with a higher bit transmission rate (whether in error or not) will have a higher BER.* For example, in Figure 6.3, with an SNR of 10 dB, BPSK modulation with a transmission rate of 1 Mbps has a BER of less than 10^{-7}, while with QAM16 modulation with a transmission rate of 4 Mbps, the BER is 10^{-1}, far too high to be practically useful. However, with an SNR of 20 dB, QAM16 modulation has a transmission rate of 4 Mbps and a BER of 10^{-7}, while BPSK modulation has a transmission rate of only 1 Mbps and a BER that is so low as to be (literally) "off the charts." If one can tolerate a BER of 10^{-7}, the higher transmission rate offered by QAM16 would make it the preferred modulation technique in this situation. These considerations give rise to the final characteristic, described next.

• *Dynamic selection of the physical-layer modulation technique can be used to adapt the modulation technique to channel conditions.* The SNR (and hence the BER) may change as a result of mobility or due to changes in the environment. Adaptive modulation and coding are used in cellular data systems and in the 802.11 WiFi and 3G cellular data networks that we'll study in Sections 6.3 and 6.4. This allows, for example, the selection of a modulation technique that provides the highest transmission rate possible subject to a constraint on the BER, for given channel characteristics.

A higher and time-varying bit error rate is not the only difference between a wired and wireless link. Recall that in the case of wired broadcast links, all nodes receive the transmissions from all other nodes. In the case of wireless links, the situation is not as simple, as shown in Figure 6.4. Suppose that Station A is transmitting to Station B. Suppose also that Station C is transmitting to Station B. With the so-called **hidden terminal problem**, physical obstructions in the environment (for example, a mountain or a building) may prevent A and C from hearing each other's transmissions, even though A's and C's transmissions are indeed interfering at the destination, B. This is shown in Figure 6.4(a). A second scenario that results in undetectable collisions at the receiver results from the **fading** of a signal's strength as it propagates through the wireless medium. Figure 6.4(b) illustrates the case where A and C are placed such that their signals are not strong enough to detect each other's transmissions, yet their signals *are* strong enough to interfere with each other at station B. As we'll see in Section 6.3, the hidden terminal problem and fading

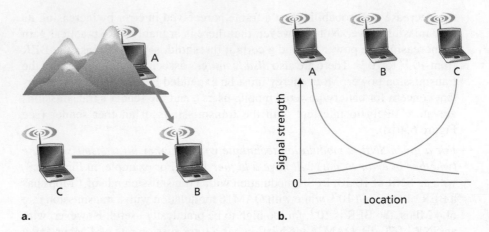

Figure 6.4 ♦ Hidden terminal problem caused by obstacle (a) and fading (b)

make multiple access in a wireless network considerably more complex than in a wired network.

6.2.1 CDMA

Recall from Chapter 5 that when hosts communicate over a shared medium, a protocol is needed so that the signals sent by multiple senders do not interfere at the receivers. In Chapter 5 we described three classes of medium access protocols: channel partitioning, random access, and taking turns. Code division multiple access (CDMA) belongs to the family of channel partitioning protocols. It is prevalent in wireless LAN and cellular technologies. Because CDMA is so important in the wireless world, we'll take a quick look at CDMA now, before getting into specific wireless access technologies in the subsequent sections.

In a CDMA protocol, each bit being sent is encoded by multiplying the bit by a signal (the code) that changes at a much faster rate (known as the **chipping rate**) than the original sequence of data bits. Figure 6.5 shows a simple, idealized CDMA encoding/decoding scenario. Suppose that the rate at which original data bits reach the CDMA encoder defines the unit of time; that is, each original data bit to be transmitted requires a one-bit slot time. Let d_i be the value of the data bit for the ith bit slot. For mathematical convenience, we represent a data bit with a 0 value as –1. Each bit slot is further subdivided into M mini-slots; in Figure 6.5, M = 8, although in practice M is much larger. The CDMA code used by the sender consists of a sequence of M values, c_m, m = 1, . . . , M, each taking a +1 or –1

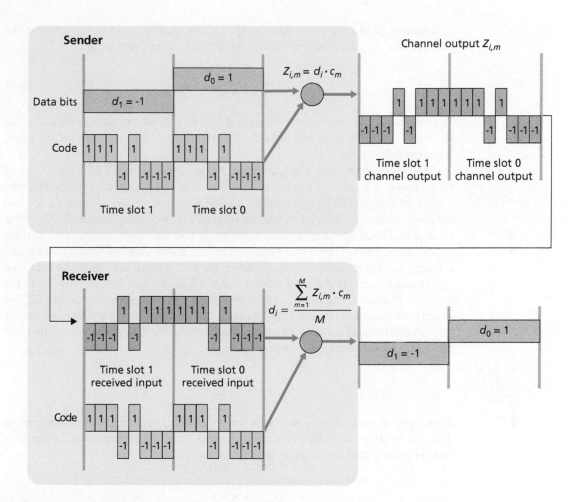

Figure 6.5 ◆ A simple CDMA example: sender encoding, receiver decoding

value. In the example in Figure 6.5, the M-bit CDMA code being used by the sender is $(1, 1, 1, -1, 1, -1, -1, -1)$.

To illustrate how CDMA works, let us focus on the ith data bit, d_i. For the mth mini-slot of the bit-transmission time of d_i, the output of the CDMA encoder, $Z_{i,m}$, is the value of d_i multiplied by the mth bit in the assigned CDMA code, c_m:

$$Z_{i,m} = d_i \cdot c_m \qquad (6.1)$$

In a simple world, with no interfering senders, the receiver would receive the encoded bits, $Z_{i,m}$, and recover the original data bit, d_i, by computing:

$$d_i = \frac{1}{M} \sum_{m=1}^{M} Z_{i,m} \cdot c_m \qquad (6.2)$$

The reader might want to work through the details of the example in Figure 6.5 to see that the original data bits are indeed correctly recovered at the receiver using Equation 6.2.

The world is far from ideal, however, and as noted above, CDMA must work in the presence of interfering senders that are encoding and transmitting their data using a different assigned code. But how can a CDMA receiver recover a sender's original data bits when those data bits are being tangled with bits being transmitted by other senders? CDMA works under the assumption that the interfering transmitted bit signals are additive. This means, for example, that if three senders send a 1 value, and a fourth sender sends a –1 value during the same mini-slot, then the received signal at all receivers during that mini-slot is a 2 (since $1 + 1 + 1 - 1 = 2$). In the presence of multiple senders, sender s computes its encoded transmissions, $Z_{i,m}^s$, in exactly the same manner as in Equation 6.1. The value received at a receiver during the mth mini-slot of the ith bit slot, however, is now the *sum* of the transmitted bits from all N senders during that mini-slot:

$$Z_{i,m}^* = \sum_{s=1}^{N} Z_{i,m}^s$$

Amazingly, if the senders' codes are chosen carefully, each receiver can recover the data sent by a given sender out of the aggregate signal simply by using the sender's code in exactly the same manner as in Equation 6.2:

$$d_i = \frac{1}{M} \sum_{m=1}^{M} Z_{i,m}^* \cdot c_m \qquad (6.3)$$

as shown in Figure 6.6, for a two-sender CDMA example. The M-bit CDMA code being used by the upper sender is $(1, 1, 1, -1, 1, -1, -1, -1)$, while the CDMA code being used by the lower sender is $(1, -1, 1, 1, 1, -1, 1, 1)$. Figure 6.6 illustrates a receiver recovering the original data bits from the upper sender. Note that the receiver is able to extract the data from sender 1 in spite of the interfering transmission from sender 2.

Recall our cocktail analogy from Chapter 5. A CDMA protocol is similar to having partygoers speaking in multiple languages; in such circumstances humans are actually quite good at locking into the conversation in the language they understand, while filtering out the remaining conversations. We see here that CDMA is a partitioning protocol in that it partitions the codespace (as opposed to time or frequency) and assigns each node a dedicated piece of the codespace.

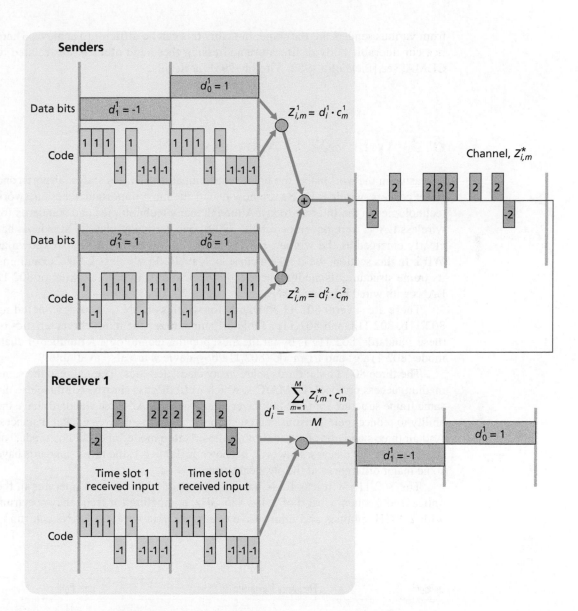

Figure 6.6 ♦ A two-sender CDMA example

Our discussion here of CDMA is necessarily brief; in practice a number of difficult issues must be addressed. First, in order for the CDMA receivers to be able to extract a particular sender's signal, the CDMA codes must be carefully chosen. Second, our discussion has assumed that the received signal strengths from various senders are the same; in reality this can be difficult to achieve. There is a considerable body of literature addressing these and other issues related to CDMA; see [Pickholtz 1982; Viterbi 1995] for details.

6.3 WiFi: 802.11 Wireless LANs

Pervasive in the workplace, the home, educational institutions, cafés, airports, and street corners, wireless LANs are now one of the most important access network technologies in the Internet today. Although many technologies and standards for wireless LANs were developed in the 1990s, one particular class of standards has clearly emerged as the winner: the **IEEE 802.11 wireless LAN**, also known as **WiFi**. In this section, we'll take a close look at 802.11 wireless LANs, examining its frame structure, its medium access protocol, and its internetworking of 802.11 LANs with wired Ethernet LANs.

There are several 802.11 standards for wireless LAN technology, including 802.11b, 802.11a, and 802.11g. Table 6.1 summarizes the main characteristics of these standards. 802.11g is by far the most popular technology. A number of dual-mode (802.11a/g) and tri-mode (802.11a/b/g) devices are also available.

The three 802.11 standards share many characteristics. They all use the same medium access protocol, CSMA/CA, which we'll discuss shortly. All three use the same frame structure for their link-layer frames as well. All three standards have the ability to reduce their transmission rate in order to reach out over greater distances. And all three standards allow for both "infrastructure mode" and "ad hoc mode," as we'll also shortly discuss. However, as shown in Table 6.1, the three standards have some major differences at the physical layer.

The 802.11b wireless LAN has a data rate of 11 Mbps and operates in the unlicensed frequency band of 2.4–2.485 GHz, competing for frequency spectrum with 2.4 GHz phones and microwave ovens. 802.11a wireless LANs can run at

Standard	Frequency Range (United States)	Data Rate
802.11b	2.4–2.485 GHz	up to 11 Mbps
802.11a	5.1–5.8 GHz	up to 54 Mbps
802.11g	2.4–2.485 GHz	up to 54 Mbps

Table 6.1 ♦ Summary of IEEE 802.11 standards

significantly higher bit rates, but do so at higher frequencies. By operating at a higher frequency, 802.11a LANs have a shorter transmission distance for a given power level and suffer more from multipath propagation. 802.11g LANs, operating in the same lower-frequency band as 802.11b and being backwards compatible with 802.11b (so one can upgrade 802.11b clients incrementally) yet with the higher-speed transmission rates of 802.11a, allows users to have their cake and eat it too.

A relatively new WiFi standard, 802.11n [IEEE 802.11n 2012], uses multiple-input multiple-output (MIMO) antennas; i.e., two or more antennas on the sending side and two or more antennas on the receiving side that are transmitting/receiving different signals [Diggavi 2004]. Depending on the modulation scheme used, transmission rates of several hundred megabits per second are possible with 802.11n.

6.3.1 The 802.11 Architecture

Figure 6.7 illustrates the principal components of the 802.11 wireless LAN architecture. The fundamental building block of the 802.11 architecture is the **basic service set (BSS)**. A BSS contains one or more wireless stations and a central

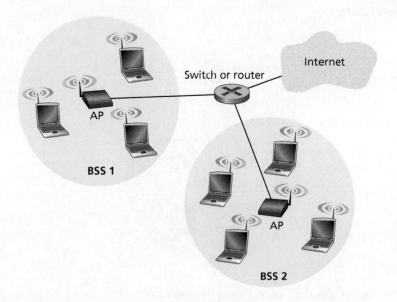

Figure 6.7 ◆ IEEE 802.11 LAN architecture

base station, known as an **access point (AP)** in 802.11 parlance. Figure 6.7 shows the AP in each of two BSSs connecting to an interconnection device (such as a switch or router), which in turn leads to the Internet. In a typical home network, there is one AP and one router (typically integrated together as one unit) that connects the BSS to the Internet.

As with Ethernet devices, each 802.11 wireless station has a 6-byte MAC address that is stored in the firmware of the station's adapter (that is, 802.11 network interface card). Each AP also has a MAC address for its wireless interface. As with Ethernet, these MAC addresses are administered by IEEE and are (in theory) globally unique.

As noted in Section 6.1, wireless LANs that deploy APs are often referred to as **infrastructure wireless LANs**, with the "infrastructure" being the APs along with the wired Ethernet infrastructure that interconnects the APs and a router. Figure 6.8 shows that IEEE 802.11 stations can also group themselves together to form an ad hoc network—a network with no central control and with no connections to the "outside world." Here, the network is formed "on the fly," by mobile devices that have found themselves in proximity to each other, that have a need to communicate, and that find no preexisting network infrastructure in their location. An ad hoc network might be formed when people with laptops get together (for example, in a conference room, a train, or a car) and want to exchange data in the absence of a centralized AP. There has been tremendous interest in ad hoc networking, as communicating portable devices continue to proliferate. In this section, though, we'll focus our attention on infrastructure wireless LANs.

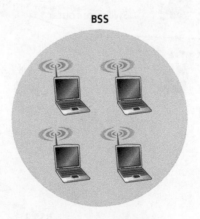

BSS

Figure 6.8 ♦ An IEEE 802.11 ad hoc network

Channels and Association

In 802.11, each wireless station needs to associate with an AP before it can send or receive network-layer data. Although all of the 802.11 standards use association, we'll discuss this topic specifically in the context of IEEE 802.11b/g.

When a network administrator installs an AP, the administrator assigns a one- or two-word **Service Set Identifier (SSID)** to the access point. (When you "view available networks" in Microsoft Windows XP, for example, a list is displayed showing the SSID of each AP in range.) The administrator must also assign a channel number to the AP. To understand channel numbers, recall that 802.11 operates in the frequency range of 2.4 GHz to 2.485 GHz. Within this 85 MHz band, 802.11 defines 11 partially overlapping channels. Any two channels are non-overlapping if and only if they are separated by four or more channels. In particular, the set of channels 1, 6, and 11 is the only set of three non-overlapping channels. This means that an administrator could create a wireless LAN with an aggregate maximum transmission rate of 33 Mbps by installing three 802.11b APs at the same physical location, assigning channels 1, 6, and 11 to the APs, and interconnecting each of the APs with a switch.

Now that we have a basic understanding of 802.11 channels, let's describe an interesting (and not completely uncommon) situation—that of a WiFi jungle. A **WiFi jungle** is any physical location where a wireless station receives a sufficiently strong signal from two or more APs. For example, in many cafés in New York City, a wireless station can pick up a signal from numerous nearby APs. One of the APs might be managed by the café, while the other APs might be in residential apartments near the café. Each of these APs would likely be located in a different IP subnet and would have been independently assigned a channel.

Now suppose you enter such a WiFi jungle with your portable computer, seeking wireless Internet acccss and a blueberry muffin. Suppose there are five APs in the WiFi jungle. To gain Internet access, your wireless station needs to join exactly one of the subnets and hence needs to **associate** with exactly one of the APs. Associating means the wireless station creates a virtual wire between itself and the AP. Specifically, only the associated AP will send data frames (that is, frames containing data, such as a datagram) to your wireless station, and your wireless station will send data frames into the Internet only through the associated AP. But how does your wireless station associate with a particular AP? And more fundamentally, how does your wireless station know which APs, if any, are out there in the jungle?

The 802.11 standard requires that an AP periodically send **beacon frames**, each of which includes the AP's SSID and MAC address. Your wireless station, knowing that APs are sending out beacon frames, scans the 11 channels, seeking beacon frames from any APs that may be out there (some of which may be transmitting on the same channel—it's a jungle out there!). Having learned about available APs from the beacon frames, you (or your wireless host) select one of the APs for association.

The 802.11 standard does not specify an algorithm for selecting which of the available APs to associate with; that algorithm is left up to the designers of the 802.11 firmware and software in your wireless host. Typically, the host chooses the AP whose beacon frame is received with the highest signal strength. While a high signal strength is good (see, e.g., Figure 6.3), signal strength is not the only AP characteristic that will determine the performance a host receives. In particular, it's possible that the selected AP may have a strong signal, but may be overloaded with other affiliated hosts (that will need to share the wireless bandwidth at that AP), while an unloaded AP is not selected due to a slightly weaker signal. A number of alternative ways of choosing APs have thus recently been proposed [Vasudevan 2005; Nicholson 2006; Sundaresan 2006]. For an interesting and down-to-earth discussion of how signal strength is measured, see [Bardwell 2004].

The process of scanning channels and listening for beacon frames is known as **passive scanning** (see Figure 6.9a). A wireless host can also perform **active scanning**, by broadcasting a probe frame that will be received by all APs within the wireless host's range, as shown in Figure 6.9b. APs respond to the probe request frame with a probe response frame. The wireless host can then choose the AP with which to associate from among the responding APs.

After selecting the AP with which to associate, the wireless host sends an association request frame to the AP, and the AP responds with an association response frame. Note that this second request/response handshake is needed with active scanning, since an AP responding to the initial probe request frame doesn't know which of the (possibly many) responding APs the host will choose to associate with, in much the same way that a DHCP client can choose from among multiple DHCP servers (see Figure 4.21). Once associated with an AP, the host will want to join the subnet (in the IP addressing sense of Section 4.4.2) to which the AP belongs. Thus, the host will typically send a DHCP discovery message (see Figure 4.21) into the subnet via the AP in order to obtain an IP address on the subnet. Once the address is obtained, the rest of the world then views that host simply as another host with an IP address in that subnet.

In order to create an association with a particular AP, the wireless station may be required to authenticate itself to the AP. 802.11 wireless LANs provide a number of alternatives for authentication and access. One approach, used by many companies, is to permit access to a wireless network based on a station's MAC address. A second approach, used by many Internet cafés, employs usernames and passwords. In both cases, the AP typically communicates with an authentication server, relaying information between the wireless end-point station and the authentication server using a protocol such as RADIUS [RFC 2865] or DIAMETER [RFC 3588]. Separating the authentication server from the AP allows one authentication server to serve many APs, centralizing the (often sensitive) decisions of authentication and access within the single server, and keeping AP costs and complexity low. We'll see

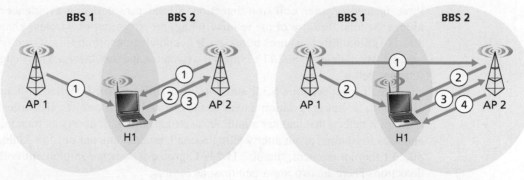

a. Passive scanning
1. Beacon frames sent from APs
2. Association Request frame sent:
   H1 to selected AP
3. Association Response frame sent:
   Selected AP to H1

a. Active scanning
1. Probe Request frame broadcast from H1
2. Probes Response frame sent from APs
3. Association Request frame sent:
   H1 to selected AP
4. Association Response frame sent:
   Selected AP to H1

Figure 6.9 ♦ Active and passive scanning for access points

in Section 8.8 that the new IEEE 802.11i protocol defining security aspects of the 802.11 protocol family takes precisely this approach.

6.3.2 The 802.11 MAC Protocol

Once a wireless station is associated with an AP, it can start sending and receiving data frames to and from the access point. But because multiple stations may want to transmit data frames at the same time over the same channel, a multiple access protocol is needed to coordinate the transmissions. Here, a **station** is either a wireless station or an AP. As discussed in Chapter 5 and Section 6.2.1, broadly speaking there are three classes of multiple access protocols: channel partitioning (including CDMA), random access, and taking turns. Inspired by the huge success of Ethernet and its random access protocol, the designers of 802.11 chose a random access protocol for 802.11 wireless LANs. This random access protocol is referred to as **CSMA with collision avoidance**, or more succinctly as **CSMA/CA**. As with Ethernet's CSMA/CD, the "CSMA" in CSMA/CA stands for "carrier sense multiple access," meaning that each station senses the channel before transmitting, and refrains from transmitting when the channel is sensed busy. Although both Ethernet and 802.11 use carrier-sensing random access, the two MAC protocols have important differences.

First, instead of using collision detection, 802.11 uses collision-avoidance techniques. Second, because of the relatively high bit error rates of wireless channels, 802.11 (unlike Ethernet) uses a link-layer acknowledgment/retransmission (ARQ) scheme. We'll describe 802.11's collision-avoidance and link-layer acknowledgment schemes below.

Recall from Sections 5.3.2 and 5.4.2 that with Ethernet's collision-detection algorithm, an Ethernet station listens to the channel as it transmits. If, while transmitting, it detects that another station is also transmitting, it aborts its transmission and tries to transmit again after waiting a small, random amount of time. Unlike the 802.3 Ethernet protocol, the 802.11 MAC protocol does *not* implement collision detection. There are two important reasons for this:

- The ability to detect collisions requires the ability to send (the station's own signal) and receive (to determine whether another station is also transmitting) at the same time. Because the strength of the received signal is typically very small compared to the strength of the transmitted signal at the 802.11 adapter, it is costly to build hardware that can detect a collision.

- More importantly, even if the adapter could transmit and listen at the same time (and presumably abort transmission when it senses a busy channel), the adapter would still not be able to detect all collisions, due to the hidden terminal problem and fading, as discussed in Section 6.2.

Because 802.11 wireless LANs do not use collision detection, once a station begins to transmit a frame, *it transmits the frame in its entirety*; that is, once a station gets started, there is no turning back. As one might expect, transmitting entire frames (particularly long frames) when collisions are prevalent can significantly degrade a multiple access protocol's performance. In order to reduce the likelihood of collisions, 802.11 employs several collision-avoidance techniques, which we'll shortly discuss.

Before considering collision avoidance, however, we'll first need to examine 802.11's **link-layer acknowledgment** scheme. Recall from Section 6.2 that when a station in a wireless LAN sends a frame, the frame may not reach the destination station intact for a variety of reasons. To deal with this non-negligible chance of failure, the 802.11 MAC protocol uses link-layer acknowledgments. As shown in Figure 6.10, when the destination station receives a frame that passes the CRC, it waits a short period of time known as the **Short Inter-frame Spacing (SIFS)** and then sends back an acknowledgment frame. If the transmitting station does not receive an acknowledgment within a given amount of time, it assumes that an error has occurred and retransmits the frame, using the CSMA/CA protocol to access the channel. If an acknowledgment is not received after some fixed number of retransmissions, the transmitting station gives up and discards the frame.

Having discussed how 802.11 uses link-layer acknowledgments, we're now in a position to describe the 802.11 CSMA/CA protocol. Suppose that a station (wireless station or an AP) has a frame to transmit.

1. If initially the station senses the channel idle, it transmits its frame after a short period of time known as the **Distributed Inter-frame Space (DIFS)**; see Figure 6.10.

2. Otherwise, the station chooses a random backoff value using binary exponential backoff (as we encountered in Section 5.3.2) and counts down this value when the channel is sensed idle. While the channel is sensed busy, the counter value remains frozen.

3. When the counter reaches zero (note that this can only occur while the channel is sensed idle), the station transmits the entire frame and then waits for an acknowledgment.

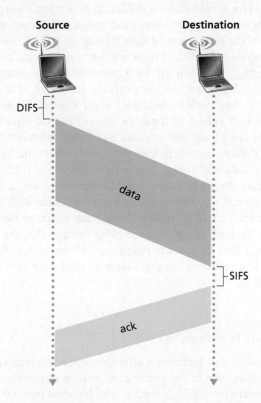

Figure 6.10 ♦ 802.11 uses link-layer acknowledgments

4. If an acknowledgment is received, the transmitting station knows that its frame has been correctly received at the destination station. If the station has another frame to send, it begins the CSMA/CA protocol at step 2. If the acknowledgment isn't received, the transmitting station reenters the backoff phase in step 2, with the random value chosen from a larger interval.

Recall that under Ethernet's CSMA/CD, multiple access protocol (Section 5.3.2), a station begins transmitting as soon as the channel is sensed idle. With CSMA/CA, however, the station refrains from transmitting while counting down, even when it senses the channel to be idle. Why do CSMA/CD and CDMA/CA take such different approaches here?

To answer this question, let's consider a scenario in which two stations each have a data frame to transmit, but neither station transmits immediately because each senses that a third station is already transmitting. With Ethernet's CSMA/CD, the two stations would each transmit as soon as they detect that the third station has finished transmitting. This would cause a collision, which isn't a serious issue in CSMA/CD, since both stations would abort their transmissions and thus avoid the useless transmissions of the remainders of their frames. In 802.11, however, the situation is quite different. Because 802.11 does not detect a collision and abort transmission, a frame suffering a collision will be transmitted in its entirety. The goal in 802.11 is thus to avoid collisions whenever possible. In 802.11, if the two stations sense the channel busy, they both immediately enter random backoff, hopefully choosing different backoff values. If these values are indeed different, once the channel becomes idle, one of the two stations will begin transmitting before the other, and (if the two stations are not hidden from each other) the "losing station" will hear the "winning station's" signal, freeze its counter, and refrain from transmitting until the winning station has completed its transmission. In this manner, a costly collision is avoided. Of course, collisions can still occur with 802.11 in this scenario: The two stations could be hidden from each other, or the two stations could choose random backoff values that are close enough that the transmission from the station starting first have yet to reach the second station. Recall that we encountered this problem earlier in our discussion of random access algorithms in the context of Figure 5.12.

Dealing with Hidden Terminals: RTS and CTS

The 802.11 MAC protocol also includes a nifty (but optional) reservation scheme that helps avoid collisions even in the presence of hidden terminals. Let's investigate this scheme in the context of Figure 6.11, which shows two wireless stations and one access point. Both of the wireless stations are within range of the AP (whose coverage is shown as a shaded circle) and both have associated with the AP. However, due to fading, the signal ranges of wireless stations are limited to the

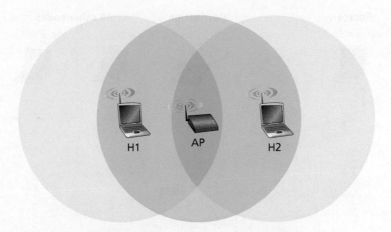

Figure 6.11 ♦ Hidden terminal example: H1 is hidden from H2, and vice versa

interiors of the shaded circles shown in Figure 6.11. Thus, each of the wireless stations is hidden from the other, although neither is hidden from the AP.

Let's now consider why hidden terminals can be problematic. Suppose Station H1 is transmitting a frame and halfway through H1's transmission, Station H2 wants to send a frame to the AP. H2, not hearing the transmission from H1, will first wait a DIFS interval and then transmit the frame, resulting in a collision. The channel will therefore be wasted during the entire period of H1's transmission as well as during H2's transmission.

In order to avoid this problem, the IEEE 802.11 protocol allows a station to use a short **Request to Send (RTS)** control frame and a short **Clear to Send (CTS)** control frame to *reserve* access to the channel. When a sender wants to send a DATA frame, it can first send an RTS frame to the AP, indicating the total time required to transmit the DATA frame and the acknowledgment (ACK) frame. When the AP receives the RTS frame, it responds by broadcasting a CTS frame. This CTS frame serves two purposes: It gives the sender explicit permission to send and also instructs the other stations not to send for the reserved duration.

Thus, in Figure 6.12, before transmitting a DATA frame, H1 first broadcasts an RTS frame, which is heard by all stations in its circle, including the AP. The AP then responds with a CTS frame, which is heard by all stations within its range, including H1 and H2. Station H2, having heard the CTS, refrains from transmitting for the time specified in the CTS frame. The RTS, CTS, DATA, and ACK frames are shown in Figure 6.12.

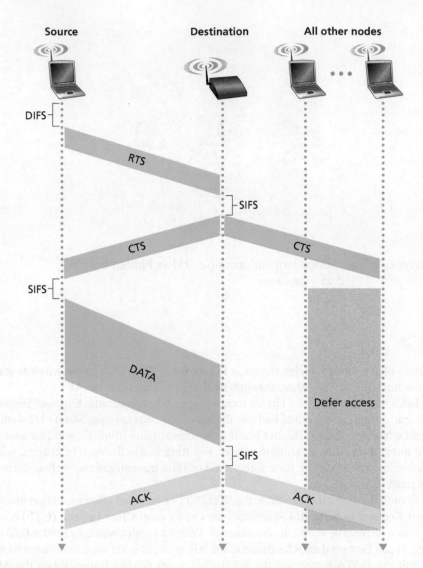

Figure 6.12 ♦ Collision avoidance using the RTS and CTS frames

The use of the RTS and CTS frames can improve performance in two important ways:

- The hidden station problem is mitigated, since a long DATA frame is transmitted only after the channel has been reserved.

- Because the RTS and CTS frames are short, a collision involving an RTS or CTS frame will last only for the duration of the short RTS or CTS frame. Once the RTS and CTS frames are correctly transmitted, the following DATA and ACK frames should be transmitted without collisions.

You are encouraged to check out the 802.11 applet in the textbook's companion Web site. This interactive applet illustrates the CSMA/CA protocol, including the RTS/CTS exchange sequence.

Although the RTS/CTS exchange can help reduce collisions, it also introduces delay and consumes channel resources. For this reason, the RTS/CTS exchange is only used (if at all) to reserve the channel for the transmission of a long DATA frame. In practice, each wireless station can set an RTS threshold such that the RTS/CTS sequence is used only when the frame is longer than the threshold. For many wireless stations, the default RTS threshold value is larger than the maximum frame length, so the RTS/CTS sequence is skipped for all DATA frames sent.

Using 802.11 as a Point-to-Point Link

Our discussion so far has focused on the use of 802.11 in a multiple access setting. We should mention that if two nodes each have a directional antenna, they can point their directional antennas at each other and run the 802.11 protocol over what is essentially a point-to-point link. Given the low cost of commodity 802.11 hardware, the use of directional antennas and an increased transmission power allow 802.11 to be used as an inexpensive means of providing wireless point-to-point connections over tens of kilometers distance. [Raman 2007] describes such a multi-hop wireless network operating in the rural Ganges plains in India that contains point-to-point 802.11 links.

6.3.3 The IEEE 802.11 Frame

Although the 802.11 frame shares many similarities with an Ethernet frame, it also contains a number of fields that are specific to its use for wireless links. The 802.11 frame is shown in Figure 6.13. The numbers above each of the fields in the frame represent the lengths of the fields in *bytes*; the numbers above each of the subfields in the frame control field represent the lengths of the subfields in *bits*. Let's now examine the fields in the frame as well as some of the more important subfields in the frame's control field.

Payload and CRC Fields

At the heart of the frame is the payload, which typically consists of an IP datagram or an ARP packet. Although the field is permitted to be as long as 2,312 bytes, it is

Frame (numbers indicate field length in bytes):

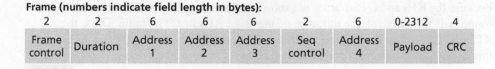

2	2	6	6	6	2	6	0–2312	4
Frame control	Duration	Address 1	Address 2	Address 3	Seq control	Address 4	Payload	CRC

Frame control field expanded (numbers indicate field length in bits):

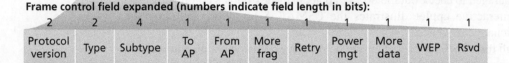

2	2	4	1	1	1	1	1	1	1	1
Protocol version	Type	Subtype	To AP	From AP	More frag	Retry	Power mgt	More data	WEP	Rsvd

Figure 6.13 ♦ The 802.11 frame

typically fewer than 1,500 bytes, holding an IP datagram or an ARP packet. As with an Ethernet frame, an 802.11 frame includes a 32-bit cyclic redundancy check (CRC) so that the receiver can detect bit errors in the received frame. As we've seen, bit errors are much more common in wireless LANs than in wired LANs, so the CRC is even more useful here.

Address Fields

Perhaps the most striking difference in the 802.11 frame is that it has *four* address fields, each of which can hold a 6-byte MAC address. But why four address fields? Doesn't a source MAC field and destination MAC field suffice, as they do for Ethernet? It turns out that three address fields are needed for internetworking purposes—specifically, for moving the network-layer datagram from a wireless station through an AP to a router interface. The fourth address field is used when APs forward frames to each other in ad hoc mode. Since we are only considering infrastructure networks here, let's focus our attention on the first three address fields. The 802.11 standard defines these fields as follows:

- Address 2 is the MAC address of the station that transmits the frame. Thus, if a wireless station transmits the frame, that station's MAC address is inserted in the address 2 field. Similarly, if an AP transmits the frame, the AP's MAC address is inserted in the address 2 field.

- Address 1 is the MAC address of the wireless station that is to receive the frame. Thus if a mobile wireless station transmits the frame, address 1 contains the MAC address of the destination AP. Similarly, if an AP transmits the frame, address 1 contains the MAC address of the destination wireless station.

- To understand address 3, recall that the BSS (consisting of the AP and wireless stations) is part of a subnet, and that this subnet connects to other subnets via some router interface. Address 3 contains the MAC address of this router interface.

   To gain further insight into the purpose of address 3, let's walk through an internetworking example in the context of Figure 6.14. In this figure, there are two APs, each of which is responsible for a number of wireless stations. Each of the APs has a direct connection to a router, which in turn connects to the global Internet. We should keep in mind that an AP is a link-layer device, and thus neither "speaks" IP nor understands IP addresses. Consider now moving a datagram from the router interface R1 to the wireless Station H1. The router is not aware that there is an AP between it and H1; from the router's perspective, H1 is just a host in one of the subnets to which it (the router) is connected.

- The router, which knows the IP address of H1 (from the destination address of the datagram), uses ARP to determine the MAC address of H1, just as in an ordinary Ethernet LAN. After obtaining H1's MAC address, router interface R1 encapsulates the datagram within an Ethernet frame. The source address field of this frame contains R1's MAC address, and the destination address field contains H1's MAC address.

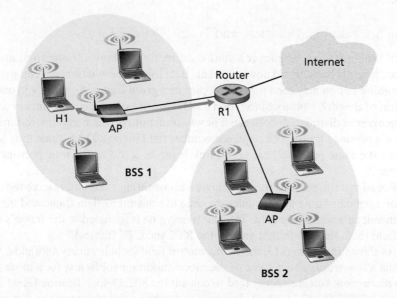

Figure 6.14 ♦ The use of address fields in 802.11 frames: Sending frames between H1 and R1

- When the Ethernet frame arrives at the AP, the AP converts the 802.3 Ethernet frame to an 802.11 frame before transmitting the frame into the wireless channel. The AP fills in address 1 and address 2 with H1's MAC address and its own MAC address, respectively, as described above. For address 3, the AP inserts the MAC address of R1. In this manner, H1 can determine (from address 3) the MAC address of the router interface that sent the datagram into the subnet.

Now consider what happens when the wireless station H1 responds by moving a datagram from H1 to R1.

- H1 creates an 802.11 frame, filling the fields for address 1 and address 2 with the AP's MAC address and H1's MAC address, respectively, as described above. For address 3, H1 inserts R1's MAC address.

- When the AP receives the 802.11 frame, it converts the frame to an Ethernet frame. The source address field for this frame is H1's MAC address, and the destination address field is R1's MAC address. Thus, address 3 allows the AP to determine the appropriate destination MAC address when constructing the Ethernet frame.

In summary, address 3 plays a crucial role for internetworking the BSS with a wired LAN.

Sequence Number, Duration, and Frame Control Fields

Recall that in 802.11, whenever a station correctly receives a frame from another station, it sends back an acknowledgment. Because acknowledgments can get lost, the sending station may send multiple copies of a given frame. As we saw in our discussion of the rdt2.1 protocol (Section 3.4.1), the use of sequence numbers allows the receiver to distinguish between a newly transmitted frame and the retransmission of a previous frame. The sequence number field in the 802.11 frame thus serves exactly the same purpose here at the link layer as it did in the transport layer in Chapter 3.

Recall that the 802.11 protocol allows a transmitting station to reserve the channel for a period of time that includes the time to transmit its data frame and the time to transmit an acknowledgment. This duration value is included in the frame's duration field (both for data frames and for the RTS and CTS frames).

As shown in Figure 6.13, the frame control field includes many subfields. We'll say just a few words about some of the more important subfields; for a more complete discussion, you are encouraged to consult the 802.11 specification [Held 2001; Crow 1997; IEEE 802.11 1999]. The *type* and *subtype* fields are used to distinguish the association, RTS, CTS, ACK, and data frames. The *to* and *from* fields are used to define the meanings of the different address fields. (These meanings change depending on whether ad hoc or infrastructure modes are used and, in the case of infrastructure mode, whether a wireless station or an AP is sending the frame.) Finally the WEP field indicates whether encryption is being used or not. (WEP is discussed in Chapter 8.)

6.3.4 Mobility in the Same IP Subnet

In order to increase the physical range of a wireless LAN, companies and universities will often deploy multiple BSSs within the same IP subnet. This naturally raises the issue of mobility among the BSSs—how do wireless stations seamlessly move from one BSS to another while maintaining ongoing TCP sessions? As we'll see in this sub-section, mobility can be handled in a relatively straightforward manner when the BSSs are part of the subnet. When stations move between subnets, more sophisticated mobility management protocols will be needed, such as those we'll study in Sections 6.5 and 6.6.

Let's now look at a specific example of mobility between BSSs in the same subnet. Figure 6.15 shows two interconnected BSSs with a host, H1, moving from BSS1 to BSS2. Because in this example the interconnection device that connects the two BSSs is *not* a router, all of the stations in the two BSSs, including the APs, belong to the same IP subnet. Thus, when H1 moves from BSS1 to BSS2, it may keep its IP address and all of its ongoing TCP connections. If the interconnection device were a router, then H1 would have to obtain a new IP address in the subnet in which it was moving. This address change would disrupt (and eventually terminate) any on-going TCP connections at H1. In Section 6.6, we'll see how a network-layer mobility protocol, such as mobile IP, can be used to avoid this problem.

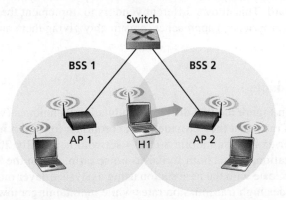

Figure 6.15 ♦ Mobility in the same subnet

But what specifically happens when H1 moves from BSS1 to BSS2? As H1 wanders away from AP1, H1 detects a weakening signal from AP1 and starts to scan for a stronger signal. H1 receives beacon frames from AP2 (which in many corporate and university settings will have the same SSID as AP1). H1 then disassociates with AP1 and associates with AP2, while keeping its IP address and maintaining its ongoing TCP sessions.

This addresses the handoff problem from the host and AP viewpoint. But what about the switch in Figure 6.15? How does it know that the host has moved from one AP to another? As you may recall from Chapter 5, switches are "self-learning" and automatically build their forwarding tables. This self-learning feature nicely handles occasional moves (for example, when an employee gets transferred from one department to another); however, switches were not designed to support highly mobile users who want to maintain TCP connections while moving between BSSs. To appreciate the problem here, recall that before the move, the switch has an entry in its forwarding table that pairs H1's MAC address with the outgoing switch interface through which H1 can be reached. If H1 is initially in BSS1, then a datagram destined to H1 will be directed to H1 via AP1. Once H1 associates with BSS2, however, its frames should be directed to AP2. One solution (a bit of a hack, really) is for AP2 to send a broadcast Ethernet frame with H1's source address to the switch just after the new association. When the switch receives the frame, it updates its forwarding table, allowing H1 to be reached via AP2. The 802.11f standards group is developing an inter-AP protocol to handle these and related issues.

6.3.5 Advanced Features in 802.11

We'll wrap up our coverage of 802.11 with a short discussion of two advanced capabilities found in 802.11 networks. As we'll see, these capabilities are *not* completely specified in the 802.11 standard, but rather are made possible by mechanisms specified in the standard. This allows different vendors to implement these capabilities using their own (proprietary) approaches, presumably giving them an edge over the competition.

802.11 Rate Adaptation

We saw earlier in Figure 6.3 that different modulation techniques (with the different transmission rates that they provide) are appropriate for different SNR scenarios. Consider for example a mobile 802.11 user who is initially 20 meters away from the base station, with a high signal-to-noise ratio. Given the high SNR, the user can communicate with the base station using a physical-layer modulation technique that provides high transmission rates while maintaining a low BER. This is one happy user! Suppose now that the user becomes mobile, walking away from the base station, with the SNR falling as the distance from the base station increases. In this case, if the modulation technique used in the 802.11 protocol operating between the base station and the user does not change, the BER will become unacceptably high as the SNR decreases, and eventually no transmitted frames will be received correctly.

For this reason, some 802.11 implementations have a rate adaptation capability that adaptively selects the underlying physical-layer modulation technique to use based on current or recent channel characteristics. If a node sends two frames in a row without receiving an acknowledgment (an implicit indication of bit errors on the channel), the transmission rate falls back to the next lower rate. If 10 frames in a row are acknowledged, or if a timer that tracks the time since the last fallback expires, the transmission rate increases to the next higher rate. This rate adaptation mechanism shares the same "probing" philosophy as TCP's congestion-control mechanism—when conditions are good (reflected by ACK receipts), the transmission rate is increased until something "bad" happens (the lack of ACK receipts); when something "bad" happens, the transmission rate is reduced. 802.11 rate adaptation and TCP congestion control are thus similar to the young child who is constantly pushing his/her parents for more and more (say candy for a young child, later curfew hours for the teenager) until the parents finally say "Enough!" and the child backs off (only to try again later after conditions have hopefully improved!). A number of other schemes have also been proposed to improve on this basic automatic rate-adjustment scheme [Kamerman 1997; Holland 2001; Lacage 2004].

Power Management

Power is a precious resource in mobile devices, and thus the 802.11 standard provides power-management capabilities that allow 802.11 nodes to minimize the amount of time that their sense, transmit, and receive functions and other circuitry need to be "on." 802.11 power management operates as follows. A node is able to explicitly alternate between sleep and wake states (not unlike a sleepy student in a classroom!). A node indicates to the access point that it will be going to sleep by setting the power-management bit in the header of an 802.11 frame to 1. A timer in the node is then set to wake up the node just before the AP is scheduled to send its beacon frame (recall that an AP typically sends a beacon frame every 100 msec). Since the AP knows from the set power-transmission bit that the node is going to sleep, it (the AP) knows that it should not send any frames to that node, and will buffer any frames destined for the sleeping host for later transmission.

A node will wake up just before the AP sends a beacon frame, and quickly enter the fully active state (unlike the sleepy student, this wakeup requires only 250 microseconds [Kamerman 1997]!). The beacon frames sent out by the AP contain a list of nodes whose frames have been buffered at the AP. If there are no buffered frames for the node, it can go back to sleep. Otherwise, the node can explicitly request that the buffered frames be sent by sending a polling message to the AP. With an inter-beacon time of 100 msec, a wakeup time of 250 microseconds, and a similarly small time to receive a beacon frame and check to ensure that there are no buffered frames, a node that has no frames to send or receive can be asleep 99% of the time, resulting in a significant energy savings.

6.3.6 Personal Area Networks: Bluetooth and Zigbee

As illustrated in Figure 6.2, the IEEE 802.11 WiFi standard is aimed at communication among devices separated by up to 100 meters (except when 802.11 is used in a point-to-point configuration with a directional antenna). Two other IEEE 802 protocols—Bluetooth and Zigbee (defined in the IEEE 802.15.1 and IEEE 802.15.4 standards [IEEE 802.15 2012]) and WiMAX (defined in the IEEE 802.16 standard [IEEE 802.16d 2004; IEEE 802.16e 2005])—are standards for communicating over shorter and longer distances, respectively. We will touch on WiMAX briefly when we discuss cellular data networks in Section 6.4, and so here, we will focus on networks for shorter distances.

Bluetooth

An IEEE 802.15.1 network operates over a short range, at low power, and at low cost. It is essentially a low-power, short-range, low-rate "cable replacement" technology for interconnecting notebooks, peripheral devices, cellular phones, and smartphones, whereas 802.11 is a higher-power, medium-range, higher-rate "access" technology. For this reason, 802.15.1 networks are sometimes referred to as wireless personal area networks (WPANs). The link and physical layers of 802.15.1 are based on the earlier **Bluetooth** specification for personal area networks [Held 2001, Bisdikian 2001]. 802.15.1 networks operate in the 2.4 GHz unlicensed radio band in a TDM manner, with time slots of 625 microseconds. During each time slot, a sender transmits on one of 79 channels, with the channel changing in a known but pseudorandom manner from slot to slot. This form of channel hopping, known as **frequency-hopping spread spectrum (FHSS),** spreads transmissions in time over the frequency spectrum. 802.15.1 can provide data rates up to 4 Mbps.

802.15.1 networks are ad hoc networks: No network infrastructure (e.g., an access point) is needed to interconnect 802.15.1 devices. Thus, 802.15.1 devices must organize themselves. 802.15.1 devices are first organized into a **piconet** of up to eight active devices, as shown in Figure 6.16. One of these devices is designated as the master, with the remaining devices acting as slaves. The master node truly rules the piconet—its clock determines time in the piconet, it can transmit in each odd-numbered slot, and a slave can transmit only after the master has communicated with it in the previous slot and even then the slave can only transmit to the master. In addition to the slave devices, there can also be up to 255 parked devices in the

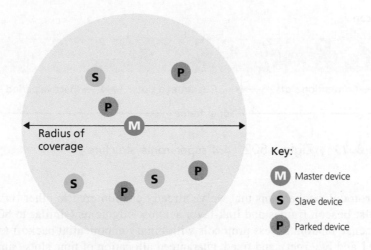

Figure 6.16 ♦ A Bluetooth piconet

network. These devices cannot communicate until their status has been changed from parked to active by the master node.

For more information about 802.15.1 WPANs, the interested reader should consult the Bluetooth references [Held 2001, Bisdikian 2001] or the official IEEE 802.15 Web site [IEEE 802.15 2012].

Zigbee

A second personal area network standardized by the IEEE is the 802.14.5 standard [IEEE 802.15 2012] known as Zigbee. While Bluetooth networks provide a "cable replacement" data rate of over a Megabit per second, Zigbee is targeted at lower-powered, lower-data-rate, lower-duty-cycle applications than Bluetooth. While we may tend to think that "bigger and faster is better," not all network applications need high bandwidth and the consequent higher costs (both economic and power costs). For example, home temperature and light sensors, security devices, and wall-mounted switches are all very simple, low-power, low-duty-cycle, low-cost devices. Zigbee is thus well-suited for these devices. Zigbee defines channel rates of 20, 40, 100, and 250 Kbps, depending on the channel frequency.

Nodes in a Zigbee network come in two flavors. So-called "reduced-function devices" operate as slave devices under the control of a single "full-function device," much as Bluetooth slave devices. A full-function device can operate as a master device as in Bluetooth by controlling multiple slave devices, and multiple full-function devices can additionally be configured into a mesh network in which full-function devices route frames amongst themselves. Zigbee shares

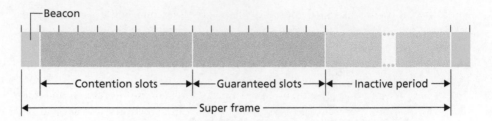

Figure 6.17 ♦ Zigbee 802.14.4 super-frame structure

many protocol mechanisms that we've already encountered in other link-layer protocols: beacon frames and link-layer acknowledgments (similar to 802.11), carrier-sense random access protocols with binary exponential backoff (similar to 802.11 and Ethernet), and fixed, guaranteed allocation of time slots (similar to DOCSIS).

Zigbee networks can be configured in many different ways. Let's consider the simple case of a single full-function device controlling multiple reduced-function devices in a time-slotted manner using beacon frames. Figure 6.17 shows the case where the Zigbee network divides time into recurring super frames, each of which begins with a beacon frame. Each beacon frame divides the super frame into an active period (during which devices may transmit) and an inactive period (during which all devices, including the controller, can sleep and thus conserve power). The active period consists of 16 time slots, some of which are used by devices in a CSMA/CA random access manner, and some of which are allocated by the controller to specific devices, thus providing guaranteed channel access for those devices. More details about Zigbee networks can be found at [Baronti 2007, IEEE 802.15.4 2012].

6.4 Cellular Internet Access

In the previous section we examined how an Internet host can access the Internet when inside a WiFi hotspot—that is, when it is within the vicinity of an 802.11 access point. But most WiFi hotspots have a small coverage area of between 10 and 100 meters in diameter. What do we do then when we have a desperate need for wireless Internet access and we cannot access a WiFi hotspot?

Given that cellular telephony is now ubiquitous in many areas throughout the world, a natural strategy is to extend cellular networks so that they support not only voice telephony but wireless Internet access as well. Ideally, this Internet access would be at a reasonably high speed and would provide for seamless mobility, allowing users to maintain their TCP sessions while traveling, for example, on a bus or a train. With sufficiently high upstream and downstream bit rates, the user could even maintain video-conferencing sessions while roaming about. This scenario is not that far-fetched. As of 2012, many cellular telephony providers in the U.S. offer their subscribers a cellular Internet access service for under $50 per month with typical downstream and upstream bit rates in the hundreds of kilobits per second. Data rates of several megabits per second are becoming available as broadband data services such as those we will cover here become more widely deployed.

In this section, we provide a brief overview of current and emerging cellular Internet access technologies. Our focus here will be on both the wireless first hop as well as the network that connects the wireless first hop into the larger telephone network and/or the Internet; in Section 6.7 we'll consider how calls are routed to a user moving between base stations. Our brief discussion will necessarily provide only a simplified and high-level description of cellular technologies. Modern cellular communications, of course, has great breadth and depth, with many universities offering several courses on the topic. Readers seeking a deeper understanding are encouraged to see [Goodman 1997; Kaaranen 2001; Lin 2001; Korhonen 2003; Schiller 2003; Scourias 2012; Turner 2012; Akyildiz 2010], as well as the particularly excellent and exhaustive reference [Mouly 1992].

6.4.1 An Overview of Cellular Network Architecture

In our description of cellular network architecture in this section, we'll adopt the terminology of the *Global System for Mobile Communications (GSM)* standards. (For history buffs, the GSM acronym was originally derived from *Groupe Spécial Mobile*, until the more anglicized name was adopted, preserving the original acronym letters.) In the 1980s, Europeans recognized the need for a pan-European digital cellular telephony system that would replace the numerous incompatible analog cellular telephony systems, leading to the GSM standard [Mouly 1992]. Europeans deployed GSM technology with great success in the early 1990s, and since then GSM has grown to be the 800-pound gorilla of the cellular telephone world, with more than 80% of all cellular subscribers worldwide using GSM.

When people talk about cellular technology, they often classify the technology as belonging to one of several "generations." The earliest generations were designed primarily for voice traffic. First generation (1G) systems were analog FDMA systems designed exclusively for voice-only communication. These 1G systems are almost extinct now, having been replaced by digital 2G systems. The original 2G systems were also designed for voice, but later extended (2.5G) to support data (i.e., Internet) as well as voice service. The 3G systems that currently are being deployed also support voice and data, but with an ever increasing emphasis on data capabilities and higher-speed radio access links.

CASE HISTORY

3G CELLULAR MOBILE VERSUS WIRELESS LANS

Many cellular mobile phone operators are deploying 3G cellular mobile systems with indoor data rates of 2 Mbps and outdoor data rates of 384 kbps and higher. These 3G systems are being deployed in licensed radio-frequency bands, with some operators paying considerable sums to governments for spectrum-use licenses. 3G systems allow users to access the Internet from remote outdoor locations while on the move, in a manner similar to today's cellular phone access. For example, 3G technology permits a user to access road map information while driving a car, or movie theater information while sunbathing on a beach. Nevertheless, one may question the extent to which 3G systems will be used, given their cost and the fact that users may often have simultaneous access to both wireless LANs and 3G:

- The emerging wireless LAN infrastructure may become nearly ubiquitous. IEEE 802.11 wireless LANs, operating at 54 Mbps, are enjoying widespread deployment. Almost all portable computers and smartphones are factory-equipped with 802.11 LAN capabilities. Furthermore, emerging Internet appliances—such as wireless cameras and picture frames—will also have small and low-powered wireless LAN capabilities.

- Wireless LAN base stations can also handle mobile phone appliances. Many phones are already capable of connecting to the cellular phone network or to an IP network either natively or using a Skype-like Voice-over-IP service, thus bypassing the operator's cellular voice and 3G data services.

Of course, many other experts believe that 3G not only will be a major success, but will also dramatically revolutionize the way we work and live. Most likely, both WiFi and 3G will both become prevalent wireless technologies, with roaming wireless devices automatically selecting the access technology that provides the best service at their current physical location.

Cellular Network Architecture, 2G: Voice Connections to the Telephone Network

The term *cellular* refers to the fact that the region covered by a cellular network is partitioned into a number of geographic coverage areas, known as **cells**, shown as hexagons on the left side of Figure 6.18. As with the 802.11WiFi standard we studied in Section 6.3.1, GSM has its own particular nomenclature. Each cell contains a **base transceiver station (BTS)** that transmits signals to and receives signals from the mobile stations in its cell. The coverage area of a cell depends on many factors, including the transmitting power of the BTS, the transmitting power of the user devices, obstructing buildings in the cell, and the height of base station antennas. Although Figure 6.18 shows each cell containing one base transceiver station residing in the middle of the cell, many systems today place the BTS at corners where three cells intersect, so that a single BTS with directional antennas can service three cells.

The GSM standard for 2G cellular systems uses combined FDM/TDM (radio) for the air interface. Recall from Chapter 1 that, with pure FDM, the channel is partitioned into a number of frequency bands with each band devoted to a call. Also recall from Chapter 1 that, with pure TDM, time is partitioned into frames with each frame further partitioned into slots and each call being assigned the use of a particular slot in the revolving frame. In combined FDM/TDM systems, the channel is partitioned into a number of frequency sub-bands; within each sub-band, time is partitioned into frames and slots. Thus, for a combined FDM/TDM system, if the channel is partitioned into F sub-bands and time is partitioned into T slots, then

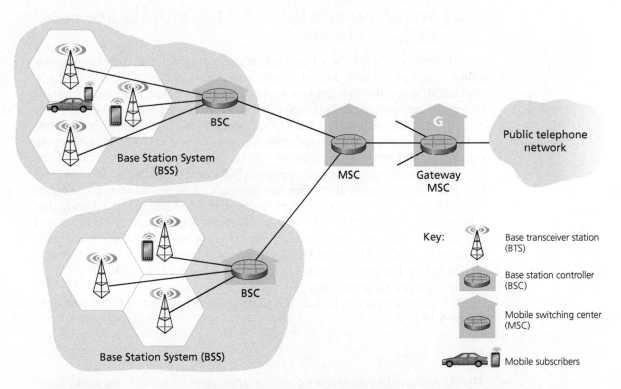

Figure 6.18 ♦ Components of the GSM 2G cellular network architecture

the channel will be able to support $F \cdot T$ simultaneous calls. Recall that we saw in Section 5.3.4 that cable access networks also use a combined FDM/TDM approach. GSM systems consist of 200-kHz frequency bands with each band supporting eight TDM calls. GSM encodes speech at 13 kbps and 12.2 kbps.

A GSM network's **base station controller (BSC)** will typically service several tens of base transceiver stations. The role of the BSC is to allocate BTS radio channels to mobile subscribers, perform **paging** (finding the cell in which a mobile user is resident), and perform handoff of mobile users—a topic we'll cover shortly in Section 6.7.2. The base station controller and its controlled base transceiver stations collectively constitute a GSM **base station system (BSS)**.

As we'll see in Section 6.7, the **mobile switching center (MSC)** plays the central role in user authorization and accounting (e.g., determining whether a mobile device is allowed to connect to the cellular network), call establishment and teardown, and handoff. A single MSC will typically contain up to five BSCs, resulting in approximately 200K subscribers per MSC. A cellular provider's network will have a number of MSCs, with special MSCs known as gateway MSCs connecting the provider's cellular network to the larger public telephone network.

6.4.2 3G Cellular Data Networks: Extending the Internet to Cellular Subscribers

Our discussion in Section 6.4.1 focused on connecting cellular voice users to the public telephone network. But, of course, when we're on the go, we'd also like to read email, access the Web, get location-dependent services (e.g., maps and restaurant recommendations) and perhaps even watch streaming video. To do this, our smartphone will need to run a full TCP/IP protocol stack (including the physical link, network, transport, and application layers) and connect into the Internet via the cellular data network. The topic of cellular data networks is a rather bewildering collection of competing and ever-evolving standards as one generation (and half-generation) succeeds the former and introduces new technologies and services with new acronyms. To make matters worse, there's no single official body that sets requirements for 2.5G, 3G, 3.5G, or 4G technologies, making it hard to sort out the differences among competing standards. In our discussion below, we'll focus on the UMTS (Universal Mobile Telecommunications Service) 3G standards developed by the 3rd Generation Partnership project (3GPP) [3GPP 2012], a widely deployed 3G technology.

Let's take a top-down look at 3G cellular data network architecture shown in Figure 6.19.

3G Core Network

The 3G core cellular data network connects radio access networks to the public Internet. The core network interoperates with components of the existing cellular voice

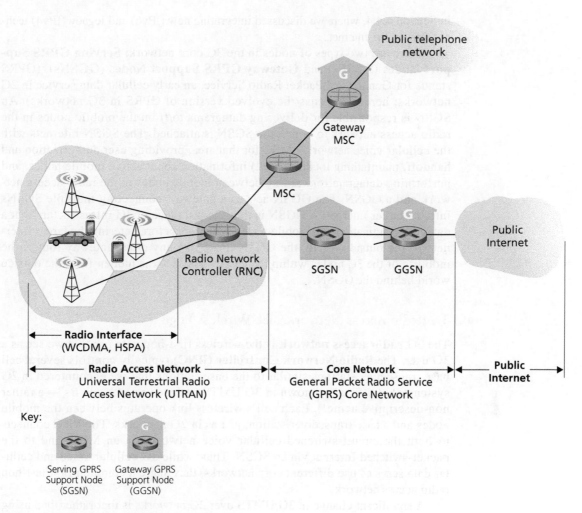

Public telephone network

Gateway MSC

MSC

Radio Network Controller (RNC)

SGSN

GGSN

Public Internet

Radio Interface
(WCDMA, HSPA)

Radio Access Network
Universal Terrestrial Radio Access Network (UTRAN)

Core Network
General Packet Radio Service (GPRS) Core Network

Public Internet

Key:

Serving GPRS Support Node (SGSN)

Gateway GPRS Support Node (GGSN)

Figure 6.19 ♦ 3G system architecture

network (in particular, the MSC) that we previously encountered in Figure 6.18. Given the considerable amount of existing infrastructure (and profitable services!) in the existing cellular voice network, the approach taken by the designers of 3G data services is clear: *leave the existing core GSM cellular voice network untouched, adding additional cellular data functionality in parallel to the existing cellular voice network*. The alternative—integrating new data services directly into the core of the existing cellular voice network—would have raised the same challenges encountered in Section 4.4.4, where we discussed integrating new (IPv6) and legacy (IPv4) technologies in the Internet.

There are two types of nodes in the 3G core network: **Serving GPRS Support Nodes (SGSNs)** and **Gateway GPRS Support Nodes (GGSNs)**. (GPRS stands for Generalized Packet Radio Service, an early cellular data service in 2G networks; here we discuss the evolved version of GPRS in 3G networks). An SGSN is responsible for delivering datagrams to/from the mobile nodes in the radio access network to which the SGSN is attached. The SGSN interacts with the cellular voice network's MSC for that area, providing user authorization and handoff, maintaining location (cell) information about active mobile nodes, and performing datagram forwarding between mobile nodes in the radio access network and a GGSN. The GGSN acts as a gateway, connecting multiple SGSNs into the larger Internet. A GGSN is thus the last piece of 3G infrastructure that a datagram originating at a mobile node encounters before entering the larger Internet. To the outside world, the GGSN looks like any other gateway router; the mobility of the 3G nodes within the GGSN's network is hidden from the outside world behind the GGSN.

3G Radio Access Network: The Wireless Edge

The 3G **radio access network** is the wireless first-hop network that we see as a 3G user. The **Radio Network Controller (RNC)** typically controls several cell base transceiver stations similar to the base stations that we encountered in 2G systems (but officially known in 3G UMTS parlance as a "Node Bs"—a rather non-descriptive name!). Each cell's wireless link operates between the mobile nodes and a base transceiver station, just as in 2G networks. The RNC connects to both the circuit-switched cellular voice network via an MSC, and to the packet-switched Internet via an SGSN. Thus, while 3G cellular voice and cellular data services use different core networks, they share a common first/last-hop radio access network.

A significant change in 3G UMTS over 2G networks is that rather than using GSM's FDMA/TDMA scheme, UMTS uses a CDMA technique known as Direct Sequence Wideband CDMA (DS-WCDMA) [Dahlman 1998] within TDMA slots; TDMA slots, in turn, are available on multiple frequencies—an interesting use of all three dedicated channel-sharing approaches that we earlier identified in Chapter 5 and similar to the approach taken in wired cable access networks (see Section 5.3.4). This change requires a new 3G cellular wireless-access network operating in parallel with the 2G BSS radio network shown in Figure 6.19. The data service associated with the WCDMA specification is known as HSP (High Speed Packet Access) and promises downlink data rates of up to 14 Mbps. Details regarding 3G networks can be found at the 3rd Generation Partnership Project (3GPP) Web site [3GPP 2012].

6.4.3 On to 4G: LTE

With 3G systems now being deployed worldwide, can 4G systems be far behind? Certainly not! Indeed, the design, early testing, and initial deployment of 4G systems are already underway. The 4G Long-Term Evolution (LTE) standard put forward by the 3GPP has two important innovations over 3G systems:

* **Evolved Packet Core (EPC)** [3GPP Network Architecture 2012]. The EPC is a simplified all-IP core network that unifies the separate circuit-switched cellular voice network and the packet-switched cellular data network shown in Figure 6.19. It is an "all-IP" network in that both voice and data will be carried in IP datagrams. As we've seen in Chapter 4 and will study in more detail in Chapter 7, IP's "best effort" service model is not inherently well-suited to the stringent performance requirements of Voice-over-IP (VoIP) traffic unless network resources are carefully managed to avoid (rather than react to) congestion. Thus, a key task of the EPC is to manage network resources to provide this high quality of service. The EPC also makes a clear separation between the network control and user data planes, with many of the mobility support features that we will study in Section 6.7 being implemented in the control plane. The EPC allows multiple types of radio access networks, including legacy 2G and 3G radio access networks, to attach to the core network. Two very readable introductions to the EPC are [Motorola 2007; Alcatel-Lucent 2009].

* **LTE Radio Access Network.** LTE uses a combination of frequency division multiplexing and time division multiplexing on the downstream channel, known as orthogonal frequency division multiplexing (OFDM) [Rohde 2008; Ericsson 2011]. (The term "orthogonal" comes from the fact the signals being sent on different frequency channels are created so that they interfere very little with each other, even when channel frequencies are tightly spaced). In LTE, each active mobile node is allocated one or more 0.5 ms time slots in one or more of the channel frequencies. Figure 6.20 shows an allocation of eight time slots over four frequencies. By being allocated increasingly more time slots (whether on the same frequency or on different frequencies), a mobile node is able to achieve increasingly higher transmission rates. Slot (re)allocation among mobile nodes can be performed as often as once every millisecond. Different modulation schemes can also be used to change the transmission rate; see our earlier discussion of Figure 6.3 and dynamic selection of modulation schemes in WiFi networks. Another innovation in the LTE radio network is the use of sophisticated multiple-input, multiple output (MIMO) antennas. The maximum data rate for an LTE user is 100 Mbps in the downstream direction and 50 Mbps in the upstream direction, when using 20 MHz worth of wireless spectrum.

The particular allocation of time slots to mobile nodes is not mandated by the LTE standard. Instead, the decision of which mobile nodes will be allowed to transmit in a given time slot on a given frequency is determined by the scheduling algorithms provided by the LTE equipment vendor and/or the network operator. With opportunistic scheduling [Bender 2000; Kolding 2003; Kulkarni 2005], matching the physical-layer protocol to the channel conditions between the sender and receiver and choosing the receivers to which packets will be sent based on channel conditions allow the radio network controller to make best use of the wireless medium. In addition, user priorities and contracted levels of service (e.g., silver, gold, or platinum) can be used in scheduling downstream packet transmissions. In addition to the LTE capabilities described above, LTE-Advanced allows for downstream bandwidths of hundreds of Mbps by allocating aggregated channels to a mobile node [Akyildiz 2010].

An additional 4G wireless technology—WiMAX (World Interoperability for Microwave Access)—is a family of IEEE 802.16 standards that differ significantly from LTE. Whether LTE or WiMAX becomes the 4G technology of choice is still to be seen, but at the time of this writing (spring 2012), LTE appears to have significantly more momentum. A detailed discussion of WiMAX can be found on this book's Web site.

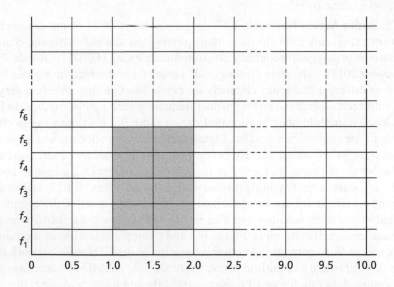

Figure 6.20 ♦ Twenty 0.5 ms slots organized into 10 ms frames at each frequency. An eight-slot allocation is shown shaded

6.5 Mobility Management: Principles

Having covered the *wireless* nature of the communication links in a wireless network, it's now time to turn our attention to the *mobility* that these wireless links enable. In the broadest sense, a mobile node is one that changes its point of attachment into the network over time. Because the term *mobility* has taken on many meanings in both the computer and telephony worlds, it will serve us well first to consider several dimensions of mobility in some detail.

• *From the network layer's standpoint, how mobile is a user?* A physically mobile user will present a very different set of challenges to the network layer, depending on how he or she moves between points of attachment to the network. At one end of the spectrum in Figure 6.21, a user may carry a laptop with a wireless network interface card around in a building. As we saw in Section 6.3.4, this user is *not* mobile from a network-layer perspective. Moreover, if the user associates with the same access point regardless of location, the user is not even mobile from the perspective of the link layer.

At the other end of the spectrum, consider the user zooming along the autobahn in a BMW at 150 kilometers per hour, passing through multiple wireless access networks and wanting to maintain an uninterrupted TCP connection to a remote application throughout the trip. This user is *definitely* mobile! In between these extremes is a user who takes a laptop from one location (e.g., office or dormitory) into another (e.g., coffeeshop, classroom) and wants to connect into the network in the new location. This user is also mobile (although less so than the BMW driver!) but does not need to maintain an ongoing connection while moving between points of attachment to the network. Figure 6.21 illustrates this spectrum of user mobility from the network layer's perspective.

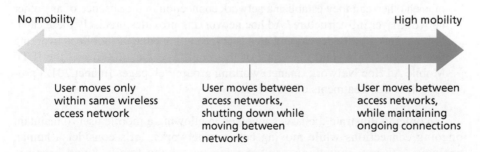

Figure 6.21 ♦ Various degrees of mobility, from the network layer's point of view

* *How important is it for the mobile node's address to always remain the same?* With mobile telephony, your phone number—essentially the network-layer address of your phone—remains the same as you travel from one provider's mobile phone network to another. Must a laptop similarly maintain the same IP address while moving between IP networks?

The answer to this question will depend strongly on the applications being run. For the BMW driver who wants to maintain an uninterrupted TCP connection to a remote application while zipping along the autobahn, it would be convenient to maintain the same IP address. Recall from Chapter 3 that an Internet application needs to know the IP address and port number of the remote entity with which it is communicating. If a mobile entity is able to maintain its IP address as it moves, mobility becomes invisible from the application standpoint. There is great value to this transparency—an application need not be concerned with a potentially changing IP address, and the same application code serves mobile and nonmobile connections alike. We'll see in the following section that mobile IP provides this transparency, allowing a mobile node to maintain its permanent IP address while moving among networks.

On the other hand, a less glamorous mobile user might simply want to turn off an office laptop, bring that laptop home, power up, and work from home. If the laptop functions primarily as a client in client-server applications (e.g., send/read e-mail, browse the Web, Telnet to a remote host) from home, the particular IP address used by the laptop is not that important. In particular, one could get by fine with an address that is temporarily allocated to the laptop by the ISP serving the home. We saw in Section 4.4 that DHCP already provides this functionality.

* *What supporting wired infrastructure is available?* In all of our scenarios above, we've implicitly assumed that there is a fixed infrastructure to which the mobile user can connect—for example, the home's ISP network, the wireless access network in the office, or the wireless access networks lining the autobahn. What if no such infrastructure exists? If two users are within communication proximity of each other, can they establish a network connection in the absence of any other network-layer infrastructure? Ad hoc networking provides precisely these capabilities. This rapidly developing area is at the cutting edge of mobile networking research and is beyond the scope of this book. [Perkins 2000] and the IETF Mobile Ad Hoc Network (manet) working group Web pages [manet 2012] provide thorough treatments of the subject.

In order to illustrate the issues involved in allowing a mobile user to maintain ongoing connections while moving between networks, let's consider a human analogy. A twenty-something adult moving out of the family home becomes mobile, living in a series of dormitories and/or apartments, and often changing addresses. If an old friend wants to get in touch, how can that friend find the address of her mobile friend? One common way is to contact the family, since a mobile adult will often register his or her current address with the family (if for no other reason than so that the parents can send money to help pay the rent!). The family home, with its permanent address, becomes that one place that others can go as a first step in communicating with the mobile adult. Later communication from the friend may be either indirect (for example, with mail being sent first to the parents' home and then forwarded to the mobile adult) or direct (for example, with the friend using the address obtained from the parents to send mail directly to her mobile friend).

In a network setting, the permanent home of a mobile node (such as a laptop or smartphone) is known as the **home network**, and the entity within the home network that performs the mobility management functions discussed below on behalf of the mobile node is known as the **home agent**. The network in which the mobile node is currently residing is known as the **foreign** (or **visited**) **network**, and the entity within the foreign network that helps the mobile node with the mobility management functions discussed below is known as a **foreign agent**. For mobile professionals, their home network might likely be their company network, while the visited network might be the network of a colleague they are visiting. A **correspondent** is the entity wishing to communicate with the mobile node. Figure 6.22 illustrates these concepts, as well as addressing concepts considered below. In Figure 6.22, note that agents are shown as being collocated with routers (e.g., as processes running on routers), but alternatively they could be executing on other hosts or servers in the network.

6.5.1 Addressing

We noted above that in order for user mobility to be transparent to network applications, it is desirable for a mobile node to keep its address as it moves from one network to another. When a mobile node is resident in a foreign network, all traffic addressed to the node's permanent address now needs to be routed to the foreign network. How can this be done? One option is for the foreign network to advertise to all other networks that the mobile node is resident in its network. This could be via the usual exchange of intradomain and interdomain routing information and would require few changes to the existing routing infrastructure. The foreign network could simply advertise to its neighbors that it has a highly specific route to the mobile node's permanent address (that is, essentially inform other networks that it has the correct path for routing datagrams to the mobile node's permanent address; see Section 4.4). These neighbors would then propagate this routing information throughout the network as part of the normal procedure of updating routing information and forwarding tables. When the mobile node leaves one foreign network and joins another, the new foreign network would advertise a new, highly specific route to the mobile node, and the old foreign network would withdraw its routing information regarding the mobile node.

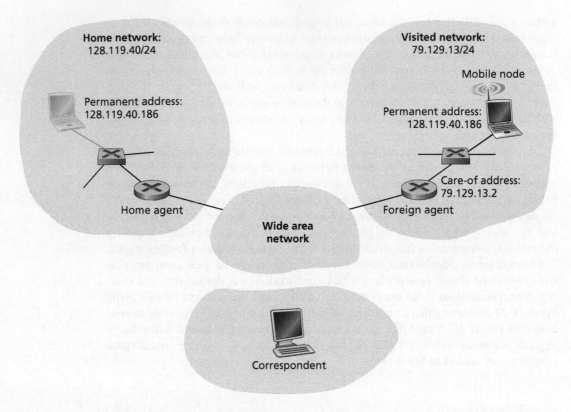

Figure 6.22 ♦ Initial elements of a mobile network architecture

This solves two problems at once, and it does so without making significant changes to the network-layer infrastructure. Other networks know the location of the mobile node, and it is easy to route datagrams to the mobile node, since the forwarding tables will direct datagrams to the foreign network. A significant drawback, however, is that of scalability. If mobility management were to be the responsibility of network routers, the routers would have to maintain forwarding table entries for potentially millions of mobile nodes, and update these entries as nodes move. Some additional drawbacks are explored in the problems at the end of this chapter.

An alternative approach (and one that has been adopted in practice) is to push mobility functionality from the network core to the network edge—a recurring theme in our study of Internet architecture. A natural way to do this is via the mobile node's home network. In much the same way that parents of the mobile twenty-something track their child's location, the home agent in the mobile node's home network can track the foreign network in which the mobile node resides. A protocol between the mobile node (or a foreign agent representing the mobile node) and the home agent will certainly be needed to update the mobile node's location.

Let's now consider the foreign agent in more detail. The conceptually simplest approach, shown in Figure 6.22, is to locate foreign agents at the edge routers in the foreign network. One role of the foreign agent is to create a so-called **care-of address (COA)** for the mobile node, with the network portion of the COA matching that of the foreign network. There are thus two addresses associated with a mobile node, its **permanent address** (analogous to our mobile youth's family's home address) and its COA, sometimes known as a **foreign address** (analogous to the address of the house in which our mobile youth is currently residing). In the example in Figure 6.22, the permanent address of the mobile node is 128.119.40.186. When visiting network 79.129.13/24, the mobile node has a COA of 79.129.13.2. A second role of the foreign agent is to inform the home agent that the mobile node is resident in its (the foreign agent's) network and has the given COA. We'll see shortly that the COA will be used to "reroute" datagrams to the mobile node via its foreign agent.

Although we have separated the functionality of the mobile node and the foreign agent, it is worth noting that the mobile node can also assume the responsibilities of the foreign agent. For example, the mobile node could obtain a COA in the foreign network (for example, using a protocol such as DHCP) and itself inform the home agent of its COA.

6.5.2 Routing to a Mobile Node

We have now seen how a mobile node obtains a COA and how the home agent can be informed of that address. But having the home agent know the COA solves only part of the problem. How should datagrams be addressed and forwarded to the mobile node? Since only the home agent (and not network-wide routers) knows the location of the mobile node, it will no longer suffice to simply address a datagram to the mobile node's permanent address and send it into the network-layer infrastructure. Something more must be done. Two approaches can be identified, which we will refer to as indirect and direct routing.

Indirect Routing to a Mobile Node

Let's first consider a correspondent that wants to send a datagram to a mobile node. In the **indirect routing** approach, the correspondent simply addresses the datagram to the mobile node's permanent address and sends the datagram into the network, blissfully unaware of whether the mobile node is resident in its home network or is visiting a foreign network; mobility is thus completely transparent to the correspondent. Such datagrams are first routed, as usual, to the mobile node's home network. This is illustrated in step 1 in Figure 6.23.

Let's now turn our attention to the home agent. In addition to being responsible for interacting with a foreign agent to track the mobile node's COA, the home agent

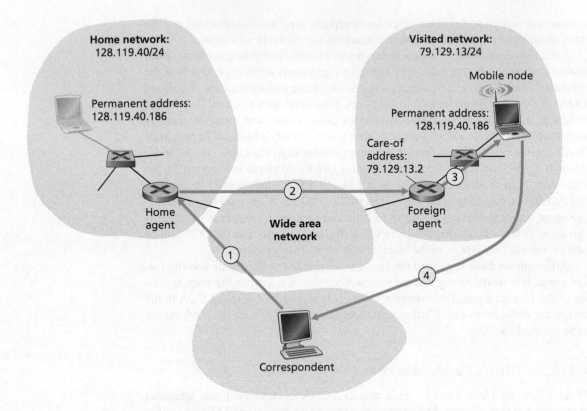

Home network:
128.119.40/24

Permanent address:
128.119.40.186

Home
agent

**Wide area
network**

Visited network:
79.129.13/24

Mobile node

Permanent address:
128.119.40.186

Care-of
address:
79.129.13.2

Foreign
agent

Correspondent

Figure 6.23 ♦ Indirect routing to a mobile node

has another very important function. Its second job is to be on the lookout for arriving datagrams addressed to nodes whose home network is that of the home agent but that are currently resident in a foreign network. The home agent intercepts these datagrams and then forwards them to a mobile node in a two-step process. The datagram is first forwarded to the foreign agent, using the mobile node's COA (step 2 in Figure 6.23), and then forwarded from the foreign agent to the mobile node (step 3 in Figure 6.23).

It is instructive to consider this rerouting in more detail. The home agent will need to address the datagram using the mobile node's COA, so that the network layer will route the datagram to the foreign network. On the other hand, it is desirable to leave the correspondent's datagram intact, since the application receiving the datagram should be unaware that the datagram was forwarded via the home agent. Both goals can be satisfied by having the home agent **encapsulate** the correspondent's original complete datagram within a new (larger) datagram. This larger datagram is addressed and delivered to the mobile node's COA. The foreign agent, who "owns" the COA, will receive and decapsulate the datagram—that is, remove the correspondent's original datagram from within the larger encapsulating datagram and forward (step 3 in Figure 6.23) the original datagram to the mobile node. Figure 6.24 shows a correspondent's original datagram being sent to the home network, an encapsulated datagram being sent to the foreign agent, and the original datagram being delivered to the mobile node. The sharp reader will note that the encapsulation/decapsulation described here is identical to the notion of tunneling, discussed in Chapter 4 in the context of IP multicast and IPv6.

Let's next consider how a mobile node sends datagrams to a correspondent. This is quite simple, as the mobile node can address its datagram *directly* to the correspondent (using its own permanent address as the source address, and the correspondent's address as the destination address). Since the mobile node knows the correspondent's address, there is no need to route the datagram back through the home agent. This is shown as step 4 in Figure 6.23.

Let's summarize our discussion of indirect routing by listing the new network-layer functionality required to support mobility.

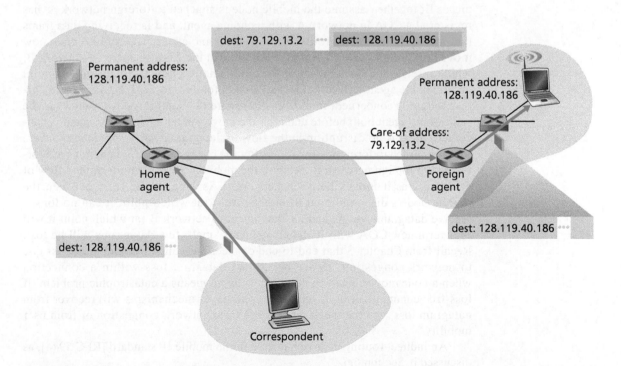

Figure 6.24 ♦ Encapsulation and decapsulation

- *A mobile-node–to–foreign-agent protocol.* The mobile node will register with the foreign agent when attaching to the foreign network. Similarly, a mobile node will deregister with the foreign agent when it leaves the foreign network.

- *A foreign-agent–to–home-agent registration protocol.* The foreign agent will register the mobile node's COA with the home agent. A foreign agent need not explicitly deregister a COA when a mobile node leaves its network, because the subsequent registration of a new COA, when the mobile node moves to a new network, will take care of this.

- *A home-agent datagram encapsulation protocol.* Encapsulation and forwarding of the correspondent's original datagram within a datagram addressed to the COA.

- *A foreign-agent decapsulation protocol.* Extraction of the correspondent's original datagram from the encapsulating datagram, and the forwarding of the original datagram to the mobile node.

The previous discussion provides all the pieces—foreign agents, the home agent, and indirect forwarding—needed for a mobile node to maintain an ongoing connection while moving among networks. As an example of how these pieces fit together, assume the mobile node is attached to foreign network A, has registered a COA in network A with its home agent, and is receiving datagrams that are being indirectly routed through its home agent. The mobile node now moves to foreign network B and registers with the foreign agent in network B, which informs the home agent of the mobile node's new COA. From this point on, the home agent will reroute datagrams to foreign network B. As far as a correspondent is concerned, mobility is transparent—datagrams are routed via the same home agent both before and after the move. As far as the home agent is concerned, there is no disruption in the flow of datagrams—arriving datagrams are first forwarded to foreign network A; after the change in COA, datagrams are forwarded to foreign network B. But will the mobile node see an interrupted flow of datagrams as it moves between networks? As long as the time between the mobile node's disconnection from network A (at which point it can no longer receive datagrams via A) and its attachment to network B (at which point it will register a new COA with its home agent) is small, few datagrams will be lost. Recall from Chapter 3 that end-to-end connections can suffer datagram loss due to network congestion. Hence occasional datagram loss within a connection when a node moves between networks is by no means a catastrophic problem. If loss-free communication is required, upper-layer mechanisms will recover from datagram loss, whether such loss results from network congestion or from user mobility.

An indirect routing approach is used in the mobile IP standard [RFC 5944], as discussed in Section 6.6.

Direct Routing to a Mobile Node

The indirect routing approach illustrated in Figure 6.23 suffers from an inefficiency known as the **triangle routing problem**—datagrams addressed to the mobile node must be routed first to the home agent and then to the foreign network, even when a much more efficient route exists between the correspondent and the mobile node. In the worst case, imagine a mobile user who is visiting the foreign network of a colleague. The two are sitting side by side and exchanging data over the network. Datagrams from the correspondent (in this case the colleague of the visitor) are routed to the mobile user's home agent and then back again to the foreign network!

  Direct routing overcomes the inefficiency of triangle routing, but does so at the cost of additional complexity. In the direct routing approach, a **correspondent agent** in the correspondent's network first learns the COA of the mobile node. This can be done by having the correspondent agent query the home agent, assuming that (as in the case of indirect routing) the mobile node has an up-to-date value for its COA registered with its home agent. It is also possible for the correspondent itself to perform the function of the correspondent agent, just as a mobile node could perform the function of the foreign agent. This is shown as steps 1 and 2 in Figure 6.25. The correspondent agent then tunnels datagrams directly to the mobile node's COA, in a manner analogous to the tunneling performed by the home agent, steps 3 and 4 in Figure 6.25.

  While direct routing overcomes the triangle routing problem, it introduces two important additional challenges:

* A **mobile-user location protocol** is needed for the correspondent agent to query the home agent to obtain the mobile node's COA (steps 1 and 2 in Figure 6.25).

* When the mobile node moves from one foreign network to another, how will data now be forwarded to the new foreign network? In the case of indirect routing, this problem was easily solved by updating the COA maintained by the home agent. However, with direct routing, the home agent is queried for the COA by the correspondent agent only once, at the beginning of the session. Thus, updating the COA at the home agent, while necessary, will not be enough to solve the problem of routing data to the mobile node's new foreign network.

  One solution would be to create a new protocol to notify the correspondent of the changing COA. An alternate solution, and one that we'll see adopted in practice in GSM networks, works as follows. Suppose data is currently being forwarded to the mobile node in the foreign network where the mobile node was located when the session first started (step 1 in Figure 6.26). We'll identify the foreign agent in that foreign network where the mobile node was first found as the **anchor foreign agent**. When the mobile node moves to a new foreign network (step 2 in Figure 6.26), the mobile node registers with the new foreign agent (step 3), and the new foreign agent provides the anchor foreign agent with the mobile node's new COA (step 4). When

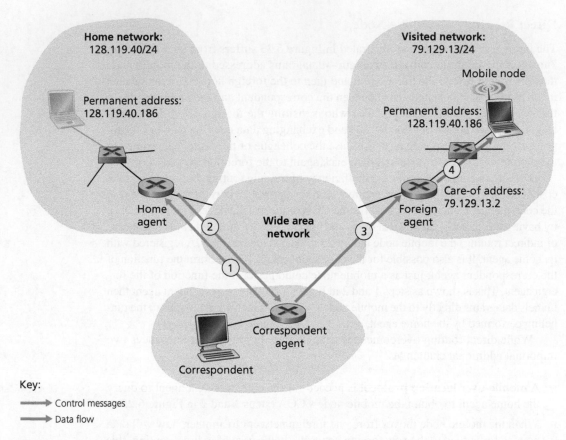

Figure 6.25 ◆ Direct routing to a mobile user

the anchor foreign agent receives an encapsulated datagram for a departed mobile node, it can then re-encapsulate the datagram and forward it to the mobile node (step 5) using the new COA. If the mobile node later moves yet again to a new foreign network, the foreign agent in that new visited network would then contact the anchor foreign agent in order to set up forwarding to this new foreign network.

6.6 Mobile IP

The Internet architecture and protocols for supporting mobility, collectively known as mobile IP, are defined primarily in RFC 5944 for IPv4. Mobile IP is a flexible standard, supporting many different modes of operation (for example, operation

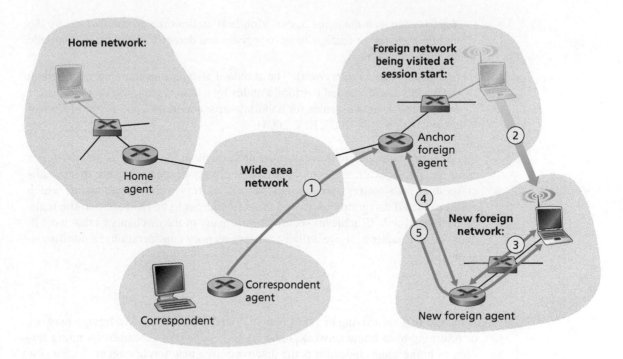

Figure 6.26 ♦ Mobile transfer between networks with direct routing

with or without a foreign agent), multiple ways for agents and mobile nodes to discover each other, use of single or multiple COAs, and multiple forms of encapsulation. As such, mobile IP is a complex standard, and would require an entire book to describe in detail; indeed one such book is [Perkins 1998b]. Our modest goal here is to provide an overview of the most important aspects of mobile IP and to illustrate its use in a few common-case scenarios.

The mobile IP architecture contains many of the elements we have considered above, including the concepts of home agents, foreign agents, care-of addresses, and encapsulation/decapsulation. The current standard [RFC 5944] specifies the use of indirect routing to the mobile node.

The mobile IP standard consists of three main pieces:

• *Agent discovery.* Mobile IP defines the protocols used by a home or foreign agent to advertise its services to mobile nodes, and protocols for mobile nodes to solicit the services of a foreign or home agent.

- *Registration with the home agent.* Mobile IP defines the protocols used by the mobile node and/or foreign agent to register and deregister COAs with a mobile node's home agent.

- *Indirect routing of datagrams.* The standard also defines the manner in which datagrams are forwarded to mobile nodes by a home agent, including rules for forwarding datagrams, rules for handling error conditions, and several forms of encapsulation [RFC 2003, RFC 2004].

Security considerations are prominent throughout the mobile IP standard. For example, authentication of a mobile node is clearly needed to ensure that a malicious user does not register a bogus care-of address with a home agent, which could cause all datagrams addressed to an IP address to be redirected to the malicious user. Mobile IP achieves security using many of the mechanisms that we will examine in Chapter 8, so we will not address security considerations in our discussion below.

Agent Discovery

A mobile IP node arriving to a new network, whether attaching to a foreign network or returning to its home network, must learn the identity of the corresponding foreign or home agent. Indeed it is the discovery of a new foreign agent, with a new network address, that allows the network layer in a mobile node to learn that it has moved into a new foreign network. This process is known as **agent discovery**. Agent discovery can be accomplished in one of two ways: via agent advertisement or via agent solicitation.

With **agent advertisement**, a foreign or home agent advertises its services using an extension to the existing router discovery protocol [RFC 1256]. The agent periodically broadcasts an ICMP message with a type field of 9 (router discovery) on all links to which it is connected. The router discovery message contains the IP address of the router (that is, the agent), thus allowing a mobile node to learn the agent's IP address. The router discovery message also contains a mobility agent advertisement extension that contains additional information needed by the mobile node. Among the more important fields in the extension are the following:

- *Home agent bit (H).* Indicates that the agent is a home agent for the network in which it resides.

- *Foreign agent bit (F).* Indicates that the agent is a foreign agent for the network in which it resides.

- *Registration required bit (R).* Indicates that a mobile user in this network *must* register with a foreign agent. In particular, a mobile user cannot obtain a care-of address in the foreign network (for example, using DHCP) and assume the functionality of the foreign agent for itself, without registering with the foreign agent.

- *M, G encapsulation bits.* Indicate whether a form of encapsulation other than IP-in-IP encapsulation will be used.

- *Care-of address (COA) fields.* A list of one or more care-of addresses provided by the foreign agent. In our example below, the COA will be associated with the foreign agent, who will receive datagrams sent to the COA and then forward them to the appropriate mobile node. The mobile user will select one of these addresses as its COA when registering with its home agent.

Figure 6.27 illustrates some of the key fields in the agent advertisement message.

With **agent solicitation**, a mobile node wanting to learn about agents without waiting to receive an agent advertisement can broadcast an agent solicitation message, which is simply an ICMP message with type value 10. An agent receiving the solicitation will unicast an agent advertisement directly to the mobile node, which can then proceed as if it had received an unsolicited advertisement.

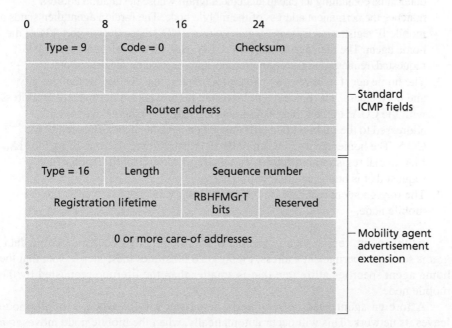

Figure 6.27 ♦ ICMP router discovery message with mobility agent advertisement extension

Registration with the Home Agent

Once a mobile IP node has received a COA, that address must be registered with the home agent. This can be done either via the foreign agent (who then registers the COA with the home agent) or directly by the mobile IP node itself. We consider the former case below. Four steps are involved.

1. Following the receipt of a foreign agent advertisement, a mobile node sends a mobile IP registration message to the foreign agent. The registration message is carried within a UDP datagram and sent to port 434. The registration message carries a COA advertised by the foreign agent, the address of the home agent (HA), the permanent address of the mobile node (MA), the requested lifetime of the registration, and a 64-bit registration identification. The requested registration lifetime is the number of seconds that the registration is to be valid. If the registration is not renewed at the home agent within the specified lifetime, the registration will become invalid. The registration identifier acts like a sequence number and serves to match a received registration reply with a registration request, as discussed below.

2. The foreign agent receives the registration message and records the mobile node's permanent IP address. The foreign agent now knows that it should be looking for datagrams containing an encapsulated datagram whose destination address matches the permanent address of the mobile node. The foreign agent then sends a mobile IP registration message (again, within a UDP datagram) to port 434 of the home agent. The message contains the COA, HA, MA, encapsulation format requested, requested registration lifetime, and registration identification.

3. The home agent receives the registration request and checks for authenticity and correctness. The home agent binds the mobile node's permanent IP address with the COA; in the future, datagrams arriving at the home agent and addressed to the mobile node will now be encapsulated and tunneled to the COA. The home agent sends a mobile IP registration reply containing the HA, MA, actual registration lifetime, and the registration identification of the request that is being satisfied with this reply.

4. The foreign agent receives the registration reply and then forwards it to the mobile node.

At this point, registration is complete, and the mobile node can receive datagrams sent to its permanent address. Figure 6.28 illustrates these steps. Note that the home agent specifies a lifetime that is smaller than the lifetime requested by the mobile node.

A foreign agent need not explicitly deregister a COA when a mobile node leaves its network. This will occur automatically, when the mobile node moves to a new network (whether another foreign network or its home network) and registers a new COA.

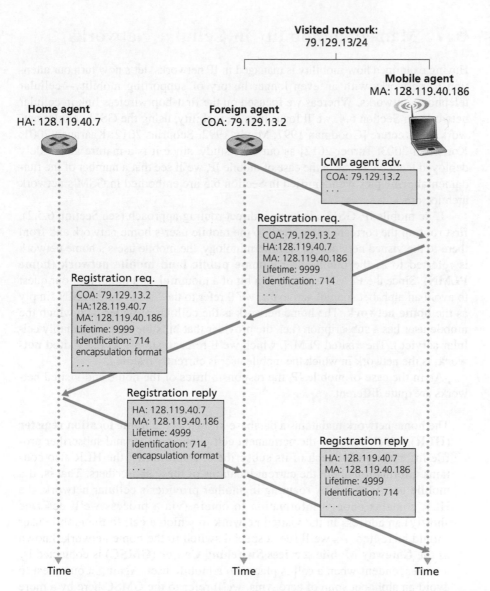

Figure 6.28 ♦ Agent advertisement and mobile IP registration

The mobile IP standard allows many additional scenarios and capabilities in addition to those described previously. The interested reader should consult [Perkins 1998b; RFC 5944].

6.7 Managing Mobility in Cellular Networks

Having examined how mobility is managed in IP networks, let's now turn our attention to networks with an even longer history of supporting mobility—cellular telephony networks. Whereas we focused on the first-hop wireless link in cellular networks in Section 6.4, we'll focus here on mobility, using the GSM cellular network architecture [Goodman 1997; Mouly 1992; Scourias 2012; Kaaranen 2001; Korhonen 2003; Turner 2012] as our case study, since it is a mature and widely deployed technology. As in the case of mobile IP, we'll see that a number of the fundamental principles we identified in Section 6.5 are embodied in GSM's network architecture.

Like mobile IP, GSM adopts an indirect routing approach (see Section 6.5.2), first routing the correspondent's call to the mobile user's home network and from there to the visited network. In GSM terminology, the mobile users's home network is referred to as the mobile user's **home public land mobile network (home PLMN)**. Since the PLMN acronym is a bit of a mouthful, and mindful of our quest to avoid an alphabet soup of acronyms, we'll refer to the GSM home PLMN simply as the **home network**. The home network is the cellular provider with which the mobile user has a subscription (i.e., the provider that bills the user for monthly cellular service). The visited PLMN, which we'll refer to simply as the **visited network**, is the network in which the mobile user is currently residing.

As in the case of mobile IP, the responsibilities of the home and visited networks are quite different.

- The home network maintains a database known as the **home location register (HLR)**, which contains the permanent cell phone number and subscriber profile information for each of its subscribers. Importantly, the HLR also contains information about the current locations of these subscribers. That is, if a mobile user is currently roaming in another provider's cellular network, the HLR contains enough information to obtain (via a process we'll describe shortly) an address in the visited network to which a call to the mobile user should be routed. As we'll see, a special switch in the home network, known as the **Gateway Mobile services Switching Center (GMSC)** is contacted by a correspondent when a call is placed to a mobile user. Again, in our quest to avoid an alphabet soup of acronyms, we'll refer to the GMSC here by a more descriptive term, **home MSC**.

- The visited network maintains a database known as the **visitor location register (VLR)**. The VLR contains an entry for each mobile user that is *currently* in the portion of the network served by the VLR. VLR entries thus come and go as mobile users enter and leave the network. A VLR is usually co-located with the mobile switching center (MSC) that coordinates the setup of a call to and from the visited network.

In practice, a provider's cellular network will serve as a home network for its subscribers and as a visited network for mobile users whose subscription is with a different cellular provider.

6.7.1 Routing Calls to a Mobile User

We're now in a position to describe how a call is placed to a mobile GSM user in a visited network. We'll consider a simple example below; more complex scenarios are described in [Mouly 1992]. The steps, as illustrated in Figure 6.29, are as follows:

1. The correspondent dials the mobile user's phone number. This number itself does not refer to a particular telephone line or location (after all, the phone number is fixed and the user is mobile!). The leading digits in the number are sufficient to globally identify the mobile's home network. The call is routed from the correspondent through the PSTN to the home MSC in the mobile's home network. This is the first leg of the call.
2. The home MSC receives the call and interrogates the HLR to determine the location of the mobile user. In the simplest case, the HLR returns the **mobile**

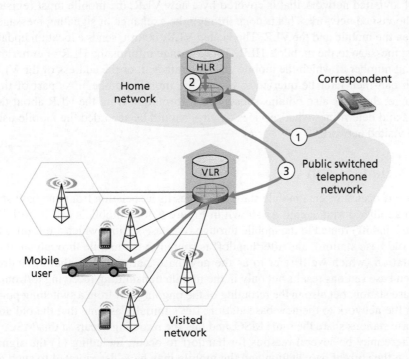

Figure 6.29 ♦ Placing a call to a mobile user: indirect routing

station roaming number (MSRN), which we will refer to as the **roaming number**. Note that this number is different from the mobile's permanent phone number, which is associated with the mobile's home network. The roaming number is ephemeral: It is temporarily assigned to a mobile when it enters a visited network. The roaming number serves a role similar to that of the care-of address in mobile IP and, like the COA, is invisible to the correspondent and the mobile. If HLR does not have the roaming number, it returns the address of the VLR in the visited network. In this case (not shown in Figure 6.29), the home MSC will need to query the VLR to obtain the roaming number of the mobile node. But how does the HLR get the roaming number or the VLR address in the first place? What happens to these values when the mobile user moves to another visited network? We'll consider these important questions shortly.

3. Given the roaming number, the home MSC sets up the second leg of the call through the network to the MSC in the visited network. The call is completed, being routed from the correspondent to the home MSC, and from there to the visited MSC, and from there to the base station serving the mobile user.

An unresolved question in step 2 is how the HLR obtains information about the location of the mobile user. When a mobile telephone is switched on or enters a part of a visited network that is covered by a new VLR, the mobile must register with the visited network. This is done through the exchange of signaling messages between the mobile and the VLR. The visited VLR, in turn, sends a location update request message to the mobile's HLR. This message informs the HLR of either the roaming number at which the mobile can be contacted, or the address of the VLR (which can then later be queried to obtain the mobile number). As part of this exchange, the VLR also obtains subscriber information from the HLR about the mobile and determines what services (if any) should be accorded the mobile user by the visited network.

6.7.2 Handoffs in GSM

A **handoff** occurs when a mobile station changes its association from one base station to another during a call. As shown in Figure 6.30, a mobile's call is initially (before handoff) routed to the mobile through one base station (which we'll refer to as the old base station), and after handoff is routed to the mobile through another base station (which we'll refer to as the new base station). Note that a handoff between base stations results not only in the mobile transmitting/receiving to/from a new base station, but also in the rerouting of the ongoing call from a switching point within the network to the new base station. Let's initially assume that the old and new base stations share the same MSC, and that the rerouting occurs at this MSC.

There may be several reasons for handoff to occur, including (1) the signal between the current base station and the mobile may have deteriorated to such an extent that the call is in danger of being dropped, and (2) a cell may have become

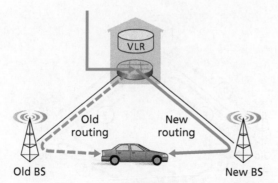

Figure 6.30 ♦ Handoff scenario between base stations with a common MSC

overloaded, handling a large number of calls. This congestion may be alleviated by handing off mobiles to less congested nearby cells.

While it is associated with a base station, a mobile periodically measures the strength of a beacon signal from its current base station as well as beacon signals from nearby base stations that it can "hear." These measurements are reported once or twice a second to the mobile's current base station. Handoff in GSM is initiated by the old base station based on these measurements, the current loads of mobiles in nearby cells, and other factors [Mouly 1992]. The GSM standard does not specify the specific algorithm to be used by a base station to determine whether or not to perform handoff.

Figure 6.31 illustrates the steps involved when a base station does decide to hand off a mobile user:

1. The old base station (BS) informs the visited MSC that a handoff is to be performed and the BS (or possible set of BSs) to which the mobile is to be handed off.
2. The visited MSC initiates path setup to the new BS, allocating the resources needed to carry the rerouted call, and signaling the new BS that a handoff is about to occur.
3. The new BS allocates and activates a radio channel for use by the mobile.
4. The new BS signals back to the visited MSC and the old BS that the visited-MSC-to-new-BS path has been established and that the mobile should be informed of the impending handoff. The new BS provides all of the information that the mobile will need to associate with the new BS.
5. The mobile is informed that it should perform a handoff. Note that up until this point, the mobile has been blissfully unaware that the network has been laying the groundwork (e.g., allocating a channel in the new BS and allocating a path from the visited MSC to the new BS) for a handoff.
6. The mobile and the new BS exchange one or more messages to fully activate the new channel in the new BS.

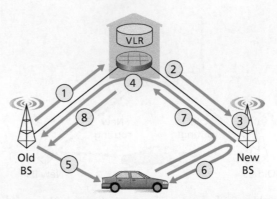

Figure 6.31 ♦ Steps in accomplishing a handoff between base stations with a common MSC

7. The mobile sends a handoff complete message to the new BS, which is forwarded up to the visited MSC. The visited MSC then reroutes the ongoing call to the mobile via the new BS.
8. The resources allocated along the path to the old BS are then released.

Let's conclude our discussion of handoff by considering what happens when the mobile moves to a BS that is associated with a *different* MSC than the old BS, and what happens when this inter-MSC handoff occurs more than once. As shown in Figure 6.32, GSM defines the notion of an **anchor MSC**. The anchor MSC is the MSC visited by the mobile when a call first begins; the anchor MSC thus remains unchanged during the call. Throughout the call's duration and regardless of the number of inter-MSC transfers performed by the mobile, the call is routed from the home MSC to the anchor MSC, and then from the anchor MSC to the visited MSC where the mobile is currently located. When a mobile moves from the coverage area of one MSC to another, the ongoing call is rerouted from the anchor MSC to the new visited MSC containing the new base station. Thus, at all times there are at most three MSCs (the home MSC, the anchor MSC, and the visited MSC) between the correspondent and the mobile. Figure 6.32 illustrates the routing of a call among the MSCs visited by a mobile user.

Rather than maintaining a single MSC hop from the anchor MSC to the current MSC, an alternative approach would have been to simply chain the MSCs visited by the mobile, having an old MSC forward the ongoing call to the new MSC each time the mobile moves to a new MSC. Such MSC chaining can in fact occur in IS-41 cellular networks, with an optional path minimization step to remove MSCs between the anchor MSC and the current visited MSC [Lin 2001].

Let's wrap up our discussion of GSM mobility management with a comparison of mobility management in GSM and Mobile IP. The comparison in Table 6.2 indicates that although IP and cellular networks are fundamentally different in many ways, they share a surprising number of common functional elements and overall approaches in handling mobility.

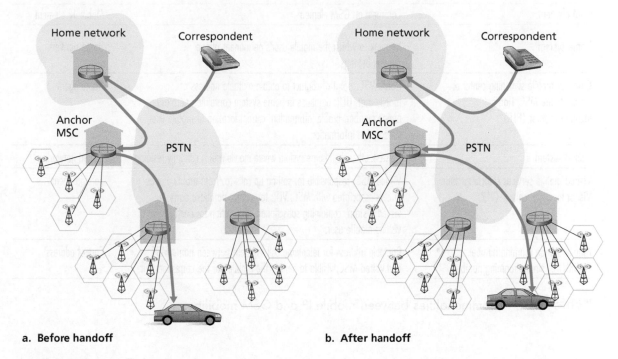

a. **Before handoff**   b. **After handoff**

Figure 6.32 ♦ Rerouting via the anchor MSC

6.8 Wireless and Mobility: Impact on Higher-Layer Protocols

In this chapter, we've seen that wireless networks differ significantly from their wired counterparts at both the link layer (as a result of wireless channel characteristics such as fading, multipath, and hidden terminals) and at the network layer (as a result of mobile users who change their points of attachment to the network). But are there important differences at the transport and application layers? It's tempting to think that these differences will be minor, since the network layer provides the same best-effort delivery service model to upper layers in both wired and wireless networks. Similarly, if protocols such as TCP or UDP are used to provide transport-layer services to applications in both wired and wireless networks, then the application layer should remain unchanged as well. In one sense our intuition is right—TCP and UDP can (and do) operate in networks with wireless links. On the other hand, transport protocols in general, and TCP in particular, can sometimes have very different performance in wired and wireless networks, and it is here, in terms of performance, that differences are manifested. Let's see why.

Recall that TCP retransmits a segment that is either lost or corrupted on the path between sender and receiver. In the case of mobile users, loss can result from either

GSM element	Comment on GSM element	Mobile IP element
Home system	Network to which the mobile user's permanent phone number belongs.	Home network
Gateway mobile switching center or simply home MSC, Home location register (HLR)	Home MSC: point of contact to obtain routable address of mobile user. HLR: database in home system containing permanent phone number, profile information, current location of mobile user, subscription information.	Home agent
Visited system	Network other than home system where mobile user is currently residing.	Visited network.
Visited mobile services switching center, Visitor location register (VLR)	Visited MSC: responsible for setting up calls to/from mobile nodes in cells associated with MSC. VLR: temporary database entry in visited system, containing subscription information for each visiting mobile user.	Foreign agent
Mobile station roaming number (MSRN) or simply roaming number	Routable address for telephone call segment between home MSC and visited MSC, visible to neither the mobile nor the correspondent.	Care-of address

Table 6.2 ♦ Commonalities between mobile IP and GSM mobility

network congestion (router buffer overflow) or from handoff (e.g., from delays in rerouting segments to a mobile's new point of attachment to the network). In all cases, TCP's receiver-to-sender ACK indicates only that a segment was not received intact; the sender is unaware of whether the segment was lost due to congestion, during handoff, or due to detected bit errors. In all cases, the sender's response is the same—to retransmit the segment. TCP's congestion-control response is *also* the same in all cases—TCP decreases its congestion window, as discussed in Section 3.7. By unconditionally decreasing its congestion window, TCP implicitly assumes that segment loss results from congestion rather than corruption or handoff. We saw in Section 6.2 that bit errors are much more common in wireless networks than in wired networks. When such bit errors occur or when handoff loss occurs, there's really no reason for the TCP sender to decrease its congestion window (and thus decrease its sending rate). Indeed, it may well be the case that router buffers are empty and packets are flowing along the end-to-end path unimpeded by congestion.

Researchers realized in the early to mid 1990s that given high bit error rates on wireless links and the possibility of handoff loss, TCP's congestion-control response could be problematic in a wireless setting. Three broad classes of approaches are possible for dealing with this problem:

• *Local recovery.* Local recovery protocols recover from bit errors when and where (e.g., at the wireless link) they occur, e.g., the 802.11 ARQ protocol we studied in Section 6.3, or more sophisticated approaches that use both ARQ and FEC [Ayanoglu 1995].

• *TCP sender awareness of wireless links.* In the local recovery approaches, the TCP sender is blissfully unaware that its segments are traversing a wireless link. An alternative approach is for the TCP sender and receiver to be aware of the existence of a wireless link, to distinguish between congestive losses occurring in the wired network and corruption/loss occurring at the wireless link, and to invoke congestion control only in response to congestive wired-network losses. [Balakrishnan 1997] investigates various types of TCP, assuming that end systems can make this distinction. [Liu 2003] investigates techniques for distinguishing between losses on the wired and wireless segments of an end-to-end path.

• *Split-connection approaches.* In a split-connection approach [Bakre 1995], the end-to-end connection between the mobile user and the other end point is broken into two transport-layer connections: one from the mobile host to the wireless access point, and one from the wireless access point to the other communication end point (which we'll assume here is a wired host). The end-to-end connection is thus formed by the concatenation of a wireless part and a wired part. The transport layer over the wireless segment can be a standard TCP connection [Bakre 1995], or a specially tailored error recovery protocol on top of UDP. [Yavatkar 1994] investigates the use of a transport-layer selective repeat protocol over the wireless connection. Measurements reported in [Wei 2006] indicate that split TCP connections are widely used in cellular data networks, and that significant improvements can indeed be made through the use of split TCP connections.

Our treatment of TCP over wireless links has been necessarily brief here. In-depth surveys of TCP challenges and solutions in wireless networks can be found in [Hanabali 2005; Leung 2006]. We encourage you to consult the references for details of this ongoing area of research.

Having considered transport-layer protocols, let us next consider the effect of wireless and mobility on application-layer protocols. Here, an important consideration is that wireless links often have relatively low bandwidths, as we saw in Figure 6.2. As a result, applications that operate over wireless links, particularly over cellular wireless links, must treat bandwidth as a scarce commodity. For example, a Web server serving content to a Web browser executing on a 3G phone will likely not be able to provide the same image-rich content that it gives to a browser operating over a wired connection. Although wireless links do provide challenges at the application layer, the mobility they enable also makes possible a rich set of location-aware and context-aware applications [Chen 2000; Baldauf 2007]. More generally, wireless and mobile networks will play a key role in realizing the ubiquitous computing environments of the future [Weiser 1991]. It's fair to say that we've only seen the tip of the iceberg when it comes to the impact of wireless and mobile networks on networked applications and their protocols!

6.9 Summary

Wireless and mobile networks have revolutionized telephony and are having an increasingly profound impact in the world of computer networks as well. With their anytime, anywhere, untethered access into the global network infrastructure, they are not only making network access more ubiquitous, they are also enabling an exciting new set of location-dependent services. Given the growing importance of wireless and mobile networks, this chapter has focused on the principles, common link technologies, and network architectures for supporting wireless and mobile communication.

We began this chapter with an introduction to wireless and mobile networks, drawing an important distinction between the challenges posed by the *wireless* nature of the communication links in such networks, and by the *mobility* that these wireless links enable. This allowed us to better isolate, identify, and master the key concepts in each area. We focused first on wireless communication, considering the characteristics of a wireless link in Section 6.2. In Sections 6.3 and 6.4, we examined the link-level aspects of the IEEE 802.11 (WiFi) wireless LAN standard, two IEEE 802.15 personal area networks (Bluetooth and Zigbee), and 3G and 4G cellular Internet access. We then turned our attention to the issue of mobility. In Section 6.5, we identified several forms of mobility, with points along this spectrum posing different challenges and admitting different solutions. We considered the problems of locating and routing to a mobile user, as well as approaches for handing off the mobile user who dynamically moves from one point of attachment to the network to another. We examined how these issues were addressed in the mobile IP standard and in GSM, in Sections 6.6 and 6.7, respectively. Finally, we considered the impact of wireless links and mobility on transport-layer protocols and networked applications in Section 6.8.

Although we have devoted an entire chapter to the study of wireless and mobile networks, an entire book (or more) would be required to fully explore this exciting and rapidly expanding field. We encourage you to delve more deeply into this field by consulting the many references provided in this chapter.

Homework Problems and Questions

Chapter 6 Review Questions

SECTION 6.1

R1. What does it mean for a wireless network to be operating in "infrastructure mode?" If the network is not in infrastructure mode, what mode of operation is it in, and what is the difference between that mode of operation and infrastructure mode?

R2. Both MANET and VANET are multi-hop infrastructure-less wireless networks. What is the difference between them?

SECTION 6.2

R3. What are the differences between the following types of wireless channel impairments: path loss, multipath propagation, interference from other sources?

R4. As a mobile node gets farther and farther away from a base station, why does the base station increase the transmission power and reduce the transmission rate?

SECTIONS 6.3 AND 6.4

R5. Describe the role of the beacon frames in 802.11.

R6. An access point periodically sends beacon frames. What are the contents of the beacon frames?

R7. Why are acknowledgments used in 802.11 but not in wired Ethernet?

R8. What is the difference between passive scanning and active scanning?

R9. What are the two main purposes of a CTS frame?

R10. Suppose the IEEE 802.11 RTS and CTS frames were as long as the standard DATA and ACK frames. Would there be any advantage to using the CTS and RTS frames? Why or why not?

R11. Section 6.3.4 discusses 802.11 mobility, in which a wireless station moves from one BSS to another within the same subnet. When the APs are interconnected with a switch, an AP may need to send a frame with a spoofed MAC address to get the switch to forward the frame properly. Why?

R12. What is the difference between Bluetooth and Zigbee in terms of data rate?

R13. What is meant by a super frame in the 802.15.4 Zigbee standard?

R14. What are the two upcoming 4G technologies?

R15. What is the role of the RNC in the 3G cellular data network architecture? What role does the RNC play in the cellular voice network?

SECTIONS 6.5 AND 6.6

R16. If a node has a wireless connection to the Internet, does that node have to be mobile? Explain. Suppose that a user with a laptop walks around her house with her laptop, and always accesses the Internet through the same access point. Is this user mobile from a network standpoint? Explain.

R17. What is the difference between a permanent address and a care-of address? Who assigns a care-of address?

R18. Consider a TCP connection going over Mobile IP. True or false: The TCP connection phase between the correspondent and the mobile host goes through the mobile's home network, but the data transfer phase is directly between the correspondent and the mobile host, bypassing the home network.

SECTION 6.7

R19. What are the purposes of the HLR and VLR in GSM networks? What elements of mobile IP are similar to the HLR and VLR?

R20. What is the role of the anchor MSC in GSM networks?

SECTION 6.8

R21. What are three approaches that can be taken to avoid having a single wireless link degrade the performance of an end-to-end transport-layer TCP connection?

 Problems

P1. Consider the single-sender CDMA example in Figure 6.5. What would be the sender's output (for the 2 data bits shown) if the sender's CDMA code were $(1, 1, -1, 1, 1, -1, -1, 1)$?

P2. Consider sender 2 in Figure 6.6. Assume that both the first two bits sent by sender 2 are -1. What are the sender's outputs to the channel (before being added to the signal from sender 1)?

P3. After selecting the AP with which to associate, a wireless host sends an association request frame to the AP, and the AP responds with an association response frame. Once associated with an AP, the host will want to join the subnet (in the IP addressing sense of Section 4.4.2) to which the AP belongs. What does the host do next?

P4. If two CDMA senders have codes $(1, 1, 1, -1, 1, -1, -1, -1)$ and $(1, -1, 1, 1, 1, 1, 1, 1)$, would the corresponding receivers be able to decode the data correctly? Justify.

P5. Suppose there are two ISPs providing WiFi access in a particular café, with each ISP operating its own AP and having its own IP address block.

   a. Further suppose that by accident, each ISP has configured its AP to operate over channel 11. Will the 802.11 protocol completely break down in this situation? Discuss what happens when two stations, each associated with a different ISP, attempt to transmit at the same time.

   b. Now suppose that one AP operates over channel 1 and the other over channel 11. How do your answers change?

P6. In step 4 of the CSMA/CA protocol, a station that successfully transmits a frame begins the CSMA/CA protocol for a second frame at step 2, rather than at step 1. What rationale might the designers of CSMA/CA have had in mind by having such a station not transmit the second frame immediately (if the channel is sensed idle)?

P7. Suppose an 802.11b station is configured to always reserve the channel with the RTS/CTS sequence. Suppose this station suddenly wants to transmit 1,000 bytes of data, and all other stations are idle at this time. Assume a transmission rate of 12 Mbps. As a function of SIFS and DIFS, and ignoring propagation delay and assuming no bit errors, calculate the time required to transmit the frame and receive the acknowledgment.

P8. Consider the scenario shown in Figure 6.33, in which there are four wireless nodes, A, B, C, and D. The radio coverage of the four nodes is shown via the shaded ovals; all nodes share the same frequency. When A transmits, it can only be heard/received by B; when B transmits, both A and C can hear/receive from B; when C transmits, both B and D can hear/receive from C; when D transmits, only C can hear/receive from D.

Suppose now that each node has an infinite supply of messages that it wants to send to each of the other nodes. If a message's destination is not an immediate neighbor, then the message must be relayed. For example, if A wants to send to D, a message from A must first be sent to B, which then sends the message to C, which then sends the message to D. Time is slotted, with a message transmission time taking exactly one time slot, e.g., as in slotted Aloha. During a slot, a node can do one of the following: (*i*) send a message; (*ii*) receive a message (if exactly one message is being sent to it), (*iii*) remain silent. As always, if a node hears two or more simultaneous transmissions, a collision occurs and none of the transmitted messages are received successfully. You can assume here that there are no bit-level errors, and thus if exactly one message is sent, it will be received correctly by those within the transmission radius of the sender.

a. Suppose now that an omniscient controller (i.e., a controller that knows the state of every node in the network) can command each node to do whatever it (the omniscient controller) wishes, i.e., to send a message, to receive a message, or to remain silent. Given this omniscient controller, what is the maximum rate at which a data message can be transferred from C to A, given that there are no other messages between any other source/destination pairs?

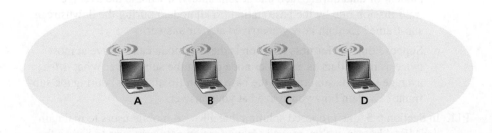

Figure 6.33 ♦ Scenario for problem P8

b. Suppose now that A sends messages to B, and D sends messages to C. What is the combined maximum rate at which data messages can flow from A to B and from D to C?

c. Suppose now that A sends messages to B, and C sends messages to D. What is the combined maximum rate at which data messages can flow from A to B and from C to D?

d. Suppose now that the wireless links are replaced by wired links. Repeat questions (a) through (c) again in this wired scenario.

e. Now suppose we are again in the wireless scenario, and that for every data message sent from source to destination, the destination will send an ACK message back to the source (e.g., as in TCP). Also suppose that each ACK message takes up one slot. Repeat questions (a) – (c) above for this scenario.

P9. Power is a precious resource in mobile devices, and thus the 802.11 standard provides power-management capabilities that allow 802.11 nodes to minimize the amount of time that their sense, transmit, and receive functions and other circuitry need to be "on." In 802.11, a node is able to explicitly alternate between sleep and wake states. Explain in brief how a node communicates with the AP to perform power management.

P10. Consider the following idealized LTE scenario. The downstream channel (see Figure 6.20) is slotted in time, across F frequencies. There are four nodes, A, B, C, and D, reachable from the base station at rates of 10 Mbps, 5 Mbps, 2.5 Mbps, and 1 Mbps, respectively, on the downstream channel. These rates assume that the base station utilizes all time slots available on all F frequencies to send to just one station. The base station has an infinite amount of data to send to each of the nodes, and can send to any one of these four nodes using any of the F frequencies during any time slot in the downstream sub-frame.

a. What is the maximum rate at which the base station can send to the nodes, assuming it can send to any node it chooses during each time slot? Is your solution fair? Explain and define what you mean by "fair."

b. If there is a fairness requirement that each node must receive an equal amount of data during each one second interval, what is the average transmission rate by the base station (to all nodes) during the downstream sub-frame? Explain how you arrived at your answer.

c. Suppose that the fairness criterion is that any node can receive at most twice as much data as any other node during the sub-frame. What is the average transmission rate by the base station (to all nodes) during the sub-frame? Explain how you arrived at your answer.

P11. In Section 6.5, one proposed solution that allowed mobile users to maintain their IP addresses as they moved among foreign networks was to have a foreign network advertise a highly specific route to the mobile user and use the existing routing infrastructure to propagate this information throughout the network. We identified scalability as one concern. Suppose that when a mobile user moves from one network to another, the new foreign network advertises a specific route to the mobile user, and the old foreign network withdraws its route. Consider how routing information propagates in a distance-vector algorithm (particularly for the case of interdomain routing among networks that span the globe).

a. Will other routers be able to route datagrams immediately to the new foreign network as soon as the foreign network begins advertising its route?

b. Is it possible for different routers to believe that different foreign networks contain the mobile user?

c. Discuss the timescale over which other routers in the network will eventually learn the path to the mobile users.

P12. Suppose the correspondent in Figure 6.22 were mobile. Sketch the additional network-layer infrastructure that would be needed to route the datagram from the original mobile user to the (now mobile) correspondent. Show the structure of the datagram(s) between the original mobile user and the (now mobile) correspondent, as in Figure 6.23.

P13. What is the role of a GSM network's base station controller (BSC)?

P14. Consider the chaining example discussed at the end of Section 6.7.2. Suppose a mobile user visits foreign networks A, B, and C, and that a correspondent begins a connection to the mobile user when it is resident in foreign network A. List the sequence of messages between foreign agents, and between foreign agents and the home agent as the mobile user moves from network A to network B to network C. Next, suppose chaining is not performed, and the correspondent (as well as the home agent) must be explicitly notified of the changes in the mobile user's care-of address. List the sequence of messages that would need to be exchanged in this second scenario.

P15. Consider two mobile nodes in a foreign network having a foreign agent. Is it possible for the two mobile nodes to use the same care-of address in mobile IP? Explain your answer.

P16. In our discussion of how the VLR updated the HLR with information about the mobile's current location, what are the advantages and disadvantages of providing the MSRN as opposed to the address of the VLR to the HLR?

 Wireshark Lab

At the companion Web site for this textbook, http://www.awl.com/kurose-ross, you'll find a Wireshark lab for this chapter that captures and studies the 802.11 frames exchanged between a wireless laptop and an access point.

AN INTERVIEW WITH...

Deborah Estrin

Deborah Estrin is Professor of Computer Science at UCLA, the Jon Postel Chair in Computer Networks, Director of the Center for Embedded Networked Sensing (CENS), and co-founder of the non-profit openmhealth.org. She received her Ph.D. (1985) in Computer Science from M.I.T., and her B.S. (1980) from UC Berkeley. Estrin's early research focused on the design of network protocols, including multicast and inter-domain routing. In 2002 Estrin founded the NSF-funded Science and Technology Center, CENS (http://cens .ucla.edu), to develop and explore environmental monitoring technologies and applications. Currently Estrin and collaborators are developing **participatory sensing** systems, leveraging the programmability, proximity, and pervasiveness of mobile phones; the primary deployment contexts are mobile health (http://openmhealth.org), community data gathering, and STEM education (http://mobilizingcs.org). Professor Estrin is an elected member of the American Academy of Arts and Sciences (2007) and the National Academy of Engineering (2009). She is a fellow of the IEEE, ACM, and AAAS. She was selected as the first ACM-W Athena Lecturer (2006), awarded the Anita Borg Institute's Women of Vision Award for Innovation (2007), inducted into the WITI hall of fame (2008) and awarded Doctor Honoris Causa from EPFL (2008) and Uppsala University (2011).

Please describe a few of the most exciting projects you have worked on during your career. What were the biggest challenges?

In the mid-90s at USC and ISI, I had the great fortune to work with the likes of Steve Deering, Mark Handley, and Van Jacobson on the design of multicast routing protocols (in particular, PIM). I tried to carry many of the architectural design lessons from multicast into the design of ecological monitoring arrays, where for the first time I really began to take applications and multidisciplinary research seriously. That interest in jointly innovating in the social and technological space is what interests me so much about my latest area of research, mobile health. The challenges in these projects were as diverse as the problem domains, but what they all had in common was the need to keep our eyes open to whether we had the problem definition right as we iterated between design and deployment, prototype and pilot. None of them were problems that could be solved analytically, with simulation or even in constructed laboratory experiments. They all challenged our ability to retain clean architectures in the presence of messy problems and contexts, and they all called for extensive collaboration.

What changes and innovations do you see happening in wireless networks and mobility in the future?

I have never put much faith into predicting the future, but I would say we might see the end of feature phones (i.e., those that are not programmable and are used only for voice and text messaging) as smart phones become more and more powerful and the primary point of Internet access for many. I also think that we will see the continued proliferation of embedded SIMs by which all sorts of devices have the ability to communicate via the cellular network at low data rates.

Where do you see the future of networking and the Internet?

The efforts in named data and software-defined networking will emerge to create a more manageable, evolvable, and richer infrastructure and more generally represent moving the role of architecture higher up in the stack. In the beginnings of the Internet, architecture was layer 4 and below, with applications being more siloed/monolithic, sitting on top. Now data and analytics dominate transport.

What people inspired you professionally?

There are three people who come to mind. First, Dave Clark, the secret sauce and unsung hero of the Internet community. I was lucky to be around in the early days to see him act as the "organizing principle" of the IAB and Internet governance; the priest of rough consensus and running code. Second, Scott Shenker, for his intellectual brilliance, integrity, and persistence. I strive for, but rarely attain, his clarity in defining problems and solutions. He is always the first person I email for advice on matters large and small. Third, my sister Judy Estrin, who had the creativity and courage to spend her career bringing ideas and concepts to market. Without the Judys of the world the Internet technologies would never have transformed our lives.

What are your recommendations for students who want careers in computer science and networking?

First, build a strong foundation in your academic work, balanced with any and every real-world work experience you can get. As you look for a working environment, seek opportunities in problem areas you really care about and with smart teams that you can learn from.

7

Multimedia Networking

People in all corners of the world are currently using the Internet to watch movies and television shows on demand. Internet movie and television distribution companies such as Netflix and Hulu in North America and Youku and Kankan in China have practically become household names. But people are not only watching Internet videos, they are using sites like YouTube to upload and distribute their own user-generated content, becoming Internet video producers as well as consumers. Moreover, network applications such as Skype, Google Talk, and QQ (enormously popular in China) allow people to not only make "telephone calls" over the Internet, but to also enhance those calls with video and multi-person conferencing. In fact, we can safely predict that by the end of the current decade almost all video distribution and voice conversations will take place end-to-end over the Internet, often to wireless devices connected to the Internet via 4G and WiFi access networks.

We begin this chapter with a taxonomy of multimedia applications in Section 7.1. We'll see that a multimedia application can be classified as either *streaming stored audio/video*, *conversational voice/video-over-IP*, or *streaming live audio/video*. We'll see that each of these classes of applications has its own unique service requirements that differ significantly from those of traditional elastic applications such as e-mail, Web browsing, and remote login. In Section 7.2, we'll examine video streaming in some detail. We'll explore many of the underlying principles behind video streaming, including client buffering, prefetching, and adapting video quality to available bandwidth. We will also investigate Content Distribution Networks (CDNs), which are used extensively today by the leading video streaming systems. We then examine the YouTube, Netflix, and Kankan systems as case studies for streaming video. In Section 7.3, we investigate conversational voice and video, which, unlike elastic applications, are highly sensitive to end-to-end delay but can tolerate occasional loss of data. Here we'll examine how techniques such as adaptive playout, forward error correction, and error concealment can mitigate against network-induced packet loss and delay. We'll also examine Skype as a case study. In Section 7.4, we'll study RTP and SIP, two popular protocols for real-time conversational voice and video applications. In Section 7.5, we'll investigate mechanisms within the network that can be used to distinguish one class of traffic (e.g., delay-sensitive applications such as conversational voice) from another (e.g., elastic applications such as browsing Web pages), and provide differentiated service among multiple classes of traffic.

7.1 Multimedia Networking Applications

We define a multimedia network application as any network application that employs audio or video. In this section, we provide a taxonomy of multimedia applications. We'll see that each class of applications in the taxonomy has its own unique set of service requirements and design issues. But before diving into an in-depth discussion of Internet multimedia applications, it is useful to consider the intrinsic characteristics of the audio and video media themselves.

7.1.1 Properties of Video

Perhaps the most salient characteristic of video is its **high bit rate**. Video distributed over the Internet typically ranges from 100 kbps for low-quality video conferencing to over 3 Mbps for streaming high-definition movies. To get a sense of how video bandwidth demands compare with those of other Internet applications, let's briefly consider three different users, each using a different Internet application. Our first user, Frank, is going quickly through photos posted on his friends' Facebook pages. Let's assume that Frank is looking at a new photo every 10 seconds, and that photos are on average 200 Kbytes in size. (As usual, throughout this discussion we make the simplifying assumption that 1 Kbyte = 8,000 bits.) Our second user, Martha, is streaming music from the Internet ("the cloud") to her smartphone. Let's assume Martha is listening to many MP3 songs, one after the other, each encoded at a rate of 128 kbps. Our third user, Victor, is watching a video that has been encoded at 2 Mbps. Finally, let's suppose that the session length for all three users is 4,000 seconds (approximately 67 minutes). Table 7.1 compares the bit rates and the total bytes transferred for these three users. We see that video streaming consumes by far

	Bit rate	Bytes transferred in 67 min
Facebook Frank	160 kbps	80 Mbytes
Martha Music	128 kbps	64 Mbytes
Victor Video	2 Mbps	1 Gbyte

Table 7.1 ♦ Comparison of bit-rate requirements of three Internet applications

the most bandwidth, having a bit rate of more than ten times greater than that of the Facebook and music-streaming applications. Therefore, when designing networked video applications, the first thing we must keep in mind is the high bit-rate requirements of video. Given the popularity of video and its high bit rate, it is perhaps not surprising that Cisco predicts [Cisco 2011] that streaming and stored video will be approximately 90 percent of global consumer Internet traffic by 2015.

Another important characteristic of video is that it can be compressed, thereby trading off video quality with bit rate. A video is a sequence of images, typically being displayed at a constant rate, for example, at 24 or 30 images per second. An uncompressed, digitally encoded image consists of an array of pixels, with each pixel encoded into a number of bits to represent luminance and color. There are two types of redundancy in video, both of which can be exploited by **video compression**. *Spatial redundancy* is the redundancy within a given image. Intuitively, an image that consists of mostly white space has a high degree of redundancy and can be efficiently compressed without significantly sacrificing image quality. *Temporal redundancy* reflects repetition from image to subsequent image. If, for example, an image and the subsequent image are exactly the same, there is no reason to re-encode the subsequent image; it is instead more efficient simply to indicate during encoding that the subsequent image is exactly the same. Today's off-the-shelf compression algorithms can compress a video to essentially any bit rate desired. Of course, the higher the bit rate, the better the image quality and the better the overall user viewing experience.

We can also use compression to create **multiple versions** of the same video, each at a different quality level. For example, we can use compression to create, say, three versions of the same video, at rates of 300 kbps, 1 Mbps, and 3 Mbps. Users can then decide which version they want to watch as a function of their current available bandwidth. Users with high-speed Internet connections might choose the 3 Mbps version; users watching the video over 3G with a smartphone might choose the 300 kbps version. Similarly, the video in a video conference application can be compressed "on-the-fly" to provide the best video quality given the available end-to-end bandwidth between conversing users.

7.1.2 Properties of Audio

Digital audio (including digitized speech and music) has significantly lower bandwidth requirements than video. Digital audio, however, has its own unique properties that must be considered when designing multimedia network applications. To understand these properties, let's first consider how analog audio (which humans and musical instruments generate) is converted to a digital signal:

- The analog audio signal is sampled at some fixed rate, for example, at 8,000 samples per second. The value of each sample is an arbitrary real number.

- Each of the samples is then rounded to one of a finite number of values. This operation is referred to as **quantization**. The number of such finite values—called quantization values—is typically a power of two, for example, 256 quantization values.

- Each of the quantization values is represented by a fixed number of bits. For example, if there are 256 quantization values, then each value—and hence each audio sample—is represented by one byte. The bit representations of all the samples are then concatenated together to form the digital representation of the signal. As an example, if an analog audio signal is sampled at 8,000 samples per second and each sample is quantized and represented by 8 bits, then the resulting digital signal will have a rate of 64,000 bits per second. For playback through audio speakers, the digital signal can then be converted back—that is, decoded—to an analog signal. However, the decoded analog signal is only an approximation of the original signal, and the sound quality may be noticeably degraded (for example, high-frequency sounds may be missing in the decoded signal). By increasing the sampling rate and the number of quantization values, the decoded signal can better approximate the original analog signal. Thus (as with video), there is a trade-off between the quality of the decoded signal and the bit-rate and storage requirements of the digital signal.

The basic encoding technique that we just described is called **pulse code modulation (PCM)**. Speech encoding often uses PCM, with a sampling rate of 8,000 samples per second and 8 bits per sample, resulting in a rate of 64 kbps. The audio compact disk (CD) also uses PCM, with a sampling rate of 44,100 samples per second with 16 bits per sample; this gives a rate of 705.6 kbps for mono and 1.411 Mbps for stereo.

PCM-encoded speech and music, however, are rarely used in the Internet. Instead, as with video, compression techniques are used to reduce the bit rates of the stream. Human speech can be compressed to less than 10 kbps and still be intelligible. A popular compression technique for near CD-quality stereo music is **MPEG 1 layer 3**, more commonly known as **MP3**. MP3 encoders can compress to many different rates; 128 kbps is the most common encoding rate and produces very little sound degradation. A related standard is **Advanced Audio Coding (AAC)**, which has been popularized by Apple. As with video, multiple versions of a prerecorded audio stream can be created, each at a different bit rate.

Although audio bit rates are generally much less than those of video, users are generally much more sensitive to audio glitches than video glitches. Consider, for example, a video conference taking place over the Internet. If, from time to time, the video signal is lost for a few seconds, the video conference can likely proceed without too much user frustration. If, however, the audio signal is frequently lost, the users may have to terminate the session.

7.1.3 Types of Multimedia Network Applications

The Internet supports a large variety of useful and entertaining multimedia applications. In this subsection, we classify multimedia applications into three broad categories: *(i) streaming stored audio/video, (ii) conversational voice/video-over-IP*, and *(iii) streaming live audio/video*. As we will soon see, each of these application categories has its own set of service requirements and design issues.

Streaming Stored Audio and Video

To keep the discussion concrete, we focus here on streaming stored video, which typically combines video and audio components. Streaming stored audio (such as streaming music) is very similar to streaming stored video, although the bit rates are typically much lower.

In this class of applications, the underlying medium is prerecorded video, such as a movie, a television show, a prerecorded sporting event, or a prerecorded user-generated video (such as those commonly seen on YouTube). These prerecorded videos are placed on servers, and users send requests to the servers to view the videos *on demand*. Many Internet companies today provide streaming video, including YouTube (Google), Netflix, and Hulu. By some estimates, streaming stored video makes up over 50 percent of the downstream traffic in the Internet access networks today [Cisco 2011]. Streaming stored video has three key distinguishing features.

- *Streaming.* In a streaming stored video application, the client typically begins video playout within a few seconds after it begins receiving the video from the server. This means that the client will be playing out from one location in the video while at the same time receiving later parts of the video from the server. This technique, known as **streaming**, avoids having to download the entire video file (and incurring a potentially long delay) before playout begins.

- *Interactivity.* Because the media is prerecorded, the user may pause, reposition forward, reposition backward, fast-forward, and so on through the video content. The time from when the user makes such a request until the action manifests itself at the client should be less than a few seconds for acceptable responsiveness.

- *Continuous playout.* Once playout of the video begins, it should proceed according to the original timing of the recording. Therefore, data must be received from the server in time for its playout at the client; otherwise, users experience video frame freezing (when the client waits for the delayed frames) or frame skipping (when the client skips over delayed frames).

By far, the most important performance measure for streaming video is average throughput. In order to provide continuous playout, the network must provide an average throughput to the streaming application that is at least as large the bit rate of the video itself. As we will see in Section 7.2, by using buffering and prefetching, it is possible to provide continuous playout even when the throughput fluctuates, as long as the average throughput (averaged over 5–10 seconds) remains above the video rate [Wang 2008].

For many streaming video applications, prerecorded video is stored on, and streamed from, a CDN rather than from a single data center. There are also many P2P video streaming applications for which the video is stored on users' hosts (peers), with different chunks of video arriving from different peers that may spread around the globe. Given the prominence of Internet video streaming, we will explore video streaming in some depth in Section 7.2, paying particular attention to client buffering, prefetching, adapting quality to bandwidth availability, and CDN distribution.

Conversational Voice- and Video-over-IP

Real-time conversational voice over the Internet is often referred to as **Internet telephony**, since, from the user's perspective, it is similar to the traditional circuit-switched telephone service. It is also commonly called **Voice-over-IP (VoIP)**. Conversational video is similar, except that it includes the video of the participants as well as their voices. Most of today's voice and video conversational systems allow users to create conferences with three or more participants. Conversational voice and video are widely used in the Internet today, with the Internet companies Skype, QQ, and Google Talk boasting hundreds of millions of daily users.

In our discussion of application service requirements in Chapter 2 (Figure 2.4), we identified a number of axes along which application requirements can be classified. Two of these axes—timing considerations and tolerance of data loss—are particularly important for conversational voice and video applications. Timing considerations are important because audio and video conversational applications are highly **delay-sensitive**. For a conversation with two or more interacting speakers, the delay from when a user speaks or moves until the action is manifested at the other end should be less than a few hundred milliseconds. For voice, delays smaller than 150 milliseconds are not perceived by a human listener, delays between 150 and 400 milliseconds can be acceptable, and delays exceeding 400 milliseconds can result in frustrating, if not completely unintelligible, voice conversations.

On the other hand, conversational multimedia applications are **loss-tolerant**—occasional loss only causes occasional glitches in audio/video playback, and these losses can often be partially or fully concealed. These delay-sensitive but loss-tolerant characteristics are clearly different from those of elastic data applications such as Web browsing, e-mail, social networks, and remote login. For elastic applications, long delays are annoying but not particularly harmful; the completeness and integrity of the transferred data, however, are of paramount importance. We will explore conversational voice and video in more depth in Section 7.3, paying particular attention to how adaptive playout, forward error correction, and error concealment can mitigate against network-induced packet loss and delay.

Streaming Live Audio and Video

This third class of applications is similar to traditional broadcast radio and television, except that transmission takes place over the Internet. These applications allow a user to receive a *live* radio or television transmission—such as a live sporting event or an ongoing news event—transmitted from any corner of the world. Today, thousands of radio and television stations around the world are broadcasting content over the Internet.

Live, broadcast-like applications often have many users who receive the same audio/video program at the same time. Although the distribution of live audio/video to many receivers can be efficiently accomplished using the IP multicasting techniques described in Section 4.7, multicast distribution is more often accomplished today via application-layer multicast (using P2P networks or CDNs) or through multiple separate unicast streams. As with streaming stored multimedia, the network must provide each live multimedia flow with an average throughput that is larger than the video consumption rate. Because the event is live, delay can also be an issue, although the timing constraints are much less stringent than those for conversational voice. Delays of up to ten seconds or so from when the user chooses to view a live transmission to when playout begins can be tolerated. We will not cover streaming live media in this book because many of the techniques used for streaming live media—initial buffering delay, adaptive bandwidth use, and CDN distribution—are similar to those for streaming stored media.

7.2 Streaming Stored Video

For streaming video applications, prerecorded videos are placed on servers, and users send requests to these servers to view the videos on demand. The user may watch the video from beginning to end without interruption, may stop watching the video well before it ends, or interact with the video by pausing or repositioning to a future or past scene. Streaming video systems can be classified into three categories: **UDP streaming**, **HTTP streaming**, and **adaptive HTTP streaming**. Although all three types of systems are used in practice, the majority of today's systems employ HTTP streaming and adaptive HTTP streaming.

A common characteristic of all three forms of video streaming is the extensive use of client-side application buffering to mitigate the effects of varying end-to-end delays and varying amounts of available bandwidth between server and client. For streaming video (both stored and live), users generally can tolerate a small several-second initial delay between when the client requests a video and when video play-out begins at the client. Consequently, when the video starts to arrive at the client, the client need not immediately begin playout, but can instead build up a reserve of video in an application buffer. Once the client has built up a reserve of several seconds of buffered-but-not-yet-played video, the client can then begin video playout. There are two important advantages provided by such **client buffering**. First, client-side buffering can absorb variations in server-to-client delay. If a particular piece of video data is delayed, as long as it arrives before the reserve of received-but-not-yet-played video is exhausted, this long delay will not be noticed. Second, if the server-to-client bandwidth briefly drops below the video consumption rate, a user can continue to enjoy continuous playback, again as long as the client application buffer does not become completely drained.

Figure 7.1 illustrates client-side buffering. In this simple example, suppose that video is encoded at a fixed bit rate, and thus each video block contains video frames that are to be played out over the same fixed amount of time, Δ. The server transmits the first video block at t_0, the second block at $t_0 + \Delta$, the third block at $t_0 + 2\Delta$, and so on. Once the client begins playout, each block should be played out Δ time units after the previous block in order to reproduce the timing of the original recorded video. Because of the variable end-to-end network delays, different video blocks experience different delays. The first video block arrives at the client at t_1 and the second block arrives at t_2. The network delay for the ith block is the horizontal distance between the time the block was transmitted by the server and the

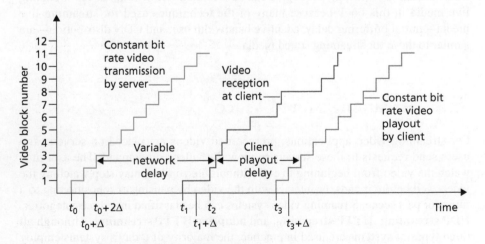

Figure 7.1 ♦ Client playout delay in video streaming

time it is received at the client; note that the network delay varies from one video block to another. In this example, if the client were to begin playout as soon as the first block arrived at t_1, then the second block would not have arrived in time to be played out at out at $t_1 + \triangle$. In this case, video playout would either have to stall (waiting for block 2 to arrive) or block 2 could be skipped—both resulting in undesirable playout impairments. Instead, if the client were to delay the start of playout until t_3, when blocks 1 through 6 have all arrived, periodic playout can proceed with *all* blocks having been received before their playout time.

7.2.1 UDP Streaming

We only briefly discuss UDP streaming here, referring the reader to more in-depth discussions of the protocols behind these systems where appropriate. With UDP streaming, the server transmits video at a rate that matches the client's video consumption rate by clocking out the video chunks over UDP at a steady rate. For example, if the video consumption rate is 2 Mbps and each UDP packet carries 8,000 bits of video, then the server would transmit one UDP packet into its socket every (8000 bits)/(2 Mbps) = 4 msec. As we learned in Chapter 3, because UDP does not employ a congestion-control mechanism, the server can push packets into the network at the consumption rate of the video without the rate-control restrictions of TCP. UDP streaming typically uses a small client-side buffer, big enough to hold less than a second of video.

Before passing the video chunks to UDP, the server will encapsulate the video chunks within transport packets specially designed for transporting audio and video, using the Real-Time Transport Protocol (RTP) [RFC 3550] or a similar (possibly proprietary) scheme. We delay our coverage of RTP until Section 7.3, where we discuss RTP in the context of conversational voice and video systems.

Another distinguishing property of UDP streaming is that in addition to the server-to-client video stream, the client and server also maintain, in parallel, a separate control connection over which the client sends commands regarding session state changes (such as pause, resume, reposition, and so on). This control connection is in many ways analogous to the FTP control connection we studied in Chapter 2. The Real-Time Streaming Protocol (RTSP) [RFC 2326], explained in some detail in the companion Web site for this textbook, is a popular open protocol for such a control connection.

Although UDP streaming has been employed in many open-source systems and proprietary products, it suffers from three significant drawbacks. First, due to the unpredictable and varying amount of available bandwidth between server and client, constant-rate UDP streaming can fail to provide continuous playout. For example, consider the scenario where the video consumption rate is 1 Mbps and the server-to-client available bandwidth is usually more than 1 Mbps, but every few minutes the available bandwidth drops below 1 Mbps for several seconds. In such a scenario, a UDP streaming system that transmits video at a constant rate of 1 Mbps over RTP/UDP would likely provide a poor user experience, with freezing or skipped frames soon after the available bandwidth falls below 1 Mbps. The second drawback of UDP streaming is that it requires a media control server, such as an RTSP server, to process client-to-server interactivity requests and to track client state (e.g., the client's playout point in the video, whether the video is being paused or played, and so on) for *each* ongoing client session. This increases the overall cost and complexity of deploying a large-scale video-on-demand system. The third drawback is that many firewalls are configured to block UDP traffic, preventing the users behind these firewalls from receiving UDP video.

7.2.2 HTTP Streaming

In HTTP streaming, the video is simply stored in an HTTP server as an ordinary file with a specific URL. When a user wants to see the video, the client establishes a TCP connection with the server and issues an HTTP GET request for that URL. The server then sends the video file, within an HTTP response message, as quickly as possible, that is, as quickly as TCP congestion control and flow control will allow. On the client side, the bytes are collected in a client application buffer. Once the number of bytes in this buffer exceeds a predetermined threshold, the client application begins playback—specifically, it periodically grabs video frames from the client application buffer, decompresses the frames, and displays them on the user's screen.

We learned in Chapter 3 that when transferring a file over TCP, the server-to-client transmission rate can vary significantly due to TCP's congestion control mechanism. In particular, it is not uncommon for the transmission rate to vary in a "saw-tooth" manner (for example, Figure 3.53) associated with TCP congestion control. Furthermore, packets can also be significantly delayed due to TCP's retransmission mechanism. Because of these characteristics of TCP, the conventional wisdom in the 1990s was that video streaming would never work well over TCP. Over time, however, designers of streaming video systems learned that TCP's congestion control and reliable-data transfer mechanisms do not necessarily preclude continuous playout when client buffering and prefetching (discussed in the next section) are used.

The use of HTTP over TCP also allows the video to traverse firewalls and NATs more easily (which are often configured to block most UDP traffic but to allow most HTTP traffic). Streaming over HTTP also obviates the need for a media control server, such as an RTSP server, reducing the cost of a large-scale deployment over the Internet. Due to all of these advantages, most video streaming applications today—including YouTube and Netflix—use HTTP streaming (over TCP) as its underlying streaming protocol.

Prefetching Video

We just learned, client-side buffering can be used to mitigate the effects of varying end-to-end delays and varying available bandwidth. In our earlier example in Figure 7.1, the server transmits video at the rate at which the video is to be played out. However, for streaming *stored* video, the client can attempt to download the video at a rate *higher* than the consumption rate, thereby **prefetching** video frames that are to be consumed in the future. This prefetched video is naturally stored in the client application buffer. Such prefetching occurs naturally with TCP streaming, since TCP's congestion avoidance mechanism will attempt to use all of the available bandwidth between server and client.

To gain some insight into prefetching, let's take a look at a simple example. Suppose the video consumption rate is 1 Mbps but the network is capable of delivering the video from server to client at a constant rate of 1.5 Mbps. Then the client will not only be able to play out the video with a very small playout delay, but will also be able to increase the amount of buffered video data by 500 Kbits every second. In this manner, if in the future the client receives data at a rate of less than 1 Mbps for a brief period of time, the client will be able to continue to provide continuous playback due to the reserve in its buffer. [Wang 2008] shows that when the average TCP throughput is roughly twice the media bit rate, streaming over TCP results in minimal starvation and low buffering delays.

Client Application Buffer and TCP Buffers

Figure 7.2 illustrates the interaction between client and server for HTTP streaming. At the server side, the portion of the video file in white has already been sent into the server's socket, while the darkened portion is what remains to be sent. After "passing through the socket door," the bytes are placed in the TCP send buffer before being transmitted into the Internet, as described in Chapter 3. In Figure 7.2,

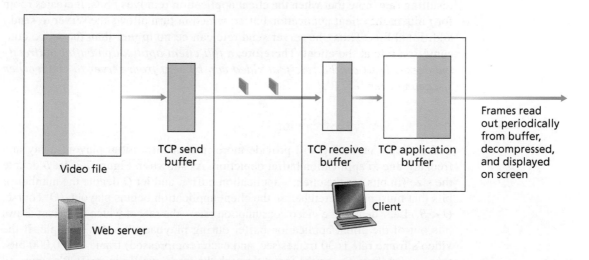

Figure 7.2 ♦ Streaming stored video over HTTP/TCP

because the TCP send buffer is shown to be full, the server is momentarily prevented from sending more bytes from the video file into the socket. On the client side, the client application (media player) reads bytes from the TCP receive buffer (through its client socket) and places the bytes into the client application buffer. At the same time, the client application periodically grabs video frames from the client application buffer, decompresses the frames, and displays them on the user's screen. Note that if the client application buffer is larger than the video file, then the whole process of moving bytes from the server's storage to the client's application buffer is equivalent to an ordinary file download over HTTP—the client simply pulls the video off the server as fast as TCP will allow!

Consider now what happens when the user pauses the video during the streaming process. During the pause period, bits are not removed from the client application buffer, even though bits continue to enter the buffer from the server. If the client application buffer is finite, it may eventually become full, which will cause "back pressure" all the way back to the server. Specifically, once the client application buffer becomes full, bytes can no longer be removed from the client TCP receive buffer, so it too becomes full. Once the client receive TCP buffer becomes full, bytes can no longer be removed from the server TCP send buffer, so it also becomes full. Once the TCP send buffer becomes full, the server cannot send any more bytes into the socket. Thus, if the user pauses the video, the server may be forced to stop transmitting, in which case the server will be blocked until the user resumes the video.

In fact, even during regular playback (that is, without pausing), if the client application buffer becomes full, back pressure will cause the TCP buffers to become full, which will force the server to reduce its rate. To determine the resulting rate, note that when the client application removes f bits, it creates room for f bits in the client application buffer, which in turn allows the server to send f additional bits. Thus, the server send rate can be no higher than the video consumption rate at the client. Therefore, *a full client application buffer indirectly imposes a limit on the rate that video can be sent from server to client when streaming over HTTP.*

Analysis of Video Streaming

Some simple modeling will provide more insight into initial playout delay and freezing due to application buffer depletion. As shown in Figure 7.3, let B denote the size (in bits) of the client's application buffer, and let Q denote the number of bits that must be buffered before the client application begins playout. (Of course, $Q < B$.) Let r denote the video consumption rate—the rate at which the client draws bits out of the client application buffer during playback. So, for example, if the video's frame rate is 30 frames/sec, and each (compressed) frame is 100,000 bits, then $r = 3$ Mbps. To see the forest through the trees, we'll ignore TCP's send and receive buffers.

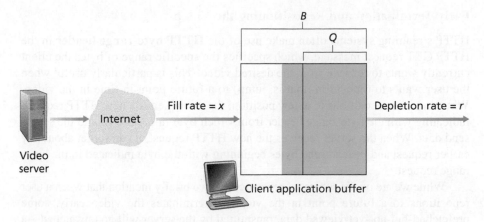

Figure 7.3 ◆ Analysis of client-side buffering for video streaming

Let's assume that the server sends bits at a constant rate x whenever the client buffer is not full. (This is a gross simplification, since TCP's send rate varies due to congestion control; we'll examine more realistic time-dependent rates $x(t)$ in the problems at the end of this chapter.) Suppose at time $t = 0$, the application buffer is empty and video begins arriving to the client application buffer. We now ask at what time $t = t_p$ does playout begin? And while we are at it, at what time $t = t_f$ does the client application buffer become full?

First, let's determine t_p, the time when Q bits have entered the application buffer and playout begins. Recall that bits arrive to the client application buffer at rate x and *no* bits are removed from this buffer before playout begins. Thus, the amount of time required to build up Q bits (the initial buffering delay) is $t_p = Q/x$.

Now let's determine t_f, the point in time when the client application buffer becomes full. We first observe that if $x < r$ (that is, if the server send rate is less than the video consumption rate), then the client buffer will never become full! Indeed, starting at time t_p, the buffer will be depleted at rate r and will only be filled at rate $x < r$. Eventually the client buffer will empty out entirely, at which time the video will freeze on the screen while the client buffer waits another t_p seconds to build up Q bits of video. *Thus, when the available rate in the network is less than the video rate, playout will alternate between periods of continuous playout and periods of freezing.* In a homework problem, you will be asked to determine the length of each continuous playout and freezing period as a function of Q, r, and x. Now let's determine t_f for when $x > r$. In this case, starting at time t_p, the buffer increases from Q to B at rate $x - r$ since bits are being depleted at rate r but are arriving at rate x, as shown in Figure 7.3. Given these hints, you will be asked in a homework problem to determine t_f, the time the client buffer becomes full. Note that *when the available rate in the network is more than the video rate, after the initial buffering delay, the user will enjoy continuous playout until the video ends.*

Early Termination and Repositioning the Video

HTTP streaming systems often make use of the **HTTP byte-range header** in the HTTP GET request message, which specifies the specific range of bytes the client currently wants to retrieve from the desired video. This is particularly useful when the user wants to reposition (that is, jump) to a future point in time in the video. When the user repositions to a new position, the client sends a new HTTP request, indicating with the byte-range header from which byte in the file should the server send data. When the server receives the new HTTP request, it can forget about any earlier request and instead send bytes beginning with the byte indicated in the byte-range request.

While we are on the subject of repositioning, we briefly mention that when a user repositions to a future point in the video or terminates the video early, some prefetched-but-not-yet-viewed data transmitted by the server will go unwatched—a waste of network bandwidth and server resources. For example, suppose that the client buffer is full with B bits at some time t_0 into the video, and at this time the user repositions to some instant $t > t_0 + B/r$ into the video, and then watches the video to completion from that point on. In this case, all B bits in the buffer will be unwatched and the bandwidth and server resources that were used to transmit those B bits have been completely wasted. There is significant wasted bandwidth in the Internet due to early termination, which can be quite costly, particularly for wireless links [Ihm 2011]. For this reason, many streaming systems use only a moderate-size client application buffer, or will limit the amount of prefetched video using the byte-range header in HTTP requests [Rao 2011].

Repositioning and early termination are analogous to cooking a large meal, eating only a portion of it, and throwing the rest away, thereby wasting food. So the next time your parents criticize you for wasting food by not eating all your dinner, you can quickly retort by saying they are wasting bandwidth and server resources when they reposition while watching movies over the Internet! But, of course, two wrongs do not make a right—both food and bandwidth are not to be wasted!

7.2.3 Adaptive Streaming and DASH

Although HTTP streaming, as described in the previous subsection, has been extensively deployed in practice (for example, by YouTube since its inception), it has a major shortcoming: All clients receive the same encoding of the video, despite the large variations in the amount of bandwidth available to a client, both across different clients and also over time for the same client. This has led to the development of a new type of HTTP-based streaming, often referred to as **Dynamic Adaptive Streaming over HTTP (DASH)**. In DASH, the video is encoded into several different versions, with each version having a different bit rate and, correspondingly, a different quality level. The client dynamically requests chunks of video segments of a few seconds in length from the different versions. When the amount of available bandwidth is high, the client naturally selects chunks from a high-rate version; and when the available bandwidth is low, it naturally selects from a low-rate version. The client selects different chunks one at a time with HTTP GET request messages [Akhshabi 2011].

On one hand, DASH allows clients with different Internet access rates to stream in video at different encoding rates. Clients with low-speed 3G connections can receive a low bit-rate (and low-quality) version, and clients with fiber connections can receive a high-quality version. On the other hand, DASH allows a client to adapt to the available bandwidth if the end-to-end bandwidth changes during the session. This feature is particularly important for mobile users, who typically see their bandwidth availability fluctuate as they move with respect to the base stations. Comcast, for example, has deployed an adaptive streaming system in which each video source file is encoded into 8 to 10 different MPEG-4 formats, allowing the highest quality video format to be streamed to the client, with adaptation being performed in response to changing network and device conditions.

With DASH, each video version is stored in the HTTP server, each with a different URL. The HTTP server also has a **manifest file**, which provides a URL for each version along with its bit rate. The client first requests the manifest file and learns about the various versions. The client then selects one chunk at a time by specifying a URL and a byte range in an HTTP GET request message for each chunk. While downloading chunks, the client also measures the received bandwidth and runs a *rate determination algorithm* to select the chunk to request next. Naturally, if the client has a lot of video buffered and if the measured receive bandwidth is high, it will choose a chunk from a high-rate version. And naturally if the client has little video buffered and the measured received bandwidth is low, it will choose a chunk from a low-rate version. DASH therefore allows the client to freely switch among different quality levels. Since a sudden drop in bit rate by changing versions may result in noticeable visual quality degradation, the bit-rate reduction may be achieved using multiple intermediate versions to smoothly transition to a rate where the client's consumption rate drops below its available receive bandwidth. When the network conditions improve, the client can then later choose chunks from higher bit-rate versions.

By dynamically monitoring the available bandwidth and client buffer level, and adjusting the transmission rate with version switching, DASH can often achieve continuous playout at the best possible quality level without frame freezing or skipping. Furthermore, since the client (rather than the server) maintains the intelligence to determine which chunk to send next, the scheme also improves server-side scalability. Another benefit of this approach is that the client can use the HTTP byte-range request to precisely control the amount of prefetched video that it buffers locally.

We conclude our brief discussion of DASH by mentioning that for many implementations, the server not only stores many versions of the video but also separately stores many versions of the audio. Each audio version has its own quality level and bit rate and has its own URL. In these implementations, the client dynamically selects both video and audio chunks, and locally synchronizes audio and video playout.

7.2.4 Content Distribution Networks

Today, many Internet video companies are distributing on-demand multi-Mbps streams to millions of users on a daily basis. YouTube, for example, with a library of hundreds of millions of videos, distributes hundreds of millions of video streams to users around the world every day [Ding 2011]. Streaming all this traffic to locations all over the world while providing continuous playout and high interactivity is clearly a challenging task.

For an Internet video company, perhaps the most straightforward approach to providing streaming video service is to build a single massive data center, store all of its videos in the data center, and stream the videos directly from the data center to clients worldwide. But there are three major problems with this approach. First, if the client is far from the data center, server-to-client packets will cross many communication links and likely pass through many ISPs, with some of the ISPs possibly located on different continents. If one of these links provides a throughput that is less than the video consumption rate, the end-to-end throughput will also be below the consumption rate, resulting in annoying freezing delays for the user. (Recall from Chapter 1 that the end-to-end throughput of a stream is governed by the throughput in the bottleneck link.) The likelihood of this happening increases as the number of links in the end-to-end path increases. A second drawback is that a popular video will likely be sent many times over the same communication links. Not only does this waste network bandwidth, but the Internet video company itself will be paying its provider ISP (connected to the data center) for sending the *same* bytes into the Internet over and over again. A third problem with this solution is that a single data center represents a single point of failure—if the data center or its links to the Internet goes down, it would not be able to distribute *any* video streams.

In order to meet the challenge of distributing massive amounts of video data to users distributed around the world, almost all major video-streaming companies make use of **Content Distribution Networks (CDNs)**. A CDN manages servers in multiple geographically distributed locations, stores copies of the videos (and other types of Web content, including documents, images, and audio) in its servers, and attempts to direct each user request to a CDN location that will provide the best user experience. The CDN may be a **private CDN**, that is, owned by the content provider itself; for example, Google's CDN distributes YouTube videos and other types of content. The CDN may alternatively be a **third-party CDN** that distributes content on behalf of multiple content providers; Akamai's CDN, for example, is a third-party CDN that distributes Netflix and Hulu content, among others. A very readable overview of modern CDNs is [Leighton 2009].

CDNs typically adopt one of two different server placement philosophies [Huang 2008]:

*   **Enter Deep.**   One philosophy, pioneered by Akamai, is to *enter deep* into the access networks of Internet Service Providers, by deploying server clusters in access ISPs all over the world. (Access networks are described in Section 1.3.)

CASE STUDY

GOOGLE'S NETWORK INFRASTRUCTURE

To support its vast array of cloud services—including search, gmail, calendar, YouTube video, maps, documents, and social networks—Google has deployed an extensive private network and CDN infrastructure. Google's CDN infrastructure has three tiers of server clusters:

- Eight "mega data centers," with six located in the United States and two located in Europe [Google Locations 2012], with each data center having on the order of 100,000 servers. These mega data centers are responsible for serving dynamic (and often personalized) content, including search results and gmail messages.
- About 30 "bring-home" clusters (see discussion in 7.2.4), with each cluster consisting on the order of 100–500 servers [Adhikari 2011a]. The cluster locations are distributed around the world, with each location typically near multiple tier-1 ISP PoPs. These clusters are responsible for serving static content, including YouTube videos [Adhikari 2011a].
- Many hundreds of "enter-deep" clusters (see discussion in 7.2.4), with each cluster located within an access ISP. Here a cluster typically consists of tens of servers within a single rack. These enter-deep servers perform TCP splitting (see Section 3.7) and serve static content [Chen 2011], including the static portions of Web pages that embody search results.

All of these data centers and cluster locations are networked together with Google's own private network, as part of one enormous AS (AS 15169). When a user makes a search query, often the query is first sent over the local ISP to a nearby enter-deep cache, from where the static content is retrieved; while providing the static content to the client, the nearby cache also forwards the query over Google's private network to one of the mega data centers, from where the personalized search results are retrieved. For a YouTube video, the video itself may come from one of the bring-home caches, whereas portions of the Web page surrounding the video may come from the nearby enter-deep cache, and the advertisements surrounding the video come from the data centers. In summary, except for the local ISPs, the Google cloud services are largely provided by a network infrastructure that is independent of the public Internet.

Akamai takes this approach with clusters in approximately 1,700 locations. The goal is to get close to end users, thereby improving user-perceived delay and throughput by decreasing the number of links and routers between the end user and the CDN cluster from which it receives content. Because of this highly distributed design, the task of maintaining and managing the clusters becomes challenging.

- **Bring Home.**   A second design philosophy, taken by Limelight and many other CDN companies, is to *bring the ISPs home* by building large clusters at a smaller number (for example, tens) of key locations and connecting these clusters using a private high-speed network. Instead of getting inside the access ISPs, these CDNs typically place each cluster at a location that is simultaneously near the PoPs (see Section 1.3) of many tier-1 ISPs, for example, within a few miles of both AT&T and Verizon PoPs in a major city. Compared with the enter-deep design philosophy, the bring-home design typically results in lower maintenance and management overhead, possibly at the expense of higher delay and lower throughput to end users.

Once its clusters are in place, the CDN replicates content across its clusters. The CDN may not want to place a copy of every video in each cluster, since some videos are rarely viewed or are only popular in some countries. In fact, many CDNs do not push videos to their clusters but instead use a simple pull strategy: If a client requests a video from a cluster that is not storing the video, then the cluster retrieves the video (from a central repository or from another cluster) and stores a copy locally while streaming the video to the client at the same time. Similar to Internet caches (see Chapter 2), when a cluster's storage becomes full, it removes videos that are not frequently requested.

CDN Operation

Having identified the two major approaches toward deploying a CDN, let's now dive down into the nuts and bolts of how a CDN operates. When a browser in a user's host is instructed to retrieve a specific video (identified by a URL), the CDN must intercept the request so that it can (1) determine a suitable CDN server cluster for that client at that time, and (2) redirect the client's request to a server in that cluster. We'll shortly discuss how a CDN can determine a suitable cluster. But first let's examine the mechanics behind intercepting and redirecting a request.

Most CDNs take advantage of DNS to intercept and redirect requests; an interesting discussion of such a use of the DNS is [Vixie 2009]. Let's consider a simple example to illustrate how DNS is typically involved. Suppose a content provider, NetCinema, employs the third-party CDN company, KingCDN, to distribute its videos to its customers. On the NetCinema Web pages, each of its videos is assigned a URL that includes the string "video" and a unique identifier for the video itself; for example, Transformers 7 might be assigned http://video.netcinema.com/6Y7B23V. Six steps then occur, as shown in Figure 7.4:

1. The user visits the Web page at NetCinema.
2. When the user clicks on the link http://video.netcinema.com/6Y7B23V, the user's host sends a DNS query for video.netcinema.com.

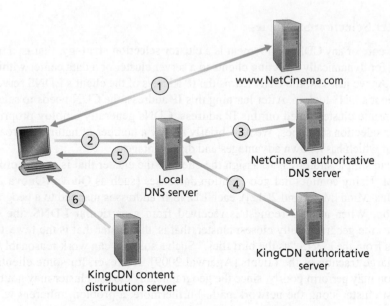

Figure 7.4 ♦ DNS redirects a user's request to a CDN server

3. The user's Local DNS Server (LDNS) relays the DNS query to an authoritative DNS server for NetCinema, which observes the string "video" in the hostname video.netcinema.com. To "hand over" the DNS query to KingCDN, instead of returning an IP address, the NetCinema authoritative DNS server returns to the LDNS a hostname in the KingCDN's domain, for example, a1105.kingcdn.com.

4. From this point on, the DNS query enters into KingCDN's private DNS infrastructure. The user's LDNS then sends a second query, now for a1105.kingcdn.com, and KingCDN's DNS system eventually returns the IP addresses of a KingCDN content server to the LDNS. It is thus here, within the KingCDN's DNS system, that the CDN server from which the client will receive its content is specified.

5. The LDNS forwards the IP address of the content-serving CDN node to the user's host.

6. Once the client receives the IP address for a KingCDN content server, it establishes a direct TCP connection with the server at that IP address and issues an HTTP GET request for the video. If DASH is used, the server will first send to the client a manifest file with a list of URLs, one for each version of the video, and the client will dynamically select chunks from the different versions.

Cluster Selection Strategies

At the core of any CDN deployment is a **cluster selection strategy**, that is, a mechanism for dynamically directing clients to a server cluster or a data center within the CDN. As we just saw, the CDN learns the IP address of the client's LDNS server via the client's DNS lookup. After learning this IP address, the CDN needs to select an appropriate cluster based on this IP address. CDNs generally employ proprietary cluster selection strategies. We now briefly survey a number of natural approaches, each of which has its own advantages and disadvantages.

One simple strategy is to assign the client to the cluster that is **geographically closest**. Using commercial geo-location databases (such as Quova [Quova 2012] and Max-Mind [MaxMind 2012]), each LDNS IP address is mapped to a geographic location. When a DNS request is received from a particular LDNS, the CDN chooses the geographically closest cluster, that is, the cluster that is the fewest kilometers from the LDNS "as the bird flies." Such a solution can work reasonably well for a large fraction of the clients [Agarwal 2009]. However, for some clients, the solution may perform poorly, since the geographically closest cluster may not be the closest cluster along the network path. Furthermore, a problem inherent with all DNS-based approaches is that some end-users are configured to use remotely located LDNSs [Shaikh 2001; Mao 2002], in which case the LDNS location may be far from the client's location. Moreover, this simple strategy ignores the variation in delay and available bandwidth over time of Internet paths, always assigning the same cluster to a particular client.

In order to determine the best cluster for a client based on the *current* traffic conditions, CDNs can instead perform periodic **real-time measurements** of delay and loss performance between their clusters and clients. For instance, a CDN can have each of its clusters periodically send probes (for example, ping messages or DNS queries) to all of the LDNSs around the world. One drawback of this approach is that many LDNSs are configured to not respond to such probes.

An alternative to sending extraneous traffic for measuring path properties is to use the characteristics of recent and ongoing traffic between the clients and CDN servers. For instance, the delay between a client and a cluster can be estimated by examining the gap between server-to-client SYNACK and client-to-server ACK during the TCP three-way handshake. Such solutions, however, require redirecting clients to (possibly) suboptimal clusters from time to time in order to measure the properties of paths to these clusters. Although only a small number of requests need to serve as probes, the selected clients can suffer significant performance degradation when receiving content (video or otherwise) [Andrews 2002; Krishnan 2009]. Another alternative for cluster-to-client path probing is to use DNS query traffic to measure the delay between clients and clusters. Specifically, during the DNS phase (within Step 4 in Figure 7.4), the client's LDNS can be occasionally directed to different DNS authoritative servers installed at the various cluster locations, yielding DNS traffic that can then be measured between the LDNS and these cluster locations.

In this scheme, the DNS servers continue to return the optimal cluster for the client, so that delivery of videos and other Web objects does not suffer [Huang 2010].

A very different approach to matching clients with CDN servers is to use **IP anycast** [RFC 1546]. The idea behind IP anycast is to have the routers in the Internet route the client's packets to the "closest" cluster, as determined by BGP. Specifically, as shown in Figure 7.5, during the IP-anycast configuration stage, the CDN company assigns the *same* IP address to each of its clusters, and *uses standard BGP* to advertise this IP address from each of the different cluster locations. When a BGP router receives multiple route advertisements for this same IP address, it treats these advertisements as providing different paths to the same physical location (when, in fact, the advertisements are for different paths to *different* physical locations). Following standard operating procedures, the BGP router will then pick the "best" (for example, closest, as determined by AS-hop counts) route to the IP address according to its local route selection mechanism. For example, if one BGP route

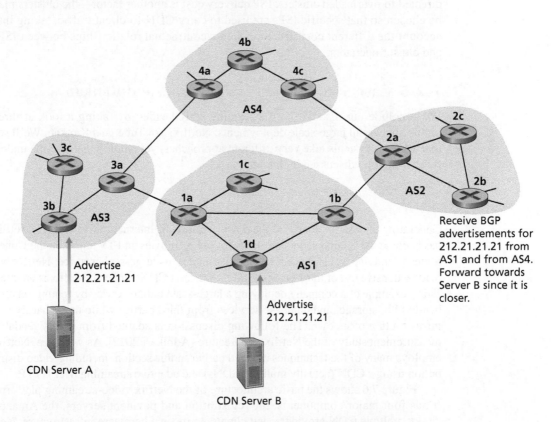

Advertise
212.21.21.21

Advertise
212.21.21.21

Receive BGP
advertisements for
212.21.21.21 from
AS1 and from AS4.
Forward towards
Server B since it is
closer.

CDN Server A

CDN Server B

Figure 7.5 ♦ Using IP anycast to route clients to closest CDN cluster

(corresponding to one location) is only one AS hop away from the router, and all other BGP routes (corresponding to other locations) are two or more AS hops away, then the BGP router would typically choose to route packets to the location that needs to traverse only one AS (see Section 4.6). After this initial configuration phase, the CDN can do its main job of distributing content. When any client wants to see any video, the CDN's DNS returns the anycast address, no matter where the client is located. When the client sends a packet to that IP address, the packet is routed to the "closest" cluster as determined by the preconfigured forwarding tables, which were configured with BGP as just described. This approach has the advantage of finding the cluster that is closest to the client rather than the cluster that is closest to the client's LDNS. However, the IP anycast strategy again does not take into account the dynamic nature of the Internet over short time scales [Ballani 2006].

Besides network-related considerations such as delay, loss, and bandwidth performance, there are many additional important factors that go into designing a cluster selection strategy. Load on the clusters is one such factor—clients should not be directed to overloaded clusters. ISP delivery cost is another factor—the clusters may be chosen so that specific ISPs are used to carry CDN-to-client traffic, taking into account the different cost structures in the contractual relationships between ISPs and cluster operators.

7.2.5 Case Studies: Netflix, YouTube, and Kankan

We conclude our discussion of streaming stored video by taking a look at three highly successful large-scale deployments: Netflix, YouTube, and Kankan. We'll see that all these systems take very different approaches, yet employ many of the underlying principles discussed in this section.

Netflix

Generating almost 30 percent of the downstream U.S. Internet traffic in 2011, Netflix has become the leading service provider for online movies and TV shows in the United States [Sandvine 2011]. In order to rapidly deploy its large-scale service, Netflix has made extensive use of third-party cloud services and CDNs. Indeed, Netflix is an interesting example of a company deploying a large-scale online service by renting servers, bandwidth, storage, and database services from third parties while using hardly any infrastructure of its own. The following discussion is adapted from a very readable measurement study of the Netflix architecture [Adhikari 2012]. As we'll see, Netflix employs many of the techniques covered earlier in this section, including video distribution using a CDN (actually multiple CDNs) and adaptive streaming over HTTP.

Figure 7.6 shows the basic architecture of the Netflix video-streaming platform. It has four major components: the registration and payment servers, the Amazon cloud, multiple CDN providers, and clients. In its own hardware infrastructure, Netflix maintains registration and payment servers, which handle registration of new

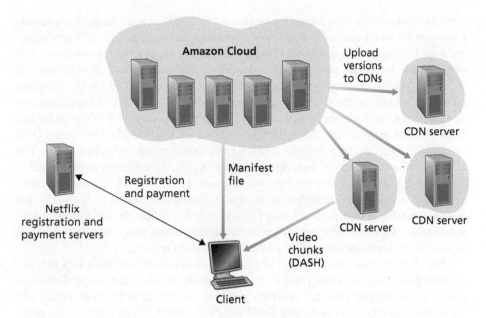

Figure 7.6 ♦ Netflix video streaming platform

accounts and capture credit-card payment information. Except for these basic functions, Netflix runs its online service by employing machines (or virtual machines) in the Amazon cloud. Some of the functions taking place in the Amazon cloud include:

- *Content ingestion.* Before Netflix can distribute a movie to its customers, it must first ingest and process the movie. Netflix receives studio master versions of movies and uploads them to hosts in the Amazon cloud.

- *Content processing.* The machines in the Amazon cloud create many different formats for each movie, suitable for a diverse array of client video players running on desktop computers, smartphones, and game consoles connected to televisions. A different version is created for each of these formats and at multiple bit rates, allowing for adaptive streaming over HTTP using DASH.

- *Uploading versions to the CDNs.* Once all of the versions of a movie have been created, the hosts in the Amazon cloud upload the versions to the CDNs.

To deliver the movies to its customers on demand, Netflix makes extensive use of CDN technology. In fact, as of this writing in 2012, Netflix employs not one but *three* third-party CDN companies at the same time—Akamai, Limelight, and Level-3.

Having described the components of the Netflix architecture, let's take a closer look at the interaction between the client and the various servers that are involved in movie delivery. The Web pages for browsing the Netflix video library are served from servers in the Amazon cloud. When the user selects a movie to "Play Now," the user's client obtains a manifest file, also from servers in the Amazon cloud. The manifest file includes a variety of information, including a ranked list of CDNs and the URLs for the different versions of the movie, which are used for DASH playback. The ranking of the CDNs is determined by Netflix, and may change from one streaming session to the next. Typically the client will select the CDN that is ranked highest in the manifest file. After the client selects a CDN, the CDN leverages DNS to redirect the client to a specific CDN server, as described in Section 7.2.4. The client and that CDN server then interact using DASH. Specifically, as described in Section 7.2.3, the client uses the byte-range header in HTTP GET request messages, to request chunks from the different versions of the movie. Netflix uses chunks that are approximately four-seconds long [Adhikari 2012]. While the chunks are being downloaded, the client measures the received throughput and runs a rate-determination algorithm to determine the quality of the next chunk to request.

Netflix embodies many of the key principles discussed earlier in this section, including adaptive streaming and CDN distribution. Netflix also nicely illustrates how a major Internet service, generating almost 30 percent of Internet traffic, can run almost entirely on a third-party cloud and third-party CDN infrastructures, using very little infrastructure of its own!

YouTube

With approximately half a billion videos in its library and half a billion video views per day [Ding 2011], YouTube is indisputably the world's largest video-sharing site. YouTube began its service in April 2005 and was acquired by Google in November 2006. Although the Google/YouTube design and protocols are proprietary, through several independent measurement efforts we can gain a basic understanding about how YouTube operates [Zink 2009; Torres 2011; Adhikari 2011a].

As with Netflix, YouTube makes extensive use of CDN technology to distribute its videos [Torres 2011]. Unlike Netflix, however, Google does not employ third-party CDNs but instead uses its own private CDN to distribute YouTube videos. Google has installed server clusters in many hundreds of different locations. From a subset of about 50 of these locations, Google distributes YouTube videos [Adhikari 2011a]. Google uses DNS to redirect a customer request to a specific cluster, as described in Section 7.2.4. Most of the time, Google's cluster selection strategy directs the client to the cluster for which the RTT between client and cluster is the lowest; however, in order to balance the load across clusters, sometimes the client is directed (via DNS) to a more distant cluster [Torres 2011]. Furthermore, if a cluster does not have the requested video, instead of fetching it from somewhere else and relaying it to the client, the cluster may return an HTTP redirect message, thereby redirecting the client to another cluster [Torres 2011].

YouTube employs HTTP streaming, as discussed in Section 7.2.2. YouTube often makes a small number of different versions available for a video, each with a different bit rate and corresponding quality level. As of 2011, YouTube does not employ adaptive streaming (such as DASH), but instead requires the user to manually select a version. In order to save bandwidth and server resources that would be wasted by repositioning or early termination, YouTube uses the HTTP byte range request to limit the flow of transmitted data after a target amount of video is prefetched.

A few million videos are uploaded to YouTube every day. Not only are YouTube videos streamed from server to client over HTTP, but YouTube uploaders also upload their videos from client to server over HTTP. YouTube processes each video it receives, converting it to a YouTube video format and creating multiple versions at different bit rates. This processing takes place entirely within Google data centers. Thus, in stark contrast to Netflix, which runs its service almost entirely on third-party infrastructures, Google runs the entire YouTube service within its own vast infrastructure of data centers, private CDN, and private global network interconnecting its data centers and CDN clusters. (See the case study on Google's network infrastructure in Section 7.2.4.)

Kankan

We just saw that for both the Netflix and YouTube services, servers operated by CDNs (either third-party or private CDNs) stream videos to clients. Netflix and YouTube not only have to pay for the server hardware (either directly through ownership or indirectly through rent), but also for the bandwidth the servers use to distribute the videos. Given the scale of these services and the amount of bandwidth they are consuming, such a "client-server" deployment is extremely costly.

We conclude this section by describing an entirely different approach for providing video on demand over the Internet at a large scale—one that allows the service provider to significantly reduce its infrastructure and bandwidth costs. As you might suspect, this approach uses P2P delivery instead of client-server (via CDNs) delivery. P2P video delivery is used with great success by several companies in China, including Kankan (owned and operated by Xunlei), PPTV (formerly PPLive), and PPs (formerly PPstream). Kankan, currently the leading P2P-based video-on-demand provider in China, has over 20 million unique users viewing its videos every month.

At a high level, P2P video streaming is very similar to BitTorrent file downloading (discussed in Chapter 2). When a peer wants to see a video, it contacts a tracker (which may be centralized or peer-based using a DHT) to discover other peers in the system that have a copy of that video. This peer then requests chunks of the video file in parallel from these other peers that have the file. Different from downloading with BitTorrent, however, requests are preferentially made for chunks that are to be played back in the near future in order to ensure continuous playback.

The Kankan design employs a tracker and its own DHT for tracking content. Swarm sizes for the most popular content involve tens of thousands of peers, typically larger than the largest swarms in BitTorrent [Dhungel 2012]. The Kankan protocols—for communication between peer and tracker, between peer and DHT, and among peers—are all proprietary. Interestingly, for distributing video chunks among peers, Kankan uses UDP whenever possible, leading to massive amounts of UDP traffic within China's Internet [Zhang M 2010].

7.3 Voice-over-IP

Real-time conversational voice over the Internet is often referred to as **Internet telephony**, since, from the user's perspective, it is similar to the traditional circuit-switched telephone service. It is also commonly called **Voice-over-IP (VoIP)**. In this section we describe the principles and protocols underlying VoIP. Conversational video is similar in many respects to VoIP, except that it includes the video of the participants as well as their voices. To keep the discussion focused and concrete, we focus here only on voice in this section rather than combined voice and video.

7.3.1 Limitations of the Best-Effort IP Service

The Internet's network-layer protocol, IP, provides best-effort service. That is to say the service makes its best effort to move each datagram from source to destination as quickly as possible but makes no promises whatsoever about getting the packet to the destination within some delay bound or about a limit on the percentage of packets lost. The lack of such guarantees poses significant challenges to the design of real-time conversational applications, which are acutely sensitive to packet delay, jitter, and loss.

In this section, we'll cover several ways in which the performance of VoIP over a best-effort network can be enhanced. Our focus will be on application-layer techniques, that is, approaches that do not require any changes in the network core or even in the transport layer at the end hosts. To keep the discussion concrete, we'll discuss the limitations of best-effort IP service in the context of a specific VoIP example. The sender generates bytes at a rate of 8,000 bytes per second; every 20 msecs the sender gathers these bytes into a chunk. A chunk and a special header (discussed below) are encapsulated in a UDP segment, via a call to the socket interface. Thus, the number of bytes in a chunk is (20 msecs)· (8,000 bytes/sec) = 160 bytes, and a UDP segment is sent every 20 msecs.

If each packet makes it to the receiver with a constant end-to-end delay, then packets arrive at the receiver periodically every 20 msecs. In these ideal conditions, the receiver can simply play back each chunk as soon as it arrives. But unfortunately, some packets can be lost and most packets will not have the same end-to-end delay, even in a lightly congested Internet. For this reason, the receiver must take more care in determining (1) when to play back a chunk, and (2) what to do with a missing chunk.

Packet Loss

Consider one of the UDP segments generated by our VoIP application. The UDP segment is encapsulated in an IP datagram. As the datagram wanders through the network, it passes through router buffers (that is, queues) while waiting for transmission on outbound links. It is possible that one or more of the buffers in the path from sender to receiver is full, in which case the arriving IP datagram may be discarded, never to arrive at the receiving application.

Loss could be eliminated by sending the packets over TCP (which provides for reliable data transfer) rather than over UDP. However, retransmission mechanisms are often considered unacceptable for conversational real-time audio applications such as VoIP, because they increase end-to-end delay [Bolot 1996]. Furthermore, due to TCP congestion control, packet loss may result in a reduction of the TCP sender's transmission rate to a rate that is lower than the receiver's drain rate, possibly leading to buffer starvation. This can have a severe impact on voice intelligibility at the receiver. For these reasons, most existing VoIP applications run over UDP by default. [Baset 2006] reports that UDP is used by Skype unless a user is behind a NAT or firewall that blocks UDP segments (in which case TCP is used).

But losing packets is not necessarily as disastrous as one might think. Indeed, packet loss rates between 1 and 20 percent can be tolerated, depending on how voice is encoded and transmitted, and on how the loss is concealed at the receiver. For example, forward error correction (FEC) can help conceal packet loss. We'll see below that with FEC, redundant information is transmitted along with the original information so that some of the lost original data can be recovered from the redundant information. Nevertheless, if one or more of the links between sender and receiver is severely congested, and packet loss exceeds 10 to 20 percent (for example, on a wireless link), then there is really nothing that can be done to achieve acceptable audio quality. Clearly, best-effort service has its limitations.

End-to-End Delay

End-to-end delay is the accumulation of transmission, processing, and queuing delays in routers; propagation delays in links; and end-system processing delays. For real-time conversational applications, such as VoIP, end-to-end delays smaller than 150 msecs are not perceived by a human listener; delays between 150 and 400 msecs can be acceptable but are not ideal; and delays exceeding 400 msecs can seriously hinder the interactivity in voice conversations. The receiving side of a VoIP application will typically disregard any packets that are delayed more than a certain threshold, for example, more than 400 msecs. Thus, packets that are delayed by more than the threshold are effectively lost.

Packet Jitter

A crucial component of end-to-end delay is the varying queuing delays that a packet experiences in the network's routers. Because of these varying delays, the time from when a packet is generated at the source until it is received at the receiver can fluctuate from packet to packet, as shown in Figure 7.1. This phenomenon is called **jitter**. As an example, consider two consecutive packets in our VoIP application. The sender sends the second packet 20 msecs after sending the first packet. But at the receiver, the spacing between these packets can become greater than 20 msecs. To see this, suppose the first packet arrives at a nearly empty queue at a router, but just before the second packet arrives at the queue a large number of packets from other sources arrive at the same queue. Because the first packet experiences a small queuing delay and the second packet suffers a large queuing delay at this router, the first and second packets become spaced by more than 20 msecs. The spacing between consecutive packets can also become less than 20 msecs. To see this, again consider two consecutive packets. Suppose the first packet joins the end of a queue with a large number of packets, and the second packet arrives at the queue before this first packet is transmitted and before any packets from other sources arrive at the queue. In this case, our two packets find themselves one right after the other in the queue. If the time it takes to transmit a packet on the router's outbound link is less than 20 msecs, then the spacing between first and second packets becomes less than 20 msecs.

The situation is analogous to driving cars on roads. Suppose you and your friend are each driving in your own cars from San Diego to Phoenix. Suppose you and your friend have similar driving styles, and that you both drive at 100 km/hour, traffic permitting. If your friend starts out one hour before you, depending on intervening traffic, you may arrive at Phoenix more or less than one hour after your friend.

If the receiver ignores the presence of jitter and plays out chunks as soon as they arrive, then the resulting audio quality can easily become unintelligible at the receiver. Fortunately, jitter can often be removed by using **sequence numbers**, **timestamps**, and a **playout delay**, as discussed below.

7.3.2 Removing Jitter at the Receiver for Audio

For our VoIP application, where packets are being generated periodically, the receiver should attempt to provide periodic playout of voice chunks in the presence of random network jitter. This is typically done by combining the following two mechanisms:

- *Prepending each chunk with a **timestamp**.* The sender stamps each chunk with the time at which the chunk was generated.

- ***Delaying playout** of chunks at the receiver*. As we saw in our earlier discussion of Figure 7.1, the playout delay of the received audio chunks must be long enough so that most of the packets are received before their scheduled playout times. This playout delay can either be fixed throughout the duration of the audio session or vary adaptively during the audio session lifetime.

We now discuss how these three mechanisms, when combined, can alleviate or even eliminate the effects of jitter. We examine two playback strategies: fixed play-out delay and adaptive playout delay.

Fixed Playout Delay

With the fixed-delay strategy, the receiver attempts to play out each chunk exactly q msecs after the chunk is generated. So if a chunk is timestamped at the sender at time t, the receiver plays out the chunk at time $t + q$, assuming the chunk has arrived by that time. Packets that arrive after their scheduled playout times are discarded and considered lost.

What is a good choice for q? VoIP can support delays up to about 400 msecs, although a more satisfying conversational experience is achieved with smaller values of q. On the other hand, if q is made much smaller than 400 msecs, then many packets may miss their scheduled playback times due to the network-induced packet jitter. Roughly speaking, if large variations in end-to-end delay are typical, it is preferable to use a large q; on the other hand, if delay is small and variations in delay are also small, it is preferable to use a small q, perhaps less than 150 msecs.

The trade-off between the playback delay and packet loss is illustrated in Figure 7.7. The figure shows the times at which packets are generated and played out for a single talk spurt. Two distinct initial playout delays are considered. As shown by the leftmost staircase, the sender generates packets at regular intervals—say, every 20 msecs. The first packet in this talk spurt is received at time r. As shown in the figure, the arrivals of subsequent packets are not evenly spaced due to the network jitter.

For the first playout schedule, the fixed initial playout delay is set to $p - r$. With this schedule, the fourth packet does not arrive by its scheduled playout time, and the receiver considers it lost. For the second playout schedule, the fixed initial playout delay is set to $p' - r$. For this schedule, all packets arrive before their scheduled playout times, and there is therefore no loss.

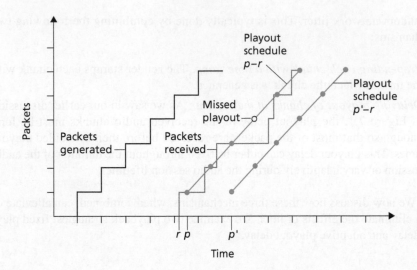

Figure 7.7 ♦ Packet loss for different fixed playout delays

Adaptive Playout Delay

The previous example demonstrates an important delay-loss trade-off that arises when designing a playout strategy with fixed playout delays. By making the initial playout delay large, most packets will make their deadlines and there will therefore be negligible loss; however, for conversational services such as VoIP, long delays can become bothersome if not intolerable. Ideally, we would like the playout delay to be minimized subject to the constraint that the loss be below a few percent.

The natural way to deal with this trade-off is to estimate the network delay and the variance of the network delay, and to adjust the playout delay accordingly at the beginning of each talk spurt. This adaptive adjustment of playout delays at the beginning of the talk spurts will cause the sender's silent periods to be compressed and elongated; however, compression and elongation of silence by a small amount is not noticeable in speech.

Following [Ramjee 1994], we now describe a generic algorithm that the receiver can use to adaptively adjust its playout delays. To this end, let

t_i = the timestamp of the ith packet = the time the packet was generated by the sender

r_i = the time packet i is received by receiver

p_i = the time packet i is played at receiver

The end-to-end network delay of the ith packet is $r_i - t_i$. Due to network jitter, this delay will vary from packet to packet. Let d_i denote an estimate of the *average* network delay upon reception of the ith packet. This estimate is constructed from the timestamps as follows:

$$d_i = (1 - u) \, d_{i-1} + u \, (r_i - t_i)$$

where u is a fixed constant (for example, $u = 0.01$). Thus d_i is a smoothed average of the observed network delays $r_1 - t_1, \ldots, r_i - t_i$. The estimate places more weight on the recently observed network delays than on the observed network delays of the distant past. This form of estimate should not be completely unfamiliar; a similar idea is used to estimate round-trip times in TCP, as discussed in Chapter 3. Let v_i denote an estimate of the average deviation of the delay from the estimated average delay. This estimate is also constructed from the timestamps:

$$v_i = (1 - u) \, v_{i-1} + u \mid r_i - t_i - d_i \mid$$

The estimates d_i and v_i are calculated for every packet received, although they are used only to determine the playout point for the first packet in any talk spurt.

Once having calculated these estimates, the receiver employs the following algorithm for the playout of packets. If packet i is the first packet of a talk spurt, its playout time, p_i, is computed as:

$$p_i = t_i + d_i + Kv_i$$

where K is a positive constant (for example, $K = 4$). The purpose of the Kv_i term is to set the playout time far enough into the future so that only a small fraction of the arriving packets in the talk spurt will be lost due to late arrivals. The playout point for any subsequent packet in a talk spurt is computed as an offset from the point in time when the first packet in the talk spurt was played out. In particular, let

$$q_i = p_i - t_i$$

be the length of time from when the first packet in the talk spurt is generated until it is played out. If packet j also belongs to this talk spurt, it is played out at time

$$p_j = t_j + q_i$$

The algorithm just described makes perfect sense assuming that the receiver can tell whether a packet is the first packet in the talk spurt. This can be done by examining the signal energy in each received packet.

7.3.3 Recovering from Packet Loss

We have discussed in some detail how a VoIP application can deal with packet jitter. We now briefly describe several schemes that attempt to preserve acceptable audio quality in the presence of packet loss. Such schemes are called **loss recovery schemes**. Here we define packet loss in a broad sense: A packet is lost either if it never arrives at the receiver or if it arrives after its scheduled playout time. Our VoIP example will again serve as a context for describing loss recovery schemes.

As mentioned at the beginning of this section, retransmitting lost packets may not be feasible in a real-time conversational application such as VoIP. Indeed, retransmitting a packet that has missed its playout deadline serves absolutely no purpose. And retransmitting a packet that overflowed a router queue cannot normally be accomplished quickly enough. Because of these considerations, VoIP applications often use some type of loss anticipation scheme. Two types of loss anticipation schemes are **forward error correction (FEC)** and **interleaving**.

Forward Error Correction (FEC)

The basic idea of FEC is to add redundant information to the original packet stream. For the cost of marginally increasing the transmission rate, the redundant information can be used to reconstruct approximations or exact versions of some of the lost packets. Following [Bolot 1996] and [Perkins 1998], we now outline two simple FEC mechanisms. The first mechanism sends a redundant encoded chunk after every n chunks. The redundant chunk is obtained by exclusive OR-ing the n original chunks [Shacham 1990]. In this manner if any one packet of the group of $n + 1$ packets is lost, the receiver can fully reconstruct the lost packet. But if two or more packets in a group are lost, the receiver cannot reconstruct the lost packets. By keeping $n + 1$, the group size, small, a large fraction of the lost packets can be recovered when loss is not excessive. However, the smaller the group size, the greater the relative increase of the transmission rate. In particular, the transmission rate increases by a factor of $1/n$, so that, if $n = 3$, then the transmission rate increases by 33 percent. Furthermore, this simple scheme increases the playout delay, as the receiver must wait to receive the entire group of packets before it can begin playout. For more practical details about how FEC works for multimedia transport see [RFC 5109].

The second FEC mechanism is to send a lower-resolution audio stream as the redundant information. For example, the sender might create a nominal audio stream and a corresponding low-resolution, low-bit rate audio stream. (The nominal stream could be a PCM encoding at 64 kbps, and the lower-quality stream could be a GSM encoding at 13 kbps.) The low-bit rate stream is referred to as the redundant stream. As shown in Figure 7.8, the sender constructs the nth packet by taking the nth chunk from the nominal stream and appending to it the $(n - 1)$st chunk from the redundant stream. In this manner, whenever there is nonconsecutive packet loss, the receiver can conceal the loss by playing out the low-bit rate encoded chunk that arrives with the subsequent packet. Of course, low-bit rate chunks give lower quality than the nominal chunks. However, a stream of mostly high-quality chunks, occasional low-quality chunks, and no missing chunks gives good overall audio quality. Note that in this scheme, the receiver only has to receive two packets before playback, so that the increased playout delay is small. Furthermore, if the low-bit rate encoding is much less than the nominal encoding, then the marginal increase in the transmission rate will be small.

In order to cope with consecutive loss, we can use a simple variation. Instead of appending just the $(n-1)$st low-bit rate chunk to the nth nominal chunk, the sender can append the $(n-1)$st and $(n-2)$nd low-bit rate chunk, or append the $(n-1)$st and $(n-3)$rd low-bit rate chunk, and so on. By appending more low-bit rate chunks to each nominal chunk, the audio quality at the receiver becomes acceptable for a wider variety of harsh best-effort environments. On the other hand, the additional chunks increase the transmission bandwidth and the playout delay.

Interleaving

As an alternative to redundant transmission, a VoIP application can send interleaved audio. As shown in Figure 7.9, the sender resequences units of audio data before transmission, so that originally adjacent units are separated by a certain distance in the transmitted stream. Interleaving can mitigate the effect of packet losses. If, for example, units are 5 msecs in length and chunks are 20 msecs (that is, four units per chunk), then the first chunk could contain units 1, 5, 9, and 13; the second chunk could contain units 2, 6, 10, and 14; and so on. Figure 7.9 shows that the loss of a single packet from an interleaved stream results in multiple small gaps in the reconstructed stream, as opposed to the single large gap that would occur in a noninterleaved stream.

Interleaving can significantly improve the perceived quality of an audio stream [Perkins 1998]. It also has low overhead. The obvious disadvantage of interleaving is that it increases latency. This limits its use for conversational applications such as VoIP, although it can perform well for streaming stored audio. A major advantage of interleaving is that it does not increase the bandwidth requirements of a stream.

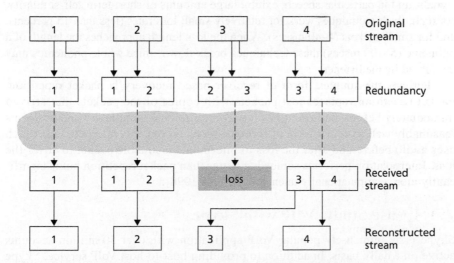

Figure 7.8 ◆ Piggybacking lower-quality redundant information

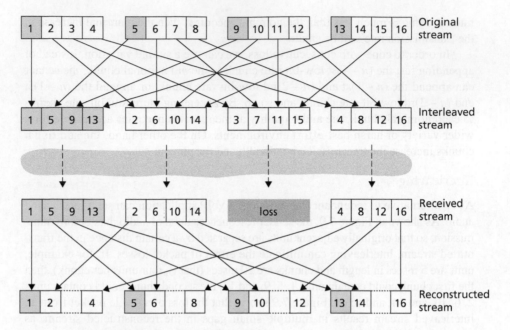

Figure 7.9 ♦ Sending interleaved audio

Error Concealment

Error concealment schemes attempt to produce a replacement for a lost packet that is similar to the original. As discussed in [Perkins 1998], this is possible since audio signals, and in particular speech, exhibit large amounts of short-term self-similarity. As such, these techniques work for relatively small loss rates (less than 15 percent), and for small packets (4–40 msecs). When the loss length approaches the length of a phoneme (5–100 msecs) these techniques break down, since whole phonemes may be missed by the listener.

Perhaps the simplest form of receiver-based recovery is packet repetition. Packet repetition replaces lost packets with copies of the packets that arrived immediately before the loss. It has low computational complexity and performs reasonably well. Another form of receiver-based recovery is interpolation, which uses audio before and after the loss to interpolate a suitable packet to cover the loss. Interpolation performs somewhat better than packet repetition but is significantly more computationally intensive [Perkins 1998].

7.3.4 Case Study: VoIP with Skype

Skype is an immensely popular VoIP application with over 50 million accounts active on a daily basis. In addition to providing host-to-host VoIP service, Skype offers host-to-phone services, phone-to-host services, and multi-party host-to-host video conferencing services. (Here, a host is again any Internet connected IP device, including PCs, tablets, and smartphones.) Skype was acquired by Microsoft in 2011 for over $8 billion.

Because the Skype protocol is proprietary, and because all Skype's control and media packets are encrypted, it is difficult to precisely determine how Skype operates. Nevertheless, from the Skype Web site and several measurement studies, researchers have learned how Skype generally works [Baset 2006; Guha 2006; Chen 2006; Suh 2006; Ren 2006; Zhang X 2012]. For both voice and video, the Skype clients have at their disposal many different codecs, which are capable of encoding the media at a wide range of rates and qualities. For example, video rates for Skype have been measured to be as low as 30 kbps for a low-quality session up to almost 1 Mbps for a high quality session [Zhang X 2012]. Typically, Skype's audio quality is better than the "POTS" (Plain Old Telephone Service) quality provided by the wire-line phone system. (Skype codecs typically sample voice at 16,000 samples/sec or higher, which provides richer tones than POTS, which samples at 8,000/sec.) By default, Skype sends audio and video packets over UDP. However, control packets are sent over TCP, and media packets are also sent over TCP when firewalls block UDP streams. Skype uses FEC for loss recovery for both voice and video streams sent over UDP. The Skype client also adapts the audio and video streams it sends to current network conditions, by changing video quality and FEC overhead [Zhang X 2012].

Skype uses P2P techniques in a number of innovative ways, nicely illustrating how P2P can be used in applications that go beyond content distribution and file sharing. As with instant messaging, host-to-host Internet telephony is inherently P2P since, at the heart of the application, pairs of users (that is, peers) communicate with each other in real time. But Skype also employs P2P techniques for two other important functions, namely, for user location and for NAT traversal.

As shown in Figure 7.10, the peers (hosts) in Skype are organized into a hierarchical overlay network, with each peer classified as a super peer or an ordinary peer. Skype maintains an index that maps Skype usernames to current IP addresses (and port numbers). This index is distributed over the super peers. When Alice wants to call Bob, her Skype client searches the distributed index to determine Bob's current IP address. Because the Skype protocol is proprietary, it is currently not known how the index mappings are organized across the super peers, although some form of DHT organization is very possible.

P2P techniques are also used in Skype **relays**, which are useful for establishing calls between hosts in home networks. Many home network configurations provide access to the Internet through NATs, as discussed in Chapter 4. Recall that a NAT prevents a host from outside the home network from initiating a connection to a host within the home network. If *both* Skype callers have NATs, then there is a problem—neither can accept a call initiated by the other, making a call seemingly impossible. The clever use of super peers and relays nicely solves this problem. Suppose that when Alice signs in, she is assigned to a non-NATed super peer and initiates a session to that super peer. (Since Alice is initiating the session, her NAT permits this session.) This session allows Alice and her super peer to

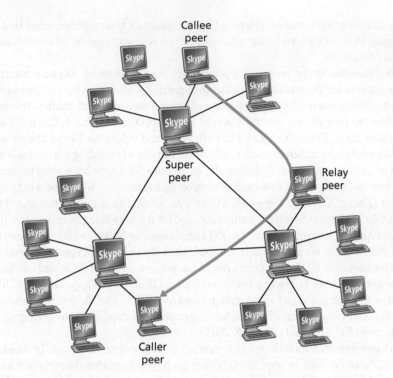

Callee peer

Super peer

Relay peer

Caller peer

Figure 7.10 ♦ Skype peers

exchange control messages. The same happens for Bob when he signs in. Now, when Alice wants to call Bob, she informs her super peer, who in turn informs Bob's super peer, who in turn informs Bob of Alice's incoming call. If Bob accepts the call, the two super peers select a third non-NATed super peer—the relay peer—whose job will be to relay data between Alice and Bob. Alice's and Bob's super peers then instruct Alice and Bob respectively to initiate a session with the relay. As shown in Figure 7.10, Alice then sends voice packets to the relay over the Alice-to-relay connection (which was initiated by Alice), and the relay then forwards these packets over the relay-to-Bob connection (which was initiated by Bob); packets from Bob to Alice flow over these same two relay connections in reverse. And *voila!*—Bob and Alice have an end-to-end connection even though neither can accept a session originating from outside.

Up to now, our discussion on Skype has focused on calls involving two persons. Now let's examine multi-party audio conference calls. With $N > 2$ participants, if each user were to send a copy of its audio stream to each of the $N - 1$ other users, then a total of $N(N - 1)$ audio streams would need to be sent into the network to support the audio conference. To reduce this bandwidth usage, Skype employs a clever distribution technique. Specifically, each user sends its audio stream to the conference initiator. The conference initiator combines the audio streams into one stream (basically by adding all the audio signals together) and then sends a copy of each combined stream to each of the other $N - 1$ participants. In this manner, the number of streams is reduced to $2(N - 1)$. For ordinary two-person video conversations, Skype routes the call peer-to-peer, unless NAT traversal is required, in which case the call is relayed through a non-NATed peer, as described earlier. For a video conference call involving $N > 2$ participants, due to the nature of the video medium, Skype does not combine the call into one stream at one location and then redistribute the stream to all the participants, as it does for voice calls. Instead, each participant's video stream is routed to a server cluster (located in Estonia as of 2011), which in turn relays to each participant the $N - 1$ streams of the $N - 1$ other participants [Zhang X 2012]. You may be wondering why each participant sends a copy to a server rather than directly sending a copy of its video stream to each of the other $N - 1$ participants? Indeed, for both approaches, $N(N - 1)$ video streams are being collectively received by the N participants in the conference. The reason is, because upstream link bandwidths are significantly lower than downstream link bandwidths in most access links, the upstream links may not be able to support the $N - 1$ streams with the P2P approach.

VoIP systems such as Skype, QQ, and Google Talk introduce new privacy concerns. Specifically, when Alice and Bob communicate over VoIP, Alice can sniff Bob's IP address and then use geo-location services [MaxMind 2012; Quova 2012] to determine Bob's current location and ISP (for example, his work or home ISP). In fact, with Skype it is possible for Alice to block the transmission of certain packets during call establishment so that she obtains Bob's current IP address, say every hour, without Bob knowing that he is being tracked and without being on Bob's contact list. Furthermore, the IP address discovered from Skype can be correlated with IP addresses found in BitTorrent, so that Alice can determine the files that Bob is downloading [LeBlond 2011]. Moreover, it is possible to partially decrypt a Skype call by doing a traffic analysis of the packet sizes in a stream [White 2011].

7.4 Protocols for Real-Time Conversational Applications

Real-time conversational applications, including VoIP and video conferencing, are compelling and very popular. It is therefore not surprising that standards bodies, such as the IETF and ITU, have been busy for many years (and continue to be busy!) at hammering out standards for this class of applications. With the appropriate standards in place for real-time conversational applications, independent companies are creating new products that interoperate with each other. In this section we examine RTP and SIP for real-time conversational applications. Both standards are enjoying widespread implementation in industry products.

7.4.1 RTP

In the previous section, we learned that the sender side of a VoIP application appends header fields to the audio chunks before passing them to the transport layer. These header fields include sequence numbers and timestamps. Since most multimedia networking applications can make use of sequence numbers and timestamps, it is convenient to have a standardized packet structure that includes fields for audio/video data, sequence number, and timestamp, as well as other potentially useful fields. RTP, defined in RFC 3550, is such a standard. RTP can be used for transporting common formats such as PCM, ACC, and MP3 for sound and MPEG and H.263 for video. It can also be used for transporting proprietary sound and video formats. Today, RTP enjoys widespread implementation in many products and research prototypes. It is also complementary to other important real-time interactive protocols, such as SIP.

In this section, we provide an introduction to RTP. We also encourage you to visit Henning Schulzrinne's RTP site [Schulzrinne-RTP 2012], which provides a wealth of information on the subject. Also, you may want to visit the RAT site [RAT 2012], which documents VoIP application that uses RTP.

RTP Basics

RTP typically runs on top of UDP. The sending side encapsulates a media chunk within an RTP packet, then encapsulates the packet in a UDP segment, and then hands the segment to IP. The receiving side extracts the RTP packet from the UDP segment, then extracts the media chunk from the RTP packet, and then passes the chunk to the media player for decoding and rendering.

As an example, consider the use of RTP to transport voice. Suppose the voice source is PCM-encoded (that is, sampled, quantized, and digitized) at 64 kbps. Further suppose that the application collects the encoded data in 20-msec chunks, that is, 160 bytes in a chunk. The sending side precedes each chunk of the audio data with an **RTP header** that includes the type of audio encoding, a sequence number, and a timestamp. The RTP header is normally 12 bytes. The audio chunk along with the RTP header form the **RTP packet**. The RTP packet is then sent into the UDP socket interface. At the receiver side, the application receives the RTP packet from its socket interface. The application extracts the audio chunk from the RTP packet and uses the header fields of the RTP packet to properly decode and play back the audio chunk.

If an application incorporates RTP—instead of a proprietary scheme to provide payload type, sequence numbers, or timestamps—then the application will more easily interoperate with other networked multimedia applications. For example, if two different companies develop VoIP software and they both incorporate RTP into their product, there may be some hope that a user using one of the VoIP products will be able to communicate with a user using the other VoIP product. In Section 7.4.2, we'll see that RTP is often used in conjunction with SIP, an important standard for Internet telephony.

It should be emphasized that RTP does not provide any mechanism to ensure timely delivery of data or provide other quality-of-service (QoS) guarantees; it does not even guarantee delivery of packets or prevent out-of-order delivery of packets. Indeed, RTP encapsulation is seen only at the end systems. Routers do not distinguish between IP datagrams that carry RTP packets and IP datagrams that don't.

RTP allows each source (for example, a camera or a microphone) to be assigned its own independent RTP stream of packets. For example, for a video conference between two participants, four RTP streams could be opened—two streams for transmitting the audio (one in each direction) and two streams for transmitting the video (again, one in each direction). However, many popular encoding techniques— including MPEG 1 and MPEG 2—bundle the audio and video into a single stream during the encoding process. When the audio and video are bundled by the encoder, then only one RTP stream is generated in each direction.

RTP packets are not limited to unicast applications. They can also be sent over one-to-many and many-to-many multicast trees. For a many-to-many multicast session, all of the session's senders and sources typically use the same multicast group for sending their RTP streams. RTP multicast streams belonging together, such as audio and video streams emanating from multiple senders in a video confer-ence application, belong to an **RTP session**.

RTP Packet Header Fields

As shown in Figure 7.11, the four main RTP packet header fields are the payload type, sequence number, timestamp, and source identifier fields.

The payload type field in the RTP packet is 7 bits long. For an audio stream, the payload type field is used to indicate the type of audio encoding (for example, PCM, adaptive delta modulation, linear predictive encoding) that is being used. If a sender decides to change the encoding in the middle of a session, the sender can inform the receiver of the change through this payload type field. The sender may want to change the encoding in order to increase the audio quality or to decrease the RTP stream bit rate. Table 7.2 lists some of the audio payload types currently supported by RTP.

For a video stream, the payload type is used to indicate the type of video encoding (for example, motion JPEG, MPEG 1, MPEG 2, H.261). Again, the sender can change video encoding on the fly during a session. Table 7.3 lists some of the video payload types currently supported by RTP. The other important fields are the following:

* *Sequence number field.* The sequence number field is 16 bits long. The sequence number increments by one for each RTP packet sent, and may be used by the

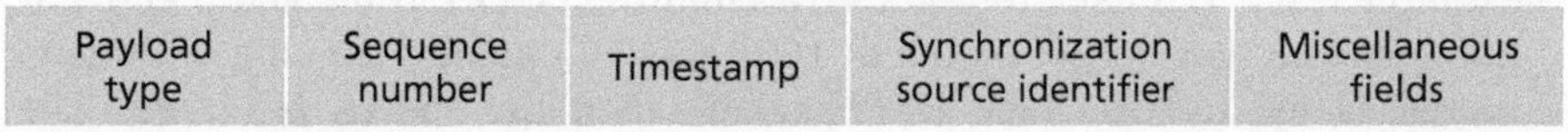

Payload type	Sequence number	Timestamp	Synchronization source identifier	Miscellaneous fields

Figure 7.11 ♦ RTP header fields

Payload-Type Number	Audio Format	Sampling Rate	Rate
0	PCM μ-law	8 kHz	64 kbps
1	1016	8 kHz	4.8 kbps
3	GSM	8 kHz	13 kbps
7	LPC	8 kHz	2.4 kbps
9	G.722	16 kHz	48–64 kbps
14	MPEG Audio	90 kHz	—
15	G.728	8 kHz	16 kbps

Table 7.2 ♦ Audio payload types supported by RTP

Payload-Type Number	Video Format
26	Motion JPEG
31	H.261
32	MPEG 1 video
33	MPEG 2 video

Table 7.3 ♦ Some video payload types supported by RTP

receiver to detect packet loss and to restore packet sequence. For example, if the receiver side of the application receives a stream of RTP packets with a gap between sequence numbers 86 and 89, then the receiver knows that packets 87 and 88 are missing. The receiver can then attempt to conceal the lost data.

• *Timestamp field.* The timestamp field is 32 bits long. It reflects the sampling instant of the first byte in the RTP data packet. As we saw in the preceding section, the receiver can use timestamps to remove packet jitter introduced in the network and to provide synchronous playout at the receiver. The timestamp is derived from a sampling clock at the sender. As an example, for audio the timestamp clock increments by one for each sampling period (for example, each 125 μsec for an 8 kHz sampling clock); if the audio application generates chunks consisting of 160 encoded samples, then the timestamp increases by 160 for each RTP packet when the source is active. The timestamp clock continues to increase at a constant rate even if the source is inactive.

• *Synchronization source identifier (SSRC).* The SSRC field is 32 bits long. It identifies the source of the RTP stream. Typically, each stream in an RTP session has a distinct SSRC. The SSRC is not the IP address of the sender, but instead is a number that the source assigns randomly when the new stream is started. The probability that two streams get assigned the same SSRC is very small. Should this happen, the two sources pick a new SSRC value.

7.4.2 SIP

The Session Initiation Protocol (SIP), defined in [RFC 3261; RFC 5411], is an open and lightweight protocol that does the following:

• It provides mechanisms for establishing calls between a caller and a callee over an IP network. It allows the caller to notify the callee that it wants to start a call. It allows the participants to agree on media encodings. It also allows participants to end calls.

• It provides mechanisms for the caller to determine the current IP address of the callee. Users do not have a single, fixed IP address because they may be assigned addresses dynamically (using DHCP) and because they may have multiple IP devices, each with a different IP address.

• It provides mechanisms for call management, such as adding new media streams during the call, changing the encoding during the call, inviting new participants during the call, call transfer, and call holding.

Setting Up a Call to a Known IP Address

To understand the essence of SIP, it is best to take a look at a concrete example. In this example, Alice is at her PC and she wants to call Bob, who is also working at his PC. Alice's and Bob's PCs are both equipped with SIP-based software for making and receiving phone calls. In this initial example, we'll assume that Alice knows the IP address of Bob's PC. Figure 7.12 illustrates the SIP call-establishment process.

In Figure 7.12, we see that an SIP session begins when Alice sends Bob an INVITE message, which resembles an HTTP request message. This INVITE message is sent over UDP to the well-known port 5060 for SIP. (SIP messages can also be sent over TCP.) The INVITE message includes an identifier for Bob (bob@193.64.210.89), an indication of Alice's current IP address, an indication that Alice desires to receive audio, which is to be encoded in format AVP 0 (PCM encoded μ-law) and encapsulated in RTP, and an indication that she wants to receive the RTP packets on port 38060. After receiving Alice's INVITE message, Bob sends an SIP response message, which resembles an HTTP response message. This response SIP message is also sent to the SIP port 5060. Bob's response includes a 200 OK as well as an indication of his IP address, his desired encoding and packetization for reception, and his port number to which the audio packets should be sent. Note that in this example Alice and Bob are going to use different audio-encoding mechanisms: Alice is asked to encode her audio with GSM whereas Bob is asked to encode his audio with PCM μ-law. After receiving Bob's response, Alice sends Bob an SIP acknowledgment message. After this SIP transaction, Bob and Alice can talk. (For visual convenience, Figure 7.12 shows Alice talking after Bob, but in truth they

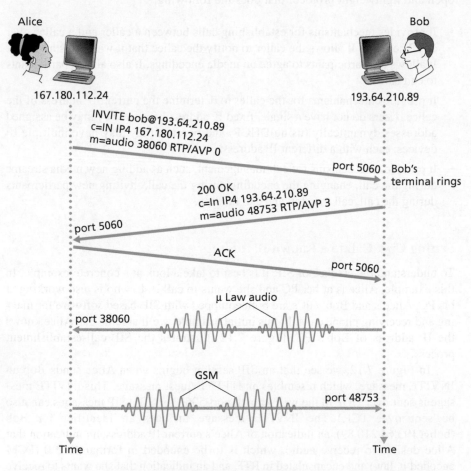

Alice

167.180.112.24

INVITE bob@193.64.210.89
c=IN IP4 167.180.112.24
m=audio 38060 RTP/AVP 0

port 5060

200 OK
c=In IP4 193.64.210.89
m=audio 48753 RTP/AVP 3

port 5060

ACK

port 5060

μ Law audio

port 38060

GSM

Time

Bob

193.64.210.89

Bob's
terminal rings

port 48753

Time

Figure 7.12 ♦ SIP call establishment when Alice knows Bob's IP address

would normally talk at the same time.) Bob will encode and packetize the audio as requested and send the audio packets to port number 38060 at IP address 167.180.112.24. Alice will also encode and packetize the audio as requested and send the audio packets to port number 48753 at IP address 193.64.210.89.

From this simple example, we have learned a number of key characteristics of SIP. First, SIP is an out-of-band protocol: The SIP messages are sent and received in sockets that are different from those used for sending and receiving the media data. Second, the SIP messages themselves are ASCII-readable and resemble HTTP messages. Third, SIP requires all messages to be acknowledged, so it can run over UDP or TCP.

In this example, let's consider what would happen if Bob does not have a PCM μ-law codec for encoding audio. In this case, instead of responding with 200 OK, Bob would likely respond with a 600 Not Acceptable and list in the message all the codecs he can use. Alice would then choose one of the listed codecs and send another INVITE message, this time advertising the chosen codec. Bob could also simply reject the call by sending one of many possible rejection reply codes. (There are many such codes, including "busy," "gone," "payment required," and "forbidden.")

SIP Addresses

In the previous example, Bob's SIP address is sip:bob@193.64.210.89. However, we expect many—if not most—SIP addresses to resemble e-mail addresses. For example, Bob's address might be sip:bob@domain.com. When Alice's SIP device sends an INVITE message, the message would include this e-mail-like address; the SIP infrastructure would then route the message to the IP device that Bob is currently using (as we'll discuss below). Other possible forms for the SIP address could be Bob's legacy phone number or simply Bob's first/middle/last name (assuming it is unique).

An interesting feature of SIP addresses is that they can be included in Web pages, just as people's e-mail addresses are included in Web pages with the mailto URL. For example, suppose Bob has a personal homepage, and he wants to provide a means for visitors to the homepage to call him. He could then simply include the URL sip:bob@domain.com. When the visitor clicks on the URL, the SIP application in the visitor's device is launched and an INVITE message is sent to Bob.

SIP Messages

In this short introduction to SIP, we'll not cover all SIP message types and headers. Instead, we'll take a brief look at the SIP INVITE message, along with a few common header lines. Let us again suppose that Alice wants to initiate a VoIP call to Bob, and this time Alice knows only Bob's SIP address, bob@domain.com, and does not know the IP address of the device that Bob is currently using. Then her message might look something like this:

```
INVITE sip:bob@domain.com SIP/2.0
Via: SIP/2.0/UDP 167.180.112.24
From: sip:alice@hereway.com
To: sip:bob@domain.com
Call-ID: a2e3a@pigeon.hereway.com
Content-Type: application/sdp
Content-Length: 885

c=IN IP4 167.180.112.24
m=audio 38060 RTP/AVP 0
```

The INVITE line includes the SIP version, as does an HTTP request message. Whenever an SIP message passes through an SIP device (including the device that originates the message), it attaches a Via header, which indicates the IP address of the device. (We'll see soon that the typical INVITE message passes through many SIP devices before reaching the callee's SIP application.) Similar to an e-mail message, the SIP message includes a From header line and a To header line. The message includes a Call-ID, which uniquely identifies the call (similar to the message-ID in e-mail). It includes a Content-Type header line, which defines the format used to describe the content contained in the SIP message. It also includes a Content-Length header line, which provides the length in bytes of the content in the message. Finally, after a carriage return and line feed, the message contains the content. In this case, the content provides information about Alice's IP address and how Alice wants to receive the audio.

Name Translation and User Location

In the example in Figure 7.12, we assumed that Alice's SIP device knew the IP address where Bob could be contacted. But this assumption is quite unrealistic, not only because IP addresses are often dynamically assigned with DHCP, but also because Bob may have multiple IP devices (for example, different devices for his home, work, and car). So now let us suppose that Alice knows only Bob's e-mail address, bob@domain.com, and that this same address is used for SIP-based calls. In this case, Alice needs to obtain the IP address of the device that the user bob@domain.com is currently using. To find this out, Alice creates an INVITE message that begins with INVITE bob@domain.com SIP/2.0 and sends this message to an **SIP proxy**. The proxy will respond with an SIP reply that might include the IP address of the device that bob@domain.com is currently using. Alternatively, the reply might include the IP address of Bob's voicemail box, or it might include a URL of a Web page (that says "Bob is sleeping. Leave me alone!"). Also, the result returned by the proxy might depend on the caller: If the call is from Bob's wife, he might accept the call and supply his IP address; if the call is from Bob's mother-in-law, he might respond with the URL that points to the I-am-sleeping Web page!

Now, you are probably wondering, how can the proxy server determine the current IP address for bob@domain.com? To answer this question, we need to say a few words about another SIP device, the **SIP registrar**. Every SIP user has an associated registrar. Whenever a user launches an SIP application on a device, the application sends an SIP register message to the registrar, informing the registrar of its current IP address. For example, when Bob launches his SIP application on his PDA, the application would send a message along the lines of:

```
REGISTER sip:domain.com SIP/2.0
Via: SIP/2.0/UDP 193.64.210.89
From: sip:bob@domain.com
To: sip:bob@domain.com
Expires: 3600
```

Bob's registrar keeps track of Bob's current IP address. Whenever Bob switches to a new SIP device, the new device sends a new register message, indicating the new IP address. Also, if Bob remains at the same device for an extended period of time, the device will send refresh register messages, indicating that the most recently sent IP address is still valid. (In the example above, refresh messages need to be sent every 3600 seconds to maintain the address at the registrar server.) It is worth noting that the registrar is analogous to a DNS authoritative name server: The DNS server translates fixed host names to fixed IP addresses; the SIP registrar translates fixed human identifiers (for example, bob@domain.com) to dynamic IP addresses. Often SIP registrars and SIP proxies are run on the same host.

Now let's examine how Alice's SIP proxy server obtains Bob's current IP address. From the preceding discussion we see that the proxy server simply needs to forward Alice's INVITE message to Bob's registrar/proxy. The registrar/proxy could then forward the message to Bob's current SIP device. Finally, Bob, having now received Alice's INVITE message, could send an SIP response to Alice.

As an example, consider Figure 7.13, in which jim@umass.edu, currently working on 217.123.56.89, wants to initiate a Voice-over-IP (VoIP) session with keith@upenn.edu, currently working on 197.87.54.21. The following steps are taken: (1) Jim sends an INVITE message to the umass SIP proxy. (2) The proxy does a DNS lookup on the SIP registrar upenn.edu (not shown in diagram) and then forwards the message to the registrar server. (3) Because keith@upenn.edu is no longer registered at the upenn registrar, the upenn registrar sends a redirect response, indicating that it should try keith@eurecom.fr. (4) The umass proxy sends an INVITE message to the eurecom SIP registrar. (5) The eurecom registrar knows the IP address of keith@eurecom.fr and forwards the INVITE message to the host 197.87.54.21, which is running Keith's SIP client. (6–8) An SIP response is sent back through registrars/proxies to the SIP client on 217.123.56.89. (9) Media is sent

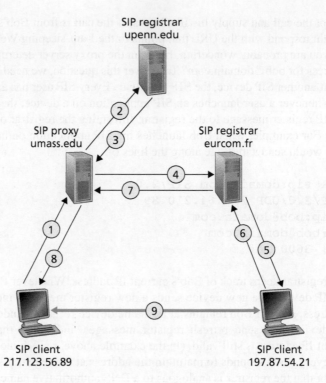

Figure 7.13 ♦ Session initiation, involving SIP proxies and registrars

directly between the two clients. (There is also an SIP acknowledgment message, which is not shown.)

Our discussion of SIP has focused on call initiation for voice calls. SIP, being a signaling protocol for initiating and ending calls in general, can be used for video conference calls as well as for text-based sessions. In fact, SIP has become a fundamental component in many instant messaging applications. Readers desiring to learn more about SIP are encouraged to visit Henning Schulzrinne's SIP Web site [Schulzrinne-SIP 2012]. In particular, on this site you will find open source software for SIP clients and servers [SIP Software 2012].

7.5 Network Support for Multimedia

In Sections 7.2 through 7.4, we learned how application-level mechanisms such as client buffering, prefetching, adapting media quality to available bandwidth, adaptive playout, and loss mitigation techniques can be used by multimedia applications to improve a multimedia application's performance. We also learned how content distribution networks and P2P overlay networks can be used to provide a *system-level* approach for delivering multimedia content. These techniques and approaches are all designed to be used in today's best-effort Internet. Indeed, they are in use today precisely because the Internet provides only a single, best-effort class of service. But as designers of computer networks, we can't help but ask whether the *network* (rather than the applications or application-level infrastructure alone) might provide mechanisms to support multimedia content delivery. As we'll see shortly, the answer is, of course, "yes"! But we'll also see that a number of these new network-level mechanisms have yet to be widely deployed. This may be due to their complexity and to the fact that application-level techniques together with best-effort service and properly dimensioned network resources (for example, bandwidth) can indeed provide a "good-enough" (even if not-always-perfect) end-to-end multimedia delivery service.

Table 7.4 summarizes three broad approaches towards providing network-level support for multimedia applications.

• *Making the best of best-effort service.* The application-level mechanisms and infrastructure that we studied in Sections 7.2 through 7.4 can be successfully used in a well-dimensioned network where packet loss and excessive end-to-end

Approach	Granularity	Guarantee	Mechanisms	Complexity	Deployment to date
Making the best of best-effort service.	all traffic treated equally	none, or soft	application-layer support, CDNs, overlays, network-level resource provisioning	minimal	everywhere
Differentiated service	different classes of traffic treated differently	none, or soft	packet marking, policing, scheduling	medium	some
Per-connection Quality-of-Service (QoS) Guarantees	each source-destination flows treated differently	soft or hard, once flow is admitted	packet marking, policing, scheduling; call admission and signaling	light	little

Table 7.4 ♦ Three network-level approaches to supporting multimedia applications

delay rarely occur. When demand increases are forecasted, the ISPs deploy additional bandwidth and switching capacity to continue to ensure satisfactory delay and packet-loss performance [Huang 2005]. We'll discuss such **network dimensioning** further in Section 7.5.1.

• *Differentiated service.* Since the early days of the Internet, it's been envisioned that different types of traffic (for example, as indicated in the Type-of-Service field in the IP4v packet header) could be provided with different classes of service, rather than a single one-size-fits-all best-effort service. With **differentiated service**, one type of traffic might be given strict priority over another class of traffic when both types of traffic are queued at a router. For example, packets belonging to a real-time conversational application might be given priority over other packets due to their stringent delay constraints. Introducing differentiated service into the network will require new mechanisms for packet marking (indicating a packet's class of service), packet scheduling, and more. We'll cover differentiated service, and new network mechanisms needed to implement this service, in Section 7.5.2.

• *Per-connection Quality-of-Service (QoS) Guarantees.* With per-connection QoS guarantees, each instance of an application explicitly reserves end-to-end bandwidth and thus has a guaranteed end-to-end performance. A **hard guarantee** means the application will receive its requested quality of service (QoS) with certainty. A **soft guarantee** means the application will receive its requested quality of service with high probability. For example, if a user wants to make a VoIP call from Host A to Host B, the user's VoIP application reserves bandwidth explicitly in each link along a route between the two hosts. But permitting applications to make reservations and requiring the network to honor the reservations requires some big changes. First, we need a protocol that, on behalf of the applications, reserves link bandwidth on the paths from the senders to their receivers. Second, we'll need new scheduling policies in the router queues so that per-connection bandwidth reservations can be honored. Finally, in order to make a reservation, the applications must give the network a description of the traffic that they intend to send into the network and the network will need to police each application's traffic to make sure that it abides by that description. These mechanisms, when combined, require new and complex software in hosts and routers. Because per-connection QoS guaranteed service has not seen significant deployment, we'll cover these mechanisms only briefly in Section 7.5.3.

7.5.1 Dimensioning Best-Effort Networks

Fundamentally, the difficulty in supporting multimedia applications arises from their stringent performance requirements—low end-to-end packet delay, delay

jitter, and loss—and the fact that packet delay, delay jitter, and loss occur whenever the network becomes congested. A first approach to improving the quality
of multimedia applications—an approach that can often be used to solve just
about any problem where resources are constrained—is simply to "throw money
at the problem" and thus simply avoid resource contention. In the case of networked multimedia, this means providing enough link capacity throughout the
network so that network congestion, and its consequent packet delay and loss,
never (or only very rarely) occurs. With enough link capacity, packets could zip
through today's Internet without queuing delay or loss. From many perspectives
this is an ideal situation—multimedia applications would perform perfectly, users
would be happy, and this could all be achieved with no changes to Internet's best-
effort architecture.

The question, of course, is how much capacity is "enough" to achieve this
nirvana, and whether the costs of providing "enough" bandwidth are practical
from a business standpoint to the ISPs. The question of how much capacity to
provide at network links in a given topology to achieve a given level of performance is often known as **bandwidth provisioning**. The even more complicated
problem of how to design a network topology (where to place routers, how to
interconnect routers with links, and what capacity to assign to links) to achieve a
given level of end-to-end performance is a network design problem often referred
to as **network dimensioning**. Both bandwidth provisioning and network dimensioning are complex topics, well beyond the scope of this textbook. We note here,
however, that the following issues must be addressed in order to predict application-level performance between two network end points, and thus provision
enough capacity to meet an application's performance requirements.

- *Models of traffic demand between network end points.*   Models may need to be
  specified at both the call level (for example, users "arriving" to the network and
  starting up end-to-end applications) and at the packet level (for example, packets
  being generated by ongoing applications). Note that workload may change over
  time.

- *Well-defined performance requirements.*   For example, a performance requirement for supporting delay-sensitive traffic, such as a conversational multimedia
  application, might be that the probability that the end-to-end delay of the packet
  is greater than a maximum tolerable delay be less than some small value
  [Fraleigh 2003].

- *Models to predict end-to-end performance for a given workload model, and techniques to find a minimal cost bandwidth allocation that will result in all user
  requirements being met.*   Here, researchers are busy developing performance
  models that can quantify performance for a given workload, and optimization
  techniques to find minimal-cost bandwidth allocations meeting performance
  requirements.

Given that today's best-effort Internet could (from a technology standpoint) support multimedia traffic at an appropriate performance level if it were dimensioned to do so, the natural question is why today's Internet doesn't do so. The answers are primarily economic and organizational. From an economic standpoint, would users be willing to pay their ISPs enough for the ISPs to install sufficient bandwidth to support multimedia applications over a best-effort Internet? The organizational issues are perhaps even more daunting. Note that an end-to-end path between two multimedia end points will pass through the networks of multiple ISPs. From an organizational standpoint, would these ISPs be willing to cooperate (perhaps with revenue sharing) to ensure that the end-to-end path is properly dimensioned to support multimedia applications? For a perspective on these economic and organizational issues, see [Davies 2005]. For a perspective on provisioning tier-1 backbone networks to support delay-sensitive traffic, see [Fraleigh 2003].

7.5.2 Providing Multiple Classes of Service

Perhaps the simplest enhancement to the one-size-fits-all best-effort service in today's Internet is to divide traffic into classes, and provide different levels of service to these different classes of traffic. For example, an ISP might well want to provide a higher class of service to delay-sensitive Voice-over-IP or teleconferencing traffic (and charge more for this service!) than to elastic traffic such as email or HTTP. Alternatively, an ISP may simply want to provide a higher quality of service to customers willing to pay more for this improved service. A number of residential wired-access ISPs and cellular wireless-access ISPs have adopted such tiered levels of service—with platinum-service subscribers receiving better performance than gold- or silver-service subscribers.

We're all familiar with different classes of service from our everyday lives—first-class airline passengers get better service than business-class passengers, who in turn get better service than those of us who fly economy class; VIPs are provided immediate entry to events while everyone else waits in line; elders are revered in some countries and provided seats of honor and the finest food at a table. It's important to note that such differential service is provided among aggregates of traffic, that is, among classes of traffic, not among individual connections. For example, all first-class passengers are handled the same (with no first-class passenger receiving any better treatment than any other first-class passenger), just as all VoIP packets would receive the same treatment within the network, independent of the particular end-to-end connection to which they belong. As we will see, by dealing with a small number of traffic aggregates, rather than a large number of individual connections, the new network mechanisms required to provide better-than-best service can be kept relatively simple.

The early Internet designers clearly had this notion of multiple classes of service in mind. Recall the type-of-service (ToS) field in the IPv4 header in Figure 4.13.

IEN123 [ISI 1979] describes the ToS field also present in an ancestor of the IPv4 datagram as follows: "The Type of Service [field] provides an indication of the abstract parameters of the quality of service desired. These parameters are to be used to guide the selection of the actual service parameters when transmitting a datagram through a particular network. Several networks offer service precedence, which somehow treats high precedence traffic as more important that other traffic." More than four decades ago, the vision of providing different levels of service to different classes of traffic was clear! However, it's taken us an equally long period of time to realize this vision.

Motivating Scenarios

Let's begin our discussion of network mechanisms for providing multiple classes of service with a few motivating scenarios.

Figure 7.14 shows a simple network scenario in which two application packet flows originate on Hosts H1 and H2 on one LAN and are destined for Hosts H3 and H4 on another LAN. The routers on the two LANs are connected by a 1.5 Mbps link. Let's assume the LAN speeds are significantly higher than 1.5 Mbps, and focus on the output queue of router R1; it is here that packet delay and packet loss will occur if the aggregate sending rate of H1 and H2 exceeds 1.5 Mbps. Let's further suppose that a 1 Mbps audio application (for example, a CD-quality audio call) shares the 1.5 Mbps link between R1 and R2 with an HTTP Web-browsing application that is downloading a Web page from H2 to H4.

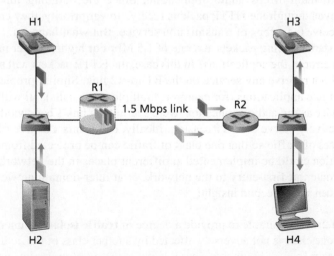

Figure 7.14 ♦ Competing audio and HTTP applications

In the best-effort Internet, the audio and HTTP packets are mixed in the output queue at R1 and (typically) transmitted in a first-in-first-out (FIFO) order. In this scenario, a burst of packets from the Web server could potentially fill up the queue, causing IP audio packets to be excessively delayed or lost due to buffer overflow at R1. How should we solve this potential problem? Given that the HTTP Web-browsing application does not have time constraints, our intuition might be to give strict priority to audio packets at R1. Under a strict priority scheduling discipline, an audio packet in the R1 output buffer would always be transmitted before any HTTP packet in the R1 output buffer. The link from R1 to R2 would look like a dedicated link of 1.5 Mbps to the audio traffic, with HTTP traffic using the R1-to-R2 link only when no audio traffic is queued. In order for R1 to distinguish between the audio and HTTP packets in its queue, each packet must be marked as belonging to one of these two classes of traffic. This was the original goal of the type-of-service (ToS) field in IPv4. As obvious as this might seem, this then is our first insight into mechanisms needed to provide multiple classes of traffic:

Insight 1: Packet marking allows a router to distinguish among packets belonging to different classes of traffic.

Note that although our example considers a competing multimedia and elastic flow, the same insight applies to the case that platinum, gold, and silver classes of service are implemented—a packet-marking mechanism is still needed to indicate that class of service to which a packet belongs.

Now suppose that the router is configured to give priority to packets marked as belonging to the 1 Mbps audio application. Since the outgoing link speed is 1.5 Mbps, even though the HTTP packets receive lower priority, they can still, on average, receive 0.5 Mbps of transmission service. But what happens if the audio application starts sending packets at a rate of 1.5 Mbps or higher (either maliciously or due to an error in the application)? In this case, the HTTP packets will starve, that is, they will not receive any service on the R1-to-R2 link. Similar problems would occur if multiple applications (for example, multiple audio calls), all with the same class of service as the audio application, were sharing the link's bandwidth; they too could collectively starve the FTP session. Ideally, one wants a degree of isolation among classes of traffic so that one class of traffic can be protected from the other. This protection could be implemented at different places in the network—at each and every router, at first entry to the network, or at inter-domain network boundaries. This then is our second insight:

Insight 2: It is desirable to provide a degree of **traffic isolation** among classes so that one class is not adversely affected by another class of traffic that misbehaves.

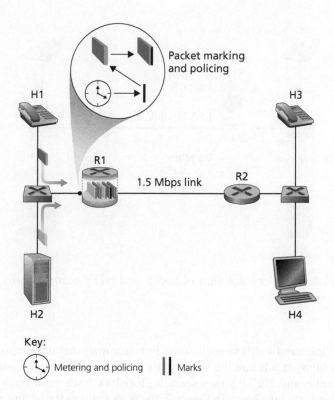

Packet marking
and policing

H1

H3

R1

1.5 Mbps link

R2

H2

H4

Key:

Metering and policing   Marks

Figure 7.15 ♦ Policing (and marking) the audio and HTTP traffic classes

We'll examine several specific mechanisms for providing such isolation among traffic classes. We note here that two broad approaches can be taken. First, it is possible to perform **traffic policing**, as shown in Figure 7.15. If a traffic class or flow must meet certain criteria (for example, that the audio flow not exceed a peak rate of 1 Mbps), then a policing mechanism can be put into place to ensure that these criteria are indeed observed. If the policed application misbehaves, the policing mechanism will take some action (for example, drop or delay packets that are in violation of the criteria) so that the traffic actually entering the network conforms to the criteria. The leaky bucket mechanism that we'll examine shortly is perhaps the most widely used policing mechanism. In Figure 7.15, the packet classification and marking mechanism (Insight 1) and the policing mechanism (Insight 2) are both implemented together at the network's edge, either in the end system or at an edge router.

A complementary approach for providing isolation among traffic classes is for the link-level packet-scheduling mechanism to explicitly allocate a fixed

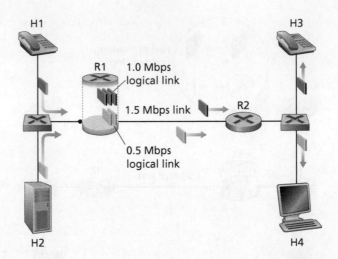

Figure 7.16 ♦ Logical isolation of audio and HTTP traffic classes

amount of link bandwidth to each class. For example, the audio class could be allocated 1 Mbps at R1, and the HTTP class could be allocated 0.5 Mbps. In this case, the audio and HTTP flows see a logical link with capacity 1.0 and 0.5 Mbps, respectively, as shown in Figure 7.16. With strict enforcement of the link-level allocation of bandwidth, a class can use only the amount of bandwidth that has been allocated; in particular, it cannot utilize bandwidth that is not currently being used by others. For example, if the audio flow goes silent (for example, if the speaker pauses and generates no audio packets), the HTTP flow would still not be able to transmit more than 0.5 Mbps over the R1-to-R2 link, even though the audio flow's 1 Mbps bandwidth allocation is not being used at that moment. Since bandwidth is a "use-it-or-lose-it" resource, there is no reason to prevent HTTP traffic from using bandwidth not used by the audio traffic. We'd like to use bandwidth as efficiently as possible, never wasting it when it could be otherwise used. This gives rise to our third insight:

> **Insight 3:** While providing isolation among classes or flows, it is desirable to use resources (for example, link bandwidth and buffers) as efficiently as possible.

Scheduling Mechanisms

Recall from our discussion in Section 1.3 and Section 4.3 that packets belonging to various network flows are multiplexed and queued for transmission at the output buffers associated with a link. The manner in which queued packets are selected for transmission on the link is known as the **link-scheduling discipline**. Let us now consider several of the most important link-scheduling disciplines in more detail.

First-In-First-Out (FIFO)

Figure 7.17 shows the queuing model abstractions for the FIFO link-scheduling discipline. Packets arriving at the link output queue wait for transmission if the link is currently busy transmitting another packet. If there is not sufficient buffering space to hold the arriving packet, the queue's **packet-discarding policy** then determines whether the packet will be dropped (lost) or whether other packets will be removed from the queue to make space for the arriving packet. In our discussion below, we will ignore packet discard. When a packet is completely transmitted over the outgoing link (that is, receives service) it is removed from the queue.

The FIFO (also known as first-come-first-served, or FCFS) scheduling discipline selects packets for link transmission in the same order in which they arrived at the output link queue. We're all familiar with FIFO queuing from bus stops (particularly in England, where queuing seems to have been perfected) or other service centers, where arriving customers join the back of the single waiting line, remain in order, and are then served when they reach the front of the line.

Figure 7.18 shows the FIFO queue in operation. Packet arrivals are indicated by numbered arrows above the upper timeline, with the number indicating the order

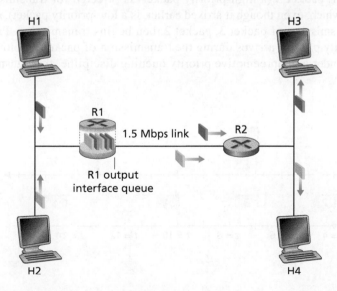

H1

H3

R1

1.5 Mbps link   R2

R1 output
interface queue

H2

H4

Figure 7.17 ♦ FIFO queuing abstraction

in which the packet arrived. Individual packet departures are shown below the lower timeline. The time that a packet spends in service (being transmitted) is indicated by the shaded rectangle between the two timelines. Because of the FIFO discipline, packets leave in the same order in which they arrived. Note that after the departure of packet 4, the link remains idle (since packets 1 through 4 have been transmitted and removed from the queue) until the arrival of packet 5.

Priority Queuing

Under **priority queuing**, packets arriving at the output link are classified into priority classes at the output queue, as shown in Figure 7.19. As discussed in the previous section, a packet's priority class may depend on an explicit marking that it carries in its packet header (for example, the value of the ToS bits in an IPv4 packet), its source or destination IP address, its destination port number, or other criteria. Each priority class typically has its own queue. When choosing a packet to transmit, the priority queuing discipline will transmit a packet from the highest priority class that has a nonempty queue (that is, has packets waiting for transmission). The choice among packets *in the same priority class* is typically done in a FIFO manner.

Figure 7.20 illustrates the operation of a priority queue with two priority classes. Packets 1, 3, and 4 belong to the high-priority class, and packets 2 and 5 belong to the low-priority class. Packet 1 arrives and, finding the link idle, begins transmission. During the transmission of packet 1, packets 2 and 3 arrive and are queued in the low- and high-priority queues, respectively. After the transmission of packet 1, packet 3 (a high-priority packet) is selected for transmission over packet 2 (which, even though it arrived earlier, is a low-priority packet). At the end of the transmission of packet 3, packet 2 then begins transmission. Packet 4 (a high-priority packet) arrives during the transmission of packet 2 (a low-priority packet). Under a nonpreemptive priority queuing discipline, the transmission of

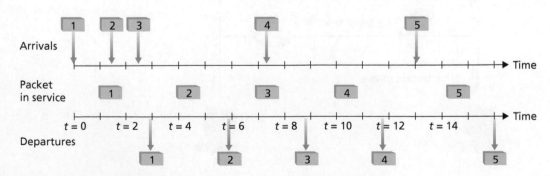

Figure 7.18 ♦ The FIFO queue in operation

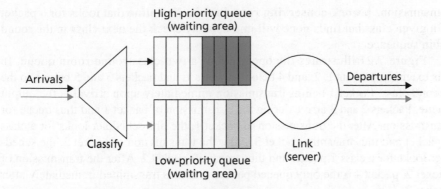

Figure 7.19 ♦ Priority queuing model

a packet is not interrupted once it has begun. In this case, packet 4 queues for transmission and begins being transmitted after the transmission of packet 2 is completed.

Round Robin and Weighted Fair Queuing (WFQ)

Under the **round robin queuing discipline**, packets are sorted into classes as with priority queuing. However, rather than there being a strict priority of service among classes, a round robin scheduler alternates service among the classes. In the simplest form of round robin scheduling, a class 1 packet is transmitted, followed by a class 2 packet, followed by a class 1 packet, followed by a class 2 packet, and so on. A so-called work-conserving queuing discipline will never allow the link to remain idle whenever there are packets (of any class) queued for

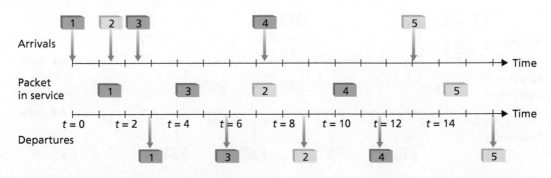

Figure 7.20 ♦ Operation of the priority queue

transmission. A **work-conserving round robin discipline** that looks for a packet of a given class but finds none will immediately check the next class in the round robin sequence.

Figure 7.21 illustrates the operation of a two-class round robin queue. In this example, packets 1, 2, and 4 belong to class 1, and packets 3 and 5 belong to the second class. Packet 1 begins transmission immediately upon arrival at the output queue. Packets 2 and 3 arrive during the transmission of packet 1 and thus queue for transmission. After the transmission of packet 1, the link scheduler looks for a class 2 packet and thus transmits packet 3. After the transmission of packet 3, the scheduler looks for a class 1 packet and thus transmits packet 2. After the transmission of packet 2, packet 4 is the only queued packet; it is thus transmitted immediately after packet 2.

A generalized abstraction of round robin queuing that has found considerable use in QoS architectures is the so-called **weighted fair queuing** (WFQ) discipline [Demers 1990; Parekh 1993]. WFQ is illustrated in Figure 7.22. Arriving packets are classified and queued in the appropriate per-class waiting area. As in round robin scheduling, a WFQ scheduler will serve classes in a circular manner—first serving class 1, then serving class 2, then serving class 3, and then (assuming there are three classes) repeating the service pattern. WFQ is also a work-conserving queuing discipline and thus will immediately move on to the next class in the service sequence when it finds an empty class queue.

WFQ differs from round robin in that each class may receive a *differential* amount of service in any interval of time. Specifically, each class, i, is assigned a weight, w_i. Under WFQ, during any interval of time during which there are class i packets to send, class i will then be guaranteed to receive a fraction of service equal to $w_i/(\Sigma w_j)$, where the sum in the denominator is taken over all classes that also have packets queued for transmission. In the worst case, even if all classes have queued packets, class i will still be guaranteed to receive a fraction $w_i/(\Sigma w_j)$ of the

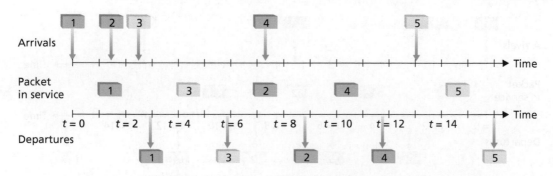

Figure 7.21 ◆ Operation of the two-class round robin queue

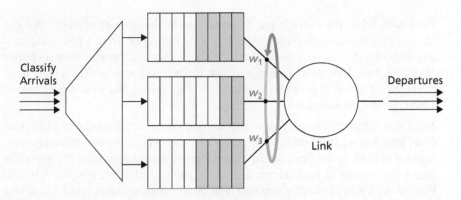

Classify
Arrivals

w_1

w_2

w_3

Link

Departures

Figure 7.22 ♦ Weighted fair queuing (WFQ)

bandwidth. Thus, for a link with transmission rate R, class i will always achieve a throughput of at least $R \cdot w_i/(\sum w_j)$. Our description of WFQ has been an idealized one, as we have not considered the fact that packets are discrete units of data and a packet's transmission will not be interrupted to begin transmission of another packet; [Demers 1990] and [Parekh 1993] discuss this packetization issue. As we will see in the following sections, WFQ plays a central role in QoS architectures. It is also available in today's router products [Cisco QoS 2012].

Policing: The Leaky Bucket

One of our earlier insights was that policing, the regulation of the rate at which a class or flow (we will assume the unit of policing is a flow in our discussion below) is allowed to inject packets into the network, is an important QoS mechanism. But what aspects of a flow's packet rate should be policed? We can identify three important policing criteria, each differing from the other according to the time scale over which the packet flow is policed:

- *Average rate.* The network may wish to limit the long-term average rate (packets per time interval) at which a flow's packets can be sent into the network. A crucial issue here is the interval of time over which the average rate will be policed. A flow whose average rate is limited to 100 packets per second is more constrained than a source that is limited to 6,000 packets per minute, even though both have the same average rate over a long enough interval of time. For example, the latter constraint would allow a flow to send 1,000 packets in a given second-long interval of time, while the former constraint would disallow this sending behavior.

- *Peak rate.* While the average-rate constraint limits the amount of traffic that can be sent into the network over a relatively long period of time, a peak-rate constraint limits the maximum number of packets that can be sent over a shorter period of time. Using our example above, the network may police a flow at an average rate of 6,000 packets per minute, while limiting the flow's peak rate to 1,500 packets per second.

- *Burst size.* The network may also wish to limit the maximum number of packets (the "burst" of packets) that can be sent into the network over an extremely short interval of time. In the limit, as the interval length approaches zero, the burst size limits the number of packets that can be instantaneously sent into the network. Even though it is physically impossible to instantaneously send multiple packets into the network (after all, every link has a physical transmission rate that cannot be exceeded!), the abstraction of a maximum burst size is a useful one.

The leaky bucket mechanism is an abstraction that can be used to characterize these policing limits. As shown in Figure 7.23, a leaky bucket consists of a bucket that can hold up to b tokens. Tokens are added to this bucket as follows. New tokens, which may potentially be added to the bucket, are always being generated at a rate of r tokens per second. (We assume here for simplicity that the unit of time is a second.) If the bucket is filled with less than b tokens when a token is generated, the newly generated token is added to the bucket; otherwise the newly generated token is ignored, and the token bucket remains full with b tokens.

Let us now consider how the leaky bucket can be used to police a packet flow. Suppose that before a packet is transmitted into the network, it must first remove a

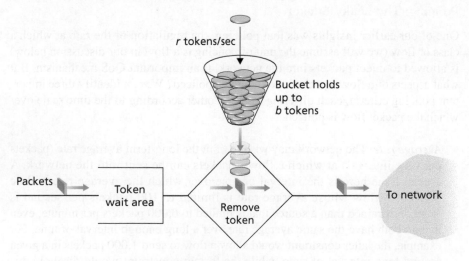

Figure 7.23 ♦ The leaky bucket policer

token from the token bucket. If the token bucket is empty, the packet must wait for a token. (An alternative is for the packet to be dropped, although we will not consider that option here.) Let us now consider how this behavior polices a traffic flow. Because there can be at most b tokens in the bucket, the maximum burst size for a leaky-bucket-policed flow is b packets. Furthermore, because the token generation rate is r, the maximum number of packets that can enter the network of *any* interval of time of length t is $rt + b$. Thus, the token-generation rate, r, serves to limit the long-term average rate at which packets can enter the network. It is also possible to use leaky buckets (specifically, two leaky buckets in series) to police a flow's peak rate in addition to the long-term average rate; see the homework problems at the end of this chapter.

Leaky Bucket + Weighted Fair Queuing = Provable Maximum Delay in a Queue

Let's close our discussion of scheduling and policing by showing how the two can be combined to provide a bound on the delay through a router's queue. Let's consider a router's output link that multiplexes n flows, each policed by a leaky bucket with parameters b_i and r_i, $i = 1, \ldots, n$, using WFQ scheduling. We use the term *flow* here loosely to refer to the set of packets that are not distinguished from each other by the scheduler. In practice, a flow might be comprised of traffic from a single end-to-end connection or a collection of many such connections, see Figure 7.24.

Recall from our discussion of WFQ that each flow, i, is guaranteed to receive a share of the link bandwidth equal to at least $R \cdot w_i/(\Sigma w_j)$, where R is the transmission

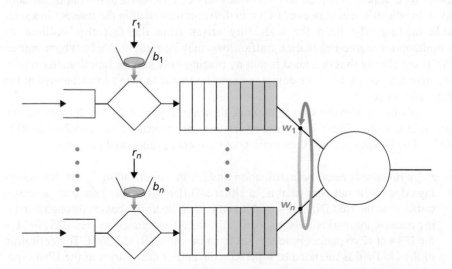

Figure 7.24 ♦ *n* multiplexed leaky bucket flows with WFQ scheduling

rate of the link in packets/sec. What then is the maximum delay that a packet will experience while waiting for service in the WFQ (that is, after passing through the leaky bucket)? Let us focus on flow 1. Suppose that flow 1's token bucket is initially full. A burst of b_1 packets then arrives to the leaky bucket policer for flow 1. These packets remove all of the tokens (without wait) from the leaky bucket and then join the WFQ waiting area for flow 1. Since these b_1 packets are served at a rate of at least $R \cdot w_i/(\sum w_j)$ packet/sec, the last of these packets will then have a maximum delay, d_{max}, until its transmission is completed, where

$$d_{max} = \frac{b_1}{R \cdot w_1/\sum w_j}$$

The rationale behind this formula is that if there are b_1 packets in the queue and packets are being serviced (removed) from the queue at a rate of at least $R \cdot w_1/(\sum w_j)$ packets per second, then the amount of time until the last bit of the last packet is transmitted cannot be more than $b_1/(R \cdot w_1/(\sum w_j))$. A homework problem asks you to prove that as long as $r_1 < R \cdot w_1/(\sum w_j)$, then d_{max} is indeed the maximum delay that any packet in flow 1 will ever experience in the WFQ queue.

7.5.3 Diffserv

Having seen the motivation, insights, and specific mechanisms for providing multiple classes of service, let's wrap up our study of approaches toward proving multiple classes of service with an example—the Internet Diffserv architecture [RFC 2475; RFC Kilkki 1999]. Diffserv provides service differentiation—that is, the ability to handle different classes of traffic in different ways within the Internet in a scalable manner. The need for scalability arises from the fact that millions of simultaneous source-destination traffic flows may be present at a backbone router. We'll see shortly that this need is met by placing only simple functionality within the network core, with more complex control operations being implemented at the network's edge.

Let's begin with the simple network shown in Figure 7.25. We'll describe one possible use of Diffserv here; other variations are possible, as described in RFC 2475. The Diffserv architecture consists of two sets of functional elements:

• *Edge functions: packet classification and traffic conditioning.* At the incoming edge of the network (that is, at either a Diffserv-capable host that generates traffic or at the first Diffserv-capable router that the traffic passes through), arriving packets are marked. More specifically, the differentiated service (DS) field in the IPv4 or IPv6 packet header is set to some value [RFC 3260]. The definition of the DS field is intended to supersede the earlier definitions of the IPv4 type-of-service field and the IPv6 traffic class fields that we discussed in Chapter 4. For example, in Figure 7.25, packets being sent from H1 to H3 might be marked

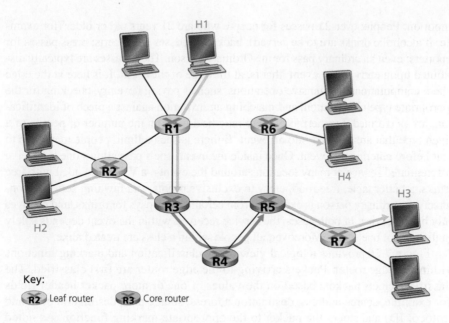

Key:

(R2) Leaf router (R3) Core router

Figure 7.25 ♦ A simple Diffserv network example

at R1, while packets being sent from H2 to H4 might be marked at R2. The mark that a packet receives identifies the class of traffic to which it belongs. Different classes of traffic will then receive different service within the core network.

• *Core function: forwarding.* When a DS-marked packet arrives at a Diffserv-capable router, the packet is forwarded onto its next hop according to the so-called per-hop behavior (PHB) associated with that packet's class. The per-hop behavior influences how a router's buffers and link bandwidth are shared among the competing classes of traffic. A crucial tenet of the Diffserv architecture is that a router's per-hop behavior will be based only on packet markings, that is, the class of traffic to which a packet belongs. Thus, if packets being sent from H1 to H3 in Figure 7.25 receive the same marking as packets being sent from H2 to H4, then the network routers treat these packets as an aggregate, without distinguishing whether the packets originated at H1 or H2. For example, R3 would not distinguish between packets from H1 and H2 when forwarding these packets on to R4. Thus, the Diffserv architecture obviates the need to keep router state for individual source-destination pairs—a critical consideration in making Diffserv scalable.

An analogy might prove useful here. At many large-scale social events (for example, a large public reception, a large dance club or discothèque, a concert, or a football game), people entering the event receive a pass of one type or another: VIP passes for Very

Important People; over-21 passes for people who are 21 years old or older (for example, if alcoholic drinks are to be served); backstage passes at concerts; press passes for reporters; even an ordinary pass for the Ordinary Person. These passes are typically distributed upon entry to the event, that is, at the edge of the event. It is here at the edge where computationally intensive operations, such as paying for entry, checking for the appropriate type of invitation, and matching an invitation against a piece of identification, are performed. Furthermore, there may be a limit on the number of people of a given type that are allowed into an event. If there is such a limit, people may have to wait before entering the event. Once inside the event, one's pass allows one to receive differentiated service at many locations around the event—a VIP is provided with free drinks, a better table, free food, entry to exclusive rooms, and fawning service. Conversely, an ordinary person is excluded from certain areas, pays for drinks, and receives only basic service. In both cases, the service received within the event depends solely on the type of one's pass. Moreover, all people within a class are treated alike.

Figure 7.26 provides a logical view of the classification and marking functions within the edge router. Packets arriving to the edge router are first classified. The classifier selects packets based on the values of one or more packet header fields (for example, source address, destination address, source port, destination port, and protocol ID) and steers the packet to the appropriate marking function. As noted above, a packet's marking is carried in the DS field in the packet header.

In some cases, an end user may have agreed to limit its packet-sending rate to conform to a declared **traffic profile**. The traffic profile might contain a limit on the peak rate, as well as the burstiness of the packet flow, as we saw previously with the leaky bucket mechanism. As long as the user sends packets into the network in a way that conforms to the negotiated traffic profile, the packets receive their priority marking and are forwarded along their route to the destination. On the other hand, if the traffic profile is violated, out-of-profile packets might be marked differently, might be shaped (for example, delayed so that a maximum rate constraint would be observed), or might be dropped at the network edge. The role of the **metering function**, shown in Figure 7.26, is to compare the incoming packet flow with the negotiated traffic profile and to determine whether a packet is within the negotiated traffic profile. The actual decision about whether to immediately remark, forward, delay, or drop a packet is a policy issue determined by the network administrator and is *not* specified in the Diffserv architecture.

So far, we have focused on the marking and policing functions in the Diffserv architecture. The second key component of the Diffserv architecture involves the per-hop behavior (PHB) performed by Diffserv-capable routers. PHB is rather cryptically, but carefully, defined as "a description of the externally observable forwarding behavior of a Diffserv node applied to a particular Diffserv behavior aggregate" [RFC 2475]. Digging a little deeper into this definition, we can see several important considerations embedded within:

• A PHB can result in different classes of traffic receiving different performance (that is, different externally observable forwarding behaviors).

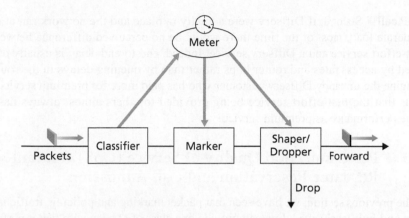

Figure 7.26 ♦ A simple Diffserv network example

- While a PHB defines differences in performance (behavior) among classes, it does not mandate any particular mechanism for achieving these behaviors. As long as the externally observable performance criteria are met, any implementation mechanism and any buffer/bandwidth allocation policy can be used. For example, a PHB would not require that a particular packet-queuing discipline (for example, a priority queue versus a WFQ queue versus a FCFS queue) be used to achieve a particular behavior. The PHB is the end, to which resource allocation and implementation mechanisms are the means.

- Differences in performance must be observable and hence measurable.

Two PHBs have been defined: an expedited forwarding (EF) PHB [RFC 3246] and an assured forwarding (AF) PHB [RFC 2597]. The **expedited forwarding** PHB specifies that the departure rate of a class of traffic from a router must equal or exceed a configured rate. The **assured forwarding** PHB divides traffic into four classes, where each AF class is guaranteed to be provided with some minimum amount of bandwidth and buffering.

    Let's close our discussion of Diffserv with a few observations regarding its service model. First, we have implicitly assumed that Diffserv is deployed within a single administrative domain, but typically an end-to-end service must be fashioned from multiple ISPs sitting between communicating end systems. In order to provide end-to-end Diffserv service, all the ISPs between the end systems must not only provide this service, but most also cooperate and make settlements in order to offer end customers true end-to-end service. Without this kind of cooperation, ISPs directly selling Diffserv service to customers will find themselves repeatedly saying: "Yes, we know you paid extra, but we don't have a service agreement with the ISP that dropped and delayed your traffic. I'm sorry that there were so many gaps in your

VoIP call!" Second, if Diffserv were actually in place and the network ran at only moderate load, most of the time there would be no perceived difference between a best-effort service and a Diffserv service. Indeed, end-to-end delay is usually dominated by access rates and router hops rather than by queuing delays in the routers. Imagine the unhappy Diffserv customer who has paid more for premium service but finds that the best-effort service being provided to others almost always has the same performance as premium service!

7.5.4 Per-Connection Quality-of-Service (QoS) Guarantees: Resource Reservation and Call Admission

In the previous section, we have seen that packet marking and policing, traffic isolation, and link-level scheduling can provide one class of service with better performance than another. Under certain scheduling disciplines, such as priority scheduling, the lower classes of traffic are essentially "invisible" to the highest-priority class of traffic. With proper network dimensioning, the highest class of service can indeed achieve extremely low packet loss and delay—essentially circuit-like performance. But can the network *guarantee* that an ongoing flow in a high-priority traffic class will continue to receive such service throughout the flow's duration using only the mechanisms that we have described so far? It cannot. In this section, we'll see why yet additional network mechanisms and protocols are required when a hard service guarantee is provided to individual connections.

Let's return to our scenario from Section 7.5.2 and consider two 1 Mbps audio applications transmitting their packets over the 1.5 Mbps link, as shown in Figure 7.27. The combined data rate of the two flows (2 Mbps) exceeds the link

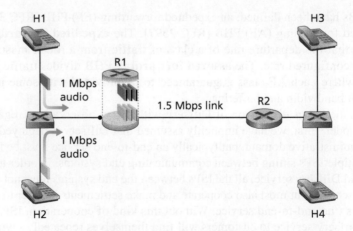

Figure 7.27 ♦ Two competing audio applications overloading the R1-to-R2 link

capacity. Even with classification and marking, isolation of flows, and sharing of unused bandwidth (of which there is none), this is clearly a losing proposition. There is simply not enough bandwidth to accommodate the needs of both applications at the same time. If the two applications equally share the bandwidth, each application would lose 25 percent of its transmitted packets. This is such an unacceptably low QoS that both audio applications are completely unusable; there's no need even to transmit any audio packets in the first place.

Given that the two applications in Figure 7.27 cannot both be satisfied simultaneously, what should the network do? Allowing both to proceed with an unusable QoS wastes network resources on application flows that ultimately provide no utility to the end user. The answer is hopefully clear—one of the application flows should be blocked (that is, denied access to the network), while the other should be allowed to proceed on, using the full 1 Mbps needed by the application. The telephone network is an example of a network that performs such call blocking—if the required resources (an end-to-end circuit in the case of the telephone network) cannot be allocated to the call, the call is blocked (prevented from entering the network) and a busy signal is returned to the user. In our example, there is no gain in allowing a flow into the network if it will not receive a sufficient QoS to be considered usable. Indeed, there is a cost to admitting a flow that does not receive its needed QoS, as network resources are being used to support a flow that provides no utility to the end user.

By explicitly admitting or blocking flows based on their resource requirements, and the source requirements of already-admitted flows, the network can guarantee that admitted flows will be able to receive their requested QoS. Implicit in the need to provide a guaranteed QoS to a flow is the need for the flow to declare its QoS requirements. This process of having a flow declare its QoS requirement, and then having the network either accept the flow (at the required QoS) or block the flow is referred to as the **call admission** process. This then is our fourth insight (in addition to the three earlier insights from Section 7.5.2) into the mechanisms needed to provide QoS.

> **Insight 4:** If sufficient resources will not always be available, and QoS is to be *guaranteed*, a call admission process is needed in which flows declare their QoS requirements and are then either admitted to the network (at the required QoS) or blocked from the network (if the required QoS cannot be provided by the network).

Our motivating example in Figure 7.27 highlights the need for several new network mechanisms and protocols if a call (an end-to-end flow) is to be guaranteed a given quality of service once it begins:

*   *Resource reservation.* The only way to *guarantee* that a call will have the resources (link bandwidth, buffers) needed to meet its desired QoS is to explicitly

allocate those resources to the call—a process known in networking parlance as **resource reservation**. Once resources are reserved, the call has on-demand access to these resources throughout its duration, regardless of the demands of all other calls. If a call reserves and receives a guarantee of x Mbps of link bandwidth, and never transmits at a rate greater than x, the call will see loss- and delay-free performance.

- *Call admission.* If resources are to be reserved, then the network must have a mechanism for calls to request and reserve resources. Since resources are not infinite, a call making a call admission request will be denied admission, that is, be blocked, if the requested resources are not available. Such a call admission is performed by the telephone network—we request resources when we dial a number. If the circuits (TDMA slots) needed to complete the call are available, the circuits are allocated and the call is completed. If the circuits are not available, then the call is blocked, and we receive a busy signal. A blocked call can try again to gain admission to the network, but it is not allowed to send traffic into the network until it has successfully completed the call admission process. Of course, a router that allocates link bandwidth should not allocate more than is available at that link. Typically, a call may reserve only a fraction of the link's bandwidth, and so a router may allocate link bandwidth to more than one call. However, the sum of the allocated bandwidth to all calls should be less than the link capacity if hard quality of service guarantees are to be provided.

- *Call setup signaling.* The call admission process described above requires that a call be able to reserve sufficient resources at each and every network router on its source-to-destination path to ensure that its end-to-end QoS requirement is met. Each router must determine the local resources required by the session, consider the amounts of its resources that are already committed to other ongoing sessions, and determine whether it has sufficient resources to satisfy the per-hop QoS requirement of the session at this router without violating local QoS guarantees made to an already-admitted session. A signaling protocol is needed to coordinate these various activities—the per-hop allocation of local resources, as well as the overall end-to-end decision of whether or not the call has been able to reserve sufficient resources at each and every router on the end-to-end path. This is the job of the **call setup protocol**, as shown in Figure 7.28. The **RSVP protocol** [Zhang 1993, RFC 2210] was proposed for this purpose within an Internet architecture for providing quality-of-service guarantees. In ATM networks, the Q2931b protocol [Black 1995] carries this information among the ATM network's switches and end point.

Despite a tremendous amount of research and development, and even products that provide for per-connection quality of service guarantees, there has been almost no extended deployment of such services. There are many possible reasons. First and foremost, it may well be the case that the simple application-level mechanisms that we studied in Sections 7.2 through 7.4, combined with proper

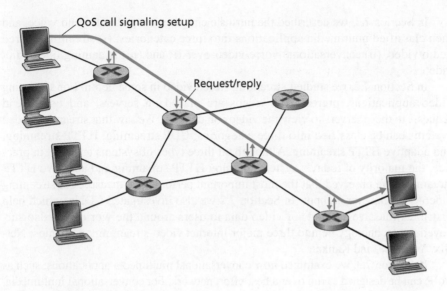

Figure 7.28 ♦ The call setup process

network dimensioning (Section 7.5.1) provide "good enough" best-effort network service for multimedia applications. In addition, the added complexity and cost of deploying and managing a network that provides per-connection quality of service guarantees may be judged by ISPs to be simply too high given predicted customer revenues for that service.

7.6 Summary

Multimedia networking is one of the most exciting developments in the Internet today. People throughout the world are spending less time in front of their radios and televisions, and are instead turning to the Internet to receive audio and video transmissions, both live and prerecorded. This trend will certainly continue as high-speed wireless Internet access becomes more and more prevalent. Moreover, with sites like YouTube, users have become producers as well as consumers of multimedia Internet content. In addition to video distribution, the Internet is also being used to transport phone calls. In fact, over the next 10 years, the Internet, along with wireless Internet access, may make the traditional circuit-switched telephone system a thing of the past. VoIP not only provides phone service inexpensively, but also provides numerous value-added services, such as video conferencing, online directory services, voice messaging, and integration into social networks such as Facebook and Google+.

In Section 7.1, we described the intrinsic characteristics of video and voice, and then classified multimedia applications into three categories: (i) streaming stored audio/video, (ii) conversational voice/video-over-IP, and (iii) streaming live audio/video.

In Section 7.2, we studied streaming stored video in some depth. For streaming video applications, prerecorded videos are placed on servers, and users send requests to these servers to view the videos on demand. We saw that streaming video systems can be classified into three categories: UDP streaming, HTTP streaming, and adaptive HTTP streaming. Although all three types of systems are used in practice, the majority of today's systems employ HTTP streaming and adaptive HTTP streaming. We observed that the most important performance measure for streaming video is average throughput. In Section 7.2 we also investigated CDNs, which help distribute massive amounts of video data to users around the world. We also surveyed the technology behind three major Internet video-streaming companies: Netflix, YouTube, and Kankan.

In Section 7.3, we examined how conversational multimedia applications, such as VoIP, can be designed to run over a best-effort network. For conversational multimedia, timing considerations are important because conversational applications are highly delay-sensitive. On the other hand, conversational multimedia applications are loss-tolerant—occasional loss only causes occasional glitches in audio/video playback, and these losses can often be partially or fully concealed. We saw how a combination of client buffers, packet sequence numbers, and timestamps can greatly alleviate the effects of network-induced jitter. We also surveyed the technology behind Skype, one of the leading voice- and video-over-IP companies. In Section 7.4, we examined two of the most important standardized protocols for VoIP, namely, RTP and SIP.

In Section 7.5, we introduced how several network mechanisms (link-level scheduling disciplines and traffic policing) can be used to provide differentiated service among several classes of traffic.

 # Homework Problems and Questions

Chapter 7 Review Questions

SECTION 7.1

R1. Reconstruct Table 7.1 for when Victor Video is watching a 5 Mbps video, Facebook Frank is looking at a new 150 Kbyte image every 25 seconds, and Martha Music is listening to 210 kbps audio stream.

R2. For 128 quantization levels, what is the size of each sample signal?

R3. Suppose an analog audio signal is sampled 8,000 times per second, and each sample is quantized into one of 512 levels. What would be the resulting bit rate of the PCM digital audio signal?

R4. Many Internet companies today provide streaming video, including YouTube (Google), Netflix, and Hulu. Streaming stored video has three key distinguishing features. List them.

SECTION 7.2

R5. What are advantages of client buffering?

R6. In video streaming applications, why is HTTP streaming more popular than UDP streaming?

R7. With HTTP streaming, are the TCP receive buffer and the client's application buffer the same thing? If not, how do they interact?

R8. Consider the simple model for HTTP streaming. Suppose the server sends bits at a constant rate of 2 Mbps and playback begins when 8 million bits have been received. What is the initial buffering delay t_p?

R9. What is prefetching video? How does it help?

R10. Several cluster selection strategies were described in Section 7.2.4. Which of these strategies finds a good cluster with respect to the client's LDNS? Which of these strategies finds a good cluster with respect to the client itself?

R11. Besides network-related considerations such as delay, loss, and bandwidth performance, there are many additional important factors that go into designing a cluster selection strategy. What are they?

SECTION 7.3

R12. What mechanisms are used at the receiver side to eliminate packet jitter?

R13. What are the two types of loss anticipation schemes used in VoIP?

R14. Section 7.3 describes two FEC schemes. Briefly summarize them. Both schemes increase the transmission rate of the stream by adding overhead. Does interleaving also increase the transmission rate?

SECTION 7.4

R15. What are the four main RTP header fields?

R16. What is the role of a SIP registrar? How is the role of an SIP registrar different from that of a home agent in Mobile IP?

SECTION 7.5

R17. In Section 7.5, we discussed non-preemptive priority queuing. What would be preemptive priority queuing? Does preemptive priority queuing make sense for computer networks?

R18. Give an example of a scheduling discipline that is *not* work conserving.

R19. What is the purpose of RSVP?

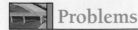 Problems

P1. Consider the figure below. Similar to our discussion of Figure 7.1, suppose that video is encoded at a fixed bit rate, and thus each video block contains video frames that are to be played out over the same fixed amount of time, $\triangle$. The server transmits the first video block at t_0, the second block at $t_0 + \triangle$, the third block at $t_0 + 2\triangle$, and so on. Once the client begins playout, each block should be played out $\triangle$ time units after the previous block.

a. Suppose that the client begins playout as soon as the first block arrives at t_1. In the figure below, how many blocks of video (including the first block) will have arrived at the client in time for their playout? Explain how you arrived at your answer.

b. Suppose that the client begins playout now at $t_1 + \triangle$. How many blocks of video (including the first block) will have arrived at the client in time for their playout? Explain how you arrived at your answer.

c. In the same scenario at (b) above, what is the largest number of blocks that is ever stored in the client buffer, awaiting playout? Explain how you arrived at your answer.

d. What is the smallest playout delay at the client, such that every video block has arrived in time for its playout? Explain how you arrived at your answer.

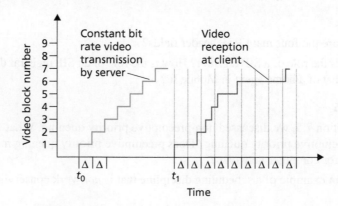

P2. Recall the simple model for HTTP streaming shown in Figure 7.3. Recall that B denotes the size of the client's application buffer, and Q denotes the number of bits that must be buffered before the client application begins playout. Also r denotes the video consumption rate. Assume that the server sends bits at a constant rate x whenever the client buffer is not full.

  a. Suppose that $x < r$. As discussed in the text, in this case playout will alternate between periods of continuous playout and periods of freezing. Determine the length of each continuous playout and freezing period as a function of Q, r, and x.

  b. Now suppose that $x > r$. At what time $t = t_f$ does the client application buffer become full?

P3. Recall the simple model for HTTP streaming shown in Figure 7.3. Suppose the buffer size is infinite but the server sends bits at variable rate $x(t)$. Specifically, suppose $x(t)$ has the following saw-tooth shape. The rate is initially zero at time $t = 0$ and linearly climbs to H at time $t = T$. It then repeats this pattern again and again, as shown in the figure below.

  a. What is the server's average send rate?

  b. Suppose that $Q = 0$, so that the client starts playback as soon as it receives a video frame. What will happen?

  c. Now suppose $Q > 0$ and $HT/2 \geq Q$. Determine as a function of Q, H, and T the time at which playback first begins.

  d. Suppose $H > 2r$ and $Q = HT/2$. Prove there will be no freezing after the initial playout delay.

  e. Suppose $H > 2r$. Find the smallest value of Q such that there will be no freezing after the initial playback delay.

  f. Now suppose that the buffer size B is finite. Suppose $H > 2r$. As a function of Q, B, T, and H, determine the time $t = t_f$ when the client application buffer first becomes full.

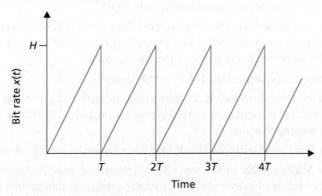

P4. Consider the following in the context of prefetching. Suppose the video consumption rate is 2 Mbps but the network is capable of delivering the video from server to client at a constant rate of 2.5 Mbps. Then the client will not only be able to play out the video with a very small playout delay, but will also be able to increase the amount of buffered video data by 500 Kbits every second. In this manner, if in the future, the client receives data at a rate of less than 2 Mbps for a brief period of time, the client will be able to continue to provide continuous playback due to the reserve in its buffer. At what throughput does streaming over TCP result in minimal starvation and low buffering delays?

P5. As an example of jitter, consider two consecutive packets in our VoIP application. The sender sends the second packet 20 msecs after sending the first packet. But at the receiver, the spacing between these packets can become greater than 20 msecs. To see this, suppose the first packet arrives at a nearly empty queue at a router, but just before the second packet arrives at the queue a large number of packets from other sources arrive at the same queue. Because the first packet experiences a small queuing delay and the second packet suffers a large queuing delay at this router, the first and second packets become spaced by more than 20 msecs. Give an analogy with driving cars on roads.

P6. In the VoIP example in Section 7.3, let h be the total number of header byte added to each chunk, including UDP and IP header.

a. Assuming an IP datagram is emitted every 40 msecs, find the transmission rate in bits per second for the datagrams generated by one side of this application.

b. What is a typical value of h when RTP is used? How much time is required to transmit the header?

P7. Consider the procedure described in Section 7.3 for estimating average delay d_i. Suppose that $u = 0.1$. Let $r_1 - t_1$ be the most recent sample delay, let $r_2 - t_2$ be the next most recent sample delay, and so on.

a. For a given audio application suppose four packets have arrived at the receiver with sample delays $r_4 - t_4$, $r_3 - t_3$, $r_2 - t_2$, and $r_1 - t_1$. Express the estimate of delay d in terms of the four samples.

b. Generalize your formula for n sample delays.

c. For the formula in Part b, let n approach infinity and give the resulting formula. Comment on why this averaging procedure is called an exponential moving average.

P8. Repeat Parts a and b in Question P7 for the estimate of average delay deviation.

P9. For the VoIP example in Section 7.3, we introduced an online procedure (exponential moving average) for estimating delay. In this problem we will examine an alternative procedure. Let t_i be the timestamp of the ith packet received; let r_i be the time at which the ith packet is received. Let d_n be our estimate of average delay after receiving the nth packet. After the first packet is received, we set the delay estimate equal to $d_1 = r_1 - t_1$.

a. Suppose that we would like $d_n = (r_1 - t_1 + r_2 - t_2 + \ldots + r_n - t_n)/n$ for all n. Give a recursive formula for d_n in terms of d_{n-1}, r_n, and t_n.

b. Describe why for Internet telephony, the delay estimate described in Section 7.3 is more appropriate than the delay estimate outlined in Part a.

P10. With the fixed-delay strategy, the receiver attempts to play out each chunk exactly q msecs after the chunk is generated. So if a chunk is timestamped at the sender at time t, the receiver plays out the chunk at time $t + q$, assuming the chunk has arrived by that time. Packets that arrive after their scheduled playout times are discarded and considered lost. What is a good choice for q?

P11. Consider the figure below (which is similar to Figure 7.7). A sender begins sending packetized audio periodically at $t = 1$. The first packet arrives at the receiver at $t = 8$.

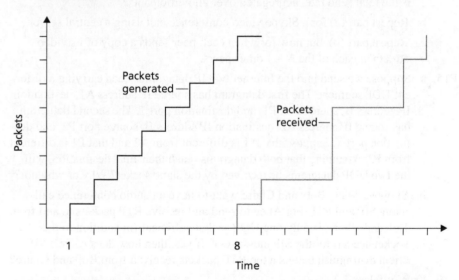

a. What are the delays (from sender to receiver, ignoring any playout delays) of packets 2 through 8? Note that each vertical and horizontal line segment in the figure has a length of 1, 2, or 3 time units.

b. If audio playout begins as soon as the first packet arrives at the receiver at $t = 8$, which of the first eight packets sent will *not* arrive in time for playout?

c. If audio playout begins at $t = 9$, which of the first eight packets sent will not arrive in time for playout?

d. What is the minimum playout delay at the receiver that results in all of the first eight packets arriving in time for their playout?

P12. Consider again the figure in P11, showing packet audio transmission and reception times.

   a. Compute the estimated delay for packets 2 through 8, using the formula for d_i from Section 7.3.2. Use a value of $u = 0.1$.

   b. Compute the estimated deviation of the delay from the estimated average for packets 2 through 8, using the formula for v_i from Section 7.3.2. Use a value of $u = 0.1$.

P13. A is at her PC and she wants to call B, who is also working at his PC. A's and B's PCs are both equipped with SIP-based software for making and receiving phone calls. Assume that A knows the IP address of B's PC. Illustrate the SIP call-establishment process.

P14. a. Consider an audio conference call in Skype with $N > 2$ participants. Suppose each participant generates a constant stream of rate r bps. How many bits per second will the call initiator need to send? How many bits per second will each of the other $N - 1$ participants need to send? What is the total send rate, aggregated over all participants?

   b. Repeat part (a) for a Skype video conference call using a central server.

   c. Repeat part (b), but now for when each peer sends a copy of its video stream to each of the $N - 1$ other peers.

P15. a. Suppose we send into the Internet two IP datagrams, each carrying a different UDP segment. The first datagram has source IP address A1, destination IP address B, source port P1, and destination port T. The second datagram has source IP address A2, destination IP address B, source port P2, and destination port T. Suppose that A1 is different from A2 and that P1 is different from P2. Assuming that both datagrams reach their final destination, will the two UDP datagrams be received by the same socket? Why or why not?

   b. Suppose Alice, Bob, and Claire want to have an audio conference call using SIP and RTP. For Alice to send and receive RTP packets to and from Bob and Claire, is only one UDP socket sufficient (in addition to the socket needed for the SIP messages)? If yes, then how does Alice's SIP client distinguish between the RTP packets received from Bob and Claire?

P16. True or false:

   a. If stored video is streamed directly from a Web server to a media player, then the application is using TCP as the underlying transport protocol.

b. When using RTP, it is possible for a sender to change encoding in the middle of a session.

c. All applications that use RTP must use port 87.

d. If an RTP session has a separate audio and video stream for each sender, then the audio and video streams use the same SSRC.

e. In differentiated services, while per-hop behavior defines differences in performance among classes, it does not mandate any particular mechanism for achieving these performances.

f. Suppose Alice wants to establish an SIP session with Bob. In her INVITE message she includes the line: m=audio 48753 RTP/AVP 3 (AVP 3 denotes GSM audio). Alice has therefore indicated in this message that she wishes to send GSM audio.

g. Referring to the preceding statement, Alice has indicated in her INVITE message that she will send audio to port 48753.

h. SIP messages are typically sent between SIP entities using a default SIP port number.

i. In order to maintain registration, SIP clients must periodically send REGISTER messages.

j. SIP mandates that all SIP clients support G.711 audio encoding.

P17. Suppose that the WFQ scheduling policy is applied to a buffer that supports three classes, and suppose the weights are 0.4, 0.4, and 0.2 for the three classes.

a. Suppose that each class has a large number of packets in the buffer. In what sequence might the three classes be served in order to achieve the WFQ weights? (For round robin scheduling, a natural sequence is 123123123 . . .)

b. Suppose that classes 1 and 3 have a large number of packets in the buffer, and there are no class 2 packets in the buffer. In what sequence might the three classes be served in to achieve the WFQ weights?

P18. Consider the figure below. Answer the following questions:

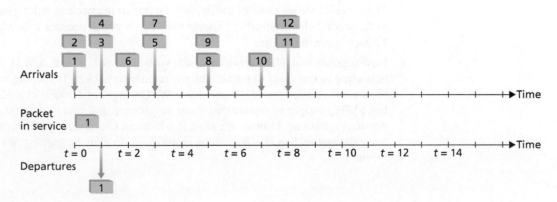

    a. Assuming FIFO service, indicate the time at which packets 2 through 12 each leave the queue. For each packet, what is the delay between its arrival and the beginning of the slot in which it is transmitted? What is the average of this delay over all 12 packets?

    b. Now assume a priority service, and assume that odd-numbered packets are high priority, and even-numbered packets are low priority. Indicate the time at which packets 2 through 12 each leave the queue. For each packet, what is the delay between its arrival and the beginning of the slot in which it is transmitted? What is the average of this delay over all 12 packets?

    c. Now assume round robin service. Assume that packets 1, 2, 3, 6, 11, and 12 are from class 1, and packets 4, 5, 7, 8, 9, and 10 are from class 2. Indicate the time at which packets 2 through 12 each leave the queue. For each packet, what is the delay between its arrival and its departure? What is the average delay over all 12 packets?

    d. Now assume weighted fair queueing (WFQ) service. Assume that odd-numbered packets are from class 1, and even-numbered packets are from class 2. Class 1 has a WFQ weight of 2, while class 2 has a WFQ weight of 1. Note that it may not be possible to achieve an idealized WFQ schedule as described in the text, so indicate why you have chosen the particular packet to go into service at each time slot. For each packet what is the delay between its arrival and its departure? What is the average delay over all 12 packets?

    e. What do you notice about the average delay in all four cases (FIFO, RR, priority, and WFQ)?

P19. Consider again the figure for P18.

    a. Assume a priority service, with packets 1, 4, 5, 6, and 11 being high-priority packets. The remaining packets are low priority. Indicate the slots in which packets 2 through 12 each leave the queue.

    b. Now suppose that round robin service is used, with packets 1, 4, 5, 6, and 11 belonging to one class of traffic, and the remaining packets belonging to the second class of traffic. Indicate the slots in which packets 2 through 12 each leave the queue.

    c. Now suppose that WFQ service is used, with packets 1, 4, 5, 6, and 11 belonging to one class of traffic, and the remaining packets belonging to the second class of traffic. Class 1 has a WFQ weight of 1, while class 2 has a WFQ weight of 2 (note that these weights are different than in the previous question). Indicate the slots in which packets 2 through 12 each leave the queue. See also the caveat in the question above regarding WFQ service.

P20. Consider the figure below, which shows a leaky bucket policer being fed by a stream of packets. The token buffer can hold at most two tokens, and is initially full at $t = 0$. New tokens arrive at a rate of one token per slot. The output link speed is such that if two packets obtain tokens at the beginning of a time slot, they can both go to the output link in the same slot. The timing details of the system are as follows:

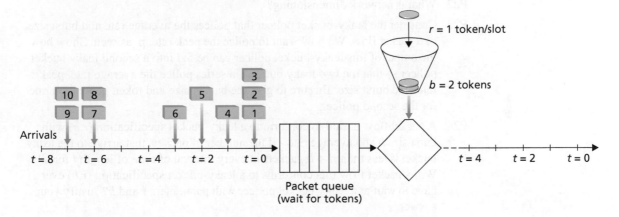

1. Packets (if any) arrive at the beginning of the slot. Thus in the figure, packets 1, 2, and 3 arrive in slot 0. If there are already packets in the queue, then the arriving packets join the end of the queue. Packets proceed towards the front of the queue in a FIFO manner.

2. After the arrivals have been added to the queue, if there are any queued packets, one or two of those packets (depending on the number of available tokens) will each remove a token from the token buffer and go to the output link during that slot. Thus, packets 1 and 2 each remove a token from the buffer (since there are initially two tokens) and go to the output link during slot 0.

3. A new token is added to the token buffer if it is not full, since the token generation rate is $r = 1$ token/slot.

4. Time then advances to the next time slot, and these steps repeat.

Answer the following questions:

   a. For each time slot, identify the packets that are in the queue and the number of tokens in the bucket, immediately after the arrivals have been processed (step 1 above) but before any of the packets have passed through the queue and removed a token. Thus, for the $t = 0$ time slot in the example above, packets 1, 2 and 3 are in the queue, and there are two tokens in the buffer.

b. For each time slot indicate which packets appear on the output after the token(s) have been removed from the queue. Thus, for the $t = 0$ time slot in the example above, packets 1 and 2 appear on the output link from the leaky buffer during slot 0.

P21. Repeat P20 but assume that $r = 2$. Assume again that the bucket is initially full.

P22. What is network dimensioning?

P23. Consider the leaky-bucket policer that polices the average rate and burst size of a packet flow. We now want to police the peak rate, p, as well. Show how the output of this leaky-bucket policer can be fed into a second leaky bucket policer so that the two leaky buckets in series police the average rate, peak rate, and burst size. Be sure to give the bucket size and token generation rate for the second policer.

P24. A packet flow is said to conform to a leaky-bucket specification (r,b) with burst size b and average rate r if the number of packets that arrive to the leaky bucket is less than $rt + b$ packets in every interval of time of length t for all t. Will a packet flow that conforms to a leaky-bucket specification (r,b) ever have to wait at a leaky bucket policer with parameters r and b? Justify your answer.

P25. Show that as long as $r_1 < R w_1/(\sum w_j)$, then d_{max} is indeed the maximum delay that any packet in flow 1 will ever experience in the WFQ queue.

 ## Programming Assignment

In this lab, you will implement a streaming video server and client. The client will use the real-time streaming protocol (RTSP) to control the actions of the server. The server will use the real-time protocol (RTP) to packetize the video for transport over UDP. You will be given Python code that partially implements RTSP and RTP at the client and server. Your job will be to complete both the client and server code. When you are finished, you will have created a client-server application that does the following:

• The client sends SETUP, PLAY, PAUSE, and TEARDOWN RTSP commands, and the server responds to the commands.

• When the server is in the playing state, it periodically grabs a stored JPEG frame, packetizes the frame with RTP, and sends the RTP packet into a UDP socket.

• The client receives the RTP packets, removes the JPEG frames, decompresses the frames, and renders the frames on the client's monitor.

The code you will be given implements the RTSP protocol in the server and the RTP depacketization in the client. The code also takes care of displaying the transmitted video. You will need to implement RTSP in the client and RTP server. This programming assignment will significantly enhance the student's understanding of RTP, RTSP, and streaming video. It is highly recommended. The assignment also suggests a number of optional exercises, including implementing the RTSP DESCRIBE command at both client and server. You can find full details of the assignment, as well as an overview of the RTSP protocol, at the Web site http://www.awl.com/kurose-ross.

Henning Schulzrinne

Henning Schulzrinne is a professor, chair of the Department of Computer Science, and head of the Internet Real-Time Laboratory at Columbia University. He is the co-author of RTP, RTSP, SIP, and GIST—key protocols for audio and video communications over the Internet. Henning received his BS in electrical and industrial engineering at TU Darmstadt in Germany, his MS in electrical and computer engineering at the University of Cincinnati, and his PhD in electrical engineering at the University of Massachusetts, Amherst.

What made you decide to specialize in multimedia networking?

This happened almost by accident. As a PhD student, I got involved with DARTnet, an experimental network spanning the United States with T1 lines. DARTnet was used as a proving ground for multicast and Internet real-time tools. That led me to write my first audio tool, NeVoT. Through some of the DARTnet participants, I became involved in the IETF, in the then-nascent Audio Video Transport working group. This group later ended up standardizing RTP.

What was your first job in the computer industry? What did it entail?

My first job in the computer industry was soldering together an Altair computer kit when I was a high school student in Livermore, California. Back in Germany, I started a little consulting company that devised an address management program for a travel agency—storing data on cassette tapes for our TRS-80 and using an IBM Selectric typewriter with a homebrew hardware interface as a printer.

My first real job was with AT&T Bell Laboratories, developing a network emulator for constructing experimental networks in a lab environment.

What are the goals of the Internet Real-Time Lab?

Our goal is to provide components and building blocks for the Internet as the single future communications infrastructure. This includes developing new protocols, such as GIST (for network-layer signaling) and LoST (for finding resources by location), or enhancing protocols that we have worked on earlier, such as SIP, through work on rich presence, peer-to-peer systems, next-generation emergency calling, and service creation tools. Recently, we have also looked extensively at wireless systems for VoIP, as 802.11b and 802.11n networks and maybe WiMax networks are likely to become important last-mile technologies for telephony. We are also trying to greatly improve the ability of users to diagnose faults in the complicated tangle of providers and equipment, using a peer-to-peer fault diagnosis system called DYSWIS (Do You See What I See).

We try to do practically relevant work, by building prototypes and open source systems, by measuring performance of real systems, and by contributing to IETF standards.

What is your vision for the future of multimedia networking?

We are now in a transition phase; just a few years shy of when IP will be the universal platform for multimedia services, from IPTV to VoIP. We expect radio, telephone, and TV to be available even during snowstorms and earthquakes, so when the Internet takes over the role of these dedicated networks, users will expect the same level of reliability.

We will have to learn to design network technologies for an ecosystem of competing carriers, service and content providers, serving lots of technically untrained users and defending them against a small, but destructive, set of malicious and criminal users. Changing protocols is becoming increasingly hard. They are also becoming more complex, as they need to take into account competing business interests, security, privacy, and the lack of transparency of networks caused by firewalls and network address translators.

Since multimedia networking is becoming the foundation for almost all of consumer entertainment, there will be an emphasis on managing very large networks, at low cost. Users will expect ease of use, such as finding the same content on all of their devices.

Why does SIP have a promising future?

As the current wireless network upgrade to 3G networks proceeds, there is the hope of a single multimedia signaling mechanism spanning all types of networks, from cable modems, to corporate telephone networks and public wireless networks. Together with software radios, this will make it possible in the future that a single device can be used on a home network, as a cordless BlueTooth phone, in a corporate network via 802.11 and in the wide area via 3G networks. Even before we have such a single universal wireless device, the personal mobility mechanisms make it possible to hide the differences between networks. One identifier becomes the universal means of reaching a person, rather than remembering or passing around half a dozen technology- or location-specific telephone numbers.

SIP also breaks apart the provision of voice (bit) transport from voice services. It now becomes technically possible to break apart the local telephone monopoly, where one company provides neutral bit transport, while others provide IP "dial tone" and the classical telephone services, such as gateways, call forwarding, and caller ID.

Beyond multimedia signaling, SIP offers a new service that has been missing in the Internet: event notification. We have approximated such services with HTTP kludges and e-mail, but this was never very satisfactory. Since events are a common abstraction for distributed systems, this may simplify the construction of new services.

Do you have any advice for students entering the networking field?

Networking bridges disciplines. It draws from electrical engineering, all aspects of computer science, operations research, statistics, economics, and other disciplines. Thus, networking researchers have to be familiar with subjects well beyond protocols and routing algorithms.

Given that networks are becoming such an important part of everyday life, students wanting to make a difference in the field should think of the new resource constraints in networks: human time and effort, rather than just bandwidth or storage.

Work in networking research can be immensely satisfying since it is about allowing people to communicate and exchange ideas, one of the essentials of being human. The Internet has become the third major global infrastructure, next to the transportation system and energy distribution. Almost no part of the economy can work without high-performance networks, so there should be plenty of opportunities for the foreseeable future.

8

Security in Computer Networks

Way back in Section 1.6 we described some of the more prevalent and damaging classes of Internet attacks, including malware attacks, denial of service, sniffing, source masquerading, and message modification and deletion. Although we have since learned a tremendous amount about computer networks, we still haven't examined how to secure networks from those attacks. Equipped with our newly acquired expertise in computer networking and Internet protocols, we'll now study in-depth secure communication and, in particular, how computer networks can be defended from those nasty bad guys.

Let us introduce Alice and Bob, two people who want to communicate and wish to do so "securely." This being a networking text, we should remark that Alice and Bob could be two routers that want to exchange routing tables securely, a client and server that want to establish a secure transport connection, or two e-mail applications that want to exchange secure e-mail—all case studies that we will consider later in this chapter. Alice and Bob are well-known fixtures in the security community, perhaps because their names are more fun than a generic entity named "A" that wants to communicate securely with a generic entity named "B." Love affairs, wartime communication, and business transactions are the commonly cited human needs for secure communications; preferring the first to the latter two, we're happy to use Alice and Bob as our sender and receiver, and imagine them in this first scenario.

We said that Alice and Bob want to communicate and wish to do so "securely," but what precisely does this mean? As we will see, security (like love) is a many-splendored thing; that is, there are many facets to security. Certainly, Alice and Bob would like for the contents of their communication to remain secret from an eavesdropper. They probably would also like to make sure that when they are communicating, they are indeed communicating with each other, and that if their communication is tampered with by an eavesdropper, that this tampering is detected. In the first part of this chapter, we'll cover the fundamental cryptography techniques that allow for encrypting communication, authenticating the party with whom one is communicating, and ensuring message integrity.

In the second part of this chapter, we'll examine how the fundamental cryptography principles can be used to create secure networking protocols. Once again taking a top-down approach, we'll examine secure protocols in each of the (top four) layers, beginning with the application layer. We'll examine how to secure e-mail, how to secure a TCP connection, how to provide blanket security at the network layer, and how to secure a wireless LAN. In the third part of this chapter we'll consider operational security, which is about protecting organizational networks from attacks. In particular, we'll take a careful look at how firewalls and intrusion detection systems can enhance the security of an organizational network.

8.1 What Is Network Security?

Let's begin our study of network security by returning to our lovers, Alice and Bob, who want to communicate "securely." What precisely does this mean? Certainly, Alice wants only Bob to be able to understand a message that she has sent, even though they *are* communicating over an insecure medium where an intruder (Trudy, the intruder) may intercept whatever is transmitted from Alice to Bob. Bob also wants to be sure that the message he receives from Alice was indeed sent by Alice, and Alice wants to make sure that the person with whom she is communicating is indeed Bob. Alice and Bob also want to make sure that the contents of their messages have not been altered in transit. They also want to be assured that they can communicate in the first place (i.e., that no one denies them access to the resources needed to communicate). Given these considerations, we can identify the following desirable properties of **secure communication**.

- *Confidentiality*. Only the sender and intended receiver should be able to understand the contents of the transmitted message. Because eavesdroppers may intercept the message, this necessarily requires that the message be somehow **encrypted** so that an intercepted message cannot be understood by an interceptor. This aspect of confidentiality is probably the most commonly perceived meaning of the term *secure communication*. We'll study cryptographic techniques for encrypting and decrypting data in Section 8.2.

- *Message integrity.* Alice and Bob want to ensure that the content of their communication is not altered, either maliciously or by accident, in transit. Extensions to the checksumming techniques that we encountered in reliable transport and data link protocols can be used to provide such message integrity. We will study message integrity in Section 8.3.

- *End-point authentication.* Both the sender and receiver should be able to confirm the identity of the other party involved in the communication—to confirm that the other party is indeed who or what they claim to be. Face-to-face human communication solves this problem easily by visual recognition. When communicating entities exchange messages over a medium where they cannot see the other party, authentication is not so simple. When a user wants to access an inbox, how does the mail server verify that the user is the person he or she claims to be? We study end-point authentication in Section 8.4.

- *Operational security.* Almost all organizations (companies, universities, and so on) today have networks that are attached to the public Internet. These networks therefore can potentially be compromised. Attackers can attempt to deposit worms into the hosts in the network, obtain corporate secrets, map the internal network configurations, and launch DoS attacks. We'll see in Section 8.9 that operational devices such as firewalls and intrusion detection systems are used to counter attacks against an organization's network. A firewall sits between the organization's network and the public network, controlling packet access to and from the network. An intrusion detection system performs "deep packet inspection," alerting the network administrators about suspicious activity.

Having established what we mean by network security, let's next consider exactly what information an intruder may have access to, and what actions can be taken by the intruder. Figure 8.1 illustrates the scenario. Alice, the sender, wants to send data to Bob, the receiver. In order to exchange data securely, while meeting the requirements of confidentiality, end-point authentication, and message integrity, Alice and Bob will exchange control messages and data messages (in much the same way that TCP senders and receivers exchange control segments and data segments). All or some of these messages will typically be encrypted. As discussed in Section 1.6, an intruder can potentially perform

- *eavesdropping*—sniffing and recording control and data messages on the channel.
- *modification, insertion,* or *deletion* of messages or message content.

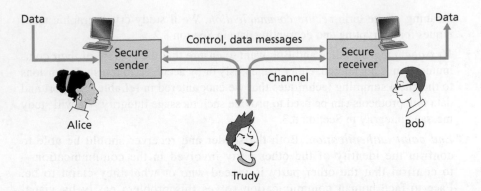

Figure 8.1 ♦ Sender, receiver, and intruder (Alice, Bob, and Trudy)

As we'll see, unless appropriate countermeasures are taken, these capabilities allow an intruder to mount a wide variety of security attacks: snooping on communication (possibly stealing passwords and data), impersonating another entitity, hijacking an ongoing session, denying service to legitimate network users by overloading system resources, and so on. A summary of reported attacks is maintained at the CERT Coordination Center [CERT 2012].

Having established that there are indeed real threats loose in the Internet, what are the Internet equivalents of Alice and Bob, our friends who need to communicate securely? Certainly, Bob and Alice might be human users at two end systems, for example, a real Alice and a real Bob who really do want to exchange secure e-mail. They might also be participants in an electronic commerce transaction. For example, a real Bob might want to transfer his credit card number securely to a Web server to purchase an item online. Similarly, a real Alice might want to interact with her bank online. The parties needing secure communication might themselves also be part of the network infrastructure. Recall that the domain name system (DNS, see Section 2.5) or routing daemons that exchange routing information (see Section 4.6) require secure communication between two parties. The same is true for network management applications, a topic we examine in Chapter 9. An intruder that could actively interfere with DNS lookups (as discussed in Section 2.5), routing computations [RFC 4272], or network management functions [RFC 3414] could wreak havoc in the Internet.

Having now established the framework, a few of the most important definitions, and the need for network security, let us next delve into cryptography. While the use of cryptography in providing confidentiality is self-evident, we'll see shortly that it is also central to providing end-point authentication and message integrity—making cryptography a cornerstone of network security.

8.2 Principles of Cryptography

Although cryptography has a long history dating back at least as far as Julius Caesar, modern cryptographic techniques, including many of those used in the Internet, are based on advances made in the past 30 years. Kahn's book, *The Codebreakers* [Kahn 1967], and Singh's book, *The Code Book: The Science of Secrecy from Ancient Egypt to Quantum Cryptography* [Singh 1999], provide a fascinating look at the long history of cryptography. A complete discussion of cryptography itself requires a complete book [Kaufman 1995; Schneier 1995] and so we only touch on the essential aspects of cryptography, particularly as they are practiced on the Internet. We also note that while our focus in this section will be on the use of cryptography for confidentiality, we'll see shortly that cryptographic techniques are inextricably woven into authentication, message integrity, nonrepudiation, and more.

Cryptographic techniques allow a sender to disguise data so that an intruder can gain no information from the intercepted data. The receiver, of course, must be able to recover the original data from the disguised data. Figure 8.2 illustrates some of the important terminology.

Suppose now that Alice wants to send a message to Bob. Alice's message in its original form (for example, "`Bob, I love you. Alice`") is known as **plaintext**, or **cleartext**. Alice encrypts her plaintext message using an **encryption algorithm** so that the encrypted message, known as **ciphertext**, looks unintelligible to any intruder. Interestingly, in many modern cryptographic systems, including those used in the Internet, the encryption technique itself is *known*—published, standardized, and available to everyone (for example, [RFC 1321; RFC 3447; RFC

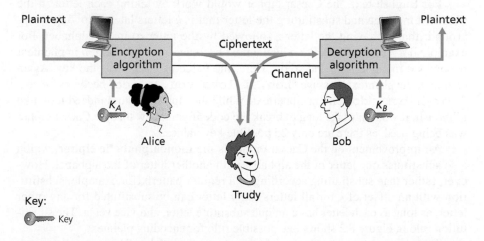

Figure 8.2 ♦ Cryptographic components

2420; NIST 2001]), even a potential intruder! Clearly, if everyone knows the method for encoding data, then there must be some secret information that prevents an intruder from decrypting the transmitted data. This is where keys come in.

In Figure 8.2, Alice provides a **key**, K_A, a string of numbers or characters, as input to the encryption algorithm. The encryption algorithm takes the key and the plaintext message, m, as input and produces ciphertext as output. The notation $K_A(m)$ refers to the ciphertext form (encrypted using the key K_A) of the plaintext message, m. The actual encryption algorithm that uses key K_A will be evident from the context. Similarly, Bob will provide a key, K_B, to the **decryption algorithm** that takes the ciphertext and Bob's key as input and produces the original plaintext as output. That is, if Bob receives an encrypted message $K_A(m)$, he decrypts it by computing $K_B(K_A(m)) = m$. In **symmetric key systems**, Alice's and Bob's keys are identical and are secret. In **public key systems**, a pair of keys is used. One of the keys is known to both Bob and Alice (indeed, it is known to the whole world). The other key is known only by either Bob or Alice (but not both). In the following two subsections, we consider symmetric key and public key systems in more detail.

8.2.1 Symmetric Key Cryptography

All cryptographic algorithms involve substituting one thing for another, for example, taking a piece of plaintext and then computing and substituting the appropriate ciphertext to create the encrypted message. Before studying a modern key-based cryptographic system, let us first get our feet wet by studying a very old, very simple symmetric key algorithm attributed to Julius Caesar, known as the **Caesar cipher** (a cipher is a method for encrypting data).

For English text, the Caesar cipher would work by taking each letter in the plaintext message and substituting the letter that is k letters later (allowing wraparound; that is, having the letter z followed by the letter a) in the alphabet. For example if $k = 3$, then the letter a in plaintext becomes d in ciphertext; b in plaintext becomes e in ciphertext, and so on. Here, the value of k serves as the key. As an example, the plaintext message "bob, i love you. alice" becomes "ere, l oryh brx. dolfh" in ciphertext. While the ciphertext does indeed look like gibberish, it wouldn't take long to break the code if you knew that the Caesar cipher was being used, as there are only 25 possible key values.

An improvement on the Caesar cipher is the **monoalphabetic cipher**, which also substitutes one letter of the alphabet with another letter of the alphabet. However, rather than substituting according to a regular pattern (for example, substitution with an offset of k for all letters), any letter can be substituted for any other letter, as long as each letter has a unique substitute letter, and vice versa. The substitution rule in Figure 8.3 shows one possible rule for encoding plaintext.

The plaintext message "bob, i love you. alice" becomes "nkn, s gktc wky. mgsbc." Thus, as in the case of the Caesar cipher, this looks like

Plaintext letter:	a b c d e f g h i j k l m n o p q r s t u v w x y z
Ciphertext letter:	m n b v c x z a s d f g h j k l p o i u y t r e w q

Figure 8.3 ♦ A monoalphabetic cipher

gibberish. A monoalphabetic cipher would also appear to be better than the Caesar cipher in that there are 26! (on the order of 10^{26}) possible pairings of letters rather than 25 possible pairings. A brute-force approach of trying all 10^{26} possible pairings would require far too much work to be a feasible way of breaking the encryption algorithm and decoding the message. However, by statistical analysis of the plaintext language, for example, knowing that the letters *e* and *t* are the most frequently occurring letters in typical English text (accounting for 13 percent and 9 percent of letter occurrences), and knowing that particular two- and three-letter occurrences of letters appear quite often together (for example, "in," "it," "the," "ion," "ing," and so forth) make it relatively easy to break this code. If the intruder has some knowledge about the possible contents of the message, then it is even easier to break the code. For example, if Trudy the intruder is Bob's wife and suspects Bob of having an affair with Alice, then she might suspect that the names "bob" and "alice" appear in the text. If Trudy knew for certain that those two names appeared in the ciphertext and had a copy of the example ciphertext message above, then she could immediately determine seven of the 26 letter pairings, requiring 10^9 fewer possibilities to be checked by a brute-force method. Indeed, if Trudy suspected Bob of having an affair, she might well expect to find some other choice words in the message as well.

When considering how easy it might be for Trudy to break Bob and Alice's encryption scheme, one can distinguish three different scenarios, depending on what information the intruder has.

- *Ciphertext-only attack.* In some cases, the intruder may have access only to the intercepted ciphertext, with no certain information about the contents of the plaintext message. We have seen how statistical analysis can help in a **ciphertext-only attack** on an encryption scheme.

- *Known-plaintext attack.* We saw above that if Trudy somehow knew for sure that "bob" and "alice" appeared in the ciphertext message, then she could have determined the (plaintext, ciphertext) pairings for the letters *a, l, i, c, e, b,* and *o.* Trudy might also have been fortunate enough to have recorded all of the ciphertext transmissions and then found Bob's own decrypted version of one of the transmissions scribbled on a piece of paper. When an intruder knows some of the (plaintext, ciphertext) pairings, we refer to this as a **known-plaintext attack** on the encryption scheme.

• *Chosen-plaintext attack.* In a **chosen-plaintext attack**, the intruder is able to choose the plaintext message and obtain its corresponding ciphertext form. For the simple encryption algorithms we've seen so far, if Trudy could get Alice to send the message, "The quick brown fox jumps over the lazy dog," she could completely break the encryption scheme. We'll see shortly that for more sophisticated encryption techniques, a chosen-plaintext attack does not necessarily mean that the encryption technique can be broken.

Five hundred years ago, techniques improving on monoalphabetic encryption, known as **polyalphabetic encryption**, were invented. The idea behind polyalphabetic encryption is to use multiple monoalphabetic ciphers, with a specific monoalphabetic cipher to encode a letter in a specific position in the plaintext message. Thus, the same letter, appearing in different positions in the plaintext message, might be encoded differently. An example of a polyalphabetic encryption scheme is shown in Figure 8.4. It has two Caesar ciphers (with $k = 5$ and $k = 19$), shown as rows. We might choose to use these two Caesar ciphers, C_1 and C_2, in the repeating pattern C_1, C_2, C_2, C_1, C_2. That is, the first letter of plaintext is to be encoded using C_1, the second and third using C_2, the fourth using C_1, and the fifth using C_2. The pattern then repeats, with the sixth letter being encoded using C_1, the seventh with C_2, and so on. The plaintext message "bob, i love you." is thus encrypted "ghu, n etox dhz." Note that the first *b* in the plaintext message is encrypted using C_1, while the second *b* is encrypted using C_2. In this example, the encryption and decryption "key" is the knowledge of the two Caesar keys ($k = 5$, $k = 19$) and the pattern C_1, C_2, C_2, C_1, C_2.

Block Ciphers

Let us now move forward to modern times and examine how symmetric key encryption is done today. There are two broad classes of symmetric encryption techniques: **stream ciphers** and **block ciphers**. We'll briefly examine stream ciphers in Section 8.7 when we investigate security for wireless LANs. In this section, we focus on block ciphers, which are used in many secure Internet protocols, including PGP (for secure e-mail), SSL (for securing TCP connections), and IPsec (for securing the network-layer transport).

Plaintext letter:	a b c d e f g h i j k l m n o p q r s t u v w x y z
$C_1(k = 5)$:	f g h i j k l m n o p q r s t u v w x y z a b c d e
$C_2(k = 19)$:	t u v w x y z a b c d e f g h i j k l m n o p q r s

Figure 8.4 ♦ A polyalphabetic cipher using two Caesar ciphers

input	output	input	output
000	110	100	011
001	111	101	010
010	101	110	000
011	100	111	001

Table 8.1 ♦ A specific 3-bit block cipher

In a block cipher, the message to be encrypted is processed in blocks of k bits. For example, if $k = 64$, then the message is broken into 64-bit blocks, and each block is encrypted independently. To encode a block, the cipher uses a one-to-one mapping to map the k-bit block of cleartext to a k-bit block of ciphertext. Let's look at an example. Suppose that $k = 3$, so that the block cipher maps 3-bit inputs (cleartext) to 3-bit outputs (ciphertext). One possible mapping is given in Table 8.1. Notice that this is a one-to-one mapping; that is, there is a different output for each input. This block cipher breaks the message up into 3-bit blocks and encrypts each block according to the above mapping. You should verify that the message 010110001111 gets encrypted into 101000111001.

Continuing with this 3-bit block example, note that the mapping in Table 8.1 is just one mapping of many possible mappings. How many possible mappings are there? To answer this question, observe that a mapping is nothing more than a permutation of all the possible inputs. There are 2^3 (= 8) possible inputs (listed under the input columns). These eight inputs can be permuted in 8! = 40,320 different ways. Since each of these permutations specifies a mapping, there are 40,320 possible mappings. We can view each of these mappings as a key—if Alice and Bob both know the mapping (the key), they can encrypt and decrypt the messages sent between them.

The brute-force attack for this cipher is to try to decrypt ciphtertext by using all mappings. With only 40,320 mappings (when $k = 3$), this can quickly be accomplished on a desktop PC. To thwart brute-force attacks, block ciphers typically use much larger blocks, consisting of $k = 64$ bits or even larger. Note that the number of possible mappings for a general k-block cipher is $2^k!$, which is astronomical for even moderate values of k (such as $k = 64$).

Although full-table block ciphers, as just described, with moderate values of k can produce robust symmetric key encryption schemes, they are unfortunately difficult to implement. For $k = 64$ and for a given mapping, Alice and Bob would need to maintain a table with 2^{64} input values, which is an infeasible task. Moreover, if Alice and Bob were to change keys, they would have to each regenerate the table. Thus, a full-table block cipher, providing predetermined mappings between all inputs and outputs (as in the example above), is simply out of the question.

Instead, block ciphers typically use functions that simulate randomly permuted tables. An example (adapted from [Kaufman 1995]) of such a function for $k = 64$ bits is shown in Figure 8.5. The function first breaks a 64-bit block into 8 chunks, with each chunk consisting of 8 bits. Each 8-bit chunk is processed by an 8-bit to 8-bit table, which is of manageable size. For example, the first chunk is processed by the table denoted by T_1. Next, the 8 output chunks are reassembled into a 64-bit block. The positions of the 64 bits in the block are then scrambled (permuted) to produce a 64-bit output. This output is fed back to the 64-bit input, where another cycle begins. After n such cycles, the function provides a 64-bit block of ciphertext. The purpose of the rounds is to make each input bit affect most (if not all) of the final output bits. (If only one round were used, a given input bit would affect only 8 of the 64 output bits.) The key for this block cipher algorithm would be the eight permutation tables (assuming the scramble function is publicly known).

Today there are a number of popular block ciphers, including DES (standing for Data Encryption Standard), 3DES, and AES (standing for Advanced Encryption Standard). Each of these standards uses functions, rather than predetermined tables, along the lines of Figure 8.5 (albeit more complicated and specific to each cipher). Each of these algorithms also uses a string of bits for a key. For example, DES uses 64-bit blocks with a 56-bit key. AES uses 128-bit blocks and can operate with keys that are 128, 192, and 256 bits long. An algorithm's key determines the specific

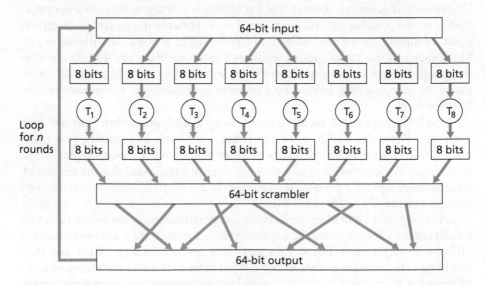

Figure 8.5 ♦ An example of a block cipher

"mini-table" mappings and permutations within the algorithm's internals. The brute-force attack for each of these ciphers is to cycle through all the keys, applying the decryption algorithm with each key. Observe that with a key length of n, there are 2^n possible keys. NIST [NIST 2001] estimates that a machine that could crack 56-bit DES in one second (that is, try all 2^{56} keys in one second) would take approximately 149 trillion years to crack a 128-bit AES key.

Cipher-Block Chaining

In computer networking applications, we typically need to encrypt long messages (or long streams of data). If we apply a block cipher as described by simply chopping up the message into k-bit blocks and independently encrypting each block, a subtle but important problem occurs. To see this, observe that two or more of the cleartext blocks can be identical. For example, the cleartext in two or more blocks could be "HTTP/1.1". For these identical blocks, a block cipher would, of course, produce the same ciphertext. An attacker could potentially guess the cleartext when it sees identical ciphertext blocks and may even be able to decrypt the entire message by identifying identical ciphertext blocks and using knowledge about the underlying protocol structure [Kaufman 1995].

To address this problem, we can mix some randomness into the ciphertext so that identical plaintext blocks produce different ciphertext blocks. To explain this idea, let $m(i)$ denote the ith plaintext block, $c(i)$ denote the ith ciphertext block, and $a \oplus b$ denote the exclusive-or (XOR) of two bit strings, a and b. (Recall that the $0 \oplus 0 = 1 \oplus 1 = 0$ and $0 \oplus 1 = 1 \oplus 0 = 1$, and the XOR of two bit strings is done on a bit-by-bit basis. So, for example, $10101010 \oplus 11110000 = 01011010$.) Also, denote the block-cipher encryption algorithm with key S as K_S. The basic idea is as follows. The sender creates a random k-bit number $r(i)$ for the ith block and calculates $c(i) = K_S(m(i) \oplus r(i))$. Note that a new k-bit random number is chosen for each block. The sender then sends $c(1), r(1), c(2), r(2), c(3), r(3)$, and so on. Since the receiver receives $c(i)$ and $r(i)$, it can recover each block of the plaintext by computing $m(i) = K_S(c(i)) \oplus r(i)$. It is important to note that, although $r(i)$ is sent in the clear and thus can be sniffed by Trudy, she cannot obtain the plaintext $m(i)$, since she does not know the key K_S. Also note that if two plaintext blocks $m(i)$ and $m(j)$ are the same, the corresponding ciphertext blocks $c(i)$ and $c(j)$ will be different (as long as the random numbers $r(i)$ and $r(j)$ are different, which occurs with very high probability).

As an example, consider the 3-bit block cipher in Table 8.1. Suppose the plaintext is 010010010. If Alice encrypts this directly, without including the randomness, the resulting ciphertext becomes 101101101. If Trudy sniffs this ciphertext, because each of the three cipher blocks is the same, she can correctly surmise that each of the three plaintext blocks are the same. Now suppose instead Alice generates the random blocks $r(1) = 001$, $r(2) = 111$, and $r(3) = 100$ and uses the above technique to generate the ciphertext $c(1) = 100$, $c(2) = 010$, and $c(3) = 000$. Note that the three ciphertext blocks are different even though the plaintext blocks are the same. Alice then sends $c(1)$, $r(1)$, $c(2)$, and $r(2)$. You should verify that Bob can obtain the original plaintext using the shared key K_S.

The astute reader will note that introducing randomness solves one problem but creates another: namely, Alice must transmit twice as many bits as before. Indeed, for each cipher bit, she must now also send a random bit, doubling the required bandwidth. In order to have our cake and eat it too, block ciphers typically use a technique called **Cipher Block Chaining (CBC)**. The basic idea is to send only *one random value along with the very first message, and then have the sender and receiver use the computed coded blocks in place of the subsequent random number.* Specifically, CBC operates as follows:

1. Before encrypting the message (or the stream of data), the sender generates a random k-bit string, called the **Initialization Vector (IV)**. Denote this initialization vector by $c(0)$. The sender sends the IV to the receiver *in cleartext*.
2. For the first block, the sender calculates $m(1) \oplus c(0)$, that is, calculates the exclusive-or of the first block of cleartext with the IV. It then runs the result through the block-cipher algorithm to get the corresponding ciphertext block; that is, $c(1) = K_S(m(1) \oplus c(0))$. The sender sends the encrypted block $c(1)$ to the receiver.
3. For the ith block, the sender generates the ith ciphertext block from $c(i) = K_S(m(i) \oplus c(i - 1))$.

Let's now examine some of the consequences of this approach. First, the receiver will still be able to recover the original message. Indeed, when the receiver receives $c(i)$, it decrypts it with K_S to obtain $s(i) = m(i) \oplus c(i - 1)$; since the receiver also knows $c(i - 1)$, it then obtains the cleartext block from $m(i) = s(i) \oplus c(i - 1)$. Second, even if two cleartext blocks are identical, the corresponding ciphertexts (almost always) will be different. Third, although the sender sends the IV in the clear, an intruder will still not be able to decrypt the ciphertext blocks, since the intruder does not know the secret key, S. Finally, the sender only sends one overhead block (the IV), thereby negligibly increasing the bandwidth usage for long messages (consisting of hundreds of blocks).

As an example, let's now determine the ciphertext for the 3-bit block cipher in Table 8.1 with plaintext 010010010 and IV = $c(0)$ = 001. The sender first uses the IV to calculate $c(1) = K_S(m(1) \oplus c(0)) = 100$. The sender then calculates $c(2) = K_S(m(2) \oplus c(1)) = K_S(010 \oplus 100) = 000$, and $c(3) = K_S(m(3) \oplus c(2)) = K_S(010 \oplus 000) = 101$. The reader should verify that the receiver, knowing the IV and K_S can recover the original plaintext.

CBC has an important consequence when designing secure network protocols: we'll need to provide a mechanism within the protocol to distribute the IV from sender to receiver. We'll see how this is done for several protocols later in this chapter.

8.2.2 Public Key Encryption

For more than 2,000 years (since the time of the Caesar cipher and up to the 1970s), encrypted communication required that the two communicating parties share a common secret—the symmetric key used for encryption and decryption. One difficulty with this approach is that the two parties must somehow agree on the shared key; but to do so requires (presumably *secure*) communication! Perhaps the parties could first meet and agree on the key in person (for example, two of Caesar's centurions might meet at the Roman baths) and thereafter communicate with encryption. In a networked world, however, communicating parties may never meet and may never converse except over the network. Is it possible for two parties to communicate with encryption without having a shared secret key that is known in advance? In 1976, Diffie and Hellman [Diffie 1976] demonstrated an algorithm (known now as Diffie-Hellman Key Exchange) to do just that—a radically different and marvelously elegant approach toward secure communication that has led to the development of today's public key cryptography systems. We'll see shortly that public key cryptography systems also have several wonderful properties that make them useful not only for encryption, but for authentication and digital signatures as well. Interestingly, it has recently come to light that ideas similar to those in [Diffie 1976] and [RSA 1978] had been independently developed in the early 1970s in a series of secret reports by researchers at the Communications-Electronics Security Group in the United Kingdom [Ellis 1987]. As is often the case, great ideas can spring up independently in many places; fortunately, public key advances took place not only in private, but also in the public view, as well.

The use of public key cryptography is conceptually quite simple. Suppose Alice wants to communicate with Bob. As shown in Figure 8.6, rather than Bob and Alice

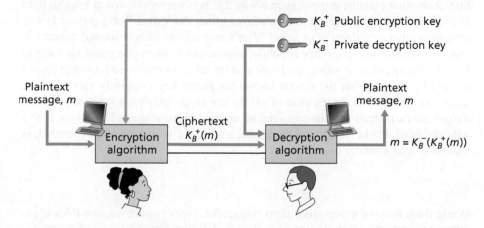

Figure 8.6 ♦ Public key cryptography

sharing a single secret key (as in the case of symmetric key systems), Bob (the recipient of Alice's messages) instead has two keys—a **public key** that is available to *everyone* in the world (including Trudy the intruder) and a **private key** that is known only to Bob. We will use the notation K_B^+ and K_B^- to refer to Bob's public and private keys, respectively. In order to communicate with Bob, Alice first fetches Bob's public key. Alice then encrypts her message, *m,* to Bob using Bob's public key and a known (for example, standardized) encryption algorithm; that is, Alice computes $K_B^+(m)$. Bob receives Alice's encrypted message and uses his private key and a known (for example, standardized) decryption algorithm to decrypt Alice's encrypted message. That is, Bob computes $K_B^-(K_B^+(m))$. We will see below that there are encryption/decryption algorithms and techniques for choosing public and private keys such that $K_B^-(K_B^+(m)) = m$; that is, applying Bob's public key, K_B^+, to a message, *m* (to get $K_B^+(m)$), and then applying Bob's private key, K_B^-, to the encrypted version of *m* (that is, computing $K_B^-(K_B^+(m))$) gives back *m*. This is a remarkable result! In this manner, Alice can use Bob's publicly available key to send a secret message to Bob without either of them having to distribute any secret keys! We will see shortly that we can interchange the public key and private key encryption and get the same remarkable result—that is, $K_B^- (_B{}^+(m)) = K_B^+ (K_B^-(m)) = m$.

The use of public key cryptography is thus conceptually simple. But two immediate worries may spring to mind. A first concern is that although an intruder intercepting Alice's encrypted message will see only gibberish, the intruder knows both the key (Bob's public key, which is available for all the world to see) and the algorithm that Alice used for encryption. Trudy can thus mount a chosen-plaintext attack, using the known standardized encryption algorithm and Bob's publicly available encryption key to encode any message she chooses! Trudy might well try, for example, to encode messages, or parts of messages, that she suspects that Alice might send. Clearly, if public key cryptography is to work, key selection and encryption/decryption must be done in such a way that it is impossible (or at least so hard as to be nearly impossible) for an intruder to either determine Bob's private key or somehow otherwise decrypt or guess Alice's message to Bob. A second concern is that since Bob's encryption key is public, anyone can send an encrypted message to Bob, including Alice or someone *claiming* to be Alice. In the case of a single shared secret key, the fact that the sender knows the secret key implicitly identifies the sender to the receiver. In the case of public key cryptography, however, this is no longer the case since anyone can send an encrypted message to Bob using Bob's publicly available key. A digital signature, a topic we will study in Section 8.3, is needed to bind a sender to a message.

RSA

While there may be many algorithms that address these concerns, the **RSA algorithm** (named after its founders, Ron Rivest, Adi Shamir, and Leonard Adleman) has become almost synonymous with public key cryptography. Let's first see how RSA works and then examine why it works.

RSA makes extensive use of arithmetic operations using modulo-n arithmetic. So let's briefly review modular arithmetic. Recall that x mod n simply means the remainder of x when divided by n; so, for example, 19 mod 5 = 4. In modular arithmetic, one performs the usual operations of addition, multiplication, and exponentiation. However, the result of each operation is replaced by the integer remainder that is left when the result is divided by n. Adding and multiplying with modular arithmetic is facilitated with the following handy facts:

$$[(a \bmod n) + (b \bmod n)] \bmod n = (a + b) \bmod n$$
$$[(a \bmod n) - (b \bmod n)] \bmod n = (a - b) \bmod n$$
$$[(a \bmod n) \cdot (b \bmod n)] \bmod n = (a \cdot b) \bmod n$$

It follows from the third fact that $(a \bmod n)^d \bmod n = a^d \bmod n$, which is an identity that we will soon find very useful.

Now suppose that Alice wants to send to Bob an RSA-encrypted message, as shown in Figure 8.6. In our discussion of RSA, let's always keep in mind that a message is nothing but a bit pattern, and every bit pattern can be uniquely represented by an integer number (along with the length of the bit pattern). For example, suppose a message is the bit pattern 1001; this message can be represented by the decimal integer 9. Thus, when encrypting a message with RSA, it is equivalent to encrypting the unique integer number that represents the message.

There are two interrelated components of RSA:

* The choice of the public key and the private key
* The encryption and decryption algorithm

To generate the public and private RSA keys, Bob performs the following steps:

1. Choose two large prime numbers, p and q. How large should p and q be? The larger the values, the more difficult it is to break RSA, but the longer it takes to perform the encoding and decoding. RSA Laboratories recommends that the product of p and q be on the order of 1,024 bits. For a discussion of how to find large prime numbers, see [Caldwell 2012].
2. Compute $n = pq$ and $z = (p - 1)(q - 1)$.
3. Choose a number, e, less than n, that has no common factors (other than 1) with z. (In this case, e and z are said to be relatively prime.) The letter e is used since this value will be used in encryption.
4. Find a number, d, such that $ed - 1$ is exactly divisible (that is, with no remainder) by z. The letter d is used because this value will be used in decryption. Put another way, given e, we choose d such that

$$ed \bmod z = 1$$

5. The public key that Bob makes available to the world, K_B^+, is the pair of numbers (n, e); his private key, K_B^-, is the pair of numbers (n, d).

The encryption by Alice and the decryption by Bob are done as follows:

- Suppose Alice wants to send Bob a bit pattern represented by the integer number m (with $m < n$). To encode, Alice performs the exponentiation m^e, and then computes the integer remainder when m^e is divided by n. In other words, the encrypted value, c, of Alice's plaintext message, m, is

$$c = m^e \bmod n$$

The bit pattern corresponding to this ciphertext c is sent to Bob.

- To decrypt the received ciphertext message, c, Bob computes

$$m = c^d \bmod n$$

which requires the use of his private key (n,d).

As a simple example of RSA, suppose Bob chooses $p = 5$ and $q = 7$. (Admittedly, these values are far too small to be secure.) Then $n = 35$ and $z = 24$. Bob chooses $e = 5$, since 5 and 24 have no common factors. Finally, Bob chooses $d = 29$, since $5 \cdot 29 - 1$ (that is, $ed - 1$) is exactly divisible by 24. Bob makes the two values, $n = 35$ and $e = 5$, public and keeps the value $d = 29$ secret. Observing these two public values, suppose Alice now wants to send the letters l, o, v, and e to Bob. Interpreting each letter as a number between 1 and 26 (with a being 1, and z being 26), Alice and Bob perform the encryption and decryption shown in Tables 8.2 and 8.3, respectively. Note that in this example, we consider each of the four letters as a distinct message. A more realistic example would be to convert the four letters into their 8-bit ASCII representations and then encrypt the integer corresponding to the resulting 32-bit bit pattern. (Such a realistic example generates numbers that are much too long to print in a textbook!)

Given that the "toy" example in Tables 8.2 and 8.3 has already produced some extremely large numbers, and given that we saw earlier that p and q should each be several hundred bits long, several practical issues regarding RSA come to mind.

Plaintext Letter	m: numeric representation	m^e	Ciphertext $c = m^e \bmod n$
l	12	248832	17
o	15	759375	15
v	22	5153632	22
e	5	3125	10

Table 8.2 ♦ Alice's RSA encryption, $e = 5$, $n = 35$

Ciphertext c	c^d	$m = c^d \bmod n$	Plaintext Letter
17	4819685721067509150915091411825223071697	12	l
15	127834039403948858939111232757568359375	15	o
22	851643319086537701956194499721106030592	22	v
10	100000000000000000000000000000000	5	e

Table 8.3 ♦ Bob's RSA decryption, $d = 29$, $n = 35$

How does one choose large prime numbers? How does one then choose e and d? How does one perform exponentiation with large numbers? A discussion of these important issues is beyond the scope of this book; see [Kaufman 1995] and the references therein for details.

Session Keys

We note here that the exponentiation required by RSA is a rather time-consuming process. By contrast, DES is at least 100 times faster in software and between 1,000 and 10,000 times faster in hardware [RSA Fast 2012]. As a result, RSA is often used in practice in combination with symmetric key cryptography. For example, if Alice wants to send Bob a large amount of encrypted data, she could do the following. First Alice chooses a key that will be used to encode the data itself; this key is referred to as a **session key**, and is denoted by K_S. Alice must inform Bob of the session key, since this is the shared symmetric key they will use with a symmetric key cipher (e.g., with DES or AES). Alice encrypts the session key using Bob's public key, that is, computes $c = (K_S)^e \bmod n$. Bob receives the RSA-encrypted session key, c, and decrypts it to obtain the session key, K_S. Bob now knows the session key that Alice will use for her encrypted data transfer.

Why Does RSA Work?

RSA encryption/decryption appears rather magical. Why should it be that by applying the encryption algorithm and then the decryption algorithm, one recovers the original message? In order to understand why RSA works, again denote $n = pq$, where p and q are the large prime numbers used in the RSA algorithm.

Recall that, under RSA encryption, a message (uniquely represented by an integer), m, is exponentiated to the power e using modulo-n arithmetic, that is,

$$c = m^e \bmod n$$

Decryption is performed by raising this value to the power d, again using modulo-n arithmetic. The result of an encryption step followed by a decryption step is thus

$(m^e \bmod n)^d \bmod n$. Let's now see what we can say about this quantity. As mentioned earlier, one important property of modulo arithmetic is $(a \bmod n)^d \bmod n = a^d \bmod n$ for any values a, n, and d. Thus, using $a = m^e$ in this property, we have

$$(m^e \bmod n)^d \bmod n = m^{ed} \bmod n$$

It therefore remains to show that $m^{ed} \bmod n = m$. Although we're trying to remove some of the magic about why RSA works, to establish this, we'll need to use a rather magical result from number theory here. Specifically, we'll need the result that says if p and q are prime, $n = pq$, and $z = (p - 1)(q - 1)$, then $x^y \bmod n$ is the same as $x^{(y \bmod z)} \bmod n$ [Kaufman 1995]. Applying this result with $x = m$ and $y = ed$ we have

$$m^{ed} \bmod n = m^{(ed \bmod z)} \bmod n$$

But remember that we have chosen e and d such that $ed \bmod z = 1$. This gives us

$$m^{ed} \bmod n = m^1 \bmod n = m$$

which is exactly the result we are looking for! By first exponentiating to the power of e (that is, encrypting) and then exponentiating to the power of d (that is, decrypting), we obtain the original value, m. Even *more* wonderful is the fact that if we first exponentiate to the power of d and then exponentiate to the power of e—that is, we reverse the order of encryption and decryption, performing the decryption operation first and then applying the encryption operation—we also obtain the original value, m. This wonderful result follows immediately from the modular arithmetic:

$$(m^d \bmod n)^e \bmod n = m^{de} \bmod n = m^{ed} \bmod n = (m^e \bmod n)^d \bmod n$$

The security of RSA relies on the fact that there are no known algorithms for quickly factoring a number, in this case the public value n, into the primes p and q. If one knew p and q, then given the public value e, one could easily compute the secret key, d. On the other hand, it is not known whether or not there *exist* fast algorithms for factoring a number, and in this sense, the security of RSA is not guaranteed.

Another popular public-key encryption algorithm is the Diffie-Hellman algorithm, which we will briefly explore in the homework problems. Diffie-Hellman is not as versatile as RSA in that it cannot be used to encrypt messages of arbitrary length; it can be used, however, to establish a symmetric session key, which is in turn used to encrypt messages.

8.3 Message Integrity and Digital Signatures

In the previous section we saw how encryption can be used to provide confidentiality to two communicating entities. In this section we turn to the equally important cryptography topic of providing **message integrity** (also known as message authentication). Along with message integrity, we will discuss two related topics in this section: digital signatures and end-point authentication.

We define the message integrity problem using, once again, Alice and Bob. Suppose Bob receives a message (which may be encrypted or may be in plaintext) and he believes this message was sent by Alice. To authenticate this message, Bob needs to verify:

1. The message indeed originated from Alice.
2. The message was not tampered with on its way to Bob.

We'll see in Sections 8.4 through 8.7 that this problem of message integrity is a critical concern in just about all secure networking protocols.

As a specific example, consider a computer network using a link-state routing algorithm (such as OSPF) for determining routes between each pair of routers in the network (see Chapter 4). In a link-state algorithm, each router needs to broadcast a link-state message to all other routers in the network. A router's link-state message includes a list of its directly connected neighbors and the direct costs to these neighbors. Once a router receives link-state messages from all of the other routers, it can create a complete map of the network, run its least-cost routing algorithm, and configure its forwarding table. One relatively easy attack on the routing algorithm is for Trudy to distribute bogus link-state messages with incorrect link-state information. Thus the need for message integrity—when router B receives a link-state message from router A, router B should verify that router A actually created the message and, further, that no one tampered with the message in transit.

In this section, we describe a popular message integrity technique that is used by many secure networking protocols. But before doing so, we need to cover another important topic in cryptography—cryptographic hash functions.

8.3.1 Cryptographic Hash Functions

As shown in Figure 8.7, a hash function takes an input, m, and computes a fixed-size string $H(m)$ known as a hash. The Internet checksum (Chapter 3) and CRCs (Chapter 4) meet this definition. A **cryptographic hash function** is required to have the following additional property:

- It is computationally infeasible to find any two different messages x and y such that $H(x) = H(y)$.

Informally, this property means that it is computationally infeasible for an intruder to substitute one message for another message that is protected by the hash function. That is, if $(m, H(m))$ are the message and the hash of the message created

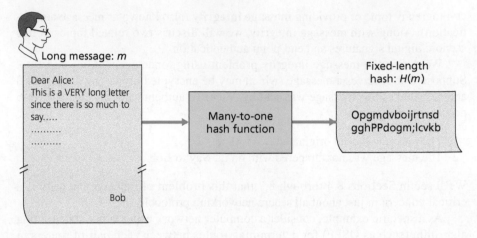

Figure 8.7 ♦ Hash functions

by the sender, then an intruder cannot forge the contents of another message, *y*, that has the same hash value as the original message.

Let's convince ourselves that a simple checksum, such as the Internet checksum, would make a poor cryptographic hash function. Rather than performing 1s complement arithmetic (as in the Internet checksum), let us compute a checksum by treating each character as a byte and adding the bytes together using 4-byte chunks at a time. Suppose Bob owes Alice $100.99 and sends an IOU to Alice consisting of the text string "IOU100.99BOB." The ASCII representation (in hexadecimal notation) for these letters is 49, 4F, 55, 31, 30, 30, 2E, 39, 39, 42, 4F, 42.

Figure 8.8 (top) shows that the 4-byte checksum for this message is B2 C1 D2 AC. A slightly different message (and a much more costly one for Bob) is shown in the bottom half of Figure 8.8. The messages "IOU100.99BOB" and "IOU900.19BOB" have the *same* checksum. Thus, this simple checksum algorithm violates the requirement above. Given the original data, it is simple to find another set of data with the same checksum. Clearly, for security purposes, we are going to need a more powerful hash function than a checksum.

The MD5 hash algorithm of Ron Rivest [RFC 1321] is in wide use today. It computes a 128-bit hash in a four-step process consisting of a padding step (adding a one followed by enough zeros so that the length of the message satisfies certain conditions), an append step (appending a 64-bit representation of the message length before padding), an initialization of an accumulator, and a final looping step in which the message's 16-word blocks are processed (mangled) in four rounds. For a description of MD5 (including a C source code implementation) see [RFC 1321].

	ASCII			
Message	Representation			
I O U 1	49	4F	55	31
0 0 . 9	30	30	2E	39
9 B O B	39	42	4F	42
	B2	C1	D2	AC	Checksum

	ASCII			
Message	Representation			
I O U 9	49	4F	55	39
0 0 . 1	30	30	2E	31
9 B O B	39	42	4F	42
	B2	C1	D2	AC	Checksum

Figure 8.8 ♦ Initial message and fraudulent message have the same checksum!

The second major hash algorithm in use today is the Secure Hash Algorithm (SHA-1) [FIPS 1995]. This algorithm is based on principles similar to those used in the design of MD4 [RFC 1320], the predecessor to MD5. SHA-1, a US federal standard, is required for use whenever a cryptographic hash algorithm is needed for federal applications. It produces a 160-bit message digest. The longer output length makes SHA-1 more secure.

8.3.2 Message Authentication Code

Let's now return to the problem of message integrity. Now that we understand hash functions, let's take a first stab at how we might perform message integrity:

1. Alice creates message m and calculates the hash $H(m)$ (for example with SHA-1).
2. Alice then appends $H(m)$ to the message m, creating an extended message $(m, H(m))$, and sends the extended message to Bob.
3. Bob receives an extended message (m, h) and calculates $H(m)$. If $H(m) = h$, Bob concludes that everything is fine.

This approach is obviously flawed. Trudy can create a bogus message m' in which she says she is Alice, calculate $H(m')$, and send Bob $(m', H(m'))$. When Bob receives the message, everything checks out in step 3, so Bob doesn't suspect any funny business.

To perform message integrity, in addition to using cryptographic hash functions, Alice and Bob will need a shared secret s. This shared secret, which is nothing more than a string of bits, is called the **authentication key**. Using this shared secret, message integrity can be performed as follows:

1. Alice creates message m, concatenates s with m to create $m + s$, and calculates the hash $H(m + s)$ (for example with SHA-1). $H(m + s)$ is called the **message authentication code (MAC)**.
2. Alice then appends the MAC to the message m, creating an extended message $(m, H(m + s))$, and sends the extended message to Bob.
3. Bob receives an extended message (m, h) and knowing s, calculates the MAC $H(m + s)$. If $H(m + s) = h$, Bob concludes that everything is fine.

A summary of the procedure is shown in Figure 8.9. Readers should note that the MAC here (standing for "message authentication code") is not the same MAC used in link-layer protocols (standing for "medium access control")!

One nice feature of a MAC is that it does not require an encryption algorithm. Indeed, in many applications, including the link-state routing algorithm described earlier, communicating entities are only concerned with message integrity and are not concerned with message confidentiality. Using a MAC, the entities can authenticate the messages they send to each other without having to integrate complex encryption algorithms into the integrity process.

As you might expect, a number of different standards for MACs have been proposed over the years. The most popular standard today is **HMAC**, which can be

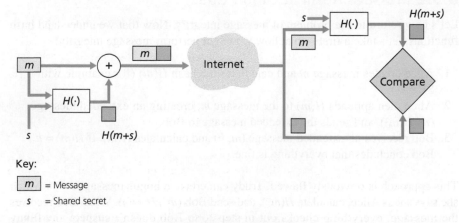

Key:

   $\boxed{m}$ = Message

   s = Shared secret

Figure 8.9 ♦ Message authentication code (MAC)

used either with MD5 or SHA-1. HMAC actually runs data and the authentication key through the hash function twice [Kaufman 1995; RFC 2104].

There still remains an important issue. How do we distribute the shared authentication key to the communicating entities? For example, in the link-state routing algorithm, we would somehow need to distribute the secret authentication key to each of the routers in the autonomous system. (Note that the routers can all use the same authentication key.) A network administrator could actually accomplish this by physically visiting each of the routers. Or, if the network administrator is a lazy guy, and if each router has its own public key, the network administrator could distribute the authentication key to any one of the routers by encrypting it with the router's public key and then sending the encrypted key over the network to the router.

8.3.3 Digital Signatures

Think of the number of the times you've signed your name to a piece of paper during the last week. You sign checks, credit card receipts, legal documents, and letters. Your signature attests to the fact that you (as opposed to someone else) have acknowledged and/or agreed with the document's contents. In a digital world, one often wants to indicate the owner or creator of a document, or to signify one's agreement with a document's content. A **digital signature** is a cryptographic technique for achieving these goals in a digital world.

Just as with handwritten signatures, digital signing should be done in a way that is verifiable and nonforgeable. That is, it must be possible to prove that a document signed by an individual was indeed signed by that individual (the signature must be verifiable) and that *only* that individual could have signed the document (the signature cannot be forged).

Let's now consider how we might design a digital signature scheme. Observe that when Bob signs a message, Bob must put something on the message that is unique to him. Bob could consider attaching a MAC for the signature, where the MAC is created by appending his key (unique to him) to the message, and then taking the hash. But for Alice to verify the signature, she must also have a copy of the key, in which case the key would not be unique to Bob. Thus, MACs are not going to get the job done here.

Recall that with public-key cryptography, Bob has both a public and private key, with both of these keys being unique to Bob. Thus, public-key cryptography is an excellent candidate for providing digital signatures. Let us now examine how it is done.

Suppose that Bob wants to digitally sign a document, m. We can think of the document as a file or a message that Bob is going to sign and send. As shown in Figure 8.10, to sign this document, Bob simply uses his private key, K_B^-, to compute $K_B^-(m)$. At first, it might seem odd that Bob is using his private key (which, as we saw in Section 8.2, was used to decrypt a message that had been encrypted

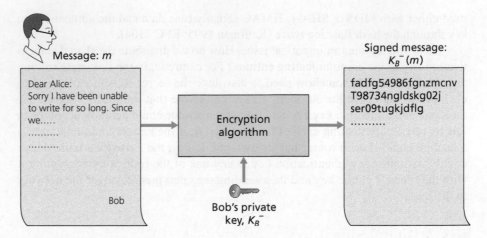

Figure 8.10 ♦ Creating a digital signature for a document

with his public key) to sign a document. But recall that encryption and decryption are nothing more than mathematical operations (exponentiation to the power of e or d in RSA; see Section 8.2) and recall that Bob's goal is not to scramble or obscure the contents of the document, but rather to sign the document in a manner that is verifiable and nonforgeable. Bob's digital signature of the document is $K_B^-(m)$.

Does the digital signature $K_B^-(m)$ meet our requirements of being verifiable and nonforgeable? Suppose Alice has m and $K_B^-(m)$. She wants to prove in court (being litigious) that Bob had indeed signed the document and was the only person who could have possibly signed the document. Alice takes Bob's public key, K_B^+, and applies it to the digital signature, $K_B^-(m)$, associated with the document, m. That is, she computes $K_B^+(K_B^-(m))$, and voilà, with a dramatic flurry, she produces m, which exactly matches the original document! Alice then argues that only Bob could have signed the document, for the following reasons:

- Whoever signed the message must have used the private key, K_B^-, in computing the signature $K_B^-(m)$, such that $K_B^+(K_B^-(m)) = m$.

- The only person who could have known the private key, K_B^-, is Bob. Recall from our discussion of RSA in Section 8.2 that knowing the public key, K_B^+, is of no help in learning the private key, K_B^-. Therefore, the only person who could know K_B^- is the person who generated the pair of keys, (K_B^+, K_B^-), in the first place, Bob. (Note that this assumes, though, that Bob has not given K_B^- to anyone, nor has anyone stolen K_B^- from Bob.)

It is also important to note that if the original document, m, is ever modified to some alternate form, m', the signature that Bob created for m will not be valid for m', since $K_B^+(K_B^-(m))$ does not equal m'. Thus we see that digital signatures also provide message integrity, allowing the receiver to verify that the message was unaltered as well as the source of the message.

One concern with signing data by encryption is that encryption and decryption are computationally expensive. Given the overheads of encryption and decryption, signing data via complete encryption/decryption can be overkill. A more efficient approach is to introduce hash functions into the digital signature. Recall from Section 8.3.2 that a hash algorithm takes a message, m, of arbitrary length and computes a fixed-length "fingerprint" of the message, denoted by $H(m)$. Using a hash function, Bob signs the hash of a message rather than the message itself, that is, Bob calculates $K_B^-(H(m))$. Since $H(m)$ is generally much smaller than the original message m, the computational effort required to create the digital signature is substantially reduced.

In the context of Bob sending a message to Alice, Figure 8.11 provides a summary of the operational procedure of creating a digital signature. Bob puts his original long message through a hash function. He then digitally signs the resulting hash

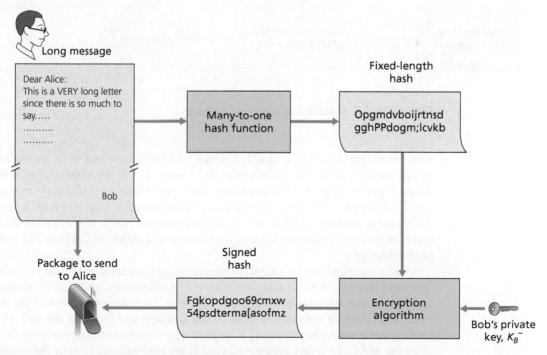

Figure 8.11 ♦ Sending a digitally signed message

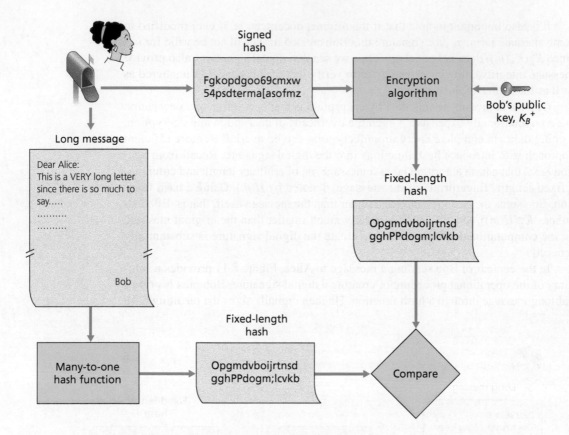

Signed hash

Fgkopdgoo69cmxw
54psdterma[asofmz

→ Encryption algorithm ←── Bob's public key, K_B^+

Long message

Dear Alice:
This is a VERY long letter
since there is so much to
say.....
....
....

Bob

Fixed-length hash

Opgmdvboijrtnsd
gghPPdogm;Icvkb

Many-to-one hash function → **Fixed-length hash** Opgmdvboijrtnsd gghPPdogm;Icvkb → Compare

Figure 8.12 ♦ Verifying a signed message

with his private key. The original message (in cleartext) along with the digitally signed message digest (henceforth referred to as the digital signature) is then sent to Alice. Figure 8.12 provides a summary of the operational procedure of the signature. Alice applies the sender's public key to the message to obtain a hash result. Alice also applies the hash function to the cleartext message to obtain a second hash result. If the two hashes match, then Alice can be sure about the integrity and author of the message.

Before moving on, let's briefly compare digital signatures with MACs, since they have parallels, but also have important subtle differences. Both digital signatures and MACs start with a message (or a document). To create a MAC out of the message, we append an authentication key to the message, and then take the hash of the result. Note that neither public key nor symmetric key encryption is involved in creating the MAC. To create a digital signature, we first take the hash of the message and then encrypt the message with our private key (using public key cryptography).

Thus, a digital signature is a "heavier" technique, since it requires an underlying Public Key Infrastructure (PKI) with certification authorities as described below. We'll see in Section 8.4 that PGP—a popular secure e-mail system—uses digital signatures for message integrity. We've seen already that OSPF uses MACs for message integrity. We'll see in Sections 8.5 and 8.6 that MACs are also used for popular transport-layer and network-layer security protocols.

Public Key Certification

An important application of digital signatures is **public key certification**, that is, certifying that a public key belongs to a specific entity. Public key certification is used in many popular secure networking protocols, including IPsec and SSL.

To gain insight into this problem, let's consider an Internet-commerce version of the classic "pizza prank." Alice is in the pizza delivery business and accepts orders over the Internet. Bob, a pizza lover, sends Alice a plaintext message that includes his home address and the type of pizza he wants. In this message, Bob also includes a digital signature (that is, a signed hash of the original plaintext message) to prove to Alice that he is the true source of the message. To verify the signature, Alice obtains Bob's public key (perhaps from a public key server or from the e-mail message) and checks the digital signature. In this manner she makes sure that Bob, rather than some adolescent prankster, placed the order.

This all sounds fine until clever Trudy comes along. As shown in Figure 8.13, Trudy is indulging in a prank. She sends a message to Alice in which she says she is Bob, gives Bob's home address, and orders a pizza. In this message she also includes her (Trudy's) public key, although Alice naturally assumes it is Bob's public key. Trudy also attaches a digital signature, which was created with her own (Trudy's) private key. After receiving the message, Alice applies Trudy's public key (thinking that it is Bob's) to the digital signature and concludes that the plaintext message was indeed created by Bob. Bob will be very surprised when the delivery person brings a pizza with pepperoni and anchovies to his home!

We see from this example that for public key cryptography to be useful, you need to be able to verify that you have the actual public key of the entity (person, router, browser, and so on) with whom you want to communicate. For example, when Alice wants to communicate with Bob using public key cryptography, she needs to verify that the public key that is supposed to be Bob's is indeed Bob's.

Binding a public key to a particular entity is typically done by a **Certification Authority (CA)**, whose job is to validate identities and issue certificates. A CA has the following roles:

1. A CA verifies that an entity (a person, a router, and so on) is who it says it is. There are no mandated procedures for how certification is done. When dealing with a CA, one must trust the CA to have performed a suitably rigorous identity verification. For example, if Trudy were able to walk into the Fly-by-Night CA

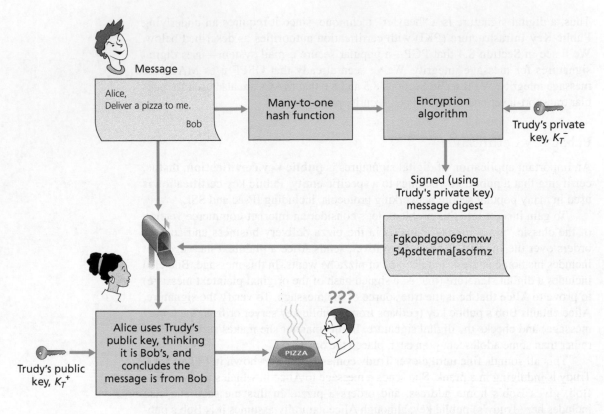

Figure 8.13 ♦ Trudy masquerades as Bob using public key cryptography

and simply announce "I am Alice" and receive certificates associated with the identity of Alice, then one shouldn't put much faith in public keys certified by the Fly-by-Night CA. On the other hand, one might (or might not!) be more willing to trust a CA that is part of a federal or state program. You can trust the identity associated with a public key only to the extent to which you can trust a CA and its identity verification techniques. What a tangled web of trust we spin!

2. Once the CA verifies the identity of the entity, the CA creates a **certificate** that binds the public key of the entity to the identity. The certificate contains the public key and globally unique identifying information about the owner of the public key (for example, a human name or an IP address). The certificate is digitally signed by the CA. These steps are shown in Figure 8.14.

Let us now see how certificates can be used to combat pizza-ordering pranksters, like Trudy, and other undesirables. When Bob places his order he also sends his CA-signed certificate. Alice uses the CA's public key to check the validity of Bob's certificate and extract Bob's public key.

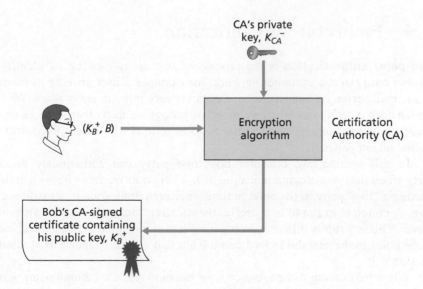

Figure 8.14 ♦ Bob has his public key certified by the CA

Both the International Telecommunication Union (ITU) and the IETF have developed standards for CAs. ITU X.509 [ITU 2005a] specifies an authentication service as well as a specific syntax for certificates. [RFC 1422] describes CA-based key management for use with secure Internet e-mail. It is compatible with X.509 but goes beyond X.509 by establishing procedures and conventions for a key management architecture. Table 8.4 describes some of the important fields in a certificate.

Field Name	Description
Version	Version number of X.509 specification
Serial number	CA-issued unique identifier for a certificate
Signature	Specifies the algorithm used by CA to sign this certificate
Issuer name	Identity of CA issuing this certificate, in distinguished name (DN) [RFC 4514] format
Validity period	Start and end of period of validity for certificate
Subject name	Identity of entity whose public key is associated with this certificate, in DN format
Subject public key	The subject's public key as well indication of the public key algorithm (and algorithm parameters) to be used with this key

Table 8.4 ♦ Selected fields in an X.509 and RFC 1422 public key

8.4 End-Point Authentication

End-point authentication is the process of one entity proving its identity to another entity over a computer network, for example, a user proving its identity to an email server. As humans, we authenticate each other in many ways: We recognize each other's faces when we meet, we recognize each other's voices on the telephone, we are authenticated by the customs official who checks us against the picture on our passport.

In this section, we consider how one party can authenticate another party when the two are communicating over a network. We focus here on authenticating a "live" party, at the point in time when communication is actually occurring. A concrete example is a user authenticating him or herself to an e-mail server. This is a subtly different problem from proving that a message received at some point in the past did indeed come from that claimed sender, as studied in Section 8.3.

When performing authentication over the network, the communicating parties cannot rely on biometric information, such as a visual appearance or a voiceprint. Indeed, we will see in our later case studies that it is often network elements such as routers and client/server processes that must authenticate each other. Here, authentication must be done solely on the basis of messages and data exchanged as part of an **authentication protocol**. Typically, an authentication protocol would run *before* the two communicating parties run some other protocol (for example, a reliable data transfer protocol, a routing information exchange protocol, or an e-mail protocol). The authentication protocol first establishes the identities of the parties to each other's satisfaction; only after authentication do the parties get down to the work at hand.

As in the case of our development of a reliable data transfer (rdt) protocol in Chapter 3, we will find it instructive here to develop various versions of an authentication protocol, which we will call **ap** (authentication protocol), and poke holes in each version as we proceed. (If you enjoy this stepwise evolution of a design, you might also enjoy [Bryant 1988], which recounts a fictitious narrative between designers of an open-network authentication system, and their discovery of the many subtle issues involved.)

Let's assume that Alice needs to authenticate herself to Bob.

8.4.1 Authentication Protocol *ap1.0*

Perhaps the simplest authentication protocol we can imagine is one where Alice simply sends a message to Bob saying she is Alice. This protocol is shown in Figure 8.15. The flaw here is obvious—there is no way for Bob actually to know

Figure 8.15 ♦ Protocol *ap1.0* and a failure scenario

that the person sending the message "I am Alice" is indeed Alice. For example, Trudy (the intruder) could just as well send such a message.

8.4.2 Authentication Protocol *ap2.0*

If Alice has a well-known network address (e.g., an IP address) from which she always communicates, Bob could attempt to authenticate Alice by verifying that the source address on the IP datagram carrying the authentication message matches Alice's well-known address. In this case, Alice would be authenticated. This might stop a very network-naive intruder from impersonating Alice, but it wouldn't stop the determined student studying this book, or many others!

From our study of the network and data link layers, we know that it is not that hard (for example, if one had access to the operating system code and could build one's own operating system kernel, as is the case with Linux and several other freely available operating systems) to create an IP datagram, put whatever IP source address we want (for example, Alice's well-known IP address) into the IP datagram, and send the datagram over the link-layer protocol to the first-hop router. From then on, the incorrectly source-addressed datagram would be dutifully forwarded to Bob. This approach, shown in Figure 8.16, is a form of IP spoofing. IP spoofing can be avoided if Trudy's first-hop router is configured to forward only datagrams containing Trudy's IP source address [RFC 2827]. However, this capability is not universally deployed or enforced. Bob would thus be foolish to assume that Trudy's network manager (who might be Trudy herself) had configured Trudy's first-hop router to forward only appropriately addressed datagrams.

Figure 8.16 ♦ Protocol *ap2.0* and a failure scenario

8.4.3 Authentication Protocol *ap3.0*

One classic approach to authentication is to use a secret password. The password is a shared secret between the authenticator and the person being authenticated. Gmail, Facebook, telnet, FTP, and many other services use password authentication. In protocol *ap3.0,* Alice thus sends her secret password to Bob, as shown in Figure 8.17.

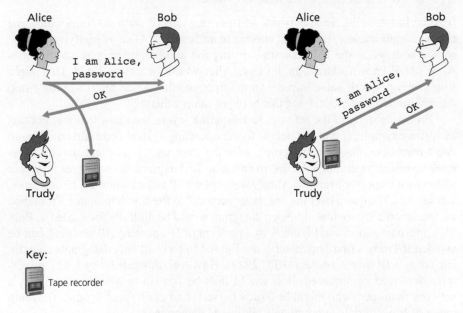

Key:

Tape recorder

Figure 8.17 ♦ Protocol *ap3.0* and a failure scenario

Since passwords are so widely used, we might suspect that protocol *ap3.0* is fairly secure. If so, we'd be wrong! The security flaw here is clear. If Trudy eavesdrops on Alice's communication, then she can learn Alice's password. Lest you think this is unlikely, consider the fact that when you Telnet to another machine and log in, the login password is sent unencrypted to the Telnet server. Someone connected to the Telnet client or server's LAN can possibly sniff (read and store) all packets transmitted on the LAN and thus steal the login password. In fact, this is a well-known approach for stealing passwords (see, for example, [Jimenez 1997]). Such a threat is obviously very real, so *ap3.0* clearly won't do.

8.4.4 Authentication Protocol *ap3.1*

Our next idea for fixing *ap3.0* is naturally to encrypt the password. By encrypting the password, we can prevent Trudy from learning Alice's password. If we assume that Alice and Bob share a symmetric secret key, K_{A-B}, then Alice can encrypt the password and send her identification message, "I am Alice," and her encrypted password to Bob. Bob then decrypts the password and, assuming the password is correct, authenticates Alice. Bob feels comfortable in authenticating Alice since Alice not only knows the password, but also knows the shared secret key value needed to encrypt the password. Let's call this protocol *ap3.1*.

While it is true that *ap3.1* prevents Trudy from learning Alice's password, the use of cryptography here does not solve the authentication problem: Bob is subject to a **playback attack**: Trudy need only eavesdrop on Alice's communication, record the encrypted version of the password, and play back the encrypted version of the password to Bob to pretend that she is Alice. The use of an encrypted password in *ap3.1* doesn't make the situation manifestly different from that of protocol *ap3.0* in Figure 8.17.

8.4.5 Authentication Protocol *ap4.0*

The failure scenario in Figure 8.17 resulted from the fact that Bob could not distinguish between the original authentication of Alice and the later playback of Alice's original authentication. That is, Bob could not tell if Alice was live (that is, was currently really on the other end of the connection) or whether the messages he was receiving were a recorded playback of a previous authentication of Alice. The very *(very)* observant reader will recall that the three-way TCP handshake protocol needed to address the same problem—the server side of a TCP connection did not want to accept a connection if the received SYN segment was an old copy (retransmission) of a SYN segment from an earlier connection. How did the TCP server side solve the problem of determining whether the client was really live? It chose an initial sequence number that had not been used in a very long time, sent that number to the client, and then waited for the client to respond with an ACK segment containing that number. We can adopt the same idea here for authentication purposes.

A **nonce** is a number that a protocol will use only once in a lifetime. That is, once a protocol uses a nonce, it will never use that number again. Our *ap4.0* protocol uses a nonce as follows:

1. Alice sends the message "I am Alice" to Bob.
2. Bob chooses a nonce, R, and sends it to Alice.
3. Alice encrypts the nonce using Alice and Bob's symmetric secret key, K_{A-B}, and sends the encrypted nonce, $K_{A-B}(R)$, back to Bob. As in protocol *ap3.1*, it is the fact that Alice knows K_{A-B} and uses it to encrypt a value that lets Bob know that the message he receives was generated by Alice. The nonce is used to ensure that Alice is live.
4. Bob decrypts the received message. If the decrypted nonce equals the nonce he sent Alice, then Alice is authenticated.

Protocol *ap4.0* is illustrated in Figure 8.18. By using the once-in-a-lifetime value, *R*, and then checking the returned value, $K_{A-B}(R)$, Bob can be sure that Alice is both who she says she is (since she knows the secret key value needed to encrypt *R*) and live (since she has encrypted the nonce, *R*, that Bob just created).

The use of a nonce and symmetric key cryptography forms the basis of *ap4.0*. A natural question is whether we can use a nonce and public key cryptography

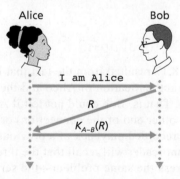

Figure 8.18 ♦ Protocol *ap4.0* and a failure scenario

(rather than symmetric key cryptography) to solve the authentication problem. This issue is explored in the problems at the end of the chapter.

8.5 Securing E-Mail

In previous sections, we examined fundamental issues in network security, including symmetric key and public key cryptography, end-point authentication, key distribution, message integrity, and digital signatures. We are now going to examine how these tools are being used to provide security in the Internet.

Interestingly, it is possible to provide security services in any of the top four layers of the Internet protocol stack. When security is provided for a specific application-layer protocol, the application using the protocol will enjoy one or more security services, such as confidentiality, authentication, or integrity. When security is provided for a transport-layer protocol, all applications that use that protocol enjoy the security services of the transport protocol. When security is provided at the network layer on a host-to-host basis, all transport-layer segments (and hence all application-layer data) enjoy the security services of the network layer. When security is provided on a link basis, then the data in all frames traveling over the link receive the security services of the link.

In Sections 8.5 through 8.8, we examine how security tools are being used in the application, transport, network, and link layers. Being consistent with the general structure of this book, we begin at the top of the protocol stack and discuss security at the application layer. Our approach is to use a specific application, e-mail, as a case study for application-layer security. We then move down the protocol stack. We'll examine the SSL protocol (which provides security at the transport layer), IPsec (which provides security at the network layer), and the security of the IEEE 802.11 wireless LAN protocol.

You might be wondering why security functionality is being provided at more than one layer in the Internet. Wouldn't it suffice simply to provide the security functionality at the network layer and be done with it? There are two answers to this question. First, although security at the network layer can offer "blanket coverage" by encrypting all the data in the datagrams (that is, all the transport-layer segments) and by authenticating all the source IP addresses, it can't provide user-level security. For example, a commerce site cannot rely on IP-layer security to authenticate a customer who is purchasing goods at the commerce site. Thus, there is a need for security functionality at higher layers as well as blanket coverage at lower layers. Second, it is generally easier to deploy new Internet services, including security services, at the higher layers of the protocol stack. While waiting for security to be broadly deployed at the network layer, which is probably still many years in the future, many application developers "just do it" and introduce security functionality into their favorite applications. A classic example is Pretty Good Privacy (PGP), which provides secure e-mail (discussed later in this section). Requiring only client and server application code, PGP was one of the first security technologies to be broadly used in the Internet.

8.5.1 Secure E-Mail

We now use the cryptographic principles of Sections 8.2 through 8.3 to create a secure e-mail system. We create this high-level design in an incremental manner, at each step introducing new security services. When designing a secure e-mail system, let us keep in mind the racy example introduced in Section 8.1—the love affair between Alice and Bob. Imagine that Alice wants to send an e-mail message to Bob, and Trudy wants to intrude.

Before plowing ahead and designing a secure e-mail system for Alice and Bob, we should consider which security features would be most desirable for them. First and foremost is *confidentiality*. As discussed in Section 8.1, neither Alice nor Bob wants Trudy to read Alice's e-mail message. The second feature that Alice and Bob would most likely want to see in the secure e-mail system is *sender authentication*. In particular, when Bob receives the message "I don't love you anymore. I never want to see you again. Formerly yours, Alice," he would naturally want to be sure that the message came from Alice and not from Trudy. Another feature that the two lovers would appreciate is *message integrity*, that is, assurance that the message Alice sends is not modified while en route to Bob. Finally, the e-mail system should provide *receiver authentication*; that is, Alice wants to make sure that she is indeed sending the letter to Bob and not to someone else (for example, Trudy) who is impersonating Bob.

So let's begin by addressing the foremost concern, confidentiality. The most straightforward way to provide confidentiality is for Alice to encrypt the message with symmetric key technology (such as DES or AES) and for Bob to decrypt the message on receipt. As discussed in Section 8.2, if the symmetric key is long enough, and if only Alice and Bob have the key, then it is extremely difficult for anyone else (including Trudy) to read the message. Although this approach is straightforward, it has the fundamental difficulty that we discussed in Section 8.2—distributing a symmetric key so that only Alice and Bob have copies of it. So we naturally consider an alternative approach—public key cryptography (using, for example, RSA). In the public key approach, Bob makes his public key publicly available (e.g., in a public key server or on his personal Web page), Alice encrypts her message with Bob's public key, and she sends the encrypted message to Bob's e-mail address. When Bob receives the message, he simply decrypts it with his private key. Assuming that Alice knows for sure that the public key is

Bob's public key, this approach is an excellent means to provide the desired confidentiality. One problem, however, is that public key encryption is relatively inefficient, particularly for long messages.

To overcome the efficiency problem, let's make use of a session key (discussed in Section 8.2.2). In particular, Alice (1) selects a random symmetric session key, K_S, (2) encrypts her message, m, with the symmetric key, (3) encrypts the symmetric key with Bob's public key, K_B^+, (4) concatenates the encrypted message and the encrypted symmetric key to form a "package," and (5) sends the package to Bob's e-mail address. The steps are illustrated in Figure 8.19. (In this and the subsequent figures, the circled "+" represents concatenation and the circled "−" represents deconcatenation.) When Bob receives the package, he (1) uses his private key, K_B^-, to obtain the symmetric key, K_S, and (2) uses the symmetric key K_S to decrypt the message m.

Having designed a secure e-mail system that provides confidentiality, let's now design another system that provides both sender authentication and message integrity. We'll suppose, for the moment, that Alice and Bob are no longer concerned with confidentiality (they want to share their feelings with everyone!), and are concerned only about sender authentication and message integrity. To accomplish this task, we use digital signatures and message digests, as described in Section 8.3. Specifically, Alice (1) applies a hash function, H (for example, MD5), to her message, m, to obtain a message digest, (2) signs the result of the hash function with her private key, K_A^-, to create a digital signature, (3) concatenates the original (unencrypted) message with the signature to create a package, and (4) sends the package to Bob's e-mail address. When Bob receives the package, he (1) applies Alice's public key, K_A^+, to the signed message digest and (2) compares the result of this operation with his own hash, H, of the message. The steps are illustrated in

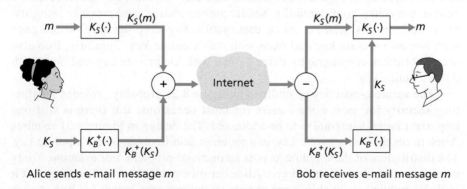

Alice sends e-mail message m Bob receives e-mail message m

Figure 8.19 ♦ Alice used a symmetric session key, K_S, to send a secret e-mail to Bob

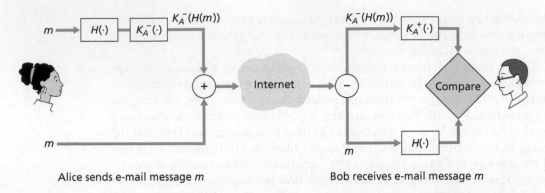

$K_A^-(H(m))$ $K_A^-(H(m))$

Alice sends e-mail message *m*   Bob receives e-mail message *m*

Figure 8.20 ♦ Using hash functions and digital signatures to provide sender authentication and message integrity

Figure 8.20. As discussed in Section 8.3, if the two results are the same, Bob can be pretty confident that the message came from Alice and is unaltered.

Now let's consider designing an e-mail system that provides confidentiality, sender authentication, *and* message integrity. This can be done by combining the procedures in Figures 8.19 and 8.20. Alice first creates a preliminary package, exactly as in Figure 8.20, that consists of her original message along with a digitally signed hash of the message. She then treats this preliminary package as a message in itself and sends this new message through the sender steps in Figure 8.19, creating a new package that is sent to Bob. The steps applied by Alice are shown in Figure 8.21. When Bob receives the package, he first applies his side of Figure 8.19 and then his side of Figure 8.20. It should be clear that this design achieves the goal of providing confidentiality, sender authentication, and message integrity. Note that, in this scheme, Alice uses public key cryptography twice: once with her own private key and once with Bob's public key. Similarly, Bob also uses public key cryptography twice—once with his private key and once with Alice's public key.

The secure e-mail design outlined in Figure 8.21 probably provides satisfactory security for most e-mail users for most occasions. But there is still one important issue that remains to be addressed. The design in Figure 8.21 requires Alice to obtain Bob's public key, and requires Bob to obtain Alice's public key. The distribution of these public keys is a nontrivial problem. For example, Trudy might masquerade as Bob and give Alice her own public key while saying that it is Bob's public key, enabling her to receive the message meant for Bob. As we learned in Section 8.3, a popular approach for securely distributing public keys is to *certify* the public keys using a CA.

CASE HISTORY

PHIL ZIMMERMANN AND PGP

Philip R. Zimmermann is the creator of Pretty Good Privacy (PGP). For that, he was the target of a three-year criminal investigation because the government held that US export restrictions for cryptographic software were violated when PGP spread all around the world following its 1991 publication as freeware. After releasing PGP as shareware, someone else put it on the Internet and foreign citizens downloaded it. Cryptography programs in the United States are classified as munitions under federal law and may not be exported.

Despite the lack of funding, the lack of any paid staff, and the lack of a company to stand behind it, and despite government interventions, PGP nonetheless became the most widely used e-mail encryption software in the world. Oddly enough, the US government may have inadvertently contributed to PGP's spread because of the Zimmermann case.

The US government dropped the case in early 1996. The announcement was met with celebration by Internet activists. The Zimmermann case had become the story of an innocent person fighting for his rights against the abuses of big government. The government's giving in was welcome news, in part because of the campaign for Internet censorship in Congress and the push by the FBI to allow increased government snooping.

After the government dropped its case, Zimmermann founded PGP Inc., which was acquired by Network Associates in December 1997. Zimmermann is now an independent consultant in matters cryptographic.

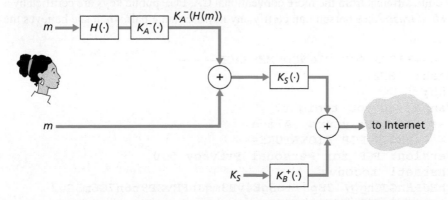

Figure 8.21 ♦ Alice uses symmetric key cyptography, public key cryptography, a hash function, and a digital signature to provide secrecy, sender authentication, and message integrity

8.5.2 PGP

Written by Phil Zimmermann in 1991, **Pretty Good Privacy (PGP)** is an e-mail encryption scheme that has become a *de facto* standard. Its Web site serves more than a million pages a month to users in 166 countries [PGPI 2012]. Versions of PGP are available in the public domain; for example, you can find the PGP software for your favorite platform as well as lots of interesting reading at the International PGP Home Page [PGPI 2012]. (A particularly interesting essay by the author of PGP is [Zimmermann 2012].) The PGP design is, in essence, the same as the design shown in Figure 8.21. Depending on the version, the PGP software uses MD5 or SHA for calculating the message digest; CAST, triple-DES, or IDEA for symmetric key encryption; and RSA for the public key encryption.

When PGP is installed, the software creates a public key pair for the user. The public key can be posted on the user's Web site or placed in a public key server. The private key is protected by the use of a password. The password has to be entered every time the user accesses the private key. PGP gives the user the option of digitally signing the message, encrypting the message, or both digitally signing and encrypting. Figure 8.22 shows a PGP signed message. This message appears after the MIME header. The encoded data in the message is $K_A^-(H(m))$, that is, the digitally signed message digest. As we discussed above, in order for Bob to verify the integrity of the message, he needs to have access to Alice's public key.

Figure 8.23 shows a secret PGP message. This message also appears after the MIME header. Of course, the plaintext message is not included within the secret e-mail message. When a sender (such as Alice) wants both confidentiality and integrity, PGP contains a message like that of Figure 8.23 within the message of Figure 8.22.

PGP also provides a mechanism for public key certification, but the mechanism is quite different from the more conventional CA. PGP public keys are certified by a *web of trust*. Alice herself can certify any key/username pair when she believes the

```
-----BEGIN PGP SIGNED MESSAGE-----
Hash:   SHA1
Bob:
Can I see you tonight?
Passionately yours, Alice
-----BEGIN PGP SIGNATURE-----
Version: PGP for Personal Privacy 5.0
Charset: noconv
yhHJRHhGJGhgg/12EpJ+lo8gE4vB3mqJhFEvZP9t6n7G6m5Gw2
-----END PGP SIGNATURE-----
```

Figure 8.22 ♦ A PGP signed message

```
-----BEGIN PGP MESSAGE-----
Version: PGP for Personal Privacy 5.0
u2R4d+/jKmn8Bc5+hgDsqAewsDfrGdszX68liKm5F6Gc4sDfcXyt
RfdS10juHgbcfDssWe7/K=lKhnMikLo0+1/BvcX4t==Ujk9PbcD4
Thdf2awQfgHbnmKlok8iy6gThlp
-----END PGP MESSAGE
```

Figure 8.23 ♦ A secret PGP message

pair really belong together. In addition, PGP permits Alice to say that she trusts another user to vouch for the authenticity of more keys. Some PGP users sign each other's keys by holding key-signing parties. Users physically gather, exchange public keys, and certify each other's keys by signing them with their private keys.

8.6 Securing TCP Connections: SSL

In the previous section, we saw how cryptographic techniques can provide confidentiality, data integrity, and end-point authentication to a specific application, namely, e-mail. In this section, we'll drop down a layer in the protocol stack and examine how cryptography can enhance TCP with security services, including confidentiality, data integrity, and end-point authentication. This enhanced version of TCP is commonly known as **Secure Sockets Layer (SSL)**. A slightly modified version of SSL version 3, called **Transport Layer Security (TLS)**, has been standardized by the IETF [RFC 4346].

The SSL protocol was originally designed by Netscape, but the basic ideas behind securing TCP had predated Netscape's work (for example, see Woo [Woo 1994]). Since its inception, SSL has enjoyed broad deployment. SSL is supported by all popular Web browsers and Web servers, and it is used by essentially all Internet commerce sites (including Amazon, eBay, Yahoo!, MSN, and so on). Tens of billions of dollars are spent over SSL every year. In fact, if you have ever purchased anything over the Internet with your credit card, the communication between your browser and the server for this purchase almost certainly went over SSL. (You can identify that SSL is being used by your browser when the URL begins with https: rather than http.)

To understand the need for SSL, let's walk through a typical Internet commerce scenario. Bob is surfing the Web and arrives at the Alice Incorporated site, which is selling perfume. The Alice Incorporated site displays a form in which Bob is supposed to enter the type of perfume and quantity desired, his address, and his payment card number. Bob enters this information, clicks on Submit, and expects to receive (via ordinary postal mail) the purchased perfumes; he also expects to receive a charge for his order in his next payment card statement. This all sounds good, but if no security measures are taken, Bob could be in for a few surprises.

• If no confidentiality (encryption) is used, an intruder could intercept Bob's order and obtain his payment card information. The intruder could then make purchases at Bob's expense.

• If no data integrity is used, an intruder could modify Bob's order, having him purchase ten times more bottles of perfume than desired.

• Finally, if no server authentication is used, a server could display Alice Incorporated's famous logo when in actuality the site maintained by Trudy, who is masquerading as Alice Incorporated. After receiving Bob's order, Trudy could take Bob's money and run. Or Trudy could carry out an identity theft by collecting Bob's name, address, and credit card number.

SSL addresses these issues by enhancing TCP with confidentiality, data integrity, server authentication, and client authentication.

SSL is often used to provide security to transactions that take place over HTTP. However, because SSL secures TCP, it can be employed by any application that runs over TCP. SSL provides a simple Application Programmer Interface (API) with sockets, which is similar and analogous to TCP's API. When an application wants to employ SSL, the application includes SSL classes/libraries. As shown in Figure 8.24, although SSL technically resides in the application layer, from the developer's perspective it is a transport protocol that provides TCP's services enhanced with security services.

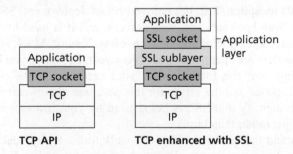

Figure 8.24 ♦ Although SSL technically resides in the application layer, from the developer's perspective it is a transport-layer protocol

8.6.1 The Big Picture

We begin by describing a simplified version of SSL, one that will allow us to get a big-picture understanding of the *why* and *how* of SSL. We will refer to this simplified version of SSL as "almost-SSL." After describing almost-SSL, in the next subsection we'll then describe the real SSL, filling in the details. Almost-SSL (and SSL) has three phases: *handshake*, *key derivation*, and *data transfer*. We now describe these three phases for a communication session between a client (Bob) and a server (Alice), with Alice having a private/public key pair and a certificate that binds her identity to her public key.

Handshake

During the handshake phase, Bob needs to (a) establish a TCP connection with Alice, (b) verify that Alice is *really* Alice, and (c) send Alice a master secret key, which will be used by both Alice and Bob to generate all the symmetric keys they need for the SSL session. These three steps are shown in Figure 8.25. Note that once the TCP connection is established, Bob sends Alice a hello message. Alice then responds with her certificate, which contains her public key. As discussed in Section 8.3, because the certificate has been certified by a CA, Bob knows for sure that the

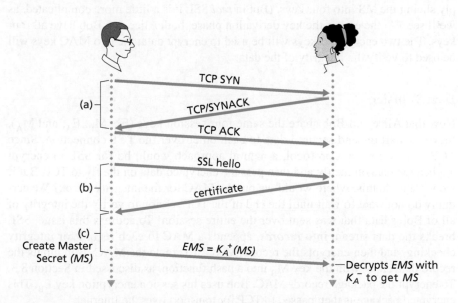

Figure 8.25 ◆ The almost-SSL handshake, beginning with a TCP connection

public key in the certificate belongs to Alice. Bob then generates a Master Secret (MS) (which will only be used for this SSL session), encrypts the MS with Alice's public key to create the Encyrpted Master Secret (EMS), and sends the EMS to Alice. Alice decrypts the EMS with her private key to get the MS. After this phase, both Bob and Alice (and no one else) know the master secret for this SSL session.

Key Derivation

In principle, the MS, now shared by Bob and Alice, could be used as the symmetric session key for all subsequent encryption and data integrity checking. It is, however, generally considered safer for Alice and Bob to each use different cryptographic keys, and also to use different keys for encryption and integrity checking. Thus, both Alice and Bob use the MS to generate four keys:

- E_B = session encryption key for data sent from Bob to Alice
- M_B = session MAC key for data sent from Bob to Alice
- E_A = session encryption key for data sent from Alice to Bob
- M_A = session MAC key for data sent from Alice to Bob

Alice and Bob each generate the four keys from the MS. This could be done by simply slicing the MS into four keys. (But in *real* SSL it is a little more complicated, as we'll see.) At the end of the key derivation phase, both Alice and Bob have all four keys. The two encryption keys will be used to encrypt data; the two MAC keys will be used to verify the integrity of the data.

Data Transfer

Now that Alice and Bob share the same four session keys (E_B, M_B, E_A, and M_A), they can start to send secured data to each other over the TCP connection. Since TCP is a byte-stream protocol, a natural approach would be for SSL to encrypt application data on the fly and then pass the encrypted data on the fly to TCP. But if we were to do this, where would we put the MAC for the integrity check? We certainly do not want to wait until the end of the TCP session to verify the integrity of all of Bob's data that was sent over the entire session! To address this issue, SSL breaks the data stream into *records*, appends a MAC to each record for integrity checking, and then encrypts the record+MAC. To create the MAC, Bob inputs the record data along with the key M_B into a hash function, as discussed in Section 8.3. To encrypt the package record+MAC, Bob uses his session encryption key E_B. This encrypted package is then passed to TCP for transport over the Internet.

Although this approach goes a long way, it still isn't bullet-proof when it comes to providing data integrity for the entire message stream. In particular, suppose Trudy is a woman-in-the-middle and has the ability to insert, delete, and replace segments in the stream of TCP segments sent between Alice and Bob. Trudy, for example, could capture two segments sent by Bob, reverse the order of the segments, adjust the TCP sequence numbers (which are not encrypted), and then send the two reverse-ordered segments to Alice. Assuming that each TCP segment encapsulates exactly one record, let's now take a look at how Alice would process these segments.

1. TCP running in Alice would think everything is fine and pass the two records to the SSL sublayer.
2. SSL in Alice would decrypt the two records.
3. SSL in Alice would use the MAC in each record to verify the data integrity of the two records.
4. SSL would then pass the decrypted byte streams of the two records to the application layer; but the complete byte stream received by Alice would not be in the correct order due to reversal of the records!

You are encouraged to walk through similar scenarios for when Trudy removes segments or when Trudy replays segments.

The solution to this problem, as you probably guessed, is to use sequence numbers. SSL does this as follows. Bob maintains a sequence number counter, which begins at zero and is incremented for each SSL record he sends. Bob doesn't actually include a sequence number in the record itself, but when he calculates the MAC, he includes the sequence number in the MAC calculation. Thus, the MAC is now a hash of the data plus the MAC key M_B *plus the current sequence number*. Alice tracks Bob's sequence numbers, allowing her to verify the data integrity of a record by including the appropriate sequence number in the MAC calculation. This use of SSL sequence numbers prevents Trudy from carrying out a woman-in-the-middle attack, such as reordering or replaying segments. (Why?)

SSL Record

The SSL record (as well as the almost-SSL record) is shown in Figure 8.26. The record consists of a type field, version field, length field, data field, and MAC field. Note that the first three fields are not encrypted. The type field indicates whether the record is a handshake message or a message that contains application data. It is also

Figure 8.26 ♦ Record format for SSL

used to close the SSL connection, as discussed below. SSL at the receiving end uses the length field to extract the SSL records out of the incoming TCP byte stream. The version field is self-explanatory.

8.6.2 A More Complete Picture

The previous subsection covered the almost-SSL protocol; it served to give us a basic understanding of the why and how of SSL. Now that we have a basic understanding of SSL, we can dig a little deeper and examine the essentials of the actual SSL protocol. In parallel to reading this description of the SSL protocol, you are encouraged to complete the Wireshark SSL lab, available at the textbook's companion Web site.

SSL Handshake

SSL does not mandate that Alice and Bob use a specific symmetric key algorithm, a specific public-key algorithm, or a specific MAC. Instead, SSL allows Alice and Bob to agree on the cryptographic algorithms at the beginning of the SSL session, during the handshake phase. Additionally, during the handshake phase, Alice and Bob send nonces to each other, which are used in the creation of the session keys (E_B, M_B, E_A, and M_A). The steps of the real SSL handshake are as follows:

1. The client sends a list of cryptographic algorithms it supports, along with a client nonce.
2. From the list, the server chooses a symmetric algorithm (for example, AES), a public key algorithm (for example, RSA with a specific key length), and a MAC algorithm. It sends back to the client its choices, as well as a certificate and a server nonce.
3. The client verifies the certificate, extracts the server's public key, generates a Pre-Master Secret (PMS), encrypts the PMS with the server's public key, and sends the encrypted PMS to the server.
4. Using the same key derivation function (as specified by the SSL standard), the client and server independently compute the Master Secret (MS) from the PMS and nonces. The MS is then sliced up to generate the two encryption and two MAC keys. Furthermore, when the chosen symmetric cipher employs CBC (such as 3DES or AES), then two Initialization Vectors (IVs)—one for each side of the connection—are also obtained from the MS. Henceforth, all messages sent between client and server are encrypted and authenticated (with the MAC).
5. The client sends a MAC of all the handshake messages.
6. The server sends a MAC of all the handshake messages.

The last two steps protect the handshake from tampering. To see this, observe that in step 1, the client typically offers a list of algorithms—some strong, some weak. This list of algorithms is sent in cleartext, since the encryption algorithms and keys have not yet been agreed upon. Trudy, as a woman-in-the-middle, could delete the stronger algorithms from the list, forcing the client to select a weak algorithm. To prevent such a tampering attack, in step 5 the client sends a MAC of the concatenation of all the handshake messages it sent and received. The server can compare this MAC with the MAC of the handshake messages it received and sent. If there is an inconsistency, the server can terminate the connection. Similarly, the server sends a MAC of the handshake messages it has seen, allowing the client to check for inconsistencies.

You may be wondering why there are nonces in steps 1 and 2. Don't sequence numbers suffice for preventing the segment replay attack? The answer is yes, but they don't alone prevent the "connection replay attack." Consider the following connection replay attack. Suppose Trudy sniffs all messages between Alice and Bob. The next day, Trudy masquerades as Bob and sends to Alice exactly the same sequence of messages that Bob sent to Alice on the previous day. If Alice doesn't use nonces, she will respond with exactly the same sequence of messages she sent the previous day. Alice will not suspect any funny business, as each message she receives will pass the integrity check. If Alice is an e-commerce server, she will think that Bob is placing a second order (for exactly the same thing). On the other hand, by including a nonce in the protocol, Alice will send different nonces for each TCP session, causing the encryption keys to be different on the two days. Therefore, when Alice receives played-back SSL records from Trudy, the records will fail the integrity checks, and the bogus e-commerce transaction will not succeed. In summary, in SSL, nonces are used to defend against the "connection replay attack" and sequence numbers are used to defend against replaying individual packets during an ongoing session.

Connection Closure

At some point, either Bob or Alice will want to end the SSL session. One approach would be to let Bob end the SSL session by simply terminating the underlying TCP connection—that is, by having Bob send a TCP FIN segment to Alice. But such a naive design sets the stage for the *truncation attack* whereby Trudy once again gets in the middle of an ongoing SSL session and ends the session early with a TCP FIN. If Trudy were to do this, Alice would think she received all of Bob's data when actuality she only received a portion of it. The solution to this problem is to indicate in the type field whether the record serves to terminate the SSL session. (Although the SSL type is sent in the clear, it is authenticated at the receiver using the record's MAC.) By including such a field, if Alice were to receive a TCP FIN before receiving a closure SSL record, she would know that something funny was going on.

This completes our introduction to SSL. We've seen that it uses many of the cryptography principles discussed in Sections 8.2 and 8.3. Readers who want to explore SSL on yet a deeper level can read Rescorla's highly readable book on SSL [Rescorla 2001].

8.7 Network-Layer Security: IPsec and Virtual Private Networks

The IP security protocol, more commonly known as **IPsec**, provides security at the network layer. IPsec secures IP datagrams between any two network-layer entities, including hosts and routers. As we will soon describe, many institutions (corporations, government branches, non-profit organizations, and so on) use IPsec to create **virtual private networks (VPNs)** that run over the public Internet.

Before getting into the specifics of IPsec, let's step back and consider what it means to provide confidentiality at the network layer. With network-layer confidentiality between a pair of network entities (for example, between two routers, between two hosts, or between a router and a host), the sending entity encrypts the payloads of all the datagrams it sends to the receiving entity. The encrypted payload could be a TCP segment, a UDP segment, an ICMP message, and so on. If such a network-layer service were in place, all data sent from one entity to the other—including e-mail, Web pages, TCP handshake messages, and management messages (such as ICMP and SNMP)—would be hidden from any third party that might be sniffing the network. For this reason, network-layer security is said to provide "blanket coverage".

In addition to confidentiality, a network-layer security protocol could potentially provide other security services. For example, it could provide source authentication, so that the receiving entity can verify the source of the secured datagram. A network-layer security protocol could provide data integrity, so that the receiving entity can check for any tampering of the datagram that may have occurred while the datagram was in transit. A network-layer security service could also provide replay-attack prevention, meaning that Bob could detect any duplicate datagrams that an attacker might insert. We will soon see that IPsec indeed provides mechanisms for all these security services, that is, for confidentiality, source authentication, data integrity, and replay-attack prevention.

8.7.1 IPsec and Virtual Private Networks (VPNs)

An institution that extends over multiple geographical regions often desires its own IP network, so that its hosts and servers can send data to each other in a secure and confidential manner. To achieve this goal, the institution could actually deploy a stand-alone physical network—including routers, links, and a DNS infrastructure—that is completely separate from the public Internet. Such a disjoint network, dedicated to a particular institution, is called a **private network**. Not surprisingly, a private network can be very costly, as the institution needs to purchase, install, and maintain its own physical network infrastructure.

Instead of deploying and maintaining a private network, many institutions today create VPNs over the existing public Internet. With a VPN, the institution's inter-office traffic is sent over the public Internet rather than over a physically independent network. But to provide confidentiality, the inter-office traffic is encrypted before it enters the public Internet. A simple example of a VPN is shown in Figure 8.27. Here

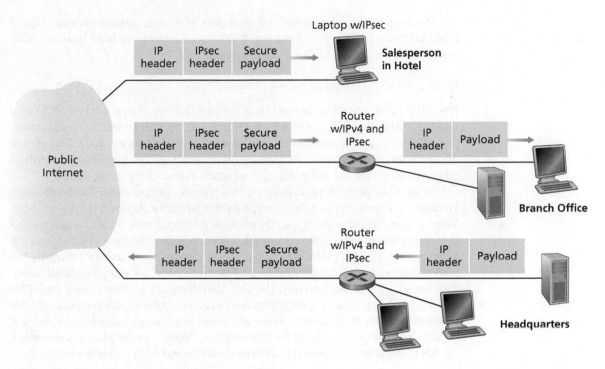

Figure 8.27 ♦ Virtual Private Network (VPN)

the institution consists of a headquarters, a branch office, and traveling salespersons that typically access the Internet from their hotel rooms. (There is only one salesperson shown in the figure.) In this VPN, whenever two hosts within headquarters send IP datagrams to each other or whenever two hosts within the branch office want to communicate, they use good-old vanilla IPv4 (that is, without IPsec services). However, when two of the institution's hosts communicate over a path that traverses the public Internet, the traffic is encrypted before it enters the Internet.

To get a feel for how a VPN works, let's walk through a simple example in the context of Figure 8.27. When a host in headquarters sends an IP datagram to a salesperson in a hotel, the gateway router in headquarters converts the vanilla IPv4 datagram into an IPsec datagram and then forwards this IPsec datagram into the Internet. This IPsec datagram actually has a traditional IPv4 header, so that the routers in the public Internet process the datagram as if it were an ordinary IPv4 datagram—to them, the datagram is a perfectly ordinary datagram. But, as shown Figure 8.27, the payload of the IPsec datagram includes an IPsec header, which is used for IPsec processing; furthermore, the payload of the IPsec datagram is encrypted. When the IPsec datagram arrives at the salesperson's laptop, the OS in the laptop decrypts the payload (and provides other security services, such as verifying data integrity) and passes the unencrypted payload to the upper-layer protocol (for example, to TCP or UDP).

We have just given a high-level overview of how an institution can employ IPsec to create a VPN. To see the forest through the trees, we have brushed aside many important details. Let's now take a closer look.

8.7.2 The AH and ESP Protocols

IPsec is a rather complex animal—it is defined in more than a dozen RFCs. Two important RFCs are RFC 4301, which describes the overall IP security architecture, and RFC 6071, which provides an overview of the IPsec protocol suite. Our goal in this textbook, as usual, is not simply to re-hash the dry and arcane RFCs, but instead take a more operational and pedagogic approach to describing the protocols.

In the IPsec protocol suite, there are two principal protocols: the **Authentication Header (AH)** protocol and the **Encapsulation Security Payload (ESP)** protocol. When a source IPsec entity (typically a host or a router) sends secure datagrams to a destination entity (also a host or a router), it does so with either the AH protocol or the ESP protocol. The AH protocol provides source authentication and data integrity but *does not* provide confidentiality. The ESP protocol provides source authentication, data integrity, *and* confidentiality. Because confidentiality is often critical for VPNs and other IPsec applications, the ESP protocol is much more widely used than the AH protocol. In order to de-mystify IPsec and avoid much of its complication, we will henceforth focus exclusively on the ESP protocol. Readers wanting to learn also about the AH protocol are encouraged to explore the RFCs and other online resources.

8.7.3 Security Associations

IPsec datagrams are sent between pairs of network entities, such as between two hosts, between two routers, or between a host and router. Before sending IPsec datagrams from source entity to destination entity, the source and destination entities create a network-layer logical connection. This logical connection is called a **security association (SA)**. An SA is a simplex logical connection; that is, it is unidirectional from source to destination. If both entities want to send secure datagrams to each other, then two SAs (that is, two logical connections) need to be established, one in each direction.

For example, consider once again the institutional VPN in Figure 8.27. This institution consists of a headquarters office, a branch office and, say, n traveling salespersons. For the sake of example, let's suppose that there is bi-directional IPsec traffic between headquarters and the branch office and bi-directional IPsec traffic between headquarters and the salespersons. In this VPN, how many SAs are there? To answer this question, note that there are two SAs between the headquarters gateway router and the branch-office gateway router (one in each direction); for each salesperson's laptop, there are two SAs between the headquarters gateway router and the laptop (again, one in each direction). So, in total, there are $(2 + 2n)$ SAs. *Keep in mind, however, that not all traffic sent into the Internet by the gateway routers or by the laptops will be IPsec secured.* For example, a host in headquarters may want to access a Web server (such as Amazon or Google) in the public Internet. Thus, the gateway router (and the laptops) will emit into the Internet both vanilla IPv4 datagrams and secured IPsec datagrams.

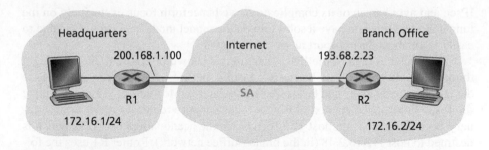

Figure 8.28 ♦ Security Association (SA) from R1 to R2

Let's now take a look "inside" an SA. To make the discussion tangible and concrete, let's do this in the context of an SA from router R1 to router R2 in Figure 8.28. (You can think of Router R1 as the headquarters gateway router and Router R2 as the branch office gateway router from Figure 8.27.) Router R1 will maintain state information about this SA, which will include:

- A 32-bit identifier for the SA, called the **Security Parameter Index (SPI)**
- The origin interface of the SA (in this case 200.168.1.100) and the destination interface of the SA (in this case 193.68.2.23)
- The type of encryption to be used (for example, 3DES with CBC)
- The encryption key
- The type of integrity check (for example, HMAC with MD5)
- The authentication key

Whenever router R1 needs to construct an IPsec datagram for forwarding over this SA, it accesses this state information to determine how it should authenticate and encrypt the datagram. Similarly, router R2 will maintain the same state information for this SA and will use this information to authenticate and decrypt any IPsec datagram that arrives from the SA.

An IPsec entity (router or host) often maintains state information for many SAs. For example, in the VPN example in Figure 8.27 with n salespersons, the headquarters gateway router maintains state information for $(2 + 2n)$ SAs. An IPsec entity stores the state information for all of its SAs in its **Security Association Database (SAD)**, which is a data structure in the entity's OS kernel.

8.7.4 The IPsec Datagram

Having now described SAs, we can now describe the actual IPsec datagram. IPsec has two different packet forms, one for the so-called **tunnel mode** and the other for the so-called **transport mode**. The tunnel mode, being more appropriate for VPNs, is more widely deployed than the transport mode. In order to further de-mystify

IPsec and avoid much of its complication, we henceforth focus exclusively on the tunnel mode. Once you have a solid grip on the tunnel mode, you should be able to easily learn about the transport mode on your own.

The packet format of the IPsec datagram is shown in Figure 8.29. You might think that packet formats are boring and insipid, but we will soon see that the IPsec datagram actually looks and tastes like a popular Tex-Mex delicacy! Let's examine the IPsec fields in the context of Figure 8.28. Suppose router R1 receives an ordinary IPv4 datagram from host 172.16.1.17 (in the headquarters network) which is destined to host 172.16.2.48 (in the branch-office network). Router R1 uses the following recipe to convert this "original IPv4 datagram" into an IPsec datagram:

- Appends to the back of the original IPv4 datagram (which includes the original header fields!) an "ESP trailer" field

- Encrypts the result using the algorithm and key specified by the SA

- Appends to the front of this encrypted quantity a field called "ESP header"; the resulting package is called the "enchilada"

- Creates an authentication MAC over the *whole enchilada* using the algorithm and key specified in the SA

- Appends the MAC to the back of the enchilada forming the *payload*

- Finally, creates a brand new IP header with all the classic IPv4 header fields (together normally 20 bytes long), which it appends before the payload

Note that the resulting IPsec datagram is a bona fide IPv4 datagram, with the traditional IPv4 header fields followed by a payload. But in this case, the payload contains an ESP header, the original IP datagram, an ESP trailer, and an ESP authentication field (with the original datagram and ESP trailer encrypted). The original IP datagram has 172.16.1.17 for the source IP address and 172.16.2.48 for the destination IP address. Because the IPsec datagram includes the original IP datagram, these addresses are included (and encrypted) as part of the payload of the IPsec packet. But what about the source and destination IP addresses that are in the new IP header, that is, in the left-most header of the IPsec datagram? As you might expect, they are set to the source and destination router interfaces at the two ends of the tunnels, namely, 200.168.1.100 and 193.68.2.23. Also, the protocol number in this new IPv4 header field is not set to that of TCP, UDP, or SMTP, but instead to 50, designating that this is an IPsec datagram using the ESP protocol.

After R1 sends the IPsec datagram into the public Internet, it will pass through many routers before reaching R2. Each of these routers will process the datagram as if it were an ordinary datagram—they are completely oblivious to the fact that the datagram is carrying IPsec-encrypted data. For these public Internet routers, because the destination IP address in the outer header is R2, the ultimate destination of the datagram is R2.

Having walked through an example of how an IPsec datagram is constructed, let's now take a closer look at the ingredients in the enchilada. We see in Figure 8.29

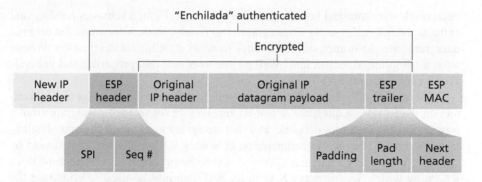

Figure 8.29 ♦ IPsec datagram format

that the ESP trailer consists of three fields: padding; pad length; and next header. Recall that block ciphers require the message to be encrypted to be an integer multiple of the block length. Padding (consisting of meaningless bytes) is used so that when added to the original datagram (along with the pad length and next header fields), the resulting "message" is an integer number of blocks. The pad-length field indicates to the receiving entity how much padding was inserted (and thus needs to be removed). The next header identifies the type (e.g., UDP) of data contained in the payload-data field. The payload data (typically the original IP datagram) and the ESP trailer are concatenated and then encrypted.

Appended to the front of this encrypted unit is the ESP header, which is sent in the clear and consists of two fields: the SPI and the sequence number field. The SPI indicates to the receiving entity the SA to which the datagram belongs; the receiving entity can then index its SAD with the SPI to determine the appropriate authentication/decryption algorithms and keys. The sequence number field is used to defend against replay attacks.

The sending entity also appends an authentication MAC. As stated earlier, the sending entity calculates a MAC over the whole enchilada (consisting of the ESP header, the original IP datagram, and the ESP trailer—with the datagram and trailer being encrypted). Recall that to calculate a MAC, the sender appends a secret MAC key to the enchilada and then calculates a fixed-length hash of the result.

When R2 receives the IPsec datagram, R2 observes that the destination IP address of the datagram is R2 itself. R2 therefore processes the datagram. Because the protocol field (in the left-most IP header) is 50, R2 sees that it should apply IPsec ESP processing to the datagram. First, peering into the enchilada, R2 uses the SPI to determine to which SA the datagram belongs. Second, it calculates the MAC of the enchilada and verifies that the MAC is consistent with the value in the ESP MAC field. If it is, it knows that the enchilada comes from R1 and has not been tampered with. Third, it checks the sequence-number field to verify that the datagram is fresh (and not a replayed datagram). Fourth, it decrypts the encrypted unit using the decryption algorithm and key associated with the SA. Fifth, it removes padding and extracts the original, vanilla IP datagram. And finally, sixth, it forwards the original datagram into the branch office network towards its ultimate destination. Whew, what a complicated recipe, huh? Well no one ever said that preparing and unraveling an enchilada was easy!

There is actually another important subtlety that needs to be addressed. It centers on the following question: When R1 receives an (unsecured) datagram from a host in the headquarters network, and that datagram is destined to some destination IP address outside of headquarters, how does R1 know whether it should be converted to an IPsec datagram? And if it is to be processed by IPsec, how does R1 know which SA (of many SAs in its SAD) should be used to construct the IPsec datagram? The problem is solved as follows. Along with a SAD, the IPsec entity also maintains another data structure called the **Security Policy Database (SPD)**. The SPD indicates what types of datagrams (as a function of source IP address, destination IP address, and protocol type) are to be IPsec processed; and for those that are to be IPsec processed, which SA should be used. In a sense, the information in a SPD indicates "what" to do with an arriving datagram; the information in the SAD indicates "how" to do it.

Summary of IPsec Services

So what services does IPsec provide, exactly? Let us examine these services from the perspective of an attacker, say Trudy, who is a woman-in-the-middle, sitting somewhere on the path between R1 and R2 in Figure 8.28. Assume throughout this discussion that Trudy does not know the authentication and encryption keys used by the SA. What can and cannot Trudy do? First, Trudy cannot see the original datagram. If fact, not only is the data in the original datagram hidden from Trudy, but so is the protocol number, the source IP address, and the destination IP address. For datagrams sent over the SA, Trudy only knows that the datagram originated from some host in 172.16.1.0/24 and is destined to some host in 172.16.2.0/24. She does not know if it is carrying TCP, UDP, or ICMP data; she does not know if it is carrying HTTP, SMTP, or some other type of application data. This confidentiality thus goes a lot farther than SSL. Second, suppose Trudy tries to tamper with a datagram in the SA by flipping some of its bits. When this tampered datagram arrives at R2, it will fail the integrity check (using the MAC), thwarting Trudy's vicious attempts once again. Third, suppose Trudy tries to masquerade as R1, creating a IPsec datagram with source 200.168.1.100 and destination 193.68.2.23. Trudy's attack will be futile, as this datagram will again fail the integrity check at R2. Finally, because IPsec includes sequence numbers, Trudy will not be able create a successful replay attack. In summary, as claimed at the beginning of this section, IPsec provides— between any pair of devices that process packets through the network layer— confidentiality, source authentication, data integrity, and replay-attack prevention.

8.7.5 IKE: Key Management in IPsec

When a VPN has a small number of end points (for example, just two routers as in Figure 8.28), the network administrator can manually enter the SA information (encryption/authentication algorithms and keys, and the SPIs) into the SADs of the endpoints. Such "manual keying" is clearly impractical for a large VPN, which may consist of hundreds or even thousands of IPsec routers and hosts. Large, geographically distributed deployments require an automated mechanism for creating the SAs. IPsec does this with the Internet Key Exchange (IKE) protocol, specified in RFC 5996.

IKE has some similarities with the handshake in SSL (see Section 8.6). Each IPsec entity has a certificate, which includes the entity's public key. As with SSL, the IKE protocol has the two entities exchange certificates, negotiate authentication and encryption algorithms, and securely exchange key material for creating session keys in the IPsec SAs. Unlike SSL, IKE employs two phases to carry out these tasks.

Let's investigate these two phases in the context of two routers, R1 and R2, in Figure 8.28. The first phase consists of two exchanges of message pairs between R1 and R2:

- During the first exchange of messages, the two sides use Diffie-Hellman (see Homework Problems) to create a bi-directional **IKE SA** between the routers. To keep us all confused, this bi-directional IKE SA is entirely different from the IPsec SAs discussed in Sections 8.6.3 and 8.6.4. The IKE SA provides an authenticated and encrypted channel between the two routers. During this first message-pair exchange, keys are established for encryption and authentication for the IKE SA. Also established is a master secret that will be used to compute IPSec SA keys later in phase 2. Observe that during this first step, RSA public and private keys are not used. In particular, neither R1 nor R2 reveals its identity by signing a message with its private key.

- During the second exchange of messages, both sides reveal their identity to each other by signing their messages. However, the identities are not revealed to a passive sniffer, since the messages are sent over the secured IKE SA channel. Also during this phase, the two sides negotiate the IPsec encryption and authentication algorithms to be employed by the IPsec SAs.

In phase 2 of IKE, the two sides create an SA in each direction. At the end of phase 2, the encryption and authentication session keys are established on both sides for the two SAs. The two sides can then use the SAs to send secured datagrams, as described in Sections 8.7.3 and 8.7.4. The primary motivation for having two phases in IKE is computational cost—since the second phase doesn't involve any public-key cryptography, IKE can generate a large number of SAs between the two IPsec entities with relatively little computational cost.

8.8 Securing Wireless LANs

Security is a particularly important concern in wireless networks, where radio waves carrying frames can propagate far beyond the building containing the wireless base station and hosts. In this section we present a brief introduction to wireless security. For a more in-depth treatment, see the highly readable book by Edney and Arbaugh [Edney 2003].

The issue of security in 802.11 has attracted considerable attention in both technical circles and in the media. While there has been considerable discussion, there has been little debate—there seems to be universal agreement that the original 802.11 specification contains a number of serious security flaws. Indeed, public domain software can now be downloaded that exploits these holes, making those who use the vanilla 802.11 security mechanisms as open to security attacks as users who use no security features at all.

In the following section, we discuss the security mechanisms initially standardized in the 802.11 specification, known collectively as **Wired Equivalent Privacy (WEP)**. As the name suggests, WEP is meant to provide a level of security similar to that found in wired networks. We'll then discuss a few of the security holes in WEP and discuss the 802.11i standard, a fundamentally more secure version of 802.11 adopted in 2004.

8.8.1 Wired Equivalent Privacy (WEP)

The IEEE 802.11 WEP protocol was designed in 1999 to provide authentication and data encryption between a host and a wireless access point (that is, base station) using a symmetric shared key approach. WEP does not specify a key management algorithm, so it is assumed that the host and wireless access point have somehow agreed on the key via an out-of-band method. Authentication is carried out as follows:

1. A wireless host requests authentication by an access point.
2. The access point responds to the authentication request with a 128-byte nonce value.
3. The wireless host encrypts the nonce using the symmetric key that it shares with the access point.
4. The access point decrypts the host-encrypted nonce.

If the decrypted nonce matches the nonce value originally sent to the host, then the host is authenticated by the access point.

The WEP data encryption algorithm is illustrated in Figure 8.30. A secret 40-bit symmetric key, K_S, is assumed to be known by both a host and the access point. In addition, a 24-bit Initialization Vector (IV) is appended to the 40-bit key to create a 64-bit key that will be used to encrypt a single frame. The IV will change from one

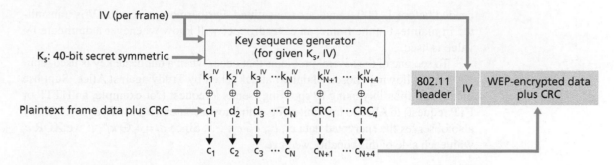

Figure 8.30 ♦ 802.11 WEP protocol

frame to another, and hence each frame will be encrypted with a different 64-bit key. Encryption is performed as follows. First a 4-byte CRC value (see Section 5.2) is computed for the data payload. The payload and the four CRC bytes are then encrypted using the RC4 stream cipher. We will not cover the details of RC4 here (see [Schneier 1995] and [Edney 2003] for details). For our purposes, it is enough to know that when presented with a key value (in this case, the 64-bit (K_S, IV) key), the RC4 algorithm produces a stream of key values, k_1^{IV}, k_2^{IV}, k_3^{IV}, . . . that are used to encrypt the data and CRC value in a frame. For practical purposes, we can think of these operations being performed a byte at a time. Encryption is performed by XOR-ing the ith byte of data, d_i, with the ith key, k_i^{IV}, in the stream of key values generated by the (K_S,IV) pair to produce the ith byte of ciphertext, c_i:

$$c_i = d_i \oplus k_i^{IV}$$

The IV value changes from one frame to the next and is included *in plaintext* in the header of each WEP-encrypted 802.11 frame, as shown in Figure 8.30. The receiver takes the secret 40-bit symmetric key that it shares with the sender, appends the IV, and uses the resulting 64-bit key (which is identical to the key used by the sender to perform encryption) to decrypt the frame:

$$d_i = c_i \oplus k_i^{IV}$$

Proper use of the RC4 algorithm requires that the same 64-bit key value *never* be used more than once. Recall that the WEP key changes on a frame-by-frame basis. For a given K_S (which changes rarely, if ever), this means that there are only 2^{24} unique keys. If these keys are chosen randomly, we can show [Walker 2000; Edney 2003] that the probability of having chosen the same IV value (and hence used the same 64-bit key) is more than 99 percent after only 12,000 frames. With 1 Kbyte frame sizes and a data transmission rate of 11 Mbps, only a few seconds are needed before 12,000 frames are transmitted. Furthermore, since the IV is transmitted in plaintext in the frame, an eavesdropper will know whenever a duplicate IV value is used.

To see one of the several problems that occur when a duplicate key is used, consider the following chosen-plaintext attack taken by Trudy against Alice. Suppose that Trudy (possibly using IP spoofing) sends a request (for example, an HTTP or FTP request) to Alice to transmit a file with known content, $d_1, d_2, d_3, d_4, \ldots$. Trudy also observes the encrypted data $c_1, c_2, c_3, c_4, \ldots$. Since $d_i = c_i \oplus k_i^{IV}$, if we XOR c_i with each side of this equality we have

$$d_i \oplus c_i = k_i^{IV}$$

With this relationship, Trudy can use the known values of d_i and c_i to compute k_i^{IV}. The next time Trudy sees the same value of IV being used, she will know the key sequence $k_1^{IV}, k_2^{IV}, k_3^{IV}, \ldots$ and will thus be able to decrypt the encrypted message.

There are several additional security concerns with WEP as well. [Fluhrer 2001] described an attack exploiting a known weakness in RC4 when certain weak keys are chosen. [Stubblefield 2002] discusses efficient ways to implement and exploit this attack. Another concern with WEP involves the CRC bits shown in Figure 8.30 and transmitted in the 802.11 frame to detect altered bits in the payload. However, an attacker who changes the encrypted content (e.g., substituting gibberish for the original encrypted data), computes a CRC over the substituted gibberish, and places the CRC into a WEP frame can produce an 802.11 frame that will be accepted by the receiver. What is needed here are message integrity techniques such as those we studied in Section 8.3 to detect content tampering or substitution. For more details of WEP security, see [Edney 2003; Walker 2000; Weatherspoon 2000] and the references therein.

8.8.2 IEEE 802.11i

Soon after the 1999 release of IEEE 802.11, work began on developing a new and improved version of 802.11 with stronger security mechanisms. The new standard, known as 802.11i, underwent final ratification in 2004. As we'll see, while WEP provided relatively weak encryption, only a single way to perform authentication, and no key distribution mechanisms, IEEE 802.11i provides for much stronger forms of encryption, an extensible set of authentication mechanisms, and a key distribution mechanism. In the following, we present an overview of 802.11i; an excellent (streaming audio) technical overview of 802.11i is [TechOnline 2012].

Figure 8.31 overviews the 802.11i framework. In addition to the wireless client and access point, 802.11i defines an authentication server with which the AP can communicate. Separating the authentication server from the AP allows one authentication server to serve many APs, centralizing the (often sensitive) decisions

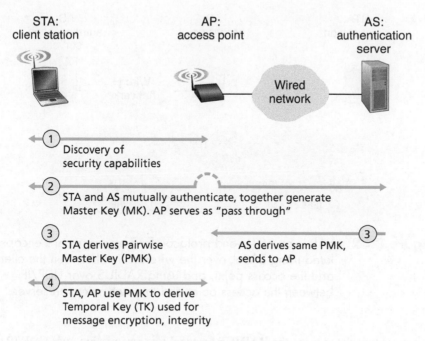

STA:
client station

AP:
access point

AS:
authentication
server

Wired
network

① Discovery of
security capabilities

② STA and AS mutually authenticate, together generate
Master Key (MK). AP serves as "pass through"

③ STA derives Pairwise
Master Key (PMK)

③ AS derives same PMK,
sends to AP

④ STA, AP use PMK to derive
Temporal Key (TK) used for
message encryption, integrity

Figure 8.31 ♦ 802.11i: four phases of operation

regarding authentication and access within the single server, and keeping AP costs
and complexity low. 802.11i operates in four phases:

1. *Discovery.* In the discovery phase, the AP advertises its presence and the forms
   of authentication and encryption that can be provided to the wireless client
   node. The client then requests the specific forms of authentication and encryption that it desires. Although the client and AP are already exchanging messages, the client has not yet been authenticated nor does it have an encryption
   key, and so several more steps will be required before the client can communicate with an arbitrary remote host over the wireless channel.
2. *Mutual authentication and Master Key (MK) generation.* Authentication takes
   place between the wireless client and the authentication server. In this phase,
   the access point acts essentially as a relay, forwarding messages between the
   client and the authentication server. The **Extensible Authentication Protocol
   (EAP)** [RFC 3748] defines the end-to-end message formats used in a simple
   request/response mode of interaction between the client and authentication
   server. As shown in Figure 8.32 EAP messages are encapsulated using
   EAPoL (EAP over LAN, [IEEE 802.1X]) and sent over the 802.11 wireless
   link. These EAP messages are then decapsulated at the access point, and then

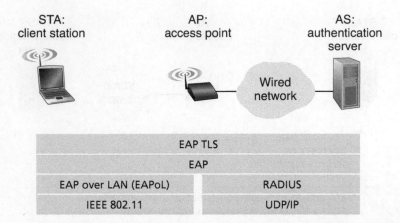

Figure 8.32 ♦ EAP is an end-to-end protocol. EAP messages are encapsulated using EAPoL over the wireless link between the client and the access point, and using RADIUS over UDP/IP between the access point and the authentication server

re-encapsulated using the **RADIUS** protocol for transmission over UDP/IP to the authentication server. While the RADIUS server and protocol [RFC 2865] are not required by the 802.11i protocol, they are *de facto* standard components for 802.11i. The recently standardized **DIAMETER** protocol [RFC 3588] is likely to replace RADIUS in the near future.

With EAP, the authentication server can choose one of a number of ways to perform authentication. While 802.11i does not mandate a particular authentication method, the EAP-TLS authentication scheme [RFC 5216] is often used. EAP-TLS uses public key techniques (including nonce encryption and message digests) similar to those we studied in Section 8.3 to allow the client and the authentication server to mutually authenticate each other, and to derive a Master Key (MK) that is known to both parties.

3. *Pairwise Master Key (PMK) generation.* The MK is a shared secret known only to the client and the authentication server, which they each use to generate a second key, the Pairwise Master Key (PMK). The authentication server then sends the PMK to the AP. This is where we wanted to be! The client and AP now have a shared key (recall that in WEP, the problem of key distribution was not addressed at all) and have mutually authenticated each other. They're just about ready to get down to business.

4. *Temporal Key (TK) generation.* With the PMK, the wireless client and AP can now generate additional keys that will be used for communication. Of particular interest is the Temporal Key (TK), which will be used to perform the link-level encryption of data sent over the wireless link and to an arbitrary remote host.

802.11i provides several forms of encryption, including an AES-based encryption scheme and a strengthened version of WEP encryption.

8.9 Operational Security: Firewalls and Intrusion Detection Systems

We've seen throughout this chapter that the Internet is not a very safe place—bad guys are out there, wreaking all sorts of havoc. Given the hostile nature of the Internet, let's now consider an organization's network and the network administrator who administers it. From a network administrator's point of view, the world divides quite neatly into two camps—the good guys (who belong to the organization's network, and who should be able to access resources inside the organization's network in a relatively unconstrained manner) and the bad guys (everyone else, whose access to network resources must be carefully scrutinized). In many organizations, ranging from medieval castles to modern corporate office buildings, there is a single point of entry/exit where both good guys and bad guys entering and leaving the organization are security-checked. In a castle, this was done at a gate at one end of the drawbridge; in a corporate building, this is done at the security desk. In a computer network, when traffic entering/leaving a network is security-checked, logged, dropped, or forwarded, it is done by operational devices known as firewalls, intrusion detection systems (IDSs), and intrusion prevention systems (IPSs).

8.9.1 Firewalls

A **firewall** is a combination of hardware and software that isolates an organization's internal network from the Internet at large, allowing some packets to pass and blocking others. A firewall allows a network administrator to control access between the outside world and resources within the administered network by managing the traffic flow to and from these resources. A firewall has three goals:

* *All traffic from outside to inside, and vice versa, passes through the firewall.* Figure 8.33 shows a firewall, sitting squarely at the boundary between the administered network and the rest of the Internet. While large organizations may use multiple levels of firewalls or distributed firewalls [Skoudis 2006], locating a firewall at a single access point to the network, as shown in Figure 8.33, makes it easier to manage and enforce a security-access policy.

* *Only authorized traffic, as defined by the local security policy, will be allowed to pass.* With all traffic entering and leaving the institutional network passing through the firewall, the firewall can restrict access to authorized traffic.

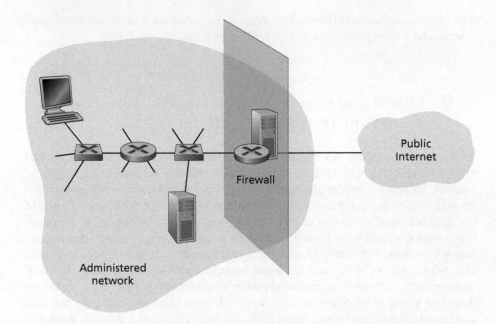

Figure 8.33 ♦ Firewall placement between the administered network and the outside world

- *The firewall itself is immune to penetration.* The firewall itself is a device connected to the network. If not designed or installed properly, it can be compromised, in which case it provides only a false sense of security (which is worse than no firewall at all!).

Cisco and Check Point are two of the leading firewall vendors today. You can also easily create a firewall (packet filter) from a Linux box using iptables (public-domain software that is normally shipped with Linux).

Firewalls can be classified in three categories: **traditional packet filters**, **stateful filters**, and **application gateways**. We'll cover each of these in turn in the following subsections.

Traditional Packet Filters

As shown in Figure 8.33, an organization typically has a gateway router connecting its internal network to its ISP (and hence to the larger public Internet). All traffic leaving and entering the internal network passes through this router, and it is at this router where **packet filtering** occurs. A packet filter examines each datagram in isolation, determining whether the datagram should be allowed to pass or should be dropped based on administrator-specific rules. Filtering decisions are typically based on:

- IP source or destination address
- Protocol type in IP datagram field: TCP, UDP, ICMP, OSPF, and so on
- TCP or UDP source and destination port
- TCP flag bits: SYN, ACK, and so on
- ICMP message type
- Different rules for datagrams leaving and entering the network
- Different rules for the different router interfaces

A network administrator configures the firewall based on the policy of the organization. The policy may take user productivity and bandwidth usage into account as well as the security concerns of an organization. Table 8.5 lists a number of possible polices an organization may have, and how they would be addressed with a packet filter. For example, if the organization doesn't want any incoming TCP connections except those for its public Web server, it can block all incoming TCP SYN segments except TCP SYN segments with destination port 80 and the destination IP address corresponding to the Web server. If the organization doesn't want its users to monopolize access bandwidth with Internet radio applications, it can block all not-critical UDP traffic (since Internet radio is often sent over UDP). If the organization doesn't want its internal network to be mapped (tracerouted) by an outsider, it can block all ICMP TTL expired messages leaving the organization's network.

A filtering policy can be based on a combination of addresses and port numbers. For example, a filtering router could forward all Telnet datagrams (those with a port number of 23) except those going to and coming from a list of specific IP addresses. This policy permits Telnet connections to and from hosts on the allowed

Policy	Firewall Setting
No outside Web access.	Drop all outgoing packets to any IP address, port 80
No incoming TCP connections, except those for organization's public Web server only.	Drop all incoming TCP SYN packets to any IP except 130.207.244.203, port 80
Prevent Web-radios from eating up the available bandwidth.	Drop all incoming UDP packets — except DNS packets.
Prevent your network from being used for a smurf DoS attack.	Drop all ICMP ping packets going to a "broadcast" address (eg 130.207.255.255).
Prevent your network from being tracerouted	Drop all outgoing ICMP TTL expired traffic

Table 8.5 ♦ Policies and corresponding filtering rules for an organization's network 130.207/16 with Web server at 130.207.244.203

list. Unfortunately, basing the policy on external addresses provides no protection against datagrams that have had their source addresses spoofed.

Filtering can also be based on whether or not the TCP ACK bit is set. This trick is quite useful if an organization wants to let its internal clients connect to external servers but wants to prevent external clients from connecting to internal servers. Recall from Section 3.5 that the first segment in every TCP connection has the ACK bit set to 0, whereas all the other segments in the connection have the ACK bit set to 1. Thus, if an organization wants to prevent external clients from initiating connections to internal servers, it simply filters all incoming segments with the ACK bit set to 0. This policy kills all TCP connections originating from the outside, but permits connections originating internally.

Firewall rules are implemented in routers with access control lists, with each router interface having its own list. An example of an access control list for an organization 222.22/16 is shown in Table 8.6. This access control list is for an interface that connects the router to the organization's external ISPs. Rules are applied to each datagram that passes through the interface from top to bottom. The first two rules together allow internal users to surf the Web: The first rule allows any TCP packet with destination port 80 to leave the organization's network; the second rule allows any TCP packet with source port 80 and the ACK bit set to enter the organization's network. Note that if an external source attempts to establish a TCP connection with an internal host, the connection will be blocked, even if the source or destination port is 80. The second two rules together allow DNS packets to enter and leave the organization's network. In summary, this rather restrictive access control list blocks all traffic except Web traffic initiated from within the organization and DNS traffic. [CERT Filtering 2012] provides a list of recommended port/protocol packet filterings to avoid a number of well-known security holes in existing network applications.

action	source address	dest address	protocol	source port	dest port	flag bit
allow	222.22/16	outside of 222.22/16	TCP	> 1023	80	any
allow	outside of 222.22/16	222.22/16	TCP	80	> 1023	ACK
allow	222.22/16	outside of 222.22/16	UDP	> 1023	53	—
allow	outside of 222.22/16	222.22/16	UDP	53	> 1023	—
deny	all	all	all	all	all	all

Table 8.6 ◆ An access control list for a router interface

Stateful Packet Filters

In a traditional packet filter, filtering decisions are made on each packet in isolation. Stateful filters actually track TCP connections, and use this knowledge to make filtering decisions.

To understand stateful filters, let's reexamine the access control list in Table 8.6. Although rather restrictive, the access control list in Table 8.6 nevertheless allows any packet arriving from the outside with ACK = 1 and source port 80 to get through the filter. Such packets could be used by attackers in attempts to crash internal systems with malformed packets, carry out denial-of-service attacks, or map the internal network. The naive solution is to block TCP ACK packets as well, but such an approach would prevent the organization's internal users from surfing the Web.

Stateful filters solve this problem by tracking all ongoing TCP connections in a connection table. This is possible because the firewall can observe the beginning of a new connection by observing a three-way handshake (SYN, SYNACK, and ACK); and it can observe the end of a connection when it sees a FIN packet for the connection. The firewall can also (conservatively) assume that the connection is over when it hasn't seen any activity over the connection for, say, 60 seconds. An example connection table for a firewall is shown in Table 8.7. This connection table indicates that there are currently three ongoing TCP connections, all of which have been initiated from within the organization. Additionally, the stateful filter includes a new column, "check connection," in its access control list, as shown in Table 8.8. Note that Table 8.8 is identical to the access control list in Table 8.6, except now it indicates that the connection should be checked for two of the rules.

Let's walk through some examples to see how the connection table and the extended access control list work hand-in-hand. Suppose an attacker attempts to send a malformed packet into the organization's network by sending a datagram with TCP source port 80 and with the ACK flag set. Further suppose that this packet has source port number 12543 and source IP address 150.23.23.155. When this packet reaches the firewall, the firewall checks the access control list in Table 8.7, which indicates that the connection table must also be checked before permitting this packet to enter the organization's network. The firewall duly checks the connection table, sees that this packet is not part of an ongoing TCP connection, and rejects

source address	dest address	source port	dest port
222.22.1.7	37.96.87.123	12699	80
222.22.93.2	199.1.205.23	37654	80
222.22.65.143	203.77.240.43	48712	80

Table 8.7 ♦ Connection table for stateful filter

action	source address	dest address	protocol	source port	dest port	flag bit	check conxion
allow	222.22/16	outside of 222.22/16	TCP	>1023	80	any	
allow	outside of 222.22/16	222.22/16	TCP	80	>1023	ACK	X
allow	222.22/16	outside of 222.22/16	UDP	>1023	53	—	
allow	outside of 222.22/16	222.22/16	UDP	53	>1023	—	X
deny	all	all	all	all	all	all	all

Table 8.8 ♦ Access control list for stateful filter

the packet. As a second example, suppose that an internal user wants to surf an external Web site. Because this user first sends a TCP SYN segment, the user's TCP connection gets recorded in the connection table. When the Web server sends back packets (with the ACK bit necessarily set), the firewall checks the table and sees that a corresponding connection is in progress. The firewall will thus let these packets pass, thereby not interfering with the internal user's Web surfing activity.

Application Gateway

In the examples above, we have seen that packet-level filtering allows an organization to perform coarse-grain filtering on the basis of the contents of IP and TCP/UDP headers, including IP addresses, port numbers, and acknowledgment bits. But what if an organization wants to provide a Telnet service to a restricted set of internal users (as opposed to IP addresses)? And what if the organization wants such privileged users to authenticate themselves first before being allowed to create Telnet sessions to the outside world? Such tasks are beyond the capabilities of traditional and stateful filters. Indeed, information about the identity of the internal users is application-layer data and is not included in the IP/TCP/UDP headers.

To have finer-level security, firewalls must combine packet filters with application gateways. Application gateways look beyond the IP/TCP/UDP headers and make policy decisions based on application data. An **application gateway** is an application-specific server through which all application data (inbound and outbound) must pass. Multiple application gateways can run on the same host, but each gateway is a separate server with its own processes.

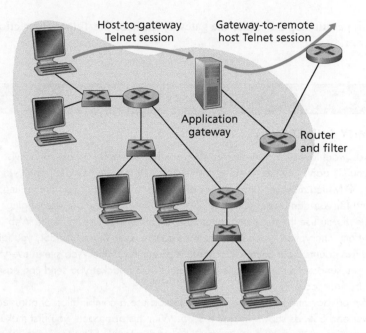

Figure 8.34 ♦ Firewall consisting of an application gateway and a filter

To get some insight into application gateways, let's design a firewall that allows only a restricted set of internal users to Telnet outside and prevents all external clients from Telneting inside. Such a policy can be accomplished by implementing a combination of a packet filter (in a router) and a Telnet application gateway, as shown in Figure 8.34. The router's filter is configured to block all Telnet connections except those that originate from the IP address of the application gateway. Such a filter configuration forces all outbound Telnet connections to pass through the application gateway. Consider now an internal user who wants to Telnet to the outside world. The user must first set up a Telnet session with the application gateway. An application running in the gateway, which listens for incoming Telnet sessions, prompts the user for a user ID and password. When the user supplies this information, the application gateway checks to see if the user has permission to Telnet to the outside world. If not, the Telnet connection from the internal user to the gateway is terminated by the gateway. If the user has permission, then the gateway (1) prompts the user for the host name of the external host to which the user wants to connect, (2) sets up a Telnet session between the gateway and the external host, and (3) relays to the external host all data arriving from the user, and relays to the user all data arriving from the external host. Thus, the Telnet application gateway not only performs user authorization but also acts as a Telnet server and a Telnet client, relaying information between the user and the remote Telnet server. Note that the filter will permit step 2 because the gateway initiates the Telnet connection to the outside world.

CASE HISTORY

ANONYMITY AND PRIVACY

Suppose you want to visit a controversial Web site (for example, a political activist site) and you (1) don't want to reveal your IP address to the Web site, (2) don't want your local ISP (which may be your home or office ISP) to know that you are visiting the site, and (3) you don't want your local ISP to see the data you are exchanging with the site. If you use the traditional approach of connecting directly to the Web site without any encryption, you fail on all three counts. Even if you use SSL, you fail on the first two counts: Your source IP address is presented to the Web site in every datagram you send; and the destination address of every packet you send can easily be sniffed by your local ISP.

To obtain privacy and anonymity, you can instead use a combination of a trusted proxy server and SSL, as shown in Figure 8.35. With this approach, you first make an SSL connection to the trusted proxy. You then send, into this SSL connection, an HTTP request for a page at the desired site. When the proxy receives the SSL-encrypted HTTP request, it decrypts the request and forwards the cleartext HTTP request to the Web site. The Web site then responds to the proxy, which in turn forwards the response to you over SSL. Because the Web site only sees the IP address of the proxy, and not of your client's address, you are indeed obtaining anonymous access to the Web site. And because all traffic between you and the proxy is encrypted, your local ISP cannot invade your privacy by logging the site you visited or recording the data you are exchanging. Many companies today (such as proxify.com) make available such proxy services.

Of course, in this solution, your proxy knows everything: It knows your IP address and the IP address of the site you're surfing; and it can see all the traffic in cleartext exchanged between you and the Web site. Such a solution, therefore, is only as good as the trustworthiness of the proxy. A more robust approach, taken by the TOR anonymizing and privacy service, is to route your traffic through a series of non-colluding proxy servers [TOR 2012]. In particular, TOR allows independent individuals to contribute proxies to its proxy pool. When a user connects to a server using TOR, TOR randomly chooses (from its proxy pool) a chain of three proxies and routes all traffic between client and server over the chain. In this manner, assuming the proxies do not collude, no one knows that communication took place between your IP address and the target Web site. Furthermore, although cleartext is sent between the last proxy and the server, the last proxy doesn't know what IP address is sending and receiving the cleartext.

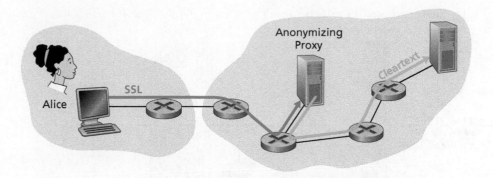

Figure 8.35 ♦ Providing anonymity and privacy with a proxy

Internal networks often have multiple application gateways, for example, gateways for Telnet, HTTP, FTP, and e-mail. In fact, an organization's mail server (see Section 2.4) and Web cache are application gateways.

Application gateways do not come without their disadvantages. First, a different application gateway is needed for each application. Second, there is a performance penalty to be paid, since all data will be relayed via the gateway. This becomes a concern particularly when multiple users or applications are using the same gateway machine. Finally, the client software must know how to contact the gateway when the user makes a request, and must know how to tell the application gateway what external server to connect to.

8.9.2 Intrusion Detection Systems

We've just seen that a packet filter (traditional and stateful) inspects IP, TCP, UDP, and ICMP header fields when deciding which packets to let pass through the firewall. However, to detect many attack types, we need to perform **deep packet inspection,** that is, look beyond the header fields and into the actual application data that the packets carry. As we saw in Section 8.9.1, application gateways often do deep packet inspection. But an application gateway only does this for a specific application.

Clearly, there is a niche for yet another device—a device that not only examines the headers of all packets passing through it (like a packet filter), but also performs deep packet inspection (unlike a packet filter). When such a device observes a suspicious packet, or a suspicious series of packets, it could prevent those packets from entering the organizational network. Or, because the activity is only deemed as suspicious, the device could let the packets pass, but send alerts to a network administrator, who can then take a closer look at the traffic and take appropriate

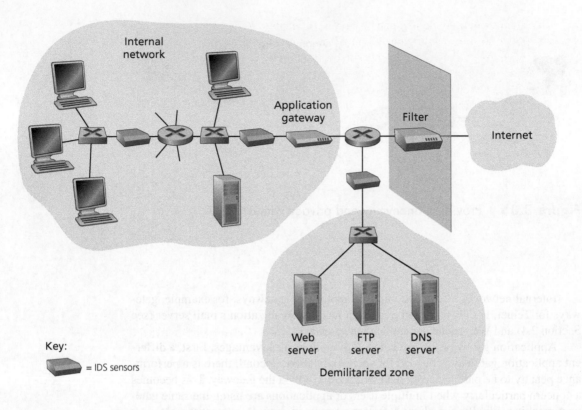

Figure 8.36 ♦ An organization deploying a filter, an application gateway, and IDS sensors

actions. A device that generates alerts when it observes potentially malicious traffic is called an **intrusion detection system (IDS)**. A device that filters out suspicious traffic is called an **intrusion prevention system (IPS)**. In this section we study both systems—IDS and IPS—together, since the most interesting technical aspect of these systems is how they detect suspicious traffic (and not whether they send alerts or drop packets). We will henceforth collectively refer to IDS systems and IPS systems as IDS systems.

An IDS can be used to detect a wide range of attacks, including network mapping (emanating, for example, from nmap), port scans, TCP stack scans, DoS bandwidth-flooding attacks, worms and viruses, OS vulnerability attacks, and application vulnerability attacks. (See Section 1.6 for a survey of network attacks.) Today, thousands of organizations employ IDS systems. Many of these deployed systems are proprietary, marketed by Cisco, Check Point, and other security equipment vendors. But many of the deployed IDS systems are public-domain systems, such as the immensely popular Snort IDS system (which we'll discuss shortly).

An organization may deploy one or more IDS sensors in its organizational network. Figure 8.36 shows an organization that has three IDS sensors. When multiple sensors are deployed, they typically work in concert, sending information about suspicious traffic activity to a central IDS processor, which collects and integrates the information and sends alarms to network administrators when deemed appropriate. In Figure 8.36, the organization has partitioned its network into two regions: a high-security region, protected by a packet filter and an application gateway and monitored by IDS sensors; and a lower-security region—referred to as the **demilitarized zone (DMZ)**—which is protected only by the packet filter, but also monitored by IDS sensors. Note that the DMZ includes the organization's servers that need to communicate with the outside world, such as its public Web server and its authoritative DNS server.

You may be wondering at this stage, why multiple IDS sensors? Why not just place one IDS sensor just behind the packet filter (or even integrated with the packet filter) in Figure 8.36? We will soon see that an IDS not only needs to do deep packet inspection, but must also compare each passing packet with tens of thousands of "signatures"; this can be a significant amount of processing, particularly if the organization receives gigabits/sec of traffic from the Internet. By placing the IDS sensors further downstream, each sensor sees only a fraction of the organization's traffic, and can more easily keep up. Nevertheless, high-performance IDS and IPS systems are available today, and many organizations can actually get by with just one sensor located near its access router.

IDS systems are broadly classified as either **signature-based systems** or **anomaly-based systems**. A signature-based IDS maintains an extensive database of attack signatures. Each signature is a set of rules pertaining to an intrusion activity. A signature may simply be a list of characteristics about a single packet (e.g., source and destination port numbers, protocol type, and a specific string of bits in the packet payload), or may relate to a series of packets. The signatures are normally created by skilled network security engineers who research known attacks. An organization's network administrator can customize the signatures or add its own to the database.

Operationally, a signature-based IDS sniffs every packet passing by it, comparing each sniffed packet with the signatures in its database. If a packet (or series of packets) matches a signature in the database, the IDS generates an alert. The alert could be sent to the network administrator in an e-mail message, could be sent to the network management system, or could simply be logged for future inspection.

Signature-based IDS systems, although widely deployed, have a number of limitations. Most importantly, they require previous knowledge of the attack to generate an accurate signature. In other words, a signature-based IDS is completely blind to new attacks that have yet to be recorded. Another disadvantage is that even if a signature is matched, it may not be the result of an attack, so that a false alarm is generated. Finally, because every packet must be compared with an extensive collection of signatures, the IDS can become overwhelmed with processing and actually fail to detect many malicious packets.

An anomaly-based IDS creates a traffic profile as it observes traffic in normal operation. It then looks for packet streams that are statistically unusual, for example, an inordinate percentage of ICMP packets or a sudden exponential growth in port scans and ping sweeps. The great thing about anomaly-based IDS systems is that they don't rely on previous knowledge about existing attacks—that is, they can potentially detect new, undocumented attacks. On the other hand, it is an extremely challenging problem to distinguish between normal traffic and statistically unusual traffic. To date, most IDS deployments are primarily signature-based, although some include some anomaly-based features.

Snort

Snort is a public-domain, open source IDS with hundreds of thousands of existing deployments [Snort 2012; Koziol 2003]. It can run on Linux, UNIX, and Windows platforms. It uses the generic sniffing interface libpcap, which is also used by Wireshark and many other packet sniffers. It can easily handle 100 Mbps of traffic; for installations with gibabit/sec traffic rates, multiple Snort sensors may be needed.

To gain some insight into Snort, let's take a look at an example of a Snort signature:

```
alert icmp $EXTERNAL_NET any -> $HOME_NET any
(msg:"ICMP PING NMAP"; dsize: 0; itype: 8;)
```

This signature is matched by any ICMP packet that enters the organization's network (`$HOME_NET`) from the outside (`$EXTERNAL_NET`), is of type 8 (ICMP ping), and has an empty payload (dsize = 0). Since nmap (see Section 1.6) generates ping packets with these specific characteristics, this signature is designed to detect nmap ping sweeps. When a packet matches this signature, Snort generates an alert that includes the message `"ICMP PING NMAP"`.

Perhaps what is most impressive about Snort is the vast community of users and security experts that maintain its signature database. Typically within a few hours of a new attack, the Snort community writes and releases an attack signature, which is then downloaded by the hundreds of thousands of Snort deployments distributed around the world. Moreover, using the Snort signature syntax, network administrators can tailor the signatures to their own organization's needs by either modifying existing signatures or creating entirely new ones.

8.10 Summary

In this chapter, we've examined the various mechanisms that our secret lovers, Bob and Alice, can use to communicate securely. We've seen that Bob and Alice are interested in confidentiality (so they alone are able to understand the contents of a transmitted message), end-point authentication (so they are sure that they are talking with each other), and message integrity (so they are sure that their messages are not altered in transit). Of course, the need for secure communication is not confined to secret lovers. Indeed, we saw in Sections 8.5 through 8.8 that security can be used in various layers in a network architecture to protect against bad guys who have a large arsenal of possible attacks at hand.

The first part of this chapter presented various principles underlying secure communication. In Section 8.2, we covered cryptographic techniques for encrypting and decrypting data, including symmetric key cryptography and public key cryptography. DES and RSA were examined as specific case studies of these two major classes of cryptographic techniques in use in today's networks.

In Section 8.3, we examined two approaches for providing message integrity: message authentication codes (MACs) and digital signatures. The two approaches have a number of parallels. Both use cryptographic hash functions and both techniques enable us to verify the source of the message as well as the integrity of the message itself. One important difference is that MACs do not rely on encryption whereas digital signatures require a public key infrastructure. Both techniques are extensively used in practice, as we saw in Sections 8.5 through 8.8. Furthermore, digital signatures are used to create digital certificates, which are important for verifying the validity of public keys. In Section 8.4, we examined endpoint authentication and introduced nonces to defend against the replay attack.

In Sections 8.5 through 8.8 we examined several security networking protocols that enjoy extensive use in practice. We saw that symmetric key cryptography is at the core of PGP, SSL, IPsec, and wireless security. We saw that public key cryptography is crucial for both PGP and SSL. We saw that PGP uses digital signatures for message integrity, whereas SSL and IPsec use MACs. Having now an understanding of the basic principles of cryptography, and having studied how these principles are actually used, you are now in position to design your own secure network protocols!

Armed with the techniques covered in Sections 8.2 through 8.8, Bob and Alice can communicate securely. (One can only hope that they are networking students who have learned this material and can thus avoid having their tryst uncovered by Trudy!) But confidentiality is only a small part of the network security picture. As we learned in Section 8.9, increasingly, the focus in network security has been on securing the network infrastructure against a potential onslaught by the bad guys. In the latter part of this chapter, we thus covered firewalls and IDS systems which inspect packets entering and leaving an organization's network.

This chapter has covered a lot of ground, while focusing on the most important topics in modern network security. Readers who desire to dig deeper are encouraged to investigate the references cited in this chapter. In particular, we recommend [Skoudis 2006] for attacks and operational security, [Kaufman 1995] for cryptography and how it applies to network security, [Rescorla 2001] for an in-depth but readable treatment of SSL, and [Edney 2003] for a thorough discussion of 802.11 security, including an insightful investigation into WEP and its flaws.

Homework Problems and Questions

Chapter 8 Review Problems

SECTION 8.1

R1. Operational devices such as firewalls and intrusion detection systems are used to counter attacks against an organization's network. What is the basic difference between a firewall and an intrusion detection system?

R2. Internet entities (routers, switches, DNS servers, Web servers, user end systems, and so on) often need to communicate securely. Give three specific example pairs of Internet entities that may want secure communication.

SECTION 8.2

R3. The encryption technique itself is known—published, standardized, and available to everyone, even a potential intruder. Then where does the security of an encryption technique come from?

R4. What is the difference between known plaintext attack and chosen plaintext attack?

R5. Consider a 16-block cipher. How many possible input blocks does this cipher have? How many possible mappings are there? If we view each mapping as a key, then how many possible keys does this cipher have?

R6. Suppose N people want to communicate with each of $N - 1$ other people using symmetric key encryption. All communication between any two people, i and j, is visible to all other people in this group of N, and no other person in this group should be able to decode their communication. How many keys are required in the system as a whole? Now suppose that public key encryption is used. How many keys are required in this case?

R7. Suppose $n = 1,000$, $a = 1,017$, and $b = 1,006$. Use an identity of modular arithmetic to calculate in your head $(a \cdot b)$ mod n.

R8. Suppose you want to encrypt the message 10010111 by encrypting the decimal number that corresponds to the message. What is the decimal number?

SECTIONS 8.3–8.4

R9. In what way does a hash provide a better message integrity check than a checksum (such as the Internet checksum)?

R10. Can you "decrypt" a hash of a message to get the original message? Explain your answer.

R11. Consider a variation of the MAC algorithm (Figure 8.9) where the sender sends $(m, H(m) + s)$, where $H(m) + s$ is the concatenation of $H(m)$ and s. Is this variation flawed? Why or why not?

R12. What does it mean for a signed document to be verifiable and non-forgeable?

R13. In the link-state routing algorithm, we would somehow need to distribute the secret authentication key to each of the routers in the autonomous system. How do we distribute the shared authentication key to the communicating entities?

R14. Name two popular secure networking protocols in which public key certification is used.

R15. Suppose Alice has a message that she is ready to send to anyone who asks. Thousands of people want to obtain Alice's message, but each wants to be sure of the integrity of the message. In this context, do you think a MAC-based or a digital-signature-based integrity scheme is more suitable? Why?

R16. What mechanism is used to defend against replay attacks?

R17. What does it mean to say that a nonce is a once-in-a-lifetime value? In whose lifetime?

R18. Is the message integrity scheme based on HMAC susceptible to playback attacks? If so, how can a nonce be incorporated into the scheme to remove this susceptibility?

SECTIONS 8.5–8.8

R19. What is the de facto e-mail encryption scheme? What does it use for authentication and message integrity?

R20. In the SSL record, there is a field for SSL sequence numbers. True or False?

R21. What is the purpose of the random nonces in the SSL handshake?

R22. Suppose an SSL session employs a block cipher with CBC. True or False: The server sends to the client the IV in the clear?

R23. Suppose Bob initiates a TCP connection to Trudy who is pretending to be Alice. During the handshake, Trudy sends Bob Alice's certificate. In what step of the SSL handshake algorithm will Bob discover that he is not communicating with Alice?

R24. Consider sending a stream of packets from Host A to Host B using IPsec. Typically, a new SA will be established for each packet sent in the stream. True or False?

R25. Suppose that TCP is being run over IPsec between headquarters and the branch office in Figure 8.28. If TCP retransmits the same packet, then the two corresponding packets sent by R1 packets will have the same sequence number in the ESP header. True or False?

R26. Is there a fixed encryption algorithm in SSL?

R27. Consider WEP for 802.11. Suppose that the data is 10001101 and the keystream is 01101010. What is the resulting ciphertext?

R28. Is the Initialization Vector (IV) appended to the secret 40-bit symmetric key in WEP protocol sent encrypted?

SECTION 8.9

R29. Stateful packet filters maintain two data structures. Name them and briefly describe what they do.

R30. Consider a traditional (stateless) packet filter. This packet filter may filter packets based on TCP flag bits as well as other header fields. True or False?

R31. In a traditional packet filter, each interface can have its own access control list. True or False?

R32. Why must an application gateway work in conjunction with a router filter to be effective?

R33. Signature-based IDSs and IPSs inspect into the payloads of TCP and UDP segments. True or False?

 Problems

P1. Using the monoalphabetic cipher in Figure 8.3, encode the message "This is a secret message." Decode the message "fsgg ash."

P2. Show that Trudy's known-plaintext attack, in which she knows the (ciphertext, plaintext) translation pairs for seven letters, reduces the number of possible substitutions to be checked in the example in Section 8.2.1 by approximately 10^9.

P3. Consider the polyalphabetic system shown in Figure 8.4. Will a chosen-plaintext attack that is able to get the plaintext encoding of the message "The quick brown fox jumps over the lazy dog." be sufficient to decode all messages? Why or why not?

P4. Consider the block cipher in Figure 8.5. Suppose that each block cipher T_i simply reverses the order of the eight input bits (so that, for example, 11110000 becomes 00001111). Further suppose that the 64-bit scrambler does not modify any bits (so that the output value of the mth bit is equal to the input value of the mth bit). (a) With $n = 3$ and the original 64-bit input equal to 10100000 repeated eight times, what is the value of the output? (b) Repeat part (a) but now change the last bit of the original 64-bit input from a 0 to a 1. (c) Repeat parts (a) and (b) but now suppose that the 64-bit scrambler inverses the order of the 64 bits.

P5. Consider the block cipher in Figure 8.5. Suppose, for a given "key," Alice and Bob would need to keep 16 tables, each 16 bits by 8 bits. For Alice (or Bob) to store all 16 tables, how many bits of storage are necessary? How does this number compare with the number of bits required for a full-table 128-bit block cipher?

P6. Consider the 3-bit block cipher in Table 8.1. Suppose the plaintext is 100100100. (a) Initially assume that CBC is not used. What is the resulting ciphertext? (b) Suppose Trudy sniffs the ciphertext. Assuming she knows that a 3-bit block cipher without CBC is being employed (but doesn't know the specific cipher), what can she surmise? (c) Now suppose that CBC is used with IV = 111. What is the resulting ciphertext?

P7. a. Using RSA, choose $p = 5$ and $q = 7$, and encode the numbers 12, 19, and 27 separately. Apply the decryption algorithm to the encrypted version to recover the original plaintext message.

   b. Choose p and q of your own and encrypt 1834 as one message m.

P8. Consider RSA with $p = 7$ and $q = 13$.

   a. What are n and z?

   b. Let e be 17. Why is this an acceptable choice for e?

   c. Find d such that $de = 1 \pmod{z}$.

   d. Encrypt the message $m = 9$ using the key (n, e). Let c denote the corresponding ciphertext. Show all work.

P9. In this problem, we explore the Diffie-Hellman (DH) public-key encryption algorithm, which allows two entities to agree on a shared key. The DH algorithm makes use of a large prime number p and another large number g less than p. Both p and g are made public (so that an attacker would know them). In DH, Alice and Bob each independently choose secret keys, S_A and S_B, respectively. Alice then computes her public key, T_A, by raising g to S_A and then taking mod p. Bob similarly computes his own public key T_B by raising g to S_B and then taking mod p. Alice and Bob then exchange their public keys over the Internet. Alice then calculates the shared secret key S by raising T_B to S_A and then taking mod p. Similarly, Bob calculates the shared key S' by raising T_A to S_B and then taking mod p.

   a. Prove that, in general, Alice and Bob obtain the same symmetric key, that is, prove $S = S'$.

   b. With $p = 11$ and $g = 2$, suppose Alice and Bob choose private keys $S_A = 5$ and $S_B = 12$, respectively. Calculate Alice's and Bob's public keys, T_A and T_B. Show all work.

   c. Following up on part (b), now calculate S as the shared symmetric key. Show all work.

   d. Provide a timing diagram that shows how Diffie-Hellman can be attacked by a man-in-the-middle. The timing diagram should have three vertical lines, one for Alice, one for Bob, and one for the attacker Trudy.

P10. Suppose Alice wants to communicate with Bob using symmetric key cryptography using a session key K_S. In Section 8.2, we learned how public-key cryptography can be used to distribute the session key from Alice to Bob. In this problem, we explore how the session key can be distributed—without public key cryptography—using a key distribution center (KDC). The KDC is a server that shares a unique secret symmetric key with each registered user. For Alice and Bob, denote these keys by $K_{A\text{-}KDC}$ and $K_{B\text{-}KDC}$. Design a scheme that uses the KDC to distribute K_S to Alice and Bob. Your scheme should use three messages to distribute the session key: a message from Alice to the KDC; a message from the KDC to Alice; and finally a message from Alice to Bob. The first message is $K_{A\text{-}KDC}(A, B)$. Using the notation, $K_{A\text{-}KDC}$, $K_{B\text{-}KDC}$, S, A, and B answer the following questions.

a. What is the second message?

b. What is the third message?

P11. Compute a third message, different from the two messages in Figure 8.8, that has the same checksum as the messages in Figure 8.8.

P12. The sender can mix some randomness into the ciphertext so that identical plaintext blocks produce different ciphertext blocks. But for each cipher bit, the sender must now also send a random bit, doubling the required bandwidth. Is there any way around this?

P13. In the BitTorrent P2P file distribution protocol (see Chapter 2), the seed breaks the file into blocks, and the peers redistribute the blocks to each other. Without any protection, an attacker can easily wreak havoc in a torrent by masquerading as a benevolent peer and sending bogus blocks to a small subset of peers in the torrent. These unsuspecting peers then redistribute the bogus blocks to other peers, which in turn redistribute the bogus blocks to even more peers. Thus, it is critical for BitTorrent to have a mechanism that allows a peer to verify the integrity of a block, so that it doesn't redistribute bogus blocks. Assume that when a peer joins a torrent, it initially gets a .torrent file from a *fully* trusted source. Describe a simple scheme that allows peers to verify the integrity of blocks.

P14. Solving factorization in polynomial time implies breaking the RSA cryptosystem. Is the converse true?

P15. Consider our authentication protocol in Figure 8.18 in which Alice authenticates herself to Bob, which we saw works well (i.e., we found no flaws in it). Now suppose that while Alice is authenticating herself to Bob, Bob must authenticate himself to Alice. Give a scenario by which Trudy, pretending to be Alice, can now authenticate herself to Bob as Alice. (*Hint*: Consider that the sequence of operations of the protocol, one with Trudy initiating and one with Bob initiating, can be arbitrarily interleaved. Pay particular attention to the fact that both Bob and Alice will use a nonce, and that if care is not taken, the same nonce can be used maliciously.)

P16. A natural question is whether we can use a nonce and public key cryptography to solve the end-point authentication problem in Section 8.4. Consider the following natural protocol: (1) Alice sends the message "I am Alice" to Bob. (2) Bob chooses a nonce, R, and sends it to Alice. (3) Alice uses her *private* key to encrypt the nonce and sends the resulting value to Bob. (4) Bob applies Alice's public key to the received message. Thus, Bob computes R and authenticates Alice.

   a. Diagram this protocol, using the notation for public and private keys employed in the textbook.

   b. Suppose that certificates are not used. Describe how Trudy can become a "woman-in-the-middle" by intercepting Alice's messages and then pretending to be Alice to Bob.

P17. Figure 8.19 shows the operations that Alice must perform with PGP to provide confidentiality, authentication, and integrity. Diagram the corresponding operations that Bob must perform on the package received from Alice.

P18. Suppose Alice wants to send an e-mail to Bob. Bob has a public-private key pair (K_B^+, K_B^-), and Alice has Bob's certificate. But Alice does not have a public, private key pair. Alice and Bob (and the entire world) share the same hash function $H(\cdot)$.

   a. In this situation, is it possible to design a scheme so that Bob can verify that Alice created the message? If so, show how with a block diagram for Alice and Bob.

   b. Is it possible to design a scheme that provides confidentiality for sending the message from Alice to Bob? If so, show how with a block diagram for Alice and Bob.

P19. Consider the Wireshark output below for a portion of an SSL session.

   a. Is Wireshark packet 112 sent by the client or server?

   b. What is the server's IP address and port number?

   c. Assuming no loss and no retransmissions, what will be the sequence number of the next TCP segment sent by the client?

   d. How many SSL records does Wireshark packet 112 contain?

   e. Does packet 112 contain a Master Secret or an Encrypted Master Secret or neither?

   f. Assuming that the handshake type field is 1 byte and each length field is 3 bytes, what are the values of the first and last bytes of the Master Secret (or Encrypted Master Secret)?

   g. The client encrypted handshake message takes into account how many SSL records?

   h. The server encrypted handshake message takes into account how many SSL records?

P20. In Section 8.6.1, it is shown that without sequence numbers, Trudy (a woman-in-the middle) can wreak havoc in an SSL session by interchanging TCP

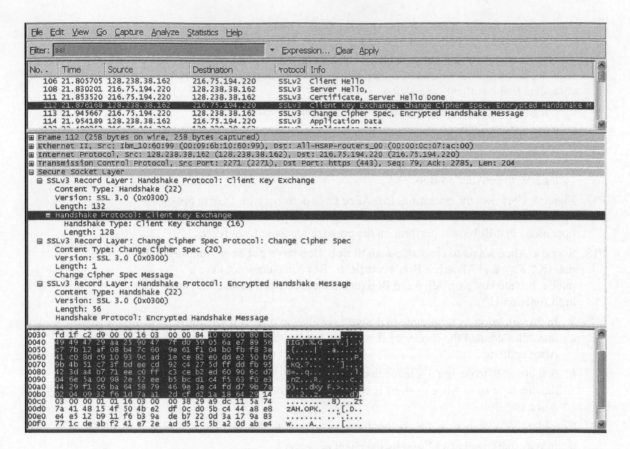

File Edit View Go Capture Analyze Statistics Help

Filter: ssl   ▼ Expression... Clear Apply

No. .	Time	Source	Destination	Protocol	Info
106	21.805705	128.238.38.162	216.75.194.220	SSLv2	Client Hello
108	21.830201	216.75.194.220	128.238.38.162	SSLv3	Server Hello,
111	21.853520	216.75.194.220	128.238.38.162	SSLv3	Certificate, Server Hello Done
112	21.876168	128.238.38.162	216.75.194.220	SSLv3	Client Key Exchange, Change Cipher Spec, Encrypted Handshake M
113	21.945667	216.75.194.220	128.238.38.162	SSLv3	Change Cipher Spec, Encrypted Handshake Message
114	21.954189	128.238.38.162	216.75.194.220	SSLv3	Application Data

⊞ Frame 112 (258 bytes on wire, 258 bytes captured)
⊞ Ethernet II, Src: Ibm_10:60:99 (00:09:6b:10:60:99), Dst: All-HSRP-routers_00 (00:00:0c:07:ac:00)
⊞ Internet Protocol, Src: 128.238.38.162 (128.238.38.162), Dst: 216.75.194.220 (216.75.194.220)
⊞ Transmission Control Protocol, Src Port: 2271 (2271), Dst Port: https (443), Seq: 79, Ack: 2785, Len: 204
⊟ Secure Socket Layer
  ⊟ SSLv3 Record Layer: Handshake Protocol: Client Key Exchange
    Content Type: Handshake (22)
    Version: SSL 3.0 (0x0300)
    Length: 132
    ⊟ Handshake Protocol: Client Key Exchange
      Handshake Type: Client Key Exchange (16)
      Length: 128
  ⊟ SSLv3 Record Layer: Change Cipher Spec Protocol: Change Cipher Spec
    Content Type: Change Cipher Spec (20)
    Version: SSL 3.0 (0x0300)
    Length: 1
    Change Cipher Spec Message
  ⊟ SSLv3 Record Layer: Handshake Protocol: Encrypted Handshake Message
    Content Type: Handshake (22)
    Version: SSL 3.0 (0x0300)
    Length: 56
    Handshake Protocol: Encrypted Handshake Message

```
0030  fd 1f c2 d9 00 00 16 03  00 00 84 10 00 00 80 bc   ........ ........
0040  49 49 47 29 aa 25 90 47  7f d0 59 05 6a e7 89 56   IIG).%.G ..Y.j..V
0050  c7 7b 12 af 08 b4 7c 60  9e 61 f1 04 b0 fb f8 3e   .{....|` .a.....>
0060  41 c0 8d c9 10 93 9c ad  1e ce 82 e0 dd e2 50 b9   A....... ......P.
0070  9b 4b 51 c7 3f bd ee cd  92 c4 27 5d ff dd fb 95   .KQ.?... ..']....
0080  42 3d a4 b7 71 ee c0 ff  c3 ce b2 ed 60 90 6c d7   B=..q... ....`.l.
0090  04 6e 5a 00 98 2e 52 ee  b5 bc d1 c4 f5 63 f0 e3   .nZ...R. .....c..
00a0  44 29 f1 c6 ba 64 58 79  46 9e 3e c4 fd d7 9b 7a   D)...dXy F.>....z
00b0  02 04 09 32 f6 1d 7a a1  2d cf d2 1a 18 64 29 14   ...2..z. -....d).
00c0  03 00 00 01 01 16 03 00  00 38 29 a9 dc 11 5a 74   ........ .8)...Zt
00d0  7a 41 48 15 4f 50 4b e2  df 0c d0 5b c4 44 a8 e8   zAH.OPK. ...[.D..
00e0  e4 e5 12 b9 11 f6 b3 9a  de b7 22 0d 3a 17 9a 83   ........ .."..:...
00f0  77 1c de ab f2 41 e7 2e  ad d5 1c 5b a2 0d ab e4   w....A.. ...[....
```

(Wireshark screenshot reprinted by permission of the Wireshark Foundation.)

segments. Can Trudy do something similar by deleting a TCP segment? What does she need to do to succeed at the deletion attack? What effect will it have?

P21. A router's link-state message includes a list of its directly connected neighbors and the direct costs to these neighbors. Once a router receives link-state messages from all of the other routers, it can create a complete map of the network, run its least-cost routing algorithm, and configure its forwarding table. One relatively easy attack on the routing algorithm is for the attacker to distribute bogus link-state messages with incorrect link-state information. How can this be prevented?

P22. The following True/False questions pertain to Figure 8.28.

  a. When a host in 172.16.1/24 sends a datagram to an Amazon.com server, the router R1 will encrypt the datagram using IPsec.

  b. When a host in 172.16.1/24 sends a datagram to a host in 172.16.2/24, the router R1 will change the source and destination address of the IP datagram.

  c. Suppose a host in 172.16.1/24 initiates a TCP connection to a Web server in 172.16.2/24. As part of this connection, all datagrams sent by R1 will have protocol number 50 in the left-most IPv4 header field.

    d. Consider sending a TCP segment from a host in 172.16.1/24 to a host in 172.16.2/24. Suppose the acknowledgment for this segment gets lost, so that TCP resends the segment. Because IPsec uses sequence numbers, R1 will not resend the TCP segment.

P23. When Bob signs a message, Bob must put something on the message that is unique to him. Bob could consider attaching a MAC for the signature, where the MAC is created by appending his key (unique to him) to the message, and then taking the hash. Will it cause any problem when Alice would try verification?

P24. Consider the following pseudo-WEP protocol. The key is 4 bits and the IV is 2 bits. The IV is appended to the end of the key when generating the keystream. Suppose that the shared secret key is 1010. The keystreams for the four possible inputs are as follows:

101000: 0010101101010101001011010100100 . . .

101001: 1010011011001010110100100101101 . . .

101010: 0001101000111100010100101001111 . . .

101011: 1111101010000000101010100010111 . . .

Suppose all messages are 8-bits long. Suppose the ICV (integrity check) is 4-bits long, and is calculated by XOR-ing the first 4 bits of data with the last 4 bits of data. Suppose the pseudo-WEP packet consists of three fields: first the IV field, then the message field, and last the ICV field, with some of these fields encrypted.

    a. We want to send the message $m = 10100000$ using the IV = 11 and using WEP. What will be the values in the three WEP fields?

    b. Show that when the receiver decrypts the WEP packet, it recovers the message and the ICV.

    c. Suppose Trudy intercepts a WEP packet (not necessarily with the IV = 11) and wants to modify it before forwarding it to the receiver. Suppose Trudy flips the first ICV bit. Assuming that Trudy does not know the keystreams for any of the IVs, what other bit(s) must Trudy also flip so that the received packet passes the ICV check?

    d. Justify your answer by modifying the bits in the WEP packet in part (a), decrypting the resulting packet, and verifying the integrity check.

P25. Provide a filter table and a connection table for a stateful firewall that is as restrictive as possible but accomplishes the following:

    a. Allows all internal users to establish Telnet sessions with external hosts.

    b. Allows external users to surf the company Web site at 222.22.0.12.

    c. But otherwise blocks all inbound and outbound traffic.

The internal network is 222.22/16. In your solution, suppose that the connection table is currently caching three connections, all from inside to outside. You'll need to invent appropriate IP addresses and port numbers.

P26. Suppose Alice wants to visit the Web site activist.com using a TOR-like service. This service uses two non-colluding proxy servers, Proxy1 and Proxy2. Alice first obtains the certificates (each containing a public key) for Proxy1 and Proxy2 from some central server. Denote $K_1^+(\ )$, $K_2^+(\ )$, $K_1^-(\ )$, and $K_2^-(\ )$ for the encryption/decryption with public and private RSA keys.

a. Using a timing diagram, provide a protocol (as simple as possible) that enables Alice to establish a shared session key S_1 with Proxy1. Denote $S_1(m)$ for encryption/decryption of data m with the shared key S_1.

b. Using a timing diagram, provide a protocol (as simple as possible) that allows Alice to establish a shared session key S_2 with Proxy2 *without revealing her IP address to Proxy2*.

c. Assume now that shared keys S_1 and S_2 are now established. Using a timing diagram, provide a protocol (as simple as possible and *not using public-key cryptography*) that allows Alice to request an html page from activist.com *without revealing her IP address to Proxy2* and *without revealing to Proxy1 which site she is visiting*. Your diagram should end with an HTTP request arriving at activist.com.

 Wireshark Lab

In this lab (available from the companion Web site), we investigate the Secure Sockets Layer (SSL) protocol. Recall from Section 8.6 that SSL is used for securing a TCP connection, and that it is extensively used in practice for secure Internet transactions. In this lab, we will focus on the SSL records sent over the TCP connection. We will attempt to delineate and classify each of the records, with a goal of understanding the why and how for each record. We investigate the various SSL record types as well as the fields in the SSL messages. We do so by analyzing a trace of the SSL records sent between your host and an e-commerce server.

 IPsec Lab

In this lab (available from the companion Web site), we will explore how to create IPsec SAs between linux boxes. You can do the first part of the lab with two ordinary linux boxes, each with one Ethernet adapter. But for the second part of the lab, you will need four linux boxes, two of which having two Ethernet adapters. In the second half of the lab, you will create IPsec SAs using the ESP protocol in the tunnel mode. You will do this by first manually creating the SAs, and then by having IKE create the SAs.

Steven M. Bellovin

Steven M. Bellovin joined the faculty at Columbia University after many years at the Network Services Research Lab at AT&T Labs Research in Florham Park, New Jersey. His focus is on networks, security, and why the two are incompatible. In 1995, he was awarded the Usenix Lifetime Achievement Award for his work in the creation of Usenet, the first newsgroup exchange network that linked two or more computers and allowed users to share information and join in discussions. Steve is also an elected member of the National Academy of Engineering. He received his BA from Columbia University and his PhD from the University of North Carolina at Chapel Hill.

What led you to specialize in the networking security area?

This is going to sound odd, but the answer is simple: It was fun. My background was in systems programming and systems administration, which leads fairly naturally to security. And I've always been interested in communications, ranging back to part-time systems programming jobs when I was in college.

My work on security continues to be motivated by two things—a desire to keep computers useful, which means that their function can't be corrupted by attackers, and a desire to protect privacy.

What was your vision for Usenet at the time that you were developing it? And now?

We originally viewed it as a way to talk about computer science and computer programming around the country, with a lot of local use for administrative matters, for-sale ads, and so on. In fact, my original prediction was one to two messages per day, from 50–100 sites at the most—ever. But the real growth was in people-related topics, including—but not limited to—human interactions with computers. My favorite newsgroups, over the years, have been things like rec.woodworking, as well as sci.crypt.

To some extent, netnews has been displaced by the Web. Were I to start designing it today, it would look very different. But it still excels as a way to reach a very broad audience that is interested in the topic, without having to rely on particular Web sites.

Has anyone inspired you professionally? In what ways?

Professor Fred Brooks—the founder and original chair of the computer science department at the University of North Carolina at Chapel Hill, the manager of the team that developed the IBM S/360 and OS/360, and the author of *The Mythical Man-Month*—was a tremendous influence on my career. More than anything else, he taught outlook and trade-offs—how to

779

look at problems in the context of the real world (and how much messier the real world is than a theorist would like), and how to balance competing interests in designing a solution. Most computer work is engineering—the art of making the right trade-offs to satisfy many contradictory objectives.

What is your vision for the future of networking and security?

Thus far, much of the security we have has come from isolation. A firewall, for example, works by cutting off access to certain machines and services. But we're in an era of increasing connectivity—it's gotten harder to isolate things. Worse yet, our production systems require far more separate pieces, interconnected by networks. Securing all that is one of our biggest challenges.

What would you say have been the greatest advances in security? How much further do we have to go?

At least scientifically, we know how to do cryptography. That's been a big help. But most security problems are due to buggy code, and that's a much harder problem. In fact, it's the oldest unsolved problem in computer science, and I think it will remain that way. The challenge is figuring out how to secure systems when we have to build them out of insecure components. We can already do that for reliability in the face of hardware failures; can we do the same for security?

Do you have any advice for students about the Internet and networking security?

Learning the mechanisms is the easy part. Learning how to "think paranoid" is harder. You have to remember that probability distributions don't apply—the attackers can and will find improbable conditions. And the details matter—a lot.

9

Network Management

Having made our way through the first eight chapters of this text, we're now well aware that a network consists of *many* complex, interacting pieces of hardware and software—from the links, switches, routers, hosts, and other devices that comprise the physical components of the network to the many protocols (in both hardware and software) that control and coordinate these devices. When hundreds or thousands of such components are cobbled together by an organization to form a network, it is not surprising that components will occasionally malfunction, that network elements will be misconfigured, that network resources will be overutilized, or that network components will simply "break" (for example, a cable will be cut or a can of soda will be spilled on top of a router). The network administrator, whose job it is to keep the network "up and running," must be able to respond to (and better yet, avoid) such mishaps. With potentially thousands of network components spread out over a wide area, the network administrator in a network operations center (NOC) clearly needs tools to help monitor, manage, and control the network. In this chapter, we'll examine the architecture, protocols, and information base used by a network administrator in this task.

9.1 What Is Network Management?

Before diving in to network management itself, let's first consider a few illustrative "real-world" non-networking scenarios in which a complex system with many interacting components must be monitored, managed, and controlled by an administrator. Electrical power-generation plants have a control room where dials, gauges, and lights monitor the status (temperature, pressure, flow) of remote valves, pipes, vessels, and other plant components. These devices allow the operator to monitor the plant's many components, and may alert the operator (with the famous flashing red warning light) when trouble is imminent. Actions are taken by the plant operator to control these components. Similarly, an airplane cockpit is instrumented to allow a pilot to monitor and control the many components that make up an airplane. In these two examples, the "administrator" *monitors* remote devices and *analyzes* their data to ensure that they are operational and operating within prescribed limits (for example, that a core meltdown of a nuclear power plant is not imminent, or that the plane is not about to run out of fuel), *reactively controls* the system by making adjustments in response to the changes within the system or its environment, and *proactively manages* the system (for example, by detecting trends or anomalous behavior, allowing action to be taken before serious problems arise). In a similar sense, the network administrator will actively monitor, manage, and control the system with which she or he is entrusted.

In the early days of networking, when computer networks were research artifacts rather than a critical infrastructure used by hundreds of millions of people a day, "network management" was unheard of. If one encountered a network problem, one might run a few pings to locate the source of the problem and then modify system settings, reboot hardware or software, or call a remote colleague to do so. (A very readable discussion of the first major "crash" of the ARPAnet on October 27, 1980, long before network management tools were available, and the efforts taken to recover from and understand the crash is [RFC 789].) As the public Internet and private intranets have grown from small networks into a large global infrastructure, the need to manage the huge number of hardware and software components within these networks more systematically has grown more important as well.

In order to motivate our study of network management, let's begin with a simple example. Figure 9.1 illustrates a small network consisting of three routers and a number of hosts and servers. Even in such a simple network, there are many scenarios in which a network administrator might benefit tremendously from having appropriate network management tools:

- *Detecting failure of an interface card at a host or a router.* With appropriate network management tools, a network entity (for example, router A) may report to the network administrator that one of its interfaces has gone down. (This is certainly preferable to a phone call to the NOC from an irate user who says the network connection is down!) A network administrator who actively monitors

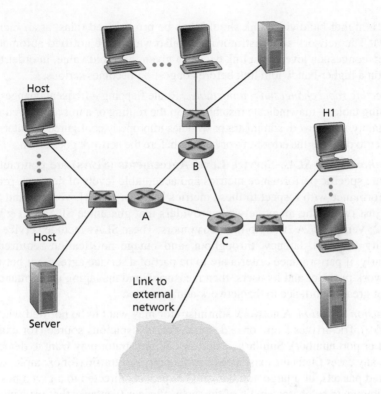

Host

Host

Server

H1

A

B

C

Link to
external
network

Figure 9.1 ♦ A simple scenario illustrating the uses of network management

and analyzes network traffic may be able to *really* impress the would-be irate user by detecting problems in the interface ahead of time and replacing the interface card before it fails. This might be done, for example, if the administrator noted an increase in checksum errors in frames being sent by the soon-to-die interface.

- *Host monitoring.* Here, the network administrator might periodically check to see if all network hosts are up and operational. Once again, the network administrator may really be able to impress a network user by proactively responding to a problem (host down) before it is reported by a user.

- *Monitoring traffic to aid in resource deployment.* A network administrator might monitor source-to-destination traffic patterns and notice, for example, that by switching servers between LAN segments, the amount of traffic that crosses multiple LANs could be significantly decreased. Imagine the happiness all around when better performance is achieved with no new equipment costs. Similarly, by monitoring link utilization, a network administrator might determine that a LAN segment or the external link to the outside world is overloaded and that a higher-bandwidth link should thus be provisioned (alas, at an increased cost). The network administrator might also want to be notified automatically when congestion levels on a link exceed a given threshold value, in order to provision a higher-bandwidth link before congestion becomes serious.

• *Detecting rapid changes in routing tables.* Route flapping—frequent changes in the routing tables—may indicate instabilities in the routing or a misconfigured router. Certainly, the network administrator who has improperly configured a router would prefer to discover the error him- or herself, before the network goes down.

• *Monitoring for SLAs.* **Service Level Agreements (SLAs)** are contracts that define specific performance metrics and acceptable levels of network-provider performance with respect to these metrics [Huston 1999a]. Verizon and Sprint are just two of the many network providers that guarantee SLAs [AT&T SLA 2012; Verizon SLA 2012] to their customers. These SLAs include service availability (outage), latency, throughput, and outage notification requirements. Clearly, if performance criteria are to be part of a service agreement between a network provider and its users, then measuring and managing performance will be of great importance to the network administrator.

• *Intrusion detection.* A network administrator may want to be notified when network traffic arrives from, or is destined for, a suspicious source (for example, host or port number). Similarly, a network administrator may want to detect (and in many cases filter) the existence of certain types of traffic (for example, source-routed packets, or a large number of SYN packets directed to a given host) that are known to be characteristic of the types of security attacks that we considered in Chapter 8.

The International Organization for Standardization (ISO) has created a network management model that is useful for placing the anecdotal scenarios above in a more structured framework. Five areas of network management are defined:

• *Performance management.* The goal of performance management is to quantify, measure, report, analyze, and control the performance (for example, utilization and throughput) of different network components. These components include individual devices (for example, links, routers, and hosts) as well as end-to-end abstractions such as a path through the network. We will see shortly that protocol standards such as the Simple Network Management Protocol (SNMP) [RFC 3410] play a central role in Internet performance management.

• *Fault management.* The goal of fault management is to log, detect, and respond to fault conditions in the network. The line between fault management and performance management is rather blurred. We can think of fault management as the immediate handling of transient network failures (for example, link, host, or router hardware or software outages), while performance management takes the longer-term view of providing acceptable levels of performance in the face of varying traffic demands and occasional network device failures. As with performance management, the SNMP protocol plays a central role in fault management.

- *Configuration management.* Configuration management allows a network manager to track which devices are on the managed network and the hardware and software configurations of these devices. An overview of configuration management and requirements for IP-based networks can be found in [RFC 3139].

- *Accounting management.* Accounting management allows the network manager to specify, log, and control user and device access to network resources. Usage quotas, usage-based charging, and the allocation of resource-access privileges all fall under accounting management.

- *Security management.* The goal of security management is to control access to network resources according to some well-defined policy. The key distribution centers that we studied in Section 8.3 are components of security management. The use of firewalls to monitor and control external access points to one's network, a topic we studied in Section 8.9, is another crucial component.

In this chapter, we'll cover only the rudiments of network management. Our focus will be purposefully narrow—we'll examine only the *infrastructure* for network management—the overall architecture, network management protocols, and information base through which a network administrator keeps the network up and running. We'll *not* cover the decision-making processes of the network administrator, who must plan, analyze, and respond to the management information that is conveyed to the NOC. In this area, topics such as fault identification and management [Katzela 1995; Medhi 1997; Labovitz 1997; Steinder 2002; Feamster 2005; Wu 2005; Teixeira 2006], anomaly detection [Lakhina 2004; Lakhina 2005; Barford 2009], and more come into consideration. Nor will we cover the broader topic of service management [Saydam 1996; RFC 3052]—the provisioning of resources such as bandwidth, server capacity, and the other computational/communication resources needed to meet the mission-specific service requirements of an enterprise.

An often-asked question is "What is network management?" Our discussion above has motivated the need for, and illustrated a few of the uses of, network management. We'll conclude this section with a single-sentence (albeit a rather long run-on sentence) definition of network management from [Saydam 1996]:

"Network management includes the deployment, integration, and coordination of the hardware, software, and human elements to monitor, test, poll, configure, analyze, evaluate, and control the network and element resources to meet the real-time, operational performance, and Quality of Service requirements at a reasonable cost."

It's a mouthful, but it's a good workable definition. In the following sections, we'll add some meat to this rather bare-bones definition of network management.

9.2 The Infrastructure for Network Management

We've seen in the preceding section that network management requires the ability to "monitor, test, poll, configure, . . . and control" the hardware and software components in a network. Because the network devices are distributed, this will, at a minimum, require that the network administrator be able to gather data (for example, for monitoring purposes) from a remote entity and effect changes at that remote entity (for example, control it). A human analogy will prove useful here for understanding the infrastructure needed for network management.

Imagine that you're the head of a large organization that has branch offices around the world. It's your job to make sure that the pieces of your organization are operating smoothly. How will you do so? At a minimum, you'll periodically gather data from your branch offices in the form of reports and various quantitative measures of activity, productivity, and budget. You'll occasionally (but not always) be explicitly notified when there's a problem in one of the branch offices; the branch manager who wants to climb the corporate ladder (perhaps to get your job) may send you unsolicited reports indicating how smoothly things are running at his or her branch. You'll sift through the reports you receive, hoping to find smooth operations everywhere but no doubt finding problems in need of your attention. You might initiate a one-on-one dialogue with one of your problem branch offices, gather more data in order to understand the problem, and then pass down an executive order ("Make this change!") to the branch office manager.

Implicit in this very common human scenario is an infrastructure for controlling the organization—the boss (you), the remote sites being controlled (the branch offices), your remote agents (the branch office managers), communication protocols (for transmitting standard reports and data, and for one-on-one dialogues), and data (the report contents and the quantitative measures of activity, productivity, and budget). Each of these components in human organizational management has a counterpart in network management.

The architecture of a network management system is conceptually identical to this simple human organizational analogy. The network management field has its own specific terminology for the various components of a network management architecture, and so we adopt that terminology here. As shown in Figure 9.2, there are three principal components of a network management architecture: a managing entity (the boss in our analogy above—you), the managed devices (the branch office), and a network management protocol.

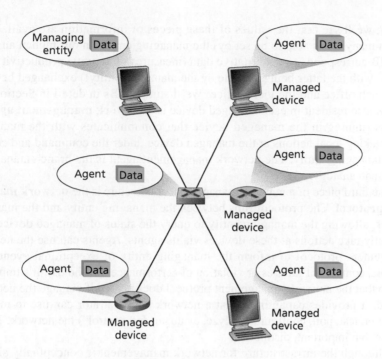

Figure 9.2 ♦ Principal components of a network management architecture

The **managing entity** is an application, typically with a human in the loop, running in a centralized network management station in the NOC. The managing entity is the locus of activity for network management; it controls the collection, processing, analysis, and/or display of network management information. It is here that actions are initiated to control network behavior and here that the human network administrator interacts with the network devices.

A **managed device** is a piece of network equipment (including its software) that resides on a managed network. This is the branch office in our human analogy. A managed device might be a host, router, bridge, hub, printer, or modem. Within a managed device, there may be several so-called **managed objects**. These managed objects are the actual pieces of hardware within the managed device (for example, a network interface card), and the sets of configuration parameters for the pieces of hardware and software (for example, an intradomain routing protocol such as RIP). In our human analogy, the managed objects might be the departments within the branch office. These managed objects have pieces of information associated with them that are collected into a **Management Information Base**

(**MIB**); we'll see that the values of these pieces of information are available to (and in many cases able to be set by) the managing entity. In our human analogy, the MIB corresponds to quantitative data (measures of activity, productivity, and budget, with the latter being settable by the managing entity!) exchanged between the branch office and the main office. We'll study MIBs in detail in Section 9.3. Finally, also resident in each managed device is a **network management agent**, a process running in the managed device that communicates with the managing entity, taking local actions at the managed device under the command and control of the managing entity. The network management agent is the branch manager in our human analogy.

The third piece of a network management architecture is the **network management protocol**. The protocol runs between the managing entity and the managed devices, allowing the managing entity to query the status of managed devices and indirectly take actions at these devices via its agents. Agents can use the network management protocol to inform the managing entity of exceptional events (for example, component failures or violation of performance thresholds). It's important to note that the network management protocol does not itself manage the network. Instead, it provides capabilities that a network administrator can use to manage ("monitor, test, poll, configure, analyze, evaluate, and control") the network. This is a subtle, but important, distinction.

Although the infrastructure for network management is conceptually simple, one can often get bogged down with the network-management-speak vocabulary of "managing entity," "managed device," "managing agent," and "Management Information Base." For example, in network-management-speak, in our simple host-monitoring scenario, "managing agents" located at "managed devices" are periodically queried by the "managing entity"—a simple idea, but a linguistic mouthful! With any luck, keeping in mind the human organizational analogy and its obvious parallels with network management will be of help as we continue through this chapter.

Our discussion of network management architecture above has been generic, and broadly applies to a number of the network management standards and efforts that have been proposed over the years. Network management standards began maturing in the late 1980s, with OSI **CMISE/CMIP** (the **Common Management Information Services Element/Common Management Information Protocol**) [Piscatello 1993; Stallings 1993; Glitho 1998] and the Internet **SNMP (Simple Network Management Protocol)** [RFC 3410; Stallings 1999; Rose 1996] emerging as the two most important standards [Subramanian 2000]. Both are designed to be independent of vendor-specific products or networks. Because SNMP was quickly designed and deployed at a time when the need for network management was becoming painfully clear, SNMP found widespread use and acceptance. Today, SNMP has emerged as the most widely used and deployed network management framework. We'll cover SNMP in detail in the following section.

PRINCIPLES IN PRACTICE

COMCAST'S NETWORK OPERATIONS CENTER

Comcast's world-class fiber-based IP network delivers converged products and services to 49 million combined video, data and voice customers. Comcast's network includes more than 618,000 plant route miles, 138,000 fiber route miles, 30,000 backbone miles, 122,000 optical nodes, and massive storage for the Comcast Content Delivery Network, which delivers a Video on Demand product of more than 134 Terabytes. Each part of Comcast's network, up to and including the customers' homes or businesses, is monitored by one of the company's Operations Centers.

Comcast operates two National Network Operations Centers that manage the national backbone, regional area networks, national applications and specific platforms supporting voice, data and video infrastructure for residential, commercial and wholesale customers. In addition, Comcast has three Divisional Operations Centers that manage the local infrastructure that supports all of their customers. Both the National and Divisional Operations Centers are accountable for proactively monitoring all aspects of their network and product performance on a 7 x 24 x 365 basis, utilizing common processes and systems. For example, various network events at the national and local levels have common pre-defined severity levels, recovery processes, and expected Mean Time to Restore objectives. The national and divisional centers can back up each other if a local issue impacts a site's operation. In addition, the National and Divisional Operations Centers have an extensive Virtual Private Network that allows engineers to securely access the network to remotely perform proactive or reactive network management activities.

Comcast's approach to network management involves five key areas: Performance Management, Fault Management, Configuration Management, Accounting Management and Security Management. **Performance Management** is focused on understanding

These screens show tools supporting correlation, threshold management, ticketing used by Comcast technicians (Courtesy of Comcast.)

(continues)

how the network/systems and applications (collectively referred to as the ecosystem) are performing with respect to pre-defined measures specific to time of day, day of week, or special events (e.g., storm surges or pay events, such as a boxing match). These pre-defined performance measures exist throughout the service path, from the customer's residence or business through the entire network, as well as the interface points to partners and peers. In addition, synthetic transactions are run to ensure the health of the ecosystem on a continual basis. **Fault Management** is defined as the ability to detect, log and understand anomalies that may impact customers. Comcast utilizes correlation engines to properly determine an event's severity and act appropriately, eliminating or remediating potential issues before they affect customers. **Configuration Management** makes sure appropriate versions of hardware and software are in place across all elements of the ecosystem. Keeping these elements at their peak "golden" levels helps them avoid unintended consequences. **Accounting Management** ensures that the operations centers have a clear understanding of the provisioning and utilization of the ecosystem. This is especially important to ensure that at all times the operations centers have the ability to re-route traffic effectively. **Security Management** ensures that the proper controls exist to ensure the ecosystem is effectively protected against inappropriate access.

Network Operations Centers and the ecosystem they support are not static. Engineering and Operations personnel are constantly re-evaluating the pre-defined performance measures and tools to ensure that the customers' expectations for operational excellence are met.

9.3 The Internet-Standard Management Framework

Contrary to what the name SNMP (Simple Network Management Protocol) might suggest, network management in the Internet is much more than just a protocol for moving management data between a management entity and its agents, and has grown to be much more complex than the word "simple" might suggest. The current Internet-Standard Management Framework traces its roots back to the Simple Gateway Monitoring Protocol, SGMP [RFC 1028]. SGMP was designed by a group of university network researchers, users, and managers, whose experience with SGMP allowed them to design, implement, and deploy SNMP in just a few months [Lynch 1993]—a far cry from today's rather drawn-out standardization process. Since then, SNMP has evolved from SNMPv1 through SNMPv2 to the most recent version, SNMPv3 [RFC 3410], released in April 1999 and updated in December 2002.

When describing any framework for network management, certain questions must inevitably be addressed:

- What (from a semantic viewpoint) is being monitored? And what form of control can be exercised by the network administrator?
- What is the specific form of the information that will be reported and/or exchanged?
- What is the communication protocol for exchanging this information?

Recall our human organizational analogy from the previous section. The boss and the branch managers will need to agree on the measures of activity, productivity, and budget used to report the branch office's status. Similarly, they'll need to agree on the actions the boss can take (for example, cut the budget, order the branch manager to change some aspect of the office's operation, or fire the staff and shut down the branch office). At a lower level of detail, they'll need to agree on the form in which this data is reported. For example, in what currency (dollars, euros?) will the budget be reported? In what units will productivity be measured? While these may seem like trivial details, they must be agreed upon, nonetheless. Finally, the manner in which information is conveyed between the main office and the branch offices (that is, their communication protocol) must be specified.

The Internet-Standard Management Framework addresses the questions posed above. The framework consists of four parts:

- Definitions of *network management objects*, known as MIB objects. In the Internet-Standard Management Framework, management information is represented as a collection of managed objects that together form a virtual information store, known as the Management Information Base (MIB). An MIB object might be a counter, such as the number of IP datagrams discarded at a router due to errors in an IP datagram header, or the number of carrier sense errors in an Ethernet interface card; descriptive information such as the version of the software running on a DNS server; status information such as whether a particular device is functioning correctly; or protocol-specific information such as a routing path to a destination. MIB objects thus define the management information maintained by a managed device. Related MIB objects are gathered into **MIB modules**. In our human organizational analogy, the MIB defines the information conveyed between the branch office and the main office.

- A *data definition language,* known as SMI (Structure of Management Information). SMI defines the data types, an object model, and rules for writing and revising management information. MIB objects are specified in this data definition language. In our human organizational analogy, the SMI is used to define the details of the *format* of the information to be exchanged.

- A *protocol, SNMP.* SNMP is used for conveying information and commands between a managing entity and an agent executing on behalf of that entity within a managed network device.

- *Security and administration capabilities.* The addition of these capabilities represents the major enhancement in SNMPv3 over SNMPv2.

The Internet network management architecture is thus modular by design, with a protocol-independent data definition language and MIB, and an MIB-independent protocol. Interestingly, this modular architecture was first put in place to ease the transition from an SNMP-based network management to a network management framework being developed by ISO, the competing network management architecture when SNMP was first conceived—a transition that never occurred. Over time, however, SNMP's design modularity has allowed it to evolve through three major revisions, with each of the four major parts of SNMP discussed above evolving independently. Clearly, the right decision about modularity was made, even if for the wrong reason!

In the following subsections, we cover the four major components of the Internet-Standard Management Framework in more detail.

9.3.1 Structure of Management Information: SMI

The **Structure of Management Information, SMI** (a rather oddly named component of the network management framework whose name gives no hint of its functionality), is the language used to define the management information residing in a managed-network entity. Such a definition language is needed to ensure that the syntax and semantics of the network management data are well defined and unambiguous. Note that the SMI does not define a specific instance of the data in a managed-network entity, but rather the language in which such information is specified. The documents describing the SMI for SNMPv3 (which rather confusingly, is called SMIv2) are [RFC 2578; RFC 2579; RFC 2580]. Let's examine the SMI in a bottom-up manner, starting with the base data types in the SMI. We'll then look at how managed objects are described in SMI, then how related managed objects are grouped into modules.

SMI Base Data Types

RFC 2578 specifies the basic data types in the SMI MIB module-definition language. Although the SMI is based on the ASN.1 (Abstract Syntax Notation One) [ISO X.680 2002] object-definition language (see Section 9.4), enough SMI-specific data types have been added that SMI should be considered a data definition language in its own right. The 11 basic data types defined in RFC 2578 are shown in Table 9.1. In addition to these scalar objects, it is also possible to impose a tabular structure on an ordered collection of MIB objects using the SEQUENCE OF construct; see RFC 2578 for details. Most of the data types in Table 9.1 will be familiar (or self-explanatory) to most readers. The one data type we will discuss in more detail shortly is the OBJECT IDENTIFIER data type, which is used to name an object.

SMI Higher-Level Constructs

In addition to the basic data types, the SMI data definition language also provides higher-level language constructs.

Data Type	Description
INTEGER	32-bit integer, as defined in ASN.1, with a value between -2^{31} and $2^{31} - 1$ inclusive, or a value from a list of possible named constant values.
Integer32	32-bit integer with a value between -2^{31} and $2^{31} - 1$ inclusive.
Unsigned32	Unsigned 32-bit integer in the range 0 to $2^{32} - 1$ inclusive.
OCTET STRING	ASN.1-format byte string representing arbitrary binary or textual data, up to 65,535 bytes long.
OBJECT IDENTIFIER	ASN.1-format administratively assigned (structured name); see Section 9.3.2.
IPaddress	32-bit Internet address, in network-byte order.
Counter32	32-bit counter that increases from 0 to $2^{32} - 1$ and then wraps around to 0.
Counter64	64-bit counter.
Gauge32	32-bit integer that will not count above $2^{32} - 1$ nor decrease beyond 0 when increased or decreased.
TimeTicks	Time, measured in 1/100ths of a second since some event.
Opaque	Uninterpreted ASN.1 string, needed for backward compatibility.

Table 9.1 ♦ Basic data types of the SMI

The OBJECT-TYPE construct is used to specify the data type, status, and semantics of a managed object. Collectively, these managed objects contain the management data that lies at the heart of network management. There are more than 10,000 defined objects in various Internet RFCs [RFC 3410]. The OBJECT-TYPE construct has four clauses. The SYNTAX clause of an OBJECT-TYPE definition specifies the basic data type associated with the object. The MAX-ACCESS clause specifies whether the managed object can be read, be written, be created, or have its value included in a notification. The STATUS clause indicates whether the object definition is current and valid, obsolete (in which case it should not be implemented, as its definition is included for historical purposes only), or deprecated (obsolete, but implementable for interoperability with older implementations). The DESCRIP-TION clause contains a human-readable textual definition of the object; this "documents" the purpose of the managed object and should provide all the semantic information needed to implement the managed object.

As an example of the OBJECT-TYPE construct, consider the `ipSystem-StatsInDelivers` object-type definition from [RFC 4293]. This object defines a 32-bit counter that keeps track of the number of IP datagrams that were received at the managed device and were successfully delivered to an upper-layer protocol.

The final line of this definition is concerned with the name of this object, a topic we'll consider in the following subsection.

```
ipSystemStatsInDelivers OBJECT-TYPE
    SYNTAX       Counter32
    MAX-ACCESS read-only
    STATUS       current
    DESCRIPTION
            "The total number of datagrams successfully
            delivered to IPuser-protocols (including ICMP).

            When tracking interface statistics, the counter
            of the interface to which these datagrams were
            addressed is incremented. This interface might
            not be the same as the input interface for
            some of the datagrams.

            Discontinuities in the value of this counter can
            occur at re-initialization of the management
            system, and at other times as indicated by the
            value of ipSystemStatsDiscontinuityTime."
    ::= { ipSystemStatsEntry 18 }
```

The MODULE-IDENTITY construct allows related objects to be grouped together within a "module." For example, [RFC 4293] specifies the MIB module that defines managed objects (including ipSystemStatsInDelivers) for managing implementations of the Internet Protocol (IP) and its associated Internet Control Message Protocol (ICMP). [RFC 4022] specifies the MIB module for TCP, and [RFC 4113] specifies the MIB module for UDP. [RFC 4502] defines the MIB module for RMON remote monitoring. In addition to containing the OBJECT-TYPE definitions of the managed objects within the module, the MODULE-IDENTITY construct contains clauses to document contact information of the author of the module, the date of the last update, a revision history, and a textual description of the module. As an example, consider the module definition for management of the IP protocol:

```
ipMIB MODULE-IDENTITY
    LAST-UPDATED "200602020000Z"
    ORGANIZATION "IETF IPv6 MIB Revision Team"
    CONTACT-INFO
            "Editor:
            Shawn A. Routhier
            Interworking Labs
            108 Whispering Pines Dr. Suite 235
```

```
         Scotts Valley, CA 95066
         USA
         EMail: <sar@iwl.com>"
DESCRIPTION
         "The MIB module for managing IP and ICMP
         implementations, but excluding their
         management of IP routes.

         Copyright (C) The Internet Society (2006).
         This version of this MIB module is part of
         RFC 4293; see the RFC itself for full legal
         notices."

REVISION          "200602020000Z"
DESCRIPTION
         "The IP version neutral revision with added
         IPv6 objects for ND, default routers, and
         router advertisements. As well as being the
         successor to RFC 2011, this MIB is also the
         successor to RFCs 2465 and 2466. Published
         as RFC 4293."

REVISION          "199411010000Z"
DESCRIPTION
         "A separate MIB module (IP-MIB) for IP and
         ICMP management objects. Published as RFC
         2011."

REVISION          "199103310000Z"
DESCRIPTION
         "The initial revision of this MIB module was
         part of MIB-II, which was published as RFC
         1213."
 ::= { mib-2 48}
```

The NOTIFICATION-TYPE construct is used to specify information regarding SNMPv2-Trap and InformationRequest messages generated by an agent, or a managing entity; see Section 9.3.3. This information includes a textual DESCRIPTION of when such messages are to be sent, as well as a list of values to be included in the message generated; see [RFC 2578] for details. The MODULE-COMPLIANCE construct defines the set of managed objects within a module that an agent must implement. The AGENT-CAPABILITIES construct specifies the capabilities of agents with respect to object- and event-notification definitions.

9.3.2 Management Information Base: MIB

As noted previously, the **Management Information Base, MIB,** can be thought of as a virtual information store, holding managed objects whose values collectively reflect the current "state" of the network. These values may be queried and/or set by a managing entity by sending SNMP messages to the agent that is executing in a managed device on behalf of the managing entity. Managed objects are specified using the OBJECT-TYPE SMI construct discussed above and gathered into **MIB modules** using the MODULE-IDENTITY construct.

The IETF has been busy standardizing the MIB modules associated with routers, hosts, and other network equipment. This includes basic identification data about a particular piece of hardware, and management information about the device's network interfaces and protocols. As of 2006 there were more than 200 standards-based MIB modules and an even larger number of vendor-specific (private) MIB modules. With all of these standards, the IETF needed a way to identify and name the standardized modules as well as the specific managed objects within a module. Rather than start from scratch, the IETF adopted a standardized object identification (naming) framework that had already been put in place by the International Organization for Standardization (ISO). As is the case with many standards bodies, the ISO had "grand plans" for its standardized object identification framework—to identify every possible standardized object (for example, data format, protocol, or piece of information) in any network, regardless of the network standards organization (for example, Internet IETF, ISO, IEEE, or ANSI), equipment manufacturer, or network owner. A lofty goal indeed! The object identification framework adopted by ISO is part of the ASN.1 (Abstract Syntax Notation One) [ISO X.680 2002] object definition language that we'll discuss in Section 9.4. Standardized MIB modules have their own cozy corner in this all-encompassing naming framework, as discussed below.

As shown in Figure 9.3, objects are named in the ISO naming framework in a hierarchical manner. Note that each branch point in the tree has both a name and a number (shown in parentheses); any point in the tree is thus identifiable by the sequence of names or numbers that specify the path from the root to that point in the identifier tree. A fun, but incomplete and unofficial, Web-based utility for traversing part of the object identifier tree (using branch information contributed by volunteers) may be found in [OID Repository 2012].

At the top of the hierarchy are the ISO and the Telecommunication Standardization Sector of the International Telecommunication Union (ITU-T), the two main standards organizations dealing with ASN.1, as well as a branch for joint efforts by these two organizations. Under the ISO branch of the tree, we find entries for all ISO standards (1.0) and for standards issued by standards bodies of various ISO-member countries (1.2). Although not shown in Figure 9.3, under (ISO member body, a.k.a. 1.2) we would find USA (1.2.840), under which we would find a number of IEEE, ANSI, and company-specific standards. These include RSA (1.2.840.11359) and Microsoft (1.2.840.113556), under which we find the Microsoft File Formats (1.2.840.113556.4) for various Microsoft products, such as

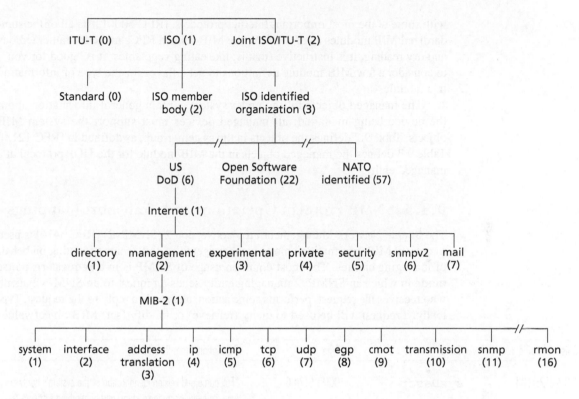

Figure 9.3 ♦ ASN.1 object identifier tree

Word (1.2.840.113556.4.2). But we are interested here in networking (*not* Microsoft Word files), so let us turn our attention to the branch labeled 1.3, the standards issued by bodies recognized by the ISO. These include the U.S. Department of Defense (6) (under which we will find the Internet standards), the Open Software Foundation (22), the airline association SITA (69), NATO-identified bodies (57), as well as many other organizations.

Under the `Internet` branch of the tree (1.3.6.1), there are seven categories. Under the `private` (1.3.6.1.4) branch, we find a list [IANA 2009b] of the names and private enterprise codes of many thousands of private companies that have registered with the Internet Assigned Numbers Authority (IANA) [IANA 2009a]. Under the `management` (1.3.6.1.2) and `MIB-2` branches (1.3.6.1.2.1) of the object identifier tree, we find the definitions of the standardized MIB modules. Whew—it's a long journey down to our corner of the ISO name space!

Standardized MIB Modules

The lowest level of the tree in Figure 9.3 shows some of the important hardware-oriented MIB modules (`system` and `interface`) as well as modules associated with some of the most important Internet protocols. [RFC 5000] lists all of the standardized MIB modules as of 2008. While MIB-related RFCs make for rather tedious and dry reading, it is instructive (that is, like eating vegetables, it is "good for you") to consider a few MIB module definitions to get a flavor for the type of information in a module.

The managed objects falling under system contain general information about the device being managed; all managed devices must support the system MIB objects. Table 9.2 defines the objects in the system group, as defined in [RFC 1213]. Table 9.3 defines the managed objects in the MIB module for the UDP protocol at a managed entity.

9.3.3 SNMP Protocol Operations and Transport Mappings

The Simple Network Management Protocol version 2 (SNMPv2) [RFC 3416] is used to convey MIB information among managing entities and agents executing on behalf of managing entities. The most common usage of SNMP is in a **request-response mode** in which an SNMPv2 managing entity sends a request to an SNMPv2 agent, who receives the request, performs some action, and sends a reply to the request. Typically, a request will be used to query (retrieve) or modify (set) MIB object values

Object Identifier	Name	Type	Description (from RFC 1213)
1.3.6.1.2.1.1.1	sysDescr	OCTET STRING	"Full name and version identification of the system's hardware type, software operating-system, and networking software."
1.3.6.1.2.1.1.2	sysObjectID	OBJECT IDENTIFIER	Vendor-assigned object ID that "provides an easy and unambiguous means for determining 'what kind of box' is being managed."
1.3.6.1.2.1.1.3	sysUpTime	TimeTicks	"The time (in hundredths of a second) since the network management portion of the system was last re-initialized."
1.3.6.1.2.1.1.4	sysContact	OCTET STRING	"The contact person for this managed node, together with information on how to contact this person."
1.3.6.1.2.1.1.5	sysName	OCTET STRING	"An administratively assigned name for this managed node. By convention, this is the node's fully qualified domain name."
1.3.6.1.2.1.1.6	sysLocation	OCTET STRING	"The physical location of this node."
1.3.6.1.2.1.1.7	sysServices	Integer32	A coded value that indicates the set of services available at this node: physical (for example, a repeater), data link/subnet (for example, bridge), Internet (for example, IP gateway), end-to-end (for example, host), applications.

Table 9.2 ♦ Managed objects in the MIB-2 system group

Object Identifier	Name	Type	Description (from RFC 4113)
1.3.6.1.2.1.7.1	`udpInDatagrams`	Counter32	"total number of UDP datagrams delivered to UDP users"
1.3.6.1.2.1.7.2	`udpNoPorts`	Counter32	"total number of received UDP datagrams for which there was no application at the destination port"
1.3.6.1.2.1.7.3	`udpInErrors`	Counter32	"number of received UDP datagrams that could not be delivered for reasons other than the lack of an application at the destination port"
1.3.6.1.2.1.7.4	`udpOutDatagrams`	Counter32	"total number of UDP datagrams sent from this entity"

Table 9.3 ♦ Selected managed objects in the MIB-2 UDP module

associated with a managed device. A second common usage of SNMP is for an agent to send an unsolicited message, known as a **trap message,** to a managing entity. Trap messages are used to notify a managing entity of an exceptional situation that has resulted in changes to MIB object values. We saw earlier in Section 9.1 that the network administrator might want to receive a trap message, for example, when an interface goes down, congestion reaches a predefined level on a link, or some other noteworthy event occurs. Note that there are a number of important trade-offs between polling (request-response interaction) and trapping; see the homework problems.

SNMPv2 defines seven types of messages, known generically as protocol data units—PDUs—as shown in Table 9.4 and described next. The format of the PDU is shown in Figure 9.4.

- The `GetRequest`, `GetNextRequest`, and `GetBulkRequest` PDUs are all sent from a managing entity to an agent to request the value of one or more MIB objects at the agent's managed device. The object identifiers of the MIB objects whose values are being requested are specified in the variable binding portion of the PDU. `GetRequest`, `GetNextRequest`, and `GetBulkRequest` differ in the granularity of their data requests. `GetRequest` can request an arbitrary set of MIB values; multiple `GetNextRequest`s can be used to sequence through a list or table of MIB objects; `GetBulkRequest` allows a large block of data to be returned, avoiding the overhead incurred if multiple `GetRequest` or `GetNextRequest` messages were to be sent. In all three cases, the agent responds with a `Response` PDU containing the object identifiers and their associated values.

- The `SetRequest` PDU is used by a managing entity to set the value of one or more MIB objects in a managed device. An agent replies with a `Response` PDU with the "noError" error status to confirm that the value has indeed been set.

SNMPv2 PDU Type	Sender-receiver	Description
`GetRequest`	manager-to-agent	get value of one or more MIB object instances
`GetNextRequest`	manager-to-agent	get value of next MIB object instance in list or table
`GetBulkRequest`	manager-to-agent	get values in large block of data, for example, values in a large table
`InformRequest`	manager-to-manager	inform remote managing entity of MIB values remote to its access
`SetRequest`	manager-to-agent	set value of one or more MIB object instances
`Response`	agent-to-manager or	generated in response to
	manager-to-manager	`GetRequest`,
		`GetNextRequest`,
		`GetBulkRequest`,
		`SetRequest` PDU, or
		`InformRequest`
`SNMPv2-Trap`	agent-to-manager	inform manager of an exceptional event

Table 9.4 ♦ SNMPv2 PDU types

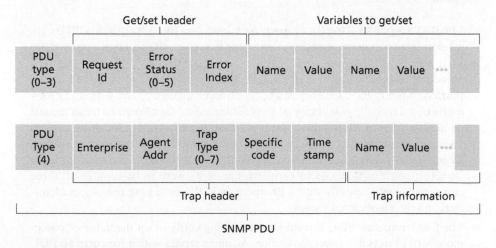

Figure 9.4 ♦ SNMP PDU format

- The `InformRequest` PDU is used by a managing entity to notify another managing entity of MIB information that is remote to the receiving entity. The receiving entity replies with a `Response` PDU with the "noError" error status to acknowledge receipt of the `InformRequest` PDU.

- The final type of SNMPv2 PDU is the trap message. Trap messages are generated asynchronously; that is, they are *not* generated in response to a received request but rather in response to an event for which the managing entity requires notification. RFC 3418 defines well-known trap types that include a cold or warm start by a device, a link going up or down, the loss of a neighbor, or an authentication failure event. A received trap request has no required response from a managing entity.

Given the request-response nature of SNMPv2, it is worth noting here that although SNMP PDUs can be carried via many different transport protocols, the SNMP PDU is typically carried in the payload of a UDP datagram. Indeed, RFC 3417 states that UDP is "the preferred transport mapping." Since UDP is an unreliable transport protocol, there is no guarantee that a request, or its response, will be received at the intended destination. The request ID field of the PDU is used by the managing entity to number its requests to an agent; an agent's response takes its request ID from that of the received request. Thus, the request ID field can be used by the managing entity to detect lost requests or replies. It is up to the managing entity to decide whether to retransmit a request if no corresponding response is received after a given amount of time. In particular, the SNMP standard does not mandate any particular procedure for retransmission, or even if retransmission is to be done in the first place. It only requires that the managing entity "needs to act responsibly in respect to the frequency and duration of retransmissions." This, of course, leads one to wonder how a "responsible" protocol should act!

9.3.4 Security and Administration

The designers of SNMPv3 have said that "SNMPv3 can be thought of as SNMPv2 with additional security and administration capabilities" [RFC 3410]. Certainly, there are changes in SNMPv3 over SNMPv2, but nowhere are those changes more evident than in the area of administration and security. The central role of security in SNMPv3 was particularly important, since the lack of adequate security resulted in SNMP being used primarily for monitoring rather than control (for example, `SetRequest` is rarely used in SNMPv1).

As SNMP has matured through three versions, its functionality has grown but so too, alas, has the number of SNMP-related standards documents. This is evidenced by the fact that there is even now an RFC [RFC 3411] that "describes an architecture for describing SNMP Management Frameworks"! While the notion of an "architecture" for "describing a framework" might be a bit much to wrap one's mind around, the goal of RFC 3411 is an admirable one—to introduce a common language for describing the functionality and actions taken by an SNMPv3 agent or managing entity. The architecture of an SNMPv3 entity is straightforward, and a tour through the architecture will serve to solidify our understanding of SNMP.

So-called **SNMP applications** consist of a command generator, notification receiver, and proxy forwarder (all of which are typically found in a managing entity); a command responder and notification originator (both of which are typically found in an agent); and the possibility of other applications. The command generator generates the `GetRequest`, `GetNextRequest`, `GetBulkRequest`, and `SetRequest` PDUs that we examined in Section 9.3.3 and handles the received responses to these PDUs. The command responder executes in an agent and receives, processes, and replies (using the `Response` message) to received `GetRequest`, `GetNextRequest`, `GetBulkRequest`, and `SetRequest` PDUs. The notification originator application in an agent generates `Trap` PDUs; these PDUs are eventually received and processed in a notification receiver application at a managing entity. The proxy forwarder application forwards request, notification, and response PDUs.

A PDU sent by an SNMP application next passes through the SNMP "engine" before it is sent via the appropriate transport protocol. Figure 9.5 shows how a PDU generated by the command generator application first enters the dispatch module,

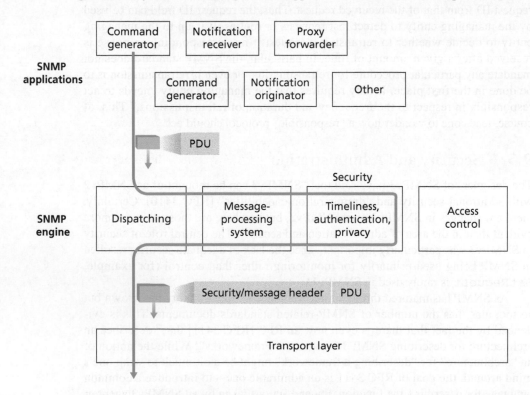

Figure 9.5 ◆ SNMPv3 engine and applications

where the SNMP version is determined. The PDU is then processed in the message-processing system, where the PDU is wrapped in a message header containing the SNMP version number, a message ID, and message size information. If encryption or authentication is needed, the appropriate header fields for this information are included as well; see [RFC 3411] for details. Finally, the SNMP message (the application-generated PDU plus the message header information) is passed to the appropriate transport protocol. The preferred transport protocol for carrying SNMP messages is UDP (that is, SNMP messages are carried as the payload in a UDP datagram), and the preferred port number for the SNMP is port 161. Port 162 is used for trap messages.

We have seen above that SNMP messages are used not just to monitor, but also to control (for example, through the `SetRequest` command) network elements. Clearly, an intruder that could intercept SNMP messages and/or generate its own SNMP packets into the management infrastructure could wreak havoc in the network. Thus, it is crucial that SNMP messages be transmitted securely. Surprisingly, it is only in the most recent version of SNMP that security has received the attention that it deserves. SNMPv3 security is known as **user-based security** [RFC 3414] in that there is the traditional concept of a user, identified by a username, with which security information such as a password, key value, or access privileges are associated. SNMPv3 provides for encryption, authentication, protection against playback attacks (see Section 8.3), and access control.

- *Encryption.* SNMP PDUs can be encrypted using the Data Encryption Standard (DES) in Cipher Block Chaining (CBC) mode. Note that since DES is a shared-key system, the secret key of the user encrypting data must be known by the receiving entity that must decrypt the data.

- *Authentication.* SNMP uses the Message Authentication Code (MAC) technique that we studied in Section 8.3.1 to provide both authentication and protection against tampering [RFC 4301]. Recall that a MAC requires the sender and receiver both to know a common secret key.

- *Protection against playback.* Recall from our discussion in Chapter 8 that nonces can be used to guard against playback attacks. SNMPv3 adopts a related approach. In order to ensure that a received message is not a replay of some earlier message, the receiver requires that the sender include a value in each message that is based on a counter in the *receiver.* This counter, which functions as a nonce, reflects the amount of time since the last reboot of the receiver's network management software and the total number of reboots since the receiver's network management software was last configured. As long as the counter in a received message is within some margin of error of the receiver's actual value, the message is accepted as a nonreplay message, at which point it may be authenticated and/or decrypted. See [RFC 3414] for details.

- *Access control.* SNMPv3 provides a view-based access control [RFC 3415] that controls which network management information can be queried and/or set by which users. An SNMP entity retains information about access rights and policies in a Local Configuration Datastore (LCD). Portions of the LCD are themselves accessible as managed objects, defined in the View-Based Access Control Model Configuration MIB [RFC 3415], and thus can be managed and manipulated remotely via SNMP.

9.4 ASN.1

In this book, we have covered a number of interesting topics in computer networking. This section on ASN.1, however, may not make the top-ten list of interesting topics. Like vegetables, knowledge about ASN.1 and the broader issue of presentation services is something that is "good for you." ASN.1 is an ISO-originated standard that is used in a number of Internet-related protocols, particularly in the area of network management. For example, we saw in Section 9.3 that MIB variables in SNMP were inextricably tied to ASN.1. So while the material on ASN.1 in this section may be rather dry, we hope the reader will take it on faith that the material *is* important.

In order to motivate our discussion here, consider the following thought experiment. Suppose one could reliably copy data from one computer's memory directly into a remote computer's memory. If one could do this, would the communication problem be "solved?" The answer to the question depends on one's definition of "the communication problem." Certainly, a perfect memory-to-memory copy would exactly communicate the bits and bytes from one machine to another. But does such an exact copy of the bits and bytes mean that when software running on the receiving computer accesses this data, it will see the same values that were stored into the sending computer's memory? The answer to this question is "not necessarily!" The crux of the problem is that different computer architectures, different operating systems, and different compilers have different conventions for storing and representing data. If data is to be communicated and stored among multiple computers (as it is in every communication network), this problem of data representation must clearly be solved.

As an example of this problem, consider the simple C code fragment below. How might this structure be laid out in memory?

```
struct {
  char code;
  int x;
  } test;
test.x = 259;
test.code = 'a';
```

The left side of Figure 9.6 shows a possible layout of this data on one hypothetical architecture: there is a single byte of memory containing the character a,

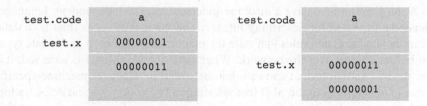

test.code	a	test.code	a
test.x	00000001		
	00000011	test.x	00000011
			00000001

Figure 9.6 ♦ Two different data layouts on two different architectures

followed by a 16-bit word containing the integer value 259, stored with the most significant byte first. The layout in memory on another computer is shown in the right half of Figure 9.6. The character a is followed by the integer value stored with the least significant byte stored first and with the 16-bit integer aligned to start on a 16-bit word boundary. Certainly, if one were to perform a verbatim copy between these two computers' memories and use the same structure definition to access the stored values, one would see very different results on the two computers!

The fact that different architectures have different internal data formats is a real and pervasive problem. The particular problem of integer storage in different formats is so common that it has a name. "Big-endian" order for storing integers has the most significant bytes of the integer stored first (at the lowest storage address). "Little-endian" order stores the least significant bytes first. Sun SPARC and Motorola processors are big-endian, while Intel processors are little-endian. As an aside, the terms "big-endian" and "little-endian" come from the book, *Gulliver's Travels,* by Jonathan Swift, in which two groups of people dogmatically insist on doing a simple thing in two different ways (hopefully, the analogy to the computer architecture community is clear). One group in the land of Lilliput insists on breaking their eggs at the larger end ("the big-endians"), while the other insists on breaking them at the smaller end. The difference was the cause of great civil strife and rebellion.

Given that different computers store and represent data in different ways, how should networking protocols deal with this? For example, if an SNMP agent is about to send a Response message containing the integer count of the number of received UDP datagrams, how should it represent the integer value to be sent to the managing entity—in big-endian or little-endian order? One option would be for the agent to send the bytes of the integer in the same order in which they would be stored in the managing entity. Another option would be for the agent to send in its own storage order and have the receiving entity reorder the bytes, as needed. Either option would require the sender or receiver to learn the other's format for integer representation.

A third option is to have a machine-independent, OS-independent, language-independent method for describing integers and other data types (that is, a data-definition language) and rules that state the manner in which each of the data types is to be transmitted over the network. When data of a given type is received, it is received in a known format and can then be stored in whatever machine-specific format is required. Both the SMI that we studied in Section 9.3 and ASN.1 adopt this third option. In ISO parlance, these two standards describe a **presentation service**—the service of transmitting and translating information from one machine-specific format to another. Figure 9.7 illustrates a real-world presentation problem; neither receiver understands the essential idea being communicated—that the speaker likes something. As shown in Figure 9.8, a presentation service can solve this problem by translating the idea into a commonly understood (by the presentation service), person-independent language, sending that information to the receiver, and then translating into a language understood by the receiver.

Table 9.5 shows a few of the ASN.1-defined data types. Recall that we encountered the INTEGER, OCTET STRING, and OBJECT IDENTIFIER data types in our earlier study of the SMI. Since our goal here is (mercifully) not to provide a complete introduction to ASN.1, we refer the reader to the standards or to the printed and online book [Larmouth 1996] for a description of ASN.1 types and constructors, such as SEQUENCE and SET, that allow for the definition of structured data types.

In addition to providing a data definition language, ASN.1 also provides **Basic Encoding Rules (BER)** that specify how instances of objects that have been defined using the ASN.1 data definition language are to be sent over the network. The BER adopts a so-called **TLV (Type, Length, Value) approach** to encoding data for transmission. For each data item to be sent, the data type, the length of the data item,

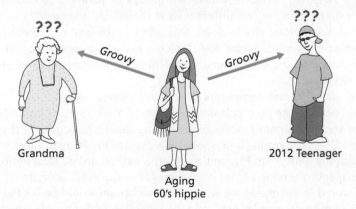

Figure 9.7 ♦ The presentation problem

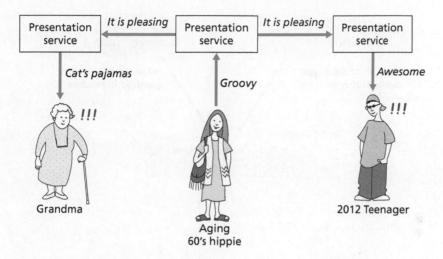

Figure 9.8 ◆ The presentation problem solved

and then the actual value of the data item are sent, in that order. With this simple convention, the received data is essentially self-identifying.

Figure 9.9 shows how the two data items in a simple example would be sent. In this example, the sender wants to send the character string "smith" followed by the value 259 decimal (which equals 00000001 00000011 in binary, or a byte value of 1 followed by a byte value of 3), assuming big-endian order. The first byte in the

Tag	Type	Description
1	BOOLEAN	value is "true" or "false"
2	INTEGER	can be arbitrarily large
3	BITSTRING	list of one or more bits
4	OCTET STRING	list of one or more bytes
5	NULL	no value
6	OBJECT IDENTIFIER	name, in the ASN.1 standard naming tree; see Section 9.2.2
9	REAL	floating point

Table 9.5 ◆ Selected ASN.1 data types

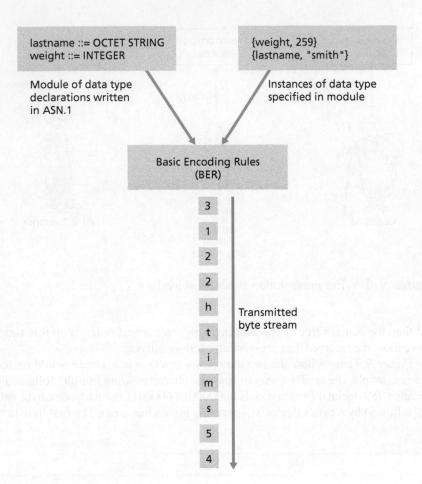

Figure 9.9 ♦ BER encoding example

transmitted stream has the value 4, indicating that the type of the following data item is an OCTET STRING; this is the "T" in the TLV encoding. The second byte in the stream contains the length of the OCTET STRING, in this case 5. The third byte in the transmitted stream begins the OCTET STRING of length 5; it contains the ASCII representation of the letter *s*. The T, L, and V values of the next data item are 2 (the INTEGER type tag value), 2 (that is, an integer of length 2 bytes), and the 2-byte big-endian representation of the value 259 decimal.

In our previous discussion, we have only touched on a small and simple subset of ASN.1. Resources for learning more about ASN.1 include the ASN.1 standards document [ISO X.680 2002], the online OSI-related book [Larmouth 2012], and the ASN.1-related Web sites, [OSS 2012] and [OID Repository 2012].

9.5 Conclusion

Our study of network management, and indeed of all of networking, is now complete!

In this final chapter on network management, we began by motivating the need for providing appropriate tools for the network administrator—the person whose job it is to keep the network "up and running"—for monitoring, testing, polling, configuring, analyzing, evaluating, and controlling the operation of the network. Our analogies with the management of complex systems such as power plants, airplanes, and human organization helped motivate this need. We saw that the architecture of network management systems revolves around five key components: (1) a network manager, (2) a set of managed remote (from the network manager) devices, (3) the Management Information Bases (MIBs) at these devices, containing data about the devices' status and operation, (4) remote agents that report MIB information and take action under the control of the network manager, and (5) a protocol for communication between the network manager and the remote devices.

We then delved into the details of the Internet-Standard Management Framework, and the SNMP protocol in particular. We saw how SNMP instantiates the five key components of a network management architecture, and we spent considerable time examining MIB objects, the SMI—the data definition language for specifying MIBs, and the SNMP protocol itself. Noting that the SMI and ASN.1 are inextricably tied together, and that ASN.1 plays a key role in the presentation layer in the ISO/OSI seven-layer reference model, we then briefly examined ASN.1. Perhaps more important than the details of ASN.1 itself was the noted need to provide for translation between machine-specific data formats in a network. While some network architectures explicitly acknowledge the importance of this service by having a presentation layer, this layer is absent in the Internet protocol stack.

It is also worth noting that there are many topics in network management that we chose *not* to cover—topics such as fault identification and management, proactive anomaly detection, alarm correlation, and the larger issues of service management (for example, as opposed to network management). While important, these topics would form a text in their own right, and we refer the reader to the references noted in Section 9.1.

 Homework Problems and Questions

Chapter 9 Review Questions

SECTION 9.1

R1. What is the frequent change in a routing table called? What does it indicate?

R2. What are Service Level Agreements (SLAs)?

R3. What is the difference between fault management and performance management?

SECTION 9.2

R4. What are two major network management protocols?

SECTION 9.3

R5. What is the role of the SMI in network management?

R6. What do SNMP applications consist of?

R7. What are the seven message types used in SNMP?

R8. What is meant by an "SNMP engine"?

SECTION 9.4

R9. What is the purpose of the ASN.1 object identifier tree?

R10. What is the role of ASN.1 in the ISO/OSI reference model's presentation layer?

R11. Does the Internet have a presentation layer? If not, how are concerns about differences in machine architectures—for example, the different representation of integers on different machines—addressed?

R12. What is meant by TLV encoding?

 Problems

P1. Consider the two ways in which communication occurs between a managing entity and a managed device: request-response mode and trapping. What are the pros and cons of these two approaches, in terms of (1) overhead, (2) notification time when exceptional events occur, and (3) robustness with respect to lost messages between the managing entity and the device?

P2. What are the questions that need to be addressed when describing any framework for network management?

P3. What does *sysUpTime* indicate in MIB?

P4. Suppose you worked for a US-based company that wanted to develop its own MIB for managing a product line. Where in the object identifier tree (Figure 9.3) would it be registered? (*Hint:* You'll have to do some digging through RFCs or other documents to answer this question.)

P5. Recall from Section 9.3.2 that a private company (enterprise) can create its own MIB variables under the private branch 1.3.6.1.4. Suppose that IBM wanted to create a MIB for its Web server software. What would be the next OID qualifier after 1.3.6.1.4? (In order to answer this question, you will need to consult [IANA 2009b]). Search the Web and see if you can find out whether such a MIB exists for an IBM server.

P6. How does SNMP provide protection against playback attack?

P7. Consider Figure 9.9. What would be the BER encoding of {`weight, 165`} {`lastname, "Michael"`}?

P8. Consider Figure 9.9. What would be the BER encoding of {`weight, 145`} {`lastname, "Sridhar"`}?

Jennifer Rexford

Jennifer Rexford is a Professor in the Computer Science department at Princeton University. Her research has the broad goal of making computer networks easier to design and manage, with particular emphasis on routing protocols. From 1996–2004, she was a member of the Network Management and Performance department at AT&T Labs–Research. While at AT&T, she designed techniques and tools for network measurement, traffic engineering, and router configuration that were deployed in AT&T's backbone network. Jennifer is co-author of the book "Web Protocols and Practice: Networking Protocols, Caching, and Traffic Measurement," published by Addison-Wesley in May 2001. She served as the chair of ACM SIGCOMM from 2003 to 2007. She received her BSE degree in electrical engineering from Princeton University in 1991, and her MSE and PhD degrees in electrical engineering and computer science from the University of Michigan in 1993 and 1996, respectively. In 2004, Jennifer was the winner of ACM's Grace Murray Hopper Award for outstanding young computer professional and appeared on the MIT TR-100 list of top innovators under the age of 35.

Please describe one or two of the most exciting projects you have worked on during your career. What were the biggest challenges?

When I was a researcher at AT&T, a group of us designed a new way to manage routing in Internet Service Provider backbone networks. Traditionally, network operators configure each router individually, and these routers run distributed protocols to compute paths through the network. We believed that network management would be simpler and more flexible if network operators could exercise *direct* control over how routers forward traffic based on a *network-wide* view of the topology and traffic. The Routing Control Platform (RCP) we designed and built could compute the routes for all of AT&T's backbone on a single commodity computer, and could control legacy routers without modification. To me, this project was exciting because we had a provocative idea, a working system, and ultimately a real deployment in an operational network.

What changes and innovations do you see happening in network management in the future?

Rather than simply "bolting on" network management on top of existing networks, researchers and practitioners alike are starting to design networks that are fundamentally easier to manage. Like our early work on the RCP, the main idea in so-called Software Defined Networking (SDN) is to run a controller that can install low-level packet-handling rules in the underlying switches using a standard protocol. This controller can run various network-management applications, such as dynamic access control, seamless user mobility, traffic engineering, server load balancing, energy-efficient networking, and so on. I believe SDN is a great opportunity to get network management right, by rethinking the relationship between the network devices and the software that manages them.

Where do you see the future of networking and the Internet?

Networking is an exciting field because the applications and the underlying technologies change all the time. We are always reinventing ourselves! Who would have predicted even five or ten years ago the dominance of smart phones, allowing mobile users to access existing applications as well as new location-based services? The emergence of cloud computing is fundamentally changing the relationship between users and the applications they run, and networked sensors are enabling a wealth of new applications. The pace of innovation is truly inspiring.

The underlying network is a crucial component in all of these innovations. Yet, the network is notoriously "in the way"—limiting performance, compromising reliability, constraining applications, and complicating the deployment and management of services. We should strive to make the network of the future as invisible as the air we breathe, so it never stands in the way of new ideas and valuable services. To do this, we need to raise the level of abstraction above individual network devices and protocols (and their attendant acronyms!), so we can reason about the network as a whole.

What people inspired you professionally?

I've long been inspired by Sally Floyd at the International Computer Science Institute. Her research is always purposeful, focusing on the important challenges facing the Internet. She digs deeply into hard questions until she understands the problem and the space of solutions completely, and she devotes serious energy into "making things happen," such as pushing her ideas into protocol standards and network equipment. Also, she gives back to the community, through professional service in numerous standards and research organizations and by creating tools (such as the widely used ns-2 and ns-3 simulators) that enable other researchers to succeed. She retired in 2009 but her influence on the field will be felt for years to come.

What are your recommendations for students who want careers in computer science and networking?

Networking is an inherently interdisciplinary field. Applying techniques from other disciplines to networking problems is a great way to move the field forward. We've seen tremendous breakthroughs in networking come from such diverse areas as queuing theory, game theory, control theory, distributed systems, network optimization, programming languages, machine learning, algorithms, data structures, and so on. I think that becoming conversant in a related field, or collaborating closely with experts in those fields, is a wonderful way to put networking on a stronger foundation, so we can learn how to build networks that are worthy of society's trust. Beyond the theoretical disciplines, networking is exciting because we create real artifacts that real people use. Mastering how to design and build systems—by gaining experience in operating systems, computer architecture, and so on—is another fantastic way to amplify your knowledge of networking to help change the world.

References

A note on URLs. In the references below, we have provided URLs for Web pages, Web-only documents, and other material that has not been published in a conference or journal (when we have been able to locate a URL for such material). We have not provided URLs for conference and journal publications, as these documents can usually be located via a search engine, from the conference Web site (e.g., papers in all *ACM SIGCOMM* conferences and workshops can be located via http://www.acm.org/sigcomm), or via a digital library subscription. While all URLs provided below were valid (and tested) in Jan. 2012, URLs can become out of date. Please consult the online version of this book (http://www.awl.com/kurose-ross) for an up-to-date bibliography.

A note on Internet Request for Comments (RFCs): Copies of Internet RFCs are available at many sites. The RFC Editor of the Internet Society (the body that oversees the RFCs) maintains the site, http://www.rfc-editor.org. This site allows you to search for a specific RFC by title, number, or authors, and will show updates to any RFCs listed. Internet RFCs can be updated or obsoleted by later RFCs. Our favorite site for getting RFCs is the original source—http://www.rfc-editor.org.

[3Com Addressing 2012] 3Com Corp., "White paper: Understanding IP addressing: Everything you ever wanted to know," http://www.3com.com/other/pdfs/infra/corpinfo/en_US/501302.pdf

[3GPP 2012] Third Generation Partnership Project homepage, http://www.3gpp.org/

[3GPP Network Architecture 2012] 3GPP, "TS 23.002: Network Architecture: Digital Cellular Telecommunications System (Phase 2+); Universal Mobile Telecommunications System (UMTS); LTE," http://www.3gpp.org/ftp/Specs/html-info/23002.htm

[Albitz 1993] P. Albitz and C. Liu, *DNS and BIND,* O'Reilly & Associates, Petaluma, CA, 1993.

[Abramson 1970] N. Abramson, "The Aloha System—Another Alternative for Computer Communications," *Proc. 1970 Fall Joint Computer Conference, AFIPS Conference,* p. 37, 1970.

[Abramson 1985] N. Abramson, "Development of the Alohanet," *IEEE Transactions on Information Theory,* Vol. IT-31, No. 3 (Mar. 1985), pp. 119–123.

[Abramson 2009] N. Abramson, "The Alohanet – Surfing for Wireless Data," *IEEE Communications Magazine*, Vol. 47, No. 12, pp. 21–25.

[Abu-Libdeh 2010] H. Abu-Libdeh, P. Costa, A. Rowstron, G. O'Shea, A. Donnelly, "Symbiotic Routing in Future Data Centers," *Proc. 2010 ACM SIGCOMM.*

[Adhikari 2011a] V. K. Adhikari, S. Jain, Y. Chen, Z. L. Zhang, "Vivisecting YouTube: An Active Measurement Study," Technical Report, University of Minnesota, 2011.

[Adhikari 2012] V. K. Adhikari, Y. Gao, F. Hao, M. Varvello, V. Hilt, M. Steiner, Z. L. Zhang, "Unreeling Netflix: Understanding and Improving Multi-CDN Movie Delivery," Technical Report, University of Minnesota, 2012.

[Afanasyev 2010] A. Afanasyev, N. Tilley, P. Reiher, L. Kleinrock, "Host-to-Host Congestion Control for TCP," *IEEE Communications Surveys & Tutorials*, Vol. 12, No. 3, pp. 304–342.

[Agarwal 2009] S. Agarwal, J. Lorch, "Matchmaking for Online Games and Other Latency-sensitive P2P Systems," *Proc. 2009 ACM SIGCOMM.*

[Ahn 1995] J. S. Ahn, P. B. Danzig, Z. Liu, and Y. Yan, "Experience with TCP Vegas: Emulation and Experiment," *Proc. 1995 ACM SIGCOMM* (Boston, MA, Aug. 1995), pp. 185–195.

[Akamai 2012] Akamai homepage, http://www.akamai.com

[Akella 2003] A. Akella, S. Seshan, A. Shaikh, "An Empirical Evaluation of Wide-Area Internet Bottlenecks," *Proc. 2003 ACM Internet Measurement Conference* (Miami, FL, Nov. 2003).

[Akhshabi 2011] S. Akhshabi, A. C. Begen, C. Dovrolis, "An Experimental Evaluation of Rate-Adaptation Algorithms in Adaptive Streaming over HTTP," *Proc. 2011 ACM Multimedia Systems Conf.*

[Akyildiz 2010] I. Akyildiz, D. Gutierrex-Estevez, E. Reyes, "The Evolution to 4G Cellular Systems, LTE Advanced," *Physical Communication,* Elsevier, 3 (2010), 217–244.

[Alcatel-Lucent 2009] Alcatel-Lucent, "Introduction to Evolved Packet Core," http://downloads.lightreading.com/wplib/alcatellucent/ALU_WP_Intro_to_EPC.pdf

[Al-Fares 2008] M. Al-Fares, A. Loukissas, A. Vahdat, "A Scalable, Commodity Data Center Network Architecture," *Proc. 2008 ACM SIGCOMM.*

[Alizadeh 2010] M. Alizadeh, A. Greenberg, D. Maltz, J. Padhye, P. Patel, B. Prabhakar, S. Sengupta, M. Sridharan, "Data Center TCP (DCTCP)," *Proc. 2010 ACM SIGCOMM.*

[Allman 2011] E. Allman, "The Robustness Principle Reconsidered: Seeking a Middle Ground," *Communications of the ACM,* Vol. 54, No. 8 (Aug. 2011), pp. 40–45.

[Anderson 1995] J. B. Andersen, T. S. Rappaport, S. Yoshida, "Propagation Measurements and Models for Wireless Communications Channels," *IEEE Communications Magazine,* (Jan. 1995), pp. 42–49.

[Andrews 2002] M. Andrews, M. Shepherd, A. Srinivasan, P. Winkler, F. Zane, "Clustering and Server Election Using Passive Monitoring," *Proc. 2002 IEEE INFOCOM.*

[Androutsellis-Theotokis 2004] S. Androutsellis-Theotokis, D. Spinellis, "A Survey of Peer-to-Peer Content Distribution Technologies," *ACM Computing Surveys,* Vol. 36, No. 4 (Dec. 2004), pp. 335–371.

[Aperjis 2008] C. Aperjis, M.J. Freedman, R. Johari, "Peer-Assisted Content Distribution with Prices," *Proc. ACM CoNEXT'08* (Madrid, Dec. 2008).

[Appenzeller 2004] G. Appenzeller, I. Keslassy, N. McKeown, "Sizing Router Buffers," *Proc. 2004 ACM SIGCOMM* (Portland, OR, Aug. 2004).

[Ash 1998] G. R. Ash, *Dynamic Routing in Telecommunications Networks,* McGraw Hill, New York, NY, 1998.

[ASO-ICANN 2012] The Address Supporting Organization home page, http://www.aso.icann.org

[AT&T SLA 2012] AT&T, "AT&T High Speed Internet Business Edition Service Level Agreements," http://www.att.com/gen/general?pid=6622

[Atheros 2012] Atheros Communications Inc. "Atheros AR5006 WLAN Chipset Product Bulletins," http://www.atheros.com/pt/AR5006Bulletins.htm

[Augustin 2009] B. Augustin, B. Krishnamurthy, W. Willinger, "IXPs: Mapped?" *Proc. Internet Measurement Conference (IMC),* November 2009.

[Ayanoglu 1995] E. Ayanoglu, S. Paul, T. F. La Porta, K. K. Sabnani, R. D. Gitlin, "AIRMAIL: A Link-Layer Protocol for Wireless Networks," *ACM ACM/Baltzer Wireless Networks Journal*, 1: 47–60, Feb. 1995.

[Bakre 1995] A. Bakre, B. R. Badrinath, "I-TCP: Indirect TCP for Mobile Hosts," *Proc. 1995 Int. Conf. on Distributed Computing Systems (ICDCS)* (May 1995), pp. 136–143.

[Balakrishnan 1997] H. Balakrishnan, V. Padmanabhan, S. Seshan, R. Katz, "A Comparison of Mechanisms for Improving TCP Performance Over Wireless Links," *IEEE/ACM Transactions on Networking* Vol. 5, No. 6 (Dec. 1997).

[Balakrishnan 2003] H. Balakrishnan, F. Kaashoek, D. Karger, R. Morris, I. Stoica, "Looking Up Data in P2P Systems," *Communications of the ACM*, Vol. 46, No. 2 (Feb. 2003), pp. 43–48.

[Baldauf 2007] M. Baldauf, S. Dustdar, F. Rosenberg, "A Survey on Context-Aware Systems," *Int. J. Ad Hoc and Ubiquitous Computing*, Vol. 2, No. 4 (2007), pp. 263–277.

[Ballani 2006] H. Ballani, P. Francis, S. Ratnasamy, "A Measurement-based Deployment Proposal for IP Anycast," *Proc. 2006 ACM Internet Measurement Conf.*

[Ballani 2011] H. Ballani, P. Costa, T. Karagiannis, Ant Rowstron, "Towards Predictable Datacenter Networks," *Proc. 2011 ACM SIGCOMM.*

[Baran 1964] P. Baran, "On Distributed Communication Networks," *IEEE Transactions on Communication Systems,* Mar. 1964. Rand Corporation Technical report with the same title (Memorandum RM-3420-PR, 1964). http://www.rand.org/publications/RM/RM3420/

[Bardwell 2004] J. Bardwell, "You Believe You Understand What You Think I Said . . . The Truth About 802.11 Signal And Noise Metrics: A Discussion Clarifying Often-Misused 802.11 WLAN Terminologies," http://www.connect802.com/download/techpubs/2004/you_believe_D100201.pdf

[Barford 2009] P. Barford, N. Duffield, A. Ron, J. Sommers, " Network Performance Anomaly Detection and Localization," *Proc. 2009 IEEE INFOCOM* (Apr. 2009).

[Baronti 2007] P. Baronti, P. Pillai, V. Chook, S. Chessa, A. Gotta, Y. Hu, "Wireless Sensor Networks: A Survey on the State of the Art and the 802.15.4 and ZigBee Standards,*"* *Computer Communications*, Vol. 30, No. 7 (2007), pp. 1655–1695.

[Baset 2006] S. A. Basset and H. Schulzrinne, "An analysis of the Skype peer-to-peer Internet Telephony Protocol," *Proc. 2006 IEEE INFOCOM* (Barcelona, Spain, Apr. 2006).

[BBC 2001] BBC news online "A Small Slice of Design," Apr. 2001, http://news.bbc.co.uk/2/hi/science/nature/1264205.stm

[BBC 2012] BBC, "Multicast," http://www.bbc.co.uk/multicast/

[Beheshti 2008] N. Beheshti, Y. Ganjali, M. Ghobadi, N. McKeown, G. Salmon, "Experimental Study of Router Buffer Sizing," *Proc. ACM Internet Measurement Conference* (October 2008, Vouliagmeni, Greece).

[Bender 2000] P. Bender, P. Black, M. Grob, R. Padovani, N. Sindhushayana, A. Viterbi, "CDMA/HDR: A bandwidth-efficient high-speed wireless data service for nomadic users," *IEEE Commun. Mag.,* Vol. 38, No. 7 (July 2000) pp. 70–77.

[Berners-Lee 1989] T. Berners-Lee, CERN, "Information Management: A Proposal," Mar. 1989, May 1990. http://www.w3.org/History/1989/proposal.html

[Berners-Lee 1994] T. Berners-Lee, R. Cailliau, A. Luotonen, H. Frystyk Nielsen, A. Secret, "The World-Wide Web," *Communications of the ACM,* Vol. 37, No. 8 (Aug. 1994), pp. 76–82.

[Bertsekas 1991] D. Bertsekas, R. Gallagher, *Data Networks, 2nd Ed.,* Prentice Hall, Englewood Cliffs, NJ, 1991.

[Biddle 2003] P. Biddle, P. England, M. Peinado, B. Willman, "The Darknet and the Future of Content Distribution," *2002 ACM Workshop on Digital Rights Management,* (Nov. 2002, Washington, D.C.) http://crypto.stanford.edu/DRM2002/darknet5.doc

[Biersack 1992] E. W. Biersack, "Performance evaluation of forward error correction in ATM networks," *Proc. 1999 ACM SIGCOMM* (Baltimore, MD, Aug. 1992), pp. 248–257.

[BIND 2012] Internet Software Consortium page on BIND, http://www.isc.org/bind.html

[Bisdikian 2001] C. Bisdikian, "An Overview of the Bluetooth Wireless Technology," *IEEE Communications Magazine*, No. 12 (Dec. 2001), pp. 86–94.

[Bishop 2003] M. Bishop, *Computer Security: Art and Science,* Boston: Addison Wesley, Boston MA, 2003.

[Black 1995] U. Black, *ATM Volume I: Foundation for Broadband Networks*, Prentice Hall, 1995.

[Black 1997] U. Black, *ATM Volume II: Signaling in Broadband Networks*, Prentice Hall, 1997.

[Blumenthal 2001] M. Blumenthal, D. Clark, "Rethinking the Design of the Internet: the End-to-end Arguments vs. the Brave New World," *ACM Transactions on Internet Technology,* Vol. 1, No. 1 (Aug. 2001), pp. 70–109.

[Bochman 1984] G. V. Bochmann, C. A. Sunshine, "Formal methods in communication protocol design," *IEEE Transactions on Communications,* Vol. 28, No. 4 (Apr. 1980) pp. 624–631.

[Bolot 1994] J-C. Bolot, T. Turletti, "A rate control scheme for packet video in the Internet," *Proc. 1994 IEEE INFOCOM,* pp. 1216–1223.

[Bolot 1996] J-C. Bolot, A. Vega-Garcia, "Control Mechanisms for Packet Audio in the Internet," *Proc. 1996 IEEE INFOCOM,* pp. 232–239.

[Bradner 1996] S. Bradner, A. Mankin, *IPng: Internet Protocol Next Generation,* Addison-Wesley, Reading, MA, 1996.

[Brakmo 1995] L. Brakmo, L. Peterson, "TCP Vegas: End to End Congestion Avoidance on a Global Internet," *IEEE Journal of Selected Areas in Communications,* Vol. 13, No. 8 (Oct. 1995), pp. 1465–1480.

[Breslau 2000] L. Breslau, E. Knightly, S. Shenker, I. Stoica, H. Zhang, "Endpoint Admission Control: Architectural Issues and Performance," *Proc. 2000 ACM SIGCOMM* (Stockholm, Sweden, Aug. 2000).

[Bryant 1988] B. Bryant, "Designing an Authentication System: A Dialogue in Four Scenes," http://web.mit.edu/kerberos/www/dialogue.html

[Bush 1945] V. Bush, "As We May Think," *The Atlantic Monthly,* July 1945. http://www.theatlantic.com/unbound/flashbks/computer/bushf.htm

[Byers 1998] J. Byers, M. Luby, M. Mitzenmacher, A. Rege, "A digital fountain approach to reliable distribution of bulk data," *Proc. 1998 ACM SIGCOMM* (Vancouver, Canada, Aug. 1998), pp. 56–67.

[Cablelabs 2012] CableLabs homepage, http://www.cablelabs.com

[CacheLogic 2012] CacheLogic homepage, http://www.cachelogic.com

[Caesar 2005a] M. Caesar, D. Caldwell, N. Feamster, J. Rexford, A. Shaikh, J. van der Merwe, "Design and implementation of a Routing Control Platform," *Proc. Networked Systems Design and Implementation* (May 2005).

[Caesar 2005b] M. Caesar, J. Rexford, "BGP Routing Policies in ISP Networks," *IEEE Network Magazine,* Vol. 19, No. 6 (Nov. 2005).

[Casado 2009] M. Casado, M. Freedman, J. Pettit, J. Luo, N. Gude, N. McKeown, S. Shenker, "Rethinking Enterprise Network Control," *IEEE/ACM Transactions on Networking (ToN),* Vol. 17, No. 4 (Aug. 2009), pp. 1270–1283.

[Caldwell 2012] C. Caldwell, "The Prime Pages," http://www.utm.edu/research/primes/prove

[Cardwell 2000] N. Cardwell, S. Savage, T. Anderson, "Modeling TCP Latency," *Proc. 2000 IEEE INFOCOM* (Tel-Aviv, Israel, Mar. 2000).

[CASA 2012] Center for Collaborative Adaptive Sensing of the Atmosphere, http://www.casa.umass.edu

[Casado 2007] M. Casado, M. Freedman, J. Pettit, J. Luo, N. McKeown, S. Shenker, "Ethane: Taking Control of the Enterprise," *Proc. 2007 ACM SIGCOMM* (Kyoto, Japan, Aug. 2007).

[Casner 1992] S. Casner, S. Deering, "First IETF Internet Audiocast," *ACM SIGCOMM Computer Communications Review,* Vol. 22, No. 3 (July 1992), pp. 92–97.

[Ceiva 2012] Ceiva homepage, http://www.cciva.com/

[CENS 2012] Center for Embedded Network Sensing, http://www.cens.ucla.edu/

[Cerf 1974] V. Cerf, R. Kahn, "A Protocol for Packet Network Interconnection," *IEEE Transactions on Communications Technology,* Vol. COM-22, No. 5, pp. 627–641.

[CERT 2001–09] CERT, "Advisory 2001–09: Statistical Weaknesses in TCP/IP Initial Sequence Numbers," http://www.cert.org/advisories/CA-2001-09.html

[CERT 2003–04] CERT, "CERT Advisory CA-2003-04 MS-SQL Server Worm," http://www.cert.org/advisories/CA-2003-04.html

[CERT 2012] CERT Coordination Center, http://www.cert.org/advisories

[CERT Filtering 2012] CERT, "Packet Filtering for Firewall Systems," http://www.cert.org/tech_tips/packet_filtering.html

[Cert SYN 1996] CERT, "Advisory CA-96.21: TCP SYN Flooding and IP Spoofing Attacks," http://www.cert.org/advisories/CA-1998-01.html

[Chao 2001] H. J. Chao, C. Lam, E. Oki, *Broadband Packet Switching Technologies— A Practical Guide to ATM Switches and IP Routers*, John Wiley & Sons, 2001.

[Chao 2011] C. Zhang, P. Dunghel, D. Wu, K. W. Ross, "Unraveling the BitTorrent Ecosystem," *IEEE Transactions on Parallel and Distributed Systems*, Vol. 22, No. 7 (July 2011).

[Chen 2000] G. Chen, D. Kotz, "A Survey of Context-Aware Mobile Computing Research," *Technical Report TR2000-381*, Dept. of Computer Science, Dartmouth College, Nov. 2000. http://www.cs.dartmouth.edu/reports/TR2000-381.pdf

[Chen 2006] K.-T. Chen, C.-Y. Huang, P. Huang, C.-L. Lei, "Quantifying Skype User Satisfaction," *Proc. 2006 ACM SIGCOMM* (Pisa, Italy, Sept. 2006).

[Chen 2010] K. Chen, C. Guo, H. Wu, J. Yuan, Z. Feng, Y. Chen, S. Lu, W. Wu, "Generic and Automatic Address Configuration for Data Center Networks," *Proc. 2010 ACM SIGCOMM*.

[Chen 2011] Y. Chen, S. Jain, V. K. Adhikari, Z. Zhang, "Characterizing Roles of Front-End Servers in End-to-End Performance of Dynamic Content Distribution," *Proc. 2011 ACM Internet Measurement Conference* (Berlin, Germany, Nov. 2011).

[Chenoweth 2010] T. Chenoweth, R. Minch, S. Tabor, "Wireless Insecurity: Examining User Security Behavior on Public Networks," *Communications of the ACM,* Vol. 53, No. 2 (Feb. 2010), pp. 134–138.

[Cheswick 2000] B. Cheswick, H. Burch, S. Branigan, "Mapping and Visualizing the Internet," *Proc. 2000 Usenix Conference* (San Diego, CA, June 2000).

[Chiu 1989] D. Chiu, R. Jain, "Analysis of the Increase and Decrease Algorithms for Congestion Avoidance in Computer Networks," *Computer Networks and ISDN Systems,* Vol. 17, No. 1, pp. 1–14. http://www.cs.wustl.edu/~jain/papers/cong_av.htm

[Christiansen 2001] M. Christiansen, K. Jeffay, D. Ott, F. D. Smith, "Tuning Red for Web Traffic," *IEEE/ACM Transactions on Networking*, Vol. 9, No. 3 (June 2001), pp. 249–264.

[Chu 2002] Y. Chu, S. Rao, S. Seshan, H Zhang, "A Case for End System Multicast," *IEEE J. Selected Areas in Communications*, Vol 20, No. 8 (Oct. 2002), pp. 1456–1471.

[Chuang 2005] S. Chuang, S. Iyer, N. McKeown, "Practical Algorithms for Performance Guarantees in Buffered Crossbars," *Proc. 2005 IEEE INFOCOM.*

[Cicconetti 2006] C. Cicconetti, L. Lenzini, A. Mingozi, K. Eklund, "Quality of Service Support in 802.16 Networks," *IEEE Network Magazine* (Mar./Apr. 2006), pp. 50–55.

[Cisco 12000 2012] Cisco Systems Inc., "Cisco XR 12000 Series and Cisco 12000 Series Routers," http://www.cisco.com/en/US/products/ps6342/index.html

[Cisco 8500 2012] Cisco Systems Inc., "Catalyst 8500 Campus Switch Router Architecture," http://www.cisco.com/univercd/cc/td/doc/product/l3sw/8540/rel_12_0/w5_6f/softcnfg/1cfg8500.pdf

[Cisco 2011] Cisco Visual Networking Index: Forecast and Methodology, 2010–2015, White Paper, 2011.

[Cisco 2012] Cisco 2012, Data Centers, http://www.cisco.com/go/dce

[Cisco NAT 2012] Cisco Systems Inc., "How NAT Works," http://www.cisco.com/en/US/tech/tk648/tk361/technologies_tech_note09186a0080094831.shtml

[Cisco QoS 2012] Cisco Systems Inc., "Advanced QoS Services for the Intelligent Internet," http://www.cisco.com/warp/public/cc/pd/iosw/ioft/ioqo/tech/qos_wp.htm

[Cisco Queue 2012] Cisco Systems Inc., "Congestion Management Overview," http://www.cisco.com/en/US/docs/ios/12_2/qos/configuration/guide/qcfconmg.html

[Cisco Switches 2012] Cisco Systems Inc, "Multiservice Switches," http://www.cisco.com/warp/public/cc/pd/si/index.shtml

[Cisco SYN 2012] Cisco Systems Inc., "Defining Strategies to Protect Against TCP SYN Denial of Service Attacks," http://www.cisco.com/en/US/tech/tk828/technologies_tech_note09186a00800f67d5.shtml

[Cisco VNI 2011] Cisco, "Visual Networking Index," http://www.cisco.com/web/solutions/sp/vni/vni_forecast_highlights/index.html

[Clark 1988] D. Clark, "The Design Philosophy of the DARPA Internet Protocols," *Proc. 1988 ACM SIGCOMM* (Stanford, CA, Aug. 1988).

[Clarke 2002] I. Clarke, T. W. Hong, S. G. Miller, O. Sandberg, B. Wiley, "Protecting Free Expression Online with Freenet," *IEEE Internet Computing* (Jan.–Feb. 2002), pp. 40–49.

[Cohen 1977] D. Cohen, "Issues in Transnet Packetized Voice Communication," *Proc. Fifth Data Communications Symposium* (Snowbird, UT, Sept. 1977), pp. 6–13.

[Cohen 2003] B. Cohen, "Incentives to Build Robustness in BitTorrent," *First Workshop on the Economics of Peer-to-Peer Systems* (Berkeley, CA, June 2003).

[Cookie Central 2012] Cookie Central homepage, http://www.cookiecentral.com/n_cookie_faq.htm

[CoolStreaming 2005] X. Zhang, J. Liu, J., B. Li, and T.-S. P. Yum, "CoolStreamingDONet/: A Data-driven Overlay Network for Peer-to-Peer Live Media Streaming," *Proc. 2005 IEEE INFOCOM* (Miami, FL, Mar. 2005).

[Cormen 2001] T. H. Cormen, *Introduction to Algorithms,* 2nd Ed., MIT Press, Cambridge, MA, 2001.

[Crow 1997] B. Crow, I. Widjaja, J. Kim, P. Sakai, "IEEE 802.11 Wireless Local Area Networks," *IEEE Communications Magazine* (Sept. 1997), pp. 116–126.

[Crowcroft 1995] J. Crowcroft, Z. Wang, A. Smith, J. Adams, "A Comparison of the IETF and ATM Service Models," *IEEE Communications Magazine* (Nov./Dec. 1995), pp. 12–16.

[Crowcroft 1999] J. Crowcroft, M. Handley, I. Wakeman, *Internetworking Multimedia,* Morgan-Kaufman, San Francisco, 1999.

[Curtis 2011] A. R. Curtis, J. C. Mogul, J. Tourrilhes, P. Yalagandula, P. Sharma, S. Banerjee, "DevoFlow: Scaling Flow Management for High-Performance Networks," *Proc. 2011 ACM SIGCOMM.*

[Cusumano 1998] M. A. Cusumano, D. B. Yoffie, *Competing on Internet Time: Lessons from Netscape and its Battle with Microsoft,* Free Press, New York, NY, 1998.

[Dahlman 1998] E. Dahlman, B. Gudmundson, M. Nilsson, J. Sköld, "UMTS/IMT-2000 Based on Wideband CDMA," *IEEE Communications Magazine* (Sept. 1998), pp. 70–80.

[Daigle 1991] J. N. Daigle, *Queuing Theory for Telecommunications,* Addison-Wesley, Reading, MA, 1991.

[Dalal 1978] Y. Dalal, R. Metcalfe, "Reverse Path Forwarding of Broadcast Packets," *Communications of the ACM*, Vol. 21, No. 12 (Dec. 1978), pp. 1040–1048.

[Davie 2000] B. Davie and Y. Rekhter, *MPLS: Technology and Applications,* Morgan Kaufmann Series in Networking, 2000.

[Davies 2005] G. Davies, F. Kelly, "Network Dimensioning, Service Costing, and Pricing in a Packet-Switched Environment," *Telecommunications Policy*, Vol. 28, No. 4, pp. 391–412.

[DEC 1990] Digital Equipment Corporation, "In Memoriam: J. C. R. Licklider 1915–1990," SRC Research Report 61, Aug. 1990. http://www.memex.org/licklider.pdf

[DeClercq 2002] J. DeClercq, O. Paridaens, "Scalability Implications of Virtual Private Networks," *IEEE Communications Magazine*, Vol. 40, No. 5 (May 2002), pp. 151–157.

[Demers 1990] A. Demers, S. Keshav, S. Shenker, "Analysis and Simulation of a Fair Queuing Algorithm," *Internetworking: Research and Experience,* Vol. 1, No. 1 (1990), pp. 3–26.

[Denning 1997] D. Denning (Editor), P. Denning (Preface), *Internet Besieged: Countering Cyberspace Scofflaws,* Addison-Wesley, Reading, MA, 1997.

[dhc 2012] IETF Dynamic Host Configuration working group homepage, http://www.ietf.org/html.charters/dhc-charter.html

[Dhungel 2012] P. Dhungel, K. W. Ross, M. Steiner., Y. Tian, X. Hei, "Xunlei: Peer-Assisted Download Acceleration on a Massive Scale," *Passive and Active Measurement Conference (PAM) 2012*, Vienna, 2012.

[Diffie 1976] W. Diffie, M. E. Hellman, "New Directions in Cryptography," *IEEE Transactions on Information Theory,* Vol IT-22 (1976), pp. 644–654.

[Diggavi 2004] S. N. Diggavi, N. Al-Dhahir, A. Stamoulis, R. Calderbank, "Great Expectations: The Value of Spatial Diversity in Wireless Networks," *Proceedings of the IEEE,* Vol. 92, No. 2 (Feb. 2004).

[Dilley 2002] J. Dilley, B. Maggs, J. Parikh, H. Prokop, R. Sitaraman, B. Weihl, "Globally Distributed Content Delivert," *IEEE Internet Computing* (Sept.–Oct. 2002).

[Ding 2011] Y. Ding, Y. Du, Y. Hu, Z. Liu, L. Wang, K. W. Ross, A. Ghose, "Broadcast Yourself: Understanding YouTube Uploaders," *Proc. 2011 ACM Internet Measurement Conference* (Berlin).

[Diot 2000] C. Diot, B. N. Levine, B. Lyles, H. Kassem, D. Balensiefen, "Deployment Issues for the IP Multicast Service and Architecture," *IEEE Network,* Vol. 14, No. 1 (Jan./Feb. 2000) pp. 78–88.

[Dischinger 2007] M. Dischinger, A. Haeberlen, K. Gummadi, S. Saroiu, "Characterizing residential broadband networks," *Proc. 2007 ACM Internet Measurement Conference*, pp. 24–26.

[Dmitiropoulos 2007] X. Dmitiropoulos, D. Krioukov, M. Fomenkov, B. Huffaker, Y. Hyun, KC Claffy, G. Riley, "AS Relationships: Inference and Validation," *ACM Computer Communication Review* (Jan. 2007).

[DOCSIS 2004] Data-over-cable service interface specifications: Radio-frequency interface specification. ITU-T J.112, 2004.

[DOCSIS 2011] Data-Over-Cable Service Interface Specifications, DOCSIS 3.0: MAC and Upper Layer Protocols Interface Specification, CM-SP-MULPIv3.0-I16-110623, 2011.

[Dodge 2012] M. Dodge, "An Atlas of Cyberspaces," http://www.cybergeography.org/atlas/isp_maps.html

[Donahoo 2001] M. Donahoo, K. Calvert, *TCP/IP Sockets in C: Practical Guide for Programmers*, Morgan Kaufman, 2001.

[Doucer 2002] J. R. Douceur, "The Sybil Attack," *First International Workshop on Peer-to-Peer Systems (IPTPS '02)* (Cambridge, MA, Mar. 2002).

[DSL 2012] DSL Forum homepage, http://www.dslforum.org/

[Dhunghel 2008] P. Dhungel, D. Wu, B. Schonhorst, K.W. Ross, "A Measurement Study of Attacks on BitTorrent Leechers," *7th International Workshop on Peer-to-Peer Systems (IPTPS 2008)* (Tampa Bay, FL, Feb. 2008).

[Droms 2002] R. Droms, T. Lemon, *The DHCP Handbook* (2nd Edition), SAMS Publishing, 2002.

[Edney 2003] J. Edney and W. A. Arbaugh, *Real 802.11 Security: Wi-Fi Protected Access and 802.11i,* Addison-Wesley Professional, 2003.

[Edwards 2011] W. K. Edwards, R. Grinter, R. Mahajan, D. Wetherall, "Advancing the State of Home Networking," *Communications of the ACM,* Vol. 54, No. 6 (June 2011), pp. 62–71.

[Eklund 2002] K. Eklund, R. Marks, K. Stanswood, S. Wang, "IEEE Standard 802.16: A Technical Overview of the Wireless MAN Air Interface for Broadband Wireless Access," *IEEE Communications Magazine* (June 2002), pp. 98–107.

[Ellis 1987] H. Ellis, "The Story of Non-Secret Encryption," http://jya.com/ellisdoc.htm

[Ericsson 2011] Ericsson, "LTE—An Introduction," www.ericsson.com/res/docs/2011/lte_an_introduction.pdf

[Ericsson 2012] Ericsson, "The Evolution of Edge," http://www.ericsson.com/technology/whitepapers/broadband/evolution_of_EDGE.shtml

[Estrin 1997] D. Estrin, M. Handley, A. Helmy, P. Huang, D. Thaler, "A Dynamic Bootstrap Mechanism for Rendezvous-Based Multicast Routing," *Proc. 1998 IEEE INFOCOM* (New York, NY, Apr. 1998).

[Falkner 2007] J. Falkner, M. Piatek, J.P. John, A. Krishnamurthy, T. Anderson, "Profiling a Million Sser DHT," *Proc. 2007 ACM Internet Measurement Conference.*

[Faloutsos 1999] C. Faloutsos, M. Faloutsos, P. Faloutsos, "What Does the Internet Look Like? Empirical Laws of the Internet Topology," *Proc. 1999 ACM SIGCOMM* (Boston, MA, Aug. 1999).

[Farrington 2010] N. Farrington, G. Porter, S. Radhakrishnan, H. Bazzaz, V. Subramanya, Y. Fainman, G. Papen, A. Vahdat, "Helios: A Hybrid Electrical/Optical Switch Architecture for Modular Data Centers," *Proc. 2010 ACM SIGCOMM.*

[Feamster 2004] N. Feamster, J. Winick, J. Rexford, "A Model for BGP Routing for Network Engineering," *Proc. 2004 ACM SIGMETRICS* (New York, NY, June 2004).

[Feamster 2005] N. Feamster, H. Balakrishnan, "Detecting BGP Configuration Faults with Static Analysis," *NSDI* (May 2005).

[Feldman 2005] M. Feldman J. Chuang, "Overcoming Free-Riding Behavior in Peer-to-peer Systems," *ACM SIGecom Exchanges* (July 2005).

[Feldmeier 1995] D. Feldmeier, "Fast Software Implementation of Error Detection Codes," *IEEE/ACM Transactions on Networking,* Vol. 3, No. 6 (Dec. 1995), pp. 640–652.

[FIPS 1995] Federal Information Processing Standard, "Secure Hash Standard," FIPS Publication 180-1. http://www.itl.nist.gov/fipspubs/fip180-1.htm

[Floyd 1999] S. Floyd, K. Fall, "Promoting the Use of End-to-End Congestion Control in the Internet," *IEEE/ACM Transactions on Networking,* Vol. 6, No. 5 (Oct. 1998), pp. 458–472.

[Floyd 2000] S. Floyd, M. Handley, J. Padhye, J. Widmer, "Equation-Based Congestion Control for Unicast Applications," *Proc. 2000 ACM SIGCOMM* (Stockholm, Sweden, Aug. 2000).

[Floyd 2001] S. Floyd, "A Report on Some Recent Developments in TCP Congestion Control," *IEEE Communications Magazine* (Apr. 2001).

[Floyd 2012] S. Floyd, "References on RED (Random Early Detection) Queue Management," http://www.icir.org/floyd/red.html

[Floyd Synchronization 1994] S. Floyd, V. Jacobson, "Synchronization of Periodic Routing Messages," *IEEE/ACM Transactions on Networking,* Vol. 2, No. 2 (Apr. 1997) pp. 122–136.

[Floyd TCP 1994] S. Floyd, "TCP and Explicit Congestion Notification," *ACM SIGCOMM Computer Communications Review,* Vol. 24, No. 5 (Oct. 1994), pp. 10–23.

[Fluhrer 2001] S. Fluhrer, I. Mantin, A. Shamir, "Weaknesses in the Key Scheduling Algorithm of RC4," *Eighth Annual Workshop on Selected Areas in Cryptography*, (Toronto, Canada, Aug. 2002).

[Fortz 2000] B. Fortz, M. Thorup, "Internet Traffic Engineering by Optimizing OSPF Weights," *Proc. 2000 IEEE INFOCOM* (Tel Aviv, Israel, Apr. 2000).

[Fortz 2002] B. Fortz, J. Rexford, M. Thorup, "Traffic Engineering with Traditional IP Routing Protocols," *IEEE Communication Magazine* (Oct. 2002).

[Fraleigh 2003] C. Fraleigh, F. Tobagi, C. Diot, "Provisioning IP Backbone Networks to Support Latency Sensitive Traffic," *Proc. 2003 IEEE INFOCOM* (San Francisco, CA, Mar. 2003).

[Freedman 2004] M. J. Freedman, E. Freudenthal, D. Mazires, "Democratizing Content Publication with Coral," *USENIX NSDI,* 2004.

[Friedman 1999] T. Friedman, D. Towsley "Multicast Session Membership Size Estimation," *Proc. 1999 IEEE INFOCOM* (New York, NY, Mar. 1999).

[Frost 1994] J. Frost, "BSD Sockets: A Quick and Dirty Primer," http://world.std.com/~jimf/papers/sockets/sockets.html

[FTTH Council 2011a] FTTH Council, "NORTH AMERICAN FTTH STATUS—MARCH 31, 2011" (March 2011), www.ftthcouncil.org

[FTTH Council 2011b] FTTH Council, "2011 Broadband Consumer Research" (June 2011), www.ftthcouncil.org

[Gallagher 1983] R. G. Gallagher, P. A. Humblet, P. M. Spira, "A Distributed Algorithm for Minimum Weight-Spanning Trees," *ACM Trans. on Programming Languages and Systems,* Vol. 1, No. 5 (Jan. 1983), pp. 66–77.

[Gao 2001] L. Gao, J. Rexford, "Stable Internet Routing Without Global Coordination," *IEEE/ACM Transactions on Networking,* Vol. 9, No. 6 (Dec. 2001), pp. 681–692.

[Garces-Erce 2003] L. Garces-Erce, K. W. Ross, E. Biersack, P. Felber, G. Urvoy-Keller, "TOPLUS: Topology Centric Lookup Service," *Fifth Int. Workshop on Networked Group Communications (NGC 2003)* (Munich, Sept. 2003) http://cis.poly.edu/~ross/papers/TOPLUS.pdf

[Gartner 2003] F. C. Gartner, "A Survey of Self-Stabilizing Spanning-Tree Construction Algorithms," *Technical Report IC/2003/38,* Swiss Federal Institute of Technology (EPFL), School of Computer and Communication Sciences, June 10, 2003. http://ic2.epfl.ch/publications/documents/IC_TECH_REPORT_200338.pdf

[Gauthier 1999] L. Gauthier, C. Diot, and J. Kurose, "End-to-end Transmission Control Mechanisms for Multiparty Interactive Applications on the Internet," *Proc. 1999 IEEE INFOCOM* (New York, NY, Apr. 1999).

[Girard 1990] A. Girard, *Routing and Dimensioning in Circuit-Switched Networks,* Addison-Wesley, Reading, MA, 1990.

[Glitho 1998] R. Glitho, "Contrasting OSI Systems Management to SNMP and TMN," *Journal of Network and Systems Management,* Vol. 6, No. 2 (June 1998), pp. 113–131.

[Gnutella 2009] "The Gnutella Protocol Specification, v0.4" http://www9.limewire.com/developer/gnutella_protocol_0.4.pdf

[Goodman 1997] David J. Goodman, *Wireless Personal Communications Systems*, Prentice-Hall, 1997.

[Google Locations 2012] Google data centers. http://www.google.com/corporate/datacenter/locations.html

[Goralski 1999] W. Goralski, *Frame Relay for High-Speed Networks,* John Wiley, New York, 1999.

[Goralski 2001] W. Goralski, *Optical Networking and WDM,* Osborne/McGraw-Hill, Berkeley, CA, 2001.

[Greenberg 2009a] A. Greenberg, J. Hamilton, D. Maltz, P. Patel, "The Cost of a Cloud: Research Problems in Data Center Networks," *ACM Computer Communications Review* (Jan. 2009).

[Greenberg 2009b] A. Greenberg, N. Jain, S. Kandula, C. Kim, P. Lahiri, D. Maltz, P. Patel, S. Sengupta, "VL2: A Scalable and Flexible Data Center Network," *Proc. 2009 ACM SIGCOMM*.

[Greenberg 2011] A. Greenberg, J. Hamilton, N. Jain, S. Kandula, C. Kim, P. Lahiri, D. Maltz, P. Patel, S. Sengupta, "VL2: A Scalable and Flexible Data Center Network," *Communications of the ACM,* Vol. 54, No. 3 (Mar. 2011), pp. 95–104.

[Griffin 2012] T. Griffin, "Interdomain Routing Links," http://www.cl.cam.ac.uk/~tgg22/interdomain/

[Guha 2006] S. Guha, N. Daswani, R. Jain, "An Experimental Study of the Skype Peer-to-Peer VoIP System," *Proc. Fifth Int. Workshop on P2P Systems* (Santa Barbara, CA, 2006).

[Guo 2005] L. Guo, S. Chen, Z. Xiao, E. Tan, X. Ding, X. Zhang, "Measurement, Analysis, and Modeling of BitTorrent-Like Systems," *Proc. 2005 ACM Internet Measurement Conference*.

[Guo 2009] C. Guo, G. Lu, D. Li, H. Wu, X. Zhang, Y. Shi, C. Tian, Y. Zhang, S. Lu, "BCube: A High Performance, Server-centric Network Architecture for Modular Data Centers," *Proc. 2009 ACM SIGCOMM*.

[Gupta 2001] P. Gupta, N. McKeown, "Algorithms for Packet Classification," *IEEE Network Magazine,* Vol. 15, No. 2 (Mar./Apr. 2001), pp. 24–32.

[Ha 2008] Ha, S., Rhee, I., L. Xu, "CUBIC: A New TCP-Friendly High-Speed TCP Variant," *ACM SIGOPS Operating System Review*, 2008.

[Halabi 2000] S. Halabi, *Internet Routing Architectures,* 2nd Ed., Cisco Press, 2000.

[Halperin 2008] D. Halperin, T. Heydt-Benjamin, B. Ransford, S. Clark, B. Defend, W. Morgan, K. Fu, T. Kohno, W. Maisel, "Pacemakers and implantable cardiac defibrillators: Software radio attacks and zero-power defenses," *Proc. 29th Annual IEEE Symposium on Security and Privacy* (May 2008).

[Halperin 2011] D. Halperin, S. Kandula, J. Padhye, P. Bahl, D. Wetherall, "Augmenting Data Center Networks with Multi-Gigabit Wireless Links," *Proc. 2011 ACM SIGCOMM*.

[Hanabali 2005] A. A. Hanbali, E. Altman, P. Nain, "A Survey of TCP over Ad Hoc Networks*," IEEE Commun. Surveys and Tutorials*, Vol. 7, No. 3 (2005), pp. 22–36.

[Hei 2007] X. Hei, C. Liang, J. Liang, Y. Liu, K. W. Ross, "A Measurement Study of a Large-scale P2P IPTV System," *IEEE Trans. on Multimedia* (Dec. 2007).

[Heidemann 1997] J. Heidemann, K. Obraczka, J. Touch, "Modeling the Performance of HTTP over Several Transport Protocols," *IEEE/ACM Transactions on Networking,* Vol. 5, No. 5 (Oct. 1997), pp. 616–630.

[Held 2001] G. Held, *Data Over Wireless Networks: Bluetooth, WAP, and Wireless LANs*, McGraw-Hill, 2001.

[Hersent 2000] O. Hersent, D. Gurle, J-P. Petit, *IP Telephony: Packet-Based Multimedia Communication Systems*, Pearson Education Limited, Edinburgh, 2000.

[Holland 2001] G. Holland, N. Vaidya, V. Bahl, "A Rate-Adaptive MAC Protocol for Multi-Hop Wireless Networks," *Proc. 2001 ACM Int. Conference of Mobile Computing and Networking (Mobicom01)* (Rome, Italy, July 2001).

[Hollot 2002] C.V. Hollot, V. Misra, D. Towsley, W. Gong, "Analysis and design of controllers for AQM routers supporting TCP flows," *IEEE Transactions on Automatic Control,* Vol. 47, No. 6 (June 2002), pp. 945–959.

[Huang 2002] C. Haung, V. Sharma, K. Owens, V. Makam, "Building Reliable MPLS Networks Using a Path Protection Mechanism," *IEEE Communications Magazine,* Vol. 40, No. 3 (Mar. 2002), pp. 156–162.

[Huang 2005] Y. Huang, R. Guerin, "Does Over-Provisioning Become More or Less Efficient as Networks Grow Larger?," *Proc. IEEE Int. Conf. Network Protocols (ICNP)* (Boston MA, November 2005).

[Huang 2007] C. Huang, Jin Li, K.W. Ross, "Can Internet VoD Be Profitable?," *Proc 2007 ACM SIGCOMM* (Kyoto, Aug. 2007).

[Huang 2008] C. Huang, J. Li, A. Wang, K. W. Ross, "Understanding Hybrid CDN-P2P: Why Limelight Needs its Own Red Swoosh," *Proc. 2008 NOSSDAV,* Braunschweig, Germany.

[Huang 2010] C. Huang, N. Holt, Y. A. Wang, A. Greenberg, J. Li, K. W. Ross, "A DNS Reflection Method for Global Traffic Management," *Proc. 2010 USENIX,* Boston.

[Huitema 1998] C. Huitema, *IPv6: The New Internet Protocol,* 2nd Ed., Prentice Hall, Englewood Cliffs, NJ, 1998.

[Huston 1999a] G. Huston, "Interconnection, Peering, and Settlements—Part I," *The Internet Protocol Journal,* Vol. 2, No. 1 (Mar. 1999).

[Huston 2004] G. Huston, "NAT Anatomy: A Look Inside Network Address Translators," *The Internet Protocol Journal,* Vol. 7, No. 3 (Sept. 2004).

[Huston 2008a] G. Huston, "Confronting IPv4 Address Exhaustion," http://www.potaroo .net/ispcol/2008-10/v4depletion.html

[Huston 2008b] G. Huston, G. Michaelson, "IPv6 Deployment: Just where are we?" http:// www.potaroo.net/ispcol/2008-04/ipv6.html

[Huston 2011a] G. Huston, "A Rough Guide to Address Exhaustion," *The Internet Protocol Journal,* Vol. 14, No. 1 (Mar. 2011).

[Huston 2011b] G. Huston, "Transitioning Protocols," *The Internet Protocol Journal,* Vol. 14, No. 1 (Mar. 2011).

[IAB 2012] Internet Architecture Board homepage, http://www.iab.org/

[IANA 2012a] Internet Assigned Number Authority homepage, http://www.iana.org/

[IANA 2012b] Internet Assigned Number Authority, "Private Enterprise Numbers" http:// www.iana.org/assignments/enterprise-numbers

[IANA Protocol Numbers 2012] Internet Assigned Numbers Authority, Protocol Numbers, http://www.iana.org/assignments/protocol-numbers/protocol-numbers.xhtml

[IANA TLD 2012] IANA Root Zone Database, http://www.iana.org/domains/root/db/

[ICANN 2012] The Internet Corporation for Assigned Names and Numbers homepage, http://www.icann.org

[IEC Optical 2012] IEC Online Education, "Optical Access," http://www.iec.org/online/ tutorials/opt_acc/

[IEEE 802 2012] IEEE 802 LAN/MAN Standards Committee homepage, http://www .ieee802.org/

[IEEE 802.11 1999] IEEE 802.11, "1999 Edition (ISO/IEC 8802-11: 1999) IEEE Standards for Information Technology—Telecommunications and Information Exchange Between Systems—Local and Metropolitan Area Network—Specific Requirements—Part 11:

Wireless LAN Medium Access Control (MAC) and Physical Layer (PHY) Specification," http://standards.ieee.org/getieee802/download/802.11-1999.pdf

[IEEE 802.11n 2012] IEEE, "IEEE P802.11—Task Group N—Meeting Update: Status of 802.11n," http://grouper.ieee.org/groups/802/11/Reports/tgn_update.htm

[IEEE 802.15 2012] IEEE 802.15 Working Group for WPAN homepage, http://grouper.ieee.org/groups/802/15/.

[IEEE 802.15.4 2012] IEEE 802.15 WPAN Task Group 4, http://www.ieee802.org/15/pub/TG4.html

[IEEE 802.16d 2004] IEEE, "IEEE Standard for Local and Metropolitan Area Networks, Part 16: Air Interface for Fixed Broadband Wireless Access Systems," http://standards.ieee.org/getieee802/download/802.16-2004.pdf

[IEEE 802.16e 2005] IEEE, "IEEE Standard for Local and Metropolitan Area Networks, Part 16: Air Interface for Fixed and Mobile Broadband Wireless Access Systems, Amendment 2: Physical and Medium Access Control Layers for Combined Fixed and Mobile Operation in Licensed Bands and Corrigendum 1," http://standards.ieee.org/getieee802/download/802 .16e-2005.pdf

[IEEE 802.1q 2005] IEEE, "IEEE Standard for Local and Metropolitan Area Networks: Virtual Bridged Local Area Networks," http://standards.ieee.org/getieee802/download/802 .1Q-2005.pdf

[IEEE 802.1X] IEEE Std 802.1X-2001 Port-Based Network Access Control, http://standards.ieee.org/reading/ieee/std_public/description/lanman/802.1x-2001_desc.html

[IEEE 802.3 2012] IEEE, "IEEE 802.3 CSMA/CD (Ethernet)," http://grouper.ieee.org/groups/802/3/

[IEEE 802.5 2012] IEEE, IEEE 802.5 homepage, http://www.ieee802.org/5/www8025org/

[IETF 2012] Internet Engineering Task Force homepage, http://www.ietf.org

[Ihm 2011] S. Ihm, V. S. Pai, "Towards Understanding Modern Web Traffic," *Proc. 2011 ACM Internet Measurement Conference* (Berlin).

[IMAP 2012] The IMAP Connection, http://www.imap.org/

[Intel 2012] Intel Corp, "Intel® 82544 Gigabit Ethernet Controller," http://www.intel.com/design/network/products/lan/docs/82544_docs.htm

[Intel WiMax 2012] Intel Corp., "WiMax Technology," http://www.intel.com/technology/wimax/index.htm

[Internet2 Multicast 2012] Internet2 Multicast Working Group homepage, http://www.internet2.edu/multicast/

[IPv6 2012] IPv6.com homepage, http://www.ipv6.com/

[ISC 2012] Internet Systems Consortium homepage, http://www.isc.org

[ISI 1979] Information Sciences Institute, "DoD Standard Internet Protocol," Internet Engineering Note 123 (Dec. 1979), http://www.isi.edu/in-notes/ien/ien123.txt

[ISO 2012] International Organization for Standardization homepage, International Organization for Standardization, http://www.iso.org/

[ISO X.680 2002] International Organization for Standardization, "X.680: ITU-T Recommendation X.680 (2002) Information Technology—Abstract Syntax Notation One (ASN.1): Specification of Basic Notation." http://www.itu.int/ITU-T/studygroups/com17/languages/X.680-0207.pdf

[ITU 1999] Asymmetric Digital Subscriber Line (ADSL) Transceivers. ITU-T G.992.1, 1999.

[ITU 2003] Asymmetric Digital Subscriber Line (ADSL) Transceivers—Extended Bandwidth ADSL2 (ADSL2Plus). ITU-T G.992.5, 2003.

[ITU 2005a] International Telecommunication Union, "ITU-T X.509, The Directory: Public-key and attribute certificate frameworks" (August 2005).

[ITU 2005b] International Telecommunication Union, *The Internet of Things,* 2005, http://www.itu.int/osg/spu/publications/internetofthings/InternetofThings_summary.pdf

[ITU 2012] The ITU homepage, http://www.itu.int/

[ITU Statistics 2012] International Telecommunications Union, "ICT Statistics," http://www.itu.int/ITU-D/icteye/Reports.aspx

[ITU 2011] ITU, "Measuring the Information Society, 2011," http://www.itu.int/ITU-D/ict/publications/idi/2011/index.html

[ITU 2011] ITU, "The World in 2010: ICT Facts and Figures," http://www.itu.int/ITU-D/ict/material/Telecom09_flyer.pdf

[ITU-T Q.2931 1995] International Telecommunication Union, "Recommendation Q.2931 (02/95) - Broadband Integrated Services Digital Network (B-ISDN)—Digital subscriber signalling system no. 2 (DSS 2)—User-network interface (UNI)—Layer 3 specification for basic call/connection control."

[Iyer 2002] S. Iyer, R. Zhang, N. McKeown, "Routers with a Single Stage of Buffering," *Proc. 2002 ACM SIGCOMM* (Pittsburgh, PA, Aug. 2002).

[Iyer 2008] S. Iyer, R. R. Kompella, N. McKeown, "Designing Packet Buffers for Router Line Cards," *IEEE Transactions on Networking*, Vol. 16, No. 3 (June 2008), pp. 705–717.

[Jacobson 1988] V. Jacobson, "Congestion Avoidance and Control," *Proc. 1988 ACM SIGCOMM* (Stanford, CA, Aug. 1988), pp. 314–329.

[Jain 1986] R. Jain, "A timeout-based congestion control scheme for window flow-controlled networks," *IEEE Journal on Selected Areas in Communications SAC-4*, 7 (Oct. 1986).

[Jain 1989] R. Jain, "A Delay-Based Approach for Congestion Avoidance in Interconnected Heterogeneous Computer Networks," *ACM SIGCOMM Computer Communications Review,* Vol. 19, No. 5 (1989), pp. 56–71.

[Jain 1994] R. Jain, *FDDI Handbook: High-Speed Networking Using Fiber and Other Media,* Addison-Wesley, Reading, MA, 1994.

[Jain 1996] R. Jain. S. Kalyanaraman, S. Fahmy, R. Goyal, S. Kim, "Tutorial Paper on ABR Source Behavior," *ATM Forum*/96-1270, Oct. 1996. http://www.cse.wustl.edu/~jain/atmf/ftp/atm96-1270.pdf

[Jaiswal 2003] S. Jaiswal, G. Iannaccone, C. Diot, J. Kurose, D. Towsley, "Measurement and Classification of Out-of-Sequence Packets in a Tier-1 IP backbone," *Proc. 2003 IEEE INFOCOM*.

[Ji 2003] P. Ji, Z. Ge, J. Kurose, D. Towsley, "A Comparison of Hard-State and Soft-State Signaling Protocols," *Proc. 2003 ACM SIGCOMM* (Karlsruhe, Germany, Aug. 2003).

[Jiang 2001] W. Jiang, J. Lennox, H. Schulzrinne, K. Singh, "Towards Junking the PBX: Deploying IP Telephony," *NOSSDAV'01* (Port Jefferson, NY, June 2001).

[Jimenez 1997] D. Jimenez, "Outside Hackers Infiltrate MIT Network, Compromise Security," *The Tech,* Vol. 117, No 49 (Oct. 1997), p. 1, http://www-tech.mit.edu/V117/N49/hackers.49n.html

[Jin 2004] C. Jin, D. X. We, S. Low, "FAST TCP: Motivation, architecture, algorithms, performance," *Proc. 2004 IEEE INFOCOM* (Hong Kong, March 2004).

[Kaaranen 2001] H. Kaaranen, S. Naghian, L. Laitinen, A. Ahtiainen, V. Niemi, *Networks: Architecture, Mobility and Services,* New York: John Wiley & Sons, 2001.

[Kahn 1967] D. Kahn, *The Codebreakers: The Story of Secret Writing,* The Macmillan Company, 1967.

[Kahn 1978] R. E. Kahn, S. Gronemeyer, J. Burchfiel, R. Kunzelman, "Advances in Packet Radio Technology," *Proc. 1978 IEEE INFOCOM*, 66, 11 (Nov. 1978).

[Kamerman 1997] A. Kamerman, L. Monteban, "WaveLAN-II: A High–Performance Wireless LAN for the Unlicensed Band," *Bell Labs Technical Journal* (Summer 1997), pp. 118–133.

[Kangasharju 2000] J. Kangasharju, K. W. Ross, J. W. Roberts, "Performance Evaluation of Redirection Schemes in Content Distribution Networks," *Proc. 5th Web Caching and Content Distribution Workshop* (Lisbon, Portugal, May 2000).

[Kar 2000] K. Kar, M. Kodialam, T. V. Lakshman, "Minimum Interference Routing of Bandwidth Guaranteed Tunnels with MPLS Traffic Engineering Applications," *IEEE J. Selected Areas in Communications* (Dec. 2000).

[Karn 1987] P. Karn, C. Partridge, "Improving Round-Trip Time Estimates in Reliable Transport Protocols," *Proc. 1987 ACM SIGCOMM.*

[Karol 1987] M. Karol, M. Hluchyj, A. Morgan, "Input Versus Output Queuing on a Space-Division Packet Switch," *IEEE Transactions on Communications,* Vol. 35, No. 12 (Dec. 1987), pp. 1347–1356.

[Katabi 2002] D. Katabi, M. Handley, C. Rohrs, "Internet Congestion Control for Future High Bandwidth-Delay Product Environments," *Proc. 2002 ACM SIGCOMM* (Pittsburgh, PA, Aug. 2002).

[Katzela 1995] I. Katzela, M. Schwartz. "Schemes for Fault Identification in Communication Networks," *IEEE/ACM Transactions on Networking,* Vol. 3, No. 6 (Dec. 1995), pp. 753–764.

[Kaufman 1995] C. Kaufman, R. Perlman, M. Speciner, *Network Security, Private Communication in a Public World,* Prentice Hall, Englewood Cliffs, NJ, 1995.

[Kelly 1998] F. P. Kelly, A. Maulloo, D. Tan, "Rate control for communication networks: Shadow prices, proportional fairness and stability," *J. Operations Res. Soc.,* Vol. 49, No. 3 (Mar. 1998), pp. 237–252.

[Kelly 2003] T. Kelly, "Scalable TCP: improving performance in high speed wide area networks," *ACM SIGCOMM Computer Communications Review,* Volume 33, No. 2 (Apr. 2003), pp 83–91.

[Kilkki 1999] K. Kilkki, *Differentiated Services for the Internet*, Macmillan Technical Publishing, Indianapolis, IN, 1999.

[Kim 2005] H. Kim, S. Rixner, V. Pai, "Network Interface Data Caching," *IEEE Transactions on Computers*, Vol. 54, No. 11 (Nov. 2005), pp. 1394–1408.

[Kim 2008] C. Kim, M. Caesar, J. Rexford, "Floodless in SEATTLE: A Scalable Ethernet Architecture for Large Enterprises," *Proc. 2008 ACM SIGCOMM* (Seattle, WA, Aug. 2008).

[Kleinrock 1961] L. Kleinrock, "Information Flow in Large Communication Networks," RLE Quarterly Progress Report, July 1961.

[Kleinrock 1964] L. Kleinrock, *1964 Communication Nets: Stochastic Message Flow and Delay,* McGraw-Hill, New York, NY, 1964.

[Kleinrock 1975] L. Kleinrock, *Queuing Systems, Vol. 1,* John Wiley, New York, 1975.

[**Kleinrock 1975b**] L. Kleinrock, F. A. Tobagi, "Packet Switching in Radio Channels: Part I—Carrier Sense Multiple-Access Modes and Their Throughput-Delay Characteristics," *IEEE Transactions on Communications,* Vol. 23, No. 12 (Dec. 1975), pp. 1400–1416.

[**Kleinrock 1976**] L. Kleinrock, *Queuing Systems, Vol. 2,* John Wiley, New York, 1976.

[**Kleinrock 2004**] L. Kleinrock, "The Birth of the Internet," http://www.lk.cs.ucla.edu/LK/Inet/birth.html

[**Kohler 2006**] E. Kohler, M. Handley, S. Floyd, "DDCP: Designing DCCP: Congestion Control Without Reliability," *Proc. 2006 ACM SIGCOMM* (Pisa, Italy, Sept. 2006).

[**Kolding 2003**] T. Kolding, K. Pedersen, J. Wigard, F. Frederiksen, P.Mogensen, "High Speed Downlink Packet Access: WCDMA Evolution," *IEEE Vehicular Technology Society News* (Feb. 2003), pp. 4–10.

[**Koponen 2011**] T. Koponen, S. Shenker, H. Balakrishnan, N. Feamster, I. Ganichev, A. Ghodsi, P. B. Godfrey, N. McKeown, G. Parulkar, B. Raghavan, J. Rexford, S. Arianfar, D. Kuptsov, "Architecting for Innovation," *ACM Computer Communications Review*, 2011.

[**Korhonen 2003**] J. Korhonen, *Introduction to 3G Mobile Communications*, 2nd ed., Artech House, 2003.

[**Koziol 2003**] J. Koziol, *Intrusion Detection with Snort,* Sams Publishing, 2003.

[**Krishnamurthy 2001**] B. Krishnamurthy, and J. Rexford, *Web Protocols and Practice: HTTP/1.1, Networking Protocols, and Traffic Measurement*, Addison-Wesley, Boston, MA, 2001.

[**Krishnamurthy 2001b**] B. Krishnamurthy, C. Wills, Y. Zhang, "On the Use and Performance of Content Distribution Networks," *Proc. 2001 ACM Internet Measurement Conference*.

[**Krishnan 2009**] R. Krishnan, H. Madhyastha, S. Srinivasan, S. Jain, A. Krishnamurthy, T. Anderson, J. Gao, "Moving Beyond End-to-end Path Information to Optimize CDN Performance," *Proc. 2009 ACM Internet Measurement Conference*.

[**Kulkarni 2005**] S. Kulkarni, C. Rosenberg, "Opportunistic Scheduling: Generalizations to Include Multiple Constraints, Multiple Interfaces, and Short Term Fairness," *Wireless Networks*, 11 (2005), 557–569.

[**Kumar 2006**] R. Kumar, K.W. Ross, "Optimal Peer-Assisted File Distribution: Single and Multi-Class Problems," *IEEE Workshop on Hot Topics in Web Systems and Technologies* (Boston, MA, 2006).

[**Labovitz 1997**] C. Labovitz, G. R. Malan, F. Jahanian, "Internet Routing Instability," *Proc. 1997 ACM SIGCOMM* (Cannes, France, Sept. 1997), pp. 115–126.

[**Labovitz 2010**] C. Labovitz, S. Iekel-Johnson, D. McPherson, J. Oberheide, F. Jahanian, "Internet Inter-Domain Traffic," *Proc. 2010 ACM SIGCOMM*.

[**Labrador 1999**] M. Labrador, S. Banerjee, "Packet Dropping Policies for ATM and IP Networks," *IEEE Communications Surveys*, Vol. 2, No. 3 (Third Quarter 1999), pp. 2–14.

[**Lacage 2004**] M. Lacage, M.H. Manshaei, T. Turletti, "IEEE 802.11 Rate Adaptation: A Practical Approach," *ACM Int. Symposium on Modeling, Analysis, and Simulation of Wireless and Mobile Systems (MSWiM)* (Venice, Italy, Oct. 2004).

[**Lakhina 2004**] A. Lakhina, M. Crovella, C. Diot, "Diagnosing Network-Wide Traffic Anomalies," *Proc. 2004 ACM SIGCOMM*.

[**Lakhina 2005**] A. Lakhina, M. Crovella, C. Diot, "Mining Anomalies Using Traffic Feature Distributions," *Proc. 2005 ACM SIGCOMM*.

[**Lakshman 1997**] T. V. Lakshman, U. Madhow, "The Performance of TCP/IP for Networks with High Bandwidth-Delay Products and Random Loss," *IEEE/ACM Transactions on Networking,* Vol. 5, No. 3 (1997), pp. 336–350.

[**Lam 1980**] S. Lam, "A Carrier Sense Multiple Access Protocol for Local Networks," *Computer Networks,* Vol. 4 (1980), pp. 21–32.

[**Larmouth 1996**] J. Larmouth, *Understanding OSI,* International Thomson Computer Press 1996. Chapter 8 of this book deals with ASN.1 and is available online at http://www.salford .ac.uk/iti/books/osi/all.html#head8.

[**Larmouth 2012**] J. Larmouth, *Understanding OSI,* http://www.business.salford.ac.uk/ legacy/isi/books/osi/osi.html

[**Lawton 2001**] G. Lawton, "Is IPv6 Finally Gaining Ground?" *IEEE Computer Magazine* (Aug. 2001), pp. 11–15.

[**LeBlond 2011**] S. LeBlond, C. Zhang, A. Legout, K. W. Ross, W. Dabbous, "Exploring the Privacy Limits of Real-Time Communication Applications," *Proc. 2011 ACM Internet Measurement Conference* (Berlin, 2011).

[**LeBlond 2011**] S. LeBlond, C. Zhang, A. Legout, K. W. Ross, W. Dabbous, "I Know Where You and What You Are Sharing: Exploiting P2P Communications to Invade Users Privacy," *Proc. 2011 ACM Internet Measurement Conference* (Berlin).

[**Leighton 2009**] T. Leighton, "Improving Performance on the Internet," *Communications of the ACM,* Vol. 52, No. 2 (Feb. 2009), pp. 44–51.

[**Leiner 1998**] B. Leiner, V. Cerf, D. Clark, R. Kahn, L. Kleinrock, D. Lynch, J. Postel, L. Roberts, S. Woolf, "A Brief History of the Internet," http://www.isoc.org/internet/history/ brief.html

[**Leung 2006**] K. Leung, V. O.K. Li, "TCP in Wireless Networks: Issues, Approaches, and Challenges," *IEEE Commun. Surveys and Tutorials,* Vol. 8, No. 4 (2006), pp. 64–79.

[**Li 2004**] L. Li, D. Alderson, W. Willinger, J. Doyle, "A First-Principles Approach to Understanding the Internet's Router-Level Topology," *Proc. 2004 ACM SIGCOMM* (Portland, OR, Aug. 2004).

[**Li 2007**] J. Li, M. Guidero, Z. Wu, E. Purpus, T. Ehrenkranz, "BGP Routing Dynamics Revisited." *ACM Computer Communication Review* (April 2007).

[**Liang 2006**] J. Liang, N. Naoumov, K.W. Ross, "The Index Poisoning Attack in P2P File-Sharing Systems," *Proc. 2006 IEEE INFOCOM* (Barcelona, Spain, April 2006).

[**Lin 2001**] Y. Lin, I. Chlamtac, *Wireless and Mobile Network Architectures,* John Wiley and Sons, New York, NY, 2001.

[**Liogkas 2006**] N. Liogkas, R. Nelson, E. Kohler, L. Zhang, "Exploiting BitTorrent For Fun (But Not Profit)," *6th International Workshop on Peer-to-Peer Systems (IPTPS 2006).*

[**Liu 2002**] B. Liu, D. Goeckel, D. Towsley, "TCP-Cognizant Adaptive Forward Error Correction in Wireless Networks," *Proc. 2002 Global Internet.*

[**Liu 2003**] J. Liu, I. Matta, M. Crovella, "End-to-End Inference of Loss Nature in a Hybrid Wired/Wireless Environment," *Proc. WiOpt'03: Modeling and Optimization in Mobile, Ad Hoc and Wireless Networks.*

[**Liu 2010**] Z. Liu, P. Dhungel, Di Wu, C. Zhang, K. W. Ross, "Understanding and Improving Incentives in Private P2P Communities," *ICDCS* (Genoa, Italy, 2010).

[**Locher 2006**] T. Locher, P. Moor, S. Schmid, R. Wattenhofer, "Free Riding in BitTorrent is Cheap," *Proc. ACM HotNets 2006 (*Irvine CA, Nov. 2006).

[**Lui 2004**] J. Lui, V. Misra, D. Rubenstein, "On the Robustness of Soft State Protocols," *Proc. IEEE Int. Conference on Network Protocols (ICNP '04)*, pp. 50–60.

[**Luotonen 1998**] A. Luotonen, *Web Proxy Servers,* Prentice Hall, Englewood Cliffs, NJ, 1998.

[**Lynch 1993**] D. Lynch, M. Rose, *Internet System Handbook,* Addison-Wesley, Reading, MA, 1993.

[**Macedonia 1994**] M. Macedonia, D. Brutzman, "MBone Provides Audio and Video Across the Internet," *IEEE Computer Magazine,* Vol. 27, No. 4 (Apr. 1994), pp. 30–36.

[**Mahdavi 1997**] J. Mahdavi, S. Floyd, "TCP-Friendly Unicast Rate-Based Flow Control," unpublished note (Jan. 1997).

[**Malware 2006**] Computer Economics, "2005 Malware Report: The Impact of Malicious Code Attacks," http://www.computereconomics.com

[**manet 2012**] IETF Mobile Ad-hoc Networks (manet) Working Group, http://www.ietf.org/html.charters/manet-charter.html

[**Mao 2002**] Z. M. Mao, C. Cranor, F. Boudlis, M. Rabinovich, O. Spatscheck, J. Wang, "A Precise and Efficient Evaluation of the Proximity Between Web Clients and Their Local DNS Servers," *Proc. 2002 USENIX ATC.*

[**MaxMind 2012**] http://www.maxmind.com/app/ip-location

[**Maymounkov 2002**] P. Maymounkov, D. Mazières. "Kademlia: A Peer-to-Peer Information System Based on the XOR Metric." *Proceedings of the 1st International Workshop on Peerto-Peer Systems (IPTPS '02)* (Mar. 2002), pp. 53–65.

[**McKeown 1997a**] N. McKeown, M. Izzard, A. Mekkittikul, W. Ellersick, M. Horowitz, "The Tiny Tera: A Packet Switch Core," *IEEE Micro Magazine* (Jan.–Feb. 1997).

[**McKeown 1997b**] N. McKeown, "A Fast Switched Backplane for a Gigabit Switched Router," *Business Communications Review,* Vol. 27, No. 12. http://tiny-tera.stanford.edu/~nickm/papers/cisco_fasts_wp.pdf

[**McKeown 2008**] N. McKeown, T. Anderson, H. Balakrishnan, G. Parulkar, L. Peterson, J. Rexford, S. Shenker, J. Turner, "OpenFlow: Enabling Innovation in Campus Networks," *ACM SIGCOMM Computer Communication Review*, Vol. 38, No. 2 (Apr. 2008).

[**McQuillan 1980**] J. McQuillan, I. Richer, E. Rosen, "The New Routing Algorithm for the Arpanet," *IEEE Transactions on Communications,* Vol. 28, No. 5 (May 1980), pp. 711–719.

[**Medhi 1997**] D. Medhi, D. Tipper (eds.), Special Issue: Fault Management in Communication Networks, *Journal of Network and Systems Management,* Vol. 5. No. 2 (June 1997).

[**Metcalfe 1976**] R. M. Metcalfe, D. R. Boggs. "Ethernet: Distributed Packet Switching for Local Computer Networks," *Communications of the Association for Computing Machinery,* Vol. 19, No. 7 (July 1976), pp. 395–404.

[**Meyers 2004**] A. Myers, T. Ng, H. Zhang, "Rethinking the Service Model: Scaling Ethernet to a Million Nodes*," ACM Hotnets Conference*, 2004.

[**MFA Forum 2012**] IP/MPLS Forum homepage, http://www.ipmplsforum.org/

[**Mirkovic 2005**] J. Mirkovic, S. Dietrich, D. Dittrich. P. Reiher, *Internet Denial of Service: Attack and Defense Mechanisms*, Prentice Hall, 2005.

[**Mockapetris 1988**] P. V. Mockapetris, K. J. Dunlap, "Development of the Domain Name System," *Proc. 1988 ACM SIGCOMM* (Stanford, CA, Aug. 1988).

[Mockapetris 2005] P. Mockapetris, Sigcomm Award Lecture, video available at http://www.postel.org/sigcomm

[Mogul 2003] J. Mogul, "TCP offload is a dumb idea whose time has come," *Proc. HotOS IX: The 9th Workshop on Hot Topics in Operating Systems* (2003), USENIX Association.

[Molinero-Fernandez 2002] P. Molinaro-Fernandez, N. McKeown, H. Zhang, "Is IP Going to Take Over the World (of Communications)?," *Proc. 2002 ACM Hotnets.*

[Molle 1987] M. L. Molle, K. Sohraby, A. N. Venetsanopoulos, "Space-Time Models of Asynchronous CSMA Protocols for Local Area Networks," *IEEE Journal on Selected Areas in Communications,* Vol. 5, No. 6 (1987), pp. 956–968.

[Moore 2001] D. Moore, G. Voelker, S. Savage, "Inferring Internet Denial of Service Activity," *Proc. 2001 USENIX Security Symposium* (Washington, DC, Aug. 2001).

[Moore 2003] D. Moore, V. Paxson, S. Savage, C. Shannon, S. Staniford, N. Weaver, "Inside the Slammer Worm," *2003 IEEE Security and Privacy Conference.*

[Moshchuck 2006] A. Moshchuk, T. Bragin, S. Gribble, H. Levy, "A Crawler-based Study of Spyware on the Web," *Proc. 13th Annual Network and Distributed Systems Security Symposium (NDSS 2006)* (San Diego, CA, Feb. 2006).

[Motorola 2007] Motorola, "Long Term Evolution (LTE): A Technical Overview," http://www.motorola.com/staticfiles/Business/Solutions/Industry%20Solutions/Service%20Providers/Wireless%20Operators/LTE/_Document/Static%20Files/6834_MotDoc_New.pdf

[Mouly 1992] M. Mouly, M. Pautet, *The GSM System for Mobile Communications*, Cell and Sys, Palaiseau, France, 1992.

[Moy 1998] J. Moy, *OSPF: Anatomy of An Internet Routing Protocol*, Addison-Wesley, Reading, MA, 1998.

[Mudigonda 2011] J. Mudigonda, P. Yalagandula, J. C. Mogul, B. Stiekes, Y. Pouffary, "NetLord: A Scalable Multi-Tenant Network Architecture for Virtualized Datacenters," *Proc. 2011 ACM SIGCOMM.*

[Mukherjee 1997] B. Mukherjee, *Optical Communication Networks*, McGraw-Hill, 1997.

[Mukherjee 2006] B. Mukherjee, *Optical WDM Networks,* Springer, 2006.

[Mydotr 2009] R. N. Mysore, A. Pamboris, N. Farrington, N. Huang, P. Miri, S. Radhakrishnan, V. Subramanya, A. Vahdat, "PortLand: A Scalable Fault-Tolerant Layer 2 Data Center Network Fabric," *Proc. 2009 ACM SIGCOMM.*

[Nadel 2011] B. Nadel, "4G shootout: Verizon LTE vs. Sprint WiMax," *Computerworld*, February 3, 2011.

[Nahum 2002] E. Nahum, T. Barzilai, D. Kandlur, "Performance Issues in WWW Servers," *IEEE/ACM Transactions on Networking*, Vol 10, No. 1 (Feb. 2002).

[Naoumov 2006] N. Naoumov, K.W. Ross, "Exploiting P2P Systems for DDoS Attacks," *Intl Workshop on Peer-to-Peer Information Management* (Hong Kong, May 2006),

[Neglia 2007] G. Neglia, G. Reina, H. Zhang, D. Towsley, A. Venkataramani, J. Danaher, "Availability in BitTorrent Systems," *Proc. 2007 IEEE INFOCOM.*

[Neumann 1997] R. Neumann, "Internet Routing Black Hole," *The Risks Digest: Forum on Risks to the Public in Computers and Related Systems,* Vol. 19, No. 12 (May 1997). http://catless.ncl.ac.uk/Risks/19.12.html#subj1.1

[Neville-Neil 2009] G. Neville-Neil, "Whither Sockets?" *Communications of the ACM,* Vol. 52, No. 6 (June 2009), pp. 51–55.

[Nicholson 2006] A Nicholson, Y. Chawathe, M. Chen, B. Noble, D. Wetherall, "Improved Access Point Selection," *Proc. 2006 ACM Mobisys Conference* (Uppsala Sweden, 2006).

[Nielsen 1997] H. F. Nielsen, J. Gettys, A. Baird-Smith, E. Prud'hommeaux, H. W. Lie, C. Lilley, "Network Performance Effects of HTTP/1.1, CSS1, and PNG," *W3C Document,* 1997 (also appears in *Proc. 1997 ACM SIGCOM* (Cannes, France, Sept 1997), pp. 155–166.

[NIST 2001] National Institute of Standards and Technology, "Advanced Encryption Standard (AES)," Federal Information Processing Standards 197, Nov. 2001, http://csrc.nist .gov/publications/fips/fips197/fips-197.pdf

[NIST IPv6 2012] National Institute of Standards, "Estimating IPv6 & DNSSEC Deployment SnapShots," http://usgv6-deploymon.antd.nist.gov/snap-all.html

[Nmap 2012] Nmap homepage, http://www.insecure.com/nmap

[Nonnenmacher 1998] J. Nonnenmacher, E. Biersak, D. Towsley, "Parity-Based Loss Recovery for Reliable Multicast Transmission," *IEEE/ACM Transactions on Networking,* Vol. 6, No. 4 (Aug. 1998), pp. 349–361.

[NTIA 1998] National Telecommunications and Information Administration (NTIA), US Department of Commerce, "Management of Internet names and addresses," Docket Number: 980212036-8146-02. http://www.ntia.doc.gov/ntiahome/domainname/6_5_98dns.htm

[O'Dell 2009] M. O'Dell, "Network Front-End Processors, Yet Again," *Communications of the ACM,* Vol. 52, No. 6 (June 2009), pp. 46–50.

[OID Repository 2012] OID Repository, http://www.oid-info.com/

[OSI 2012] International Organization for Standardization homepage, http://www.iso.org/iso/en/ISOOnline.frontpage

[OSS 2012] OSS Nokalva, "ASN.1 Resources," http://www.oss.com/asn1/

[Padhye 2000] J. Padhye, V. Firoiu, D. Towsley, J. Kurose, "Modeling TCP Reno Performance: A Simple Model and its Empirical Validation," *IEEE/ACM Transactions on Networking,* Vol. 8 No. 2 (Apr. 2000), pp. 133–145.

[Padhye 2001] J. Padhye, S. Floyd, "On Inferring TCP Behavior," *Proc. 2001 ACM SIGCOMM* (San Diego, CA, Aug. 2001).

[Pan 1997] P. Pan, H. Schulzrinne, "Staged Refresh Timers for RSVP," *Proc. 2nd Global Internet Conference* (Phoenix, AZ, Dec. 1997).

[Parekh 1993] A. Parekh, R. Gallagher, "A generalized processor sharing approach to flow control in integrated services networks: the single-node case," *IEEE/ACM Transactions on Networking,* Vol. 1, No. 3 (June 1993), pp. 344–357.

[Partridge 1992] C. Partridge, S. Pink, "An Implementation of the Revised Internet Stream Protocol (ST-2)," *Journal of Internetworking: Research and Experience*, Vol. 3, No. 1 (Mar. 1992).

[Partridge 1998] C. Partridge, et al. "A Fifty Gigabit per second IP Router," *IEEE/ACM Transactions on Networking,* Vol. 6, No. 3 (Jun. 1998), pp. 237–248.

[Pathak 2010] A. Pathak, Y. A. Wang, C. Huang, A. Greenberg, Y. C. Hu, J. Li, K. W. Ross, "Measuring and Evaluating TCP Splitting for Cloud Services," *Passive and Active Measurement (PAM) Conference* (Zurich, 2010).

[Paxson 1997] V. Paxson, "End-to-End Internet Packet Dynamics," *Proc. 1997 ACM SIGCOMM* (Cannes, France, Sept. 1997).

[Perkins 1994] A. Perkins, "Networking with Bob Metcalfe," *The Red Herring Magazine* (Nov. 1994).

[Perkins 1998] C. Perkins, O. Hodson, V. Hardman, "A Survey of Packet Loss Recovery Techniques for Streaming Audio," *IEEE Network Magazine* (Sept./Oct. 1998), pp. 40–47.

[Perkins 1998b] C. Perkins, *Mobile IP: Design Principles and Practice*, Addison-Wesley, Reading, MA, 1998.

[Perkins 2000] C. Perkins, *Ad Hoc Networking*, Addison-Wesley, Reading, MA, 2000.

[Perlman 1999] R. Perlman, *Interconnections: Bridges, Routers, Switches, and Internetworking Protocols,* 2nd ed., Addison-Wesley Professional Computing Series, Reading, MA, 1999.

[PGPI 2012] The International PGP Home Page, http://www.pgpi.org

[Phifer 2000] L. Phifer, "The Trouble with NAT," *The Internet Protocol Journal,* Vol. 3, No. 4 (Dec. 2000), http://www.cisco.com/warp/public/759/ipj_3-4/ipj_3-4_nat.html

[Piatek 2007] M. Piatek, T. Isdal, T. Anderson, A. Krishnamurthy, A. Venkataramani, "Do Incentives Build Robustness in Bittorrent?," *Proc. NSDI* (2007).

[Piatek 2008] M. Piatek, T. Isdal, A. Krishnamurthy, T. Anderson, "One hop Reputations for Peer-to-peer File Sharing Workloads," *Proc. NSDI* (2008).

[Pickholtz 1982] R. Pickholtz, D. Schilling, L. Milstein, "Theory of Spread Spectrum Communication—a Tutorial," *IEEE Transactions on Communications,* Vol. 30, No. 5 (May 1982), pp. 855–884.

[PingPlotter 2012] PingPlotter homepage, http://www.pingplotter.com

[Piscatello 1993] D. Piscatello, A. Lyman Chapin, *Open Systems Networking,* Addison-Wesley, Reading, MA, 1993.

[Point Topic 2006] Point Topic Ltd., *World Broadband Statistics Q1 2006,* http://www.pointtopic.com

[Potaroo 2012] "Growth of the BGP Table–1994 to Present," http://bgp.potaroo.net/

[PPLive 2012] PPLive homepage, http://www.pplive.com

[Quagga 2012] Quagga, "Quagga Routing Suite," http://www.quagga.net/

[Quittner 1998] J. Quittner, M. Slatalla, *Speeding the Net: The Inside Story of Netscape and How it Challenged Microsoft,* Atlantic Monthly Press, 1998.

[Quova 2012] www.quova.com

[Raiciu 2011] C. Raiciu , S. Barre, C. Pluntke, A. Greenhalgh, D. Wischik, M. Handley, "Improving Datacenter Performance and Robustness with Multipath TCP," *Proc. 2011 ACM SIGCOMM.*

[Ramakrishnan 1990] K. K. Ramakrishnan, R. Jain, "A Binary Feedback Scheme for Congestion Avoidance in Computer Networks," *ACM Transactions on Computer Systems,* Vol. 8, No. 2 (May 1990), pp. 158–181.

[Raman 1999] S. Raman, S. McCanne, "A Model, Analysis, and Protocol Framework for Soft State-based Communication," *Proc. 1999 ACM SIGCOMM* (Boston, MA, Aug. 1999).

[Raman 2007] B. Raman, K. Chebrolu, "Experiences in using WiFi for Rural Internet in India," *IEEE Communications Magazine,* Special Issue on New Directions in Networking Technologies in Emerging Economies (Jan. 2007).

[Ramaswami 2010] R. Ramaswami, K. Sivarajan, G. Sasaki, *Optical Networks: A Practical Perspective*, Morgan Kaufman Publishers, 2010.

[Ramjee 1994] R. Ramjee, J. Kurose, D. Towsley, H. Schulzrinne, "Adaptive Playout Mechanisms for Packetized Audio Applications in Wide-Area Networks," *Proc. 1994 IEEE INFOCOM.*

[Rao 1996] K. R. Rao and J. J. Hwang, *Techniques and Standards for Image, Video and Audio Coding,* Prentice Hall, Englewood Cliffs, NJ, 1996.

[Rao 2011] A. S. Rao, Y. S. Lim, C. Barakat, A. Legout, D. Towsley, W. Dabbous, "Network Characteristics of Video Streaming Traffic," *Proc. 2011 ACM CoNEXT* (Tokyo).

[RAT 2012] Robust Audio Tool, http://www-mice.cs.ucl.ac.uk/multimedia/software/rat/

[Ratnasamy 2001] S. Ratnasamy, P. Francis, M. Handley, R. Karp, S. Shenker, "A Scalable Content-Addressable Network," *Proc. 2001 ACM SIGCOMM* (San Diego, CA, Aug. 2001).

[Ren 2006] S. Ren, L. Guo, and X. Zhang, "ASAP: an AS-aware peer-relay protocol for high quality VoIP," *Proc. 2006 IEEE ICDCS* (Lisboa, Portugal, July 2006).

[Rescorla 2001] E. Rescorla, *SSL and TLS: Designing and Building Secure Systems,* Addison-Wesley, Boston, 2001.

[RFC 001] S. Crocker, "Host Software," RFC 001 (the *very first* RFC!).

[RFC 768] J. Postel, "User Datagram Protocol," RFC 768, Aug. 1980.

[RFC 789] E. Rosen, "Vulnerabilities of Network Control Protocols," RFC 789.

[RFC 791] J. Postel, "Internet Protocol: DARPA Internet Program Protocol Specification," RFC 791, Sept. 1981.

[RFC 792] J. Postel, "Internet Control Message Protocol," RFC 792, Sept. 1981.

[RFC 793] J. Postel, "Transmission Control Protocol," RFC 793, Sept. 1981.

[RFC 801] J. Postel, "NCP/TCP Transition Plan," RFC 801, Nov. 1981.

[RFC 826] D. C. Plummer, "An Ethernet Address Resolution Protocol—or—Converting Network Protocol Addresses to 48 bit Ethernet Address for Transmission on Ethernet Hardware," RFC 826, Nov. 1982.

[RFC 829] V. Cerf, "Packet Satellite Technology Reference Sources," RFC 829, Nov. 1982.

[RFC 854] J. Postel, J. Reynolds, "TELNET Protocol Specification," RFC 854, May 1993.

[RFC 950] J. Mogul, J. Postel, "Internet Standard Subnetting Procedure," RFC 950, Aug. 1985.

[RFC 959] J. Postel and J. Reynolds, "File Transfer Protocol (FTP)," RFC 959, Oct. 1985.

[RFC 977] B. Kantor, P. Lapsley, "Network News Transfer Protocol," RFC 977, Feb. 1986.

[RFC 1028] J. Davin, J.D. Case, M. Fedor, M. Schoffstall, "A Simple Gateway Monitoring Protocol," RFC 1028, Nov. 1987.

[RFC 1034] P. V. Mockapetris, "Domain Names—Concepts and Facilities," RFC 1034, Nov. 1987.

[RFC 1035] P. Mockapetris, "Domain Names—Implementation and Specification," RFC 1035, Nov. 1987.

[RFC 1058] C. L. Hendrick, "Routing Information Protocol," RFC 1058, June 1988.

[RFC 1071] R. Braden, D. Borman, and C. Partridge, "Computing The Internet Checksum," RFC 1071, Sept. 1988.

[RFC 1075] D. Waitzman, C. Partridge, S. Deering, "Distance Vector Multicast Routing Protocol," RFC 1075, Nov. 1988.

[RFC 1112] S. Deering, "Host Extension for IP Multicasting," RFC 1112, Aug. 1989.

[RFC 1122] R. Braden, "Requirements for Internet Hosts—Communication Layers," RFC 1122, Oct. 1989.

[RFC 1123] R. Braden, ed., "Requirements for Internet Hosts—Application and Support," RFC-1123, Oct. 1989.

[RFC 1142] D. Oran, "OSI IS-IS Intra-Domain Routing Protocol," RFC 1142, Feb. 1990.

[RFC 1190] C. Topolcic, "Experimental Internet Stream Protocol: Version 2 (ST-II)," RFC 1190, Oct. 1990.

[RFC 1191] J. Mogul, S. Deering, "Path MTU Discovery," RFC 1191, Nov. 1990.

[RFC 1213] K. McCloghrie, M. T. Rose, "Management Information Base for Network Management of TCP/IP-based internets: MIB-II," RFC 1213, Mar. 1991.

[RFC 1256] S. Deering, "ICMP Router Discovery Messages," RFC 1256, Sept. 1991.

[RFC 1320] R. Rivest, "The MD4 Message-Digest Algorithm," RFC 1320, Apr. 1992.

[RFC 1321] R. Rivest, "The MD5 Message-Digest Algorithm," RFC 1321, Apr. 1992.

[RFC 1323] V. Jacobson, S. Braden, D. Borman, "TCP Extensions for High Performance," RFC 1323, May 1992.

[RFC 1422] S. Kent, "Privacy Enhancement for Internet Electronic Mail: Part II: Certificate-Based Key Management," RFC 1422.

[RFC 1546] C. Partridge, T. Mendez, W. Milliken, "Host Anycasting Service," RFC 1546, 1993.

[RFC 1547] D. Perkins, "Requirements for an Internet Standard Point-to-Point Protocol," RFC 1547, Dec. 1993.

[RFC 1584] J. Moy, "Multicast Extensions to OSPF," RFC 1584, Mar. 1994.

[RFC 1633] R. Braden, D. Clark, S. Shenker, "Integrated Services in the Internet Architecture: an Overview," RFC 1633, June 1994.

[RFC 1636] R. Braden, D. Clark, S. Crocker, C. Huitema, "Report of IAB Workshop on Security in the Internet Architecture," RFC 1636, Nov. 1994.

[RFC 1661] W. Simpson (ed.), "The Point-to-Point Protocol (PPP)," RFC 1661, July 1994.

[RFC 1662] W. Simpson (ed.), "PPP in HDLC-Like Framing," RFC 1662, July 1994.

[RFC 1700] J. Reynolds and J. Postel, "Assigned Numbers," RFC 1700, Oct. 1994.

[RFC 1752] S. Bradner, A. Mankin, "The Recommendations for the IP Next Generation Protocol," RFC 1752, Jan. 1995.

[RFC 1918] Y. Rekhter, B. Moskowitz, D. Karrenberg, G. J. de Groot, E. Lear, "Address Allocation for Private Internets," RFC 1918, Feb. 1996.

[RFC 1930] J. Hawkinson, T. Bates, "Guidelines for Creation, Selection, and Registration of an Autonomous System (AS)," RFC 1930, Mar. 1996.

[RFC 1938] N. Haller, C. Metz, "A One-Time Password System," RFC 1938, May 1996.

[RFC 1939] J. Myers and M. Rose, "Post Office Protocol—Version 3," RFC 1939, May 1996.

[RFC 1945] T. Berners-Lee, R. Fielding, H. Frystyk, "Hypertext Transfer Protocol—HTTP/1.0," RFC 1945, May 1996.

[RFC 2003] C. Perkins, "IP Encapsulation within IP," RFC 2003, Oct. 1996.

[RFC 2004] C. Perkins, "Minimal Encapsulation within IP," RFC 2004, Oct. 1996.

[RFC 2018] M. Mathis, J. Mahdavi, S. Floyd, A. Romanow, "TCP Selective Acknowledgment Options," RFC 2018, Oct. 1996.

[RFC 2050] K. Hubbard, M. Kosters, D. Conrad, D. Karrenberg, J. Postel, "Internet Registry IP Allocation Guidelines," RFC 2050, Nov. 1996.

[RFC 2104] H. Krawczyk, M. Bellare, R. Canetti, "HMAC: Keyed-Hashing for Message Authentication," RFC 2104, Feb. 1997.

[RFC 2131] R. Droms, "Dynamic Host Configuration Protocol," RFC 2131, Mar. 1997.

[RFC 2136] P. Vixie, S. Thomson, Y. Rekhter, J. Bound, "Dynamic Updates in the Domain Name System," RFC 2136, Apr. 1997.

[RFC 2153] W. Simpson, "PPP Vendor Extensions," RFC 2153, May 1997.

[RFC 2205] R. Braden, Ed., L. Zhang, S. Berson, S. Herzog, S. Jamin, "Resource ReSerVation Protocol (RSVP)—Version 1 Functional Specification," RFC 2205, Sept. 1997.

[RFC 2210] J. Wroclawski, "The Use of RSVP with IETF Integrated Services," RFC 2210, Sept. 1997.

[RFC 2211] J. Wroclawski, "Specification of the Controlled-Load Network Element Service," RFC 2211, Sept. 1997.

[RFC 2215] S. Shenker, J. Wroclawski, "General Characterization Parameters for Integrated Service Network Elements," RFC 2215, Sept. 1997.

[RFC 2326] H. Schulzrinne, A. Rao, R. Lanphier, "Real Time Streaming Protocol (RTSP)," RFC 2326, Apr. 1998.

[RFC 2328] J. Moy, "OSPF Version 2," RFC 2328, Apr. 1998.

[RFC 2420] H. Kummert, "The PPP Triple-DES Encryption Protocol (3DESE)," RFC 2420, Sept. 1998.

[RFC 2453] G. Malkin, "RIP Version 2," RFC 2453, Nov. 1998.

[RFC 2460] S. Deering, R. Hinden, "Internet Protocol, Version 6 (IPv6) Specification," RFC 2460, Dec. 1998.

[RFC 2475] S. Blake, D. Black, M. Carlson, E. Davies, Z. Wang, W. Weiss, "An Architecture for Differentiated Services," RFC 2475, Dec. 1998.

[RFC 2578] K. McCloghrie, D. Perkins, J. Schoenwaelder, "Structure of Management Information Version 2 (SMIv2)," RFC 2578, Apr. 1999.

[RFC 2579] K. McCloghrie, D. Perkins, J. Schoenwaelder, "Textual Conventions for SMIv2," RFC 2579, Apr. 1999.

[RFC 2580] K. McCloghrie, D. Perkins, J. Schoenwaelder, "Conformance Statements for SMIv2," RFC 2580, Apr. 1999.

[RFC 2597] J. Heinanen, F. Baker, W. Weiss, J. Wroclawski, "Assured Forwarding PHB Group," RFC 2597, June 1999.

[RFC 2616] R. Fielding, J. Gettys, J. Mogul, H. Frystyk, L. Masinter, P. Leach, T. Berners-Lee, R. Fielding, "Hypertext Transfer Protocol—HTTP/1.1," RFC 2616, June 1999.

[RFC 2663] P. Srisuresh, M. Holdrege, "IP Network Address Translator (NAT) Terminology and Considerations," RFC 2663.

[RFC 2702] D. Awduche, J. Malcolm, J. Agogbua, M. O'Dell, J. McManus, "Requirements for Traffic Engineering Over MPLS," RFC 2702, Sept. 1999.

[RFC 2827] P. Ferguson, D. Senie, "Network Ingress Filtering: Defeating Denial of Service Attacks which Employ IP Source Address Spoofing," RFC 2827, May 2000.

[RFC 2865] C. Rigney, S. Willens, A. Rubens, W. Simpson, "Remote Authentication Dial In User Service (RADIUS)," RFC 2865, June 2000.

[RFC 2961] L. Berger, D. Gan, G. Swallow, P. Pan, F. Tommasi, S. Molendini, "RSVP Refresh Overhead Reduction Extensions," RFC 2961, Apr. 2001.

[RFC 3007] B. Wellington, "Secure Domain Name System (DNS) Dynamic Update," RFC 3007, Nov. 2000.

[RFC 3022] P. Srisuresh, K. Egevang, "Traditional IP Network Address Translator (Traditional NAT)," RFC 3022, Jan. 2001.

[RFC 3022] P. Srisuresh, K. Egevang, "Traditional IP Network Address Translator (Traditional NAT)," RFC 3022, Jan. 2001.

[RFC 3031] E. Rosen, A. Viswanathan, R. Callon, "Multiprotocol Label Switching Architecture," RFC 3031, Jan. 2001.

[RFC 3032] E. Rosen, D. Tappan, G. Fedorkow, Y. Rekhter, D. Farinacci, T. Li, A. Conta, "MPLS Label Stack Encoding," RFC 3032, Jan. 2001.

[RFC 3052] M. Eder, S. Nag, "Service Management Architectures Issues and Review," RFC 3052, Jan. 2001.

[RFC 3139] L. Sanchez, K. McCloghrie, J. Saperia, "Requirements for Configuration Management of IP-Based Networks," RFC 3139, June 2001.

[RFC 3168] K. Ramakrishnan, S. Floyd, D. Black, "The Addition of Explicit Congestion Notification (ECN) to IP," RFC 3168, Sept. 2001.

[RFC 3209] D. Awduche, L. Berger, D. Gan, T. Li, V. Srinivasan, G. Swallow, "RSVP-TE: Extensions to RSVP for LSP Tunnels," RFC 3209, Dec. 2001.

[RFC 3221] G. Huston, "Commentary on Inter-Domain Routing in the Internet," RFC 3221, Dec. 2001.

[RFC 3232] J. Reynolds, "Assigned Numbers: RFC 1700 is Replaced by an On-line Database," RFC 3232, Jan. 2002.

[RFC 3246] B. Davie, A. Charny, J.C.R. Bennet, K. Benson, J.Y. Le Boudec, W. Courtney, S. Davari, V. Firoiu, D. Stiliadis, "An Expedited Forwarding PHB (Per-Hop Behavior)," RFC 3246, Mar. 2002.

[RFC 3260] D. Grossman, "New Terminology and Clarifications for Diffserv," RFC 3260, Apr. 2002.

[RFC 3261] J. Rosenberg, H. Schulzrinne, G. Carmarillo, A. Johnston, J. Peterson, R. Sparks, M. Handley, E. Schooler, "SIP: Session Initiation Protocol," RFC 3261, July 2002.

[RFC 3272] J. Boyle, V. Gill, A. Hannan, D. Cooper, D. Awduche, B. Christian, W.S. Lai, "Overview and Principles of Internet Traffic Engineering," RFC 3272, May 2002.

[RFC 3286] L. Ong, J. Yoakum, "An Introduction to the Stream Control Transmission Protocol (SCTP)," RFC 3286, May 2002.

[RFC 3346] J. Boyle, V. Gill, A. Hannan, D. Cooper, D. Awduche, B. Christian, W. S. Lai, "Applicability Statement for Traffic Engineering with MPLS," RFC 3346, Aug. 2002.

[RFC 3376] B. Cain, S. Deering, I. Kouvelas, B. Fenner, A. Thyagarajan, "Internet Group Management Protocol, Version 3," RFC 3376, Oct. 2002.

[RFC 3390] M. Allman, S. Floyd, C. Partridge, "Increasing TCP's Initial Window," RFC 3390, Oct. 2002.

[RFC 3410] J. Case, R. Mundy, D. Partain, "Introduction and Applicability Statements for Internet Standard Management Framework," RFC 3410, Dec. 2002.

[RFC 3411] D. Harrington, R. Presuhn, B. Wijnen, "An Architecture for Describing Simple Network Management Protocol (SNMP) Management Frameworks," RFC 3411, Dec. 2002.

[RFC 3414] U. Blumenthal and B. Wijnen, "User-based Security Model (USM) for Version 3 of the Simple Network Management Protocol (SNMPv3)," RFC 3414, December 2002.

[RFC 3415] B. Wijnen, R. Presuhn, K. McCloghrie, "View-based Access Control Model (VACM) for the Simple Network Management Protocol (SNMP)," RFC 3415, Dec. 2002.

[RFC 3416] R. Presuhn, J. Case, K. McCloghrie, M. Rose, S. Waldbusser, "Version 2 of the Protocol Operations for the Simple Network Management Protocol (SNMP)," Dec. 2002.

[RFC 3439] R. Bush and D. Meyer, "Some internet architectural guidelines and philosophy," RFC 3439, Dec. 2003.

[RFC 3447] J. Jonsson, B. Kaliski, "Public-Key Cryptography Standards (PKCS) #1: RSA Cryptography Specifications Version 2.1," RFC 3447, Feb. 2003.

[RFC 3468] L. Andersson, G. Swallow, "The Multiprotocol Label Switching (MPLS) Working Group Decision on MPLS Signaling Protocols," RFC 3468, Feb. 2003.

[RFC 3469] V. Sharma, Ed., F. Hellstrand, Ed, "Framework for Multi-Protocol Label Switching (MPLS)-based Recovery," RFC 3469, Feb. 2003. ftp://ftp.rfc-editor.org/in-notes/rfc3469.txt

[RFC 3501] M. Crispin, "Internet Message Access Protocol—Version 4rev1," RFC 3501, Mar. 2003.

[RFC 3550] H. Schulzrinne, S. Casner, R. Frederick, V. Jacobson, "RTP: A Transport Protocol for Real-Time Applications," RFC 3550, July 2003.

[RFC 3569] S. Bhattacharyya (ed.), "An Overview of Source-Specific Multicast (SSM)," RFC 3569, July 2003.

[RFC 3588] P. Calhoun, J. Loughney, E. Guttman, G. Zorn, J. Arkko, "Diameter Base Protocol," RFC 3588, Sept. 2003.

[RFC 3618] B. Fenner, D. Meyer, Ed., "Multicast Source Discovery Protocol (MSDP)," RFC 3618, Oct. 2003.

[RFC 3649] S. Floyd, "High Speed TCP for Large Congestion Windows," RFC 3649, Dec. 2003.

[RFC 3748] B. Aboba, L. Blunk, J. Vollbrecht, J. Carlson, H. Levkowetz, Ed., "Extensible Authentication Protocol (EAP)," RFC 3748, June 2004.

[RFC 3782] S. Floyd, T. Henderson, A. Gurtov, "The NewReno Modification to TCP's Fast Recovery Algorithm," RFC 3782, Apr. 2004.

[RFC 3973] A. Adams, J. Nicholas, W. Siadak, "Protocol Independent Multicast—Dense Mode (PIM-DM): Protocol Specification (Revised)," RFC 3973, Jan. 2005.

[RFC 4022] R. Raghunarayan, Ed., "Management Information Base for the Transmission Control Protocol (TCP)," RFC 4022, Mar. 2005.

[RFC 4113] B. Fenner, J. Flick, "Management Information Base for the User Datagram Protocol (UDP)," RFC 4113, June 2005.

[RFC 4213] E. Nordmark, R. Gilligan, "Basic Transition Mechanisms for IPv6 Hosts and Routers," RFC 4213, Oct. 2005.

[RFC 4271] Y. Rekhter, T. Li, S. Hares, Ed., "A Border Gateway Protocol 4 (BGP-4)," RFC 4271, Jan. 2006.

[RFC 4272] S. Murphy, "BGP Security Vulnerabilities Analysis," RFC 4274, Jan. 2006.

[RFC 4274] Meyer, D. and K. Patel, "BGP-4 Protocol Analysis", RFC 4274, January 2006.

[RFC 4291] R. Hinden, S. Deering, "IP Version 6 Addressing Architecture," RFC 4291, February 2006.

[RFC 4293] S. Routhier, Ed. "Management Information Base for the Internet Protocol (IP)," RFC 4293, Apr. 2006.

[RFC 4301] S. Kent, K. Seo, "Security Architecture for the Internet Protocol," RFC 4301, Dec. 2005.

[RFC 4302] S. Kent, "IP Authentication Header," RFC 4302, Dec. 2005.

[RFC 4303] S. Kent, "IP Encapsulating Security Payload (ESP)," RFC 4303, Dec. 2005.

[RFC 4305] D. Eastlake, "Cryptographic Algorithm Implementation Requirements for Encapsulating Security Payload (ESP) and Authentication Header (AH)," RFC 4305, Dec. 2005.

[RFC 4340] E. Kohler, M. Handley, S. Floyd, "Datagram Congestion Control Protocol (DCCP)," RFC 4340, Mar. 2006.

[RFC 4443] A. Conta, S. Deering, M. Gupta, Ed., "Internet Control Message Protocol (ICMPv6) for the Internet Protocol Version 6 (IPv6) Specification," RFC 4443, Mar. 2006.

[RFC 4346] T. Dierks, E. Rescorla, "The Transport Layer Security (TLS) Protocol Version 1.1," RFC 4346, Apr. 2006.

[RFC 4502] S. Waldbusser, "Remote Network Monitoring Management Information Base Version 2," RFC 4502, May 2006.

[RFC 4514] K. Zeilenga, Ed., "Lightweight Directory Access Protocol (LDAP): String Representation of Distinguished Names," RFC 4514, June 2006.

[RFC 4601] B. Fenner, M. Handley, H. Holbrook, I. Kouvelas, "Protocol Independent Multicast—Sparse Mode (PIM-SM): Protocol Specification (Revised)," RFC 4601, Aug. 2006.

[RFC 4607] H. Holbrook, B. Cain, "Source-Specific Multicast for IP," RFC 4607, Aug. 2006.

[RFC 4611] M. McBride, J. Meylor, D. Meyer, "Multicast Source Discovery Protocol (MSDP) Deployment Scenarios," RFC 4611, Aug. 2006.

[RFC 4632] V. Fuller, T. Li, "Classless Inter-domain Routing (CIDR): The Internet Address Assignment and Aggregation Plan," RFC 4632, Aug. 2006.

[RFC 4960] R. Stewart, ed., "Stream Control Transmission Protocol," RFC 4960, Sept. 2007.

[RFC 4987] W. Eddy, "TCP SYN Flooding Attacks and Common Mitigations," RFC 4987, Aug. 2007.

[RFC 5000] RFC editor, "Internet Official Protocol Standards," RFC 5000, May 2008.

[RFC 5109] A. Li (ed.), "RTP Payload Format for Generic Forward Error Correction," RFC 5109, Dec. 2007.

[RFC 5110] P. Savola, "Overview of the Internet Multicast Routing Architecture," RFC 5110, Jan. 2008.

[RFC 5216] D. Simon, B. Aboba, R. Hurst, "The EAP-TLS Authentication Protocol," RFC 5216, Mar. 2008.

[RFC 5218] D. Thaler, B. Aboba, "What Makes for a Successful Protocol?," RFC 5218, July 2008.

[RFC 5321] J. Klensin, "Simple Mail Transfer Protocol," RFC 5321, Oct. 2008.

[RFC 5322] P. Resnick, Ed., "Internet Message Format," RFC 5322, Oct. 2008.

[RFC 5348] S. Floyd, M. Handley, J. Padhye, J.Widmer, "TCP Friendly Rate Control (TFRC): Protocol Specification," RFC 5348, Sept. 2008.

[RFC 5411] J Rosenberg, "A Hitchhiker's Guide to the Session Initiation Protocol (SIP)," RFC 5411, Feb. 2009.

[RFC 5681] M. Allman, V. Paxson, E. Blanton, "TCP Congestion Control," RFC 5681, Sept. 2009.

[RFC 5944] C. Perkins, Ed., "IP Mobility Support for IPv4, Revised," RFC 5944, November 2010.

[RFC 5996] C. Kaufman, P. Hoffman, Y. Nir, P. Eronen, "Internet Key Exchange Protocol Version 2 (IKEv2)," RFC 5996, Sept. 2010.

[RFC 6071] S. Frankel, S. Krishnan, "IP Security (IPsec) and Internet Key Exchange (IKE) Document Roadmap," RFC 6071, Feb. 2011.

[RFC 6265] A Barth, "HTTP State Management Mechanism," RFC 6265, Apr. 2011.

[RFC 6298] V. Paxson, M. Allman, J. Chu, M. Sargent, "Computing TCP's Retransmission Timer," RFC 6298, June 2011.

[Rhee 1998] I. Rhee, "Error Control Techniques for Interactive Low-Bit Rate Video Transmission over the Internet," *Proc. 1998 ACM SIGCOMM* (Vancouver BC, Aug. 1998).

[Roberts 1967] L. Roberts, T. Merril, "Toward a Cooperative Network of Time-Shared Computers," *AFIPS Fall Conference* (Oct. 1966).

[Roberts 2004] J. Roberts, "Internet Traffic, QoS and Pricing," *Proc. 2004 IEEE INFOCOM*, Vol. 92, No. 9 (Sept. 2004), pp. 1389–1399.

[Rodriguez 2010] R. Rodrigues, P. Druschel, "Peer-to-Peer Systems," *Communications of the ACM,* Vol. 53, No. 10 (Oct. 2010), pp. 72–82.

[Rohde 2008] Rohde and Schwarz, "UMTS Long Term Evolution (LTE) Technology Introduction," Application Note 1MA111.

[Rom 1990] R. Rom, M. Sidi, *Multiple Access Protocols: Performance and Analysis,* Springer-Verlag, New York, 1990.

[Root Servers 2012] Root Servers homepage, http://www.root-servers.org/

[Rose 1996] M. Rose, *The Simple Book: An Introduction to Internet Management, Revised Second Edition,* Prentice Hall, Englewood Cliffs, NJ, 1996.

[Ross 1995] K. W. Ross, *Multiservice Loss Models for Broadband Telecommunication Networks,* Springer, Berlin, 1995.

[Rowston 2001] A. Rowston, P. Druschel, "Pastry: Scalable, Distributed Object Location and Routing for Large-Scale Peer-to-Peer Systems," *Proc. 2001 IFIP/ACM Middleware* (Heidelberg, Germany, 2001).

[RSA 1978] R. Rivest, A. Shamir, L. Adelman, "A Method for Obtaining Digital Signatures and Public-key Cryptosystems," *Communications of the ACM,* Vol. 21, No. 2 (Feb. 1978), pp. 120–126.

[RSA Fast 2012] RSA Laboratories, "How Fast is RSA?" http://www.rsa.com/rsalabs/node .asp?id=2215

[RSA Key 2012] RSA Laboratories, "How large a key should be used in the RSA Crypto system?" http://www.rsa.com/rsalabs/node.asp?id=2218

[Rubenstein 1998] D. Rubenstein, J. Kurose, D. Towsley, "Real-Time Reliable Multicast Using Proactive Forward Error Correction," *Proceedings of NOSSDAV '98* (Cambridge, UK, July 1998).

[Rubin 2001] A. Rubin, *White-Hat Security Arsenal: Tackling the Threats,* Addison-Wesley, 2001.

[Ruiz-Sanchez 2001] M. Ruiz-Sánchez, E. Biersack, W. Dabbous, "Survey and Taxonomy of IP Address Lookup Algorithms," *IEEE Network Magazine,* Vol. 15, No. 2 (Mar./Apr. 2001), pp. 8–23.

[Saltzer 1984] J. Saltzer, D. Reed, D. Clark, "End-to-End Arguments in System Design," *ACM Transactions on Computer Systems (TOCS),* Vol. 2, No. 4 (Nov. 1984).

[Sandvine 2011] "Global Internet Phenomena Report, Spring 2011," http://www.sandvine. com/news/global broadband trends.asp, 2011.

[Sardar 2006] B. Sardar, D. Saha, "A Survey of TCP Enhancements for Last-Hop Wireless Networks," *IEEE Commun. Surveys and Tutorials,* Vol. 8, No. 3 (2006), pp. 20–34.

[Saroiu 2002] S. Saroiu, P.K. Gummadi, S.D. Gribble, "A Measurement Study of Peer-to-Peer File Sharing Systems," *Proc. of Multimedia Computing and Networking (MMCN)* (2002).

[Saroiu 2002b] S. Saroiu, K. P. Gummadi, R. J. Dunn, S. D. Gribble, and H. M. Levy, "An Analysis of Internet Content Delivery Systems," *USENIX OSDI* (2002).

[Saydam 1996] T. Saydam, T. Magedanz, "From Networks and Network Management into Service and Service Management," *Journal of Networks and System Management,* Vol. 4, No. 4 (Dec. 1996), pp. 345–348.

[Schiller 2003] J. Schiller, *Mobile Communications* 2nd edition, Addison Wesley, 2003.

[Schneier 1995] B. Schneier, *Applied Cryptography: Protocols, Algorithms, and Source Code in C,* John Wiley and Sons, 1995.

[Schulzrinne 1997] H. Schulzrinne, "A Comprehensive Multimedia Control Architecture for the Internet," *NOSSDAV'97 (Network and Operating System Support for Digital Audio and Video)* (St. Louis, MO, May 1997).

[Schulzrinne-RTP 2012] Henning Schulzrinne's RTP site, http://www.cs.columbia.edu/~hgs/rtp

[Schulzrinne-RTSP 2012] Henning Schulzrinne's RTSP site, http://www.cs.columbia.edu/~hgs/rtsp

[Schulzrinne-SIP 2012] Henning Schulzrinne's SIP site, http://www.cs.columbia.edu/~hgs/sip

[Schwartz 1977] M. Schwartz, *Computer-Communication Network Design and Analysis*, Prentice-Hall, Englewood Cliffs, N.J., 1997.

[Schwartz 1980] M. Schwartz, *Information, Transmission, Modulation, and Noise,* McGraw Hill, New York, NY 1980.

[Schwartz 1982] M. Schwartz, "Performance Analysis of the SNA Virtual Route Pacing Control," *IEEE Transactions on Communications,* Vol. 30, No. 1 (Jan. 1982), pp. 172–184.

[Scourias 2012] J. Scourias, "Overview of the Global System for Mobile Communications: GSM." http://www.privateline.com/PCS/GSM0.html

[Segaller 1998] S. Segaller, *Nerds 2.0.1, A Brief History of the Internet,* TV Books, New York, 1998.

[Shacham 1990] N. Shacham, P. McKenney, "Packet Recovery in High-Speed Networks Using Coding and Buffer Management," *Proc. 1990 IEEE INFOCOM* (San Francisco, CA, Apr. 1990), pp. 124–131.

[Shaikh 2001] A. Shaikh, R. Tewari, M. Agrawal, "On the Effectiveness of DNS-based Server Selection," *Proc. 2001 IEEE INFOCOM.*

[Sharma 2003] P. Sharma, E, Perry, R. Malpani, "IP Multicast Operational Network management: Design, Challenges, and Experiences," *IEEE Network Magazine* (Mar. 2003), pp. 49–55.

[Singh 1999] S. Singh, *The Code Book: The Evolution of Secrecy from Mary, Queen of Scotsto Quantum Cryptography,* Doubleday Press, 1999.

[SIP Software 2012] H. Schulzrinne Software Package site, http://www.cs.columbia.edu/IRT/software

[Skoudis 2004] E. Skoudis, L. Zeltser, *Malware: Fighting Malicious Code*, Prentice Hall, 2004.

[Skoudis 2006] E. Skoudis, T. Liston, *Counter Hack Reloaded: A Step-by-Step Guide to Computer Attacks and Effective Defenses (2nd Edition)*, Prentice Hall, 2006.

[Skype 2012] Skype homepage, www.skype.com

[SMIL 2012] W3C Synchronized Multimedia homepage, http://www.w3.org/AudioVideo

[Smith 2009] J. Smith, "Fighting Physics: A Tough Battle," *Communications of the ACM,* Vol. 52, No. 7 (July 2009), pp. 60–65.

[Snort 2012] Sourcefire Inc., Snort homepage, http://http://www.snort.org/

[Solari 1997] S. J. Solari, *Digital Video and Audio Compression,* McGraw Hill, New York, NY, 1997.

[Solensky 1996] F. Solensky, "IPv4 Address Lifetime Expectations," in *IPng: Internet Protocol Next Generation* (S. Bradner, A. Mankin, ed.), Addison-Wesley, Reading, MA, 1996.

[Spragins 1991] J. D. Spragins, *Telecommunications Protocols and Design,* Addison-Wesley, Reading, MA, 1991.

[Srikant 2004] R. Srikant, *The Mathematics of Internet Congestion Control,* Birkhauser, 2004

[Sripanidkulchai 2004] K. Sripanidkulchai, B. Maggs, and H. Zhang, "An analysis of live streaming workloads on the Internet," *Proc. 2004 ACM Internet Measurement Conference* (Taormina, Sicily, Italy), pp. 41–54.

[Stallings 1993] W. Stallings, *SNMP, SNMP v2, and CMIP The Practical Guide to Network Management Standards,* Addison-Wesley, Reading, MA, 1993.

[Stallings 1999] W. Stallings, *SNMP, SNMPv2, SNMPv3, and RMON 1 and 2,* Addison-Wesley, Reading, MA, 1999.

[Steinder 2002] M. Steinder, A. Sethi, "Increasing robustness of fault localization through analysis of lost, spurious, and positive symptoms," *Proc. 2002 IEEE INFOCOM.*

[Stevens 1990] W. R. Stevens, *Unix Network Programming,* Prentice-Hall, Englewood Cliffs, NJ.

[Stevens 1994] W. R. Stevens, *TCP/IP Illustrated, Vol. 1: The Protocols,* Addison-Wesley, Reading, MA, 1994.

[Stevens 1997] W.R. Stevens, *Unix Network Programming, Volume 1: Networking APIs-Sockets and XTI,* 2nd edition, Prentice-Hall, Englewood Cliffs, NJ, 1997.

[Stewart 1999] J. Stewart, *BGP4: Interdomain Routing in the Internet,* Addison-Wesley, 1999.

[Stoica 2001] I. Stoica, R. Morris, D. Karger, M.F. Kaashoek, H. Balakrishnan, "Chord: A Scalable Peer-to-Peer Lookup Service for Internet Applications," *Proc. 2001 ACM SIGCOMM* (San Diego, CA, Aug. 2001).

[Stone 1998] J. Stone, M. Greenwald, C. Partridge, J. Hughes, "Performance of Checksums and CRC's Over Real Data," *IEEE/ACM Transactions on Networking,* Vol. 6, No. 5 (Oct. 1998), pp. 529–543.

[Stone 2000] J. Stone, C. Partridge, "When Reality and the Checksum Disagree," *Proc. 2000 ACM SIGCOMM* (Stockholm, Sweden, Aug. 2000).

[Strayer 1992] W. T. Strayer, B. Dempsey, A. Weaver, *XTP: The Xpress Transfer Protocol,* Addison-Wesley, Reading, MA, 1992.

[Stubblefield 2002] A. Stubblefield, J. Ioannidis, A. Rubin, "Using the Fluhrer, Mantin, and Shamir Attack to Break WEP," *Proceedings of 2002 Network and Distributed Systems Security Symposium* (2002), pp. 17–22.

[Subramanian 2000] M. Subramanian, *Network Management: Principles and Practice,* Addison-Wesley, Reading, MA, 2000.

[Subramanian 2002] L. Subramanian, S. Agarwal, J. Rexford, R. Katz, "Characterizing the Internet Hierarchy from Multiple Vantage Points," *Proc. 2002 IEEE INFOCOM.*

[Sundaresan 2006] K.Sundaresan, K. Papagiannaki, "The Need for Cross-layer Information in Access Point Selection," *Proc. 2006 ACM Internet Measurement Conference* (Rio De Janeiro, Oct. 2006).

[Su 2006] A.-J. Su, D. Choffnes, A. Kuzmanovic, and F. Bustamante, "Drafting Behind Akamai" *Proc. 2006 ACM SIGCOMM.*

[Suh 2006] K. Suh, D. R. Figueiredo, J. Kurose and D. Towsley, "Characterizing and detecting relayed traffic: A case study using Skype," *Proc. 2006 IEEE INFOCOM* (Barcelona, Spain, Apr. 2006).

[Sunshine 1978] C. Sunshine, Y. Dalal, "Connection Management in Transport Protocols," *Computer Networks,* North-Holland, Amsterdam, 1978.

[Tariq 2008] M. Tariq, A. Zeitoun, V. Valancius, N. Feamster, M. Ammar, "Answering What-If Deployment and Configuration Questions with WISE," *Proc. 2008 ACM SIGCOMM* (Aug. 2008).

[TechnOnLine 2012] TechOnLine, "Protected Wireless Networks," online webcast tutorial, http://www.techonline.com/community/tech_topic/internet/21752

[Teixeira 2006] R. Teixeira and J. Rexford, "Managing Routing Disruptions in Internet Service Provider Networks," *IEEE Communications Magazine* (Mar. 2006).

[Thaler 1997] D. Thaler and C. Ravishankar, "Distributed Center-Location Algorithms," *IEEE Journal on Selected Areas in Communications,* Vol. 15, No. 3 (Apr. 1997), pp. 291–303.

[Think 2012] Technical History of Network Protocols, "Cyclades," http://www.cs.utexas.edu/users/chris/think/Cyclades/index.shtml

[Tian 2012] Y. Tian, R. Dey, Y. Liu, K. W. Ross, "China's Internet: Topology Mapping and Geolocating," *IEEE INFOCOM Mini-Conference 2012* (Orlando, FL, 2012).

[Tobagi 1990] F. Tobagi, "Fast Packet Switch Architectures for Broadband Integrated Networks," *Proc. 1990 IEEE INFOCOM,* Vol. 78, No. 1 (Jan. 1990), pp. 133–167.

[TOR 2012] Tor: Anonymity Online, http://www.torproject.org

[Torres 2011] R. Torres, A. Finamore, J. R. Kim, M. M. Munafo, S. Rao, "Dissecting Video Server Selection Strategies in the YouTube CDN," *Proc. 2011 Int. Conf. on Distributed Computing Systems.*

[Turner 1988] J. S. Turner "Design of a Broadcast packet switching network," *IEEE Transactions on Communications,* Vol. 36, No. 6 (June 1988), pp. 734–743.

[Turner 2012] B. Turner, "2G, 3G, 4G Wireless Tutorial," http://blogs.nmscommunications.com/communications/2008/10/2g-3g-4g-wireless-tutorial.html

[UPnP Forum 2012] UPnP Forum homepage, http://www.upnp.org/

[van der Berg 2008] R. van der Berg, "How the 'Net works: an introduction to peering and transit," http://arstechnica.com/guides/other/peering-and-transit.ars

[Varghese 1997] G. Varghese, A. Lauck, "Hashed and Hierarchical Timing Wheels: Efficient Data Structures for Implementing a Timer Facility," *IEEE/ACM Transactions on Networking,* Vol. 5, No. 6 (Dec. 1997), pp. 824–834.

[Vasudevan 2012] S. Vasudevan, C. Diot, J. Kurose, D. Towsley, "Facilitating Access Point Selection in IEEE 802.11 Wireless Networks," *Proc. 2005 ACM Internet Measurement Conference*, (San Francisco CA, Oct. 2005).

[Verizon FIOS 2012] Verizon, "Verizon FiOS Internet: FAQ," http://www22.verizon.com/residential/fiosinternet/faq/faq.htm

[Verizon SLA 2012] Verizon, "Global Latency and Packet Delivery SLA," http://www.verizonbusiness.com/terms/global_latency_sla.xml

[Verma 2001] D. C. Verma, *Content Distribution Networks: An Engineering Approach,* John Wiley, 2001.

[Villamizar 1994] C. Villamizar, C. Song. "High performance tcp in ansnet," *ACM SIGCOMM Computer Communications Review*, Vol. 24, No. 5 (1994), pp. 45–60.

[Viterbi 1995] A. Viterbi, *CDMA: Principles of Spread Spectrum Communication,* Addison-Wesley, Reading, MA, 1995.

[Vixie 2009] P. Vixie, "What DNS Is Not," *Communications of the ACM,* Vol. 52, No. 12 (Dec. 2009), pp. 43–47.

[W3C 1995] The World Wide Web Consortium, "A Little History of the World Wide Web" (1995), http://www.w3.org/History.html

[Wakeman 1992] I. Wakeman, J. Crowcroft, Z. Wang, D. Sirovica, "Layering Considered Harmful," *IEEE Network* (Jan. 1992), pp. 20–24.

[Waldrop 2007] M. Waldrop, "Data Center in a Box," *Scientific American* (July 2007).

[Walker 2000] J. Walker, "IEEE P802.11 Wireless LANs, Unsafe at Any Key Size; An Analysis of the WEP Encapsulation," Oct. 2000, http://www.drizzle.com/~aboba/IEEE/0-362.zip

[Wall 1980] D. Wall, *Mechanisms for Broadcast and Selective Broadcast,* Ph.D. thesis, Stanford University, June 1980.

[Wang 2004] B. Wang, J. Kurose, P. Shenoy, D. Towsley, "Multimedia Streaming via TCP: An Analytic Performance Study," *Proc. 2004 ACM Multimedia Conference* (New York, NY, Oct. 2004).

[Wang 2008] B. Wang, J. Kurose, P. Shenoy, D. Towsley, "Multimedia Streaming via TCP: An Analytic Performance Study," *ACM Transactions on Multimedia Computing Communications and Applications (TOMCCAP)*, Vol. 4, No. 2 (Apr. 2008), pp. 16:1–22.

[Wang 2010] G. Wang, D. G. Andersen, M. Kaminsky, K. Papagiannaki, T. S. E. Ng, M. Kozuch, M. Ryan, "c-Through: Part-time Optics in Data Centers," *Proc. 2010 ACM SIGCOMM.*

[Weatherspoon 2000] S. Weatherspoon, "Overview of IEEE 802.11b Security," *Intel Technology Journal* (2nd Quarter 2000), http://download.intel.com/technology/itj/q22000/pdf/art_5.pdf

[Wei 2005] W. Wei, B. Wang, C. Zhang, J. Kurose, D. Towsley, "Classification of Access Network Types: Ethernet, Wireless LAN, ADSL, Cable Modem or Dialup?," *Proc. 2005 IEEE INFOCOM* (Apr. 2005).

[Wei 2006] W. Wei, C. Zhang, H. Zang, J. Kurose, D. Towsley, "Inference and Evaluation of Split-Connection Approaches in Cellular Data Networks," *Proc. Active and Passive Measurement Workshop* (Adelaide, Australia, Mar. 2006).

[Wei 2007] D. X. Wei, C. Jin, S. H. Low, S. Hegde, "FAST TCP: Motivation, Architecture, Algorithms, Performance," *IEEE/ACM Transactions on Networking* (2007).

[Weiser 1991] M. Weiser, "The Computer for the Twenty-First Century," *Scientific American* (Sept. 1991): 94–10. http://www.ubiq.com/hypertext/weiser/SciAmDraft3.html

[White 2011] A. White, K. Snow, A. Matthews, F. Monrose, "Hookt on fon-iks: Phonotactic Reconstruction of Encrypted VoIP Conversations," *IEEE Symposium on Security and Privacy*, Oakland, CA, 2011.

[Wigle.net 2012] Wireless Geographic Logging Engine, http://www.wigle.net

[Williams 1993] R. Williams, "A Painless Guide to CRC Error Detection Algorithms," http://www.ross.net/crc/crcpaper.html

[Wilson 2011] C. Wilson, H. Ballani, T. Karagiannis, A. Rowstron, "Better Never than Late: Meeting Deadlines in Datacenter Networks," *Proc. 2011 ACM SIGCOMM.*

[WiMax Forum 2012] WiMax Forum, http://www.wimaxforum.org

[Wireshark 2012] Wireshark homepage, http://www.wireshark.org

[Wischik 2005] D. Wischik, N. McKeown, "Part I: Buffer Sizes for Core Routers," *ACM SIGCOMM Computer Communications Review*, Vol. 35, No. 3 (July 2005).

[Woo 1994] T. Woo, R. Bindignavle, S. Su, S. Lam, "SNP: an interface for secure network programming," *Proc. 1994 Summer USENIX* (Boston, MA, June 1994), pp. 45–58.

[Wood 2012] L. Wood, "Lloyds Satellites Constellations," http://www.ee.surrey.ac.uk/Personal/L.Wood/constellations/iridium.html

[Wu 2005] J. Wu, Z. M. Mao, J. Rexford, J. Wang, "Finding a Needle in a Haystack: Pinpointing Significant BGP Routing Changes in an IP Network," *Proc. USENIX NSDI* (2005).

[Xanadu 2012] Xanadu Project homepage, http://www.xanadu.com/

[Xiao 2000] X. Xiao, A. Hannan, B. Bailey, L. Ni, "Traffic Engineering with MPLS in the Internet," *IEEE Network* (Mar./Apr. 2000).

[Xie 2008] H. Xie, Y.R. Yang, A. Krishnamurthy, Y. Liu, A. Silberschatz, "P4P: Provider Portal for Applications," *Proc. 2008 ACM SIGCOMM* (Seattle, WA, Aug. 2008).

[Yannuzzi 2005] M. Yannuzzi, X. Masip-Bruin, O. Bonaventure, "Open Issues in Interdomain Routing: A Survey," *IEEE Network Magazine* (Nov./Dec. 2005).

[Yavatkar 1994] R. Yavatkar, N. Bhagwat, "Improving End-to-End Performance of TCP over Mobile Internetworks," *Proc. Mobile 94 Workshop on Mobile Computing Systems and Applications* (Dec. 1994).

[YouTube 2009] YouTube 2009, Google container data center tour, 2009.

[Yu 2006] H. Yu, M. Kaminsky, P. B. Gibbons, and A. Flaxman, "SybilGuard: Defending Against Sybil Attacks via Social Networks," *Proc. 2006 ACM SIGCOMM* (Pisa, Italy, Sept. 2006).

[Zegura 1997] E. Zegura, K. Calvert, M. Donahoo, "A Quantitative Comparison of Graph-based Models for Internet Topology," *IEEE/ACM Transactions on Networking,* Vol. 5, No. 6, (Dec. 1997). See also http://www.cc.gatech.edu/projects/gtim for a software package that generates networks with a transit-stub structure.

[Zhang 1993] L. Zhang, S. Deering, D. Estrin, S. Shenker, D. Zappala, "RSVP: A New Resource Reservation Protocol," *IEEE Network Magazine,* Vol. 7, No. 9 (Sept. 1993), pp. 8–18.

[Zhang 2007] L. Zhang, "A Retrospective View of NAT," *The IETF Journal,* Vol. 3, Issue 2 (Oct. 2007).

[Zhang M 2010] M. Zhang, W. John, C. Chen, "Architecture and Download Behavior of Xunlei: A Measurement-Based Study," *Proc. 2010 Int. Conf. on Educational Technology and Computers (ICETC).*

[Zhang X 2102] X. Zhang, Y. Xu, Y. Liu, Z. Guo, Y. Wang, "Profiling Skype Video Calls: Rate Control and Video Quality," *IEEE INFOCOM* (Mar. 2012).

[Zhao 2004] B. Y. Zhao, L. Huang, J. Stribling, S. C. Rhea, A. D. Joseph, J. Kubiatowicz, "Tapestry: A Resilient Global-scale Overlay for Service Deployment," *IEEE Journal on Selected Areas in Communications,* Vol. 22, No. 1 (Jan. 2004).

[Zimmerman 1980] H. Zimmerman, "OS1 Reference Model-The ISO Model of Architecture for Open Systems Interconnection," *IEEE Transactions on Communications,* Vol. 28, No. 4 (Apr. 1980), pp. 425–432.

[Zimmermann 2012] P. Zimmermann, "Why do you need PGP?" http://www.pgpi.org/doc/whypgp/en/

[Zink 2009] M. Zink, K. Suh, Y. Gu, J. Kurose, "Characteristics of YouTube Network Traffic at a Campus Network - Measurements, Models, and Implications," *Computer Networks,* Vol. 53, No. 4 (2009), pp. 501–514.

Index